MAZD

MIATA MX5

ENTHUSIAST'S SHOP MANUAL

By Rod Grainger & Pete Shoemark

VELOCE PUBLISHING PLC
PUBLISHERS OF FINE AUTOMOTIVE BOOKS

To MP, without whom this project would not have been possible.

First published in 1994 by Veloce Publishing Plc., 33 Trinity Street, Dorchester, Dorset DT1 1TT, England. Fax 01305 268864. Reprinted 1995, 1996 (twice), 1997.

ISBN 1 874105 06 5
ISBN 1 874105 16 2 (US edition)
ISBN 1 874105 59 6 (US edition softback)
UPC 36847 00059 2

Readers with ideas for automotive books, or books on other transport or related hobby subjects, are invited to write to the editorial director of Veloce Publishing at the above address.

British Library Cataloguing in Publication Data -
A catalogue record for this book is available from the British Library.

Typesetting, design and page make-up all by Veloce on AppleMac.

Printed and bound in England.

Cover front panel photograph by David Sparrow.

10 9 8 7 6

CONTENTS

CHAPTER 5: ENGINE MANAGEMENT, FUEL, IGNITION & EXHAUST SYSTEMS

CHAPTER 6: COOLING, HEATING & AIR CONDITIONING SYSTEMS

CHAPTER 7: ELECTRICAL SYSTEM

CHAPTER 8: SUSPENSION & STEERING

CHAPTER 9: BRAKES, WHEELS & TIRES

CHAPTER 10: INTERIOR

CHAPTER 11: BODY

CHAPTER 12: UNDERBODY & RUSTPROOFING

CHAPTER 13: PERFORMANCE TUNING

CHAPTER 14: COSMETIC ACCESSORIES

CHAPTER 15: TROUBLESHOOTING, CLUBS & SPECIALISTS

AMERICAN/ENGLISH GLOSSARY OF AUTOMOTIVE TERMS

INTRODUCTION & ACKNOWLEDGE-MENTS

When Mazda launched the Miata/MX5, the motoring world was astonished to see something that had been presumed extinct: the sports roadster was back. The Miata/MX5 was hailed as a future classic as soon as it hit the streets, and we figured that as a sports car enthusiast and Miata/MX5 driver, you'd want to keep your car in peak condition. It seems to us that Mazda threw away the conventional car maker's shackles and produced a true sports car: therefore, in producing this book, we have endeavored to provide a true enthusiast's manual for a real enthusiast's car.

Our working environment was an ordinary domestic garage equipped with ordinary tools. Because of this, you can be sure we encountered the same problems you will and, more importantly, that our workarounds will work for you too. All of the strip and rebuild work and photography was carried out by Pete, Judith, 'Wally' and myself (Rod). Wally is a fictional technical adviser of dubious ability, so we allowed him to make all the mistakes: we figured this would make the rest of us look better and allow us to tell you how to avoid potential mistakes in your own work.

We've gone to great lengths to make this the most friendly, easy to use and detailed workshop manual for owners that's ever existed. If you think we've succeeded, like our work and want to show your appreciation, send us an old (non-British) license plate for our garage wall. Of course you can just write and tell us what you think of the manual and how we can make future editions even better - we'll be pleased to hear from you.

Acknowledgements

This project has taken well over two years to complete and really would not have been possible without the help and support of many people. I'd like to thank Judith St Clair-Pedroza who, as well as enduring many, many hours of cold mid-winter work on the project car, typed out dictated notes and has had to put up with anti-social behavior while I've spent what seems like a lifetime at the keyboard of my Apple Mac producing this manual. Pete Shoemark came to my rescue when I simply ran out of time: he wrote around half of the chapters and built some photographic lights to help with the photography - thanks Pete! My Dad kindly loaned me the camera and lenses which produced the photographs in this book. Tim Parker helped out by obtaining US literature and generally being 'our man in America'. Tim Watson of Mazda UK has been very supportive of this project and has assisted in many ways. Norman Garrett of the Miata Club of America and a concept engineer during the Miata's/MX5's creation, has been very enthusiastic about this manual and helped enormously with information for the chapter on performance tuning. Thanks a lot, all of you.

Rod Grainger

The crew. From left to right, Rod, Judith and Pete. We think Wally's probably sleeping under there! Bottom left is puppy Hubble.

1

WORKING PROCEDURES & TECHNICAL SPECIFICATIONS

1. USING THIS MANUAL

Sorry about this, but we're not a huge Intergalactic Corporation. We're just a bunch of enthusiasts with the ability to publish this manual so, in today's litigation crazy world, we need to draw your attention to the following -

IMPORTANT NOTE. While we have prepared this manual with great diligence and care, it is possible that it contains errors or ommisions. Also, we cannot foresee every possible area of personal danger or possibility of mechanical damage and warn our readers accordingly. The authors, publishers and retailers therefore accept no responsibility for personal injury or mechanical damage which is in any way related to the use of this publication. If you use the information contained within this manual, you accept full personal responsibility for the consequences: if this is not acceptable to you, return the pristine book to your supplier for a refund.

As the majority of Miatas are in the USA we've written this manual in American English. We don't think different spellings will lead to any problems for other English speakers but different terminology might: we have therefore included a glossary of terms which you can consult if necessary.

In chapter 2, we cover the basic maintenance operations necessary to keep your Miata/MX5 in peak condition. Most of these tasks are relatively simple to do, and if they're not, we tell you. In the chapters which follow we look in detail at the various major assemblies and systems which together make up your car. Some chapters discuss ways of enhancing and uprating your Miata/MX5, together with information on how to maintain it in optimum condition for years to come.

We reasoned that a car like this would appeal to a broad spectrum of individuals who would approach the maintenance and repair of their car in a variety of ways. Some of you may have no intention of ever lifting the hood (bonnet), while others may want to become familiar with the innermost secrets of the car. We hope that we have provided a manual with something of real value to *all* owners.

Wherever possible, we have placed emphasis on diagnosing suspected faults before giving detailed information on how to track down and resolve specific problems. With complex electronic sensing and control systems it is often difficult to locate problems using traditional methods, and unless you work methodically and logically you can easily waste hours without result, or worse still, introduce further problems by tinkering with adjustments.

We have concentrated on descriptive and diagnostic information because we feel strongly that you need to understand your Miata/MX5 before you attempt to work on it. This gives you the opportunity to understand what is likely to have caused any particular breakdown or difficulty, and with this information, make your decision about how best to deal with the situation. Despite its obvious affinity with European sports roadsters of the 1950s and 1960s, make no mistake, this is very much a car of the 1990s with all that this implies; crammed into that tiny bodyshell is all the technical sophistication of its era.

In some respects, the Miata/MX5 can seem a daunting prospect for home maintenance and repair. It has a sophisticated engine management system, which when hooked up to the equally sophisticated diagnostic equipment available to Mazda dealers, offers fast identification of many system faults. When we wrote this book, it would have been easy just to relate the official test procedures, but we were determined to base the book on normal home workshop tools and working methods.

This might seem to suggest that home diagnosis is not possible, but in many cases you can use alternative methods to avoid the need for expensive test equipment, and we made strenuous efforts to pack in as much of this type of information as we could. Where home testing and diagnosis really is out of the question, we indicate this in the text. Equally, where many hours of painstaking work could easily be avoided with a few minutes dealer attention, we say so; after all, you bought your Miata/MX5 for the fun and exhilaration that comes from driving it.

CONVENTIONS

The various chapter headings should be reasonably self-explanatory - we grouped together related assemblies and systems in a fairly logical way. You may realize, however, that linking the disparate aspects of the car to a surprising degree is the engine management system. This is more extensive than the term suggests, because the electronic control unit (ECU) reads data from all over the vehicle, processing this as part of its control function. In this sense, *chapter 5, Fuel, Ignition & Exhaust systems* forms the core of the book, and it is here that you should look first if you experience just about any problem. Even if it seems like a straightforward engine fault, there are tests and procedures given here which will identify the nature of the fault and then point you elsewhere in the book if more detailed information is required.

Within each chapter, you will find the text subdivided into sections, these being further subdivided into numbered paragraphs, with subsection headings to tell you which part of a procedure you are dealing with.

Right and left. All references to right and left are from the point of view of someone standing behind the car and looking forward.

SYMBOLS & CROSS-REFERENCES

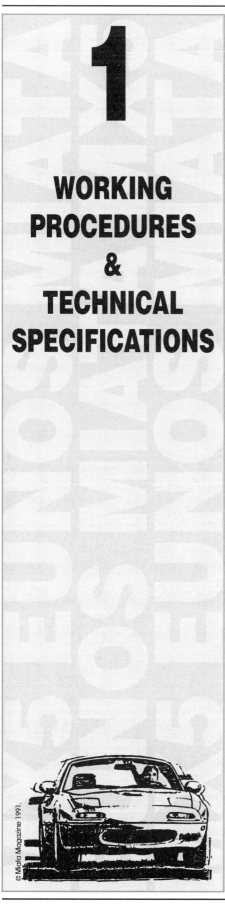

While we have tried to avoid the irritation of cross-references as far as possible, in some cases this was unavoidable if the book was to be kept to a reasonable size and price. We have adopted a number of conventions to help you find your way around: where a particular procedure requires you to carry out operations described in detail elsewhere in the book, you will find a symbol like this appearing in the text -

☞ 3/4/1-51.

This tells you that at this point in the current procedure, you should carry out work described in chapter 3, section 4, paragraphs 1 to 51. You should move to the part of the book indicated, carry out the operations detailed there, and then resume the current task where you left off. Please note that the first number is always the chapter number, even when the cross-reference is in the same chapter.

Where a data table/data chart accompanies a particular piece of text, you will find it nearby and numbered appropriately. For example, table T1/10 relates to section 1, paragraph 10 of the chapter in which it appears. A symbol appears in the text to tell you to look at a useful data table: if the symbol's followed by a + sign, there's more than one table. This is the table symbol -

Drawings are numbered in relation to the appropriate text. For example, D22/1 relates to section 22, paragraph 1 of the chapter in which the drawing appears. To help you, we have included a symbol in any text where reference to a particular drawing will be helpful: if the symbol's followed by a + sign, there's more than one drawing. The symbol looks like this -

Photographs will be found close to the text to which they relate, and illustrate part or all of the specific procedure being described. Each photograph is numbered in relation to the appropriate text. For example a photo caption beginning 7/47 indicates that the photo relates to section 7, paragraph 47 of the chapter in which it appears. We have created a text symbol to tell you when reference to a particular photo will be helpful: if the symbol's followed by a + sign, there is more than one relevant photo. Here is the photo symbol -

HEY! WATCH OUT!

We have assumed that you will be working responsibly at all times, and taking appropriate precautions to avoid damage or personal injury. On occasions where a particular procedure may carry a special risk to the operator's safety, we have drawn attention to this by placing a **Warning!** in the text. If you see this, be aware that it is there to draw attention to a serious risk of personal injury if special care or precautions are not observed. Don't ignore these warnings - we put them in because there is a **real** risk of injury. **Don't assume that tasks which don't carry this warning are safe, we cannot possibly foresee every potential danger in every situation.** Try to be aware of potential dangers whenever working on or around your car. Don't think just in terms of the obvious, go a little deeper. Here are just five examples of the level of awareness you should maintain. 1) Remember that most fluids used by the car or for maintenance/cleaning are in some way dangerous - so read the maker's instructions and don't make assumptions. 2) Old engine oil has been proved to cause skin cancer in mice - so protect your skin with gloves or barrier cream and wash contaminated areas quickly. 3) If you're working on the car's fuel system in your garage, remember that if the garage contains a house heating boiler the ignition sequence may occur while there are gas (petrol) fumes in the air - it's also possible the boiler has a constant pilot flame. 4) Slipping on spilled oil, or other fluids, could put you in hospital for a long time. 5) A metal watch strap, bracelet or even a ring could cause a short between a live terminal and ground (earth).

In other cases, there may be some risk of serious damage to the car if special care is not taken. We have identified such instances by placing **Caution!** in the text. What we mean here is that you need to take even more care than usual if you are to avoid accidentally damaging some component of the car or, perhaps, your tools. These messages mean business, so please don't just skip past them. **Don't assume that tasks which don't carry this warning are safe, we cannot possibly foresee every potential danger in every situation.**

Other specific information of special note, but which does not pose a serious risk of personal injury or damage to the car will be highlighted by the less dramatic 'Note:' You should take note of the information which follows - it could save you making mistakes in a procedure.

2. WORKING PROCEDURES

GENERAL

1 Before you start **any** operation on your car, read through the details carefully. Check any drawings or photographs relating to the task, and compare this information with your own car. If necessary reread the section until you are confident that you know what you will be doing. Not only does this minimize mistakes, it will actually save you time when you do the job for real - you won't need to constantly refer back to the manual for procedural details. We find that it helps to sit somewhere comfortable and quiet to do this.

2 You should remember that the project car for this book was a UK specification model, which means right-hand drive. There are instances where this affects the procedure described to some degree. For example, the power steering pipe routing is the same on all cars, except where it connects into the steering rack - there are extra-long pipes on the RHD version. We have tried to cover these differences throughout the book, and where necessary we have shown a drawing of the LHD version for comparison with the photographs, but there may be further minor variations which were not apparent during the photographic project.

THE WORK AREA AND STORAGE FACILITIES

3 On occasions, you may need to work on your car on the roadside in the event of a breakdown, or if you do not have access to a garage. For simple procedures this may be acceptable, but if a major repair or overhaul is envisaged, you should make strenuous efforts to find somewhere under cover. If absolutely unavoidable, you could remove major assemblies outside, but any dismantling work should take place under some sort of roof.

4 Most of us will be working inside a normal domestic garage with restricted floor area and ceiling height. Before you start work, make sure that you have sufficient room to work comfortably. If you have the same kind of garage that most of us have to use, clear out as much junk as you can (especially on or around the bench area), and arrange your garden tools, bicycles, ski equipment or whatever neatly, and well away from your work area. Try to keep at least one side of the garage clear of domestic items.

5 You will need plenty of light as well. Make sure you have adequate general lighting, with extra lighting over the workbench, plus one or two inspection lights for use around and under the car and a flashlight for use in confined spaces.

6 Don't forget that you will need somewhere to store removed parts safely, and this requirement will vary according to what you intend to do. In most cases, you can lay out the parts on shelves or in boxes, though some of the bigger assemblies, especially things like the dash panel, seats or the hood will obviously require much more space.

7 If you are going to undertake a major overhaul which entails removal of the engine and transmission, you will need around twice the area required to park the car, plus adequate access to allow the engine/transmission assembly to be removed. You will need to assess the likely space requirement and make suitable arrangements before you start work.

8 Set aside an area where you can leave major parts or assemblies safely, with no risk of accidental damage. You will know best how you can arrange this according to your own circumstances. You may be planning to carry out major work over an extended period, maybe over the Winter months. If so, plan some kind of long-term storage for removed parts, with dust sheets to cover removed major assemblies or body parts until they are needed again. We won't bother describing some utopian home workshop - just try to give it a little thought before you start.

9 The seasoned home mechanic will instinctively collect handy containers - plastic tubs and resealable plastic bags are great for tiny, easily lost parts, and cardboard cartons are good for bigger parts. If money is no object, get some stackable plastic bins.

10 Use PVC electrical tape or masking tape to identify parts, hose and wiring connections, etc as they are removed - you can write on the tape or on the part itself with a fine-point indelible marker pen. You can also use card or paper labels for this. Have a notepad handy for making simple sketches of how specific parts fit together or how wiring or hoses are routed. Avoid pens that use water-based inks which will rub off easily. Also avoid using glass jars for storage - they break easily.

11 If you are unfamiliar with car repair work, the value of marking things cannot be overstressed - you will be surprised how easily it is to get confused about which wire or bolt goes where, just

a few hours after you disconnected them. In many cases you can make life easier for yourself by refitting bolts and screws as you remove them, either screwing them loosely back into position after removing the component they retain, or in the case of covers, pushing the screw back through the cover and through a piece of corrugated card. When you get round to installing the part, the fasteners will be in the correct relative positions - this is especially important where you have similar screws or bolts of varying length.

HOSE CONNECTIONS

12 You will encounter hose connections during many procedures on the car, and the way you deal with them will depend to some extent on the function of the hose.

Cooling system hoses

13 **Warning!** If the engine has been run within the last hour or so, the engine coolant will be hot and under pressure. Removing the radiator filler or coolant reservoir caps, or disconnecting any hose can result in the water boiling as pressure is released, resulting in scalding steam being ejected. Always allow the engine to cool before removing either cap. Wear eye protection, gloves and overalls for safety if there is any doubt. Place some thick rag over the radiator cap and turn it slowly counterclockwise until it reaches the first stop position. Wait until pressure has vented before removing the cap completely.

14 **Caution!** Before you disconnect any hose, you will need to drain the cooling system ☞ 6/2.

15 The coolant hoses are generally secured by spring clips, and these should be moved clear of the stub over which the hose is fitted before you attempt to remove the hose. Use pliers to grasp the clip ends, squeezing them together to release the grip on the hose. Slide the clip an inch or so along the hose until it lies clear of the stub, then release it.

16 To free the hose from its stub, always try to push it off, using a screwdriver blade to lever it. If you try pulling on the hose you will only tighten the grip on the stub, and hoses rarely come off this way. If it has been in place a long time, the hose may be stuck on the stub. If necessary, try working a small screwdriver blade under the hose end if access permits.

17 As a last resort, cut off the old hose by slitting it lengthways with a craft knife (**Warning!** Watch your fingers!) being careful not to score into the stub end. Of course, if you have to do this the hose will be destroyed, so make sure that you have a new hose of the correct type before you take drastic action ☞ 6/4.

Fuel system hoses

18 The fuel system hoses can be approached in much the same way as described above for the cooling system, though of course they are considerably smaller in size. Although the contents are not hot, they are normally under a lot of pressure, and you must always depressurize the fuel system before you start.

19 **Warning!** Whenever the fuel system is disconnected, fuel vapor will be present. Be aware of the potential fire hazard. Have available a fire extinguisher of the type approved for automotive fires. Make sure that the working area is well ventilated - working in a poorly ventilated building will increase the risk of a dangerous buildup of fuel vapor. We do not recommend that you carry out fuel system work with the vehicle over an access pit - fuel vapor is heavier than air and will collect in the access pit where it will persist for some time, presenting a significant fire hazard.

20 **Warning!** Before commencing work which requires disconnection of the fuel hoses or related parts it is essential to release fuel system pressure. Even if the engine has not been run for a while, high pressure remains in the system until the following procedure has been undertaken.

21 Working inside the car, remove the two screws which secure the access cover around the lower section of the steering column. Unclip and remove the cover to gain access to the fuel circuit opening relay. On our UK market project car, the relay could be identified by its yellow color. On cars built for other markets, the relay may differ slightly in appearance, and might be confused with other relays in the vicinity.

22 Start the engine, then unplug the wiring connector from the relay assumed to be the opening relay and wait for about a minute. If you've got the right relay, the engine will stall due to fuel starvation - if necessary, repeat this process on the other relays until you get the right one. Once the engine has stalled, the fuel system is depressurized.

23 Turn off the ignition switch and plug the relay back into the connector, then refit the inspection cover. Isolate the electrical system by disconnecting the battery negative (-) terminal in the trunk after disabling the stereo security system. Open the fuel filler flap and release the fuel filler cap to prevent fuel vapor pressure building up in the tank.

24 When disconnecting any fuel line, cover it with a rag to catch any fuel spray. Once a fuel line is disconnected, plug the open end to prevent dirt getting into the system. Golf tees work fine for this, or if you don't play golf, try using small bolts of the appropriate diameter.

25 If you need to connect a fuel pressure gauge to the system for a check under pressure, **always** secure the connection with a suitable hose clip or it may be forced apart under system pressure - this applies equally to plugged hose ends which are under fuel system pressure.

26 After work on the fuel system is complete, it is preferable to prime the fuel system to avoid excessive engine cranking - remember that the standard Miata/MX5 battery is tiny by normal automotive standards, and has little reserve capacity.

27 Check that all residual fuel vapor has dispersed, then reconnect the battery negative (-) terminal. Open the diagnosis socket cover (mounted on the left inner wing near the suspension turret and clearly marked). Refer to the table inside the cover, and connect pins **F/P** and **GND** using a short insulated jumper wire.

28 Turn on the ignition switch for about ten seconds and check for fuel leaks around any connection which has been disturbed. If you want to check that the pump is running, open the fuel filler and listen at the opening while the system is priming. A high-pitched whine indicates pump operation. Turn the ignition switch off, disconnect the jumper wire and close the diagnosis socket cover.

29 For full details of fuel system working procedures ☞ 5/13.

Brake hoses

30 Before disconnecting any part of the brake system, make sure that you have any necessary replacement parts ready, or the car will be immobilized until you can obtain them. You will also need a supply of fresh hydraulic fluid of the correct specification; SAE J1703 or FMVSS 116, DOT-3. You will also need to bleed air from the brake system after making any disconnection ☞ 9/2.

31 **Warning!** Hydraulic fluid is harmful if swallowed or if it gets into the eyes or bloodstream. If any of this things happen, get prompt medical attention. Avoid skin contact with the fluid and wash contaminated skin promptly. Wear protective gloves when working with brake fluid - particularly if you have open cuts.

32 **Caution!** Hydraulic fluid may damage any painted finish or plastic parts it contacts. Take care to avoid contact, and wash off any accidental spills immediately using detergent or denatured alcohol (meths).

33 If you need to disconnect any of the metal brake pipes, be aware of the risk of corrosion at the union. In cases of severe corrosion, it is not uncommon for the pipe to be frozen (seized) inside the union, in which case it is likely that the pipe will twist off as the union is unscrewed - this is no real problem if you were intending to fit a new pipe anyway, but beware of the union twisting off if you don't have a new pipe ready to fit. As the union is freed, there will be a little fluid leakage. Don't worry too much about this, but use some rag to catch the spills to avoid damage to the paintwork or plastic parts in the vicinity.

34 Where a brake hose is to be removed, Slacken the flare nut which secures it to the body bracket, then withdraw the retaining clip to release the chassis end. Once this is free, unscrew the hose union bolt at the caliper end and remove the hose.

35 Install the hose using new copper washers at the union. Make sure the union locating peg engages correctly, then tighten the union bolt to the specified torque figure. Be sure that suspension or steering movement will not cause damage to the hose. Bleed air from the system.

36 For detailed information on the brake hydraulic system ☞ 9/1-4.

GASKETS AND SEALS

37 You will normally need to fit new gaskets and seals whenever you disturb them, unless advised differently in the text. With this in mind, make sure that you get the appropriate parts ready *before* you start.

38 You will need to remove all traces of old

gaskets before you fit new ones. You can use a gasket remover for this (available from auto parts stores) or you can carefully scrape off any residue, using a soft metal scraper. Beware of using an old screwdriver to remove gaskets - this often causes scoring of the joint surfaces, and will usually result in subsequent leaks.

39 Unless advised to the contrary, fit the new gasket dry. Gasket cement or jointing compound is rarely required, though we like to keep a tube of silicone rubber sealant handy. This can be used to seal a joint where a new gasket or O-ring is not available, or in cases where light damage to a sealing face is discovered, but must be used with discretion; it will not withstand direct combustion heat, and is dissolved by fuel.

40 Note also that if it gets into the engine it can obstruct oil passages with catastrophic results; never apply more than a thin film, and wipe excess away from the inside edge of the joint face before assembly. You should also leave the sealant to harden slightly for around ten minutes before you assemble the parts.

41 O-rings are used extensively to seal passages and small components, and again should be replaced if disturbed. Even if they seem to be in good condition, the rubber will have compressed and hardened, and it is very likely that they will leak if reused. It is well worth having a selection of O-rings in the workshop; these can be purchased from auto parts stores and are inexpensive.

42 You can also buy O-ring kits which allow you to make up your own O-rings of any diameter. The material is cut to size with a craft knife or scalpel blade, and then joined using an isocyanate adhesive. This system is reputed to work very well, though we would have some reservations where the seal is of vital importance.

43 Oil seals lead a particularly hard life, and should always be replaced during an overhaul. As with O-rings, the rubber material hardens with age and the effects of heat, and in addition, the fine seal lip will wear down and so will grip the shaft less securely. If the old seal is badly damaged, rather than just worn down, check the shaft or component on which it was fitted for damage. If necessary, replace the damaged part before you fit a new seal, or you will find yourself repeating the overhaul in a short while.

44 Make a note of the fitting direction of the seal during removal, and make sure that you fit the new one in the same position. In most cases, the seal case is located by a shoulder or rib in the outer bore, but if this is not present, normal practice is to fit the seal flush with the outer face of the casting or component which carries it. Before you refit the shaft through the seal, lubricate it and the seal lip to prevent damage during installation and to provide lubrication in use.

45 A seal should be pressed home carefully, making sure that it enters its bore squarely. If you force the seal in at an angle, the usual result is damage to the seal's metal casing and this will often result in leakage. Use a blunt tubular drift to press the seal home - sockets of the appropriate diameter are very useful for this.

SCREWS, BOLTS & NUTS

46 All threaded fasteners should be checked carefully before they are reused, rejecting any which show signs of wear or damage to the threads. If you need to fit new bolts, it is preferable to obtain these through a Mazda dealer; this way you know that not only is the bolt of the right size, it is also of the correct material - something not readily apparent from casual examination. If you purchase new bolts or nuts elsewhere, a reputable supplier will be able to check that the replacement is of the correct material if you take along the old one when ordering.

47 Where the bolt or screw fits directly into a casting or captive nut, clean out any dirt or oil from the threads with degreasing solvent, then blow the threads clear with compressed air. Failure to do so can prevent the bolt or screw seating fully, or can damage the bolt/screw or casting threads. Even a small amount of dirt on the threads can prevent the correct torque setting being applied. In some instances, the bolt threads should be given a light coating of copper grease during installation. This is especially important where they are subject to high temperatures, as is the case with exhaust system fasteners.

48 Plain nuts can be reused if they are in good condition, but special nuts should normally be replaced. This includes Nyloc and other self-locking nuts, which rely on the plastic ring insert to prevent them loosening in service; once used, the insert's grip is much diminished.

49 In most cases, you will find specific torque wrench settings in the text, and these should be adhered to closely. The settings assume clean, dry and undamaged threads; you cannot accurately torque-tighten where there is any sort of damage or obstruction. If you accidentally overtighten a fastener, or in cases where you need to check-tighten after an earlier overhaul, back the fastener off by a quarter turn, then tighten to the specified setting.

50 Where castellated nuts are fitted, always tighten to the lower end of the specified torque range and check whether the cotter (split) pin can be fitted. If necessary, tighten a little more until the pin can be slid home; never back the nut off unless instructed to the contrary.

51 Mechanical locking methods, like locking tabs, or cotter pins used to secure castellated nuts should always be replaced. Use a locking tab or cotter pin of the correct size or diameter, and always bend it over correctly to ensure security. With cotter pins, use pliers to bend over the pin ends, and cut off any excess with side cutters. In the case of locking tabs, bend the tab up against the side of the bolt or nut hexagon, then tap it firmly into position with a small hammer.

TORQUE-TIGHTENING BY FEEL

52 There are many occasions when working on your car that you will run into problems when attempting to tighten down fasteners to a specified torque setting. Usually, this is because you are unable to reach the fastener in question using a torque wrench.

53 Once upon a time, professional mechanics took pride in being able to tighten even vital fasteners like head nuts or bearing cap bolts by feel, with no ill effects. These guys were good. Because they did this day in, day out, for years: they got to be pretty accurate with this approach. They may have wrecked a few threads as apprentices, but the machinery that they worked on was so tough and forgiving that a bit of practice usually meant that they could tighten down reliably and without damage ninety nine times in a hundred.

54 However, times and technology change, and modern vehicles are designed and built to much finer tolerances. The use of light alloy castings in place of cast iron gives little room for making mistakes; the old approach of over-engineering, with the resulting latitude in torque ranges is long gone. If you try to tighten a bolt until it 'feels about right' you stand a good chance of stripping threads or worse.

55 If you've ever sheared off a bolt by overtightening, you will have a good idea of how much time-wasting and hassle results from a simple mistake. Here are a few tips (we know what we're talking about here - we've seen Wally shear off those bolts and strip those threads!) -

- ***Rule 1: Use the torque wrench.*** *Always make the effort to use the torque wrench where a tightening torque is specified.*
- ***Rule 2: Are you sure you can't reach the bolt?*** *- try a shorter extension and try again. You may need to play around with your socket accessories a little. Try using flexible joints. You may find that special ball-end sockets and accessories would give that little bit of movement you need, or you could try using 3/8 in drive parts instead of 1/2 in drive.*
- ***Rule 3: OK, you can't use the torque wrench.*** *So make one that you can use. If you can't get in there with a conventional torque wrench, improvise. We have made our own 'torque crescent wrench' before - here's how:*

  Get a strip of steel and drill a hole in one end so that you can hook a spring balance into it. Fix it onto a crescent wrench / open ended spanner / combination wrench or whatever you can fit on the bolt head, using a couple of worm-drive hose clips. Position the strip so that the hole for the spring balance is 12 inches from the center of the jaws. Fit the tool to the bolt head, hook up the spring balance.

  Now, if you need to apply 24 lbf ft (used to be expressed as foot-pounds) remember a foot-pound is a force of one pound applied to a lever one foot in length: pull on the spring balance until you see 24 lb on the scale and you've done it.
- ***Rule 4: Use your brain instead.*** *Let us explain that. Your brain is pretty good at remembering things, especially short-term. If you really can't get to that bolt head with anything but a wrench, find a nut and bolt*

of the same size and clamp the nut in a vise. Screw in the bolt and torque-tighten it to the specified pressure. Hold the torque wrench in a position that corresponds with the length of the wrench you intend to use on the real thing, and try to gauge how hard you need to pull it.

Do this a few times with the torque wrench, then try it using the plain wrench. Use the torque wrench to check how much torque you applied. Repeat until you get good at attaining the correct pressure every time. Now rush over to the car before you forget, and apply precisely the right torque to your inaccessible fastener.

ELECTRICAL CONNECTIONS AND WIRE COLOR CODING

56 The Mazda's wiring is color coded to make tracing and troubleshooting easier, and to assist identification. We have used Mazda's abbreviations throughout this book, so that there should be no confusion on this point. The wire colors and their abbreviations are shown in this table:

CODE	COLOR	CODE	COLOR
B	Black	O	Orange
BR	Brown	P	Pink
G	Green	R	Red
GY	Gray	V	Violet
L	Blue	W	White
LB	Light blue	Y	Yellow
LG	Light green		

T2/56 STANDARD MAZDA WIRE COLOR CODING.

Note that where more than one color is indicated, for example LB/Y, the main wire color is shown first (light blue) and the second, or tracer, color is shown after the slash (yellow). Physical tracing of an individual wire is next to impossible on a system of this complexity (we reckoned that some of the main harness sections we encountered must have held a hundred or more individual wires, all tightly bound into a harness, but spurring off here and there. You can check continuity between each end of a wire, but you can't be certain of its route through the harness. If you come across a broken wire, your only alternative to fitting a new harness section is to cut off each end of the wire in question, and to add a new wire to bypass the damaged one.

57 In fairness, modern wiring is of such high quality that you would be unlucky to experience problems in the life of the car. In most cases any fault will be found at the wire ends - usually at the connector terminal, or will turn out to be a component failure. If you do find an internally broken or intermittent wire, try to trace the route of that part of the harness, and tape a new wire of the same size and, preferably, of the same color as the original to the outside of the harness with PVC electrical tape.

58 If you want to add electrical accessories to the car, try to do so intelligently. When fitting accessory items it is tempting to do the minimum of dismantling to get access, and this invariably means that later access to some part of the car will be difficult because of straggling wires. Try to use connectors of the type already used on the car, so that panels or assemblies can still be removed for servicing.

59 Be aware that if you patch into existing wiring using Scotchloks or similar snap-together wire connectors, you may be imposing too much load on that circuit or fuse. Patching in like this is just about unavoidable, but think about what you are doing - for example, if you hook into the instrument panel lighting circuit to run the rear window demister on your new hardtop, you will be drawing power through a 10A fuse, so don't be surprised when it blows.

60 If you need to cut an accessory wire in the course of removing other components, you should reconnect it in a way that allows for subsequent dismantling. We prefer to use screw-type connectors - they seem to work more reliably than the Scotchlok type. Cut the wire and bare the ends using an insulation stripping tool. Fit the bared ends into the connector and tighten the screws to secure them. If you use Scotchloks, make sure that you use the correct size - if too small you will cut through some of the conductor strands and restrict the carrying capacity of the circuit. Conversely, if the connector is too big it will be a loose fit on the conductor and may cause intermittent contact.

WRESTLING WITH PLASTIC TWO-PIECE PANEL FASTENERS

Crosshead type

61 When you work on some areas of the car, it seems as if the Mazda Miata/MX5 is held together with these fasteners. They look for all the world like crosshead screws through cup washers, but once you look closely, they are actually two parts of a widely-used fastener arrangement for holding access covers and the like. The idea is that during assembly, the cross-headed center pin pushes into a split outer part which is wedge shaped internally. As the pin is pushed home it forces the outer part to expand in its hole and lock the panel (or whatever) in position. The crossheaded pin actually has a thread of sorts, and presumably is intended to unscrew to permit removal. Great idea, except that it doesn't really work!

62 What really happens is that the screw part just turns in the outer section, and that means that you can't shift either of them without destroying them. We came across so many of these little devils that we took the trouble to work out a surefire method of shifting them. We figured that the outer wedge-shaped piece was failing to grip the screw thread because it was a slack fit in the panel hole. What you need to do is work a flat screwdriver blade under the 'washer' part. This pulls it down and makes it grip the screw, which can then be (very carefully) removed.

63 Don't push on the screwdriver when turning the crosshead pin, or you will just force it back into the outer part. You have to be careful though, the screw slot is very soft and easily damaged.

Plain head type

64 This type of fastener is similar to the crosshead type described above, but it has no thread on the pin and a plain head. To remove the fastener, you need to pry out the center pin, using a small screwdriver under the head. Take care not to damage the pin head or surround when you do this, especially where the fastener is in a prominent position.

65 Once the center pin has been popped out, the grip of the surround is released and you will find that it can be lifted out easily. When installing this type of fastener, grip the top of the pin so that it can be pushed back into place, then depress the pin head to lock it there.

General purpose trim fasteners

66 These are low-tech, low cost versions of the types described above, and are widely used to secure odd bits of trim and the carpet sections. They have broad circular heads and are a simple push-fit in the associated panel. The only thing to remember with this type of fastener is that you need to lift them out from under the heads, near the shank of the pin; if you do this near the outside of the head you'll probably find that it breaks off.

67 You can use a pair of screwdriver blades to lever them out, or if you have a pair of snipe (needle)-nose pliers with cranked ends, these work very well instead. Where the fasteners are used to hold carpets, do not attempt to get them out by pulling on the carpet; this usually just pulls the carpet over the head of the pin, and you will then have to remove it by levering anyway.

Specialized plastic clips

68 There are many examples of plastic clips and stops which are pushed through holes in the bodywork. In most cases we note how they are best removed, but as a general rule, they will be found to have small tabs which spring out to lock them in place. Always check around the back of the pin for these tabs, and squeeze them together to free the clip.

Screw covers and blanking pieces

69 Where a visible screw head would be considered unsightly, you will probably find a small blanking cover fitted into the trim panel secured by the screw underneath. Again, we have generally described how these fit and how you need to remove them - the exact method varies a little.

70 Mostly, you can pry them out with a fine screwdriver blade, but be very careful not to lose them as they fly off - keep your hand or a finger over them to prevent this.

71 In some cases, these covers should only be fitted in one direction, and need to be removed at a specific point. In one or two examples, they are

locked in position and need to be freed by depressing a locking pin or tab. It is not always obvious exactly where or how to do this.

72 We think that we have found and described all such fittings, but if we missed one or two types and there are no specific instructions in the text, do as we did, and work around the clip or cover to establish where it is held, and from this deduce how to go about freeing it. Usually, if you can't reach behind to free a locking tab, you need to lift the edge of a panel and free a hidden tab below it.

3. JACKING AND SUPPORTING THE CAR

1 There are a number of operations described in this manual which will require you to work under the car, and you will need to make some provision for this. In an ideal world, we would all have vehicle lifts, but most of us must make do with less exotic equipment. When we worked on our project vehicle, we deliberately restricted ourselves to the use of equipment available to the average enthusiast owner, even though this made photographic access more difficult.

2 Unless you happen to have an access pit in the floor of your garage, you'll need to raise the car high enough to permit good working access below the body, while preserving a good level of safety. **Warning!** Don't forget that a car is heavy - if it collapses while you're under it, you will be killed or badly injured, so don't take chances.

3 We used a normal small wheeled hydraulic jack and four large safety stands to achieve good access during the project. You can purchase a suitable jack from tool or auto parts stores, or from mail order sources. We recommend that you avoid the smallest of the jacks supplied for home use. These have a capacity of 1500 Kg / 1 1/2 tons, which is adequate, but have a restrictive lift range of only around 200 mm / 8 inches. The type we used had a capacity of 2000 Kg / 2 tons and a lift range of just under 300 mm / 12 inches.

4 You'll find that the lift range is significant when you need to raise the car enough to work underneath. The further the jack can lift, the less you will need to jack in stages, which will save you a lot of time. As rule of thumb, buy the biggest lift capacity you can afford.

5 The safety stands come in various sizes too, and again, the rule is the bigger the better. These are not only stronger than the smaller types, they allow you to raise the vehicle much higher, and every extra inch helps. There are a few operations on the car which will require around 460 mm / 18 inches clearance underneath, and in all cases, more space means more comfortable working conditions. Remember that if you use a crawler board, you lose a little clearance.

6 + Jacking the vehicle to any height takes time because it needs to be done in stages. We jacked each end of the vehicle in turn, supporting it on a pair of stands placed under the vehicle jacking points with small wood blocks to prevent damage to the sill area. Once we had raised one

3/6a Use wood strips to protect paint.

3/6b Chock wheels.

end part way, we positioned the first pair of stands, lowered the jack so that the vehicle was supported on the stands, and then moved to the other end of the car. **Warning!** If you are only jacking one end or side of the car, remember to chock those wheels which remain on the ground.

7 Next, we repeated the jacking operation and fitted a second pair of stands. Then we moved back to the other end and repeated the process until we had the car high enough to be able to work underneath. **Warning!** Don't be tempted to jack too much at each stage, because the vehicle will become unstable, and you may run out of jacking range.

8 + On one or two occasions we had to use large pieces of lumber positioned under the jack wheels to get enough lift to raise the vehicle fully, because the small hydraulic jack we had could only lift around a foot or so each time. This is safe enough if you take great care to position the blocks accurately and make sure that the jack is kept at the exact center of the car. At the front of the car we positioned the jack pad under the crossmember to the rear of the engine. At the back we used the differential casing as a lifting point. As luck would have it, the heavy finning at the bottom of

3/8a Jack pad at center of crossmember.

3/8b Jack pad at center of diff. casing.

the casing fitted neatly into the jack pad, locating it very securely.

9 If you decide to use our method, work carefully and methodically, checking that the supports are absolutely secure at each stage. Also, be sure to place wooden chocks on each side of the road wheels before starting, and remember that once all four wheels have been raised clear of the ground, excessive jacking at either end might topple the car off its stands.

10 We suggest that you proceed cautiously, raising each end in turn by a few inches so that the car stays more or less level and minimizes this risk. It may be tempting to go for the maximum lift each time, but you increase the risk of toppling if you do so. Finally, give the car a really good shake to check that there is no danger of it collapsing on top of you, before you venture underneath.

11 **Caution!** Finally, a word on where not to jack. The car has four reinforced jacking points located near the ends of each sill. These are mostly intended for wheel changing, and the small scissor jack supplied with the car has a slotted pad which fits over the reinforced seam sections. You will rarely use these points for jacking during mainte-

3/10 Car safely supported.

nance, because this would only allow you to raise one corner of the car. These jack points also provide ideal positions for safety stands, however.

12 You may have noted the longitudinal box sections just inboard of the jacking points. These are strengthening sections which give rigidity to the floor. They are definitely not suitable for jacking, and any attempt to raise the car at these points will simply collapse the box section.

13 There are a few operations which will require you to have the car raised enough for access underneath, but with the car supported on

its wheels. An example of this is where work is carried out on the suspension. After completing the overhaul you will need to have the car resting on its wheels while the suspension pivots are tightened. For this you need to use fabricated steel wheel ramps. You will need to fit the wheels, position the ramps below them and then lower the car onto the ramps.

14 For other tasks where temporary access is required and access to the suspension is not necessary, you can in theory, drive the car up onto the ramps. In practice, however, the ramps usually skid across the floor as you attempt to do this, and

3/14 Ramps allow good access.

we would advise jacking the car and then lowering it onto the stands. When doing this, position the ramp end nearest the garage door. That way you can drive the car off when work is finished.

4. CLEANING COMPONENTS

1 With just about any overhaul procedure on the car it is advisable to clean down the area concerned before you start. Not only will this make the work more pleasurable, it will minimize the risk of dirt getting into the assembly in question.

2 For large areas, such as the underside of the car or engine compartment, a hot pressure wash is a good starting point. You can either use this type of facility at a local carwash, or you could use a domestic pressure wash instead. Take care to protect vulnerable areas like electrical components or connectors from the ingress of water. These are usually splashproof, but will not withstand direct high pressure jets.

3 Tape up such areas or cover vulnerable components with plastic bags before you start. **Caution!** Remember that if you saturate connectors under the hood you stand a good chance of damaging electronic components if power is applied while they are wet. If you think this may have happened, disconnect and dry out the affected part before attempting to start the engine.

4 If you pressure wash the suspension, try to keep the water away from the brake components, or you may find that the brakes will not work until they have dried out. If you think that you have soaked the brakes, drive very slowly with the brake pedal depressed lightly. The heat generated will dry off the disc and pads.

5 During dismantling, use a proprietary degreasing solvent to clean parts off as you work. Follow the maker's directions when using these products, and never use gasoline for cleaning purposes unless specifically advised in the text; it is dangerous and illegal to use gasoline as a cleaning solvent in some areas. When disposing of used solvents, do so responsibly with regard to the environment. In most areas, your local authority will be happy to advise about disposal methods and may provide such facilities.

6 When working on brake parts, use only brake cleaner or denatured alcohol (methylated spirit). Use of any other type of solvent may cause damage or deterioration of the seals, with a consequent risk of brake failure. **Warning!** Brake friction materials usually contain asbestos which is hazardous if inhaled as dust. Wear gloves when handling dirty brake parts, and clean down only with brake cleaner, disposing of contaminated rags or wipes safely. Never use compressed air to clean any brake part.

5. BUYING NEW PARTS

1 When buying parts you will need to make a few decisions about where you source them. In the main, you will probably want to obtain parts through your Mazda dealer, and this is certainly the safest option; you know that the parts you buy will fit correctly and be of good quality. If the car is still under warranty, use of non-genuine parts may invalidate it, so bear this in mind too.

2 + + Major parts and assemblies will probably have to be obtained through a Mazda dealer throughout the life of the car. To save time when ordering parts, and to make sure that you get the correct part for your particular car, have ready as much information as possible. The main things to note are the VIN (Vehicle Identification Number) and the engine model and number. On automatic transmission cars, you should also note the model

5/2a VIN number here and ...

5/2b ... stamped into firewall (bulkhead).

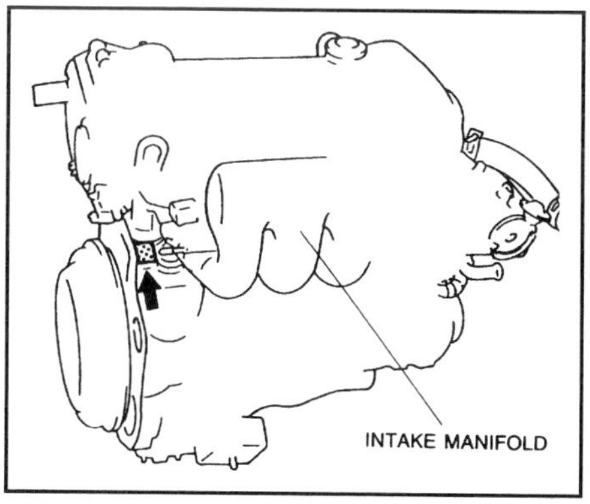

D5/2A ENGINE MODEL & NUMBER ARE HERE.

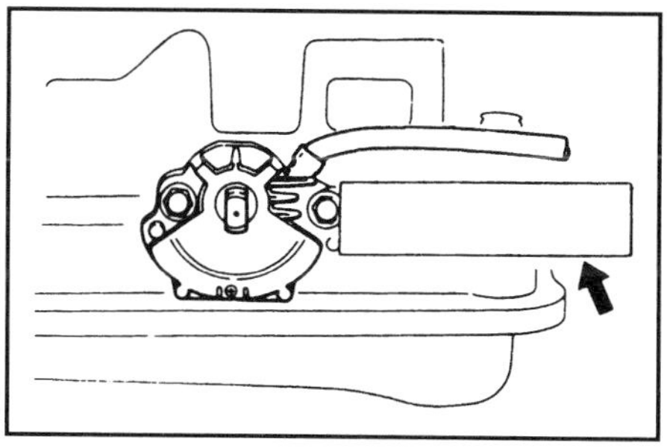

D5/2B AUTO. TRANS. MODEL & NUMBER HERE.

and number of the transmission. You will find this information in the locations pictured.

3 Your Mazda dealer can tell a lot about your car from these numbers. For example, they will indicate any instances where a modification is required to rectify minor defects found after the car was built (major defects will have been covered by the normal recall procedures operating in most countries). If you order a part and a revised fitment is available, your dealer will be able to advise on this. This type of information is not generally available from other suppliers, and this alone helps offset the slightly higher prices charged by dealers.

4 You can purchase consumable items needed for maintenance procedures from other sources. Items such as spark plugs, oil, and light bulbs can be found in most auto parts stores and some gas stations, and this may be more convenient and less expensive than a visit to your dealer. Remember that you will need to check that any parts or materials obtained from such sources are suitable for use in your Mazda.

5 Auto parts stores will carry application charts and lists for many of the products they stock, and these will provide some guidance about suitability. Don't forget though, that these lists are compiled by third-party manufacturers, and may not be 100% reliable in all cases. The store is unlikely to be able to make too much sense of the vehicle details, but you should take these with you anyway - they may help. If at all possible, take with you the old part and check that the new component is identical.

6 The bigger auto parts stores may also carry things like clutches, brake parts, pistons and valves, though they tend to concentrate more on parts for mainstream vehicles than for cars like the Miata.

Prices are often lower than they would be from a franchised dealer, and the quality of the parts is generally good. The down side is that you can never be sure if non-original parts will perform or last as well as genuine parts. If you fit a non-original clutch disc, it may wear out more quickly than the original, and this will mean you need to fit another one sooner.

7 With items like brake pads, you can rarely tell by looking at them if the pad material is of the correct grade, and in extreme cases this has been known to be downright dangerous. We are not saying that non-original parts are no good; many are fine, and reputable stores will not sell you substandard parts. Do use your discretion, however, and don't be tempted to spoil a finely balanced car by using poor quality parts just to save a little money.

8 Finally, don't forget specialist suppliers like auto-electrical specialists, tire specialists and performance car and tuning specialists. The range of services offered by these companies is very wide and very variable, but often they may be able to supply parts or services that even franchised dealers have trouble with. We cannot give specific recommendations here - the best policy is to use tried and trusted local companies. Personal recommendation counts for far more than impressive trading premises in this respect.

6. TOOLS & EQUIPMENT

1 We've tried to base this manual on the type of tools that most enthusiasts will already have, and this is a difficult thing to define. You will not get very far using the tools which came with the car - they are intended for the most simple roadside repairs only, and few enthusiast owners will wish to travel far without a better selection in the trunk. On the other hand, only the most dedicated owner will have a fully equipped professional workshop at their disposal.

2 If you are experienced in home car repairs and maintenance, you will already have the basic hand tools you need for almost any job on the Miata/MX5 (we assume that you will have metric sized tools). Where you need more specialized tools, this is indicated in the text.

3 If you are a newcomer to the delights of home maintenance and repair, we suggest that you begin building your tool set slowly. Don't be tempted by offers of hundreds of tools for next to nothing - they are badly made from inferior materials, and are usually worse than useless. Buy only quality tools as and when you can afford and need them, sticking to known, quality brands - you won't regret it.

4 Wrenches should cover the range 8 mm to around 19 mm - you will rarely need larger or smaller sizes than this. You will need both crescent and box end wrenches, and if money is tight, you can get both in the form of combination wrenches, with a box end and crescent wrench combined in the same tool.

5 You will also need a 1/2 in drive socket set covering the range 8 mm to around 30 mm. The set will come with a range of extensions, T-bars and a ratchet, and you can expand on this as the need arises. Again, go for quality in preference to quantity, or you will eventually end up buying the set over again in replacement parts - a very expensive way of buying sockets. Just about every fastener will require torque tightening, so you will need a torque wrench. The preset type are best, but if money is tight, the simple beam type wrenches will suffice.

6 A range of screwdrivers with both slotted and crosshead tips will be required. Be especially careful with crosshead screwdrivers; these come in a variety of tip profiles, and you need to be careful that the type you choose fits snugly in the Japanese pattern screws. Many cheap brands will be a sloppy fit and will tear out the screw heads. You will need several sizes in each type, and on occasions you may also need specialized screwdrivers to reach awkward or inaccessible screws.

7 In addition to the above, you will require pliers, needle-nosed pliers and a pair of electrical side cutters, plus self-grip pliers (Vise Grip or similar). On infrequent occasions you will need snap ring pliers, and this is one area where a cheap set with interchangeable tips will be adequate. You will also need items like Allen (socket) screw wrenches, feeler gauges and a spark plug gapping / adjusting tool.

8 To supplement the basic list of hand tools described above, there are other pieces of equipment that you will find essential for all but the most simple dismantling and installation work. We suggest that you acquire these as and when you need them to spread the cost a little. In most instances, we have indicated where these tools will be required:

General workshop tools

Wheeled hydraulic jack
Safety stands
Fabricated steel wheel ramps
Bench (with engineer's vise)
Large and small hammers (ball pein type)
1/2 in cold chisel
Assorted drifts and punches (as required)
Plastic or rubber faced hammer
Steel straight edge and scribing tool
Hacksaw and blades
Assorted files and abrasive papers
Inspection light

Specialized tools

Multipurpose puller
Valve spring compressor
Piston ring compressor
Impact driver
Balljoint separator
Engine hoist

Measuring equipment

Vernier caliper
Internal and external micrometer
Dial gauge and stand, with clamp or magnetic base
Steel tape rule

Test equipment

Ohmmeter, voltmeter and ammeter (or a multimeter, which will cover ohms, volts amps and more besides)
Jumper leads and continuity tester
Timing light (xenon tube type)
Engine compression tester
Thermometer
Spring scale

7. DEALING WITH BREAKDOWNS

INITIAL SAFETY

1 **Warning!** If your car suffers a roadside breakdown, the first consideration is safety - yours, your passenger's and that of other road users. If you can, get the car off the road, or at least try to stop where visibility is good. Don't forget that what might appear to be a clear view for a good distance while you are stationary, may seem a lot different from another vehicle approaching at speed. If your car has hazard warning lights, use them, even in daylight. In many European countries, all cars have to carry warning triangles by law. These should be placed well in advance of your car. Anything which catches the attention of approaching drivers is a good thing.

CHECK THE PROBLEM

2 Try to work out why the car has stopped. In some cases (punctured tires or an empty fuel tank) this will be pretty obvious, but if there has been some mechanical failure, it will help you or the recovery driver if you can give some indication of what went wrong. If you heard any unusual noises, felt vibration or smelt or saw smoke just before the car broke down, it is likely to be significant. For more information on troubleshooting ☞ 15.

GETTING HELP

3 In all but the simplest cases you will need professional assistance to repair or recover your car. How you go about getting that help will depend on your circumstances at the time. If you have a carphone, or there is a phone nearby, there is no real problem. If, on the other hand, you have broken down miles from anywhere at night, you'll need help getting help!

4 **Warning!** Unfortunately, you can never be quite sure of the motives of the driver who may stop when you have broken down. It is beyond the scope of this book to get into this difficult area in detail, but the bottom line is to be wary, especially if you are a lone female. Try to stay in, or very close to the car, and don't be afraid to lock yourself in if you need to. If the other driver is genuinely trying to help you, they won't mind if you ask them to phone or go for help on your behalf, though if you have a bad feeling about the person, it may be better to say that help is already on its way, even if this means you may have to wait longer for help.

TOWING THE CAR

5 This may not be your problem, and a professional recovery driver should know how to deal with your car, but be aware of a couple of important points about your Miata/MX5 which affect towing procedures. We assume that you will comply with any local laws regarding safe towing practice.

Automatic transmission models

6 You should get the car recovered on a breakdown truck if possible. If it has to be towed, you should arrange to have a suspended tow with the **rear** wheels clear of the road. If the car has to be towed from the front, a towing dolly must be fitted under the rear wheels.

7 If you have no option but to tow with all four wheels on the ground, do not tow at more than 35 mph (56 kph) or for more than 35 miles (56 km) or you will damage the transmission. Note also that you should release the parking brake, shift into **N** (neutral) and set the ignition switch to **ACC** before towing commences. If you need to tow any automatic Miata/MX5 for longer distances without a towing dolly, you will have to disconnect the propshaft to isolate the transmission and prevent damage.

Manual transmission models

8 This is generally less of a problem than towing an auto transmission car - you won't damage the transmission by towing. You should, however, release the parking brake, shift into neutral and set the ignition switch to **ACC** before towing commences.

All models

9 Mazda caution that the hooks at the front and rear of the car are for tie-down purposes only and are not designed for towing. They state that damage to the car bodywork may result if these points are used for towing, and they may well be right. The front tie-down hooks lie inside the air intake, and there is every chance that a jerking tow rope would damage the surrounding bodywork. Unfortunately, there is no better towing point that we could find. Mazda acknowledge the problem, but do not suggest any alternative to the tie-down hooks. We can only suggest that you use great caution if you tow from these hooks.

10 If you are steering your Miata/MX5 while being towed by another vehicle (check that it is legal to do this in your area first!), remember that without the engine running, there will be no power to the car's electrical system. You will need electrical power to operate your brake and turn signal lights, but the Mazda's reserve battery capacity is limited. Try not to use the headlights which would rapidly discharge the battery, and where possible, avoid towing at night.

11 Another problem is that without the engine running, the power brake system and the power steering (where fitted) will be inoperative. The steering and brakes will still work, but will require more effort and be less effective, so be prepared for this.

12 Being towed by another car requires a little skill, and unless you trust the driver of the tow car, can be a frightening experience. Before you start out, agree your route and speed, and arrange some sort of signal (such as flashing the headlights) to indicate to the tow car that you wish to stop.

13 When you move off, the tow car should creep forward until the slack in the tow rope is taken up. The driver of the car being towed should use the brakes to make sure that the rope stays taut at all times, and this means that he will have to anticipate when the driver of the tow car is likely to start slowing. To some extent, the car being towed should be braking for both cars. If you can get this to work smoothly, you are unlikely to suffer from the rope breaking, but get it wrong and you will be stopping to join the rope with monotonous regularity. Note also the comments about the risk of damage to the bodywork if you tow from the tie-down hooks - you will minimize this risk if you keep the rope taut.

© Miata Magazine 1990.

8. TECHNICAL SPECIFICATIONS

GENERAL

Dimensions and weights

Overall length .... 3,948 mm (155.4 in)
Overall width .... 1,676 mm (65.9 in)
Overall height .... 1,224 mm (48.2 in)
Wheelbase .... 2,266 mm (89.2 in)
Headroom .... 942 mm (37.1 in)
Legroom .... 1,085 mm (42.7 in)
Shoulder room .... 1,280 mm (50.4 in)
Track:
 Front .... 1,410 mm (55.5 in)
 Rear .... 1,428 mm (56.2 in)
Curb weight
 Manual transmission .... 1,008 kg (2,222 lb)
 Automatic transmission .... 1,034 kg (2,280 lb)

Transmission

Type
 Standard .... 5-speed manual
 Optional .... 4-speed automatic with lockup

Chassis

Type .... Unitary steel body, steel and plastic panels
Suspension .... Fully independent front and rear. Adjustable double-wishbone Coils springs, gas-filled shock absorbers. Front & rear stabilizer bars
Steering .... Rack-and-pinion, optional engine speed-sensing power steering
Brakes .... Power-assisted disc, dual circuit hydraulics
Tires .... P185/60R 14 82H steel-belted radial

Engine - general

Type .... In-line 4-cylinder, dohc
Displacement .... 1597 cc (97 cu in)
Bore .... 78 mm (3.07 in)
Stroke .... 83.6 mm (3.29 in)
Compression ratio
 Manual transmission 9.4:1
 Automatic transmission 9.0:1
Horsepower (SAE net)
 Manual transmission .... 116 @ 6,500 rpm
 Automatic transmission .... 105 @ 6,000 rpm
Torque (SAE net)
 Manual transmission .... 100 lb ft @ 5,500 rpm
 Automatic transmission .... 100 lb ft @ 4,000 rpm
Fuel system .... Multi-port electronic fuel injection
Ignition system .... Electronic (distrubutorless, twin coil)
Control system .... Full ECU control system

ENGINE - DETAIL

Type B6
Combustion chamber type .... Pentroof
Valve system .... Belt-driven, dohc 16 valve
Bore and stroke .... 78.0 X 83.6 mm (3.07-3.29 in)
Total displacement .... 1,597 cc (97.42 cu in)
Compression ratio
 Manual 9.4:1
 Automatic 9.0:1
Valve timing (manual)
 Intake opens at .... 5° BTDC
 Intake closes at .... 51° ABDC
 Exhaust opens at .... 53° BBDC

Exhaust closes at	15° ATDC
Valve timing (automatic)	
Intake opens at	5° BTDC
Intake closes at	40° ABDC
Exhaust opens at	55° BBDC
Exhaust closes at	5° ATDC
Valve clearances	0 (hydraulic lifters)

Cylinder head

Material Aluminum alloy	
Height	133.8-134.0 mm (5.268-5.276 in)
Maximum distortion	0.15 mm (0.006 in)
Grinding limit	0.20 mm (0.008 in)
Cylinder head to HLA clearance	
Standard	0.025-0.066 mm (0.0010-0.0026 in)
Maximum	0.18 mm (0.0071 in)

Valves and guides

Valve head diameter	
Intake	30.9-31.1 mm (1.217-1.224 in)
Exhaust	26.1-26.3 mm (1.028-1.035 in)
Valve head margin width	
Intake	0.9 mm (0.035 in)
Exhaust	1.0 mm (0.039 in)
Valve face angle	45°
Valve length - standard	
Intake	105.29 mm (4.1452 in)
Exhaust	105.39 mm (4.1492 in)
Valve length - minimum	
Intake	104.79 mm (4.1256 in)
Exhaust	104.89 mm (4.1295 in)
Valve stem diameter	
Intake	5.970-5.985 mm (0.2350-0.2356 in)
Exhaust	5.965-5.980 mm (0.2348-0.2354 in)
Valve guide bore diameter	6.01-6.03 mm (0.2366-0.2374 in)
Valve stem to guide clearance	
Intake	0.025-0.060 mm (0.0010-0.0024 in)
Exhaust	0.030-0.065 mm (0.0012-0.0026 in)
Service limit	0.020 mm (0.008 in)
Valve guide projection above head surface	
Intake & exhaust	16.8-17.4 mm (0.0661-0.0685 in)

Valve seats

Valve seat angle	45°
Contact width	0.8-1.4 mm (0.031-0.055 in)
Rebate in head	
Standard	43.5 mm (1.713 in)
Maximum	45.0 mm (1.772 in)

Valve springs

Free length (standard)	
Intake	48.1 mm (1.893 in)
Exhaust	48.3 mm (1.902 in)
Free length (service limit)	
Intake	47.0 mm (1.893 in)
Exhaust	47.3 mm (1.902 in)
Minimum length	
Intake	40.0 mm (1.575 in) under 22.13-25.05 kg load
Exhaust	40.0 mm (1.575 in) under 17.67-20.00 kg load
Out-of-square limit	
Intake	1.68 mm (0.0661 in)
Exhaust	1.69 mm (0.0665 in)
Installed load / height	
Intake	217-246 N (22.1-25.1 kg, 48.6-55.2 lb) / 40 mm (1.575 in)
Exhaust	174-196 N (17.7-20.0 kg, 39.8-44.0 lb) / 40 mm (1.575 in)

Camshafts

Cam height (manual transmission)	
Intake	40.888 mm (1.6098 in)
Service limit	40.688 mm (1.6019 in)
Exhaust	40.889 (1.6098 in)
Service limit	40.689 mm (1.6019
Cam height (automatic transmission)	
Intake	39.984 mm (1.5741 in)
Service limit	39.784 mm (1.5662 in)
Exhaust	40.888 mm (1.6098 in)
Service limit	40.688 mm (1.6019 in)
Camshaft journal diameter	
Standard	25.940-25.965 mm (1.0213-1.0222 in)
Out-of-round limit (US/Canada)	0.03 mm (0.001 in)
Out-of-round limit (except US/Canada)	0.05 mm (0.002 in)
Camshaft bearing oil clearance	
Standard	0.035-0.081 mm (0.0014-0.0032 in)
Service limit	0.15 mm (0.006 in)
Camshaft runout (maximum)	0.03 mm (0.0012 in)
Camshaft end float	
Standard	0.07-0.19 mm (0.0028-0.0075 in)
Service limit	0.20 mm (0.008 in)

Cylinder block

Height	221.5 mm (8.720 in)
Maximum distortion	0.15 mm (0.006 in)
Grinding limit	0.20 mm (0.008 in)
Cylinder bore diameter	
Standard	78.006-78.013 mm (3.0711-3.0714 in)
+0.25 mm (0.010 in)	78.256-78.263 mm (3.0809-3.0812 in)
+0.50 mm (0.020 in)	78.506-78.513 mm (3.0908-3.0911 in)
Maximum bore taper / ovality	0.019 mm (0.0007 in)

Pistons

Piston diameter (90° to pin bore, 16.5 mm below oil ring)	
Standard	77.954-77.974 mm (3.0690-3.0698 in)
+0.25 mm (0.010 in)	78.211-78.217 mm (3.0792-3.0794 in)
+0.50 mm (0.020 in)	78.461-78.467 mm (3.0890-3.0892 in)
Piston to bore clearance	
Standard	0.039-0.052 mm (0.0015-0.0020 in)
Service limit	0.15 mm (0.006 in)
Piston ring groove width	
Top	1.52-1.54 mm (0.0598-0.0606 in)
2nd	1.52-1.54 mm (0.0598-0.0606 in)
Oil	4.02-4.04 mm (0.1583-0.1591 in)

Piston rings

Thickness	
Top	1.47-1.49 mm (0.0579-0.0587 in)
2nd	1.47-1.49 mm (0.0579-0.0587 in)
End gap (ring installed in bore)	
Top	0.15-0.30 mm (0.006-0.012 in)
2nd	0.30-0.45 mm (0.012-0.018 in)
Oil (rail)	0.20-0.70 mm (0.008-0.028 in)
Service limit (all rings)	1.0 mm (0.039 in)
Piston ring groove width	
Top	1.52-1.54 mm (0.0599-0.0606 in)
2nd	1.52-1.54 mm (0.0599-0.0606 in)
Oil	4.02-4.04 mm (0.1583-0.1590 in)
Piston ring to groove clearance	
Top	0.03-0.07 mm (0.0012-0.0028 in)
2nd	0.03-0.07 mm (0.0012-0.0028 in)
Service limit	0.15 mm (0.006 in)

Piston pins

Diameter	19.987-19.993 mm (0.7869-0.7871 in)

Pin to piston clearance	-0.005-0.013 mm (-0.0002-0.0005 in)
Connecting rod bush to piston clearance	0.010-0.027 mm (0.0004-0.0011 in)

Connecting rods

Length between centers	132.85-132.95 mm (5.230-5.234 in)
Bend limit	0.075 mm (0.003 in) per 50 mm (1.97 in)
Small end bush ID	20.003-20.014 mm (0.7875-0.7880 in)
Big end (crankpin) bore	48.000-48.016 mm (1.8898-1.8904 in)
Big end (crankpin) width	21.838-21.890 mm (0.8598-0.8618 in)
Side clearance (at crankpin)	
Standard	0.110-0.262 mm (0.0043-0.0103 in)
Service limit	0.30 mm (0.012 in)

Crankshaft

Runout (maximum)	0.04 mm (0.0016 in)
Main bearing journal diameter	
Standard	49.938-49.956 mm (1.9661-1.9668 in)
Service limit	49.904 mm (1.9647 in)
-0.25 mm (-0.010 in)	49.704-49.708 mm (1.9568-1.9570 in)
Service limit	49.652 mm (1.9548 in)
-0.50 mm (-0.020 in)	49.454-49.458 mm (1.9470-1.9472 in)
Service limit	49.402 mm (1.9450 in)
-0.75 mm (-0.30 in)	49.204-49.208 mm (1.9372-1.9373 in)
Service limit	49.152 mm (1.9351 in)
Main bearing journal taper & ovality limit	0.05 mm (0.0020 in)
Crankpin diameter	
Standard	44.940-49.956 mm (1.7693-1.7699 in)
Service limit	44.908 mm (1.7680 in)
-0.25 mm (-0.010 in)	44.690-44.706 mm (1.7594-1.7601 in)
Service limit	44.658 mm (1.7582 in)
-0.50 mm (-0.020 in)	44.440-44.456 mm (1.7496-1.7502 in)
Service limit	44.408 mm (1.7483 in)
-0.75 mm (-0.30 in)	44.190-44.206 mm (1.7398-1.7404 in)
Service limit	44.158 mm (1.7385 in)
Crankpin taper & ovality limit	0.05 mm (0.0020 in)

Main bearings

Oil clearance	
Standard	0.018-0.036 mm (0.0007-0.0014 in)
Service limit	0.10 mm (0.004 in)
Available undersizes	-0.25, -0.50 & -0.75 mm (-0.010, -0.020 & -0.030 in)

Crankpin

Oil clearance	
Standard	0.028-0.068 mm (0.0011-0.0027 in)
Service limit	0.10 mm (0.004 in)
Available undersizes	-0.25, -0.50 & -0.75 mm (-0.010, -0.020 & -0.030 in)

Crankshaft thrust bearings

Crankshaft end play	
Standard	0.080-0.282 mm (0.0031-0.0111 in)
Service limit	0.30 mm (0.012 in)
Thrust bearing width	
Standard	2.500-2.550 mm (0.0984-0.1004 in)
+0.25 mm (+0.010 in)	2.625-2.675 mm (0.1033-0.1053 in)
+0.50 mm (+0.020 in)	2.750-2.800 mm (0.1083-0.1102 in)
+075 mm (+0.030 in)	2.875-2.925 mm (0.1132-0.1152 in)

Camshaft drive (timing) belt

Deflection @ 98 N (10 kg / 22 lb)	9.0-11.5 mm (0.35-0.45 in)

LUBRICATION SYSTEM (ENGINE)

Oil pump

Type	Trochoid

Relief pressure	343-441 kPa (3.5-4.5 kg cm^2 / 50-64 psi)
Oil pressure	
At 1,000 rpm	194-294 kPa (2.0-3.0 kg cm^2 / 28-43 psi)
At 3,000 rpm	294-392 kPa (3.0-4.0 kg cm^2 / 43-57 psi)
Inner rotor tip to outer rotor clearance	
Standard	0.02-0.16 mm (0.0008-0.0063 in)
Service limit	0.20 mm (0.0079 in)
Outer rotor to body clearance	
Standard	0.09-0.18 mm (0.0035-0.0071 in)
Service limit	0.22 mm (0.0087 in)
Side clearance	
Standard	0.03-0.11 mm (0.0012-0.0043 in)
Service limit	0.14 mm (0.0055 in)

Oil filter

Type	Full-flow, paper element, canister type
Relief pressure	78-118 kPa (0.8-1.2 kg cm^2 / 11-17 psi)

Engine oil

Capacity	
Dry engine	3.6 liters (3.8 US qt / 3.2 Imp qt)
Oil pan	3.2 liters (3.4 US qt / 2.8 Imp qt)
Oil filter	0.17 liters (0.18 US qt / 0.15 Imp qt)
Grade	API Service SG energy conserving II (ECII)
Viscosity (US and Canada)	
Above -25°C (-13°F)	SAE 10W-30
Below 0°C (32°F)	SAE 5W-30
Viscosity (UK and Europe)	
Above 30°C (86°F)	SAE 40
Below 0-40°C (32-104°F)	SAE 30
-10-20°C (14--68°F)	SAE 20W-20
Above -10°C (14°F)	SAE 20W-40 or 20W-50
-25-30°C (-13-86°F)	SAE10W-30
Above -25°C (-13°F)	SAE 10W-40 or 10W-50
Below 0°C (32°F)	SAE 5W-30
Below -20°C (-4°F)	SAE 5W-20

COOLING SYSTEM

General

Type	Pump assisted thermosyphon, electric cooling fan
Coolant capacity	6.0 liters (6.3 US qt / 5.5 Imp qt)
Coolant mixture percentages & specific gravity	
Above -16°C (3°F)	65% water, 35% antifreeze (SG 1.054)
Above -26°C (-15°F)	55% water, 45% antifreeze (SG 1.066)
Above -40°C (-40°F)	45% water, 55% antifreeze (SG 1.078)

Water pump

Pump type	Belt-driven centrifugal
Impeller diameter	75 mm (2.95 in)
Number of blades	6
Pump drive ratio	1.05:1
Pump seal	mechanical

Thermostat

Type	Wax
Opening temperature (US and Canada)	
Sub	83.5-86.5 °C (182-188°F)
Main	86.5-89.5°C (188-193°F)
Opening temperature (UK and Europe)	80.5-83.5°C (177-182°F)
Full-open temperature	
US and Canada	100°C (212°F)
UK and Europe	95°C (203°F)
Full-open lift (US and Canada)	

Sub	1.5 mm (0.06 in) minimum
Main	8.0 mm (0.31 in) minimum
Full-open lift (UK and Europe)	8.5 mm (0.33 in) minimum

Radiator

Type	Corrugated fin
Cap opening pressure	74-103 kPa (0.75-1.05 kg cm^2 / 11-15 psi)
Cooling system checking pressure	103 kPa (1.05 kg cm^2 / 15 psi)
Fan type	Electric
Number of blades	5
Fan diameter	320 mm (12.6 in)
Fan switches on at	97°C (207°F)
Fan motor rating	12 volt, 70W, 5.3-6.5 A

FUEL AND EMISSION CONTROL SYSTEMS

General

dle speed (during self test)	850 ± 50
gnition timing (during self test)	
Manual transmission	10° ± 1°
Automatic transmission	8° ± 1°

hrottle body

ype	Side draft
hroat diameter	55 mm (2.2 in)

ashpot

djustment speed	2,500 ± 150 rpm

irflow meter resistances

$_2$ - V_S	
Fully closed	200-600
Fully open	20-1,000
$_2$ - V_C	200-400
$_2$ - THA_A (intake air thermosensor)	
at -20°C (-4°F)	13,600 - 18,400
at 20°C (68°F)	2,210 - 2,690
at 60°C (140°F)	493-667
$_1$ - F_C	
Fully closed	(Infinity)
Fully open	zero

uel pump

ype	Impeller type (in fuel tank)
utput pressure	441-589 kPa (4.5-6.0 kg cm^2 / 64-85 psi)

uel filter

ype	
Low pressure	Nylon strainer
High pressure	Paper element

uel pressure regulator

ype	Diaphragm
egulating pressure	265-314 kPa (2.7-3.2 kg cm^2 / 38-46 psi)

njectors

ype	High ohmic
rive type	Voltage
esistance	12-16 @ 20°C (68°F)

SC (Idle Speed Control) valve

esistance	11-13 @ 20°C (68°F)

Circuit opening relay

Resistances

STA - E_1 21-43

B - F_C 109-226

B - F_P .... (Infinity)

Solenoid (Purge control) valve

Resistance .... 23-27 @ 20°C (68°F)

Crank angle sensor

Type .... Optical or Hall effect

Water thermosensor

Resistances

-20°C (-4°F) 14.6-17.8k

20°C (68°F) 2.2-2.7k

80°C (176°F) 0.29-0.35k

Air valve

Opening temperature .... Below 40°C (104°F)

Fuel tank

Capacity .... 45 liters (11.9 US gal / 9.9 Imp gal)

Air cleaner

Type .... Disposable paper element

Accelerator cable

Lash (free play) .... 1-3 mm (0.039-0.118 in)

Fuel

Specified grade

US and Canada .... Unleaded regular (RON 87 or higher)

UK and Europe .... Unleaded regular (RON 90 or higher)

ELECTRICAL SYSTEM (ENGINE)

Battery

Type .... S46A24L(S), Maintenance-free

Capacity .... 32 Ah

Voltage & polarity .... 12 volt, negative (-) ground

Dark current .... 20.0 mA (Ignition switch off)

Alternator

Type .... AC

Output

Manual transmission .... 12-60 V-A

Automatic transmission .... 12-65 V-A

Regulator type .... Built-in IC regulator

Regulated voltage

US and Canada .... 14.3-14.9 volts

UK and Europe .... 14.1-14.7 volts

Brush length

Standard .... 21.5 mm (0.85 in)

Service limit .... 8 mm (0.31 in)

Drive belt deflection

New .... 8-9 mm (0.31-0.35 in)

Used .... 9-10 mm (0.35-0.39 in)

Starter motor

Type .... Direct

Output .... 12.0 volts, 0.95 kW

Brush length

Standard .... 17.0 mm (0.67 in)

Service limit	11.5 mm (0.45 in)

Ignition system

Type	Electronic, electronic ignition advance
Advance control	By ECU
Ignition timing (during self test)	
Manual transmission	9-11° BTDC
Automatic transmission	7-9° BTDC
Ignition coil	Twin, molded
Primary winding resistance	0.78-0.94 k
Secondary winding resistance	11.2-15.2 k
Spark plugs - standard fitment	
Manual transmission	NGK BKR6E-11 or ND K20PR-U11
Automatic transmission	ND K20PR-U11
Spark plugs - alternative fitments	
NGK	BKR5E-11, BKR7E-11
NIPPONDENSO	K16PR-U11, K22PR-U11
Plug gap	1.0-1.1 mm (0.038 - 0.043 in)
Firing order	1-3-4-2

CLUTCH

Type	Single dry plate
Control type	Hydraulic
Pedal type	Pendant
Pedal ratio	6.13
Pedal stroke	120 mm (4.72 in)
Pedal height (from carpet)	175-185 mm (6.89-7.28 in)
Pedal free play	0.6-3.1 mm (0.02-0.12 in)
Pedal height from carpet when fully disengaged	68 mm (2.68 in) minimum
Flywheel runout limit	0.2 mm (0.008 in)
Clutch disc runout limit	0.7 mm (0.028 in)
Clutch disc minimum thickness	0.3 mm (0.012 in) above rivet head
Clutch disc OD	200 mm (7.87 in)
Clutch disc ID	130 mm (5.12 in)
Friction material thickness	
Flywheel side	3.5 mm (0.14 in)
Clutch side	3.5 mm (0.14 in)
Clutch cover type	Diaphragm spring
Installed pressure	4.022 N (410 kg / 902 lb)

TRANSMISSION (MANUAL)

Oil capacity	2.0 liters (2.1 US qt / 1.8 Imp qt)
Oil grade	
Above 10°C (50°F)	API Service GL-4 or GL-5 SAE 80W-90
All seasons	API Service GL-4 or GL-5 SAE 75W-90
Gear ratios	
1st	3.136:1
2nd	1.888:1
3rd	1.330:1
4th	1.000:1
5th	0.814:1
Reverse	3.758:1
Mainshaft	
Max. runout	0.03 mm (0.0012 in)
Shaft to gear/bush clearance	0.15 mm (0.006 in) max.
Reverse idle gear	
Bush to shaft clearance	0.5 mm (0.020 in) max.
Shift fork & rod	
Fork to clutch sleeve clearance	0.5 mm (0.020 in) max.
Shift rod gate to control lever clearance	0.8 mm (0.032 in) max.
Synchronizer ring to gear face clearance (installed)	
Standard	1.5 mm (0.059 in)
Service limit	0.8 mm (0.032 in)

Shift rod 5th/ reverse spring
 Free length .... 75 mm (2.953 in)
1st/2nd detent ball spring
 Free length .... 22.5 mm (0.886 in)
3rd/4th detent ball spring
 Free length .... 22.5 mm (0.886 in)
5th/reverse detent ball spring
 Free length .... 17.0 mm (0.669 in)

TRANSMISSION (AUTOMATIC)

Oil capacity
 Total .... 6.7 liters (7.1 US qt / 5.9 Imp qt)
 Oil pan .... 4.0 liters (4.2 US qt / 3.5 Imp qt)
Oil grade .... Dexron®II or M-III
Gear ratios
 1st 2.841:1
 2nd 1.541:1
 3rd 1.000:1
 OD (4th) 0.720:1
 Reverse 2.400:1
Torque converter stall torque ratio 1.9:1
Engine stall speed
 D, 2, 1 and R ranges .... 2,600-3,000 rpm
Time lag
 N to D range .... 0.5-1.0 seconds
 N to R range .... 0.5-1.0 seconds
Line pressure at idle
 D and 1 ranges .... 294-392 kPa (3.0-4.0 kg cm^2 / 43-57 psi)
 2 range .... 1,020-1,138 kPa (10.4-11.6 kg cm^2 / 148-166 psi)
 R range .... 697-834 kPa (7.1-8.5 kg cm^2 / 101-121 psi)
Line pressure at stall
 D and 1 ranges .... 932-1,282 kPa (9.5-11.5 kg cm^2 / 135-164 psi)
 2 range .... 981-1,177 kPa (10.0-12.0 kg cm^2 / 142-171 psi)
 R range .... 2,246-2,541 kPa (22.9-25.9 kg cm^2 / 326-369 psi)
Governor pressure
 at 19 mph (30 kph) .... 78-137 kPa (0.8-1.4 kg cm^2 / 11-20 psi)
 at 34 mph (55 kph) .... 157-235 kPa (1.6-2.4 kg cm^2 / 23-34 psi)
 at 53 mph (85 kph) .... 334-434 kPa (3.4-4.4 kg cm^2 / 48-63 psi)
Governor cutback point
 at atmospheric pressure .... 108-167 kPa (1.1-17 kg cm^2 / 16-24 psi)
 at 200 mmHg (7.87 inHg) .... 59-118 kPa (0.6-1.2 kg cm^2 / 9-17 psi)

Oil pump
Oil pump body clearance
 Standard .... 0.02-0.04 mm (0.0008-0.0016 in)
 Service limit .... 0.08 mm (0.0031 in)
Oil pump tip clearance
 Standard .... 0.14-0.21 mm (0.0055-0.0083 in)
 Service limit .... 0.25 mm (0.0098 in)
Oil pump side clearance
 Standard .... 0.05-0.20 mm (0.0020-0.0079 in)
 Service limit .... 0.25 mm (0.0098 in)
Drum support seal ring and groove clearance
 Standard .... 0.04-0.16 mm (0.0016-0.0063 in)
 Service limit .... 0.40 mm (0.016 in)

Direct clutch
Drive plate quantity 2
Driven plate quantity 2
Drive plate thickness
 Standard .... 1.6 mm (0.063 in)
 Service limit .... 1.4 mm (0.055 in)
Clutch clearance (maximum) .... 0.2 mm (0.008 in)
Side plate sizes (mm) .... 0.4, 0.6, 0.8, 1.0 & 1.2

Side plate sizes (in)	0.016, 0.024, 0.031, 0.039 & 0.047
End play	0.5-0.8 mm (0.020-0.031 in)
Thrust washer sizes (mm)	1.3, 1.5, 1.7, 1.9, 1.2, 2.3 & 2.7
Thrust washer sizes (in)	0.051, 0.059, 0.067, 0.075, 0.098 & 0.106

Overdrive planetary gear unit

Pinion clearance	
Standard	0.2-0.7 mm (0.008-0.028 in)
Service limit	0.8 mm (0.031 in)
Total end play	0.25-0.50 mm (0.0098-0.0197 in)
Bearing race sizes (mm)	1.2, 1.4, 1.6, 1.8, 2.0 & 2.2
Bearing race sizes (in)	0.047, 0.055, 0.063, 0.071, 0.079 & 0.087

Front clutch

Number of drive plates	4
Number of driven plates	5
Drive plate thickness	
Standard	1.6 mm (0.063 in)
Service limit	1.4 mm (0.055 in)
Clutch clearance	0.9-1.1 (0.035-0.043 in)
Retaining plate sizes (mm)	5.6, 5.8, 6.0, 6.2, 6.4, 6.6, 6.8 & 7.0
Retaining plate sizes (in)	0.220, 0.228, 0.236, 0.244, 0.252, 0.260, 0.268 & 0.276
End play	0.5-0.8 mm (0.020-0.031 in)
Thrust washer sizes (mm)	1.3, 1.5, 1.7, 1.9, 1.2, 2.3 & 2.7
Thrust washer sizes (in)	0.051, 0.059, 0.067, 0.075, 0.098 & 0.106

Rear clutch

Number of drive plates	6
Number of driven plates	6
Drive plate thickness	
Standard	1.6 mm (0.063 in)
Service limit	1.4 mm (0.055 in)
Clutch clearance	0.8-1.0 mm (0.031-0.039 in)
Retaining plate sizes (mm)	6.2, 6.4, 6.6, 6.8, 7.0, 7.2, 7.4 & 7.6
Retaining plate sizes (in)	0.244, 0.252, 0.260, 0.268, 0.276, 0.238, 0.291 & 0.299
End play	0.25-0.50 mm (0.0098-0.0197 in)
Thrust washer sizes (mm)	1.3, 1.5, 1.7, 1.9, 1.2, 2.3 & 2.7
Thrust washer sizes (in)	0.051, 0.059, 0.067, 0.075, 0.098 & 0.106
Bearing race sizes (mm)	1.2, 1.4, 1.6, 1.8, 2.0 & 2.2
Bearing race sizes (in)	0.047, 0.055, 0.063, 0.071, 0.079 & 0.087

Low and reverse brake

Number of drive plates	4
Number of driven plates	4
Drive plate thickness	
Standard	2.0 mm (0.079 in)
Service limit	1.8 mm (0.071 in)
Clutch clearance	0.8-1.05 mm (0.031-0.041 in)
Retaining plate sizes (mm)	7.8, 8.0, 8.2, 8.4, 8.6 & 8.8
Retaining plate sizes (in)	0.307, 0.315, 0.323, 0.331, 0.339 & 0.346

Front planetary gear

Pinion clearance	
Standard	0.2-0.7 mm (0.008-0.028 in)
Service limit	0.8 mm (0.031 in)

Rear planetary gear

Pinion clearance	
Standard	0.2-0.7 mm (0.008-0.028 in)
Service limit	0.8 mm (0.031 in)

Parking gear (oil distributor)

Seal ring and groove clearance	
Standard	0.04-0.16 mm (0.0016-0.0063 in)
Service limit	0.40 mm (0.0157 in)

Springs

Control valve

Second lock outer diameter	5.55 mm (0.219 in)
Second lock free length	33.5 mm (1.319 in)
Second lock number of coils	18.0
Second lock wire diameter	0.55 mm (0.022 in)
Pressure regulator outer diameter	11.7 mm (0.461 in)
Pressure regulator free length	43.0 mm (1.692 in)
Pressure regulator number of coils	15.0
Pressure regulator wire diameter	1.2 mm (0.047 in)
Down shift outer diameter	5.55 mm (0.219 in)
Down shift free length	21.9 mm (0.862 in)
Down shift number of coils	14.0
Down shift wire diameter	0.55 mm (0.022 in)
Throttle backup outer diameter	7.3 mm (0.287 in)
Throttle backup free length	36.0 mm (1.417 in)
Throttle backup number of coils	16.0
Throttle backup wire diameter	0.80 mm (0.031 in)
3-4 shift outer diameter	6.6 mm (0.260 in)
3-4 shift free length	30.3 mm (1.193 in)
3-4 shift number of coils	14.6
3-4 shift wire diameter	0.80 mm (0.031 in)
2-3 shift outer diameter	6.4 mm (0.252 in)
2-3 shift free length	39.2 mm (1.543 in)
2-3 shift number of coils	20.0
2-3 shift wire diameter	0.70 mm (0.028 in)
1-2 shift outer diameter	6.65 mm (0.262 in)
1-2 shift free length	26.9mm (1.059 in)
1-2 shift number of coils	12.2
1-2 shift wire diameter	0.65 mm (0.026 in)
Pressure modifier outer diameter	8.60 mm (0.339 in)
Pressure modifier free length	15.5 mm (0.610 in)
Pressure modifier number of coils	7.5
Pressure modifier wire diameter	0.60 mm (0.024 in)
3-2 timing outer diameter	7.50 mm (0.295 in)
3-2 timing free length	23.2 mm (0.913 in)
3-2 timing number of coils	11.0
3-2 timing wire diameter	0.80 mm (0.031 in)
Throttle relief outer diameter	6.50 mm (0.256 in)
Throttle relief free length	26.8 mm (1.055 in)
Throttle relief number of coils	16.0
Throttle relief wire diameter	0.90 mm (0.035 in)
Orifice check outer diameter	5.00 mm (0.197 in)
Orifice check free length	15.5 mm (0.610 in)
Orifice check number of coils	12.0
Orifice check wire diameter	0.23 mm (0.009 in)

Governor valve

Primary outer diameter	8.75 mm (0.344 in)
Primary free length	21.8 mm (0.858 in)
Primary number of coils	7.0
Primary wire diameter	0.45 mm (0.018 in)
Secondary outer diameter	9.25 mm (0.364 in)
Secondary free length	26.7 mm (1.051 in)
Secondary number of coils	9.0
Secondary wire diameter	0.75 mm (0.030 in)

Oil pump

Lockup control outer diameter	5.50 mm (0.217 in)
Lockup control free length	25.0 mm (0.984 in)
Lockup control number of coils	15.0
Lockup control wire diameter	0.70 mm (0.028 in)

Drum support

OD accumulator outer diameter	16.0 mm (0.630 in)
OD accumulator free length	40.4 mm (1.591 in)
OD accumulator number of coils	9.8
OD accumulator wire diameter	2.60 mm (0.102 in)
OD cancel outer diameter	4.95 mm (0.195 in)

OD cancel free length	23.0 mm (0.906 in)
OD cancel number of coils	14.8
OD cancel wire diameter	0.65 mm (0.026 in)
Band servo	
OD outer diameter	26.8 mm (1.055 in)
OD free length	47.0 mm (1.850 in)
OD number of coils	8.4
OD wire diameter	2.90 mm (0.114 in)
2nd outer diameter	28.25 mm (1.112 in)
2nd free length	37.0 mm (1.457 in)
2nd number of coils	5.4
2nd wire diameter	3.5 mm (0.138 in)
Direct, front & rear clutches	
outer diameter	8.0 mm (0.315 in)
free length	30.5 mm (1.201 in)
Number of coils	14.5
wire diameter	1.30 mm (0.051 in)
Low and reverse brake	
free length	5.9-6.2 mm (0.232-0.244 in)
Parking rod	
outer diameter	7.2 mm (0.283 in)
free length	32.0 mm (1.260 in)
Number of coils	14.0
wire diameter	0.70 mm (0.028 in)

Vehicle speeds at gear shift points

Range D, throttle fully open	
D_1-D_2	31-35 mph (50-56 kph)
D_2-D_3	58-61 mph (93-99 kph)
OD-D_3	Above 58 mph (93 kph)
D_3-D_2	54-58 mph (87-93 kph)
D_2-D_1	23-27 mph (37-43 kph)
Range D, half throttle (200 mmHg / 7.87 inHg)	
D_1-D_2	11-14 mph (17-23 kph)
D_2-D_3	16-19 mph (25-31 kph)
D_3-OD	27-31 mph (44-50 kph)
Lockup ON (OD)	41-45 mph (66-72 kph)
Lockup OFF (OD)	37-41 mph (60-66 kph)
OD-D_3	17-20 mph (27-33 kph)
D_3-D2	6-9 mph (9-15 kph)
D_2-D_1	6-9 mph (9-15 kph)
Range D, throttle fully closed	
D1-D_2	7-11 mph (12-18 kph)
D_2-D_3	14-17 mph (22-28 kph)
D_3-OD	25-29 mph (41-47 kph)
OD-D_3	17-20 mph (27-33 kph)
D_3-D_2	6-9 mph (9-15 kph)
D_2-D_1	6-9 mph (9-15 kph)
Range 1	
1_2-1_1	24-27 mph (38-44 kph)

PROPSHAFT

Maximum runout	0.4 mm (0.016 in)

FRONT AXLE

Type	Double wishbone
Bearing type	Angular ball, integral with hub
Maximum bearing play	0.05 mm (0.002 in)

REAR AXLE

Type	Double wishbone
Bearing type	Angular ball
Maximum bearing play	0.05 mm (0.002 in)

DIFFERENTIAL

Type	Bevel (Optional viscous limited-slip differential)
Reduction gear type	Hypoid gear
Reduction ratio	4.300:1
Differential gear type	Straight-cut bevel
Ring gear size	162.16 mm (6.38 in)
Drive pinion preload (oil seal removed)	0.3-0.7 Nm (3-7 kgf cm / 2.6-6.1 lbf in)
Backlash	
Side and pinion gears	0-0.1 mm (0-0.004 in)
Final gear	0.09-0.11 (0.0035-0.0043 in)
Length (between pilot sections)	150.137-150.200 mm (5.9105-5.9130 in)
Oil	
Grade	API service GL-5
Viscosity (above -18°C / 0°F)	SAE 90
Viscosity (Below -18°C / 0°F)	SAE 80W
Capacity	0.65 liter (0.69 US qt / 0.57 Imp qt)

STEERING

Steering wheel

Outer diameter	370 mm (14.6 in)
Free play	0-30 mm (0-1.18 in)
Wheel effort	
Manual	4.9-29.4 N (0.5-3.0 kg / 1.1-6.6 lb)
Power	23.5-35.3 N (2.4-3.6 kg / 5.3-8.0 lb)
Turns, lock-to-lock	
Manual	3.36
Power	2.80

Steering column assembly

Type	Collapsible
Joint type	2-cross joints

Power steering system

Type	Engine speed sensing
Mechanism	Rack-and-pinion
Gear ratio	
Rack stroke	121.0 mm (4.76 in)
Fluid type	ATF Dexron®II or M-III
Capacity	0.8 liter (0.85 US qt / 0.70 Imp qt)
Fluid pressure	7,603-8,339 kPa (77.5-85.0 kg cm^2 / 1,102-1,209 psi)

BRAKING SYSTEM

Hydraulic fluid

Fluid type	SAEJ1703 or FMVSS116, DOT-3

Brake pedal

Height (carpet installed)	171-181 mm (6.73-7.13 in)
Free play	4-7 mm (0.16-0.28 in)
Reserve travel*	95 mm (3.74 in)

(*Carpet removed, clearance with pedal depressed with force of 589 N (60 kg / 132 lb)

Master cylinder

Type	Tandem

Bore .... 22.22 mm (0.87 in)

Front brakes

Type .... Ventilated disc
Pad thickness
    Standard .... 9.5 mm (0.37 in)
    Service limit .... 1.0 mm (0.04 in)
Disc thickness
    Standard .... 18.0 mm (0.71 in)
    Service limit .... 16.0 mm (0.63 in)
Disc maximum runout .... 0.1 mm (0.004 in)
Caliper bore diameter .... 51.1 mm (2.01 in)

Rear brakes

Type .... Disc
Pad thickness
    Standard .... 8.0 mm (0.31 in)
    Service limit .... 1.0 mm (0.04 in)
Disc thickness
    Standard .... 9.0 mm (0.35 in)
    Service limit .... 7.0 mm (0.28 in)
Disc maximum runout .... 0.1 mm (0.004 in)
Caliper bore diameter .... 31.75 mm (1.25 in)

Parking brake

Type .... Cable operated, on rear wheels
Adjustment .... 5-7 notches with 98 N (10 kg / 22 lb) pull

Power brake (servo) unit

Type .... Single diaphragm
Diameter .... 214 mm (8.0 lb)
Pushrod to piston clearance* .... 0.1-0.4 mm (0.004-0.016 in)
(* Vacuum of approx. 500 mmHg / 19.7 inHg applied to unit)

Fluid pressure per pedal force
    at 0 mmHg (0 inHg) .... 1,079-1,177 kPa (11-12 kg cm^2 / 156-171 psi
    at 500 mmHg (19.7 inHg) .... 5,199-5,494 kPa (53-56 kg cm^2 / 754-796 psi)

WHEELS AND TIRES

Wheels

Size
    Standard .... 14 X $5^1/_2$-JJ
    Temporary spare .... 14 X 4T
Offset .... 45 mm (1.77 in)
Pitch circle diameter .... 100 mm (3.94 in)
Material
    Standard .... Aluminum alloy
    Temporary spare .... Steel

Tires

Size
    Standard P185/60R14 82H
    Temporary spare T115/70D14
Air pressure (US and Canada)
    Standard .... 179 kPa (1.8 kg cm^2 / 26 psi)
    Temporary spare .... 415 kPa (4.2 kg cm^2 / 60 psi)
Air pressure (UK and Europe)
    Standard .... 177 kPa (1.8 kg cm^2 / 26 psi)
    Temporary spare .... 412 kPa (4.2 kg cm^2 / 60 psi)

Wheel & tire

Runout limit
    Horizontal .... 2.0 mm (0.079 in)

Vertical	1.5 mm (0.059 in)
Maximum imbalance	10g (0.35 oz)

SUSPENSION

Front

Type	Double wishbone
Stabilizer bar diameter	
US '92	21 mm (0.82 in)
US '93 on, UK & Europe	19 mm (0.75 in)
Other markets	Check with dealer
Shock absorber type	Double-acting, low-pressure gas-charged
Coil spring color code	
Manual	Red
Automatic	White
Coil wire diameter	
Manual	10.8 mm (0.43 in)
Automatic	11.0 mm (0.43 in)
Coil inner diameter	
Manual	83 mm (3.27 in)
Automatic	83 mm (3.27 in)
Free length	
Manual	282.5 mm (11.12 in)
Automatic	292.5 mm (11.52 in)
Number of coils	
Manual	5.91
Automatic	6.32

Rear

Type	Double wishbone
Stabilizer bar diameter	
US '92	14 mm (0.55 in)
US '93 on	11 mm (0.43 in)
UK & Europe	12 mm (0.47 in)
Other markets	Check with dealer
Shock absorber type	Double-acting, low-pressure gas-charged
Coil spring color code - US '92, UK and Europe models (Other markets - check with dealer)	
Manual	Blue
Automatic	Orange
Coil spring color code - US '93 on	
Manual	Yellow
Automatic	Green
Coil wire diameter	
Manual	10.1 mm (0.40 in)
Automatic	10.2 mm (0.40 in)
Coil inner diameter	
Manual	83 mm (3.27 in)
Automatic	83 mm (3.27 in)
Free length -US '92, UK and Europe models (Other markets - check with dealer)	
Manual	339.5 mm (13.37 in)
Automatic	347.5 mm (13.68 in)
Free length -US '93 on	
Manual	348.5 mm (13.727 in)
Automatic	356.5 mm (14.04 in)
Number of coils	
Manual	7.68
Automatic	7.96

Wheel alignment - front[*1]

Total toe-in	
mm (in)	3 ± 3 mm (0.12 ± 0.12 in)
Degrees	0°18' ± 18'
Maximum steering angle	
Inner	37°23' ± 2°
Outer (US and Canada)	32°23' ± 2°

Outer (UK and Europe)	32°32' ± 2°
Outer (Other markets)	Check with vehicle handbook
Camber angle	0°24' ± 45' *2
Caster angle	
US and Canada	4°26' ± 45 *3
UK and Europe	4°30' ± 45 *3
Other markets	Check vehicle handbook
King pin angle	11°20'

Wheel alignment - rear *1

Total toe-in	
mm (in)	3 ± 3 mm (0.12 ± 0.12 in)
Degrees	0°18' ± 18'
Camber angle	
US and Canada	0°24' ± 45' *2
UK and Europe	0°43' ± 30' *2
Other markets	Check vehicle handbook

**1 Measured with full fuel tank, correct coolant and engine oil levels, spare tire, jack and tools in correct position in trunk and no passenger or other load in car.*

**2 Difference between left and right sides must not exceed 1°*

**3 Difference between left and right sides must not exceed 1°30'*

ELECTRICAL SYSTEM (BODY)

Instrument panel lamps (all 12 volt)

High beam warning	3.4W
Turn signal	3.4W
Illumination	3.4W
Engine check	1.4W
Brake	1.4W
Charge	1.4W
Belts	1.4W
Air bag	1.4W
Headlight retractor	1.4W
O/D off	1.4W
ABS system	1.4W
Washer low	1.4W
Rear window defrost	1.4W

Exterior lights

Note: for markets other than US, Canada and Europe check car handbook for bulb specification.

Headlights	
US and Canada	60/40W
UK and Europe	60/55W
Front turn signal/parking (US and Canada)	27/8W
Front turn signal (UK and Europe)	21W
Front side marker (US and Canada)	3.8W
Side turn signal (UK and Europe)	5W
License plate	
US and Canada	7.5W
UK and Europe	5W
Rear turn signal	
US and Canada	27W
UK and Europe	21W
Rear side marker	3.8W
Stop/tail	
US and Canada	27/8W
UK and Europe	21/5W
Backup	
US and Canada	27W
UK and Europe	21W
Hi-mount stoplight	18.4W

Interior lights

Courtesy lights	5W
Ashtray	3.4W
Heater control panel	1.4
A/C switch	1.4W
Hazard switch	1.4W
Cruise control switch	1.4W

AIR CONDITIONING SYSTEM

Refrigerant quantity	800 g (28.24 oz)
Compressor oil quantity	80-100 cc (4.88-6.1 cu in)
Refrigerant pressure	
Low	147-294 kPa (1.5-3.0 kg cm^2 / 21-43 psi)
High	1,117-1,1619 (12.0-16.5 kg cm^2 / 171-235 psi

2

2 TUNE-UP & MAINTENANCE

1. INTRODUCTION

Regular maintenance is vitally important for the long term health of your vehicle. Ignoring the recommended maintenance procedures will invariably lead to a general deterioration of the vehicle as many areas of minor wear or incorrect adjustment mount up. In the longer term, high repair bills become inevitable. More significantly, the inexorable decline of any vehicle in which maintenance is neglected means that driving enjoyment and fuel economy are impaired, resale value is adversely affected, and eventually the safety of the driver and other road users is compromised.

By definition, most Miata/MX5 owners are enthusiasts and, as such, will want to ensure that the vehicle is kept in optimum condition. We suggest that you approach the necessary mechanical maintenance procedures along with regular cleaning and waxing. The two go hand in hand; as you wash the vehicle down, you automatically give it a close visual inspection, and this is fundamental to basic maintenance operations.

Once you start to get into regular maintenance checks you will find that you will begin to spot potential trouble spots before problems develop. Very often these will be outside conventional maintenance procedures, but the fact that general scrutiny is required during maintenance tasks ensures that incidental items like burned out bulbs or damaged wiring get spotted along the way.

In most cases, the procedures required to carry out your own maintenance work are straightforward and require no special tools or skills; even where this is not the case, or if you decide to let a professional mechanic take care of the work for you, be aware of the various tasks required. That way you can be sure that the necessary work has been carried out correctly.

Please note that we have included the maintenance procedures which would normally be carried out on new vehicles by the supplying dealer as part of the warranty. Be aware that maintenance operations during the warranty period usually have to be carried out by an authorized dealer - if you do the work yourself, you may void the warranty. Our purpose in including these operations is to ensure that you have the necessary information to perform these tasks after major reconditioning work where, for all practical purposes, the car should be treated as if it were new.

In the maintenance schedules which follow, we have adhered closely to Mazda's recommendations, which means that you will be able to maintain the car as the makers intended. Each maintenance item is marked to indicate to which markets or conditions it applies:

❍ Denotes an official Mazda maintenance operation applicable to US market cars under normal operating conditions.
◆ Denotes an official Mazda maintenance operation applicable to US market cars under abnormal operating conditions
✱ Denotes an official Mazda maintenance operation applicable to Canadian market cars.
❑ Denotes a Veloce-recommended maintenance operation in addition to the official schedule.

Where necessary, each maintenance operation is described in greater detail later in this chapter - see the references at the end of the operation. If you want more information on a particular component, system or procedure, you'll usually find more to read in the relevant chapter.

Owners of US market cars may care to peruse the additional items outlined for non-US cars. You'll note that the breadth of coverage is significantly greater than that recommended for US models, and mileage intervals are usually shorter. In part, this takes into account variations in operating conditions, which in some cases may be harsher, but it is difficult not to conclude that it is mainly due to a requirement to keep servicing times (and thus costs) to a minimum in the USA.

While we do not intend to suggest that the US maintenance schedule is in any way inadequate, US owners performing their own maintenance may wish to incorporate some of the additional checks outlined for other markets - after all, a Miata is a Miata wherever it operates, and given similar conditions the cars will wear out at the same rate. The extra checks won't cost you money if you are doing the work yourself, and will help keep your Miata in perfect condition at all times.

In addition to the scheduled maintenance operations listed in this chapter, we further suggest that you try to arrange to have the car raised on a vehicle lift for a full underbody inspection in early spring and early fall each year. Before you do this, get the underside cleaned really thoroughly using a pressure wash facility so that you can see what you're checking without the usual coating of road dirt getting in the way. The pressure wash treatment will also remove any buildup of corrosive road chemicals like road salt.

Note that if your car has a wax-type underbody coating, do not use steam cleaning or the coating will be stripped away. Having said that, if your car's wax coating is beginning to deteriorate, it is a good idea to steam clean the underside to remove the remainder and have a new wax coat applied.

THE BASIS OF MAINTENANCE INTERVALS

Mazda's maintenance schedule for the Miata/MX5 is based on an anticipated average monthly mileage for the market area in which the car was originally sold. In addition to this factor, there is a minimum time interval at which each maintenance operation must be undertaken. Also taken into consideration are other factors, such as the prevailing operating conditions, plus local conventions about maintenance intervals in each market.

In the case of the US market, the basic anticipated monthly mileage for a Miata is 1,000 miles (1,600 km). This, combined with a time interval of 7.5 months, produces a basic maintenance interval of 7.5 months / 7,500 miles (12,000 km), later intervals being multiples of this. Where US-spec cars are used in abnormal conditions, the time interval is reduced to 5 months, and this also applies to Canadian market cars.

ABNORMAL OPERATING CONDITIONS - US MARKET CARS

Owners of US market cars should follow the maintenance schedule laid out in section 2A below wherever normal operating conditions apply. In areas where unusually harsh environmental conditions apply, or where the type of usage might cause accelerated wear, Mazda have prescribed a revised set of mileage/time intervals and operations. These appear within the maintenance schedule described in section 2B and are marked ◆ to distinguish them as being specific to these conditions. Mazda's list of criteria for abnormal operating conditions follows. If your car is subject to any of these criteria, use the schedule in section 2B to maintain your car and include all the items marked ◆

Repeated short distance driving
Driving in dusty conditions
Driving in areas where road salt or other corrosive materials are used
Driving on rough or muddy roads
Extended periods of idling and/or low-speed operation
Driving for prolonged periods in cold temperatures and/or extremely humid conditions

HOW TO INTERPRET THE SCHEDULES

Whichever schedule is applicable to your car and market, note that each heading comprises both a time and distance factor. It is important that you carry out the prescribed maintenance operation at **whichever** of these points is reached **first.**

Apart from the weekly and annual checks, all maintenance operations are based around the time/mileage intervals described earlier. As soon as you reach either one of these points, you need to carry out all the operations listed under that heading. This means, for example, that if your car does a lot of miles, you may end up doing the 7.5 month/ 7,500 mile (12,000 km) maintenance sequence every four or five months. Conversely, if you do lots of short journeys, you may need to carry out these tasks after only 4,000 miles, if the six month time interval has been reached.

As time and miles pass, you will reach the next specified interval. If, for example, you are carrying out the operations listed under the 15 month/15,000 mile (24,000 km) heading, note that this is **in addition** to the earlier intervals - so at this interval you will need to carry out the operations listed, plus all those listed under earlier headings except, of course, there is no point in carrying out fluid level checks if the fluids are due to be replaced at the interval you have reached.

Although it may appear that the maintenance schedule comes to an end at 60,000 miles, (96,000 km), this does not mean that your car has ceased to require maintenance! What you have to do here is start over at the beginning of the cycle. Remember that in the first and subsequent repetitions of the cycle, you will need to be increasingly vigilant when it comes to inspecting components and checking systems; age and use will begin to have a more marked effect, particularly upon things like hoses, HT leads, wheel bearings and brake parts, etc. You should also pay even closer attention to the main body structure, watching out for signs of corrosion and ageing.

2A. MAINTENANCE SCHEDULE: USA

Note: This schedule relates to US market cars used under normal driving conditions. If you use your car in harsh conditions (see earlier description) follow the schedule described in section 2B.

☞ 1/1,2 & 2/1.

WEEKLY/250 MILES (400 KM)

ENGINE

❑ Check the engine oil level ☞ 2/3
❑ Check the coolant level ☞ 2/14

ELECTRICAL

❑ Check the operation of the electrical components ☞ 2/15
❑ Raise and clean the headlights ☞ 2/15
❑ If you suspect a problem, remove and check the battery ☞ 2/11

BODY

❑ Wash the bodywork and wheels, checking and rectifying any paint or trim defects noted ☞ 2/17
❑ Clean the windshields, side windows and mirrors ☞ 2/15
o Wipers ☞ 2/15.6
❑ Check and top up the windshield washer reservoir ☞ 2/15
❑ Check and top up the headlight washer reservoir ☞ 2/15
❑ Check the tires and tire pressures ☞ 2/16

3 MONTHS/3,000 MILES (4,800 KM)

◆ Note. This interval is specified by Mazda only for cars sold in Puerto Rica. Owners operating their cars in similarly hostile conditions may wish to include this in their schedule, however.

ENGINE

◆ Change the engine oil and filter ☞ 2/3

7.5 MONTHS/7,500 MILES (12,000 KM)

ENGINE

❍ Change the engine oil and filter ☞ 2/3
❑ Power steering fluid level ☞ 2/18/18

AUTOMATIC TRANSMISSION

❑ Check the automatic transmission fluid (ATF) level

Note: Mazda specify **no** interval for checking the automatic transmission fluid. We suggest, however, that you check the fluid level at this interval.

BRAKES

❑ Inspect the brake lines, hoses & connections ☞ 9/4
❑ Inspect/replace the brake pads ☞ 9/10 & 9/15
❑ Check the brake discs for wear or damage ☞ 9/12 & 9/17
❑ Check the operation and adjustment of the parking brake ☞ 9/20

BODY

❍ Check and lubricate locks and hinges ☞ 2/17
❑ Check the condition of the convertible top ☞ 2/17
❑ Check that rear window zipper operates smoothly ☞ 2/17
❑ Wash the exterior of the car thoroughly ☞ 2/17
❑ Pressure-wash the underbody [see 2/17]

ANNUALLY (IRRESPECTIVE OF MILEAGE)

AIR CONDITIONING SYSTEM

❍ Have the air conditioning system checked by a Mazda dealer or air conditioning specialist. Specifically, check refrigerant (quantity and check for contamination), system pressure and compressor operation. **Warning!** Do not attempt these checks at home ☞ 6/16
❑ Check that seatbelts and fasteners are in good, undamaged condition and that the inertia lock system operates correctly.

30 MONTHS/30,000 MILES (48,000 KM)

ENGINE

❍ Inspect and replace or adjust external drive belts ☞ 2/4
❍ Replace the air cleaner element ☞ 2/5

TRANSMISSION

❑ Change the automatic transmission fluid (ATF)

Note: Mazda specify **no** interval for changing the automatic transmission fluid. We suggest, however, that you change the ATF at this interval.

❑ Check manual transmission oil level ☞ 2/8

IGNITION SYSTEM

❍ Replace the spark plugs ☞ 2/6

FUEL SYSTEM

❍ Check and adjust idle speed ☞ 2/7

Note: Up to model year 1992, this operation is specified by Mazda for all states except California, but Mazda recommend that it is also carried out on California market cars.

For model year 1993 on, Mazda recommend that this operation is carried out for all states including California, but point out that it is not necessary for emission warranty coverage or manufacturer recall liability.

❍ Check fuel lines and connections for leaks*2 ☞ 5/13 and 5/14
Replace fuel filter ☞ 5/20

COOLING SYSTEM

❍ Replace the engine coolant ☞ 2/14
❍ check cooling system ☞ 6/3

❍ check hose condition ☞ 6/4

BRAKES

❍ Inspect the brake lines, hoses & connections ☞ 9/4
❍ Inspect/replace the brake pads ☞ 9/10 & 9/15
❍ Check the brake discs for wear or damage ☞ 9/12 & 9/17

STEERING AND SUSPENSION

❍ Check manual steering system ☞ 2/18
❍ Check power steering system ☞ 2/18
❍ Check power steering for leaks ☞ 2/16
❍ Check the front suspension balljoints and dust boots for wear or damage ☞ 2/18

CHASSIS & BODY

❍ Check and tighten loose fittings and fasteners

EXHAUST SYSTEM

❍ Inspect the exhaust system, heatshields and catalytic converter ☞ 2/19

60 MONTHS/60,000 MILES (96,000 KM)

ENGINE

❍ Replace the camshaft drivebelt*1 ☞ 3/13

Note: From 1993 model year, this operation is required for all states except California. For Californian market cars, Mazda recommend inspection of the drivebelt at this interval*2

❍ Check and adjust idle speed*1 ☞ 2/7

MANUAL TRANSMISSION

❍ Replace the transmission oil ☞ 2/8

REAR AXLE

❍ Replace the differential oil ☞ 2/10

FUEL SYSTEM

❍ Check and adjust idle speed*3 ☞ 2/7
❍ Check emission system lines and connections for leaks*2 ☞ 5/23
❍ Check fuel lines and connections for leaks*2 ☞ 5/14
❍ Replace the fuel filter ☞ 5/20

Note: From model year 1993, Mazda specify this operation for all states except California, but recommend that it is carried out on California market cars.

EVERY 105,000 MILES (168,000 KM) - CALIFORNIA MARKET CARS ONLY

ENGINE

❍ Replace the camshaft drivebelt*1 ☞ 3/13

FUEL AND EMISSION SYSTEMS

❍ Fit new fuel hoses ☞ 5/14
❍ Check emission system lines and connections for leaks*2 ☞ 5/23

Notes (see text references) -

*1 **Caution!** Do not skip this operation. Camshaft drivebelt failure can result in engine damage. The operation requires extensive preliminary dismantling for access - you may prefer to have this work carried out by your Mazda dealer.

*2 This operation is recommended by Mazda, but is not necessary for emission warranty coverage or manufacturer recall liability.

*3 This operation is required in all states except California. Mazda recommend that it is also carried out on California vehicles.

2B. MAINTENANCE SCHEDULE: CANADA (& USA ABNORMAL OPERATING CONDITIONS)

Note. This schedule relates to all Canadian market cars, plus US market cars used under abnormal driving conditions (definition ☞ 2/1).

☞ 1/1,2 & 2/1.

WEEKLY/250 MILES (400 KM)

ENGINE

❑ Check the engine oil level ☞ 2/3
❑ Check the coolant level ☞ 2/14

ELECTRICAL

❑ Check the operation of the electrical components ☞ 2/15
❑ Raise and clean the headlights ☞ 2/15
❑ If you suspect a problem, remove and check the battery ☞ 2/11

BODY

❑ Wash the bodywork and wheels, checking and rectifying any paint or trim defects noted ☞ 2/17
❑ Clean the windshields, side windows and mirrors ☞ 2/15
❑ Check and top up the windshield washer reservoir ☞ 2/15
o Check wipers ☞ 2/15.6
❑ Check and top up the headlight washer reservoir ☞ 2/15
❑ Check the tires and tire pressures ☞ 2/16

3 MONTHS/3,000 MILES (4,800 KM)

Puerto Rican cars: carry out operations detailed in the following (5 months/5000 mile) schedule.

Note. Although this interval is specified by Mazda only for cars sold in Puerto Rica, other owners operating their cars in similarly tough conditions may wish to include it in their schedule.

5 MONTHS/5,000 MILES (8,000 KM)

ENGINE

*◆ Change the engine oil and filter ☞ 2/3
* Inspect and replace or adjust external drive belts ☞ 2/4
* Check the coolant level ☞ 2/14

TRANSMISSION

* Check the automatic transmission fluid (ATF) level
❑ Check manual transmission oil level

CLUTCH

* Check the clutch fluid level and condition ☞ 2/20

REAR AXLE

* Check the differential oil condition and level ☞ 2/10

BRAKES

❑ Inspect the brake lines, hoses & connections ☞ 9/4
❑ Inspect/replace the brake pads ☞ 9/10 & 9/15
❑ Check the brake discs for wear or damage ☞ 9/12 & 9/17
❑ Check the operation and adjustment of the parking brake ☞ 9/20
* Check the brake fluid level and condition ☞ 2/20

TIRES

* Check the tires and tire pressures ☞ 2/16

STEERING AND SUSPENSION

* Check power steering fluid level ☞ 2/16

BODY

* Check and top up the washer reservoir ☞ 2/15
*◆ Check and lubricate locks and hinges ☞ 2/17
* Raise and clean the headlights ☞ 2/15
* Check and clean all external lights ☞ 2/15
❑ Check the condition of the convertible top ☞ 2/17
❑ Check that rear window zipper operates smoothly ☞ 2/17
❑ Wash the exterior of the car thoroughly ☞ 2/17
❑ Pressure-wash the underbody ☞ 2/17

ANNUALLY (IRRESPECTIVE OF MILEAGE)

AIR CONDITIONING SYSTEM

*◆ Have the air conditioning system checked by a Mazda dealer or air conditioning specialist. Specifically, check refrigerant (quantity and check for contamination), system pressure and compressor operation. **Warning!** Do not attempt these checks at home ☞ 6/16
❑ Check that seatbelts are in good, undamaged condition and that the inertia system is operating correctly.

15 MONTHS/15,000 MILES (24,000 KM)

FUEL SYSTEM

*◆ Inspect the air cleaner element ☞ 2/5
* Inspect and adjust the idle speed ☞ 2/7

COOLING SYSTEM

* Inspect and top up the coolant level ☞ 2/14
* Inspect and top up the coolant level ☞ 2/14

BRAKES

*◆ Inspect/replace the brake pads ☞ 9/10 & 9/15

2

✱◆ Check the brake discs for wear or damage ☞ 9/12 & 9/17

CHASSIS & BODY

✱◆ Check and tighten loose fittings and fasteners

TIRES

✱ Rotate the tires ☞ 2/16

30 MONTHS/30,000 MILES (48,000 KM)

AUTOMATIC TRANSMISSION

❑ Change the automatic transmission fluid (ATF) ☞ 2/9

MANUAL TRANSMISSION

✱◆ Change the transmission oil ☞ 2/8

REAR AXLE

✱ Change the differential oil ☞ 2/10

IGNITION SYSTEM

✱◆ Replace the spark plugs ☞ 2/6

FUEL SYSTEM

✱◆ Replace the air cleaner element ☞ 2/5
✱ Inspect and adjust the idle speed ☞ 2/7
◆ Inspect and adjust the idle speed*[2] ☞ 2/7
✱ Replace the fuel filter ☞ 5/20
✱◆ Check fuel lines and connections for leaks*[2] ☞ 5/13 and 5/14

EXHAUST SYSTEM

✱◆ Inspect the exhaust system, heatshields and catalytic converter ☞ 2/19

COOLING SYSTEM

✱◆ Replace the engine coolant ☞ 2/14
✱◆ Check cooling system ☞ 6/3
✱◆ Check hose condition ☞ 6/4

BRAKES

✱◆ Inspect the brake lines, hoses & connections ☞ 9/4
✱◆ Inspect/replace the brake pads ☞ 9/10 & 9/15
✱◆ Check the brake discs for wear or damage ☞ 9/12 & 9/17
✱ Change the brake fluid*[5] ☞ 2/20

STEERING AND SUSPENSION

✱◆ Check manual steering system ☞ 2/18
✱◆ Check power steering system ☞ 2/18
✱◆ Check power steering for leaks ☞ 2/16
✱◆ Check the front suspension balljoints and dust boots for wear or damage ☞ 2/18
✱ Have wheel alignment checked (all four wheels) ☞ 8/3
✱◆ Check drive shaft dust boots ☞ 4/13

60 MONTHS/60,000 MILES (96,000 KM)

ENGINE

✱ Replace the camshaft drivebelt*[1] ☞ 3/13
◆ Replace the camshaft drivebelt*[1] ☞ 3/13

Note: From 1993 model year, this operation is required for all states except California. For Californian market cars, Mazda recommend inspection of the drivebelt at this interval*[2]

FUEL AND EMISSIONS SYSTEMS

✱◆ Check fuel lines and connections for leaks*[3] ☞ 5/13 and 5/14
✱◆ Inspect and adjust the idle speed*[3] ☞ 2/7
✱◆ Replace the fuel filter*[3] ☞ 5/20
✱ Check emission system lines and connections for leaks*[2] ☞ 5/23
◆ Check emission system lines and connections for leaks*[4] ☞ 5/23

EVERY 105,000 MILES (168,000 KM) - CALIFORNIA CARS ONLY

ENGINE

◆ Replace the camshaft drivebelt*[1] ☞ 3/13

FUEL AND EMISSION SYSTEMS

◆ Fit new fuel hoses ☞ 5/14
◆ Check emission system lines and connections for leaks*[2] ☞ 5/23

Notes (see text references) -

*[1] **Caution!** Do not skip this operation. Camshaft drivebelt failure can result in engine damage. The operation requires extensive preliminary dismantling for access - you may prefer to have this work carried out by your Mazda dealer.

*[2] This operation is recommended by Mazda, but is not necessary for emission warranty coverage or manufacturer recall liability.

*[3] This operation is required in Canada and all US states except California. Mazda recommend that it is also carried out on California vehicles.

*[4] This operation is required all US states except California. Mazda recommend that it is also carried out on California vehicles.

*[5] This operation is recommended by Mazda.

2C. MAINTENANCE SCHEDULE: EUROPE & OTHER MARKETS

☞ 1/1, 2 & 2/1.

WEEKLY/250 MILES (400 KM)

ENGINE

❑ Check the engine oil level ☞ 2/3
❑ Check the coolant level ☞ 2/14

ELECTRICAL

❑ Check the operation of the electrical components ☞ 2/15
❑ Raise and clean the headlights ☞ 2/15
❑ If you suspect a problem, remove and check the battery ☞ 2/11

BODY

❑ Wash the bodywork and wheels, checking and rectifying any paint or trim defects noted ☞ 2/17
❑ Clean the windshields, side windows and mirrors ☞ 2/15
❑ Check and top up the windshield washer reservoir ☞ 2/15
❑ Check the wipers ☞ 2/15.6
❑ Check and top up the headlight washer reservoir ☞ 2/15
❑ Check the tires and tire pressures ☞ 2/16

INITIAL 600 MILES (1,000 KM) - NEW/REBUILT ENGINE

ENGINE

❍ Check tighten the intake manifold and exhaust manifold (header) nuts/bolts ☞ 2/13
❍ Inspect and adjust the external drive belts ☞ 2/4
❍ Change the engine oil and filter ☞ 2/3

INITIAL 600 MILES (1,000 KM) - NEW CAR OR AFTER MAJOR CHASSIS WORK

CHASSIS/BODY

❍ Check for for loose fittings and fasteners, tighten as necessary.

6 MONTHS/6,000 MILES (10,000 KM)

ENGINE

❍ Change the engine oil and filter ☞ 2/3

CLUTCH

❍ Check and adjust clutch pedal height and free play (lash) ☞ 3/28
❍ Top up the clutch fluid reservoir ☞ 2/20

BRAKES

❍ Check the brake pedal operation and adjustment ☞ 9/5
❍ Top up the brake fluid reservoir*[7] ☞ 2/20
❑ Inspect/replace the brake pads ☞ 9/10 & 9/15
❑ Check operation and adjustment of parking brake ☞ 9/20
❑ Inspect brakelines, hoses and connections ☞ 9/4

POWER STEERING

❍ Check the power steering fluid level ☞ 2/18

*ELECTRICAL SYSTEM *[6]*

❍ Inspect the operation of all electrical and related mechanical parts, including lights, horn, wipers etc. ☞ 2/15, chapter 7

BODY

❑ Check the condition of the convertible top (where fitted) ☞ 2/17
❑ Pressure-wash the underside of the car ☞ 2/17
❑ Wash and wax the exterior of the car ☞ 2/17

YEARLY/12,000 MILES (20,000 KM)

Carry out the operations outlined under the previous headings in this section then, after the work is complete, road test the car and make any further adjustments that this might indicate.

ENGINE

❍ Inspect and adjust the external drive belts ☞ 2/4

COOLING SYSTEM

❍ Check and top up the engine coolant ☞ 2/14,

FUEL & CONTROL SYSTEMS

❍ Check and adjust idle speed ☞ 2/7
❍ Check and adjust the throttle sensor*8 ☞ 5/32
❍ Check the operation of the PCV valve*8 ☞ 5/22
❍ Check the Evaporative Emission Control (EEC) system*8 ☞ 5/23
❍ Check and adjust the throttle dashpot*8 ☞ 5/24

*IGNITION SYSTEM *8*

❍ Check, clean and adjust or replace the spark plugs as required p 5/27/3 on

ELECTRICAL SYSTEM

❍ Check battery electrolyte level and specific gravity.

Note: Although this check is specified by Mazda, it is not possible to carry out on the maintenance-free battery supplied with the car. For details of battery maintenance where your car is fitted with the original or official replacement type battery, ☞ 7/5. If you have a replacement battery with removable cell caps on your car ☞ 2/11

❍ Check headlight alignment ☞ 7/25

Note: We suggest that you get this done professionally using headlight alignment equipment, and observing local laws regarding headlight settings.

BRAKES

❍ Inspect/replace the brake pads ☞ 9/10 and 9/15
❍ Check the brake discs for wear or damage ☞ 9/12 and 9/17
❍ Inspect the brake lines, hoses and connections ☞ 9/4
❍ Adjust the parking brake ☞ 9/20
❍ Check operation of power brake unit (servo) and hoses ☞ 9/8

STEERING & SUSPENSION

❍ Check power steering fluid level ☞ 2/16
❍ Check power steering system ☞ 2/18
❍ Check manual steering system ☞ 2/18
❍ Check front suspension balljoints and dust boots for wear or damage ☞ 2/18

CHASSIS AND BODY

❍ Check and tighten loose fittings and fasteners
❍ Check and lubricate locks and hinges ☞ 2/17
❍ Check vehicle underside (corrosion or damage) ☞ 11/2 & 12/3
❍ Check condition, operation and security of seat belts ☞ 10/14

TIRES

❍ Check the tires and tire pressures ☞ 2/16

TWO-YEARLY/24,000 MILES (40,000 KM)

In addition to the operations described above, carry out the following tasks.

ENGINE

❍ Check tighten the intake manifold and exhaust manifold nuts/bolts ☞ 2/13
❍ Replace the air cleaner element ☞ 2/5

COOLING SYSTEM

❍ Change the engine coolant ☞ 2/14
❍ Check cooling system ☞ 6/3
❍ Check hose condition ☞ 6/4

FUEL SYSTEM

❍ Check fuel lines and connections for leaks ☞ 5/13 and 5/14
❍ Replace the fuel filter ☞ 5/20

IGNITION SYSTEM

❍ Check the ignition timing ☞ 5/26

BRAKES

❍ Change the brake fluid ☞ 2/20

MANUAL TRANSMISSION

❍ Check and top up the manual transmission oil ☞ 2/8

DIFFERENTIAL

❍ Check and top up the differential oil level ☞ 2/10

SUSPENSION

❍ Check the rear suspension joints ☞ 2/18

EXHAUST SYSTEM

❍ Inspect the exhaust system, heatshields and catalytic converter ☞ 2/19

4-YEARLY/48,000 MILES (80,000 KM)

In addition to the operations described above, carry out the following tasks.

MANUAL TRANSMISSION

❍ Change the manual transmission oil ☞ 2/8

REAR AXLE

❍ Change the differential oil ☞ 2/10

EVERY 60,000 MILES (100,000 KM)

ENGINE

❍ Replace the camshaft drivebelt*3 ☞ 3/13

Notes (see text references) -

*1 Major service interval of 12 months (12,000 miles / 20,000 km). Lubrication interval based on mileage, irrespective of time interval.

*2 This operation relates to the inspection and adjustment of alternator / water pump drive belt, plus power steering and air conditioning system belts, where fitted.

*3 Camshaft drivebelt must be replaced at 60,000 miles (96,000 km). Failure to observe this operation may lead to belt failure in service and serious engine damage.

*4 This interval should be reduced if the vehicle is operated under adverse conditions, including:

Driving in dusty conditions
Extended periods of idling, or low-speed operation
Driving for prolonged periods in low temperatures, or regular short journeys.

*5 If the vehicle is used in abnormally sandy or dusty areas, replace more frequently than recommended.

*6 Full functional check of all electrical systems and related mechanical parts.

*7 Replace every two years. Under adverse conditions, or if the vehicle has been driven hard on a continuous basis, reduce this interval to yearly.

*8 This operation should be carried out at 18,000 mile (30,000 km) intervals - Swedish market cars only.

3. ENGINE OIL & OIL FILTER - CHANGING

☞ 1/1, 2 & 2/1.

1 The engine oil should be changed with the engine at normal operating temperature, preferably after a journey of several miles. This ensures that the oil drains easily and that any contaminants are held in suspension in the oil and are flushed out. You will need a drain tray or similar container able to take around 4 liters (4 US/Imp quarts) of oil. You will also need fresh oil and a replacement oil filter, of course. The oil pan will take around 3.2 liters (3.4 US qt, 2.8 Imp qt) and the filter a further 0.17 liters (0.18 US qt, 0.15 Imp qt).

2 The type of oil specified by the manufacturer varies to some extent according to operating conditions, and you will find details of any special requirements in the vehicle handbook. For most areas, any good quality SAE 10W-40, 10W-50, 20W-40 or 20W-50 grade Type SD, SE or SF oil will be appropriate. In excessively cold or hot climates, consult the vehicle handbook or seek advice from a local Mazda dealer.

3 + Remove the oil filler cap from the cambox cover. Place the drain tray below the drain plug and carefully unscrew the 19 mm drain plug. Once you have loosened the plug with a wrench or socket, continue unscrewing it by hand, holding

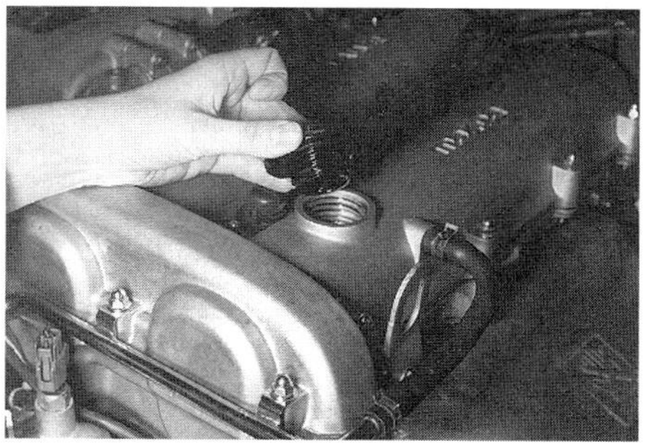

3/3a Remove engine oil filler cap ...

3/3b ... loosen the oil pan drain plug ...

3/3c ... and allow the oil to drain.

the plug up against the oil pan. Once the last thread has come free, remove the plug quickly to avoid having used oil running down your arm - **Warning!** Remember it will be quite hot.

4 Leave the oil to drain. Meanwhile, remove the oil filter using a commercially available oil filter wrench. There are numerous types of wrench available, including versions for use with socket set drive bars. The filter is located on the side of the block, just to the rear of the alternator. Access is not too easy - you will have to work around the alternator and the engine mounting, so it is impor-

3/4 Use a strap wrench to loosen filter ...

tant that the wrench you use will work in the confined space available. If you need to buy a wrench, we suggest you purchase it from your Mazda dealer, or at least ask where they got theirs - that way you'll get one that works.

5 Place some rag below the filter to catch any oil spillage, then loosen the filter with the wrench and remove it by hand - **Warning!** The oil may be hot. Carefully clean around the mounting face with clean rag, and while you're doing this, remove the oil dipstick and wipe it clean. Once the old oil has drained fully, clean the drain plug and oil

3/5 ... then unscrew and remove by hand.

pan threads, then screw the drain plug in by hand. Tighten the plug to 21-41 Nm (3.0-4.2 m-kg, 22-30 ft-lb). Now fit the new oil filter. Smear some oil on the sealing gasket, then screw it in place and hand tighten only. (Never use a wrench to tighten a filter - you will either damage the threads or find it impossible to remove when the next filter change is due).

6 Add the fresh oil slowly. After about 3 liters have been added, start checking the level using the dipstick. Take care not to overfill the engine - if you do you will have to drain off the

3/6 Refill the engine with oil - don't overfill!

excess. Refit the dipstick and filler cap, start the engine and let it idle for a few minutes, then switch it off and allow it to stand for a further minute or two. Recheck the oil level and top up if required - the oil level will have dropped slightly as the oil filter filled.

4. DRIVEBELTS (EXTERNAL) - INSPECTION, REPLACEMENT & ADJUSTMENT

☞ 1/1, 2 & 2/1.

INSPECTION

1 The drive belt arrangement varies from model to model and is dependent on the options fitted (power steering and/or air conditioning). Note that the camshaft drivebelt is dealt with separately, later in this chapter - in this section we are dealing with the external V-belts or V-ribbed belts. The checking and adjustment is similar for all configurations.

2 Start by examining the belt carefully for signs of wear or damage. Excessive wear is often due to incorrect adjustment, but eventually all belts wear out and must be replaced. Indications are obvious scuffing or fraying of the belt structure. In time, the belt material will begin to break down and cracking will begin to form on the working area of the belt.

3 Traditional V-belts work by being pinched between the pulley faces and must be tensioned correctly to achieve sufficient grip. Eventually, wear on the working faces of the belt may allow the belt to bottom out in the pulley groove. Any belt that gets this worn can never be made to work properly and will slip even if excessive tension is applied.

4 V-ribbed belts are thinner and wider in section, using a number of smaller V-sections working in corresponding grooves on the pulley face. They rely on their greater surface area to achieve grip, and are generally more flexible and less prone to cracking. Make sure that they sit on the pulleys correctly - it is easy to fit them so they are displaced by one rib either way.

REPLACEMENT

5 Regardless of the type of belt used, if you find signs of wear or damage, fit a new belt right away - don't wait until the belt breaks in service. The basic configuration is a single belt driven from the crankshaft and running around the alternator and water pump pulleys. Where either power steering, air conditioning or both are fitted, you will need to remove this belt first to gain access to the alternator belt.

6 Where power steering only is fitted a second, outer, belt runs from the crankshaft up around the power steering pump. Refer to the accompanying line drawing. Slacken bolt (A) and

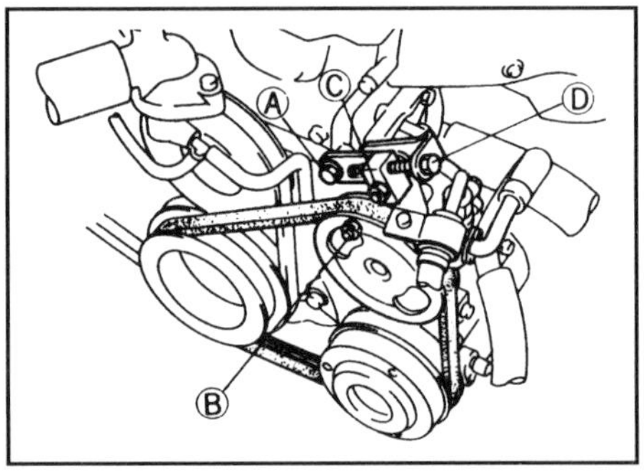

D4/6 DRIVEBELT ARRANGEMENT (POWER STEERING & AIR CON).

nuts (B) and (C). Back off the adjuster bolt (D) and remove the belt.

7 If the car has power steering and air conditioning, a longer outer belt is used to accommodate the extra pulley, but the removal procedure is essentially the same as described above.

8 If the car has air conditioning but no power steering, the belt runs around an idler pulley, occupying the position normally used for the power steering pump, and then around the air conditioning pump. On these vehicles, slacken the locknut at the centre of the idler pulley, then back off the adjuster bolt and remove the belt.

9 Once the outer belt, where fitted, has been removed, you can remove the inner alternator belt. Slacken the alternator mounting bolts positioned above and below the alternator body. Back off the

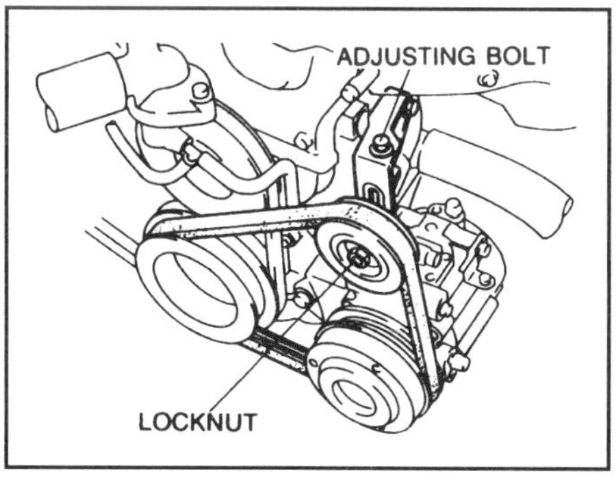

D4/8 DRIVEBELT ARRANGEMENT (AIR CON ONLY).

alternator adjuster bolt to release belt tension and remove the belt.

10 Clean off the pulleys using a solvent cleaner and dry them thoroughly. Place the new belt in position over the pulley. Make sure that V-ribbed type belts sit centrally over the ribbed pulleys - it is easy to get it one groove out of line if you fail to check this.

ADJUSTMENT

11 The belt tension can be checked either by measuring the amount of deflection possible on a specified run, or by using a special service tool (49 9200 020) to measure belt tension. Unless you happen to be a Mazda dealer, we assume that you won't have access to the special tool, so we will concentrate on the deflection method.

12 To check the deflection of the alternator belt, press the belt inward with your thumb midway between the crankshaft and alternator pulleys. You need to apply moderate pressure - specifically 98 N (10 kg, 22 lb) though absolute accuracy is not vital. A new belt should be set to allow 8-9 mm (0.32-0.35 in) deflection, while a used belt is set to give 9-10 mm (0.36-0.39 in). Refer to the accompanying drawing and set the belt tension using bolt (C), then tighten the remaining bolts as follows:

(A) 19-25 Nm (1.9-2.6 kgf m / 14-19 lbf ft)
(B) 37-52 Nm (3.8-5.3 kgf m / 27-38 lbf ft)

4/12 Use thumb to check belt tension.

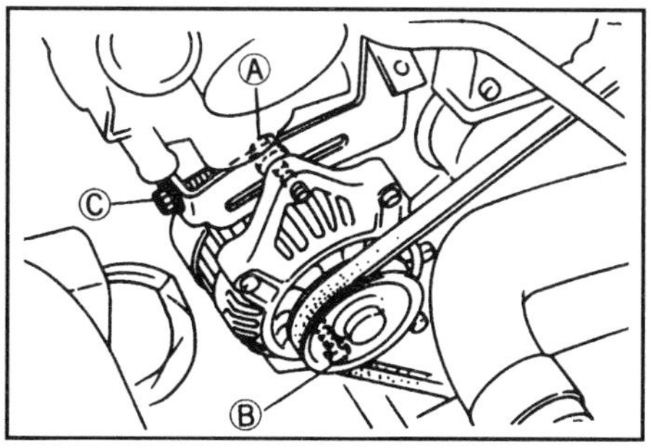

D4/12 ADJUSTING DRIVEBELT.

13 If your car has a secondary belt driving either power steering, air conditioning or both, check its tension midway between the crankshaft pulley and the power steering pump or idler pulley. Press the belt inward with your thumb midway between the two pulleys. You need to apply moderate pressure - actually 98 N (10 kg, 22 lb) though absolute accuracy is not vital. A new belt should be set to allow 8-9 mm (0.32-0.35 in) deflection, while a used belt is set to give 9-10 mm (0.36-0.39 in).

14 (D4/6) To adjust the belt tension, make sure that you slacken off the pivot bolt(s) or nut(s) before setting the tension using the adjuster bolt. If you omit to do this you will almost certainly cause damage. On cars with power steering, slacken (A), (B) and (C) and set the belt tension with the adjuster bolt (D). Once the correct tension has been set, tighten the various fasteners shown in the accompanying line drawing to the following torque figures:

(A) 32-46 Nm (3.2-4.7 kgf-m, 24-33 lbf-ft)
(B) 37-53 Nm (3.7-5.5 kgf-m, 27-39 lbf-ft)
(C) 19-25 Nm (1.9-2.6 kgf-m, 14-18 lbf-ft)

15 (D4/8) If your car has air conditioning with manual steering, there is an idler pulley in place of the power steering pump. On these cars, slacken the idler pulley locknut, and turn the adjusting bolt to set belt tension. Once set correctly, tighten the pulley locknut to 37-52 Nm (3.8-5.3 kgf m / 27-38 lbf ft).

16 If you happen to have access to the special service tool (49 9200 020) you can check belt tension between any two pulleys. Grip the handle and depress the center shaft against spring pressure. Fit the tool over the belt and release the shaft. Read off the tension indicated on the scale and compare it with the following specified tension settings:

New: 491-589 N (50-60 kg, 110-132 lb)
Used: 422-491 N (43-50 kg, 95-110 lb)

Adjustment is carried out as described above, leaving the tool in place on the belt so that the tension can be read off as the adjustment is made.

5. AIR CLEANER ELEMENT - REPLACEMENT

☞ 1/1, 2 & 2/1.

1 The air cleaner element will normally require replacement at the intervals specified at the beginning of this chapter. If the vehicle operates in unusually dusty areas, it will probably require more frequent replacement. Also, any time the element gets contaminated with oil or water it must be replaced. Note that it is not possible to clean the element - even blowing it through with compressed air is not permissible.

2 + You can gain access to the element after removing the cover of the air cleaner casing. Start by disconnecting the hose clip which secures the trunking to the airflow meter, and pull the trunking clear. Unplug the electrical connector from the airflow meter (you can leave the meter attached to the air cleaner cover). Remove the cover securing 10 mm screws and lift the cover and airflow meter clear. The air cleaner element can now be removed.

3 Fit the new element into the casing and refit the cover. Tighten the securing screws to 7.8-11 Nm (80-110 cm-kg, 69-95 in-lb). Plug in the airflow meter electrical connector. Reconnect the air intake trunking and tighten the hose clip which secures it.

5/2a Remove air cleaner cover.

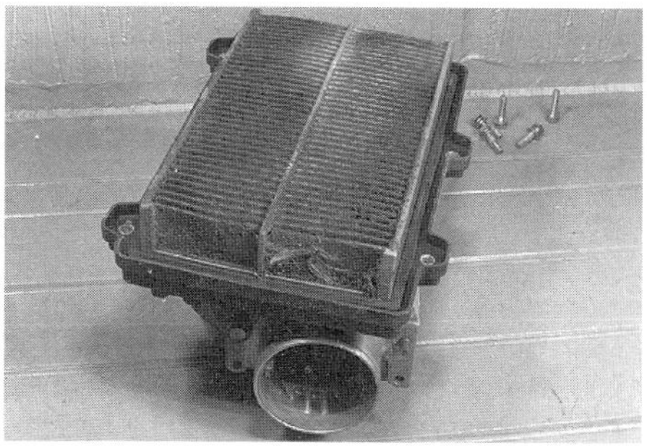

5/2b Dirty air cleaner element.

5/3 Fit the new element in place.

6. SPARK PLUGS - CHECKING, CLEANING & ADJUSTING

☞ 1/1, 2 & 2/1.

1 The spark plugs should be replaced at the prescribed service intervals. Between these inter-

vals it is permissible to clean and re-gap the plugs, though you may feel as we do that so much depends on the correct operation of these relatively inexpensive consumable items, that it is preferable to fit new plugs whenever their operation is suspect. If you need to check, clean and re-gap the plugs between changes, the procedure is outlined below. Even if you intend to fit new plugs, read through this section; you can assess engine condition from the appearance of the used plugs.

2 Remove each plug in turn and examine the working end for signs of eroded electrodes. Check for indications of cracks on the porcelain insulator nose or on the ribbed external insulator between the plug body and terminal. If severe wear or damage is noted, replace the plug.

3 You can tell quite a lot about engine condition by examining the business end of spark plugs, but only if the car has been on a decent length run and not allowed to idle for more than a few seconds before they are removed. Normal operation will produce an even grey/brown deposit on the electrodes and on the porcelain insulator around the center electrode. A sooty black deposit is indicative of an excessively rich fuel/air mixture, and an oily black appearance indicates oil fouling, often discovered in a worn engine where a significant amount of engine oil is getting burnt as it works past worn rings or valve guides.

4 At the other extreme, very light deposits and a glazed appearance on the electrodes is indicative of overheating - if the correct plug grade is in use, this could be due to a weak fuel/air mixture, the wrong grade of fuel or incorrect ignition timing. For details of the recommended plug types see the specifications in chapter 1. Note that optional plug grades are included here. They are primarily for use in abnormal operating conditions, and as a rule you should stick to the standard types listed. If you use the car in unusual climatic conditions, or intend to go racing in it, consult a Mazda dealer or a recognized tuning specialist for specific advice on plug grades. Note that you may need to change the plug grade if you have modified the engine or fitted performance parts.

5 It is permissible to remove light deposits from the plug electrodes using fine abrasive paper - hold the plug with the electrode end downwards so that any debris drops away and not into the recess around the insulator. Use a wire brush to clean the plug threads.

6 Once you have checked and cleaned the plug electrodes, or before new plugs are installed, check the electrode gap. It is worth buying a plug gapping tool for this task; these have wire-type feeler gauges and special tools for setting the gap by bending the ground (earth) electrode. Note that you should never attempt to bend the center electrode. If you do, you are likely to break the insulator nose. Set the electrode gap to 1-1.1 mm (0,039-0.043 in).

7 Before installing the new or cleaned plugs, apply a small trace of copper-based anti-seize compound or molybdenum disulfide grease to the plug threads; this will make removal easier next time, and lessens the risk of a seized plug tearing

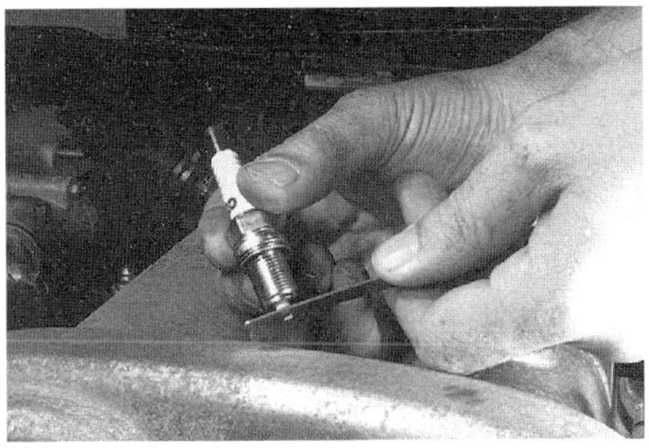

6/6 Measuring spark plug electrode gap.

out the plug threads in the cylinder head. **Caution!** Do not overtighten the spark plugs.

7. IDLE SPEED - CHECKING & ADJUSTMENT

☞ 1/1, 2 & 2/1.

1 To carry out the idle speed check you will require an accurate external tachometer, and ideally, the System Selector (service tool No. 49 B019 9A0). You can get by without the tool, but the vehicle's own tachometer is not sufficiently accurate to be able to set the idle speed precisely (it is also difficult to work with during the test procedure!) The engine should be at normal operating temperature during the test.

2 Locate the diagnosis connector and open the cover. Connect the System Selector to the diagnosis connector, and set the selector to the **SELF TEST** position. If you don't have access to the System Selector, use an insulated jumper wire to connect terminals **TEN** and **GND**.

3 If your tachometer requires an external power feed, connect this to the blue power connection terminal. Take care not to allow the power connection terminal to be grounded (earthed) or you will burn out the 20A wiper fuse. Connect the tachometer probe to the **IG** terminal on the diagnosis connector.

4 On manual transmission cars, check that neutral is selected. In the case of automatic transmission models, select P (Park). **Warning!** Apply the parking brake. Start the engine and note the idle speed reading on the tachometer. If outside the range 800-900 rpm, pull off the blanking cap on the throttle body and turn the adjustment screw until the idle speed is within this range. Refit the blanking cap and switch off the ignition. Disconnect the tachometer, and also the System Selector or jumper wire and close the diagnosis connector cover.

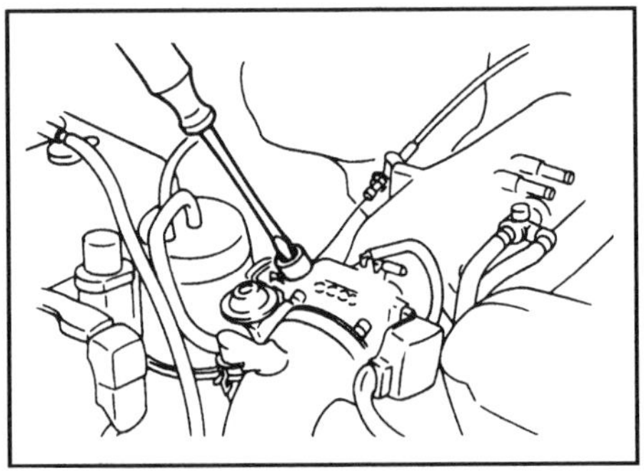

D7/4 ADJUSTING IDLE SPEED.

8. TRANSMISSION OIL (MANUAL TRANS) - CHECKING LEVEL & CHANGING

☞ 1/1, 2 & 2/1.

1 Checking or changing the transmission oil requires the car to be raised so you can get access underneath to the filler and drain plugs. This can be achieved by placing the car on safety stands or on fabricated steel wheel ramps, noting that the car should be raised to a level position to ensure the resulting oil level is correct. If you have access to a vehicle lift, or can get the oil changed by a Mazda dealer or service station, we suggest that you do so. Unless you need to do other work under the car, you need to do a lot of preparatory work to gain access. For details of jacking and supporting the car ☞ 1/3

CHECKING LEVEL

2 With the car safely supported, unscrew and remove the transmission oil level/filler plug (A) which is situated halfway up the transmission casing on the lefthand side.

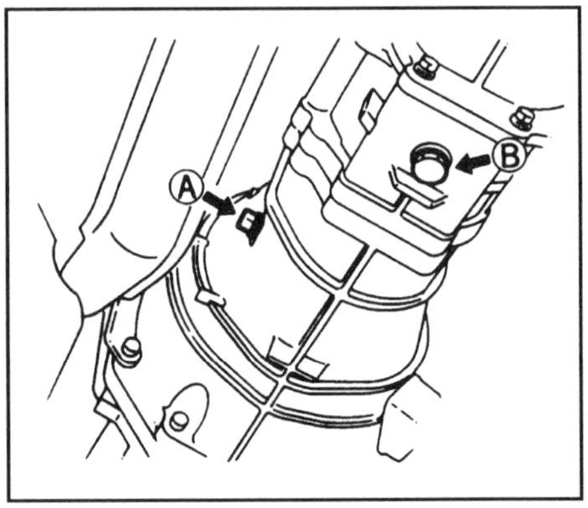

D8/2 LOCATION OF MANUAL TRANSMISSION DRAIN AND LEVEL/FILLER PLUGS.

3 Add fresh oil through the filler/level plug hole until the oil is level with the hole - allow any excess to drain out. The correct oil grade is as follows:

Above 10 C (50 F): API Service GL-4 or GL-5 SAE 80W-90

8/3 Topping-up transmission oil.

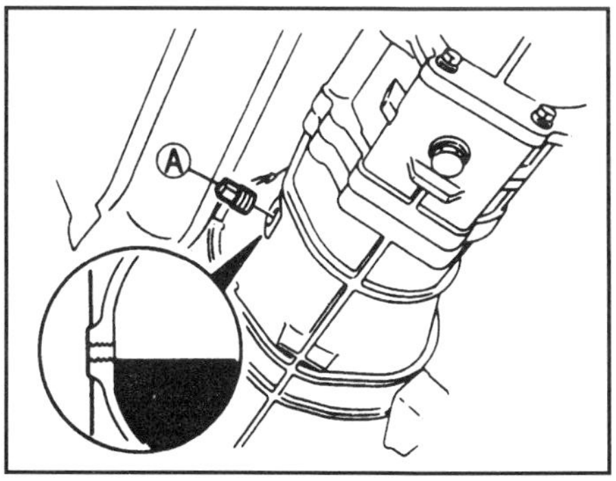

D8/4 CORRECT OIL LEVEL FOR MANUAL TRANSMISSION.

All seasons:API Service GL-4 or GL-5 SAE 75W-80

4 Once the oil level is correct, install the filler/level plug and tighten it to 25-39 Nm (2.5-4.0 kgf m / 18-29 lbf ft).

CHANGING TRANSMISSION OIL

5 With the car safely supported, position a drain tray under the transmission drain plug, then remove the filler plug (A) followed by the drain plug (B). The transmission holds 2.0 liters (2.1 US qt / 1.8 Imp qt) of oil, so have a container of at least this capacity ready. The transmission oil is viscous and will take a while to drain completely. It will drain quicker, and more contaminants will be flushed out, if the car has been driven and the transmission is warm. **Warning!** Take care to avoid burns from the hot oil or the exhaust system.

6 When the oil has finished draining, clean the drain plug and drain hole threads, and then install the plug using a new sealing washer. Tighten the plug to 39-59 Nm (4.0-6.0 kgf m / 29-43 lbf ft).

7 Add fresh oil (see specification in step 3) through the filler/level plug hole until the oil is level with the hole - allow any excess to drain out.

8 Once the oil level is correct, install the filler plug and tighten it to 25-39 Nm (2.5-4.0 kgf m / 18-29 lbf ft).

9. TRANSMISSION OIL (AUTO TRANS) - CHECKING LEVEL & CHANGING

☞ 1/1, 2 & 2/1.

1 The automatic transmission oil should be checked and changed at the specified intervals or transmission performance will deteriorate, and in the longer term, wear or damage may result.

CHECKING

2 Position the car on a flat, level surface. **Warning!** Make sure that the parking brake is applied and that the rear wheels are secured by chocks; the car must be unable to move during the checking procedure.

3 Start the engine and wait until the engine is at normal temperature before commencing the test. The transmission oil must be at 60-70 C (140-158 F) during the test, and the best way to ensure this is to carry out the check after a run of several miles.

4 Apply the brake, holding the pedal down firmly while shifting into each range in turn, leaving the shift lever in each position for several seconds. This distributes the oil around the transmission, leaving the level as it would normally be during driving. Shift back to **P** (Park) and leave the engine idling.

5 Withdraw the transmission dipstick, wipe it clean, then reinsert it, pushing it fully home. Withdraw the dipstick again and note the level indicated. This must lie between the **F** (Full) and **L** (Low) marks. Examine the oil on the dipstick for discoloration or abnormal smells.

6 Heavy discoloration may indicate burning of the drive plates, while an abnormal smell can suggest general overheating of the transmission (or oil in bad need of changing). In either case, try changing the oil as described below and see if the condition improves, before having the transmission checked professionally.

7 Top up the transmission if required by adding fresh oil through the dipstick guide tube. The oil is usually supplied in plastic packs with flexible filler tubes to facilitate this. The correct oil grade is ATF (Automatic Transmission Fluid): Dexron® II or M-III.

CHANGING

8 During the oil change procedure the car must be level, but raised clear of the ground to allow access to the underside of the transmission. You will need to jack the car and support it on safety stands, ensuring that it is secure before venturing underneath ☞ 1/3.

9 Note also that the oil change should be carried out after a run, while the oil in the transmission is hot. This will ensure that it drains quickly and completely, and that any contaminants are in suspension and thus flushed out. You will need a drain tray with a capacity of around a gallon to catch the used oil.

10 Position the drain tray under the transmission oil pan, then loosen the oil pan bolts by around one turn each. Leave one bolt loosely in place at each corner and remove the rest. You will need to take care during the next stage - the oil in the transmission is hot and could burn if you get it on your arms.

11 Support the oil pan with one arm and remove the remaining bolts, then quickly lower one end of the oil pan so that the oil drains into the drain tray. Leave any residual oil to drain off and remove the oil pan for cleaning.

12 Carefully clean out the oil pan, removing all traces of old oil and contaminants from it and its magnet. Clean the transmission case gasket face, then install the oil pan using a new gasket. Tighten the oil pan bolts evenly and progressively to 5.9-7.8 Nm (60-80 kgf cm / 52-69 lbf in).

13 Add around 4.0 liters (4.2 US qt / 3.5 Imp qt) of ATF (Automatic Transmission Fluid): Dexron® II or M-III. After lowering the car to the ground and chocking the rear wheels, apply the parking brake and go through the oil level check described above. If necessary, add a little extra oil to bring the level to within the prescribed range on the dipstick.

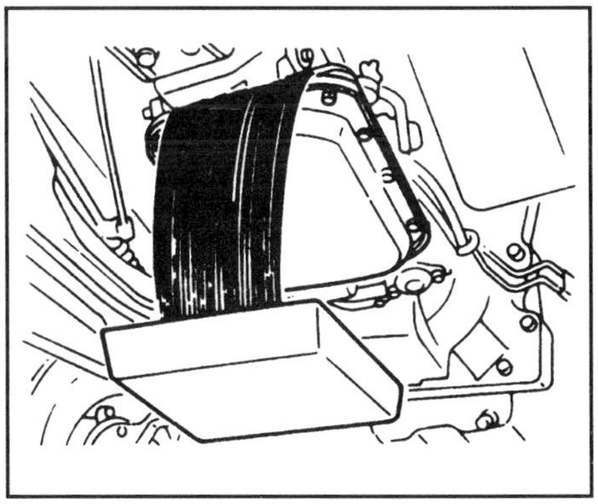

D9/11 DRAINING THE AUTOMATIC TRANSMISSION UNIT.

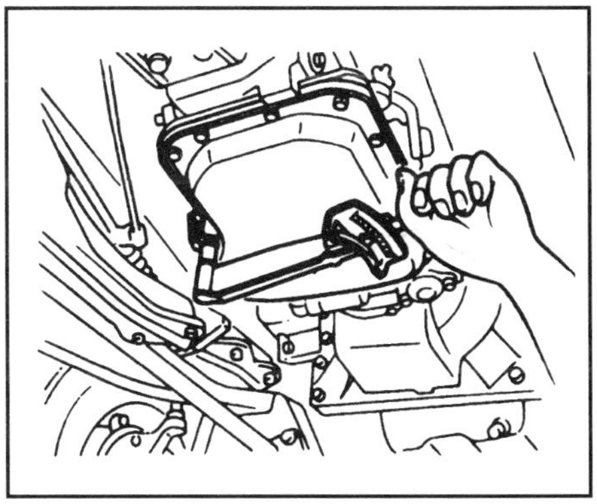

D9/12 TORQUE TIGHTEN OIL PAN BOLTS.

14 **Caution!** Take care not to overfill the transmission. If you do, you will need to remove the excess, using a hand operated pump or syringe and a long tube introduced down the dipstick guide tube. Failing this, you will have to remove the oil pan again to drain off the excess oil.

10. DIFFERENTIAL OIL - CHECKING LEVEL & CHANGING

☞ 1/1, 2 & 2/1.

CHECKING

1 The way you go about tacking this operation will depend on your agility and facilities. The car needs to be resting on a level surface during the check, either on its wheels, or raised and supported on safety stands. If you can reach the filler/level plug on the back of the differential housing without having to jack and support the car, so much the better, but if you cannot reach the plug this way, ☞ 1/3.

2 Unscrew and remove the combined 23 mm filler/level plug - this is the higher of the two plugs on the back of the differential housing. Verify that oil is level with the bottom edge of the hole. If necessary, add oil until it is at the correct level, but do not overfill; leave any excess to drain out before

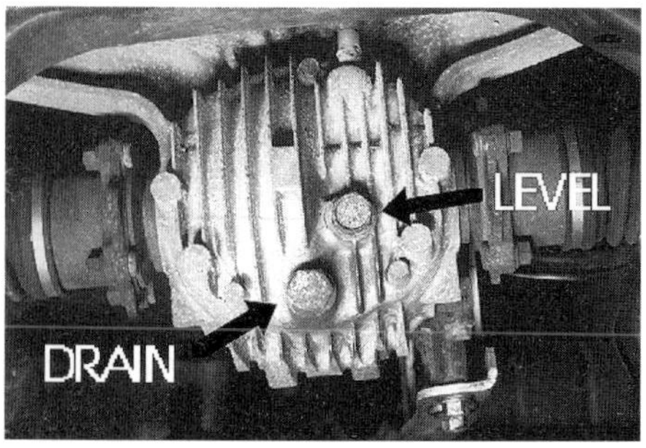

10/2 Axle drain and level/filler plugs.

installing the plug. The specified oil types and capacity are as follows:

Above -18 C (0 F): API GL-5, SAE 90
Below -18 C (0 F): API GL-5, SAE 80W
Total capacity: 0.65 liter (0.69 US qt / 0.57 Imp qt)

3 Clean the plug and threads in the filler hole, then install the plug using a new sealing washer, tightening it to 39-54 Nm (4.0-5.5 kgf m / 29-40 lbf ft). Wipe off any residual oil from the outside of the differential housing.

CHANGING

4 Place a drain tray of around 1 liter (1.06 US qt / 0.88 Imp qt) capacity below the differential housing and remove the combined 23 mm filler/level (upper) plug and the 24 mm drain (lower) plug. **Warning!** The oil could be hot. Leave the oil to drain. This may take a while due to the viscosity of the oil, and will be speeded up a little if the car has been used recently and the oil is still warm.

5 When the old oil has finished draining, clean the drain plug, filler/level plug and the casing hole threads, then install the drain plug using a new sealing washer. Tighten it to 39-54 Nm (4.0-5.5 kgf m / 29-40 lbf ft).

6 Add oil through the filler/level hole until it is just level with the bottom of the hole; do not overfill. Leave any excess oil to drain out before installing the plug. The specified oil types and capacity are as follows:

Above -18 C (0 F): API GL-5, SAE 90
Below -18 C (0 F): API GL-5, SAE 80W
Total capacity: 0.65 liter (0.69 US qt / 0.57 Imp qt)

7 Install the filler/level plug using a new sealing washer, tightening it to 39-54 Nm (4.0-5.5 kgf m / 29-40 lbf ft). Wipe off any residual oil from the outside of the differential housing.

11. BATTERY - CHECKING CHARGE LEVEL, SPECIFIC GRAVITY & ELECTROLYTE LEVEL

☞ 1/1, 2 & 2/1.

Warning! Battery electrolyte is extremely corrosive. Take care not to drop the battery or damage its casing. Take care to avoid eye or skin contact during handling (use disposable plastic gloves and eye protection). If electrolyte splashes on the skin, wash immediately with copious amounts of water and get medical assistance if burning is noted. If splashes enter the eyes, wash immediately with copious amounts of water and summon immediate medical assistance. Contact between electrolyte and clothing will quickly cause damage - wash immediately in water to minimize damage.

1 Mazda describe this operation as part of the maintenance schedule on cars sold in Europe. However, this check can be applied only where a replacement battery with removable cell caps is fitted. The original, maintenance-free battery supplied with the car contains gel and does not have removable cell caps: it should not be tampered with. Most replacement batteries are also of the maintenance-free type and, again, this section should be ignored. For information on checking and charging the original battery ☞ 7/5.

REMOVAL AND CHECKING

2 Disable the audio unit security system (where fitted). Open the trunk and remove the cover over the battery. It is held by snap fasteners to the trunk floor. Disconnect the battery leads, negative (-) lead first, followed by the positive (+) lead. Each terminal is clamped in place - use a 10 mm wrench to release it. **Warning!** When loosening the negative (-) terminal connector take great care not to short the tool you are using against the positive (+) terminal.

3 📷 + Using a 10 mm wrench or socket, remove the two bolts which secure the battery end bracket and lift this away. Unscrew and remove the single 10 mm clamp nut and unhook the upper part of the clamp from the threaded rod. The clamp mechanism can be removed by rotating it toward the center of the trunk and unhooking it.

4 Pull off the nearest of the two vent hoses from the end of the battery vent manifold. The battery can now be lifted partway out of its recess, and the remaining vent hose disconnected. Note that replacement batteries may have a different vent hose arrangement. Lift the battery out of the trunk and place it on the bench for examination and charging.

11/3a battery with cover removed.

11/3b Gently lift battery out.

5 If you detect signs of electrolyte on the exterior of the battery, it may be that the casing has been damaged, in which case a new battery must be fitted. If electrolyte has leaked into the trunk, you must remove and neutralize any traces, or serious corrosion will result. With luck, any leakage will be confined in the plastic tray which the battery sits in. Given the battery's location in the trunk, if you have any reason to suspect casing damage, fit a new battery immediately.

6 You will need to wash the affected area with an alkaline solution to neutralize the acidic electrolyte. Make up a solution of warm water to which a couple of tablespoons of sodium bicarbonate have been added and dissolved. You can get sodium bicarbonate from pharmacies and general stores, where it is sold as a raising agent for home baking. The solution will fizz as it contacts the electrolyte. Don't breathe the fumes produced, and wear eye and skin protection throughout the operation.

7 If the battery is undamaged, wipe over its casing with a rag or paper wipe dampened with the sodium bicarbonate solution. This will clean the casing and remove any acid residue. The terminal posts can be cleaned using abrasive paper or a small wire brush (or you can buy special cleaning tools from auto parts stores). Once clean, coat the terminals with petroleum jelly or battery terminal grease to prevent corrosion - don't use regular grease for this.

8 Remove each cell cap in turn and use a commercially available battery hydrometer to measure the specific gravity of the electrolyte in each cell. The specific gravity readings found should be compared with the following:

Battery electrolyte specific gravity at 20 C (68 F)
Fully charged: 1.270-1.290
Half charged: 1.190-1.210
Discharged: 1.110-1.130

9 It will be noted that the specific gravity varies according to the state of charge of the battery, and will also be affected by variations in ambient temperature. A low reading on all cells is indicative of a low state of charge. More significantly, a low reading on only one cell indicates that the cell may be defective, and if you have experienced starting problems it may be preferable to fit a new battery, or at least to have it checked out professionally.

10 If the battery requires charging, do so, then recheck the specific gravity of each cell before installing it in the trunk. **Warning!** Excessively high charging rates could explode the battery due to gas buildup. Any form of charging releases hydrogen and oxygen from the battery. This is a potentially

explosive mixture - keep well away from any potential source of ignition, and make sure the charging area is well ventilated. When handling the battery, take care to avoid short circuits - they can be dramatic and dangerous.

11 The standard S46A24L(S) battery fitted to all new Miatas/MX5s should normally be recharged at 3A or less. This slow charging procedure is always preferable where time allows. If you need to fast-charge the battery as described above, never exceed 20A, and note that repeated fast charging shortens battery life. If the battery becomes hot to the touch during charging, discontinue charging and allow it to cool down, or reduce the charge rate. Replacement batteries with similar capacities will require a similar charge rate - consult the battery supplier for further information.

12 It is always preferable to use a current-controlled charger if possible - if you intend to buy a charger, try to get one of these units if you can. A current-controlled charger allows you to set the charge rate. Cheaper voltage-controlled units find their own charging current - the current starts out high, then slowly falls back to zero as the battery reaches full charge. With this type of charger it is harder to gauge how long you need to perform the charging operation.

13 Check that the battery terminals are clean, then connect the charger clamps to the battery terminal posts, positive (+) to positive and negative (-) to negative. **Warning!** Reconnect the positive (+) clamp first and cover it with its insulator. **Warning!** When reconnecting the negative clamp take great care not to short the tool you are using against the positive (+) terminal. Switch on the charger at the selected rate and charge for the prescribed amount of time. On cheaper chargers, just switch on and charge until the charger meter falls to zero, then disconnect the charger and recheck the voltage of the battery. If you find that the battery gets hot during charging, switch off and allow it to cool, then resume charging for a while if required.

14 When charging is complete, check the battery electrolyte specific gravity as described above. If the electrolyte specific gravity fails to reach the correct level, it indicates that it is at or nearing the end of its useful life.

TOPPING UP

15 If the battery electrolyte level is low, top up using distilled or demineralized water only. Do not overfill the cells or excess electrolyte may be expelled in service - the correct electrolyte level is around 5 mm (0.25 in) above the top edge of the plates. Always top up the battery just before a run to ensure that the extra liquid mixes thoroughly with the electrolyte - this is especially important in winter, and will reduce the risk of the battery freezing and splitting while the car is parked.

BATTERY INSTALLATION

16 With the battery clean and fully charged, place it in its tray in the trunk, remembering to install the vent hoses as it is maneuvered into position. Reassemble and secure the clamp (do not overtighten it). Install the end bracket, then connect the battery leads, positive (+) lead first, negative (-) lead last. **Warning!** Take care not to short the battery to ground with the wrench during installation. Install the battery cover.

INSTALLING A NEW BATTERY

17 It is not possible to purchase a straight replacement battery for the Miata/MX5. The official replacement unit is physically larger, and you will also need an installation kit to suit the new unit - ask for the Mazda battery replacement kit, Part No. NAY1 56 020A, or equivalent at your Mazda dealer. The kit consists of a new battery tray, plus a new clamp and clamp bolt. Note that you should not install any battery that just happens to fit the mounting area. The correct battery must have a vent manifold, or electrolyte vapor will be released into the trunk in service. You must verify that this is the case if you plan to purchase a battery other than through a Mazda dealer.

18 To install the replacement battery, you will first need to remove the battery clamp bolt anchor plate, turn it through 180°, and then reinstall it. The position of the battery end bracket also has to be changed. Install the new battery tray, then fit the new battery, connecting the vent pipes to the manifold stubs. Secure the battery using the new clamp arrangement from the fitting kit. Finally, you will need to trim part of the battery cover to fit the new battery. For more information on this and other aspects of battery maintenance ☞ 7/5.

12. IGNITION TIMING - CHECKING & ADJUSTING

☞ 1/1, 2 & 2/1.

1 The ignition timing check should be carried out at the specified intervals in conjunction with the idle speed check - the two procedures overlap to some degree. Before starting you should ensure that all electrical accessories are switched off - they could produce spurious signals which might in turn affect the test. The spark plugs must be in good condition and correctly adjusted, and the fuel system should be functioning normally; there is no point conducting the timing check if the normal running of the engine is being impaired by some other factor. Before starting the engine, you should also identify the marks used during the timing check and ensure that they are clean and easily visible. There is a yellow timing mark on the crankshaft pulley which aligns with a scale on the camshaft drivebelt cover.

2 You will require a xenon timing light, an accurate external tachometer and, ideally, the System Selector (service tool No. 49 B019 9A0). You can get by without the System Selector, but the vehicle's own tachometer is not sufficiently accurate to be able to measure the idle speed precisely (it is also difficult to see while working under the hood!) The engine should be at normal operating temperature during the test.

3 Locate the diagnosis connector and open the cover. Connect the System Selector to the diagnosis connector, and set the selector to the **SELF TEST** position. If you don't have access to the System Selector, use an insulated jumper wire to connect terminals **TEN** and **GND**.

4 If your tachometer and/or timing light requires an external power feed, connect this to the blue power connection terminal. Take care not to allow the power connection terminal to be grounded (earthed) or you will burn out the 20A wiper fuse. Connect the tachometer probe and the timing light trigger lead to the IG terminal on the diagnosis connector.

5 (D7/4) On manual transmission cars, check that neutral is selected. In the case of automatic transmission models, select **P** (Park). **Warning!** Make sure the parking brake is applied and wheels chocked. Start the engine and note the idle speed reading on the tachometer. If outside the range 800-900 rpm, pull off the blanking cap on the throttle body and turn the adjustment screw until the idle speed is within this range. Refit the blanking cap.

6 With the engine idling, aim the timing light at the crankshaft pulley and note the position of the timing mark in relation to the scale on the cover. It should be within one degree of the 10° mark. If the setting is incorrect, slacken the crank angle sensor 12 mm lock bolt and carefully turn the sensor until the marks are correctly aligned. Once correct, tighten the sensor lock bolt to 19-25 Nm (1.9-2.6 m-kg, 14-19 ft-lb). Disconnect the System Selector or jumper wire, and the tachometer and timing light, and refit the diagnosis connector cover.

12/6 Strobe-lit ignition timing marks.

13. MANIFOLD FASTENERS - CHECKING TIGHTNESS

☞ 1/1, 2 & 2/1.

1 Because they may loosen slightly as the gasket beds in, the intake manifold and exhaust manifold (header) nuts/bolts should be check-tightened after the recommended interval on new or rebuilt engines, and at the intervals specified above in the case of engines which have covered higher mileages. It is interesting to note that while this is a scheduled maintenance item on European market cars, no such requirement applies to other market cars.

2 Access to the intake manifold nuts/bolts is extremely restricted using normal socket accessories, and depending on your socket set, some preliminary dismantling may be inevitable before

you can reach all of the fasteners. We found that we were able to reach most of the individual nuts and bolts retaining the manifold using a 12 mm socket on a 250 mm (9.5 in) extension. This was only possible after we had maneuvered the socket between the individual intake trunks until we found a gap large enough for it to pass through.

3 There are two extremely awkward bolts alongside the pillars which support the fuel rail. We got to these by fitting a socket and universal joint to the bolt head from above and then inserting the extension between the intake tracts and engaging it in the universal joint: this was with a 1/2 inch

13/3 Tightening intake manifold bolts -tricky!

drive socket set. If you use a smaller drive socket system, access may be improved, but it will need to be of extremely good quality because these bolts are tight. Loosen the nuts and bolts a little and then retighten in the sequence of an outward spiral from the center to the specified torque figure of 19-25 Nm (1.9-2.6 kgf m / 14-19 lbf ft). For further information regarding the intake manifold nuts and bolts ☞ 3

4 The exhaust manifold nuts are considerably easier to access. You will need to remove the air cleaner casing together with the air cleaner and airflow meter in order to be able to detach the manifold heatshield. **Warning!** The heatshield and manifold could be very hot.

5 Working inside the engine compartment, detach the air hose from the airflow meter and air pipe stubs and remove it - the hose is secured by a worm-drive clip at each end.

6 Disconnect the airflow meter wiring connector, lifting the locking wire with a screwdriver blade. Unhook the wiring from the guide clip on the side of the air cleaner / plenum casing.

7 Remove the air cleaner / plenum casing complete with the airflow meter. The casing is held by two 12 mm bolts and a 12 mm nut, plus a single

13/7 Remove air cleaner body ...

10 mm bolt holding the end of the intake pipe. On our project car, there was an adjacent electrical unit which also needed to be swung clear to allow removal.

8 The next task is to remove the manifold heat shield - this is held by four 10 mm bolts, all of which are easy to reach. The heatshield is a double-skinned component, and on our car had obviously suffered the combined effects of heat and vibration; when we removed it, a section round one of the bolt holes broke away. You may wish to check yours for damage before starting this procedure so that a new unit can be obtained.

13/8 ... and heatshield.

9 With the heatshield removed you can reach the manifold nuts easily. These should be slackened slightly and then retightened evenly and progressively to 38-46 Nm (3.9-4.7 kgf m / 28-34 lbf ft). Use a tightening sequence that spirals outward from the center.

10 When you fit the manifold heatshield, use copper grease on the threads to prevent them from seizing in the manifold brackets - this could cause you problems later if ignored - the retaining bolts will tend to freeze in their threads due to the effects of repeated heating. To conclude this sequence,

13/9 Checking exhaust manifold nuts.

install the air cleaner casing / plenum chamber and reconnect the airflow meter wiring and air hose.

14. ENGINE COOLANT - TOPPING-UP & CHANGING

☞ 1/1, 2 & 2/1.

Warning! If the engine has been run within the last hour or so, the engine coolant will be hot and under pressure. Removing the radiator filler or coolant reservoir caps can result in the water boiling as pressure is released, resulting in scalding steam being ejected. Always allow the engine to cool before removing either cap. Wear eye protection, gloves and overalls for safety.

1 Place some rag over the radiator cap and turn it slowly counterclockwise until it reaches the first stop position. Wait until pressure has vented before removing the cap completely.

2 The engine coolant level should be checked and topped up as required regularly - we suggest that you give the level a quick visual check on a weekly basis. The check should be carried out with the engine cold, to avoid any risk of scalding

14/1 Careful when removing rad cap - see text.

14/2 Topping-up coolant reservoir.

(see warning above). Check that the radiator coolant level is just below the filler neck, and that the coolant level in the reservoir is between the **FULL** and **LOW** level marks. Add only pre-mixed coolant to adjust the levels as necessary.

MIXING ENGINE COOLANT

Warning! Keep antifreeze away from children and pets - it may be harmful or even fatal if swallowed. Do not allow skin contact with antifreeze. Store antifreeze in a sealed container well out of children's reach.

Caution! Do not allow antifreeze to come into contact with painted surfaces - color or surface damage may result. Wipe up coolant spills immediately.

3 It is important to use coolant made up in the correct proportions from distilled or demineralized water and ethylene glycol antifreeze. Never use tap water or you risk corrosion and scale deposits in the cooling system. Never use alcohol-based or methanol-based antifreeze.

4 To check the existing coolant mixture you will need a thermometer and a coolant hydrometer. The specific gravity of the coolant mixture varies according to ambient temperature and

Coolant protection down to	Water (%)	Antifreeze (%)	Specific gravity at 20°C (68°F)
-16°C (3°F)	65	35	1.054
-26°C (-15°F)	55	45	1.066
-40°C (-40°F)	45	55	1.078

T14/4 COOLANT MIXTURE PERCENTAGES.

the water / antifreeze ratio. The recommended proportions for frost protection down to various air temperatures is shown in the table:

5 Note the point made above about how ambient temperature will affect the specific gravity. The accompanying table illustrates this relationship.

6 Having checked the specific gravity required for operation in your area, mix the appropriate proportions of antifreeze and distilled / demineralized water in a clean container. Store the mixture in a sealed plastic drum or similar for use when topping up the cooling system (see warning notes above).

TOPPING UP THE COOLING SYSTEM

7 Before adding fresh coolant, check the general condition of the existing coolant. Look for signs of scale buildup around the filler neck, and also for signs of oil contamination. If the coolant is dirty or contaminated, you should drain the system, flush it out with a hose, and then add fresh coolant. Note that if oil contamination was present, this may indicate a failed seal or gasket in the engine, especially if there has been a significant coolant loss recently. If the head gasket, for example, blows between the cooling system passages and one of the combustion chambers, combustion pressure may well force coolant out of the system and cause the oil contamination of the remainder. Always investigate and monitor such incidents closely - you could avoid more expensive repair bills if you act quickly.

CHANGING THE COOLANT

8 The engine coolant should be changed at the specified intervals, or more frequently if there have been signs of contamination or deterioration of the existing coolant (see above). This task should be undertaken with the engine cold. The cooling system capacity is 6.0 liters (6.3 US qt / 5.3 Imp qt), so you will need a drain container of at least this capacity.

9 Remove the radiator filler cap and position the drain container below the drain plug on the underside of the radiator. Loosen and remove the plug and allow the coolant to drain. **Warning!** The coolant could be hot.

10 Place a hose in the radiator filler neck and allow the system to flush through for a while, until the emerging water is completely clear, then allow the system to drain completely. While this is taking place, remove, empty and refit the coolant reservoir, washing out any dirt or sediment at the same time. Refit the drain plug and tighten it securely.

14/11 Refilling radiator.

11 📷 Add fresh coolant to the radiator until the level is just below the filler neck. Run the engine at idle for a while with the radiator cap removed. When the top hose feels hot to the touch, top up to bring the coolant level to just below the filler neck and refit the radiator cap. Top up the coolant reservoir to between the **FULL** and **LOW** marks.

15. LIGHTS, HORN, WIPERS & WASHERS - CHECKING

☞ 1/1, 2 & 2/1.

1 Periodically, you should check that the main electrical subsystems are functioning normally. We recommend a weekly general inspection, though you should be aware of any developing problem, such as burned out bulbs, while you drive. You should also check around the car before undertaking any long journey.

LIGHTS CHECK

2 In some countries, it is compulsory to carry a set of replacement bulbs in the car, a practice we would recommend in all areas. Although storage space is at a premium in the Miata/MX5, you'll find that there are a few small recesses in the trunk which would be suitable for this purpose. You may be able to obtain a boxed set of bulbs from an auto parts store. Alternatively, have a set made up by your Mazda dealer, parts store or auto-electrical shop. We further suggest that you purchase a replacement fuse of each type used on the car (you only need one of each rating) and keep this with your spare bulbs.

3 It is pretty easy to monitor the condition of all external lights on your car with minimum effort. If you position an old mirror on the back wall of your garage, you can check the operation of the tail, brake and rear turn signal lights as you park the car. Alternatively, if you regularly park in front of a large window, such as a shop front, you can use this in the same way. It is usually pretty obvious if a headlight bulb has failed, and you can also check these and the other lights while driving, as you approach buildings with lots of glass in the frontage. If you live miles from civilization and there is nothing more reflective than a tree around, you'll need to walk around the car and check each light in turn. An assistant makes this check a lot easier, especially in the case of brake lights.

4 Of special importance to Miata/MX5 owners is a regular check on the headlight lenses. Because these are normally retracted while the car is parked, it is easy for dirt buildup or damage to go unnoticed. Use the manual control to raise the lights for checking and cleaning. While water works fine for cleaning, a silicone-based spray polish will help prevent dirt sticking to the lens surface.

HORN

5 This is easy enough to check while driving (depending on where you live, you probably get to check this most days!) Note that it is illegal to have a non-functioning horn in many countries/states.

WIPERS AND WASHERS

6 Check that the wiper and washer systems function normally. Have you ever noticed how washer reservoirs run out only on days when you really need them and there is no water around? Check that the reservoir is full, and remember to add a screenwash additive for better dirt and bug removal.

7 📷 On most cars, the windshield washer reservoir is mounted on the firewall, the exact location and design varying according to market. On ABS-equipped cars, the reservoir is relocated under the wheelarch, with a filler point under the hood, connected to the reservoir by a hose.

15/7 Topping-up windshield washer reservoir.

8 Cars for some European markets also have headlight washer systems. The reservoir will be found in the nose of the car, with a remote filler point accessible under the hood.

9 If the washer system does not operate normally, check that the reservoir is full and that the washer motor can be heard running when the system is operated. If this does not resolve the problem, check that the washer jet(s) are clear. Blockages can usually be cleared using a pin or fine wire. You can also adjust the jet angle using a pin - locate the pin in the jet and swivel it to the desired angle. Check the adjustment while driving the car - note that the airflow over the car will affect the way the water hits the windshield, and you may need to compensate a little for this.

10 If the wipers leave streaks across the windshield, check for an oil film on the glass. This is often caused by diesel fumes, and can be removed by washing with a detergent solution. Once the dirt is removed, dry the windshield with a handful of newspaper - this will leave the surface really clean

2

and grease-free.

11 If cleaning the windshield fails to improve the operation of the wipers, check the blade condition, and fit new blades if the wiping edge is worn or damaged. Note that the blades will last a lot longer if you clean the screen regularly - dirt and bug remains are abrasive and will soon damage the fine blade edge.

16. TIRE PRESSURES AND CHECKS

☞ 1/1, 2 & 2/1.

PRESSURE CHECKS AND ADJUSTMENT

1 Tire pressures need to be maintained regularly, and should be checked when the tires are cold. The Miata/MX5 is known to be especially sensitive to pressure settings, and if these are not kept at the correct settings, the car's handling characteristics will be affected. **Warning!** Incorrect tire pressures can put your life and that of other road users at risk ...

2 It is preferable to check tire pressures at home, after the car has been standing for some hours. An accurate pressure reading can only be made while the tires are at ambient temperature. When you drive the car, the tire temperature rises, and this means that a pressure reading taken at a gas station will be misleading. Also, gas station gauges can vary in accuracy.

3 We recommend that you use a simple pressure gauge, which can be carried in the car for this purpose. You can buy inexpensive pocket pressure gauges at auto parts stores, and if you don't have compressed air in your garage, you can use either a footpump, or a small electric compressor to inflate the tires - these can also be obtained from auto parts stores.

16/3 Checking tire pressure.

4 The specified tire pressure (front and rear) is 177 kPa (1.8 kgf cm2 / 26 psi). In the case of the temporary spare tire, inflate to 412 kPa (4.2 kgf cm2 / 60 psi). The temporary spare is of much smaller section than the normal tire, and this is why it needs the extra pressure. **Warning!** If you ever need to use the temporary spare, note the speed restriction label and get the normal wheel installed again as soon as you can.

TIRE CONDITION CHECKS

5 As mentioned above, the tires and wheels have a significant effect on the car's handling and roadholding, and should be checked regularly as detailed below. Note also that if you have reason to suspect possible damage, as might be caused by running over an object in the road, or accidentally kerbing the wheels, make a point of checking for damage as soon as possible.

6 Once each week, make a point of checking over each wheel and tire. Inspect the tire generally for wear, splits or other damage, and for foreign objects like stones or nails embedded in the tire treads. The tire condition and tread wear limit laws vary from one country to another, and you should be aware of and conform with local laws applicable to your car. In addition to these requirements, the tires must be replaced when the tread depth falls to 1.6 mm (0.063 in) or less, or whenever the tread has worn down enough to reach the wear indicator bars at any point.

7 You should also take into consideration seasonal factors. A part-worn tire with around 2 mm or so tread remaining might be acceptable during dry summer weather, but the same tire should be discarded if noted during late fall - at this time of year, much more reliance is placed on the tire's ability to deal with water and mud, and with the approach of winter, snow and ice may be a problem in some areas. As with pressures, the MX5-Miata is especially sensitive to tire condition, and you will notice a significant improvement in the way the car steers and handles after new tires have been installed.

8 While checking the tread, take note of *how* the tread is wearing - this can tell you a lot about potential tire and suspension problems. This topic is covered in detail later in this manual ☞ 9/24.

9 During the tire check, look out for stones, nails or other items embedded in the tire. If found, pry out the object with an old screwdriver or similar tool. Modern tire construction methods give us tires which are pretty resistant to punctures, but if an object has penetrated the tire sufficiently for it to be punctured (you should hear the leak hissing as the object is pulled out) mark the site of the puncture, then fit the emergency spare wheel and get the damaged tire repaired or replaced.

10 Examine the tire tread and both sidewalls (don't forget the inner wall!) for splits, cuts or bulges. Splits or cuts are usually caused by running over road debris - steel strapping from packing cases is a common culprit. Bulges in either the tread or sidewall denote a structural failure of the tire casing, and in extreme cases you may find the casing plies, fine steel strands, sticking out of the tire. If you find damage of this type, again, install the temporary spare and get a new tire fitted.

TIRE ROTATION

11 To maximize tire life, the tires (and wheels) should be rotated at the intervals specified in the relevant maintenance schedule. Even if the schedule for your car doesn't list tire rotation as an operation, you can carry this out on an annual basis.

12 The purpose of tire rotation is to get better tire mileage by evening out wear. Front and rear tires wear differently; the front ones tend to scrub out on the edges, while the rear ones wear out faster, and down the centerline. By interchanging the tires front to rear, you even out this wear and get better mileage overall.

13 Jack the car on one side, having loosened the lug nuts by a turn each on both wheels. Move the front wheel to the back and install the rear wheel on the front, then tighten the lug nuts provisionally. Lower the car to the ground and check-tighten the lug nuts, then check the tire pressure, which should be set at 177 kPa (1.8 kgf cm2 / 26 psi) on all wheels.

17. GENERAL BODY MAINTENANCE

☞ 1/1, 2 & 2/1.

LOCKS AND HINGES

1 The various locks, catches and hinges around the body require occasional maintenance to ensure smooth operation and to minimize wear. This applies to the door hinges and locks, the hood and trunk hinges and catches and minor mechanical parts like the seat hinges and runners.

2 It also applies to the moving parts of the convertible top. In predominantly hot and dry areas, it is likely that the car will be used with the top down for much of the time. Conversely, in colder or wetter areas, the top may remain up a lot of the time. Either way, the moving parts will be static for long periods, and this can lead to them freezing (seizing) in one position.

2 Operate the catch or hinge concerned and check that it moves smoothly and easily. If dirt has built up, this should be cleaned off. Electrical switch cleaner is often effective for this purpose, but care should be taken that this does not cause discoloration of nearby paint or upholstery.

3 Lubrication can be carried out with a number of products. General-purpose lubricating oil is fine if used carefully, though most areas where this would have been used traditionally can usually be treated with a more modern silicone-based lubricant like WD40. On the heavier pivots, grease is preferable. This can either be plain grease from a can, or an aerosol grease.

4 If using the latter, beware of overspray on adjacent trim or upholstery. We have found motorcycle chain lube to be good on heavier items like door hinges. This product is formulated to penetrate into the mechanism. Its solvent then evaporates, leaving a specially sticky grease coating which lasts well and resists the effects of weather.

5 After lubrication, operate the catch or pivot repeatedly to distribute the grease or oil evenly, then wipe away any excess. This is especially important in areas like the door catches and strikers, where excess is likely to get on your clothing.

CLEANING THE BODYWORK

6 Wash the car using plenty of water - a hose or domestic pressure wash is ideal for this. Alternatively, use water from a bucket, but remember to change it regularly before the dirt turns it into an

abrasive. To avoid any risk of damage to the paint finish, soak the bodywork thoroughly to soften the film of dirt, then gently hose it away using a soft brush agitate the dirt and loosen it. Don't scrub at the paintwork during this stage, or you will cause tiny scratches to form, dulling the finish.

7 By all means use a detergent additive in moderation - this will help shift the greasy road dirt which builds up where the car is used in areas of high traffic density (in other words, just about everywhere). Beware of using too much detergent or you will remove any body wax as well as the dirt. Whatever method and solution you use for the job, always wash the car on an overcast day if possible, or park it in the shade while you work; if the sun is shining on the car and the paintwork heats up, you'll find that you will have problems with spotting as the water keeps drying out too fast.

8 All external parts of the car should be cleaned in this way, including the plastic body parts, the hard or soft top and the wheels. Follow up by rinsing thoroughly with clean water. When rinsing down, check how the water lies on the hood or trunk lid - if it forms small beads, the wax coating is still good, while a continuous film tells you that it's time to wax the car. The paintwork can be dried off using an old (clean!) towel to prevent marking from the water droplets - some owners may prefer to use a traditional chamois leather; expensive, but effective. You may wish to try out some of the newer synthetic chamois leathers (the old ones were next to useless, but we hear that they've got better).

9 In the case of the wheels, note that they are lacquer-coated; don't use abrasive cleaners or you will damage the lacquer film and then rapid corrosion will set in. Never, ever, use a wire brush to clean them. If your car has signs of peeling lacquer, or damage has resulted from stone chips, have the wheels blasted and re-lacquered professionally before the alloy surface gets pitted by corrosion. If you encounter stubborn staining or marking of the wheels, you could try one of the specialist products formulated for use on alloy wheels. Check with the store that it will not damage your lacquer coating before use.

10 Don't forget the wheel wells (wheelarches) or the lower edges of the rockers (sills) during regular washes. These areas are easily overlooked, and this explains why they are often the first areas to suffer corrosion problems - don't just deal with the easy-to-reach parts, or you'll get a nasty surprise when you do get round to them. Pay special attention to the lip which lies inside the edge of many panels. These are here to give strength and rigidity. Unfortunately, they also provide tiny ledges where dirt can often build up unnoticed until the paint begins to blister.

11 Inside each wheel well you'll notice plastic liners attached with 10 mm bolts. Be aware that road dirt can get behind these and build up - this can lead to corrosion problems if left too long. It is a good idea to remove the liners each spring and fall and clean out any buildup of dirt, especially to the rear of the wheels where most of it gets thrown by the tires. You can guard against corrosion here (and elsewhere) by applying a wax-based underbody coating before the liners are reinstalled.

12 Don't forget that road dirt contains all kinds of pollutants, many of which are corrosive. In northern areas where the winter roads are salted to clear snow, salt corrosion is a real problem. If you drive your car all year and live in such an area, you need to wash the bodywork at least as often as during the summer.

POLISHING THE BODY

13 We recommend that you polish your Miata/MX5 at least twice a year, or whenever water stops beading on the paint. Spring and Fall are the best times - that way you get protection from summer sun and winter rain and snow. Polishing takes a little time to do, especially if you use a traditional, quality wax. On the other hand, we are talking about the Miata here, not a 30 foot RV - so you can afford to lavish attention on the body.

14 The choice of polish is up to you. There are hi-tech wax-in-30-seconds products, and wax-as-you-wash additives. We've used them, and don't rate them highly. The way we figure it, if the instant shine products work, why are there still expensive, labor-intensive traditional waxes on sale? Take our advice, and use a traditional nonabrasive paste or cream body wax - you'll work hard a couple of times a year, but the rest of the time you can rest easy about your paint.

15 As with washing, polishing should be carried out on a dull day, or under shade, *never* in full sun or while the bodywork is still hot. Be sure to use really soft, clean rag for polishing and buffing the paint. Work on a small area at a time (we like to complete one panel at a time and then move to the next - that way, nothing gets missed). Apply the wax sparingly with a light circular action - if the paint has not been waxed for a long time and it soaks in, apply a little more. When it has dried to a white color, use a clean rag to buff to a good finish. Don't skip seams and crevices - they need waxing more than the flat areas. Finally, hand waxing is always preferable than using a power polisher. Frankly, on the Miata/MX5, you don't need anything else.

TAR SPOTS

16 Road tar spotting on your paint can be removed using a proprietary solvent. Always follow the maker's directions, and we further suggest you try out the product on an unobtrusive area first to check for paint discoloration. Note that tar spots are much easier to remove from waxed paintwork than neglected and faded paint.

COLOR RESTORERS

17 Most of these products are nothing less than fine abrasives, and are designed to remove the surface layer of the paint to expose the unoxidized layer below. If you need to use them, do so sparingly, or you could cut through to the primer or bare metal - and the paint finish on the Miata/MX5 is none too thick. On the whole, steer clear. That said, if you've just bought a used Miata with dull paint at a bargain price - try a color restorer before booking a paint job - you could be pleasantly surprised. You might also like to try one of the color-impregnated polishes - these are designed to cover minor scratches and blemishes in the paint finish. In either case, follow the maker's directions for use, and with any abrasive restorer or wax, don't rub too hard, especially near edges.

CLEANING AND RESTORING THE CONVERTIBLE TOP AND TRIM

18 You can purchase a wide range of products which are specifically designed for cleaning items like the convertible top, dash panel, interior trim and the various body seals and the like. They make these parts look like new and offer a degree of protection from sun damage and chemical attack. We have used 'Armor All' and 'Son of a Gun' to good effect. This type of cleaner also works well on tire sidewalls.

19 When dealing with the convertible top, remember it is an expensive part to replace - regular maintenance will get the best out of it. Mechanical maintenance of the frame and catch parts is described earlier in this section. You should also check the fabric regularly, especially if your car is normally used with the top permanently raised or lowered. If the top is kept stowed over long periods, it is a good idea to raise it once in a while, and then re-stow it, checking that the window is laid flat and the top fabric is folded carefully to avoid puckers and creases.

PRESSURE WASHING THE UNDERBODY

20 About twice each year you should pressure-wash the underside of the car to remove accumulated road dirt and any chemical pollutants such as road salt. It helps if you can raise the car on safety stands (☞ 1/3) and remove the wheels to improve access. Where the underbody has a wax coating for corrosion protection, judicious pressure washing will do no damage, though you should be aware that hot pressure washing or steam cleaning may damage or remove this coating, which will then need to be reapplied.

21 Inspect the underbody after pressure washing (**Warning!** Make certain that the car is supported safely, and ***never*** get under a car supported only by a jack). Check for signs of damage to the underbody coating or of developing corrosion. **Caution!** Repair any such damage promptly to prevent it from getting worse.

18. STEERING & SUSPENSION CHECKS

☞ 1/1, 2 & 2/1.

1 The steering and suspension components should be checked at the intervals specified above, preferably after the underside of the car has been pressure-washed to remove road dirt. It should be noted that the Miata/MX5 is sensitive to incorrect steering or suspension adjustment, and such misalignment will impair handling and may result in rapid or uneven tire wear.

2 If you note such symptoms, carry out a check right away, even if this is not due on the maintenance schedule for some time. This could

improve the car's driveability, reduce tire wear, and maybe even save your life. Preliminary checks can be carried out with the car sat on its wheels, but for a full check you will need to jack the car and support it on safety stands.

CHECKS WITH THE CAR ON THE GROUND

3 Preliminary checks on the steering can be carried out without dismantling. Sit in the driver's seat with the front wheel in the straight ahead position, and gently turn the wheel to and fro to gauge the amount of free play (lash) before any slack in the steering mechanism is taken up. You can gauge this better by leaning out of the car and noting when the road wheel begins to move.

4 Allowable freeplay at the steering wheel rim is 0-30 mm (0-1.18 in) before the road wheels begin to move. Excessive play normally indicates wear in the steering balljoints, steering column universal joints or the rack mechanism. Less likely causes are loose steering column clamps or rack mountings.

5 Next, try pulling the steering wheel left and right, then up and down, at right angles in relation to the steering column. There should be no play felt here. If there is, check for wear in the steering column and joints and check the security of the steering wheel and the clamps at the upper and lower ends of the intermediate shaft.

6 Relatively little can be determined about suspension condition while the car is resting on its wheels - the weight of the car will tend to disguise wear or stiffness in the suspension joints and pivots. You can, however, perform a quick check of shock absorber condition as follows.

7 Press down firmly on each corner of the car in turn and release it. The car should return to its normal height quickly and stop - if it continues to bounce like a 20 year old Oldsmobile, read this as un-Miata-like behavior. The chances are that the shock absorber seals have failed and this will be confirmed if you can see the damper oil leaking out of them. If you discover this problem, note that the units must be replaced as an axle set as a minimum. You might like to take the opportunity to upgrade all four units.

CHECKS WITH THE CAR RAISED ON SAFETY STANDS

8 Park the car on a smooth, level surface, then jack it so that all four wheels are raised clear of the ground. **Warning!** Support the car securely on safety stands before proceeding further ☞ 1/3.

9 On manual steering cars, turn the steering from lock to lock at least five times to settle the steering components. While doing so, note any unusually slack or tight spots which might indicate wear or damage in the intermediate shaft joints or the rack mechanism, possibly as a result of impact damage. If noted, these faults should be investigated and rectified.

10 In the case of cars with power steering, the engine should be running during the check (ensure adequate ventilation of the working area), and you will need a thermometer to measure the power steering fluid temperature. Before you check the steering resistance, check and top up the power steering fluid and make sure that there is no air in the system, as described below.

11 With the engine running on power steering cars, turn the steering wheel from lock to lock until the fluid temperature in the reservoir reaches 50-60 C (122-140 F) - you can check this using the thermometer inserted into the fluid reservoir.

12 If the steering feels abnormally stiff with the wheels clear of the ground, the rack mechanism may be at fault, or the steering balljoints may be badly worn or damaged. Hook a pull scale (spring balance) to the outer edge of one of the steering wheel spokes and check the effort needed to turn the wheel during one complete revolution.

13 On manual steering cars this should be in the range 4.9-29.4 N (0.5-3.0 kg / 1.1-6.6 lb), while for power steering cars, the normal resistance should be in the range 23.5-35.3 N (2.4-3.6 kg / 5.3-8.0 lb). If it is outside these limits a problem is indicated. If steering resistance is outside the relevant limit a problem is indicated. For more information on manual steering systems ☞ 8/10, 8/12 & 8/13. In the case of power steering systems, refer to the fluid level checks described below. If this fails to resolve the fault ☞ 8/17 to 8/20.

14 While you've got the car raised on safety stands, check the steering and suspension parts visually. Obvious signs of wear or damage, like torn dust boots, should be investigated and repaired immediately, or further deterioration will result ☞ 8/12.

15 Push and pull on the steering balljoints and steering/suspension knuckles and feel for freeplay. You can determine minute amounts of wear this way, though you will probably not be able to *see* any movement. Try to establish which component is responsible for any movement, then turn to chapter 8 for a more detailed account of repair procedures.

16 It is not easy to detect wear or incorrect adjustment in the suspension wishbones with the suspension fully assembled; the assembly rides on rubber bushes and this tends to mask wear a little. If you suspect that there may be wear, or if you know that a wheel has been 'kerbed', we suggest that you check this more thoroughly, or have a Mazda dealer check and set up the suspension for you. Refer to chapter 8 for detailed checking and overhaul procedures.

17 You should also check the wheel bearings for play while you are in the neighborhood. Grab hold of the top and bottom of the wheel and rock it to and fro. Now grasp the front and back of the wheel and do the same. Even a minute amount of freeplay in the bearing will be magnified at the wheel rim, but 2 mm or more at the wheel rim means trouble ☞ 9/29.

POWER STEERING - CHECKING FLUID LEVEL AND AIR BLEEDING

18 Fluid level in the power steering fluid reservoir should be checked periodically according to the maintenance schedule, and whenever abnormal steering operation is suspected. Note that low fluid level or air in the hydraulic system can result in excessive steering effort being required, or abnormal noise from the steering system. Pull out the combined filler plug and dipstick, and check that the fluid level lies between the high and low marks. **Caution!** If you need to add fluid, use only ATF Dexron®II or M-III.

18/18 Checking power steering fluid level.

19 To bleed air from the hydraulic system, jack the front of the car so the wheels are just clear of the ground, supporting the car on safety stands placed under the front jacking points - we suggest that you place small wood blocks between the car and the stands to prevent damage to the paint finish ☞ 1/3.

20 With the engine off, turn the steering fully to the left and then back to the right several times, and check whether the fluid level in the power steering fluid reservoir drops. If it does, top up the fluid in the reservoir and repeat this procedure until the level remains stable.

21 Next start the engine and allow it to idle. Turn the steering wheel fully to the left and then back to the right several times, and check whether the fluid level in the power steering fluid reservoir drops or becomes foamy. If it does, top up the fluid in the reservoir as necessary, then repeat the procedure until the level remains stable, indicating that any air has been expelled.

CHECKING FOR POWER STEERING SYSTEM LEAKS

22 In the event of power steering problems, it is a good idea to check the system for possible leakage between the steering rack and pump. Start by jacking the front of the car and supporting it on safety stands as described above.

23 Start the engine and let it idle. Turn the steering from lock to lock a few times, then hold it at full lock in each direction to place the system under pressure. **Caution!** Do not keep the steering fully turned for more than 15 seconds or damage may result. Check for signs of leakage along both pipes and at their unions. If leakage is found, check and tighten the affected union, or replace worn or damaged hoses as required. For full details ☞ 8/17

19. EXHAUST SYSTEM - CHECKING

☞ 1/1, 2 & 2/1.

1 The exhaust system should be checked at the specified intervals, and whenever unusual ex-

haust noise, or rattles from underneath the car might indicate a problem. **Warning!** You should only carry out the check when the exhaust system is completely cold, and the car needs to be raised clear of the ground and supported on safety stands before you start ☞ 1/3.

2 Lying under the car (and wearing safety glasses to protect your eyes), check the system from front to back, remembering to check the top surface nearest the body underside - a small mirror helps here.

3 Look out for signs of corrosion. This may not be readily apparent - the metal-sprayed exhaust components tend to look nice and shiny right up to the time they perforate through from the inside.

4 Check the exhaust and body-mounted heatshields. If these are loose or damaged, they should be repaired or replaced as necessary. The exhaust manifold heatshield can be checked from under the hood. Check also the exhaust system hangers, and fit new ones if they are torn or perished.

5 For more information on checking the exhaust system ☞ 5/38.

20. BRAKE & CLUTCH FLUID - CHECKING LEVEL & CHANGING

☞ 1/1, 2 & 2/1.

CHECKING

1 The level and condition of the hydraulic fluid in the brake and clutch reservoirs should be checked at the specified intervals, or whenever there is concern over the operation of the hydraulic system concerned.

2 + Remove the reservoir top, taking care to avoid spilling the fluid. Note that the reservoirs may have secondary caps. **Caution!** Hydraulic fluid will discolor and damage painted and plastic parts. In the event of spillage, wash off all traces immediately.

20/2a Ready to top-up brake fluid (rhd car).

20/2b Clutch master cylinder reservoir (rhd car).

20/2c ... Don't forget secondary cap (rhd car).

3 Check visually for signs of contamination of the fluid. If it looks dirty and discolored, you should change the fluid as a precaution. If you note bubbles in the fluid, or the operation of the brake or clutch seems spongy and imprecise, you may have air in the system, possibly as a result of seal failure.

4 For details of bleeding air from the clutch hydraulic system ☞ 3/26.

5 For information on bleeding air from the brake hydraulic system ☞ 9/2.

6 If repair of either the brake or clutch hydraulic system components is required, you'll find details of overhaul procedures for the brake and clutch assemblies in their respective chapters.

7 Top up to the **MAX** level line using only fresh hydraulic fluid conforming to SAE J1703 or FMVSS116 DOT 3. After topping up, refit the reservoir top securely and wipe up any traces of fluid on the reservoir.

20/7 Topping-up clutch fluid reservoir (rhd car).

CHANGING

8 If you need to change the hydraulic fluid, either as the result of reaching the appropriate maintenance operation, or due to contamination of the existing fluid, this can be done as an extension of the air bleeding procedure.

9 In the case of the clutch hydraulic system ☞ 3/26.

10 In the case of the brake hydraulic system ☞ 9/2.

AMERICAN/ENGLISH GLOSSARY OF AUTOMOTIVE TERMS

American	English
A-arm	Wishbone (suspension)
Antenna	Aerial
Axleshaft	Halfshaft
Back-up	Reverse
Barrel	Choke/venturi
Block	Chock/wedge
Box end wrench	Ring spanner
Bushing	Bush
Clutch hub	Synchro hub
Coast	Freewheel
Convertible	Drop head
Cotter pin	Split pin
Counterclockwise	Anti-clockwise
Countershaft	Layshaft (of gearbox)
Crescent wrench	Open-ended spanner
Curve	Corner
Dashboard	Facia
Denatured alcohol	Methylated spirit
Dome lamp	Interior light
Driveaxle	Driveshaft
Driveshaft	Propeller shaft
Fender	Wing/mudguard
Firewall	Bulkhead
Flashlight	Torch
Float bowl	Float chamber
Freeway, turnpike, etc.	Motorway
Frozen	Seized
Gas tank	Petrol tank
Gas pedal	Accelerator pedal
Gasoline (gas)	Petrol
Gearshift	Gearchange
Generator (DC)	Dynamo
Ground	Earth (electrical)
Header/manifold	Manifold (exhaust)
Heat riser	Hot spot
High	Top gear
Hood	Bonnet (engine cover)
Idle	Tickover
Intake	Inlet
Jackstands /Safety stands	Axle stands
Jumper cable	Jump lead
Keeper	Collet
Kerosene	Paraffin
Knock pin	Roll pin
Lash	Freeplay/Clearance
Latch	Catch
Latches	Locks
License plate /tag plate	Number plate
Light	Lamp
Lock (for valve spring retainer)	Split cotter (for valve cap)
Lopes	Hunts
Lug nut	Wheel nut
Metal chips or debris	Swarf
Misses	Misfires
Muffler	Silencer
Oil pan	Sump
Open flame	Naked flame
Panel wagon/van	Van
Parking light	Sidelight
Parking brake	Handbrake
Piston pin or wrist pin bearing/bush	Small (little) end bearing
Piston pin or wrist pin	Gudgeon pin
Pitman arm	Drop arm
Power brake booster	Servo unit
Primary shoe	Leading shoe (of brake)
Prussian blue	Engineer's blue
Pry	Prise (force apart)
Prybar	Crowbar
Prying	Levering
Quarter window	Quarterlight
Recap	Retread
Release cylinder	Slave cylinder
Repair shop	Garage
Replacement	Renewal
Ring gear (of differential)	Crownwheel
Rocker panel	Sill panel
Rod bearing	Big-end bearing
Rotor/disk	Disc (brake)
Secondary shoe	Trailing shoe (of brake)
Sedan	Saloon
Setscrew, Allen screw	Grub screw
Shift fork	Selector fork
Shift lever	Gearlever/gearstick
Shift rod	Selector rod
Shock absorber, shock	Damper/shocker
Snap-ring	Circlip
Soft top	Hood
Spacer	Distance piece
Spare tire	Spare wheel
Spark plug wires	HT leads
Spindle arm	Steering arm
Stablizer or sway bar	Anti-roll bar
Station wagon	Estate car
Stumbles	Hesitates
Tang or lock	Tab
Taper pin	Cotter pin
Teardown	Strip(down)/dismantle
Throw-out bearing	Thrust bearing
Tie-rod (or connecting rod)	Trackrod (of steering)
Transmission	Gearbox
Troubleshooting	Fault finding/diagnosis
Trunk	Boot
Tube wrench	Box spanner
Turn signal	Indicator
Valve lifter	Tappet
Valve lifter or tappet	Cam follower or tappet
Valve cover	Rocker cover
VOM (volt ohmmeter)	Multimeter
Wheel cover	Roadwheel trim
Wheel well	Wheelarch
Whole drive line	Transmission
Windshield	Windscreen
Wrench	Spanner

3

ENGINE & CLUTCH

1. MAJOR WORK POSSIBLE WITH ENGINE IN CAR

1 You can undertake the following tasks without removing the engine from the car -

Camshaft drivebelt: renewal
Camshafts, camshaft pulleys and camshaft followers: removal and installation
Cylinder head and gasket: removal and fitting
Crankshaft/oil pump oil seal (front): renewal
**Crankshaft oil seal (rear): renewal*
**Starter ring gear: removal and installation*
**Clutch and clutch release bearing: removal and installation*
Water (coolant) pump: removal and installation

*These tasks require removal of transmission.

2. MAJOR WORK REQUIRING ENGINE REMOVAL

1 The following tasks can only be accomplished by removing the engine from the car -

Oil pan and baffle plate: removal and installation
Connecting rod (big-end) bearings: renewal
Main bearings & crankshaft thrust washers: renewal
Crankshaft: removal and installation
Pistons and connecting rods: removal and installation
Oil pump: removal and installation

3. ENGINE REMOVAL METHODS AND PREPARATION

1 The engine can be removed by itself or as a unit with the transmission. The latter is probably easier as the procedure is more straightforward, particularly when it comes to installation. However, the weight of engine and transmission combined is considerable and this should be borne in mind. We didn't have a means of weighing the engine and transmission but would estimate that, together, they weigh between 136 and 181 kg (300 and 400 lb), with the transmission alone accounting for between a quarter and a third of the total.

2 You'll need a hoist capable of lifting double this weight - as a safety margin - and capable of a vertical lift of not less than 650 mm (25.6 in) from a starting point of 810 mm (32 in) above the ground, plus whatever height you have the car jacked above the ground. The hoist also needs to be mounted on wheels or castors so that it can easily be moved back and forth - even when it is carrying the weight of the engine or engine and transmission. We hired a hoist from a tool/machinery hire company of the kind you find in every small town. The hire charge was small and the whole hoist could be quickly dismantled to fit into the trunk of an ordinary family car. These hire companies usually deliver, too, if it's more convenient. Don't forget to hire a suitable rope or chain at the same time to sling the engine.

3 Before you remove the engine, think about where and how you're going to work on it once it's out. Bear in mind not only the weight of the engine, but also its height of around 610 mm (24 in). It's no use putting it on the workbench only to find that you can't comfortably reach the top of the engine to work on the cams and head! With manifolds in place the engine's overall size is 610 mm long, 610 mm high and 560 mm wide (24 in x 24 in x 22 in). In addition, the transmission is 1020 mm (40 in) long. A good plan of action might be to place the engine on top of a couple of securely stacked pallets for major dismantling, moving individual components to the workbench for further work. You'll need a block of hardwood 305 mm (12 in) long by 100 x 100 mm (4 x 4 in) or 125 x 125 mm (5 x 5 in) to place under the shallow end of the engine's oil pan to make it stable on your work surface.

4 If the engine/engine and transmission unit is dirty you'll be well advised to clean its exterior before dismantling starts: you could even get it steam cleaned before the car's immobilized. Make sure you've got solvents, brushes, scrapers, rags and old newsprint ready. **Warning!** Do not use gasoline/petrol as a cleaning solvent.

5 Read through the whole procedure *before* starting the job.

6 The specific tool requirements are detailed in the relevant text but you'll find the following useful: plastic bags and twist wire (the sort you use for gardening) for keeping, identifying and tying back components; adhesive tape to wrap over the end of open pipes, etc.; a magnet and stiff wire for picking up dropped small components; a torch for looking into nooks and crannies and containers for the oil and coolant which will be drained.

7 Don't forget that when the engine is out you'll have great access to the engine compartment. Plan to fix that chipped paint, weeping hydraulic joint, etc., whilst you have the opportunity ...

4. ENGINE - REMOVAL (WITHOUT TRANSMISSION)

☞ First read 1/1, 2.

1 Before any other work takes place, it's necessary to release the fuel system's pressure by temporarily disconnecting the fuel system opening relay. The relay is housed inside the car above the access panel which covers the lower section of the steering column. The exact location and form of the relay varies according to market and, in all probability, between models of different years. It's common for car manufacturers to source components like relays from a number of suppliers so small physical variations are rarely documented. On our UK market car, the relay was easy to identify - it was bright yellow. We know that in the case of cars sold in other European countries and in North America the relay is mounted on the left of the car above the steering column access panel: unfortunately, we can't be precise in its description or location (or color!) This is not a big problem ...

2 From the driver's footwell, remove the access panel from beneath the steering column - it's

held by sheet metal screws. Using a torch - and contortionist's techniques - examine the exposed area. You'll see two or three plastic boxes with multi-pin plugs: one of these will be the fuel system opening relay. Start the car's engine and allow it to idle, after releasing the locking clips pull the wire connector from each suspect 'relay' in turn and wait one minute before reconnecting it. Disconnecting one of these units will cause the engine to stall after some seconds as it is starved of fuel. After the engine has stalled turn off the ignition and then reconnect the multi-pin plug, making sure it clicks home securely. Install the access panel.

3 First jack the vehicle from the ground and support on safety stands as described in Chapter 1. The higher you can safely raise the car the better.

4 + Isolate the battery by disconnecting its ground/earth (-) negative lead. Open the trunk lid and undo the wing-nutted bolt holding the spare wheel to the floor of the compartment. Lift out the spare wheel. On the right-hand side of the luggage compartment you'll see a black moulding covering the battery. First, undo the two 13 mm plastic nuts which should be finger-tight and no wrench will be required. Next, release the row of stud fasteners at the bottom of the moulding and lift the moulding

4/4a Remove securing bolt ...

4/4b ... and lift out spare wheel.

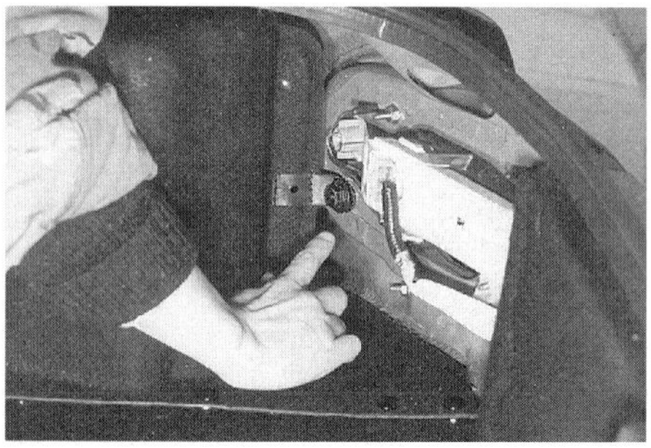

4/4c Remove this plastic 'nut' and ...

4/4d ... this one, then unclip base and ...

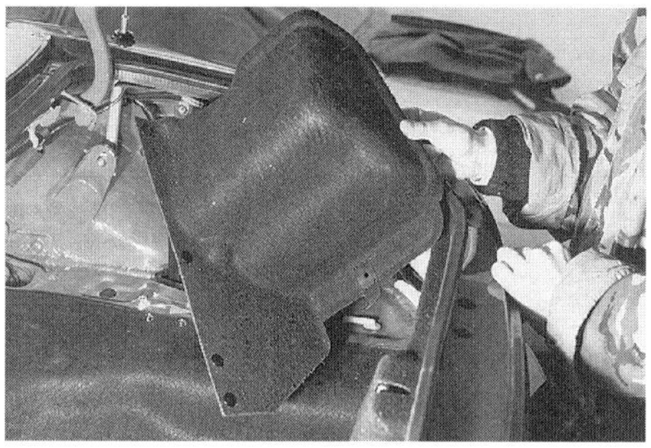

4/4e ... lift out battery cover.

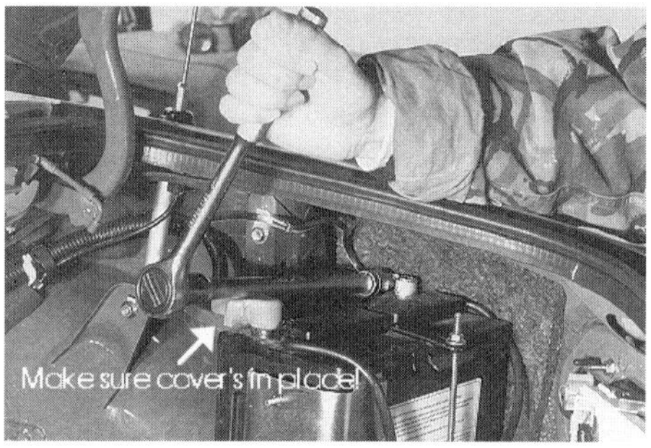
Make sure cover's in place!

4/4f Slacken negative (-) terminal clamp.

clear. Slacken the 10 mm nut on the negative terminal of the battery and then lift the terminal clear. **Warning!** If you use a socket and extension to reach the negative terminal retaining nut, make sure that the positive terminal of the battery is protected by its plastic cover otherwise the extension could short across the two terminals. Move the disconnected terminal away from the battery post and push it down behind the battery securely out of harm's way.

5 Open the engine hood (bonnet) and support with its stay. Protect the paintwork around the engine compartment with thick cloth (old towels are ideal). To improve access during engine removal, remove the hood as follows.

6 Disconnect the windshield washer jet pipework at the first union by pulling on the pipe and moving it to and fro until the pipe is free.

7 Mark the relative position of the hood and hinge on each side of the car with a marker pen so that the hood can be exactly realigned when installed. With an assistant holding the hood steady, release the two 14 mm nuts on each side and then carefully lift the hood away from the car. Replace the four nuts finger-tight on the projecting studs for safekeeping and then store the hood safely until it

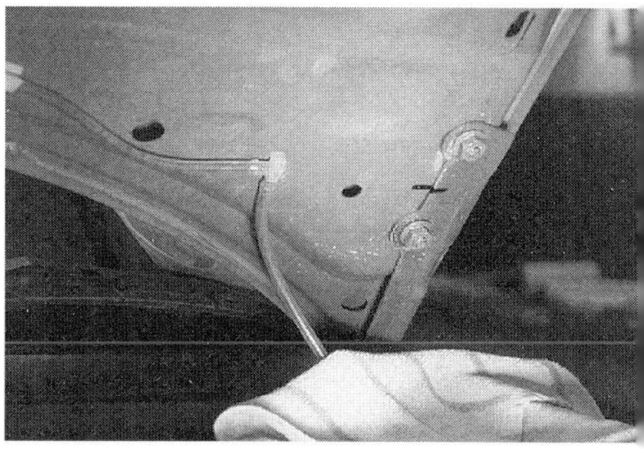

4/7 Mark hinge position.

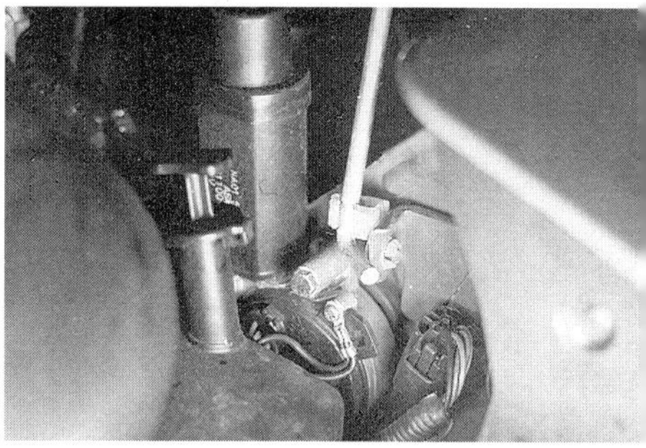

4/8 Release hood (bonnet) stay.

is required again.

8 Remove the hood support stay by pulling back the outer tag of its nylon swivel clip and levering the clip open with a screwdriver blade. After this the stay can be pulled out of the clip and removed from the car.

9 Moving to the underside of the car, the next job is to remove the plastic undertray from beneath the front of the engine. All fixings are 10 mm. First, remove the three self-tapping screws from the front of the tray. Then remove the bolt next to the top swinging arm on each side of the car, the bolt on the side of the chassis member in the wheelwell from each side and, finally, the nut on each side holding not only the tray but also the front valence stay. Once the nut is removed the stay can be pulled from the stud and moved out of the way to give enough clearance to remove the plastic undertray, It's recommended that you put all of the screws and the two nuts back in place finger-tight once the tray is removed.

10 + If the engine is to be dismantled after removal its oil should be drained. Temporarily remove the oil filter cap on top of the cambox cover. Place a container capable of taking 4 liters (4 US or Imp. quarts) of engine oil beneath the oil pan

4/10a Engine oil pan drain plug.

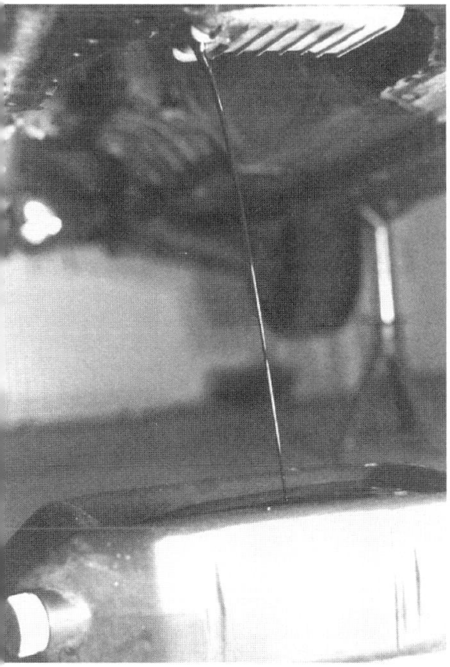

4/10b Draining engine oil into drain can.

drain plug and then unscrew and remove the 19 mm plug. Use your fingers to undo the plug for its last few turns so that it can be held in place as long as possible. When completely unthreaded pull the plug away quickly to prevent oil splattering everywhere. **Caution!** Initially, the oil will shoot out in a jet, so place the receptacle towards the right-hand front wheel to take this into account. Used engine oil should be disposed of safely; please do not be tempted to re-use it. Install the oil filler cap.

11 The next task is to drain the cooling system. Remove the cap on top of the radiator.

4/11 Release radiator drain plug.

Caution! If the car has been running up to an hour before this point, cover the cap with cloth and wear protective gloves before releasing the cap in case scalding coolant is ejected. Place a receptacle beneath the radiator drain plug; it will need to be capable of holding 6.5 liters (6.5 US or 6.1 Imp. quarts) and, if you intend to re-use the coolant, should be spotlessly clean. Once again protecting your hands if the coolant is hot, unscrew the radiator drain plug with a medium sized crosshead screwdriver until the plug drops and the coolant flows.

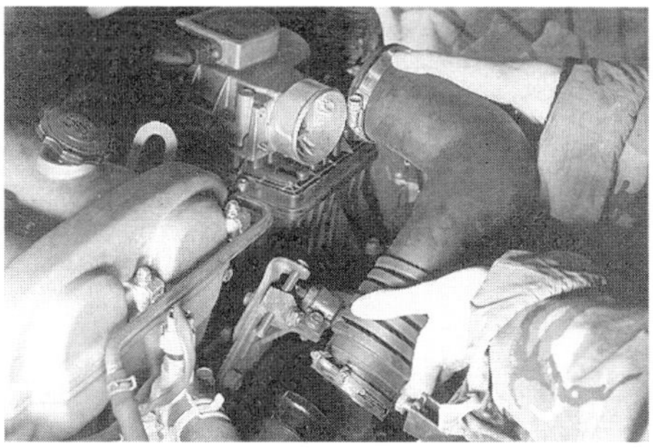

4/12 Release clips and remove air trunking.

12 Remove the flexible air intake trunking at the front of the engine. The piece of trunking is retained at one end by a hose clip with a medium sized crosshead drive 10 mm hex and, at the other end, another oval-shaped worm drive clip with a crosshead drive 8 mm hex.

13 Removing the electric fan (there will be two on some models) from the radiator. First release the electrical wire from the clip in the fan housing by pulling back the catch on the side of the clip and thereby releasing the wire retainer. The electrical connector block can now be separated by

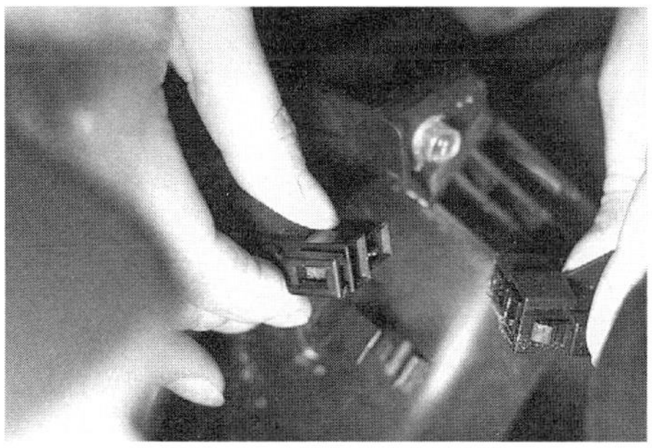

4/13 Unplug wiring connector.

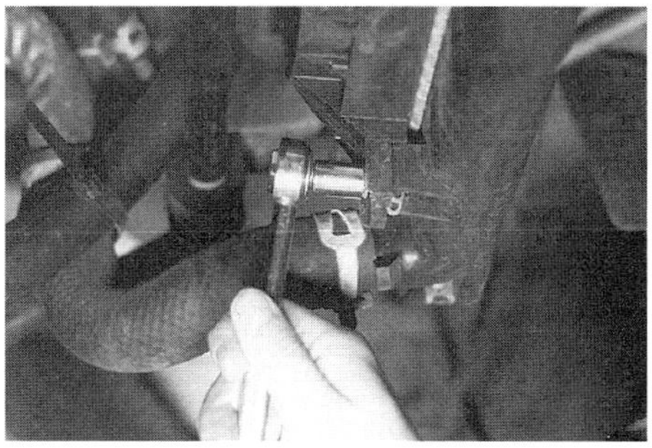

4/14a Release fan lower mountings ...

pushing the outer catch inwards and pulling the two halves apart.

14 + The electric fan housing is fixed to the radiator body by four 10 mm bolts, threaded into spring clips. Note: you may find, as we did, that the bottom retaining bolts and their clips are considerably corroded. If this is the case, a soaking with penetrating oil some time before the bolts are removed will help. Once the two top bolts have been removed and the two bottom bolts loosened, the cooling fan assembly can be lifted away from the car.

4/14b ... upper mountings and ...

4/14c ... lift fan from radiator.

15 + Remove the radiator top hose by squeezing the ears of each spring clip with pliers and moving the clips back until they stop clamping the union. The hose can then be worked off of both the radiator union and the thermostat housing union. **Caution!** Behind the top hose there is a small rubber coolant hose which goes from the thermostat housing to the manifold air valve. This, too, has a spring clip which, on our car, was digging into the back of the top hose and actually beginning to cut a hole. If necessary, reposition the offending clip and replace the damaged hose.

4/15a Release clip at radiator end and ...

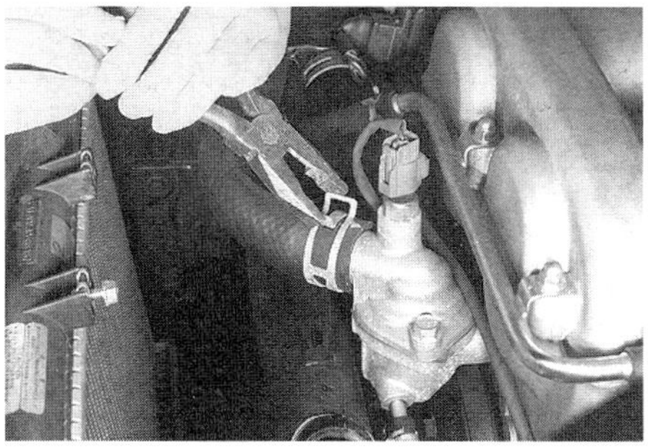

4/15b ... thermostat end, then remove hose.

16 Note: you may find that coolant hoses are difficult to release from metal stubs and pipes - we did, even though our project car was less than two years old. The problem is caused by a combination of very tight-fitting pipes and metal corrosion. Generally it is better to push the hoses off than to pull them. Often, working a screwdriver into and around the joint - taking care not to gouge either hose or union stub - helps; simultaneously squirting silicone based water repellent lubricant such as WD40 will help greatly, too. If the hose simply refuses to budge, carefully slit it lengthways along the union joint with a craft knife, taking care not to

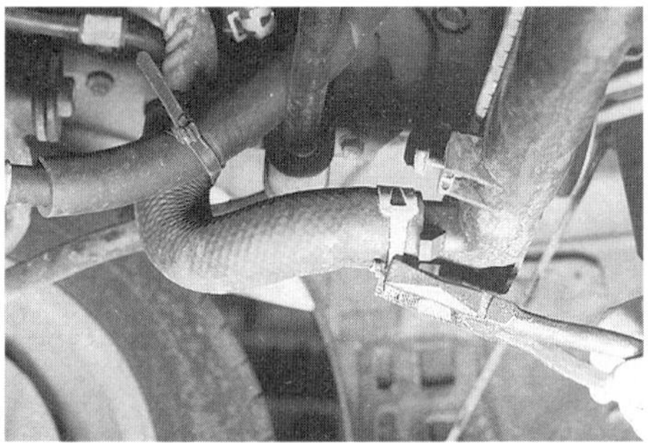

4/17 Release clips and remove bottom hose.

gouge the union stub. This method means, of course, that you'll have to buy a new hose.

17 Next remove the bottom hose after releasing the plastic tie holding the power steering pump hose against the radiator hose. To release the tie pull back the locking tab with a finger nail and then slide the tail of the tie through the clip. The bottom hose can be removed after releasing both of its spring clips and working the hose off of its unions. Easier said than done, but persevere and the hose will come free.

18 Remove the overflow pipe from its union

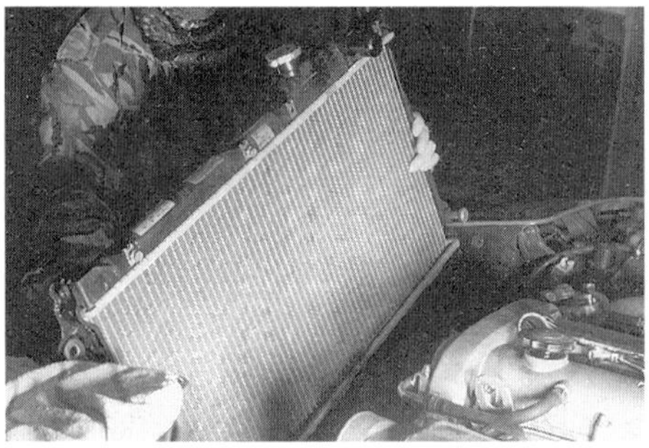

4/19 Lift out radiator and store safely.

just beneath the radiator filler cap.

19 Remove the two 12 mm headed bolts towards the top and on each side of the radiator. Once two screws have been removed the radiator can be lifted upward out of its bottom brackets and removed from the car. Store in a safe place.

20 + Release the plastic tie holding the airflow sensor electrical wire to the air cleaner body. Then remove the connector plug from the sensor body after pushing the wire spring clips with a screwdriver and gently pulling on the female connector. Move the wire and connector out of the

4/20a Release plastic tie (arrowed).

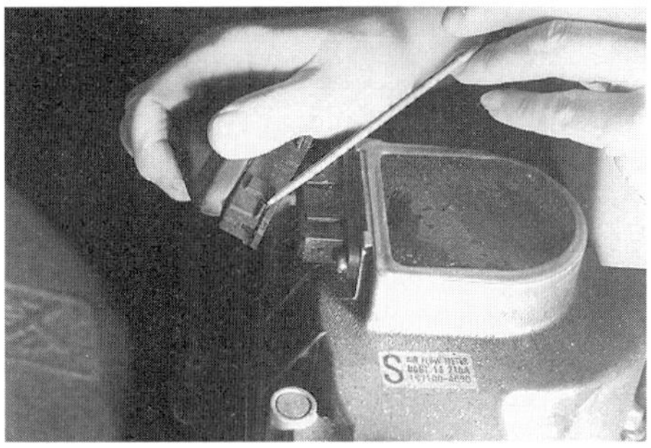

4/20b Release clips and remove sensor's plug.

way.

21 + Release the screw holding the extreme end of the plastic air intake (officially a 'resonator'!) to the top of the left-hand inner wing. Next, undo and remove the two 12 mm bolts and 12 mm nut fixing the air cleaner to the inner wing. The bracket which carries an electrical component will need to be lifted and swivelled to one side in order to lift the air cleaner. The air cleaner assembly can now be lifted away from the car.

22 + Release the throttle cable by turning the butterfly spindle wheel clockwise far enough to

4/21a Release this screw & air cleaner fixings ...

4/21b ... and lift away air cleaner body.

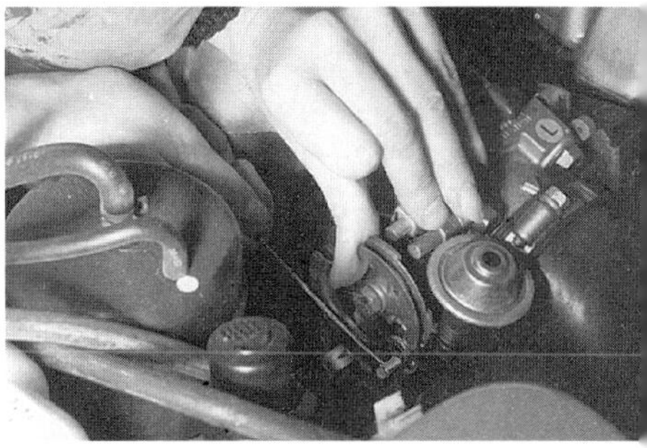

4/22a Release accelerator cable ...

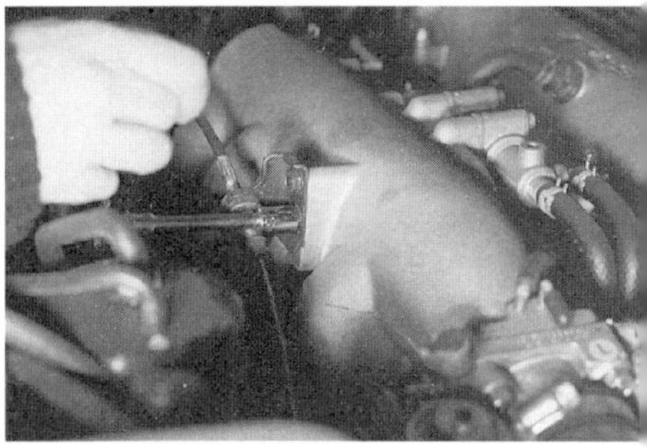

4/22b ... and remove cable bracket.

give sufficient slack to allow the cable and nipple to be slid from its location. Rather than upset the throttle cable setting, remove the cable stop bracket from the intake manifold by removing the two 10 mm bolts. Fix the end of the throttle cable out of harm's way by tying it to another component.

23 + Removal of power steering pump (if fitted). First, remove the electrical wire to the pressure switch at the top of the pump simply by lifting the plastic connector block. Tuck the cable end out of the way. Using a 14 mm socket and a short extension, slacken the pump pivot bolt nut

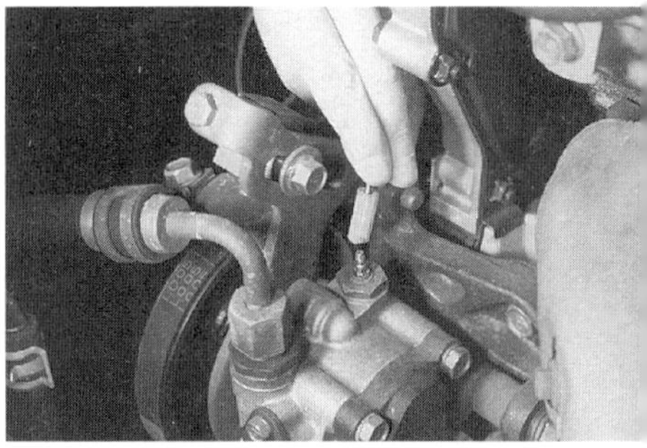

4/23a Disconnect pump's wiring ...

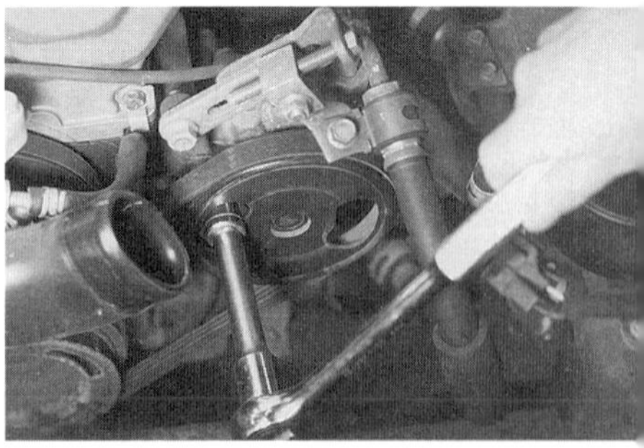

4/23b ... slacken pivot bolt thru pulley ...

4/23c ... slacken adjuster and then ....

4/23d ... swing pump to release drivebelt.

via one of the cutouts in the pump pulley. Next, slacken the adjustment bracket lower bolt. Slacken the adjuster lock bolt and then the adjuster bolt itself. Then remove the lock bolt completely. The pump body can then be pushed downwards to slacken the drivebelt and the drivebelt lifted off of the drive pulley.

24 + Remove the 14 mm nut from the pump pivot bolt via the pulley cutout and then push the pivot bolt backward until the whole pivot bolt can be pulled out from the rear: you might need to use a hammer and thin brass drift just to get it moving. The pump can now be pulled from its bracket, but if it's the same as the one on our car, it will still be very stiff and will need to be worked up and down until it comes free. Once the pump is free, leave it connected to its piping but move it down to the stabilizer/anti-roll bar and tie or tape it in place so that it does not get in the way during engine removal.

4/24a Lift pump away from mounting ...

4/24b ...and tie to stabilizer bar.

25 If an air conditioning compressor is fitted, it should be removed from its mounting on the lower left-hand side of the cylinder block, without disconnecting its hoses, and tied away from the engine. Our car did not have a compressor so we cannot give full details of fixings, but believe four bolts secure the unit to its cradle. Note: if your car has air-conditioning but does not have power steering, you'll have to slacken the belt adjuster mechanism above the compressor to release the drivebelt. **Warning!** Do not, under any circumstances, try to slacken or disconnect air conditioning pipe unions and take great care not to damage the pipes with sharp tools - the gas/liquid in the system can be extremely dangerous.

26 Release the electrical connector on top of the thermostat housing by squeezing the catch inward and lifting the connector block.

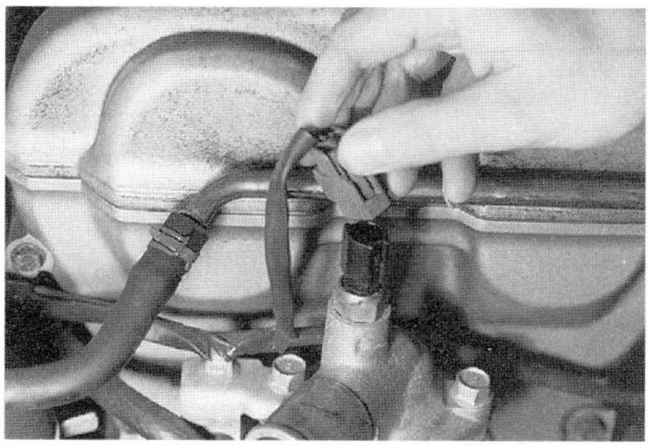

4/26 Release thermostat's connector.

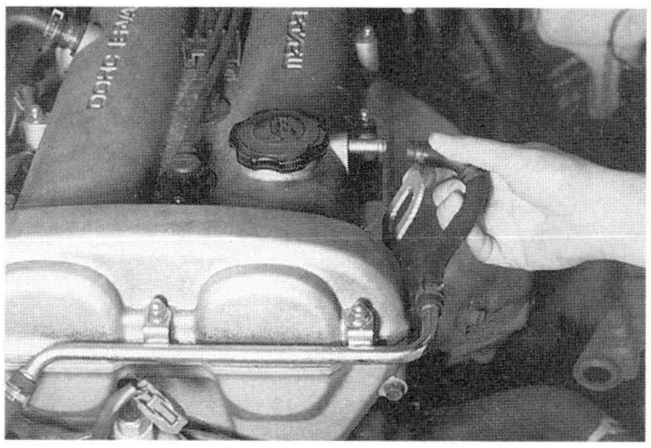

4/27a Release breather pipe from stub ...

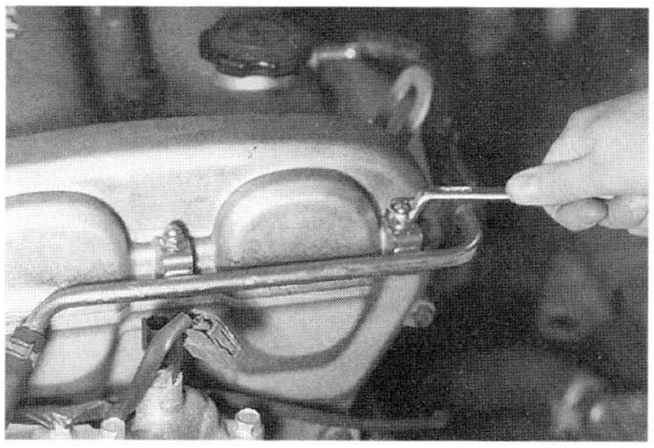

4/27b ... and mountings.

27 + Release the breather pipe from the cambox cover after releasing its spring clip with pliers. The breather's metal pipe can be removed from the front of the cambox by undoing the two chrome headed 10 mm bolts holding it in place. At the intake manifold end release the spring clip from the rubber tube of the cambox breather and pull the tube from the trunking. The whole breather pipe assembly can then be removed.

28 Looking from the front of the car there is a pipe of approximately 13 mm (0.5 in) bore between the rigid plastic intake ('resonator') pipe and an anodized pipe under the throttle body on the nose of the intake manifold. Release the clip at the manifold end and slide the rubber pipe off of the anodized pipe. Slacken the clip retaining the air pipe to the manifold body using a medium sized crosshead screwdriver or 10 mm socket.

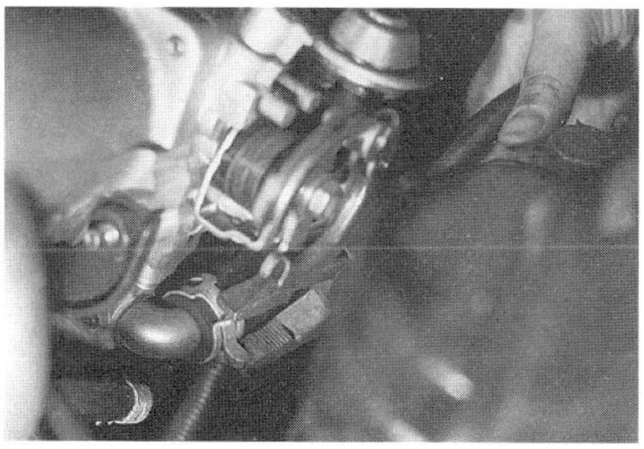

4/28 Release clip.

29 + Remove the 10 mm bolt retaining the rigid intake pipe assembly to the alternator mounting bracket. The pipe assembly can now be pulled off its manifold connection and mounting bracket, then the whole thing can be twisted sufficiently to give access to the black plastic cable clip on the side of the rectangular-shaped resonance chamber. This

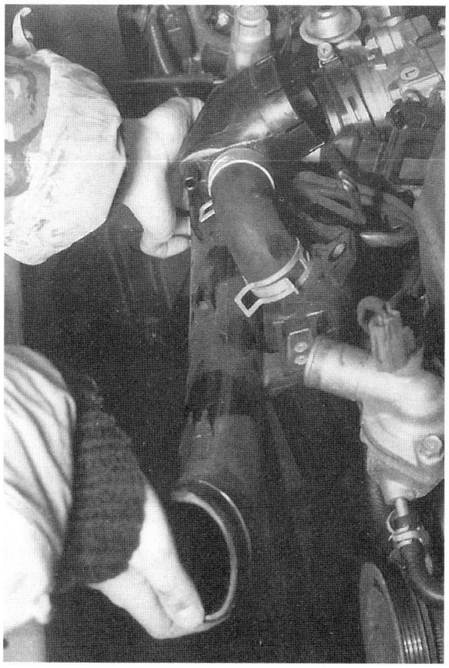

4/29a Release pipe and twist to ...

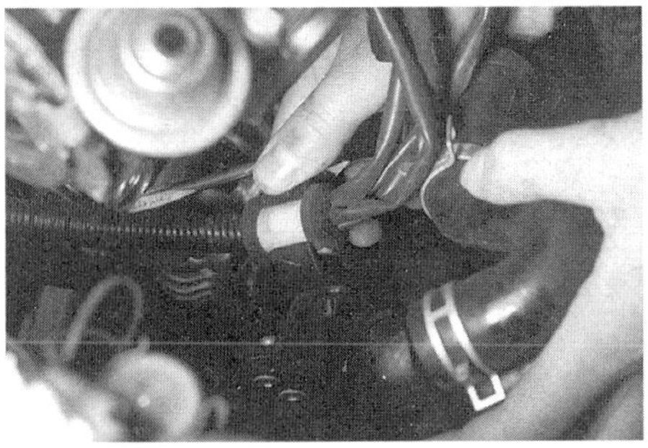

4/29b ... give access to last clip.

ratchet-type clip can be released by inserting a screwdriver into the exposed slot and twisting the screwdriver blade to release the ratchet. When the clip is opened the whole air pipe and resonance box assembly can be removed from the car.

30 Remove the electrical connector block from the throttle body after springing its spring clip with the blade of a screwdriver.

31 Remove the electrical connector block from the ISC (Idle Speed Control) by squeezing the tag at the top of the block and simultaneously pulling.

4/30 Release connector block's clip.

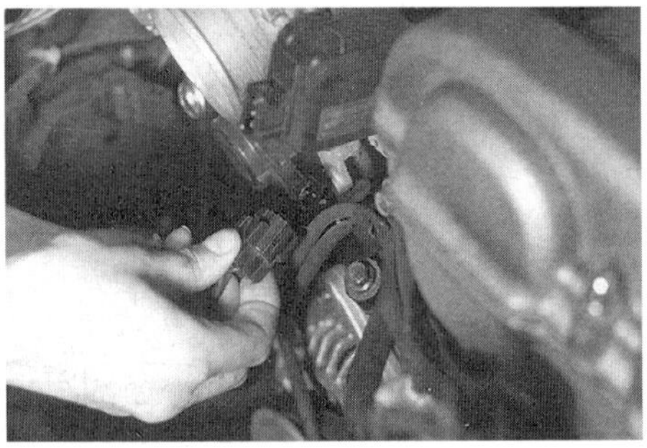

4/31 Release ISC connector.

32 Bend open the electrical cable clamp on the side of the cambox to release the bunch of electrical cables. Release the cables from the clip on the side of the thermostat housing, after pushing down the locking tang and opening the nylon clip. The cables can then be pushed to the side of the engine compartment and tied out of harm's way.

33 + At the rear end of the cambox cover, above the crank-angle sensor, are the connector blocks for the ignition coil and the exhaust manifold oxygen sensor. Disconnect both blocks by pressing on the release tags and separating the two halves.

4/32 Release wires from clip.

4/33a Release locking tab ...

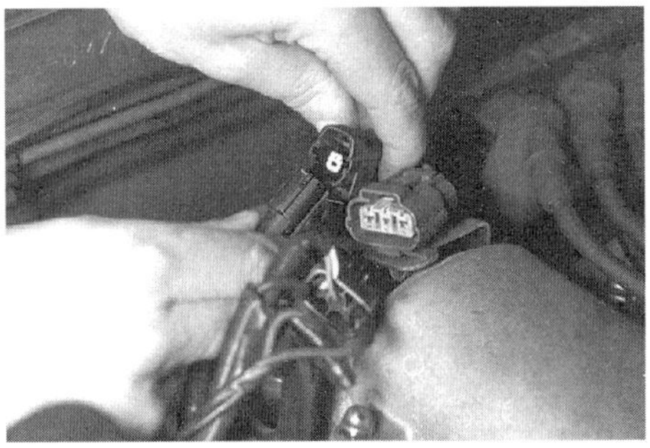

4/33b ... and unplug ...

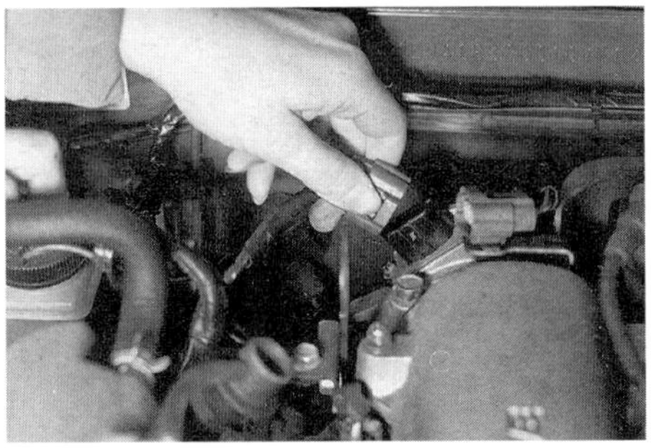

4/34 .... both connectors.

34 Release the electrical connector from the top of the crank-angle sensor by pushing in the release tag and pulling the connector upwards at the same time.

35 With a 10 mm socket release the bolt securing the ground/earth wire connection to the engine lifting bracket at the rear of the cambox cover on the right-hand side. Replace the bolt finger-tight once the terminal has been removed.

36 At the rear of the intake manifold, on the right-hand side adjacent to the injector electrical connector block, there is a cable tie on a bracket.

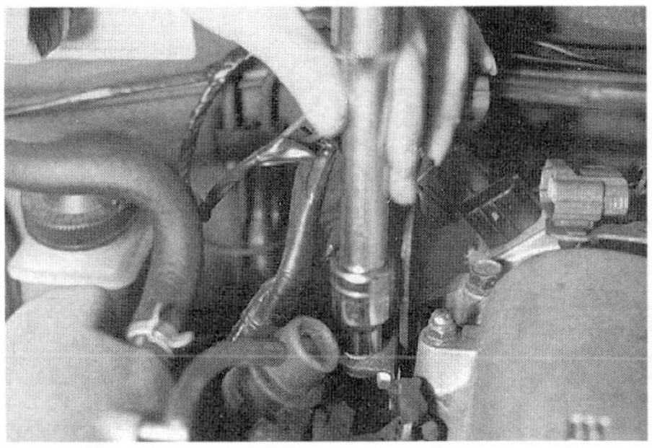

4/35 Release ground wire connection.

This tie can be released by pulling back the locking tongue and pulling the cable free which will allow easier access to the injector connector.

37 Press its tab and pull the Lucar connector from the ground/earth terminal at the firewall end of the intake manifold. The male half of the injector loom electrical connector block can be pulled from the bracket mounted female part after inserting a screwdriver into the slot on the side of the female part.

38 The free wiring loom can now be pulled upwards and tied back for safekeeping.

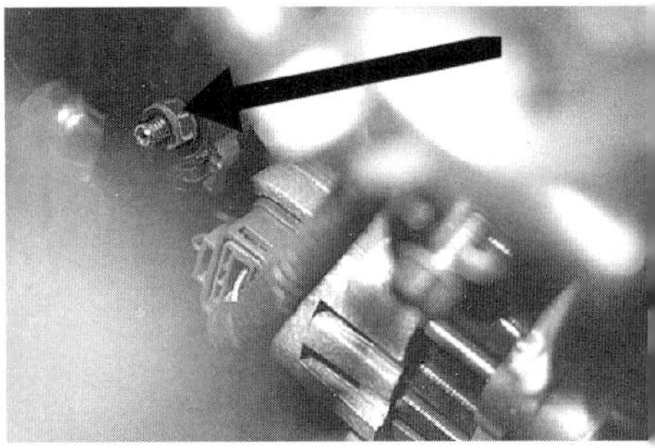

4/39 Permanent live connection arrowed.

39 There are two electrical connections to the alternator: first, the permanent live, which is retained by a 10 mm nut within a plastic cover. Unclip the plastic cover and unscrew the nut; the terminal comes away from the alternator complete with the plastic cover assembly.

40 The second connection is via a grey connector block in the side of the alternator body and this is released by pressing the spring clip on the side of the body inwards, whilst pulling the connector block outwards.

41 Halfway along the right-hand side of the cylinder block is the oil pressure sensor. The electrical wire can be disconnected from this sensor by pressing the tag on the side of the connector block and pulling the connector block free of the Lucar-type terminal.

42 Looking down between the right-hand inner wing and the intake manifold, you can just about see the electrical connections on the back of the starter motor solenoid. There's one Lucar connector which is easy to remove once its retaining clip has been pressed, then you must pull back the rubber cover and undo the 12 mm nut retaining the larger cables from the loom. Once the cable is free the nut should be replaced finger-tight. Re-

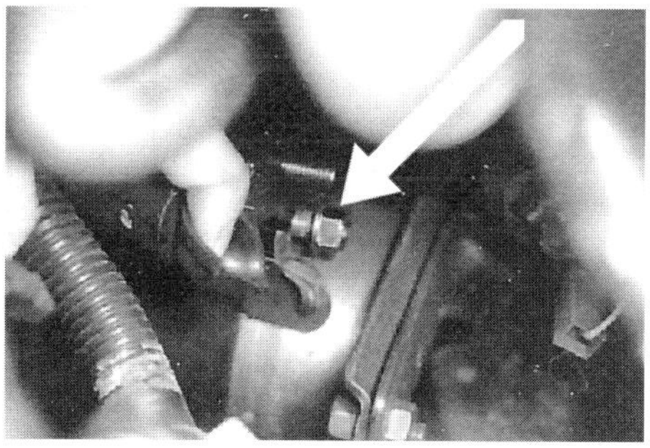

4/42 Starter motor terminal nut.

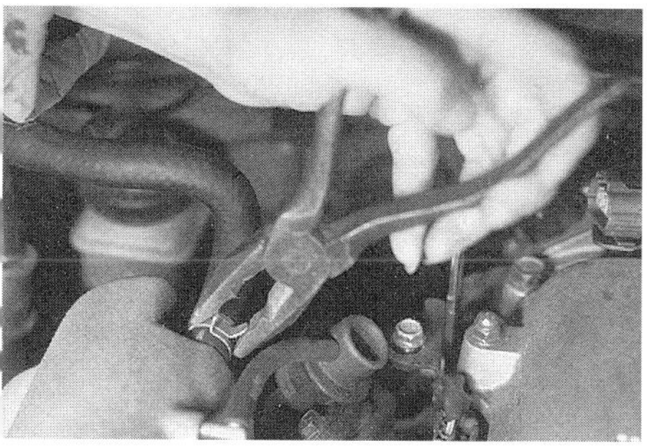

4/43 Release servo vacuum pipe.

lease the cable harness from its clip on the right-hand side of the cylinder block and pull the harness through the manifold support behind the alternator. Once it's clear, bring it up to the right-hand side of the bulkhead and tie it back out of the way.

43 Release the clip on the manifold end of the brake servo vacuum pipe and pull the pipe away from the manifold, then tie it back out of the way.

44 + Open the fuel filler flap and remove the fuel filler cap and then close the flap. Next, disconnect the flexible fuel hoses from the rigid fuel pipes mounted on the chassis rail on the right-hand side of the engine compartment. Pack cloth around the rigid pipes because when the flexible pipes are disconnected there will be some fuel leakage. Use tape to identify one matching pair of rigid and flexible pipes. Release the clips and work the flexible hoses off of the rigid pipes.

45 When the flexible hoses are free hold them downwards to drain residual fuel and then tie them up against the manifold having taped over their ends to stop debris entering; also wrap insulation tape around the top of both open rigid fuel pipes for the same reason.

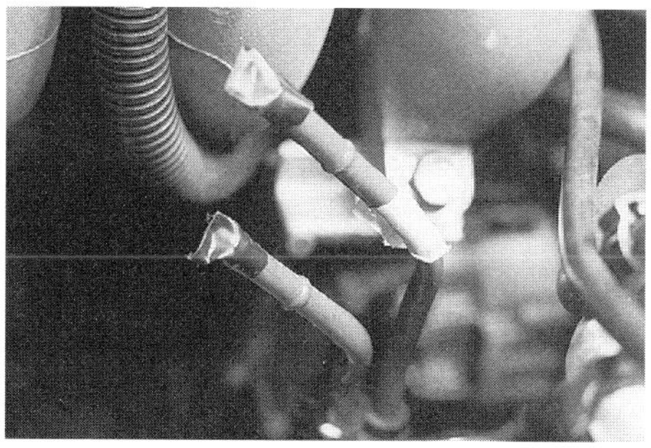

4/45 Tape over open pipe ends.

46 **Warning!** If the fuel filler cap is not left off, residual pressure can continue to push fuel from the pipes for hours, and even days: this could be extremely dangerous.

47 Disconnect the vacuum hose from the purge control at its connection at the top of the intake manifold.

48 Moving back to the left-hand side of the engine compartment, remove the water inlet hose after releasing both hose clips.

49 Toward the back of the engine compartment still on the left-hand side, you will see two rubber heater hoses between the engine and the bulkhead. Release the clips at the bulkhead end and pull both pipes free of the connector's stubs.

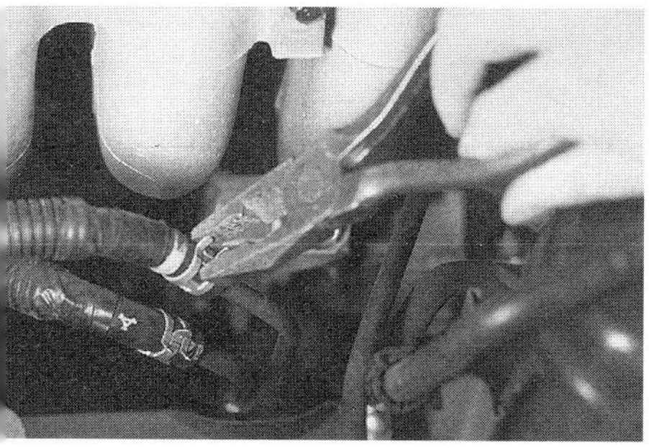

4/44a Release fuel pipe clips.

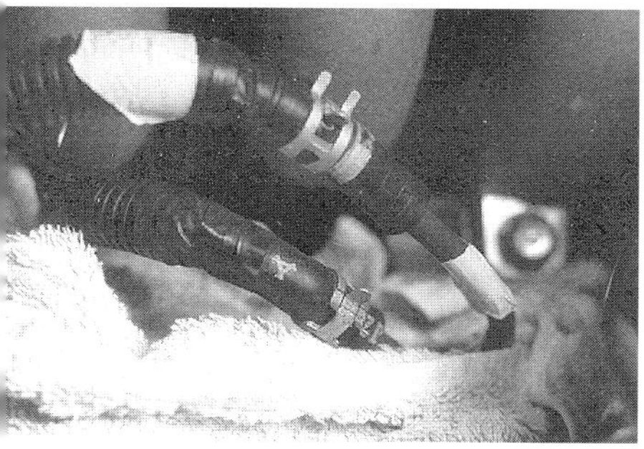

4/44b Wrap tape around one pipe.

4/47 Release vacuum pipe.

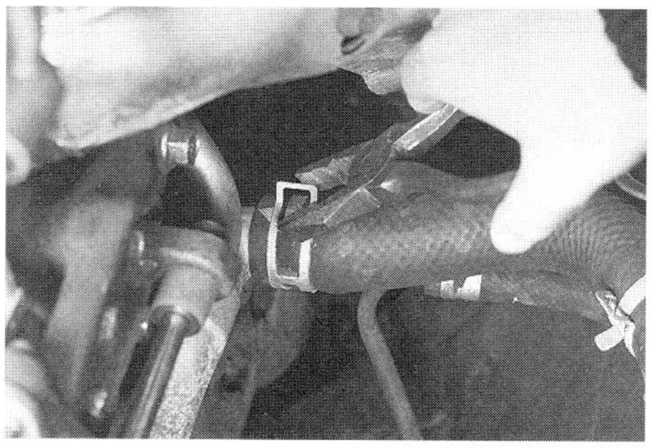

4/48 Remove water inlet hose.

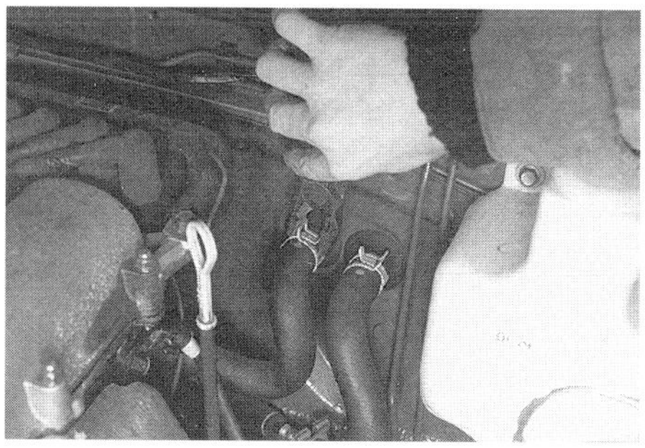

4/49 Release heater hoses.

50 Between the rear left of the cambox and the chassis frame of the car you will see a short ground/earth strap. Undo and remove the 12 mm bolt at the cambox end and release the strap. Tuck the strap back out of the way and replace the bolt finger-tight.

51 From beneath the car you can gain access to the 14 mm nuts securing the engine mountings to the subframe. The nuts are located in

4/50 Release ground (earth) strap.

4/51 Engine mount from beneath car.

recesses each side of the subframe between the pivots of the lower swinging arm. Undo and remove the nuts and keep together with their washers.

52 The next task is to remove the complete exhaust system. ☞ 5/38.

53 Cars with automatic transmission only. Using the access hole in the bottom of the bellhousing reach up into the bellhousing and release the four bolts which fix the torque convertor to the driveplate: you can lock the driveplate by wedging a large screwdriver into the starter teeth. We cannot give more details as our project car was equipped with manual transmission.

54 Removal of bellhousing bolts and nuts. Note: you'll need 14 mm and 17 mm sockets, a universal joint and extension(s) of around 450 mm (18 in) to reach these fixings, which are also very tight! Start by removing the nut and bolt holding the starter motor. Both nut and bolt are 14 mm (smaller than the rest of the bellhousing bolts) and are situated about halfway up the right-hand side of the bellhousing. The head of the lower bolt holding the starter motor will have to be held by a second person and can be accessed via the space above the front subframe in the right-hand front wheelwell. Once a helper is holding the bolt head, the nut can be released from the transmission side. There are no nuts for the top starter motor bolts and these can be unscrewed and removed from the transmission side. Note: both of these bolts also secure brackets fixing wiring and (manual cars) hydraulic pipe. Once free, tie these brackets and their wiring/pipework to one side away from the bellhousing. You are now left with seven 17 mm bolts and one 17 mm nut and bolt holding the transmission bellhousing to the engine. Using a diagonal sequence, first of all loosen each of these bolts and one nut by half a turn. Then remove all of the bolts and the nut.

55 Place a jack beneath the forward end of the transmission and raise its pad until it just takes the weight of the unit.

56 + Get the engine crane in position and lower the boom as near to the top of the engine cam cover as it will go. Fix a sturdy nylon rope or chain through the two lifting eyes at each end and on opposite sides of the cambox and over the hook of the lifting arm. Knot the rope securely.

57 **Caution!** Make one careful final check using a lead light or torch to check all around the engine to ensure that everything is disconnected from the unit and it really is ready to lift.

4/56a Engine crane in position.

4/56b Take the strain ....

58 + Lift the engine vertically a couple of inches (50 mm) until the engine mountings spring clear of their seats. You can then move the engine crane backwards so that the engine moves forward in its bay until the crankshaft pulley is just touching the suspension stabilizer bar and the clutch has disengaged from the transmission input shaft. Hold the engine steady and lift vertically until it is clear of the engine compartment. The engine crane can then be moved backward, drawing the engine clear of the car, and the engine placed wherever it is to be first worked upon.

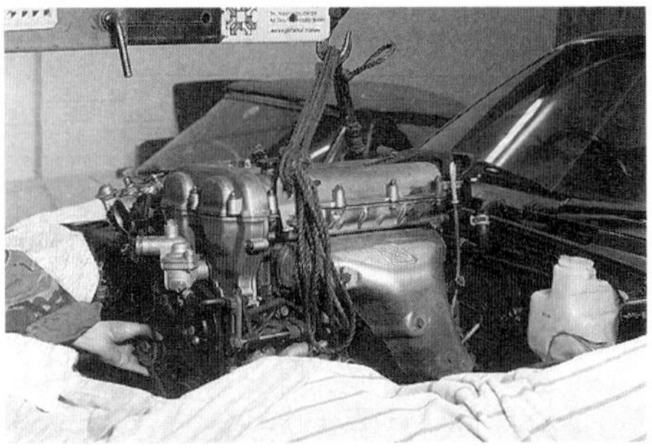

4/58a ... and lift carefully until ....

4/58b ... clear!

5. ENGINE - REMOVAL (WITH TRANSMISSION)

☞ First read 1/1, 2.

☞ 3/3.

1 ☞ 3/4/1-51.

2 Manual transmission cars. ☞ 4/2/3-9, 12-23.

2 Automatic transmission cars. ☞ 4/3/5-14 and 3/2/17-23.

3 Remove the two 14 mm bolts (one of which fixes the top of the starter motor to the bellhousing) which are about halfway up on the right-hand side of the bellhousing. These two bolts also secure brackets carrying wiring looms and the hydraulic pipe for the clutch release cylinder (if fitted). Tie all wiring and the hydraulic pipe safely away from the bellhousing.

4 Cars with automatic transmission only and if the auto trans is to be separated from the engine after removal. Using the access hole in the bottom of the bellhousing, reach up into the bellhousing and release the four bolts which fix the torque convertor to the driveplate: you can lock the driveplate by wedging a large screwdriver into the starter teeth. Unfortunately, we cannot give more details as our project car was equipped with manual transmission.

5 Release the sling (if applicable) around the tailhousing of the transmission after placing a jack under the unit. Lower the transmission as far as it will go without squashing the ignition coil and crank-angle sensor against the firewall.

6 Manual trans only. There should now be enough space above the lowered transmission to disconnect the wiring to the neutral and reverse switches. One of the switches has two plastic clip type connectors which can each be released once the locking tab is depressed; the other switch has two bullet-type connectors which can simply be pulled apart. The wiring loom can now be pulled to one side and tied to the brake pipes alongside the chassis rail out of the way.

7 Auto trans only. ☞ 4/3/17.

8 Get the engine crane in position and lower the boom as near to the top of the engine cam cover as it will go. Fix a sturdy nylon rope or chain through the two lifting eyes at either end and on opposite sides of the cambox and over the hook of the lifting arm. Knot the rope securely.

9 **Caution!** Make one final check with a lead light or torch around the engine and transmission to ensure that everything is disconnected from the unit and it is ready to lift.

10 Lower the jack beneath the transmission and remove it. Lay some cardboard or fiberboard beneath the car between the end of the transmission and the engine compartment: this will enable the tail of the transmission to skid along the ground without damage, during removal.

11 You'll need an assistant to hold things steady during the lift. In the first instance, simply lift the engine vertically a couple of inches until the engine mountings spring clear of their seats. You can then move the engine crane backward so that the engine and transmission unit moves forward in

its bay until the crankshaft pulley is just touching the suspension stabilizer bar. Tilt the whole engine and transmission assembly in its sling to an angle of about 45 degrees, then lift vertically until it is clear of the engine compartment. The engine crane can then be moved backward, drawing the unit clear of the car, and placing it wherever it is to be worked upon. **Caution!** Take care that the transmission, which will tend to hang down, does not damage the car's bodywork as it clears the engine bay.

12 Lower the engine and transmission until the unit just rests on the workplace. Now is a good time to separate the engine from the transmission by removing the 17 mm bolts and one 17 mm nut and bolt (if still fitted) holding them together. Initially, slacken each fastening half a turn working in a diagonal sequence. Before removing the last bolt, make sure the transmission is supported, otherwise the transmission input shaft will be strained. Once the last bolt is removed the transmission - which weighs around 45 kg /100 lb (auto: 75 kg /150 lb) - should be pulled straight back until free of locating spigots. **Caution!** With manual transmission units, make sure input shaft is clear of the clutch before tilting transmission unit.

13 Automatic transmission only. **Caution!** During and after removal, the transmission unit must not be turned on its side or inverted as such action would allow sediment and debris from the oil pan to contaminate fine oilways and valves.

6. ENGINE TEARDOWN - GENERAL ADVICE

☞ First read 1/1, 2.

1 You'll find the teardown of the engine is made much easier if all external oil and dirt is cleaned off first. There will also be less risk of contaminating and damaging components with bearings or fine operating clearances.

2 Place the engine on a bed of several thicknesses of newspaper or cardboard which will absorb solvents and oil.

3 Use a combination of proprietary solvent or kerosene (paraffin) and brushes and scrapers to remove congealed oil and dirt. Wipe off excess cleaning fluid with a rag once the exterior of the engine and its fittings are clean. **Warning!** Do not use gasoline/petrol as a cleaning solvent. Take care not to let cleaning fluid run into the alternator through its cooling slots. Don't forget you have the opportunity to clean up the engine bay whilst the engine's out.

4 Obtain a complete set of engine gaskets before beginning the engine teardown. Note: see the advice on ordering parts in Chapter 1.

5 Don't throw away any of the old gaskets or seals removed during the engine teardown; they might be useful as patterns or reference if there are any shortcomings in your new gasket/seal kit.

6 Have plenty of plastic bags or other transparent containers for storing bits and pieces as they are removed. Identify the components and where they've come from. Adhesive tape and gardening wire will also be useful.

7 Make it a habit to reinstall bolts, screws and nuts (with attendant washers, spacers and brackets) finger-tight after components are dismantled. You'll be surprised how much head scratching and confusion this will prevent when it comes to the rebuild.

7. ENGINE TEARDOWN

☞ First read 1/1, 2.

Warning! The complete unit should be at a comfortable working height and supported by wooden blocks to make it stable. If you have access to one, an engine dismantling stand will make life easier. We managed without and didn't hit any big problems.

7/0 Engine unit secure on bench.

Note: It's a good idea to place the engine on an opened-out cardboard box, this not only provides a nonslip surface but will also absorb the small amounts of oil, fuel and coolant which will be released as the engine is disassembled.

1 Start at the right-hand side of the engine.

INTAKE MANIFOLD & INJECTOR RAIL REMOVAL

2 + Release the clip at the manifold end of the small coolant hose between the airvalve on the intake manifold and the thermostat unit base. Pull the hose away from the manifold and tie it back out of the way; this is easier if the clip on the side of the thermostat housing is also released. **Caution!** We found that the hose on our car had chafed against the clip at the front of the cambox - check that yours is not similarly damaged.

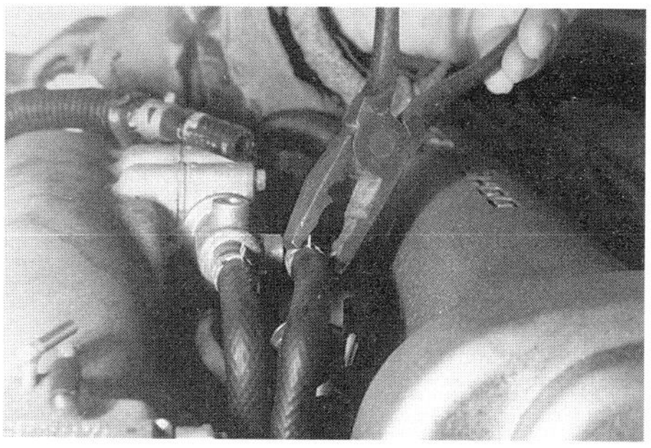

7/2a Release airvalve hose.

7/2b Hose can get damaged here (see text).

3 The PCV (Positive Crankcase Ventilation) hose between the cam cover and the intake manifold should be freed by releasing the spring clips at both ends and lifting the hose away.

4 Remove the engine sling bracket, retained by a single 14 mm bolt, from the rear right-hand side of the cambox: once the bracket is removed install the bolt finger-tight.

7/3 Remove PCV hose.

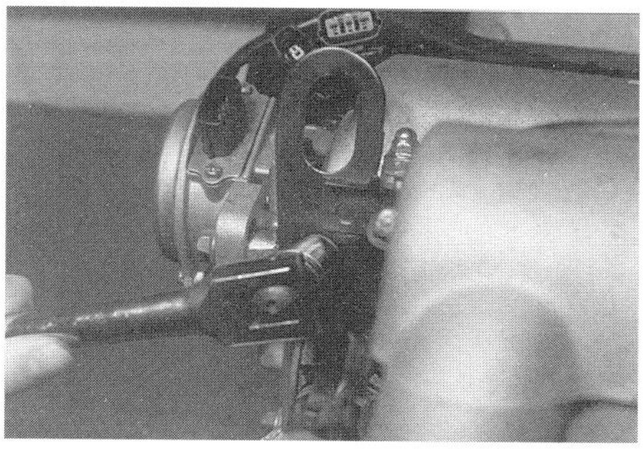

7/4 Remove engine sling bracket.

5 Disconnect the second small coolant hose from the airvalve on the manifold after releasing its retaining clip. The airvalve itself is then held to the intake manifold by four 8 mm-headed bolts: these bolts also have crossheads for a screwdriver if preferred, although you'll need an angled screwdriver to reach the lower bolts. The four bolts should be loosened slightly in a diagonal sequence before they are fully unscrewed. Note: both lower retaining bolts are difficult to access with a socket and should be undone with an 8 mm box end

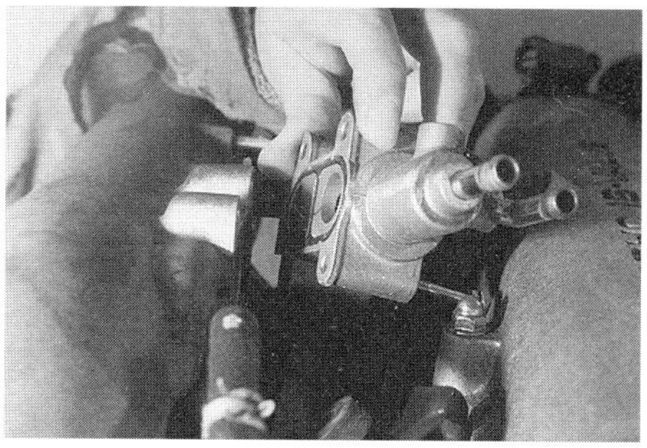

7/5 Lift away airvalve.

spanner. One of the lower retaining bolts cannot be withdrawn completely because its head contacts a boss on the cam cover; therefore, it must be loosened completely but left in position until the airvalve is pulled away from the manifold. The four bolts have loose spring washers.

6 + Disconnection of injector wiring loom. At the rear of the cylinder head you'll see a protruding boss carrying the heater hose outlet union. On the union casting is a green plastic wiring connector block: spring its wire clip with a screwdriver blade and separate the two parts of the connector. Nearby, on the side of the alloy boss, is another electrical

7/6a Undo this connector ...

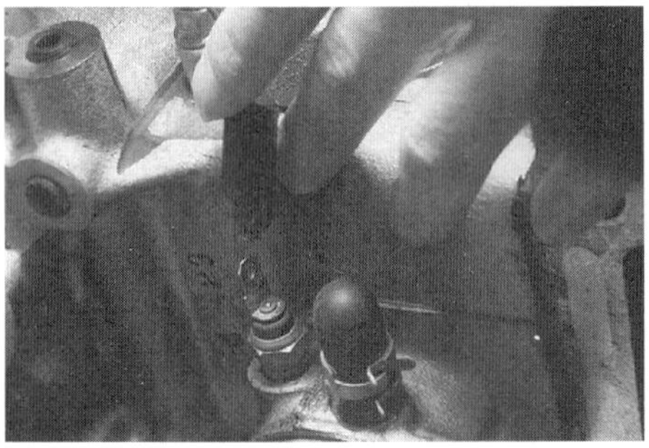
7/6b ... and release this one.

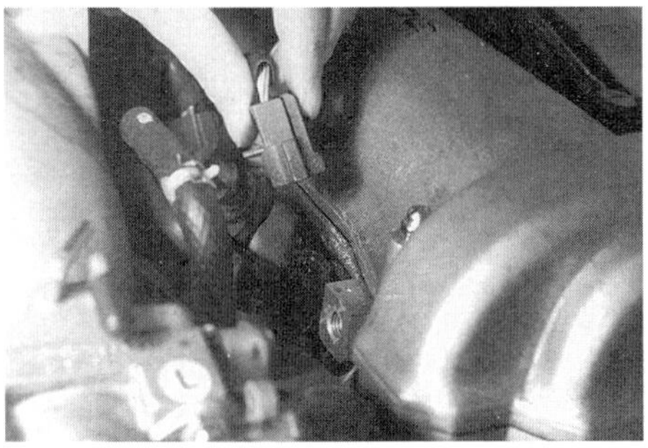
7/7 Squeeze tags & release injector connectors.

connection. The tab on top of the connector block needs to be pushed down and then the connector can be withdrawn.

7 Release the electrical connector block at each individual injector. This is done by squeezing the tag at the top of the connector block inwards, after which the connector block can be pulled away from the side of the injector body.

8 Release the injector loom connector block from its mounting bracket at the rear end of the intake manifold. Squeeze the lugs on the retaining pin with pliers and then the connector block can

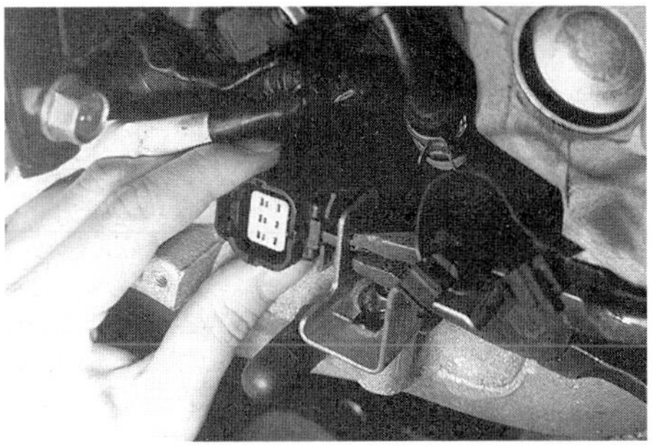
7/8 Unplug injector loom connector.

be freed from the bracket.

9 There is a small vacuum hose running between the pressure regulator valve on the fuel rail and a stub on the manifold. This hose should be disconnected simply by pulling it from either of its unions: there are no spring clips.

10 The fuel rail itself is fixed to the manifold casting by two 12 mm bolts. These should be undone with a box end or crescent wrench as there's no real access for sockets. Withdraw the bolts leaving the fuel rail free for removal. **Caution!** There are locating collars, between the rail and its two mountings, which will be dislodged as the fuel rail is moved and could easily be lost or damaged.

11 Pull the rail assembly away from the manifold to release the injectors from their bores and then move the whole thing towards the rear of the engine and manipulate it up between the cambox and intake manifold plenum chamber, at the same time push the fuel hoses up through the gaps between the individual intake manifolds and pull the injector wiring loom clear as necessary. **Caution!** As the injectors clear the manifold their individual insulators will come away with them, be careful not to lose these.

7/11 Lift away injector fuel rail.

12 + Manifold removal. Undo and remove the single 14 mm bolt holding the manifold to the aluminum support bracket. Now, using a 12 mm socket on a 250 mm (9.5 in) extension, you will be able to reach most of the individual nuts and bolts retaining the manifold once you have maneuvered the socket between the individual intake trunks until you find a gap large enough for it to pass through. There are two extremely awkward bolts alongside the pillars which support the fuel rail. We got to these by fitting a socket and universal joint to the bolt head from above and then inserting the

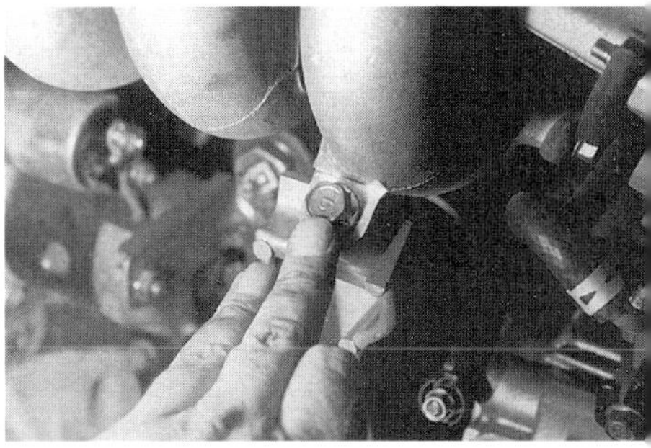
7/12a Remove support bracket bolt ...

7/12b ... unscrew manifold nuts ...

7/12c ... and lift manifold away from head.

extension between the intake tracts and engaging it in the universal joint: this was with a 1/2 inch drive socket set. If you use a smaller drive socket system it will need to be of extremely good quality because these bolts are tight. The nuts and bolts should be loosened in a diagonal sequence and, once the bolts and nuts have been removed, the manifold can be slid off the three studs left protruding from the cylinder head. If the gasket stays fixed to the head, or manifold face, peel it off. **Caution!** Don't damage the cylinder head by trying to free the old gasket with a sharp tool and don't try to re-use the gasket, it's a false economy.

ALTERNATOR & MOUNTING BRACKET REMOVAL

13 With a 12 mm socket or box end wrench slacken the alternator locking bolt at the back of the sliding block.

14 Using a 14 mm socket at the pulley end and a crescent or box end wrench at the other end slacken the alternator pivot bolt. Note: if the area around the pivot bolt is corroded, you may need to coat the bolt with penetrating oil and allow it to soak in before going further.

7/13 Slacken alternator locking bolt.

7/14 Slacken alternator pivot bolt.

7/15a Slacken alternator adjuster bolt ...

7/15b ... and lift from its bracket.

7/15c Lift adjuster block away.

15 + Turn the alternator adjusting bolt anti-clockwise until it is loose enough to swing upwards out of its bracket. With the screw lifted from its bracket, the alternator can be pushed towards the engine giving enough slack to remove the drivebelt. Fully undo the lock bolt retaining the adjuster block. Lift the block and two bolts away.

16 + Remove its nut and withdraw the alternator swivel bolt forwards. The alternator can then be lifted away from the engine. You may have to rock it backwards and forwards a little just to free the alternator from its mounting bracket.

17 Slacken and remove the 14 mm bolt holding the manifold support bracket to the base of the cylinder block. The bracket can then be lifted away.

7/16a Remove alternator swivel bolt ...

7/16b ... and lift alternator from its bracket.

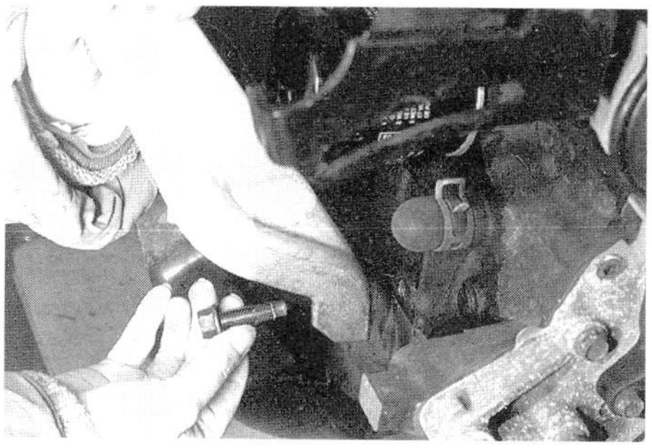
7/17 Remove manifold support bracket.

18 The alternator adjuster bracket is fixed to the cylinder block by two 17 mm bolts. Slacken and remove both bolts and the bracket can then be lifted away. Note the two large bolts will be fairly tight so you'll need to ensure the engine is held securely as they are first loosened. Note that the rearmost bolt also holds a cable clip which, of course, should be kept with the bracket.

7/18 Remove alternator adjustment bracket.

7/19a Release starter motor rear bracket ...

7/19b ... and lift starter motor away.

STARTER MOTOR REMOVAL.

19 + Unscrew and remove the single 14 mm bolt holding the starter motor rear bracket to the cylinder block (the bellhousing bolts should already have been removed when the engine was separated from the transmission), the starter motor can then be lifted away from the engine.

ENGINE MOUNTING BRACKET REMOVAL

20 Undo and remove the two 14 mm bolts (assuming the starter motor retaining bracket has been removed - otherwise there will be three). The engine mounting bracket can then be lifted away

7/20 Remove engine mounting bracket bolts.

7/21 Unscrew oil filter cannister.

7/22 Remove oil pressure sender unit.

from the cylinder block.

21 Unscrew the oil filter canister which should be hand-tight. If it's not, use a strap wrench. Note: oil is likely to spill from the filter canister as it comes free.

22 Using a 17 mm crescent wrench on the hexagonal section between the back of the oil pressure sender unit and the cylinder block, undo and remove the unit. **Caution!** The hexagonal section at the top of the unit must not be used to undo the sender.

23 Move to the left-hand side of the engine.

7/24a Remove 4 bolts ....

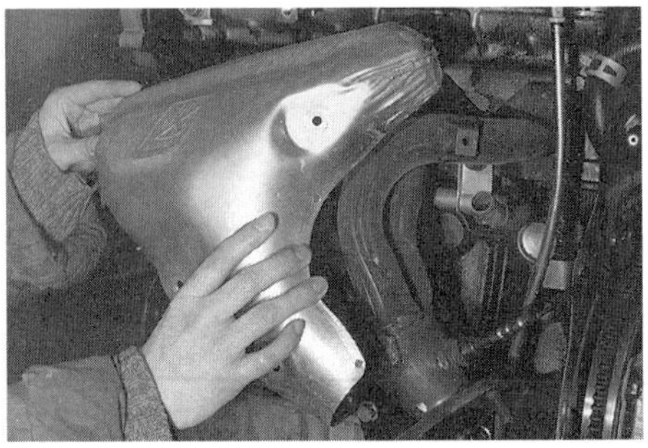

7/24b ... and lift away heatshield.

EXHAUST MANIFOLD, HEATSHIELD & OXYGEN SENSOR REMOVAL

24 + Remove the exhaust manifold heatshield after unscrewing the four 10 mm headed retaining bolts.

25 Unclip the oxygen sensor electrical cable from the engine backplate. Then unscrew and remove oxygen sensor from the exhaust manifold with a 22 mm crescent wrench.

26 + Using 14 mm socket with a 125 mm/5 in extension, undo and remove the nine nuts fixing the exhaust manifold to the cylinder head. Note the studs may be rusty and therefore cleaning with a small wire brush, followed by a dousing of penetrating oil, may well be helpful.

27 After removing the manifold flange nuts, the water pipe bracket fixed to the second stud from the rear on the lower edge of the exhaust flange should be pulled off the stud to give clearance for removal of the exhaust manifold. This is fiddly but it's possible!

28 Once the manifold has been removed, lift the three-piece exhaust gasket off of the studs.

COOLANT INLET CASTING REMOVAL

29 Undo the securing clip on the forward elbow of the coolant inlet casting and release the small hose that connects to the thermostat housing.

30 + Using a 12 mm socket and a 75 mm/3 in extension, undo and remove the two bolts securing the coolant inlet casting flange to the side of the water pump body at the front of the cylinder block. Once the two bolts are removed the casting will need a sharp tug to release the adhesion of its gasket.

7/25 Unscrew and remove oxygen sensor.

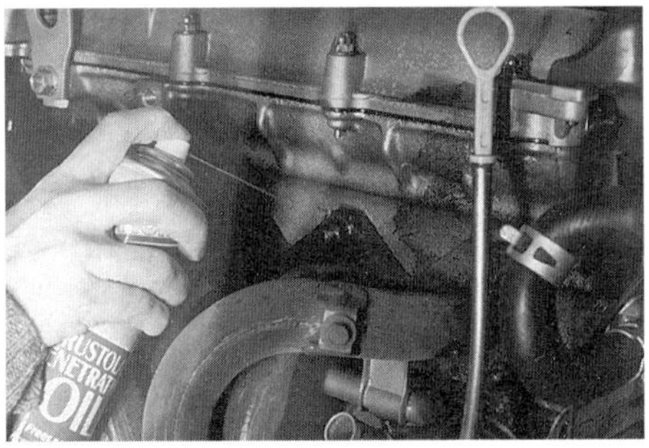

7/26a Spray with penetrating oil ...

7/26b ... then undo exhaust manifold nuts.

7/27 Release water pipe bracket.

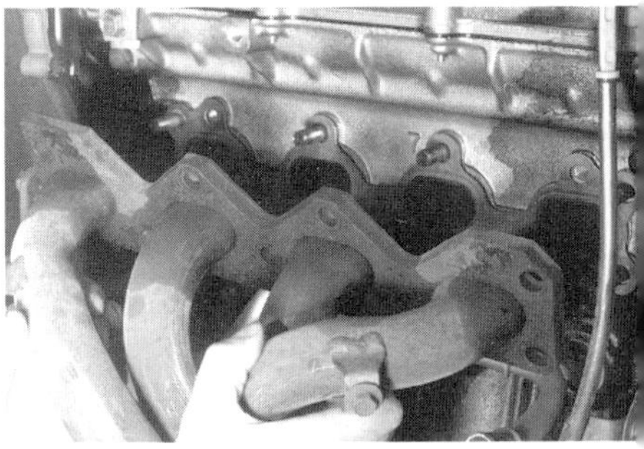

7/28 Lift manifold away.

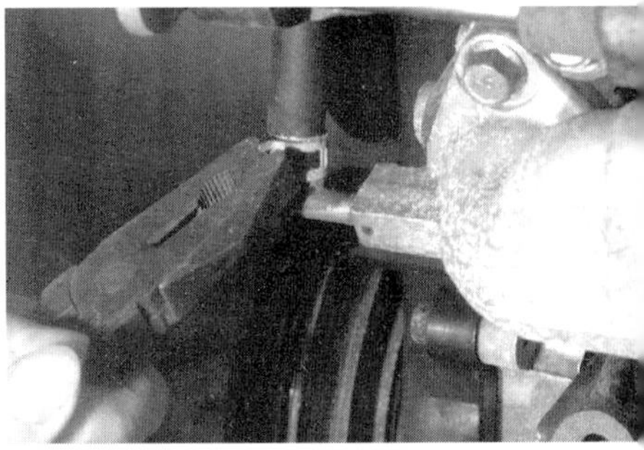

7/29 Release small hose at elbow.

ENGINE MOUNTING BRACKET REMOVAL

31 + Using a 14 mm socket with a 125 mm/5 in extension, unscrew and remove the three

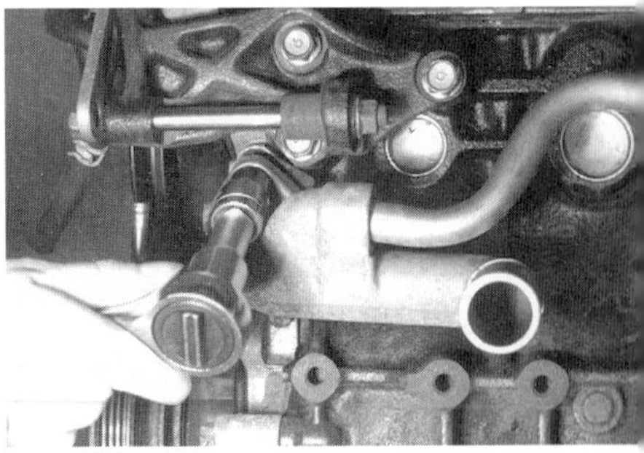

7/30a Remove inlet casting bolts ...

7/30b ... and lift casting away.

7/31a Release bolts ...

7/31b ... & lift engine mounting bracket away.

bolts securing the engine mounting to the left-hand side of the cylinder block.

DIPSTICK TUBE REMOVAL

32 + Undo and remove the 10 mm nut holding the dipstick tube bracket to the engine backplate. Run a little oil down around the base of the dipstick tube and then, pulling quite hard whilst simultaneously working the dipstick tube backwards and forwards, pull the tube from its mounting in the side of the oil pan. **Warning!** It will come free quite suddenly.

7/32a Release dipstick tube bracket ....

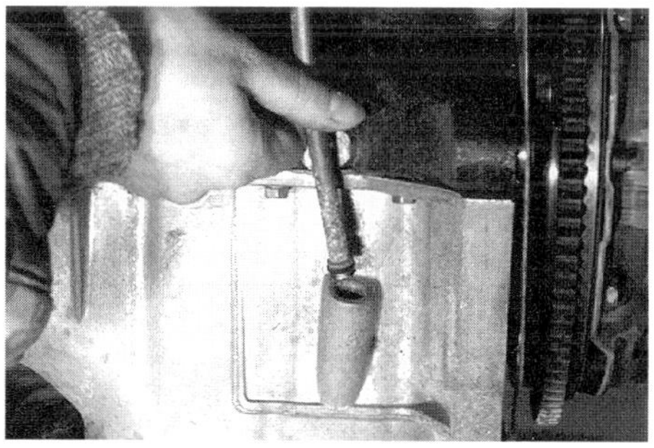

7/32b ... and pull tube out of oil pan.

POWER STEERING PUMP MOUNTING BRACKET REMOVAL

33 + The bracket is retained by three 14 mm headed bolts. The top two bolts are easily accessible by socket; however, the lower bolt is obscured by the spacer for the power steering pump pivot bolt. The spacer can be driven out of the bracket by pushing it forward with a brass drift and hammer. However, before doing this its position relative to the bracket should be marked with a small hacksaw cut which will ensure that there is no difficulty in installing the power steering pump when the time comes. Ideally, the drift needs to have a diameter of 15 or 16 mm /0.6 in. Once the three bolts have been unscrewed the mounting bracket can be lifted away from the cylinder block.

7/33a Mark spacer position ...

7/33b ... drift spacer out ...

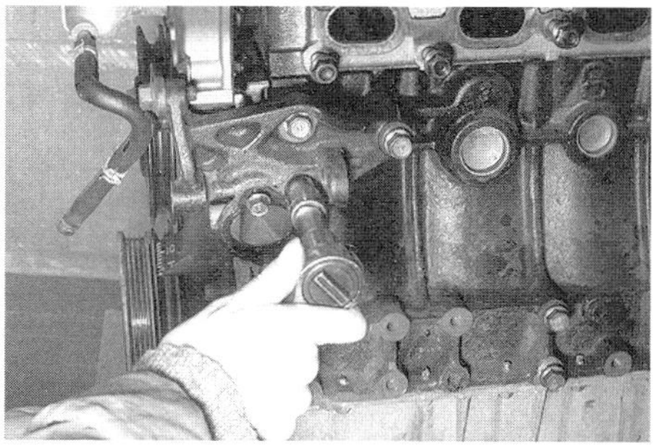

7/33c .... remove bolts ...

7/33d ... & lift away p/s pump bracket.

7/34 Remove engine lifting eye.

34 Remove the engine lifting eye from the front left-hand side of the cylinder head after removing the 14 mm bolt that secures it.

35 Move to the rear of the engine.

HEATER OUTLET COVER REMOVAL

36 The cover is held by one 12 mm bolt

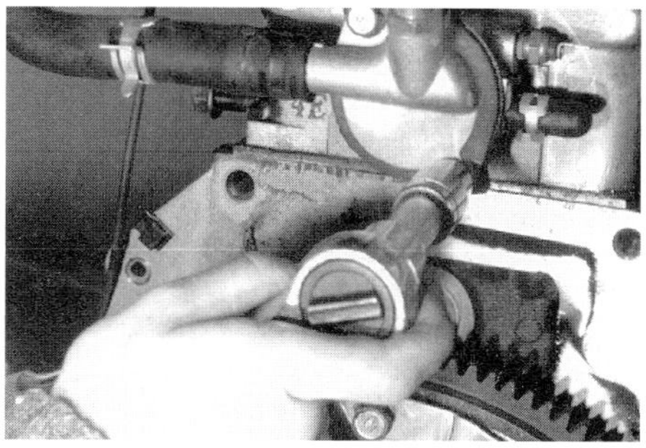

7/36a Release nut and bolt ...

7/36b ... and pull cover free.

and one 12 mm nut. Unscrew both and pull the cover free: it will come away suddenly as it will have stuck to the gasket. **Caution!** Don't use sharp instruments to pry the cover loose.

IGNITION COIL & HT LEADS REMOVAL

37 Pull each of the HT connectors from its spark plug bore using your fingers only: start at the front of the engine and work backwards. As each spark plug connector is released, free its cable from the clips in the valley of the cambox. Leave all four connectors lying on top of the cambox for the moment

7/38a Release bolts ...

7/38b ... and lift coil unit away.

38 + Undo and remove the three 12 mm bolts retaining the coil assembly to the cambox/ cylinder head. Once the bolts are removed the coil assembly can be lifted away from the rear of the cylinder head/cambox. Note: the right-hand coil unit retaining bolt also holds an electrical connector bracket.

CRANK-ANGLE SENSOR REMOVAL

39 + The crank-angle sensor is driven from the rear of the intake camshaft so it's located at the rear of the cambox/cylinder head on the right-hand side. First, mark the relative position of the angle

7/39a Make a reference mark ....

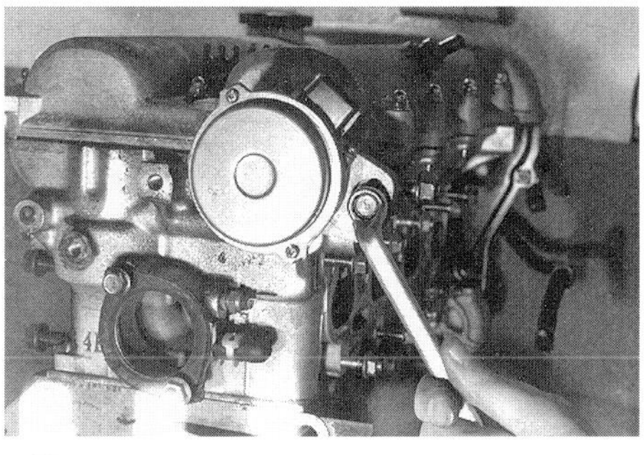

7/39b ... undo single bolt and lift ...

7/39c .... away crank-angle sensor.

sensor body and the cambox, using an indelible pen. Then unscrew and remove the single 12 mm bolt from the adjustment slot on the right-hand side. Once the bolt is removed the crank angle sensor can be pulled backwards until it is clear of its housing in the cambox/cylinder head. **Warning!** It may come free suddenly.

CLUTCH REMOVAL FROM FLYWHEEL (MANUAL TRANSMISSION CARS ONLY)

40 The cover/pressure plate is retained by 12 mm bolts which should be gradually unscrewed

7/40 Lock flywheel as shown.

by half of a turn at a time each, in a diagonal sequence, until the pressure exerted by the cover plate is completely relieved. To lock the flywheel you'll need to temporarily install one of the bell-housing bolts and then jam a screwdriver wedged into the ring gear teeth against it. **Warning!** Failure to undo all of the bolts progressively could easily result in the one or two bolts left under tension suddenly shearing and the cover plate flying off the flywheel. When the cover plate bolts have been removed lift away the cover plate and clutch disc together.

41 Move to the front of the engine.

THERMOSTAT COVER & THERMOSTAT REMOVAL

42 Undo and remove the two 12 mm studs holding the thermostat cover to the thermostat housing. Once the screws are removed the cover can be pulled away from the housing, but be careful as it will come away suddenly once the gasket releases. **Caution!** Do not use a sharp instrument to lever the cover from the housing. Note: the right-hand cover retaining screw also holds a hose bracket. With the cover removed the

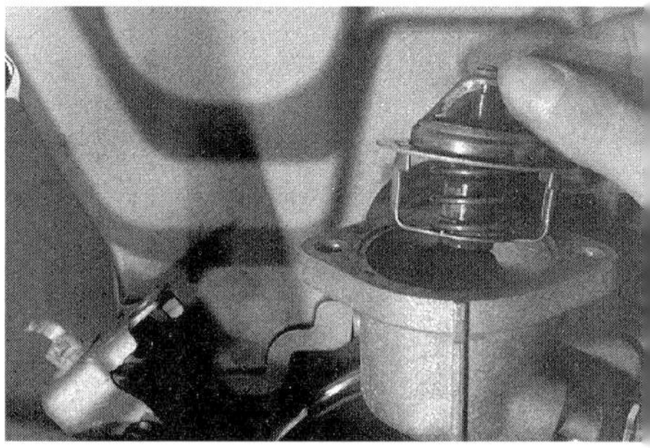

7/42 Lift out thermostat.

thermostat can be lifted from its housing.

CAMBOX COVER REMOVAL

43 + Unscrew and remove the thirteen 10 mm chrome dome-headed bolts which hold the cambox cover to the cylinder head. Unscrew the bolts progressively in a diagonal sequence until they are all loose enough to unscrew with your fingers. Note: a short 75 mm /3 inch extension is also needed. There are four cambox cover bolts down each side of the cambox, three down in the center valley and two at the front. Note: the two

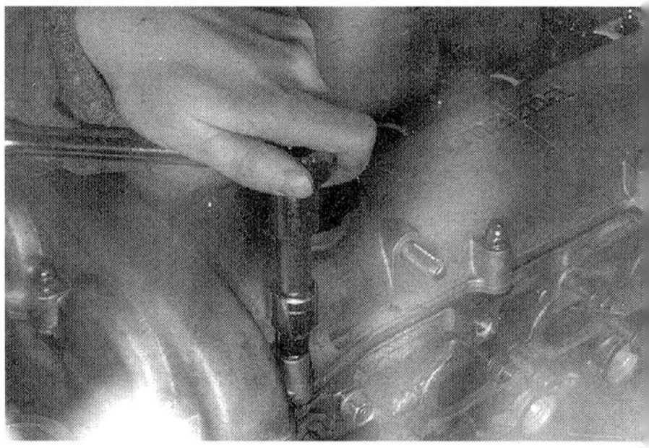

7/43a Release nuts ...

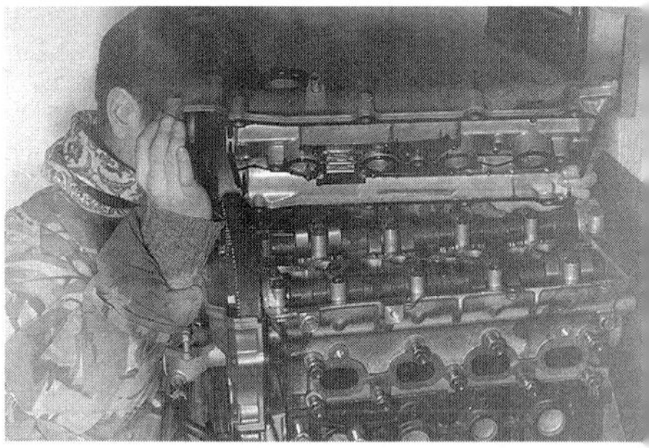

7/43b ... and lift off cambox cover.

front bolts are shorter than the others. Once the bolts have been removed the cambox cover can be lifted clear of the cylinder head.

CAMSHAFT DRIVEBELT COVERS, WATER PUMP PULLEY & CRANKSHAFT OUTER PULLEY REMOVAL

44 + The upper drivebelt cover is retained by four 10 mm bolts which can be undone with a socket and 75 mm /3 inch extension. The cover can be lifted away once the four screws have been removed but note that the bottom left-hand and top right-hand bolts also hold clips.

7/44a Remove bolts ...

7/44b ... & lift away upper drivebelt cover.

45 Wrap the drivebelt around the water pump pulley and clamp with fingers or pliers to hold the pulley still whilst the three 10 mm bolts are loosened and removed from its center. The pulley can then be withdrawn from its mounting flange.

46 The crankshaft outer pulley has a central 21 mm bolt surrounded by four small 10 mm bolts and a plate. To remove the pulley it is only necessary to unscrew and remove the four small bolts. If necessary, lock the crankshaft by once more temporarily replacing one of the bellhousing bolts and using this and a screwdriver to jam the ring gear. Once the four bolts are removed the crankshaft pulley can be withdrawn, together with its front and rear washers and the dished camshaft drivebelt guide plate.

7/46 Undo 4 small bolts to free pulley.

47 There are four 10 mm bolts retaining the middle and lower drivebelt covers. One of these is adjacent to the water pump center boss and is longer than the other three. Once the bolts retaining the drivebelt cover have been removed, the cover can be withdrawn in two pieces. Note that the bolt close to the water pump central boss is longer than the other three.

CAMSHAFT DRIVEBELT REMOVAL

48 **Warning!** Mazda have provided various markings to assist in making sure that the two camshafts and crankshaft are correctly positioned when fitting a camshaft drivebelt and thus critical valve timing is preserved. Frankly, we found these manufacturer's markings hard to use and open to error. Therefore, whilst we do describe use of the manufacturer's markings in our book, we strongly recommend you use the following backup procedure before removing the existing camshaft drivebelt.

49 Using a 21 mm socket on the crankshaft nose bolt, rotate the crankshaft (removing the spark plugs will make this easier) until the cutout in the rear flange of the crankshaft drivebelt pulley is vertical and aligns with the arrow-shaped boss in the oil pump body. Simultaneously, the letter "E" on the exhaust (left-hand) cam pulley and the letter "I" on the intake cam pulley are both more-or-less vertical. Note: this coincidence of relative positions will occur only once in every two revolutions of the crankshaft. When all is correctly positioned, use a straight edge running from the center of the crankshaft pulley and across the center of each camshaft pulley in turn, to make alignment marks with a scriber or indelible pen at the two points where the straight edge crosses the rim of each camshaft pulley - don't allow the pulleys to move at all until all alignment marks have been made. Identify the exhaust cam pulley with the letter "E" written in indelible ink.

50 If the camshaft drivebelt is to be re-used - a false economy unless the belt has been in place for less than 50,000 km /30,000 miles and is completely damage-free - mark the outward edge of the belt with a white dot (typist's correction fluid is good for this) so that the belt can be installed to run in the same direction. Slacken the central locking bolt on the tensioner jockey wheel and pull the wheel backwards as far as possible to relieve the tension on the drivebelt. Whilst holding the wheel back, retighten the central screw. The drivebelt will now be loose enough to withdraw from the crankshaft and camshaft pulleys. **Caution!** Avoid rotating the crankshaft whilst the drivebelt is removed. If you must turn the crankshaft do it very slowly and carefully, stopping at the least sign of contact between valve heads and pistons - which could result in bent valve stems. In fact, our engine showed no signs of such contact when we checked by turning the crank with the cams in various different positions, but it's possible tolerances will vary from engine to engine, particularly if high-performance camshafts are fitted.

7/50 Slacken tensioner jockey wheel.

CAMSHAFT DRIVEBELT TENSIONER WHEEL, TENSIONER SPRING & IDLER WHEEL REMOVAL

51 + Slacken and remove the tensioner wheel 14 mm lockbolt whilst holding the wheel against spring tension sufficiently to prevent the bolt binding. Unclip the tensioner spring from the tensioner wheel bracket and from its anchor pin then lift away the tensioner wheel assembly and the spring. Unscrew and remove the 14 mm bolt securing the idler wheel and lift the wheel away.

7/51a Remove tensioner wheel bolt ...

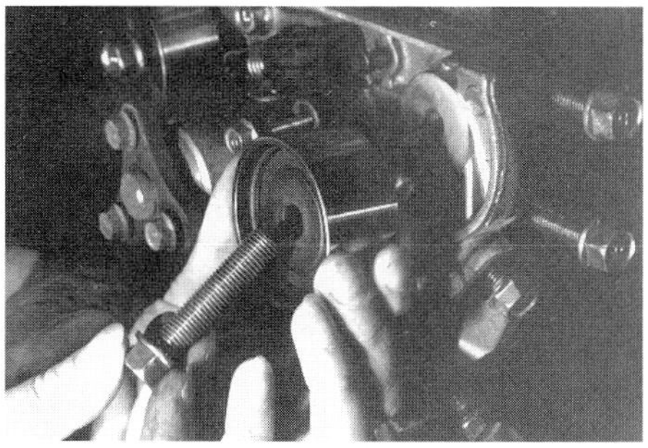

7/51b ... and idler wheel bolt.

CAMSHAFT PULLEYS REMOVAL

52 There is a hex-shaped section on each of the two camshafts between bearings two and three, counting from the front of the engine. Use a 24 mm crescent wrench to hold each cam in a locked position whilst the drive pulley retaining 14 mm bolt is slackened and removed. **Caution!** Do not wedge the open-ended wrench locking the cam against the side of the cambox - it's a fragile casting which could easily be broken. Before removing the pulleys, note that they are apparently interchange-

able: mark an "E" on the exhaust pulley so that it can be installed on the same cam. Once the bolt is removed the drive pulley can be pulled forward off of the mounting spigot.

CYLINDER HEAD FRONT SEALING PLATE REMOVAL

53 After undoing the six 10 mm retaining bolts, the seal plate can be lifted away from the front of the cylinder head. Note: there is a rubber seal which fits around the thermostat housing casting and which should not be lost.

THERMOSTAT HOUSING REMOVAL

54 Unscrew and remove the two 12 mm bolts holding the thermostat housing to the front of the cylinder head. This will be difficult with sockets as there is little room, so use a box end spanner. Once the two bolts have been removed the housing can be pulled forward off of the cylinder head. **Warning!** It will probably come free rather suddenly. Note: the thermostat housing connection is sealed by an O-ring which should be replaced and take care of the strip of sealing rubber which should be adhering to the casting's base.

7/55 Just water pump & pulley to go!

WATER PUMP REMOVAL

55 First, using a 14 mm socket, undo and remove the bolt securing the camshaft drivebelt idler wheel (if still fitted) and lift the wheel away from the water pump body. This will then give clearance to reach a partially obscured water pump retaining bolt.

56 Slacken and then unscrew - in a diagonal sequence - the four 12 mm bolts holding the water pump body to the front of the cylinder block. Once the bolts are clear the pump body can be pulled away. **Warning!** It will come free suddenly

7/56 Remove the water pump.

as the gasket seal breaks. **Caution!** You can tap the back of the casting with a wooden hammer handle or soft-faced mallet to help break the joint's adhesion, but don't use a sharp implement to lever the casting away from the cylinder block.

CRANKSHAFT INNER PULLEY REMOVAL

57 + Unscrew and remove the 21 mm headed pulley retaining bolt. This will require considerable force and it will be necessary to lock the flywheel as previously described. Once the pulley retaining bolt has been removed, spray a little penetrating oil into the end of the pulley to lubricate the area between the pulley and crankshaft nose. Reach in with a pair of needle-nosed pliers and pull out the key locking the pulley to the crank. We found with our engine that replacing two of the small outer pulley retaining bolts gave sufficient purchase just to pull the toothed pulley from the crankshaft nose with fingers. If necessary, these same bolts will give enough purchase for an ordinary two-pronged puller. Alternatively, you could drill two holes in a small flat plate placed across a protruding spacer - such as a socket - and then screw two of the small screws through the plate

7/57a Unscrew pulley retaining bolt ...

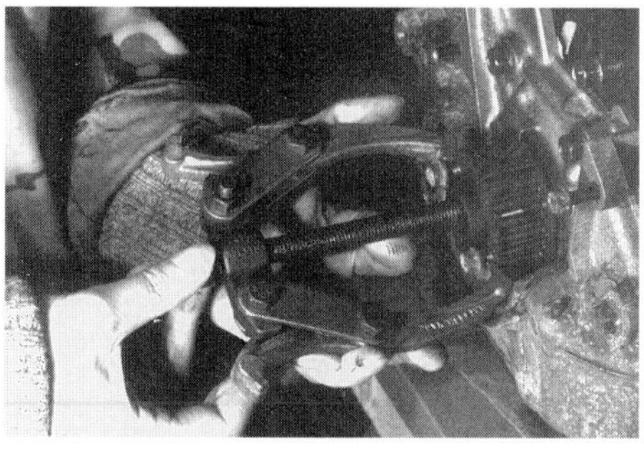
9/57b ... and withdraw pulley ...

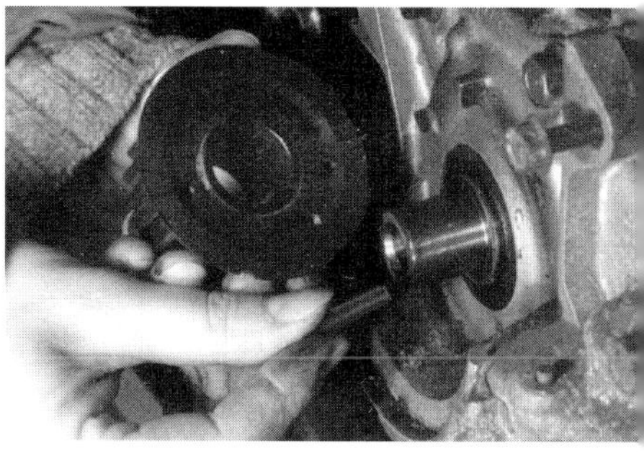
9/57c ... lift out locking key.

until the pulley is pulled off the crankshaft nose. Note: it might seem logical to remove the oil pump at this point but, in fact, it can't be done until the oil pan/sump has been removed.

CAMSHAFTS REMOVAL

58 Each camshaft is retained by five bearing caps and each cap is numbered from the front of the engine backwards. The first cap is simply marked with an "E" for the exhaust camshaft and an "I" for the intake camshaft; each subsequent cap is marked "E2", "E3" etc. Each cap is also

7/58 Camshaft bearing cap markings.

marked with an arrow shape pointing toward the front of the engine so that the caps are installed the correct way around.

59 + Undo and remove the ten 10 mm bolts retaining the bearing caps for each camshaft. **Caution!** The bolts must be undone in sequence to prevent distortion and it is suggested that, initially, they are undone by half a turn on the first pass, followed by a full turn on the second pass and then removed completely on the third pass. The sequence is simply a spiral that works inward from the outer caps of each cam. Once all of the cap bolts have been removed for a complete camshaft, the

7/59a Remove bearing cap bolts ...

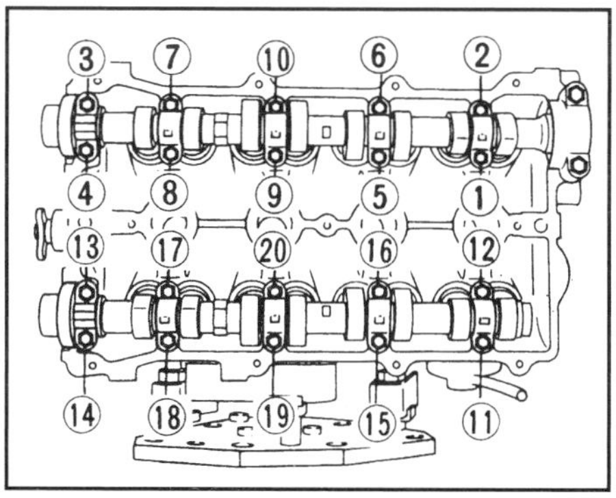

D7/59 CAM CAP LOOSENING SEQUENCE.

individual caps can be lifted. They will be a little tight as they are located on close-fitting spigots. The front cap of each cam really is rather difficult to remove: not only is it mounted on spigots but there is sealing compound around its edges and the cap also tends to get held by the oil seal. Very gently tapping the caps backwards and forwards with a nylon or leather-faced mallet will eventually loosen them. **Caution!** Do not insert sharp implements between the base casting and the cap. Once all the

7/59b ... lift away caps ...

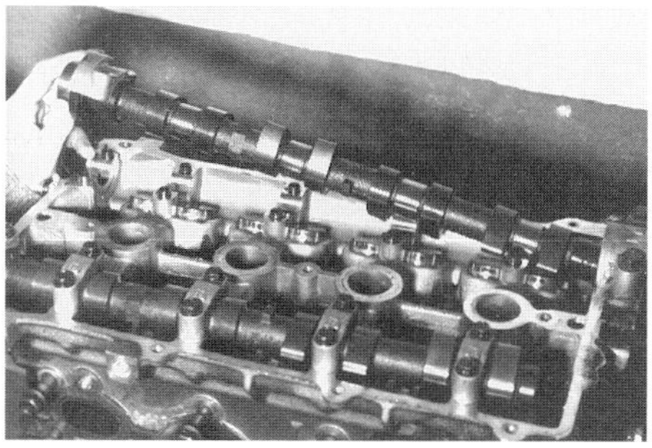

7/59c ... followed by camshaft.

caps are removed, each camshaft can be lifted away from the cylinder head taking care not to scratch the bearing surfaces with the cam lobes.

CAM-FOLLOWER REMOVAL

60 + Once the camshafts are removed the hydraulic cam-followers should be wiped clean, numbered with indelible ink and removed. **Caution!** It is essential, when the engine is reassembled, that each cam-follower is replaced in the bore from which it was taken. If there is any danger at all that the numbers will be erased during cleaning or

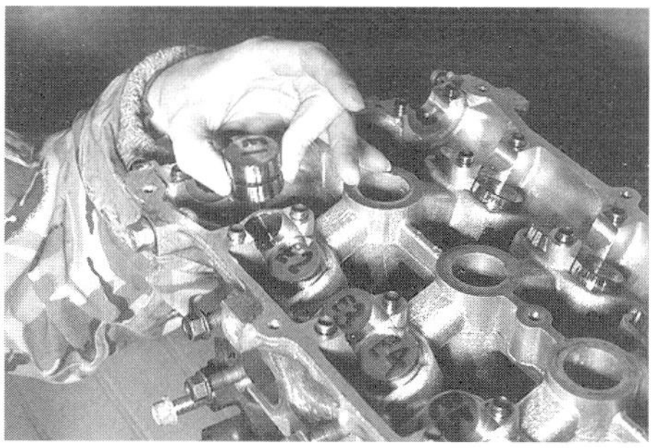

7/60a Lift out cam-followers ....

7/60b ... and number them individually.

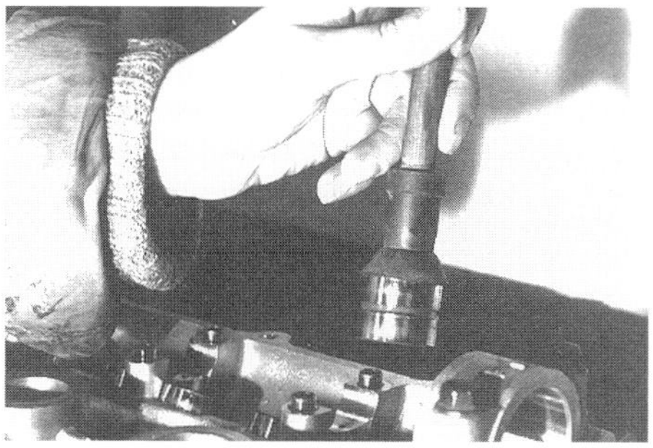

7/60c Sometimes a valve grinding tool helps.

storage, and a good idea anyway, is to place the cam-followers in an egg tray or similar with numbered compartments. If you find the followers difficult to remove with your fingers you can use a valve grinding suction tool to remove them.

CYLINDER HEAD REMOVAL.

61 + There are ten 12 mm bolts holding the cylinder head to the cylinder block. **Caution!** The bolts must be loosened in a sequence which spirals inward from the outer bolts of the head - this

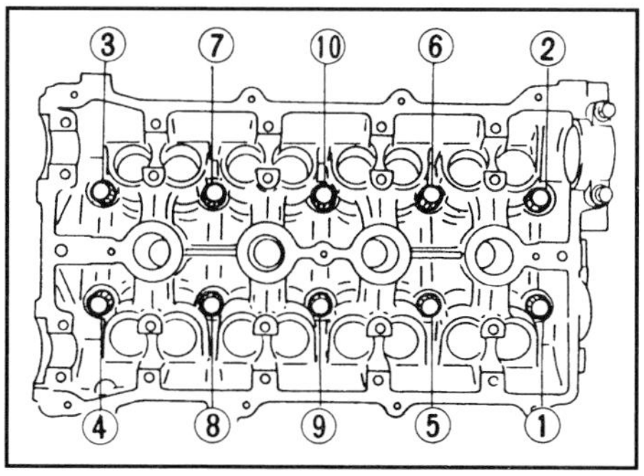

D7/61 CYLINDER HEAD BOLT LOOSENING SEQUENCE.

7/61a Slacken and remove bolts ...

7/61b ... then lift off cylinder head.

7/61c Cover oilway with adhesive tape.

minimizes distortion. Initially loosen each bolt half a turn, then a whole turn, followed by full removal. A 125 mm/5 inch extension will be needed with the socket as the bolts are quite deeply recessed in the cambox. Note: it doesn't matter that the bolts have splined heads - your ordinary socket will still work. Once the ten bolts holding the cylinder head have been loosened and removed, the cylinder head can be lifted. It may be necessary to use a leather or other soft-faced mallet just to tap the head gently upwards to loosen it. **Caution!** Do not be tempted to break the head from the block using a sharp instrument as a wedge or lever. Once the head is removed, protect the oilway in the cylinder block by covering it with tape.

VALVES REMOVAL

62 In order to remove a valve, its valve spring must be compressed sufficiently to free the two valve keepers (split collets) around the upper part of its stem. If you don't have one already, you'll be able to buy, borrow or hire a universal valve spring compressing tool. Unfortunately, like us, you're likely to find that the tool won't operate properly on the head because the valve springs and stems are so deeply recessed in the cambox.

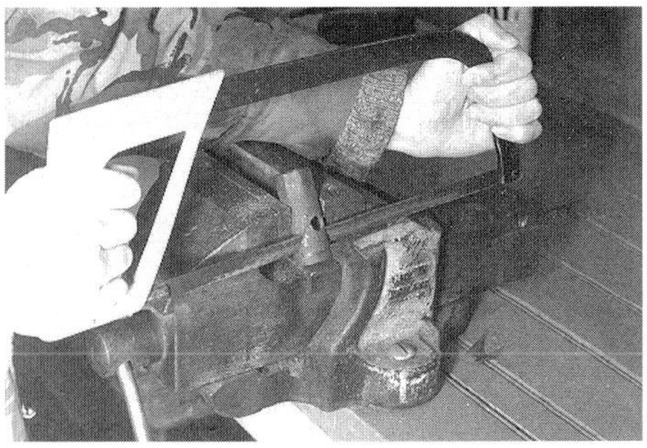

7/63a Making valve keeper removal tool.

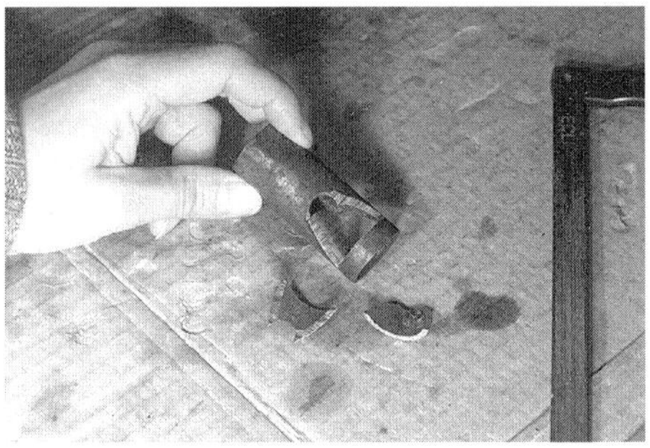

7/63b The finished tool.

63 To get around the problem of reach we made a spacer out of an old tube (box) spanner. To give better access to the valve keepers we cut triangular 'windows' in each side of the tube using a hacksaw; cleaning up rough edges with a file. The original tube spanner had an external diameter of 25 mm/1 inch and a length of 60 mm/2.4 in - in fact, another 12.5 mm/0.5 inch would have been better.

64 Mount the cylinder head horizontally in a vise (fitted with jaw protectors) so that you have access to all of the valves on one side of the head. **Caution!** Don't overtighten the vice, it should be just tight enough to grip the head.

7/65a Position keeper removal tool ...

7/65b ... and use valve spring compressor.

65 Place the spacer tube on the valve spring cap and then locate the spring compressor in position so that it is bearing centrally on both spacer rim and valve head. Tighten the compressor until you see that the spring cap has been pushed far enough down the valve stem to free the valve keepers. Remove the keepers with needle-nosed pliers, a screwdriver with a magnetic tip or a screwdriver with a small blob of sticky grease on the tip.

66 Carefully release the compressor until the spring has reached its full free length. **Warning!** Whilst releasing the compressor, make sure it stays squarely seated on both spacer and valve head; if it slips off after the keepers have been removed the spring and cap are free to fly off the valve stem with very considerable force. With the compressor removed, the spring cap, spring and spring seat can be withdrawn over the valve stem. Thread a length of gardening wire through these components to keep them together and correctly orientated. Withdraw the valve from the combustion chamber side of the head.

7/66 Remove valve.

67 **Caution!** It's essential that not only are each valve and spring set kept together - assuming the components will be reused - but also that you know exactly where each valve came from so that it can be installed in original position. It's suggested that the stem of each valve is pushed through a piece of cardboard and that the cardboard is marked "E1" (exhaust 1) - counting from the front of the head - until you have a row of valves in the card sheet, each with a position ID. Of course, the spring sets should be tagged and marked using the same ID system.

68 Lever the valve stem oil seal from the top of the valve guide using a screwdriver. You should have new seals with your new gasket set.

69 Use the same process to remove the other valves from the head.

7/68 Remove stem guide seals.

7/69 Valve and spring components.

VALVE GUIDES REMOVAL & FITTING

70 Don't remove the valve guides unless inspection shows that they need to be renewed: 3/8/14.

71 Mazda dealers have a special tool set numbered "SST - 49 L012 0A0" which is a kit of tools designed specifically for the safe and easy removal and installation of Miata/MX5 valve guides: borrow the set if you can. Otherwise you'll have to get your local small machine shop to machine a drift. It will need to be 150 mm/6 in long or longer and initially of 12.5 mm/0.5 inch diameter. The first 51 mm/2 in should be machined to a diameter of 5.985 mm/ 0.2356 inch, the next 51 mm/2 in should be machined to a diameter of 9 mm/0.3543 inch with only a small radius in the corner of the shoulder. Using the drift, inserted narrowest end first into the guide from the combustion chamber end, drive the guide out into the cambox. Repeat the process for the other guides.

72 The new guides can be driven in from the cambox side using the same tool but check the guide height frequently as dimension "A" (see picture) must be between 16.8 - 17.4 mm /0.661 - 0.685 in. Note that the replacement valve guides will all be of the exhaust type but they can also be used for intake valves.

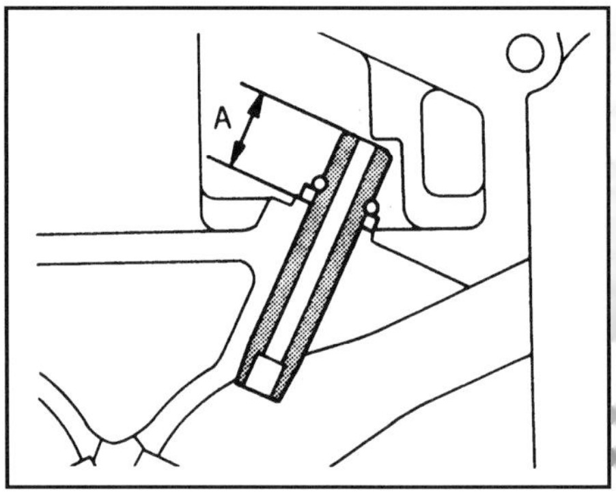

D7/72 VALVE GUIDE CORRECT POSITION.

OIL PAN REMOVAL

73 Turn the engine upside-down. There are nine 10 mm bolts on each side of the oil pan securing it to the bottom of the cylinder block; two of these are long bolts situated close to the flywheel. Access to the bolt on the oil pan flange closest to the starter motor mounting is difficult with

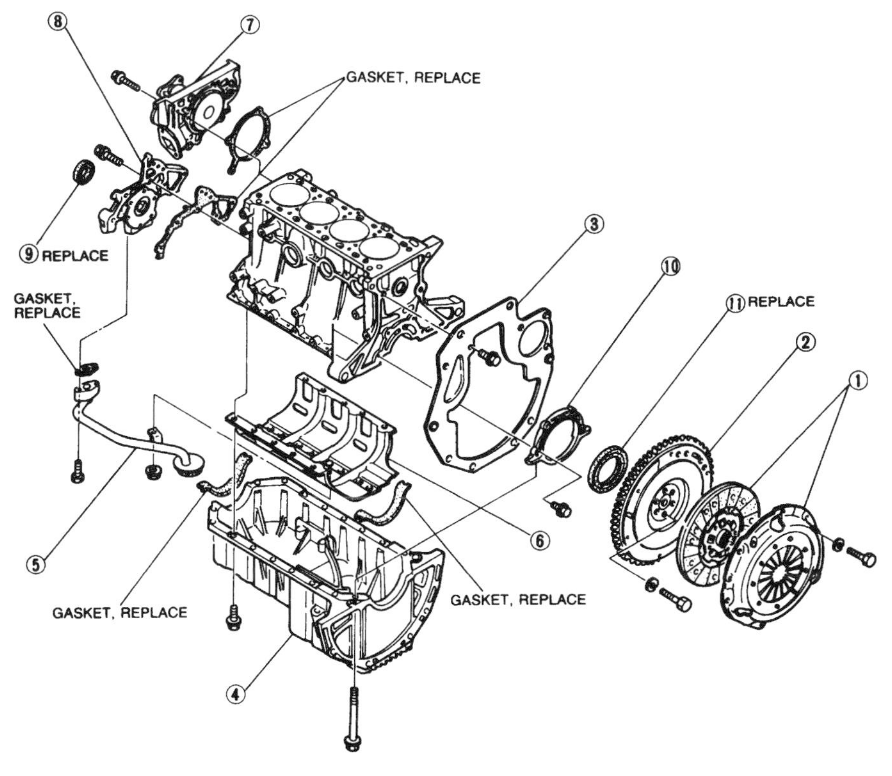

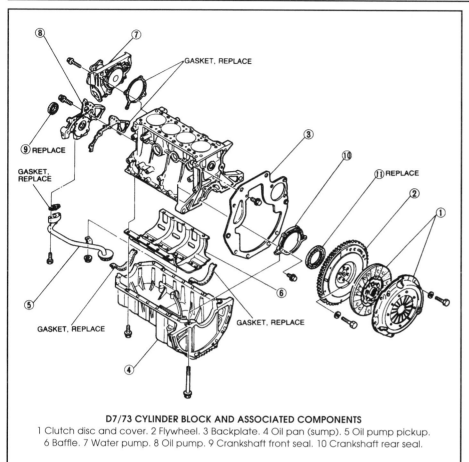

D7/73 CYLINDER BLOCK AND ASSOCIATED COMPONENTS
1 Clutch disc and cover. 2 Flywheel. 3 Backplate. 4 Oil pan (sump). 5 Oil pump pickup. 6 Baffle. 7 Water pump. 8 Oil pump. 9 Crankshaft front seal. 10 Crankshaft rear seal.

1/2 inch drive sockets. It can either be undone progressively with a box end wrench or you could choose to use a socket system with a smaller drive.

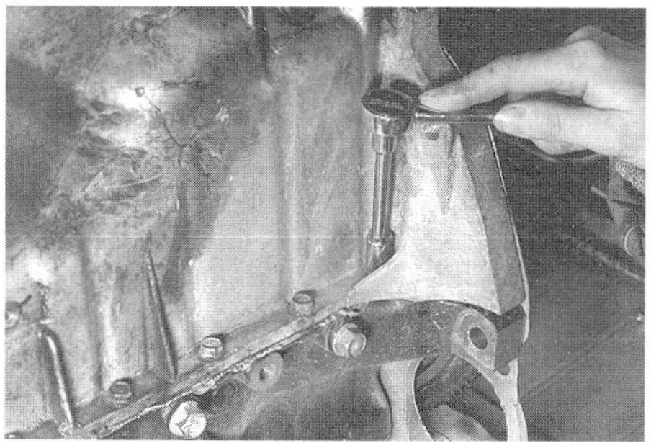

7/73a Oil pan bolts ...

7/73b ... include these long ones.

Once all of the bolts have been removed, you can begin to break the seal between the oil pan and cylinder block by using a screwdriver as a lever at

7/73c Safe levering point.

7/73d Break seal carefully ...

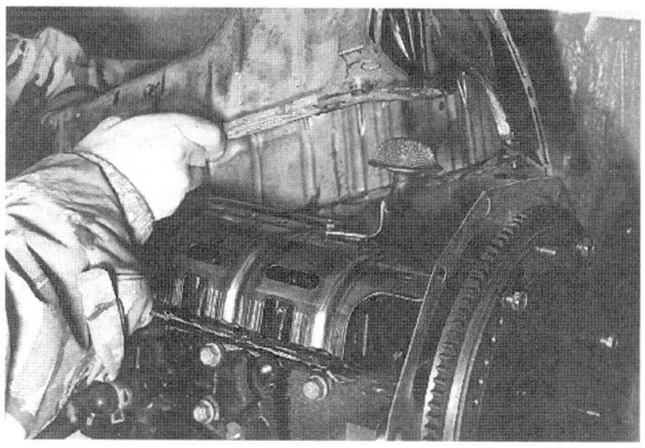

7.73e ... and lift oil pan away.

the point shown in the photograph: there is one of these points on each side of the engine. **Caution!** On no account should you try to insert a sharp implement elsewhere in an attempt to lever off the oil pan. You'll find that the oil pan is well 'glued' in place by the gasket cement used to seal it, but suddenly the seal will break and the pan can be removed. If you find that once the seal is broken the pan still will not lift clear, as with our engine, it's because the baffle flange is stuck to the oil pan flange rather than the cylinder block. If this is the case, gently work a chisel in between the face of the oil pan flange and the underside of the baffle flange. You can see from the photograph where the baffle will be in relation to the oil pan flange. Take great care not to bend the baffle's thin flange more than necessary as it will have to be straightened before the engine is rebuilt.

OIL PUMP, PICKUP PIPE & OIL PAN BAFFLE REMOVAL

74 The oil pump is retained by six 12 mm bolts in its face and four 10 mm bolts around the oil pan flange (which will have been removed). Unscrew and remove the four 10 mm bolts using a box end wrench as there is hardly enough room for a socket, unless you use a small drive system. Note: the topmost bolt is the shortest and the lowest two bolts are both extra long.

75 + Two 10 mm bolts hold the pickup union to the oil pump body and a 10 mm nut holds the pickup pipe bracket to the oil pan baffle. Undo and remove all three. Once the two securing bolts and nut have been removed the pickup assembly can be lifted away, followed by the baffle itself.

76 The oil pump body can now be pulled away from the front of the cylinder block and off over the nose of the crankshaft. If you have trouble breaking the gasket seal, use light blows from a

7/75a Release oil pump pickup here ...

7/75b ... and at baffle bracket, then ...

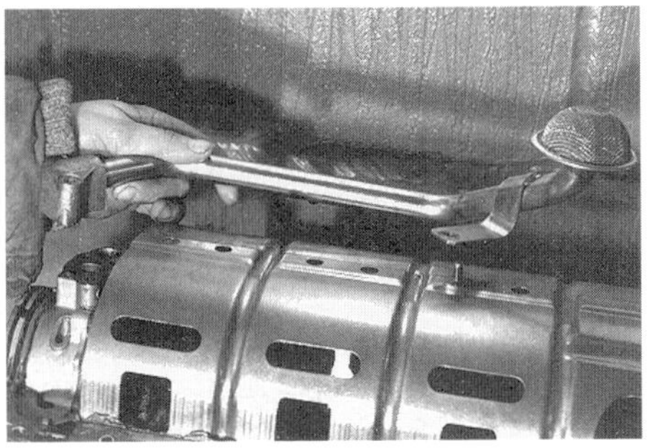

7/75c ... lift pickup away ...

7/75d ... followed by baffle.

7/76 Remove the oil pump.

soft-faced mallet to start the pump moving. **Caution!** Do not force a sharp tool into the joint as a wedge or lever.

OIL PUMP & OIL PRESSURE RELIEF VALVE TEARDOWN

77 Place the oil pump on the bench with the backplate upward. You'll see that the backplate is held to the oil pump body by six countersunk crosshead screws. You'll need an ordinary impact screwdriver to loosen them. Select the crosshead bit which fits the screws best, and don't use an

7/78 Oil pump rotors.

undersize bit.

78 Slacken and remove the screws in a diagonal sequence. Once the cover is off the pump, the rotors can be removed.

79 The oil pressure relief valve can be dismantled by pushing the spring cap down with a screwdriver whilst withdrawing the straightened split pin, then removing the spring retaining cap spring and domed top from the pressure relief valve bore.

FLYWHEEL (DRIVEPLATE - AUTO TRANS CARS) REMOVAL

80 Lock the crankshaft by wedging a hammer handle between a crank web and the side of the cylinder block. Undo and remove the six bolts holding the flywheel to the crankshaft flange. Note: the bolts should be loosened half a turn each initially and in a diagonal sequence. **Caution!** It's a good idea to make sure that the same relationship between crankshaft and flywheel position is kept on reassembly to maintain balance. Mark the top of the flywheel and mark the top of the crankshaft (once the flywheel has been removed) using indelible ink so that the flywheel can be installed in exactly the same position. Once the bolts have been removed the flywheel can be lifted away- it's heavy!

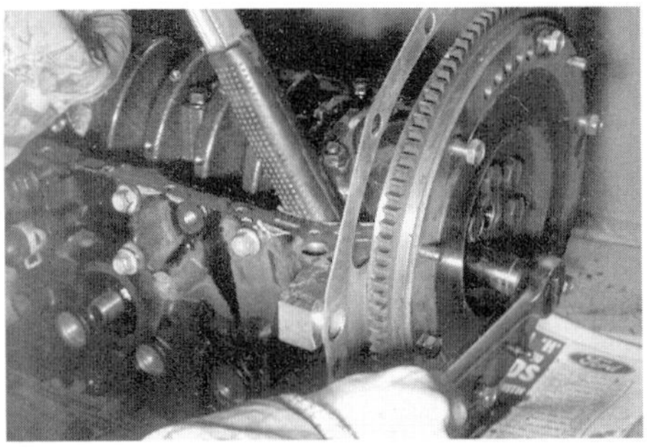

7/80a Lock crank & undo flywheel bolts, then ...

7/80b ... remove flywheel - it's heavy!

81 The procedure for automatic transmission cars, which will be fitted with a torque converter driveplate, is the same as the flywheel removal procedure, except that the driveplate will be lighter and there will be a backing plate between the bolt heads and the face of the driveplate and an adaptor between the crank and driveplate.

D7/81 DRIVEPLATE REMOVAL (AUTOMATIC TRANSMISSION MODELS)

ENGINE BACKPLATE REMOVAL

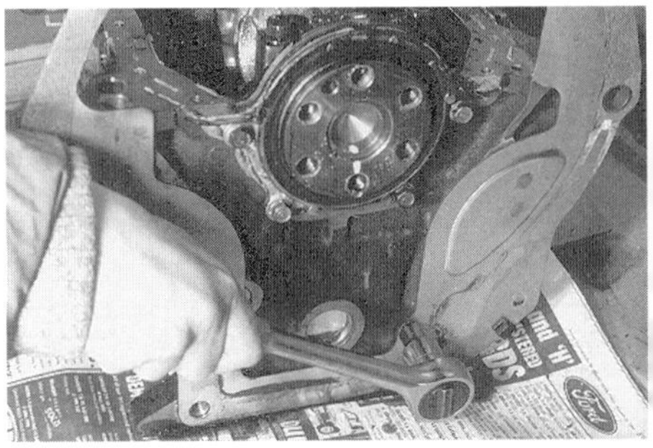

7/82a Remove single bolt ...

7/82b ... and lift backplate away.

82 With the flywheel out of the way the single 10 mm bolt now holding the backplate to the cylinder block can be unscrewed and the backplate removed.

CRANKSHAFT REAR OIL SEAL HOUSING REMOVAL

83 The housing is fixed to the cylinder block by four 10 mm headed bolts. Unscrew and remove the four bolts. Note that the two lower bolts closest to the oil pan flange are slightly longer and are, in fact, set screws. Once the four bolts have

7/83a Unscrew bolts ...

been removed the housing can be pulled away from the cylinder block. If necessary, gentle leverage can be applied by inserting a screwdriver between the rearmost main bearing cap and the back of the seal housing.

CONNECTING ROD (BIG END) CAPS, CONNECTING RODS & PISTONS REMOVAL

84 The connecting rod caps are marked across their joint with the con-rod by Mazda - our engine had a V-shaped device stamped in it. This is fine to tell you which cap goes with which rod, but won't tell you which rod and cap come from which bore! We recommend that you use a center punch to mark each connecting rod and cap with an appropriate number of dots to ensure that they remain a pair and are installed on the correct crank web. Note that the cap and con-rod ID marks should be stamped on the right-hand side of the units. Note: before removing the connecting rod caps, it would be a good idea to check con-rod bearing side clearance. ☞ 3/8/50.

85 + Each connecting rod cap is retained by two 14 mm nuts which should be slackened alternately and progressively. Once the nuts have been removed each cap can be lifted off of the con-

7/83b ... and lift seal housing away.

7/84 Mark conrods and caps.

7/85a Unscrew cap nuts ...

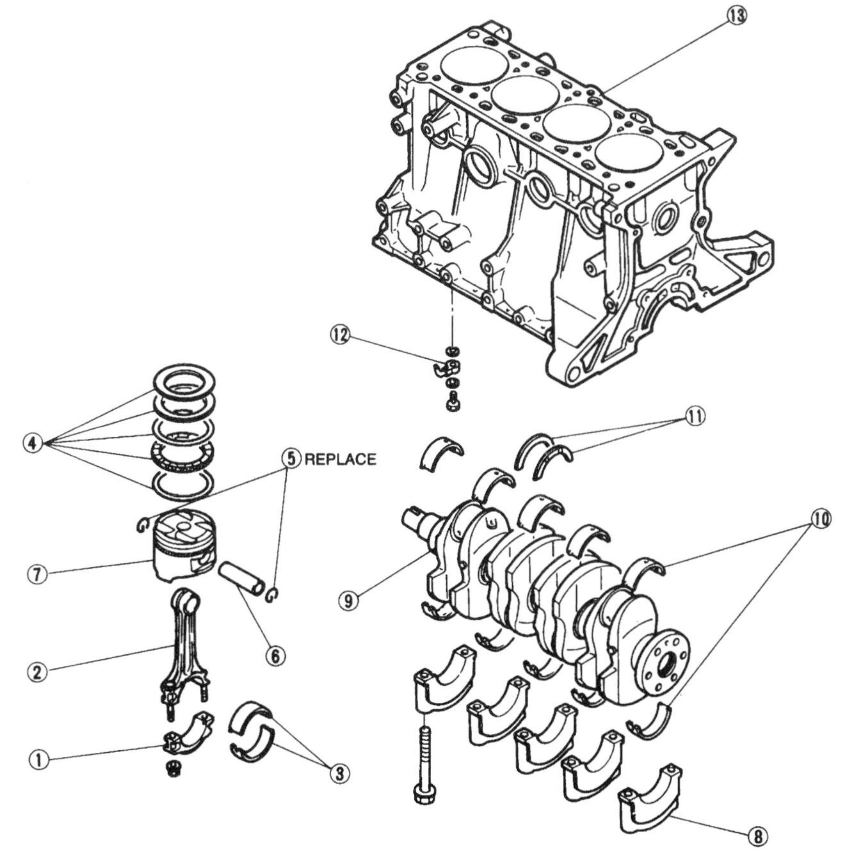

D7/84 CYLINDER BLOCK INTERNAL PARTS

1 Connecting rod (big end) cap. 2 Connecting rod. 3 Connecting rod (big end) bearing shells. 4 Piston rings. 5 Piston pin clips. 6 Piston (Wrist/Gudgeon) pin. 7 Piston. 8 Main bearing caps. 9 Crankshaft. 10 Crankshaft (Main) bearings. 11 Thrust washers. 12 Oil jet, sealing washers & banjo bolt. 13 Cylinder block.

7/85b ... and lift caps away.

rod studs: if its bearing shell sticks to the crankshaft gently lift the shell off and keep it with the correct cap. Note: it's easier to rotate the crankshaft if the flywheel bolts are lightly screwed back into the crankshaft rear flange and then a screwdriver can be inserted between the bolts to lever the crank around. **Caution!** Make sure the con-rod studs don't scrape or gouge the crank journals as the crank is rotated.

86 Note: if there's a ring of carbon around the top of the bore, above the piston's travel, scrape it away with a sharp-edged tool - this will make piston removal easier. Each piston and con-

7/86 Withdraw piston and conrod from bore.

rod assembly can now be pushed out through the top of the cylinder block using a wooden hammer handle. **Caution!** Be careful that the piston doesn't come out of the bore suddenly and drop to the floor.

87 Remove the shell bearings from con-rods and caps and, if they are to be re-used, wipe clean and number their backs with indelible ink so that they can be installed in original positions. **Caution!** It's essential that shells are not mixed up if they are to be re-used, but if the shells have done more than 48,000 km /30,000 miles they should be replaced even if they look fine. Temporarily install bearing caps to con-rods and retain with finger-tightened screws.

MAIN BEARING CAPS & CRANKSHAFT REMOVAL

88 There are five main bearing caps, none of which are marked to indicate position; however, each bearing cap does have an arrow cast into its bottom, pointing towards the front of the engine. It's a good idea to punch an appropriate number of dots into the right-hand side of each main bearing cap so that they can be installed in exactly the positions they were taken from. Note: before removing the caps, it would be a good idea to check crankshaft lash (endfloat): ☞ 3/8/56.

7/88 Bearing cap markings.

89 + Each main bearing cap is held by two 14 mm headed bolts. The ten main bearing cap bolts must be undone in a sequence that spirals inward starting front left, front right, rear right, rear left, cap 2 left, etc. Undo each bolt half a turn initially, followed by a full turn on the next sequence, after which they can be loosened completely. It's suggested you leave the loose bolts in place as they can be used to lever the caps backwards and forwards to loosen them: then each cap and its pair of bolts can be lifted off together. If a bearing shell sticks to the crankshaft journal, remove it and keep it with its original main bearing cap. **Caution!** It's essential that shells are not mixed up if they are to be re-used but, if the shells have done more than 50,000 km /30,000 miles, it's our advice that they should be replaced even if they look fine.

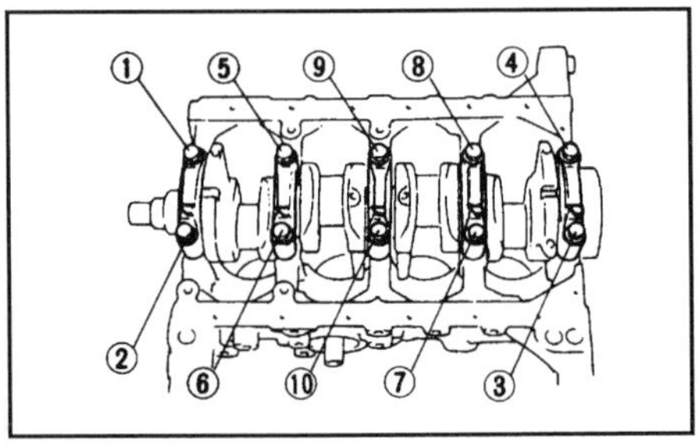
D7/89 MAIN BEARING CAP LOOSENING SEQUENCE.

7/89a Unscrew bolts ...

7/89b ... and lift caps away.

90 When the five main bearing caps have been removed the crankshaft can be lifted clear of the cylinder block. Once again, if bearing shells adhere to the crank journals, lift them off carefully noting which journal they belong to. Two semicircular thrust washers should be stuck, one each side, of main bearing number 4: these can be lifted from their recesses and kept with the bearing shells.

7/90 Lift crankshaft from cylinder block.

91 The bearing shells can be removed one at a time, wiped clean and then their position number marked on their backs with an indelible pen. **Caution!** Do not attempt to stamp numbers or punch dots into bearing shells.

PISTON OIL JETS REMOVAL

92 The piston oil jet at the base of each cylinder bore can be removed with a 14 mm socket and 125 mm/5 inch extension. Lift away the jet complete with banjo bolt and two copper washers.

PISTONS REMOVAL FROM CONNECTING RODS

93 The skirt of each piston is asymmetrical, having a section cutaway on one side to clear the oil jet in the base of each cylinder bore. To make sure that the piston will be installed, or a new piston fitted, with the same orientation, mark the side of each con-rod which is adjacent to the piston skirt cutaway. If the old pistons are to be reused, mark the skirt of each in indelible ink to indicate which cylinder the piston came from.

7/93 Mark conrods.

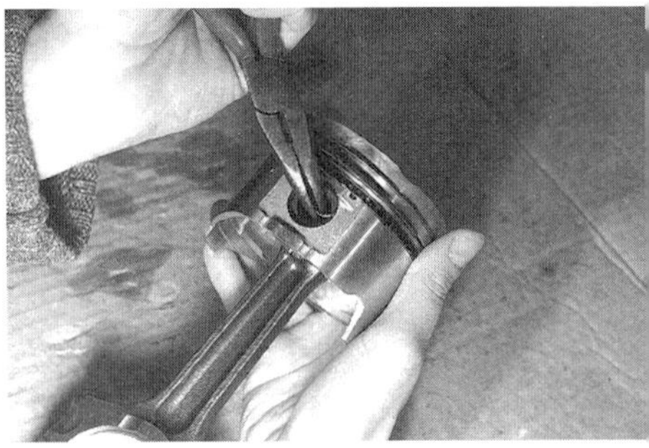
7/94 Remove piston pin clips.

94 Using a pair of needle-nosed pliers grasp the wire spring clips which will be found on each side of the piston retaining the piston pin (wrist/gudgeon pin). Discard the clips as new ones should be used on rebuild.

95 + The piston pin is an interference fit in the piston and, therefore, warming the piston to expand the aluminum will make it easier to push the slower expanding steel piston pin out. Mount the connecting rod in a vise with jaw protectors. Using a normal domestic butane torch, heat the

7/95a Heat piston ...

7/95b ... then drift out piston pin.

piston evenly and quickly: it doesn't need to be seriously hot and you should avoid heating the piston pin itself. As soon as the piston is hot enough to make a drop of water sizzle, use a metal drift - it can be a solid rod or, say, a tube (box) spanner - of 15-16 mm /0.6 inches outside diameter and at least 100 mm/4 inches in length, to push the pin through the piston and connecting rod until it emerges from the other side of the piston. You'll need a rag to catch it as it may well be fairly hot by now. You'll find that using this method will allow you to push out the piston pin without using any more than hand pressure. The piston can now be removed from the connecting rod.

PISTON RINGS REMOVAL

96 **Caution!** It's important that the rings are removed carefully; if they are twisted too much or opened too far they will snap. Remove the topmost ring first and work your way down. If the rings are likely to be re-used, place each set in a bag marked with the number of the piston from which they were removed.

97 You can buy a piston ring removal tool from your local tool shop and it will make life easier,

7/97 Use old hacksaw blades or metal strips.

or you can use the following method as we did. Use three old feeler gauge blades or three pieces of hacksaw blade as groove bridges to remove the rings without twisting them. The trick is to pull the ring out far enough with your fingers to insert two strips between the piston ring and the piston on the opposite side to the piston ring gap. Then, hold one of the strips in that position and slide the other around until it is supporting one end of the ring. Slide a third strip between the ring and piston on the opposite side of the piston to the ring gap and then slide that strip around until it supports the other end of the ring. With the ring held clear of its ring groove by the three strips, it can be slid evenly upwards to remove it from the piston. You don't need to use this procedure for the three-piece oil scraper ring as the thin rings above and below the corrugated spacer are so thin that they can be opened with your fingers and carefully slid off of the piston. Again, be careful not to twist the rings as they could snap. The corrugated spacer is easily removed by fingers.

ENGINE TEARDOWN CONCLUSION

98 Phew, that's it - the engine is now completely disassembled! Individual components need to be thoroughly cleaned and then inspected as described in the following sections of this chapter. If the engine is to be left in a dismantled state for longer than a few days double check that you've ID'd components which have to go back in original positions and spray all components with silicone-based lubricant to keep corrosion at bay.

8 ENGINE COMPONENTS - CHECKING AND REPAIR

First read 1/1, 2.

CHECKING & REPAIR GENERAL

1 **Caution!** It's important that all of the items mentioned in this section are checked thoroughly for excessive wear or damage. One small faulty component is all it takes to destroy the value of an otherwise good engine rebuild. Don't believe it? Wally once rebuilt an engine with a re-ground crankshaft and forgot to check that the crank's oilways were clear. They weren't, they contained swarf from the machining: the engine ran for just 320 km /200 miles before the bearings started to knock and the whole job had to be done again ...

2 All components should be thoroughly clean before inspection occurs.

3 Micrometers. Some components simply have to be measured with a micrometer to establish whether or not they are serviceable. A set of micrometers is not hugely expensive and will prove a worthwhile investment if you intend to do a lot of mechanical work. If you can't use a micrometer, you're bound to know an engineer or mechanic who can and who you can invite to help you: it won't take long if you have all the components cleaned and together.

8/4 Clean combustion chambers.

CYLINDER HEAD & VALVES REMOVING CARBON

4 Place the cylinder head cambox side down on your workbench. Cover the oilway with tape as shown. Using a small diameter - around 25 mm/1 inch - wire brush mounted in an electric drill, brush away all traces of carbon buildup. **Caution!** This process should not remove any metal from the combustion chambers; take care not to scratch the gasket surface of the head or the valve seats if the valves are not in place.

5 Mount each valve, by its stem, in a vise fitted with jaw protectors. The same combination of wire brush and electric drill can be used to remove all traces of carbon from the valve head and lower part of stem. **Caution!** Take care not to scratch the valve seat with the wire brush.

CYLINDER HEAD CHECKING & REPAIR

6 Visually check the combustion chambers for cracking between valve openings and the percussive damage which can result from bits of broken ring, valve or piston entering the combustion chamber. Also check the machined face between each combustion chamber for erosion or burning. If your car's head is suffering from any of these problems, you'll need to consult a machine shop which will advise on the possibility of repair. Maximum head machining tolerance is given in the next step.

7 Using a straightedge longer than the cylinder head and a set of feeler gauges check the machined gasket face of the head for distortion. Check in straight and diagonal planes and also crosswise at each end. If you find a gap of more than 0.15 mm/0.006 inch the head will have to be machined flat by your local machine shop. No more than 0.20 mm/0.008 inch should be removed and the minimum total head height is 133.8 mm/5.268 in. If the head can't be brought back within tolerance before you run out of metal, you'll have to buy a new one.

8 Use the same measuring method to check

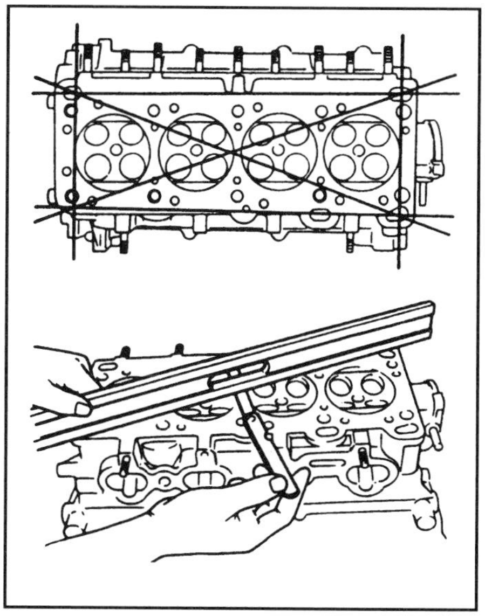

D8/7 MEASURING CYLINDER HEAD DISTORTION.

for longitudinal distortion in the head flanges for intake and exhaust manifolds. Again 0.15 mm/ 0.006 inch is the maximum. These faces can be re-ground until the definition of the gasket seating area begins to be lost.

9 Before having a distorted head machined, check that other wear areas like camshaft bearings and valve seats are within tolerance, otherwise you may have the work done for nothing ...

VALVES, GUIDES & VALVE SEATS CHECKING, REPAIR & VALVE LAPPING

10 Inspect each valve for obvious signs of damage such as a chipped or cracked face or bent stem. Also check the stem tip, where the follower bears, for chipping or uneven wear. Any of these faults will mean a new valve is needed.

11 Check the section of the valve stem which slides back and forth in the guide: you should not be able to see or feel, with a fingernail, a lip at either end of the wearing section. If you have access to a micrometer, check the thicker portion of the valve stem at top, bottom and center to ensure that it's in tolerance at between 5.970 - 5.985 mm/0.2350 - 0.2356 inch for intake valves and 5.965 - 5.980

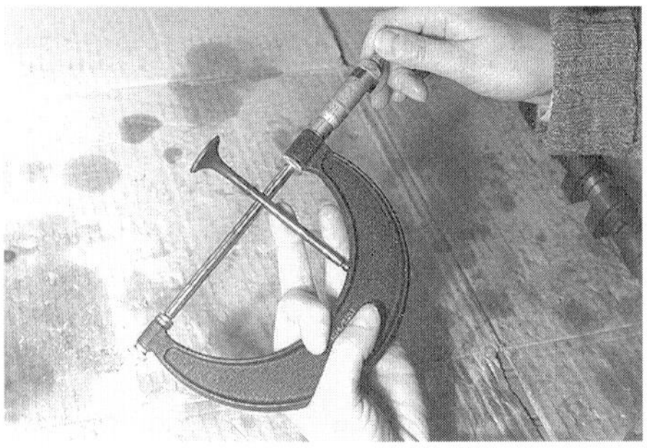

8/11 Checking valve stem.

mm/0.2348 - 0.2354 inch for exhaust valves. If a valve's out of tolerance or shows visible wear replace it.

12 Check that the overall length of the valve is not less than 104.79 mm/4.1256 in for intake valves and 104.89 mm/4.1295 in for exhaust valves. Too short? Throw it away!

13 Check the margin of the valve head; it's the bit between the face and the beginning of the seat on the back of the head. The margin must not be less than 1 mm/0.039 inch for both intake and exhaust valves. Less margin than this means that the valve has been ground too much or has simply worn and must be renewed.

14 If you have access to an internal micrometer small enough to measure at top, bottom and center of the internal bore of the valve guides they should be within the following tolerances: 6.01 - 6.03 mm/0.2366 - 0.2374 inch for both intake and exhaust guides. If you don't have a micrometer, insert the valve (having checked it's in tolerance) into the guide until the valve head is around 6 mm/ 0.25 inch from its seat. With your fingers rock the valve head back and forth: anything more than barely perceptible play means that the guide should be renewed.

15 + Place two small blobs of fine valve grinding paste on opposite sides of the valve face. Lightly lubricate the valve stem and lower the valve onto its seat (the head should be combustion chamber side up on your bench). Press the rubber suction cup of a valve grinding tool lightly against the valve head and then, by moving the palms of your hands to-and-fro either side of the tool's handle, impart a reciprocating motion to the valve head. After every 5 or 6 back-and-forth movements lift the valve head and turn it through 90 degrees, and repeat this process until the valve

8/15a Apply grinding paste and then grind ...

8/15b ... valve seat using to-and fro action.

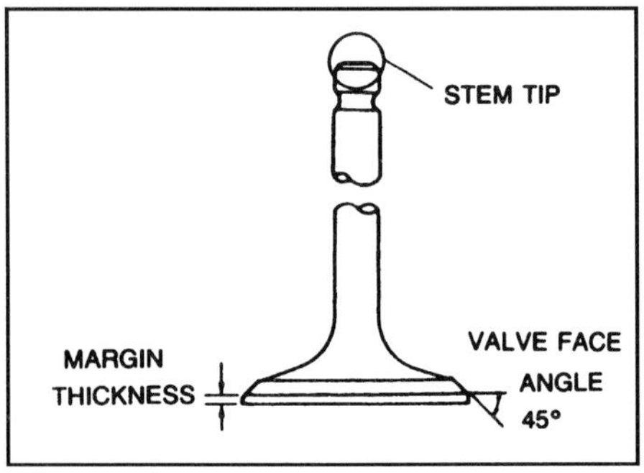

D8/13 CHECKING VALVE HEAD.

head has been turned a full 360 degrees. Lift the valve out and wipe the grinding paste from valve head and seat.

16 Inspect the seat on the back of the valve first, it should be unbroken and free of pitting, should be in the center of the angled face on the back of the valve head and should not be wider than 0.8 - 1.4 mm/0.031 - 0.055 inch. If the seat is not continuous repeat the grinding process, only this time use coarse grinding paste first followed by fine. If you still cannot achieve a continuous seat it indicates some distortion in the valve head or valve

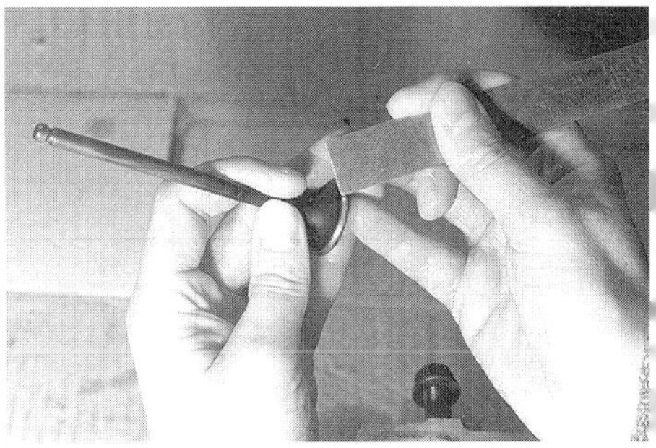

8/16 An unbroken bright ring.

8/17 Another unbroken bright ring.

seat. Too wide a seat on the valve head or a seat that's off-center indicates the need to recut the corresponding seat in the combustion chamber.

17 Now inspect the seat in the valve port in the combustion chamber. It, too, should be unbroken and free of pitting, in the center of the seat area and about the same width as the seat on the valve. If the seat is not continuous, try re-grinding with coarse and fine paste as described in the previous step.

18 If you still haven't achieved a continuous seat it's most likely that the valve seat in the combustion chamber needs to be recut. In cross-section the standard seat is actually comprised of three differently angled faces made with different cutting tools in order to achieve a centrally positioned 45 degree valve seat that's not too wide. We strongly recommend taking the head to a machine shop for seat recutting as it's really easy to make a mistake and end up trashing the head. If, after the port seats have been recut you still can't get a continuous seat on a valve, throw the valve away and start again with a new one. **Caution!** All new valves have to be lapped in with grinding paste as previously described.

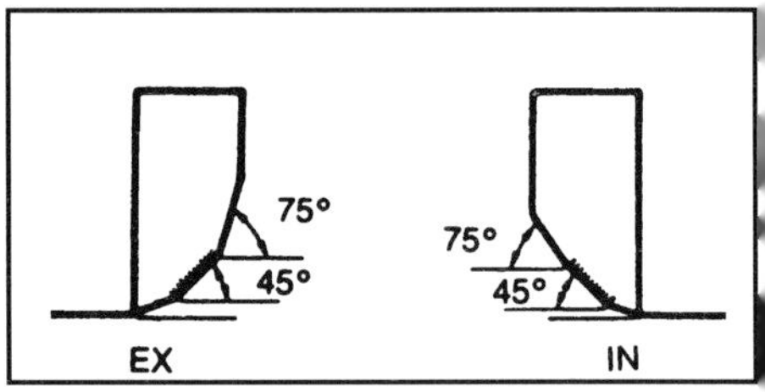

D8/18 VALVE SEAT DETAIL.

19 After valve lapping, or seat recutting, check that the valve seats are not now recessed too far into the head. Hold the valve against its seat and

8/19 Measuring valve stem protrusion.

then, using the tail of a vernier gauge, measure the protrusion of the valve stem from the head as shown. 43.4 - 44.0 mm/1.713 - 1.732 inch is OK, between 44.1 - 45.0 mm/1.736 - 1.772 inch needs a shim washer on the valve seat area of the head of between 0.7 - 1.0 mm/0.023 - 0.040 inch to bring it back in tolerance: more than 45.1 mm/1.776 inch means buying a new cylinder head ...

20 **Caution!** Ensure all traces of grinding paste are removed from valves, valve stems and valve seats once valve seating has been satisfactorily completed.

VALVE SPRINGS CHECKING & REPAIR

21 Visually inspect the springs, spring seats, spring caps and valve keepers for obvious damage or wear. These are high stress components so, if in any doubt about serviceability, renew.

22 Using a vernier gauge, measure the free length of each spring. Less than 47.0 mm/ 1.850 in for an intake and 47.3 mm/1.862 in for an exhaust valve means that a new spring is needed. Buy a complete set, even if some of the old springs are in tolerance.

23 Place a set square on a flat surface and then stand each spring alongside the vertical section of the square. Turn the spring until it shows the greatest deviation from vertical whilst the base of the spring is still touching the set square. Maximum deviation at the top of the spring must not exceed 1.68 mm/0.0661 inch for intake, and 1.69 mm/ 0.0665 inch for exhaust valve springs.

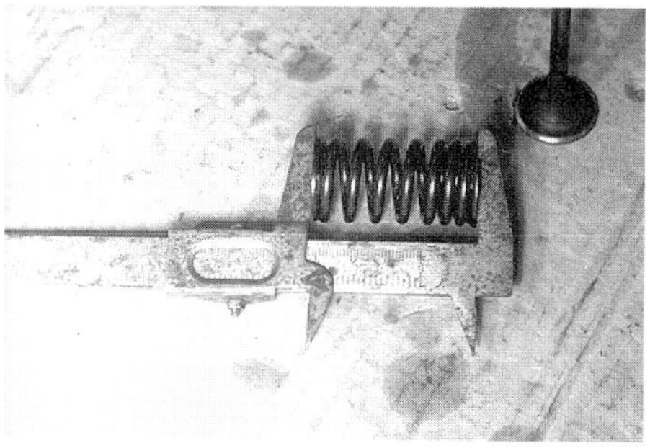

8/22 Checking valve spring length.

8/23 Checking valve spring distortion.

CAMSHAFTS & CAMSHAFT BEARINGS CHECKING & REPAIR

24 If you have access to V-blocks, use them to support the front and rear bearing journals of a camshaft. Set up a dial gauge to read from the center bearing journal and then rotate the camshaft in the blocks to measure runout. If runout exceeds 0.03 mm/0.0012 inch discard the cam. Repeat the process with the second cam. If you haven't got this measuring equipment, don't worry too much as it's unlikely that a cam will bend in service.

25 Visually inspect the cam bearing journals and lobes for wear. The lobe faces should be blackish in color which shows that the surface hardening is still intact. Bright shiny areas, wear that can clearly be seen or felt with a fingernail indicate that the cam should be renewed. Bearing surfaces should be shiny, smooth and free of scratches or gouges. If you want to double check and have the equipment, use a micrometer to read the maximum height of each cam lobe from base circle to lobe tip taking a reading from each side. Bearing journals, too, can be measured with a micrometer taking readings from each side and at two positions around the circumference of each journal. Minimum lobe heights are 40.688 mm/ 1.6019 in for both intake and exhaust cams. Minimum bearing journal diameter is 25.940 mm/ 1.0213 in and out of round maximum is 0.05 mm/ 0.002 inch.

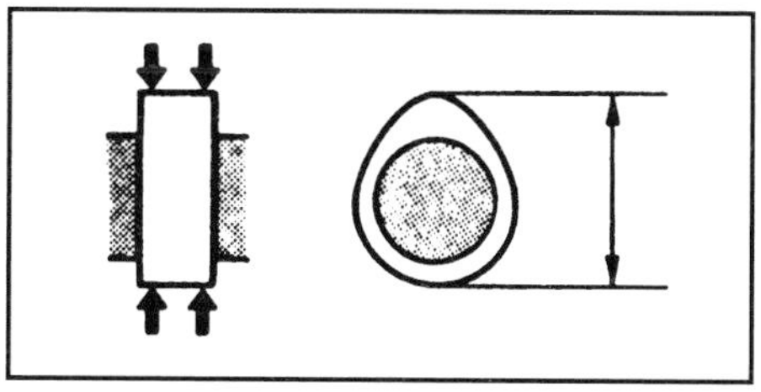

D8/25 CHECKING CAM LOBES.

8/25 Checking cam bearing journals.

26 Lubricate the cam bearing journals in the head and rest the two cams in place - they're marked "I" and "E" so you'll know which is which - without fitting the cam-followers. Lubricate the bearing caps and temporarily replace them in their correct positions - each cap is marked with a number and an arrow (see rebuild instructions for more detail). Tighten the retaining bolts in three stages to a torque of 11.3 - 14.2 Nm /1.15 - 1.45 kgf m /100 - 126 lbf in using a sequence which spirals outward from the center of each cam.

27 Measure the lash (endplay) of each cam. You can do this with feeler gauges between the thrust face at the back of each front bearing and the cam, or by mounting a dial gauge at the front of the cambox. Either way, lash (endfloat) should not exceed 0.20 mm/0.008 inch and if it does replace the camshaft. If this doesn't fix the problem you'll need to buy a new head too.

8/27 Checking cam endfloat.

28 You'll need some "Plastigage" to measure the camshaft bearing wear; you can get it and the measuring strip from your Mazda parts shop or a good tool shop. Remove the two intermediate bearing caps from each camshaft. Wipe the journal and bearing cap dry, then lay a strip of Plastigage parallel with the cam across the journal: take care

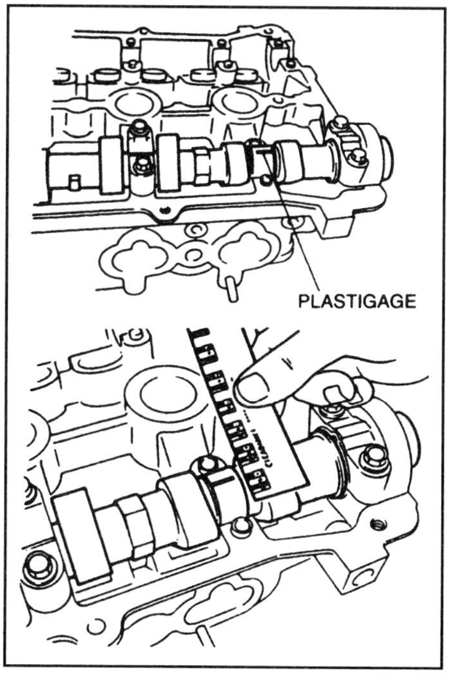

D8/28 USING PLASTIGAGE TO MEASURE CAM BEARING WEAR.

not to squeeze or damage the Plastigage strip. Repeat the process on the other three journals. Install the bearing caps and tighten each to the correct torque. Remove the four intermediate bearing caps again to reveal four strips of squashed Plastigage. Match the width of each strip to a bar on the measuring tool which will give a corresponding clearance measurement. Maximum bearing clearance is 0.15 mm/0.006 inch; more than that and a new head is needed. Remove the remaining bearing caps using a sequence which spirals in from the ends of each cam. Clean off any residue of Plastigage.

29 **Caution!** If you have to fit new camshafts, fit new cam-followers too - otherwise rapid wear will result.

CAM-FOLLOWERS CHECKING & REPAIR

30 Inspect the surface upon which the cam lobe bears: it should be shiny but not scratched or gouged. Clearly visible wear means replacement and you should think of renewing the cams at the same time. It's not really possible to check if the hydraulics of the follower are working properly. Therefore if followers have done 62,000 km / 40,000 miles it's probably wise to replace them whilst you have the opportunity.

CYLINDER BLOCK CHECKING & REPAIR: CORE PLUG RENEWAL

31 Make a visual inspection of the block, looking for obvious damage. If you find any cracks, you should discuss them with a machine shop in case the block is salvageable. Deep scratches in the bore or a pronounced wear ridge at the top of the bore will necessitate a re-bore and new pistons.

32 If any of the core (Welch) plugs appear to have been leaking they should be renewed. Drive a small chisel through the old plug and lever it out. Clean up the plug housing thoroughly. Coat the rim of a new plug with gasket cement and place the plug, dished-side out, over its housing. Cover the plug with a block of hardwood and then use a hammer to drive the plug fully and evenly into its housing.

33 Check the cylinder block deck lengthways, crosswise and diagonally using a straightedge and feeler gauges. A gap under the straightedge exceeding 0.15 mm/0.006 inch means the deck will need to be re-ground by your local machine shop. The maximum amount of metal which can be removed to rectify distortion is 0.20 mm/0.008 inch. Minimum total block height is 221.5 mm/8.720 inch.

34 Take a commonsense attitude to bore wear. If the engine's done 80,000 km /50,000 miles or more and prior to dismantling was burning oil and showing poor compression, the chances are that the bores and piston rings will be well worn. Have your local machine shop re-bore the cylinders to the next nearest oversize and supply new pistons and rings to suit. Recommended re-bore oversizes go up in increments of 0.25 mm/0.010 inch. If the engine's already been re-bored, you'll usually be able to find the oversize stamped in the piston crowns. Failing this, measure the bottom of

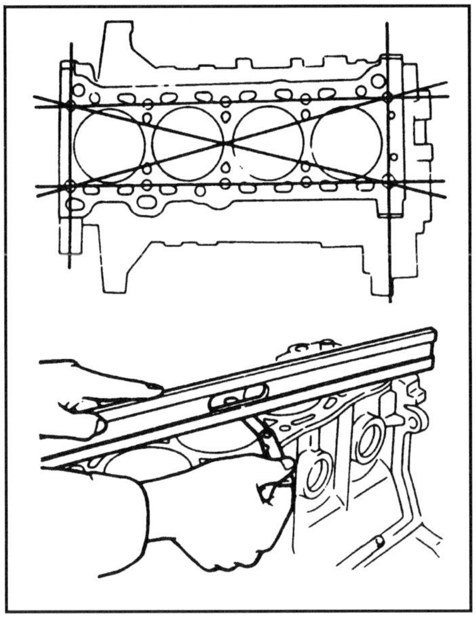

D8/33 MEASURING CYLINDER BLOCK HEAD FACE DISTORTION.

a cylinder bore with an internal micrometer: the standard original bore size is in the range 78.006 - 78.013 mm/3.0711 - 3.0714 in.

35 If you're not sure whether the bores are serviceable, then bore wear needs to be measured carefully. If you have access to an internal micrometer this is the best and most accurate tool. Measure the diameter of each bore around 25 mm/ 1 inch below the deck and again at the very base of the cylinder where no wear will have occurred. At each of these depths take a reading across the bore in line with the crankshaft centerline and another at 90 degrees to the first to establish ovality. The maximum difference between the worn and unworn sections of the bore is 0.019 mm/0.0007 inch. These figures are also the maximum for ovality.

PISTONS: REMOVING CARBON

36 If the piston is still on its con-rod you can clamp the rod in a vise fitted with jaw protectors so that the piston skirt rests on top of the jaws. If you have to fit the piston itself between the vise jaws wrap it first with cardboard or thick rag and only apply the very minimum pressure needed to provide grip.

37 If the rings are still fitted, wrap adhesive tape around them to minimize contamination with carbon dust. **Caution!** After the removal of carbon is completed the rings and grooves should be brushed liberally with kerosene/paraffin to ensure that all carbon dust is removed.

38 Mount a small diameter - 25 mm/1 inch approx - wire brush in an electric drill. Use the brush to clean all traces of carbon from the piston crown, valve cutouts and the area of the piston above the top ring groove. **Caution!** The pistons are made of a pretty hard aluminum alloy, but the cleaning process must not be allowed to remove any metal.

39 Carbon can be scraped carefully from

8/38 Clean piston crown and, very carefully, ...

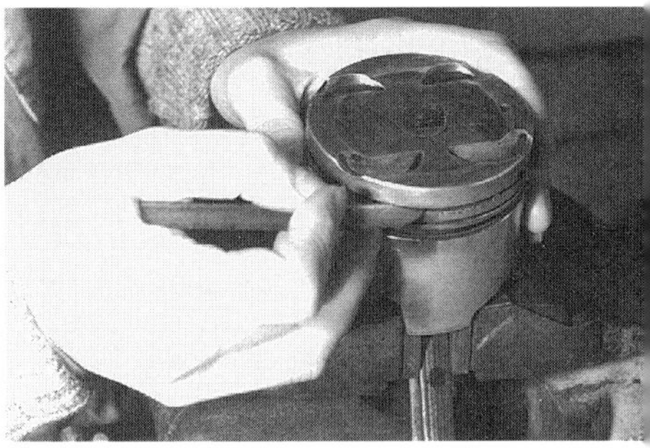

8/39 ... piston ring grooves.

the ring grooves with a fine-bladed screwdriver, or with a piece of broken piston ring. **Caution!** Take great care not to gouge or enlarge the grooves.

40 The rings, once removed from the pistons, can be cleaned with fine wire wool.

PISTONS, PISTON RINGS & PISTON PINS CHECKING & REPAIR

41 The first thing to say is that if you're having the cylinder block re-bored you'll have to fit new pistons and rings of appropriate oversize, so there's no point in checking the old ones.

8/42 Check piston for damage and wear.

42 Inspect each piston visually. Percussion damage to the crown, cracks or any pieces broken off - no matter how small - will mean discarding the component. Likewise deep scratches in, or bad burning of, the piston sides.

43 Having checked first that bore wear is within tolerance, slide each piston (without rings) into its bore until the crown is 50 mm/2 in below the deck. The piston should be normally orientated, *i.e.*, skirt cutout over oil jet. Using feeler gauges at various points around the circumference of the piston, establish the biggest clearance between

8/43 Check piston to bore clearance.

piston and bore. More than 0.15 mm/0.006 inch means the piston must be replaced and, even if the bore is within tolerance, a re-bore will be a good idea because it will bring piston and bore tolerances back to as new standards

44 **Caution!** Pistons should only be replaced as complete sets. Note: the new pistons will come complete with rings and piston pins.

45 Check a random selection of the piston rings - at least eight - by pushing them, one at a time, into a cylinder bore. Position each ring about 50 mm/2 in from the deck - you'll find that using an

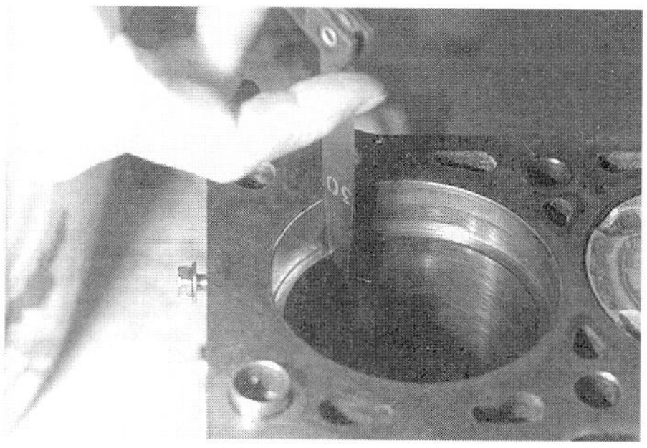

8/45 Checking piston ring gaps.

8/46 Check piston pin and conrod.

inverted piston to push the ring down the bore will help to keep it square with the deck. Measure the ring gap with feeler gauges: more than 1.0 mm/0.039 inch shows that a ring is worn out and that it, and all the other rings, must be renewed.

46 The piston pin should be a tight fit in the piston when both are cold. If the pin moves freely it, and its piston, should be renewed.

47 Slide the piston pin into the con-rod bushing until it's central. There should be no perceptible up and down movement of the pin. If you have access to micrometers measure the diameter of the center of the piston pin at two points 90 degrees apart: the tolerance is 19.987 - 19.993 mm/0.7869 - 0.7871 inch. Measure the internal diameter of the con-rod bushing which should be in the tolerance range 20.003 - 20.014 mm/0.7875 - 0.7880 inch. Calculate the difference between the two measurements you have taken to work out the clearance which should be in the tolerance range of 0.010 - 0.027 mm/0.0004 - 0.0011 inch. Replace components which are worn beyond tolerance.

CONNECTING RODS CHECKING & REPAIR

48 Checking of the piston pin bushing was described in the previous step.

49 If you suspect that a connecting rod is bent or twisted - which could be caused by a broken or seized piston, water entering the combustion chamber or the camshaft drivebelt breaking and allowing valve to piston contact - you'll have to arrange for a machine shop to make the necessary measurements. The same shop can advise on the salvageability of damaged rods.

50 If not done during the engine teardown, temporarily fit each rod complete with lubricated bearing shells to its original journal on the crank. Tighten the cap retaining nuts progressively to a torque of 50 Nm /5.1 kgf m /37 lbf ft. Measure the maximum gap between the side of the bearing housing and the flange of the crank web. Maximum connecting rod side clearance is 0.30 mm/0.012 inch.

CRANKSHAFT & CRANKSHAFT BEARINGS CHECKING & REPAIR

51 If there were symptoms of crankshaft bearing wear - knocking, rumbling and/or low oil pressure - before the engine was dismantled, then all of the crankshaft bearing journals should be re-ground by your local machine shop. Re-grinding is undertaken in increments of 0.25 mm/0.010 inch, and undersized main and con-rod bearings are available to suit. Normally, the machine shop will decide which undersize to go for and will supply appropriate new bearings. **Caution!** Tell your machine shop that they must preserve the 1.5 mm/0.060 inch fillet roll at each side of each journal.

52 Crankshaft shell bearings are not hugely expensive, therefore if the engine has covered more than 50,000 km /30,000 miles you would be wise to fit new bearings of the same size. Undersize bearings usually have their size marked on the backs of the shells, whilst standard shells are unmarked. If in doubt check journal diameters as described later.

53 Inspect the crankshaft visually. Any scratching of the bearing journals will necessitate a regrind.

54 If the engine has been subjected to a major breakage like a smashed piston or has seized at speed, it would be a good idea to have your local machine shop crack test the crank and check it for straightness.

55 Measure the bearing journals with a micrometer. Take two measurements at 90 degrees to one another on both sides of each journal, in other words four measurements per journal. Tolerances are as follows:

Standard main	*49.938 - 49.956 mm/1.9661 - 1.9668 in.*
-0.25 mm/0.010 in.	*49.704 - 49.708 mm/1.9568 - 1.9570 in.*
-0.50 mm/0.020 in.	*49.454 - 49.458 mm/1.9470 - 1.9472 in.*
-0.75 mm/0.030 in.	*49.204 - 49.208 mm/1.9372 - 1.9373 in.*
Standard con	*44.940 - 44.956 mm/1.7693 - 1.7699 in.*
-0.25 mm/0.010 in.	*44.690 - 44.706 mm/1.7594 - 1.7601 in.*
-0.50 mm/0.020 in.	*44.440 - 44.456 mm/1.7496 - 1.7502 in.*
-0.75 mm/0.030 in.	*44.190 - 44.206 mm/1.7398 - 1.7404 in.*
Maximum ovality (all journals)	*0.05 mm/0.0020 in.*

If any of the journals measured are close to or beyond maximum tolerance in any size range, the crank will have to be re-ground to the next undersize. If the tolerance for maximum undersize is exceeded you'll need to replace the crank or talk to your local machine shop about having the journals built up. **Caution!** While it's OK to have main and con-rod bearings in different undersizes, all of the bearings in each category should be of the same size.

56 Place the cylinder block upside-down on your workbench. Fit the main bearing shells into

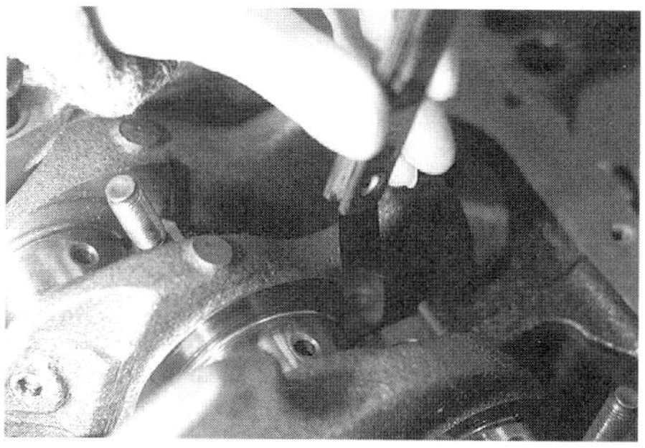

8/56a Measuring crankshaft endfloat.

8/56b You can use a dial gauge instead.

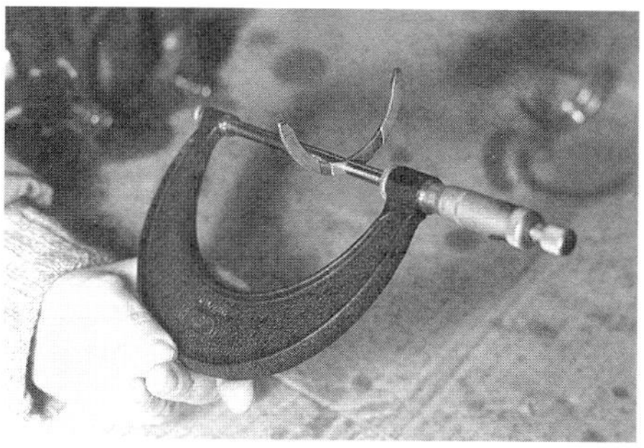

8/56c Measure thrust washer thickness.

their housings and fit the two thrust washers, cut-outs outward, into their recesses in the side of the bearing housing. Lubricate the bearings and then carefully lower the crankshaft into place making sure the thrust washers don't get knocked out of place. When the crank is properly seated, measure the maximum gap between thrust washer and crank flange with feeler gauges. This only needs to be done on one side of the main bearing, but constant downward pressure must be applied to the crank which must also be pulled or pushed hard up against the thrust washer on the other side of the main bearing. Normal tolerances are 0.080 - 0.282 mm/0.0031 - 0.0111 inch and maximum lash (endfloat) is 0.30 mm/0.012 inch. If lash is excessive, remove the crank and check the thickness of the thrust washers with a micrometer. Thickness tolerances are as follows for standard and undersized washers:

Standard	*2.500 - 2.550 mm/0.0984 - 0.1004 in.*
-0.25 mm/0.010 in.	*2.625 - 2.675 mm/0.1033 - 0.1053 in.*
-0.50 mm/0.020 in.	*2.750 - 2.800 mm/0.1083 - 0.1102 in.*
-0.75 mm/0.030 in.	*2.875 - 2.925 mm/0.1132 - 0.1152 in.*

If fitting new standard or oversized thrust washers will bring the endplay back into normal tolerance do that. If not, have the crank thrust faces re-ground to the next undersize.

57 If you're re-using used bearing shells/thrust washers because they've only done a small mileage and the crank journals are not worn, check them very carefully for scratches, heat blueing or uneven wear - if in any doubt, renew.

58 Use pipe cleaners to ensure that the crankshaft oil drillings are clear and clean. **Caution!** If you've had the crank journals re-ground, insist the machine shop verifies that the crankshaft drillings have been cleaned thoroughly and all swarf removed before accepting delivery.

CAMSHAFT DRIVEBELT, TENSIONER, IDLER & PULLEYS CHECKING & REPAIR

59 If the camshaft drivebelt has covered 50,00 km /30,000 miles or more it would sensible to replace it whilst you have the opportunity. Otherwise, check the belt for delamination, cracking and damaged teeth. Also check for contamination by oil or grease - if any of these problems are evident replace the belt. **Caution!** Do not twist, bend or turn the belt inside-out. Do not attempt to clean the belt with any fluids.

60 Check that both tensioner and idler wheels run freely and without noise and that the wheel surface is free of serious scratches. Replace if in doubt. **Caution!** Don't clean the wheels with any fluid, use a soft dry cloth only.

61 Measure the free length of the tensioner spring. If it exceeds 58.8 mm/2.315 in it's old and tired and should be renewed.

62 Check crankshaft and camshaft pulleys for obvious damage and wear. Replace if the 'teeth' are losing their profile or if there are faults which might damage the belt. **Caution!** Do not clean the pulleys with any fluid; use a soft, dry cloth only.

OIL PUMP CHECKING & REPAIR

63 Check that the inner face of the rotor cover is flat and unscratched.

64 Using a straightedge placed across the pump body, check the side clearance of both rotors. Maximum permissible is 0.14 mm/0.0055 inch.

65 Using feeler gauges determine the clearance between the outer rotor and chamber walls, as shown. Maximum is 0.20 mm/0.0079 inch.

66 Measure the gap between rotor tooth tips, as shown, using feeler gauges. More than 0.20

8/66 Check tooth tip clearance.

mm/0.0079 inch is too much.

67 **Caution!** If the pump components are worn outside of the tolerances given, replace the whole pump: a weak pump will have a detrimental effect by allowing general engine wear to accelerate.

68 Using a vernier gauge, measure the free length of the oil pressure relief valve spring. It should not be shorter than 45.5 mm/1.791 in otherwise oil pressure will fall.

69 Check that the relief valve plunger moves freely in its bore and that neither the plunger or

8/68 Check relief valve spring.

8/57 Check bearing shells & thrust washers.

8/64 Check rotor side clearance.

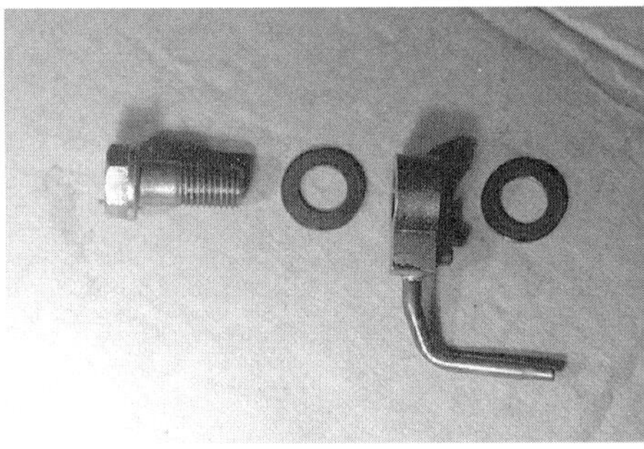

8/70 Oil jet components - use new washers.

bore are scratched or otherwise damaged.

OIL JETS CHECKING & REPAIR

70 Using a screwdriver press the ball valve in the banjo bolt: be sure it springs back freely Blow through the jet pipe from the jet end to make sure it is clear. Get new copper washers.

FLYWHEEL, PILOT BEARING & STARTER RING GEAR CHECKING & REPAIR

71 Check the friction surface of the flywheel for obvious wear or damage. Minor blueing o

8/58 Clean crankshaft oilways thoroughly.

8/65 Check rotor to wall clearance.

scratching can be removed with progressively finer grades of emery paper mounted on a flat rubbing block. Deep scratches or a worn area perceptibly below the original surface of the flywheel will have to be machined out by your local machine shop. **Caution!** If you don't rectify such damage clutch wear will be very rapid and smooth engagement impossible.

72 If you suspect the flywheel is distorted, you should have it checked by a local machine shop. Maximum runout is 0.2 mm/0.008 inch. Replace or re-machine as necessary.

73 Rotate the pilot bearing with a finger whilst simultaneously applying sideways pressure. Noise or stickiness of operation indicate the need for renewal. Replacement would be sensible if the engine has covered 80,000 km /50,000 miles or more.

74 Pilot bearing removal. Obtain a piece of solid round bar of exactly the same diameter as the spigot of the transmission input shaft - sorry, we forgot to measure it! Fill the pilot bearing center with grease. Engage the bar in the bearing and then give the bar a sharp blow with a hammer: hydraulic pressure will force the bearing out.

75 Pilot bearing fitting. The new bearing can be gently drifted into place using a suitably-sized socket or tube.

76 Check the ring gear teeth for severe wear or damage such as broken or missing teeth. If a new ring gear is needed, remove the old item by sawing partway through it with a hacksaw and then splitting it with a chisel.

77 Heat the new ring gear to a temperature of 250-300 degrees C/480-570 degrees F - a conventional domestic oven / cooker will reach the lower range of these temperatures. When the ring gear has reached the desired temperature, pick it up with tongs or protective hand gear and place it into position on the flywheel as quickly as possible, ensuring that the side with chamfered teeth is towards the engine. If the ring gear is hot enough it may go fully and evenly home with just a few light taps of a hide mallet. Failing this, a soft metal drift and hammer should do the job. Work quickly before the flywheel draws heat from the ring gear.

DRIVEPLATE (AUTO-TRANS CARS) & STARTER RING GEAR CHECKING & REPAIR

78 There's not too much to go wrong with a driveplate, but check it visually for obvious damage such as cracking or distortion. Replace if serious faults are evident.

79 Inspect the starter ring gear. ☞ 3/8/76-77.

CLUTCH COVER, DISC, RELEASE BEARING & RELEASE FORK CHECKING & REPAIR

80 First of all let's say that it wouldn't be sensible to re-use any of these components if they've covered 40,000 km /25,000 miles or more.

81 Check the friction surface of the cover plate for blueing, scratching and cracking. The first two types of damage can often be removed with emery paper wrapped around a flat-faced block, but if cracking is in evidence, trash the cover.

8/81 Check friction face of cover.

Check the fingers of the diaphragm spring: broken, bent, cracked or heavily worn fingers all point (forgive the pun!) to the need for renewal.

82 Check the thickness of lining material on the disc; as a minimum it must be 0.3 mm/0.012 inch above the rivet heads - but that's not going to give you much more service. If lining thickness is OK, check for burning, oil contamination, obvious distortion and loose linings, rivets or torsion rubbers. Also check the central hub splines for obvious wear or damage. Any of these faults should be enough to make you dig in your pocket.

83 Release bearing. Grasp the inner race and turn it whilst pushing it inwards as hard as you can. Noise or stickiness indicate the need for a new bearing.

84 Release fork. Check the tips of the two prongs where they bear against the back of the release bearing and the inside of the recess which fits over the pivot head. There should be plenty of metal left and no signs of severe wear. Replace the fork if serious wear is evident. Check the spring clip which grips the back of the pivot pin: apart from the circular section the spring should snap closed.

9. ENGINE REBUILD

☞ First read 1/1, 2.

ENGINE REBUILD GENERAL

1 To ensure maximum life and reliability from a rebuilt engine not only must the work be done with great care and thoroughness, but also in a clean environment with completely clean components and tools. Also, all internal moving components must be thoroughly lubricated with engine oil as they are reassembled/installed.

2 Before the rebuild begins replace any bolts, screws, studs or nuts the threads of which are in any way damaged. All threads must be clean and torque wrench settings strictly observed.

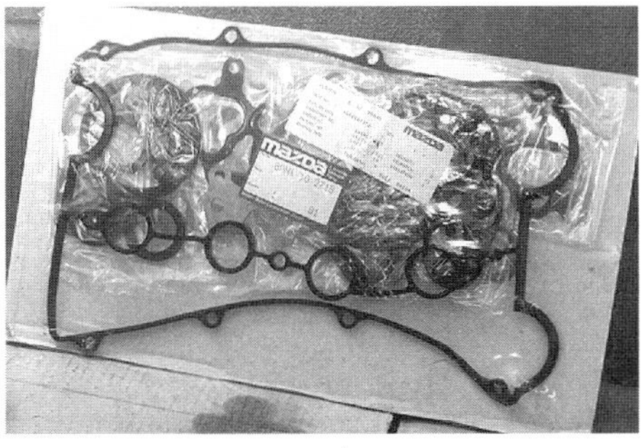

9/3 Engine gasket set - check crank seal size.

3 Have a complete set of new gaskets and seals ready before work starts, together with silicone based fluid gasket material and thread locking fluid.

4 If a component won't fit, don't force it. Stop, stand back, think about the problem and resolve it properly before proceeding.

5 Take your time, get it right and keep your personal safety and the safety of others in mind at all times.

9/6 Fit piston rings very carefully!

PISTONS & PISTON RINGS REBUILD

6 First fit the corrugated oil scraper ring spacer into the lowest of the three piston grooves. **Caution!** It is essential the ring is installed so that the final corrugation is closed side downwards. Fit the thin oil scraper rings one above and one below the corrugated spacer. Before doing this adjust the spacer ring so that the ring gap is over one end of the piston pin. Fit the lower oil rail ring first and set its gap 30 degrees anti-clockwise from

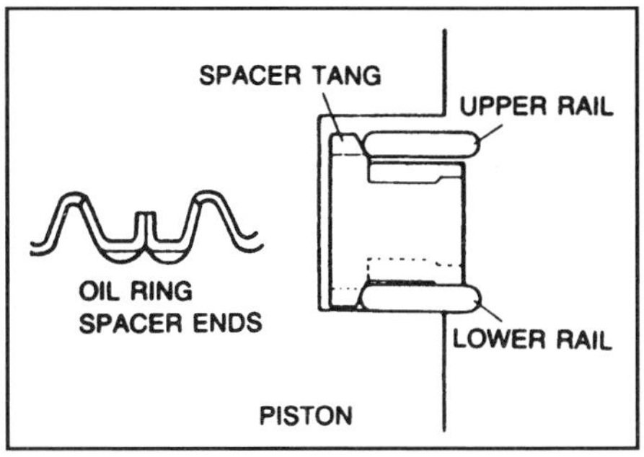

D9/6A CORRECT INSTALLATION OF SCRAPER RINGS.

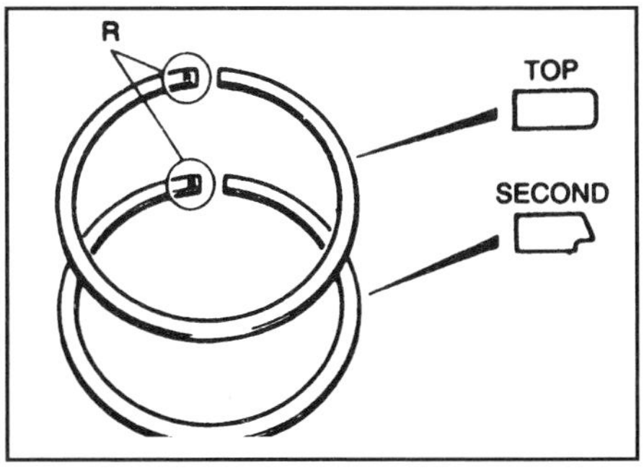

D9/6B PISTON RING MARKINGS AND PROFILES.

the corrugated ring gap, then fit the top rail ring and set its gap 30 degrees clockwise of the corrugated ring gap.

7 Using three old feeler gauge blades, three strips of hacksaw blade or other thin metal strips, slide the middle piston ring into its groove. Note that the top of the ring is marked with the letter "R", which must face upwards. Also notice that the lower edge of this piston ring is notched. Set the gap of the center ring 30 degrees clockwise from one end of the piston pin.

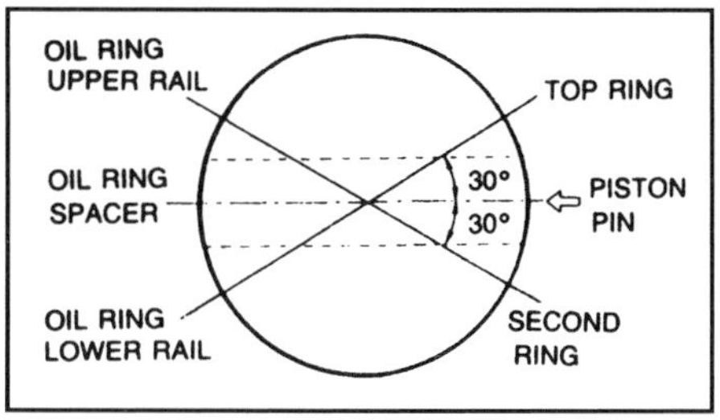

D9/7 CORRECT ORIENTATION OF FITTED RINGS.

8 The top ring is of plain section but must be installed with the letter "R" upwards. Set this piston ring so that its gap is 60 degrees anti-clockwise from the middle ring's gap. Repeat this procedure with the other three pistons.

PISTONS & CONNECTING RODS REBUILD & INSTALLATION

9 Mount the connecting rod in a vise fitted with jaw protectors; the rod needs to protrude from the jaws by 75 mm/3 in or so. Make sure you know which side of the rod is the oil jet side and don't forget to apply oil liberally to the connecting rod piston pin bearing, the pin itself and the piston pin bore in the piston.

10 Fit one new spring clip into its groove in the piston pin bore. Make sure you know which way the piston will go on the con-rod so that the cutout in the skirt will be over the oil jet. Heat the piston with a butane torch for around a minute until it's too hot to touch - but don't overdo it. Wrap the piston in rag and quickly fit it over the con-rod and then push the piston pin home through the piston and con-rod bearing until it contacts the spring clip. Fit the second spring clip to retain the pin. **Caution!** Double check that both pin retaining clips are seated fully and securely in their grooves and that the con-rod swings freely on the piston pin.

11 Stand the cylinder block on end or on its side. Lubricate the rings, grooves and piston pin/con-rod bearing thoroughly before installing each piston; also rub oil around the cylinder bore with your fingers. **Caution!** Make sure you know to which bore each piston/con-rod assembly belongs.

12 Guide the rod and piston into the bore until the lowest piston ring is approximately half an inch from the top of the cylinder block. Make sure that the piston and connecting rod assembly is fitted so that the cutout in the piston skirt is over the oil jet (if your engine still has original pistons, you'll probably find that there is a dot on the piston crown indicating the side of the piston which should face toward the front of the engine). You also need to

9/12 Slide piston and rod into bore.

check that the piston ring gaps are still correctly positioned as described earlier. **Caution!** If the crankshaft is in place, great care must be taken to guide the connecting rod studs away from the crankshaft bearing journal as the piston is pushed into the bore. A gouge or bad scratch will necessitate a crankshaft re-grind ...

13 Use an ordinary piston ring compressor to squeeze all of the piston rings fully into their grooves so that the piston can be pushed home into its bore. Don't forget to lubricate the inner part of the ring compressor thoroughly before clamping

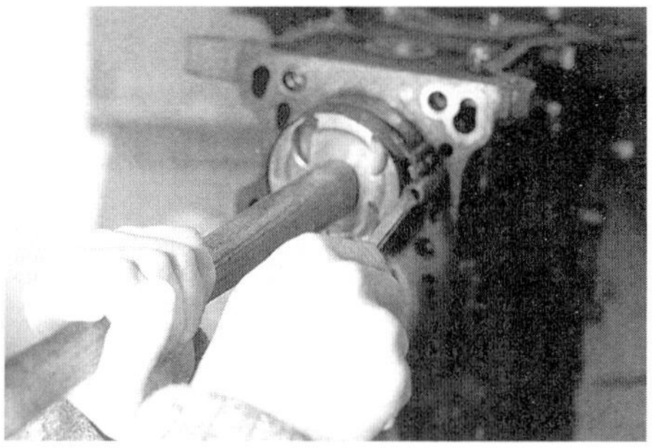

9/13 Piston ring compressor is needed.

the piston and rings. **Caution!** Don't try to fit pistons without a ring compressor: the likely result will be a broken ring. Compressors are not expensive and are available in the same places that you buy your parts and tools.

14 Repeat the process for the other three pistons.

OIL JETS REBUILD & INSTALLATION

15 Assemble each oil jet in the following sequence. Fit a new copper washer to the banjo bolt followed by the oil jet union (jet pointing away from bolt head) and another new copper washer. Screw the banjo bolt loosely into its threaded recess in the cylinder block and move the jet union from side-to-side until its locating pin locks it in place. The banjo bolt can then be tightened to its correct torque of 12-18 Nm/1.2-1.8 kgf m /104-156 lbf in.

CRANKSHAFT & BEARING SHELLS INSTALLATION

16 Turn the cylinder block upside-down on your bench. Check that the main bearing seats are scrupulously clean, as even the slightest amount of debris could lift the shells and create a tight spot.

9/15 Fit oil jets, using new washers.

9/17 Fit crankshaft bearing shells.

Ensure, too, that the bearing shells are equally clean.

17 Fit the main bearing shell halves in place in the cylinder block and bearing caps, making sure that the tongue in each shell is engaged with the cutout in the seat and also that each end of the shell is flush with the top of the housing. If you are re-using serviceable shells, make sure they are installed in their original positions.

18 Fit the two semicircular thrust washers into the side recesses of the fourth main bearing. The cutaways in the thrust washers should be

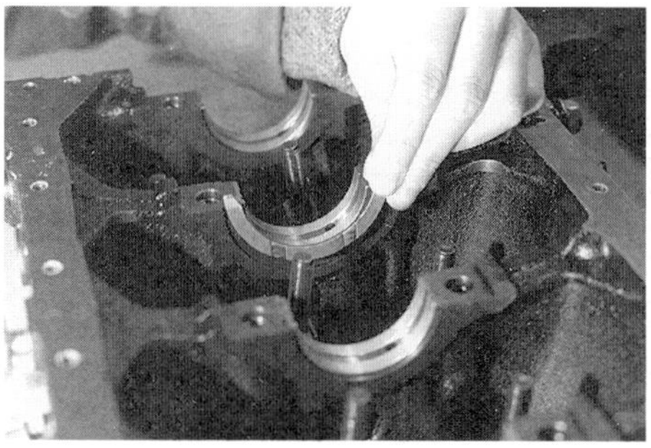

9/18 Fit thrust washers.

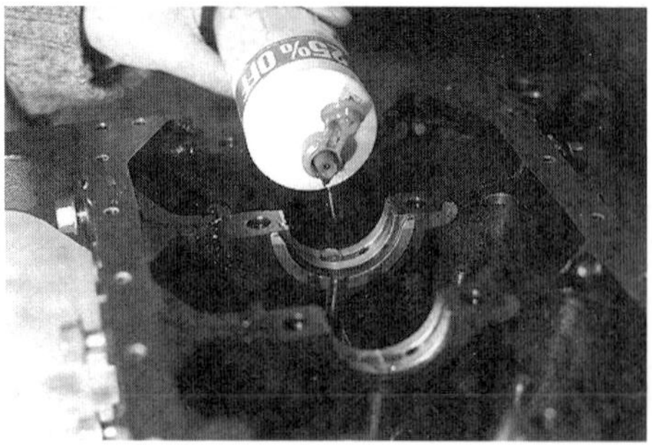

9/19 Lubricate generously.

facing outward, away from the bearing.

19 Check that all of the crankshaft bearing journals are spotlessly clean and that the oilways are clear. Push all of the pistons to the tops of their bores. Lubricate all of the bearings and thrust washers thoroughly before lowering the crankshaft gently into position, taking great care not to knock out the thrust washers sitting each side of the fourth main bearing, also not to scratch journals on the connecting rod studs.

20 **Caution!** Make sure that the threaded holes for the main bearing cap retaining bolts are clean and completely free of oil or debris. A doubled

9/20 Bolt holes MUST be clean.

over pipe cleaner is a good tool for this job.

21 Lubricate the bearing shells in the main bearing caps thoroughly and then, noting the dot-punched location ID, lower each bearing cap into its correct position and finger-tighten its retaining bolts which should have clean dry threads. Remember, the arrow cast into each bearing cap points toward the front of the engine.

22 The final torque for the main bearing cap 14 mm bolts is 54 - 59 Nm /5.5 - 6.0 kgf m /40 - 43 lbf ft. Tighten the bolts in three stages using a sequence which spirals outward from the central cap: *i.e.*, start with the nearest bolt of the center bearing, move to the furthest bolt of the center bearing and then to the furthest bolt of bearing number four (or two) and so on. If the connecting rods are not yet in place, the crankshaft should be free to rotate under hand pressure after the bearing caps have been torqued. If it won't rotate, remove the caps again and check that there is no foreign matter between bearing shell backs and seats. If the problem persists, you'll need to consult the bearing supplier or the machine shop which carried out the re-grind.

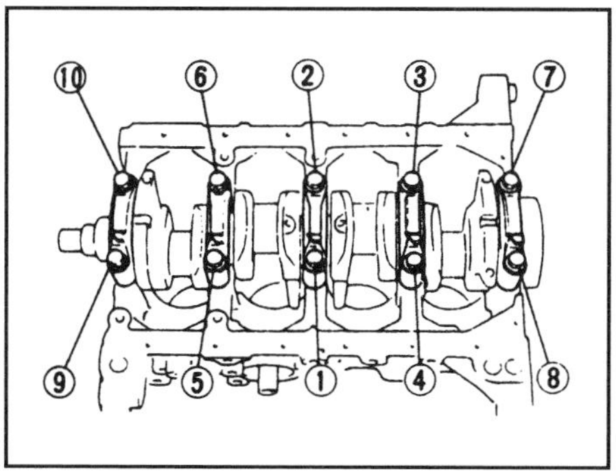

D9/22 MAIN BEARING CAPS TIGHTENING SEQUENCE.

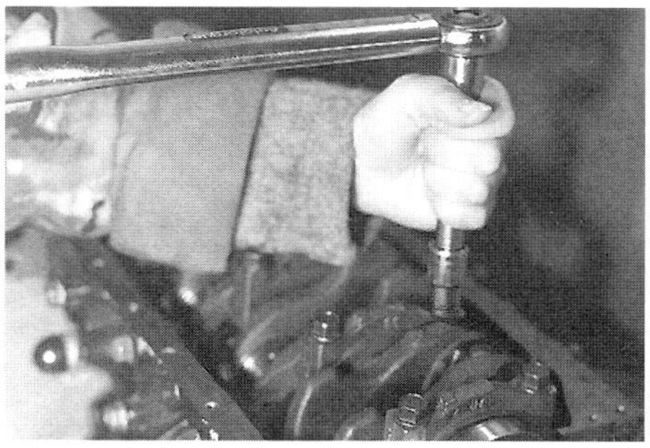

9/22 Torque tighten cap bolts.

CONNECTING RODS & CAPS FITTING TO CRANKSHAFT

23 Make sure that the bearing housings of both the connecting rods and their caps are spotlessly clean. Ensure, too, that the bearing shells are equally clean before fitting them to rods and caps and be sure to engage the shell tabs in the seat cutout.

24 Lubricate the connecting rod bearing shells thoroughly, then pull the connecting rods onto their crankshaft journals - it's best if all four crank webs are at more or less the same height rather than two being up and two being down.

9/25 Connecting rod caps.

25 You'll have no trouble identifying which bearing cap goes with which connecting rod if, as recommended, you dot punched their position numbers into the side of the caps and connecting rods during the engine teardown. If not, all may not be lost! On our engine the manufacturers had stamped a "V" device across the joint of each connecting rod and cap so, by matching the two parts of the "V", you can identify which cap goes with which connecting rod.

26 Lubricate the crank con-rod journals liberally and dribble oil into the oilways which should be facing upwards. Fit the caps and tighten the two 14 mm nuts retaining each cap in three stages until a final torque of 50-54 Nm /5.1-5.5 kgf m /37-40 lbf ft is reached. Check that the crankshaft is free to rotate once all of the cap nuts have been torqued. You'll find that rotation will be stiff because of the friction created by the pistons in their bores. If the crank won't rotate remove the caps and check that there is not foreign material between shells and seats. Should the problem persist, consult your bearing shell supplier or the machine shop which re-ground the crank.

9/27 Drift out the old seal.

CRANKSHAFT REAR COVER FITTING NEW OIL SEAL

27 Mount the cover on top of a vise as shown and, using a blunt chisel or punch, drive the old oil seal through the housing.

28 Lubricate the outer lip of the new oil seal and lightly tap it into position with a nylon or rubber-faced hammer whilst supporting the cover casting on the vise and turning it a little after each blow so that the seal is driven evenly home. **Caution!** The closed side of the oil seal must face outward from the rear of the engine and must be flush with the outer face of the housing.

CRANKSHAFT REAR COVER INSTALLATION

29 Apply a bead of silicone gasket cement to the area shown. Lubricate the inner lip of the seal and the flange of the flywheel mounting where the seal bears on the crank.

30 Fit the cover to the rear of the cylinder block, feeding it carefully over the flywheel boss on the crankshaft end. Fit the four retaining bolts, noting that the two longer bolts must be positioned

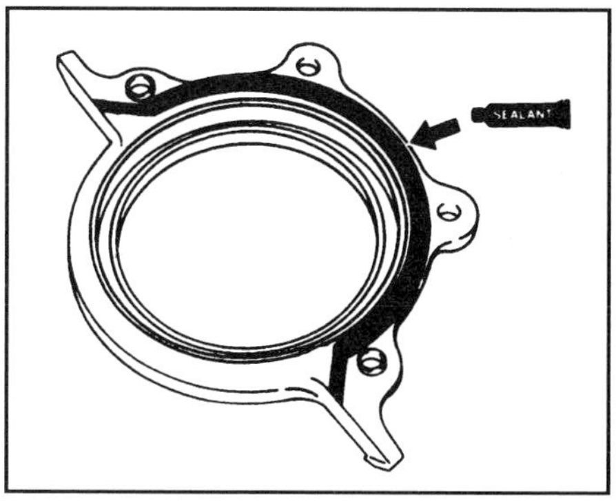

D9/29 APPLY SEALANT AS SHOWN.

9/29 Allow sealant to dry a little.

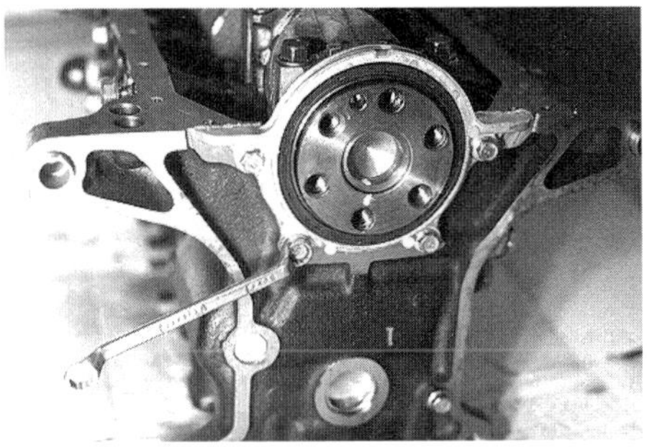

9/30 Tighten seal housing bolts.

closest to the oil pan flange. Tighten the cover retaining 10 mm bolts to a torque of 7.8-11 Nm / 80-110 kgf cm /69-95 lbf in. If you don't have a torque wrench capable of reading such small torque levels, use a box end wrench and finger tip pressure only to tighten the bolts.

OIL PUMP REBUILD & FITTING NEW OIL SEAL

31 Lubricate the rotors thoroughly, then fit the cover to the rear of the oil pump body without using any sealing compound. The crosshead screws should be tightened to a torque of 5.9-8.8 Nm /60-90 kgf cm /52-78 lbf in. If you have a hexagonal-shaped crosshead bit from an impact driver you will be able to mount this in a socket and use a torque wrench conventionally. **Caution!** It is important that the crosshead bit you use is a good fit in the screw heads and that constant downward pressure is applied during tightening.

32 Before fitting the oil pump to the crankshaft nose it will be necessary to fit a new oil seal in the pump housing. Turn the pump housing face down on a vise or hard work surface and, using a small diameter chisel or punch from behind, drive out the old seal. Turn the pump body over so that

9/32 Drive out old seal.

the pump backplate is on your bench. Lubricate the outer lip of the new oil seal and, after positioning it carefully closed side facing outward, drive it home with evenly spaced light blows from a nylon or rubber faced hammer. **Caution!** The face of the seal must be flush with the face of the housing.

OIL PUMP INSTALLATION

33 Fit a new paper gasket onto the back of the oil pump body casting, locating it over the two projecting spigots. No gasket cement is necessary.

34 Lubricate the oil seal inner lip and the

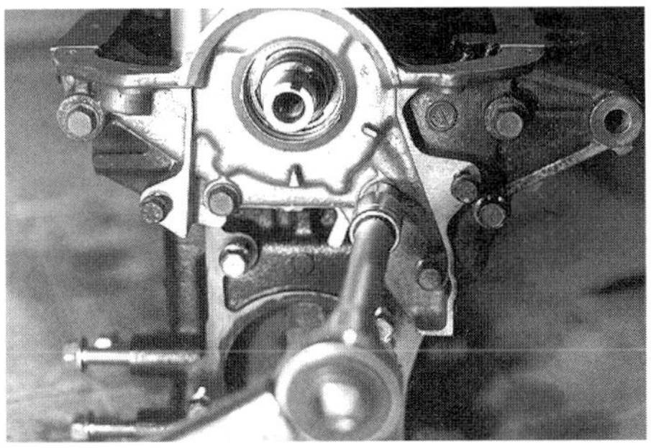

9/34 Install oil pump.

area of the crankshaft nose that the seal bears upon. Line up the flats on the oil pump central rotor with the flats on the crankshaft and then slide the whole oil pump into position against the front of the cylinder block. The pump body casting is secured to the cylinder block by six 12 mm bolts. The longest bolts fit the bolt holes closest to the oil pan flange on each side of the pump body. The shortest bolt fits the single hole closest to the water pump. Tighten the screws by hand and then progressively in a diagonal sequence to a final torque of 19-25 Nm /1.9-2.6 kgf m /14-19 lbf ft. Note: the seal is

9/35 Trim gasket.

missing in our photo because the one supplied in our gasket set turned out to be too small and we had to fit the correct item later.

35 If any of the gasket protrudes into the oil pan flange, trim it off with a craft knife or razor blade.

OIL PAN BAFFLE, OIL PUMP PICKUP PIPE & OIL PAN INSTALLATION

36 If the baffle flanges were bent during removal, carefully straighten them using a flat surface and a flat-faced hammer.

37 Apply a bead of silicone-based jointing compound along the flanges - cylinder block side - of the baffle. The bead should run down the center of the flange diverting around the inside of each hole. **Caution!** Once the sealing compound has been applied, no more than 30 minutes must elapse before the oil pan is fitted to the cylinder block.

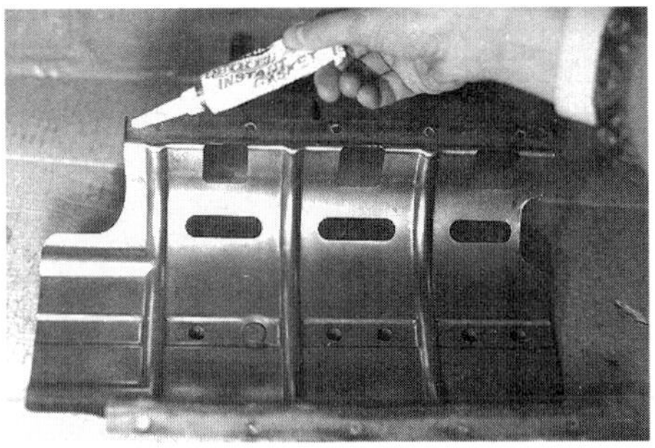

9/37 Apply jointing compound to baffles.

38 Fit the baffle into position on the inverted cylinder block and line up with the oil pan bolt holes.

39 You'll notice that there are grooved bridges over both crank rear seal housing and oil pump body. Starting and ending approx 12 mm/

9/38 Fit baffle in place.

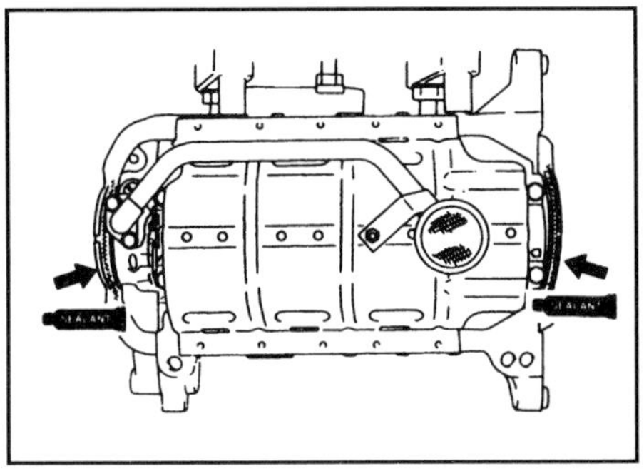

D9/39 APPLY SEALANT TO BRIDGES AS SHOWN.

0.5 inch each side of these bridges, run a continuous bead of sealant over each bridge.

40 Whilst the sealant in the grooves is still tacky, fit the appropriate new rubber seal in each bridge. Make sure that the tab in each seal is located in the notch in the side of the housing.

41 Apply a continuous bead of sealant to the flange of the oil pan. The bead should run along the center of the flange, diverting around the inside of holes as necessary.

42 Fill the oil pump body with engine oil, then

9/40 Fit rubber seals (arrowed).

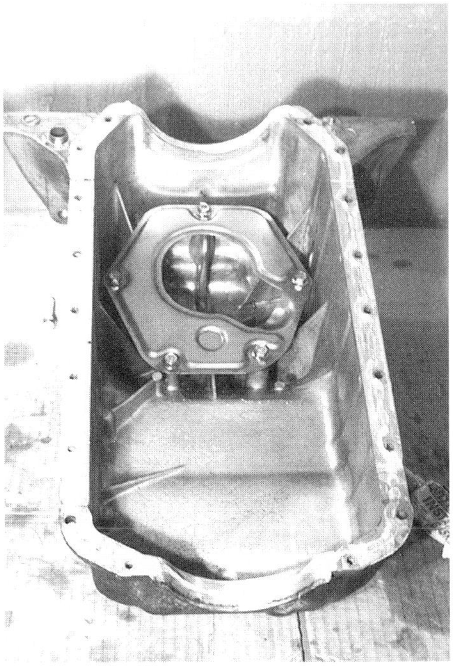

9/41 Apply sealant to oil pan flange.

place a new gasket on the pickup flange of the pump body - no gasket cement is needed. Position the pickup assembly and fit the two 10 mm bolts and one 10 mm nut that secure it to the pump and baffle. Tighten the bolts and nut to a torque of 7.8-11 Nm /80-110 kgf cm /69-95 lbf in. Tightening with a box end wrench and finger tip pressure is OK.

43 Fit the oil pan and the eighteen 10 mm bolts that secure it, including the two long bolts adjacent to the flywheel. Tighten the bolts in three stages and in a sequence which spirals outward from the center bolts to a final torque of 7.8-11 Nm /80-110 kgf cm /69-95 lbf in.

44 Fit a new copper sealing washer to the oil pan drain plug and tighten the plug securely.

ENGINE BACKPLATE INSTALLATION

45 Turn the engine over so that it is resting on the oil pan base and place a block of wood between the shallow end of the pan and the bench to stabilize the unit.

46 Position the engine backplate so that it locates over the two projecting spigots and secure it with a single 10 mm bolt toward the top left of the plate. Tighten the bolt with a box end wrench and finger tip pressure only.

9/46 Install backplate.

FLYWHEEL (DRIVEPLATE - AUTO TRANS) INSTALLATION

47 Check that the threaded bolt holes in the crankshaft rear flange are clear and clean, a doubled over pipe cleaner is a good tool for this purpose.

48 Flywheel (manual transmission) installation. Apply thread locking fluid to the threads of each of the flywheel retaining bolts. Hold the flywheel in position over the rear of the crankshaft and fit the retaining bolts finger-tight.

9/47 Bolt holes MUST be clean.

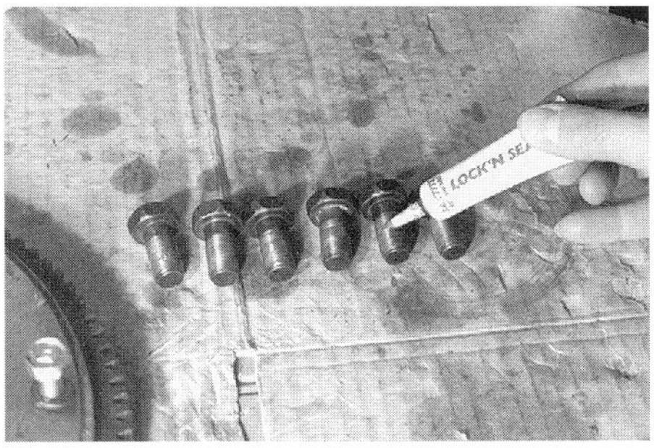

9/48 Apply locking fluid to bolts.

49 Driveplate (auto transmission) installation. Apply thread locking fluid to the threads of each of the flywheel retaining bolts. Fit the adaptor collar to the rear of the crankshaft, followed by the driveplate and its backing plate. Fit bolts fingertight.

50 Lock the flywheel or driveplate by temporarily fitting a bellhousing bolt and then wedging a screwdriver into the ring gear teeth and against the bolt. Tighten the flywheel or driveplate retaining bolts progressively, and in a diagonal sequence, to a final torque of 100 Nm /10 kgf m / 74 lbf ft.

9/50 Lock flywheel & torque tighten bolts.

9/51 Fit a new gasket to the water pump.

WATER PUMP INSTALLATION

51 Fit a new gasket to the face of the water pump - no gasket cement is necessary. Hold the water pump in position at the front of the cylinder block and retain by fitting the four bolts finger-tight. Tighten the 12 mm retaining bolts, in a diagonal sequence, to a final torque of 22 Nm /2.2 kgf m /17 lbf ft.

VALVES, SPRINGS & VALVE STEM OIL SEALS INSTALLATION

52 Fitting new valve stem seals. Place the cylinder head, combustion chambers down, on your workbench. Fitting seals is a fiddly job because access is restricted; however, using fingers only, push the new oil seal over the top of the valve guide until the seal seems to be fully seated. Using the depth gauge section of a vernier gauge check that the shoulder of the seal is 18.3-18.5 mm/ 0.720-0.728 inch above the surface of the head. Adjust as necessary, then repeat the process until a new seal has been fitted to every guide.

53 **Caution!** The following procedures assume that the individual valves have been checked and lapped: ☞ 3/8/10-20. Mount the cylinder head horizontally in a vise (fitted with jaw protectors) in such a way that you have access to a complete row of valves from both sides of the head. Tighten the vise just enough to grip the head.

54 From the combustion chamber side insert the valve, having first lubricated its stem thoroughly. **Caution!** If re-using valves previously removed it is essential that they are each returned to their original locations and the seat with which they were lapped. Even new valves must be fitted to the seat with which they were lapped.

55 From the other side of the head, fit the spring seat followed by the spring itself. **Caution!** If you look closely at the spring you will see that the coils at one end are closer pitched (together): this end of the spring must be closest to the cylinder head. Fit the spring cap.

56 You'll need the spacer constructed earlier and an ordinary valve spring compressor. Make sure the compressor is fitted centrally and securely over both valve head and spacer, then compress the spring until enough of the recess in the valve stem is revealed to fit the keepers.

57 Now the fun really begins! Stick each keeper in turn to a small screwdriver with a blob of grease, then position the keeper, taper down-

9/57 Refit the valve keepers.

wards, into the spring cap. Repeat the process with the second keeper, so that both keepers are contained within the spring cap and the heads of the keepers are below the top of the recess in the valve stem. You'll find this much more difficult than it sounds, but patience will be rewarded with success.

58 Gradually release the compressor making sure that the two keepers slide up the valve stem and then engage positively in the stem recess. Release the compressor completely and remove it. **Warning!** Stay out of the line of fire, whilst giving the valve stem tip three sharp blows with a small hammer to seat the keepers. **Caution!** Check, and double check, that the keepers are securely and properly seated in the valve stem recess - still keeping out of the line of fire.

59 Repeat the valve fitting process until all valves are in place.

CYLINDER HEAD INSTALLATION

60 Check that all of the threaded bolt holes in the top of the cylinder block are clean to their full depth, a doubled over pipe cleaner's a good tool for this. Turn the crankshaft, via the

9/60 Bolt hole MUST be clean.

flywheel, until all of the pistons are approximately half way down their bores. Pour a little engine oil into each cylinder and spread it around the rim of the pistons and over the cylinder walls with your fingers.

61 Position a new cylinder head gasket over the dowels on the deck of the cylinder block. Make sure the gasket is the right way up so that the oilway on the right of the engine is left open. No gasket cement is needed.

62 Lower the cylinder head into position until it positively locates over the two protruding

9/61 Position new head gasket.

9/62 Fit the cylinder head.

dowels. Lightly oil their threads and their head shoulders, then replace the ten bolts which secure the head and screw them in finger-tight.

63 Using a 12 mm socket, short extension and torque wrench tighten the cylinder head bolts to a final torque of 80 Nm /8 kgf m /58 lbf ft. Tighten the bolts in three stages and in a sequence which spirals outward from the two central bolts.

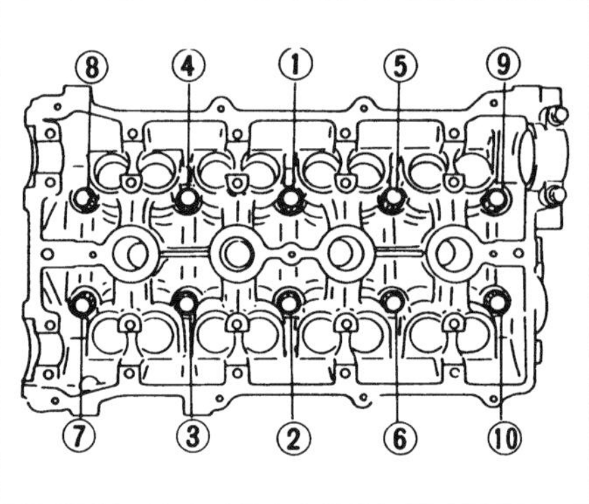

D9/63 CYLINDER HEAD TIGHTENING SEQUENCE.

9/63 Torque tighten cylinder head bolts.

THERMOSTAT HOUSING INSTALLATION

64 Fit a new rubber sealing ring into the groove in the flange of the thermostat housing, no sealant is necessary.

65 Hold the housing in position against the front of the cylinder head and replace the two retaining bolts finger-tight. Tighten the 12 mm bolts to a torque of 20 Nm /2 kgf m /16 lbf ft.

CYLINDER HEAD SEAL PLATE INSTALLATION

66 Fit a new rubber seal into the section of the seal plate which fits around the thermostat housing. Position the seal plate at the front of the cylinder head making sure it's properly positioned, clipped over the water pump body and that the bolt holes line up. Fit the six retaining screws but don't tighten them yet.

67 Fit a new rubber sealing strip along the base of the plate and onto the underside of the thermostat housing. Now tighten the 10 mm plate retaining bolts with a box end wrench using only finger tip pressure.

CAM-FOLLOWERS INSTALLATION

68 Generously lubricate the valve springs

9/67 Fit seal plate.

and rub oil around the bores in which the cam-followers fit. **Caution!** If you're re-using cam-followers it is essential that they are returned to the position from which they were originally taken.

69 Slide each cam-follower, open side downwards, into its bore and make sure it moves freely.

CAMSHAFTS INSTALLATION

70 Check that the cap bolt holes in the head are completely free of debris and fluid. Thoroughly lubricate the camshaft bearings in the head and the tops of the cam-followers, ensuring that none of the oil runs into the cleaned bolt holes.

71 Gently lay each camshaft into its bearings taking care not to damage the bearings with the sharp edges of the cam lobes. Note: the intake cam is the longer of the two because it carries the drive slot for the crank-angle sensor and it fits on the right.

72 Apply a bead of silicone sealant to the cambox flange over about 12 mm/half an inch each side of each camshaft front bearing journal as shown. **Caution!** Take care not to get any sealant on the cam journals. Allow the sealant to harden for around five minutes.

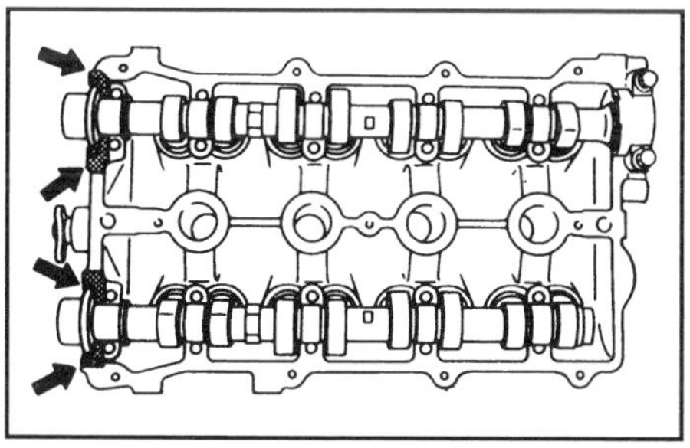

D9/72 APPLY SEALANT AS SHOWN.

73 Lubricate all of the camshaft bearing caps and fit them into position. The caps must be fitted in their original positions and be correctly orientated. Each cap is embossed with an arrow which must point toward the front of the engine, and stamped with the letter "I" or "E" in combination with a number. Therefore, for example, cap "E/3" is the third cap from the front of the exhaust camshaft.

74 Fit the cap bolts and tighten them finger-tight for the moment.

75 Tighten the camshaft bearing cap bolts in three stages to a final torque of 13 Nm /1.30 kgf m

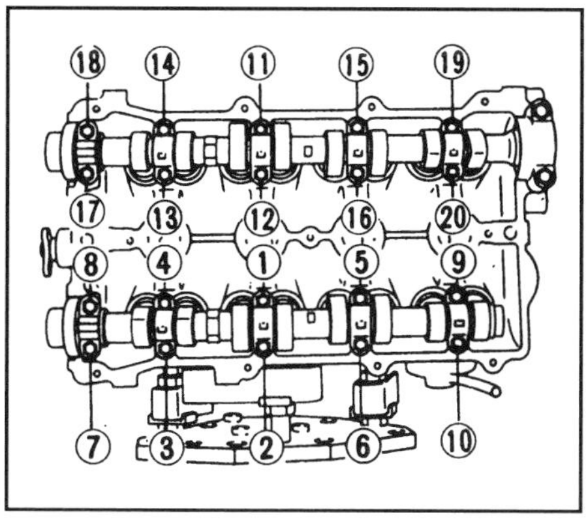

D9/74 CAMSHAFTS BEARING CAPS TIGHTENING SEQUENCE.

/115 lbf in. **Caution!** These bolts must be tightened in a sequence which spirals outward from the central cap of each camshaft. Start with the central bolt closest to the side of the cambox and tighten the caps of one cam at a time. Be especially careful to tighten the caps down evenly, particularly where you find the caps are initially prevented from engaging with their locating dowels because of the need for the cam lobes to partially force open some of the valves.

CAMSHAFT OIL SEALS FITTING

76 Lightly lubricate the inner lip and outer circumference of a new oil seal. Slide the seal over the nose of the camshaft and then, with a very light flat-faced hammer, tap the seal fully into its housing, making sure that the blows are applied evenly around the circumference so that the seal is driven home square. The face of the seal must be flush with the front of its housing when it's finally in position. Make sure you keep the face of the

9/76 Tap new seals into place.

hammer square to the seal so that neither the seal nor alloy housing are damaged. You may need to use a flat-ended drift just to tap the lower part of the seal into place where it is partially shrouded by the seal plate. Repeat the process for the second camshaft seal.

CAMSHAFT PULLEYS INSTALLATION

77 Using a 24 mm crescent wrench on the hex-shaped section, rotate each cam until the spigot on the pulley boss is almost vertically above the bolt hole. You'll find each cam will 'rest' in this

9/78 Fit camshaft pulleys.

position.

78 Fit the intake cam pulley first, locating it over the camshaft boss and positioning the center cutaway over the spigot so that the letter "I" on one of the pulley spokes is almost vertical. Do the same for the exhaust camshaft pulley except, of course, this time the letter "E" should be almost vertical. Note: we marked the exhaust camshaft pulley on removal so that it would be reinstalled on the same cam.

79 Put a dab of thread locking fluid on each camshaft pulley retaining bolt and then screw it home finger-tight. Use a spanner on the hexagonal section of the camshaft, between caps two and three, to lock the camshaft whilst each 14 mm pulley bolt is tightened to a torque of 55 Nm /6 kgf m /40 lbf ft. **Caution!** Do not allow the crescent wrench used to lock the cams to wedge against the sides of the cambox which will be very easily damaged.

9/79 Torque tighten retaining bolts.

CAMSHAFT DRIVEBELT IDLER, TENSIONER WHEELS & TENSIONER SPRING INSTALLATION

80 Place a blob of copper-based grease on the tensioner pulley pivot pin. Also spread a thin

9/80 Smear copper-based grease onto boss.

smear of the same grease on the alloy boss on which the tensioner pulley bracket slides.

81 Place the tensioner wheel and bracket in position and screw in the 14 mm retaining bolt, but leave it loose enough for the tensioner wheel to move back-and-forth.

82 Hold the tensioner spring so that the hook at the wheel end is open downwards, and the closed section of the spring shroud is toward the anchor pin near the location of the idler wheel. Clip the spring into the recess in the tensioner wheel bracket and, using needle-nosed pliers, stretch the

9/82 Fit tensioner spring.

9/83 Lock tensioner wheel.

spring back until the other end can be clipped over the anchor pin. Make sure both ends of the spring are securely located in their respective cutout and groove.

83 Pull the tensioner wheel outward, against the spring tension, as far as it will go and then tighten the 14 mm center bolt to lock it in this position until the drivebelt is fitted.

84 Fit the idler wheel to the left-hand side of the engine and tighten its 14 mm retaining bolt to 45 Nm /4.5 kgf m /32 lbf ft.

CRANKSHAFT INNER (CAM DRIVEBELT) PULLEY INSTALLATION

85 Temporarily fit the 21 mm-headed crankshaft center bolt, and using a socket and T-bar to apply leverage, rotate the crankshaft until the keyway in its nose is facing upward. A sharp tap on the T-bar in the reverse direction will slacken the bolt once more without moving the crankshaft. Remove the bolt. **Caution!** Take care when turning the crank in case the valve heads come into contact with the pistons, although this couldn't be made to happen with our engine.

86 Rub a smear of oil over the crankshaft nose and in the keyway. Fit the cam drivebelt

9/86 Fit cam drivebelt pulley and ...

9/87 ... don't forget key.

pulley over the nose of the crankshaft - flanged side toward the rear - and rotate it until the cutout in the pulley aligns with the cutout in the crankshaft.

87 Hold the locking key so that the chamfered end points toward the oil pump body and the chamfer is toward the crankshaft. Push the key into its slot with your fingers.

88 Lock the key in position by fitting the crankshaft pulley lock bolt and tightening it to a torque of 100 Nm /11.5 kgf m /84 lbf ft. You can lock the crankshaft by wedging a screwdriver between a bellhousing bolt which has been temporarily installed and the starter ring gear teeth.

CAMSHAFT DRIVEBELT FITTING & VALVE TIMING

89 If the pulley spokes with the "I" on the intake pulley and "E" on the exhaust pulley are not topmost and almost vertical, use a ratchet and 14 mm socket to rotate the cams clockwise until they are. You'll notice that the second letter mark on each pulley now, more-or-less, lines up with the matching embossed pointers in the seal plate.

90 If necessary, rotate the crankshaft (if they're fitted, removing the spark plugs will make

9/89 Correct camshaft pulley positions.

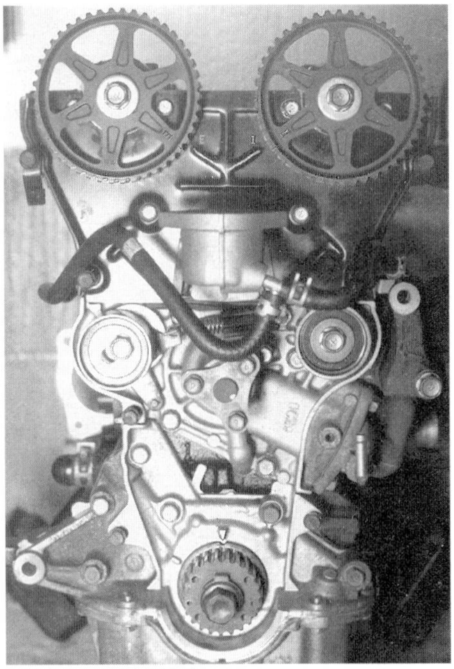

9/90 Ready to fit drivebelt.

this easier) using the 21 mm pulley locking bolt until the notch in the flange at the back of the crankshaft inner pulley aligns with the triangular pointer cast into the oil pump body. This represents TDC (Top Dead Centre).

91 Begin fitting the drivebelt by first sliding it half on to the crankshaft drive pulley, threading it up past the idler wheel on the exhaust side of the engine and then halfway onto the exhaust camshaft pulley. **Caution!** It's important that there is no slack on this, the 'pulling' side, of the cam drive system. Keeping the belt taut between the crank pulley and the exhaust cam pulley, pull the belt onto the intake cam pulley until it's about halfway on. Feed the belt around the tensioner wheel and then push it fully home onto the three pulleys. Don't release the tensioner wheel lock bolt yet.

92 The marked section of each pulley flange adjacent to the letter "I" or "E" should be in alignment with the center of the pointer embossed in the seal plate behind the camshaft pulleys and bearing the same ID letter. On our project engine the exhaust pulley lined up OK, but we had to turn the intake pulley a little with a 14 mm spanner and move the belt one notch.

93 Frankly, it's hard to tell with Mazda's system whether or not you've got everything lined up exactly as it should be - which is why we recommended adding additional reference marks before removing the original drivebelt. If you added those extra marks, carry out the procedure outlined so far and then place a straightedge over the centers of the crank and exhaust cam pulley retaining bolts. Check that with the drivebelt taut between these pulleys, your marks line up with the straightedge. When satisfied, move the straightedge to cover the centers of the crank and intake cam pulleys to make sure the marks on that side also line up. If they don't, without moving the other pulleys, or losing the tension of the belt between the crank and exhaust cam pulleys, reposition the intake pulley, tooth-by-tooth, until you are satisfied all is in alignment. Double check that the crank pulley is still aligned with the TDC marker and that the "I" of the intake cam and "E" of the exhaust cam are still more or less vertical.

94 If you think you've got it right, using a socket on the crankshaft nose bolt, rotate the crankshaft through four complete turns until the TDC notch in the pulley rear flange once again aligns with the indicator in the oil pump body. Check that both camshaft drive pulleys still register correct alignment. If the alignment is not right, repeat the valve timing procedure until you're satisfied that all is correct.

95 Turn the crankshaft 1 and 5/6ths turns clockwise (looking at the crankshaft nose), at which point the cutout in the rear flange of the crankshaft pulley will be aligning with the belt tension setting marker, which is about 60 degrees anti-clockwise of the TDC pointer.

96 Slacken the camshaft belt tensioner wheel locking bolt until it springs forward and takes up the belt's slack. Tighten the tensioner locking bolt to a torque of 45 Nm /4.5 kgf m /34 lbf ft.

9/95 Correctly aligned crankshaft pulley.

9/97a Checking drivebelt tension.

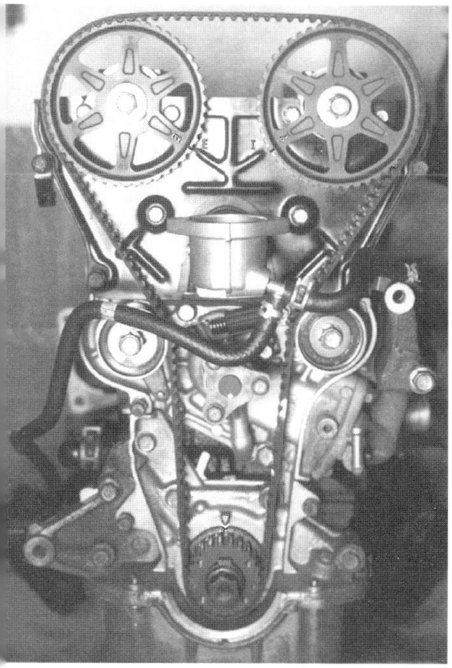

9/97b How it should look.

97 Check that the cam drivebelt is correctly tensioned by placing a straightedge on the top of the cam belt where it stretches between the two cam pulleys and then, using the T-bar of a socket set, press the cam drivebelt down between the two pulleys and measure how far the cam belt can be deflected from the straightedge. With a pressure of 10 kg or 22 lb applied, the cam belt deflection should be 9-11.5 mm /0.35-0.45 inch. If necessary, repeat the tensioning procedure.

CAMSHAFT DRIVEBELT COVERS, WATER PUMP PULLEY & CRANKSHAFT PULLEY INSTALLATION

98 Start by fitting the lowest cover first. Slide the section of the cover that covers the cam drivebelt jockey wheel into place between the jockey wheel and the power steering pump mounting bracket. You will then find that the rest of the cover can be swung around the boss of the water pump and into position. Engage the protecting spigots of the cover into the bolt holes of the water pump body.

99 Before fixing the lower cover in position, slide the center cover over the water pump center boss and engage it with the bottom cover, then fit the four 10 mm headed retaining bolts that secure both covers and tighten them with a box end wrench using finger tip pressure only. Note that the bolt which fits closest to the water pump central boss is longer than the other three.

100 Fit the top section of the cover in place, flexing it just a little to clear the thermostat housing body. Note: the cover is held by four 10 mm bolts and the bolt at bottom left and the bolt at top right both also secure pipe/cable clips. If the small bore water pipe from the thermostat housing to the water inlet on the left-hand side of the cylinder block was detached for any reason, it should now

9/100 Covers refitted.

9/101 Cam drivebelt guide and spacer.

be reconnected and placed in its clip alongside the power steering pump bracket.

101 Fitting the crankshaft pulley. Before fitting the pulley itself, there is a cam drivebelt guide plate and, on our car, a thin spacer, to go between the cam belt pulley and the back of the large V-belt pulley which is to be fitted. Install the belt guide plate, dished side facing outward, then the spacer: engage the cutouts of both with the square boss on the toothed pulley.

102 Fit the large V-belt pulley over the crankshaft nose, engaging its cutout with the square shaped boss. Then fit the large washer through which the four pulley retaining bolts pass, once again making sure the large washer engages with the square boss.

103 Place a drop of thread locking fluid on each of the four 10 mm pulley retaining bolts and screw them home to a torque of 15 Nm /1.50 kgf m /140 lbf ft. If the engine's out of the car you can lock the crankshaft, either by wedging a screwdriver into the teeth of the flywheel ring gear as described before or, alternatively, by looping the power steering pump drivebelt around the crankshaft pulley and gripping it tightly. Of course, if the

9/102 Tighten pulley retaining bolts.

engine's in the car, you only need to engage a gear and apply the parking brake.

104 Fitting the water pump pulley. Place the water pump pulley on the flange of the water pump, noting that the recessed side of the pulley should face toward the engine. Put a drop of thread lock on each of the three retaining bolts and then tighten them to a torque of 9 Nm /90 kgf cm /85 lbf in - about finger tip pressure tight using a box end spanner. You can lock the pulley to tighten the bolts by wrapping the drivebelt around the pulley and gripping the belt firmly in one hand.

CAMBOX COVER INSTALLATION

105 Apply beads of silicone sealant in the corners of the crank-angle sensor housing and the two front camshaft bearing cap shrouds, as shown.

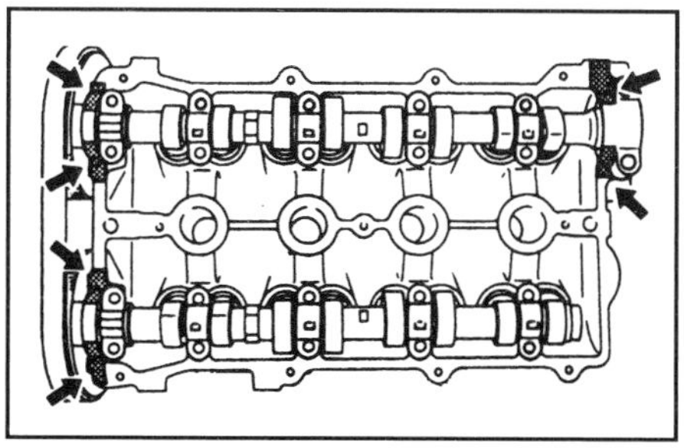

D9/105 APPLY SEALANT AS SHOWN.

Allow the silicone sealant to harden for at least five minutes before fitting the cover.

106 Fit a new seal into the groove on the underside of the cambox cover. This is a complex seal which also encompasses sealing for the spark plug access tubes.

107 Douse all of the camshaft lobes with oil and then lower the cambox cover into place. Make sure the front of the cambox cover engages prop-

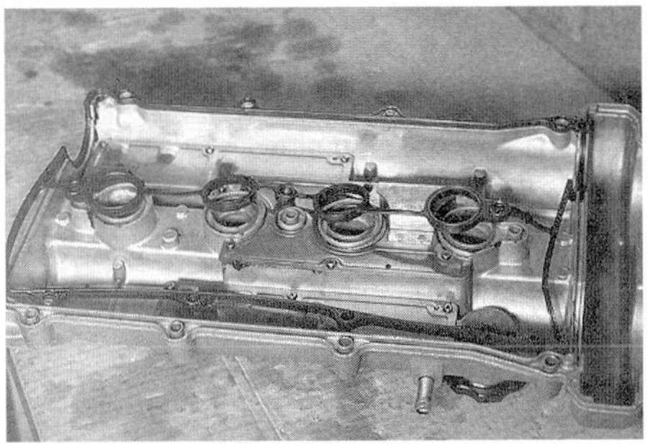

9/106 Fit a new seal to the cambox cover.

erly with the top of the cam drivebelt cover on the front of the cylinder head. Tighten the eleven 10 mm dome-headed bolts to a torque of 7 Nm /70 kgf cm /55 lbf in.

108 If you don't have a torque wrench that reads this low you'll find that moderate finger pressure against a spanner is sufficient and will compress the rubber seal enough to seal the cambox. It is suggested you tighten the cambox cover retaining bolts in three stages, working in an outward spiral from the center bolt.

THERMOSTAT & THERMOSTAT HOUSING COVER INSTALLATION

109 Lower the thermostat into the thermostat housing and make sure the thermostat center lip sits down in the recess in the housing. The part of the thermostat with the spring should be downward.

110 Fit a new gasket to the housing and note that on one side of the gasket there is a thin plastic ring. This should be positioned to lie on top of the thermostat flange. No gasket cement should be necessary if both sealing flanges have been thoroughly cleaned. Fit the thermostat housing cover,

9/109 Lower thermostat into place.

and tighten the two 12 mm retaining bolts to a torque of 22 Nm /2.3 kgf m /17 lbf ft. Note: the bolt on the right-hand side of the housing should also retain a hose clip.

111 Turn the engine so that you can work on the left-hand side.

ENGINE MOUNTING BRACKET (LEFT-HAND) INSTALLATION

112 These brackets are handed so there can be no confusion as to which side of the engine

9/112 Fit engine mounting bracket.

they fit. The bracket is retained by three 14 mm bolts which should be tightened to a torque of 50 Nm /5 kgf m /36 lbf ft. Note: engine installation may be easier if the installation of this bracket is left until the engine is in place.

POWER STEERING PUMP BRACKET INSTALLATION

113 The power steering pump bracket is fixed to the left-hand side of the cylinder block by three 14 mm bolts, which should be tightened to a torque of 50 Nm /5 kgf m /36 lbf ft.

114 Once the three securing bolts have been torqued the pivot pin spacer can be driven back into its correct position in the bracket. Oil the section of the spacer which will slide into the bracket. Fit the pivot bolt through the front eye of the mounting, screw its retaining nut on backwards so that the washer surface is facing the spacer and then screw the nut fully up the threaded section until it jams against the unthreaded portion of the bolt.

115 The bolt can now be used as a drift to push the spacer back into its housing in the bracket. Hit the head of the bolt with a nylon or copper-

9/115 Install spacer in original position.

faced hammer and drift the spacer home slowly until the position mark made before removal aligns once more with the bracket.

COOLANT INLET CASTING INSTALLATION

116 Hold a new gasket over the water inlet casting flange and then pass the two 12 mm bolts through the holes in the flange to hold the gasket in position. Fit the casting to the water pump inlet and tighten the retaining bolts to a torque of 22 Nm /2.2 kgf m /17 lbf ft. No gasket cement should be necessary if the water pump and inlet pipe flanges are clean and free of all old gasket material. Note: for the moment, leave the metal bypass pipe free.

EXHAUST MANIFOLD, HEATSHIELD & OXYGEN SENSOR INSTALLATION

117 First, position a new metal gasket over the exhaust manifold studs. The gasket is actually made of three separate pieces of metal spot-welded at one point so that the three parts are held together in the correct order. One side of the gasket is totally flat, whilst the other has indentations around the portholes. The flat side should be against the

9/117 Fit a new manifold gasket.

cylinder head. Once again, if the mating faces are completely clean and free of old gasket material no gasket cement will be needed.

118 Screw on the nine 14 mm nuts which retain the manifold, not forgetting to put the wate bypass pipe bracket in place on the relevant ex haust manifold stud first. The nuts are all 14 mm and should be tightened to a torque of 42 Nm /4. kgf m /32 lbf ft. Once the nuts are pinched up do th final torquing in a sequence that spirals outwar from the central nut.

119 Place the exhaust manifold heatshiel

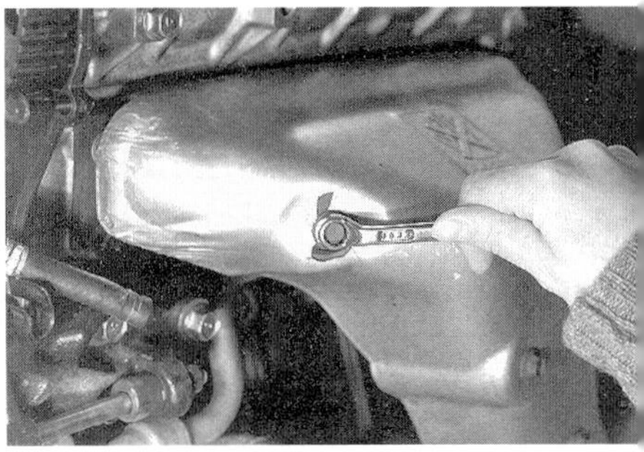

9/119 Fit exhaust heatshield.

in position over the manifold and then, having pu a dab of copper-based grease on the threads c each, replace the four bolts which secure the shiel in position. Tighten the bolts with a box en wrench and finger tip pressure only. Note that o our low mileage engine the heatshield was broke and cracked around the foremost top retainin bolt. If this is a common problem and your engin is worse affected than ours, you could conside placing a large diameter washer under the bolt t make sure it continues to grip the shield.

120 Fitting oxygen sensor. Smear a trace

9/120 Fit oxygen sensor.

copper-based grease on the threads of the oxygen sensor body. Wind up the electrical wire a little - as the sensor doesn't rotate independently of the cable - and then screw the sensor home into its exhaust manifold housing. Tighten the sensor body with a 22 mm crescent wrench. Finally, clip the sensor wire into the spring clip on the left-hand side of the engine backplate, just above the dipstick tube bracket.

DIPSTICK TUBE INSTALLATION

121 Fit a new rubber seal ring over the end

9/121 Fit new sealing ring to dipstick tube.

of the dipstick tube and then smear it with engine oil. Gently push the tube into its recess in the oil pan until you feel the seal slide into position and the tube support bracket stud aligns with, and passes through, its hole in the engine backplate. Put a blob of thread lock on the stud and tighten its 10 mm retaining nut with a box end wrench and finger tip pressure only. Fit the dipstick in its tube.

LIFTING EYE (LEFT-HAND) INSTALLATION

122 Fit the silver painted engine lifting eye to the front left-hand side of the cylinder head. Note that the tangs at the base of the bracket should face inward, toward the cylinder head, and that the retaining 14 mm bolt should be torqued to 44 Nm /4.5 kgf m/34 lbf ft.

123 Turn the engine so you can work on the back.

CLUTCH COVER & DISC INSTALLATION

124 Place the disc on the friction surface of the cover with the protruding side of the disc facing the diaphragm. Hold both together by inserting a finger from the back of the coverplate.

125 Push the clutch assembly against the fly-

9/124 Fit clutch disc and cover.

wheel face and locate it in position over the pins projecting from the flywheel. Fit the six cover retaining bolts and finger-tighten.

126 The next bit can be tricky! It's important that the splined center hub of the disc is centered in relation to the pilot/spigot bearing so that the transmission input shaft slides through the former into the latter - otherwise installing the transmission will be difficult. Whilst the cover retaining bolts are only finger-tight you'll still be able to move the disc, so now's the time to get it right. You can buy or hire a universal mandrel designed

9/126 Align disc carefully ...

for clutch centering then simply select sleeves suitable to fit the pilot bearing and clutch hub: move the disc around until the mandrel slides into place easily. If you don't have a mandrel align the disc by eye as we did. Using one eye only ensure that the disc hub and pilot bearing are concentric with the ring formed by the diaphragm spring fingers.

127 When you're satisfied that the disc is centered, tighten the 12 mm cover retaining bolts in a diagonal sequence, and in a minimum of three stages, to a torque of 22 Nm /2.2 kgf m/17 lbf ft. To lock the flywheel, temporarily install a bellhousing bolt then use a screwdriver wedged against the bolt

9/127 ... then torque tighten retaining bolts.

9/128 Fit water outlet cover.

and into the ring gear teeth.

HEATER OUTLET COVER INSTALLATION

128 Fit a new gasket over the stud protruding from the water outlet in the rear of the cylinder head - no gasket cement is needed. Fit the cover in place, screw in the one retaining bolt and fit the nut on the projecting stud. Tighten both 12 mm nut and bolt to 22 Nm /2.2 kgf m/17 lbf ft.

CRANK-ANGLE SENSOR INSTALLATION

129 Look at the back end of the intake

9/129a Correct cam position.

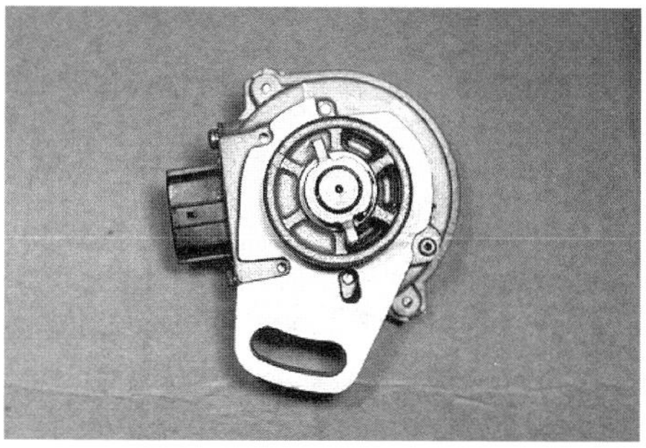

9/129b Offset dogs on angle sensor.

camshaft and see how the cutouts which drive the angle sensor are angled. If you have just installed the cam drivebelt and the engine has not been turned since, then the slot in the rear end of the intake camshaft should be vertical. You'll find that the drive dogs on the spindle of the crank-angle sensor are slightly offset, which means that it will only fit into its recess when it has the correct relationship with the camshaft and therefore cannot be fitted 180 degrees out.

130 Fit a new rubber oil seal into the groove in the sensor boss and lubricate the seal and the drive

dogs with a little engine oil. Set the drive dogs to match the slots in the cam and then slide the angle sensor into position: if it won't go home with a little to-and-fro twisting, then pull it out and rotate the drive spindle 180 degrees and try again. Once the drive dogs engage the rear of the camshaft , push the angle sensor body fully home against the rear of the cylinder head and loosely install the retaining bolt.

131 If you marked the relationship of the crank-angle sensor body to the cylinder head, realign the marks and tighten the 12 mm lock bolt to a torque of 22 Nm /2.2 kgf m/17 lbf ft.

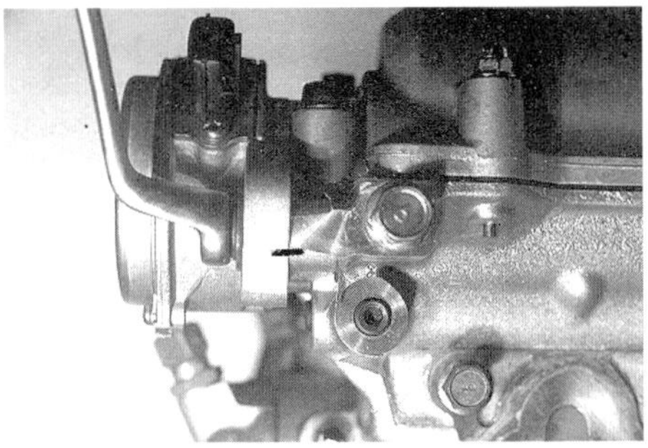

9/131 Align marks and tighten bolt.

132 If you didn't mark the setting of the crank-angle sensor, then set it in mid position and follow the ignition timing adjustment procedure: ☞ 5.

IGNITION COIL & HIGH-TENSION LEADS INSTALLATION

Note: If you intend to install the engine and transmission as a single unit, consider leaving the fitting of the coil unit until after the engine is back in place, otherwise you'll find that the coil unit hits the engine compartment firewall/bulkhead because of the acute angle taken by the engine/transmission assembly during installation.

133 Fit the coil assembly in position on the back of the cylinder head and replace the two 12 mm headed bolts which hold the coil bracket to the top rear of the cambox cover. There is a further 12 mm bolt underneath the coil assembly and this, too, needs to be installed. Tighten the bolts to a torque of 22 Nm /12.2 kgf m/17 lbf ft.

134 For the moment leave the HT leads and connectors loose on top of the cambox.

135 If necessary, turn the whole engine so that you can work on the right-hand side.

ENGINE MOUNTING BRACKET (RIGHT-HAND) INSTALLATION

136 The bracket is retained by three 14 mm bolts which are of three different lengths. The shortest bolt should be at the front of the bracket in the lowest position and the longest bolt in the topmost position. For the moment leave the top bolt loosely threaded, but tighten the two lower bolts to a torque of 50 Nm /5 kgf m/36 lbf ft.

OIL PRESSURE GAUGE SENDER UNIT INSTALLATION

137 The oil pressure gauge sender unit screws into a threaded drilling on the right-hand side of the cylinder block immediately adjacent to a core plug and just slightly above, and to the left of, the oil filter boss.

138 Using your fingers screw the sensor body into the drilling. Do the final tightening with a 17 mm crescent wrench bearing on the hexagonal section of the sensor just above the threaded stem. **Caution!** Do not try to tighten the sensor by using the hexagonal section just below the electrical connector blade.

ALTERNATOR BRACKET INSTALLATION

139 Position the alternator bracket at the

9/139 Torque tighten bracket bolts.

front right-hand side of the cylinder block, just beneath the cylinder head, and install the two 17 mm bolts. Note: don't forget the clip which is located under the head of the rearmost alternator bracket bolt. Tighten the bolts to a torque of 50 Nm /5 kgf m/36 lbf ft.

INTAKE MANIFOLD & SUPPORT BRACKET INSTALLATION

140 Fit a new gasket over the three studs projecting from the side of the cylinder head. Note that the gasket must be fitted so that the portion

9/140 Fit new manifold gasket.

which surrounds the water jacket opening between intakes three and four is correctly positioned. No gasket cement is necessary if the sealing faces of cylinder head and intake manifold are both thoroughly clean and free of all traces of old gasket.

141 Gently slide the intake manifold into position over the three projecting studs and secure by fitting and finger-tightening the three 12 mm nuts.

142 Fit the six 12 mm-headed manifold retaining bolts, some of which are tricky to install although there is access between the individual manifold tracts. All the nuts and bolts should be tight-

9/143 Torque tighten support bracket bolt.

ened in three stages using a sequence that spirals outward from the center bolts. Note: you'll need a universal joint and extension bar to tighten the two bolts closest to the pillars supporting the fuel rail. Tighten all nuts and bolts to a final torque of 22 Nm /2.2 kgf m/17 lbf ft.

143 The manifold support bracket is secured by two 14 mm bolts, the longer of which goes at the top of the bracket. Tighten the bolts to a torque of 50 Nm /5 kgf m/36 lbf ft.

FUEL INJECTORS & FUEL RAIL INSTALLATION

144 Fit the four new insulating seal rings into the fuel injector apertures in the manifold flange. Fit the two locating collars in the tops of the fuel rail support pillars. Feed the fuel feed and return pipes down between intake tracts one and two and three and four. Tuck the wiring loom injector connector blocks out of the way and carefully lower the fuel rail into position, gently feeding each injector's nose into its port. It will seem a bit of a fiddle, but with a little gentle maneuvering and pressure you'll find that the fuel rail suddenly slips into place and you can guide the injectors home. Make sure that neither the insulator rings nor the rail locating collars are knocked out of position during this process. As soon as all of the injectors and the fuel rail sit down into their respective seats, install the two 12 mm headed bolts that secure the fuel rail to the support pillars on the intake manifold. Tighten the two 12 mm bolts to 2 Nm /2.2 kgf m/17 lbf ft. **Warning!** Do not overtighten - a damaged rail insulators or seals could allow fuel leakage.

145 Reconnect the vacuum hose from the valve on the rear of the fuel rail to the adjacent stub at the top rear of the intake manifold.

146 Connect the four terminals of the injection system wiring loom to the blue male connectors on each injector. Start at the rear end of the engine with the shortest spur and move forward to the second shortest, and so on - an audible click indicates the connection is properly made.

AIRVALVE INSTALLATION

147 Fit the airvalve to the side of the intake manifold, having first checked that its rubber seal is still resilient and intact. Tighten the four retaining bolts with an 8 mm wrench/spanner or socket using modest finger pressure only.

148 Once the airvalve has been installed, reconnect the small diameter coolant pipe that comes

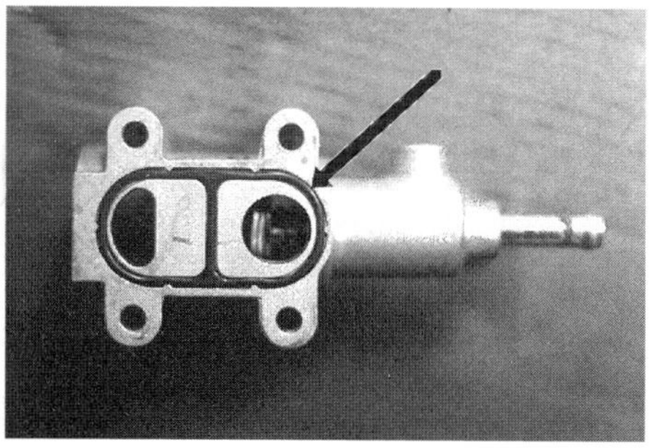

9/147 Check airvalve's seal.

from the ISC valve beneath the throttle body to the stub that projects forward from the central part of the airvalve. Spread a little silicone lubricating fluid over the stub before pushing on the pipe. Once the pipe is in place, grab the ears of the pipe clip with a pair of pliers and return the clip to its original position, squeezing its body for added security.

149 Repeat this process with the second small diameter coolant hose coming from the thermostat housing body, ensuring that the hose is also safely clipped into the small bracket on the right-hand side of the cambox. Make sure the bracket is not going to chafe the hose, which it can do if badly positioned.

PCV HOSE INSTALLATION

150 Fit the short length of hose that connects the stub just behind the airvalve on the intake manifold to the PCV (Positive Crankcase Ventilation) valve body located in the side of the cambox. Close the ears of both hose clips and move them into their original positions. Squeeze the clip bodies after positioning for extra security.

OIL FILTER INSTALLATION

151 The filter canister screws onto a projecting boss on the right-hand side of the cylinder block behind the aluminum manifold support bracket.

152 Take the new oil filter and smear engine oil around the sealing ring in its face. Screw the filter fully home by hand only.

STARTER MOTOR INSTALLATION

153 Slide the nose of the starter motor through the hole in the backplate until the front face of the starter motor body closes right up to the backplate: the hole in the starter motor bracket should be in alignment with the bolt hole in the engine mounting bracket. Fit the 14 mm retaining bolt through the starter motor rear bracket and engine mounting bracket and tighten to a torque of 50 Nm /5 kgf m/ 36 lbf ft.

ALTERNATOR INSTALLATION

154 Slide the alternator mounting lugs over the projecting bosses of the cylinder block and oil pump. It may be quite a tight fit and you may need to work the alternator to-and-fro until it slides fully into position. Once the pivot pin holes in the mounting and boss line up, smear the pivot bolt with grease and push it home from the front of the alternator. Finger tighten the bolt retaining nut for the time being.

155 With the pivot bolt in place, push the alternator body right up against the side of the cylinder block. This will allow the alternator drivebelt to be fitted over the alternator, water pump and crankshaft pulleys.

156 Install the threaded sliding block which contains both adjuster and lock bolts, noting that the axis of the lock bolt (which passes through the adjustment slot in the alternator bracket) should be lower than the axis of the adjuster bolt. To retain the sliding block, tighten the lock bolt with your fingers until the alternator is just free to slide back

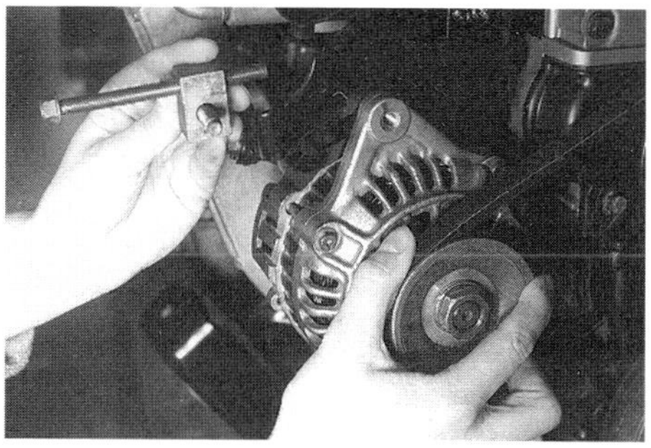

9/156 Fit alternator adjuster block.

9/159 Fit engine lifting eye.

and forth along the adjustment slot.

157 The adjustment bolt head should have dropped into its recess in the bracket. Tighten the 12 mm adjuster bolt with a until there's about 12 mm/half an inch of deflection when strong thumb pressure is applied to the belt midway between the water pump and alternator pulleys.

158 Tighten the 12 mm alternator pivot bolt and 12 mm nut and the 14 mm locking bolt at the top of the alternator.

ENGINE LIFTING EYE (RIGHT-HAND) INSTALLATION

159 Fit the black painted engine lifting eye with its integral bracket to the rear of the cylinder head on the right-hand side of the engine. The eye should be vertical and the two tangs in its bottom edge should face inward toward the cylinder head. Tighten the retaining bolt to a torque of 44 Nm /4.5 kgf m/34 lbf ft.

10. TRANSMISSION - FITTING TO ENGINE (OUT OF CAR)

☞ First read 1/1, 2.

1 Manual transmission only. Spread a thin smear of copper-based lubricant on the nose and splines of the transmission input shaft - don't overdo it!

2 Manual transmission only. Bring the engine and transmission unit together, making sure that the transmission input shaft enters the center of the clutch and that the bellhousing is correctly lined up with the engine backplate. If the clutch disc has been well centered, the transmission bellhousing should go fully home against the engine backplate with no more than a little joggling around. Life will be more difficult if the clutch disc has not been well centered and, in extreme cases, you'll have to withdraw the transmission, slacken the clutch cover plate and re-center the friction disc before attempting again to make the transmission fit. Once the transmission bellhousing slides fully home, make sure it engages on the hollow spigots projecting from the rear of the cylinder block.

3 Automatic transmission only. Bring the engine and transmission unit together, making sure that the bellhousing is correctly lined up with the engine backplate. Once the transmission bellhousing slides fully home, make sure it engages on the hollow spigots projecting from the rear of the cylinder block.

4 Fit the two topmost bellhousing bolts which are 17 mm (x 60 mm) and screw them into place finger-tight. This will be enough to stop the transmission coming away from the back of the engine.

5 With the help of an assistant, tilt the whole engine/transmission unit a little to one side and then the other, in order to allow the fitting of the two lowermost 17 mm (x 60 mm) bolts which, again, should be screwed in finger-tight at this stage.

6 Position the exhaust pipe support bracket over the two bolt holes on the left-hand side of the bellhousing. Secure the bracket, with flange facing rearward, with two 17 mm bolts, the upper of which is longer at 70 mm, although there seems no good reason for this. Screw the bolts home finger-tight. Note: the remaining fasteners in the starter motor area will be fitted later.

7 Tighten all of the 17 mm bellhousing bolts to 80 Nm /8 kgf m/58 lbf ft.

11. ENGINE & TRANSMISSION - INSTALLATION AS A UNIT

☞ First read 1/1, 2.

1 **Caution!** Check that the engine bay is clear and that all pipes, wires and cables are tied back out of the way so that the engine and transmission unit will not become entangled as they pass through the engine compartment. This particularly applies to the clutch flexible hydraulic pipe (right-hand drive cars with manual transmission) which runs across the top of the bellhousing and shares a clip with the main wiring loom. Tie this bracket high up on the right of the compartment. As with engine removal, the car will need to be raised and securely supported high enough above the ground to give good access to the underside: ☞ 1/3.

2 Spread old towels over the nose of the car and the fender (wing) tops: this will help to protect the paintwork from accidental damage.

3 You'll need at least one assistant to help you install the engine and transmission units as an assembly, as well as a small mobile engine crane of the type that can be hired from the tool and plant hire companies you find in every medium-sized and bigger town. **Warning!** Sorry, we weren't able to weigh them, but we believe the engine and transmission together weigh up to 181 kg (400 lb) so the rope and crane you use should be capable of lifting twice this weight as a safety margin. Also, the lifting hook of the crane's boom should be capable of reaching a height of around 1830 mm (6 ft) above the ground.

4 Tie several strands of very strong nylon rope tightly between the two lifting eyes positioned on each side of the cylinder head, one toward the front of the engine and one toward the back. It's important to keep the rope as tight as possible; you'll be surprised how much the rope will stretch once the crane takes the strain.

5 Engage the crane's hook with the rope sling and lift the engine/transmission unit far enough from the ground to clear the front edge of the engine compartment opening. Line the crane and engine up in front of the car.

6 With an assistant holding the transmission tailshaft extension to stop the engine/transmission unit swaying, gently roll the crane forward until the tailshaft end is approximately over the center of the engine compartment. Now, the transmission end of the unit needs to be pushed downward to achieve the steepest angle possible, as the engine/transmission is simultaneously pushed further back into the compartment and lowered. **Caution!** Take great care not to crush or snag any components, pipework, etc.

11/4 Lift engine & transmission from bench.

7 Once the rear of the cylinder head gets close to the firewall/bulkhead - put an old towel or similar between the two - begin to level up the engine/transmission unit. (**Caution!** If the coil and crank-angle sensor units are fitted, take great care not to bang them against the firewall). Levelling the unit will allow you to push the whole thing further into the compartment as the transmission moves beneath the floorpan.

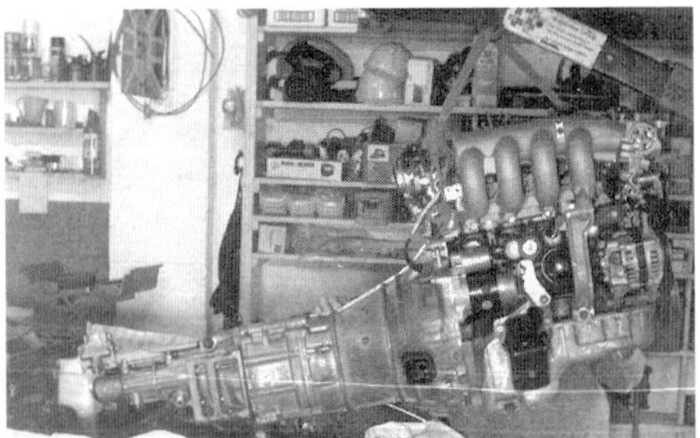

11/6a Position over car ...

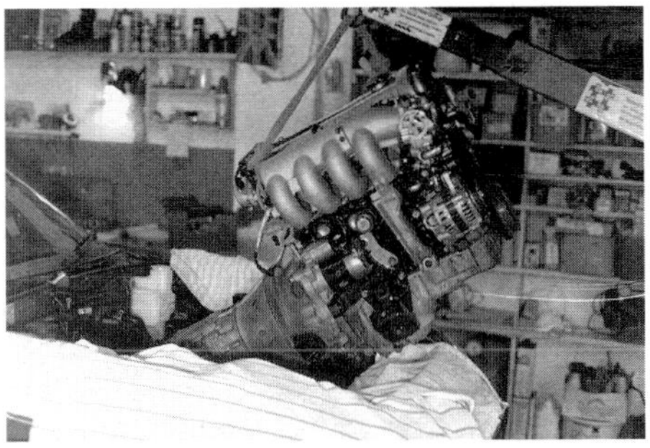

11/6b ... and lower very carefully ...

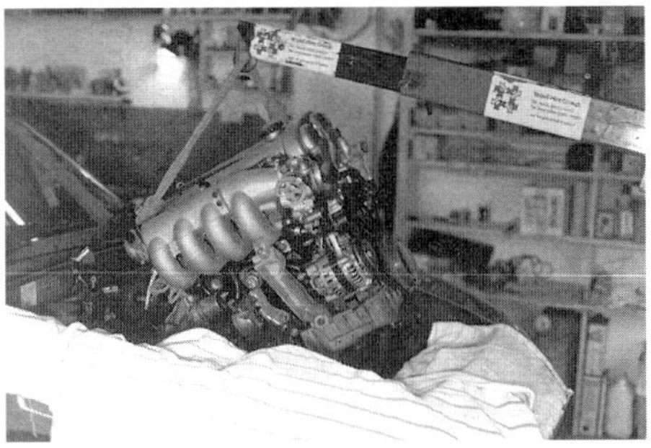

11/6c ... into position.

8 When the engine/transmission unit is almost in final position it can be carefully maneuvered until the studs protruding from the engine mountings pass through the hole and slot in the subframe. Note: you may find it necessary, as we did, to remove the left-hand engine mounting bracket from the engine and to fasten the mounting to the subframe independently of the engine. This allowed us to maneuver the engine sufficiently to engage the stud of the right-hand mounting in its slot, at which point the retaining nut and washer were immediately screwed into place. Then, the engine was twisted and lowered until the mounting bracket on the left-hand side aligned once more with the bolt holes in the side of the engine. The three bolts were fitted and tightened to a torque of 45 Nm /4.5 kgf m/34 lbf ft. As the engine reached its final location, we also found it helpful (manual transmission cars only) to tie the transmission tailshaft extension to a crossbar bridging the gearshift lever hole in the transmission tunnel so that the transmission end of the unit was held as high as possible, but was still free to move backwards and forwards a little. You can, of course, use a wheeled jack to support the transmission as it moves backwards. Note: if you do leave both engine mountings in place on the engine during installation, you wil need to push the studs the last 13 mm (half inch), or so, toward their holes with a long screwdriver o similar, but you're going to find it a tricky task. Taking the mounting bracket off will save a lot o sweat and swearing ...

11/8 Rope sling for transmission.

9 Once the engine is sitting safely on its mountings, the crane can be released and withdrawn.

10 Temporarily, lower the jack or rope sling supporting the transmission unit. Above the transmission case you'll see that several wires sprout from the main loom (four connectors man trans./six connectors auto. trans.), these are the connectors for the sensors and switches mounted in the transmission outer casing. You'll see tha they have different types of connector so there car be no confusion over which connections are fo which switch or sensor and, as the switches with two wires simply complete a circuit, it doesn' matter which way round the two wires for each ar connected; but do make sure all the connector click securely into place.

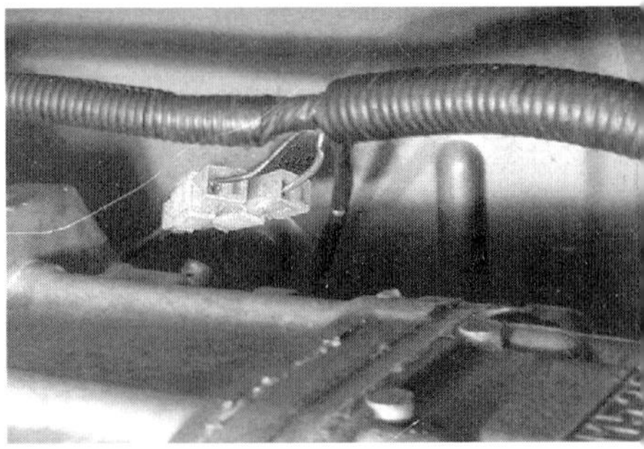

11/10 Remake transmission's wiring connections.

11 From beneath the car put the PPF in place by sliding it forward onto its mounting on the righ side of the transmission, then pushing it up around the side of the differential unit until it slides onto it mounting. Note: you may have to lift the propshaf flange end of the differential slightly to get the PPF to slide into engagement. The end of the PPF frame with round drillings is the differential end.

12 With the PPF roughly positioned, insta the two 17 mm-headed bolts that pass through th lower flange of the PPF, up through the transmission casing and then screw into the top flange of th PPF. For the moment, these bolts should be le finger-tight.

13 Move to the rear end of the PPF an install the 17 mm through bolts that clamp the PP to the side of the differential casing. Fit the bo without a collar first, followed by the bolt with th collar. It's suggested that you spray the shanks c both bolts with WD40 or similar silicone-base lubricant as they seem prone to corrosion. Yo may need to lift the nose of the diff. casing a little t align the holes in the differential casing and th

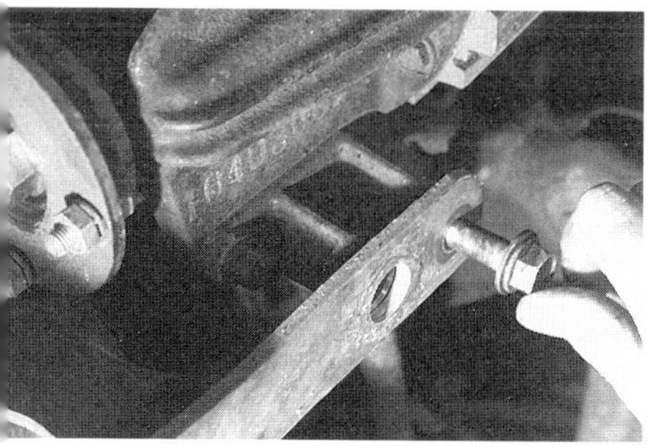

11/13 Fit PPF through bolts.

PPF. Tighten the two bolts snugly but not fully at this stage.

14 Move once again to the forward end of the PPF and install the transmission extension housing support bracket between the PPF and the tailhousing of the transmission. If there's a rope supporting the transmission and it's in the way, you should remove it before installing the bracket. Hold the bracket in place above the lower flange of the PPF and finger-tighten the 17 mm retaining bolt. Insert the two 14 mm bolts that secure the bracket to the transmission tailshaft and, once again, tighten

11/14 Install transmission bracket.

them finger-tight. You may need to lift the tail of the transmission slightly to make the bracket align with the threaded holes in the transmission casing. Tighten the two 17 mm PPF to transmission side bolts to a torque of 115 Nm /11.5 kgf m/85 lbf ft.

15 Next, tighten the PPF to differential 17 mm side bolts to the same torque. Make sure the collar on the forward bolt is properly engaged in the recess in the PPF.

16 Move to the tailshaft support bracket and tighten the 17 mm bolts to the same torque as the other 17 mm bolts. Then tighten the bracket's 14 mm bolts to a final torque of 45 Nm /4.5 kgf m/35 lbf ft.

17 From within the engine compartment release the wires, brackets, etc., for the bellhousing area which were tied out of harm's way. Then, from beneath the car, position the two wiring loom brackets (one of which also carries a pipe clip on manual transmission cars) toward the top right-hand side of the bellhousing. This is fiddly as there's not enough room to swing a mouse, let alone a cat, but a little perseverance will pay dividends. Once the brackets are in place, fix by fitting the 14 mm retaining bolts finger-tight; the outer of these bolts also secures the starter motor.

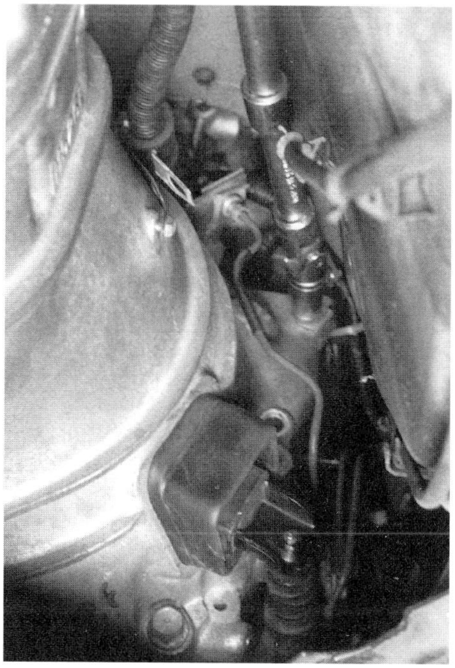

11/17 Fit bracket bolt.

Whilst in the vicinity, install the 14 mm bolt and nut which also secures the starter motor.

18 Manual trans only. Place a dab of molybdenum disulfide or copper-based grease on the ball end of the release cylinder pushrod. Engage the ball with the recess in the clutch operating arm and pull the body of the release cylinder toward the clutch operating arm until the two release cylinder retaining screws can be got into place and engaged with their threads in the bellhousing. This is pretty fiddly if you're lying on your back, but a little patience will see it done one bolt at a time.

19 Before tightening the clutch release cylinder retaining bolts, fit the bracket that holds the coiled loop of the rigid hydraulic pipe which connects to the release cylinder. This is most easily done by reaching down from above through the engine compartment and pushing the long 17 mm bolt through the bracket, then through the bellhousing and finally screwing the nut on the back of the bolt with your fingers. The procedure for fitting this bolt and nut will be the same for auto trans cars.

20 From beneath the car tighten the various bellhousing bolts fitted during the last few steps. Tighten 17 mm fasteners to 80 Nm /8 kgf m/60 lbf ft and the 14 mm fasteners to 45 Nm /4.5 kgf m/57 lbf ft. Note: access to these fasteners is not easy so you'll need an appropriate socket attached to a universal joint in turn attached to extensions of around 350 mm (14 in) and then a ratchet handle. A couple of these bolts also have nuts and the nut or bolt head on the engine side can be locked with a wrench/spanner via the opening in the inner wheelwell.

21 Manual transmission cars. Next, the two 12 mm clutch release cylinder retaining bolts (manual transmission cars) should be tightened. The upper bolt can be accessed through the hole in the inner wheelwell using socket, universal joint, 250 mm (10 inch) extension bar and ratchet handle. The lower bolt can be tightened only with an open-ended spanner. Correct torque is 22 Nm /2.2 kgf m/16 lbf ft.

22 Automatic transmission cars: ☞ 4/9/8, 11-13.

23 Start to secure the loom by fixing its support bracket to the side of the transmission with the short, self-tapping screw provided.

24 Work your way along the PPF, pushing each loom retaining clip into place as you go. Note that the first clip, at the engine end, is at the top of the PPF and the second clip about halfway down the side of the frame. The following clips run along the frame about two thirds of the way down on the right-hand side, whilst the last two clips, at the axle end of the PPF, are at the top.

25 Toward the rear end of the PPF there is a ground/earth wire sprouting from the loom which should be re-secured to the PPF by tightening its 10 mm retaining bolt. Note: before fastening the ground/earth strap clean the eye and the contact area of the PPF with emery paper. Smear both with petroleum jelly (Vaseline) and then replace and tighten the screw.

26 Whilst you're in the area, pass the end

11/25 Fit ground wire to PPF.

11/26 Fit speedo drive cable.

of the speedo drive cable through the first slot in the PPF and screw the knurled retaining nut home onto the speedo drive gear housing. Note: you may have difficulty in engaging the end of the speedo cable: if so, simply rotate it with your fingers a few degrees at a time until it slips home into the drive gear. Finger-tightness is enough for the knurled nut.

27 Rub engine oil over the section of the propshaft that enters the transmission tailhousing and engages with the transmission mainshaft splines. This ensures that the transmission tailshaft oil seal

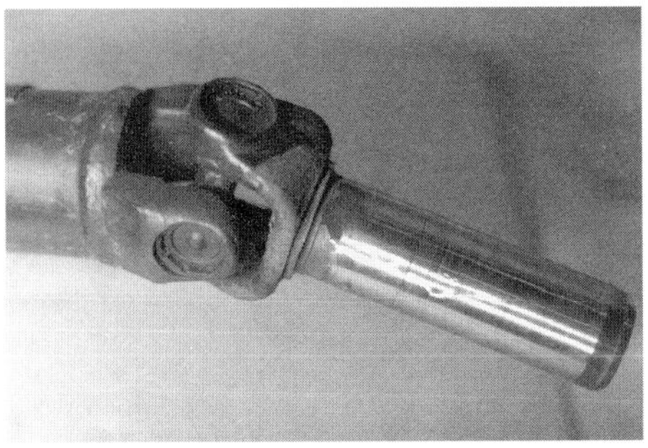

11/27 Lubricate propshaft nose.

is well lubricated.

28 Slide the front end of the propshaft into the tail end of the transmission unit: you may have to rotate the propshaft just a little to allow the splines to engage. Then, lift up the rear end of the propshaft and engage its flange with the differential drive flange, lining up the marks you made when the propshaft was removed. Install the four 12 mm bolts and 14 mm nuts (nuts toward the front of the car) and tighten to a torque of 29 Nm /2.9 kgf m/ 21 lbf ft. **Warning!** If the spring washers show any signs of having become flattened, they should be renewed. Note: you'll need to apply the parking brake (handbrake) if the rear wheels are off the ground in order to stop the propshaft rotating when you try to torque the nuts.

29 Automatic transmission cars only: reconnect the shift lever to the shaft in the transmission casing and secure with nut and washer; tighten the nut with a wrench/spanner and finger pressure only.

30 Tighten both engine mounting retaining nuts from beneath the car after making sure their spring washers are still in good shape. The correct torque for the 14 mm nuts is 70 Nm /7 kgf m/50 lbf ft. You'll need a 125 mm (5 inch) extension behind the socket in order to reach into the subframe turret in which the nut is housed.

31 Now's a good time to refill the transmission with oil if it has been emptied. Manual transmission: first check that the 24 mm drain plug is tight, then remove the filler plug halfway up the left-hand side of the transmission case. Add 2 liters (0.43 Imp gal/0.52 US gal) of the approved gear oil and then replace and tighten the filler plug. If the transmission oil was not emptied, check oil level and top up as necessary. Automatic transmission: for the moment, just check that the oil pan securing bolts have been retightened.

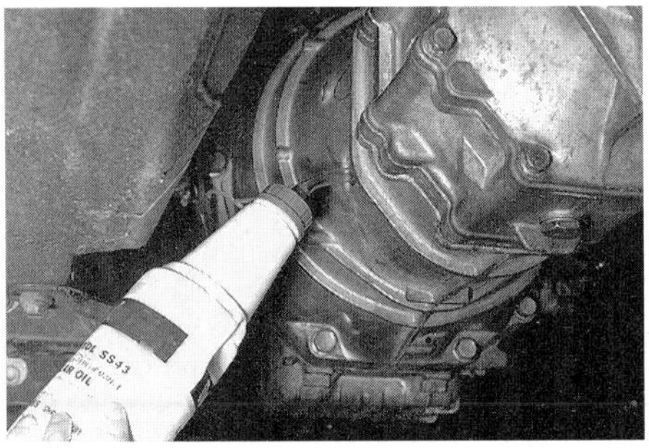

11/31 Fill transmission with oil to level hole.

32 The next task is to install the whole exhaust system: ☞ 5/38. After smearing its threads with copper-based grease install the 12 mm bolt that fixes the exhaust pipe clamp to the bracket on the side of the bellhousing. The bolt can be inserted and tightened through the gap between the subframe and chassis rail in the left-hand front wheelwell. Torque the bolt to 24 Nm /2.4 kgfm /17 lbf ft.

33 That concludes most of the installation work beneath the car, but don't lower it to the ground yet! Move to the left-hand side of the engine compartment, working from above.

34 Reconnect the two heater hoses, either to their junctions on the bulkhead or at the engine. The pipe on the left connects with the extension from the main water inlet, which runs along the left-hand side of the engine and exits behind the exhaust manifold, whilst the pipe on the right connects with the heater outlet at the back of the cylinder head. Clean all unions with a little wire wool or one of those nylon abrasive pads you can buy for scrubbing household pots. Then spray with WD40 or similar as this will make installation of hoses much simpler.

35 Note: if possible, return clips to their exact

11/34 Reconnect heater hoses.

original positions and squeeze their bodies with a pair of pliers to make sure that they are as securely fitted as possible. If the clips have been re-used more than twice it is recommended that you replace them, either with the same self-tightening type or with worm drive hose clips. Note that the original heater hoses have white dots to indicate the end that fits the bulkhead and the dots also represent the top of the hose.

36 Whilst in the area reconnect the short ground/earth strap that runs between the chassis frame and a 12 mm bolt behind the dipstick tube and just above the back edge of the exhaust manifold. Make sure the eye and its contact area are clean, using emery paper if necessary, then smear a little Vaseline on the eye terminal before fitting the bolt and tightening.

37 Moving forward a little, clean the union of the water inlet pipe on the left-hand side of the cylinder block and the rearmost end of the short section of rigid pipe mounted on the left-hand chassis rail. Again, spray the stubs that the hose will fit over with a little WD40 or similar. Install the hose and clips, again taking care to fit them as closely as possible in their original positions and giving them a squeeze to make them as tight as possible.

38 If your car is fitted with factory air conditioning, position the compressor (which will still be connected to its hoses) on its mounting, install the securing bolts and tighten them to a torque of 18 Nm /1.8 kgf m /14 lbf ft.

39 If your car is fitted with power steering, bring the pump (which should still be connected to its hoses) up to its mounting on the left-hand side of the engine and, after lubricating the pivot pin with a smear of engine oil, slide the pin through the bracket and pump body to fix the pump to the cylinder block. Replace the pin's nut and tighten finger-tight only at this stage. Note that the 14 mm pivot bolt has to be fed through one of the cutouts in the compressor pulley in order to go into position.

40 Lift the power steering pump body upwards and then pass the locking bolt through the front of the adjuster bolt block (below the tensioner bolt), through the strap from the front of the alternator bracket and through the elongated slot of the pipe support bracket on the front of the pump. Tighten the nut on the back of the lock bolt finger-tight for the moment.

41 Turn the 12 mm tensioner bolt anti-clockwise until the pulley has swung toward the engine

11/40 Fit power steering pump.

far enough to allow you to install the power steering pump drivebelt. **Note.** If your car is fitted with air conditioning, the same drivebelt also fits over the a.c compressor pulley.

42 Once the belt is in position, screw the tensioner bolt clockwise until there is about half an inch of deflection at the mid point between the two pulleys when the belt is depressed by firm thumb pressure. Once the correct belt tension is achieved tighten the 14 mm pivot bolt nut, the 12 mm lock bolt on the sliding adjustment mechanism and the 14 mm bolt holding the adjuster strap to the front of the pump bracket.

11/42 Check belt tension.

13 Move around to the right-hand side of the ɜngine compartment.
14 Reconnect the green connector block at he end of the injector loom (*i.e.* the one that's :radled in the intake manifold) to the socket on top ɔf the heater outlet casting at the very rear of the :ylinder head. At the same time, connect the spade erminal to the connector blade on the right-hand ide of the heater outlet cover. This is a lot easier to ay than to do. If you reach round the back of the :ylinder head and feel for the terminal you may be ble to make the multi-pin connection, followed by he simple spade terminal connection. The writer ɔund it easier to lie beneath the car and reach pward around the left-hand side of the bellhous-ıg because, this way, it's actually possible to see vhat you're doing. It probably would be helpful to ave someone manipulating the wire in the engine :ompartment to assist you. Note: if you get into real rouble you can always remove the crank-angle ensor, having first carefully marked its position in elation to the cambox so that you can install it vithout re-timing the engine.
5 If you didn't fit the ignition coils and the rank-angle sensor during the engine rebuild, now's good time to do so. ☞ 3/9/129-135.
6 You'll find a heavy loom with a corrugated over projecting from the firewall/bulkhead on the ght-hand side of the car - between the clutch eservoir (if fitted) and servo body on right-hand rive cars. First, lower the loom into position on the etaining bracket bolted to the rear end of the nanifold. You'll find that the loom has a rubber ısulator wrapped around it at this point. Set the ısulator down in the bracket and then tighten the ylon clip to hold the loom in position. In this icinity you'll have the following connections to ıake -
7 Take the spade-type connector which has lack and black/green wires down to the ground/ arth blade connector at the base of the loom racket and make the connection.
8 Then take the black male connector block ith six internal pins and push it into the female ɔnnector block connected into the fuel injection ɔom. Push the male part into the connector until clicks home.
9 Smear its brass eye with a little Vaseline ıen connect the ground/earth terminal with its two lack wires to the side of the engine lifting eye. ighten its 10 mm fixing bolt.
0 Next, select the grey female connector ith four internal terminals and fix it to the male ug protruding from the crank-angle sensor. You'll ear a click as it locks into place.
1 Take the black male connector with single ɾrminal and fix it to the corresponding female ɔnnector on the coil side bracket.
2 Lastly, in this area, connect the three-ɾrminal grey male connector to the corresponding ɔnnector on the coil bracket at the rear of the ımbox.
3 📷 Take the pipe which runs from the ack colored bellows unit of the brake servo and ɔnnect it to the projecting section of metal pipe at e rear top of the intake manifold. Note that this

11/53 Fit servo vacuum pipe.

hose has an arrow and the words "to engine"; this is because the hose contains a one-way valve and must therefore be fitted the right way round. Squeeze the tangs of the hose clip and slide it into its original position, then squeeze the clip body to make sure it is as tight as possible. Replace the clip if it has been loosened more than twice.
54 Moving along the intake manifold, install the accelerator cable stop bracket which secures the cable to the side of the manifold and fix with two 10 mm bolts which should be tightened by no more than finger pressure on the wrench/spanner.
55 📷 Having fitted the bracket, pull the accelerator inner cable forward and, gripping the nipple firmly, rotate the throttle spindle wheel clockwise until the recess in the wheel comes far enough around to enter the cable nipple completely, and then to place the cable in the grooved outer section of the wheel. Allow the wheel to return under its own spring tension. Note that the cable runs beneath the wheel, not over the top.
56 Reach down beneath the intake manifold toward the back of the engine and fit the copper terminal of the starter motor feed wire onto the top terminal stud of the solenoid. Smear the stud and

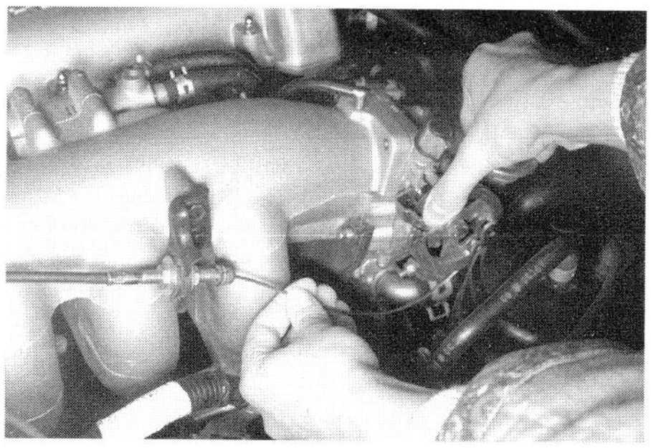
11/55 Fit accelerator cable.

connector eye with Vaseline before fitting. Replace the spring washer and nut and tighten with a 12 mm box end spanner, then spring the rubber protecting cap back over the terminal.
57 Take the black spade-type connector and fix it to the blade projecting from the rear of the solenoid on top of the starter motor.
58 There is a spur loom which leaves the main loom at the bracket fixed to the bellhousing. Take this spur and run it along beneath the intake manifold and behind the manifold support bracket. Fix the spur loom into the clip at the rear of the alternator support bracket just above the oil filter. A number of wires sprout from the spur loom and these need to be connected as follows -
59 Take the single red and white wire with its spade-type connector block and connect it to the projecting blade on the top of the oil pressure sensor.
60 The spur loom terminates at the alternator with two types of connector. First, position the black-bodied connector over the brass stud projecting from the rear of the alternator body. Note that the plastic body of the connector will only slot fully into place when its tail is vertical. Fit the 10 mm brass nut together with a split washer and tighten. When the nut is tight, snap the cover of the terminal closed, having first sprayed a little water repellent fluid over the brass components.
61 Finally, plug the grey connector block into the recess in the side of the alternator. Make sure it clicks firmly home.
62 Fit the fuel pipe which comes from the front of the fuel rail between intake tracts one and two to the rigid fuel pipe attached to the chassis rail nearest to the rear of the engine compartment. The hose will be a tight fit so a smear of WD40 or other silicone fluid may be helpful. Push the flexible pipe fully onto the rigid pipe until it meets the collar. Grasp the ears of the pipe clip and slide the pipe clip forward to its original position so that it clamps the flexible fuel pipe onto the rigid fuel pipe. Squeeze the body of the clip with pliers to make it as tight as possible. If the clip has been used more than twice, discard it and obtain a new replacement.
63 Connect the second fuel pipe in exactly the same way.
64 Move around to the front of the engine compartment.
65 📷 Gently slide the radiator into position. It's in its correct location when the two pegs pro-

11/65 Install radiator.

jecting from the rear face of the radiator, one each side, engage with the clips on the chassis rails. The radiator can now be secured by fitting the two 12 mm headed bolts - one each side - that retain the top of the radiator to the chassis side rail brackets. Torque the bolts to 22 Nm /2.2 kgf m/17 lbf ft.
66 Install the bottom radiator hose between the radiator and the section of rigid tubing fixed to the left-hand chassis side rail. Clean both pipe stubs as previously described and lubricate with a little WD40 or similar. With the hose in position, return the clips to their original locations and then

squeeze their bodies a little to ensure maximum tightness. If the clips have been used more than twice discard them and replace with new ones. Note: you'll probably find it easier to fit the bottom hose from beneath the car.

67 Lower the electric cooling fan into position against the rear face of the radiator (note that some cars will be fitted with two fans). The bottom of the fan has open brackets which slide over the projecting bolts in the base of the radiator. With the fan correctly seated, replace the two 10 mm bolts which fix it to the radiator header tank then, from beneath the car, using a wrench/span-

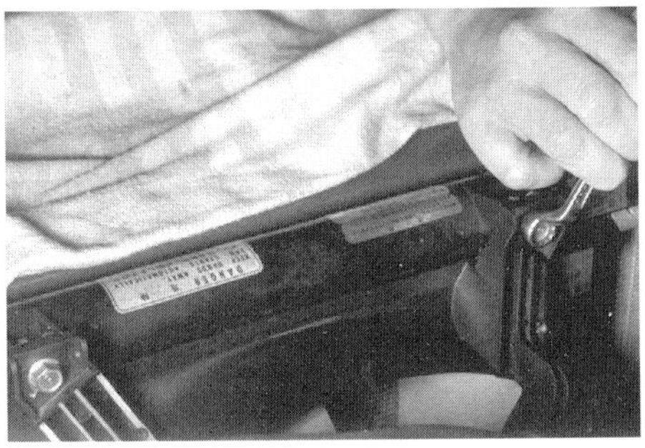

11/67 Install electric fan/fans.

ner and finger pressure only, tighten the two 10 mm bolts that secure the base of the fan.

68 Clip the radiator overflow pipe into the clip on the right-hand side of the radiator and then push it over the stub beneath the radiator filler cap.

69 There is a short spur wire projecting from the wiring loom alongside the left-hand headlight body at chassis rail level. Clip this spur into the bracket on the left-hand side of the radiator top, then make a connection with the female part of the same connector block, which is on the end of the wire coming from the fan motor. Make sure the

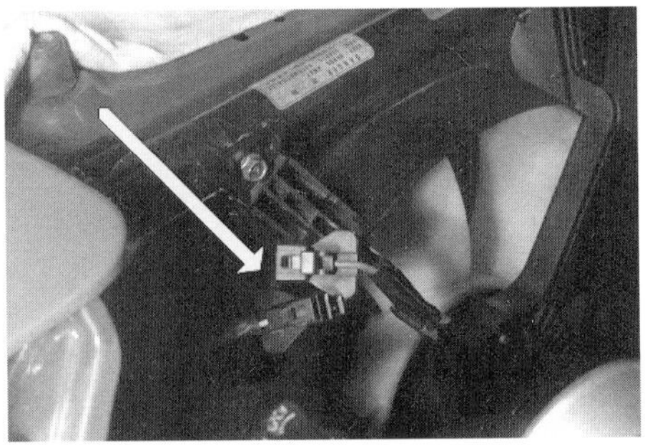

11/69 Reconnect fan/s wiring.

terminals click together securely.

70 Move to the left-hand side of the engine compartment.

71 Lower the air filter box into position on the left-hand chassis rail, noting that the rubber lug in its base has to engage in the bracket which projects slightly into the engine area from the chassis rail. (Our project car had a small electrical box - which we could not identify - mounted on a metal bridge between the airbox and inner wing. This had to be temporarily swung out of the way to allow the airbox's central side mounting to fit down over the stud on the side of the suspension turret). Once the air filter box is seated in its correct position, fit the two 12 mm retaining bolts and the single 12 mm retaining nut. Tighten the fixings - but not too tight, it's not necessary.

72 The air intake behind the airbox can be fixed to the inner wing by fitting the single 10 mm bolt it shares with the diagnostics plug bracket. The grey sleeved loom that connects to the airflow meter on top of the air filter box should be clipped to the bracket on the rear of the air filter box and the nylon clip refastened - don't overtighten!

73 Plug the 7-pin female connector of the loom to the male connector projecting from the side of the airflow meter toward the engine. You'll hear a click as the connection is properly made.

74 Move back to the front of the engine compartment.

75 Fit the air intake assembly to the front of the intake manifold. Note that, apart from the clamped connection on the nose of the intake manifold, this assembly is retained by a single 10 mm bolt in the top of the alternator support bracket. Once the large part of the hose is over the nose of the intake manifold, maneuver the assembly until the 10 mm screw can be returned to the alternator support bracket. Tighten the 10 mm bolt in the support bracket and also the 10 mm-headed hose clip securing the assembly to the nose of the intake manifold.

76 Reconnect the flexible hose from the air intake body moulding to the ISC valve beneath the throttle body assembly. Grip the ears of its hose clip with pliers and slide the hose clip back into its original position. Squeeze the body of the clip to make sure it's as tight as possible. Make sure that the hose goes fully on to the stub from the ISC valve otherwise it will be kinked and restricted.

77 There is a wiring loom which projects toward the engine from the top of the right-hand chassis leg, just forward of the suspension turret. Carefully feed this loom through the gap between the black plastic air intake trunking that you've just fitted and the base of the ISC valve beneath the throttle body. Once you've got the loom into position you'll find that the protective rubber grommet around the loom will fall into position alongside its supporting clip on the black plastic body of the air intake trunking assembly. Open the clip, secure the loom and lock the clip again with its ratchet. Connect the four electrical terminals at the end of the loom -

78 The 2-pin female terminal with black body goes onto its male counterpart on the ISC valve - you'll see it between the intake manifold and the cambox. Fiddly to get to, but make sure it clicks home securely.

79 Connect the black-bodied female connector with three terminals to its male counterpart on the side of the throttle body adjacent to the cam cover. Again, make sure the connector clicks home securely.

80 The remaining two longer wires should be fed across the face of the cambox and secured to the bracket on the side of the thermostat housing with a nylon clip. Do not overtighten the clip.

81 Connect the grey bodied female connector with the single terminal to its male counterpart on the top of the thermostat housing. Click it home.

82 The last connector, with white nylon body, fits over the brass stud projecting from the top of the power steering pump body (if fitted).

83 Your car's engine compartment should now be looking pretty complete - we're almost there!

84 Move to the right-hand side of the engine compartment.

85 Between the top of the suspension turret and the inner wing is a metal bracket carrying two electrical components - the one nearest the front is the solenoid valve (purge control). Take the loose vacuum hose from this assembly, pass it beneath the throttle cable and between the throttle body and first intake tract, up over the top of the manifold. Plug the hose into the stub projecting backward at the top of the intake manifold, just behind the mounting flange for the throttle body.

86 Fit the radiator top hose, again smearing both the radiator stub and the thermostat housing stub with a little silicone spray, having first cleaned away any corrosion or sediment. Wriggle

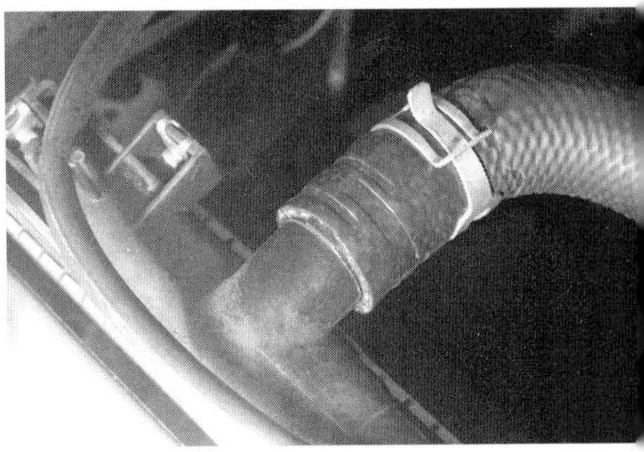

11/86 Fit top hose and clip firmly.

the hose into place, making sure it is not at all stressed, and then squeeze the ears of the hose clips with pliers and slide the clips into their original positions. Squeeze the bodies of the clips with the pliers just to make sure they are as tight as possible. If the clips have been used more than twice, throw them away and replace with new items.

87 Fit the hard rubber moulded tube that connects the airflow meter with the black plastic air intake moulding crossing the front of the engine. Push the oval end of the tube onto the air intake plastic moulding first, then work the round end onto the stub of the airflow meter. Make sure the tube's not kinked, then tighten the hose clips at each end to secure the tube in place. At the airflow meter end the worm drive screw is 10 mm, while the screw in the clip at the other end of the hose is 8 mm but can also be tightened with a crosshead screwdriver.

88 Fit the short section of chrome tubing, with its associated rubber hoses, to the front of the cambox, securing it with the two 8 mm dome-headed bolts. Fit one end of the rubber hose to the plastic intake moulding in front of the intake manifold and the other to the metal stub projecting from the left-hand side of the cambox. In both cases

grasp the clip ears with pliers and move the clips back into their original positions then squeeze the clip body for good measure.

89 Fit a set of spark plugs and reconnect the HT leads: ☞ 5.

90 Check that the 19 mm oil pan drain plug is tight. Assuming that the engine is 'dry', that is has been completely drained of oil and has a new (empty) oil filter, add 3.6 liters/3.8 US quarts/3.2 Imp quarts of fresh engine oil. The oil should be poured slowly into the oil filler on top of the cambox. Do not overfill. If the engine is not dry, check oil level and top-up: ☞ 2.

11/90 Refill engine with oil to correct level.

91 + Double check that all hoses have been reconnected and properly clipped, then refill the cooling system with coolant fluid: ☞ 6. **Caution!** don't forget to replace and tighten radiator and reservoir caps.

92 Installing the hood/bonnet stay. The gold colored end of the stay with the longer leg fits in the hinge clip. The clip is located high on the left chassis rail, just behind the headlight assembly. Make sure the nylon clip is open and pass the leg of the stay through the circular section of the clip and metal bracket, then close the latch over the

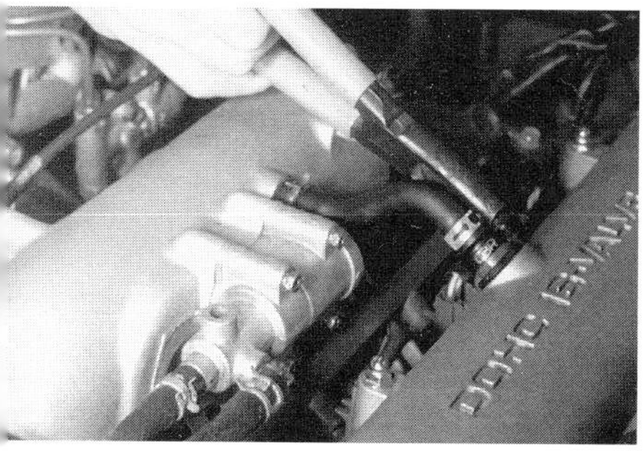

1/91a Double check all hose connections.

1/91b Should look like this ...

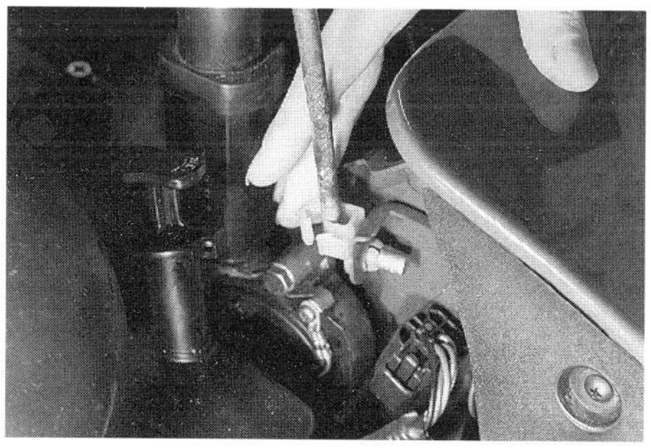

11/92 Fit hood stay.

vertical section of the stay. Lay the stay across the front of the engine compartment and fix the other end into its clip.

93 Fitting hood/bonnet. With the help of an assistant carefully position the hood so that its rear corners are wedged into the gap on each side of the car between the windshield lower rail and the fender/wing. Quickly lift the hinges and push them over the protruding studs on the underside of the hood and then tighten the two 14 mm nuts on each side finger-tight. Prop the hood open with its stay. If there are positional marks on the hinges, manipulate the hood/hinge relationship until the marks realign and then tighten the 14 mm nuts to 22 Nm /2.2 kgf m/17 lbf ft. Repeat the process with the second hinge. If the hinges do not have positional marks, you'll have to slide the hood backwards and forwards in the hinges until you are able to close the hood and obtain even gaps all the way around, then tighten the retaining nuts.

94 Reconnect the windshield washer pipe to the pipework union stub on the underside of the bonnet.

95 Manual transmission cars. From inside of the car, fit the shift lever (gearstick) and console:

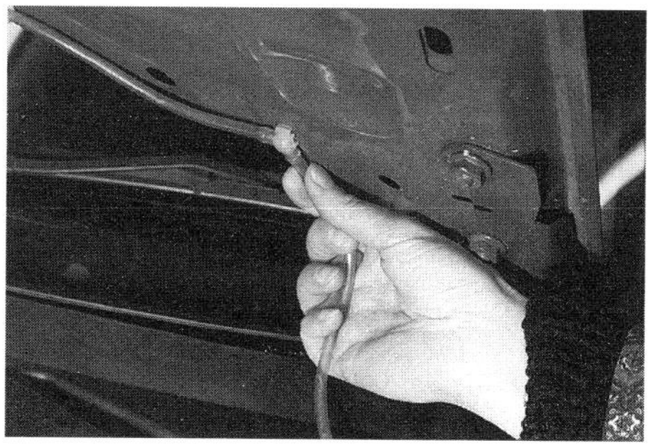

11/94 Reconnect windshield washer pipe.

☞ 4/8/8-15.

96 Automatic transmission cars. If appropriate, refill the transmission unit with ATF: ☞ 2. If the ATF level just requires checking and topping up, wait until after a short test run: ☞ 2.

97 Fit and tighten the fuel filler cap.

98 **Warning!** double check that all electrical connections have been remade, that there is no damage to electrical wiring or components and that the ignition is turned off. From inside the trunk reconnect the ground/earth cable to the battery's negative (-) terminal and tighten the clamp nut with a 10 mm socket on an extension to restore the car's electrical power. **Warning!** The extension bar will cross the battery's positive (+) terminal to reach the negative terminal clamp, so make absolutely sure the positive terminal is fully insulated otherwise a dangerous dead short can occur. Note: it's possible that if your car is fitted with an audible security alarm system, it will sound off as the battery is reconnected - check the system manufacturer's instructions.

99 If you want to check that everything works before the car is lowered to the ground and easy access is lost, now's the time to do it: ☞ 3/11/102-108. Note: because the car is rigidly supported on a hard surface it has lost the sound and vibration deadening properties of rubber mounts, suspension and tires, in other words it will sound terrible because every small mechanical knock and whir is magnified: you've been warned!

100 Check for fluid leaks and then install the engine undertray. The tray is secured by three 10 mm self-tapping screws at the front edge, two 10 mm bolts on the front suspension/engine subframe, two 10 mm bolts into the chassis rail on each side of the car, together with one 10 mm nut on the stud the tray shares with a front body support stay on each side of the car. To fit the tray, first slide one side up around the stabilizer bar and secure by tightening a couple of the fastenings finger-tight. Repeat the process on the other side of the car, at the same time making sure that the projecting tab in the front of the suspension/engine subframe locates in the indent of the undertray. You can now install and tighten all of the securing screws, bolts and nuts: finger pressure on a wrench/spanner is sufficient.

101 Carefully lower the car to the ground: ☞ 1/3.

102 Start up time! **Warning!** First, check the following - drain and filler plugs tight; engine and transmission oil level; brake and, if applicable, clutch master cylinder fluid levels; coolant level, hoses, radiator and reservoir caps tight; fuel level, fuel filler cap tight and fuel pipes; spark plugs fitted; all wiring reconnected; drivebelts correctly tensioned?

103 Ensure that the gearshift lever is in the neutral position; 'N' or 'P' for cars with automatic transmission. Have a car or garage-type fire extinguisher handy.

104 It's a good idea to prime the fuel system to avoid excessive engine cranking - remember that the Miata/MX5 original battery is tiny by normal automotive standards, and has little reserve capacity. Open the diagnosis socket cover (mounted on the left inner wing near the suspension turret and clearly marked). Refer to the table inside the cover, and temporarily connect terminal pins **F/P** and **GND** using a short insulated jumper wire bent into a 'U' shape - a 75 mm /3 in length of domestic wire of the type with a solid copper core would be ideal (after baring and sharpening each end). When the terminals are bridged, turn on the ignition switch and quickly check for fuel leaks around any connection which has been disturbed. **Warning!** If a leak is detected turn off the ignition immediately,

then dispose safely of spilled fuel and rectify the fault before turning the ignition on again. If, during the priming there's a smell of burning insulation or fuses blow, then immediately turn off the ignition and if necessary disconnect the battery. Do not turn the ignition on again until the fault has been found and rectified. If all's well check that the pump is running by opening the fuel filler and listen at the opening while the system is priming - a high-pitched whine indicates that the pump is operating and priming the fuel system. After about 10 seconds turn the ignition switch off, disconnect the jumper wire and close the diagnosis socket cover.

105 Start the engine in the usual way. It may not fire as quickly as usual, but should start within 15 seconds of continuous cranking. When the engine first starts after a rebuild, there will be a considerable amount of mechanical noise until oil under pressure circulates fully. It's also quite normal for new gaskets and components to create burning smells. **Caution!** If no oil pressure is registered within 15 seconds of start-up, stop the engine, investigate and rectify the problem; likewise if oil, water or fuel leaks become evident. **Caution!** Do not rev the engine, instead allow it to idle until normal operating temperature is registered on the temperature gauge.

106 If the starter does not operate check its wiring and terminals carefully. If it still doesn't work: ☞ 7.

107 If the starter operates but the engine fails to start and there is no obvious reason, like an empty gas tank, run through all of the steps detailed in the engine installation procedure to double check that all work has been completed. If before the engine was removed you temporarily disconnected the fuel circuit opening relay, check that you really did reconnect it fully! Should the engine still fail to start, check ignition timing and, if that doesn't solve the problem, valve timing (via camshaft drivebelt) by referring to the appropriate parts of this book.

108 In the trunk, check that the breather pipe is properly connected to the battery and that terminal insulators are in place. Install the battery cover moulding and secure by fitting the two plastic 13 mm nuts and then clipping it to the row of stud fasteners on the trunk floor. Install the spare wheel and secure with its collar and wing-nutted bolt.

109 Road test the car to ensure performance is normal and for the first week, or so, check fluid levels often. Reset the clock!

110 **Caution!** If the engine has been rebuilt, don't use the car's full performance right away, instead gradually increase your use of potential performance over 3-5000 km /2-3000 miles. Avoid laboring the engine, sustained high revs and constant speed. After 1000 km /600 miles replace the engine's oil and oil filter, re-torque the exhaust and intake manifolds retaining bolts/nuts after slackening them half a turn first.

111 Note: in some markets the car will be fitted with a security coded radio. If your car has such a radio, after battery disconnection you'll need to re-enter your personal security number before the radio will work. Consult the radio manufacturer's handbook.

12. ENGINE - INSTALLATION (WITHOUT TRANSMISSION)

☞ First read 1/1, 2.

1 You'll need an assistant to help you install the engine, as well as a small mobile engine crane of the type that can be hired from the tool and plant hire companies you find in every medium-sized and bigger town. **Warning!** Sorry, we weren't able to weigh it, but we believe the engine weighs around 136 kg /300 lb so the rope and crane you use should be capable of lifting twice this weight as a safety margin. Also, the lifting hook of the crane's boom should be capable of reaching a height of around 1830 mm (6 ft) above the ground.

2 Tie several strands of very strong nylon rope tightly between the two lifting eyes positioned on each side of the cylinder head, one toward the front of the engine and one toward the back. It's important to keep the rope as tight as possible; you'll be surprised how much the rope will stretch once the crane takes the strain.

3 **Caution!** check that the engine bay is clear and that all pipes, wires and cables are tied back out of the way so that the engine will not become entangled as it is moved into position within the engine compartment. This particularly applies to the clutch flexible hydraulic pipe on right-hand drive cars which runs across the top of the bellhousing and shares a clip with the main wiring loom. Tie this bracket high up on the right of the compartment.

4 As with engine removal, the car will need to be safely supported high enough above the ground to give good, safe access to the underside and you'll find it much easier if the raised car is level: ☞ 1/3.

5 Place a jack beneath the transmission bellhousing and lift the unit as high as possible without it coming into contact with the floorpan.

6 Manual transmission cars only. Rub a thin smear of copper-based lubricant on the nose and splines of the transmission input shaft - don't overdo it!

7 Spread old towels over the nose of the car and the fender (wing) tops: this will help to protect the paintwork from accidental damage.

8 Engage the crane's hook with the rope sling and lift the engine far enough from the ground to clear the front edge of the engine compartment opening. Line the crane and engine up in front of the car.

9 With an assistant holding the engine to stop it swaying, gently roll the crane forward until the unit is approximately over the center of the engine compartment. Gently lower the engine until it is approximately level with the transmission, then tilt the engine just a little so that its longitudinal axis is roughly the same as the transmission's. Move the engine toward the transmission, adjusting its height simultaneously, until the transmission input shaft is about to enter the clutch cover (manual transmission cars). Adjust the vertical and lateral position of the engine so that the input shaft is centered on the clutch (manual transmission cars).

10 **Caution!** Once the rear of the cylinder head gets close to the firewall/bulkhead put an old towel or similar between the two as a cushion and if the coil and crank-angle sensor units are fitted take great care not to bang them against the firewall.

11 Manual transmission cars. Bring the engine and transmission unit together, making sure that the transmission input shaft enters the center of the clutch and that the bellhousing is correctly lined up with the engine backplate. If the clutch disc has been well centered, the transmission bellhousing should go fully home against the engine backplate with no more than a little joggling around. Life will be more difficult if the clutch disc has not been well centered and, in extreme cases, you'll have to withdraw the engine, slacken the clutch cover and re-center the disc before attempting again to make the connection. As the engine backplate goes fully home against the transmission bellhousing make sure that the hollow spigots projecting from the rear of the cylinder block engage with their locating holes in the bellhousing.

12 Automatic transmission cars. Bring the engine and transmission unit together, making sure that the transmission is correctly lined up with the engine backplate. As the engine backplate goes fully home against the transmission bellhousing ensure that the hollow spigots projecting from the rear of the cylinder block engage with their locating holes in the bellhousing.

13 From beneath the car quickly fit the two lowermost 17 mm (x 60 mm) bellhousing bolts. Screw the bolts in just enough to prevent any movement between the engine backplate and transmission bellhousing.

14 Lower and remove the jack that was supporting the bellhousing.

15 The threaded studs of both engine mountings should now be directly above their fixing hole and slot in the subframe. Lower the engine unit gently until you can maneuver the left-hand mounting stud through its hole, after which the stud of the right-hand mounting can be fed through its slot in the subframe. Note: you may find it necessary, as we did, to remove the left-hand engine mounting bracket from the engine and to fasten the mounting to the subframe independently of the engine. This allowed us to maneuver the engine sufficiently to engage the stud of the right-hand mounting in its slot, at which point the retaining nut and washer were immediately screwed into place. Then, the engine was twisted and lowered until the mounting bracket on the left-hand side aligned once more with the bolt holes in the side of the engine. The three bolts were fitted and tightened to a torque of 45 Nm /4.5 kgf m/34 lbf ft.

16 Once the engine is sitting safely on its mountings, the crane can be released and withdrawn.

17 Fit the two topmost bellhousing bolts which are 17 mm (x 60 mm) and screw them into place finger-tight. Note: you'll need 14 mm and 17 mm sockets, universal joint and extensions of around 450 mm (18 in) to reach some of the bellhousing fasteners.

18 Position the exhaust pipe support bracke

over the two bolt holes on the left-hand side of the bellhousing. Secure the bracket, with flange facing rearward, with two 17 mm bolts the upper of which is longer at 70 mm, although there seems no good reason for this. Screw the bolts home finger-tight.

19 Automatic transmission cars. Fit and finger-tighten the 17 mm (x 60 mm) bolt at lower right of the bellhousing.

20 From within the engine compartment release the wires, brackets, etc., for the bellhousing area which were tied out of harm's way. Then, from beneath the car, position the two wiring loom (and clutch pipe manual transmission) brackets toward the top right-hand side of the bellhousing. This is fiddly as there's not enough room to swing a mouse, let alone a cat, but a little perseverance will pay dividends. Once the brackets are in place, fix by fitting the 14 mm retaining bolts finger-tight; the outer of these bolts also secures the starter motor. Whilst in the vicinity, install the 14 mm bolt and nut which also secures the starter motor.

21 Manual trans cars. Place a dab of molybdenum disulfide or copper-based grease on the ball end of the clutch release cylinder pushrod. Engage the ball with the recess in the clutch operating arm and pull the body of the release cylinder toward the clutch operating arm until the two release cylinder retaining screws can be got into place and engaged with their threads in the bellhousing. This is pretty fiddly if you're lying on your back, but a little patience will see it done one bolt at a time.

22 Before tightening the clutch release cylinder retaining bolts, fit the bracket that holds the coiled loop of the rigid hydraulic pipe which connects to the release cylinder. This is most easily done by reaching down from above through the engine compartment and pushing the long 17 mm bolt through the bracket, then through the bellhousing and then screwing the nut on the back of the bolt with your fingers. The procedure for fitting this bolt and nut will be the same for auto trans cars.

23 Tighten the various bellhousing bolts fitted during the last few steps. Tighten 17 mm fasteners to 80 Nm /8 kgf m/60 lbf ft and the 14 mm fasteners to 45 Nm /4.5 kgf m/57 lbf ft. Note: access to these fasteners is not easy so you'll need an appropriate socket attached to a universal joint in turn attached to extensions of around 350 mm (14 in) and then a ratchet handle. A couple of these bolts also have nuts and the nut or bolt head on the engine side which can be locked with a wrench/spanner via the opening in the inner wheelwell.

24 Manual transmission cars. Next, the two 12 mm release cylinder retaining bolts should be tightened. The upper bolt can be accessed through the hole in the inner wheelwell using socket, universal joint, 250 mm (10 inch) extension bar and ratchet handle. The lower bolt can be tightened only with an open-ended spanner. Correct torque is 22 Nm /2.2 kgf m/16 lbf ft.

25 Automatic transmission cars. If applicable, reach up into the bellhousing, via the access hole in its base, and install the four bolts which secure the torque convertor to the driveplate. Lock the driveplate by wedging a large screwdriver into the starter teeth, then tighten the bolts to a torque of 50 Nm /5.0 kgf m/36 lbf ft. If there is one, install the cover to the bellhousing access hole.

26 Fit and tighten both engine mounting retaining nuts from beneath the car after making sure their spring washers are still in good shape. The correct torque for the 14 mm nuts is 70 Nm /7 kgf m/50 lbf ft. You'll need a 125 mm (6 inch) extension behind the socket in order to reach into the subframe turret in which the nut is housed.

27 ☞ 3/11/32-94, 97-112.

13. CAMSHAFT DRIVEBELT - REPLACEMENT (ENGINE IN CAR)

☞ First read 1/1, 2.

CAMSHAFT DRIVEBELT REMOVAL

1 It's best if the car's on level ground. Apply the parking brake and if the ground is not level use wheel chocks too.

2 Disconnect the battery: ☞ 3/4/4.

3 Open the hood/bonnet and support with its stay. Protect the paintwork around the engine compartment with thick cloth - old towels are ideal.

4 Drain around 4.5 liters/1 gallon of coolant from the radiator: ☞ 6. Collect the coolant in a clean container as it can be re-used.

5 Using pliers, release the clips at both end of the top hose by squeezing their ears together and then sliding them back 50 mm/2 in or so. Pull the top hose off both radiator and thermostat housing stubs. If it's really stuck, cut the hose lengthways on the stub connection using a craft knife and taking care not to gouge the stub: of course, a new hose will be needed.

6 Release the electrical connector on top of the thermostat housing by squeezing the catch inward and lifting the connector block.

7 Using a crosshead screwdriver, slacken the hose clip fixing the intake hose moulding to the air filter unit on the left-hand side of the engine compartment. Pull the pipe off the stub.

8 Free the small bore breather pipe from the front left-hand side of the cambox cover by releasing its spring clip with pliers. The breather's metal pipe can be released from the front of the cambox by undoing the two chrome-headed 10 mm bolts holding it in place. At the intake manifold end release the spring clip from the rubber tube of the cambox breather and pull the tube from the trunking. The whole breather pipe assembly can then be removed.

9 Looking from the front of the car there is a pipe of approximately 13 mm (0.5 in) bore between the rigid black plastic intake ('resonance') pipe and an anodized pipe under the throttle body on the nose of the intake manifold. Release the clip at the manifold end and slide the rubber pipe off of the anodized pipe. Slacken the clip retaining the air pipe to the manifold body using a medium sized crosshead screwdriver or 10 mm socket.

10 Remove the 10 mm bolt retaining the rigid intake pipe assembly to the alternator mounting bracket. The pipe assembly can now be pulled off its manifold connection and mounting bracket , then the whole thing can be twisted sufficiently to give access to the black plastic cable clip on the side of the rectangular-shaped resonance chamber. This ratchet-type clip can be released by inserting a screwdriver into the exposed slot and twisting the screwdriver blade to release the ratchet. When the clip is opened the whole air pipe and resonance box assembly can be removed from the car.

11 Removing the electric fan (there will be two on some models) from the radiator. First release the electrical wire from the clip in the fan housing by pulling back the catch on the side of the clip and thereby releasing the wire retainer. The electrical connector block can now be separated by pushing the outer catch inwards and pulling the two halves apart.

12 The electric fan housing is fixed to the radiator body by four 10 mm bolts, threaded into spring clips. Note: you may find, as we did, that the bottom retaining bolts and their clips are considerably corroded. If this is the case, a soaking with penetrating oil some time before the bolts are removed will help. Once the two top bolts have been removed and the two lower bolts loosened, the cooling fan assembly can be lifted away from the car.

13 Remove the power steering pump/air conditioning compressor (if fitted) drivebelt followed by the alternator drivebelt: ☞ 2. If the drivebelts are in good condition they can be re-used

14 Remove the electrical connection to the top of the power steering pump by lifting the connector from its terminal. Release the wire from the clip on the thermostat body and tie the wire out of harm's way.

15 Release both of the mini-hoses from their connections on the thermostat housing using the method described for the top hose.

16 Ignition coil and HT leads removal. Pull each of the HT connectors from its spark plug bore using your fingers only: start at the front of the engine and work backwards. As each spark plug connector is released, free its cable from the clips in the valley of the cambox. Leave all four connectors lying on top of the cambox for the moment. Release the spring clip and separate the two halves of the coil's loom connector above the crank-angle sensor unit.

17 Using a crescent or box end wrench slacken the single 12 mm bolt fixing the base of the coil unit to the rear of the cambox/cylinder head, then with a socket undo and remove the two 12 mm bolts fixing the unit to the top of the cambox. Once the bolts are removed the coil assembly can be lifted a little and then moved away from cambox.

18 Remove the small hose between the intake manifold and the PCV valve on the right-hand side of the cambox. The clips are slackened by squeezing their ears together.

19 Cambox cover removal. Unscrew and remove the thirteen 10 mm chrome dome-headed bolts which hold the cambox cover to the cylinder head. Unscrew the bolts progressively in a diagonal sequence until they are all loose enough to unscrew with your fingers. Note: a short 75 mm /3 inch extension is also needed. There are four

cambox cover bolts down each side of the cambox: three down in the center valley and two at the front. Note: the two front bolts are shorter than the others. Once the bolts have been removed the cambox cover can be lifted clear of the cambox/ cylinder head. Cover the open cambox with a clean cloth to prevent contamination.

20 The upper drivebelt cover is retained by four 10 mm bolts which can be undone with a socket and 75 mm /3 inch extension. The cover can be lifted away once the four screws have been removed but note that the bottom left-hand and top right-hand bolts also hold clips.

21 Wrap the drivebelt around the water pump pulley and clamp with fingers or pliers to hold the pulley still whilst the three 10 mm bolts are loosened and removed from its center. The pulley can then be withdrawn from its mounting flange.

22 The crankshaft outer pulley has a central 21 mm bolt surrounded by four small 10 mm bolts and a plate. To remove the pulley it is only necessary to unscrew and remove the four small bolts. If necessary, lock the crankshaft by engaging 1st gear. You'll have to jar the bolts loose on cars with auto trans. Once the four bolts are removed the crankshaft pulley can be withdrawn, together with its front and rear washers and the dished camshaft drivebelt guide plate.

23 There are four 10 mm bolts retaining the middle and lower drivebelt covers. One of these is adjacent to the water pump center boss and is longer than the other three. Once the bolts retaining the drivebelt cover have been removed, the cover can be withdrawn in two pieces. Note that the bolt close to the water pump central boss is longer than the other three.

24 Remove the cam drivebelt: ☞ 3/7/48-50. Note: it's recommended that you also remove the tensioner wheel and spring because if the drivebelt is due for replacement it makes good sense to fit a new tensioner spring at the same time: ☞ 3/6/51

CAMSHAFT DRIVEBELT, TENSIONER, IDLER & PULLEYS CHECKING & REPAIR

25 ☞ 3/8/59-62. **Caution!** These checks are important: don't be tempted to skip them.

CAMSHAFT DRIVEBELT FITTING & VALVE TIMING

26 If the new (where applicable) camshaft drivebelt is marked with a direction arrow, it's important to make sure it's fitted correctly. When looking at the front of the engine, the camshaft drivebelt runs in a clockwise direction.

27 If it's not already in the correct position, slacken its 14 mm locking bolt and pull the drivebelt tensioner wheel outward, against spring tension, as far as it will go: lock by retightening the bolt.

28 ☞ 3/9/89-108. You can skip the bit about dousing the camshafts with oil, unless they have been removed or have had the lubricant wiped from them.

29 Reconnect the small hose between the intake manifold and the cambox PCV valve.

30 Fit the coil unit and tighten its three 12 mm retaining bolts to a torque of 22 Nm /2.2 kgf m/17 lbf ft. Push together the two parts of the coil's loom connector until an audible click is heard. Using fingers only, reconnect the HT lead connectors to the spark plugs, starting with the plug nearest the coil and working forwards. Push the HT leads into their clips in the cambox valley.

31 Fit and tension the alternator and, if fitted, power steering/air-conditioning compressor drive-belts: ☞ 2.

32 Reconnect the two small bore hoses to the thermostat housing and reposition their retaining clips in the original positions. Squeeze the clip bodies with pliers for extra security. Make sure both hoses are installed in their support clips.

33 Remake the electrical connections to both power steering pump and thermostat housing. Resecure the power steering pump wire to the clip on the thermostat housing.

34 Reposition the electric fan housing (two of them on some cars) over the two protruding bolts at the back of the radiator and then install the top two bolts. Tighten the four 10 mm bolts using finger pressure only on a wrench/spanner.

35 Remake the fan's electrical connection by pushing the two halves of the connector block together; an audible click indicates the connection is secure.

36 Maneuver the black plastic intake pipe onto the nose of the intake manifold and install the 10 mm bolt which secures the assembly to the alternator mounting bracket. At the other end of the intake pipe, push the hard rubber moulding over the stub of the air filter assembly on the left side of the engine compartment. Once all is correctly positioned, tighten the worm drive clips at both ends to secure. The clips have 8 mm and 10 mm crosshead drives. Tighten the 10 mm securing bolt also and don't forget to fit the wiring loom spur into its bracket on the intake pipe.

37 Reconnect the hose between the intake piping and the anodized pipe stub below the throttle body of the manifold. Replace the securing clip in its original position, and squeeze its body with pliers.

38 Fit the small breather pipe to its stub on the intake pipe and, at its other end, to the stub on the cambox. Fit and tighten - using a wrench/spanner and finger pressure only - the two chrome-headed bolts which secure the rigid section of the pipe to the front of the cambox. Replace the two pipe securing clips in their original positions and squeeze the clip bodies for added security.

39 Fit the radiator top hose and secure by placing the hose clips in their original positions. Squeeze the clip bodies for extra security. Note: a little silicone-based lubricant sprayed onto the radiator and thermostat housing stubs will make fitting of the hose easier.

40 If you only partially drained the coolant, pour the coolant that you have saved back into the radiator and fit the radiator cap. Note: if the radiator won't accept all of the coolant, pour the balance into the coolant reservoir on the right-hand inner wing. If in doubt, if you need to refill the system completely or if you didn't save the coolant you drained: ☞ 6.

41 Remake the battery connection: ☞ 3/11/ 98, 108.

42 **Caution!** Before starting the engine: ☞ 3/11/100-111.

14. CAMSHAFTS & FOLLOWERS - REMOVAL & INSTALLATION (ENGINE IN CAR)

☞ First read 1/1, 2.

1 ☞ 3/13/1-24. This will take you to the point where the camshaft drivebelt has been removed.

2 Camshaft pulley removal: ☞ 3/7/52.

3 The crank-angle sensor is driven from the rear of the intake camshaft so it's located at the rear of the cambox/cylinder head on the right-hand side. Release its spring clip and pull the loom connector from the crank-angle sensor unit. Mark the relative position of the angle sensor body and the cambox, using an indelible pen. Then unscrew and remove the single 12 mm bolt from the adjustment slot on the right-hand side. Once the bolt is removed the angle sensor can be pulled backwards until it is clear of its housing in the cambox/cylinder head. **Warning!** It may come free suddenly.

4 Camshaft and followers removal: ☞ 3/7/ 58.

5 Checking components: ☞ 3/8/24-30. **Caution!** These checks are important: don't be tempted to skip them.

6 Camshafts, camshaft pulleys and cam-followers installation. Note: if you're fitting new camshafts, it's always advisable to fit new cam-followers at the same time unless the existing followers have been in use for a negligible mileage. This advice is particularly important if you're fitting high performance camshafts. New cams and old followers, or vice-versa, are likely to produce rapid wear and loss of performance.

7 ☞ 3/9/68-75.

8 Fitting new camshaft oil seals: ☞ 3/9/76.

9 Crank-angle sensor fitting. You'll find that the drive dogs on the spindle of the crank-angle sensor are slightly offset, which means that it will only fit into its recess when it has the correct relationship with the camshaft and therefore cannot be fitted 180 degrees out.

10 Fit a new rubber oil seal into the groove in the sensor boss and lubricate the seal and the drive dogs with a little engine oil. Set the drive dogs to match the slots in the cam (if you can see how the slot's orientated) and then slide the angle sensor into position: if it won't go home with a little to-and fro twisting, then pull it out and rotate the drive spindle a few degrees and try again. Once the drive dogs engage the rear of the camshaft , push the angle sensor body fully home against the rear of the cylinder head and loosely install the retaining bolt. Push together the unit's loom connector plug and socket until you hear an audible click.

11 If, as advised, you marked the relationship of the crank-angle sensor body with the cylinder head, realign your marks and tighten the 12 mm

lock bolt to a torque of 22 Nm /2.2 kgf m/17 lbf ft. If you didn't mark the setting of the crank-angle sensor, you'll have to reset the ignition timing: ☞ 5.

12 Camshaft pulleys installation. **Caution!** If you're fitting high performance pulleys with an adjustable timing facility, follow the manufacturer's advice on fitting. Otherwise: ☞ 3/9/77-79.

13 Camshaft drivebelt installation, valve timing and general rebuild: ☞ 3/13/26-42.

15. CYLINDER HEAD - REMOVAL & INSTALLATION (ENGINE IN CAR)

☞ First read 1/1, 2.

CYLINDER HEAD REMOVAL

1 Relieve fuel system pressure: ☞ 3/4/1-2.

2 Remove the camshaft drivebelt: ☞ 3/13/1-24.

3 Release the throttle cable by turning the butterfly spindle wheel clockwise far enough to give sufficient slack to allow the cable and nipple to be slid from its location. Remove the cable stop bracket from the intake manifold by removing the two 10 mm bolts. Fix the end of the throttle cable out of harm's way by tying it to one side

4 Disconnect the following hoses, most of which are secured by the usual spring hose clips or have no clip at all. The heater hose which connects between the firewall/bulkhead and the heater outlet at the rear of the cylinder head (either end). The brake vacuum hose which connects between the rear of the intake manifold and the servo unit piping (lhd cars)/servo bellows unit (rhd cars): again either end will do. The vacuum hose to the purge control at the manifold end near the throttle body: pull the hose out through the manifold, and tie to one side. The vacuum hose to the cruise control (if fitted): disconnect at the manifold end, release from any clips and tie out of harm's way at the side of the engine compartment.

5 Open the fuel filler flap and remove the fuel filler cap and then close the flap. Next, disconnect the flexible fuel hoses from the rigid fuel pipes mounted on the chassis rail on the right-hand side of the engine compartment. Pack cloth around the rigid pipes because when the flexible pipes are disconnected there will be some fuel leakage. Use tape to identify one matching pair of rigid and flexible pipes. Release the clips and work the flexible hoses off of the rigid pipes. When the flexible hoses are free hold them downwards to drain residual fuel and then tie them up against the manifold having first taped over their ends to stop debris entering; wrap insulation tape around the top of both open rigid fuel pipes for the same reason. **Warning!** If the fuel filler cap is not left off, residual pressure can continue to push fuel from the pipes for hours, and even days: this could be extremely dangerous.

6 The following few steps detail harness connectors which have to be disconnected: most have spring clip latches. In all cases, after disconnection, release the wires or looms from any clips and tie them back out of the way.

7 Remove the electrical connector block from the throttle body after springing its spring clip with the blade of a screwdriver. In the same area, remove the electrical connector block from the ISC (Idle Speed Control) by squeezing the tag at the top of the block and simultaneously pulling.

8 At the rear end of the cambox cover, above the crank-angle sensor, are the connector blocks for the ignition coil and the exhaust manifold oxygen sensor. Disconnect both blocks (if both are still connected) by pressing on the release tags and separating the two halves.

9 Release the electrical connector from the top of the crank-angle sensor by pushing in the release tag and pulling the connector upwards at the same time.

10 With a 10 mm socket release the bolt securing the ground/earth wire connection to the engine lifting bracket at the rear of the cambox cover on the right-hand side and then, from the other side of the car, the bolt securing the ground/earth connection just above the rear of the exhaust manifold flange. Replace the bolts finger-tight once the terminals have been removed.

11 At the rear of the intake manifold on the right-hand side adjacent to the injector electrical connector block, there is a cable tie on a bracket. This tie can be released by pulling back the locking tongue and pulling the cable free. This will allow easier access to the injector connector.

12 Pull the connector from the ground/earth terminal at the bulkhead end of the intake manifold. The male half of the injector loom electrical connector block can be pulled from the bracket mounted female part after inserting a screwdriver into the slot on the side of the female part. The free wiring loom can now be pulled upwards and tied back for safekeeping.

13 There are two electrical connections to the alternator: first, the permanent live, which is retained by a 10 mm nut within a plastic cover. Unclip the plastic cover and unscrew the nut; the terminal comes away from the alternator complete with the plastic cover assembly. The second connection is via a grey connector block in the side of the alternator body and this is released by pressing inwards the spring clip on the side of the body, whilst pulling the connector block outwards.

14 Unscrew and remove the four 10 mm bolts which retain the exhaust manifold heatshield. Lift the shield away.

15 Release the oxygen sensor wire from its clip on the engine backplate.

16 Looking through the branches of the exhaust manifold, you will see that the small bore rigid heater spur of the water inlet pipe is fixed to the exhaust manifold flange by a single 14 mm nut. Remove the nut using a 125 mm/5 inch extension and release the bracket.

17 To gain best access to the exhaust manifold flange nuts it will be necessary to raise the front or left-hand side of the car and support securely: ☞ 1/3.

18 From beneath the car you can just about see three 14 mm nuts which hold the exhaust downpipe to the exhaust manifold. To get at and undo these nuts you need to put together extensions of at least 360 mm (14 in) and a universal joint. The combination should be socket, universal joint, extension or extensions, then the T-bar or ratchet handle. Two of the nuts can be accessed from the gap between the transmission and subframe, whilst the third nut can be reached from the gap above the subframe in the left-hand front wheelwell. It would be advisable to spray these three nuts and their studs with penetrating oil and allow it to soak in for half-an-hour, or so, before attempting to remove the nuts. Once the nuts have been removed the car can be lowered to the ground.

19 Undo and remove the two 14 mm bolts which secure the intake manifold support bracket to the manifold and cylinder block, the bracket can then be lifted away.

20 There are ten 12 mm bolts holding the cylinder head to the cylinder block. **Caution!** The bolts must be loosened in a sequence which spirals inward from the outer bolts of the head - this minimizes distortion. Initially loosen each bolt half a turn, then a whole turn, followed by full removal. A 125 mm/5 inch extension will be needed with the socket as the bolts are quite deeply recessed in the cambox. Note: it doesn't matter that the bolts have splined heads - your ordinary socket will still work. Once the ten bolts holding the cylinder head have been loosened and removed, the cylinder head can be lifted. It may be necessary to use a leather or other soft-faced mallet to gently tap the head upwards to loosen it. **Caution!** Do not be tempted to break the head from the block using a sharp instrument as a wedge or lever.

21 If you wish to dismantle the cylinder head further, you'll find all the information you need in the full engine teardown and rebuild sequences elsewhere in this Chapter.

CHECKING & REPAIR OF CYLINDER HEAD

22 ☞ 3/8/1-9.

23 Also inspect the piston tops for damage and the bores for serious scratching. If damage is evident, it might be as well to teardown the engine further and rectify it.

24 If you wish to remove carbon from the piston tops, bring each piston in turn to the top of its bore. Pack the gap between the piston and bore with grease and then scrape off the carbon with a brass or aluminum scraper. When you've finished, use a plastic or wooden spatula to scrape the contaminated grease from around the piston. **Caution!** Take great care not to allow debris to fall into oilways or waterways.

CYLINDER HEAD & GASKET INSTALLATION

25 Check that all of the threaded bolt holes in the top of the cylinder block are clean to their full depth; a doubled over pipe cleaner's a good tool for this. Turn the crankshaft, via the flywheel, until all of the pistons are approximately half way down their bores. Pour a little engine oil into each cylin-

der and spread it around the rim of the pistons and over the cylinder walls with your fingers.

26 Position a new cylinder head gasket over the dowels on the deck of the cylinder block. Make sure the gasket is the right way up so that the oilway on the right of the engine is left open. No gasket cement is needed.

27 Place a new gasket over the studs of the exhaust manifold.

28 Lower the cylinder head into position until it positively locates over the two protruding dowels and the studs of the exhaust manifold flange engage with the exhaust pipe flange. Lightly oil their threads and their head shoulders, then replace the ten bolts which secure the head and screw them in finger-tight.

29 Using a 12 mm socket, short extension and torque wrench tighten the cylinder head bolts to a final torque of 80 Nm /8 kgf m/58 lbf ft. Tighten the bolts in three stages and in a sequence which spirals outward from the two central bolts.

30 Fit the intake manifold support bracket and secure with its two 14 mm bolts which should be torqued to 45 Nm /4.5 kgf m /34 lbf ft.

31 To gain best access to the exhaust manifold flange nuts it will be necessary to raise the front or left-hand side of the car and support securely: ☞ 1/3.

32 From beneath the car push the exhaust system flange fully home against the manifold flange. Note: the three manifold flange nuts and washers are very difficult to get into place. The easiest nut to place is the one for the topmost stud, it can be fitted by reaching through the gap between the front subframe and chassis from the left-hand front wheelwell. Once you have a nut in place it becomes comparatively easy to fit the others.

33 You'll find the only way to tighten the manifold flange nuts is with a 14 mm socket attached to a universal joint attached to an extension of at least 360 mm (14 in), and then a ratchet or T-bar. Both of the lower nuts can be tightened from beneath the car; the top nut is most easily accessible via the left-hand front inner wheelwell. Torque the three nuts to 38 Nm /3.8 kgf m/30 lbf ft. Once the nuts are tight the car can be lowered to the ground.

34 Fit the rigid heater pipe bracket to the exhaust manifold flange, and tighten its 14 mm securing nut to a torque of 42 Nm /4.2 kgf m/31 lbf ft.

35 Fit the exhaust manifold heatshield after clipping the oxygen sensor wire to the engine backplate. Tighten the four 10 mm bolts which secure the shield using a wrench/spanner and finger pressure only.

36 During dismantling a number of individual wires and wiring looms were disconnected at connector blocks or terminals and then tied back out of harm's way. Lay the wires and looms back in their original positions and, where appropriate, fasten to support clips, then remake electrical connections in the following order -

37 At the alternator, first, position the black-bodied connector over the brass stud projecting from the rear of the alternator body. Note that the plastic body of the connector will only slot fully into place when its tail is vertical. Install the 10 mm brass nut together with a split washer and tighten. When the nut is tight, snap the cover of the terminal closed, having first sprayed a little water repellent fluid over the brass components. Plug the grey connector block into the recess in the side of the alternator. Make sure it clicks firmly home.

38 Push together the two parts of the fuel injection loom connector (at the rear end of the intake manifold): an audible click indicates a secure joint. Connect the ground/earth wire to its spade-type connector next to the injection connector block.

39 Using a 10 mm socket secure the ground/earth wire terminal to the engine lifting eye and then, from the other side of the car, another ground/earth terminal just above the rear of the exhaust manifold flange. There needs to be metal to metal contact at both these connections so ensure the surfaces are clean, bright and protected with a little petroleum jelly.

40 Push together the two parts of the electrical connector blocks of the crank-angle sensor and oxygen sensor (both connectors at rear of cambox) followed by the throttle body and ISC units (on the nose of the manifold) - an audible click means a good connection has been made.

41 Fit the fuel pipe which comes from the front of the fuel rail between intake tracts one and two to the rigid fuel pipe attached to the chassis rail nearest to the rear of the engine compartment. The hose will be a tight fit so a smear of WD40 or other silicone fluid may be helpful. Push the flexible pipe fully onto the rigid pipe until it meets the collar. Grasp the ears of the pipe clip and slide the pipe clip forward to its original position so that it clamps the flexible fuel pipe onto the rigid fuel pipe. Squeeze the body of the clip with pliers to make it as tight as possible. If the clip has been used more than twice, discard it and obtain a new replacement. Connect the second fuel pipe in exactly the same way. Fit and tighten the fuel filler cap at the rear of the car.

42 Reconnect the following hoses having first lubricated the union stubs with a little silicone-based lubricant. In all cases where spring hose clips are used, they should be returned to their original positions and then their bodies squeezed with pliers for extra security - vacuum hose to cruise control (if fitted), purge control vacuum hose, brake servo unit vacuum hose and heater hose.

43 Install the accelerator cable stop bracket which secures the cable to the side of the manifold and fix with two 10 mm bolts which should be tightened by no more than finger pressure on the wrench/spanner.

44 Having fitted the bracket, pull the accelerator inner cable forward and, gripping the nipple firmly, rotate the throttle spindle wheel clockwise until the recess in the wheel comes far enough around to enter the cable nipple completely, and then to place the cable in the grooved outer section of the wheel. Allow the wheel to return under its own spring tension. Note that the cable runs beneath the wheel, not over the top.

45 ☞ 3/13/26-42.

16. CRANKSHAFT FRONT OIL SEAL - REPLACEMENT (ENGINE IN CAR)

☞ First read 1/1, 2.

1 Remove the camshaft drivebelt: ☞ 3/13/1-24.

2 Unscrew and remove the 21 mm headed pulley retaining bolt. This will require considerable initial force so use a good quality socket with the longest possible lever hanging down toward the ground. If your car has manual transmission, engage a gear but also be sure to apply the brakes and chock all wheels. Leave automatic cars in "Park" or "Neutral" and install spark plugs if they've been removed. Strike the lever hard and fast blows with a soft-faced mallet and from an anti-clockwise direction (looking from the front of the car) until it loosens.

3 At this point you may find it helpful to raise the front of the car and support it securely: this will improve access to the seal area. ☞ 1/3.

4 Once the pulley retaining bolt has been removed, spray a little penetrating oil into the end of the pulley to lubricate the area between the pulley and crankshaft nose. Reach in with a pair of needle-nosed pliers and pull out the key locking the pulley to the crank.

5 We found with our engine that replacing two of the small outer pulley retaining bolts gave sufficient purchase to pull the toothed pulley from the crankshaft nose with fingers. If necessary, these same bolts will give enough purchase for an ordinary two-pronged puller. Alternatively, you could drill two holes in a small flat plate placed across a protruding spacer - such as a socket - and then screw two of the small screws through the plate until the toothed pulley is pulled off the crankshaft nose.

6 You will now be able to see the oil seal which is located in the oil pump body and surrounds the nose of the crankshaft.

7 Using a small chisel or an old screwdriver and fairly gentle hammer blows, force the sides of the seal away from its housing at one or more points until the seal is sufficiently buckled to be able to lever it free of the housing. Alternatively, you can drive the tip of the tool right through the front of the seal and, once the seal is impaled, lever it out of the housing. Use a small piece of wood or plastic at the lever's fulcrum point to prevent damage to the oil pump body **Caution!** Be careful not to hammer your screwdriver or chisel blade against the machined surface of the crankshaft where the

16/7 Remove old seal carefully.

oil seal lip bears or against the seal's seat in the oil pump body.

8 Lubricate the outer circumference and inner lip of a new oil seal and position it in the oil seal housing with your fingers.

9 Using a soft-faced hammer and a socket (32 mm on our car, but we know some cars have a seal of different diameter) or a piece of metal tubing of close to the same outer diameter as the seal, gently drift the seal fully home into its housing. If you don't have an appropriate piece of tubing or socket, you can drift the seal into its housing with direct but light blows from a very small hammer. If

16/9 Drift new seal into position.

you use this method, make sure you tap the seal home squarely and that you keep the hammer face flat against the seal, otherwise damage will result. The seal is properly installed when its face is flush with the lip of its housing in the oil pump.

10 Check components: ☞ 3/8/59-62. **Caution!** These checks are important: don't be tempted to skip them.

11 If necessary, temporarily install the 21 mm-headed crankshaft center bolt and, using a socket and T-bar to apply leverage, rotate the crankshaft until the keyway in its nose is facing upward. A sharp tap on the T-bar in the reverse direction will slacken the bolt once more without moving the crankshaft. Remove the bolt. **Caution!** Take care when turning the crank in case the valve heads come into contact with the pistons, although this couldn't be made to happen with our engine.

12 Rub a smear of oil over the crankshaft nose and in the keyway. Fit the cam drivebelt pulley over the nose of the crankshaft - flanged side toward the rear - and rotate it until the cutout in the pulley aligns with the cutout in the crankshaft.

13 Hold the locking key so that the chamfered end points toward the oil pump body and the chamfer is toward the crankshaft. Push the key into its slot with your fingers.

14 Lock the key in position by fitting the crankshaft pulley lock bolt and tightening it to a torque of 110 Nm /11.5 kgf m/84 lbf ft. If you have a car with automatic transmission, and are therefore unable to lock the crankshaft, smear the threads of the pulley lock bolt with thread locking fluid before installation and use the same method and force to tighten the bolt as was used to release it (including, if they've been removed, installation the spark plugs). If the front of the car has been raised, it can now be lowered to the ground.

15 ☞ 3/13/26-42.

17. CRANKSHAFT REAR OIL SEAL - REPLACEMENT (ENGINE IN CAR)

☞ First read 1/1, 2.

1 The first task is to remove the transmission unit. Manual: ☞ 4/1, 2. Auto: ☞ 4/1, 3.

2 Manual transmission cars only. The cover/pressure plate is retained by 12 mm bolts which should be gradually unscrewed by half of a turn at a time each, in a diagonal sequence, until the pressure exerted by the cover plate is completely relieved. To lock the flywheel you'll need to temporarily install one of the bellhousing bolts and then jam a screwdriver wedged into the ring gear teeth against it. **Warning!** Failure to undo all of the bolts progressively could easily result in the one or two bolts left under tension suddenly shearing and the cover plate flying off the flywheel. When the cover plate bolts have been removed lift away the cover plate and clutch disc together.

3 Flywheel (manual transmission cars) removal. Lock the flywheel as described in the previous step, then undo and remove the six bolts holding the flywheel to the crankshaft flange. Note: the bolts should be loosened half a turn each initially, in a diagonal sequence. **Caution!** It's a good idea to make sure that the same relationship between crankshaft and flywheel position is kept on reassembly to maintain balance. Mark the top of the flywheel and mark the top of the crankshaft (once the flywheel has been removed) using indelible ink so that the flywheel can be installed in exactly the same position. Once the bolts have been removed the flywheel can be lifted away - it's heavy!

4 Driveplate (auto transmission cars) removal. The procedure is the same as the flywheel removal procedure in the previous step, except that the driveplate will be lighter, there will be a backing plate between the bolt heads and the face of the driveplate and an adaptor between the crank and driveplate.

5 Using a small chisel or an old screwdriver and fairly gentle hammer blows, force the sides of the seal away from its housing at one or more points until the seal is sufficiently buckled to be able to lever it free of the housing. Alternatively, you can drive the tip of the tool right through the front of the seal and, once the seal is impaled, lever it out of the housing. Use a small piece of wood or plastic at the lever's fulcrum point to prevent damage to the seal housing. **Caution!** Be careful not to hammer your screwdriver or chisel blade against the machined surface of the crankshaft where the oil seal lip bears or against the seal's seat in its housing.

6 Lubricate the outer circumference and inner lip of a new oil seal and position it in the oil seal housing with your fingers, noting that the closed side of the seal should face outward.

7 Drift the seal into its housing with direct but light blows from a small hammer making sure that the seal is driven home evenly. If you use this method, make sure you keep the hammer face flat against the seal, otherwise damage will result. The seal is properly installed when its face is flush with the lip of its housing in the oil pump.

8 Inspect flywheel or driveplate and clutch components: ☞ 3/8/78-84. **Caution!** Don't be tempted to skip these checks: they're important.

9 Check that the threaded bolt holes in the crankshaft rear flange are clear and clean: a doubled over pipe cleaner is a good tool for this purpose.

10 Flywheel (manual transmission) installation. Apply thread locking fluid to the threads of each of the flywheel retaining bolts. Hold the flywheel in position over the rear of the crankshaft and fit the retaining bolts finger-tight.

11 Driveplate (auto transmission) installation. Apply thread locking fluid to the threads of each of the flywheel retaining bolts. Fit the adaptor collar to the rear of the crankshaft, followed by the driveplate and its backing plate. Fit the retaining bolts finger-tight.

12 Lock the flywheel or driveplate by temporarily fitting a bellhousing bolt and then wedging a screwdriver into the ring gear teeth and against the bolt. Tighten the flywheel or driveplate retaining bolts progressively, and in a diagonal sequence, to a final torque of 100 Nm /10 kgf m/74 lbf ft.

13 Fit the clutch (manual transmission cars): ☞ 3/9/124-127.

14 Fit the transmission. Manual: ☞ 4/8. Auto: ☞ 4/9.

18. STARTER RING GEAR - REPLACEMENT (ENGINE IN CAR)

☞ First read 1/1, 2.

1 The first task is to remove the transmission and flywheel /driveplate: ☞ 3/17/1-4.

2 For information on how to replace the ring gear and about inspecting flywheel or driveplate and clutch components: ☞ 3/8/71-84. **Caution!** Don't skip these checks: they're important.

3 Fit the flywheel and clutch /driveplate and transmission: ☞ 3/17/9-14.

19. CLUTCH & RELEASE BEARING - REMOVAL & INSTALLATION (ENGINE IN CAR)

☞ First read 1/1, 2.

1 The first task is to remove the transmission and the clutch: ☞ 3/17/1-2.

2 Release its rubber boot, then pull the clutch release fork outwards which will release it from its pivot and simultaneously from the back of

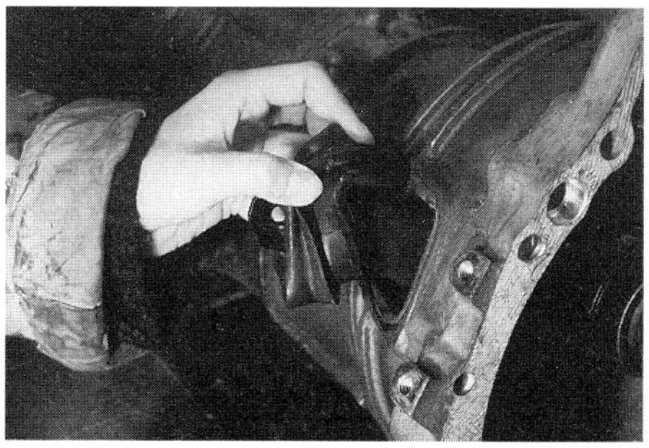

19/2 Remove fork's rubber boot.

the release bearing. The release bearing can now be pulled forward off the transmission input shaft sleeve. The release fork can be pulled inward through the square hole in the side of the bellhousing.

3 Pull the release bearing off over the nose of the input shaft.

4 Inspect the flywheel and clutch components: ☞ 3/8/78-84. **Caution!** Don't skip these checks: they're important.

5 Smear high melting point copper or molybdenum grease thinly over the sleeve of the transmission input shaft and spread a little of the same in the pivot socket on the back of the clutch release fork and the two pads which bear upon the release bearing.

6 Pull the release fork tail out through the square hole in the side of the bellhousing. Take the release bearing and place it on the input shaft sleeve with arms facing towards the back of the transmission.

7 Now the tricky bit is to push the arm against its pivot ball so that the retaining clip springs open and locks around the back of the ball whilst, simultaneously, the arm fork tips engage with the arms on the back of the release bearing. In fact, it's easier than it sounds!

19/6 Pull out release fork.

8 Fit the clutch to the flywheel: ☞ 3/9/124-127.

9 Fit the transmission. Manual: ☞ 4/8. Auto: ☞ 4/9

20. WATER PUMP - REMOVAL & INSTALLATION (ENGINE IN CAR)

☞ First read 1/1, 2.

1 Remove the camshaft drivebelt: ☞ 3/13/1-24.

2 Remove the power steering pump (if fitted). Using a 14 mm socket and a short extension, remove the nut from the pump pivot bolt via the pulley cutout. Next remove the 14 mm nut securing the pump's adjustment strap to the pump mounting bracket. Push the pivot bolt backward until the whole pivot bolt can be removed from the rear: you might need to use a thin brass drift and hammer just to get it moving. The pump can now be pulled from its bracket, but if it's the same as the one on our car, it will be very stiff and will need to be worked up and down until it comes free. Once the pump is free, leave it connected to its piping but move it down to the anti-sway bar and tie or tape it in place so that it does not get in the way.

3 Using a 12 mm socket and a 75 mm /3 in extension, undo and remove the two bolts securing the coolant inlet casting flange to the side of the water pump body at the front of the cylinder block. Once the two bolts are removed the casting will need a sharp tug to release the adhesion of its gasket.

4 Using a 14 mm socket, undo and remove the bolt securing the camshaft drivebelt idler wheel (if still fitted) and lift the wheel away from the water pump body. This will then give clearance to reach a partially obscured water pump retaining bolt.

5 Slacken and then unscrew - in a diagonal sequence - the four 12 mm bolts holding the water pump body to the front of the cylinder block. Once the bolts are clear, the pump body can be pulled away. **Warning!** It will come free suddenly as the gasket seal breaks. **Caution!** You can tap the back of the casting with a wooden hammer handle or soft-faced mallet to help break the joint's adhesion, but don't use a sharp implement to lever the casting away from the cylinder block.

6 The water pump cannot be dismantled further so, if it's faulty, replace the whole unit.

7 Clean all traces of old gasket material from joint faces thoroughly, taking great care not to gouge the metal.

8 Check the condition of the camshaft drivebelt and associated components: ☞ 3/8/59-62. **Caution!** Don't skip these checks: they're important.

9 Fit a new gasket to the face of the water pump - no gasket cement is necessary. Hold the water pump in position at the front of the cylinder block - making sure that the (new) sealing strip between the top of the pump and the cylinder head seal plate stays in place - and fix by installation the four bolts finger-tight. Tighten the 12 mm retaining bolts, in a diagonal sequence, to a final torque of 22 Nm /2.2 kgf m/17 lbf ft.

10 Hold a new gasket over the water inlet casting flange and then pass the two 12 mm bolts through the holes in the flange to hold the gasket in position. Fit the casting to the water pump inlet and tighten the retaining bolts to a torque of 22 Nm /2.2 kgf m/17 lbf ft. No gasket cement should be necessary if the water pump and inlet pipe flanges are clean and free of all old gasket material.

11 Lift the power steering pump (if fitted) into position and reinsert its long pivot bolt then, via a cutout in the pulley, loosely install the 14 mm nut which retains the pivot bolt. Secure the pump's adjustment strap to the pump mounting bracket with its 14 mm bolt and leave the bolt fingertight until later.

12 ☞ 3/13/26-42.

21. ENGINE MOUNTINGS - REPLACEMENT (ENGINE IN CAR)

☞ First read 1/1, 2.

1 You'll need enough room beneath the car to access the undersides of the engine mountings. Raise the front of the car and support securely: ☞ 1/3.

2 Centre a jack beneath the oil pan/sump, place a piece of protective wooden packing on its pad and raise the pad until it just contacts the underside of the pan. Raise the pad a further 6-7 mm/quarter inch to take the weight from the engine mountings. **Caution!** Don't jack the engine any higher.

3 Each of the mounting brackets is held to the cylinder block by three 14 mm bolts which are a little inaccessible but otherwise not too difficult to undo: you'll find a short extension will help. Note that one of the bolts on the right-hand mounting also passes through the starter motor mounting.

4 From beneath the car, undo and remove the 14 mm nuts and spring washers which secure the mountings to the subframe: you'll need a 125 mm/5 inch extension to reach up inside the turrets.

5 You should now be able to withdraw the mounting brackets, complete with mountings and mounting covers from the sides of the engine: the right-hand bracket will need to be worked out from beneath the starter mounting bracket. The mounting covers should fall off.

6 + Place the engine mounting in a vise and, using a 14 mm socket with a 125 mm/5 inch extension, undo the nut that holds the mounting to its bracket.

21/6a Remove mounting from bracket.

21/6b Engine mounting components.

7 Fit the new mounting in the vice, noting that there is a square boss on the back of the mounting which should engage with the square recess in the mounting bracket. Tighten the retaining nut to a torque of 100 Nm /10 kgf m/74 lbf ft. Repeat the process for the second mounting.

8 Fit the outer covers, noting that the two large drain holes should be at the bottom when the mountings are *in situ*. Hold the outer cover in place

whilst lowering the threaded stud of each mounting through its hole or slot in the subframe. When both mountings are resting in place fit securing washers and nut finger-tight from beneath the car.

9 You should now be able to fit the mounting brackets to the cylinder block sides, remembering that the right-hand one has to be pushed under the starter bracket. A further peculiarity of the right-hand bracket (on our car at least!) is that the three bolts are all of different lengths: the shortest bolt should be in the forwardmost position and the longest in the topmost position; you can guess where the third one goes ... Note: you may have to manipulate the engine's height a little, using the jack, to achieve bracket alignment with the bolt holes in the cylinder block. Tighten the 14 mm bolts which retain the brackets to a torque of 50 Nm /5 kgf m/36 lbf ft.

10 Lower and remove the jack supporting the engine.

11 From beneath the car tighten the mounting nuts to a torque of 70 Nm /7 kgf m/50 lbf ft.

12 That's it, lower the car to the ground.

22. CLUTCH MASTER CYLINDER - REMOVAL & INSTALLATION

☞ First read 1/1, 2.

REMOVAL

1 **Caution!** Clutch hydraulic fluid - which is the same as brake fluid - is an extremely effective paint stripper so, whenever disconnecting hydraulic pipes or removing hydraulic components, make sure you have placed rags to catch and absorb spillages. Wipe off any spillages on paintwork immediately.

2 The master cylinder is mounted on the engine side of the firewall/bulkhead immediately in front of the clutch pedal position.

3 Unscrew the cylinder's reservoir cap and stretch a piece of thin polyethylene (one skin of a bag or food wrap) across the open reservoir before replacing the cap. This simple procedure will stop the cylinder leaking fluid when its union is undone.

4 Unscrew the 10 mm union nut which fixes the rigid hydraulic pipe to the side of the cylinder and when it's completely unscrewed gently pull the rigid pipe out of the cylinder. Plug, cap or tape wrap the open end of the pipe to reduce fluid spillage.

5 The mounting flange of the master cylinder is fixed to the firewall/bulkhead by two 12 mm nuts. We believe that on most cars these nuts will be on the engine side of the firewall but, on our left-hand drive car, one of the nuts was on the driver's side of the firewall. Undo and remove the nut, or nuts , on the engine side of the firewall using a socket and short extension. If there's a retaining nut inside the car, you'll find that access is made easier by removing the large plastic cover beneath the steering wheel; it's held by two medium cross-head screws. Even so you'll almost have to stand on your head to reach up to the offending nut: you might even consider removing the seat ...

6 The master cylinder can now be removed. Note: there's an insulating gasket against the cylinder's mounting flange: if it's damaged replace it.

INSTALLATION

7 Place a dab of white brake grease on the tip of the pushrod - which should be protruding from the firewall. As you fit the cylinder into position, reengage the pushrod from the pedal. Tighten the two 12 mm retaining nuts to a torque of 22 Nm /2.2 kgf m/17 lbf ft. If you had to remove the cover beneath the steering wheel, install it and secure with its two crosshead screws. **Warning!** Make sure the cover is properly installed: you don't want it to drop down on your feet when you're driving.

8 Remove the plug or cap - leaving absolutely no blockage or debris behind in the pipe - and then fit the pipe union into its recess in the side of the cylinder. **Caution!** It's very easy to cross-thread these unions so screw the union nut home with your fingers (not possible if cross-threaded) whilst holding the pipe square to the cylinder body. Finally tighten the union using the pull of two fingers at the end of an ordinary wrench/spanner.

9 Remove the polyethylene sheet from beneath the reservoir cap, then bleed the hydraulic system: ☞ 3/26.

10 Check clutch pedal height and free play adjustments: ☞ 3/28.

23. CLUTCH MASTER CYLINDER - TEARDOWN & REBUILD

☞ First read 1/1, 2.

1 **Caution!** It is our advice that you replace a faulty master cylinder with a new or exchange unit. However, if you wish to rebuild the master cylinder yourself, or you're fitting new seals to a serviceable unit as part of a maintenance program, then the procedure is as follows -

TEARDOWN

2 **Caution!** You must not rebuild the master cylinder using the old seals so, before you start, check that the overhaul kit you've purchased contains a new cup-shaped main seal, piston seal, reservoir seal and snap ring/circlip.

3 Remove the master cylinder: ☞ 3/22. Unscrew the reservoir cap, the protective cover beneath and the cap sealing ring. Tip the fluid contents of the cylinder into your garage's old oil

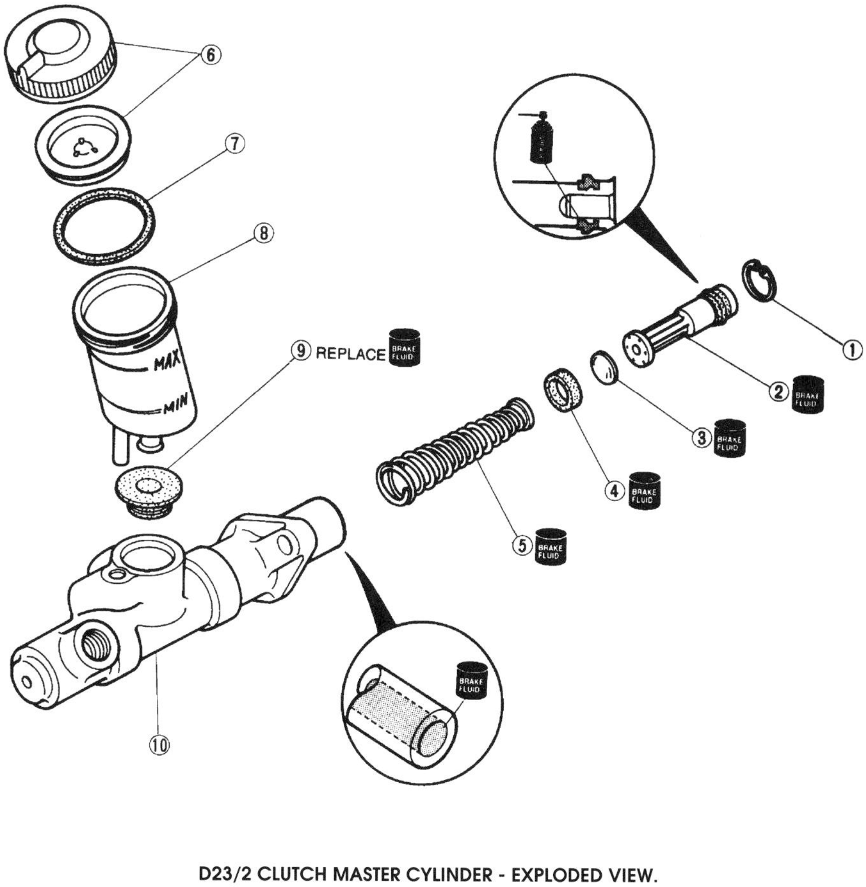

D23/2 CLUTCH MASTER CYLINDER - EXPLODED VIEW.
1 Snapring (Circlip). 2 Piston. 3 Spacer disc. 4 Primary cup seal. 5 Spring. 6 Reservoir cap & cover. 7 Sealing ring. 8 Reservoir body. 9 Reservoir seal. 10 Master cylinder body.

container ready for safe disposal.

4 Mount the cylinder in a vise fitted with jaw protectors so that the mounting flange faces upward.

5 Using snap ring/circlip pliers whilst simultaneously pushing the piston down the bore with a screwdriver, release and withdraw the snap ring/ circlip from the cylinder bore. Gently release the screwdriver and, if the piston emerges from the bore, pull it out.

6 Remove the cylinder from the vise and try shaking out the bore's contents. If this doesn't work you'll have to apply compressed air to the pipe terminal on the side of the cylinder having first installed the reservoir cap and wrapped the whole thing in rag to catch the parts as they are expelled. **Warning!** Point the open end of the cylinder away from yourself and others when using compressed air.

7 Pull the plastic reservoir body from the cylinder body.

8 Discard the main seal, reservoir seal, piston seal and snap ring/circlip; you'll need to lever the piston seal off with a screwdriver, taking great care not to damage the piston. Using methylated spirit only, clean every component that is to be reused until it is spotless.

9 Inspect the cylinder bore for damage in the form of scratching or corrosion. If such damage is evident, scrap the cylinder. Check, too, that the spring is not corroded and that the piston is undamaged: again, damage dictates renewal.

REBUILD

10 **Caution!** Work on a totally clean surface - newspaper is ideal.

11 Pour a little fresh brake fluid into the cylinder bore and rub it around the bore with your fingers. Lubricate the new cup seal with hydraulic fluid and then fit its open side over the cap at the small end of the spring. Whilst holding the cylinder closed end upwards, feed the larger diameter end of the spring into the bore and then push the spring and seal together as far into the bore as they will go. **Caution!** It's important that the spring pad stays seated in the seal cup during this process and that the cup does not get turned inside out as it enters the bore.

12 Using your fingers only, fit a new seal into the groove at the pushrod end of the piston: the chamfered side of the protruding seal lip should face the pushrod end of the piston.

13 Rub brake fluid all over the piston and the spacer disc. Place the spacer disc on the thrust pad of the piston (opposite end to pushrod recess) and, whilst holding the cylinder closed end upwards, push the spacer and piston into the bore.

14 Mount the cylinder in the vise as before and, whilst pushing the piston down into the bore, fit a new snap ring/circlip into the groove at the pushrod end of the cylinder bore. Keep the piston pushed into the bore and, using a cotton bud, apply a smear of white brake grease around the bore just below the snap ring. Release the piston and place a dab of the same lubricant into the pushrod recess of the piston.

15 After lubricating it with brake fluid, fit a new reservoir seal into the top of the cylinder body and then push the reservoir into the seal until it is firmly home. Temporarily install the reservoir's cap seal, cover and cap. Tape over the cylinder's outlet to prevent the ingress of dirt until it's installed. Install the master cylinder ☞ 3/22.

24. CLUTCH RELEASE (SLAVE) CYLINDER - REMOVAL & INSTALLATION

☞ First read 1/1, 2.

REMOVAL

1 **Caution!** Clutch hydraulic fluid - which is the same as brake fluid - is an extremely effective paint stripper so, whenever disconnecting hydraulic pipes or removing hydraulic components, make sure you have placed rags to catch and absorb spillages. Wipe off any spillages from paintwork immediately.

2 Remove the cap from the clutch master cylinder, stretch a thin piece of polyethylene sheet over the reservoir top and then fit and tighten the cap. This will prevent the leakage of fluid when the release cylinder is removed.

3 You'll need good, safe access to the underside of the car in the vicinity of the bellhousing. Raise the right-hand side of the car and support securely: ☞ 1/3.

4 You'll find the release cylinder bolted to the lower right-hand side of the bellhousing.

5 Using a 10 mm wrench/spanner unscrew the pipe union nut from the cylinder's body. Once the nut is completely free, pull the pipe from the union and then plug, cap or tape over the pipe end to prevent the ingress of dirt.

6 Free the clutch release cylinder from its mounting by removing the two 12 mm retaining bolts. Access to these bolts is difficult but the lower bolt can be reached from beneath with a wrench/ spanner while the upper bolt can be undone with a socket mounted on a 350 mm/14 inch extension inserted through the gap above the subframe in the right-hand front inner wheel arch.

INSTALLATION

7 Place a dab of copper-based or molybdenum grease on the pushrod recess in the clutch release lever. Position the release cylinder on its mounting bosses whilst simultaneously engaging the pushrod with the release fork.

8 Fit and tighten the 12 mm bolts which retain the cylinder. Tighten to a torque of 20 Nm / 2 kgf m/15 lbf ft.

9 Remove the plug or cap - leaving absolutely no blockage or debris behind in the pipe - and then fit the pipe union into its recess in the side of the cylinder. **Caution!** It's very easy to cross-thread these unions so screw the union nut home with your fingers (not possible if cross-threaded) whilst holding the pipe square. Finally, tighten the union using the pull of two fingers at the end of an ordinary wrench/spanner.

10 Remove the polyethylene sheet from beneath the reservoir cap, then bleed the hydraulic system: ☞ 3/26.

25. CLUTCH RELEASE (SLAVE) CYLINDER - TEARDOWN & REBUILD

☞ First read 1/1, 2.

1 **Caution!** It is our advice that you replace a faulty clutch release cylinder with a new or exchange unit. However, if you wish to rebuild the cylinder yourself, or you're fitting new seals to a serviceable unit as part of a maintenance program, then the procedure is as follows -

TEARDOWN

2 **Caution!** You must not rebuild the cylinder using the old seal so, before you start, make sure you have a new piston seal available. The kit should also contain a new pushrod boot and a cover for the bleed valve.

3 Remove the cylinder from the bellhousing: ☞ 3/24. Pull the pushrod from its boot and then pull the boot off of the cylinder. Discard the boot.

4 Shake the piston from the cylinder bore taking care not to drop it on the ground. If it won't come out, apply compressed air to the pipe terminal having first wrapped the cylinder in rag to catch the ejected parts. **Warning!** Point the open end of the cylinder away from yourself and others when using compressed air.

5 Using a small screwdriver and taking great care not to scratch the piston, lever the old piston seal off and discard it.

6 Using an 8 mm wrench/spanner, unscrew and remove the bleed valve from the cylinder. Note: beneath the valve there's a steel ball which

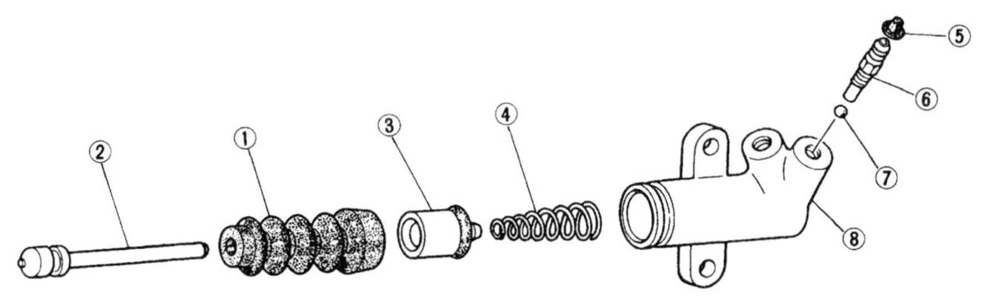

D25/4 CLUTCH RELEASE (SLAVE) CYLINDER - EXPLODED VIEW.
1 Boot. 2 Pushrod. 3 Piston & seal. 4 Spring. 5 Bleed valve cap. 6 Bleed valve. 7 Steel ball. 8 Cylinder body.

you should now tip out into your hand.

7 Using methylated spirit only, clean every component that is to be re-used until it is spotless.

8 Inspect the cylinder bore for damage in the form of scratching or corrosion. If such damage is evident, scrap the cylinder. Check, too, that the spring is not corroded and that the piston is undamaged: again, damage dictates renewal.

REBUILD

9 **Caution!** Work on a totally clean surface - newspaper is ideal.

10 Lubricate the seal and the piston with brake fluid and then, using your fingers only, fit the new seal to the piston. **Caution!** The chamfered side of the seal should face the pushrod end of the cylinder.

11 Pour a little fresh brake fluid into the cylinder bore and rub it around the bore with your fingers. Once more lubricate the piston and seal assembly with brake fluid and then engage the small end of the spring with the boss at the seal end of the piston. Spring first, feed the piston and spring assembly into the cylinder bore.

12 Smear white brake grease into the pushrod recess of the piston and around the exposed end of the bore. Fit the pushrod boot over the end of the cylinder until it engages with its groove and then slide the pushrod into the boot, ball end outward.

13 Drop the steel ball into the bleed valve's threaded bore and then install the bleed valve which can be left fingertight until the cylinder is bled.

26. CLUTCH HYDRAULIC SYSTEM - AIR BLEEDING

☞ First read 1/1, 2.

1 If air bubbles are trapped in the hydraulic system you may well find that you need to pump the clutch pedal to make the clutch work at all. This is because air is much more compressible than brake fluid (which is the hydraulic fluid used by your car's clutch system) and therefore a reduced amount of movement is transmitted to the clutch release fork. These same symptoms can be created by aged brake fluid which has absorbed water vapor from the atmosphere.

2 **Caution!** Brake fluid is an extremely effective paint stripper so, whenever working on an hydraulic system, make sure you have placed rags to catch and absorb spillages. Wipe off any spillages from paintwork immediately.

3 The clutch release cylinder is bolted to the lower right-hand side of the bellhousing and to bleed the hydraulic system constant access to the cylinder's bleed valve is required. Therefore, raise the right-hand side of the car and support securely: ☞ 1/3. Note: do not raise the car any higher than is necessary for comfortable access because, if the car is too far from level, bleeding will not be so effective.

4 Gather together a good supply of fresh, high quality brake fluid, a 500 mm/20 inch length of bleed tubing (any flexible tubing that will fit tightly over the ball-shaped end of the bleed valve) a 8 mm wrench/spanner, a clear plastic bottle or jar that will hold around a half liter or pint of fluid, oh, and three beers. Three beers? Yep, one for yourself, and one each for the two assistants you're going to need for about ten minutes.

5 Remove the cap and cover from the master cylinder reservoir and make one assistant responsible for keeping the fluid level topped up above the "Min" level at all times during the bleeding process and starting now.

6 Your other assistant gets to sit comfortably behind the wheel and pump the clutch pedal when required.

7 You get the dirty job! Pour brake fluid into the clear container until it reaches a depth of around 50 mm /2 in. Take this, the wrench/spanner and the bleed tube with you beneath the car. Fit the wrench on the bleed valve and check that it's closed (tight). Leave the wrench in place whilst pushing one end of the bleed tube firmly onto the bleed valve head. Immerse the other end of the tube in the brake fluid in the clear container and note that the tube end must stay immersed through the whole process, otherwise air will be sucked back into the system.

8 Get your friend in the driving seat to pump the pedal slowly 4-5 times. Let the pedal rise and then, on your instruction, your pal should begin to depress the pedal at a speed that will take 2-3 seconds before the pedal hits the floor. At the start of the stroke, open the bleed valve around half a turn: you'll immediately see bubbles and fluid shooting out the end of the bleed tube. As soon as the stroke is complete, close the bleed valve (your friend should keep the pedal against the floor until you've closed the valve and shouted "OK"). Let the pedal return to its normal height.

9 Repeat the process detailed in step 8 until the fluid emerging from the bleed tube is completely free of bubbles. Then close the bleed valve, remove the bleed tube and fit the protective cover over the bleed valve. **Caution!** Do not re-use brake fluid bled from the system; instead dispose of it safely as you would old oil.

10 Lower the car to the ground, top up the master cylinder to the "Max" mark, fit the reservoir cover and cap. You've finished, so you can all drink your beer!

27. CLUTCH HYDRAULIC LINES/HOSES - REPLACEMENT

☞ First read 1/1, 2.

1 The hydraulic line system for the clutch is comprised of rigid and flexible pipes joined together by bracket-mounted unions. The pipework connects the master and release cylinders. Whether your car is left or right-hand drive, it seems that the pipework is identical between the union mounted on the firewall at the left-hand side of the engine compartment and the release cylinder - which means that on right-hand drive cars, the pipework doubles back on itself!

2 **Warning!** Clutch hydraulic fluid must not be swallowed nor allowed to enter the bloodstream: seek medical aid if this happens. **Caution!** Clutch hydraulic fluid - which is the same as brake fluid - is an extremely effective paint stripper so, whenever disconnecting hydraulic pipes or removing hydraulic components, make sure you have placed rags to catch and absorb spillages. Wipe any spillages from paintwork immediately.

3 **Caution!** If you're renewing rigid hydraulic pipes, we advise you to buy preformed replacements. However, if you do intend to bend straight replacement piping to fit: ☞ 9/3.

4 Before you disconnect any pipework stretch a piece of thin polyethylene sheet across the top of the master cylinder reservoir, then fit and tighten its cap: this will minimize fluid loss when pipes are separated.

5 The only piece of clutch pipework that's easy to replace is the rigid section between the master cylinder and the union at the left-hand rear firewall. Unscrew the pipe's 10 mm union at the master cylinder, then using pliers pull the spring locking clip from the union bracket at the other end of the pipe. Push the union through the bracket sufficiently to give access to the 17 mm hex on the flexible pipe. Lock the flexible pipe's collar with a 17 mm wrench/spanner whilst undoing the 10 mm union nut with another. Pull the pipe from its firewall clips.

6 The problem with the remaining bits of pipework is access to the second union above the starter motor on the bellhousing. If you're extremely dexterous or have some fancy tools it's possible you can separate the union in order to replace the length of flexible pipe which crosses the firewall behind the engine. However, for mere mortals we recommend removing the rigid (union to release cylinder) and flexible pipes together and then separating the two. The procedure is detailed in the following steps 7 to 10.

7 The clutch release/release cylinder and associated piping is bolted to the right-hand side of the bellhousing and to gain access the right-hand side of the car will have to be raised and supported securely: ☞ 1/3.

8 From beneath the car, reach up to the pipe union bracket on the right and, using pliers, pull the locking spring clip from the bracket. Push the union upward sufficiently to allow the rigid pipe to be pulled through the slot in the bracket. You might just have enough room now to undo the union with 10 mm and 12 mm wrenches, if not carry on to the next step.

9 You will see that the coiled section of the rigid pipe is fixed to the bellhousing by a bracket. Remove the 17 mm nut from the transmission side of the bellhousing and then withdraw the bracket securing bolt from the engine side.

10 Unscrew the 10 mm union nut on the release cylinder to free the pipe or pipes which can now be removed from the car.

11 Renew the section or sections of piping as necessary noting that the pipe unions should not be tightened with more pressure than the pull of two fingers at the end of an ordinary wrench/spanner. Install the lower rigid pipe and the flexible hose first making sure they are safely secured in their brack-

ets. Retighten the pipe bracket bellhousing bolt to a torque of 80 Nm /8 kgf m/60 lbf ft.

12 Fit the top section of rigid piping, making sure it is firmly secured in the firewall spring clips.

13 **Caution!** Union bracket spring clips must be installed so that the bowed side faces away from the bracket; also make sure the spring clips are fully home.

14 **Caution!** When connecting unions to master or release cylinders, screw the union nuts home with your fingers before final tightening: this simple precaution will prevent cross-threading.

15 Remove the polyethylene sheet from the master cylinder reservoir and bleed air from the hydraulic system: ☞ 3/26. Lower the car to the ground: ☞ 1/3.

28. CLUTCH PEDAL HEIGHT & LASH - CHECKING & ADJUSTMENT

☞ First read 1/1, 2.

PEDAL HEIGHT

1 With the pedal in its normal position, measure the distance between the center of the pedal's footpad and the carpet surface on the vertical firewall/bulkhead behind the pedal. The correct height is 175 to 185 mm/6.9 to 7.25 in.

2 The height of the pedal is dictated by the threaded stop of the electrical switch which senses when the clutch is engaged and which is mounted in the top of the pedal box.

3 Access to the clutch pedal box area is easier if the plastic cover beneath the steering wheel is removed: it's retained by two medium sized crosshead screws. By standing on your head in the driver's footwell, and generally adopting a position that would make a contortionist proud, you'll be able to reach the switch.

4 Release the switch's 16 mm locknut and then screw the 21 mm switch body backwards or forwards until the correct pedal height is achieved. Retighten the locknut and check pedal lash (free play).

PEDAL LASH (FREE PLAY)

5 Lash is the distance between the pedal footpad's highest position and the position at which clutch resistance is first felt when the pedal is pressed by hand. This measurement should be between 5 and 13 mm/0.2 and 0.5 inch.

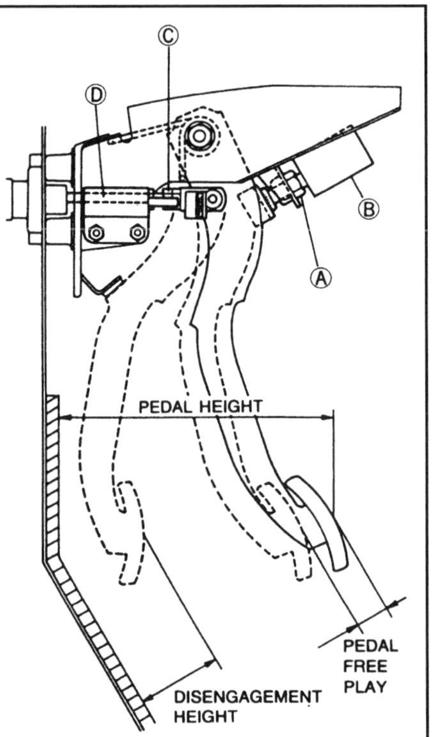

D28/1 CLUTCH PEDAL HEIGHT ADJUSTMENT. A Locknut. B Clutch switch body. C Locknut. D Pushrod.

6 If you want to adjust the lash, take up the contortionist's position again, slacken the 12 mm locknut on the clutch cylinder pushrod and then, using a 10 mm wrench/spanner, rotate the pushrod clockwise or anti-clockwise until the desired free play is achieved.

7 Now ensure that the pedal's disengagement height is correct. At the point at which the clutch disengages measure the distance between the center of the pedal's footpad and the carpet of the sloping section of the firewall behind the pedal. The dimension should be 68 mm/2.68 in: if necessary, readjust the length of the pushrod. When you are satisfied with both lash and disengagement height, retighten the pushrod locknut.

8 If you had to remove the cover beneath the steering wheel, fit it and secure with its two crosshead screws. **Warning!** Make sure the cover is properly installed: you don't want it to drop down on your feet when you're driving.

29. CLUTCH PEDAL REMOVAL & INSTALLATION

☞ First read 1/1, 2.

1 It's likely you want to remove the clutch pedal because the pivot bushings are worn or the pedal return spring has broken, therefore, it's only necessary to withdraw the pedal's pivot pin having first released its 12 mm nut and spring washer. Of course, this is easier said than done because of the pivot pin's position high up behind the dash panel. Access to the clutch pedal box area is easier if the plastic cover beneath the steering wheel is removed: it's retained by two medium sized crosshead screws. By standing on your head in the driver's footwell, and generally adopting a position that would make a contortionist proud, you'll be able to reach the pivot pin.

2 Once the pin is withdrawn, it should be possible to remove the pedal complete with pushrod. Fit well greased new bushings inside and a new spring outside the pedal pivot tube and then slide the pedal and pushrod back into position.

3 Fit the pivot bolt and secure with its nut. Using needle nosed pliers, a screwdriver and infinite patience, lock the tang end of the return spring in place and hook the hooked end of the spring behind the pedal so that tension is restored. When you've successfully located the spring tighten the pivot bolt locknut to a torque of 27 Nm /2.7 kgf m /20 lbf ft.

4 If you had to remove the cover beneath the steering wheel, fit it and secure with its two crosshead screws. **Warning!** Make sure the cover is properly fitted: you don't want it to drop down on your feet when you're driving.

4 TRANSMISSION & DRIVELINE

1. TRANSMISSION (GEARBOX) - PREPARATION FOR REMOVAL

☞ First read 1/1, 2.

1 The transmission unit, whether manual or automatic, can be removed by itself or in unit with the engine. If removal of the engine would allow you to do some beneficial work on that unit it's worth considering removal of both components together for the small amount of extra work it will entail: ☞ 3/4.

2 To remove and install the transmission unit you'll need easy access to much of the car's underside. If you have access to, or can hire, a garage pit or whole vehicle hoist, go for it - your life will then be much easier. Otherwise, as a sensible minimum, you're going to need four strong safety stands and a hard and level surface as your workplace: ☞ 1/3.

3 **Caution!** If your car has a faulty automatic transmission unit, have the problem professionally diagnosed before the transmission is removed.

4 📷 **Warning!** The transmission unit is a heavy and large item; you'll need occasional assistance ... unless your name's Schwartzenegger.

5 After removal, and before any dismantling

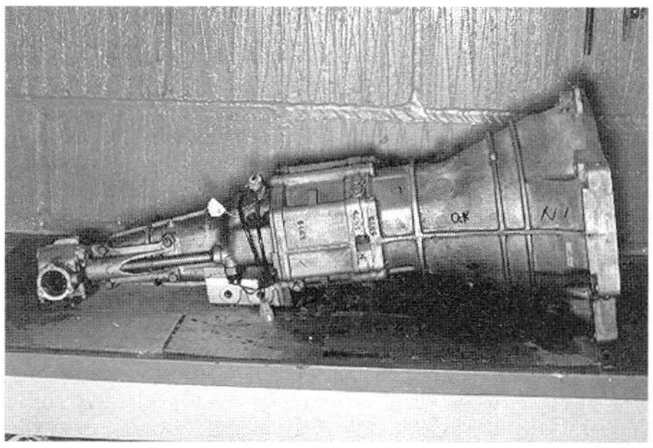

1/4 Ready to begin work.

begins, the outside of the unit will need to be thoroughly cleaned. Make sure you've got solvents (proprietary brands or kerosene/paraffin), brushes, scrapers, rags and old newsprint ready. **Warning!** Do not use gasoline/petrol as a cleaning solvent.

6 Specific tool requirements are described in the text.

7 Read through the whole procedure before starting the job.

2/3 Unscrew gearshift knob.

2/4a Lift out ashtray.

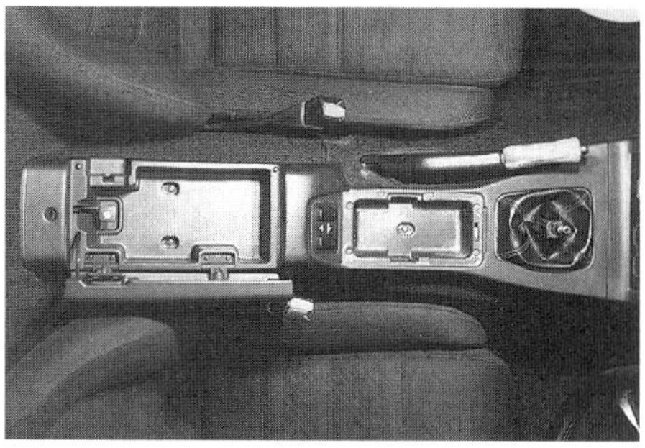

2/4b Remove retaining screws ...

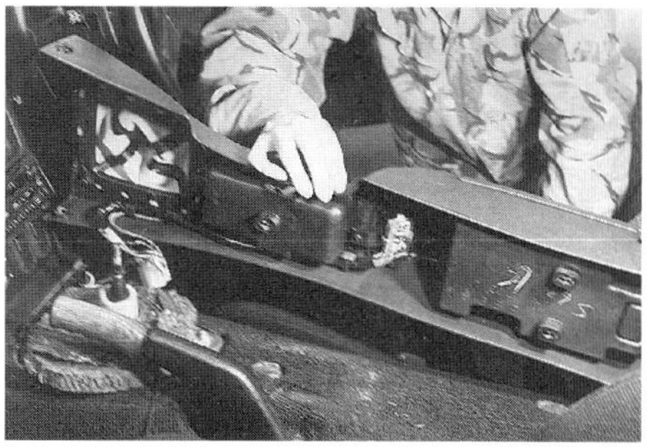

2/4c ... and lift away console.

2. TRANSMISSION (GEARBOX), MANUAL - REMOVAL

☞ First read 1/1, 2.

1 Isolate the battery: ☞ 3/4/4.

2 Raise and support the whole car securely and at a height sufficient to give easy access to the underside: ☞ 1/3.

3 📷 From inside the car unscrew the knob from the gearshift lever.

4 📷+ Lift the ashtray from the center console: it's held by spring clips. Lift the lid of the cassette compartment. All of the crosshead screws retaining the transmission tunnel console are now exposed; two in the cassette compartment, one beneath the ashtray and one on each side of the moulding adjacent to the shift lever. Once the five screws are removed, spring the front side pieces of the console outwards slightly, then lift the console enough to move it forward and off of the fuel filler flap release lever. **Caution!** Do not attempt to remove the console completely before disconnecting the wiring. For transmission removal, it's sufficient to leave the wiring in place and lay the plastic console alongside the tunnel, having lifted it off the shift lever.

5 Remove the insulating material and foam

2/6 Remove gaiter unit bolts.

collar from around the shift lever base.

6 There are four 10 mm bolts holding the gearshift lever's rubber gaiter to the transmission tunnel. You'll need a 10 mm wrench to get to one of the bolts which is partly recessed beneath the center console.

7 + Once the lever gaiter is released from the tunnel, it can be lifted high enough to give access to the three 10 mm bolts fixing the shift lever base pivot to the transmission extension. Once the three bolts are removed, the whole shift lever assembly, complete with gaiter, can be lifted away.

2/7a Remove three bolts ...

2.7b ... and lift lever from housing.

Caution! The lever assembly may drip oil, so have a rag ready to wipe the lever swivel pin before oil is dripped onto upholstery or carpets.

8 + Next you'll need a bowl or a drainer can capable of holding at least 3 liters (6 pints) of fluid that will be drained from the transmission unit. Place the bowl directly beneath the transmission drain plug and undo the plug with a 24 mm socket. It's best to do the final unscrewing by hand so that the plug can be held in place until the last moment and then quickly removed so that oil doesn't spray everywhere.

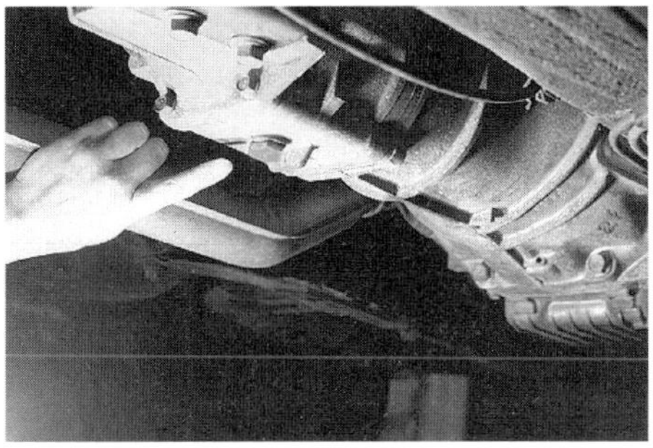

2/8a Remove transmission drain plug ...

2.8b ... and drain oil completely.

9 Note: the drain plug is magnetic so that it will collect any metal fragments in the transmission lubricant. If the plug has never been removed and cleaned, it's quite normal for there to be a small amount of deposited fine metal debris, but if there are any large pieces of swarf it is possible that one of the transmission components is damaged and wearing rapidly. Once the oil has drained the plug can be installed finger-tight to stop residual oil dripping to the ground. Discard the oil you have drained by taking it to a local oil disposal/recycling point. Do not attempt to re-use the oil.

10 Moving to the underside of the car the next job is to remove the plastic undertray from beneath the front of the engine. All fixings are 10mm. First remove the three self-tapping screws from the front of the tray, followed by the bolts at the back of the tray. Then, at each side of the car, remove the bolt next to the top swinging arm, the bolt on the side of the chassis member in the wheelarch and, finally, the nut holding the tray and the front valence stay. Once the nut is removed the stay can be pulled from the stud and moved out of the way to give enough clearance to remove the plastic undertray. It's recommended that you put all of the screws and the two nuts back in place, finger-tight, once the tray has been removed.

11 Remove the complete exhaust system: ☞ 5/38.

12 + The next job is to remove the propshaft. Before undoing the four nuts and bolts holding the shaft flange to the differential flange, use a blob of white paint to mark the relative positions of both flanges. Alternatively, a small groove can be filed across the joint for the same purpose. It is important to mark the relative position of the two components because the propshaft may be out of balance in another position. The bolts have 12 mm heads, whilst the nuts are 14mm,

2/12a Mark propshaft flange ...

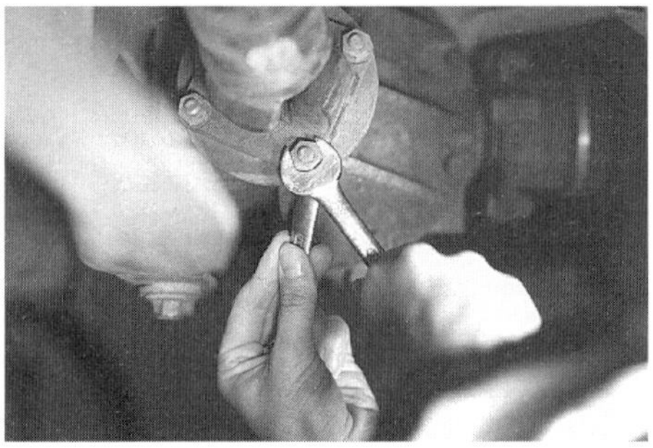

2/12b ... & remove retaining nuts & bolts.

so you'll need a combination of two wrenches/spanners to release each nut and bolt. Using a diagonal sequence, slacken in turn each of the nuts and bolts a little before removing them completely. You may need to apply the parking brake to lock the propshaft.

13 Once the four nuts and bolts have been released, separate the propshaft and differential flanges by pushing the shaft forward further onto the transmission tailshaft and then lowering the axle end of the shaft before withdrawing the shaft's nose from the tail of the transmission. Note: some oil will drip from the transmission end once the

2/13 Slide shaft forward.

propshaft is removed; place a plastic bag over the end of the transmission tail and secure with an elastic band.

14 Once the propshaft has been removed completely, replace the bolts, locking washers and nuts finger-tight in the differential flange for safe-keeping.

15 Free the clutch release cylinder from its mounting on the bellhousing by removing the two 12 mm retaining bolts. Access to these bolts is difficult but the lower bolt can be reached with a 12 mm wrench from beneath the car, and the upper bolt with a 12 mm socket mounted on a 360 mm

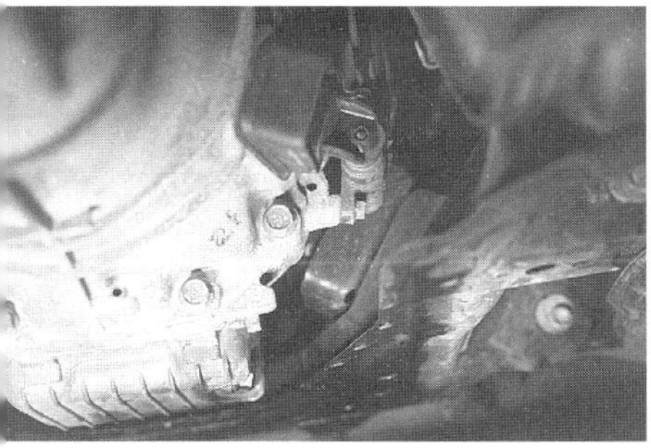

2/15a Remove release cylinder bolts ...

2/15b ... one accessible thru wheel well.

(14 inch) extension via the gap above the subframe accessible in the right-hand front wheelarch. The clutch cylinder can be left to hang loose. **Caution!** Remember not to press the clutch pedal until the cylinder is once again bolted in position.

16 The speedometer drive cable needs to be removed from the rear end of the transmission casing. Simply unscrew the large knurled nut with your fingers - you may need to use pliers just to get it started. Once the nut is fully loosened the speedometer cable can be withdrawn from the transmission and tied to the brake pipes running alongside the chassis member.

2/16 Disconnect speedo cable.

17 Release the wiring loom from the side of the PPF (the Power Plant Frame running from transmission to diff housing) by squeezing the retaining ears of each plastic clip with your fingers or pliers and then, whilst the ears are squeezed together, pulling the clip free of the frame. Some of these clips are very fiddly but with care they can all be removed without breaking them. Don't forget to release the ground wire held by a 10 mm bolt toward the rear end of the PPF and the loom clip on the side of the bellhousing which is held by a 10 mm screw. There is some more wiring above the transmission; however, this cannot be disconnected

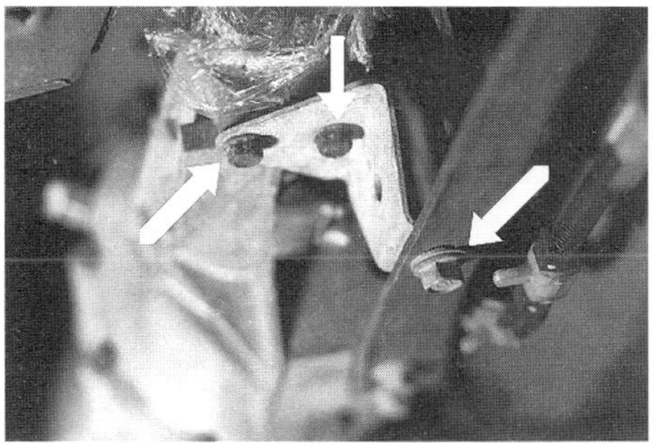

2/18a Release these bolts ...

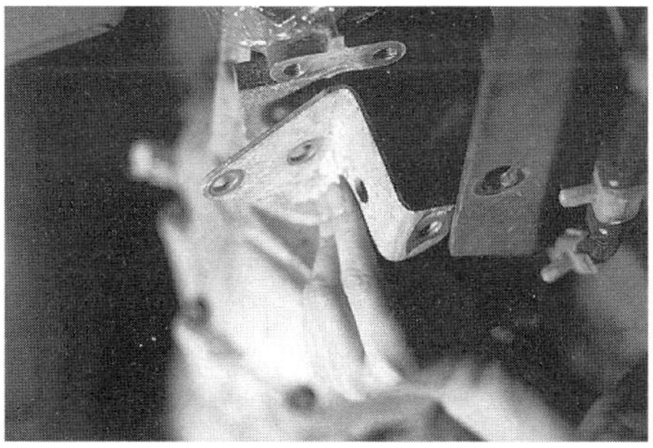

2/18b ... and remove bracket.

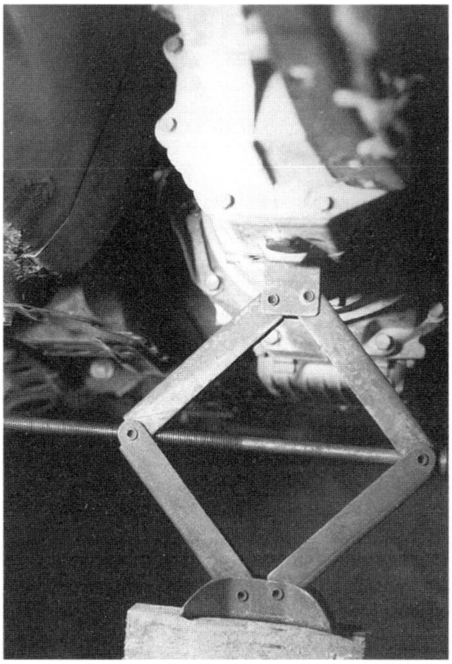

2/19 Lift rear of transmission unit.

until a little later.

18 Remove the support bracket between the PPF and the transmission tail casting by first unscrewing the 17 mm headed bolt holding the bracket to the PPF, followed by the two 14 mm headed bolts holding the bracket to the transmission. Remove the bracket and install the bolts finger-tight in their appropriate places for safe-keeping.

19 Place a jack beneath the transmission, just ahead of the front end of the PPF. Raise the jack until the rear of the transmission is supported and very slightly lifted: this will relieve the strain on

2/20 Remove front PPF bolts.

the PPF.

20 At the very front of the PPF there are two 17 mm headed bolts which pass upward, right through the transmission casing, and screw into the top of the PPF. Slacken and remove both of these bolts, which are 198 mm (8 inches) long!

21 At the rear end of the PPF there are two more long bolts, this time passing through the differential casting. Slacken and remove both bolts with a 17 mm socket wrench. You will notice that the forward bolt has a collar. Note: before removal of the long bolts and collar holding the PPF to the

2/21 Remove rear PPF bolts.

diff, it's a good idea to soak the whole area with penetrating oil as the collared bolt is a tight fit in the spacer and its shaped bore in the diff: even on our low mileage car the forward bolt was pretty well corroded in place.

22 When the bolts have been removed the collar in the forward bolt position also has to be removed. If you look carefully at the shoulders of the collar you will see a couple of cutouts. Initially, tap a chisel or an old screwdriver into these recesses until the collar begins to move away from the PPF. Once movement has started you can lever

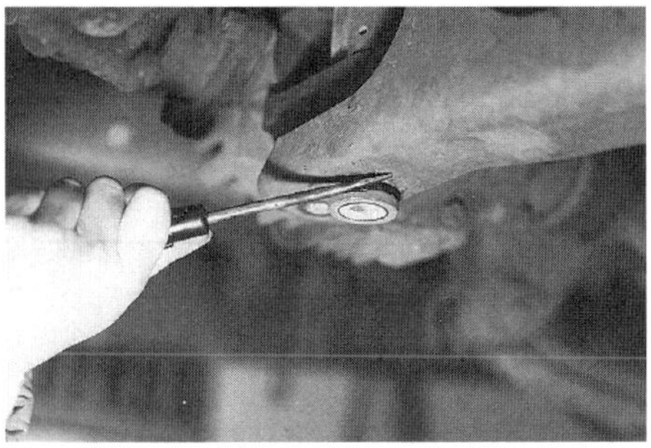

2/22 Lever out collar.

the collar out with a screwdriver, moving from side to side and working it out gradually.

23 Once the collar is removed the rear of the PPF can be moved sideways until clear of the differential casing and then pulled backward, freeing it from the transmission casing, after which the PPF can be removed from the car.

24 The next task is to remove the bolts and nuts around the periphery of the bellhousing. However, the jack supporting the transmission will probably be in the way, so here's a method which will allow its temporary removal. Place a T-bar or

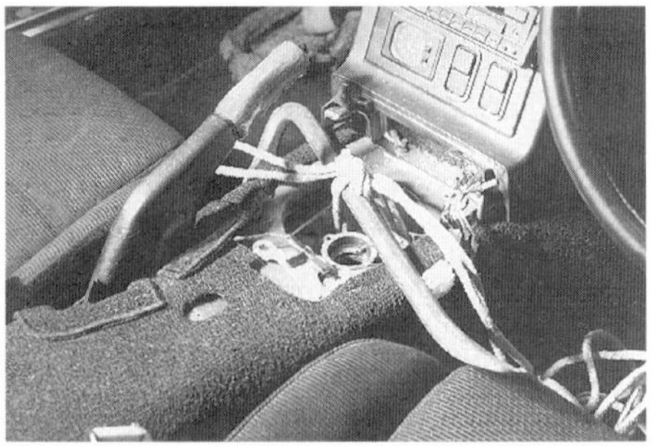

2/24 Place sling around transmission.

crowbar over the empty gearshift lever hole inside of the car, then thread a piece of rope down around the transmission tailhousing and back up through the hole and tie it to the supporting bar. Ensure the rope used is strong enough to support the weight of the transmission. Once the rope is in place and tight, the jack can be removed to allow the removal of the bellhousing bolts.

25 Removal of bellhousing bolts and nuts. Note: you'll need 14 mm and 17 mm sockets, a universal joint and extension(s) of at least 450 mm (18 inches) to reach these fixings, which are also very tight!

26 Start by removing the nut and bolt holding the starter motor. Both nut and bolt are 14 mm (smaller than most of the bellhousing bolts) and are situated about halfway up the right-hand side of the bellhousing. The head of the lower bolt holding the starter motor will have to be held by a second person and can be accessed via the space above the front subframe in the right-hand front wheelarch. Once a helper is holding the bolt head, the nut can be released from the transmission side. There are no nuts for the other two 14 mm bolts, one of which secures the top of the starter motor: these bolts can be unscrewed and removed from

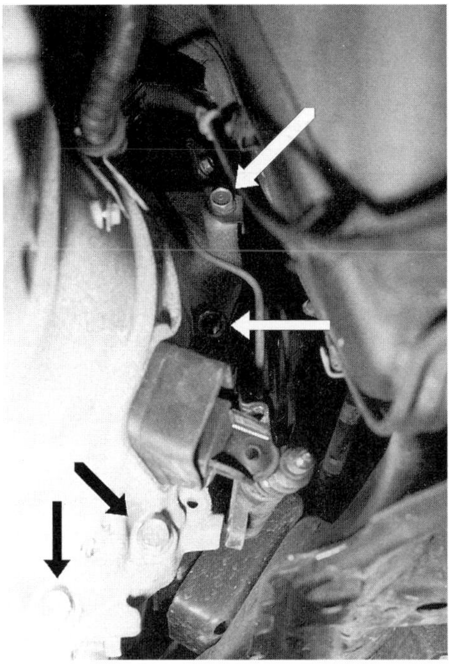

2/27 Location of some of the bellhousing bolts.

the transmission side. Note: both of these bolts also secure brackets fixing wiring and hydraulic pipe. Once free, tie these brackets and their wiring/pipework to one side away from the bellhousing.

27 You are now left with seven 17 mm headed bolts and one 17 mm nut and bolt holding the transmission bellhousing to the engine. Using a diagonal sequence, first of all loosen each of these bolts by half a turn. Then remove all of the bolts except two, one top and one bottom, which should be left in place but loosened by half a turn.

28 Release the sling around the tailhousing of

2/29 Disconnect transmission wiring.

the transmission (if applicable) after placing the jack back under the transmission. Lower the transmission as far as it will go and then jack it up again just 13 mm/half an inch so that the engine mountings are not strained.

29 There should now be enough space above the lowered transmission to disconnect the wiring to the neutral and reverse switches. One of the switches has two plastic clip-type connectors which can be released once the locking tab of each is depressed; the other switch has two bullet-type connectors which can simply be pulled apart.

30 The whole wiring loom can now be pulled to one side and tied to the brake pipes alongside the chassis rail out of harm's way. Carefully undo and remove the last two bellhousing bolts.

31 Using a wooden packing piece, place a jack under the rear end of the engine oil pan/sump adjacent to the bellhousing and jack upwards until the weight of the transmission is just released from the existing jack. **Caution!** Don't jack the sump any higher than this. The jack which was used to support the transmission should now be removed unless it's a wheeled jack.

32 With the help of a strong assistant, or

2/32 Clutch accesible if attention required.

by supporting the weight of the transmission on a wheeled jack, pull the transmission backward whilst supporting the weight of the unit - which we think is around 46kg (100lb). **Warning!** If you and your assistant are doing this job without a wheeled jack, neither of you should position yourselves directly beneath the transmission in case it drops. Once the input shaft is clear of the clutch, the whole transmission unit can be lowered to the ground and then removed from beneath the car. Note: there will probably be a considerable amount of oil left in the transmission gearshift lever turret so tip the unit onto its side and drain that oil into a suitable container.

3. TRANSMISSION (GEARBOX), AUTOMATIC - REMOVAL

Note: we were not able to carry out this work as the automatic version of the Miata/MX5 was not available in our market at the time of writing. The following is Mazda's official advice with further advice from us where we feel it appropriate. Use your own common sense to make sure that no obvious points are overlooked.

☞ First read 1/1, 2.

1 Isolate the battery: ☞ 3/4/4.

2 Raise and support the whole car securely and at a height sufficient to give easy access to the underside: ☞ 1/3.

3 Moving to the underside of the car the next job is to remove the plastic undertray from beneath the front of the engine. All fixings are 10mm. First remove the three self-tapping screws from the front of the tray, followed by the bolts at the back of the tray. Then, at each side of the car, remove the bolt next to the top swinging arm, the bolt on the side of the chassis member in the wheelarch and, finally, the nut holding the tray and the front valence

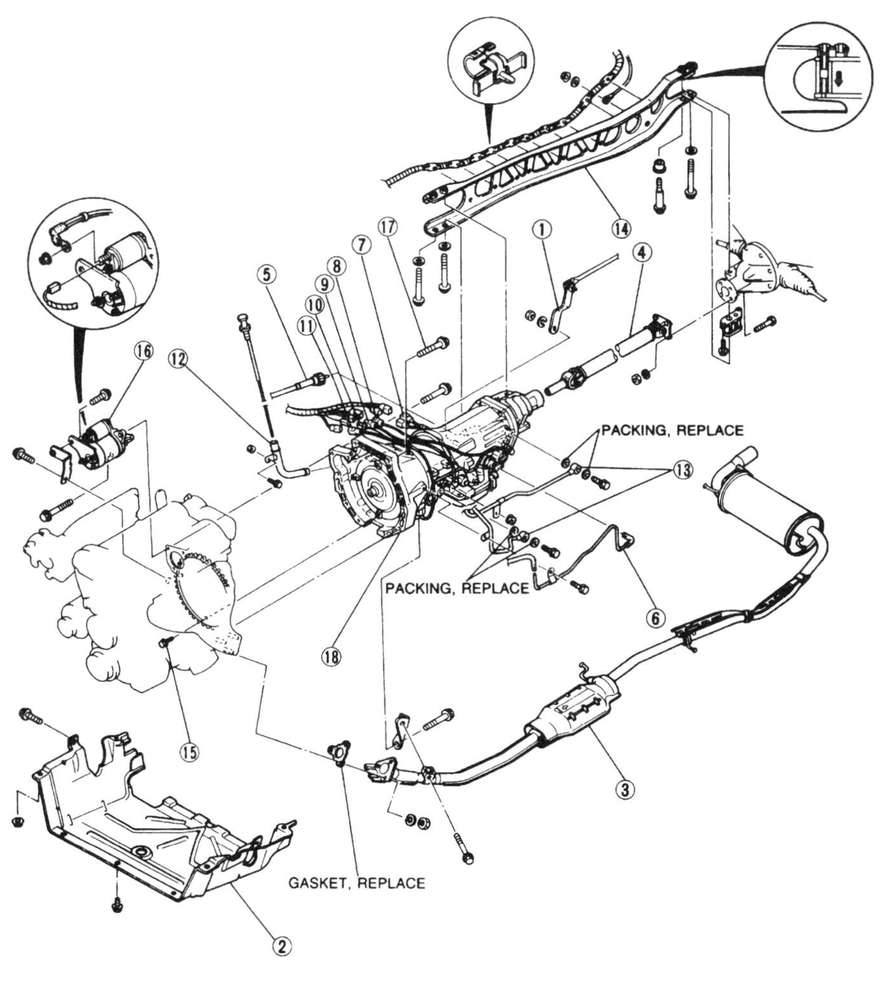

D3/6 AUTOMATIC TRANSMISSION REMOVAL SEQUENCE
Text gives full sequence and explains key numbers: ☞ 4/3/6 - 20.

stay. Once the nut is removed the stay can be pulled from the stud and moved out of the way to give enough clearance to remove the plastic undertray. It's recommended that you put all of the screws and the two nuts back in place, finger-tight, once the tray has been removed.

4 Remove the complete exhaust system: ☞ 5/38.

5 Draining the ATF (Automatic Transmission Fluid). You'll need a bowl or tray larger than the transmission's oil pan/sump and capable of holding 7 liters/6.2 Imp. quarts/7.4 US quarts. Slacken the oil pan bolts until their heads are protruding by around 6 mm/a quarter inch and then gently pull one end of the pan away from the transmission unit; this will allow the fluid to drain. When draining is complete nip up the bolts and wipe ATF from the pan's exterior.

6 Take a look at the drawing, it will help to clarify all of the following steps -

7 Disconnect the selector lever (1) from the right-hand side of the unit.

8 The next job is to remove the propshaft (4): ☞ 4/2/12-14.

9 Unscrew the large knurled nut holding the speedo drive cable (5) to the transmission casing and then withdraw the cable. Tie the cable end to the brake pipes alongside the chassis rail.

10 Remove the single bolt securing the rigid section of the small bore vacuum pipe (6) to the left-hand side of the casing. Pull the rubber section of the pipe from its union stub.

11 Also on the left of the unit you'll see the oil cooler feed and return pipes (13). Both are secured to the transmission casing and bellhousing by clips and then at their unions by banjo bolts. Remove the bolts securing the clips and the banjo bolts, then fix the loose pipes out of the way.

12 At the front of the unit on the right-hand side you'll see the transmission dipstick tube (12). Unscrew the nut and bolt securing the tube's support bracket and then pull the tube from the transmission case.

13 ☞ 4/2/17-63.

14 Remove the cover, if fitted, of the access hole in the bottom of the bellhousing. Reach up into the bellhousing and unscrew and remove the four bolts (15) fixing the torque convertor to the driveplate. You can lock the driveplate by jamming a large screwdriver into the starter ring gear teeth and simultaneously wedging it against the side of the access hole.

15 ☞ 4/2/25-27.

16 Lower the transmission as far as it will go until the jack pad just comes free and then jack it back up just 13 mm/half an inch so that the engine mountings are not too strained.

17 There should now be sufficient room above the transmission to reach and separate the six electrical connector blocks (7,8,9,10,11). **Caution!** Before disconnecting, check the color coding of the wires each side of each connector: if necessary, tag wires so you know what goes with what on refit. The wiring loom can now be pulled to the side and tied to the brake pipes out of harm's way.

18 Carefully undo and remove the last two bellhousing bolts.

19 Using a wooden packing piece, place a jack under the rear end of the engine oil pan/sump adjacent to the bellhousing and jack upwards until the weight of the transmission is just released from the existing jack. **Caution!** Don't jack the sump any higher than this. The jack which was used to support the transmission should now be removed unless it's a wheeled jack.

20 With the help of a strong assistant, or by supporting the weight of the transmission on a wheeled jack, pull the transmission backward whilst supporting the weight of the unit - which we think is around 70kg (155lb). **Warning!** If you and your assistant are doing this job without a wheeled jack, neither of you should position yourselves directly beneath the transmission in case it drops. Once the spigots in the bellhousing joint face are clear, the whole transmission unit can be lowered to the ground and then removed from beneath the car. **Caution!** It is essential that the automatic transmission unit is kept the right way up at all times, otherwise sediment and debris from the oil pan can be dislodged and allowed to contaminate fine drillings and valves.

4. TRANSMISSION (GEARBOX), MANUAL - TEARDOWN AND REBUILD GENERAL

☞ First read 1/1, 2.

1 Read the text on teardown and rebuild before you start the job so that you have a good idea of what's involved: ☞ 4/5, 6, 7.

2 Most of the work can be undertaken with ordinary tools but there are a few tasks requiring some inventiveness to get round the lack of Mazda's special tools: our solutions are described, but maybe you can do better?

3 It is recommended that the teardown is carried out on top of several thicknesses of newsprint: you'll be amazed at how much oil there is to soak up.

4 As dismantling proceeds, clean all components in batches using proprietary oil/grease remover or kerosene/paraffin and making sure all components are thoroughly dried afterwards. **Warning!** Do not use gasoline/petrol for cleaning purposes. **Caution!** Don't immerse bearings in

4/5 Keep shaft components together.

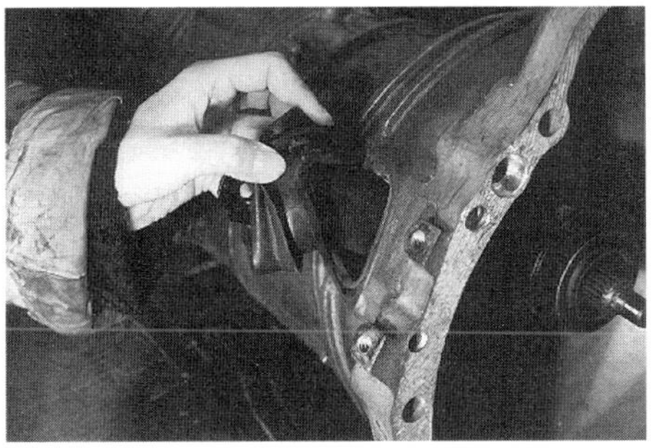
5/1 Remove rubber boot.

5/2a Release spring clips ...

cleaning fluid: they should simply be wiped with a cloth.

5 Immediately after cleaning, it's a good idea to slide components removed from transmission shafts on to lengths of metal tube or wire. This system removes any confusion about the order in which parts should be reassembled and their correct orientation. You'll need three tubes or wires representing the transmission's three shafts.

6 Have a supply of small transparent bags for the storage of groups of small components and don't forget to label the bags. A felt-tipped pen with indelible ink will also prove very useful.

7 Don't throw away any old components, including gaskets and seals, until you have the correct replacements. It's surprising how often an old component is a useful pattern or source of reference.

8 For the rebuild you'll need a strong workbench and a vise fitted with jaw protectors.

9 To ensure maximum life and reliability from a rebuilt transmission, not only must the work be done with great care and thoroughness, but also in a clean environment and with completely clean tools and components. Also all internal moving components must be thoroughly lubricated with transmission oil as they are reassembled/installed.

10 Before the rebuild begins replace any bolts, screws, studs or nuts the threads or heads of which are in any way damaged. All threads must be clean and torque wrench settings strictly observed.

11 Have a complete set of new gaskets and seals ready before work starts, together with silicone-based fluid gasket cement. Also buy the new components and tools that you know you'll need ahead of time.

12 If a component won't fit, don't force it. Stop, stand back, think about the problem and resolve it properly before proceeding.

13 Take your time, get it right and keep your personal safety and the safety of others in mind at all times.

5. TRANSMISSION (GEARBOX), MANUAL - TEARDOWN

First read 1/1, 2.

1 Start by removing the rubber boot around the clutch operating arm: squeeze the base of the boot to release it from the bellhousing casting.

2 + With two pairs of pliers pull the two

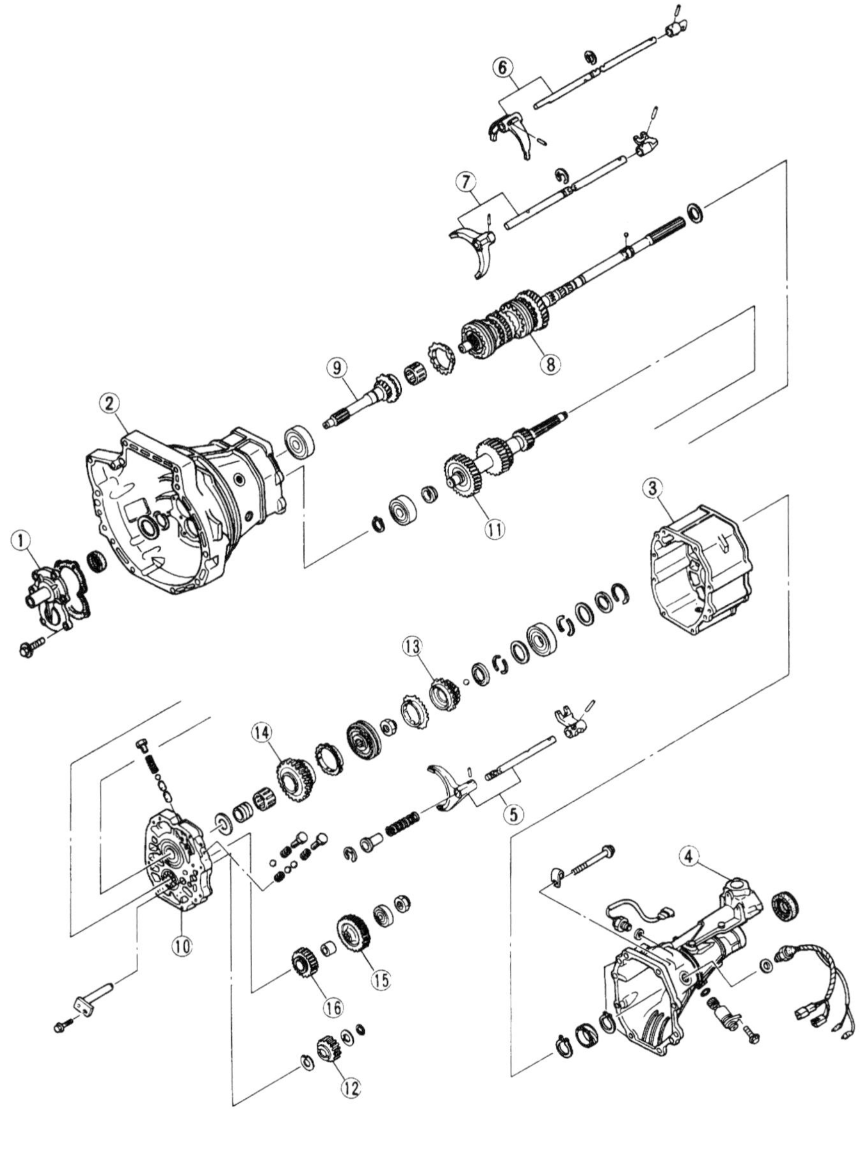

D5/1 EXPLODED VIEW OF MANUAL TRANSMISSION (GEARBOX)

1 Front cover. 2 Bellhousing and front casing. 3 Main casing. 4 Extension housing and tailshaft casing. 5 Shift fork and rod: 5th/reverse. 6 Shift fork and rod: 1st/2nd. 7 Shift fork and rod: 3rd/4th. 8 Mainshaft/ tailshaft and gear cluster. 9 Input shaft. 10 Central bearing carrier. 11 Countershaft. 12 5th gear. 13 Reverse gear. 14 Countershaft 5th gear. 15 Countershaft reverse gear.

5/2b ... and pull out fork.

5/3 Remove release bearing.

spring tags protruding from the clutch release fork outwards, the arm can then be pulled off of its pivot pin and out of the release bearing. Once clear of the bearing and pivot pin the arm should be withdrawn from inside the bellhousing.

3 The clutch release bearing can now be pulled off the transmission input shaft.

4 + The transmission front cover, which incorporates input shaft sleeve and release fork pivot, is fixed by six 12 mm bolts and you'll need a 250 mm/10 inch extension with the socket to reach them. Slacken each of these by half a turn, in a diagonal sequence, before unscrewing them completely and then pulling the front cover from the transmission casting. **Warning!** The cover may come free suddenly, as the gasket's adhesion breaks. **Caution!** Don't use a sharp tool between the bellhousing and cover in order to lever it free. Draw the front cover forward carefully on the input shaft as you don't want to damage the rubber oil seal it contains on the input shaft splines. Behind the front cover and on top of the input shaft bearing there is a spacer washer. This, too, should be removed and kept with the housing.

5 Remove the snap ring/circlip from the input shaft in front of the bearing. This is a fiddly task and is probably best accomplished by springing the clip with a pair of expanding snap ring pliers and working a small, thin-bladed screwdriver between the snap ring and bearing face until the snap ring is fully free of its groove in the input shaft and can be drawn forward and off the shaft. You'll probably find this easier if one person uses the snap ring pliers and another fits the screwdriver blade behind the snap ring.

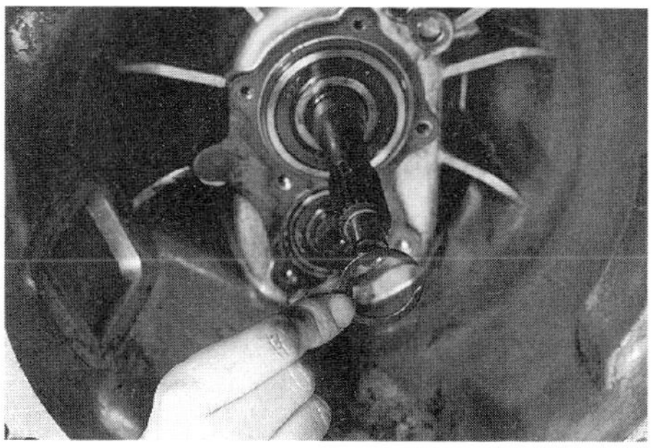
5/5 Remove input shaft snapring (circlip).

6 + Speedometer drive gear removal. The speedometer drive gear is retained in the transmission tail casing by a single 10 mm bolt. Undo and remove the bolt and withdraw the speedometer drive gear. **Warning!** The gear will come away suddenly as it's a tight fit in its housing.

7 + Unscrew and remove the neutral switch from the top of the transmission tail casing. You'll need a 24 mm crescent wrench/spanner.

8 Unscrew and remove the back up/reversing light switch from the left-hand side of the transmission tail casing, again using a 24 mm crescent wrench.

9 + Transmission tailshaft/extension casing removal. The tailshaft casing is held to the

5/4a Release bolts ...

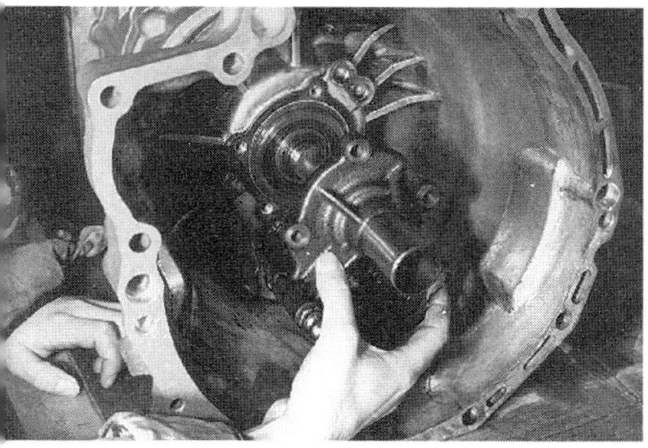
5/4b ... and withdraw cover.

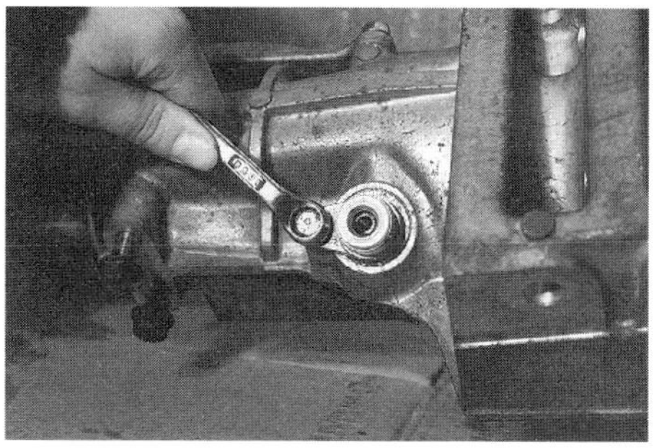
5/6a Undo retaining bolt ...

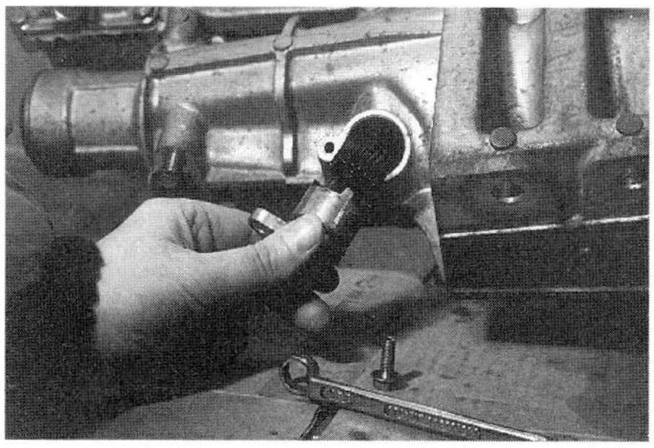
5/6b ... & withdraw speedo drive gear.

5/7a Unscrew and ...

5.7b ... remove neutral switch.

5/8 Remove backup (reversing) light switch.

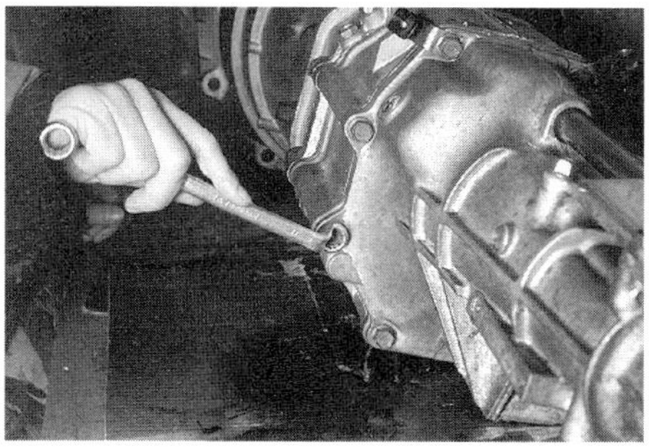
5/9a Slacken tailshaft casing bolts ...

5/9b ... including these two.

central part of the transmission by a ring of eight 12 mm bolts. These should be loosened progressively in a diagonal sequence and then removed completely. Two of the bolts are accessible to a socket and extension via holes in the PPF mounting on the right-hand side of the transmission. You'll need an extension of at least 570m/5 inches to reach these bolts, although you could get to them with a box end spanner. Note: if you do use a socket set through the PPF mounting casting you need to put the socket on the bolt first and then feed the extension through. Don't try to undo the bolts

5/10a Remove tailshaft casing bolts ...

5/10b ... and withdraw casing.

completely with a socket as you'll find that once the two offending bolts are loose there's no longer sufficient room to withdraw the socket from the PPF bracket casting! Note that both of the top bolts also have wire clips under their heads.

10   ■+ Once the through bolts have been removed, pull the extension housing backwards to free it from the main transmission casing. As soon as the joint is broken, turn the extension housing clockwise, looking from the rear, which will then allow the whole unit to be drawn off of the transmission tailshaft. **Caution!** Pull the unit over the

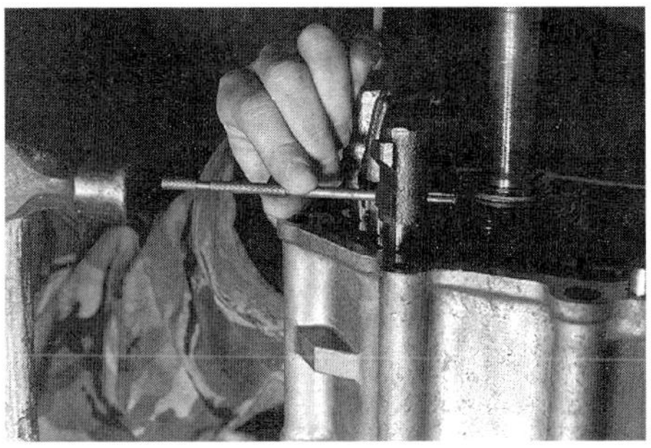

5/11a Drift out roll pins ...

5/11b ... and remove shift rod arms.

tailshaft carefully so as not to damage the rubber oil seal.

11   ■+ Stand the transmission unit on its nose and remove the three shift rod arms. Each arm is held in place by a single roll pin which can be pushed out with a 4 mm drift and a light hammer. Get someone else to hold the roll pin as it emerges otherwise it might drop into the transmission. Once the roll pin is out, the shift rod arm can be removed. Repeat the process for the other two arms.

12   Once the three arms are off, lift away the main casing. **Warning!** It may free suddenly.

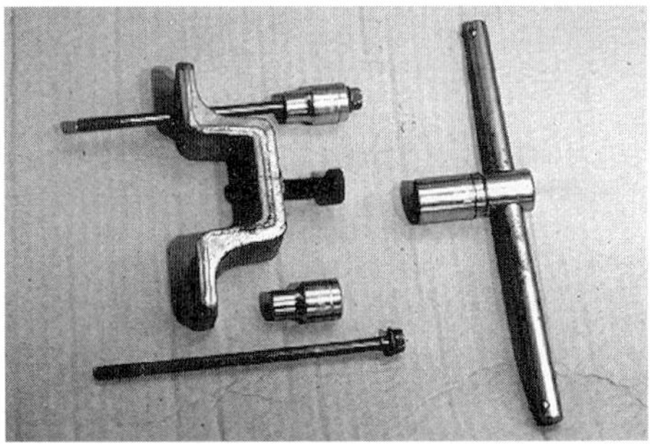

5/13a Components of puller used to ...

5/13b ... pull bellhousing off.

13   ■+ The next step is to pull the bellhousing/front casing off. Create a simple puller, like the one we show, using a proprietary brake drum/hub puller, a couple of sockets and two of the transmission through bolts which were removed earlier. Fit the puller, as shown, and tighten the two long bolts to take up any slack. Screw the center bolt inward which will pull the casing over the countershaft bearing and the input shaft through its bearing. Once it's free, lift the bellhousing/gearbox front casing away to reveal a large part of the gear train.

14   ■ If you want to see how the transmission works now's a good time to experiment. Bear in

5/14 The naked transmission!

mind that drive comes into the transmission via the single gearwheel on the input shaft and is transmitted to the countershaft. Now try moving a clutch hub sleeve backwards or forwards until it locks with the adjacent gear; turn the input shaft and watch what happens. Play around, try reverse, and very quickly, despite its apparent complexity, you'll see what a simple mechanism the transmission really is.

15   ■ Back to work! Each of the three shift forks is locked to its shift rod by a roll pin: drive the pins out with a 4 mm drift and light hammer whilst,

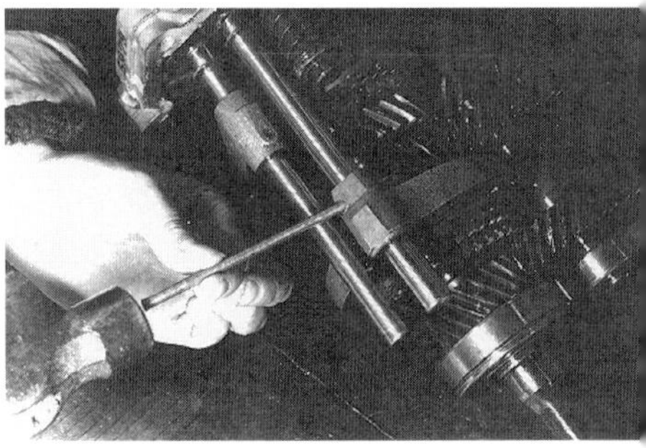

5/15 Drift out shift fork roll pin.

where possible, supporting the shift fork.

16   ■+ Around the central bearing carrier of the transmission there are three detents operating on the three shift rods. Each detent is held in place by a 14 mm bolt which should be unscrewed and removed, then the spring and ball should be collected from each detent. Note: the spring on the shortest shaft is lighter and the bolt does not have a copper washer, unlike the other two bolts. The long shift rod with the central fork selects first and second gears, the other long shift rod third and fourth and, of course, the short shift rod fifth and

5/16a Remove detents but ...

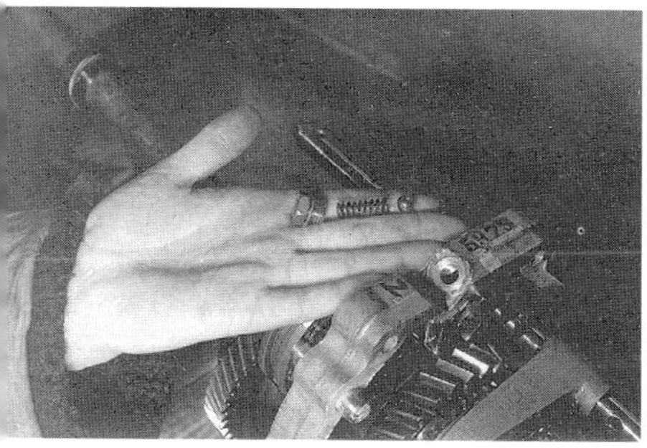
5/16b ... watch out for flying balls!

5/17 Remove 1st/2nd shift rod snapring.

reverse.

17 Remove the snap ring from the first/second shift rod. With some difficulty, it can be pushed off with two screwdrivers.

18 The first/second shift rod can now be pulled through the shift fork and through the transmission bearing carrier casting.

19 Remove the snap ring from the third/fourth shift rod, then withdraw the rod from the bearing carrier casting and the shift fork in the same way as for the first/second shift rod. The shift forks can now be lifted from the clutch hubs.

20 + The fifth/reverse shift rod can then be pulled forward through the shift fork and transmission bearing carrier, complete with collar and spring. Note that as the rod is withdrawn from the bearing carrier casting, a second detent ball and spring will pop out.

5/19 Withdraw 3rd/4th shift rod.

5/20a Withdraw 5th/rev shift rod ...

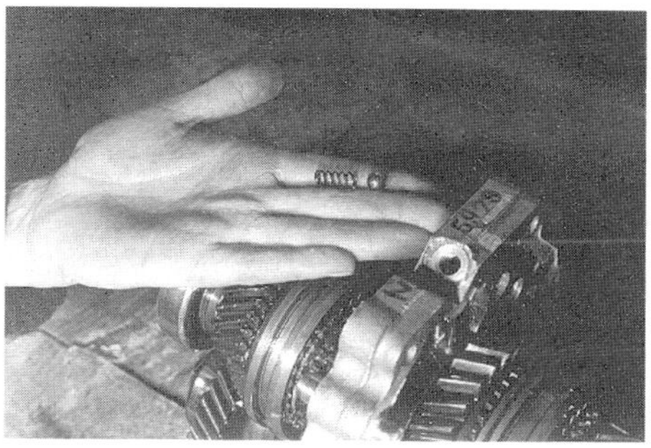
5/20b ... releasing this detent.

21 If you look at the transmission's bearing carrier casting, the three shift rod bores lie side by side and you'll see that there are elongated detents in a bore between the two outer rods and the inner rod. These detents can be pushed out through the bore vacated by the first/second shift rod detent.

22 + Speedo drive gear removal from output shaft. Using a pair of snap ring pliers on the snap ring nearest the end of the output shaft, open the snap ring and slide it out of its groove, over the splines and off the shaft. Do the same with the nylon drive gear itself. There is a ball-bearing in a recess in the output shaft which locks the speedo driven gear in position: remove the ball-bearing and keep it together with the gear and its snap rings. Remove the second snap ring in the same way as the first.

5/22a Remove snapring and ...

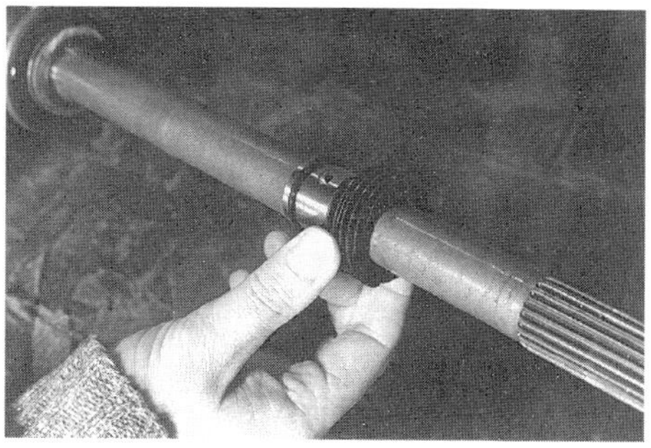
5/22b ... withdraw speedo gear.

23 Using snap ring pliers and a screwdriver, open the mainshaft bearing retaining snap ring and slide it out of its groove and then along and off of the end of the mainshaft. The snap ring should be followed by the thick spacing washer and the thin ring which retains the two C-shaped sections of the selective C-washer.

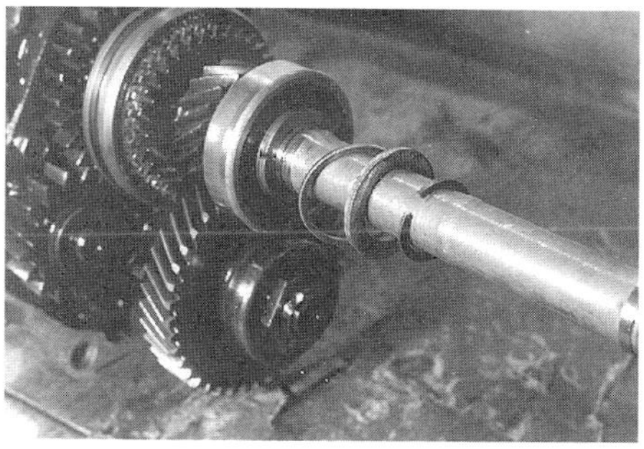
5/23a Remove snapring, spacer and ring ...

5/23b ... followed by C-washers.

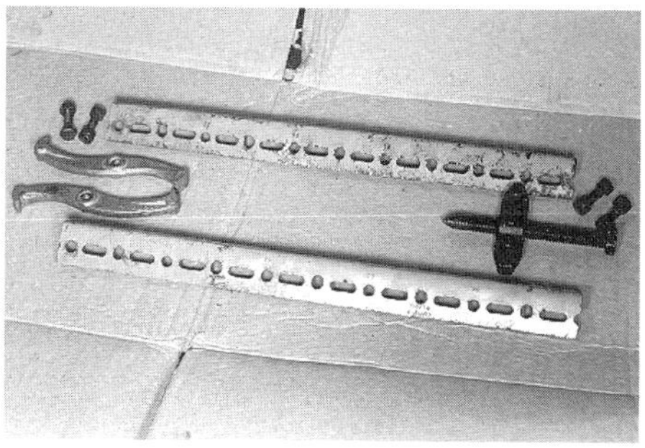
5/24 Homemade mainshaft bearing puller.

24 Now the mainshaft bearing needs to be pulled off which is a bit of a problem as the bearing's so far down the shaft. We made a puller for this job by dismantling our ordinary two pronged puller and then reassembling it with two lengths of slotted shelving framework between the puller's yoke and arms. Okay, it looks pretty rough but it does work ... Perfectly!

4

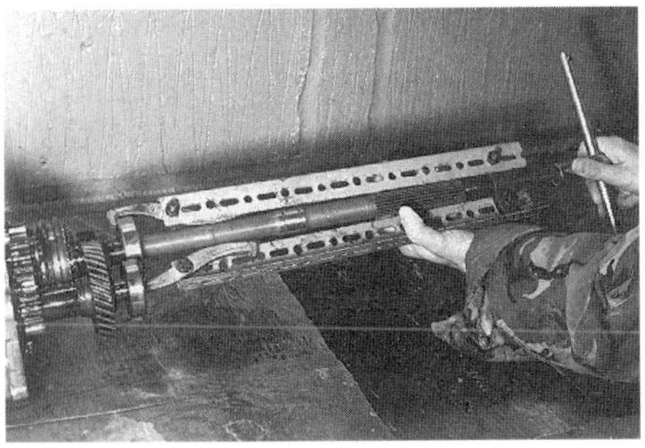

5/25a Use puller to free bearing ...

5/25b ... then slide bearing off mainshaft.

25 + Using a long reach bearing puller, pull the mainshaft bearing off its seat and then off the mainshaft. Wipe the bearing clean and mark its identity and orientation on the outer race with an indelible pen.

26 With the mainshaft rear bearing removed, pull off the washer which retains the two C-washer segments, which will then fall clear of the mainshaft. Next, pull off the thick washer which abuts the fifth gearwheel and remove the single ball-bearing which locks the washer on the shaft. **Caution!** Keep ball-bearing, C-washers, C-washer

5/26 C-washers, retainer, spacer and ball.

locking ring and the thick spacing washer together as a set: they need to go back in exactly the same position and must not be confused with similar components removed earlier from the mainshaft. It's a good idea to put all of these components in a small plastic bag, seal it and then write an identification on the outside.

27 + Note: the four photos relating to the next two steps wrongly show the mainshaft rear bearing still in place - we all have bad days! Using a screwdriver, lever the dimple in the countershaft/layshaft locknut's rim out of the groove in the shaft.

5/27a Release locknut locking tab ...

5/27b ... and remove nut.

5/27c Lock countershaft.

Then use a 32 mm socket to unscrew and remove the nut. The countershaft can be locked by clamping the fifth gearwheel in vise jaws, but do ensure you have protectors mounted in the vise jaws otherwise the hardened gear teeth could be chipped. You can actually lock the countershaft by moving the two synchromesh hubs shown towards each other to engage first and reverse gears simultaneously. **Warning!** The nut is very tight and will give very suddenly, so be careful.

28 After removing the locknut from the countershaft, the countershaft bearing should be removed using a puller. However, it's difficult to

5/28 Using puller to free 5th gearwheel.

get a proprietary puller to do this job because there is little space to get the hooked legs of the puller between the rear face of the bearing and the fifth gearwheel. Instead it is recommended that, as shown, you use a conventional proprietary puller to release the fifth gearwheel and countershaft bearing simultaneously. Wipe the bearing clean and mark its identity and orientation on the outer race with an indelible pen.

29 Pull the countershaft fifth gear from the splines on the countershaft. Note: the forward side of the gear is marked with a white spot; however, if no such orientation mark is present use an

5/29 Pull spacer from countershaft.

5/30a Withdraw 5th gear pinion ...

5/30b ... followed by synchro ring.

indelible pen to mark the gear pinion for correc reassembly. The spacer between the fifth gear an the countershaft reverse gear can now be pulle free of the countershaft.

30 + Pull the fifth gear pinion along th mainshaft until it can be removed. Next, pull off th fifth gear synchro ring.

31 Release the locking tab of the larg mainshaft locknut from the cutout in the shaft usin a screwdriver as shown. Slide first and revers clutch hubs towards the transmission center cast ing to simultaneously engage both gears and there

5/31 Release locknut's locking tab.

5/32 Unscrew locknut (see text) & slide off ...

fore lock the mainshaft.

32 Undo the mainshaft locknut with a 41 mm tube wrench slid down the mainshaft and over the nut: a pipe wrench on the exterior of the tube wrench should then release the nut. If, like us, you cannot obtain such a large tube wrench, then a cold chisel and light blows from a hammer can be used to rotate the nut until it is slack enough to turn by hand. The idea, of course, is to get the chisel just behind one of the nut corners and then to drive the nut around by holding the chisel at an oblique angle.

5/33 ... hub, synchro ring, rev pinion & cage.

33 Once loose the locknut can be undone with fingers and pulled off of the transmission mainshaft, followed by the clutch hub which should be slid off of its locking splines on the mainshaft. **Caution!** Take care not to pull the clutch hub's sleeve too far out of position, otherwise you could have springs and keys flying everywhere ... Remove the second synchro ring, followed by the reverse gear pinion, together with its roller bearing cage.

34 Remove the inner race of the reverse gear pinion, followed by the thick selective washer.

5/34 Remove inner race & selective washer.

5/35 Pull off countershaft reverse pinion.

35 The countershaft reverse gear can now be pulled off of the splined section of the countershaft (it was only left in place to enable the mainshaft to be locked).

36 + Remove the snap ring on the end of the reverse idler shaft, followed by the tabbed washer and then the gear pinion itself (noting that, in the case of our transmission, there is a white spot on the side of the pinion facing the rear of the transmission) and, finally, the thrust washer from the bearing plate side of the pinion.

37 Undo and remove the five 12 mm bolts

5/36a Release snapring and remove ...

5/36b tabbed washer and gear pinion.

5/38 Remove bearing retainer.

holding the bearing retaining plate to the central bearing carrier. Note that the five bolts all have spring washers.

38 With the bolts removed the bearing retaining plate can be pulled over the main- and countershafts.

39 Take the weight of the countershaft gear cluster and, with the aid of a screwdriver but without using any real force, lever out the center race of the countershaft bearing. If this proves difficult leave the race in place for the moment.

40 Once the inner race is removed you

5/39 Lever out bearing center race.

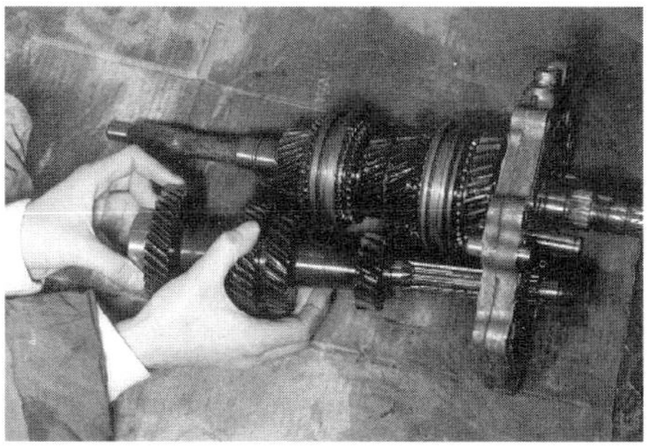

5/40 If possible, remove countershaft.

may find that the countershaft can be disengaged from the input shaft and mainshaft gears to allow its removal. If not, don't worry.

41 With an assistant taking the weight of the gear clusters so that they're not straining the bearings, grasp the bearing carrier firmly and use a copper or nylon-faced hammer to tap the countershaft and mainshaft back through their bearings. You'll find that the countershaft does not need to be tapped back very far (particularly if you were successful in removing the bearing center race) before it can be removed. **Caution!** Make sure that

both shafts move back through the bearing carrier by more or less the same amount, otherwise the gears on the two shafts will foul each other and damage may result. As soon as it is free enough remove the countershaft from the central bearing housing.

42 Once the countershaft is removed the input shaft can be pulled forward to disengage it from the transmission mainshaft. **Caution!** Take care not to drop the synchro ring attached to the main drive gear pinion. Make sure, too, that the bearing in the tail of the input shaft doesn't fall out and become damaged.

5/42 Remove input shaft.

5/43a Withdraw mainshaft from carrier ...

5/43b ... then selective spacer.

43 + With your assistant holding the gear cluster to take the strain from the bearing, continue to tap the mainshaft through its bearing in the central carrier. As soon as the bearing boss clears the bearing's inner race, the shaft becomes very loose and can be withdrawn completely. Note that on the back of the bearing there is a large spacer which is selective.

44 The first gear pinion, together with its needle bearing cage and inner race, can be slid along the mainshaft and removed from the splined end. Remove the synchro ring from the back of the

5/44 Remove 1st gear pinion & bearing.

5/45 Remove snapring.

first/second gear clutch hub and slide it off of the tail of the mainshaft.

45 Turning to the front of the mainshaft you'll see that there is a snap ring retaining the clutch hub for third and fourth gears. Using snap ring pliers open and remove the snap ring.

46 Wrap the first and second gear clutch hub in rag and pull its outer sleeve forward and off, dislodged springs and keys will be caught within the rag. Collect together the pieces and store them in a safe place.

47 + You'll now find that you can use an

5/47a Use puller to remove ...

5/47b ... clutch hub & 3rd gear pinion.

ordinary proprietary puller to pull the clutch hub, synchro ring and third gear pinion off the mainshaft together.

48 + Using inverted jaw protectors, mount the transmission mainshaft in a vise so that the shoulders of the second gear pinion assembly are supported by the vise but the mainshaft is free. Then, using only light blows from a copper or nylon hammer on the splined end of the mainshaft, drive the mainshaft downwards through the pinion. **Caution!** Keep hold of the mainshaft as it will suddenly come free and should not be allowed to drop to the floor.

5/48a Drive mainshaft thru 2nd gear pinion ...

5/48b ... and withdraw these components.

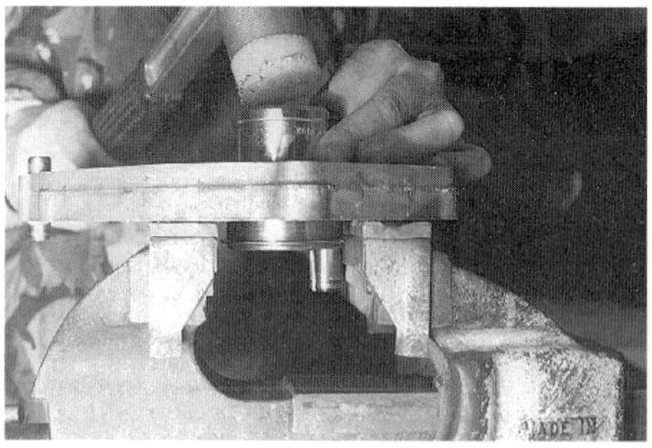

5/49 Drift out countershaft bearing.

49 Removal of the countershaft bearing from the bearing carrier. Fit jaw protectors to the top of your bench vise. Then set the jaws so that there is just sufficient room for the bearing to pass between them. **Caution!** Drive the bearing through the carrier from the opposite side of the bearing to that which has a retaining snap ring/circlip. Using a length of metal piping (or a socket of a diameter great enough to bear evenly on the outer race of the bearing) and using a soft-faced hammer, drive the bearing gently through the carrier until it is removable. If the bearing is a very tight fit in the bearing carrier you can apply a little heat to the aluminum casting using a butane torch: this will have the effect of expanding the aluminum slightly and should make the bearing easier to remove. **Caution!** If you use heat on the plate don't play it on the plastic side pieces of the mainshaft bearing. Note that there may be a spacing shim behind the snap ring/circlip.

50 Removal of the mainshaft bearing from the bearing carrier is a similar procedure to that described for the countershaft bearing except that access to the outer race of the bearing is via two cutouts. Therefore, the bearing should be driven out by using a brass or copper drift against the outer

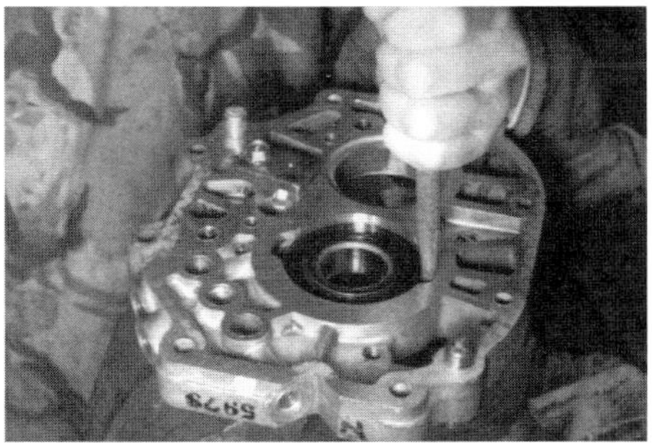

5/50 Drift out mainshaft bearing.

race, and alternating from cutout to cutout with every other blow so that the bearing remains square in its bore as it moves through the bearing housing. **Note**. There is likely to be a shim between the bearing and its seat.

51 The input shaft bearing can be removed from the bellhousing casting using the techniques just described. The bearing should be driven outward from the transmission side.

52 If you wish to remove the reverse idler gearshaft from the center casting, first remove its single fixing bolt. Position the center casting over inverted vise jaw protectors and then, using a nylon- or copper-faced hammer, drift the shaft out of the casting.

53 From this point, to the end of this section, the text describes the teardown of the extension housing and, therefore, need only be followed if you wish to service components in the extension.

54 From the rear of the shift turret, remove the 19 mm bolt, washer, spring and steel ball. Keep the components together in a bag.

55 From the underside of the shift turret, undo and remove the two 10 mm securing bolts and then remove the spring cap, gasket, spring and plunger of the shift lock. Keep the small parts together in a bag.

56 In the turret side cover plate, angled downwards, is a 21 mm bolt which should be removed, followed by washer, spring and plunger. Again, keep the components together.

57 Unscrew and remove the four bolts securing the turret side cover plate. Remove the plate.

58 Angle the control lever cup advantageously and then, using a 4 mm metal drift and light hammer blows, drive the roll pin far enough through the cup to release the shift rod. Pull the shift rod out from inside the extension casing. Withdraw the cup from the turret and mount it in a vise to drive the pin out completely.

59 Lift the nylon ball seat bearing, and the wave washer beneath, from the turret top.

60 Unscrew and remove the four 12 mm bolts which secure the turret to the extension body. Lift away the turret pulling it backwards at the same time to free the shift rod cover tube.

61 Remove the oil supply rail from within the extension housing after releasing the single 10 mm bolt securing its bracket.

6. TRANSMISSION (GEARBOX), MANUAL - COMPONENTS CHECKING & REPAIR

☞ First read 1/1, 2.

1 After thorough cleaning it's essential that all transmission components are checked thoroughly for damage or excessive wear. The following steps cover standard areas of wear and common faults, but be on the lookout for the unexpected too and, if in the slightest doubt about any component, replace it for the sake of your own peace of mind.

2 Take a commonsense attitude to new parts. If your car's done over 100,000km/60,000 miles the chances are that the wearable bits in the transmission are showing their age even if, technically they're not worn out. It's not worth putting such components back into a rebuilt transmission. For a really good rebuild to restore the car's original slick gearshift and quietness replace bearings, synchro rings, clutch hubs, shift forks and detent springs

3 **Caution!** All roll pins, snap rings, locknuts and gaskets must be replaced.

MAINSHAFT GEAR PINIONS

4 Inspect the individual teeth which should be unchipped, uncracked and have nice squarish edges to the tooth tips. Heavy wear of gear pinions would have manifested itself as gear whine when the transmission was in use and should now show up as unevenness in tooth shape and bright patches of obvious wear.

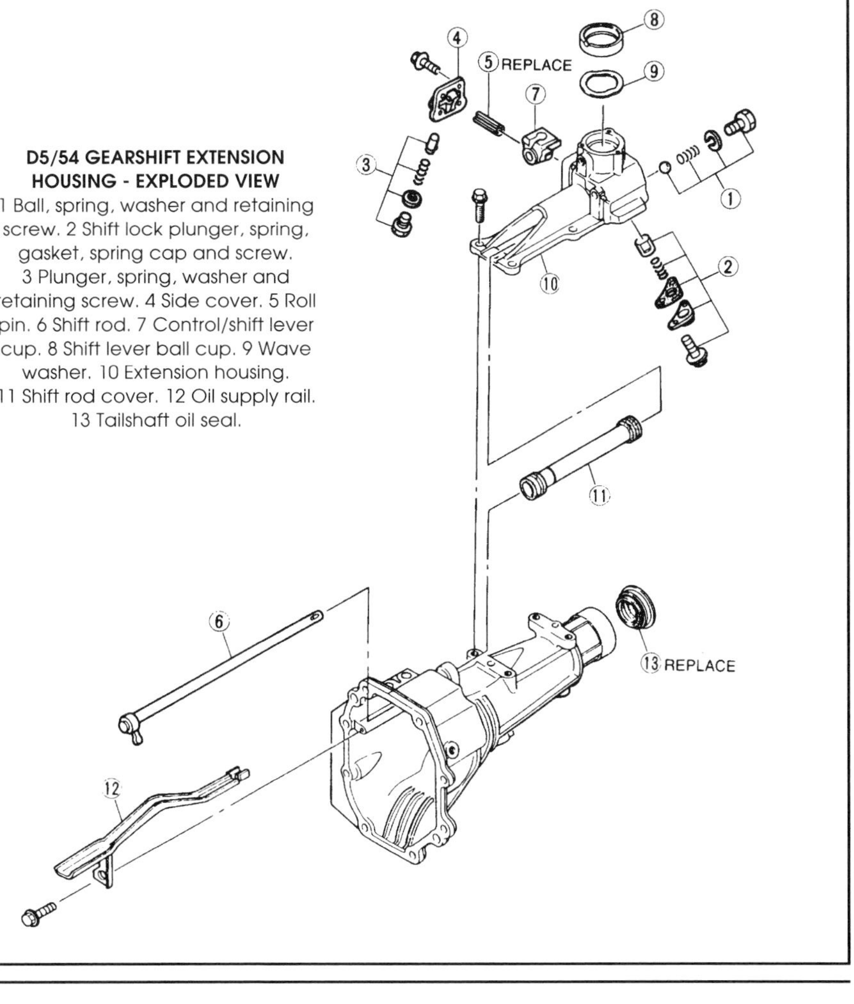

D5/54 GEARSHIFT EXTENSION HOUSING - EXPLODED VIEW
1 Ball, spring, washer and retaining screw. 2 Shift lock plunger, spring, gasket, spring cap and screw. 3 Plunger, spring, washer and retaining screw. 4 Side cover. 5 Roll pin. 6 Shift rod. 7 Control/shift lever cup. 8 Shift lever ball cup. 9 Wave washer. 10 Extension housing. 11 Shift rod cover. 12 Oil supply rail. 13 Tailshaft oil seal.

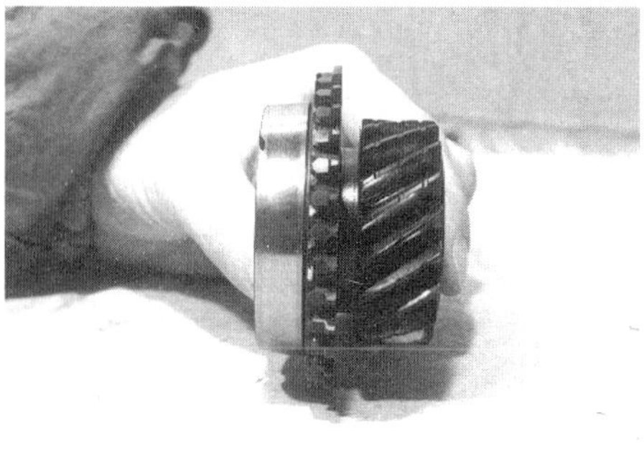

6/4-5 Check pinion, synchro boss & teeth (dogs).

5 On one side of each pinion is the conical boss upon which the synchro ring affects its braking action and ring of teeth or dogs with which the clutch hub sleeve locks when the gear is selected. There is unlikely to be any wear on the boss as the synchro ring is made of softer material; however, it's possible the dogs will be worn or damaged: check each one carefully.

6 Place each of the mainshaft gears in its normal position on the mainshaft and, using feeler gauges, check that the clearance between gear and shaft does not exceed 0.15 mm/0.006 in.

MAINSHAFT

7 Check for obvious damage to splines, gear and bearing seats. If you have the facilities, check that the shaft's runout does not exceed 0.03 mm/ 0.0012 in.

INPUT SHAFT AND COUNTERSHAFT

8 Check for obvious damage to splines, gear and bearing seats. Check condition of gear teeth as described in step 1.

CLUTCH/SELECTOR HUBS AND SELECTOR

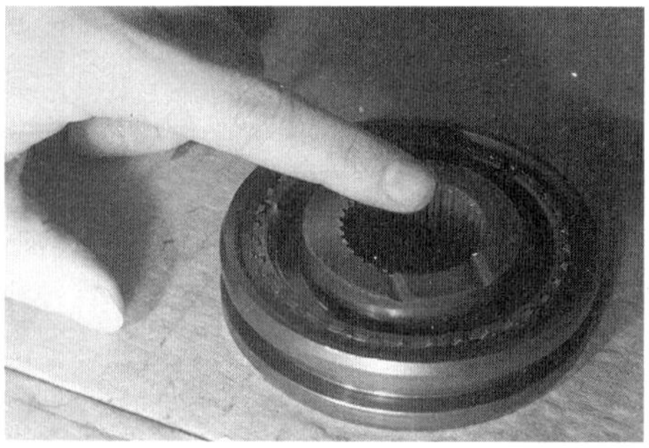

6/9 Check clutch hub including inner splines.

FORKS

9 Check that the outer sleeve of the clutch hub moves freely and defaults to central position. Pull the hub apart, having wrapped it in rag to catch the bits, and inspect the inner hub's inner and outer splines, the sleeve's inner splines and the keys for obvious damage or wear.

10 Fit the relevant shift fork into the sleeve's outer groove. Push the fork finger to one side of the groove and then, using feeler gauges, measure the gap between the finger's thrust pad and the wall of the groove on the other side of the same finger. Ideal clearance is between 0.2 and 0.3 mm/0.008 and 0.012 in and will mean a very long serviceable life ahead. Maximum permissible clearance is 0.5 mm/0.020 in but such a clearance will result in lower quality gearshift and short service life.

SYNCHRO RINGS

11 Check the teeth (or dogs) around the periphery of each ring for wear or obvious damage: the teeth should have good squarish edges. Look at the conical center of each ring, it should be covered with uniformly crisp but tiny oil retaining grooves: if these have disappeared severe wear is indicated.

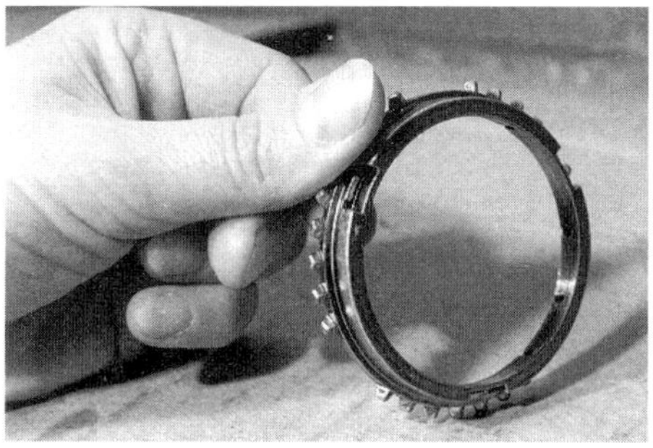

6/11 Check synchro rings.

12 Place each synchro ring on the relevant gear's boss, making sure it is evenly seated. Using a feeler gauge, measure the gap between the back of the synchro ring and the flank of the gear. Standard clearance is 1.5 mm/0.059 in and minimum clearance is 0.8 mm/0.031 in: the latter will mean a short service life and poorer quality gearchanges.

BEARINGS

13 Rotate each bearing with your fingers. Any noisiness or stickiness indicates the need for replacement.

14 The surface of built-in oil seals, where applicable, should be undamaged.

15 The races should not be corroded, cracked or chipped.

SPRINGS

16 + Serviceable free length of springs is as follows (shorter means replacement): fifth and reverse shift rod spring, 75 mm/2.953 in; short detent springs (x2), 17.0 mm/0.669 in; long detent springs (x2), 22.5 mm/0.886 in.

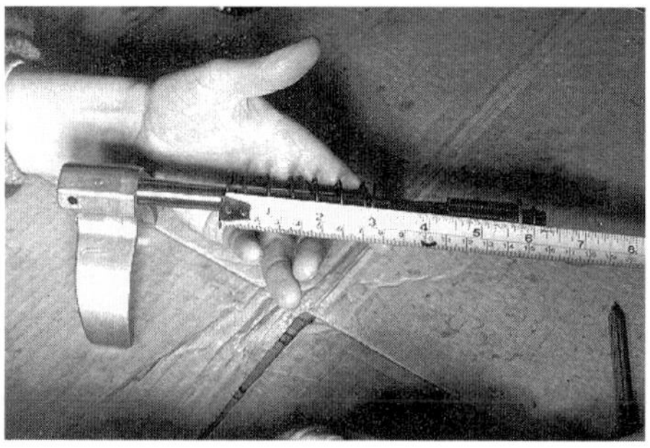

6/16a Check rod and ...

6/16b ... detent springs.

CASINGS

17 Inspect visually for obvious damage. Check joint faces and remove light scratches with fine emery paper.

7. TRANSMISSION (GEARBOX), MANUAL - REBUILD

☞ First read 1/1, 2.

1 Note: as it's likely the transmission is being rebuilt with a number of new components it's also more than likely that some tolerances will have to be adjusted with shims and selective washers as the rebuild proceeds. Unfortunately it's not possible to predict what thicknesses of shims will be required before the rebuild starts, therefore you should expect to have to stop the rebuild at least twice whilst you obtain suitable replacement shims. Transmission rebuilding is a job best done at a relaxed pace over a few evenings. Don't be tempted to cut corners, you'll end up with a noisy, notchy, short-life transmission unit.

2 Lubricate all components with fresh transmission oil as they are installed and keep tools, components and workplace clean at all times. If you have the slightest doubt about the serviceability of a component replace it; you'll be glad you did, even if it hurts your pocketbook for a while ... ☞ 4/4.

3 Fit the bearings to the transmission bearing carrier remembering to install any shims that were originally fitted. Drive each bearing into place with either a tube or socket large enough to bear against the outer race, or by placing a block of hardwood over the whole bearing face and then hammering on that. **Caution!** Whichever method you choose, drive each bearing home squarely.

4 Check by how much the bearing face stands proud of the bearing carrier by placing a

7/4 Check bearing protrusion.

straightedge across the bearing face and then measuring the gap between the straightedge and bearing carrier (or bearing if it's sunk in its housing) with a feeler gauge. You should do this for both countershaft and mainshaft bearings. Note that the bearing face can be flush with the bearing housing or proud by up to 0.1 mm (0.004 inches) but no more. If the bearing is protruding from the carrier too much you will need to remove it as previously described and then fit an appropriately thinner shim behind the bearing in place of the original so that it seats further into the bearing carrier. If the bearing face was found to be below the face of the housing, then a thicker packing washer is needed. Replacement shims are available in sizes of 0.1 mm (0.004 inches), 0.15 mm (0.006 inches) and 0.3 mm (0.012 inches). When correct bearing fit has been achieved carry on with transmission assembly.

5 Fit the bearing carrier bearing retaining plate in place and refit, finger-tight, the five bolts and spring washers which hold the plate to the carrier. **Caution!** If the spring washers have become flattened they must be replaced. Using a diagonal sequence tighten the five bolts to a torque of 22 Nm/2.2 kgf m/17lbf ft.

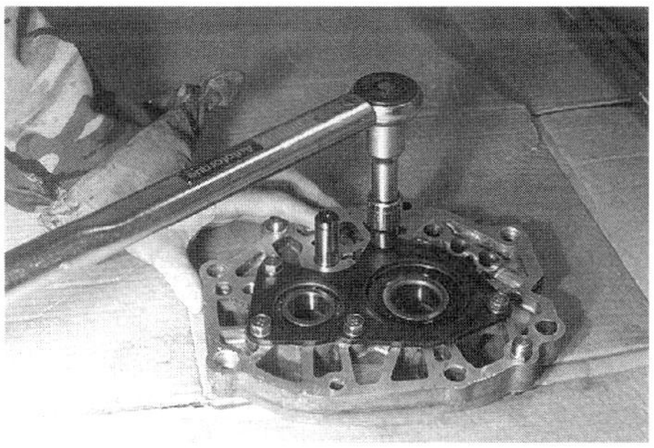

7/5 Torque tighten retainer plate bolts.

6. If the reverse idler gearshaft is being installed, after pressing the shaft into position its retaining bolt should be tightened to 12 Nm/120 kgf cm/100 lbf in.

7 Reassemble the reverse idler gear components by first fitting the thrust washer on the gearshaft, followed by the idler pinion (white spot toward rear of transmission), after having lubricated the gearshaft. Next fit the spacer washer with its center tang in the shaft's groove and, finally, fit a new snap ring to the groove at the end of the shaft making sure the snap ring is fully seated.

8 Using a feeler gauge check that the free play between the spacer washer and snap ring does not exceed 0.1 mm (0.004 inches). If the clearance is greater than the maximum allowed then remove the snap ring and substitute a new spacer washer of a thickness appropriate to give the desired clearance. Replacement washers are available in sizes of 2.6 mm (0.102 inches)/2.8 mm (0.110 inches) and 3.0 mm (0.118 inches). When the correct clearance has been achieved, transmission reassembly can continue.

7/8 Check lash (freeplay).

9 Mount the mainshaft in a vise so that the splined tail section is upward. **Caution!** You must use soft jaw protectors to ensure that the shaft is not damaged. Lubricate the whole of the mainshaft and then fit the second gear pinion, sliding it down the shaft until it meets the flange which separates it from third gear on the nose of the shaft. The pinion should be fitted so that the selector dogs are toward the rear of the transmission.

7/9 Fit 2nd gear pinion.

10 Next, fit the second gear synchro ring so that the cutouts face toward the rear end of the transmission.

11 If you've managed to get your clutch/selector hub mixed up, you will find it useful to know that the largest hub (approximately 97 mm/3.8 inches diameter) is the first/second hub, the second largest (90 mm/3.54 inches diameter) is the hub for third and fourth gears and finally the smallest hub (84 mm/3.3 inches diameter) is for fifth and reverse.

7/10 Fit 2nd gear synchro ring.

12 Fit the first/second clutch hub over the splines at the end of the mainshaft and slide it down the shaft into position. Note that the chamfered side of the hub's splined section should face toward the front of the transmission. Also, if you've dismantled the hub, ensure that the hub sleeve is fitted so that the side with the slight extension faces toward the rear of the transmission. Lastly, make sure the synchro keys on the clutch hub are lined up with the cutouts in the already positioned synchro ring before the clutch hub is pushed fully home onto its splines.

13 Ideally, a length of metal piping of at least 560 mm/22 inches in length and 35 mm/1.37 inches internal diameter, should be used to drift the hub fully onto its splines. Alternatively, you can temporarily remove the shaft from the vise and then, using the inverted jaw protectors as a seat for the clutch hub, tap the nose of the shaft until the hub is fully home on its splines. **Caution!** Don't forget to align the synchro keys and the cutouts in the synchro ring. Drive the hub home until there is no perceptible backward and forward play in the second gear pinion. Leave the mainshaft sitting on the clutch hub for the next procedure.

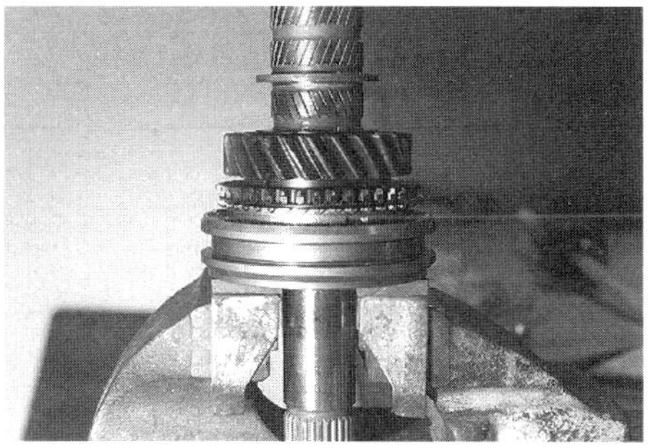

7/13 Drive mainshaft into position.

14 Having lubricated its seating, slide the third gear pinion over the nose of the mainshaft with the selector dogs facing toward the front of the transmission. Fit the synchro ring over the conical boss on the pinion with its cutouts facing toward the front of the transmission.

15 In our case, the third/fourth clutch hub had come apart during transmission dismantling and needed to be reassembled. A clutch hub is comprised of the central splined hub, an outer sliding sleeve, three keys and two synchro key retaining springs.

16 Slide the central hub into the outer sliding sleeve. Then slide the three keys - which look like tiny cars in profile - into the hub slots with their 'roofs' facing outward. Leave each key protruding slightly into the recess in the central hub.

17 Take one of the key retaining springs and fit its angled end into the hole in the side of the center hub's recess, then push the spring into position so that it holds each of the three keys in

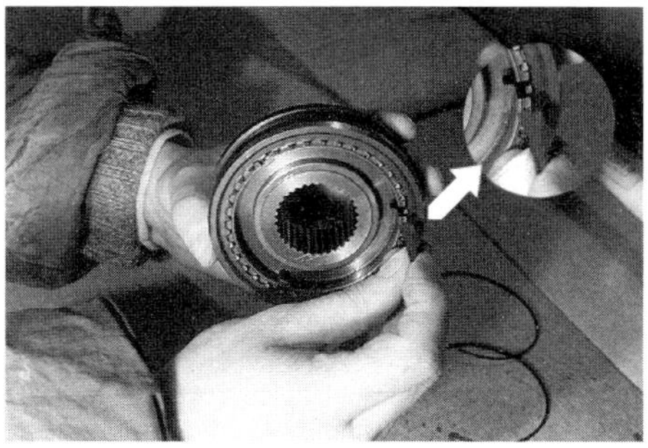

7/16 Correct fitting of keys ...

7/17 ... and springs.

place. Note that the spring will only press against all three keys, which it must do, when it is fitted a certain way round. Carefully turn the hub assembly around and fit the spring on the other side, once again ensuring that it contacts all three keys when in the fully seated position.

18 Double check on each side of the hub that each spring is in contact with all three keys and that the spring lies against the recessed part of each key so that neither the keys nor the spring can fall out.

19 + Fit the third/fourth clutch hub over the nose of the mainshaft, ensuring that the cham-

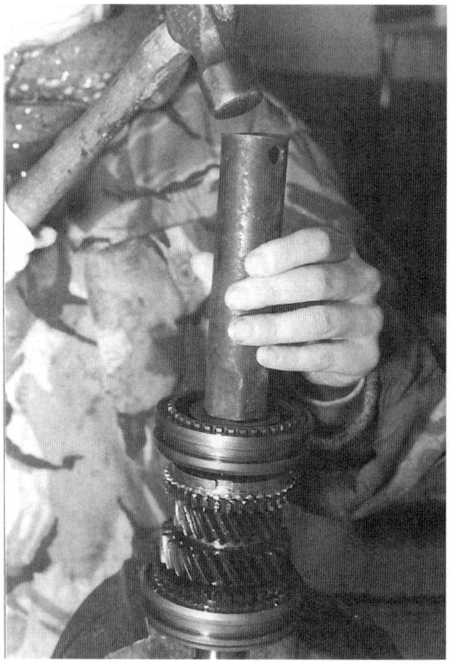
7/19a Drift 3rd/4th clutch hub into place ...

fered side of the splined center faces toward the rear of the transmission. Make sure the splined section of the mainshaft is well lubricated. Engage the splines of the hub and then, using a length of metal piping or a tube wrench of suitable diameter to bear on the central part of the clutch hub, drive the hub fully home on its splines. **Caution!** Make sure that the cutouts in the synchro ring align with the keys in the clutch hub, otherwise both could be damaged and neither will work properly. The tube wrench or metal pipe used as a drift needs to have an internal diameter of 35 mm/1.37 inches to clear

7/19b ... until snapring groove is exposed.

the boss of the mainshaft. You can tell when the hub is fully home as the snap ring groove in the mainshaft boss will be fully exposed.

20 Spring the snap ring into place, making sure that it is firmly and completely seated in its groove.

21 Turn the mainshaft assembly over in the vise and clamp the forward end of the mainshaft between jaw protectors.

22 Slide the second synchro ring for the first/second clutch hub over the shaft and into position with the ring cutouts engaged with the

7/22 Align ring cutouts with keys.

keys in the clutch hub.

23 Slide the inner race for the first gear bearings down the mainshaft and into position against the hub of the clutch.

24 + Slide the bearing cage for the first gear pinion over the central race, having lubricated it thoroughly. Fit the first gear pinion with its selector dogs facing toward the front of the transmission, having first oiled the synchro ring which is already in position. Put the spacing washer over the mainshaft until it is in position against the rearward facing side of the first gear pinion. The whole

7/24a Fit bearing cage ...

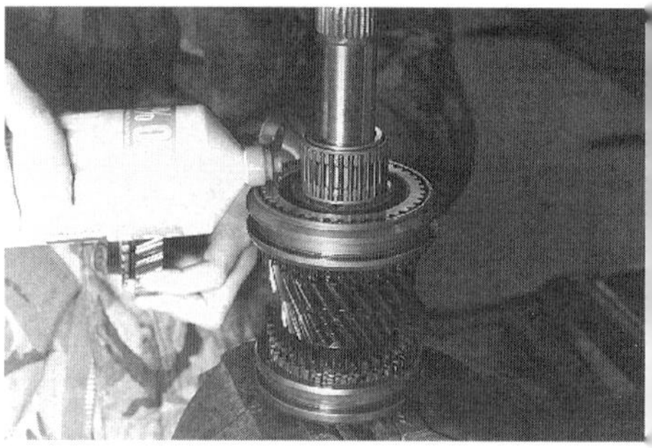
7/24b ... lubricate ...

7/24c ... and fit 1st gear pinion.

7/25 Fit selective washer to countershaft.

assembly should now look like this.

25 Fit the selective washer over the splined section of the countershaft so that it is pushed right up against the gear pinion. Remove the mainshaft assembly from the vise and lay it on your bench.

26 If the front bearing is not fitted to the countershaft now's the best time to do it. Mount the countershaft in a vise fitted with jaw protectors and then, using a metal tube or tube wrench of appropriate size to bear against the bearing's inner race, drift the bearing squarely, and fully, home. Fit a new snap ring, making sure it's fully seated in its

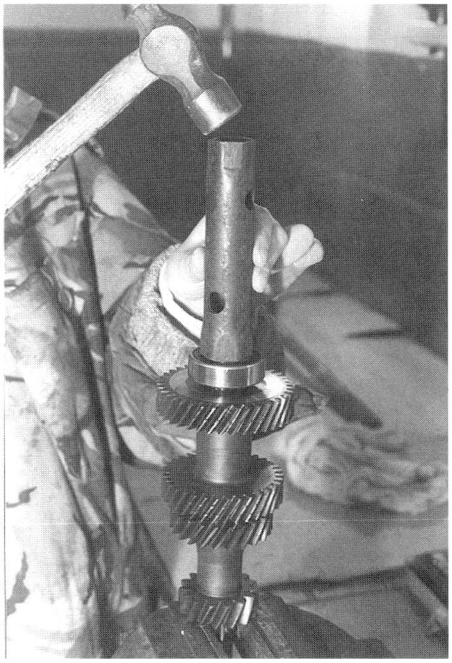

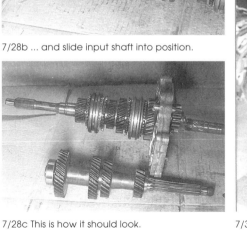

7/26 Drift bearing into place.

groove.

27 Place a block of wood on your workbench. Stand the nose of the mainshaft on the block of wood. Slide the transmission bearing carrier down the mainshaft (with the reverse idler pinion facing the rear of the transmission) until resistance is felt. Using a nylon-faced hammer tap alternately on each side of the bearing retaining plate until the bearing carrier is fully home against the back of the first gear pinion.

28 Pick up the transmission input shaft and place a dab of molybdenum disulfide grease

7/27 Drift bearing carrier onto shaft.

7/28a Grease bearing recess ...

7/28b ... and slide input shaft into position.

7/28c This is how it should look.

into the base of the bearing recess at the back end of the shaft. Grease the bearing cage with the same grease and fit it into place in the end of the shaft. Lubricate the conical boss behind the selector dogs of the primary drive gear and then position the synchro ring. Slide the input shaft over the boss on the front end of the mainshaft, making sure that the cutouts in the synchro ring are engaged with the keys in the third/fourth clutch hub. The mainshaft and countershaft assemblies should now look like this.

29 Install the countershaft. The fact that

7/29 Fit countershaft.

the countershaft's bearing is missing its inner race allows the countershaft to be introduced at such an angle it can be meshed with all of the gears on the input and mainshaft. You might find that you have to tap the mainshaft back through its central bearing slightly just to give clearance past the selector dogs of third gear: we were just able to do it without having to knock back the mainshaft. **Caution!** If you do have to tap the mainshaft back through its bearing, don't forget to return it to the correct position as soon as the countershaft is in place.

30 Mount the whole gear assembly in a

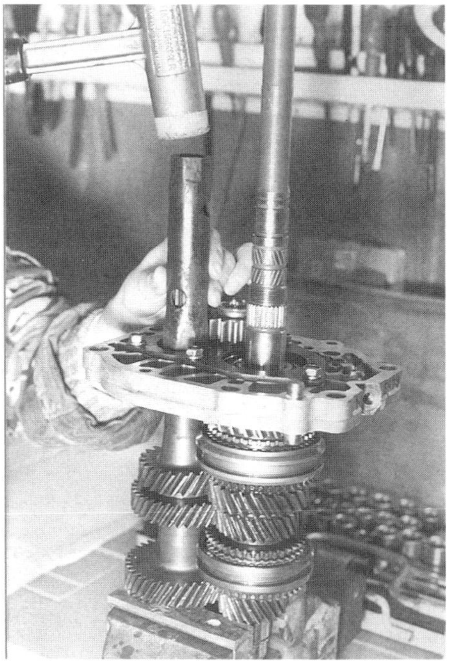

7/30 Gently drift in inner race.

vise with the face of the large pinion on the countershaft sitting on jaw protectors. From the rear of the center casting slide the countershaft bearing inner race down over the splined section (with collar towards rear of transmission) and, if necessary, using a tube wrench or metal pipe of appropriate dimensions drift the inner race gently home.

31 Lubricate the splines of the countershaft and slide the countershaft reverse gear pinion down over the splines, collar side toward the front of the transmission, until it engages with the idler pinion teeth and finally goes home against the

inner race of the center bearing.

32 Fit the large selective washer over the mainshaft and let it drop onto the face of the mainshaft center bearing. Fit the inner race of the reverse gear pinion bearing onto the mainshaft. Drop it down until it abuts the washer.

33 Note: don't forget to keep lubricating the mainshaft and individual components as they are fitted.

34 Fit the reverse gear pinion bearing cage over the inner race, having lubricated it well.

35 Fit the mainshaft reverse gear pinion with the selector dogs facing toward the rear of the transmission. You'll need to engage the teeth of the pinion with the reverse idler pinion before it will go fully home against the large washer.

36 Next fit the reverse synchro ring with the cutouts facing toward the rear of the transmission. The ring seats over the conical boss on the back of the gear pinion.

37 Slide the first and reverse clutch hub down the mainshaft making sure that the side with the central boss is toward the front of the transmission (this is also the side with the slight chamfer to the splined center section). Slide the clutch hub down the mainshaft until it engages with the shaft splines. Rotate the synchro ring until its cutouts align with the keys in the clutch hub.

7/37 Fit 1st/rev clutch hub.

38 The clutch hub now has to be driven fully onto the splined section of the mainshaft. Ideally, you'll have a piece of hollow metal pipe that's 432 mm/17 inches long and has an internal diameter of 35 mm/1.37 inches. However, if you don't have such a piece of metal piping you'll find that a shorter tube wrench will do almost as well but don't forget to tap evenly around the top of the tube wrench, or pipe, so that the clutch hub does not tilt and jam.

39 Slide a new 41 mm locknut down the mainshaft, collar toward the rear of the transmission, and finger-tighten it on the threaded section of the shaft until it contacts the inner hub of the clutch hub. It's going to be tricky to tighten this nut unless you have access to Mazda's special tool, which amounts to an elongated socket, but which does allow controlled tightening of the nut to 128-235 Nm, 13-24 kgf m or 94-174lbf ft. This really is pretty tight, so if you're using a 41 mm tube wrench and pipe wrench - which is the second favored method after the official special tool - you'll need to tighten the nut as much as you can without applying additional leverage to the wrench. When we rebuilt our transmission we were working in a small community near to a fairly large town where we tried tool specialists and even agricultural suppliers for a 41 mm tube wrench, but no-one had such a tool in stock. You may well find the same problem. Therefore, we had to resort to a chisel to tighten the nut. The technique for tightening a nut with a chisel is to set the chisel point behind one of the corners of the nut and then to drive that corner forward or, in other words, around. Continue this process until the nut will not move any further using moderate blows from a 1lb hammer.

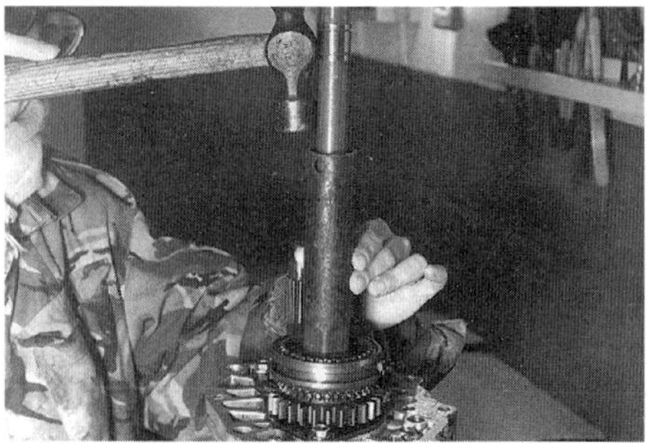

7/38 Drift clutch hub into place.

40 Using the corner of the chisel or a center punch, push a section of the nut's collar into the cutout in the mainshaft to lock the nut in place.

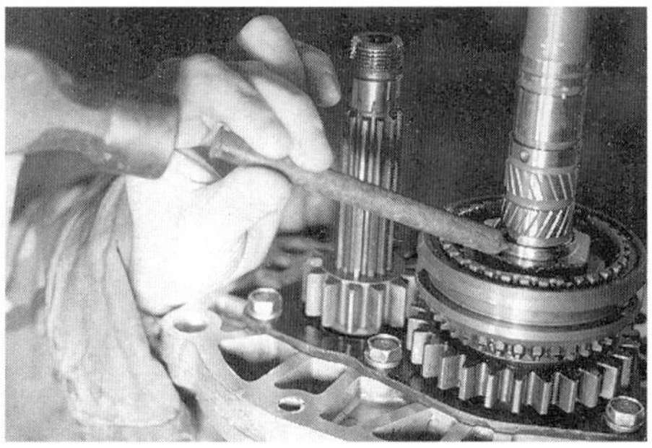

7/40 Stake the locknut.

41 Fit the first reverse clutch hub synchro ring, cutouts toward the front of the transmission, ensuring that the three cutouts are aligned with the three keys in the clutch hub.

42 Slide the fifth gear pinion down over the mainshaft, selector dogs toward the front of the transmission, until it sits snugly in the synchro ring of the clutch hub.

43 Carefully push the ball-bearing into its recess just behind the fifth gear pinion. Then slide the thick selective washer with central cutout down the shaft and engage the cutout with the ball-bearing to prevent the washer from rotating. Position the two halves of the C-washer on top of the washer you have just installed so that they are seated in the groove in the shaft. Then slide the large retaining ring down the shaft and over the outside of the C-washer halves to keep them together.

7/43 Fit ball and selective washer.

44 + Using a feeler gauge measure the space between the C-washers and the selective washer behind. This represents fifth gear lash/endfloat. The clearance should be in the range 0.1 - 0.3 mm (0.00 - 0.012 inches) and, if not, then a replacement selective washer should be obtained of appropriate size to correct the discrepancy. Selective washers are available in four sizes: 6.2 mm (0.244 inches), 6.4 mm (0.252 inches), 6.5 mm (0.256 inches) and 6.6 mm (0.260 inches).

7/44a Check gear lash (endfloat).

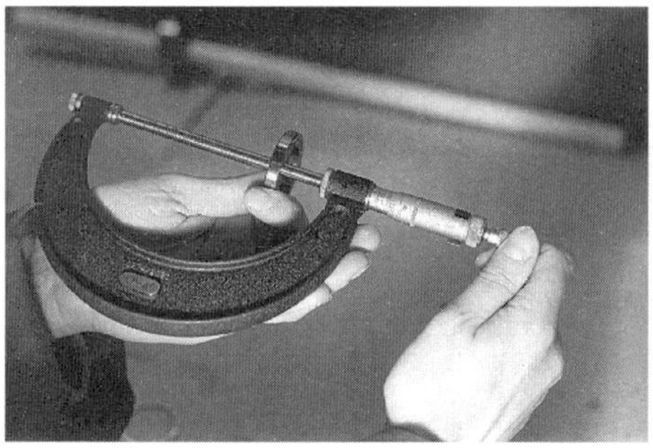

7/44b Measuring selective washer.

45 Slide the spacer down the countershaft until it sits on the reverse pinion.

46 Slide the countershaft fifth gear into position, protruding boss toward the front of the transmission.

47 Fit the mainshaft rear bearing by sliding it down over the shaft until it will go no further. The bearing will need to be driven the rest of the way home against the C-washers using the piece of metal piping previously used or an appropriate tube wrench.

48 Fit the two C-washers into the slot behind the mainshaft rear bearing, followed by their retaining ring.

49 + Using a feeler gauge check that there is no lash/endfloat between the inner race of the mainshaft rear bearing and the C-washers. There should be no play at all, but up to 0.1 mm (0.004 inches) is permissible. If there is a discrepancy this should be corrected by fitting C-washers of different thicknesses. Replacement washers are avail-

7/49a Check lash (endfloat).

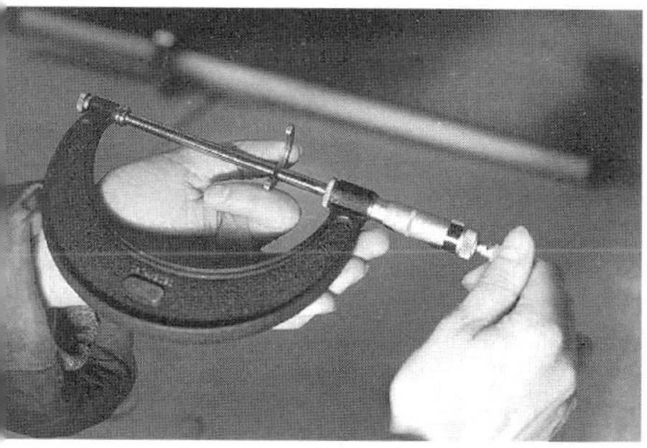

7/49b Measuring thickness of C-washer.

able in thicknesses of 2.9 mm (0.114 inches), 3.0 mm (0.118 inches), 3.1 mm (0.122 inches) and 3.2 mm (0.126 inches).

50 Fit the large spacing washer over the mainshaft and against the C-washers. Fit a new snap ring into the groove behind the washer and make sure it's fully seated and secure.

51 Fit the countershaft rear bearing in place and drive it home against the fifth gear pinion using a 20 mm socket and a nylon or copper-faced hammer.

52 Lock the countershaft by engaging first and reverse gears simultaneously (shift their respective clutch hub sleeves toward the center bearing carrier plate).

7/51 Drift countershaft bearing home.

53 Screw a new 32 mm locknut onto the end of the countershaft with your fingers, then torque the nut to a torque of 170 Nm/1.7 kgf m/125ft lbs.

54 Using a center punch or small chisel, peen the locking ring of the countershaft locknut into the groove in the shaft.

55 Disengage first and reverse gears by moving both synchro rings back to a central position and thus setting the transmission in neutral.

56 Reassembling detents. Remove the whole gear cluster assembly from the vise and place on your workbench so that the countershaft is at the bottom and the mainshaft on top. Now looking at the rear side of the center casting you'll see the three holes through which the shift rods slide. The lowest hole carries the shift rod for reverse and fifth gear, the middle hole the shift rod for third and fourth gear and the top hole the shift rod for first and second. Using blocks of wood, support the bearing plate and transmission input shaft so that the detent bores for shift rods reverse/five and three/four are vertical in both planes.

7/54 Stake locknut.

7/56 Ready to refit detents.

57 Take the spring for the lower part of the fifth/reverse detent (you have two long and two short springs; both short springs are used in the fifth/reverse detent bore). Drop the spring into the top of the detent bore and, if necessary, guide it into position below the shift rod bore. The spring should be followed by the round detent ball. With a little luck you should end up with the ball sitting on top of the spring. If not, using fingers or screwdrivers, manipulate the ball until it is sitting on top of the spring.

7/57 Drop spring & ball into detent bore.

58 Lubricate the fifth/reverse gear shift rod (it's the shortest rod with a spring and spring collar butting against a snap ring at one end). Using a screwdriver inserted from the rear side of the center casting, press down the ball in the shift rod bore whilst inserting the nose of the rod from the other side of the casting until the screwdriver is displaced and the rod itself is holding the ball and spring in place. For the moment the fifth/reverse shift rod should only protrude about half an inch through the rear side of the center casting.

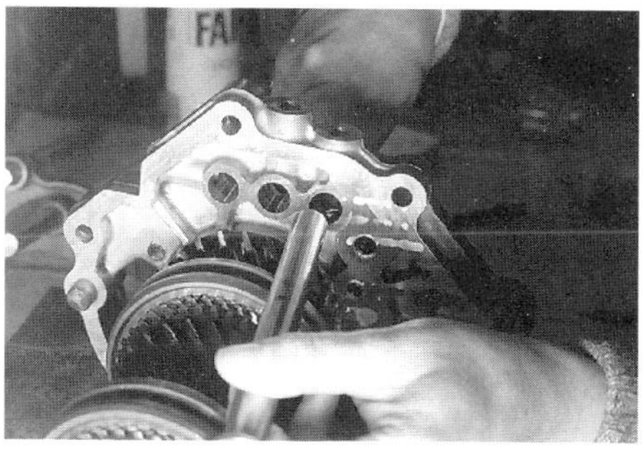

7/58 Hold down detent & fit shift rod.

59 Position the fifth/reverse shift fork on the fifth/reverse clutch hub. Then feed the shift rod through the fork until the roll pin holes align. Note that the side of the shaft with three detent notches should be facing away from the gear train. Note that the protruding side of the fork boss should point toward the rear of the transmission.

7/59 Feed shift rod thru fork.

60 Drive a new roll pin, seam facing forward, into position to lock the fork to the shift rod. Use a light hammer to drive the pin home whilst holding a heavier hammer against the other side of the yoke to absorb the hammer blows.

61 Rotate the bearing carrier plate until the bore for the first/second detent is vertical in both planes.

62 Take one of the elongated detent balls

7/60 Drive in new roll pin.

7/62 Drop in detent 'ball'.

and drop it into the top of the first/second detent bore and hopefully it will drop right the way down through to sit on top of the fifth/reverse shift rod. If it doesn't you'll need to manipulate it into position with your fingers.

63 Push the third/fourth shift rod into its bore from the rear side of the bearing carrier, making sure that the end with a flattened section is toward the front of the transmission. Hold the third/fourth shift fork in position on its clutch hub so that the rod can also be pushed through the fork's mounting boss.

7/63 Fit 3rd/4th shift rod.

64 Make sure that the three detent notches in the third/fourth shift rod face away from the mainshaft gear train. Line up the roll pin drilling in both fork and shift rod then drive a new roll pin home, seam facing forward, as previously described.

65 Drop the second elongated detent ball into the detent bore for the first/second shift rod. With luck it should drop right the way through to bear against the newly installed third/fourth shift rod. If necessary, you can manipulate the ball with fingers or a screwdriver until it drops into place. **Caution!** Don't forget to lubricate the detent bores

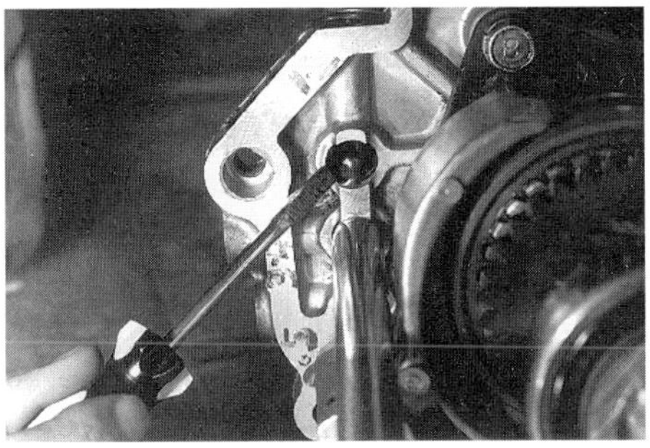

7/65 Drop in detent 'ball'.

and detent balls during assembly.

66 Insert the first/second shift rod from the rear of the bearing plate, whilst holding the first/second fork in position on its clutch hub so that the shaft also passes through the fork. Set the three detent grooves so that they face away from the third/fourth shift rod and then align the roll pin bore in the shift fork and rod, before driving the pin home as described previously. **Caution!** It's important that the slot in the pin faces toward the front or rear of the transmission and not toward the side.

67 Rotate the bearing carrier so that the

7/66 Fit 1st/2nd shift rod.

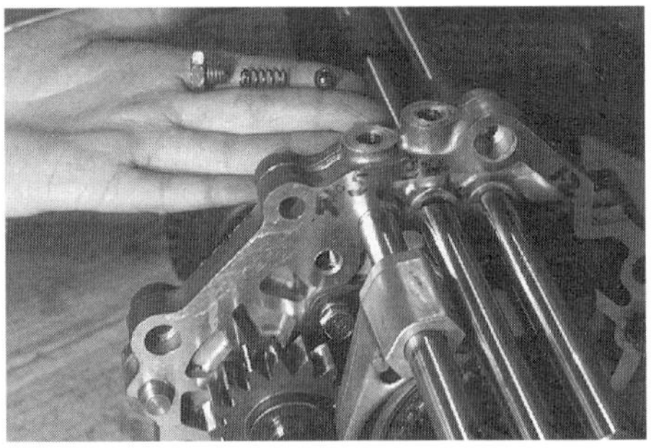

7/67 Fit detent ball, spring and bolt.

bore for the fifth/reverse shift rod detent is vertical in both planes. Put a drop of oil into the detent bore, followed by a round detent ball, the second short spring and, finally, the retaining bolt, to which I suggest you apply a little thread locking fluid for the sake of security. Tighten the retaining bolt to a torque of 22 Nm/2.2 kgf m/17lbf ft.

68 Repeat this procedure using the remaining balls and two long springs for the detent bores of the third/fourth shift rod and the first/second shift rod. Note that the retaining bolts for these two detents both have copper washers, whilst

7/68 Fit new snaprings.

that for the fifth/reverse detent does not. Again, it's suggested you put a little thread lock on the retaining bolt threads for the sake of security. Torque wrench settings are the same as before. Fit the snap rings/circlips to the shift rods for first/second and third/fourth gears. Make sure that the new clips are firmly and securely seated in their grooves.

69 Set all of the clutch hub sleeves in their central 'relaxed' position so that no gears are engaged. Using feeler gauges measure the gaps between the shift fork thrust pads and the sides of the clutch sleeves; make and record this measure-

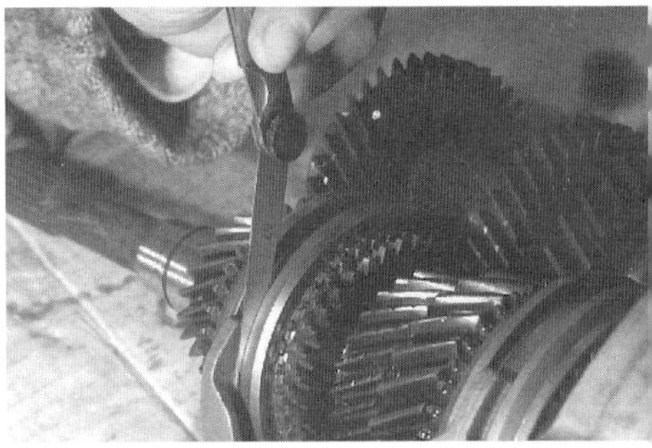

7/69 Measuring fork clearance.

ment both sides of the same shift fork tip (only measure one tip for each fork) and for each of the three shift forks.

70 It is important that the clutch hub sleeves run centrally on the shift fork tips. The measurements you have just recorded should show that the hub sleeves are centered on the fork tips or are, at least, within 0.3 mm/0.012 in of being so. If the hubs are not central enough the very bad news is that you'll have to dismantle the mainshaft again to reset the whole shaft, and therefore the clutch hub sleeves, further forward or backward as appropriate.

71 The mainshaft's longitudinal position is adjusted by the selective spacers to be found on each side of the shaft's center casting bearing. The total thickness of the two spacers must be between 5.9 and 6 mm/0.2323-0.2362 in. Individual spacer washers are available in the following thicknesses: 2.2 mm/0.0866 in; 2.7 mm/0.1063 in; 3.0 mm/0.1181 in; 3.2 mm/0.1260 in; 3.7 mm/0.1457 in.

72 Whoa, don't panic! It's not as complex as it sounds. Here's how. Say the measurements you took showed that the whole mainshaft was too far forward by 0.3 mm/0.012 in (the gap on the side of the shift fork tip is bigger, by 0.3 mm/0.012 in, on

the side that faces the front of the transmission) then the required adjustment is a thinner spacer in front of the center casting bearing to move the mainshaft back by 0.3 mm/0.012 in. Comprendez vous? Tres bon!

73 Record the adjustment required and then teardown down the gearshafts, as you've done before, until you've got the mainshaft out of the center casting. Measure the individual thickness of the existing spacers, making sure you know which spacer came from which position. To make it easy in our example we'll say that we found both existing spacers to be 3.0 mm/0.1181 in thick. To move the mainshaft backwards through the bearing we need a forward spacer 0.3 mm/0.012 in thinner, *i.e.*, a new spacer that's 2.7 mm/0.1063 in thick. Remember that the total thickness of both spacers must be between 5.9-6.0 mm/0.2323-0.2362 in, therefore, the second new washer that's appropriate from the range available is of 3.2 mm/0.1260 in thickness. This time, when you've reassembled the transmission, you should find the shift fork fingers slap bang in the middle of the clutch hub sleeve grooves.

74 Stand the whole gear cluster assembly on its nose in an open vise with the front face of the countershaft first gear resting on jaw protectors.

75 Spread a thin, but continuous, bead of silicone sealant around the flange of the bearing carrier and allow it to dry for around five minutes. Rub oil over the three shift rods, the rims of the countershaft and mainshaft rear bearings and also liberally oil the whole gear train. Lower the transmission main casing into position, carefully feeding it over the three shift rods and making sure that the mainshaft and countershaft bearings are aligned with their housings in the back end of the casting.

76 Fit the three shift rod end arms in the arrangement shown in the photograph. As when

7/75 Fit main casing.

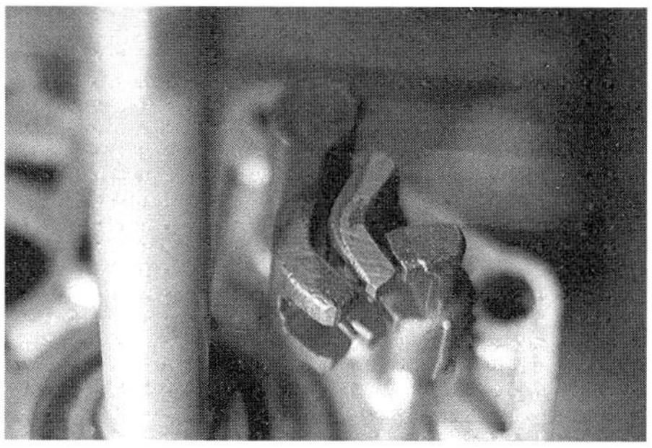

7/76 Correct arrangement of shiftrod arms.

fitting the shift forks, use a large hammer to absorb the blows when driving roll pins home. Make sure that the roll pin openings face toward the front of the transmission. Fit the shift rod end with the shortest pawl first and the one with the longest pawl last. **Caution!** Be careful not to drop the roll pins into the transmission center housing.

77 Stretch a rag over the transmission center housing so that you cannot drop components into the casing, then fit a new snap ring into the groove of the mainshaft nearest the center casing. Make sure the snap ring is securely located in its groove. Fit the small ball-bearing into the

7/77 Fit locking ball and speedo drive.

recess in the mainshaft; this bearing will lock the speedometer drive gear in position and prevent it rotating. Slide the speedometer drive gear over the mainshaft and align one of its internal grooves with the ball-bearing so that the speedometer drive gear can be pushed fully home against the snap ring that has already been fitted. Fit the second new snap ring to retain the speedometer drive gear, ensuring the snap ring is securely seated in its groove.

78 Steps 80 to 88 describe the rebuild of the transmission extension housing and only apply if the unit is disassembledped.

79 Fit the oil rail inside the extension housing a fix with the single 10 mm bracket bolt. Tighten the bolt with a wrench using finger pressure only.

80 Lubricate the rubber seals of the shift rod tube with oil and then push the end of the tube with the forward mark into position in the extension housing.

81 Spread silicone sealant over the turret mounting pads on top of the extension and then fit the turret in place, taking care to engage it with the free end of the shift rod cover tube. Fit the turret's four 12 mm retaining bolts and tighten the bolts to a torque of 22 Nm/2.2 kgf m/17lbf ft.

82 From inside the extension housing, slide

7/81 Torque tighten turret bolts.

the lubricated shift rod back into position and simultaneously engage it with the shift cup in the turret. Check that the shift finger of the rod is pointing downward and then align the roll pin hole in the cup with that in the rod. Drive a new roll pin home making sure that its seam faces the front of the transmission.

83 Spread a thin, but continuous, smear of silicone sealant around the side flange of the shift turret. Four 10 mm bolts retain the cover plate on the side of the turret and these, too, should each be smeared with silicone sealant before they are fitted. Once the bolts are in place and finger-tight, tighten

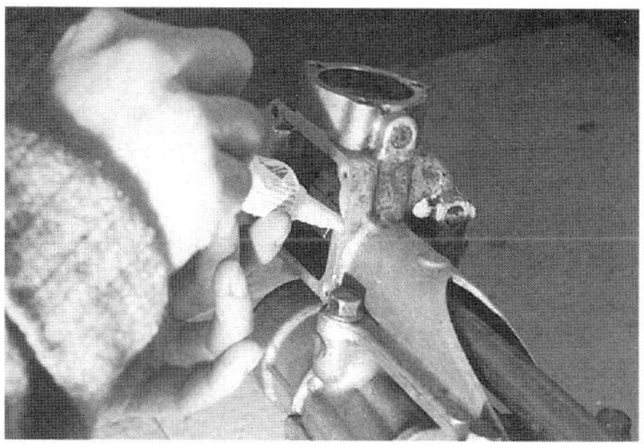

7/83 Apply silicone sealant.

them fully using just a box end wrench and finger-pressure. Note that the cover should be fitted with the angled threaded bore facing downwards.

84 + Oil them first, then slide the thrust pin and spring up into the bore in the side of the turret cover - the domed part of the thrust pin first. Fit and tighten the 21 mm retaining bolt by wrench and finger pressure only. Do not overtighten.

85 Turn the extension housing upside down and from the base of the shift turret insert the spring-loaded locking plunger, dome end first, making absolutely sure that the side with three flats

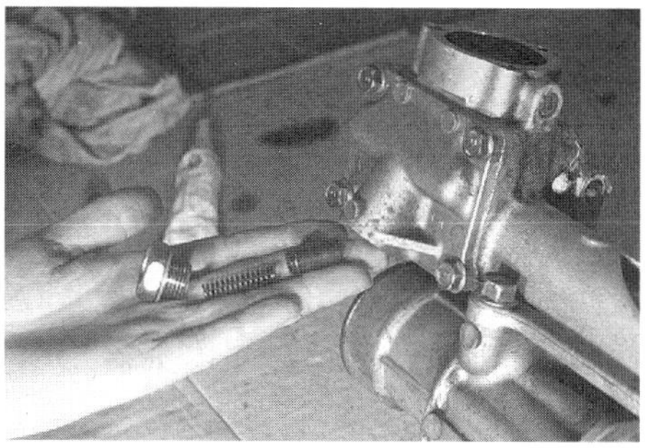

7/84a Fit thrust pin and spring ...

7/84b ... then retaining bolt.

7/85 Locking plunger components.

faces toward the detent bore; in other words, toward the back of the transmission. Oil the plunger before installing it. With the plunger in position, insert the spring into its center followed by the thrust cap which, of course, should be sealed with a new gasket. Tighten the two 10 mm bolts securing the thrust cap using a wrench and finger pressure only.

86 Oil the spring and ball for the shift lock detent and then insert the ball, followed by the spring, into the detent bore at the rear of the shift turret. Smear the whole threaded area of the retaining hollow bolt with silicone sealant. Engage the protruding spring end with the hollow center of the bolt and screw the 19 mm bolt home. Tighten with a wrench and finger pressure only. Do not overtighten.

7/86 Shift lock detent components.

87 Fit the wave washer, followed by the nylon ball seat into the top of the turret.

88 Spread a thin, but continuous, bead of silicone sealant around the rear flange of the transmission main casing and allow it to dry for around five minutes.

89 Using a screwdriver or your fingers, move the shift cup in the transmission extension housing to the reverse position. In other words, looking from the rear of the transmission it will be laid over as far as possible to the left and pushed as far as possible forward. Hold it in this position and then lower the extension gently into position and twist it slightly to the right. As the gap between the center housing and extension housing closes to about 13 mm/half an inch, you should be able to see the extension housing shift engage with the shift arms on the end of the shift rods and, as soon as that happens, twist the extension casing to the left and lower it into final position. Before going further, check that the shift is working by temporarily installing the gearshift lever and gently selecting gears. You may need to lift the assembly out of the vise to do this so that the gear train is free to rotate a little.

7/88 Apply silicone sealant.

90 + If the input shaft front bearing was removed from the bellhousing now is the time to refit, or fit a new bearing. First, fit a new snap ring into the groove in the outer race of the bearing, making sure the snap ring is securely seated in the groove. Lubricate the outer race of the bearing and position it over its housing in the bellhousing casting (from the open bellhousing end). Using a 200 mm/8 inch length of hardwood timber of 75x75 mm/3x3 inches or more square or a piece of metal pipe with an outside diameter matching the bearing's outer race, drift the bearing home until the snap ring contacts the bellhousing casting. Remember to tap the wood block or drift in a circular pattern so that the bearing is driven home evenly.

7/90a Fit new snapring ...

7/90b ... position bearing ...

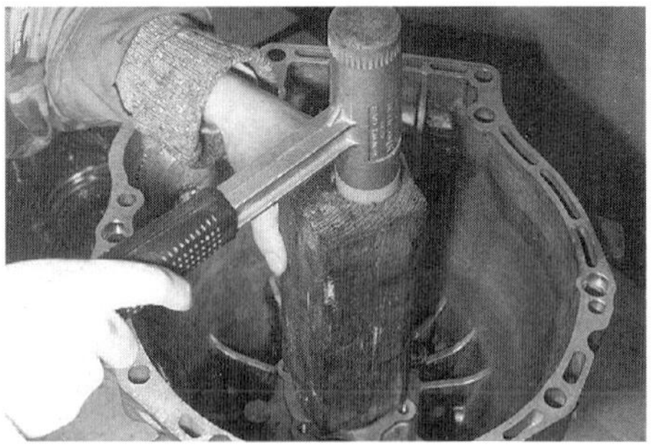

7/90c ... then drift home.

91 Using a vernier depth gauge, or a straightedge and feeler gauges, measure the height of the bearing face above the face of its housing and make a note of the measurement as 'B'. Then, using the same tools, measure the depth of the second recess (almost same diameter as the input shaft bearing) in the rear of the input shaft cover and note this measurement as 'A'. The input shaft cover serves as a bearing retainer which should secure the input shaft bearing with virtually no lash/endfloat. Measurement 'B' can be between 0 and 0.1 mm/0 and 0.004 in smaller than measurement 'A': it must not be larger. Adjustment shims, which fit between the bearing's front face and the back of the cover, are available in three sizes: 0.10 mm/0.004 in; 0.15 mm/0.006 in; 0.30 mm/0.012 in.

92 Place the bellhousing casting clutch end down on your bench, then spread a thin but continuous bead of silicone sealant around the rear flange of the transmission bellhousing casting.

7/93 Fit transmission assembly to bellhousing.

93 Lubricate the forward ends of the shift rods and also liberally oil the whole gear train. Gently lower the transmission assembly into the bellhousing until the joint flanges meet. Be careful to ensure that the shift rods have lined up with their supporting bores in the back of the bellhousing and also that the input shaft is lined up with its bearing and the countershaft bearing with its housing. Once you are confident all is correctly lined up, you can use a rubber or nylon-faced hammer around the forward flange of the extension housing to tap the whole assembly together.

94 Once the gap between the bellhousing casting rear flange and the front flange of the central bearing carrier is no more than 6-7 mm/a quarter inch apart, you can insert the transmission casing through bolts and, in a diagonal sequence, gradually tighten them to evenly close and seal all of the transmission joints. Note: before inserting the bolts, a bead of sealant should be put under the head of each and remember that the two uppermost bolts retain wiring clips. Final torque for the 12 mm through bolts is 20 Nm/2.0 kgf m/15lbf ft.

95 Input shaft front cover oil seal replacement (if required).

7/95 Buckle old seal ...

Mount the input shaft cover in a vise, clamping the input shaft sleeve between jaw protectors. Using gentle blows, drive a screwdriver blade between the outer rim of the seal and the casting.

96 You'll then find you can lever the buckled seal out of its seat. Lubricate the outer rim of the new seal.

97 Place the seal over its housing and, using very gentle taps from a rubber or nylon-faced hammer against the outer rim of the seal only, gently tap it home into its housing.

98 Transmission rebuild continued. Place

7/96 ... and lever out.

7/97 Tap new seal into position.

7/98 Fit a new gasket.

a new gasket in position on the front housing flange inside the bellhousing, having first smeared the back of the gasket with oil to make it stick in place. Smear the flange of the housing with oil and also lubricate the inner lip of the oil seal and the area of the input shaft the seal lip bears upon. If bearing shims are required (see step 82) fit them into the rear of the housing.

99 Slide the housing into position inside the bellhousing casting and tighten its six retaining bolts finger-tight. It's recommended you put a smear of silicone sealant around the threads of

7/99 Slide housing into position.

each of the bolts before inserting them. Tighten the bolts to a torque of 22/2.2 kgf m/17lbf ft. Don't forget to tighten in a diagonal sequence.

100 + Smear high melting point copper-based, or organic molybdenum grease on the input shaft sleeve and on the clutch release fork pivot. Put another blob in the socket on the back of the release fork and more on the tips of the release arm's fork fingers.

101 Pass the release fork tail out through the square hole in the side of the bellhousing. Take the clutch release bearing and place it on the input shaft sleeve with its arms facing toward the back of

7/100a Grease input shaft sleeve ...

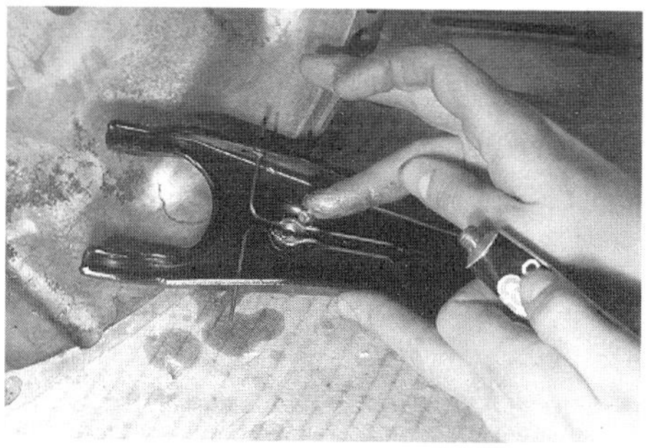

7/100b and release fork pivot socket.

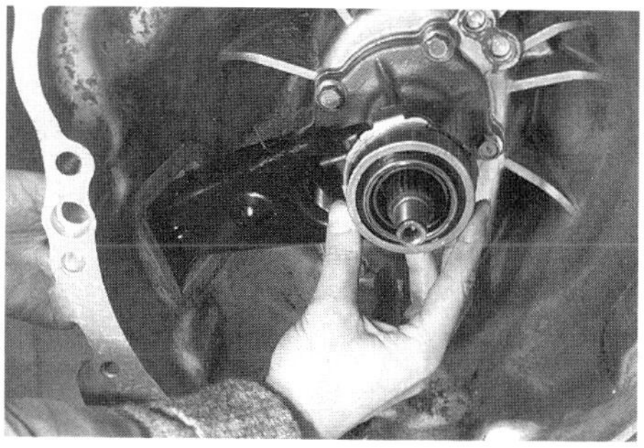

7/101 Fit release bearing and fork.

the transmission. Note that the fork tips of the release fork must engage with these arms once the whole assembly is in place. Now the tricky bit is to push the arm against its pivot so that the spring opens and retains the arm, whilst at the same time the fork tips of the arm engage with the extensions on the back of the thrust washer. It's easier than it sounds!

102 Replace the rubber boot around the protruding part of the clutch release arm, making sure its lip is engaged with the bellhousing casting.

103 Fit the backup/reverse light switch to the left-hand side of the transmission rear extension. This is the switch with red cables and enscapulation around the top. Tighten the 24 mm hexagonal section of the switch using an crescent wrench and finger pressure only. Do not overtighten. Don't forget the copper sealing ring which should be replaced every time the switch is removed.

104 Fit the neutral sensor switch at the top right of the extension casing. Once again, don't forget a new sealing washer and tighten the switch's 24 mm hexagonal section by hand pressure only.

105 Turn the transmission onto its left-hand side and on the right-hand side of the transmission extension casing you'll see an opening for the speedometer driven gear. Lubricate the gearwheel thoroughly and gently slide the driven gear assembly down into its housing. When the driven gear is fully home in its housing, fit the 10 mm bolt which retains it and tighten with a wrench using finger pressure only.

106 That concludes the transmission rebuild. If it's the first one you've ever done, you should celebrate!

8. TRANSMISSION (GEARBOX), MANUAL - INSTALLATION

☞ First read 1/1, 2.

1 Spread a thin smear of copper-based lubricant on the nose and splines of the transmission input shaft - don't overdo it!

2 Using protective packing on the jack's pad, jack the front of the engine 50 mm/2 inches which will have the effect of tilting the rear of the engine slightly downwards. **Caution!** Don't jack so far that the crank-angle sensor or coil contact the firewall and check that hoses and looms are not getting stretched.

3 With the help of a strong assistant or, better still, by supporting the weight of the transmission on a wheeled jack, bring the engine and transmission unit together. Make sure that the transmission input shaft enters the center of the clutch cover and that the bellhousing is correctly lined up with the engine backplate. If the clutch disc is well centered, the transmission bellhousing should go fully home against the engine backplate with no more than a little joggling around. Life will be a little more difficult if the clutch disc isn't well centered and, in extreme cases, you'll have to withdraw the transmission, slacken the clutch cover and re-center the disc before attempting again to make the transmission fit. Once the transmission bellhousing slides fully home, make sure it engages on the hollow spigots projecting from the rear of the cylinder block.

4 Fit the two topmost bellhousing bolts which are 17 mm (x 60 mm) and screw them into place finger-tight which, for the moment, will be enough to stop the transmission coming away from the back of the engine again. Fit the two lowermost 17 mm (x 60 mm) bolts which, again, should be screwed in finger-tight at this stage.

5 Position the exhaust pipe support bracket over the two bolt holes on the left-hand side of the bellhousing. Secure the bracket, flange facing rearward, with two 17 mm bolts the upper of which is longer at 70 mm although there seems no good reason for this. Screw the bolts home finger-tight. Note: The four remaining fasteners in the starter motor area will be fitted later.

6 Tighten all of the 17 mm bellhousing bolts to 80 Nm/8 kgf m/58lbf ft.

7 ☞ 3/11/10-28, 30-32.

8 📷 From inside the car, pour 90 ccs/5.4 cu in. of transmission oil into the shift turret of the transmission. Spread a little of the same lubricant

8/8a Add oil to turret ...

8/8b ... and lubricate pivot ball.

over the gearshift lever pivot ball and the nylon swivel at the stick's base.

9 Smear a little silicone gasket sealant or conventional gasket sealant around the top flange of the shift turret and then carefully lower the lever assembly into position, making sure that the cutout in the pivot ball engages with the peg in the turret.

10 Fit the three 10 mm bolts which hold the gearshift lever securing plate to the top of the turret and tighten them using only moderate pressure.

11 Having first made sure no carpet or wiring is trapped underneath, fit and tighten with moderate pressure the four 10 mm bolts which retain the shift lever gaiter to the top of the transmission tunnel. Don't forget the bridging piece which goes on top of the gaiter at the rear.

12 📷+ Once the gaiter is secured wrap the long thin piece of insulation around the outside of the gaiter turret. Place the foam tube over the shift lever and then place the large piece of insulation over the gearshift lever too.

13 Lay the central console on its side alongside the gearshift lever and remake the electrical connections by pushing the connector blocks together. Slide the fuel cap release lever through the

8/12a Refit insulation ...

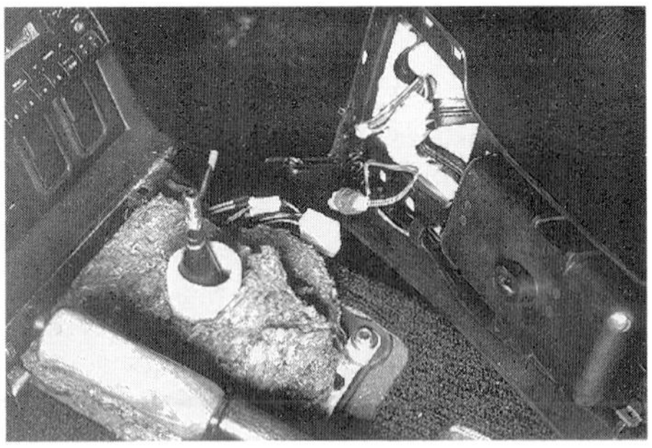

8/12b ... as shown.

recess in the rear of the console and then maneuver the console into position over the gearshift lever. Make sure all wires are tucked within the console body and that the strip of carpet surrounding the parking/hand brake is also fixed under the console, then fit the five crosshead, self-tapping screws which retain the console to the transmission tunnel. Tighten the five screws.

14 Lower the ashtray into its recess and close the lid of the cassette box.

15 Screw the gearshift knob onto the lever and don't forget to leave it correctly orientated so that the shift pattern on its top makes sense!

16 Fit the engine undertray. The tray is secured by three 10 mm sheet metal (self-tapping) screws at the front edge, two 10 mm bolts on the front suspension/engine subframe, two 10 mm bolts into the chassis rail on each side of the car, together with one 10 mm nut on the stud the tray shares with a front body support stay on each side of the car. To fit the tray, first slide one side up around the stabilizer bar and secure by tightening a couple of the fastenings finger-tight. Repeat the process on the other side of the car, at the same time making sure that the projecting tab in the front of the suspension/engine subframe locates in the indent of the undertray. You can now fit and tighten all of the securing screws, bolts and nuts: finger pressure on a wrench is sufficient.

17 Carefully lower the car to the ground: ☞ 1/3.

18 Reconnect the battery: ☞ 3/11/98, 108.

9. TRANSMISSION (GEARBOX), AUTOMATIC - INSTALLATION

☞ First read 1/1, 2.

1 Using protective packing on the jack's pad, jack the front of the engine 50 mm/2 inches which will have the effect of tilting the rear of the engine slightly downwards. **Caution!** Don't jack so far that the crank-angle sensor or coil contact the firewall and check that hoses and looms are not getting stretched.

2 With the help of a strong assistant or, better still, by supporting the weight of the transmission on a wheeled jack, bring the engine and transmission unit together. Make sure that the transmission bellhousing is correctly lined up with the engine backplate.

3 Once the transmission bellhousing slides fully home on the hollow spigots projecting from the rear of the cylinder block, quickly fit the two topmost 17 mm (x 60 mm) bellhousing bolts and screw them into place finger-tight This, for the moment, will be enough to stop the transmission coming away from the back of the engine again. Fit the two lowermost 17 mm (x 60 mm) bolts which, again, should be screwed in finger-tight at this stage.

4 Position the exhaust pipe support bracket over the two bolt holes on the left-hand side of the bellhousing. Secure the bracket, with flange facing rearward, with two 17 mm bolts the upper of which is longer at 70 mm although there seems no good reason for this. Screw the bolts home finger-tight.

5 Fit, and finger-tighten, the 17 mm (x 60 mm) bolt at lower right of the bellhousing. Note: the remaining fasteners in the starter motor area will be fitted later.
6 Tighten all of the 17 mm bellhousing bolts to 80 Nm/8 kgf m/58Ibf ft.
7 Reach up into the bellhousing, via the access hole in its base, and fit the four bolts which secure the torque convertor to the driveplate. Lock the driveplate by wedging a large screwdriver into the starter teeth, then tighten the bolts to a torque of 50 Nm/5.0 kgf m/36Ibf ft. If there is one, fit the cover to the bellhousing access hole.
8 If used, lower and remove the jack which was supporting the transmission, then reach up around the top of the transmission and remake the six electrical connections. If the wires were held in clips, refix them.
9 Lower and remove the jack supporting the front of the engine.
10 ☞ 3/11/11-16.
11 Fit a new O-ring to the base of the transmission dipstick tube and smear it with ATF. Push the base of the tube into position in the transmission unit, and then fit the bolt and nut which secure the tube's bracket. Tighten to a torque of 22 Nm/ 2.2 kgf m/17Ibf ft.
12 On the left of the transmission, reconnect the two oil cooler pipes by installing their banjo bolts complete with new, ATF lubricated, sealing washers. Fit the bolts fixing the pipe's support brackets to the side of the transmission and bellhousing and tighten with a wrench and finger pressure only. The banjo bolts should be tightened to a torque of 30 Nm/3.0 kgf m/22Ibf ft.
13 Also on the left is the vacuum pipe. Push the rubber end of the pipe over the union stub in the transmission case and secure the rigid section of pipe by installing its clip bolt and tightening with a wrench and finger pressure only.
14 ☞ 3/11/17-28 (ignoring references to the clutch release cylinder and its piping), 32.
15 Reconnect the selector lever to the shaft in the transmission casing and secure with nut and washer; tighten the nut with a wrench and finger pressure only.
16 Fit the engine undertray. The tray is secured by three 10 mm self-tapping screws at the front edge, two 10 mm bolts on the front suspension/engine subframe, two 10 mm bolts into the chassis rail on each side of the car, together with one 10 mm nut on the stud the tray shares with a front body support stay on each side of the car. To fit the tray, first slide one side up around the stabilizer bar and secure by tightening a couple of the fastenings finger-tight. Repeat the process on the other side of the car, at the same time making sure that the projecting tab in the front of the suspension/engine subframe locates in the indent of the undertray. You can now fit and tighten all of the securing screws, bolts and nuts: finger pressure on a wrench is sufficient.
17 Check that the transmission's oil pan bolts have been tightened. If the transmission unit is 'dry', fill it with around 4 liters/4.2 US qt/3.5 Imp qt of new ATF: ☞ 2. Otherwise check and replenish the ATF level: ☞ 2.
18 Carefully lower the car to the ground: ☞ 1/3.
19 Reconnect the battery: ☞ 3/11/98, 108 .

10. PROPSHAFT - REMOVAL, CHECKING, REPAIR & INSTALLATION

☞ First read 1/1, 2.

REMOVAL

1 Raise, and securely support, the rear of the car high enough to give good access to the underside as far forward as the transmission unit: ☞ 1/ 3. If you raise the rear of the car as opposed to the left-hand side, you can avoid having to drain, or partially drain, the transmission oil/ATF.
2 Remove the rear section of the exhaust system: ☞ 5/38.
3 ☞ 4/2/12-14.

CHECKING AND REPAIR

4 Clean the propshaft with oil solvent or kerosene/paraffin and wipe dry before making a visual inspection. **Warning!** Do not use gasoline/ petrol for cleaning purposes. **Caution!** Do not immerse the U-joints/universal joints in solvent. The propshaft is not a serviceable item so any significant fault will necessitate replacement.
5 If you suspect the propshaft is bent, take it to a machine shop and have them check the runout. If you have two large V-blocks, a long flat surface and a dial gauge you can easily check the runout yourself. Maximum runout is 0.4 mm/0.016 in.
6. Mount the shaft in a vise, but don't squeeze it too tightly. One at a time, grasp the drive flange at one end of the shaft and then the sliding sleeve at the other and try to twist them backwards and forwards. If you feel a significant amount of lash/ freeplay then the bad news is it's time to replace the shaft as the UJs cannot be repaired.

INSTALLATION

7 ☞ 3/11/27-28.
8 Fit the exhaust system rear section: ☞ 5/ 38.
9 Lower the car to the ground: ☞ 1/3.

11. TRANSMISSION (GEARBOX) REAR OIL SEAL - REPLACEMENT

☞ First read 1/1, 2.
1 Remove the propshaft: ☞ 4/10/1-3.
2 Using a small chisel and a light hammer drive the oil seal out of the housing. Don't forget to work from side-to-side so that the seal comes out evenly.
3 Spread oil (ATF for auto. trans.) around the outer periphery of the new seal and around the inner lip. Position the new seal in the tailhousing, spring side inward. When you are satisfied that it is square to its housing, use a length of metal tubing with a diameter to match the rim of the seal, or a block of wood, and a hammer to drive it evenly home into the transmission tailshaft housing.

11/2 Drive old seal out.

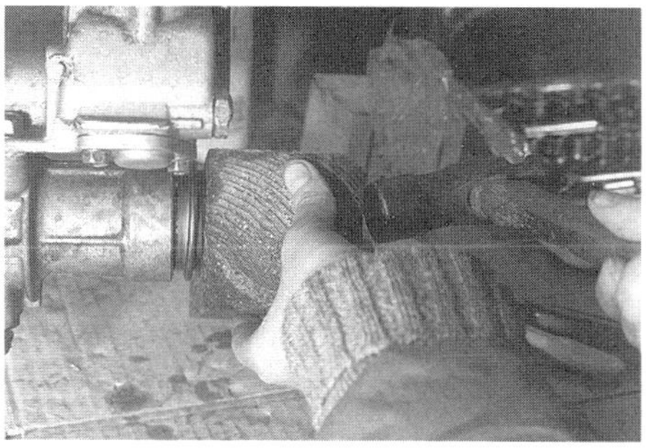

11/3 Drift new seal in.

4 Install the propshaft: ☞ 4/10/7-9.

12. PPF (POWER PLANT FRAME) - REMOVAL & INSTALLATION

☞ First read 1/1, 2.

REMOVAL

1 You'll need good access to much of the car's underside to carry out this work, so raise the whole car to a suitable height and support securely: ☞ 1/3.
2 ☞ 4/2/16-23.
3 **Warning!** The PPF makes a fundamental contribution to your car's good handling but is, unfortunately, not a component that can be repaired. If the PPF is bent, cracked or seriously corroded it should be replaced. Take the old PPF to a scrap metal dealer: that much alloy has to have some value.

INSTALLATION

4 ☞ 3/11/11-16, 23-26.
5 Lower the car to the ground: ☞ 1/3.

13. DRIVESHAFT - REMOVAL, CHECKING, REPAIR & INSTALLATION

☞ First read 1/1, 2.

REMOVAL

1 Remove the hubcap from the appropriate wheel. Use a narrow chisel or an old screwdriver to release the staking of the hub locknut from the groove in the driveshaft/halfshaft.
2 With the footbrake applied, unscrew and remove the 29 mm hub locknut: it'll be real tight so you may need to use a heavy duty socket and drive and to extend the socket's T-bar with a length of

hollow steel pipe. **Warning!** The locknut's likely to release suddenly, so be ready! Leave the nut in position once it has freed. **Warning!** Do not use the car until the nut has been retightened and re-staked.

3 Slacken the wheelnuts of the appropriate wheel or wheels and then jack and safely support the rear of the car high enough to give easy access to the differential unit and driveshafts: ☞ 1/3.

4 Unscrew and remove the wheelnuts, then lift away the road wheel to expose the hub and brake disk.

5 Using an indelible marker pen or a center punch, mark the relative positions of the driveshaft flange and the differential flange.

6 With the parking brake applied, unscrew and remove the four 14 mm nuts and spring washers securing the driveshaft flange to the diff. flange. Withdraw the driveshaft unit from the car. Repeat the process on the other side of the car if both driveshafts are to be removed.

7 📷+ Behind the brake caliper, low down, you'll see a black plastic cover over the head of the caliper's lower mounting pin: prise the cover off with your fingers or pliers. Unscrew and remove the pin using a 10 mm box-end wrench or socket.

13/7a Remove cover and ...

13/7b ... unscrew and remove pin.

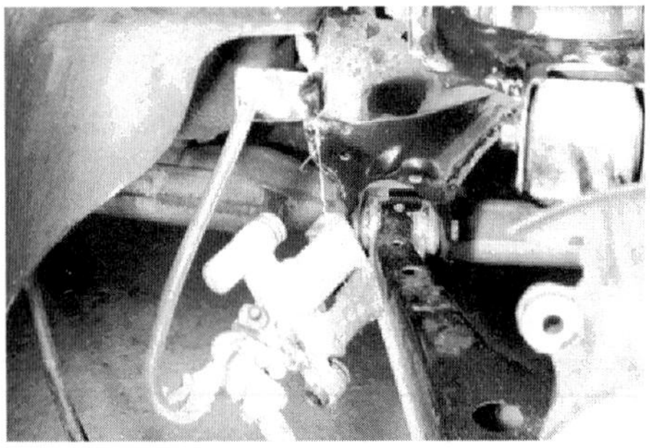

13/8 Tie caliper out of harm's way.

8 📷 Swivel the caliper body upward thru 90 degrees and then slide the caliper off of its top mounting pin. Tie the caliper out of harm's way and so that the brake hose is not strained. **Caution!** Don't press the car's brake pedal until the caliper is back in place over the disc.

9 Lift away the brake disc. Then remove the already loosened hub locknut. Pull the hub flange from the splined section of the driveshaft (if it sticks, see note in step 11).

10 📷 Unscrew and remove the 14 mm nut of swivel pin connecting the top wishbone to the hub upright: withdraw the pin.

13/10 Remove nut and swivel pin.

11 Swing the hub carrier outward and over the end of the driveshaft. Note: if the driveshaft sticks in the hub bearings, Install the old locknut so that its top is flush with the end of the driveshaft. Gently tap the nut and shaft end with a nylon-faced hammer, while supporting the carrier, until the shaft begins to slide through the hub bearings. Remove the nut.

CHECKING & REPAIR

12 Check the rubber boots/gaiters at both ends of the shaft for cracks and holes. Don't attempt to repair such damage, instead replace the whole boot. Check that the boot retaining straps are tight and in good condition.

13 If the shaft itself has sustained obvious damage it should be replaced.

INSTALLATION

14 Place the driveshaft flange over the studs and against the flange of the differential making sure the mating marks are aligned (not applicable if a new shaft is being fitted) and fit the four new spring washers and four securing nuts. Leave the nuts fingertight for the moment.

12 Feed the splined end of the shaft through the hub having first smeared a little copper-, or molybdenum-based grease over the splines and bearing seat. Push the hub carrier backward until the shaft protrudes through the wheel side of the hub.

13 Smear copper-based grease over the shaft of the wishbone to hub upright swivel bolt and, having lined up the upright and wishbone, push the bolt home. Install and tighten the bolt's 14 mm retaining nut to a torque of 60 Nm/6.0 kgf m/42lbf ft.

14 Slide the hub flange over the splines of the driveshaft and then Install the brake disc over the wheel mounting studs.

15 Smear a little copper-based grease over the top caliper swivel pin and then slide the caliper body over the pin. Swing the caliper body downwards until the disc is once more properly sandwiched between the pads. Smear a little copper-based grease on its shank and then fit the lower caliper mounting pin and tighten it to a torque of 52 Nm /5.1 kgf m / 38lbf ft. Install the pin's plastic cover.

16 Apply the parking brake and then screw a new hub locknut into position - leave final tightening until later.

15 Tighten the driveshaft to differential flange 14 mm nuts to a torque of 60 Nm/6.0 kgf m/44ft lb using a diagonal sequence.

16 Release the parking brake and fit the roadwheel. Lower the car to the ground: ☞ 1/3. **Warning!** Don't forget to tighten the roadwheel nuts.

17 Have someone apply the footbrake whilst you tighten the hub locknut to a torque of 260 Nm/ 26 kgf m/190lbf ft. Phew! Using a blunt punch or chisel stake the locknut flange ring into the groove in the shaft. **Warning!** The staking should be at least 4 mm/0.16 in deep for security. Fit the hubcap.

14. DRIVESHAFT - TEARDOWN & REBUILD

☞ First read 1/1, 2.

1 Each driveshaft has two constant velocity joints; one at each end. Unfortunately the CV joint at the wheel end is not repairable so there seems little point in describing the dismantling and overhaul of the CV joint at the other end of the shaft as both joints will wear at approximately the same rate. If either of the CV joints is worn and has become noisy in service fit a complete new or exchange reconditioned driveshaft.

2 New original type boots/gaiters cannot be fitted without dismantling the differential end CV joint. However, for this kind of situation, aftermarket manufacturers usually design and market replacement boots which can be split and refastened once in position. **Caution!** Once in place CV joint boots should be filled with molybdenum disulfide grease and then new retaining bands fitted (tongue facing away from the direction of normal rotation).

15. DIFFERENTIAL UNIT AND CARRIER - REMOVAL & INSTALLATION

☞ First read 1/1, 2.

REMOVAL

1 Slacken the wheelnuts of the two rear wheels and then jack the car high enough to give easy access to the whole of the underside: ☞ 1/3. If you have access to a workshop pit or a vehicle hoist they will make this task much easier.

2 Unscrew and remove the wheelnuts, then lift away each rear road wheel to expose the hub and brake disk.

3 Remove the rear section of the exhaust system: ☞ 5/38.

4 ☞ 4/2/12-14. Note: there is no need to withdraw the front of the propshaft from the gearbox tailhousing which would cause oil to leak.

5 At this point the official Mazda procedure is to remove the whole of the PPF frame, however it seems to the writer that it would probably be sufficient simply to release the differential end of the frame and then, when the time comes, to slide the diff. unit out of the frame. Unfortunately this is a piece of supposition which cannot be verified. If you want to remove the whole PPF: ☞ 4/2/16-23. Otherwise just follow the appropriate steps of the same section to release the diff end of the PPF.

6 Have a container of at least 1 liter/2 pint capacity handy and then unscrew and remove the differential's 23 mm filler plug and 24 mm drain plug. Unscrew the last few threads of the drain plug with your fingers, holding the plug in position until it's completely unthreaded and then withdrawing it suddenly to minimize oil seepage. Allow the oil to drain and then fit the plugs finger-tight.

7 Using an indelible marker pen or a centre punch, mark the relative positions of the driveshaft flange and the differential flange of each driveshaft.

8 Unscrew and remove the four 14 mm nuts and spring washers securing each driveshaft flange to its diff. flange: apply the parking brake if necessary. If you cannot release the driveshafts from their diff. flanges unscrew and remove the 14 mm nut of the swivel pin connecting each top wishbone to the hub upright and withdraw the pin. Swing the hub upright outward to free the driveshaft.

9 Support the weight of the differential unit on a wheeled jack and then unscrew and remove the single 17 mm nut and two 12 mm nuts from each of its mountings. Lower the differential unit and wheel it out from beneath the car. Note: if the PPF is still in place it will be necessary to lower the diff. sufficiently to allow it to be disengaged from the PPF, before the diff. unit can be withdrawn (the transmission unit will need to be supported whilst the diff. unit is out of the car).

INSTALLATION

10 Support the differential unit on a wheeled jack and raise into position until the mountings engage with the three studs on each side. Note: if the PPF frame is still in place, engage the diff. with the frame before raising fully.

11 Fit the three nuts securing each mounting. Tighten the central 17 mm nut of each mounting to 92 Nm/9.2 kgf m/68ft.lb and the two outer 12 mm nuts to 22 Nm/2.2 kgf m/17lbf ft.

12 Place a driveshaft flange over the studs and against the flange of the differential making sure the mating marks are aligned and fit the four new spring washers and four securing nuts. Tighten the 14 mm nuts to a torque of 60 Nm/6.0 kgf m/44ft lb using a diagonal sequence. You may need to have an assistant apply the footbrake during this process. Repeat the process for the other driveshaft.

13 If you released the top wishbones, smear copper-based grease over the shaft of a wishbone to hub upright swivel bolt and, having lined up the upright and wishbone, push the bolt home. Fit and tighten the bolt's 14 mm retaining nut to a torque of 60 Nm/6.0 kgf m/42lbf ft. Repeat the process on the other side of the car.

14 ☞ 3/11/11-16, 23-26. If only the rear end of the PPF was disengaged, follow the relevant parts of the same text.

15 Lift up the rear end of the propshaft and align its flange with the mating marks on the diff. flange. Fit the four 12 mm bolts, new spring washers and 14 mm nuts (nuts toward the front of the car). Apply the parking/handbrake to prevent the shaft from turning and tighten the nuts in a diagonal sequence to a torque of 29 Nm/2.9 kgf m/21lbf ft.

16 Replenish the diff. unit with the specified oil: ☞ 2. **Caution!** Remember to tighten both drain and filler plugs.

17 Fit the roadwheels and lower the car to the ground: ☞ 1/3. **Warning!** Don't forget to tighten the roadwheels' nuts.

16. DIFFERENTIAL SIDE (OUTPUT SHAFT) OIL SEALS - REPLACEMENT

First read 1/1, 2.

1 Remove the appropriate rear driveshaft: ☞ 4/13/1-11.

2 Have a container of at least 1 liter/2 pint capacity handy and then unscrew and remove the differential's 23 mm filler plug and 24 mm drain plug. Unscrew the last few threads of the drain plug with your fingers, holding the plug in position until it's completely unthreaded and then withdrawing it suddenly to minimize oil seepage. Allow the oil to drain and then fit the plugs finger-tight.

3 Using a couple of tire levers or old screwdrivers wedged against the diff. casing, lever the output shaft flange outwards until its shaft is free enough to be totally withdrawn.

4 Drive a thin chisel or screwdriver through

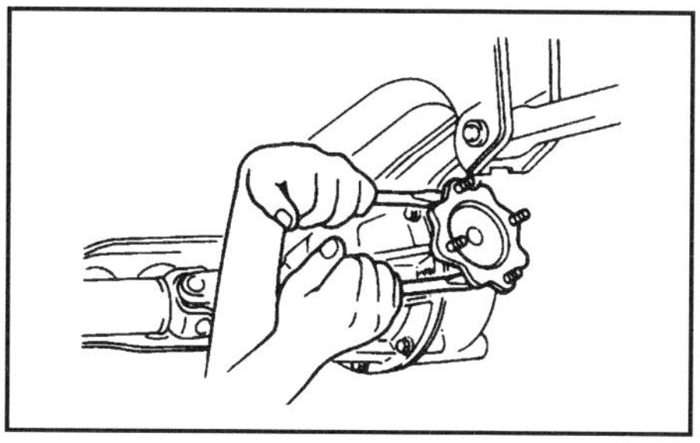

D16/3 LEVER OFF OUTPUT FLANGE AS SHOWN.

the face of the old oil seal and lever it out of its housing.

5 Smear the outer circumference of a new seal with oil and position it squarely over its housing, closed side of the seal facing out. Place a flat block of hardwood over the seal's complete face and then, using moderate hammer blows, drive the new seal squarely home until its face is flush with the housing.

6 **Caution!** If your car is fitted with a limited slip differential (LSD) and you've removed both output shafts, the longer of the two fits on the right. Fit a new spring ring to the output shaft and then

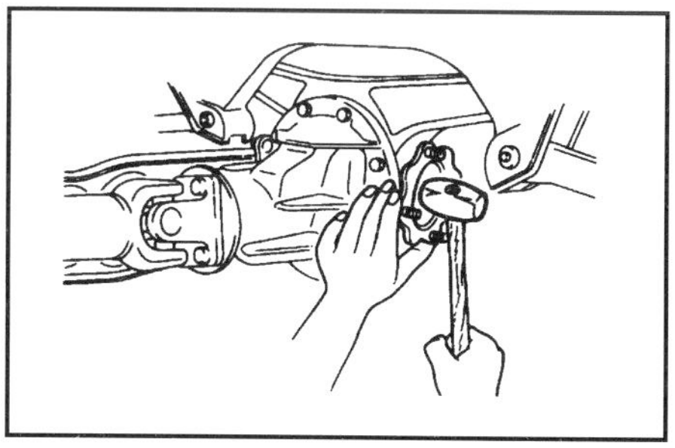

D16/7 TAP HOME THE OUTPUT SHAFT AS SHOWN.

smear the shaft with axle oil. Gently, push the shaft through the seal.

7 Tap the shaft fully home using a nylon- or copper-faced hammer against the center of its flange. You'll know when the spring clip has locked as you'll no longer be able to withdraw the shaft with your fingers.

8 Replenish the diff. unit with the specified oil: ☞ 2. **Caution!** Remember to tighten both drain and filler plugs.

9 Fit the driveshaft/s: ☞ 4/13/14-17.

17. DIFFERENTIAL NOSE (PINION) OIL SEAL - REPLACEMENT

☞ First read 1/1, 2.

1 Partially remove the propshaft: ☞ 4/2/12-14. There is no need to pull the front of the shaft out of the transmission which would lead to some oil loss.

2 Apply the parking brake - you may need an assistant to operate the footbrake at the same time - and then unscrew and remove the large nut (sorry, forgot to record its size ...) and washer retaining the differential pinion flange. **Warning!** The nut will be tight, and will probably loosen suddenly: be prepared.

3 Using an ordinary proprietary two- or three-legged puller, pull the pinion flange off the pinion shaft.

4 Drive a thin chisel or screwdriver through the face of the oil seal and then lever it out of its housing. Note: there may be some oil loss if the car is not level.

5 Smear the periphery of the new seal with oil and then position it squarely over its housing. Use a piece of metal tube of the same outer diameter as the seal to drift it squarely home until the seal's face is flush with the housing. If you don't have an appropriate piece of tube, use a nylon-faced hammer to tap around the face of the seal until it's fully home: take care to keep the face of the hammer square to the face of the seal.

6 Smear the outer circumference of the pinion flange with oil and then push the flange home onto the pinion shaft. Fit the washer and a new nut. Apply the parking brake and then tighten the nut to a torque of 160 Nm/16 kgf m/110lbf ft.

7 ☞ 3/11/27-28.

8 If there was any loss of oil when the seal was removed, check the differential oil level and top up as necessary: ☞ 2.

9 Lower the car to the ground: ☞ 1/3.

18. DIFFERENTIAL UNIT CARRIER MOUNTINGS - REPLACEMENT

☞ First read 1/1, 2.

1 You will need to replace these rubber/ metal composite mountings if the rubber section has broken away from the metal or has become over compliant through age and use.

2 Remove the differential unit: ☞ 4/15.

3 Clamp the 'eye' of the diff. carrier casting which contains the mounting in a vise so that the side of the mounting without an external flange is facing upwards. Using a piece of metal tubing of slightly smaller diameter than the mounting's outer sleeve, drive the mounting downwards and out of the diff. carrier casting.

4 Note: in the previous step we made it sound easy but the mounting was pressed into the carrier by a force of 2000kg/2 tons so after a few years it may be reluctant to move. If in difficulty, drill through and around the rubber section of the mounting until it can be pushed out of the outer sleeve. Using a small chisel you should now be able to buckle the outer sleeve inward until it is loose enough to push out of the carrier 'eye'.

5 Position the 'eye' of the diff. carrier casting (diff. downwards) centrally over vise jaws closed to a gap of around 25 mm/1 in. Lubricate the exterior of the new mounting with silicone-based lubricant like WD40, then position the mounting squarely over the eye so that its external flange is on top and the two voids in the rubber section face front and back of the car.

6 Using a piece of metal tube of the same diameter as the flange and a hammer, or moderate blows from a nylon- or copper-faced hammer around the periphery of the flange, drive the mounting into the carrier until the flange is in full contact with the carrier.

7 Fit the differential unit: ☞ 4/15.

19. DIFFERENTIAL UNIT - TEARDOWN AND REBUILD

☞ First read 1/1, 2.

1 We hope you won't think we've taken a soft option, but we strongly advise you not to attempt a differential teardown and rebuild. A number of specialist tools are required and the whole unit must be reassembled with precise regard to adjustments and tolerances if it is to work efficiently and quietly.

2 Unless some manufacturing fault comes to light, which would almost certainly happen within the warranty period, the differential should last the life of the car. However, if your car's differential does require attention or you want to have a limited slip differential (LSD) fitted or different ratio gears then remove the diff. carrier (complete with diff.) and take it to your Mazda dealer or engineering shop for the work to be done.

20. ELECTRONIC DEVICES, AUTO TRANS - GENERAL

1 If a fault develops with the operation of your car's automatic transmission - and you've checked that the ATF level is OK - it is most likely to be caused by a failing electronic component. Therefore it is worth carrying out the tests and rectifications detailed in the following sections before assuming that the unit has an internal fault: ☞ 4/21-25. If the tests do fail to locate the fault you should consult your Mazda dealer or an auto trans specialist for further advice.

21. O/DRIVE ELECTRICAL SYSTEM, A/T - TESTING & COMPONENT REPLACEMENT

☞ First read 1/1, 2.

FUNCTION TESTING

1 Drive the car with "D" selected at a speed where the auto trans has shifted into top gear - but not faster than 87 mph /140 kph. Operate the overdrive switch and verify that overdrive and lockup are provided, then depress the o/d switch and verify that overdrive and lockup are disengaged. If the system does not operate correctly check the overdrive off switch, overdrive cancel solenoid and the lockup solenoid.

O/D OFF SWITCH TESTING, REPLACEMENT

2 Remove the console between the seats and lay it to one side of the transmission tunnel - you don't need to disconnect its wiring: ☞ 3/2/4.

3 Turn the ignition on - but don't start the car - and use a multimeter between terminal "A" and ground to make the test shown in the drawing. When the overdrive switch is released (out) the meter should show battery voltage and, when the switch is depressed (in), no voltage. If the switch fails this test check continuity as detailed next. Turn the ignition off.

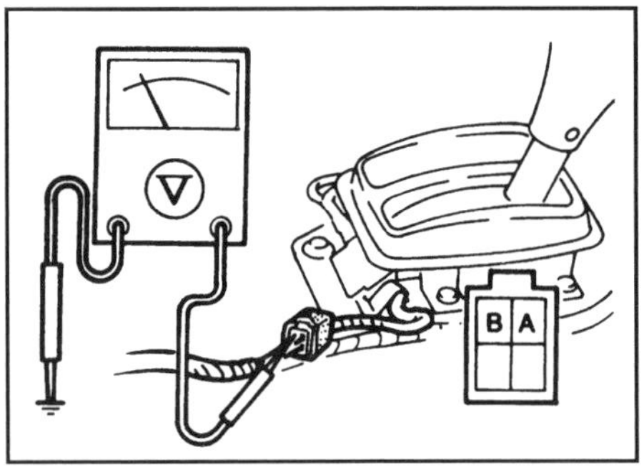

D21/3 O/D OFF SWITCH TESTING.

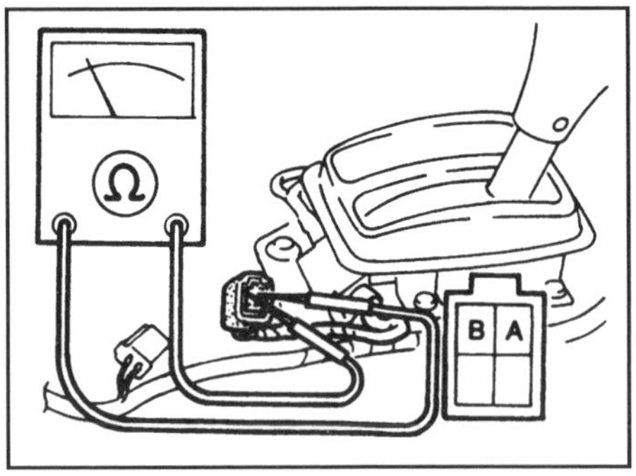

D21/4 O/D OFF SWITCH TESTING.

4 Press its locking tang and pull the male part from the switch connector. Test terminals "A" and "B" of the female part as shown in the drawing. With the overdrive switch pressed in there should be no circuit; with the switch released there should be continuity.

5 If the switch fails either or both these tests, replace the shift lever knob (it contains the actual switch): it's fixed to the lever by two screws. If the switch is OK check the overdrive cancel solenoid.

6 Fit the console between the seats: ☞ 4/8/13-14.

O/D CANCEL SOLENOID TESTING, REPLACEMENT

7 You'll need easy access to the underside so raise the car and support securely: ☞ 1/3.

8 Drain approximately 1 liter / 1.1 US qt / 0.9 Imp qt of ATF from the auto trans and then retighten the oil pan bolts: ☞ 4/3/5.

9 Unscrew the o/d cancel solenoid and withdraw it from the transmission case as shown in the drawing.

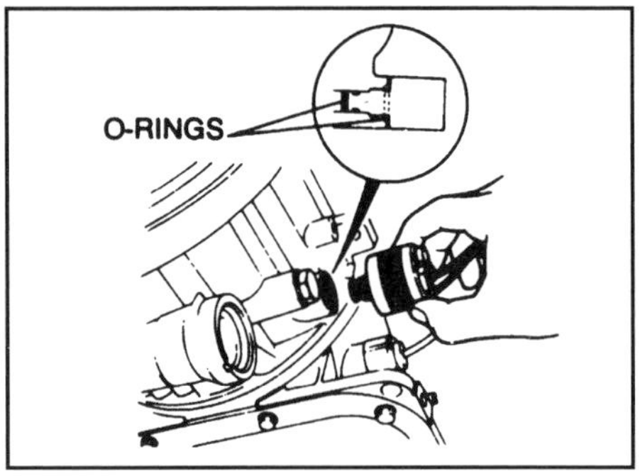

D21/9 O/D CANCEL SOLENOID REMOVAL.

10 Disconnect the solenoid's electrical connector and apply battery voltage to the solenoid - you should hear a click as the solenoid operates. Note that there is an oil passage between the end and side of the solenoid's threaded nose. This passage should be open when battery voltage is applied to the solenoid and closed when there is no voltage. Replace the solenoid if it fails to operate. If the solenoid is OK go on to test the lockup solenoid.

11 You'll need new O-rings if you're reusing the old solenoid. Smear the nose of the solenoid with ATF and screw it home into the transmission case - it doesn't need to be very tight. Reconnect its wiring.

12 Skip the next two steps if you need to test the lockup solenoid.

13 Lower the car to the ground: ☞ 1/3.

14 Check and replenish the automatic transmission fluid (ATF): ☞ 2.

LOCKUP SOLENOID TESTING & REPLACEMENT

15 The procedure for removing, testing and renewing the lockup solenoid is identical to that for the o/d cancel solenoid, except that the lockup solenoid is located as shown in the drawing.

16 Lower the car to the ground: ☞ 1/3.

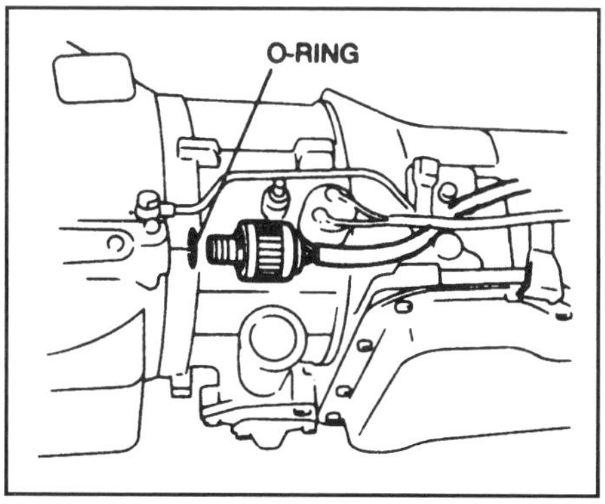

D21/15 LOCKUP SOLENOID REMOVAL.

17 Check and replenish the automatic transmission fluid (ATF): ☞ 2.

22. KICKDOWN & 4-3 SWITCH, AUTO TRANS - TESTING & REPLACEMENT

☞ First read 1/1, 2.

TESTING KICKDOWN FUNCTION

1 Drive the car with "D" selected at a speed where the auto trans has shifted into top gear - but not faster than 87 mph /140 kph. Quickly push the accelerator pedal right to the floor and verify that the transmission kicks down a gear. If kickdown doesn't work, check the kickdown switch, kickdown relay and kickdown solenoid.

TESTING 4-3 SWITCH FUNCTION

2 Drive the car with "D" selected and overdrive engaged in the 50-60 mph / 80-97 kph range. Depress the accelerator thru three-quarters of its maximum travel and verify that overdrive gets cancelled. If the 4-3 function isn't working properly check the 4-3 switch.

KICKDOWN & 4-3 SWITCH TESTING

3 The kickdown and 4-3 switching functions are combined in a single switch mounted near the top of the accelerator pedal. To gain access to the switch remove the access panel below the steering

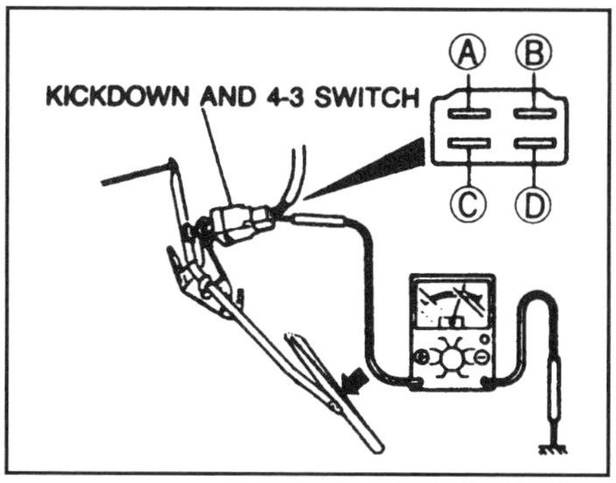

D22/4 TESTING KICKDOWN SWITCK OPERATION.

column; it's held by two sheet metal screws.

4 To test kickdown switch operation, turn on the ignition - but don't start the engine - and using a grounded multimeter test the switch terminal "C" voltage as shown in the drawing. With the accelerator pedal fully depressed the reading should show battery voltage and in the first eighth of the pedal's downward travel there should be no reading. If the readings are wrong check the switch's continuity. Switch the ignition off.

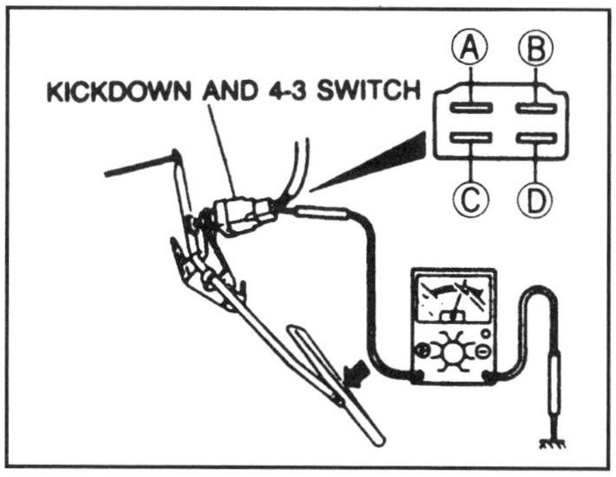

D22/5 TESTING 4-3 SWITCH OPERATION.

5 To test 4-3 switch operation, turn on the ignition - but don't start the engine - and using a grounded multimeter test the switch terminal "A" voltage as shown in the drawing. With the accelerator pedal fully depressed the reading should show battery voltage and in the first five eighths of the pedal's downward travel there should be no reading. If the readings are wrong check the switch's continuity. Switch the ignition off.

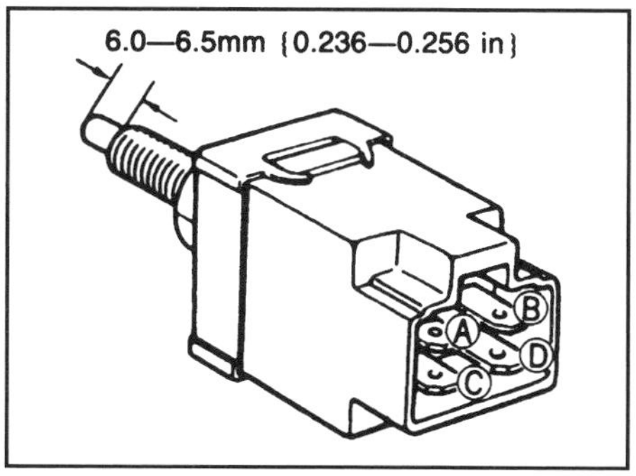

D22/6 TESTING KICKDOWN SWITCH CONTINUITY.

6 To test kickdown switch continuity release the catch and pull the wiring connector from the switch. Check that there is continuity between terminals "C" and "D" (as shown in drawing) when the switch pushrod is depressed 6-6.5 mm / 0.23 to 0.25 in. If the reading is wrong replace the switch. Whether fitting a new switch or not, adjust the switch as described later.

7 To test 4-3 switch continuity release the catch and pull the wiring connector from the switch. Check that there is continuity between terminals "A" and "B" (as shown in drawing) when the switch pushrod is depressed 3.5-4.5 mm / 0.14 to 0.17 in. If the reading is wrong replace the switch. Whether fitting a new switch or not, adjust the switch as described later.

KICKDOWN & 4-3 SWITCH ADJUSTMENT & REPLACEMENT

8 Disconnect the switch's wire connector.

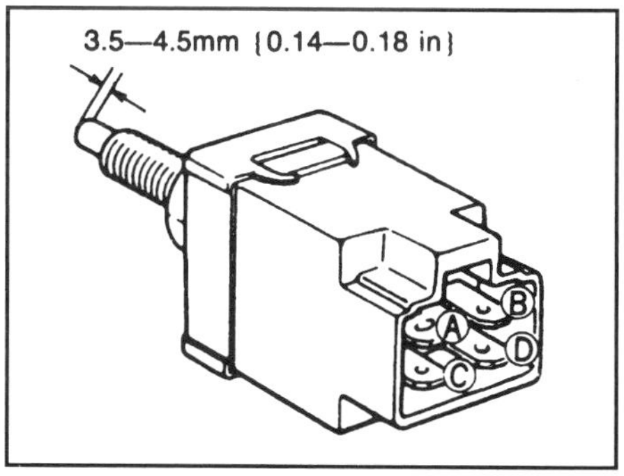

D22/7 TESTING 4-3 SWITCH CONTINUITY.

9 Loosen the locknuts and back the switch out fully, or if you've fitted a new switch set it in this same position.

10 Press the accelerator pedal to the floor and hold it there: turn the switch body clockwise until you hear a click (the switch turning on) and then turn the switch body a further quarter turn clockwise.

11 Holding the switch in this position, tighten the locknuts and then release the accelerator.

12 Fit the switch's wire connector.

13 Depress the accelerator pedal and verify that the switch clicks as the pedal reaches full travel.

KICKDOWN RELAY TESTING, REPLACEMENT

14 Pull the kickdown relay from the relay board - see drawing for location.

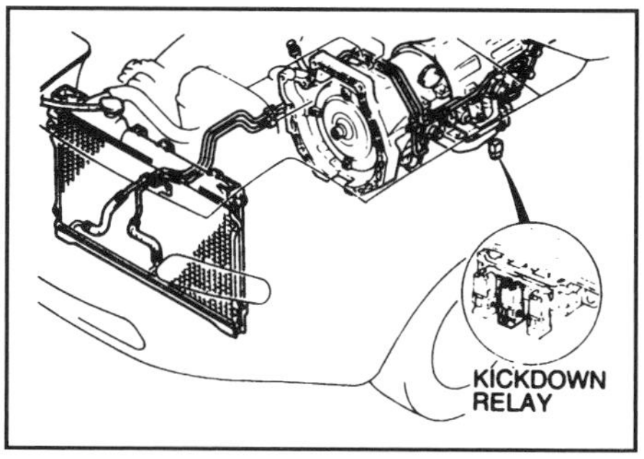

D22/14 LOCATION OF KICKDOWN RELAY ON SIDE OF ENGINE COMPARTMENT.

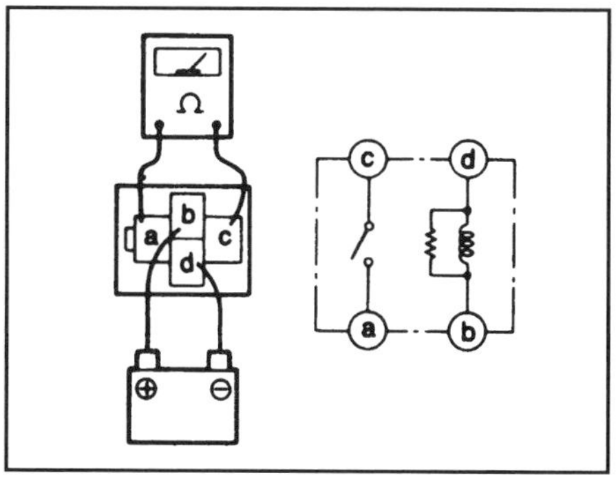

D22/15 KICKDOWN RELAY CONTINUITY TESTING.

15 Connect battery voltage and an ohmmeter to the relay's terminals as shown in drawing. There should be continuity when battery voltage is

applied and no circuit when battery voltage is disconnected. Replace the relay if it is faulty, otherwise fit the existing unit.

KICKDOWN SOLENOID TESTING, REPLACEMENT

16 The procedure for removing, testing and renewing the kickdown solenoid is identical that for the o/d cancel solenoid, except that the lockup solenoid is located as shown in the drawing and has a protruding pin instead of an oilway: ☞ 4/20/7-11.

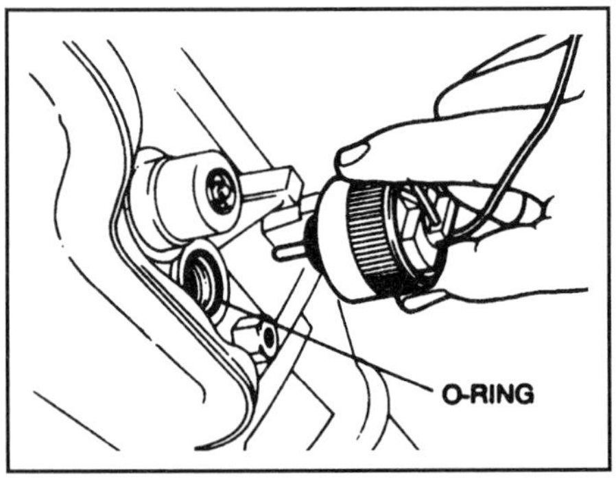

D22/16 KICKDOWN SOLENOID REMOVAL.

17 Lower the car to the ground: ☞ 1/3.
18 Check and replenish the automatic transmission fluid (ATF): ☞ 2.

23. STARTER INHIBITOR, AUTO TRANS - TESTING, ADJUSTMENT & REPLACEMENT

☞ First read 1/1, 2.

SYSTEM FUNCTION TESTING

1 The purpose of this system is to prevent the engine being started while a gear is engaged. **Warning!** To test the system park the car where there is no obstruction front or rear and apply the parking and footbrake - don't touch the accelerator. Try starting the engine with the shift lever in each of its possible positions. The engine should only start when "P" or "N" is selected.
2 With the ignition switched on, move the shift lever to "R" and verify that the backup (reversing) lights operate.
3 If the inhibitor system fails these tests check the inhibitor switch.

INHIBITOR SWITCH TESTING & ADJUSTMENT

4 The switch is located on the right-hand side of the auto trans unit so you'll need to raise the car high enough to give easy and safe access to the underside: ☞ 1/3.
5 + Separate the two parts of each of the inhibitor switch's wiring connectors and using a multimeter as shown (drawing 4:17) test the terminals shown (drawing 4:18) for continuity as follows -
6 With the shift lever in "P" terminals "1" - "2" should give continuity and likewise with the shift lever in "N" - shift lever positions "R", "D", "1" and

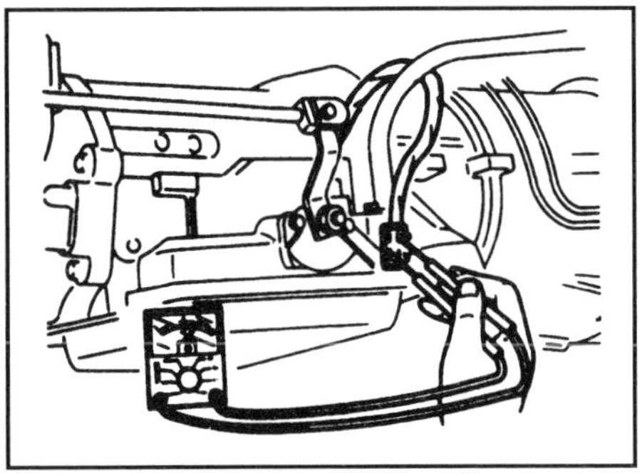

D23/5A INHIBITOR SWITCH TESTING.

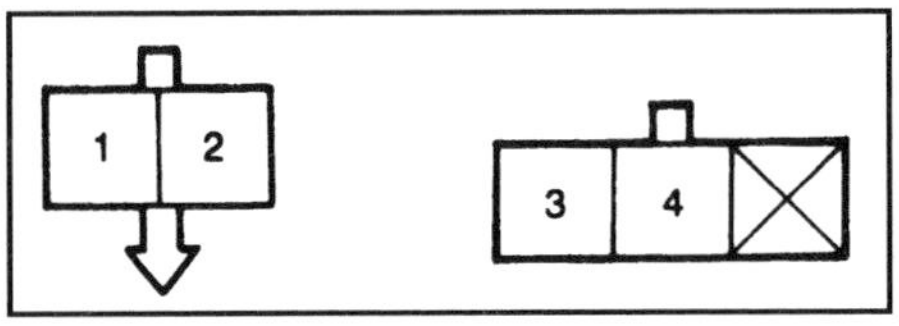

D23/5B INHIBITOR SWITCH TERMINALS.

"2" should give no reading.
7 With the shift lever in "R" there should be continuity between terminals "3" and "4", all other shift lever positions should give no reading.
8 If the test readings are not correct, try adjusting the switch and repeating the tests. If it still fails replace the switch.
9 Remake the inhibitor switch's wiring connections making sure the two halves of the connectors snap together securely.
10 Lower the car to the ground: ☞ 1/3.

INHIBITOR SWITCH ADJUSTMENT

11 First move the shift lever to "N" and then loosen the inhibitor switch mounting bolts a little.
12 Remove the small screw at the bottom of the switch body and then move the switch body until the screw hole is aligned with the hole inside the switch. Check their alignment by inserting the end of a piece of 2 mm /0.79 in wire (a suitable

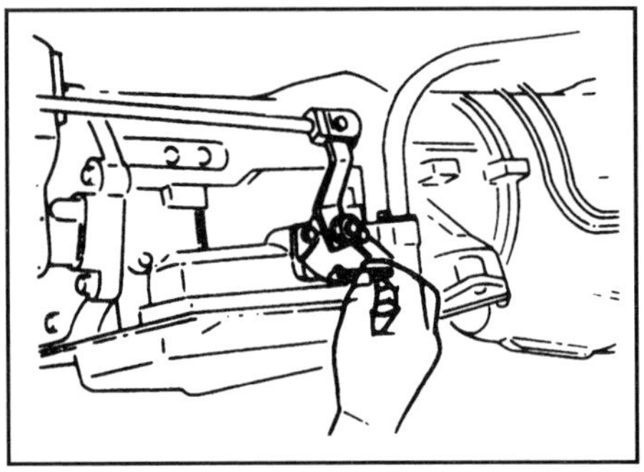

D23/12 INHIBITOR SWITCH ADJUSTMENT.

round nail would be fine) thru both the screw hole and the hole inside the switch.
13 With the wire in place, retighten the switch securing bolts using finger pressure only on the wrench. Pull out the wire and replace the blanking screw. Retest the switch as described earlier.
14 Lower the car to the ground: ☞ 1/3.

INHIBITOR SWITCH REPLACEMENT

15 The switch is located on the right-hand side of the auto trans unit so you'll need to raise the car high enough to give easy and safe access to the underside: ☞ 1/3.
16 First move the shift lever to "N" and then release the shift mechanism's bellcrank arm from the spindle which passes thru the inhibitor switch after unscrewing the retaining nut.

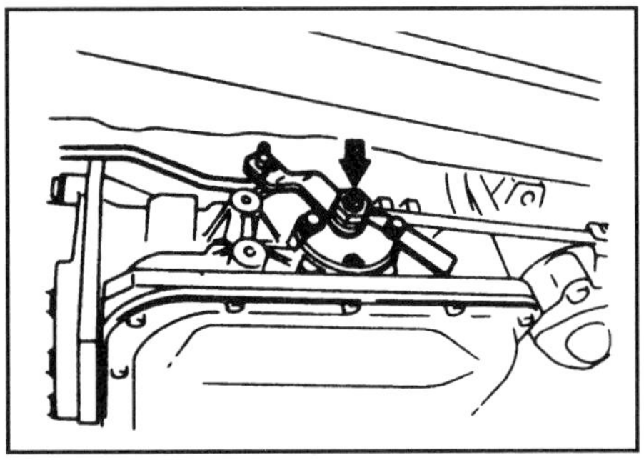

D23/16 INHIBITOR SWITCH REMOVAL.NUT RETAINS BELLCRANK.

17 Release the inhibitor switch's wiring connectors.
18 Unscrew and remove the two bolts securing the switch to the auto trans body. Note: Mazda recommend that new bolts are used to fit the new switch. Slide the switch body off the shift spindle without rotating the spindle.
19 Fit the new switch - again without rotating the spindle - and fit the new retaining bolts loosely.
20 Fit the bellcrank arm over the shift spindle and tighten its securing nut to 30 Nm / 3-4 kgf m / 25 lbf ft.
21 Adjust the switch: ☞ 4/21/11-13.
22 Remake the wiring connections securely.
23 Lower the car to the ground: ☞ 1/3.

24. SHIFTLOCK ACTUATOR & P-RANGE SWITCHES, A/T - TESTING & REPLACEMENT

☞ First read 1/1, 2.
1 The shift lock system prevents the shift lever being moved from "P" unless the brake pedal is pressed first; it also prevents the ignition key being turned to the lock position if "R" is selected. This system is not fitted for all markets. If your car has an override button at the front of the shift lever gear indicator panel the system is fitted.

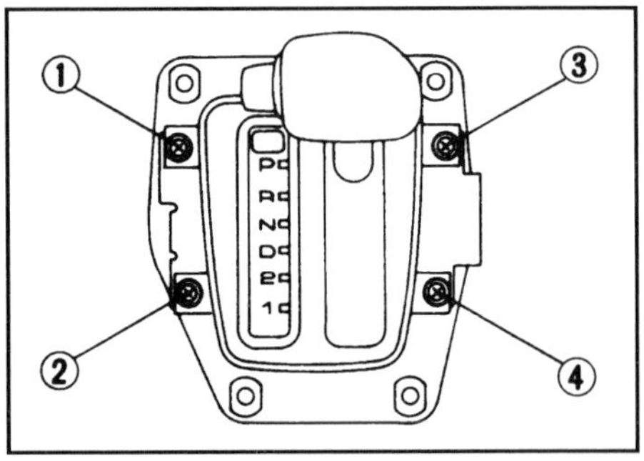

D24/3 GEAR INDICATOR PANEL SCREWS.

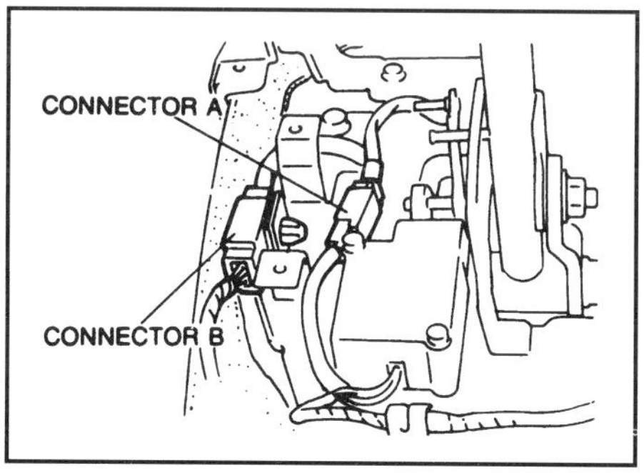

D24/7 P-RANGE (A) & SHIFT LOCK ACTUATOR (B) SWITCH CONNECTORS.

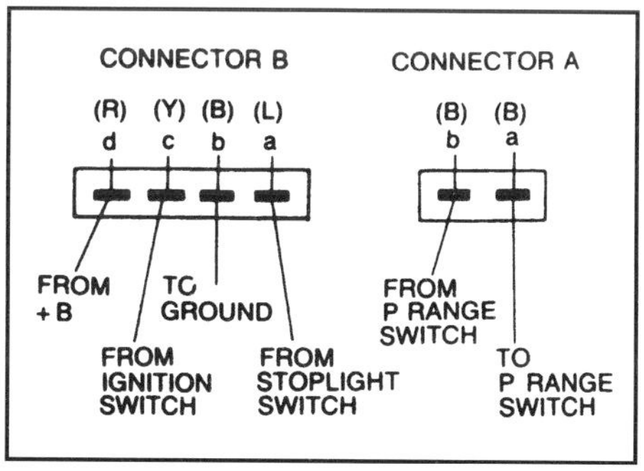

D24/8 SHIFTLOCK & P-RANGE CONNECTORS TERMINALS.

VB: Battery voltage

Connector	Terminal	⊖ terminal connected to	Condition	Correct measurement value
A	a	B—b	P range, selector lever release button not depressed	0Ω
A	b	B—b	Constant	0Ω
B	a	B—b	Brake pedal released → depressed	0V → VB
B	b (harness side)	Body	Constant	0Ω
B	c	B—b	Ignition switch ON	VB
B	d	B—b	Ignition switch OFF	VB

T24/9 SHIFT LOCK ACTUATOR & P-RANGE SWITCHES CONTINUITY & VOLTAGE TESTS.

2 Remove the console between the seats and lay it to one side of the transmission tunnel - you don't need to disconnect its wiring: ☞ 3/2/4.

3 Select "P" then remove four securing screws with a crosshead screwdriver and lift up the gear indicator panel. If you need more space remove its two securing screws and then lift the gear lever knob a little - don't lift it too far as its connected to wiring which runs thru the shift lever center.

4 Separate the two halves of the P-range switch connector ("A" in drawing).

5 Using a multimeter check for continuity between the two terminals on the switch side of the connector. With "P" selected there should be continuity when the shift lever release button is released but no circuit when the release button is pressed. There should be no continuity when other ranges are selected whether or not the release button is pressed. If the test is failed replace the P-range switch: it's held to the lever quadrant by a single screw.

6 (D21/3). Separate the two halves of the overdrive switch connector: see drawing for identification.

7 Separate the two halves of the shift lock actuator switch ("B" in drawing).

8 Using a multimeter test the two terminal halves linked to the shift actuator switch (Connectors "A" & "B" in drawing).

9 With the ignition switched on - but without the engine running - make the terminal voltage and continuity checks detailed in the table.

10 If the readings are faulty replace the shift lock actuator which is held to the shift lever baseplate by two bolts and nuts.

11 Remake all electrical connections securely.

12 If the shift knob was released, push it back into position whilst gently pulling on the wiring passing up thru the shift lever. Fasten the knob with its two screws having first smeared them with a little thread locking compound. Reposition the indicator panel and tighten its four retaining screws.

13 Fit the console between the seats: ☞ 4/8/13-14.

25. 4AT CONTROL UNIT, AUTO TRANS - TESTING

1 The 4AT control unit is a circuit board or processor which coordinates electronic aspects of the automatic transmission's performance. There is an electrical test procedure for the device but, unfortunately, it requires the use of a rolling road to be carried out safely: it is therefore deemed to be beyond the scope of this publication. If you've checked all the other auto trans electronic devices as detailed in this chapter and still have an unresolved electrical fault consult your Mazda dealer who will be happy to test the 4AT control unit for you.

AMERICAN/ENGLISH GLOSSARY OF AUTOMOTIVE TERMS

American	English
A-arm	Wishbone (suspension)
Antenna	Aerial
Axleshaft	Halfshaft
Back-up	Reverse
Barrel	Choke/venturi
Block	Chock/wedge
Box end wrench	Ring spanner
Bushing	Bush
Clutch hub	Synchro hub
Coast	Freewheel
Convertible	Drop head
Cotter pin	Split pin
Counterclockwise	Anti-clockwise
Countershaft	Layshaft (of gearbox)
Crescent wrench	Open-ended spanner
Curve	Corner
Dashboard	Facia
Denatured alcohol	Methylated spirit
Dome lamp	Interior light
Driveaxle	Driveshaft
Driveshaft	Propeller shaft
Fender	Wing/mudguard
Firewall	Bulkhead
Flashlight	Torch
Float bowl	Float chamber
Freeway, turnpike, etc.	Motorway
Frozen	Seized
Gas tank	Petrol tank
Gas pedal	Accelerator pedal
Gasoline (gas)	Petrol
Gearshift	Gearchange
Generator (DC)	Dynamo
Ground	Earth (electrical)
Header/manifold	Manifold (exhaust)
Heat riser	Hot spot
High	Top gear
Hood	Bonnet (engine cover)
Idle	Tickover
Intake	Inlet
Jackstands /Safety stands	Axle stands
Jumper cable	Jump lead
Keeper	Collet
Kerosene	Paraffin
Knock pin	Roll pin
Lash	Freeplay/Clearance
Latch	Catch
Latches	Locks
License plate /tag plate	Number plate
Light	Lamp
Lock (for valve spring retainer)	Split cotter (for valve cap)
Lopes	Hunts
Lug nut	Wheel nut
Metal chips or debris	Swarf
Misses	Misfires
Muffler	Silencer
Oil pan	Sump
Open flame	Naked flame
Panel wagon/van	Van
Parking light	Sidelight
Parking brake	Handbrake
Piston pin or wrist pin bearing/bush	Small (little) end bearing
Piston pin or wrist pin	Gudgeon pin
Pitman arm	Drop arm
Power brake booster	Servo unit
Primary shoe	Leading shoe (of brake)
Prussian blue	Engineer's blue
Pry	Prise (force apart)
Prybar	Crowbar
Prying	Levering
Quarter window	Quarterlight
Recap	Retread
Release cylinder	Slave cylinder
Repair shop	Garage
Replacement	Renewal
Ring gear (of differential)	Crownwheel
Rocker panel	Sill panel
Rod bearing	Big-end bearing
Rotor/disk	Disc (brake)
Secondary shoe	Trailing shoe (of brake)
Sedan	Saloon
Setscrew, Allen screw	Grub screw
Shift fork	Selector fork
Shift lever	Gearlever/gearstick
Shift rod	Selector rod
Shock absorber, shock	Damper/shocker
Snap-ring	Circlip
Soft top	Hood
Spacer	Distance piece
Spare tire	Spare wheel
Spark plug wires	HT leads
Spindle arm	Steering arm
Stablizer or sway bar	Anti-roll bar
Station wagon	Estate car
Stumbles	Hesitates
Tang or lock	Tab
Taper pin	Cotter pin
Teardown	Strip(down)/dismantle
Throw-out bearing	Thrust bearing
Tie-rod (or connecting rod)	Trackrod (of steering)
Transmission	Gearbox
Troubleshooting	Fault finding/diagnosis
Trunk	Boot
Tube wrench	Box spanner
Turn signal	Indicator
Valve lifter	Tappet
Valve lifter or tappet	Cam follower or tappet
Valve cover	Rocker cover
VOM (volt ohmmeter)	Multimeter
Wheel cover	Roadwheel trim
Wheel well	Wheelarch
Whole drive line	Transmission
Windshield	Windscreen
Wrench	Spanner

5

ENGINE MANAGEMENT, FUEL, IGNITION & EXHAUST SYSTEMS

1. INTRODUCTION

1 This chapter covers fuel, air, exhaust, and emissions control systems along with the engine control unit (ECU) and related sensing and regulating subsystems. For convenience, we will refer to these collectively as the engine management system (EMS). These systems and devices interrelate to such an extent that there is little point in dealing with them in isolation; to check one you invariably need to deal with another to some extent.

2 Viewed overall, the engine management system is extremely complicated, and this makes methodical diagnosis of a suspected fault essential. There is absolutely no point going on a hunch unless you are sufficiently familiar with the vehicle and its various electronic systems to be able to bypass some of the diagnosis sequence and go straight to the source of the trouble. It is very easy to jump to the wrong conclusion and, at best, waste a lot of time checking the wrong area. At worse, you could actually introduce further problems, making diagnosis even more difficult.

3 Before getting into the business of locating faults and resolving them, it is important to have a clear grasp of the various components and subsystems which make up the engine management system. Some of these are quite simple, and their function obvious, others less so, but they all affect each other to some degree.

2. ENGINE MANAGEMENT SYSTEM - COMPONENT SUMMARY

1 Let's start with a summary of the engine management system components. We suggest that you spend a little time getting familiar with what each component and subsystem does and the terminology used. You can also refer back to this section as a glossary of terms if you encounter something unfamiliar in later sections.

2 Like many other areas in automotive terminology, component names are to some extent arbitrary. We have deliberately kept closely to Mazda's choice in this respect - we figured that it would be helpful if you spoke the same language as your Mazda dealer in these matters!

Air cleaner

3 This, as you might expect, filters the incoming air to remove dust particles which would otherwise enter the engine and cause premature wear. As long as the air cleaner element is clean and uncontaminated by oil or water, it will function correctly. If damaged or clogged with dirt it will adversely affect the fuel/air mixture and make normal engine operation impossible.

Airflow meter

4 This device monitors the volume of air flowing through the intake system in response to changes in the throttle valve opening and engine load. This information is then fed to the engine control unit (ECU).

Airvalve

5 The airvalve is housed in the intake manifold, where it varies the bypass air fed to the engine in response to engine temperature. It is automatic in operation, responding directly to engine temperature, and functioning independently of the rest of the engine management system.

Atmospheric Pressure Sensor

6 The amount of fuel required by the engine in relation to the volume of air is affected by the air pressure around the vehicle. This changes with altitude and is also affected to a lesser degree by weather conditions. The pressure sensor is an integral part of the ECU, and allows it to compensate for these variations.

Catalytic converter

7 Most vehicles sold around the world are cat-equipped. The catalytic converter helps reduce harmful emissions of hydrocarbons, carbon monoxide and nitrous oxide in the exhaust gases. The 'cat' brings about high-temperature reactions in the exhaust gases, converting the more toxic elements into relatively harmless gases.

Charcoal canister

8 Another emissions-related item, the charcoal canister acts as a holding area for unburned hydrocarbons in the form of fuel vapor. These are later purged through the engine and burnt normally.

Circuit Opening Relay

9 This device controls the operation of the fuel delivery subsystem, shutting off the electrical supply to the fuel pump when the engine is switched off.

Clutch switch

10 This is a simple switch which allows the ECU to detect whether or not the clutch is engaged.

Diagnosis Connector

11 A multi-pin connector providing access for a number of service checks on the engine management system. (You will find this in the engine compartment on the left side. It is clearly marked DIAGNOSIS on the cover, and the pin positions are shown on a label inside the cover).

Crank angle sensor

12 This device enables the ECU to determine that cylinder No.1 is at top dead center (TDC) and sends a crank angle signal every 180 degrees. The ECU utilizes this information to calculate the ignition and injection timing.

Engine Control Unit (ECU)

13 This is in effect a small dedicated computer located under an access panel in the vehicle floor. It is fundamental to the operation of the engine management system; if the ECU is out of action, so is the vehicle. It reads information from the various sensors throughout the engine management system, and applies this information to pre-pro-

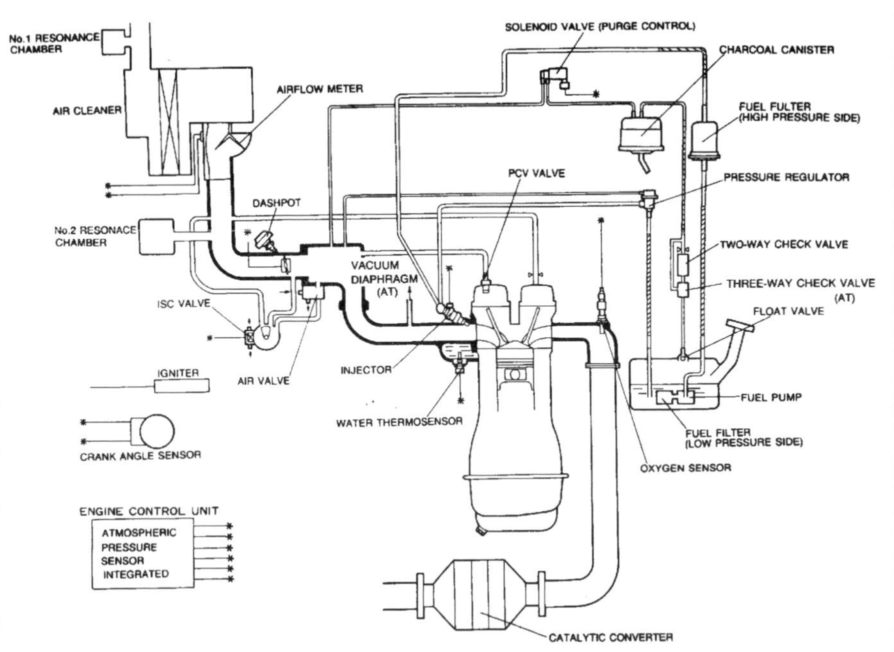

D3/1 THE ENGINE MANAGEMENT SYSTEM.

grammed data to derive control signals which are fed back to the relevant parts of the engine management system. In addition, it provides diagnostic information when interrogated by the appropriate service tool.

Fuel vapor valve

14 A simple shut-off valve which prevents fuel running from the fuel tank into the charcoal canister in the event that the vehicle is rolled in an accident.

Fuel filter

15 Removes small particles from the fuel pumped from the fuel tank to prevent damage or obstruction of the injectors.

Fuel pump

16 Maintains constant pressure in the fuel system while the engine is running. The pump supplies fuel via the main fuel filter and delivery line to the injector rail, then back through a pressure regulator to the tank.

Igniter

17 This device generates the high voltage pulse fed to the ignition coils under control of the ECU. It also detects the ignition pulse in each coil, and relays this as low-voltage information back to the ECU.

Ignition switch

18 Applies power to the engine management system and electrical system when turned on. Also sends 'engine cranking' signal to the ECU while turned to the START position.

Injector

19 A precision device for atomizing and injecting fuel under high pressure into the intake port. Each injector opens and closes in response to electronic control signals from the ECU, passing a controlled amount of fuel to its cylinder.

Intake Air Thermosensor

20 Housed inside the airflow meter, this device measures ambient air temperature and relays this information back to the ECU.

Idle Speed Control (ISC) Valve

21 Mounted on the underside of the throttle body, this device controls bypass air volume during warm-up at all engine speeds. It is controlled by the ECU.

Solenoid Valve (Purge Control Valve)

22 Feeds accumulated fuel vapor from the charcoal canister to the engine under control of the ECU.

Main Relay

23 Controls current to the main subassemblies of the engine management system (injectors, ECU, etc.). It is located in the main fuse block in the engine compartment.

Neutral Switch

24 Detects when transmission is in neutral, sends information to ECU.

Oxygen Sensor

25 Detects oxygen concentration in the exhaust gases and relays this information to ECU.

Positive Crankcase Ventilation (PCV) Valve

26 This emissions-related valve controls evacuation of blowby gases from the engine and feeds them back for combustion.

Power Steering (PS) pressure switch

27 Detects operation of power steering (where fitted) and relays operational information back to ECU.

Pressure Regulator

28 Maintains constant fuel pressure at the injectors by imposing a controlled resistance in the return line to the tank.

Resonance Chamber

29 Part of intake system. Smooths out pulses in the intake air and improves mid-range torque.

Stoplight switch

30 Apart from its obvious function, sends signal back to ECU to indicate braking (deceleration).

Throttle body

31 This is where you come in! The throttle body provides the driver's means of regulating engine speed (with a little help from the ECU) by controlling intake air volume. Also has sensors for throttle angle and Idle Speed Control (ISC) valve and feeds this data back to ECU.

Throttle sensor

32 Senses when throttle valve is closed and sends IDL (idle) signal back to ECU. Also senses when throttle valve has opened to a predetermined angle and sends POW (power) signal back to the ECU.

Two-way check valve (three-way check valve, automatic transmission models)

33 Controls air pressure in fuel tank.

Water thermosensor

34 Monitors coolant temperature and sends signal back to ECU.

3. ENGINE MANAGEMENT SYSTEM - OVERVIEW

1 In *section 2* we looked at the system components in turn, with a brief summary of what each one does. In this section we will look at how the system operates and how each component fits into the overall scheme of things. Use this section in conjunction with the accompanying diagram.

Fuel circuit

2 The fuel circuit is powered by a submersed pump housed in the fuel tank. The pump draws fuel through a low-pressure inlet filter to remove any contaminants which might otherwise damage the pump. The outgoing fuel passes through an external high pressure filter which removes fine contaminants which could obstruct the injectors.

3 Fuel flows along the fuel feed line to the injector rail, then back along a return line to a pressure regulator. This device maintains a constant fuel pressure, allowing excess fuel to pass back to the fuel tank.
4 The individual injectors are controlled by the ECU, which regulates the amount of fuel passing through each one in response to varying engine demands. It does so by controlling the duration of the injector opening.

Air intake system
5 The air intake system cleans and controls the incoming air fed to the engine. Air is admitted via a resonance chamber and air filter. From here it passes through the airflow meter and a second resonance chamber to the throttle body, where the engine speed is regulated by a butterfly throttle assembly before being passed to the intake manifold.
6 An additional automatic idle speed control system ensures smoothness at idle speed. This comprises an idle speed control (ISC) valve and airvalve. The ECU-controlled ISC valve regulates the volume of bypass air throughout the engine speed range, and this is supplemented by the temperature sensitive airvalve which operates until the engine reaches its normal working temperature.

Emission control and exhaust system
7 The **Positive Crankcase Ventilation (PCV) system** utilizes a valve controlled by intake manifold vacuum to control blowby gases from the engine. These gases, which for the most part contain unburned or part-burnt fuel and oil vapor, are passed by the PCV valve back to the intake system where they are drawn into the engine, burnt and expelled trough the exhaust system. The PCV valve is closed when the engine is off. At idle speeds, small amounts of blowby gas are passed back to the intake system, this volume increasing as engine speed rises and engine vacuum increases.
8 The **Evaporative Emission Control System** utilizes a charcoal canister to contain fuel vapor given off by the fuel tank while the vehicle is parked. Fuel vapor passes through a fuel vapor valve at the tank. This device prevents fuel spillage should the vehicle overturn in an accident. From here it is passed through a two-way (three-way, automatic transmission models) check valve to the charcoal canister, where the vapor is held in temporary storage.
9 When the engine is next started, the ECU monitors the engine operating conditions and, when it judges conditions to be appropriate to do so, opens the solenoid valve (purge control valve) to allow the accumulated fuel vapor to be fed back into the engine and burnt normally. Purging will only take place after the engine has warmed up, and the ECU can sense that the vehicle is being driven in gear, with the throttle above idle speed and when the oxygen sensor detects normal oxygen levels.
10 The **Deceleration Control System** controls the rate at which the throttle valve closes and also cuts fuel delivery during deceleration to improve fuel economy and uneven running during deceleration. A dashpot unit acts as a damper on the throttle, preventing sudden closing. The ECU reads data from the crank angle sensor, the throttle sensor and the water thermosensor to determine the fuel cutoff speed.
11 A **Dechoke Control System** is fitted to allow the engine to be cleared after accidental flooding with fuel. The ECU monitors the crank angle sensor and water thermosensor, and will prevent injection of fuel if the throttle is held fully open during cranking, when the engine is cold.
12 Like most vehicles sold worldwide, the Miata/MX5 has a **Catalytic Converter** as part of its exhaust system. Its function is to reduce emissions of unburned hydrocarbons, carbon monoxide and nitrous oxide. The cat is fitted in-line between the exhaust manifold (header) and the main muffler/silencer.
13 The **Ignition System** is operated by the igniter unit, under the control of the ECU. The ECU reads the engine operating condition and uses this data to determine the exact point of ignition for each cylinder. Once triggered by the ECU, the igniter feeds a pulse through the ignition coil primary windings, inducing a high tension spark at the plug electrodes.
14 The **Engine Control Unit (ECU)** is the main control element in the engine management system - the Miata/MX5's brain, if you like. Tucked safely away under the vehicle floor, it constantly monitors engine operating conditions through the battery of sensors described above. It uses a basic pre-programmed set of instructions overlaid by the varying conditions it reads from the rest of the vehicle to control the above subsystems.

4. ENGINE MANAGEMENT SYSTEM - TROUBLESHOOTING

PART 1 - INITIAL CHECKS

1 In the preceding sections we've looked at what makes up the engine management system, so you should have a pretty good idea of what we are dealing with. Unlike the European sports roadsters which inspired its designers, the Miata/MX5 is a modern and sophisticated vehicle, and virtually any engine-related problem will involve some aspect of the engine management system. This poses a problem for the home mechanic with the usual range of tools and equipment in the garage - you've probably got everything you'll need to fix the fault, but not to diagnose it in the first place.
2 Almost all of the troubleshooting checks described in this section involve the use of two SSTs; a Self-Diagnosis Checker (49 H018 9A1), and a System Selector (49B019 9A0). These tools interrogate the engine management system and report any faults found in the form of a two-digit code. We have described this procedure later in this section for the benefit of owners with access to these SSTs.
3 You could probably obtain the necessary SSTs through your dealer, but this is not really a cost-effective option for even the most enthusiastic owner; the equipment is expensive and will be needed only occasionally. We would suggest that you have these checks carried out by your dealer. Alternatively, if you belong to a Miata/MX5 club, it may be that the club will want to invest in these two pieces of equipment; they are probably the most useful pieces of test equipment for the car.
4 Before you get to the stage where you get your hands dirty, it is a very good idea to sit down quietly and figure out exactly what you are looking for. It helps to list any symptoms. For example, "Engine keeps stalling when I stop at junctions". Try to elaborate - does it stall *all* the time? Is it worse when the engine is warming up, or does it only happen after you have been driving for a while? Time spent at this stage is worthwhile; when you start your troubleshooting procedure on the vehicle, you'll have a clear idea of the nature of the fault to work with.
5 Armed with your notes on the problem, run through the initial checklist below. This is not comprehensive, but it will give you a starting point. If you find a symptom described which is similar to one you have listed, start checking at this point. **Caution!** Most of these checks require testing of ECU terminal voltages, a procedure requiring further SSTs. Before attempting any such test, read about the correct test procedure ☞ 5/28. Incorrect testing could permanently damage the ECU. If you are uncertain about the procedures described, have your Mazda dealer carry out the diagnosis operation for you.

STAGE 1: ENGINE FAILS TO CRANK, OR CRANKS VERY SLOWLY
6 Is the battery serviceable, fully charged and connected correctly?
7 Is there a fault in the starter system? For further information ☞ 7.

STAGE 2: ENGINE CRANKS NORMALLY, BUT DOES NOT FIRE
8 You have either got no ignition spark (or a weak spark) at the plugs or you've got no fuel at the injectors. Make sure you have fuel in the tank and that the battery is fully charged.
9 Remember that the dechoke control system prevents the injectors from working if the accelerator pedal is depressed and the engine is cold.
10 If you have access to the requisite SSTs, perform the self-diagnosis test sequence (☞ 5/4: Part 2), or have your dealer carry out this check for you. If you get a malfunction code, follow the checking procedure described for that code. If the display shows **88**, check that battery voltage is present on ECU terminal 1F when the ignition switch is turned on - check the wiring between the ECU and diagnosis connector, and between the connector and SSTs. If the display shows **00**, check out the ignition system ☞ 5/27.
11 Connect a jumper wire between terminals

F/P and **GND** of the diagnosis connector. If the engine will start with the jumper in place, the circuit opening relay may be at fault ☞ 5/17.

12 Check the fuel system ☞ 5/14.

13 Check engine compression ☞ 5/5. Excessively low compression could make starting difficult or impossible.

14 Fit new spark plugs and see if the engine will now start normally.

15 Have the ECU checked by your Mazda dealer ☞ 5/28.

STAGE 3: ENGINE CRANKS NORMALLY BUT FIRES INTERMITTENTLY - ENGINE COLD

16 If you have access to the requisite SSTs, perform the self-diagnosis test sequence (☞ 5/4: Part 2), or have your dealer carry out this check for you. If you get a malfunction code, follow the checking procedure described for that code. If the display shows **88**, check that battery voltage is present on ECU terminal 1F when the ignition switch is turned on - check the wiring between the ECU and diagnosis connector, and between the connector and SSTs.

17 Disconnect each plug lead in turn, remove the spark plug and refit it to the lead. Using insulated pliers, hold the plug about 5 mm (0.2 in) away from the cambox cover and crank the engine. A strong, blue spark should be visible. If it is weak or yellowish in color, try repeating the check with new plugs. If no improvement is found ☞ 5/27.

18 Carry out the fuel system pressure checks ☞ 5/14.

19 Fuel/air mixture may be too rich: the air cleaner element may be blocked (☞ 5/6) or the airflow meter may be stuck, fooling the ECU into delivering excessive fuel (☞ 5/30). The fuel/air mixture may be too lean, possibly due to a fault in the idle speed control (ISC) or airvalves ☞ 5/11,12. Check also the fuel circuit and injection systems (☞ 5/14,19) and intake system (☞ 5/6).

20 Have your Mazda dealer check out your ECU, either by testing it on the appropriate SST or by substituting a known good ECU.

STAGE 4: ENGINE CRANKS NORMALLY, BUT FIRES INTERMITTENTLY - ENGINE WARM

21 Start with general checks on the fuel injection system (☞ 5/14) and test the injectors for leakage (☞ 5/19). Could be due to vapor lock - check fuel system pressure ☞ 5/14. Make sure you are not using a winter grade (high RPV) fuel in warmer weather.

22 If you have access to the requisite SSTs, perform the self-diagnosis test sequence (☞ 5/4: Part 2), or have your dealer carry out this check for you. If you get a malfunction code, follow the checking procedure described for that code. If the display shows **88**, check that battery voltage is present on ECU terminal 1F when the ignition switch is turned on - check the wiring between the ECU and diagnosis connector, and between the connector and SSTs. If **00** is not displayed, have the ECU bench-tested or substitute a known good ECU to see if this resolves the problem.

23 Check ECU terminals 2D and 2Q for voltages. 2D is a ground terminal and should read zero volts. If not, check for a bad connection or open circuit between the ECU and the chassis. 2Q relates to the water thermosensor, and the voltage read should vary between approximately 2.5 volts (coolant at 20°C / 68°F) and around 0.4 volts after warm-up. If not as specified, check the water thermosensor ☞ 5/31.

STAGE 5: ENGINE CRANKS NORMALLY, BUT IS ALWAYS HARD TO START

24 If the battery is in good condition and fully charged, but the engine always requires excessive cranking (more than 5 seconds or so) before it starts, the likely causes are incorrect fuel/air mixture (too rich or too lean) or a weak ignition spark.

25 If you have access to the requisite SSTs, perform the self-diagnosis test sequence (☞ 5/4: Part 2), or have your dealer carry out this check for you. If you get a malfunction code, follow the checking procedure described for that code. If the display shows **88**, check that battery voltage is present on ECU terminal 1F when the ignition switch is turned on - check the wiring between the ECU and diagnosis connector, and between the connector and SSTs. If **00** is not displayed, have the ECU bench-tested or substitute a known good ECU to see if this resolves the problem.

26 Connect a vacuum gauge to the intake manifold - there is a capped takeoff point just to the rear of the throttle body provided for this purpose. Check the intake vacuum at idle. If this is less than 450 mm Hg (17.7 in Hg) check the intake system for air leaks ☞ 5/6.

27 Check the air filter and replace it (☞ 2/5) if dirty or contaminated with oil or water.

28 Carry out fuel system pressure checks ☞ 5/14.

29 Check ECU terminals 2D, 2O and 2Q voltages. 2D is a ground terminal and should read zero volts. If not, check for a bad connection or open circuit between the ECU and the chassis. 2O relates to the airflow meter and should read approximately 3.8 volts with the ignition switch turned on, or with the engine at idle - if not as specified ☞ 5/30. 2Q relates to the water thermosensor, and the voltage read should vary between approximately 2.5 volts (coolant at 20°C / 68°F) and around 0.4 volts after warm-up. If not as specified, check the water thermosensor ☞ 5/31.

30 Disconnect each plug lead in turn, remove the spark plug and refit it to the lead. Using insulated pliers, hold the plug about 5 mm (0.2 in) away from the cambox cover and crank the engine. A strong, blue spark should be visible. If it is weak or yellowish in color, try repeating the check with new plugs. If no improvement is found, for full details of ignition system checks ☞ 5/27.

31 Perform an injector operation check ☞ 5/14/14-15.

32 Check engine compression ☞ 5/5. Excessively low compression could make starting difficult or impossible.

33 Have your Mazda dealer check out your ECU, either by testing it on the appropriate SST or by substituting a known good ECU.

STAGE 6: ENGINE CRANKS NORMALLY, BUT IS HARD TO START ONLY WHEN COLD

34 If the battery is in good condition and fully charged, but the engine always requires excessive cranking (more than 5 seconds or so) before it starts from cold, the likely causes are incorrect fuel/air mixture (too rich or too lean). In cold operating environments, check that a low RVP (summer grade) fuel is not being used in cold weather, leading to poor fuel atomization.

35 If you have access to the necessary SSTs, perform the self-diagnosis test sequence (☞ 5/4: Part 2), or have your dealer carry out this check for you. If you get a malfunction code, follow the checking procedure described for that code. If the display shows **88**, check that battery voltage is present on ECU terminal 1F when the ignition switch is turned on - check the wiring between the ECU and diagnosis connector, and between the connector and SSTs. If **00** is not displayed, have the ECU bench-tested or substitute a known good ECU to see if this resolves the problem.

36 Check ECU terminals 1C, 2D, 2O and 2Q voltages. 1C monitors the ignition switch and should show around 10 volts while the engine is cranking, and zero volts when the key is released from the START position. If zero volts are read during cranking, check for an open circuit between the starter interlock switch and the ECU.

37 2D is a ground terminal and should read zero volts. If not, check for a bad connection or open circuit between the ECU and the chassis.

38 2O relates to the airflow meter and should read approximately 3.8 volts with the ignition switch turned on, or with the engine at idle - if not as specified ☞ 5/30.

39 2Q relates to the water thermosensor, and the voltage read should vary between approximately 2.5 volts (coolant at 20°C / 68°F) and around 0.4 volts after warm-up. If not as specified, check the water thermosensor ☞ 5/31.

40 Check if the engine can be started easily from cold if the accelerator pedal is depressed. If it can, check the ISC and airvalves ☞ 5/10, 11.

41 Connect a vacuum gauge to the intake manifold - there is a capped takeoff point just to the rear of the throttle body provided for this purpose. Check the intake vacuum at idle. If this is less than 450 mm Hg (17.7 in Hg) check the intake system for air leaks ☞ 5/6.

42 Check the air filter and replace it (☞ 2/5) if dirty or contaminated with oil or water.

43 Have your Mazda dealer check out your ECU, either by testing it on the appropriate SST or by substituting a known good ECU.

STAGE 7: ENGINE CRANKS NORMALLY, BUT IS HARD TO START AFTER WARM-UP

44 If the battery is in good condition and fully charged, but the engine always requires excessive cranking (more than 5 seconds or so) before it starts after reaching normal operating temperature, but will start normally from cold, the likely causes are fuel/air mixture too rich (due to an injector control malfunction or injector leakage) or vapor lock (loss of fuel system pressure while

engine stopped or high RPV winter grade fuel used during summer).

45 If you have access to the necessary SSTs, perform the self-diagnosis test (☞ 5/4: Part 2), or have your dealer carry out this check for you. If you get a malfunction code, follow the checking procedure described for that code. If the display shows **88**, check that battery voltage is present on ECU terminal 1F when the ignition switch is turned on - check the wiring between the ECU and diagnosis connector, and between the connector and SSTs. If **00** is not displayed, have the ECU bench-tested or substitute a known good ECU to see if this resolves the problem.

46 Check ECU terminals 2D and 2Q voltages.

47 2D is a ground terminal and should read zero volts. If not, check for a bad connection or open circuit between the ECU and the chassis.

48 2Q relates to the water thermosensor, and the voltage read should vary between approximately 2.5 volts (coolant at 20°C / 68°F) and around 0.4 volts after warm-up. If not as specified, check the water thermosensor ☞ 5/31.

49 Carry out the fuel system pressure hold check ☞ 5/14.

50 Have your Mazda dealer check out your ECU, either by testing it on the appropriate SST or by substituting a known good ECU.

STAGE 8: ROUGH OR ERRATIC IDLE - AT ALL ENGINE TEMPERATURES

51 If the engine idle is always erratic, with excessive vibration, and possibly stalling, check for the following. Fuel/air mixture may be too lean (due to air leaks, and injection control problem or low fuel system pressure). One or more injectors may be clogged or inoperative. One or more spark plugs may be inoperative or erratic in operation. Ignition timing may be set incorrectly. Engine compression may be low (mechanical wear).

52 Connect a vacuum gauge to the intake manifold - there is a capped takeoff point just to the rear of the throttle body provided for this purpose. Check the intake vacuum at idle. If this is less than 450 mm Hg (17.7 in Hg) check the intake system for air leaks ☞ 5/6.

53 Check the air filter and replace it (☞ 2/5) if dirty or contaminated with oil or water.

54 If you have access to the necessary SSTs, perform the self-diagnosis test sequence (☞ 5/4: Part 2), or have your dealer carry out this check for you. If you get a malfunction code, follow the checking procedure described for that code. If the display shows **88**, check that battery voltage is present on ECU terminal 1F when the ignition switch is turned on - check the wiring between the ECU and diagnosis connector, and between the connector and SSTs. If **00** is not displayed, have the ECU bench-tested or substitute a known good ECU to see if this resolves the problem.

55 If you have access to the necessary SSTs, perform the switch monitor function test sequence (☞ 5/4: Part 2), or have your dealer carry out this check for you. Rectify any switch or wiring faults which show up under test.

56 Check ECU terminals 2D, 2O and 2Q voltages:

57 2D is a ground terminal and should read zero volts. If not, check for a bad connection or open circuit between the ECU and the chassis.

58 2O relates to the airflow meter and should read approximately 3.8 volts with the ignition switch turned on, or with the engine at idle - if not as specified ☞ 5/30.

59 2Q relates to the water thermosensor, and the voltage read should vary between approximately 2.5 volts (coolant at 20°C / 68°F) and around 0.4 volts after warm-up. If not as specified, check the water thermosensor ☞ 5/31.

60 Hold a screwdriver against each injector in turn and listen at the handle end while the engine idles. If you can hear each injector operating, skip to the next step.

61 If one or more injectors seems inoperative, check for battery voltage on the (W/R) wire of each injector connector. If battery voltage is not present on one or more connectors, check the wiring back to the ECU.

62 If battery voltage was present on all connectors, measure the resistance of each injector. If outside the range 12-16Ω replace the injector(s).

63 Using insulated pliers, pull off each spark plug terminal cap in turn while the engine idles and check whether the idle speed drops by the same amount each time. If not, fit a new set of plugs and see if this resolves the problem.

64 If the drop in idle speed was the same in each check, try disconnecting each injector wiring connector in turn and noting whether the idle speed drops by the same amount each time. If it does, skip to the next step. If not, check the injectors for leakage ☞ 5/19.

65 Check the ignition timing at idle using a timing light ☞ 5/26.

66 Carry out the fuel system pressure hold check ☞ 5/14.

67 Have your Mazda dealer check out your ECU, either by testing it on the appropriate SST or by substituting a known good ECU.

STAGE 9: ROUGH OR ERRATIC IDLE - DURING WARM-UP

68 If the engine idle is erratic while warming up, with excessive vibration, and possibly stalling, check for the following:

- *Incorrect intake air volume due to stuck airflow meter, clogged or contaminated air filter element, ISC or airvalve fault.*
- *Insufficient fuel injected due to control malfunction (incorrect correction for coolant temperature).*
- *Poor fuel atomization (may be due to low RPV, summer grade fuel used in cold weather).*

69 If you have access to the necessary SSTs, perform the self-diagnosis test sequence (☞ 5/4: Part 2), or have your dealer carry out this check for you. If you get a malfunction code, follow the checking procedure described for that code. If the display shows **88**, check that battery voltage is present on ECU terminal 1F when the ignition switch is turned on - check the wiring between the ECU and diagnosis connector, and between the connector and SSTs. If **00** is not displayed, have the ECU bench-tested or substitute a known good ECU to see if this resolves the problem.

70 If you have access to the necessary SSTs, perform the switch monitor function test sequence (☞ 5/4: Part 2), or have your dealer carry out this check for you. Rectify any switch or wiring faults which show up under test.

71 Check ECU terminals 2D, 2O and 2Q voltages:

- *2D is a ground terminal and should read zero volts. If not, check for a bad connection or open circuit between the ECU and the chassis.*
- *2O relates to the airflow meter and should read approximately 3.8 volts with the ignition switch turned on, or with the engine at idle - if not as specified.* ☞ *5/30.*
- *2Q relates to the water thermosensor, and the voltage read should vary between approximately 2.5 volts (coolant at 20°C / 68°F) and around 0.4 volts after warm-up. If not as specified, check the water thermosensor* ☞ *5/31.*

72 Connect a vacuum gauge to the intake manifold - there is a capped takeoff point just to the rear of the throttle body provided for this purpose. Check the intake vacuum at idle. If this is less than 450 mm Hg (17.7 in Hg) check the intake system for air leaks 5/6.

73 Check the air filter and replace it (☞ 2/5) if dirty or contaminated with oil or water.

74 With the engine cold, open the diagnosis connector cover and connect a jumper wire between terminals **TEN** and GND. Start the engine, and check that the idle speed gradually falls as the engine warms up. If it does not do so, check the airvalve ☞ 5/11.

75 Check the ignition timing at idle using a timing light ☞ 5/26.

76 Have your Mazda dealer check out your ECU, either by testing it on the appropriate SST or by substituting a known good ECU.

STAGE 10: ROUGH OR ERRATIC IDLE - AT NORMAL OPERATING TEMPERATURE

77 If the engine idle is erratic at normal operating temperature, but normal while cold and during warm-up, check the following:

- *ISC malfunction.*
- *Fuel / air mixture too lean (due to air leakage or low fuel system pressure).*
- *Fuel / air mixture too rich (injection control fault due to incorrect coolant temperature correction).*
- *Weak ignition spark.*
- *Low engine compression (mechanical wear or damage).*

78 If you have access to the necessary SSTs, perform the self-diagnosis test sequence (☞ 5/4: Part 2), or have your dealer carry out this check for you. If you get a malfunction code, follow the checking procedure described for that code. If the display shows **88**, check that battery voltage is

present on ECU terminal 1F when the ignition switch is turned on - check the wiring between the ECU and diagnosis connector, and between the connector and SSTs. If **00** is not displayed, have the ECU bench-tested or substitute a known good ECU to see if this resolves the problem.

79 If you have access to the necessary SSTs, perform the switch monitor function test sequence (5/4: Part 2), or have your dealer carry out this check for you. Rectify any switch or wiring faults which show up under test.

80 Disconnect the ISC valve wiring connector while the engine is idling, and check that clicking is heard from valve - if not, replace the valve 5/10.

81 Connect a vacuum gauge to the intake manifold - there is a capped takeoff point just to the rear of the throttle body provided for this purpose. Check the intake vacuum at idle. If this is less than 450 mm Hg (17.7 in Hg) check the intake system for air leaks 5/6.

82 Check ECU terminals 2D, 2O and 2Q voltages:

- *2D is a ground terminal and should read zero volts. If not, check for a bad connection or open circuit between the ECU and the chassis.*
- *2O relates to the airflow meter and should read approximately 3.8 volts with the ignition switch turned on, or with the engine at idle - if not as specified ☞ 5/30.*
- *2Q relates to the water thermosensor, and the voltage read should vary between approximately 2.5 volts (coolant at 20°C / 68°F) and around 0.4 volts after warm-up. If not as specified, check the water thermosensor ☞ 5/31.*

83 Check the ignition timing at idle using a timing light ☞ 5/26.

84 Carry out fuel system checks ☞ 5/14.

85 Disconnect each plug lead in turn, remove the spark plug and refit it to the lead. Using insulated pliers, hold the plug about 5 mm (0.2 in) away from the cambox cover and crank the engine. A strong, blue spark should be visible. If it is weak or yellowish in color, try repeating the check with new plugs. If no improvement is found ☞ 5/27.

86 Check engine compression ☞ 5/5. Excessively low compression could make starting difficult or impossible.

87 Have your Mazda dealer check out your ECU, either by testing it on the appropriate SST or by substituting a known good ECU.

STAGE 11: ABNORMALLY HIGH IDLE SPEED - AT NORMAL OPERATING TEMPERATURE

88 If the engine idle speed is abnormally high after the engine has reached normal operating temperature, but normal while cold and during warm-up, check the following:

- *Throttle valve sticking partially open.*
- *ISC malfunction.*
- *Airvalve is not closing.*
- *ISC valve is stuck.*
- *Incorrect coolant temperature signal being fed to ECU.*

89 Check that throttle valve moves smoothly and closes normally when accelerator pedal is released ☞ 5/7.

90 Check that you can feel resistance when depressing the throttle dashpot rod with a finger, and that it returns quickly when released. Connect a test tachometer to the engine, start the engine and run it at 4,000 rpm. Slowly reduce the engine speed to 2,500 rpm and verify that the throttle lever just touches the dashpot rod at this speed. If necessary, adjust the dashpot height after slackening its locknut.

91 If you have access to the necessary SSTs, perform the self-diagnosis test sequence (☞ 5/4: Part 2), or have your dealer carry out this check for you. If you get a malfunction code, follow the checking procedure described for that code. If the display shows **88**, check that battery voltage is present on ECU terminal 1F when the ignition switch is turned on - check the wiring between the ECU and diagnosis connector, and between the connector and SSTs. If **00** is not displayed, have the ECU bench-tested or substitute a known good ECU to see if this resolves the problem.

92 If you have access to the necessary SSTs, perform the switch monitor function test sequence (☞ 5/4: Part 2), or have your dealer carry out this check for you. Rectify any switch or wiring faults which show up under test.

93 With the engine cold, open the diagnosis connector cover and connect a jumper wire between terminals **TEN** and GND. Start the engine, and check that the idle speed gradually falls as the engine warms up. If it does not do so, check the airvalve ☞ 5/11.

94 Disconnect the ISC valve wiring connector while the engine is idling, and check that clicking is heard from valve - if not, replace the valve ☞ 5/10.

95 Wrap some rag around the PCV hose and clamp it with pliers, noting whether the idle speed falls. If it does, check the PCV valve ☞ 5/22.

96 Check ECU terminals 2D, 2O and 2Q voltages:

- *2D is a ground terminal and should read zero volts. If not, check for a bad connection or open circuit between the ECU and the chassis.*
- *2O relates to the airflow meter and should read approximately 3.8 volts with the ignition switch turned on, or with the engine at idle - if not as specified ☞ 5/30.*
- *2Q relates to the water thermosensor, and the voltage read should vary between approximately 2.5 volts (coolant at 20°C / 68°F) and around 0.4 volts after warm-up. If not as specified, check the water thermosensor ☞ 5/31.*

97 Have your Mazda dealer check out your ECU, either by testing it on the appropriate SST or by substituting a known good ECU.

STAGE 12: ABNORMALLY LOW IDLE SPEED - WHEN POWER STEERING, AIR CONDITIONING, HEADLIGHTS, COOLING OR BLOWER FANS ARE OPERATING

98 If the engine idle speed falls when the above systems are working, but is normal otherwise, check the following:

- *Idle speed control (ISC) malfunction (erroneous engine speed feedback to ECU, or ISC valve stuck).*

99 If you have access to the necessary SSTs, perform the self-diagnosis test sequence (☞ 5/4: Part 2), or have your dealer carry out this check for you. If you get a malfunction code, follow the checking procedure described for that code. If the display shows **88**, check that battery voltage is present on ECU terminal 1F when the ignition switch is turned on - check the wiring between the ECU and diagnosis connector, and between the connector and SSTs. If **00** is not displayed, have the ECU bench-tested or substitute a known good ECU to see if this resolves the problem.

100 If you have access to the necessary SSTs, perform the switch monitor function test sequence (☞ 5/4: Part 2), or have your dealer carry out this check for you. Rectify any switch or wiring faults which show up under test.

101 Check if continuity exists between the diagnosis connector terminal **TEN** and ground. If so, check for a wiring short between terminal **TEN** and ground, repairing or rewiring as necessary.

102 Disconnect the ISC valve wiring connector while the engine is idling, and check that clicking is heard from valve - if not, replace the valve ☞ 5/10..

103 Have your Mazda dealer check out your ECU, either by testing it on the appropriate SST or by substituting a known good ECU.

STAGE 13: ROUGH IDLE IMMEDIATELY AFTER STARTING

104 If the engine starts normally, but vibrates excessively immediately after starting, check the following:

- *Injection control or idle speed control malfunction (START signal not relayed to the ECU).*
- *Incorrect idle speed adjustment.*
- *Incorrect ignition timing adjustment.*

105 If you have access to the necessary SSTs, perform the self-diagnosis test sequence (☞ 5/4: Part 2), or have your dealer carry out this check for you. If you get a malfunction code, follow the checking procedure described for that code. If the display shows **88**, check that battery voltage is present on ECU terminal 1F when the ignition switch is turned on - check the wiring between the ECU and diagnosis connector, and between the connector and SSTs. If **00** is not displayed, have the ECU bench-tested or substitute a known good ECU to see if this resolves the problem.

106 If you have access to the necessary SSTs, perform the switch monitor function test sequence (☞ 5/4: Part 2), or have your dealer carry out this check for you. Rectify any switch or wiring faults which show up under test.

107 Check ECU terminal 1C voltage:

- *1C monitors the ignition switch and should show around 10 volts while the engine is cranking, and zero volts when the key is released from the START position. If zero volts are read during cranking, check for an open circuit between the starter interlock switch and the ECU.*

108 Check the ignition timing at idle using a timing light ☞ 5/26.

109 Have your Mazda dealer check out your ECU, either by testing it on the appropriate SST or by substituting a known good ECU.

STAGE 14: IDLE SPEED FLUCTUATES PERIODICALLY

110 If the engine idle speed varies up and down, check the following:

- *Fuel cut occurring during idle (airvalve not closing properly after warm-up).*
- *Fuel injection amount fluctuating (poor contact point in airflow meter).*
- *Air leaks in intake system.*
- *Weak or erratic ignition spark.*
- *Fuel / air mixture too rich (fault in evaporative emission control system).*
- *Low engine compression (mechanical wear or damage).*

111 If you have access to the necessary SSTs, perform the self-diagnosis test sequence (☞ 5/4: Part 2), or have your dealer carry out this check for you. If you get a malfunction code, follow the checking procedure described for that code. If the display shows **88**, check that battery voltage is present on ECU terminal 1F when the ignition switch is turned on - check the wiring between the ECU and diagnosis connector, and between the connector and SSTs. If **00** is not displayed, have the ECU bench-tested or substitute a known good ECU to see if this resolves the problem.

112 Open the diagnosis connector cover and connect terminals **TEN** and **GND** with a jumper wire. Connect a test tachometer and check that the idle speed is 850 ± 50 rpm. Adjust where necessary using the air screw on the throttle body.

113 Check the ignition timing at idle using a timing light ☞ 5/26.

114 Connect a vacuum gauge to the intake manifold - there is a capped takeoff point just to the rear of the throttle body provided for this purpose. Check the intake vacuum at idle. If this is less than 450 mm Hg (17.7 in Hg) check the intake system for air leaks ☞ 5/6.

115 Carry out fuel system checks ☞ 5/14.

116 Disconnect each plug lead in turn, remove the spark plug and refit it to the lead. Using insulated pliers, hold the plug about 5 mm (0.2 in) away from the cambox cover and crank the engine. A strong, blue spark should be visible. If it is weak or yellowish in color, try repeating the check with new plugs. If no improvement is found ☞ 5/27.

117 Check ECU terminals 2D, 2Q and 2X voltages:

- *2D is a ground terminal and should read zero volts. If not, check for a bad connection or open circuit between the ECU and the chassis.*
- *2Q relates to the water thermosensor, and the voltage read should vary between approximately 2.5 volts (coolant at 20°C / 68°F) and around 0.4 volts after warm-up. If not as specified, check the water thermosensor ☞ 5/31.*
- *2X is the solenoid valve (purge control) output terminal and should read battery voltage if the ignition switch is turned on or if the engine is at idle.*

118 Check that vacuum can be felt at the solenoid valve with the engine at idle - if not, fit a new valve ☞ 5/23.

119 Check engine compression ☞ 5/5. Excessively low compression could make it impossible to obtain a regular idle.

120 Have your Mazda dealer check out your ECU, either by testing it on the appropriate SST or by substituting a known good ECU.

STAGE 15: ENGINE STALLS AT IDLE - ALL CONDITIONS

121 If the engine repeatedly stalls from idle, irrespective of operating conditions or temperature, check the following:

- *Incorrect idle speed (incorrect adjustment or control malfunction).*
- *Fuel / air mixture incorrect (injector blocked or inoperative, low fuel system pressure or intake system fault).*
- *Weak ignition spark.*

122 Connect a vacuum gauge to the intake manifold - there is a capped takeoff point just to the rear of the throttle body provided for this purpose. Check the intake vacuum at idle. If this is less than 450 mm Hg (17.7 in Hg) check the intake system for air leaks ☞ 5/6.

123 Check the air filter element, replacing it (☞ 2/5) if it is dirty or contaminated with oil or water.

124 If you have access to the necessary SSTs, perform the self-diagnosis test sequence (☞ 5/4: Part 2), or have your dealer carry out this check for you. If you get a malfunction code, follow the checking procedure described for that code. If the display shows **88**, check that battery voltage is present on ECU terminal 1F when the ignition switch is turned on - check the wiring between the ECU and diagnosis connector, and between the connector and SSTs. If **00** is not displayed, have the ECU bench-tested or substitute a known good ECU to see if this resolves the problem.

125 If you have access to the necessary SSTs, perform the switch monitor function test sequence (☞ 5/4: Part 2), or have your dealer carry out this check for you. Rectify any switch or wiring faults which show up under test.

126 Check ECU terminals 2D, 2O and 2Q voltages:

- *2D is a ground terminal and should read zero volts. If not, check for a bad connection or open circuit between the ECU and the chassis.*
- *2O relates to the airflow meter and should read approximately 3.8 volts with the ignition switch turned on, or with the engine at idle - if not as specified ☞ 5/30.*
- *2Q relates to the water thermosensor, and the voltage read should vary between approximately 2.5 volts (coolant at 20°C / 68°F) and around 0.4 volts after warm-up. If not as specified, check the water thermosensor ☞ 5/31.*

127 Disconnect each plug lead in turn, remove the spark plug and refit it to the lead. Using insulated pliers, hold the plug about 5 mm (0.2 in) away from the cambox cover and crank the engine. A strong, blue spark should be visible. If it is weak or yellowish in color, try repeating the check with new plugs. If no improvement is found ☞ 5/27.

128 Carry out fuel system checks ☞ 5/14.

129 Have your Mazda dealer check out your ECU, either by testing it on the appropriate SST or by substituting a known good ECU.

STAGE 16: ENGINE STALLS AT IDLE - ENGINE COLD OR WARMING UP

130 If the engine starts normally, but stalls during the warm-up period, check the following:

- *Insufficient intake air volume (idle speed control malfunction, blocked air filter element or sticking airflow meter).*
- *Fuel / air mixture too lean (intake system air leak).*
- *Poor fuel atomization (low RPV, summer grade fuel used in cold conditions).*

131 If you have access to the necessary SSTs, perform the self-diagnosis test sequence (☞ 5/4: Part 2), or have your dealer carry out this check for you. If you get a malfunction code, follow the checking procedure described for that code. If the display shows **88**, check that battery voltage is present on ECU terminal 1F when the ignition switch is turned on - check the wiring between the ECU and diagnosis connector, and between the connector and SSTs. If **00** is not displayed, have the ECU bench-tested or substitute a known good ECU to see if this resolves the problem.

132 If you have access to the necessary SSTs, perform the switch monitor function test sequence (☞ 5/4: Part 2), or have your dealer carry out this check for you. Rectify any switch or wiring faults which show up under test.

133 Check ECU terminals 2D, 2O and 2Q voltages:

- *2D is a ground terminal and should read zero volts. If not, check for a bad connection or open circuit between the ECU and the chassis.*
- *2O relates to the airflow meter and should read approximately 3.8 volts with the ignition switch turned on, or with the engine at idle - if not as specified ☞ 5/30.*
- *2Q relates to the water thermosensor, and the voltage read should vary between approximately 2.5 volts (coolant at 20°C / 68°F) and around 0.4 volts after warm-up. If not as specified, check the water thermosensor ☞ 5/31.*

134 Connect a vacuum gauge to the intake manifold - there is a capped takeoff point just to the rear of the throttle body provided for this purpose. Check the intake vacuum at idle. If this is less than 450 mm Hg (17.7 in Hg) check the intake system for air leaks ☞ 5/6.

135 Check the air filter element, replacing it

(☞ 2/5) if it is dirty or contaminated with oil or water.

136 With the engine cold, disconnect the ISC valve wiring connector, start the engine and note the idle speed, which should decrease as the engine warms up. If not, check the ISC valve ☞ 5/10.

137 Have your Mazda dealer check out your ECU, either by testing it on the appropriate SST or by substituting a known good ECU.

STAGE 17: ENGINE STALLS AT IDLE - ENGINE AT NORMAL OPERATING TEMPERATURE

138 If the engine idles normally during the warm-up period, but stalls or runs roughly when warm, check the following:

- *Fuel / air mixture too lean (intake system air leak).*
- *Insufficient intake air volume (idle speed control malfunction).*

139 Check for intake system air leaks ☞ 5/6.

140 Disconnect the ISC valve wiring connector while the engine is idling, and check that clicking is heard from valve - if not, replace the valve ☞ 5/10.

141 If fault persists ☞ 5/4: Stage 10: *Rough or erratic idle - at normal operating temperature.*

STAGE 18: ENGINE STALLS UNEXPECTEDLY WHEN MOVING OFF

142 If the engine suddenly stalls when moving away from a standstill, check the following:

- *Misfire when pulling away (fuel / air mixture incorrect, Ignition timing incorrect or poor ignition spark).*
- *Insufficient engine torque (fuel / air mixture incorrect, insufficient intake air, or low engine compression).*

143 Check for dragging brakes ☞ 9.

144 If you have access to the necessary SSTs, perform the self-diagnosis test sequence (☞ 5/4: Part 2), or have your dealer carry out this check for you. If you get a malfunction code, follow the checking procedure described for that code. If the display shows **88**, check that battery voltage is present on ECU terminal 1F when the ignition switch is turned on - check the wiring between the ECU and diagnosis connector, and between the connector and SSTs. If **00** is not displayed, have the ECU bench-tested or substitute a known good ECU to see if this resolves the problem.

145 If you have access to the necessary SSTs, perform the switch monitor function test sequence (☞ 5/4: Part 2), or have your dealer carry out this check for you. Rectify any switch or wiring faults which show up under test.

146 Trace and disconnect wiring from oxygen sensor. If fault improves, check oxygen sensor ☞ 5/33.

147 Check ECU terminal voltages.

148 Check for free and smooth operation of the throttle linkage.

149 Connect a vacuum gauge to the intake manifold - there is a capped takeoff point just to the rear of the throttle body provided for this purpose. Check the intake vacuum at idle. If this is less than 450 mm Hg (17.7 in Hg) check the intake system for air leaks ☞ 5/6.

150 Check the air filter element, replacing it (☞ 2/5) if it is dirty or contaminated with oil or water.

151 Check the ignition timing at idle using a timing light ☞ 5/26.

152 Carry out the fuel system checks described in ☞ 5/14.

153 Check engine compression ☞ 5/4. Excessively low compression could make it impossible to obtain a regular idle.

154 Have your Mazda dealer check out your ECU, either by testing it on the appropriate SST or by substituting a known good ECU.

STAGE 19: ENGINE STALLS UNEXPECTEDLY DURING DECELERATION

155 If the engine suddenly stalls during or immediately after deceleration, check the following:

- *Idle speed control malfunction.*
- *Fuel cut control malfunction.*
- *Engine feedback malfunction.*
- *Incorrect idle speed adjustment.*

156 If you have access to the necessary SSTs, perform the self-diagnosis test sequence (☞ 5/4: Part 2), or have your dealer carry out this check for you. If you get a malfunction code, follow the checking procedure described for that code. If the display shows **88**, check that battery voltage is present on ECU terminal 1F when the ignition switch is turned on - check the wiring between the ECU and diagnosis connector, and between the connector and SSTs. If **00** is not displayed, have the ECU bench-tested or substitute a known good ECU to see if this resolves the problem.

157 If you have access to the necessary SSTs, perform the switch monitor function test sequence (☞ 5/4: Part 2), or have your dealer carry out this check for you. Rectify any switch or wiring faults which show up under test.

158 Trace and disconnect wiring from oxygen sensor. If fault improves, check oxygen sensor ☞ 5/33.

159 Check ECU terminals 2D, 2O, 2U, 2V and 2Q voltages:

- *2D is a ground terminal and should read zero volts. If not, check for a bad connection or open circuit between the ECU and the chassis.*
- *2O relates to the airflow meter and should read approximately 3.8 volts with the ignition switch turned on, or with the engine at idle - if not as specified ☞ 5/30.*
- *2U and 2V are the injector output terminals. With the ignition switch turned on, battery voltage should be shown. At idle, and during deceleration from 3,000 to 1,900 rpm, approximately 12 volts should be shown. If zero volts is indicated, check for a main relay fault or open or shorted wiring to these ECU terminals. If battery voltage is always shown, an ECU fault is indicated.*
- *2Q relates to the water thermosensor, and the voltage read should vary between approximately 2.5 volts (coolant at 20°C / 68°F) and around 0.4 volts after warm-up. If not as specified, check the water thermosensor ☞ 5/31.*

160 Disconnect the ISC valve wiring connector while the engine is idling, and check that clicking is heard from valve - if not, replace the valve ☞ 5/10.

161 Open the diagnosis connector cover and connect terminals **TEN** and **GND** with a jumper wire. Connect a test tachometer and check that the idle speed is 850 ± 50 rpm. Adjust where necessary using the air screw on the throttle body.

162 Have your Mazda dealer check out your ECU, either by testing it on the appropriate SST or by substituting a known good ECU.

STAGE 20: ENGINE STALLS UNEXPECTEDLY FROM IDLE WHEN AIR CONDITIONING, POWER STEERING, HEADLIGHTS, COOLING FAN OR HEATER BLOWER FAN OPERATES

163 If the engine suddenly stalls during operation of the above systems, check the following:

- *Idle speed control malfunction (no input signal from switch, incorrect idle speed adjustment, ISC valve stuck).*

164 If you have access to the necessary SSTs, perform the self-diagnosis test sequence (☞ 5/4: Part 2), or have your dealer carry out this check for you. If you get a malfunction code, follow the checking procedure described for that code. If the display shows **88**, check that battery voltage is present on ECU terminal 1F when the ignition switch is turned on - check the wiring between the ECU and diagnosis connector, and between the connector and SSTs. If **00** is not displayed, have the ECU bench-tested or substitute a known good ECU to see if this resolves the problem.

165 If you have access to the necessary SSTs, perform the switch monitor function test sequence (☞ 5/4: Part 2), or have your dealer carry out this check for you. Rectify any switch or wiring faults which show up under test.

166 Check ECU terminals 1G, 1P, 1U, 2D, 2Q and 2W voltages:

- *1G is the igniter output. This should show zero volts with the ignition switch turned on and around 0.2 volts during idling.*
- *1P is the input from the power steering switch. You should read battery voltage with the ignition switch or the engine idling, with zero volts shown if the steering is turned.*
- *1U is the input from the headlight system. With the lights on (in any position) around 12 volts should be indicated, with zero volts shown when the lights are switched off.*
- *2D is a ground terminal and should read zero volts. If not, check for a bad connection or open circuit between the ECU and the chassis.*
- *2Q relates to the water thermosensor, and the voltage read should vary between approximately 2.5 volts (coolant at 20°C /*

68°F) and around 0.4 volts after warm-up. If not as specified, check the water thermosensor ☞ 5/31.

- *2W is the output to the ISC valve, and should show around 7 volts when the ignition is on with the engine stopped, and approximately 9 volts with the engine idling.*

167 Open the diagnosis connector cover and connect terminals **TEN** and **GND** with a jumper wire. Connect a test tachometer and check that the idle speed is 850 ± 50 rpm. Adjust where necessary using the air screw on the throttle body.

168 Disconnect the ISC valve wiring connector while the engine is idling, and check that clicking is heard from valve - if not, replace the valve ☞ 5/10.

169 Have your Mazda dealer check out your ECU, either by testing it on the appropriate SST or by substituting a known good ECU.

STAGE 21: ENGINE STALLS SUDDENLY - INTERMITTENT FAULT

170 If the engine runs normally most of the time, but occasionally stalls for no obvious reason, check the following:

- *Intermittent wiring fault (injection or ignition systems).*

171 If you have access to the necessary SSTs, perform the self-diagnosis test sequence (☞ 5/4: Part 2), or have your dealer carry out this check for you. If you get a malfunction code, follow the checking procedure described for that code. If the display shows **88**, check that battery voltage is present on ECU terminal 1F when the ignition switch is turned on - check the wiring between the ECU and diagnosis connector, and between the connector and SSTs. If **00** is not displayed, have the ECU bench-tested or substitute a known good ECU to see if this resolves the problem.

172 If you have access to the necessary SSTs, perform the switch monitor function test sequence (☞ 5/4: Part 2), or have your dealer carry out this check for you. Rectify any switch or wiring faults which show up under test.

173 Check ECU terminals 1B, 2A, 2B, and 2C voltages:

- *1B is the main relay input and should read zero volts when the ignition switch is off, and battery voltage when it is on.*
- *2A is the injector ground and should show a constant zero volts.*
- *2B is the output ground and should show a constant zero volts.*
- *2C is the CPU ground and should show a constant zero volts.*

174 When checking these terminal voltages, try moving the connectors to check for an intermittent connection. Use switch cleaner to restore normal operation, and check the associated wiring for damage or shorts.

STAGE 22: ENGINE HESITATES OR STUMBLES DURING ACCELERATION

175 If you have a flat spot during acceleration, or you notice mild jerking during acceleration, check the following:

- *Weak fuel /air mixture during acceleration (injection control malfunction, intake air leak, low fuel system pressure or spark advance malfunction).*

176 If you have access to the necessary SSTs, perform the self-diagnosis test sequence (☞ 5/4: Part 2), or have your dealer carry out this check for you. If you get a malfunction code, follow the checking procedure described for that code. If the display shows **88**, check that battery voltage is present on ECU terminal 1F when the ignition switch is turned on - check the wiring between the ECU and diagnosis connector, and between the connector and SSTs. If **00** is not displayed, have the ECU bench-tested or substitute a known good ECU to see if this resolves the problem.

177 If you have access to the necessary SSTs, perform the switch monitor function test sequence (☞ 5/4: Part 2), or have your dealer carry out this check for you. Rectify any switch or wiring faults which show up under test.

178 Temporarily disconnect the oxygen sensor wiring. If fault improves, check the oxygen sensor ☞ 5/33.

179 Check the ECU terminal voltages, or have these checked by a Mazda dealer ☞ 5/28.

180 Check that the throttle linkage operates smoothly and freely.

181 Check that intake air system is undamaged and connected correctly.

182 Connect a vacuum gauge to the intake manifold - there is a capped takeoff point just to the rear of the throttle body provided for this purpose. Check the intake vacuum at idle. If this is less than 450 mm Hg (17.7 in Hg) check the intake system for air leaks ☞ 5/6.

183 Check that the air filter element is clean and uncontaminated ☞ 2/5.

184 Check the ignition timing at idle using a timing light ☞ 5/26.

185 Carry out a fuel system check. You need to check the fuel system pressure at idle with the pressure regulator vacuum hose disconnected - this should be 265-314 kPa (2.7-3.2 kg cm2 / 38-46 psi). If within specification, accelerate the engine and note whether the pressure drops. If it does, check the fuel pump maximum pressure, replacing the pump if out of specification.

186 If the system pressure at idle reads low, try pinching the return hose. If this causes pressure to rise rapidly, the regulator may be faulty and should be checked. If it rises only slowly, check for obstructions or pipe damage between the pump and pressure regulator ☞ 5/14.

187 Check exhaust system for obstructions or damage ☞ 5/38.

188 Have your Mazda dealer check out your ECU, either by testing it on the appropriate SST or by substituting a known good ECU.

STAGE 23: ENGINE SURGES DURING CRUISE

189 If the engine surges while the accelerator pedal is kept in a constant position - the surging effect is often repetitive or cyclical in nature - check the following:

- *Incorrect fuel / air mixture (injection control malfunction, intake air system leak, low fuel system pressure, evaporative emission control system malfunction or ignition advance control malfunction).*

190 If you have access to the necessary SSTs, perform the self-diagnosis test sequence (☞ 5/4: Part 2), or have your dealer carry out this check for you. If you get a malfunction code, follow the checking procedure described for that code. If the display shows **88**, check that battery voltage is present on ECU terminal 1F when the ignition switch is turned on - check the wiring between the ECU and diagnosis connector, and between the connector and SSTs. If **00** is not displayed, have the ECU bench-tested or substitute a known good ECU to see if this resolves the problem.

191 If you have access to the necessary SSTs, perform the switch monitor function test sequence (5/4: Part 2), or have your dealer carry out this check for you. Rectify any switch or wiring faults which show up under test.

192 Temporarily disconnect the oxygen sensor wiring. If fault improves, check the oxygen sensor 5/33.

193 Check the ECU terminal voltages, or have these checked by a Mazda dealer 5/28.

194 Check that the throttle linkage operates smoothly and freely.

195 Connect a vacuum gauge to the intake manifold - there is a capped takeoff point just to the rear of the throttle body provided for this purpose. Check the intake vacuum at idle. If this is less than 450 mm Hg (17.7 in Hg) check the intake system for air leaks 5/6.

196 Check that the air filter element is clean and uncontaminated ☞ 2/5.

197 Check the ignition timing at idle using a timing light 5/26.

198 Carry out a fuel system check. You need to check the fuel system pressure at idle with the pressure regulator vacuum hose disconnected - this should be 265-314 kPa (2.7-3.2 kg cm2 / 38-46 psi). If within specification, accelerate the engine and note whether the pressure drops. If it does, check the fuel pump maximum pressure, replacing the pump if out of specification.

199 If the system pressure at idle reads low, try pinching the return hose. If this causes pressure to rise rapidly, the regulator may be faulty and should be checked. If it rises only slowly, check for obstructions or pipe damage between the pump and pressure regulator 5/14.

200 Check exhaust system for obstructions or damage 5/38.

201 Have your Mazda dealer check out your ECU, either by testing it on the appropriate SST or by substituting a known good ECU.

STAGE 24: ENGINE LACKS POWER

202 If the engine obviously lacks power, with poor performance under load and reduced maximum speed, check the following:

- *Other mechanical problems (clutch slip, dragging brakes, incorrect tire pressures or excessive load in car - refer to appropriate chapters for details).*

- *Reduced intake air volume (throttle valve not opening properly, obstructed intake system).*
- *Incorrect fuel / air mixture (low fuel system pressure, impaired fuel injection).*
- *Ignition system fault.*
- *Low engine compression (wear or damage).*

203 Check that the throttle valve opens fully in response to accelerator pedal operation - check and adjust as necessary 5/8.

204 If you have access to the necessary SSTs, perform the self-diagnosis test sequence (5/4: Part 2), or have your dealer carry out this check for you. If you get a malfunction code, follow the checking procedure described for that code. If the display shows **88**, check that battery voltage is present on ECU terminal 1F when the ignition switch is turned on - check the wiring between the ECU and diagnosis connector, and between the connector and SSTs. If **00** is not displayed, have the ECU bench-tested or substitute a known good ECU to see if this resolves the problem.

205 If you have access to the necessary SSTs, perform the switch monitor function test sequence (☞ 5/4: Part 2), or have your dealer carry out this check for you. Rectify any switch or wiring faults which show up under test.

206 Check the ignition timing at idle using a timing light ☞ 5/26.

207 Disconnect each spark plug terminal cap in turn, remove the spark plug and refit it to the cap. Using insulated pliers, hold the plug about 5 mm (0.2 in) away from the cambox cover and crank the engine. A strong, blue spark should be visible. If it is weak or yellowish in color, try repeating the check with new plugs. If no improvement is found ☞ 5/27.

208 Check resistances of plug leads ☞ 5/27.

209 Check resistances of ignition coils ☞ 5/27.

210 Check engine compression ☞ 5/5. Excessively low compression could make it impossible to obtain a regular idle.

211 Connect a vacuum gauge to the intake manifold - there is a capped takeoff point just to the rear of the throttle body provided for this purpose. Check the intake vacuum at idle. If this is less than 450 mm Hg (17.7 in Hg) check the intake system for air leaks ☞ 5/6.

212 Check that the air filter element is clean and uncontaminated - replace as necessary (☞ 2/5). Check intake system for obstruction (collapsed hoses or trunking, etc.).

213 Place a screwdriver against each injector in turn with the engine idling, and listen for the click as the injector operates.

214 If one or more injectors seems inoperative, check for battery voltage on the (W/R) wire of each injector connector. If battery voltage is not present on one or more connectors, check the wiring back to the ECU.

215 If battery voltage was present on all connectors, measure the resistance of each injector. If outside the range 12-16Ω replace the injector(s).

216 Check ECU terminals 2D, 2O, and 2Q voltages:

- *2D is a ground terminal and should read zero volts. If not, check for a bad connection or open circuit between the ECU and the chassis.*
- *2O relates to the airflow meter and should read approximately 3.8 volts with the ignition switch turned on, or with the engine at idle - if not as specified ☞ 5/30.*
- *2Q relates to the water thermosensor, and the voltage read should vary between approximately 2.5 volts (coolant at 20°C / 68°F) and around 0.4 volts after warm-up. If not as specified, check the water thermosensor ☞ 5/31.*

217 Carry out a fuel system check. You need to check the fuel system pressure at idle with the pressure regulator vacuum hose disconnected - this should be 265-314 kPa (2.7-3.2 kg cm2 / 38-46 psi). If within specification, accelerate the engine and note whether the pressure drops. If it does, check the fuel pump maximum pressure, replacing the pump if out of specification.

218 If the system pressure at idle reads low, try pinching the return hose. If this causes pressure to rise rapidly, the regulator may be faulty and should be checked. If it rises only slowly, check for obstructions or pipe damage between the pump and pressure regulator ☞ 5/14.

219 With the engine idling, disconnect each injector wiring connector in turn and check that the idle speed slows by a similar amount. If an injector has little or no effect on idle speed it may be blocked or inoperative ☞ 5/19.

220 Have your Mazda dealer check out your ECU, either by testing it on the appropriate SST or by substituting a known good ECU.

STAGE 25: POOR ACCELERATION

221 If performance is poor during acceleration ☞ 5/4: Stage 24: *Engine lacks power.*

STAGE 26: ENGINE RUNS ROUGHLY DURING DECELERATION

222 If the engine runs roughly during deceleration, and abnormal combustion (backfiring) in the exhaust is noted, check the following:

- *Fuel / air mixture incorrect (air filter element clogged, fuel injection control malfunction, injector leakage or ignition timing fault.*

223 If you have access to the necessary SSTs, perform the self-diagnosis test sequence (☞ 5/4: Part 2), or have your dealer carry out this check for you. If you get a malfunction code, follow the checking procedure described for that code. If the display shows **88**, check that battery voltage is present on ECU terminal 1F when the ignition switch is turned on - check the wiring between the ECU and diagnosis connector, and between the connector and SSTs. If **00** is not displayed, have the ECU bench-tested or substitute a known good ECU to see if this resolves the problem.

224 If you have access to the necessary SSTs, perform the switch monitor function test sequence (☞ 5/4: Part 2), or have your dealer carry out this check for you. Rectify any switch or wiring faults which show up under test.

225 Check the ignition timing at idle using a timing light ☞ 5/26.

226 Check if the fuel cut function is operating normally. With the engine at full operating temperature, raise the engine speed well above 1,900 rpm while holding a screwdriver against an injector. Release the accelerator pedal and check that the clicking from the injector ceases as the engine speed falls. If the fuel cut function is inoperative, have your Mazda dealer check the ECU, or substitute a known good ECU and repeat the fuel cut check.

227 Perform a fuel system pressure hold check. The system pressure must be above 147 kPa (1.5 kg cm2 / 21 psi) five minutes after the engine is stopped, having first run the engine at idle for several minutes. If pressure does not hold correctly, check the injectors for leakage ☞ 5/14, 19.

228 Check that the air filter element is clean and uncontaminated - replace as necessary (☞ 2/5). Check intake system for obstruction (collapsed hoses or trunking, etc.).

229 Have your Mazda dealer check out your ECU, either by testing it on the appropriate SST or by substituting a known good ECU.

STAGE 27: KNOCKING FROM ENGINE

230 In the event of knocking from the engine (by which we mean detonation, not mechanical clatter) check the following:

- *Fuel / air mixture too lean (incorrect injection amount, fuel system pressure drop during acceleration).*
- *Ignition timing too advanced.*
- *Engine overheated.*
- *Carbon deposits in engine.*

231 If you have access to the necessary SSTs, perform the self-diagnosis test sequence (☞ 5/4: Part 2), or have your dealer carry out this check for you. If you get a malfunction code, follow the checking procedure described for that code. If the display shows **88**, check that battery voltage is present on ECU terminal 1F when the ignition switch is turned on - check the wiring between the ECU and diagnosis connector, and between the connector and SSTs. If **00** is not displayed, have the ECU bench-tested or substitute a known good ECU to see if this resolves the problem.

232 If you have access to the necessary SSTs perform the switch monitor function test sequence (☞ 5/4: Part 2), or have your dealer carry out this check for you. Rectify any switch or wiring faults which show up under test.

233 Check ECU terminals 2D, 2O, and 2Q voltages:

- *2D is a ground terminal and should read zero volts. If not, check for a bad connection or open circuit between the ECU and the chassis.*
- *2O relates to the airflow meter and should read approximately 3.8 volts with the ignition switch turned on, or with the engine at idle - if not as specified ☞ 5/30.*
- *2Q relates to the water thermosensor,*

and the voltage read should vary between approximately 2.5 volts (coolant at 20°C / 68°F) and around 0.4 volts after warm-up. If not as specified, check the water thermosensor ☞ 5/31.

234 Connect a vacuum gauge to the intake manifold - there is a capped takeoff point just to the rear of the throttle body provided for this purpose. Check the intake vacuum at idle. If this is less than 450 mm Hg (17.7 in Hg) check the intake system for air leaks ☞ 5/6.

235 Check that the air filter element is clean and uncontaminated - replace as necessary (☞ 2/5). Check intake system for obstruction (collapsed hoses or trunking, etc.).

236 Check engine compression ☞ 5/5. Excessively low compression could make it impossible to obtain a regular idle.

237 Carry out a fuel system check. You need to check the fuel system pressure at idle with the pressure regulator vacuum hose disconnected - this should be 265-314 kPa (2.7-3.2 kg cm2 / 38-46 psi). If within specification, accelerate the engine and note whether the pressure drops. If it does, check the fuel pump maximum pressure, replacing the pump if out of specification.

238 If the system pressure at idle reads low, try pinching the return hose. If this causes pressure to rise rapidly, the regulator may be faulty and should be checked. If it rises only slowly, check for obstructions or pipe damage between the pump and pressure regulator☞ 5/14.

239 Check the ignition timing at idle using a timing light ☞ 5/26.

240 Carry out a full check of the cooling system if overheating is indicated. Rare occurrences of overheating due to abnormal operating conditions are allowable, but if the problem is recurrent, check for cooling system problems ☞ 6.

241 Have your Mazda dealer check out your ECU, either by testing it on the appropriate SST or by substituting a known good ECU.

STAGE 28: FUEL VAPOR IN OR AROUND CAR

242 If there is an abnormal smell of gasoline in or around the car, check the following:

- *Damaged or leaking fuel or evaporative emission control line.*
- *Charcoal canister overflow (evaporative emission control system malfunction).*

243 If you have access to the necessary SSTs, perform the self-diagnosis test sequence (☞ 5/4: Part 2), or have your dealer carry out this check for you. If you get a malfunction code, follow the checking procedure described for that code. If the display shows **88**, check that battery voltage is present on ECU terminal 1F when the ignition switch is turned on - check the wiring between the ECU and diagnosis connector, and between the connector and SSTs. If **00** is not displayed, have the ECU bench-tested or substitute a known good ECU to see if this resolves the problem.

244 Check for vacuum at solenoid valve stub with the engine running (neutral switch wiring disconnected). Apply battery voltage to solenoid (purge control) valve and check that air can be passed through it ☞ 5/23.

245 Check ECU terminal 2X (purge control output) voltage. This should show battery voltage with the ignition switch turned on, or with the engine idling.

246 Have your Mazda dealer check out your ECU, either by testing it on the appropriate SST or by substituting a known good ECU.

STAGE 29: ABNORMAL SMELL OF SULFUR FROM EXHAUST

247 If you notice an abnormal sulfur smell from the exhaust, gasoline with a high sulfur content is indicated. Change to another brand of gasoline.

STAGE 30: ENGINE OIL CONSUMPTION ABNORMALLY HIGH

248 If the engine is using oil at an unusually high rate, check the following:

- *PCV malfunction.*
- *Engine wear or damage (engine oil being burnt or leaking).*

249 Check PCV system for loose connections or damaged hoses. Repair or replace as necessary.

250 Disconnect vent hose from stub just forward of throttle body. Check for air or oil emerging from hose with engine running. If found, check for possible wear or damage in valve stems, guides or oil seals.

251 Pull out the PCV valve from the cambox cover. With the engine idling, check for vacuum by placing finger over valve end. If vacuum is felt, check for worn piston rings, pistons or cylinder bores.

STAGE 31: FUEL CONSUMPTION ABNORMALLY HIGH

252 If the car is consuming fuel at an unusually high rate, assess whether any unusual driving conditions have applied during recent use. For example, if you normally use the car on fairly long runs on open roads, its fuel economy will be far better than the same car used in the city or for numerous short stop-start journeys. Different drivers of the same car may get significantly differing consumption figures due to individual driving techniques. If circumstances and drivers are the same as usual, and consumption increases suddenly, however, check the following:

- *Heavier than normal use of accelerator pedal to compensate for abnormally low engine power (ignition, intake air, clutch or exhaust malfunctions, or dragging brakes, incorrect tire pressures or vehicle overloading).*
- *Fuel / air mixture too rich (injection system malfunction, excessive fuel system pressure).*
- *Wrong fuel grade / type or fuel leaks.*
- *Fuel cut control malfunction.*
- *Abnormally high idle speed.*

253 Eliminate non engine related areas first (see above) referring to the appropriate chapters of this book.

254 Check intake air system for leaks or loose or damaged hoses ☞ 5/6.

255 Check air filter element for dirt or contamination with oil or water and replace as necessary (☞ 2/5).

256 If you have access to the necessary SSTs, perform the self-diagnosis test sequence (☞ 5/4: Part 2), or have your dealer carry out this check for you. If you get a malfunction code, follow the checking procedure described for that code. If the display shows **88**, check that battery voltage is present on ECU terminal 1F when the ignition switch is turned on - check the wiring between the ECU and diagnosis connector, and between the connector and SSTs. If **00** is not displayed, have the ECU bench-tested or substitute a known good ECU to see if this resolves the problem.

257 If you have access to the necessary SSTs, perform the switch monitor function test sequence (☞ 5/4: Part 2), or have your dealer carry out this check for you. Rectify any switch or wiring faults which show up under test

258 Check ECU terminals 2D, 2N, 2O, 2P, 2Q, 2U and 2V voltages:

- *2D is a ground terminal and should read zero volts. If not, check for a bad connection or open circuit between the ECU and the chassis.*
- *2N is the oxygen sensor input. With the ignition switch on and the engine stopped, zero volts should be shown. At idle with a cold engine, zero volts should be shown. At idle with the engine warmed up, you should see 0-1 volt. As you increase engine speed (engine warm) 0.5-1.0 should be indicated. During deceleration, a reading of 0-0.4 volts should be found.*
- *2O relates to the airflow meter and should read approximately 3.8 volts with the ignition switch turned on, or with the engine at idle - if not as specified ☞ 5/30.*
- *2P is the input from the intake air thermosensor. At 20°C (68°F) you should read around 2.5 volts.*
- *2Q relates to the water thermosensor, and the voltage read should vary between approximately 2.5 volts (coolant at 20°C / 68°F) and around 0.4 volts after warm-up. If not as specified, check the water thermosensor ☞ 5/31.*
- *2U and 2V are the injector output terminals. With the ignition switch turned on, battery voltage should be shown. At idle, and during deceleration from 3,000 to 1,900 rpm, approximately 12 volts should be shown. If zero volts is indicated, check for a main relay fault or open or shorted wiring to these ECU terminals. If battery voltage is always shown, an ECU fault is indicated.*

259 Check if the fuel cut function is operating normally. With the engine at full operating temperature, raise the engine speed well above 1,900 rpm while holding a screwdriver against an injector. Release the accelerator pedal and check that the clicking from the injector ceases as the engine

speed falls. If the fuel cut function is inoperative, have your Mazda dealer check the ECU, or substitute a known good ECU and repeat the fuel cut check.

260 Check the ignition timing at idle using a timing light ☞ 5/26.

261 Carry out a fuel system check. You need to check the fuel line pressure at idle - this should be 216-265 kPa (2.2-2.7 kg cm2 / 31-38 psi). If above the specified pressure, check for a loose or damaged regulator vacuum hose, replacing it as required. If the fault persists, fit a new pressure regulator.

262 Check the fuel system hold pressure after running the engine for several minutes and then switching off. After 5 minutes, pressure should remain at 147 kPa (1.5 kg cm^2 / 21 psi) or more. If not, you will need to check the injectors for possible leakage ☞ 5/14, 19.

STAGE 32: MALFUNCTION INDICATOR LAMP (MIL) ALWAYS ON

263 If the MIL is always on, but the self-diagnosis checker indicates no malfunction code, check first for a wiring short. If the problem persists, disconnect the (Y/B) wire from the ECU connector and check if the light goes off. If it does, have the ECU checked by a Mazda dealer and replace it if required.

STAGE 33: MALFUNCTION INDICATOR LAMP (MIL) DOES NOT WORK

264 If the MIL does not come on despite a malfunction code being indicated by the self-diagnosis checker, and the remaining warning lights work normally, check first for a burned out bulb. Next, check for an open circuit in the MIL wiring. Finally, ground the ECU (Y/B) wire and see if the light comes on. If it does, check the ECU connector. If not, check the (Y/B) wire between the connector and the instrument panel, rewiring as necessary. If you cannot resolve the fault, have the ECU tested by a Mazda dealer and replace it as necessary.

STAGE 34: AIR CONDITIONING SYSTEM INOPERATIVE

265 ☞ 6/16 plus the following supplementary ECU-related checks.

266 Ground the A/C relay (L/B) wire and check if the air conditioning condenser fan runs when the ignition switch is turned on. If not ☞ 6/16.

267 Ground the (L/B) wire at the ECU and check if the air conditioning condenser fan runs when the ignition switch is turned on. If not, repair or rewire the (L/B) wire between the A/C relay and the ECU.

268 Check the A/C switch and wiring. If this is OK, get the ECU checked by a Mazda dealer, or substitute a known good unit and see if this resolves the fault.

PART 2: SELF-DIAGNOSIS CODES & CHECKS

269 As mentioned in *Part 1* of this section, the Miata/MX5 is capable of some degree of self-diagnosis, and this procedure is almost essential in the event of abnormal engine operation. To a limited extent, you could check each suspect area in the hope of eliminating the fault, but this would be a highly time-consuming approach with no guarantee of success.

270 Performing the self-diagnosis checks described here will usually pinpoint the source of the trouble quickly. To carry out the self-diagnosis procedure you will need access to two SSTs; a *Self-Diagnosis Checker (49 H018 9A1)*, and a *System Selector (49B019 9A0)*. If you do not have the use of these two pieces of equipment, take the car in to your Mazda dealer for the checks to be carried out.

271 Isolate the car's battery ☞ 7/2.

272 Open the cover of the diagnosis connector - this is located on the left side of the engine compartment and is clearly marked. Plug the System Selector into the diagnosis connector and set the rotary selector switch to position 1, and the test switch to **SELF TEST**. Plug the Self-Diagnosis Checker into the remaining system selector connector and attach the ground lead clip to an engine ground point. Set the selector switch to position A.

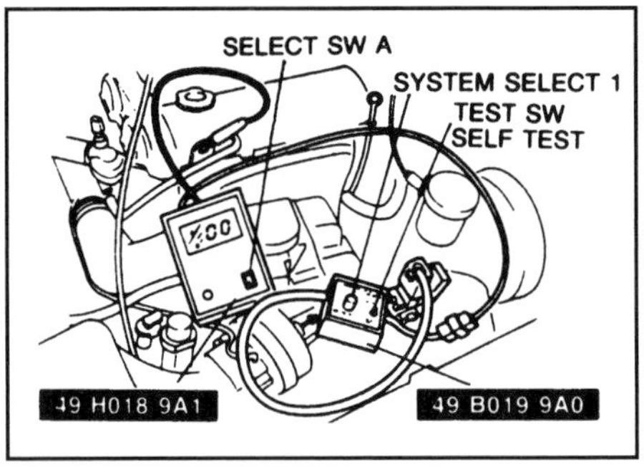

D4/272 HOW TO CONNECT THE 'SYSTEM SELECTOR' & 'SELF-DIAGNOSIS CHECKER' DEVICES.

273 Reconnect the vehicle's battery and turn the ignition switch on. Check that **88** flashes on the checker's display and that the buzzer sounds for 3 seconds after the ignition is switched on.

274 If **88** does not flash on the display, check the SST wiring connections. If these are connected correctly, check whether the main relay (located in the main fuse block in the engine compartment) clicks when the ignition switch is turned on and off. Unplug the relay, and check for continuity between terminals **C** and **D** while applying battery voltage across terminals **A** and **B** as indicated in the accompanying diagram. You should read continuity while battery voltage is applied, and no continuity when the battery is disconnected. If the relay does not operate as described, fit a new one.

275 If **88** flashes, but the buzzer sounds for 20 seconds or more, check for a short circuit between the diagnosis socket and the ECU terminal 1F (For details of ECU location ☞ 5/28). If necessary, have the ECU condition checked, and replace the ECU unit if faulty. In view of the cost of this unit we suggest that you have a Mazda dealer confirm your diagnosis.

276 If there is a system fault detectable by the self-diagnosis function, this will be indicated by a two-digit numeric code on the self-diagnosis checker's display. If there is more than one fault present, they will show up in ascending numeric sequence. The rest of this section describes the fault codes and the associated checks required.

277 Once you have traced and rectified any fault, disconnect the battery negative (-) lead **for at least 20 seconds** to erase the malfunction code from the ECU's memory. Leaving the SSTs connected, turn on the ignition switch, but **do not** start the engine for at least 6 seconds. Start the engine and allow it to reach normal operating temperature, then run it at 2,000 rpm for 3 minutes. Check that no code numbers are displayed (**00** should be shown if no malfunctions are detected).

CODE 01 (IGF SIGNAL)

278 Check for bad connections at the ignition coils and igniter.

279 Check if tachometer is operating normally. If not, check for open circuit between the igniter and ECU terminal 2I.

280 Check the ignition coil primary and secondary resistances.

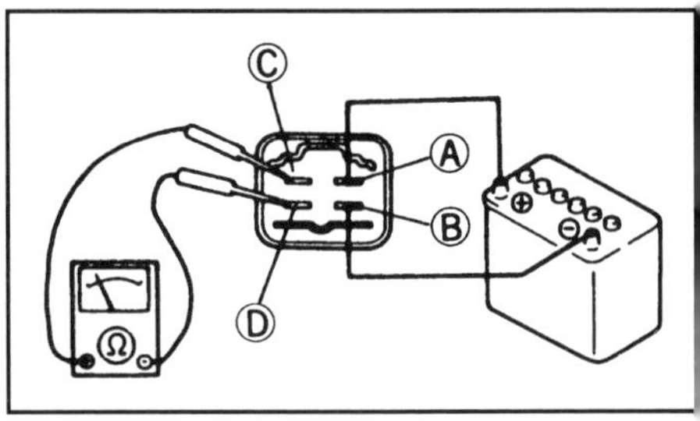

D4/274 TESTING MAIN (FUEL INJECTOR) RELAY.

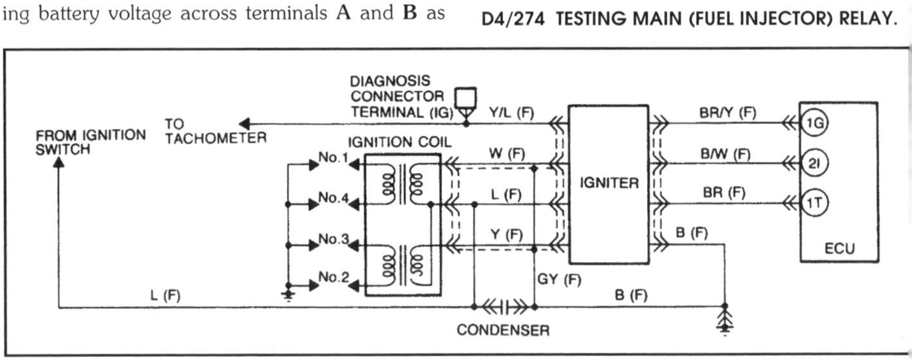

D4/278-286 'IGF-SIGNAL' TEST CIRCUIT.

281 Check for continuity between the ignition coils and igniter.
282 Check for battery voltage at the ignition coil (L) wire terminal.
283 Check for battery voltage at the igniter (L) wire terminal.
284 Check that continuity exists between the igniter and ground.
285 Check the igniter and replace if necessary.
286 For further information on the above checks ☞ 5/27.

CODE 02 (NE SIGNAL)

287 Check connections in crank angle sensor circuit.
288 If CODE 03 is also shown, check continuity between crank angle sensor (B/LG) wire and ground and repair or replace as necessary.
289 If CODE 03 is also shown, check for battery voltage on crank angle sensor (W/R) wire. If battery voltage is not present, check and repair wiring between sensor and main relay.
290 Check for continuity on the (W) wire between the crank angle sensor and the ECU 2E terminal. If you read an open circuit, repair or replace the wire.
291 With the crank angle sensor disconnected, check for approximately 5V on terminal 2E of the ECU. If 5V is not shown, have the ECU checked and replace it as necessary.
292 Check for 5V (approx) on the crank angle sensor (W) wire (harness side, connector unplugged). If you read around 5V, replace the crank angle sensor. If you read zero volts, check for a short between the sensor wiring connector and the ECU.
293 For further information ☞ 5/28, 29.

CODE 03 (G SIGNAL)

294 Check connections in crank angle sensor circuit - repair or replace the connector or wiring as necessary.
295 If CODE 02 is also present, check continuity between crank angle sensor (B/LG) wire and ground and repair or replace as necessary.
297 If CODE 02 is also shown, check for battery voltage on crank angle sensor (W/R) wire. If battery voltage is not present, check and repair wiring between sensor and main relay.

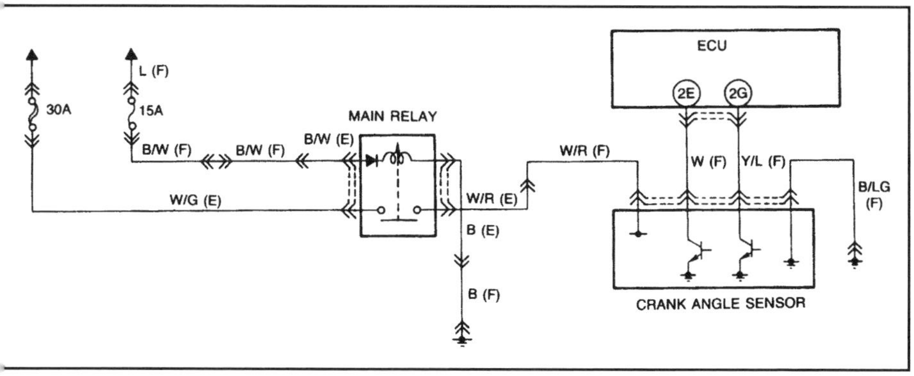

D4/294-301 'G-SIGNAL' TEST CIRCUIT.

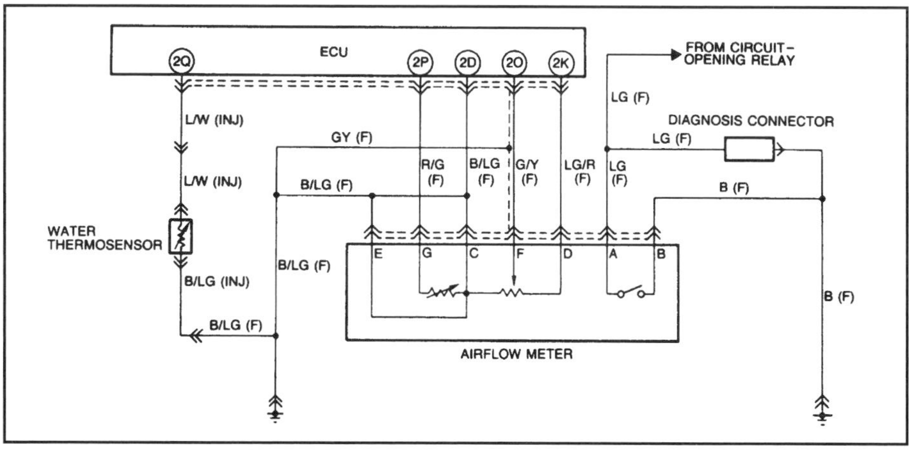

D4/302-309 AIRFLOW METER TEST CIRCUIT.

298 Check for continuity on the (Y/L) wire between the crank angle sensor and the ECU 2G terminal. If you read an open circuit, repair or replace the wire.
299 With the crank angle sensor disconnected, check for approximately 5V on terminal 2E of the ECU. If 5V is not shown, have the ECU checked and replace it as necessary.
300 Check for 5V (approx) on the crank angle sensor (Y/L) wire (harness side, connector unplugged). If you read around 5V, replace the crank angle sensor. If you read zero volts, check for a short between the sensor wiring connector and the ECU.
301 For further information ☞ 5/28, 29.

CODE 08 (AIRFLOW METER)

302 Check connections in airflow meter circuit - repair or replace the connector or wiring as necessary.
303 If CODE 10 is also present, check for an open circuit between the airflow meter (B/LG) wire and ground.
304 Check the airflow meter resistances ☞ 5/30.
305 Check for continuity between the airflow meter (LG/R) wire and terminal 2K of the ECU.
306 Check for continuity between the airflow meter (R) wire and terminal 2O of the ECU.
307 Check that zero volts is present on the ECU terminal 2D.
308 Check that 4.5-5.5 volts is present on the ECU terminal 2K.
309 For further information ☞ 5/28, 30.

CODE 09 (WATER THERMOSENSOR)

310 Check connections in water thermosensor circuit - repair or replace the connector or wiring as necessary.
311 Check that continuity exists between the water thermosensor (L/W) wire and ECU terminal 2Q. Repair or rewire as necessary.
312 Check that continuity exists between the water thermosensor (B/LG) wire and ECU terminal 2D. Repair or rewire as necessary.
313 Check the thermosensor resistances (☞ 5/31) and replace the thermosensor if required.
314 Disconnect the battery negative (-) terminal for at least 20 seconds. Reconnect the battery and check whether CODE 09 appears. If CODE 09 no longer shows, the problem has been resolved. If it does, move to the next two checks.
315 Check the voltage shown at terminal 2D of the ECU. If anything other than zero volts is indicated, have the ECU checked and replace it as necessary.
316 Check the voltage shown at terminal 2Q of the ECU. With the engine coolant at 20°C (68°F) approx 2.5 volts should be shown, falling to around 0.4 volts at normal operating temperature. If other than indicated, have the ECU checked and replace it as necessary.
317 For further information ☞ 5/28, 31.

CODE 10 (INTAKE AIR THERMOSENSOR (HOUSED IN AIRFLOW METER))

318 Check connections in intake air thermosensor circuit - repair or replace the connector or wiring as necessary.
319 Check for continuity between the intake air thermosensor (B/LG) wire and ECU terminal 2D. If no continuity is shown, repair or rewire as required.
320 Check for continuity between the intake air thermosensor (R/G) wire and ECU terminal 2P. If no continuity is shown, repair or rewire as required.

321 Measure the resistance between the intake air thermosensor (B/LG) and (R/G) wires. At -20°C (-4°F) a reading of 13.6-18.4 kΩ should be indicated. At 20°C (68°F) you should read 2.21-2.69 kΩ, and at 60°C (140°F) 493-667Ω should be found. If outside the prescribed range, a new airflow meter assembly should be fitted. (It is not possible to dismantle the unit and replace the intake air sensor alone).

322 Disconnect the battery negative (-) terminal for at least 20 seconds. Reconnect the battery and check whether CODE 10 appears. If CODE 10 no longer shows, the problem has been resolved. If it does, move to the next two checks.

323 Check the voltage shown at terminal 2D of the ECU. If anything other than zero volts is indicated, have the ECU checked and replace it as necessary.

324 Check the voltage shown at terminal 2P of the ECU. With the engine coolant at 20°C (68°F) approx 2.5 volts should be shown. If other than indicated, have the ECU checked and replace it as necessary.

325 For further information ☞ 5/28, 31.

CODE 12 (THROTTLE SENSOR-4A/T)

326 Check connections throttle sensor circuit - repair or replace the connector or wiring as necessary.

327 Check for continuity between the throttle sensor (LG/R) wire and ECU terminal 2K. If no continuity is shown, repair or rewire as required.

328 Check for continuity between the throttle sensor (R/B) wire and ECU terminal 2M. If no continuity is shown, repair or rewire as required.

329 Check for continuity between the throttle sensor (B/LG) wire and ECU terminal 2D. If no continuity is shown, repair or rewire as required.

330 Check the resistance between the throttle sensor (R/B) and (B/LG) wires. With the throttle fully closed a reading of less than 1 kΩ should be shown, while at the fully open position, approx 5 kΩ should be indicated. If not as specified, adjust or replace the throttle sensor.

331 Check the voltage on terminal 2M of the ECU. With the accelerator pedal released, around 0.5 volts should be shown. With the pedal fully depressed, you should read 4.0 volts approx. If not as described, have the ECU checked and replace it if necessary.

332 For further information ☞ 5/7, 28.

CODE 14 (ATMOSPHERIC PRESSURE SENSOR)

333 If CODE 14 shows up, this means that the atmospheric pressure sensor in the ECU has failed. Have this verified by a Mazda dealer and replace the ECU - it is not possible to repair the sensor.

334 For further information ☞ 5/28.

CODE 15 (OXYGEN SENSOR)

335 Check connections in the oxygen sensor circuit - repair or replace the connector or wiring as necessary.

336 Check the oxygen sensor terminal voltage ☞ 5/33. If not as specified, replace the sensor.

337 Check for continuity between the oxygen sensor and ECU terminal 2N.

338 Check the ECU terminal 2N voltage. With the engine cold and stopped, but the ignition switch turned on, and at idle with a cold engine, you should read zero volts. With a warm engine at idle, 0-1 volts should be shown, and as the engine speed is increased after warm-up, 0.5-1.0 volts should be indicated. During deceleration you should see 0-0.4 volts.

339 Have your Mazda dealer check the sensitivity of the oxygen sensor for you, or check this by substituting a new or known good sensor.

340 For further information ☞ 5/33.

CODE 17 (FEEDBACK SYSTEM)

341 Warm the engine up by running it at 2,500-3,000 rpm for 3 minutes.

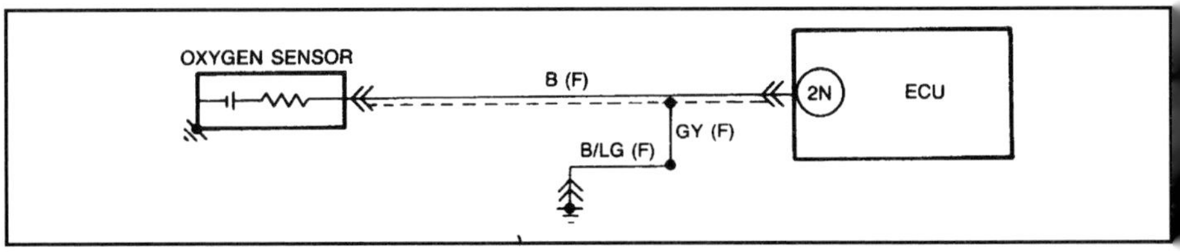

D4/341-347 FEEDBACK SYSTEM TEST CIRCUIT.

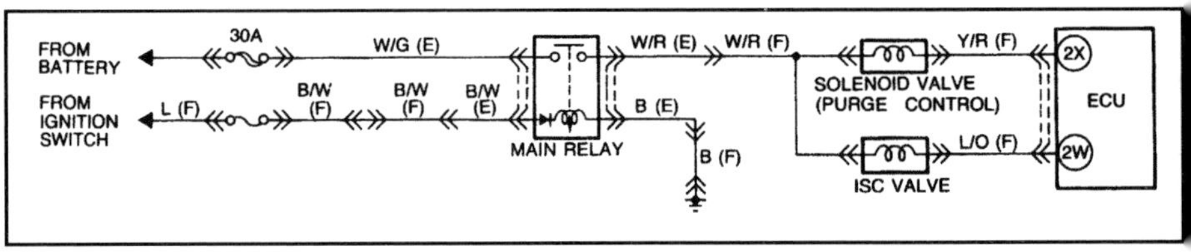

D4/348-353 SOLENOID VALVE-PURGE CONTROL TEST CIRCUIT.

342 Check that the monitor lamp on the self-diagnosis checker illuminates when the engine is idling. If it does not do so, check for air leaks in the engine vacuum hoses, intake system or emission control components (for more information ☞ 5/6, 21), check for a contaminated oxygen sensor and replace it if required (☞ 5/33) and check the fuel injection system ☞ 5/13 onwards.

343 Check the spark plugs and clean or replace as required.

344 Check the oxygen sensor terminal voltage ☞ 5/33. If not as specified, replace the sensor.

345 Disconnect the battery negative (-) terminal for at least 20 seconds. Reconnect the battery and check whether CODE 17 reappears. If CODE 17 no longer shows, check for a short in the wiring between the oxygen sensor and ECU terminal 2N.

346 Check the ECU terminal 2N voltage. With the engine cold and stopped, but the ignition switch turned on, and at idle with a cold engine, you should read zero volts. With a warm engine at idle, 0-1 volts should be shown, and as the engine speed is increased after warm-up, 0.5-1.0 volts should be indicated. During deceleration you should see 0-0.4 volts.

347 If you have been unable to resolve the fault, have your Mazda dealer check the ECU and replace it if necessary.

CODE 26 (SOLENOID VALVE-PURGE CONTROL)

348 Check for bad connections in the solenoid valve circuit and repair or rewire as required.

349 Check the solenoid valve resistances ☞ 5/23. Fit a new unit if required.

350 Check for battery voltage on the (W/R) wire of the solenoid valve - repair or rewire if voltage is not indicated.

351 Check for continuity between the solenoid valve (Y/R) wire and ECU terminal 2X. Repair or rewire as necessary if no continuity is found.

352 Check that battery voltage is indicated on the ECU 2X terminal with the engine at idle, or stopped with the ignition switch turned on.

353 If you have been unable to resolve the fault, have your Mazda dealer check the ECU and replace it if necessary.

CODE 34 (ISC VALVE)

354 Check for bad connections in the ISC valve circuit and repair or rewire as required.

355 Check the ISC valve resistances ☞ 5/10. Fit a new unit if required.

356 Check for battery voltage on the (W/R) wire of the ISC valve - repair or rewire if voltage is not indicated.

357 Check for continuity between the ISC valve (L/O) wire and ECU terminal 2W. Repair or rewire as necessary if no continuity is found.

358 Check that battery voltage is indicated on the ECU 2W terminal. If no voltage is found, repair or rewire as necessary.

359 If you have been unable to resolve the fault, have your Mazda dealer check the ECU and replace it if necessary.

Switch monitor function

360 With the SSTs connected as described above, you can also check the various system switches as follows. Note that the ignition switch should be turned on during these checks, but the engine should not be started. Note also that if any one switch remains on, the monitor lamp will also remain on - check each switch in turn and make sure it is off before proceeding to the next.

361 First, check that all switches are off and

that the monitor lamp is extinguished. If the lamp is on, make sure that all accessories are turned off, that the transmission is in neutral and that all pedals are released fully. If the lamp remains illuminated, check the following:

- *Clutch switch and wiring (☞ 5/36).*
- *Neutral switch and wiring (☞ 5/37).*
- *Throttle sensor IDL switch and wiring (☞ 5/32).*
- *Throttle sensor POW switch and wiring (☞ 5/32).*
- *Stoplight switch and wiring (☞ 7/33).*
- *Headlight switch and wiring (☞ 7/12).*
- *Blower switch and wiring (☞ 6/15).*
- *A/C switch and wiring (☞ 6/16).*
- *Water thermoswitch and wiring (☞ 5/31).*

362 Next, check each switch in turn. Start by checking the **neutral and clutch switches** (manual transmission cars). Shift the transmission into gear and check that the monitor light comes on when the clutch pedal is released, and extinguishes when it is depressed. If the light fails to operate as described, check the clutch and neutral switches and their associated wiring ☞ 5/36, 37. If the fault remains, check ECU terminal 1V for voltage. There should be zero volts shown while the transmission is shifted to neutral or the clutch pedal is depressed, with battery voltage being shown otherwise.

363 On automatic transmission cars, check the **inhibitor switch** operation as follows. Shift into the L, S, D and P ranges and check that the lamp comes on in each position. If not as described, you should check and adjust as required the inhibitor switch (for details ☞ 4/23). If the switch is operating normally and correctly adjusted, but the fault persists, check the voltage at the ECU 1V terminal. This should show zero volts when shifted to N or P, and battery voltage at all other positions. If not as specified, an ECU fault is indicated - have this checked by your Mazda dealer, and fit a new ECU if necessary.

364 On all cars, check the operation of the **throttle sensor** as described below. Partially depress the accelerator pedal and check that the monitor lamp comes on. If not, check the throttle sensor ☞ 5/32. If the sensor checks out OK, look for a short in the wiring between the sensor and the ECU. If this does not resolve the problem, measure the voltage at ECU terminal 1N. With the accelerator pedal released, zero volts should be shown, while battery voltage should be read when the pedal is depressed. If the fault remains, an ECU fault is indicated - have this checked by your Mazda dealer, and fit a new ECU if necessary.

365 Next, depress the accelerator pedal fully and check that the monitor lamp goes out. If it fails to do so, check the throttle sensor ☞ 5/32. If the sensor checks out OK, look for an open circuit in the wiring between the sensor and the ECU. Finally, check the voltage at the appropriate ECU terminal as follows. On manual transmission cars, you should read approximately 5 volts at terminal 2L with the accelerator pedal released, and zero volts when it is depressed. In the case of automatic transmission cars, there should be a reading of approximately 0.5 volts at terminal 2M with the accelerator pedal released, and around 4 volts when it is depressed.

366 Now check that the **stoplight switch** is operational by depressing the brake pedal. If the monitor lamp fails to come on, check the switch and its wiring ☞ 7/33. If this fails to locate the fault, check for battery voltage at the ECU terminal 1O when the brake pedal is depressed, and zero volts when it is released.

367 Turn on the **headlight switch** and verify that the monitor lamp illuminates. If not, check the switch and its wiring ☞ 7/12 onwards. If the switch and wiring are in good condition, check terminal 1U of the ECU - you should read battery voltage with the lights on in any position, and zero volts when off.

368 Turn the **heater blower switch** to the medium position and check that the monitor lamp illuminates. If there is a problem, for details of further tests ☞ 6/10. If the fault remains unresolved, check the voltage on terminal 1S of the ECU. If the blower switch is set to OFF or LOW, you should read 12 volts, with zero volts indicated at all other positions.

369 Turn the **air conditioning switch** on and set the fan to the low position. Check that the monitor lamp illuminates. If not, for details of further tests on the blower switch circuit ☞ 6/10. If the fault remains unresolved, check the voltage on terminal 1Q of the ECU. When the air conditioning switch is turned on (blower motor running and ignition switch turned on), you should read less than 2.5 volts. Battery voltage should be indicated when the air conditioning switch is turned off.

370 The final check in this sequence relates to the **water thermoswitch circuit**, and is not included in the above sequence. During the test you need to connect the diagnosis connector terminals TFA and **GND** using a jumper wire. This bypasses the thermoswitch and switches the cooling fan on. **Warning!** Take care to avoid the moving fan blades during this check.

371 If the monitor lamp fails to illuminate, check for a relay or wiring fault ☞ 6/8. If this checks out OK, test the voltage at terminal 1R of the ECU. With the jumper wire in place (or if the engine coolant temperature is above 97°C (207°F)) you should read zero volts. With the jumper wire removed or at lower temperatures, battery voltage should be shown.

5. ENGINE COMPRESSION CHECK

☞ 1/1,2.

1 If the engine is worn the loss of compression will affect the operation of the engine management system and can produce a number of faults which might otherwise be attributed to it. Eliminate engine wear as a problem by carrying out a compression check, using a proprietary compression gauge. Check that the battery is fully charged and in good condition, and that the engine is at normal operating temperature.

2 📷 Disconnect the ignition coil connector to disable the ignition system, then remove all the spark plugs. Fit the compression gauge to cylinder No.1, hold down the accelerator pedal and crank the engine until the maximum pressure reading stabilizes. Note the reading and then repeat the check on the remaining cylinders.

5/2 Cylinder compression test.

3 The normal compression pressure in a new engine is 1,324 kPa (13.5 kg/cm2, 192 psi) at 300 rpm. On a used engine, a pressure above 932 kPa (9.5 kg/cm2, 135 psi) is acceptable, with less than 196 kPa (2.0 kg/cm2, 28 psi) difference between cylinders.

4 If you find one cylinder reading low, add a small quantity of oil through the spark plug hole and repeat the check. If the reading improves, piston ring or bore wear is indicated. If the reading is unchanged, suspect a cylinder head or valve problem. Either way, you should investigate and remedy the problem before investigating the Engine Management System further.

5 You should note that though a compression check is useful for identifying a number of mechanical faults without having to dismantle the engine, it does not provide an exhaustive test of engine condition. If you are convinced that you have mechanical problems, consider getting a dyno check carried out. This will provide more information than a simple compression check, and will probably either identify the fault or set your mind at rest about general engine condition.

6. AIR INTAKE SYSTEM CHECKS

☞ 1/1, 2.

1 📷 If you suspect a fault in the intake system, it is well worth carrying out a simple preliminary check before serious investigation is undertaken. First, make sure that the air filter element is clean and serviceable - a dirty or contaminated element will adversely affect performance and fuel

6/1 Dirty air cleaner element.

5

efficiency. Note that the element cannot be cleaned, even with compressed air. If it is dirty, damaged or contaminated with oil or water, fit a new one ☞ 2/5.

2 It is also important that there are no air leaks in the intake system. If there are, you will find it impossible to get the engine to run smoothly and predictably, because misleading data will be fed to the ECU from its sensors. Inspect the various connections visually, and fit new hoses if they appear aged or damaged. Check the hose clips for security.

3 You might find it helpful to spray WD40 on

6/2 Check hose clip security.

a suspected leak while the engine is running. If a leak is present, the lubricant will be drawn into the intake system and burnt as it passes into the engine, the resulting exhaust smoke helping to confirm the leak. This method can often locate obscure leaks in areas like the manifold to head joint. This test is only relevant to the part of the intake system from throttle valve to cylinder head. **Caution!**: Don't spray WD40 onto other parts of the intake system if you try this technique as it could contaminate the air cleaner.

4 Another point to be aware of is the noise sometimes caused by intake system leaks. Any unusual squealing or hissing noises when the engine is running may be due to air leaking past a damaged gasket or seal. This type of noise is likely to be more obvious when the engine is under load.

7. THROTTLE BODY - REMOVAL, INSPECTION & INSTALLATION

☞ 1/1, 2.

REMOVAL

1 Before attempting removal of the throttle body, disconnect the battery negative (-) terminal to isolate the electrical system ☞ 7/2. Clean the external surfaces of the throttle body to prevent contamination.

2 The next task is to drain the cooling system. Remove the cap on top of the radiator. **Warning!:** If the car has been running up to an hour before this point, cover the cap with thick cloth and wear protective gloves and safety glasses before releasing the cap in case scalding coolant is ejected. Turn the cap counterclockwise until it reaches the first stop - this allows residual pressure to be released safely. The cap can then be turned again and removed. Place a receptacle beneath the radiator drain plug; it will need to be capable of holding 6.5 liters (6.5 US or 6.1 imp. quarts) and, if you intend to reuse the coolant, should be spotlessly clean. Once again protecting your hands if the coolant is hot, unscrew the radiator drain plug with a medium sized crosshead screwdriver until the plug drops and the coolant flows.

3 Disconnect the breather hose which runs from the cambox cover, via a metal pipe across the front of the engine to a stub on the intake air pipe. Release the clip which secures the air pipe and resonance chamber assembly to the throttle body and pull it off the connecting stub. As it comes

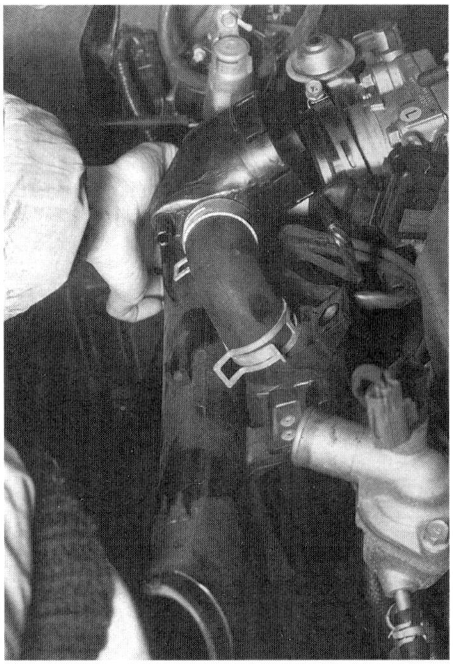

7/3 Pull off air pipe & resonance chamber.

away, disconnect at the air pipe end the smaller air hose which runs to the ISC valve stub on the underside of the throttle body. Note that the ISC (Idle Speed Control) valve is secured to the underside of the throttle body and will be removed with it.

4 Disconnect the water hose which runs from the underside of the intake manifold to a cranked stub below the ISC valve - you can reach this best at the ISC valve end. A second water hose runs from the inner side of the ISC valve up to the airvalve (nearest the cambox cover). Disconnect this at the airvalve end.

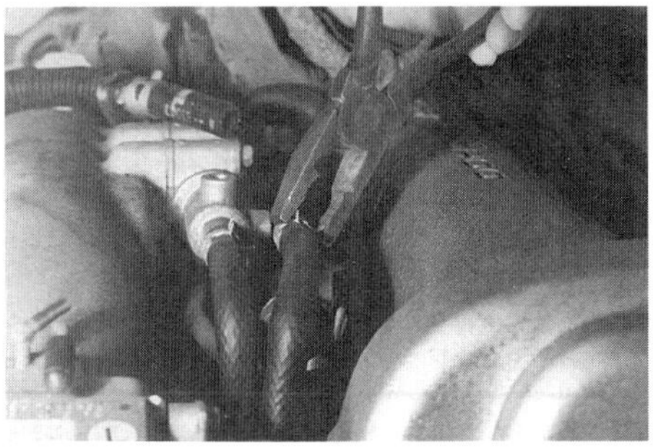

7/4 Disconnect hose at airvalve.

5 + Twist the throttle body pulley and release the accelerator cable from the pulley. Disconnect the ISC valve and throttle sensor connectors. Using a 12 mm mm socket, remove the four bolts which secure the throttle body to the intake manifold and lift the unit clear.

INSPECTION

6 Check that the throttle butterfly valve is fully closed. Turn the throttle pulley and check that the valve moves smoothly and easily to the fully open position. There should be no sign of tight spots. If found, these could indicate that the throttle

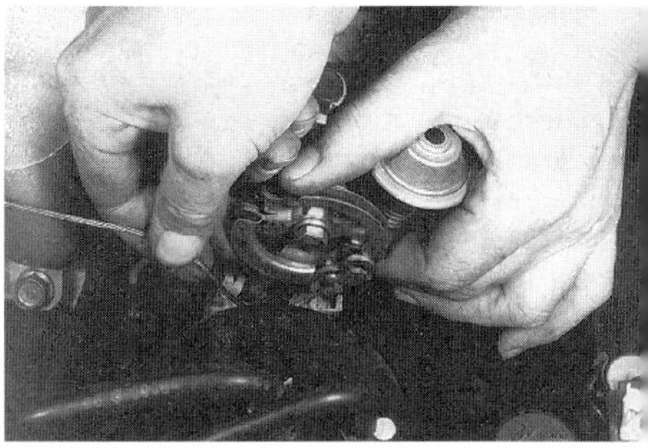

7/5a Release accelerator cable ...

7/5b ... unplug connectors ...

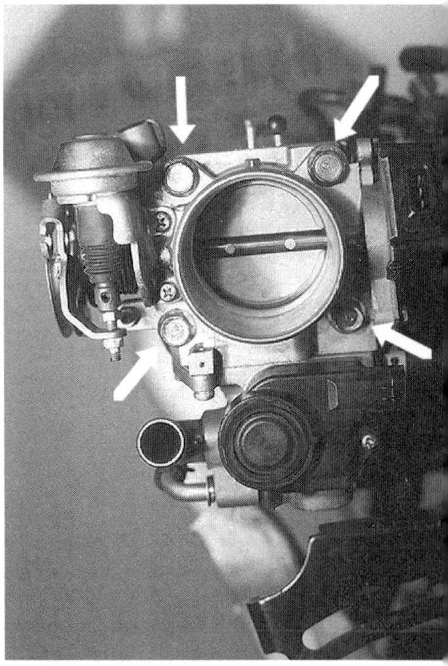

7/5c ... remove throttle body bolts.

ody has become distorted. Check for lash in the ırottle spindle. Excessive clearance here indicates ir leakage which would upset the air fuel mixture nd cause erratic running.

Repair possibilities are limited; the official emedy to any malfunction of the throttle body is eplacement and, generally speaking, this is the nly practical course of action. You may find a pecialist machine shop who could undertake limed repair work, but this is unlikely to prove cost ffective. Note also that the throttle butterfly valve nd throttle body bore are coated with a thin ealing compound; this must not be removed.

INSTALLATION

Clean the gasket faces of the throttle body nd intake manifold and fit a new gasket over the owel pins on the manifold mounting face. Position the throttle body and fit the four holding bolts nger tight. Tighten the bolts evenly and progresvely to 19-25 Nm (1.9-2.6 kgf m, 14-19 lbf ft).

Reconnect the throttle cable and check ıat it operates smoothly. Set the throttle cable lash ɔ 1-3 mm (0.039-0.118 in) using the adjuster at ıe end of the outer cable. Fit the ISC valve and ırottle sensor wiring connectors and the water oses. Install the air pipe and reconnect the smaller ose from the ISC valve. Fit and tighten the radiaɔr drain plug, then fill the cooling system with thylene glycol based coolant to the bottom of the adiator filler neck. Don't fit the radiator filler cap et.

0 Start the engine and check for correct ırottle operation, then let the engine idle until the adiator top hose gets hot. This will allow the water evel to stabilize and any air in the cooling system ɔ work out. If necessary, top up the radiator and ıe coolant reservoir, and then fit the radiator cap. eave the engine running for a while to allow the ystem to reach normal operating pressure, then heck the water hose connections at the throttle ody for leaks.

3. ACCELERATOR CABLE & PEDAL - ADJUSTMENT & CABLE REPLACEMENT

☞ 1/1, 2.

The accelerator cable is a normally a durable component of little or no interest to anyone. Jntil it breaks, that is. Cables always like to break t night, miles from home, and usually when its aining. They never break right outside your local Aazda dealership on a sunny afternoon when you ave a couple of hours to kill. It is well worth giving a quick visual check from time to time. Watch for igns of fraying of the inner cable strands; this is the rst warning of impending failure. The broken trands can also catch in the inner cable causing the ccelerator to stick. Depending on circumstances, his can be inconvenient, scary or downright dangerous. The rule here is if the inner cable is frayed r kinked, fit a new one before it lets you down.

Wally, our technical adviser, says that it is good idea to keep a spare cable in the car - they're mall enough to stow in the trunk, even on a Miata/ AX5! Maybe so, but we disagree. We reckon it is much better to fit the new cable as soon as you note signs of fraying on the old one, because it rates highly on our list of difficult jobs and, believe us, you won't ever want to attempt this on the roadside. We recommend that before attempting this feat, you become proficient in yoga. This will both improve your physical flexibility and your ability to remain comfortably upside down for long periods - you will need to be accomplished in both these respects. It will also impart the inner calmness you will find essential during the later stages of the removal operation.

3 📷 First, the easy part. Start work under the hood, by turning the throttle valve pulley and unhooking the cable inner. Next, back off the cable adjuster locknut and free the cable adjuster from the bracket on the intake manifold. The bracket has a keyhole slot in it, and a sharp tug will allow the rubber grommet to be pulled clear. Follow the cable back to the firewall and release any cable ties or support blocks. Most of the cable ties used on the Miata/MX5 have small release tabs on the buckle, and if you lift or press these with a finger nail (depending on the type fitted) it can be slid apart and re-used later. You may encounter non-releasing cable ties; these will have to be cut off with wire

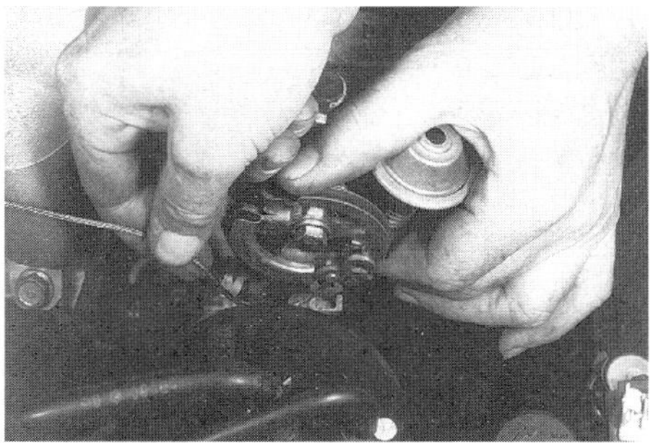

8/3 Release accelerator cable.

cutters or a craft knife and a new one fitted during installation. Support blocks are retained in their brackets by small tabs which should be squeezed together to release them.

4 Moving inside the car, remove the two screws which retain the access cover below the steering wheel, and unclip and remove the cover. Grab the accelerator pedal pad, then feel with one hand up the pedal until you reach the lever end. When you get to the cable, work back along it to the firewall where you'll find a plastic cable stop recessed in the sound insulation and clipped firmly into the firewall. This is the part which is going to cause you BIG TROUBLE.

5 📷 To have any chance of seeing what you are doing here, you will need to assume the Veloce MX5 Accelerator Cable Removal Position™, an advanced yoga-like position not recommended for couch potatoes. **Warning!** If you suffer from claustrophobia, we recommend that you do not attempt this operation (actually, don't even read the rest of this section). You will also need an assistant who you can trust to pass tools to you without laughing or making provocative remarks. (Better still, read through the following procedure, then get your assistant to do the work while *you* pass the tools

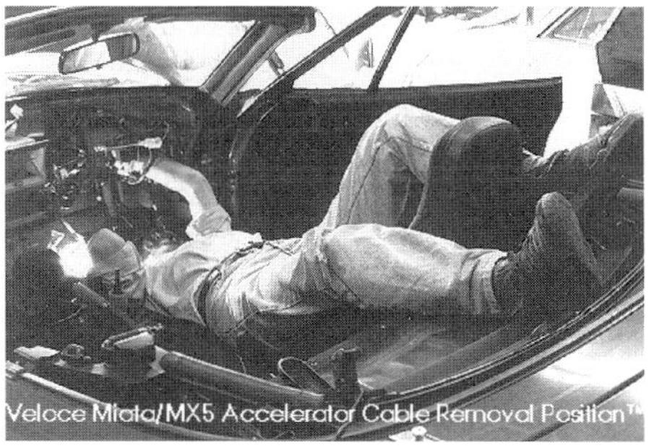

8/5 Know a good chiropractor?

and give instructions). If you know a good chiropractor, invite them round before you start. Sit on the drivers seat facing backwards (yes, really) and maneuver your head under the steering wheel and into the aperture below the steering column. Place your feet either side of the seat back, resting them on the rear deck. With your head somewhere near the pedals (and using a flashlight or inspection lamp) you should be able to locate the cable stop in the firewall.

6 📷 Around the back of the pedal lever you will feel two small tabs; these lock the cable in the

8/6 Release cable from back of lever.

lever end and can be released by squeezing them until the plastic clip pops free. Pull the clip clear of the pedal lever end and disengage it from the slot. Similar tabs lock the cable stop in the firewall; all you need to do is squeeze them together and push the stop and cable through the firewall and withdraw it from under the hood. The problem here is that you need to compress four fairly stiff tabs simultaneously in a confined space. We tried different combinations of fingers and every pair of pliers we had, but to no avail.

7 You can improve access a little by moving the sound insulation away from the firewall and removing the accelerator pedal. The sound insulation is held in place by large flanged plastic retainers which can be unscrewed from their studs as required - you can probably do this by hand unless they are unusually tight. The pedal pivot is secured by one of those tiny clips which, when dislodged with a screwdriver, travel at near light speed to the nearest inaccessible recess, where they defy all attempts at recapture. Try to hold some rag around the clip as it is levered off the pivot (better still, purchase one or two new ones before starting the job). Note the relative positions of the pedal spring and its fitting direction, then slide the pedal out of

its mounting. The spring will come off the pedal as it is removed, so fit it back on the pivot and place both parts to one side. You can now peel back the sound insulation to get a clearer view of the cable stop. Access may be further improved by detaching any relay(s) which are obstructing your view of the stop. If you can now depress the tabs enough by hand to push the stop back through the firewall, great. Wally couldn't, so we devised the Veloce Cable Stop Removal Method™ as follows.

8 Get your assistant to pass you two 16 mm crescent wrenches. On each side of the stop there are two tabs, with a solid section at the center.

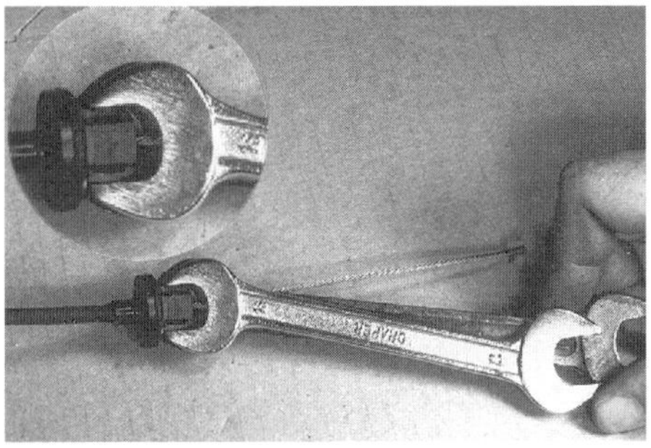

8/8 How to compress cable stop tags.

What you need to do is push the crescent wrenches over the pairs of tabs so that they are held compressed, allowing you to push the stop into the firewall. Yep! it really does work. Once the tabs have passed through the firewall, have your assistant check that the cable is free by pulling it through from the engine compartment. You can now attempt to escape from under the dashboard - don't rush this. We suggest that you sit quietly until you feel normal again, and don't worry, installation is easy by comparison.

9 Thread the new cable into position, securing the cable outer in the firewall by clicking the stop into position. Climb under the dashboard, taking with you the pedal and pedal spring and the securing clip. When reassembling the pedal, lubricate the pin with molybdenum grease, because you don't ever want it to wear out and need changing. Fit the retaining clip carefully, making sure that it is fully seated in its groove. Check that the return spring is correctly positioned and that the pedal moves smoothly before reconnecting the cable. Hook the cable end over the pedal lever and click its stop into place. Working under the hood, fit the cable clips and connect the cable at the throttle body end. Set the adjuster nuts so that you have 1-3 mm (0.039-0.118 in) lash in the cable inner. Finally, have someone floor the accelerator pedal and check that the throttle valve reaches the fully open position. If you need to, you can set the pedal travel by moving the stop bolt just above the pivot pin.

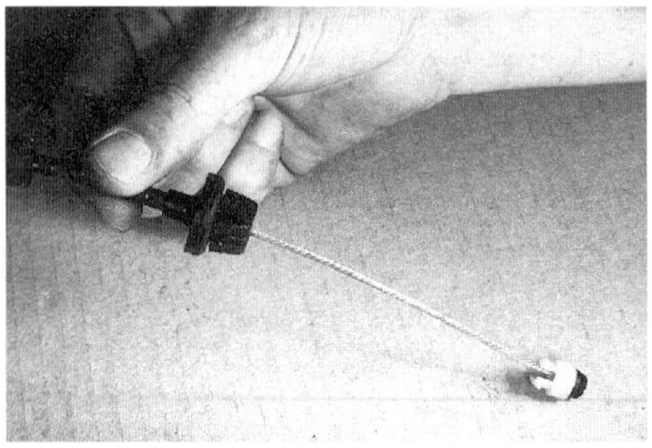

8/9 The cable stop and clip devices.

10 That's about it. Wally said that as soon as he's out of traction he's going to learn how to do this job by feel alone and make a fortune fitting MX5 accelerator cables. Meanwhile, next time you're at your Mazda dealer, just mention casually that you changed the accelerator cable, and look at the *awe* on their faces.

9. INTAKE MANIFOLD - REMOVAL, INSPECTION & INSTALLATION

☞ 1/1, 2.

Warning! Before commencing removal of the intake manifold it is essential to release fuel system pressure. Even if the engine has not been run for a while, high pressure remains in the system until this procedure has been undertaken. Before proceeding further ☞ 5/13. Note also that the cooling system must be drained before the intake manifold water hose connections are disturbed.

REMOVAL

1 + Remove the throttle body and the airvalve ☞ 5/7, 11. Disconnect the vacuum hoses (one small bore hose near the throttle body mounting, plus the larger bore hose from the brake servo which connects to the rear of the manifold) and cambox breather hose (center of intake manifold to PCV valve in cambox cover). Release the two 10 mm bolts which secure the accelerator cable bracket to the side of the manifold and lodge the cable clear of the working area.

2 + Mark one of the fuel lines and its connecting pipe using PVC tape or a paint mark as a guide during installation. Using a rag to catch any residual fuel spray, disconnect the fuel lines and plug the open ends to exclude dirt.

9/1a Remove throttle body vacuum hose ...

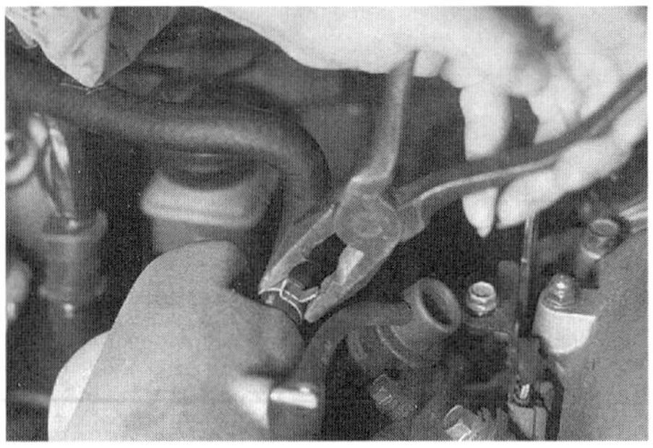

9/1b ... and servo vacuum hose ...

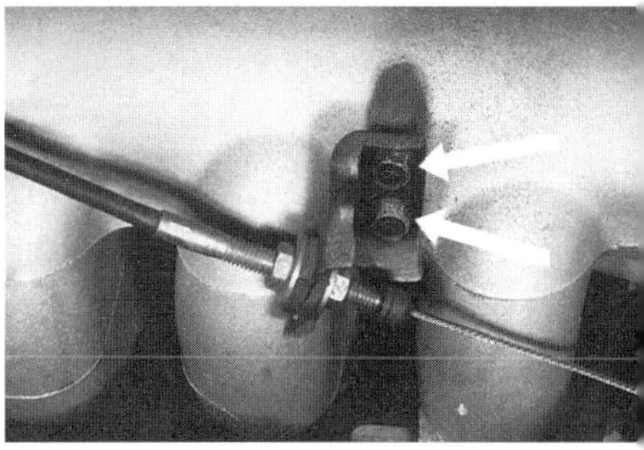

9/1c ... then release cable bracket.

3 Release the electrical connector block at each individual injector. This is done by squeezing the tag at the top of the connector block inwards after which the connector block can be pulled away from the side of the injector body.

4 Release the injector loom connector block from its mounting bracket at the rear end of the intake manifold. Squeeze the lugs on the retaining pin with pliers and then the connector block can be freed from the bracket.

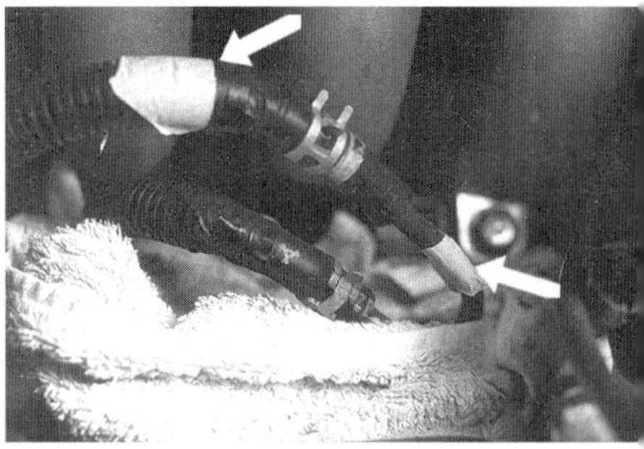

9/2a Mark fuel lines then disconnect.

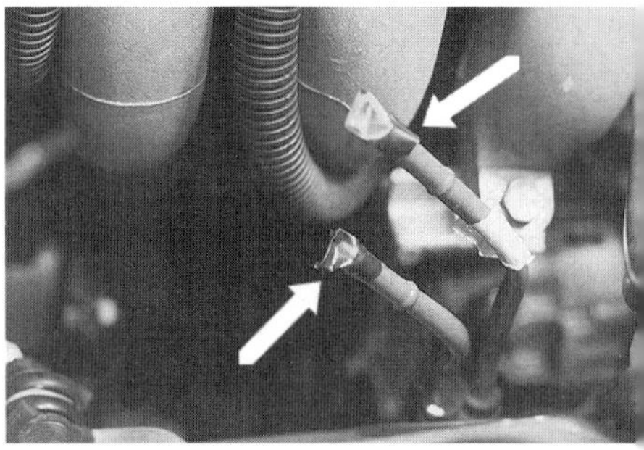

9/2b Tape over pipe ends.

5 There is a small vacuum hose running between the pressure regulator valve on the fuel rail and a stub on the manifold. This hose should be disconnected simply by pulling it from either of its unions: there are no spring clips.

6 The fuel rail itself is fixed to the manifold casting by two 12 mm bolts. These should be undone with a box end or crescent wrench as there's no real access for sockets. Withdraw the bolts leaving the fuel rail free for removal. **Caution**

There are locating collars, between the rail and its two mountings, which will be dislodged as the fuel rail is moved and could easily be lost or damaged.

7 Pull the rail assembly away from the manifold to release the injectors from their bores and then move the whole thing towards the rear of the engine and manipulate it up between the cambox and intake manifold plenum chamber, at the same time push the fuel hoses up through the gaps between the individual intake manifolds and pull the injector wiring loom clear as necessary. **Caution!** As the injectors clear the manifold their individual insulators will come away with them, be careful not to lose these.

8 Undo and remove the single 14 mm bolt holding the manifold to the aluminum support bracket. Now, using a 12 mm socket on a 250 mm (9.5 in) extension, you will be able to reach most of the individual nuts and bolts retaining the manifold once you have maneuvered the socket between the individual intake trunks until you find a gap large enough for it to pass through. There are two extremely awkward bolts alongside the pillars which support the fuel rail. We got to these by fitting a socket and universal joint to the bolt head from above and then inserting the extension between the intake tracts and engaging it in the universal joint: this was with a 1/2 In drive socket set. If you use a smaller drive socket system it will need to be of extremely good quality because these bolts are tight. The nuts and bolts should be loosened in a diagonal sequence and once the bolts and nuts have been removed, the manifold can be slid off the three studs left protruding from the cylinder head. If the gasket stays fixed to the head, or manifold face, peel it off. **Caution!** Don't damage the cylinder head by trying to free the old gasket with a sharp tool and don't try to reuse the gasket, it's a false economy.

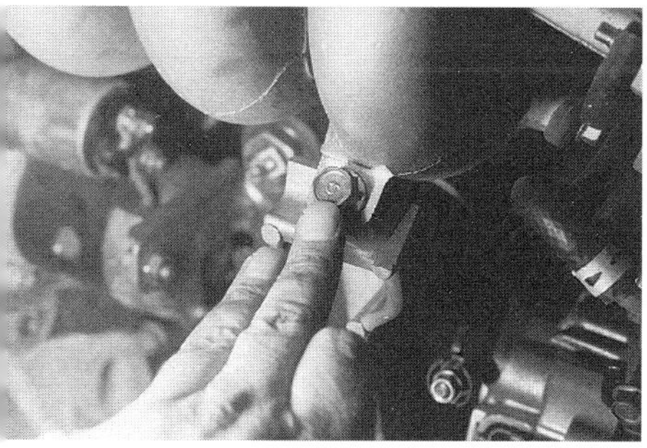

9/8a Remove support bracket bolt ...

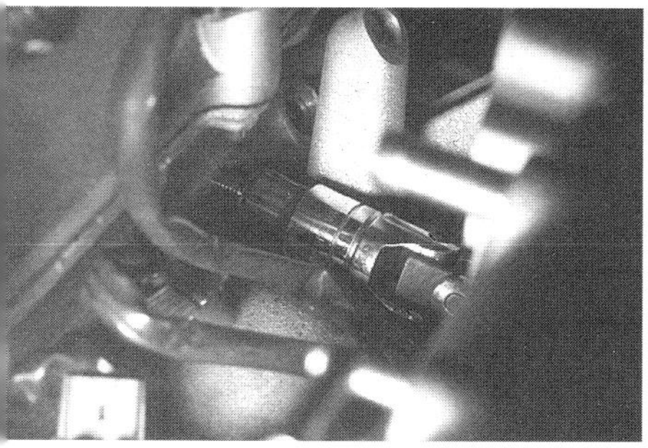

9/8b ... and undo manifold nuts.

INSPECTION

9 Clean the manifold using either kerosene (paraffin) or a proprietary solvent. The staining and deposits from the fuel are best removed using an aerosol carburettor cleaner. Once you've got it clean, check carefully for signs of cracking or other damage. Any cracks will allow air leakage into the manifold and will make it impossible to get the engine to run normally.

10 Check the gasket faces using a straight-edge placed across each one at various angles. Again, if the gasket face is warped it will be impossible to get the manifold to seal correctly. You should also consider why the warping has occurred; it may have been due to an isolated case of overheating, but be sure to check that the engine is not running hot due to the fuel/air mixture ratio being incorrect. (Remember that once the air leak has occurred, the mixture will be weak anyway, until the fault is corrected, compounding the problem).

11 If you discover damage, the easiest option is to fit a new manifold. If you want to keep costs down, consult a reputable engineering shop, who will be able to advise whether any cracks can be repaired by welding, and whether warped gasket faces can safely be machined flat again. Don't be tempted to reuse a manifold which you know is damaged; if you do you will never get the engine to run correctly and you could risk further engine damage due to the weakened mixture.

INSTALLATION

12 Install the manifold using new gaskets. Fit the mounting bolts and tighten them evenly, finally torque-tightening them to 19-25 Nm (1.9-2.6 kgf m / 14-19 lbf ft). Fit the injector rail and injectors, noting that the injector harness and bracket bolts are tightened to 7.8-11 Nm (80-110 kgf cm / 69-95 lbf in). Fit the fuel delivery hose and make sure it is secured with its clip.

9/12a Fit a new gasket ...

9/12b ... then install manifold.

13 Reconnect the injector wiring harness. Install the fuel pressure regulator, tightening the bolts to 7.8-11 Nm (80-110 kgf cm / 69-95 lbf in) and reconnect the vacuum and fuel return hoses, noting that the latter must be secured with a retaining clip. Fit the throttle body and airvalve using new gaskets ☞ 5/7, 11. Install the accelerator cable bracket, tightening the retaining bolts to 7.8-11 Nm (80-110 kgf cm / 69-95 lbf in).

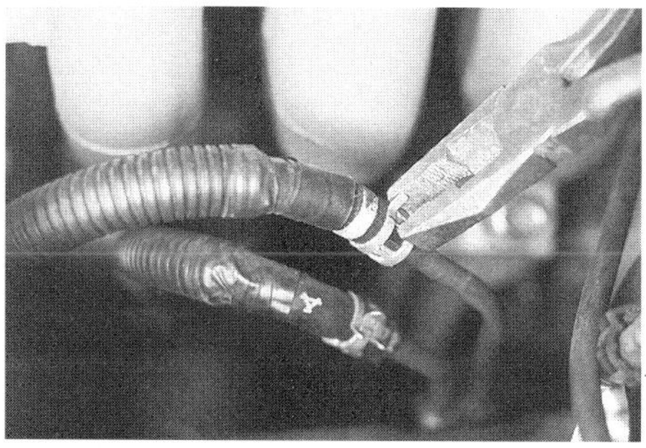

9/13 Connect fuel lines and clip securely.

14 Reconnect the throttle cable and check that it operates smoothly. Set the throttle cable lash to 1-3 mm (0.039-0.118 in) using the adjuster at the end of the outer cable. Fit the ISC valve and throttle sensor wiring connectors and the water hoses. Fit and tighten the radiator drain plug, then fill the cooling system with ethylene glycol based coolant to the bottom of the radiator filler neck. Don't fit the radiator filler cap yet. Check and fit the breather and vacuum hoses at the rear of the manifold. Install the resonance chamber and secure it with its hose clips.

9/14 Fit cable bracket.

15 The next job is to prime the fuel system. Locate the diagnosis connector which is mounted on the left-hand inner wing near the suspension turret. Open the connector cover and identify terminals **F/P** and **GND** as shown on the chart inside the connector cover. Make up a short jumper wire from a piece of insulated electrical wire with the ends bared. Connect together the two terminals and switch on the ignition for around ten seconds to allow the system to pressurize. Turn the ignition switch off, remove the jumper wire and close the connector cover.

16 Start the engine and check for correct throttle operation, and for indications of air leakage anywhere around the manifold (indicated by unusual hissing or squealing noises), and investigate and repair as required. Note that if the manifold or mounting gasket(s) were found to be damaged when the manifold was removed, it is worth getting the vehicle checked out on an analyzer to make sure that the fuel/air mixture ratio is now correct at all engine speeds and loads.

17 Let the engine idle until the radiator top hose gets hot. This will allow the water level to stabilize and any air in the cooling system to work out. If necessary, top up the radiator and the coolant reservoir, and then fit the radiator cap. Leave the engine running for a while to allow the system to reach normal operating pressure, then check all water hose connections disturbed during the procedure for leaks.

10. IDLE SPEED CONTROL (ISC) SYSTEM - CHECKING

☞ 1/1, 2.

WHAT IS IT?

1 The ISC system is responsible for the automatic control of idling at various engine temperatures. Without it, the engine idle speed would be erratic at low temperatures. It consists of the Airvalve, which is mounted in the intake manifold, and Idle Speed Control (ISC) valve, which is mounted on the underside of the throttle body. The two units sense engine temperature from a coolant feed. The Airvalve is 'dumb' - it responds directly to changes in coolant temperature to regulate bypass air entering the engine through the intake manifold. The ISC valve responds to information fed from the Engine Control Unit (ECU).

CHECKING

2 This checking procedure should be carried out with the engine cold. The coolant temperature should be at 20°C (68°F). You will need an external tachometer, and either the Mazda System Selector (SST No. 49 B019 9A0) or a short insulated jumper wire.

3 Open the Diagnosis Connector and connect the tachometer probe to the IG terminal. If the tachometer requires an external power feed, connect it to the blue single-pin power connector, taking care not to allow it to short to ground (earth). Next, either plug the System Selector into the Diagnosis Connector and set its switch to 'SELF TEST' or alternatively connect the jumper wire between terminals **TEN** and **GND** of the Diagnosis Connector.

4 Start the engine and monitor the engine speed reading on the external tachometer. The engine idle speed should gradually decrease as the engine reaches normal operating temperature, indicating that the Airvalve is functioning normally. If all is well, move on to the ISC valve check which is described next.

5 Once the engine is at full operating temperature, allow it to continue idling and then disconnect the wiring connector from the ISC valve. Engine idle speed should now increase to around 1,200 rpm and the ISC valve should click.

6 If either the Airvalve or the ISC valve do not conform to the results described, you will have to replace them. The procedure is described below.

11. AIRVALVE - REMOVAL, INSPECTION & INSTALLATION

☞ 1/1, 2.

REMOVAL

1 Before you can remove the airvalve it will be necessary to drain the cooling system. Remove the cap on top of the radiator. **Warning!:** If the car has been running up to an hour before this point, cover the cap with cloth and wear protective gloves before releasing the cap in case scalding coolant is ejected.

2 Place a receptacle beneath the radiator drain plug; it will need to be capable of holding 6.5 liters (6.5 US or 6.1 Imp. quarts) and, if you intend to reuse the coolant, should be spotlessly clean. Once again protecting your hands if the coolant is hot, unscrew the radiator drain plug with a medium sized crosshead screwdriver until the plug drops and the coolant flows.

3 Disconnect the water hoses from the airvalve stubs, using a rag to catch any residual coolant. The airvalve itself is then held to the intake manifold by four 8 mm-headed bolts: these bolts also have crossheads for a screwdriver if preferred, although you'll need an angled screwdriver to reach the lower bolts. The four bolts should be loosened slightly in a diagonal sequence before they are fully unscrewed. Note: both lower retaining bolts are difficult to access with a socket and should be undone with an 8 mm box end wrench. One of the lower retaining bolts cannot be withdrawn completely because its head contacts a boss on the cam cover; therefore, it must be loosened completely but left in position until the airvalve is pulled away from the manifold. The four bolts have loose spring washers.

INSPECTION

4 You can check the operation of the airvalve as follows. Clean the valve and place it in a plastic bag, then put it in a domestic freezer for an hour or so to cool it to 0°C (32°F). Remove the valve from the bag and make a mark on the internal

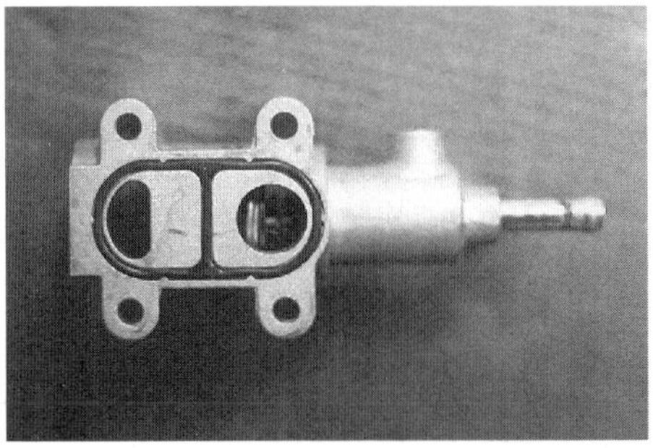

11/4 The airvalve.

shaft using an indelible marker through the port on the side of the valve. Using a hot air gun, warm the valve and note the movement of the shaft. If it is working correctly, the shaft should move away from the water hose stub end of the valve body as it warms up. If the valve fails to operate, you will have to fit a new unit.

INSTALLATION

5 Fit the airvalve, using a new O-ring seal. Fit the four mounting bolts finger-tight, then torque down to 4.9-7.8 Nm (50-80 kgf cm / 43-69 lbf in). Reconnect and secure the water hoses. Fit

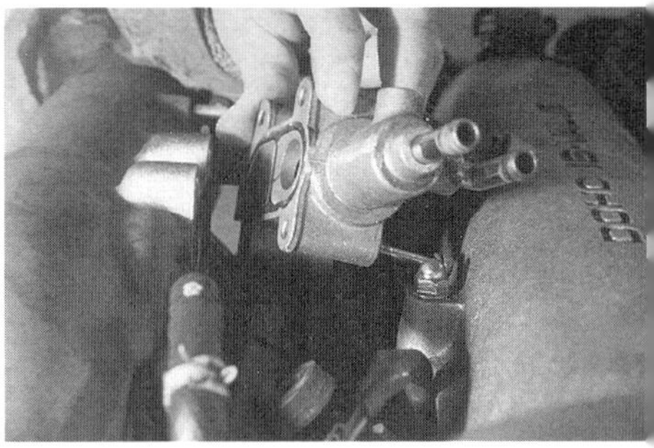

11/5 Fit airvalve to manifold.

and tighten the radiator drain plug, then fill the cooling system with ethylene glycol based coolant to the bottom of the radiator filler neck. Don't fit the radiator filler cap just yet.

6 The next job is to prime the fuel system. Locate the diagnosis connector which is mounted on the left-hand inner wing near the suspension turret. Open the connector cover and identify terminals **F/P** and **GND** as shown on the inside of the connector cover. Make up a short jumper wire from a piece of insulated electrical wire with the ends bared. Connect together the two terminals and switch on the ignition for around ten seconds to allow the system to pressurize. Turn the ignition switch off, remove the jumper wire and close the connector cover.

7 Start the engine and leave it to idle until the radiator top hose gets hot. This will allow the water level to stabilize and any air in the cooling system to work out. If necessary, top up the radiator and then fit the radiator cap. Leave the engine running for a while to allow the system to reach normal operating pressure, then check the water hose connections at the airvalve for leaks.

12. IDLE SPEED CONTROL (ISC) VALVE - INSPECTION, REMOVAL & INSTALLATION

☞ 1/1, 2.

INSPECTION

1 You can check the ISC valve *in situ* using an ohmmeter. Disconnect the ISC valve wiring connector, and check the resistance between the valve terminals. At 20°C (68°F) a reading of 12 ± 1Ω should be shown. If the reading obtained does not correspond with this figure, replace the valve as follows.

REMOVAL

2 Before attempting removal of the ISC valve, disconnect the battery negative (-) terminal to isolate the electrical system ☞ 7/2. Clean the external surfaces of the ISC valve and the throttle body to prevent dirt entering the intake system.

3 The next task is to drain the cooling system. Remove the cap on top of the radiator. **Warning!:** If the car has been running up to an hour before this point, cover the cap with cloth and wear protective gloves before releasing the cap in case scalding coolant is ejected.

4 Place a receptacle beneath the radiator drain plug; it will need to be capable of holding 6.5 liters (6.5 US or 6.1 Imp. quarts) and, if you intend to reuse the coolant, should be spotlessly clean. Once again protecting your hands if the coolant is hot, unscrew the radiator drain plug with a medium sized crosshead screwdriver until the plug drops and the coolant flows.

5 Release the clip which secures the air pipe to the throttle body and pull the hose off the connecting stub. As it comes away, detach the smaller hose at the ISC valve stub, and the vent hose from the cambox cover. Disconnect the water hoses from the ISC valve stubs. Disconnect the ISC valve wiring connector.

6 The ISC valve is held on the underside of the throttle body by crosshead screws. The two outer screws can be reached without too much trouble, but the single (maybe two) inner screw is much more difficult to reach. If you have a cranked screwdriver of the correct size you may be able to remove it. Otherwise, it is relatively easy to remove the throttle body first, and then remove the ISC valve from the throttle body. Note that the throttle cable should normally be disconnected before the throttle body is removed, though it can be left connected if it is not necessary to move the throttle body from the engine compartment.

12/6 ISC valve location.

INSTALLATION

7 Clean the throttle body and ISC valve joint faces and fit a new sealing gasket. Position the ISC valve and fit the three securing screws. These should be tightened to 2.8 - 4.0 Nm (29 - 41 kgf cm / 25 - 35 lbf in).

8 If the throttle body was removed to improve access to the ISC valve screws, clean the gasket faces of the throttle body and intake manifold and fit a new gasket over the dowel pins on the manifold mounting face. Position the throttle body and fit the four holding bolts finger tight. Tighten the bolts evenly and progressively to 19-25 Nm (1.9-2.6 kgf m / 14-19 lbf ft).

9 Reconnect the throttle cable and check that it operates smoothly. Set the throttle cable lash to 1-3 mm (0.039-0.118 in) using the adjuster at the end of the outer cable. Fit the ISC valve and throttle sensor wiring connectors and the water hoses. Fit and tighten the radiator drain plug, then fill the cooling system with ethylene glycol based coolant to the bottom of the radiator filler neck. Don't fit the radiator filler cap yet.

10 Start the engine and check for correct throttle operation, then let the engine idle until the radiator top hose gets hot. This will allow the water level to stabilize and any air in the cooling system to work out. If necessary, top up the radiator and coolant reservoir, and then fit the radiator cap. Leave the engine running for a while to allow the system to reach normal operating pressure, then check the water hose connections at the throttle body for leaks.

13. FUEL SYSTEM - SAFETY PRECAUTIONS & WORKING PROCEDURES

☞ 1/1, 2.

1 Before undertaking any work which necessitates disconnecting any part of the fuel system, read through this section - it contains information on safety precautions which must be adopted before work commences, plus general information on working procedures.

2 **Warning!** Whenever the fuel system is disconnected, fuel vapor will be present. Be aware of the potential fire hazard. Have available a fire extinguisher of the type approved for automotive fires. Make sure that the working area is well ventilated - working in a poorly ventilated building will increase the risk of a dangerous buildup of fuel vapor. We do not recommend that you carry out fuel system work with the vehicle over an access pit - fuel vapor is heavier than air and will collect in the access pit where it will persist for some time, presenting a significant fire hazard. Whenever possible, work with the car's battery disconnected (☞ 7/2).

3 **Warning!** Before commencing work which requires disconnection of the fuel hoses or related parts it is essential to release fuel system pressure. Even if the engine has not been run for a while, high pressure remains in the system until the following procedure has been undertaken.

RELEASING FUEL SYSTEM PRESSURE

4 Working inside the car, remove the two screws which secure the access cover around the lower section of the steering column. Unclip and remove the cover to gain access to the fuel circuit opening relay. On our UK market project car, the relay could be identified by its yellow color. On cars built for other markets, the relay may differ slightly in appearance, and might be confused with other relays in the vicinity. Start the engine, then unplug the wiring connector from the relay thought to be the opening relay and wait for about a minute. If you've got the right relay, the engine will stall due to fuel starvation - if necessary, repeat this process on the other relays until you get the right one. Once the engine has stalled, the fuel system is depressurized. Turn off the ignition switch and plug the relay back into the connector, then fit the inspection cover.

13/4 Our car's uel circuit opening relay

DISCONNECTING FUEL LINES

5 Release fuel system pressure ☞ 5/13/4. Disconnect the battery ☞ 7/2.

6 When disconnecting any fuel line, cover it with a rag to catch fuel spray. Once a fuel line is disconnected, plug the open end to prevent dirt getting into the system. Golf tees work fine for this or, if you don't play golf, try using small bolts of the appropriate diameter. **Warning!** If you need to connect a fuel pressure gauge to the system for a check under pressure, **always** secure the connection with a suitable hose clip or it may be forced apart under system pressure - this applies equally to plugged hose ends which are under fuel system pressure.

PRIMING THE FUEL SYSTEM

7 After work on the fuel system is complete, it is preferable to prime the fuel system to avoid excessive engine cranking - remember that the Miata/MX5 battery is tiny by normal automotive standards, and has little reserve capacity. Ensure that all residual fuel vapor has dispersed, then reconnect the battery negative (-) terminal ☞ 7/2. Open the diagnosis socket cover (mounted on the left inner wing near the suspension turret and clearly marked). Refer to the table inside the cover, and connect pins **F/P** and **GND** using a short insulated jumper wire.

8 Turn on the ignition switch for about ten

13/7 Bridge terminals in diagnosis socket.

seconds and check for fuel leaks around any connection which has been disturbed. If you want to check that the pump is running, open the fuel filler and listen at the opening while the system is priming. A high-pitched whine indicates pump operation. Turn the ignition switch off, disconnect the jumper wire and close the diagnosis socket cover.

14. FUEL SYSTEM CHECKS

☞ 1/1, 2 & 5/13.

1 If the engine fails to start and you suspect that fuel is not reaching the injectors, you can perform a quick check to see if the pump is operating. You first need to bypass the fuel circuit opening relay so that the pump will operate as soon as the ignition switch is turned on. Open the diagnosis connector cover and connect terminals **GND** and **F/P** using an insulated jumper wire.

2 Turn the ignition switch on and remove the fuel filler cap. Listen carefully at the fuel filler opening to see if the pump is running. You will need somewhere quiet for this. If you can hear the high-pitched whine from the pump, try starting the engine. If it now starts normally, you will need to check the circuit opening relay.

CIRCUIT OPENING RELAY

3 Remove the two screws which secure the access cover around the lower section of the steering column. Unclip and remove the cover. On our UK market project car, the relay could be identified by its yellow color. On cars built for other markets, the relay may differ slightly in appearance, and might be confused with other relays in the vicinity. Start the engine, then unplug the wiring connector from the relay thought to be the opening relay and wait for about a minute. If you've got the right relay, the engine will stall due to fuel starvation - if necessary, repeat this process on the other relays until you get the right one. Once the engine has stalled, the fuel system is depressurized (to repressurize ☞ 5/13/7). Unplug the relay and remove the single 10 mm headed bolt which retains it to its bracket, then take it to the workbench for checking. You will need a 12 volt battery, some insulated jumper leads with miniature clip probes, and volt and ohmmeters (or a multimeter).

4 Refer to the accompanying diagram for terminal identification. Using jumper leads, apply battery voltage as shown in the following

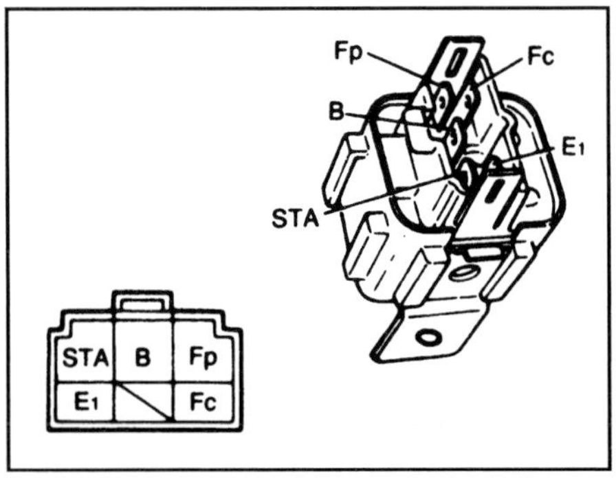

D14/4 TESTING FUEL CIRCUIT OPENING RELAY.

12 Volts	Ground (Earth)	Correct result
STA	E1	B-Fp = continuity
B	Fc	Fp = battery voltage

T14/4 FUEL CIRCUIT OPENING RELAY OPERATION.

table; also check relay operation as shown. If you don't get the right results, fit a new relay.

5 With the relay installed and connected, check the voltage between the various terminals and ground (earth) using a voltmeter. Check the voltages by connecting the meter negative (-) probe to ground (earth) and then introducing the meter positive (+) probe to the terminal to be tested through the back of the wiring connector. If the readings obtained are not as shown in the table, check the wiring harness to locate the source of the problem.

Test conditions	Fp	Fc	B	STA	E1
Ignition switch: ON	0V	12V	12V	0V	0V
Ignition switch: START	12V	0V	12V	12V	0V
Engine idling	12V	0V	12V	0V	0V

T14/5 FUEL CIRCUIT OPENING RELAY CIRCUIT VOLTAGES.

6 With the relay removed, check the resistances between terminals with an ohmmeter, comparing the readings obtained with the accompanying table. If any of the readings are not as indicated, replace the relay.

Check between terminals	Resistance (Ω)
STA-E1	21-43
B-Fc	109-226
B-Fp	∞

T14/6 FUEL CIRCUIT OPENING RELAY RESISTANCE TEST.

FUEL PUMP OPERATION

7 Open the diagnosis connector cover and connect terminals **GND** and **F/P** using an insulated jumper wire (this allows the fuel pump to run as soon as the ignition switch is turned on by bypassing the circuit opening relay). Turn the ignition switch on and remove the fuel filler cap. Listen carefully at the fuel filler opening to see if the pump is running. You will need somewhere quiet for this. If you can hear the high-pitched whine which indicates that the pump is running, suspect the opening relay (see above). If not, check for battery voltage on the pump supply wire as follows.

8 Working inside the car, carefully lever out the black plastic clips which secure the carpet to the rear deck. We found that the best technique for this was to use two flat-bladed screwdrivers to lift the clips. Don't be tempted to pull up on the carpet - it will just pull off over the clip heads. You need to remove sufficient clips to allow the carpet to be rolled back clear of the access cover above the fuel tank. You'll find that there are three bright metal access covers. Ignore the long cover at the front edge of the deck - we are interested in the larger of the two remaining covers. Remove the 10 mm screws which retain the cover and remove it. Lo-

14.8 Covers removed to give access.

cate and separate the fuel pump wiring connector. Connect the positive (+) probe of a voltmeter to the **L/R** terminal and the negative (-) probe to ground (earth). The **L/R** terminal will be found at bottom left, with the connector held with the key uppermost. Turn on the ignition switch. If 12 volts is shown, you know that battery voltage is reaching the pump. Next, check for continuity between the pump connector **B** terminal (positioned bottom right on the connector) and ground (earth) using an ohmmeter. If continuity is shown, the pump circuit is fine, which means that you will have to replace the fuel pump. If not, repair the ground (earth) circuit from the pump to the **B** terminal.

FUEL SYSTEM PRESSURE CHECKS

9 To carry out these checks, you will need a fuel pressure gauge which can be clamped in place in the fuel delivery line. Before starting you will need to release residual pressure from the system. Be aware that pressure can remain in the fuel system for an hour or more after the engine is stopped, and must be released before any part of the system is disconnected. Before you do this, get the car in position for the check to be carried out. The easiest access point for gauge connection is under the hood, where the fuel delivery line connects to the injector rail.

10 Start the engine and, while it is idling remove the opening relay connector to stop the fuel pump. After the engine stalls, turn off the ignition switch and reconnect the opening relay wiring (full details ☞ 5/13). Open the fuel tank filler to prevent any buildup of air pressure in the tank.

FUEL PUMP HOLD PRESSURE

11 Start by depressurizing the fuel system ☞ 5/13. Once pressure has been released, disconnec

the battery negative (-) terminal (☞ 7/2) to isolate the electrical system. Working inside the engine compartment, identify the fuel delivery hose which connects to the front of the injector rail. Have some rag handy to catch any residual fuel leakage as the delivery line is pulled off. Disconnect the fuel hose and fit the fuel pressure gauge to the open hose end and a plug to the gauge outlet, using hose clamps to secure both connections. **Warning!** Don't skip the hose clips - there's a lot of pressure involved. Reconnect the battery negative (-) terminal. Moving to the diagnosis connector, open the cover and fit an insulated jumper wire between terminals **F/P** and **GND**. Turn the ignition switch on for ten seconds to allow the fuel system to pressurize, then switch off. You now need to wait for five minutes, after which a pressure reading of at least 343 kPa (3.5 kg/cm2, 50 psi) should be shown on the gauge. If the hold pressure is below specification you should check that there are no fuel system leaks. If no leaks are found between the pump outlet at the top of the tank and the gauge connection point, there is excessive back-leakage through the pump, indicating the need for replacement.

FUEL PUMP MAXIMUM PRESSURE

12 With the gauge and jumper wire fitted as described above for the hold pressure check, switch on the ignition and note the maximum pressure reading shown on the gauge. This should be 441-589 kPa (4.6-6.0 kg/cm2, 64-85 psi). If below the lower figure specified, a new pump should be fitted.

13 After the hold and maximum pressure checks are completed, wrap some rag around the gauge connections to catch any fuel spray, then disconnect the gauge. Reconnect the fuel pipe, making sure that the hose clip is secure. Switch on the ignition for a few seconds to allow the system to prime, then switch off and remove the jumper wire from the diagnosis connector.

INJECTOR OPERATION CHECKS

14 Have an assistant crank the engine while you listen to each injector in turn. Use a long screwdriver with the tip held against the injector and listen at the handle end. You should be able to hear the click as the injector discharges. (Remember not to depress the accelerator pedal during this check - if the engine is cold the dechoke system will disable the injectors). If the injectors appear to operate normally but the problem persists, you may have a low fuel system pressure problem - check the pressure regulator as described below.

15 If the injectors seem inoperative or intermittent, check each injector wiring connector for battery voltage on the **W/R** terminal with the ignition switch on. If you read zero volts, check the wiring and connections back to the main relay and repair or replace as necessary. If you read 12 volts and the injectors are still inoperative, check the resistance of each injector with an ohmmeter. This should be 12-16 Ω. If the injector is out of the specified range, fit a new one. Note that if the above check fails to isolate the problem the fault is likely to lie with the ECU. Have a full test carried out by a Mazda dealer or ☞ 5/28.

PRESSURE REGULATOR CHECKS

16 If a pressure regulator fault is suspected, you can carry out a preliminary check of the system pressure as follows. You will need a fuel pressure gauge which can be clamped in place in the fuel delivery line. Before starting you will need to release residual pressure from the system. Be aware that pressure can remain in the fuel system for an hour or more after the engine is stopped, and must be released (☞ 5/13) before any part of the system is disconnected.

17 Disconnect the battery negative (-) terminal to isolate the electrical system ☞ 7/2. If you have just carried out the fuel pump pressure checks discussed above, you can make these checks at the same connection point under the hood, where the fuel feed pipe connects to the injector rail. Reconnect the battery negative (-) terminal.

18 Start the engine and note the fuel system pressure reading. This should be 216-265 kPa (2.2-2.7 kg/cm2, 31-38 psi). If the reading is low, try clamping the fuel line return hose to impede the flow of fuel back to the tank. If the pressure reading rises quickly, a regulator fault is indicated. A gradual increase in pressure indicates a partial blockage somewhere between the fuel pump and the regulator.

19 With the fuel pressure gauge still connected in-line as described above, check the fuel system hold pressure. Moving to the diagnosis connector, open the cover and fit an insulated jumper wire between terminals **F/P** and **GND**. Turn the ignition switch on for ten seconds to allow the fuel system to pressurize. Turn the ignition switch off and wait for five minutes, after which a pressure reading of at least 147 kPa (1.5 kg/cm2, 21 psi) should be shown on the gauge. If the hold pressure is below specification a new pressure regulator should be fitted.

15. FUEL TANK - REMOVAL & INSTALLATION

☞ 1/1, 2 & 5/13.

1 This operation is complicated, even if you have access to a 2-post vehicle lift and a transmission jack. Without this equipment we would advise you to consider having the work done professionally. We're not saying that you couldn't do it at home, but it will entail a lot of work. Read through the procedure first, and then decide for yourself if you want to attempt it. You will have to remove the rear subframe assembly to obtain clearance for fuel tank removal, so if there is anything else requiring attention in this area, this would be a good time to do it.

PREPARATION

2 Before you start work, note that it will be necessary to drain the tank before you remove it. It follows that it would be advantageous to run the tank low before you start this procedure. The first task is to get the car raised high enough for access to the underside ☞ 1/3. Once you're satisfied that the car is raised sufficiently to give reasonable access, and that it is secure on its stands, you must depressurize the fuel system ☞ 5/13. Having done this, disconnect the battery negative (-) terminal to isolate the electrical system ☞ 7/2.

DRAINING THE FUEL TANK

3 Moving under the car, locate the plastic cover which conceals the fuel filter. This is on the right side of the car at the rear of the floorpan, and is held onto the body by cunningly designed plastic clips. At first sight, you might be forgiven for thinking that they were crosshead screws seated in cup washers. On closer examination, however, they turn out to be two-piece plastic fasteners and are more complicated to deal with than you might think: for more advice ☞ 1/2 (*Wrestling with two-piece plastic panel fasteners*).

4 Back to the job in hand. Remove all the fasteners which hold the filter cover in place. Lift the cover away to reveal the filter and fuel hose connections. In theory, you can now remove the bolts securing the filter bracket to the body, leaving the fuel hose connections undisturbed. The next step, however, is to drain the fuel from the tank, and this is best done by disconnecting the fuel delivery hose at the filter as described below.

5 Draining the fuel tank at the filter connection point is pretty easy, because the fuel will siphon out of the tank once you've disconnected the delivery pipe. Find a clean, sealable container suitable for gasoline and place it under the car. If the tank is full, you will need something with a capacity of at least 45 liters (12 US gallons / 10 Imp. gallons). A funnel would be useful here, too. The next stage is messy, and we know of no method of avoiding getting your arm soaked in gasoline. Wear coveralls to keep the gasoline off the skin. We further suggest that you wear safety glasses to keep gasoline splashes out of your eyes.

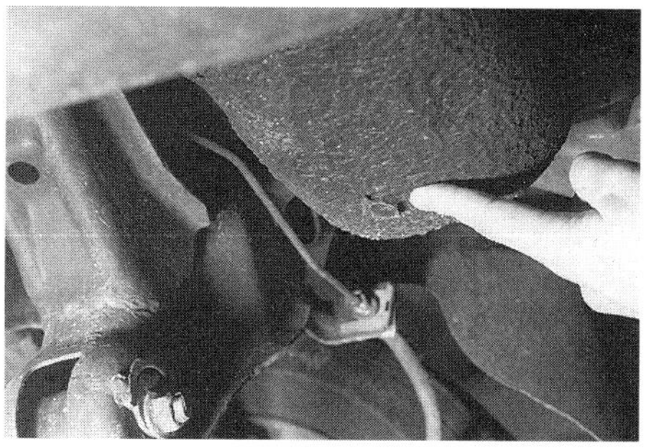

15/5 Fuel tank drain plug.

Other than that, we can only suggest that you try to disconnect the pipe quickly to minimize the mess. Alternatively, you'll find a drain plug on the underside of the tank. Clean off the underbody sealant before you attempt removal. If the plug seems abnormally tight, we recommend that you drain the tank as described below - you could tear the plug out of the tank base if you apply too much pressure, and that will mean fitting a new tank.

6 Using pliers, grip the ends of the fuel delivery pipe clip and slide it up the pipe and clear of the stub on the filter. The stub is quite long -

move the clip away by at least an inch or so, or it will still grip the stub. Using a screwdriver, push the hose off the stub (don't try pulling it off or it will just grip the stub tighter). The fuel system hoses are a tight fit on the metal pipes - they have to be because of the high fuel pressure they contain. If the hose won't yield to gentle screwdriver pressure, try fitting a pair of pliers loosely around the metal pipe and using the sides of the jaws to apply pressure to the hose end. Don't grip the pipe with the pliers, just let it slide over the pipe.

7 As the hose comes away, quickly position the end in the container or funnel and allow gravity to do the rest - you can leave the fuel to siphon out of the tank while you get cleaned up. (Remember to release the fuel filler cap so that the air can enter the tank as the fuel runs out). Once the tank has drained completely, remove the drain container, fit its cap and store it safely away from any source of fire, in a well-ventilated area. Plug the open end of the fuel hose with a golf tee or similar to prevent dirt entering the fuel system. We suggest that you check your service schedule for the car and see whether it is about due for a new fuel filter - if so, this is a great time to fit one - remember that if you don't do it now, you will have to endure the arm-soaked-in-gasoline procedure all over again when the time comes!

REMOVING THE EXHAUST SYSTEM

8 You need to drop the exhaust system clear of the underside of the car to get access to the PPF and propshaft (actually, you may be able to get by if you just remove the main muffler, but access is much better with the system out of the way, and it takes little extra time to do). Disconnect the front downpipe, then free the system from the hangers and lift it away ☞ 5/38.

REMOVING THE POWER PLANT FRAME (PPF)

9 The next step is to remove the Power Plant Frame (PPF). Unless you have access to SST 49 0259 440, which prevents oil leakage from the transmission housing when the propshaft coupling is detached, you will need to drain the oil from the transmission ☞ 2/8 or 9.

10 Start by disconnecting and removing the propshaft. Before undoing the four nuts and bolts holding the shaft flange to the differential flange, use a blob of white paint to mark the relative positions of both flanges. Alternatively, a small groove can be filed across the joint for the same purpose. It is important to mark the relative position of the two components because the propshaft may be out of balance in another position.

11 The bolts have 12 mm heads, while the nuts are 14 mm, so you'll need a combination of two wrenches to release each nut and bolt. Using a diagonal sequence, slacken in turn each of the nuts and bolts a little before removing them completely. You may need to apply the parking brake to lock the propshaft while each nut and bolt is freed, turning the shaft and reapplying the brake to gain access to all four fasteners.

12 Once the four nuts and bolts have been released, separate the driveshaft and differential flanges by pushing the shaft forward further onto the transmission tailshaft and then lowering the axle end of the shaft before withdrawing the shaft's nose from the tail of the transmission. Note: some residual oil will drip from the transmission end once the propshaft is removed; place a plastic bag over the end of the transmission tail and secure with an elastic band to contain the drips and prevent dirt getting into the transmission bearings.

13 Once the driveshaft has been removed completely, replace the bolts, locking washers and nuts finger-tight in the differential flange for safe-keeping.

14 📷+ Release the wiring loom from the side of the PPF by squeezing the retaining ears of each plastic clip with your fingers or pliers and then, while the ears are squeezed together, pulling the clip free of the frame. Some of these clips are very fiddly but with care they can all be removed without breaking them. Don't forget to release the ground wire held by a 10 mm bolt toward the rear end of the PPF and the loom clip on the side of the bellhousing which is held by a 10 mm screw.

15 Remove the support bracket between the PPF and the transmission tail casting by first unscrewing the 17 mm headed bolt between the PPF and the bracket, followed by the two 14 mm headed bolts holding the bracket to the transmission. Remove the bracket and fit the bolts finger-tight in their appropriate places for safekeeping.

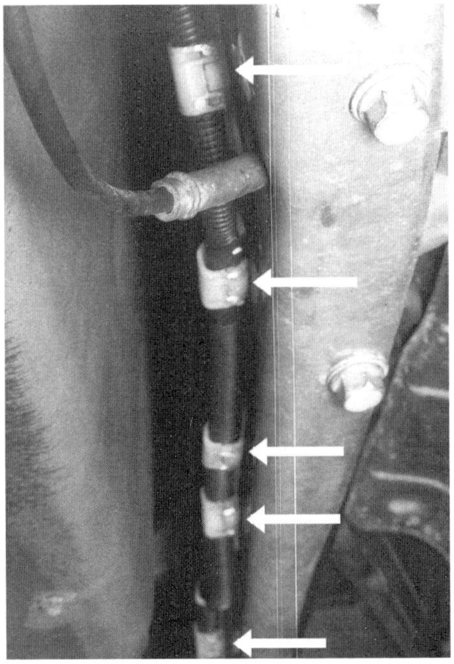

15/14a Release wiring from PPF clips ...

15/14b ... don't forget ground terminal.

16 Place a jack beneath the transmission, just ahead of the front end of the PPF. Raise the jack until the rear of the transmission is supported and very slightly lifted: this will relieve the strain on the PPF.

17 At the very front of the PPF there are two 17 mm headed bolts which pass upward, right through the transmission casing, and screw into the top of the PPF. Slacken and remove both of these bolts, which are 198 mm (8 in) long!

18 At the rear end of the PPF there are two more long bolts, this time passing through the differential casting. Slacken and remove both bolts with a 17 mm socket wrench. You will notice that the forward bolt has a shoulder. Note: before removal of the long bolts and collar holding the PPF to the diff, it's a good idea to soak the whole area with penetrating oil as the collared bolt is a tight fit in the spacer and its shaped bore in the diff: even on our low mileage car, the forward bolt was pretty well corroded in place.

19 When the bolts have been removed the collar in the forward bolt position also has to be removed. If you look carefully at the shoulders of the collar you will see a couple of cutouts. Initially, tap a chisel or an old screwdriver into these recesses until the collar begins to move away from the PPF. Once movement has started you can lever the collar out with a screwdriver, moving from side to side and working it out gradually.

20 Once the collar is removed the rear of the PPF can be moved sideways until clear of the differential casing and then pulled backward, freeing it from the transmission casing, after which the PPF can be removed from the car.

REAR SUBFRAME REMOVAL

21 If you lie under the rear of the car, you can see the fuel tank mounted above the rear subframe assembly. The tank is wedge-shaped, and during removal must be moved forward and then rotated around the front edge of the subframe. As you will see, there is not enough room to do this with the subframe bolted in position; you have to lower it enough to permit the tank to be removed. In theory, you don't have to remove the subframe completely, but doing so confers some advantages. Firstly, you get unrestricted access to the tank and, secondly, you can check over the subframe and the normally-hidden areas of the bodyshell, so you have a great opportunity for inspection and rustproofing. The extra work required to detach the subframe completely, rather than just lowering it, is worth the extra time taken on this job if you need to check or repair these areas.

22 What we will be doing here is supporting the rear subframe as an assembly on a normal wheeled hydraulic jack, and lowering it from under the car. As well as the jack, you will need a couple of assistants, one on each side of the subframe, to steady and support it as it is lowered and to help maneuver it out. The first step is to remove the rear

wheels and place them to one side. If you just want to lower the subframe enough to get the tank out, proceed as described below. If you want to remove the subframe so you can check over the subframe components and body underside, skip down to paragraph 26.

23 From under the car, locate the brake pipe distribution block on the subframe. Remove the two nuts which secure the block to the subframe, but leave the brake lines connected. Next to the distribution block you will see the battery cables and other wiring running though a square-section guide. Disconnect this from the subframe by pulling it out carefully.

24 Position a wheeled hydraulic jack below the differential housing, making sure that the finned area sits squarely in the jack pad. Raise the jack slightly to take the weight of the subframe assembly. Working from each side of the car through the wheel arch, slacken and remove the subframe fasteners. On each side there are two 19 mm headed nuts at the front and rear mounting points, with a single 19 mm headed bolt between the two (it's possible that the center bolt is not fitted on all vehicles). You will need a fairly long socket extension to reach them, the center bolt being accessed through the gap in the upper wishbone. As you remove the fasteners, note that the subframe will come free, and you should have an assistant at each side to steady it and prevent it from toppling off the jack.

25 Slowly lower the jack, with your assistants guiding it downwards on each side. As it moves down, keep a close eye on the wiring, brake lines, fuel lines and parking brake cables - these are easily strained if they get caught up as the crossmember descends. Get the assembly as low as you can without risking damage to the above connections, then support the ends of the assembly by positioning strong crates or pieces of lumber under the lower wishbones. Make sure that it sits securely and is in no danger of toppling off the supports. Note that because the suspension is still connecting the subframe and body, it should be pretty stable, but try not to place undue stress on the suspension parts.

26 If you want to get the subframe out completely to allow a detailed inspection as discussed above, there are a few additional steps to follow. From inside the car, back off the parking brake adjuster to allow plenty of slack in the cable. You can turn the hexagonal adjuster with a screwdriver; you'll find the adjuster at the side of the parking brake lever. At the wheel end of the parking brake cable, slacken the cable locknut and disengage the cable adjuster from its bracket. You can now free the cable inner from the operating lever and disengage the cable assembly. Repeat this procedure on the remaining wheel.

27 Working below the car, disconnect the brake pipe which runs from the front of the car at its union with the distributor block. Free the pipe end, and plug the distributor block thread and cap the pipe end to keep dirt out of the hydraulic system. Disconnect the square-section guide which carries the battery cables and wiring along the crossmember and lodge them clear of the working area. On each side of the car, remove the suspension unit lower mounting bolt from the lower wishbone, passing a 17 mm socket through the access hole (when you remove the subframe the suspension units will be left hanging from their top mountings, reducing the weight and overall height of the subframe assembly).

28 Position a wheeled hydraulic jack below the differential housing, making sure that the finned area sits squarely in the jack pad. Raise the jack slightly to take the weight of the subframe assembly. Working from each side of the car through the wheel arch, slacken and remove the subframe fasteners. On each side there are two 19 mm headed nuts at the front and rear mounting points, with a single 19 mm headed bolt between the two. (The center bolt may not be fitted on all cars). You will need a fairly long socket extension to reach them, the center bolt being accessed through the gap in the upper wishbone. As you remove the fasteners, note that the subframe will come free, and you should have an assistant at each side to steady it and prevent it from toppling off the jack.

29 Slowly lower the jack, with your assistants guiding it downwards on each side. As it moves down, keep a close eye on the wiring, brake lines, fuel lines and parking brake cables - these are easily strained if they get caught up as the crossmember descends. Note that if your car is wired differently to ours, or if aftermarket wiring has been added in the vicinity of the subframe, you may need to disconnect or reroute it.

30 Once the subframe has been lowered enough to clear the body, it can be removed from the rear of the car. Wheel it out on the jack, with your assistants steadying each end. You will need to arrange some kind of support for the subframe by positioning strong crates or pieces of lumber under the lower wishbones. Make sure that it sits securely and is in no danger of toppling off the supports.

TANK REMOVAL

31 + With the subframe removed or lowered for access, we can at last begin to remove the fuel tank. Start by lifting the rear deck carpet and removing all of the inspection covers above the tank (for more information ☞ 5/14/8). At the back of the deck, removal of the smallest of the three covers will reveal the fuel filler and vent pipes connected to tank stubs. Free the vent pipe by squeezing together the tabs on the retaining clip

15/31a Remove cover ...

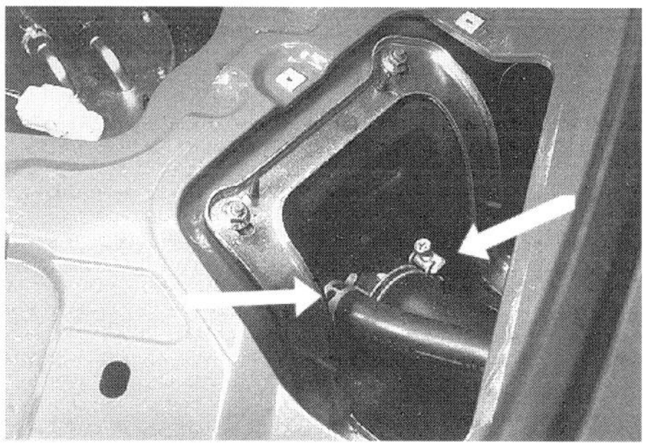

15/31b ... to reveal pipe connections.

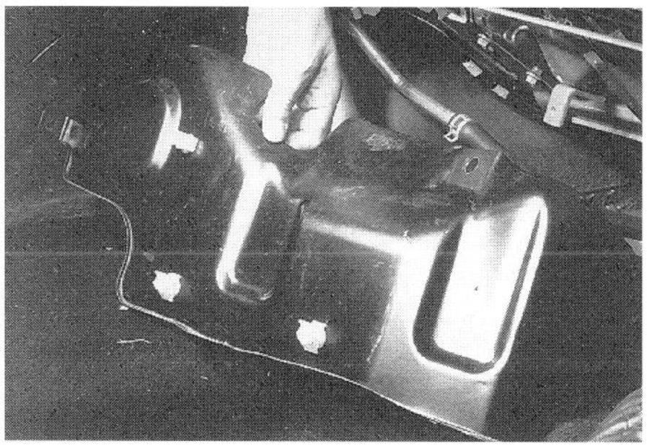

15/31c This cover in the trunk (boot) ...

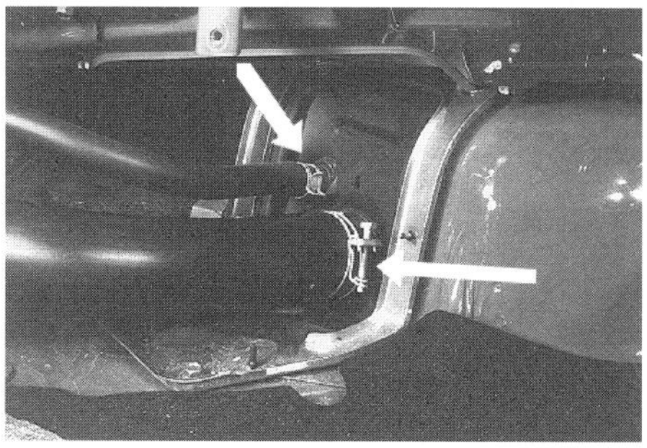

15/31d ... also gives access.

with pliers and sliding the clip back along the pipe. The pipe can then be worked off its stub. The filler pipe can be removed in the same way, except that it is secured by a screw-type clip. If you have difficulty reaching the hose connections, note that you can also reach them from inside the trunk, after you have removed the access cover forward of the tool recess. Note that this is the access point for the filler and vent hose upper connection points, should you need to replace them. There is a rubber closing seal around the stubs, and it and its metal surround should be removed after releasing the 10 mm headed nuts and bolts which retain them. Note that if there is still fuel in the tank, now is the time to remove it. We recommend one of those hand pumps sold in auto parts stores. Once you have started the flow of fuel from the tank filler opening into a sealable container suitable for gasoline, it should continue to siphon out as long as the container is below tank level.

32 Working through the larger aperture above the tank, disconnect the fuel gauge sender/fuel pump wiring connector and lodge the connector clear of the tank. (It's a good idea to pull the wiring out of the tank recess and tape it to the body so that it won't accidentally get trapped under the

15/32 Remove wiring and hoses.

tank during installation). Grasp the fuel delivery and return hose clips with pliers and slide them away from their stubs, then push the hoses off using the flat blade of a screwdriver, having first marked one of the hose ends and its stub with paint or typists correcting fluid as a guide during installation. Plug the hose ends with golf tees or similar, and cap the stub ends to exclude dirt from the fuel system. The vent hose can similarly be disconnected and taped up outside the access aperture.

33 Moving back under the car, you can now remove the four fixing bolts, making a note of the plates and rubber gaskets fitted either side of the tank flange. Since these are all that now hold the tank, be ready to support it as the fasteners are released. The tank can now be lowered and removed, maneuvering it round the subframe if this is still below the car.

INSPECTION AND REPAIR

34 Examine the tank for corrosion or damage and assess the best course of action. If the damage or corrosion is serious, a new tank should be fitted and, in view of the work needed to remove and install a tank, we would be inclined to fit a new one whatever the problem, just to make sure that you won't need to repeat the procedure in the near future. Minor damage may be repaired, but this **must** be entrusted to a professional welder. **Warning!** Fuel tanks are notoriously dangerous to repair by welding, for obvious reasons, and it is essential that it is steam cleaned first to remove any residual fuel vapor. (We know a guy who is very relaxed about welding fuel tanks. "No problem", he says, "You just put the torch to the tank filler and let the vapor burn away". He's an odd-looking guy, with no eyebrows or eyelashes).

35 Whatever you choose to do, you will first have to teardown the tank. Remove the crosshead screws which secure the fuel pump flange to the tank. Carefully free the flange and its seal from the top of the tank. The seal is pegged into the pump flange, but may be stuck to the tank; if so, work a screwdriver around the edge of the seal to free it.

36 Carefully remove the pump and fuel gauge sender as an assembly, noting that you will have to maneuver the assembly as it is lifted out so the fuel gauge sender float comes free of the tank. Don't bend the float arm, or the fuel gauge readings will be affected. Once you have removed the assembly, cover the hole in the tank with clean cloth to exclude dirt and minimize the escape of fuel vapor.

37 Next, remove the fuel vapor valve from the tank by removing the four crosshead screws which secure the valve to the tank. Release the single 10 mm headed bolt which retains the two-way check valve (three-way check valve, automatic transmission models) and lift away the two components leaving them connected together by the vent hose. If you intend to reuse the tank, make sure that it is clean inside, with no sediment lying around to block up the pump.

38 Install the removed components on the repaired or new tank, noting that the bolt securing the two-way check valve (three-way check valve, automatic transmission models) should be tightened to 3.9-5.9 Nm (40-60 kgf cm / 34-52 lbf in). When you fit the pump/sender assembly, be careful not to bend the float arm or you will get incorrect gauge readings. The fuel pump / fuel gauge sender flange screws have a torque range of 7.8-11 Nm (80-110 Kgf cm / 69-95 lbf in) and the fuel vapor valve screws should be tightened down to 1.1-1.6 Nm (11-17 kgf cm / 9.5-14.8 lbf in).

INSTALLATION

40 Fit the tank in the car, securing it with the bolts and retainer plates, noting that the bolts should be tightened to 22-30 Nm (2.1-3.1 Kgf m / 16-22 lbf ft). Remember to check during installation that any wiring or hoses have not become trapped under the tank. Reconnect the fuel pump and vent hoses, installing the securing clips where fitted, and ensuring that the hoses are pushed onto the stubs by at least 25 mm (1 in). Install the closing seal and its surround at the rear of the tank, tightening the fasteners to 7.8-11 Nm (80-110 Kgf cm / 69-95 lbf in). Reconnect the fuel filler and vent hoses, pushing the filler hose onto its stub by at least 35 mm (1.4 in) to ensure a good seal. Fit the hose retaining clips making sure that they are secure. Reconnect the fuel pump / sender wiring connector. Leave the access panels and deck carpet removed at this stage.

41 Working under the car, install the (preferably new) fuel filter and reconnect the hoses, securing them with their spring clips. It is a good idea to check all the disturbed connections at this stage. Fill the fuel tank, then temporarily reconnect the battery ☞ 7/2. Prime the fuel system (for details ☞ 5/13) which will show that the pump is operating correctly. Next, check all fuel line connection points for leaks - if necessary, depressurize the system and remake connections or fit new hoses if leaks are found. Check the fuel filler hose

15/41 Make sure hoses are secure.

for leaks, and check that the fuel gauge operates normally (check the wiring connections at the fuel tank flange if there is no response from the gauge). When you are satisfied that all is well, disconnect the battery negative (-) lead (☞ 7/2) and resume reassembly. Start by installing the rear deck inspection covers, and then fit the deck carpet.

42 Reposition the rear subframe and carefully jack it back into position, checking that nothing gets trapped or strained as it is raised. Install the subframe mounting bolts and nuts, tightening them evenly to 93-117 Nm (9.5-11.9 kgf m / 69-86 lbf ft). Where they were removed, make sure that you guide the bottoms of the suspension units into their recesses in the lower wishbone. Fit the suspension unit lower mounting bolts and tighten them to 73-93 Nm (7.4-9.5 kgf m / 54-69 lbf ft).

43 If the brake hydraulic system was disconnected, fit and secure the pipe unions, then bleed the hydraulic system at each rear caliper ☞ 9/2. Otherwise, fit the distributor block, tightening the mounting nuts to 13-22 Nm (1.3-2.2 kgf m / 9.4-16 lbf ft) Reposition the fuel filter cover and secure it with the two-piece plastic fasteners. Fit the wiring harness / battery cable guide to the subframe. Fit the brake cables, if removed, and secure

15/43 Install fuel filter cover.

their locknuts. Check and adjust the parking brake ☞ 9/20. Check that any accessory wires disconnected during removal are reconnected properly.

PPF INSTALLATION

44 From beneath the car put the PPF in place by sliding it forward onto its mounting on the right side of the transmission, then pushing it up around the side of the differential unit until it slides onto its mounting. Note: you may have to lift the propshaft flange end of the differential slightly to get the PPF to slide into engagement. The end of the PPF with round drillings is the differential end.

45 With the PPF roughly positioned, install the two 17 mm-headed bolts that pass through the lower flange of the PPF, up through the transmission casing and then screw into the top flange of the PPF. For the moment, these bolts should be left finger-tight.

46 Move to the rear end of the PPF and install the 17 mm through bolts that clamp the PPF to the side of the differential casing. Fit the bolt without a collar first, followed by the bolt with the collar. It's suggested that you spray the shanks of both bolts with WD40 or similar silicone-based lubricant as they seem prone to corrosion. You

may need to lift the nose of the diff casing a little to align the holes in the differential casing and the PPF. Tighten the two bolts snugly but not fully at this stage.

47 Move once again to the forward end of the PPF and install the transmission extension housing support bracket between the PPF and the tailhousing of the transmission. If you've used a rope or a jack to support the transmission, and it's in the way, you should remove it before installing the bracket. Hold the bracket in place above the lower flange of the PPF and finger-tighten the 17 mm retaining bolt. Insert the two 14 mm bolts that secure the bracket to the transmission tailshaft and, once again, tighten them finger-tight. You may need to lift the tail of the transmission slightly to make the bracket align with the threaded holes in the transmission casing. Tighten the two 17 mm PPF to transmission side bolts to a torque of 115 Nm (11.5 kgf m / 85 lbf ft).

48 Next, tighten the PPF to differential 17 mm side bolts to the same torque. Make sure the collar on the forward bolt is properly engaged in the recess in the PPF.

49 Move to the tailshaft support bracket and tighten the 17 mm bolts to the same torque as the other 17 mm bolts. Then tighten the bracket's 14 mm bolts to a final torque of 45 Nm / 4.5 kgf m/ 35 lbf ft.

WIRING LOOM FITTING TO PPF

50 Start to secure the loom by fixing its support bracket to the side of the transmission with the short, sheet metal screw provided.

51 Work your way along the PPF, pushing each loom retaining clip into place as you go. Note that the first clip, at the engine end, is at the top of the PPF and the second clip about halfway down the side of the frame. The following clips run along the frame about two thirds of the way down on the right-hand side, while the last two clips, at the axle end of the PPF, are at the top.

52 Toward the rear end of the PPF there is a ground (earth) wire sprouting from the loom which should be re-secured to the PPF by tightening its 10 mm retaining bolt. Note: before fastening the ground (earth) strap clean the eye and the contact area of the PPF with abrasive paper. Smear both with petroleum jelly (Vaseline) and then replace and tighten the screw.

PROPSHAFT INSTALLATION

53 Rub engine oil over the section of the propshaft that enters the transmission tailhousing and engages with the transmission mainshaft splines. This ensures that the transmission tailshaft oil seal is well lubricated.

54 Slide the front end of the propshaft into the tail end of the transmission unit: you may have to rotate the propshaft just a little to allow the splines to engage. Then, lift up the rear end of the propshaft and engage its flange with the differential drive flange, lining up the marks you made when the propshaft was removed. Fit the four bolts and nuts (nuts toward the front of the car) and tighten to a torque of 29 Nm (2.9 kgf m / 21 lbf ft). **Warning!** If the spring washers show any signs of having become flattened, they should be replaced. Note: you'll need to apply the parking brake in order to stop the propshaft rotating when you try to torque the nuts.

TRANSMISSION OIL

55 Now's a good time to refill the transmission with oil if it has been emptied. Manual transmission: first check that the 24 mm drain plug is tight, then remove the filler plug halfway up the left hand side of the transmission case. Add 2 liters (0.43 Imp gal / 0.52 US gal) of the approved gear oil and then replace and tighten the filler plug. If the transmission oil was not emptied, check oil level and top up as necessary ☞ 2/8 or 9. On automatic transmission cars, remember to check the transmission fluid level after installation is complete (☞ 2/9).

EXHAUST SYSTEM - INSTALLATION AS A ONE-PIECE ASSEMBLY

56 The following procedure deals with fitting the complete exhaust system as opposed to fitting a new system in parts. It is assumed that the whole exhaust, from manifold (header) flange to rear tailpipe, is in one piece and is exactly as it was when removed. It would, of course, be a false economy to fit a broken or corroded system. If you removed only part of the system in the course of this procedure, refer to the appropriate paragraphs of the installation sequence.

57 Slide the exhaust system along the ground until it is in approximately the correct position beneath the car. Note that the heatshields on top of various sections of the exhaust system should be in good condition and, where so marked, be correctly orientated.

58 Lubricate the studs on the exhaust manifold with copper-based grease. Slide a - preferably new - metal gasket over the studs, noting that no sealing compound is necessary if both mating faces are clean.

59 Have an assistant support the rear end of the system, while from beneath the car you begin to maneuver it into position. You'll find that you'll have to twist the system to one side a little in order to work the exhaust pipe flange past the bellhousing bracket, but once past the bracket it will comfortably slide up roughly into position.

60 When the flange at the front of the exhaust system engages with the three manifold studs, quickly spin on any one of the three nuts by a few turns and just leave it at that for the moment. Note: each of the three retaining nuts has a spring washer which should be replaced if it has become flattened.

61 Your assistant should now lift the rear exhaust box and fix it to the underside of the car by pushing the eyes of the rubber supports over pegs and hangers: this process is made so much easier by spraying the rubber supports with silicone-based lubricant, that it can then be done without tools.

62 Moving back to the front of the system, it should now be easy to push the exhaust system flange fully home against the manifold flange. Note: the three manifold flange nuts and washers are very difficult to get into place. I spent quite a lot of time cursing and trying to get one of the two lower nuts to nip the threads when, in fact, the easiest nut to place - and it can be without its washer initially - is the top nut. What you need here is an assistant who will reach through the gap between the front subframe and chassis from the left-hand front wheelarch to fit the nut to the top stud. Once you have a nut in place it becomes comparatively easy to fit the others.

63 You'll find the only way to tighten the manifold flange nuts is with a 14 mm socket attached to a universal joint attached to an extension of at least 360 mm (14 in), and then a ratchet or T-bar. Both of the lower nuts can be tightened from beneath the car; the top nut is most easily accessible via the left-hand front inner wheelarch. Torque the three nuts to 38 Nm (3.8 kgf m / 30 lbf ft).

64 Once the manifold flange nuts have been tightened, work your way back along the exhaust system fitting all of the rubber hangers. As mentioned before, a quick spray with silicone fluid will make this job so easy you can just push each rubber hanger over its pin with your fingers.

65 When all of the hangers are in place, come back to the front of the system and, after lubricating it with copper-based grease, insert the 12 mm bolt that fixes the exhaust pipe clamp to the bracket on the side of the bellhousing. The bolt can be inserted and tightened through the gap between the subframe and chassis rail in the left-hand front wheelarch. Torque the bolt to 24 Nm (2.4 kgf m/ 17 lbf ft).

66 That's about it. Mazda recommend that the rear suspension adjustment is checked and reset as required (☞ 7). We suggest that you get the alignment checked by a tire specialist, but there should be no reason why these settings would have been altered as a result of the procedures described above.

16. FUEL PUMP - REMOVAL & INSTALLATION

☞ 1/1, 2 & 5/13.

1 The fuel injection system is powered by a high-pressure electric fuel pump housed in the fuel tank. It is in practice a sealed-for-life unit, so the only reason you will need to remove it is for replacement, or for access to the low-pressure filter in the event of fuel contamination.

2 You should depressurize the fuel system (☞ 5/13) before starting work, and also remove the fuel filler cap to prevent any pressure buildup in the tank. **Warning!**: Have a fire extinguisher to hand, and make sure that you take sensible precautions to avoid any potential fire risk - the fuel tank will be open once the pump is removed, and there will inevitably be a lot of fuel vapor around. Disconnect the battery negative (-) terminal ☞ 7/2.

3 Working inside the car, carefully lever out the black plastic clips which secure the carpet to the rear deck. We found that the best technique for this was to use two flat-bladed screwdrivers or

cranked needle-nosed pliers to lift the clips. Don't be tempted to pull up on the carpet - it will just pull off over the clip heads. You need to remove sufficient clips to allow the carpet to be rolled back clear of the access cover above the fuel tank. You'll find that there are three bright metal access covers. Ignore the long cover at the front edge of the deck - we are interested in the larger of the two remaining covers. Remove the 10 mm screws which retain the cover and lift it away.

4 You now have access to the top of the fuel tank, and the fuel pump mounting flange, the fuel hoses and the associated check valve and

16/3 Remove this access cover.

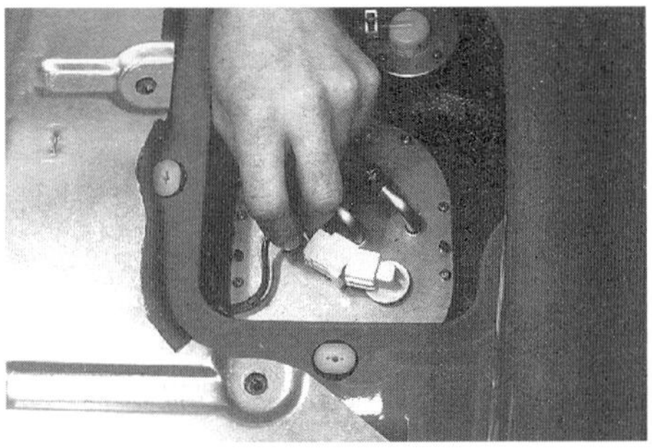

16/4 Unplug wiring connector.

vapor valve will be visible. Mark one of the fuel pipes and its stub with paint as a guide during reassembly, then release the hose clips with pliers and push the hoses off their stubs. Have some rag handy to catch any residual fuel; try not to let any fuel spills run down the tank or the car, and especially the trunk, will smell of gasoline. Disconnect the fuel pump wiring connector.

5 Remove the crosshead screws which secure the fuel pump flange to the tank. Carefully free the flange and its seal from the top of the tank. The seal is pegged into the pump flange, but may be stuck to the tank; if so, work a screwdriver

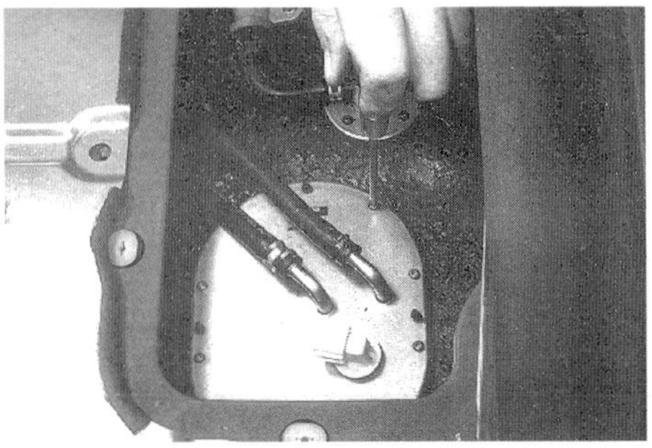

16/5 Remove hoses and then screws.

around the edge of the seal to free it.

6 Carefully remove the pump and fuel gauge sender as an assembly, noting that you will have to maneuver the assembly as it is lifted out so the fuel gauge sender float comes free of the tank. Don't bend the float arm, or the fuel gauge readings will be affected. Once you have removed the assembly, cover the hole in the tank with clean cloth to exclude dirt and minimize the escape of fuel vapor.

7 + Moving to a clean workbench, commence dismantling by removing the single screw which holds the metal baseplate to the pump

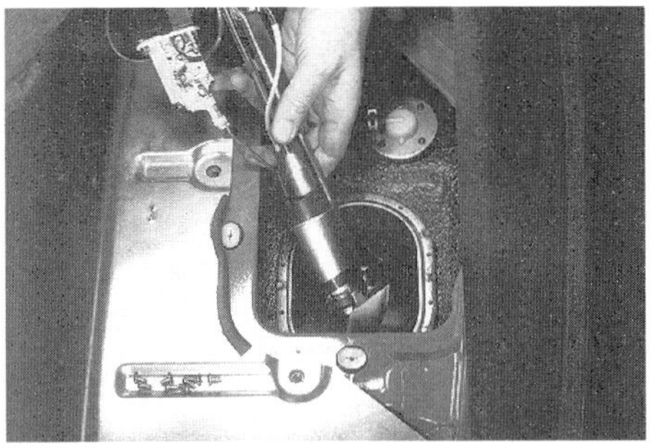

16/6 Lift out pump/sender unit.

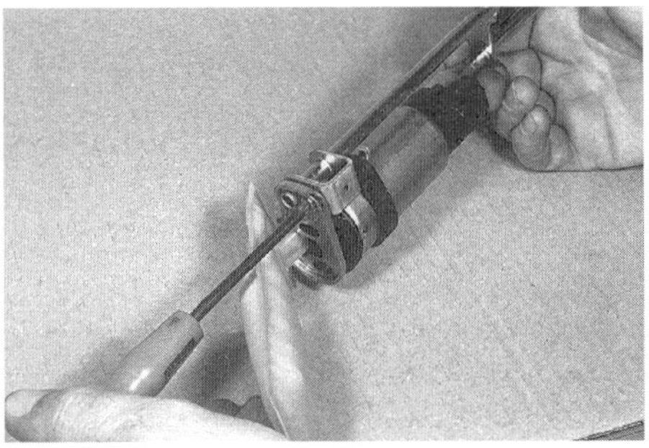

16/7a Remove screw ...

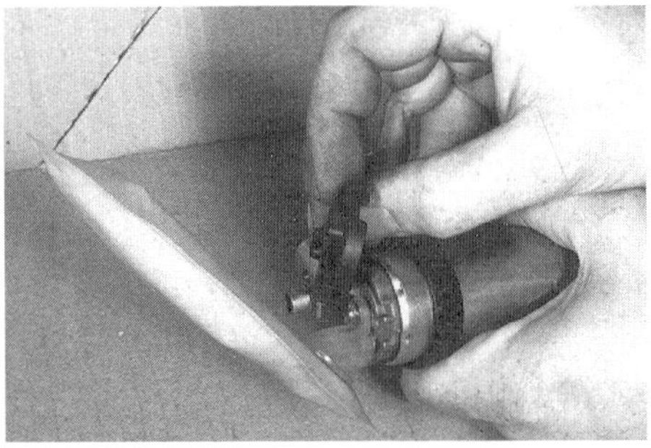

16/7b ... pull plate away ...

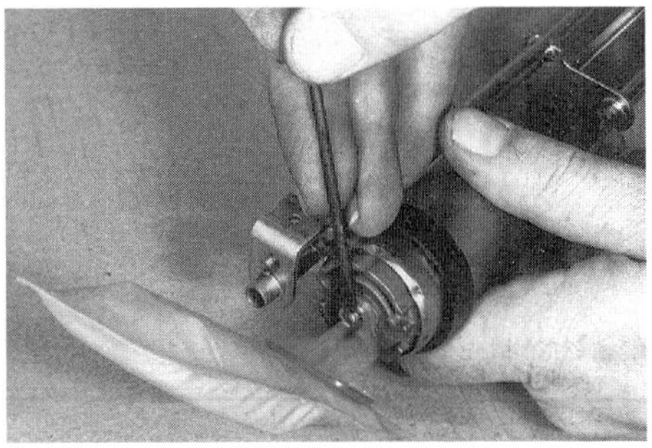

16/7c ... release spring clip ...

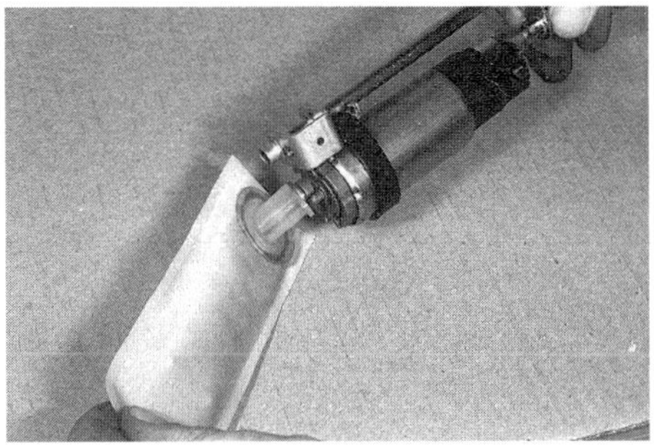

16.7d ... and remove filter.

support. The plate and the rubber pump seating can now be lifted away. The low pressure filter takes the form of a nylon gauze strainer and is held in place by a tiny spring clip. Be warned, this is another of those parts which will attempt escape when you try to remove it, so place some rag in front of it to impede its flight as you pry it loose. Carefully work it off the peg with a small flat-bladed screwdriver, moving it a little at a time to avoid damage.

8 Unplug the pump wiring connector from the top of the fuel pump. The connector will

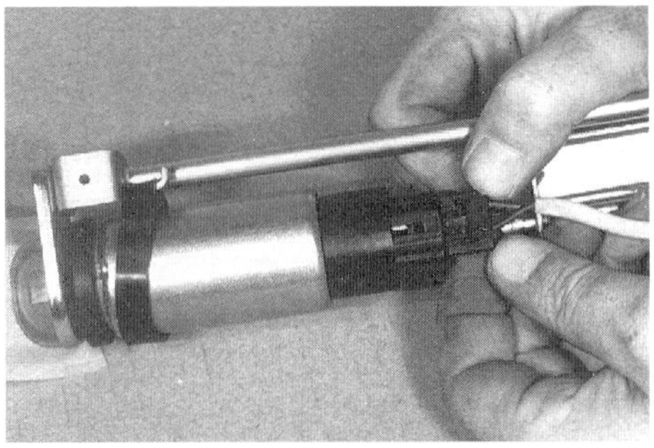

16/8 Unplug wiring connector.

be a particularly tight fit - we assume that this is intentional on the part of the manufacturer, and that it is meant to minimize the risk of the wiring coming unplugged in service and the consequent risk of an electrical spark in the fuel tank (Boom!). Now remove the serrated rubber band which supports the pump body on the side of the pickup pipe - note how this locates around the pump and pickup pipe as a guide during installation. You can now disengage the pump from its seating by pulling it down until it comes free of the socket.

9 + Whether or not you intend to fit a new pump, you must use a new O-ring seal during

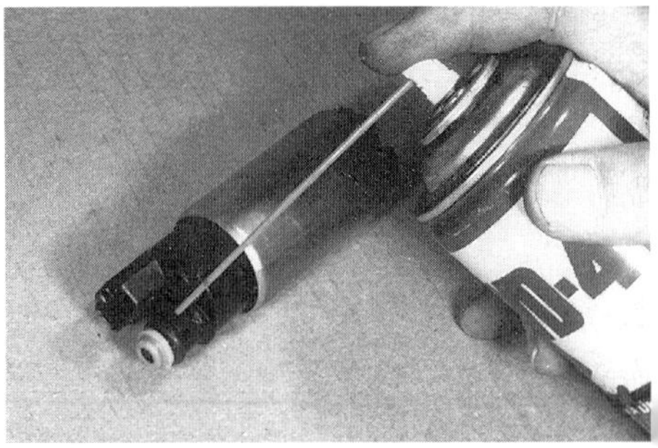

16/9a Lubricate O-ring.

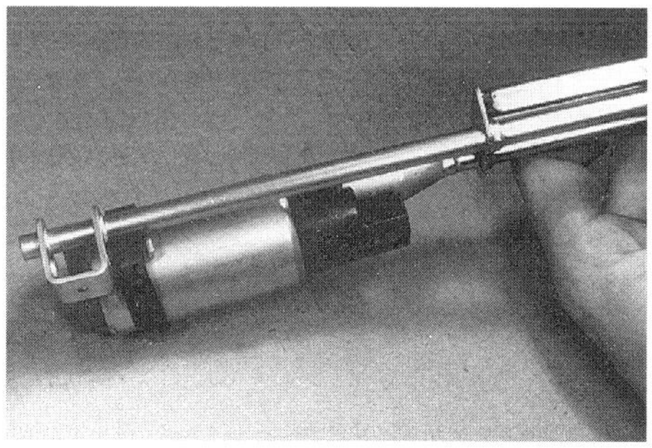

16/9b ... and fit pump to socket.

installation, or you may get leakage occurring. Apply a little oil to the O-ring to lubricate it during pump installation, and be sure to check that the pump seats securely and squarely. Fit the serrated band around the pump body and hook it over the bracket on the pickup pipe.

10 Clean the low pressure filter in a little clean gasoline. Allow it to dry off, then check it very carefully for holes or splits - if you find any, fit a new filter to avoid the risk of damage to the pump. Fit the filter, and carefully push the retaining clip fully home to secure it.

11 Place the pump seating in position, then fit the retaining plate and screw. We recommend that you apply a drop of nonpermanent thread-locking compound to the screw threads. Pull down on the pump body to make sure it seats correctly. Once assembled, it is a good idea to check that the pump is sealed correctly by blowing compressed air down the delivery pipe and making sure that it doesn't leak at the pump to pickup pipe joint. Plug in the pump wiring connector, ensuring that it snaps into place securely.

12 Check that the pump flange seal is correctly positioned and that it locating pegs are pushed though the holes in the flange. Maneuver the pump and fuel gauge sender back into the tank, again taking care not to bend the float arm. Fit the mounting screws, pulling them down evenly. Reconnect the fuel hoses and the external wiring connector. Note that the fuel hoses must be pushed onto their stubs by at least 25 mm (1 in) and their clips fitted securely to ensure a good seal.

13 It makes sense to check that everything works at this stage, before fitting the rear deck components. If there's no fuel vapor around, reconnect the battery negative (-) terminal (☞ 7/2), then go through the fuel system priming routine ☞ 5/13. While the jumper is in place during priming, you should hear the whine from the pump, indicating normal operation. Listen at the fuel filler opening with the filler cap removed. Assuming that all is well, fit the access panel and screws, then roll back the carpet and fit the retaining clips.

17. FUEL CIRCUIT OPENING RELAY - REMOVAL & INSTALLATION

☞ 1/1, 2.

1 The opening relay is housed inside the car, behind the access panel which covers the lower section of the steering column. Remove the two screws which secure the panel, unclip it from the dash panel and lift it away. The exact appearance of the opening relay varies according to market and, in all probability, will vary between models of different years. It is not uncommon for car manufacturers to source components like these from a number of suppliers, and insignificant variations like this are rarely documented.

2 In the case of UK market vehicles, including the one that the book is based on, the arrangement certainly differs from other European

17/2 Our car's fuel circuit opening relay.

market models. Mostly, this is due to the UK cars being right-hand drive, but in addition a different relay appears to be used in the UK. On our car, the relay was easy to identify - it is bright yellow, and is held by a single bolt to a bracket on the body. The multi-pin wiring connector can be unplugged with the relay in place, if required.

3 We know that in the case of cars sold in other European countries and in North America, the relay is mounted on the left of the car, again behind the steering column access panel. It seems to be of a different shape. We assume it to be functionally identical, but we cannot be precise in its description or location (or color!). It is relatively easy to pinpoint the opening relay as follows. Start the engine, and disconnect the wiring connector from what you think is the opening relay, leaving it disconnected for a few moments. If you have unplugged the opening relay, the fuel pump will cut off and the engine will stall.

4 If you need to fit a new relay, be sure to obtain it through a Mazda dealer, and let him know the vehicle's engine and chassis numbers to be sure of getting the correct part.

18. FUEL PRESSURE REGULATOR - REMOVAL & INSTALLATION

☞ 1/1, 2 & 5/13.

1 The fuel pressure regulator is held by two bolts to the rearmost end of the injector rail. If the fuel system checks described earlier in this chapter have indicated that replacement is required, first depressurize the fuel system ☞ 5/13.

2 Using a flat-bladed screwdriver, push off the small vacuum hose. Release the return hose clip, then push off the clip, using a rag to catch any residual fuel. Plug the hose with a golf tee, or similar, to prevent dirt entering the fuel system.

3 Remove the two screws and lift away the regulator, taking care to catch the O-ring which will drop free as you lift it clear of the injector rail.

4 Once removed, you only have two choices - reuse the old one or install a new one. Either way, use a new O-ring to seal it against the injector rail. Fit the return hose to its stub, securing it by sliding the hose clip back into position. Fit the vacuum hose.

5 Repressurise the fuel system ☞ 5/13. While the system is priming, check for signs of leakage at the return pipe to regulator joint. If there is a leak, depressurize the system and check the connection. Once you've checked and primed the system, remove the jumper wire from the diagnosis connector and close its cover. Fit the fuel filler cap, and check that the engine starts and runs normally.

19. FUEL INJECTORS & RAIL - REMOVAL, LEAK TESTING & INSTALLATION

☞ 1/1, 2 & 5/13.

1 Before starting work on the injector components, depressurize the fuel system (☞ 5/13), then disconnect the battery negative (-) terminal to isolate the electrical system ☞ 7/2.

2 Next, remove the airvalve (☞ 5/11) to gain working access around the injectors. You don't need to disconnect the airvalve hoses - just lodge the assembly out of the way. Disconnect the PCV (Positive Crankcase Ventilation) and vacuum hoses. Disconnect each of the injector wiring connectors.

3 Have some rag handy to catch any fuel spills. Mark one of the fuel hoses and its stub as a guide during installation, using tape or a paint mark. Release the fuel delivery and return hose

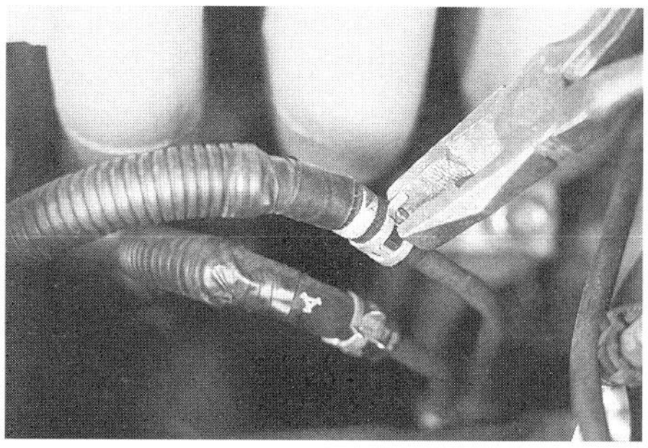

19/3 Disconnect fuel pipes.

clips, gripping the ends with a pair of pliers and sliding them up the hoses, clear of the stubs. Using a flat-bladed screwdriver, work the hoses off the stubs, pushing rather than pulling them. As the hoses come free, plug the open ends to exclude dirt. Golf tees make good plugs, or you can tape over the open ends.

4 Remove the two 12 mm headed bolts which hold the injector rail in place. These should be undone with a box end or crescent wrench as there's no real access for sockets. Withdraw the bolts leaving the fuel rail free for removal. **Caution!**

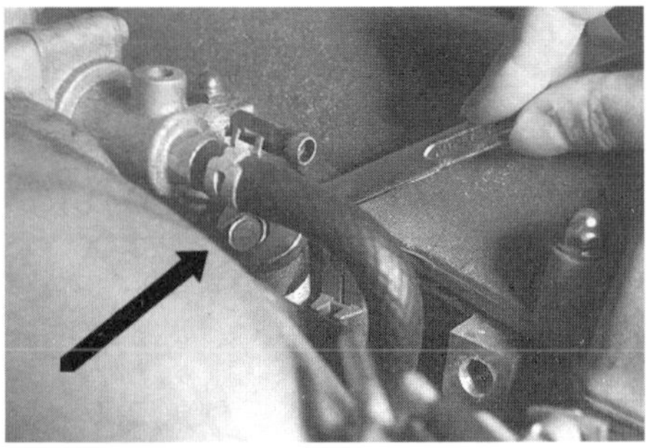
19/4 Remove injector rail bolts.

There are locating collars, between the rail and its two mountings, which will be dislodged as the fuel rail is moved and could easily be lost or damaged. Pull the rail assembly away from the manifold to release the injectors from their bores and then move the whole thing towards the rear of the engine and manipulate it up between the cambox and intake manifold plenum chamber, at the same time pull the injector wiring loom clear as necessary. **Caution!** As the injectors clear the manifold their individual insulators will come away with them, be careful not to lose these. Place the assembly on the workbench. It is a good idea to mark each injector and its position on the rail with blobs of paint - if you reuse the injectors it is preferable to install them in the same relative positions.

5 + The injectors can be checked for leakage as follows. Assemble the injectors on the injector rail, remembering to fit the grommet as the injector is installed. Secure the injectors in position using lengths of wire to hold them firmly against the rail. Temporarily reconnect the fuel hoses. Connect the battery negative (-) terminal (☞ 7/2), then prime the fuel system ☞ 5/13. While the system is priming, hold the injector rail with the

19/5a Wire injectors to rail ...

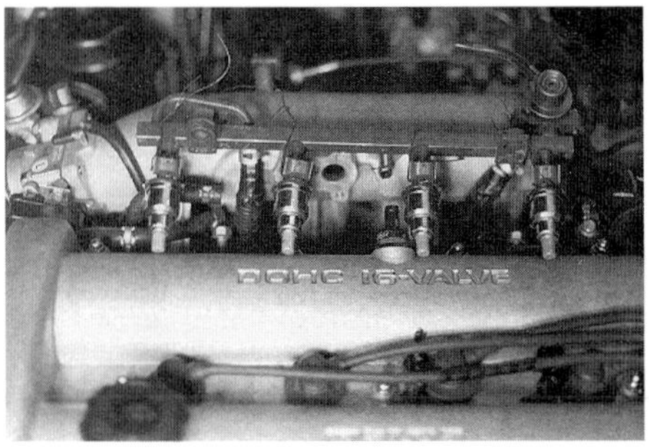

19/5b ... before testing.

injector pointing downwards at about 60°. There should be no obvious sign of leakage from any injector, though a single drop leaking after one minute is considered acceptable. If one or more injectors is leaking, replacement will be required, and it is good practice to replace them as a set.

6 After completing the leak check, depressurize the fuel system again, and then turn off the ignition switch and disconnect the battery negative (-) terminal. A little fuel may leak out when you disconnect the fuel hoses - prepare for this by wrapping the hose end in rag as it is pushed of its stub. **Warning!** Wear overalls and protective glasses to fend off any fuel spray.

7 Each injector is sealed to the injector rail by an O-ring seal fitted in a groove at the top of the injector. The O-ring should be replaced each time it is disturbed, using a small amount of oil to lubricate it during installation. Do not omit to fit the grommet which seals the base of the injector top. Make sure that the injector enters its bore squarely, or the injector or its O-ring may be damaged. You will also need a set of insulators to seal the injectors where they enter the injection ports.

8 During installation, tighten the injector rail bolts to 19-25 Nm (1.9-2.6 kgf m / 14-19 lbf ft).

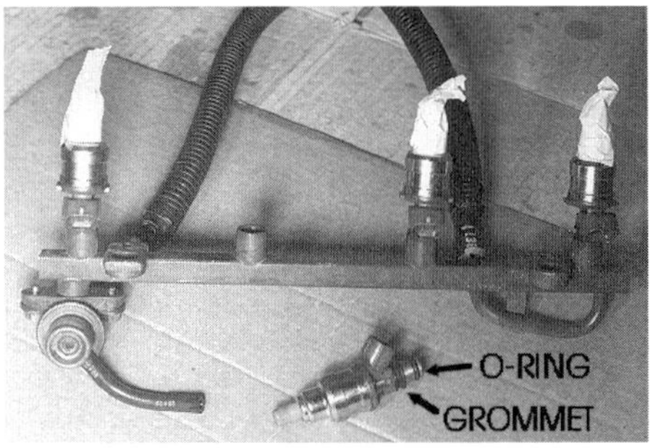

19/7 Injector removed from rail.

Reconnect the injector wiring, the fuel hoses and the PCV and vacuum hoses remembering to reposition the clips on the fuel hoses to secure them. Fit the airvalve. Prime the fuel system (☞ 5/13) and check for leaks. If all is well, remove the jumper wire from the diagnosis connector, start the engine and check that it runs normally.

20. FUEL FILTER - REMOVAL & INSTALLATION

☞ 1/1, 2 & 5/13.

1 This section deals with the removal and installation of the high-pressure fuel filter. For information relating to the low pressure filter attached to the fuel pump ☞ 5/16.

2 The main reason for removing the fuel filter is as part of the normal servicing schedule. The job is not in itself too difficult but the location of the filter, on the underside of the car, means that an inspection pit is needed or the car will have to be safely raised to get access: ☞ 1/3.

3 Moving under the car, locate the plastic cover at the rear of the floorpan which conceals the fuel filter. This is on the right side of the car, and is

20/3 Remove fuel filter cover.

held onto the body by cunningly designed plastic clips. At first sight, you might be forgiven for thinking that they were crosshead screws seated in cup washers. On closer examination, however, they turn out to be two-piece fasteners and they're not easy to remove: ☞ 1/2 (*Wrestling with two-piece plastic panel fasteners)*.

4 Back to the job in hand. Remove all the clips which hold the filter cover in place. Lift the cover away to reveal the filter and fuel hose connections.

5 Before you attempt to disconnect the hoses, be warned that any residual pressure in the tank will force fuel out at a surprising rate. You should remove the fuel filler cap to prevent pressure building up, but even then, once the hose is disconnected, fuel will siphon out of the tank. There is no way of avoiding this problem, but you can take measures to deal with it. Arm yourself with something to plug the open hose ends as soon as they are pulled off - golf tees worked well for us. Wear overalls to keep the gasoline off the skin. We further suggest that you wear safety glasses to keep gasoline splashes out of your eyes. Have everything ready so that once the hose is disconnected it can be plugged quickly to keep spillage to a minimum.

6 Using pliers, grip the ends of the fuel delivery pipe clip and slide it up the pipe and clear of the stub on the filter. (Note: check that you disconnect the hose running down from the fuel tank to the filter first). The stub is quite long - move the clip away by at least an inch or so. Using a screwdriver, push the hose off the stub (don't try pulling it off or it will just grip the stub tighter). The fuel system hoses are a tight fit on the metal pipes - they have to be because of the high fuel pressure they contain. If the hose won't yield to gentle screwdriver pressure, try fitting a pair of pliers loosely around the metal pipe and using the sides of the jaws to apply pressure to the hose end. Don't grip the pipe with the pliers, just let it slide over the pipe). As the hose comes away, quickly fit a golf tee to plug the end and prevent the tank contents siphoning out.

7 Next, repeat the procedure to free the outlet hose where it connects to the delivery pipe which runs forward to the engine compartment. There will only be a little residual fuel in the line, but plug it anyway to keep out any dirt. The filter unit is held by a bracket which is in turn bolted to the body. Remove the two 10 mm bolts which retain

the bracket to the body and lift away the filter with its bracket attached.

8 + The new filter comes complete with a mounting bracket and can be bolted to the body, preferably after you have connected the hoses. Fit the outlet hose first, followed by the inlet hose, securing both by sliding the clips back into position. Note that both hoses should be slid onto their stubs until they stop against the raised collar. Fit and tighten the two 10 mm mounting bolts to 7.8-11 Nm (80-110 kgf cm / 69-95 lbf in).

9 Before proceeding further, repressurise the fuel system (☞ 5/13) and check the hose

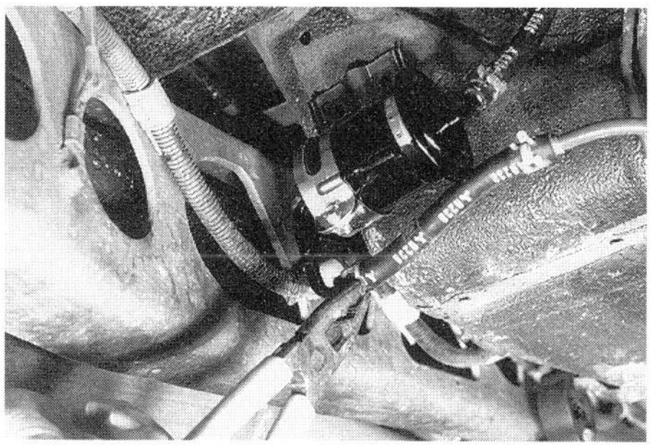

20/8a Reconnect hoses & clip securely ...

20/8b ... before securing new filter.

connections for leaks. If you need to check or fit either hose, remember to depressurize the fuel system first, or things get very messy! When all is well, fit the filter cover, securing it with the pesky plastic clips, then lower the vehicle to the ground.

21. EMISSION CONTROL SYSTEM - INTRODUCTION

1 The following sections describe work on the emissions-related systems and components. While it is tempting to overlook these areas of the car, they are fitted to minimize the pollution hazard presented by all motor vehicles, and in most parts of the world, fully operational emissions control systems are a legal requirement. Note also that if certain emissions-related subsystems are not working, or working inefficiently, the fuel economy and performance of the engine will be adversely affected. Most aspects of the emission control system are covered in the sections which follow; for details of catalytic converter inspection and replacement ☞ 5/38.

22. PCV VALVE - INSPECTION & REPLACEMENT

☞ 1/1, 2.

1 The PCV (Positive Crankcase Ventilation) valve is a passive device, operating under engine vacuum to draw crankcase gases from the cambox and allowing them to be drawn into the intake system, where they pass into the engine and are burnt. While the engine is switched off, the valve remains closed, trapping the gases in the engine. At idle, the valve opens slightly, drawing a small amount of crankcase gas back into the intake system. As engine speed rises, the valve opens wider to admit a greater volume of crankcase gases.

2 To perform a quick check of the valve's operation, disconnect it from the cambox cover by pulling it out of its rubber seat, leaving the vacuum hose in place. Start the engine and allow it to idle. If you now place a finger over the open end of the valve you should be able to feel the vacuum.

3 +Disconnect the valve from the hose, after releasing the retaining clip, and wipe it clean. The valve has stubs of unequal size; if you blow through the valve from the larger (cambox side)

22/3a To remove valve release clip ...

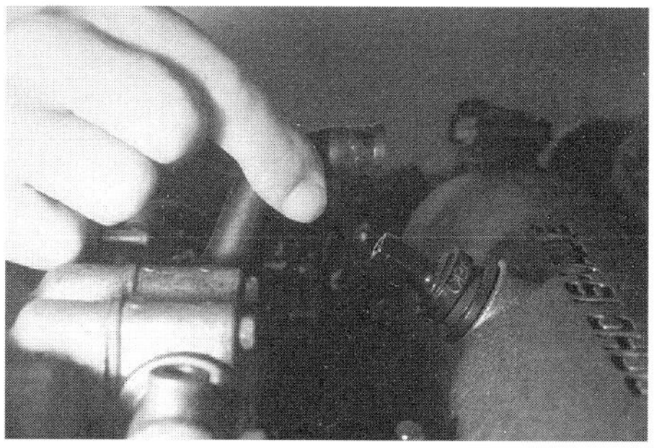

22/3b ... pull off hose & pull valve out.

stub, air should pass easily through the valve. If you now blow from the other end, air should not pass through the valve. If the valve is either completely blocked, or if it passes air both way, it should be replaced.

4 When installing the PCV valve note that it can only be fitted in one direction. Fit the valve to the vacuum hose and secure it with its hose clip, then fit the remaining end into the cambox cover.

23. EEC SYSTEM - COMPONENT INSPECTION & REPLACEMENT

☞ 1/1, 2 & 5/13.

1 The EEC (Evaporative Emission Control) system relates to the control of unburned hydrocarbons in the form of fuel vapor. For many years, the fuel system on motor vehicles incorporated various vents to allow for expansion and contractions within the fuel tank and carburettor, due to changes in the fuel level in the tank and variations in atmospheric temperature. Along with other manufacturers, Mazda employ a system which prevents the venting of fuel vapor to the atmosphere, and so reduces this aspect of atmospheric pollution.

2 One of the main problems is dealing with fuel vapor which would normally be expelled from the fuel tank while the vehicle is parked. This is accomplished by routing the vapor from the tank to a charcoal canister under the hood. The canister acts as a temporary store for the vapor. When the engine is next started, the ECU assesses operating conditions, and when certain criteria are met, allows the vapor to be purged by drawing it through the engine, where it is burnt along with the normal combustion mixture. The purge process is controlled by the ECU through a purge control valve. The ECU reads operating conditions from its various sensors, and uses this data to determine the rate at which purging takes place. This ensures that the process does not itself cause undue pollution by upsetting the combustion mixture.

3 In this section we look at the various EEC components, starting at the fuel tank and working forwards. The fuel vapor valve, the two-way check valve (three-way check valve, automatic transmission models), the charcoal canister and the associated pipework require attention during normal service intervals.

FUEL VAPOR VALVE

4 **Warning!** You must depressurize the fuel system (☞ 5/13) before starting work, and also remove the fuel filler cap to prevent any air pressure buildup in the tank . Have a fire extinguisher to hand, and make sure that you take sensible precautions to avoid any potential fire risk - there will inevitably be a lot of fuel vapor around.

5 Working inside the car, carefully lever out the black plastic clips which secure the carpet to the rear deck. We found that the best technique for this was to use two flat-bladed screwdrivers or a pair of cranked needle-nosed pliers to lift the clips. Don't be tempted to pull up on the carpet - it will just pull off over the clip heads. You need to remove sufficient clips to allow the carpet to be rolled back clear of the access cover above the fuel tank. You'll find that there are three bright metal access covers. Ignore the long cover at the front edge of the deck - we are interested in the larger of the two remaining covers. Remove the 10 mm screws which retain the cover and lift it away.

6 You now have access to the top of the fuel tank, and the fuel pump mounting flange, the fuel hoses and the associated check valve and vapor

valve will be visible. Have some rag handy to catch any residual fuel; try not to let any fuel spills run down the tank or into the car, especially the trunk, it will smell for weeks afterwards.

7 The fuel vapor valve's purpose is to allow vapor to pass through it, but to shut off this outlet in the event that the car rolls over in an accident. You can check that this is the case after removing the valve from the tank by disconnecting the hose (held by a spring clip) and then removing the screws which secure the valve to the tank.

8 With the valve removed, hold it in its normal position (pipe stub at the top) and blow

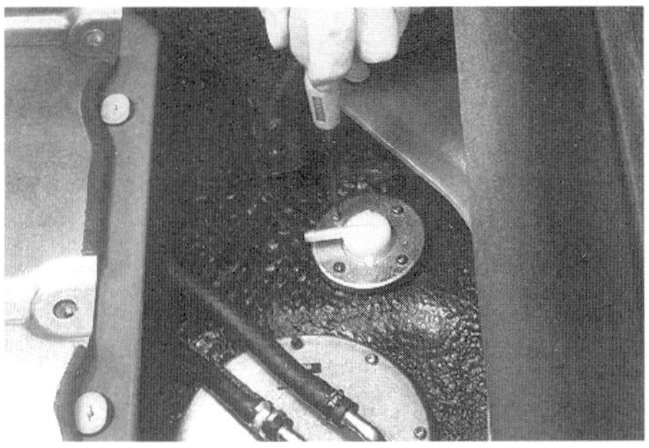

23/7 Remove vapor valve's screws.

through the stub. Air should pass with little resistance. Now turn the valve over so that the stub is at the bottom and repeat the check. The valve should be closed, obstructing the flow of air.

9 If the valve does not work as described, the official remedy is to fit a new one. We found that the valve is both simple to dismantle and in construction, so if it is not working, you may as well check to see if the problem can be fixed before fitting a new one. Unclip the metal cover from the end of the valve body and tip out the spring and valve plunger. Check the conical tip of the plunger

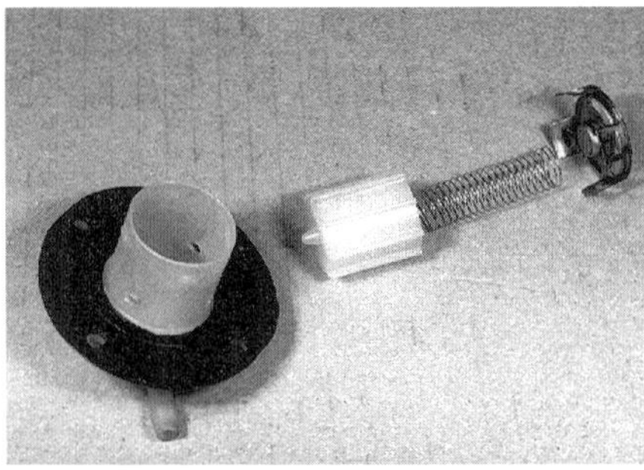

23/9 Components of the vapor valve.

and its seat in the body for dirt - if the valve was not sealing this could well be the cause. Make sure that the plunger slides freely in the body, and that there are no obvious signs of damage at the sealing point. If the problem was dirt, cleaning the valve components will probably cure the fault. If damage was discovered, replace the valve. If you are intending to reuse the valve after cleaning, reassemble carefully, making sure that the end cover is clipped into place over the body.

10 Fit the valve to the tank and secure it with its four retaining screws. Do not fit the access

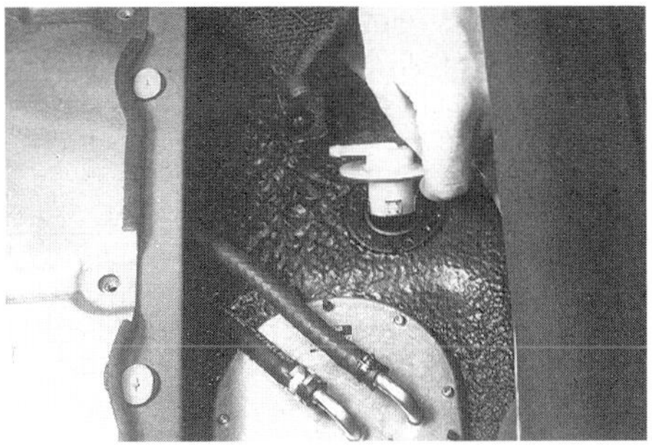

23/10 Refit vapor valve.

panel yet - you need to check the operation of the two-way check valve as described below.

TWO-WAY CHECK VALVE (THREE-WAY CHECK VALVE, AUTO TRANS MODELS)

11 + The check valve is accessed through the fuel pump access panel, the removal of which is described above. Disconnect the pipes after sliding back the retaining clips, then remove the single 10 mm bolt which retains the valve.

12 The official checking procedure is to apply a specified vacuum from a vacuum pump at

23/11a Release hose and then ...

23/11b ... unscrew check valve's bolt.

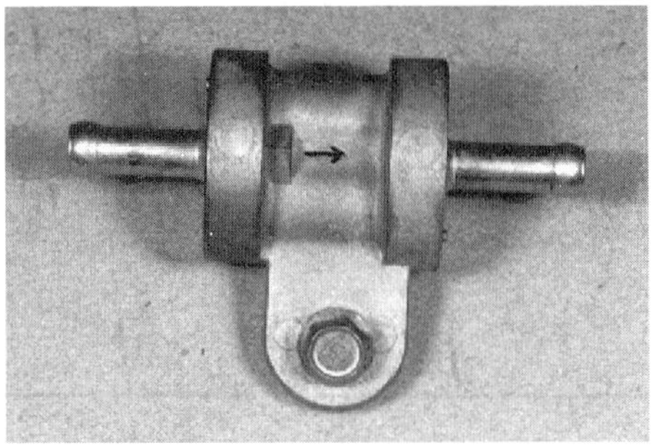

23/12 Two-way check valve.

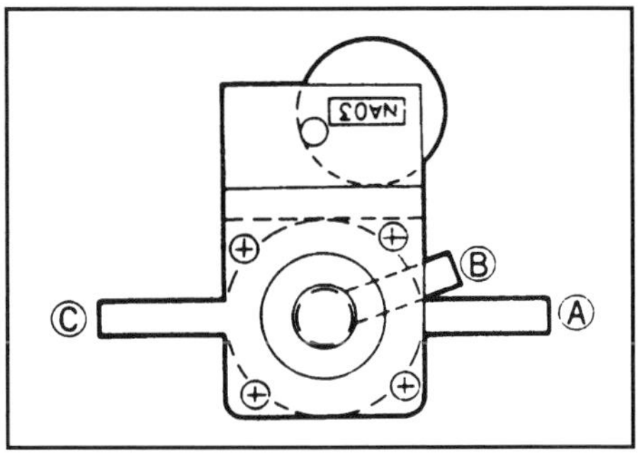

D23/12 THREE-WAY CHECK VALVE.

the valve stubs. Note the arrow mark on the valve body. If you apply approx 37 mm Hg (1.46 in Hg) at the stub furthest from the arrow head, air should flow through the valve. Applying 44 mm Hg (1.73 in Hg) at the other stub should produce the same result. Not having a vacuum pump handy, we translated this into blowing through the valve and noting that there was a greater resistance in one direction than the other. Not precise, but a fair indication. If the valve is either completely blocked, or shows no resistance, replace it. On cars fitted with automatic transmission, a three-way check valve is used. Referring to the accompanying diagram, plug port **C** and apply vacuum to ports **A** and **B** in turn. Air should flow when approximately 37 mm Hg (1.46 in Hg) is applied to port **A**, and when 70 mm Hg (2.76 in Hg) is applied to port **B**.

13 After fitting the valve (tighten the single bolt to 3.9-5.9 Nm (40-60 Kgf cm / 34-52 lbf in), make a final check of the various hose connections, then fit the access cover and rear deck carpet.

EEC HOSES

14 Make a visual check of the EEC hoses running from the check valve, along the underside of the car, and up to the charcoal canister, purge control valve and intake system. Replace the hose(s) if damaged or if they appear aged.

CHARCOAL CANISTER

15 Working under the hood, locate the charcoal canister which fits into a bracket near the coolant reservoir. Disconnect the vent and smaller vacuum hoses from the canister top, then pull the canister up and clear of its mounting bracket. Disconnect the remaining hose, and remove the canister for inspection.

16 Check the canister body for damage and signs of leakage. Check also for indications of

23/15 Charcoal canister location.

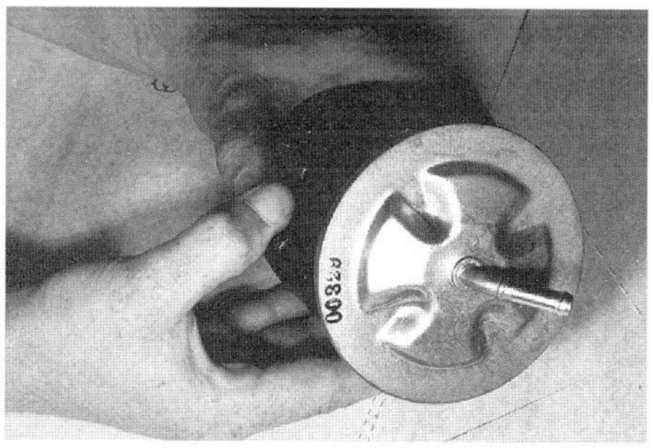

23/16 Check canister body.

corrosion on the metal end plate. If found, a new canister must be fitted - repair is not practical. Fit the canister, noting that the lower hose should be fitted before the canister is installed in its bracket. Once in position, connect the remaining vent hose and the vacuum hose.

SOLENOID (PURGE CONTROL) VALVE

17 The solenoid valve is operated by the ECU and controls the venting of the charcoal canister. It is located close to the canister on the right side inner wing. Check the valve with the

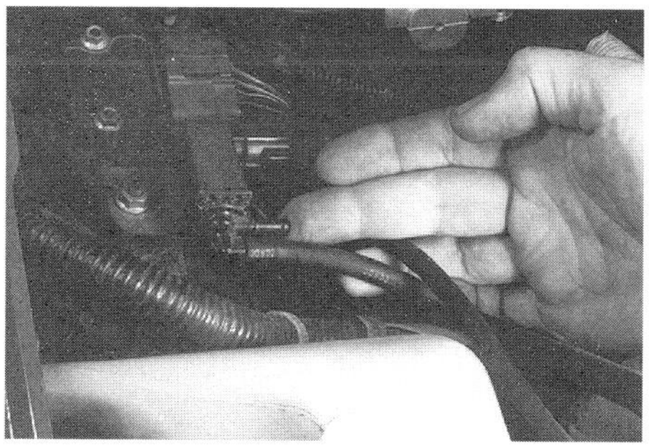

23/17 Testing purge valve.

engine at normal operating temperature. With the engine idling, disconnect the vacuum hose (upper stub) and place a finger over the open stub. Check that no vacuum can be felt. Turn the ignition switch off.

18 With both hoses and the wiring connector disconnected, remove the single mounting bolt and lift the valve away for inspection. Check that with no power applied, the valve does not allow air to flow in either direction.

19 With the unit on the bench, connect a 12 volt supply to the wiring terminals, the positive (+) lead to the terminal pin nearest the end of the valve unit, negative (-) to the remaining terminal. The valve should produce an audible click, and air should now flow through it. It is not possible to repair the valve - if it doesn't work as described, fit a new one.

24. DECELERATION CONTROL SYSTEM - CHECKS & ADJUSTMENT

☞ 1/1, 2.

1 The deceleration control system is designed to improve fuel economy and to reduce uneven running during deceleration. A fuel cut function is controlled by the ECU, drawing readings from the crank angle sensor, the throttle sensor and the cooling system thermosensor to determine at what point the fuel supply to the injectors should be cut. In addition, a small dashpot device is employed to prevent the throttle valve snapping shut when the accelerator pedal is released, smoothing the transition back to idle.

2 Check the fuel cut function ☞ 5/4/226. Check the operation of the crank angle sensor (☞ 5/29), the throttle sensor (☞ 5/32) and the cooling system thermosensor (☞ 5/31).

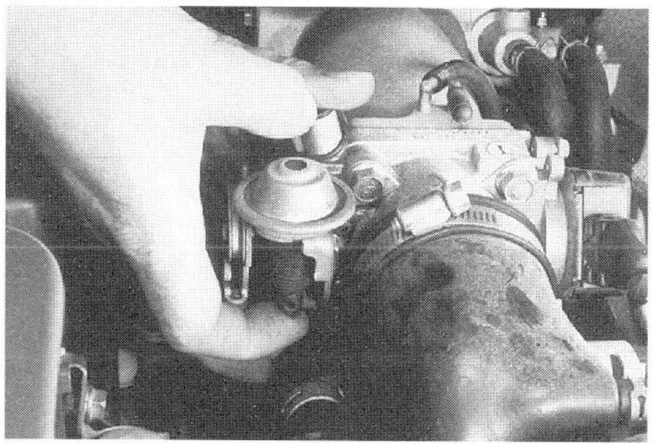

24/3 Testing dashpot.

3 To check the dashpot, hold open the throttle pulley with one hand, and press in the dashpot rod with a finger. It should offer resistance when depressed, but should move back quickly when released. We tried this check and, although the dashpot seemed to be working normally, we found it impossible to say for sure that it conformed to this check. In practice, you may be better off removing the dashpot and comparing it with a new one - be nice to your Mazda dealer: he should be able to help out here.

4 To check the dashpot adjustment, proceed as follows. Open the Diagnosis Connector and connect an external tachometer probe to the IG terminal. If the tachometer requires an external power feed, connect it to the blue single-pin power connector, taking care not to allow it to short to ground (earth).

24/5 Dashpot detail.

5 With the engine warmed up and idling, raise the engine speed to 4,000 rpm, then slowly reduce it until the throttle pulley lever touches the dashpot rod, noting the tachometer reading. The specified engine speed at this point is 2,500 ± 150 rpm. If necessary, adjust the dashpot by slackening the locknut and turning the dashpot body. Repeat the check, and once the dashpot is set correctly, tighten the locknut.

25. DECHOKE CONTROL SYSTEM - DESCRIPTION

☞ 1/1, 2.

1 The Miata/MX5 features a dechoke control system designed to allow a flooded engine to be cleared. If a cold engine is inadvertently flooded with gasoline while attempting to start it, depress the accelerator fully. This locks out the injection system, allowing the excess fuel to be cleared quickly (hopefully, before you flatten the battery). Note that the system only works with a cold engine.

2 There are no general checks of this sub-system, but given the marginal battery capacity, we thought you might like to be reminded of its existence, should you get the engine gassed up one morning.

26. IGNITION SYSTEM - INTRODUCTION & TIMING ADJUSTMENT

☞ 1/1, 2.

1 The ignition system on the Miata/MX5 forms part of the Engine Management System (EMS). The ECU controls the igniter, which in turn feeds ignition pulses to each of the two coil assemblies in turn. These pulses discharge through the primary windings of the coils, inducing the high-tension ignition at the plug electrodes. The ECU also reads back data from the igniter, which provides it with information on engine speed. The igniter also drives the vehicle's electronic tachometer.

2 There are few regular maintenance tasks to be performed on modern electronic ignition systems. Apart from periodic checking and adjustment of the ignition timing, which we cover below, maintenance is confined to fitting new spark plugs at the prescribed service interval, and making sure that wiring connections are kept clean and dry. If you have an ignition problem, it is worth performing the timing check first. If this fails to resolve the fault, there is a range of system and component checks to help you track down the cause ☞ 5/27.

CHECKING AND ADJUSTING THE IGNITION TIMING

3 To carry out this check, you will need an accurate test tachometer and a timing light. You should also check the timing marks on the lower

(crankshaft) pulley and the nearby scale. Clean the marks and, if necessary, use typists correction fluid to make them more visible. The test should be conducted at normal operating temperature, so run the engine for a while before starting the test, or do it after a run.

4 Open the diagnosis connector cover and connect the timing light and tachometer trigger leads to the **IG** terminal. Note that if your tachometer needs an external power feed, connect this to the single-pin blue power connector (take care not to short this to ground (earth).

5 If you are the lucky owner of SST 49 B019

26/4 Location of power connector.

9A0, connect it to the diagnosis socket and set the main switch to position 1 and the test switch to **SELF TEST**. Mere mortals (like us) can skip the SST and just fit a jumper wire between terminals **TEN** and **GND** in the diagnosis socket instead.

6 + Start the engine, and if necessary adjust the idle speed to the specified 850 ± 50 rpm. **Warning!** Keep the timing light and your fingers clear of the drivebelts. Aim the light at the timing marks near the bottom pulley at the front of the engine. The mark on the pulley should appear frozen at 10° ± 1° against the scale. If adjustment is needed, slacken the crank angle sensor 12mm lock

26/6a Where you'll find strobe timing marks.

26/6b Using a strobe light.

26/6c Timing marks 'frozen' by strobe.

bolt just enough to allow it to be moved, adjust the sensor position until the timing is correct, then retighten the lock bolt to 19-25 Nm (1.9-2.6 kgf m / 14-19 lbf ft).

7 Recheck the timing setting, then gradually increase engine speed and confirm that the ignition timing mark advances in relation to the scale. If it fails to do so, you will need to check the ignition system as described below. Finally, disconnect the tachometer and timing light, remove the jumper lead (or SST) and close the diagnosis connector cover.

27. IGNITION SYSTEM CHECKS

☞ 1/1, 2.

Warning! High voltages are present in the ignition system, and shocks from the plugs or plug leads can be dangerous. During any check, handle the plugs, leads and terminal caps with insulated pliers only.

SELF-DIAGNOSIS CHECKS

1 The Miata/MX5 has provision for self-diagnosis, assuming that you have the required SSTs (Special Service Tools). We have assumed that this type of equipment is going to be confined to Mazda dealers, and suggest that if you have an ignition fault, you could save a lot of time and effort by getting your Mazda dealer to run the self-diagnosis sequence for you. This should pinpoint the cause of the problem quite quickly. If you have access to the required equipment and wish to carry out the self-diagnosis sequence ☞ 5/4.

2 If you don't have access to the SSTs or a Mazda dealer, you can follow the checking sequence outlined below. This will cover most of the likely ignition faults, but not ECU-related problems, but at least you will have done what you can to avoid professional involvement. We're inclined to be philosophical about this situation. We figure that if you know you have a fault, it is cost effective to get it checked out by your dealer, rather than waste a lot of time trying to figure it out at home. (Wally, our technical adviser, often complains that technical sophistication is bad news for the enthusiast owner, but we bet he complained when coil ignition replaced hot tubes). We digress ...

SPARK PLUGS

3 + Welcome back all you non-SST owners! If you suspect an ignition problem, start by checking for a spark at the plugs. Remove one plug

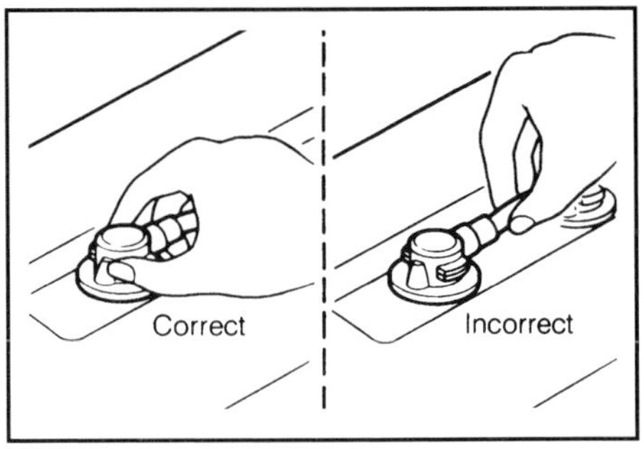

D27/3 HOW TO REMOVE PLUG CAPS.

27/3a Pull off terminal cap ...

27/3b ... and unscrew spark plug.

lead by pulling off the terminal cap and unscrew and remove the plug. Fit the plug into its terminal cap after removal.

4 Using insulated pliers, hold the plug so that the plug body is 5-10 mm (0.2-0.4 in) from the cambox cover - the plug terminals should be visible and not grounded (earthed). **Warning!** Ignition systems generate high voltages which can be dangerous if mishandled - be sure that your insulated pliers are undamaged and dry before use. Have an assistant crank the engine while you observe the

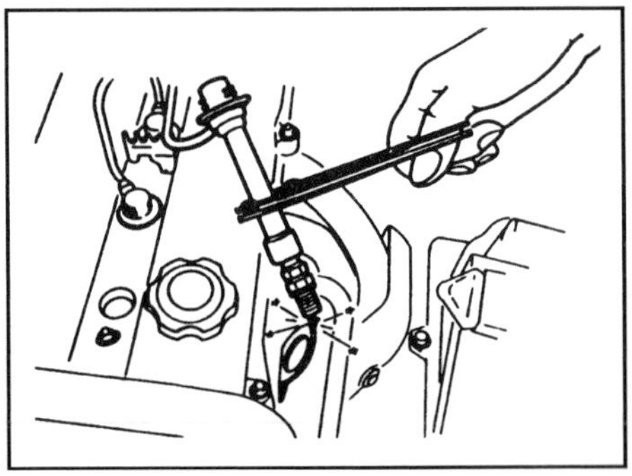

D27/4 TESTING SPARK PLUG.

plug. A strong, blue spark should jump across from the plug to the cambox cover if all is well.

5 If the spark is absent or a weak yellowish color, try a new plug and repeat the check. If you now have a strong spark, you can assume that the original plug is faulty. Don't assume that the plug is serviceable just because it looks OK; plugs can look fine, and even spark convincingly at atmospheric pressure, but once under combustion pressures can fail or operate intermittently. Plugs are cheap - our advice is to fit new ones whenever you suspect a fault. That way you can be reasonably certain that you have eliminated one possible source of trouble. Repeat the check on the remaining plugs, noting that it is preferable to replace the plugs as a set.

6 + Check the electrode gap with feeler gauges or a plug electrode gauge before you fit the new (or used) plugs - this should be set to 1.0-1.1 mm (0.039-0.043 in). If you need to adjust the gap, we recommend that you use a commercially available plug gapping tool. Set the gap by bending the outer, ground electrode only - if you put pressure on the center electrode you will almost certainly damage the porcelain insulator nose. Fit the new plugs using an anti-seize compound on the threads and tightening them to 15-32 Nm (1.5-2.3 kgf m, 11-17 lbf ft) and see whether this has resolved the problem.

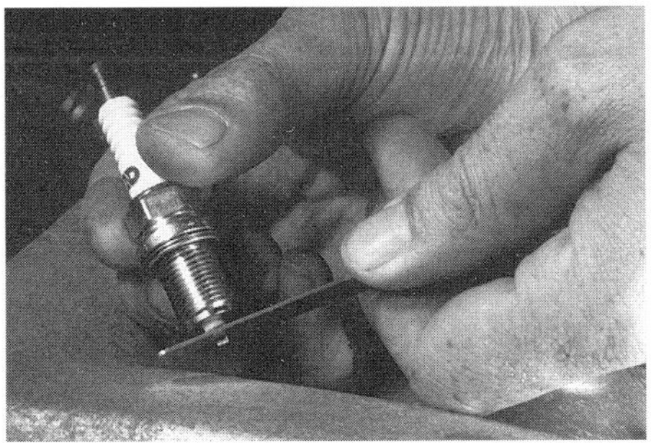

27/6a Measure and adjust plug gap ...

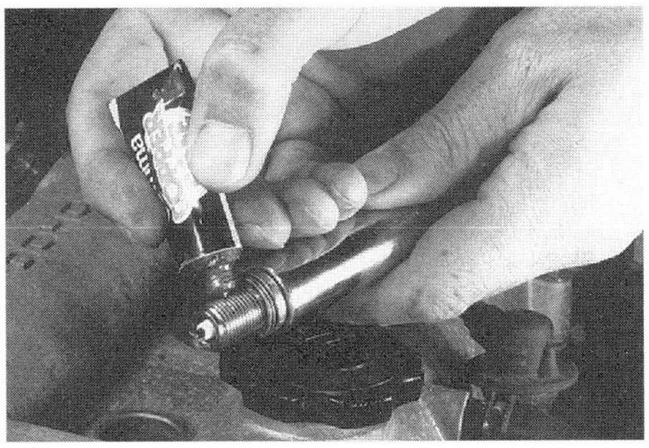

27/6b ... copper-based grease on threads ...

27/6c ... torque tighten.

7 Note that if you find a strong spark on two plugs, and a weak or nonexistent spark on the remaining two, this points to a coil failure. The Miata/MX5 utilizes a 'spare spark' ignition system. There are two double-ended coils, each coil operating two plugs simultaneously. This means that the plugs each spark twice during an engine cycle, one of the sparks being wasted, or 'spare' during the exhaust phase. It follows that if you discover a fault on two plugs you are likely to find that they share the same, defective, coil.

SPARK PLUG LEADS

8 Next check the plug lead resistances using an ohmmeter. Disconnect and remove each lead in turn and check the resistance between the terminals at each end. The correct resistance figure is 16 kΩ per meter - you'll have to measure the length of the lead to calculate the appropriate value; for example a 45 mm lead should read 7.2 kΩ. You can expect a little variation from the recommended figure, but if the resistance is very high, assume that the lead needs replacement. Note that if one plug (HT) lead has failed, the others are likely to follow suit; replace them as a set.

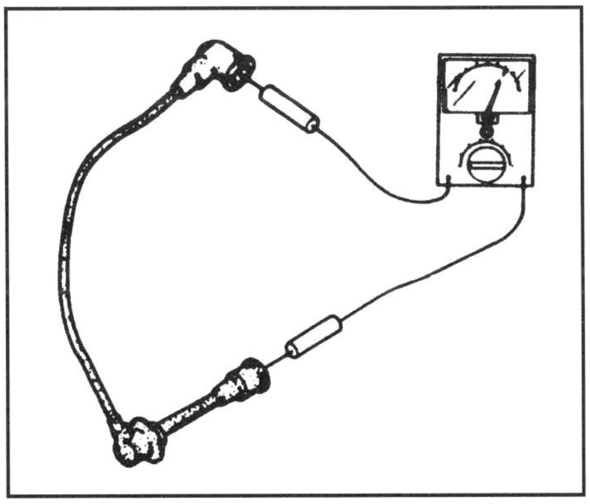

D27/8 CHECKING HT LEAD RESISTANCE.

IGNITION COILS

9 Disconnect the three-pin connector from the ignition coil. Using a voltmeter, check for battery voltage (12 volts) between the positive (+) terminal of the wiring side of the connector and ground (earth). If no reading is shown, check back through the main fuse, ignition switch and wiring harness until you locate the cause of the failure.

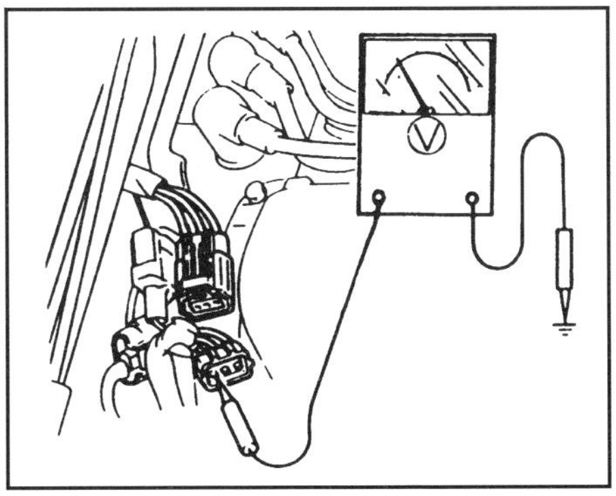

D27/9 CHECKING COIL CONNECTOR - WIRING SIDE.

10 On the coil side of the three-pin connector, check the resistance of the coil primary windings with an ohmmeter. Refer to the accompanying diagram and measure the resistance of each coil. At 20°C (68°F) this should be 0.78-0.94Ω.

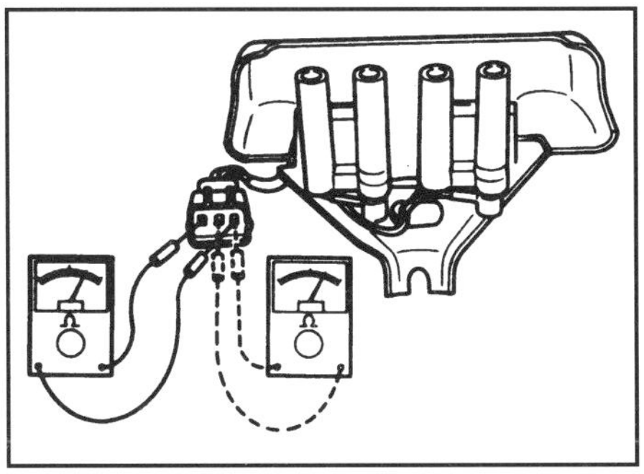

D27/10 CHECKING COIL CONNECTOR - COIL

11 Next, you need to check the coil secondary winding resistances. This measurement is made between adjacent pairs of HT terminals on the coil unit. The correct resistance figure is 11.2-15.2 kΩ at 20°C (68°F).

12 The final coil check is to measure insulation resistance between the coil primary terminals and the coil casing as shown in the accompanying diagram. You will need a 500V megger to perform the test. This is specialized equipment, unlikely to be readily available to most owners, so it is probably best to remove the coils and get an automotive electrical specialist to do the test for you. The specified resistance is 10MΩ.

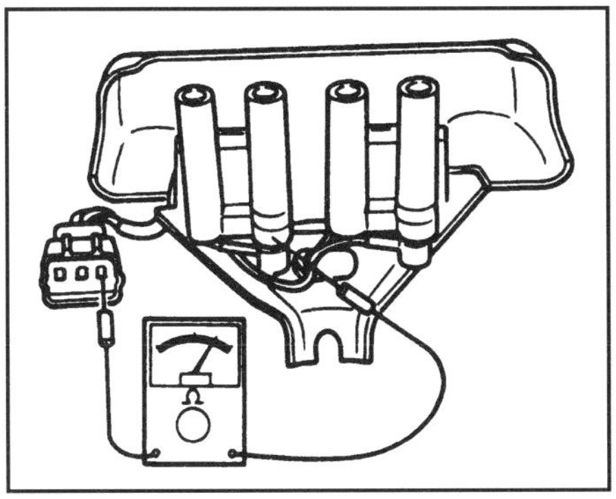

D27/12 CHECKING COIL INSULATION RESIS-

IGNITER

13 To check the igniter you will need two special service tools and a voltmeter. We describe the procedure here for reference, but in practice it is probably better to take the vehicle to a Mazda dealer to have the test done (the test is done on-vehicle).

14 Disconnect the igniter wiring connector. Connect the Igniter Checker (49 F018 002) to the Adaptor Harness (49 N018 001). Plug the

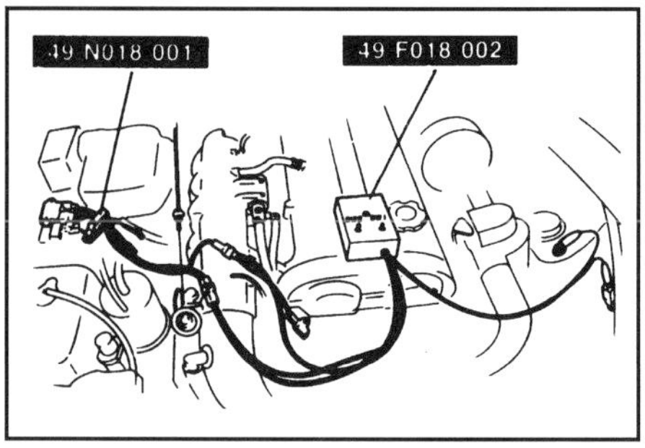

D27/14 CHECKING THE IGNITER/1.

adaptor harness between the igniter and its wiring connector as shown in the diagram, then connect the Adaptor Harness power lead to the vehicle's single-pin blue power connector. (Be careful not to accidentally ground (earth) the power connector. Connect the voltmeter positive (+) probe to the brown wire of the Adaptor Harness, and the voltmeter negative (-) probe to ground (earth).

15 Turn on the ignition switch and check that you have 12 volts showing. If not, check the wiring connections. Once 12 volts are showing,

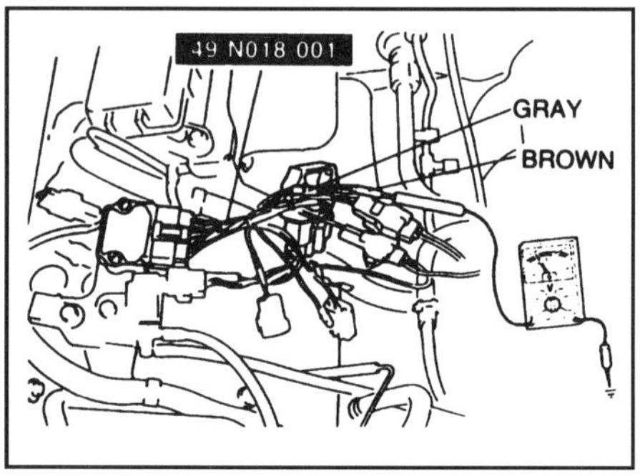

D27/15 CHECKING THE IGNITER/2.

press SW2 on the Igniter Checker **for no more than two seconds. Caution!** Exceeding the two second limit for this test could itself cause damage. The voltmeter reading should drop to around 8 volts. Switch off the ignition.

16 Now disconnect the voltmeter positive (+) probe from the brown wire, and connect it to the

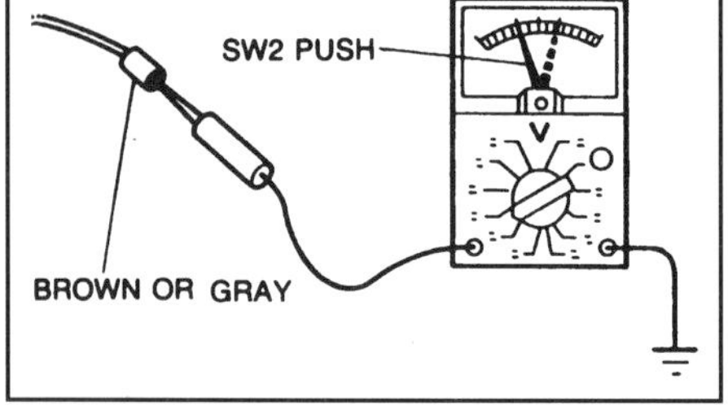

D27/17 CHECKING THE IGNITER/3.

gray wire of the Adaptor Harness. Repeat step 16.

17 If the reading obtained is out of specification, fit a new igniter.

28. ECU - LOCATION & TESTING

☞ 1/1, 2.

1 The Engine Control Unit (ECU) can be regarded as the 'brain' of the vehicle. As we have described earlier in the chapter, the ECU is a dedicated microcomputer. It reads in data from a range of sensors around the vehicle, and uses this information to control the Engine Management System (EMS).

2 As a subject for home diagnosis, the ECU poses something of a problem. To do the job correctly, you would need the following special

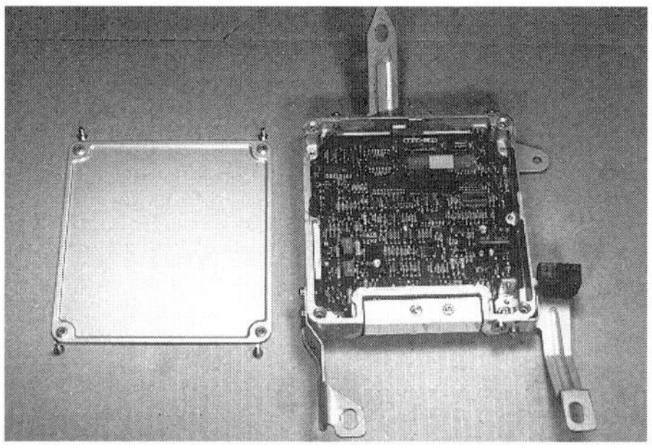

28/1 Inside the ECU.

service tools (SSTs): Engine Signal Monitor (49 9200 162), Adaptor (49 G018 903) and overlay sheet for the monitor (49 G018 904). This equipment costs serious money, and is not something you would normally consider buying for occasional use. However, without the right equipment, there is no way you can undertake diagnosis of the ECU. Be warned that the use of the wrong test equipment could cause irreparable damage to an otherwise functional ECU, so don't start fooling around with test meters unless you know what you're doing.

3 We reckon that the best course of action if you suspect an ECU fault is to take the car into a Mazda dealer for the diagnosis work to be carried out. This may offend the real enthusiasts out there, but it is the only really cost-effective option - working at home you are forced to work on a trial-and-error basis, and with a modern engine management system you could be doing it for ever! The dealer may go through the full check sequence, though it is common practice in the automotive trade simply to substitute a new (or known good) ECU to localize the problem. That way, the operator can quickly say "Yep - the ECU is burned out" - or not as the case may be - without a laborious and complex diagnostic procedure to follow.

4 This last procedure might possibly offer an option for the enthusiast owner; if you know another Miata/MX5 owner *really* well, you may be able to persuade them to let you swap ECUs to check a fault, but be warned, if the problem that damaged your ECU remains unresolved, it could do the same to the substitute, and so you could end up buying two new ones ...

5 So what approach should you take with ECU problems - is it really 'take it to your dealer' time? Well, maybe. Before you do, there are two basic rules to note. First, there is a good chance that the fault is in a related sensor, solenoid or whatever, not the ECU itself, so if you've got a fault, check what you can first. Go back over the outline at the beginning of the chapter, and try to figure out which sensor(s) could be responsible, and check it out. Secondly, the fate of supposedly dead ECUs in the automotive trade is interesting - across most manufacturers that operate a service exchange deal with their dealers, *less than 20%* of the returned ECUs prove to have a fault when tested. Strange but true - but how can this be?

6 What seems to happen is that the car comes in with a fault, the dealer tries a fresh ECU and Hey Presto! the fault is cured. The mysterious recovery of over 80% of returned units is easily explained. When the technician unplugs the suspect unit and plugs in a new one, he or she disturbs the multi-pin connectors. If there was a problem with corrosion or a loose contact on the terminal pins, this action cleans them, so the substituted unit works normally. The technician, reasonably enough, assumes that the old ECU is no good. Of course, unless this is a warranty return, guess who ends up paying the bill for the new ECU ...

7 We suggest that before you take the car in, you simply remove and refit the ECU to check this possibility. Lift the carpet on the passenger side of the car to reveal the ECU access panel. To get the carpet up, you will have to unscrew the screws holding the kick panel on the top of the door sill. Lift the inner edge of the panel and unhook the carpet edge retainers from underneath, then pull the carpet back.

8 + Remove the 10 mm bolts which secure the panel and lift it out of the footwell. With the battery negative (-) terminal disconnected to isolate the electrical system, disconnect the ECU wiring. Check the terminals for signs of corrosion. Do not attempt to clean the gold-plated terminal

28.8a Remove cover panel ...

28/8b ... to expose ECU.

pins, but by all means use a switch cleaning lubricant on them, reconnect the wiring and check whether the fault has disappeared. If so, great - you just saved yourself a significant parts bill. If not, at least you will know that the fault really is down to the ECU (but don't forget to check the rest of the system components - see below).

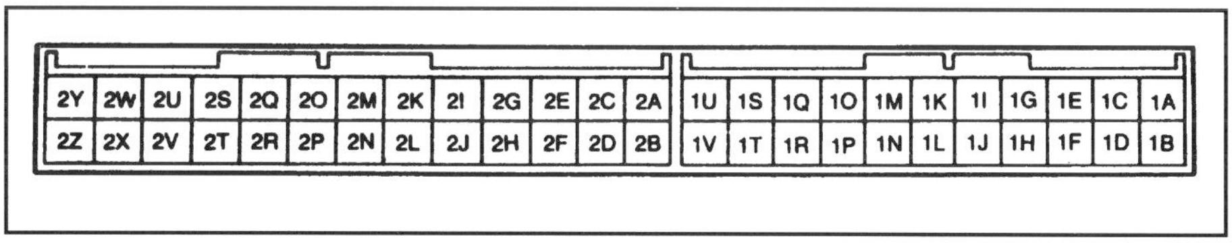

D28/10 ECU TERMINAL IDENTIFICATION.

ECU TERMINAL VOLTAGE CHECKS

9 If you happen to have access to the Engine Signal Monitor, Adaptor and overlay sheet

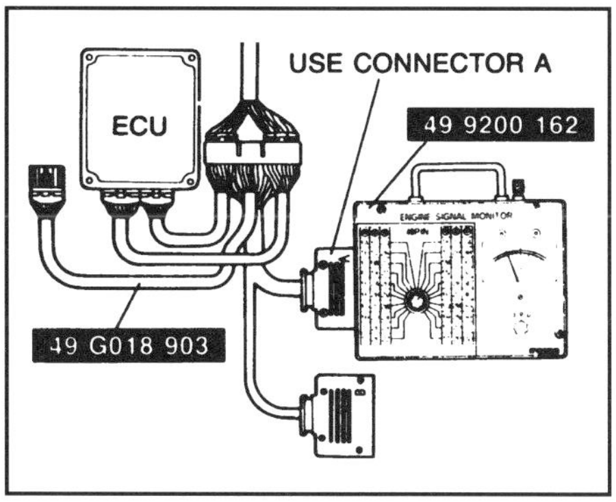

D28/9 ECU VOLTAGE CHECKS.

described earlier, or are skilled in electronic diagnostics and have suitable alternative test equipment, you can perform voltage checks at the ECU to determine whether the ECU and related sensing and control systems are operating correctly. If using the Engine Signal Monitor and Adaptor, unplug the ECU wiring and connect the adaptor and monitor as shown in the accompany diagram.

10 While we do not recommend this course of action, if you are suitably skilled in this sort of work and have appropriate equipment, it would seem reasonable to make each voltage check at the terminal concerned, noting that the ECU must be connected normally during the test. You will need to introduce the meter positive (+) probe through the back of the wiring connector, so a fine-tipped probe will be needed, and care must be taken to avoid damage to the terminal pins. The meter negative (-) probe should be connected to a suitable ground point. The terminal locations are as shown in the diagram.

11 If the readings obtained at one or more terminals are not as shown in the above table, make a note of the reading found and refer to the table for details of abnormal readings and suggested causes.

Terminal	Input	Output	Connection to	Test condition	Voltage	Remark
1A	○	—	Battery	Constant	V_B	For backup
1B	○		Main relay	Ignition switch OFF	0V	—
				Ignition switch ON	V_B	
1C	○		Ignition switch (Start position)	While cranking	Approx. 10V	—
				Ignition switch ON	0V	
1D		○	Diagnosis connector (MEN terminal)	Test switch at "SELF-TEST" Lamp illuminated for 3 sec. after ignition switch OFF→ON	4.5—5.5V	With Self-Diagnosis Checker and System Selector
				Lamp not illuminated after 3 sec.	V_B	
				Test switch at "O_2 MONITOR" at idle Monitor lamp illuminated	4.5—5.5V	
				Test switch at "O_2 MONITOR" at idle Monitor lamp not illuminated	V_B	
1E		○	Malfunction indicator lamp	Lamp illuminated for 3 sec. after ignition switch OFF→ON	Below 2.5V	With System Selector test switch at "SELF-TEST."
				Lamp not illuminated after 3 sec.	V_B	
				Lamp illuminated	Below 2.5V	
				Lamp not illuminated	V_B	
1F		○	Diagnosis connector (FEN terminal)	Buzzer sound for 3 sec. after ignition switch OFF→ON	Below 2.5V	• With Self-Diagnosis Checker and System Selector • With System Selector test switch at "SELF-TEST"
				Buzzer not sounded after 3 sec.	V_B	
				Buzzer sounded	Below 2.5V	
				Buzzer not sounded	V_B	
1G		○	Igniter	Ignition switch ON	0V	—
				Idle	Approx. 0.2V	
1H		○	Igniter	Ignition switch ON	0V	—
				Idle	Approx. 0.2V	
1I		○	4AT control unit (California AT)	Ignition switch ON	0V	—
1J		○	A/C relay	Ignition switch ON	V_B	—
				A/C switch ON at idle	Below 2.5V	
				A/C switch OFF at idle	V_B	
1K	○		Diagnosis connector (TEN terminal)	System Selector test switch at "O_2 MONITOR"	V_B	—
				System Selector test switch at "SELF-TEST"	0V	
1L	—	—	—	—	—	—
1M	○		Vehicle speed sensor (California)	While driving	2—5V	—
				Vehicle stopped	1 or 7V	
1N	○		Throttle sensor (Idle point)	Accelerator pedal released	0V	Ignition switch ON
				Accelerator pedal depressed	V_B	
1O	○		Stoplight switch (MT)	Brake pedal released	0V	—
				Brake pedal depressed	V_B	
1P	○		P/S pressure switch	Ignition switch ON	V_B	—
				P/S ON (at idle)	0V	
				P/S OFF (at idle)	V_B	
1Q	○		A/C switch	A/C switch ON (Ignition switch ON)	Below 2.5V	Blower motor ON
				A/C switch OFF (Ignition switch ON)	V_B	

T28/10A ECU TERMINAL VOLTAGE TEST TABLE.

Terminal	Input	Output	Connection to	Test condition	Voltage	Remark
1R	○		Fan switch	Fan operating (Engine coolant temperature over 97°C {207°F} or diagnosis connector terminal TFA grounded)	0V	—
				Fan not operating (Idle)	V_B	
1S	○		Blower control switch	Blower control switch at mid, high or super high position	Approx. 0V	Ignition switch ON
				Blower control switch OFF or low	Approx. 12V	
1T	○		Rear window defroster switch (California)	Rear window defroster switch OFF	Below 1.0V	Ignition switch ON
				Rear window defroster switch ON	V_B	
1U	○		Headlight switch	Headlights ON (Tail, parking, low beam/ high beam)	Approx. 12V	—
				Headlights OFF	0V	
1V	○		Neutral or clutch switch (MT)	Neutral position or clutch pedal depressed	0V	—
				Other conditions	V_B	
			Inhibitor switch (AT)	N or P range	0V	
				Other conditions	V_B	
2A	—	—	Ground (Injector)	Constant	0V	—
2B	—	—	Ground (Output)	Constant	0V	—
2C	—	—	Ground (CPU)	Constant	0V	—
2D	—	—	Ground (Input)	Constant	0V	—
2E	○		Crank angle sensor (Ne-signal)	Ignition switch ON	0V or 5V	—
				Idle	Approx. 2V	
2F	—	—	—	—	—	—
2G	○		Crank angle sensor (G-signal)	Ignition switch ON	0V or 5V	—
				Idle	Approx. 1.5V	
2H	—	—	Ground (Federal)	Constant	0V	—
2I	○		Igniter ·	Ignition switch ON	Below 0.5V	—
				Idle	Approx. 1V	
2K		○	Airflow meter	Constant	4.5—5.5V	—
2L	○		Throttle sensor (Power terminal)	Accelerator pedal released	Approx. 5V	—
				Accelerator pedal fully depressed	0V	
2M	○		Throttle sensor (AT)	Accelerator pedal released	Approx. 0.5V	—
				Accelerator pedal fully depressed	Approx. 4.0V	
2N	○		Oxygen sensor	Ignition switch ON	0V	—
				Idle (Cold engine)	0V	
				Idle (After warm-up)	0—1V	
				Increase engine speed (After warm-up)	0.5—1V	
				Deceleration	0—0.4V	
2O	○		Airflow meter	Ignition switch ON	Approx. 3.8V	—
				Idle	Approx. 3.3V	
2P	○		Intake air thermosensor	At 20°C {68°F}	Approx. 2.5V	Built in airflow meter
2Q	○		Water thermosensor	Engine coolant temperature 20ºC {68ºF}	Approx. 2.5V	—
				After warm-up	Approx. 0.4V	
2R	—	—	—	—	—	—

T28/10B ECU TERMINAL VOLTAGE TEST TABLE.

Terminal	Input	Output	Connection to	Test condition	Voltage	Remark
2S	—	—	—	—	—	—
2T	—	—	—	—	—	—
2U		○	Injector Nos. 1, 3 (Federal and Canada) No.1 (California)	Ignition switch ON	V_B	* Engine Signal Monitor: Green and red lights flash
				Idle	Approx. 12V*	
				Deceleration from 3,000 rpm to 1,900 rpm (After warm-up)	Approx. 12V	
2V		○	Injector Nos. 2, 4 (Federal and Canada) No.2 (California)	Ignition switch ON	V_B	* Engine Signal Monitor: Green and red lights flash
				Idle	Approx. 12V*	
				Deceleration from 3,000 rpm to 1,900 rpm (After warm-up)	Approx. 12V	
2W		○	ISC valve	Ignition switch ON	Approx. 7V	—
				Idle	Approx. 9V	
2X		○	Solenoid valve (Purge control)	Ignition switch ON	V_B	—
				Idle	V_B	
2Y		○	Injector No. 3 (California)	Ignition switch ON	V_B	* Engine Signal Monitor: Green and red lights flash
				Idle	Approx. 12V*	
				Deceleration from 3,000 rpm to 1,900 rpm (After warm-up)	Approx. 12V	
2Z		○	Injector No. 4 (California)	Ignition switch ON	V_B	* Engine Signal Monitor: Green and red lights flash
				Idle	Approx. 12V*	
				Deceleration from 3,000 rpm to 1,900 rpm (After warm-up)	Approx. 12V	
			4AT control unit (Federal and Canada AT)	Ignition switch ON	0V	—

T28/10C ECU TERMINAL VOLTAGE TEST TABLE.

Terminal	Connection to	Abnormal voltage	Possible cause
1A	Battery	Always 0V (Battery OK)	• ROOM 10A fuse burned • Open circuit in wiring from ROOM 10A fuse to ECU terminal 1A
1B	Main relay	Always 0V	• Main relay malfunction • Open circuit in wiring from main relay to ECU terminal 1B
1C	Ignition switch (Start position)	Always 0V (Starter turns)	• Open circuit in wiring from starter interlock switch to ECU terminal 1C
1D	Self-Diagnosis Checker (Monitor lamp)	Always 0V	• Main relay malfunction • Open circuit in wiring from main relay to diagnosis connector terminal +B • Open or short circuit in wiring from diagnosis connector terminal MEN to ECU terminal 1D
		Always VB	• Poor connection at ECU connector • ECU malfunction
		Always approx. 5V	• ECU malfunction
1E	Malfunction indicator lamp (MIL)	Always below 2.5V (MIL always ON)	• Short circuit in wiring from combination meter to ECU terminal 1E • ECU malfunction
		Always below 2.5V (MIL never ON)	• Open circuit in wiring from combination meter to ECU terminal 1E
		Always VB	• Poor connection at ECU connector • ECU malfunction
1F	Self-Diagnosis Checker (Code No.)	Always below 2.5V (No display on Self-Diagnosis Checker)	• Main relay malfunction • Open circuit in wiring from main relay to diagnosis connector terminal +B
		Always below 2.5V ("88" is displayed and buzzer sounds continuously)	• Open or short circuit in wiring from diagnosis connector terminal FEN to ECU terminal 1F
		Always VB	• Poor connection at ECU connector • ECU malfunction
1G 1H	Igniter	Always 0V	Refer to Code No.01 troubleshooting
1I	4AT control unit (California AT)	Always VB	• ECU malfunction
1J	A/C relay	Always below 2.5V (A/C does not operate)	• A/C relay malfunction • Open circuit in wiring from main relay to A/C relay • Open circuit in wiring from A/C relay to ECU terminal 1J
		Always below 2.5V (A/C switch OFF but A/C operates)	• Short circuit in wiring from A/C relay to ECU terminal 1J • ECU malfunction
		Always VB	• A/C switch malfunction • Poor connection at ECU connector • ECU malfunction
1K	Diagnosis connector (Terminal TEN)	Always 0V	• Short circuit in wiring from ECU terminal 1K to diagnosis connector terminal TEN
		Always VB	• Open circuit in wiring from ECU terminal 1K to diagnosis connector terminal TEN • Open circuit in wiring from diagnosis connector terminal GND to ground
1M	Vehicle speed sensor (California)	Always approx. 1V	• Vehicle speed sensor malfunction • Short circuit in wiring from vehicle speed sensor to ECU terminal 1M
		Always approx. 7V	• Vehicle speed sensor malfunction • Open circuit in wiring from vehicle speed sensor to ECU terminal 1M

T28/11A ECU TERMINAL VOLTAGE TEST - ABNORMAL READING CHECK LIST.

Terminal	Connection to	Abnormal voltage	Possible cause
1N	Throttle sensor (Idle terminal)	Always 0V	• Throttle sensor misadjustment • Short circuit in wiring from ECU terminal 1N to throttle sensor • ECU malfunction
		Always VB	• Throttle sensor misadjustment • Open circuit in wiring from ECU terminal 1N to throttle sensor • Open circuit in wiring from throttle sensor to ground
1O	Stoplight switch	Always 0V (Stoplights OK)	• Open circuit in wiring from stoplight switch to ECU terminal 1O
1P	P/S pressure switch	Always 0V	• P/S pressure switch malfunction • Short circuit in wiring from ECU terminal 1P to P/S pressure switch • ECU malfunction
		Always VB	• P/S pressure switch malfunction • Open circuit in wiring from ECU terminal 1P to P/S pressure switch • Open circuit in wiring from P/S pressure switch to ground
1Q	A/C switch	Always 0V (with blower switch ON)	• A/C switch malfunction • Short circuit in wiring from ECU terminal 1Q to A/C switch • Poor connection at ECU connector • ECU malfunction
		Always VB (with blower switch ON) (Blower fan OK)	• A/C switch malfunction • Open circuit in wiring from ECU terminal 1Q to A/C switch • Open circuit in wiring from A/C switch to blower control switch
1R	Fan switch	Always 0V (Cooling fan OK)	• Open or short circuit in wiring from electric cooling fan relay to ECU terminal 1R • ECU malfunction
1S	Blower control switch	Always 0V (Blower fan OK)	• Short circuit in wiring from blower control switch to ECU terminal 1S • Poor connection at ECU connector • ECU malfunction
		Always VB (Blower fan OK)	• Open circuit in wiring from blower control switch to ECU terminal 1S
1T	Rear window defroster switch (California)	Always below 1.0V — Illumination lamp ON when rear window defroster switch ON	• Open or short circuit in wiring from rear window defroster switch to ECU terminal 1T
		Always below 1.0V — Illumination lamp never ON	• Open circuit in wiring from ignition switch to rear window defroster switch • Rear window defroster switch malfunction
1U	Headlight switch	Always 0V (Headlights OK)	• Open or short circuit in wiring from headlight relay to ECU terminal 1U

T28/11B ECU TERMINAL VOLTAGE TEST - ABNORMAL READING CHECK LIST.

Terminal	Connection to	Abnormal voltage	Possible cause
1V	Neutral switch Clutch switch (MT)	Always 0V (MT)	• Neutral switch malfunction • Clutch switch malfunction • Short circuit in wiring from ECU terminal 1V to neutral or clutch switch
		Always VB (MT)	• Neutral switch malfunction • Clutch switch malfunction • Open circuit in wiring from ECU terminal 1V to neutral or clutch switch • Poor connection at ECU connector
	Inhibitor switch (AT)	Always 0V (AT)	• Inhibitor switch malfunction • Short circuit in wiring from inhibitor switch to ECU terminal 1V
		Always VB (AT)	• Inhibitor switch malfunction • Open circuit in wiring from inhibitor switch to ECU terminal 1V
2A 2B 2C 2D	Ground	More than 0V	• Poor contact at ground terminal • Open circuit in wiring from ECU to ground
2E	Crank angle sensor (Ne-signal)	Always 0V or approx. 5V	• Refer to Code No.02 troubleshooting
2G	Crank angle sensor (G-signal)	Always 0V or approx. 5V	• Refer to Code No.03 troubleshooting
2I	Igniter	Always 0V	• Refer to Code No.01 troubleshooting
2K	Airflow meter	Always 0V	• Short circuit in wiring from ECU terminal 2K to airflow meter • Poor connection at ECU connector • ECU malfunction
		Below 4.5V or above 5.5V	• ECU malfunction
2L	Throttle sensor (Power terminal) (MT)	Always 0V	• Throttle sensor malfunction • Short circuit in wiring from ECU terminal 2L to throttle sensor • Poor connection at ECU connector • ECU malfunction
		Always approx. 5V	• Throttle sensor misadjustment • Open circuit in wiring from ECU terminal 2L to throttle sensor • Open circuit in wiring from throttle sensor to ground
2M	Throttle sensor (AT)	Always constant	• Open circuit in wiring from ECU terminal 2M to throttle sensor • Open circuit in wiring from ECU terminal 2K to throttle sensor • Open circuit in wiring from ECU terminal 2D to throttle sensor
		Always above 1V	• Throttle sensor misadjustment
2N	Oxygen sensor	0V after warm-up	• Refer to Code No.15 troubleshooting
		Always approx. 1V after warm-up	• Refer to Code No.17 troubleshooting
2O	Airflow meter	Always 0V or approx. 5V	• Refer to Code No.08 troubleshooting
2P	Airflow meter (Intake air thermosensor)	Always 0V or approx. 5V	• Refer to Code No.10 troubleshooting
			• Intake air thermosensor malfunction

T28/11C ECU TERMINAL VOLTAGE TEST - ABNORMAL READING CHECK LIST.

Terminal	Connection to	Abnormal voltage	Possible cause
2Q	Water thermosensor	Always 0V or approx. 5V	• Refer to Code No.09 troubleshooting
			• Water thermosensor malfunction
2U 2V	Injector	Always 0V	• Main relay malfunction • Open or short circuit in wiring from injector to ECU terminal 2U or 2V
		Always VB	• ECU malfunction
2W	ISC valve	Always 0V or VB	• Refer to Code No.34 troubleshooting
			• ISC valve malfunction
2X	Solenoid valve (Purge control)	Always 0V or VB	• Refer to Code No.26 troubleshooting
			• Solenoid valve (Purge control) malfunction
2Y	Injector (California)	Always 0V	• Main relay malfunction • Open or short circuit in wiring from injector to ECU terminal 2Y
		Always VB	• ECU malfunction
2Z	Injector (California)	Always 0V	• Main relay malfunction • Open or short circuit in wiring from injector to ECU terminal 2Z
		Always VB	• ECU malfunction
	4AT control unit (Federal and Canada)	Always VB	• ECU malfunction

T28/11D ECU TERMINAL VOLTAGE TEST - ABNORMAL READING CHECK LIST.

29. CRANK ANGLE SENSOR - REMOVAL, INSPECTION & INSTALLATION

☞ 1/1, 2.

1 The crank angle sensor is located at the back of the cambox cover. Note that it is adjustable - its position sets the ignition timing - so apply a paint mark between the slotted adjuster and the adjacent casting, so you can refit it without affecting the timing.

29/1 Mark position of crank angle sensor.

29/2a Disconnect wiring ...

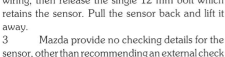

29/2b ... then remove crank angle sensor.

2 Disconnect the crank angle sensor wiring, then release the single 12 mm bolt which retains the sensor. Pull the sensor back and lift it away.

3 Mazda provide no checking details for the sensor, other than recommending an external check of condition. If it is obviously damaged or badly worn, fit a new sensor.

4 When installing the sensor, note that the drive dogs on the sensor and intake camshaft are each slightly offset, which means that it will only fit into its recess when it has the correct relationship with the camshaft and therefore cannot be fitted 180° out.

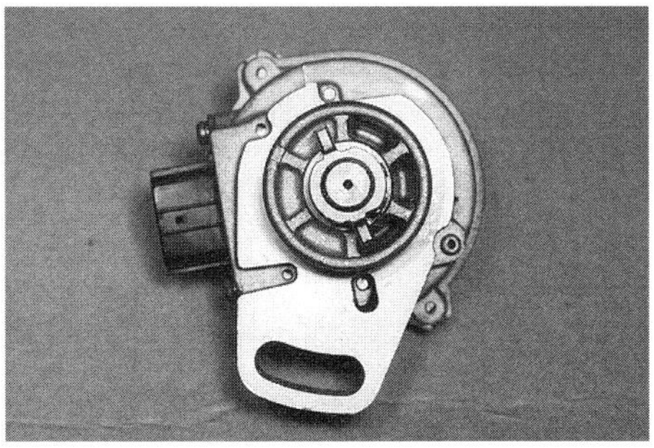

29/4a Sensor's offset drive dogs ...

29/4b ... & cam's offset cutouts mean ...

29/4c ... sensor cannot be incorrectly fitted.

5 Fit a new rubber oil seal into the groove in the sensor boss and lubricate the seal and the drive dogs with a little engine oil. Set the drive dogs to match the slots in the cam and then slide the angle sensor into position: if it won't go home with a little to-and-fro twisting, pull it out and rotate the drive spindle 180° and try again. Once the drive dogs engage the rear of the camshaft , push the angle sensor body fully home against the rear of the cylinder head and loosely fit the retaining bolt.

6 If, as advised, you marked the relationship of the crank angle sensor body with the cylinder head, realign your marks and tighten the 12 mm lock bolt to a torque of 22 Nm (2.2 kgf m / 17 lbf ft).

7 If you didn't mark the setting of the crank angle sensor, set it temporarily in mid position and then follow the ignition timing adjustment procedure ☞ 5/26.

30. AIRFLOW METER - REMOVAL, TESTING & INSTALLATION

☞ 1/1, 2.

1 The airflow meter is mounted on the top of the air cleaner assembly, and can be removed after the air trunking has been detached. The trunking is secured by a single hose clip and can be pulled away after this has been slackened. Unplug the wiring connector, noting that you need to lift the wire retainer on the connector to unlock it - use a small screwdriver to do this. Remove the four 12 mm flanged nuts which retain the airflow meter and remove it together with its gasket.

2 The chamber housing the airflow meter mechanism is sealed and cannot be accessed for repair. Inside, there is a rheostat arrangement attached to the external vane. It also houses the

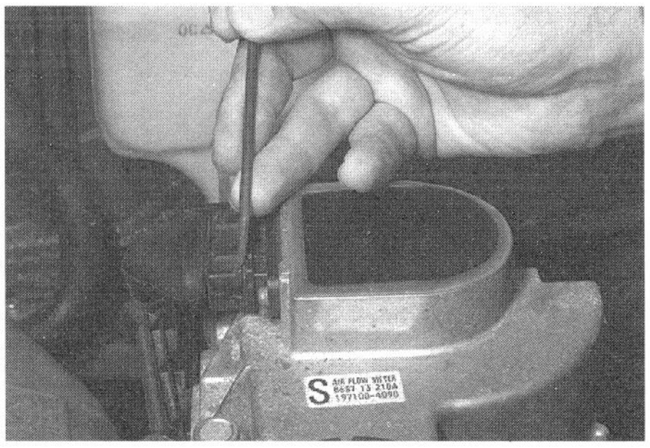

30/1a Release clip and ...

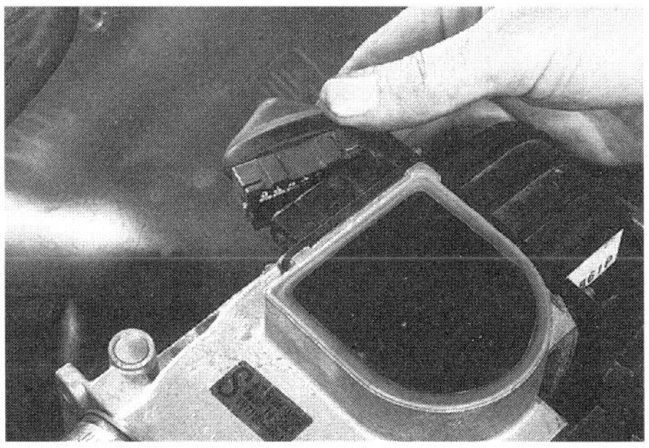

30/1b ... unplug wiring connector ...

30/1c ... remove air trunking ...

30/1d ... unscrew four retaining bolts ...

30/1e ... lift airflow meter away.

5

intake air thermosensor and the fuel pump switch. When the engine is running, intake air passes through the airflow meter, pushing the sensor vane against spring pressure. As the vane moves in response to the varying airflow, it moves the rheostat. This in turn allows the ECU to determine the airflow through the intake system.

3 Using the accompanying table, and referring to the terminal positions shown, measure the resistances of the unit at the vane positions indicated. We did the test, and found that although the readings we got were in broad agreement with those specified, we got some wild fluctuations as the vane was moved. Since the operation of the sensor on our project car was in no way suspect, we assume these variations to be normal, and due to intermittent contact within the rheostat. However, it is undeniably the case that any 'drop-out' in the resistance readings from the sensor can feed erroneous data to the ECU - this is a common cause of problems with engine management systems. Unfortunately, with no means of access, we were unable to investigate this further.

30/3 Testing airflow meter.

4 From our own experience, we would advise that these fluctuations need not be of concern unless the range of resistances obtained between E_2 and V_S is significantly outside that specified. Equally, when measuring the intake air thermosensor resistances (E_2 and THA_A) remember to correct for atmospheric temperature - it will make a lot of difference to the reading. When checking the resistance between E_2 and V_C, note that this represents the rheostat windings - a reading of infinite resistance usually means that the windings are broken, while a abnormally low reading means a partial short circuit.

5 When installing the airflow meter, use a new sealing gasket. Fit the four 12 mm retaining nuts and tighten down evenly to 7.8-11 Nm (80-

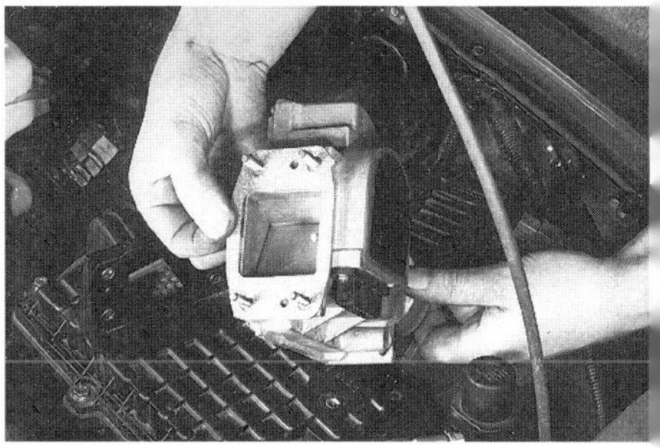

30/5 Refit airflow meter.

110 kgf m / 69-95 lbf in). Fit the intake air trunking and tighten the securing clip.

31. WATER THERMOSENSOR - REMOVAL, TESTING & INSTALLATION

☞ 1/1, 2.

1 Before attempting to remove this sensor, depressurize the cooling system by releasing the radiator filler cap. **Warning!** If the engine has been run within an hour or so, take precautions against scalding as the cap is removed - wrap rag around it and turn it just enough for pressure to escape, the remove the cap completely. The sensor is positioned high up in relation to the cooling system, so there should be no significant water loss as it is removed, (unless you forgot to depressurize the system, that is) but check and top up if necessary when the radiator cap is refitted after the check.

2 The thermosensor is screwed into a

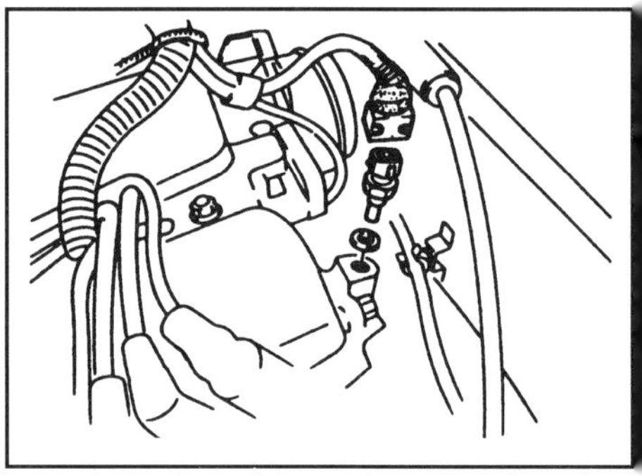

D31/2 THERMOSENSOR UNIT LOCATION.

housing mounted at the back of the cylinder head, just to the rear of the exhaust side of the cambox cover. You will need to detach the coil assembly to gain access to it. Disconnect the sensor wiring and unscrew the sensor, retrieving the sealing washer.

3 To check the sensor, you will need an ohmmeter (or multimeter) and some means of cooling the sensor to a measured -20°C (-4°F) and heating it to 80°C (176°F). The cooling method poses a problem for most of us - Mazda offer no suggestions as to how this might be achieved. You could try a freezing aerosol spray, but maintaining the correct temperature could prove impossible. Alternatively, put it and the thermometer in your freezer in a plastic bag for an hour or so and see how cold you can get it - you may have to guess-timate a correction for a higher temperature than

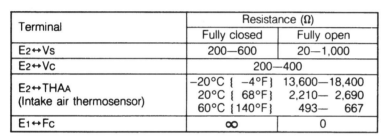

Terminal	Resistance (Ω)	
	Fully closed	Fully open
E2↔Vs	200—600	20—1,000
E2↔Vc	200—400	
E2↔THAA (Intake air thermosensor)	−20°C {−4°F} 20°C {68°F} 60°C {140°F}	13,600—18,400 2,210—2,690 493—667
E1↔Fc	∞	0

T30/3 AIRFLOW METER RESISTANCE TABLE.

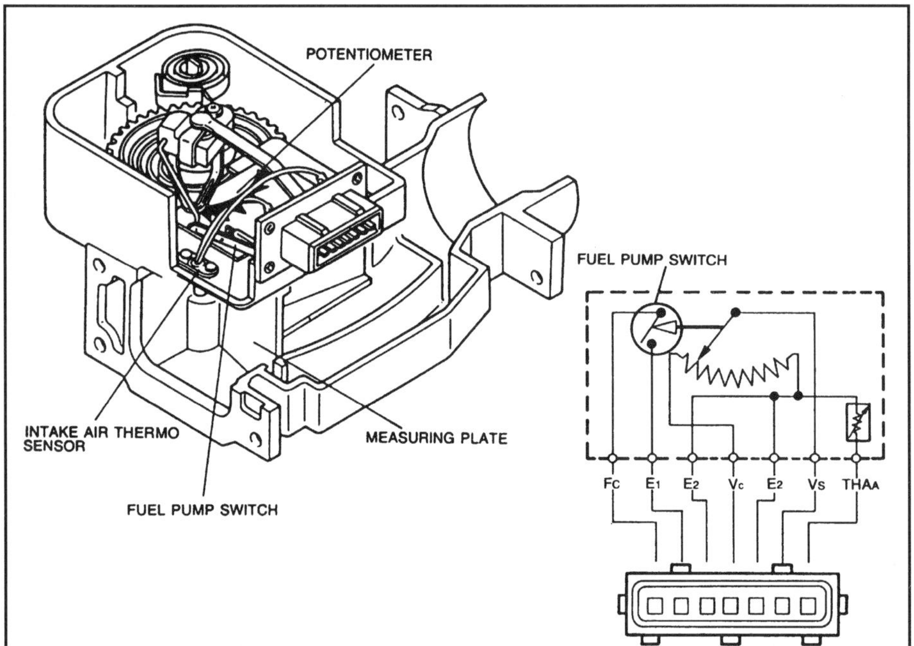

D30/3 AIRFLOW METER CUTAWAY AND TERMINAL IDENTIFICATION.

that specified.

4 We are inclined to ignore the low-temperature part of the test (lets face it, if you're driving around with your cooling system at -20°C, you've got bigger problems to deal with than incorrect thermosensor resistances) and just check at the two higher temperatures. To reach the higher temperature, suspend a thermometer and the thermosensor in a pan of water (keep the wiring connections dry and out of the water, and hook them up to the ohmmeter before you start). Make sure that the sensor and thermometer are kept clear of the sides or base of the pan. Heat the water over a stove or gas burner until you reach the prescribed temperature, and note the reading.

5 Now cool the water in the pan by pouring in cold water until you get a temperature of

Coolant temp.	Resistance (kΩ)
-20°C (-4°F)	14.6 - 17.8
20°C (68°F)	2.2 - 2.7
80°C (176°F)	0.29 - 0.35

T31/5 COOLANT THERMOSENSOR RESISTANCES.

20°C (68°F) and repeat the measurement. If you can think of some way to get the sensor down to a stable -20° (-4°F), do it (and maybe you could fax us and let us know how you did it!).

6 If the thermosensor is significantly outside specifications, fit a new one. You should remember that the sensor provides the engine temperature readings on which the ECU bases numerous control decisions. If the sensor is malfunctioning, it will affect the way the engine runs to a significant degree, so if you're uncertain about its condition, and running faults indicate that the sensor may be the problem, we suggest that you fit a new one to eliminate this possibility. When installing the sensor, whether the old one or a new one, fit a new sealing washer. Tighten the sensor to 25-29 Nm (2.5-3.0 kgf m / 18-22 lbf ft) and connect the wiring. Fit the coil assembly. Check that the coolant level is correct and fit the filler cap.

32. THROTTLE SENSOR - CHECKING, ADJUSTMENT, REMOVAL & INSTALLATION

☞ 1/1, 2.

1 The throttle sensor feeds information about the position of the throttle butterfly valve back to the ECU. It is mounted on the side of the throttle body and presents no access problems.

2 To check the operation of the throttle sensor you will need a set of feeler gauges and a continuity sensor (either a test lamp or a multimeter set to one of the resistance ranges).

3 Disconnect the sensor wiring and note the sensor terminal identification - from top to bottom the terminal pins are POW, TL and IDL. POW and TL are connected when the throttle is fully open, while IDL and TL are connected (you guessed it) at idle.

4 Connect the continuity tester probes between POW and TL and check that no continuity is shown. Now turn the throttle pulley to the fully open position, at which point continuity should be indicated.

5 Next, connect the test probes between IDL and TL. Continuity should be shown with the throttle pulley at rest. Insert a 0.4 mm (0.016 in) feeler gauge between the throttle stop screw and

32/4 Testing throttle sensor.

stop lever (the insertion point is accessed from the back of the throttle pulley - its easiest to identify the right place for the feeler gauge if you peer around the back while opening and closing the throttle a few times).

6 Continuity should be indicated with a 0.4 mm feeler gauge blade in position. If you now insert a 0.7 mm (0.027 in) blade, no continuity should be shown. If this is not the case, adjust the sensor as follows.

7 Slacken the throttle sensor mounting screws just enough to allow it to be rotated - the

32/7 Slacken retaining screws.

screws should apply just enough pressure to grip the sensor lightly. Back off the sensor by turning it clockwise by about 30°. Fit the 0.4 mm feeler gauge blade, then carefully turn the sensor counterclockwise until continuity is just indicated. Hold the sensor in position and tighten the screws, then fit the 0.7 mm blade and check that no continuity is shown. Open and close the throttle a few times and repeat the check with both blades to verify that adjustment is now correct. Tighten the mounting screws to 1.6-2.4 Nm (16-24 kgf cm / 13.9-20.8 lbf in).

REMOVAL AND INSTALLATION

8 The sensor can be removed by unplugging the wiring connector and removing the two mounting screws. When fitting the sensor, note that you must carry out the adjustment procedure described above.

33. OXYGEN SENSOR - TESTING, REMOVAL & REPLACEMENT

☞ 1/1, 2.

1 The oxygen sensor responds to the proportion of oxygen in the exhaust gases, feeding

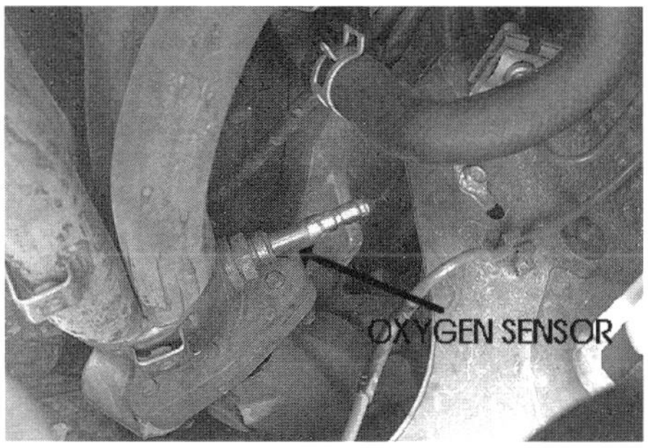

33/1 Oxygen sensor location.

information back to the ECU in the form of a varying voltage. The sensor is tested in position, with the engine at normal operating temperature. First locate the sensor - it is just visible at the back of the exhaust manifold (header) - you can just see it if you peer behind the manifold heatshield. Trace the wire back from the sensor to its connector (the wire runs behind the coil assembly and cambox) and separate the connector.

2 Make the check using a voltmeter capable of reading low voltages - the sensor produces only about 1 volt maximum. Connect a voltmeter positive (+) probe to the sensor wire, and ground (earth) the negative (-) probe. Start the engine and run it at about 3000 rpm until the meter shows a reading of about 0.55 volts. Open and close the throttle several times and check that when the engine speed rises a reading of 0.5-1.0 volts is shown. As the engine speed falls, the reading should drop to 0-0.4 volts. If the readings shown are outside this range, fit a new sensor.

3 It is possible to make further checks on the sensitivity, using an armful of Mazda Special Service Tools. If you feel that further testing may be warranted, take the car in to your Mazda dealer and have him perform these tests for you.

REMOVAL AND INSTALLATION

4 Disconnect the sensor wiring, and feed the wire back to the left side of the engine compartment, disconnecting it from any wiring ties along the way. It is important that the wire is free to turn as the sensor is unscrewed. You will be working on the exhaust manifold, so if the engine has been run recently, go and do something else while it cools down (access is restricted around the sensor, so we recommend that you spend the time doing exercises to improve the flexibility of hands and fingers). It is worth applying a little releasing fluid to

the sensor once the manifold is cool.

5 Working behind the rear edge of the exhaust manifold heatshield, unscrew and remove the sensor, checking that the sensor wire is free to turn with the sensor or the wire may be twisted off. Remove the sensor and its sealing washer.

6 When installing the sensor, use a new sealing washer, and apply a copper-based heat-resistant grease to the sensor threads. Screw in the sensor by hand, then tighten with a wrench. It is not realistic to try to torque-tighten the sensor (you can't use a socket, and access is too restricted anyway) so try to get as close to the prescribed

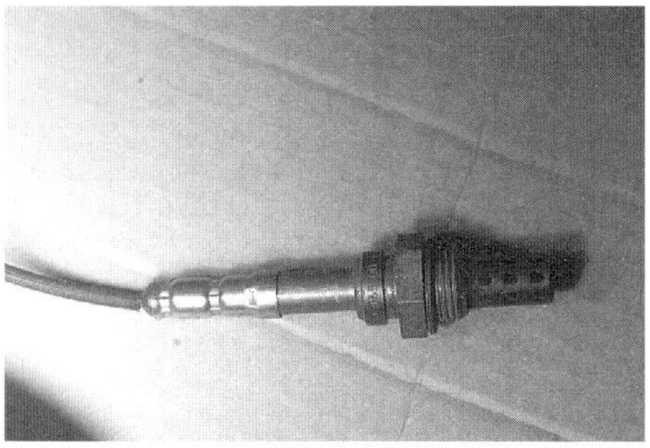

33/5 The oxygen sensor unit.

figure of 29-49 Nm (3-5 kgf m / 22-36 lbf ft). For further information on how to tighten fasteners by feel ☞ 1/2/52-55.

34. POWER STEERING PRESSURE SWITCH - CHECKING, REMOVAL & INSTALLATION

☞ 1/1, 2.

1 This section applies only to those vehicles with power steering! The power steering pressure switch feeds information back to the ECU to indicate whether the steering is being turned. It is a simple on-off switch, and can be checked using a continuity tester or a multimeter set to a resistance range.

2 Disconnect the pressure switch wire, and connect the meter or tester between the switch terminal and ground (earth). Have an assistant start the engine and, while it is running, alternately turn slightly then release the steering wheel. When the wheel is turned, the tester or meter should show continuity, while at rest no continuity should be indicated.

REMOVAL AND INSTALLATION

3 With the switch wire disconnected, unscrew the switch and remove it and its sealing washer(s) - note the position and order of the washers as they are removed. If the switch is faulty, fit a new one - you cannot repair this component. Fit the new switch, making sure that the sealing washers are in the right positions.

34/2 Testing power steering pressure switch.

35. MAIN RELAY (FUEL INJECTOR RELAY) - INSPECTION & REPLACEMENT

☞ 1/1, 2.

1 This relay is housed in the main fuse

35/1 Location of fuel injector relay.

block in the engine compartment (there is a second fuse box under the facia, inside the car). It is the larger of the two relays and so easily identified.

2 The first check is to see that the relay clicks when the ignition switch is turned on - a simple check but often a good indicator as to whether the unit is serviceable.

3 The next stage is to unplug the relay for bench tests. For these you will need a continuity tester or a multimeter set to the resistance range, plus a 12 volt battery and a pair of jumper leads. Refer to the accompanying line drawing for details of the relay terminal positions.

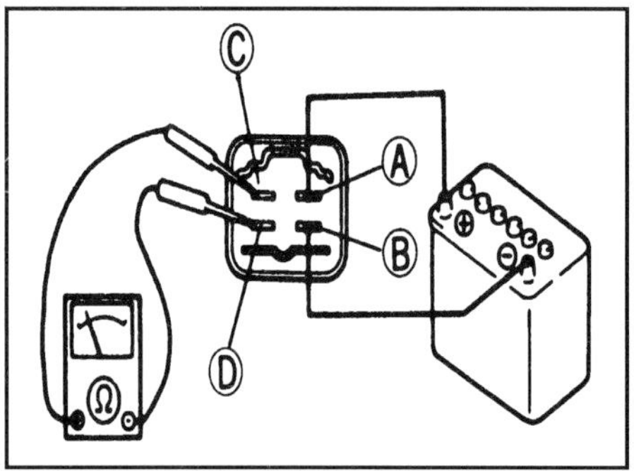

D35/3 CHECKING MAIN (FUEL INJECTOR) RELAY.

4 Using the jumper leads, connect the battery positive (+) terminal to the relay terminal **A**, and the battery negative (-) terminal to the relay **B** terminal. Connect the continuity tester or multimeter between relay terminals **C** and **D**. While 12 volts is applied to the relay, continuity should be indicated. With the battery disconnected, no continuity should be shown. If the relay does not conform to the expected results, fit a new one, seating it firmly in its recess in the fuse box.

36. CLUTCH SWITCH - CHECKING, REMOVAL & INSTALLATION

☞ 1/1, 2.

1 This section relates to manual transmission cars only. The clutch switch is used by the ECU to determine whether or not the clutch is engaged. From inside the car remove the access panel under the steering column (two screws, then unclip it), unplug the clutch switch wire and connect a continuity tester, or a multimeter set to the resistance range, across the switch terminals (you may need to adopt something close to the Veloce

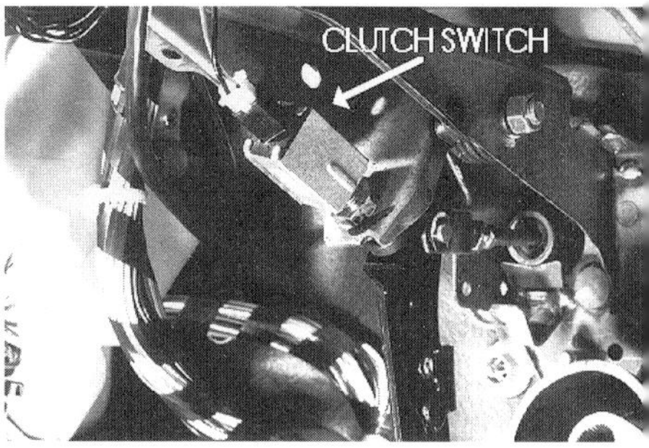

36/1 Location of clutch switch.

MX5 Accelerator Cable Removal Position™ ☞ 5/ 8). Check that continuity is shown when the pedal is depressed, and that no continuity exists when the pedal is released. If not as specified, fit a new switch.

2 To remove the switch, unplug the wiring connector, then back off the 16 mm locknut on the switch body side of the mounting bracket and unscrew the 21 mm switch body. After the new switch has been fitted (or old one refitted), check the clutch pedal height adjustment. Measure the distance between the rearmost edge of the pedal horizontally back to the carpet on the firewall. If this is outside the range 175-185 mm (6.89-7.28 in), unplug the switch wiring connector, back off the locknut and adjust the switch position until within specification. Tighten the locknut and reconnect the switch wiring.

3 Now check the clutch pedal lash (free play). Move the pedal with your hand until resistance is just felt. There should be 0.6-3.1 mm (0.02-0.12 in) lash measured at the pedal end. If incorrect, locate the 12 mm locknut on the pushrod, and back it off a turn. Now rotate the pushrod by hand until the correct lash is obtained and secure the locknut.

4 Mazda suggest that after setting the pedal height, you must adjust the pedal lash, which seems fine by us. But then they say that after you adjust the pedal lash you need to check the pedal height. Of course, when you've done that you need to ... yep, you guessed it! Our technical adviser, Wally, spent three days locked in a continuous cycle of adjustment until someone heard groaning noises coming from the garage. He was discovered babbling, frozen permanently into the Veloce MX5 Accelerator Cable Removal Position™ and had to be winched to safety. Even after months of therapy, he won't open that access panel again. Don't be

fooled like poor Wally was - just do the job once.

37. NEUTRAL SWITCH - CHECKING, REMOVAL & INSTALLATION

☞ 1/1, 2.

1 This section relates to manual transmission cars only. The neutral switch is used by the ECU to determine when neutral is selected. To check the operation of the switch you will need to raise the car safely ☞ 1/3. You will also need an assistant to operate the gearshift while you make the test.

2 With the car raised and securely supported on safety stands, climb underneath armed with an ohmmeter or multimeter set to a resistance range (a continuity checker will do the job too). You'll find the switch screwed into the right side of the transmission casing, fairly near the top towards the tail extension. Trace the wiring back and separate the connector.

3 Connect the tester probes to the switch terminal wires and check that continuity is shown when neutral is selected, and that no continuity is shown in any other position. If not as specified, fit a new switch. The switch, which is simply screwed

37/3 Neutral switch location (trans removed).

into place, is located near the top of the transmission casing, just forward of the tail extension.

38. EXHAUST SYSTEM - INSPECTION & COMPONENT REPLACEMENT

☞ 1/1, 2.

1 The exhaust system comprises four main parts; the exhaust manifold (header), the downpipe, the catalytic converter and the main muffler/silencer. In addition, there are a number of related minor parts - heatshields, brackets and gaskets, for example, which form the rest of the system.

2 Inspection or dismantling of the exhaust system requires access to the underside of the car. This is easiest if a vehicle lift is available, but if not, the car can be raised by jacks and supported securely on safety stands ☞ 1/3. You should leave the rear of the car clear so that the system can be slid out from underneath. If you're working in your garage, drive the car in front first, or you may not have room to pull the exhaust system out from underneath. **Warning!** The catalytic converter gets extremely hot in service, and even though it is covered by a heatshield will cause severe burns if touched. It also retains heat longer than other parts of the system. Wait until the system is stone cold before starting work.

3 Inspection of the system is pretty straightforward, but take care not to forget its top surface, nearest the bodywork. Holes will be immediately evident, but check carefully for smaller cracks, especially near the various joints. Sooty marks on the vehicle underside indicate leaks - due either to failure or incorrect assembly. If you know you have a leak somewhere but can't track it down, get an assistant to run the engine at idle and partially block off the muffler outlet with a rag. The increased pressure in the system should show up any leak. You should also check for impact damage along the system. This may have resulted from grounding the exhaust on a rock or similar, and the resulting restriction can have an adverse effect on engine performance. **Warning!** Be sure that the working area is well ventilated and on no account touch the catalytic converter during the check. Leave the system to cool down fully before proceeding.

4 In many areas, exhaust system repair products are available. These take the form of pastes and bandages which harden when heated. We feel that these products have their place in emergency repairs, but don't regard them as permanent, whatever the packaging says. That said, if the system is nearly worn out, you may be able to postpone the expense of replacing it by judicious use of these products. Check whether such repairs are legal in your area. In our experience, repair by welding falls into the same category; fine for a while, but normally another hole or split will appear soon. Given the proximity of the fuel tank and pipes, and the risk of damage to the electrical system and electronics (arc welders can easily zap your ECU), you must remove the system before attempting this type of repair.

5 It is unusual to have to remove the exhaust system in its entirety; the manifold section normally outlasts the rest of the pipework by a considerable margin, and is removed from the engine compartment in any case. So for now we will deal with the rest of the system, from the downpipe back to the main muffler, all of which is removed from under the car.

6 We recommend that you remove the whole of this assembly in one piece - it is easier, for a start, but there are other good reasons. Firstly, once you have removed the assembly, you will find it much easier to work on cleaning and separating the individual parts than would be the case if you were under the car. Secondly, even if you are only replacing a single component in the system, you should dismantle everything first, then reassemble loosely (with the new section in place) leaving final tightening until it is all back on the car. This ensures that the system is not under stress, which might lead to premature failure of joints, or put undue stress on the hangers. There are instances, however, where you will want to remove only the rear section of the system, from the catalytic converter back, to gain access to other components or assemblies. If this is the case, you will not need to separate the system at the (rather inaccessible) downpipe to manifold (header) joint. Instead, start the dismantling process by separating the system at the catalytic converter.

7 Start by arming yourself with overalls, safety glasses, a wire brush and some penetrating oil. Position yourself under the car, get as comfortable as you can (an old cushion will save you a lot of neck ache) and get busy with the brush, removing dirt and loose rust around the joints and brackets. Once you've got them clean, soak the nuts in penetrating fluid and leave to soak in as long as possible - overnight would be great, but a half hour or so will probably work.

8 + From beneath the car you can just about see three 14 mm nuts which hold the exhaust downpipe to the exhaust manifold. To get at and undo these nuts you need to put together extensions of at least 360 mm (14 in) and a universal joint. The combination should be socket, universal joint, extension or extensions, then the T-bar or ratchet handle. Two of the nuts can be accessed from the gap between the transmission and subframe, while the third nut can be reached from the gap above the subframe in the left-hand front wheelarch.

9 + Next release the exhaust downpipe

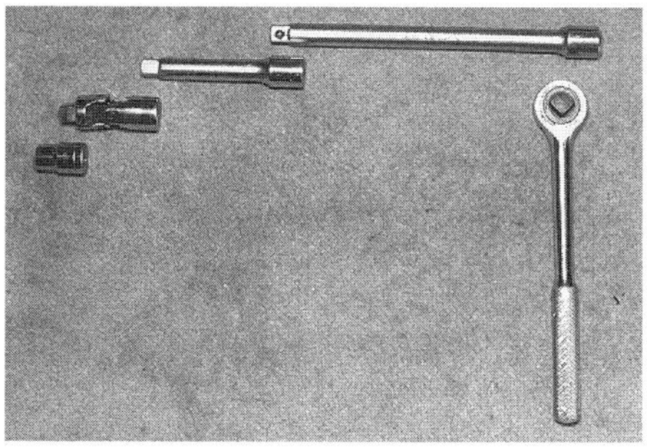

38/8a Tools you'll need to access ...

38/8b ... nuts at manifold/downpipe joint.

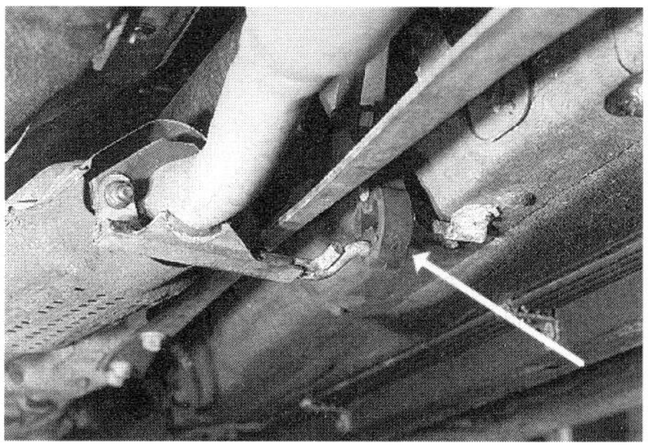

38/9a Release this support ...

5

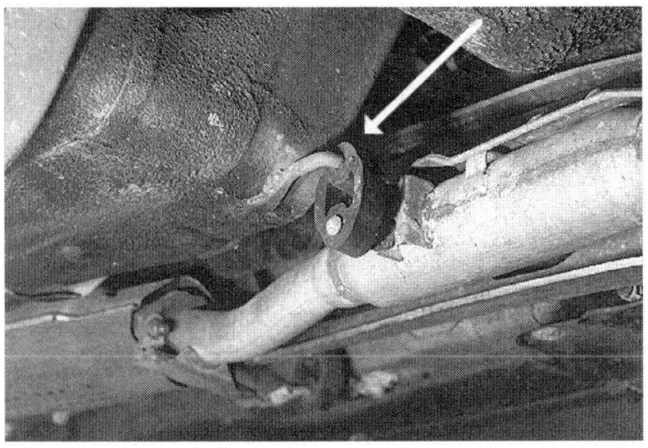

38/9b ... and this one ...

38/9c ... and this one ...

38/9d ... and these by levering ...

38/9e ... rubber supports over pins.

bracket attached to the bellhousing. There is a captive nut on the bellhousing bracket and the pinch-bolt can be undone through the gap above the front subframe in the front left-hand wheelarch. The bolt has a 12 mm head. Despite the penetrating oil, our bolt still sheared! Working backward from the bellhousing there are five rubber supports for the exhaust system. With the use of a screwdriver the rubber can be stretched over either the body or exhaust system hanger pin. The technique is to push the blade of the screwdriver through the hole in the rubber mounting alongside the hanger pin - from the back of the pin, of course, - and once the blade tip is past the mushroomed end of the hanger pin use the screwdriver like a tire lever to lever the rubber mounting over the head of the pin.

10 The complete exhaust system can now be lowered toward the ground and the downpipe manipulated through the gap between the subframe and bellhousing. The writer managed this single-handed: two people would make it a whole lot easier. If you are working alone, you may find it helps to prop the front of the system on a cardboard carton while you free the remainder.

11 Once the system is out from the underside of the car you will find it much easier to work on. Clean off any remaining dirt and rust, and reapply the penetrating fluid as required. Separate the catalytic converter from the downpipe and main muffler, releasing the two nuts which secure each flange.

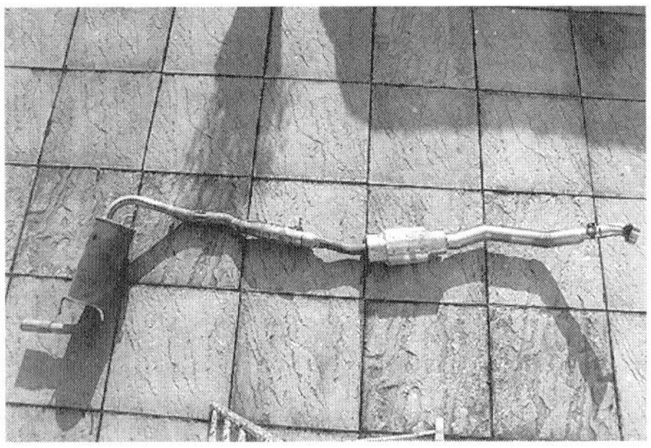

38/11 The exhaust system.

12 Inspect each part for damage or deterioration. You will have to assess whether the system parts are serviceable, or in imminent danger of blowing - bearing in mind that if they do so a week after you fit the system, you'll be doing this all over again. External rusting tends to take place along seams and welded joints, and even where plating or metal spraying has kept the system generally intact, it is at these point that corrosion shows up first. Less easy to spot is corrosion from the inside of the system. Most exhausts have low spots where moisture condenses when the system cools down, and combined with acidic gases, this produces the corrosive effects which eventually eat through and form holes. Probe any areas which look to be on the verge of perforation with a screwdriver to check this.

13 The catalytic converter in particular, leads a stressful existence. It is subject to extremes of temperature, alternately heating up and cooling each time you use the car. Climate and the type of journeys undertaken will affect the life of the system, but 2-3 years life should be considered about average. Note that the heatshield around the catalytic converter seems to be one of the first things to burn through, and indicates that the converter body will be doing the same thing fairly soon. In some areas it is illegal to use the vehicle in this condition - it is easy to start a fire by parking on tall grass which can ignite under the car with expensive consequences. Check your local laws for details, but in general, fit a new converter rather than run this sort of risk. Note the 'FRONT' marking on the upper surface of the converter when installing a new one.

38/13 'CAT' is behind heatshield.

14 Non-original replacement parts are generally inadvisable - they usually don't last as long as the originals, may not fit well, and may affect engine performance noticeably. Aftermarket performance systems are a different matter. Those from reputable suppliers should be as good or better than the original, and the price will undoubtedly reflect this. If you use them, note any installation advice supplied, and check whether you need to modify any other part of the car to suit.

15 When fitting the system, assemble it loosely using new gaskets at each joint. Check the hanger rubbers, replacing any that are damaged or aged. Slide the system under the car and prop the front end on the carton (you did keep it, didn't you?).

16 Slide the exhaust system along the ground until it is in approximately the correct position beneath the car, and if working alone, prop it in position on the carton you used during removal. Note that the heatshields on top of various sections of the exhaust system should, where so marked, be correctly orientated. Where there are body heatshields fitted, check for corrosion and security before you install the system.

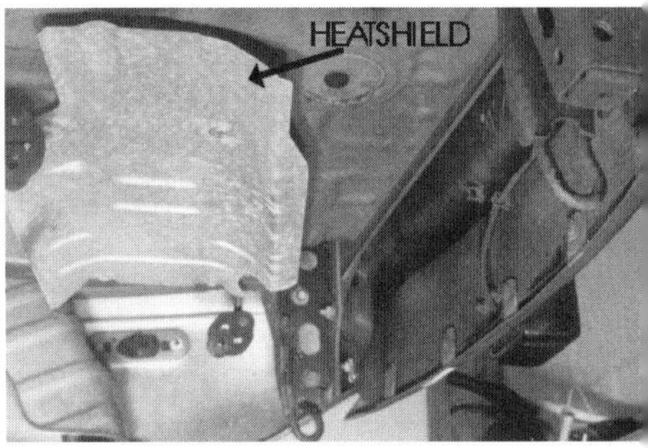

38/16 Check body mounted heatshields.

17 Lubricate the studs on the exhaust manifold with copper-based grease. Slide a new - metal gasket over the studs, noting that no sealing compound is necessary if both mating faces are clean.

18 Have an assistant support the rear end of the system, while from beneath the car you begin to maneuver it into position. You'll find that you'll have to twist the system to one side a little in order to work the exhaust pipe flange past the bellhousing bracket, but once past the bracket it will comfortably slide up roughly into position.

19 When the flange at the front of the

exhaust system engages with the three manifold studs, quickly spin on any one of the three nuts by a few turns and just leave it at that for the moment. Note: each of the three retaining nuts has a spring washer which should be replaced if it has become flattened.

20 Your assistant should now lift the rear muffler and fix it to the underside of the car by pushing the eyes of the rubber supports over pegs and hangers: this process is made so much easier by spraying the rubber supports with silicone-based lubricant, that it can then be done without tools.

21 Moving back to the front of the system, it should now be easy to push the exhaust system flange fully home against the manifold flange. Note: the three manifold flange nuts and washers are very difficult to get into place. I spent quite a lot of time cursing and trying to get one of the two lower nuts to nip the threads when, in fact, the easiest nut to place - and it can be without its washer initially - is the top nut. What you need here is an assistant who will reach through the gap between the front subframe and chassis from the left-hand front wheelarch to fit the nut to the top stud. Once you have a nut in place it becomes comparatively easy to fit the others.

22 You'll find the only way to tighten the manifold flange nuts is with the same tools you used during removal; a 14 mm socket attached to a universal joint attached to an extension of at least 360 mm (14 in), and then a ratchet or T-bar. Both of the lower nuts can be tightened from beneath the car; the top nut is most easily accessible via the left-hand front inner wheelarch. Torque the three nuts to 38 Nm (3.8 kgf m / 30 lbf ft).

23 Once the manifold flange nuts have been tightened, work your way back along the exhaust system fitting all of the rubber hangers. As mentioned before, a quick spray with silicone fluid will make this job so easy you can just push each rubber hanger over its pin with your fingers.

24 When all of the hangers are in place, come back to the front of the system and, after lubricating it with copper-based grease, insert the 12 mm bolt that fixes the exhaust pipe clamp to the bracket on the side of the bellhousing. The bolt can be inserted and tightened through the gap between the subframe and chassis rail in the left-hand front wheelarch. Torque the bolt to 24 Nm (2.4 kgf m/ 17 lbf ft).

EXHAUST HEADER/MANIFOLD REMOVAL AND INSTALLATION

25 If you need to remove the exhaust header/ manifold assembly, most of the work is done from the engine compartment, but note that you will first need to detach the front downpipe at the flange joint as described earlier in this section.

26 Working inside the engine compartment, detach the air hose from the airflow meter and air pipe stubs and remove it - the hose is secured by a worm-drive clip at each end.

27 Disconnect the airflow meter wiring connector, lifting the locking wire with a screwdriver blade. Unhook the wiring from the guide clip

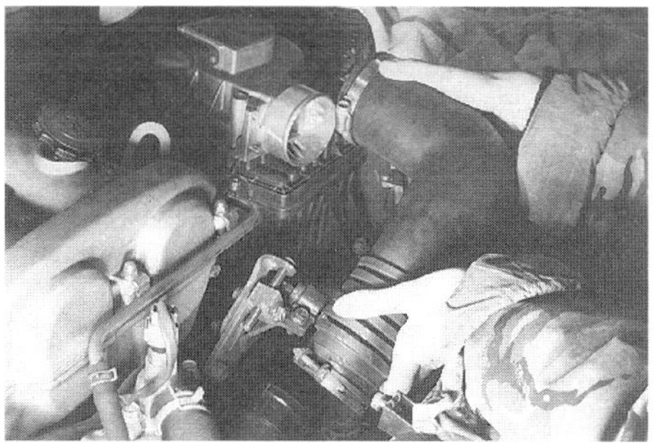
38/26 Detach air hose and ...

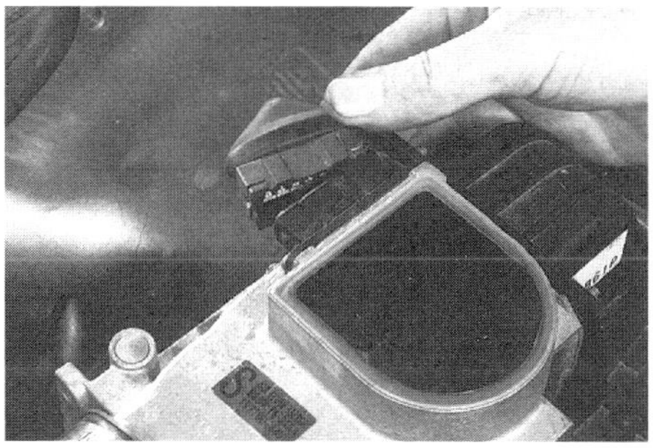
38/27 ... disconnect wiring.

on the side of the air cleaner / plenum casing.

28 + Remove the air cleaner / plenum casing complete with the airflow meter. The casing is held by two 12 mm bolts and a 12 mm nut, plus a single 10 mm bolt holding the end of the intake pipe. On our project car, there was an adjacent electrical unit (which we never did identify!) which also needed to be swung clear to allow removal.

29 The next task is to remove the manifold heatshield - this is held by four 10 mm bolts, all of which are easy to reach. The heatshield is a double-skinned component, and on our car had obviously

38/28a Don't forget this bolt when ...

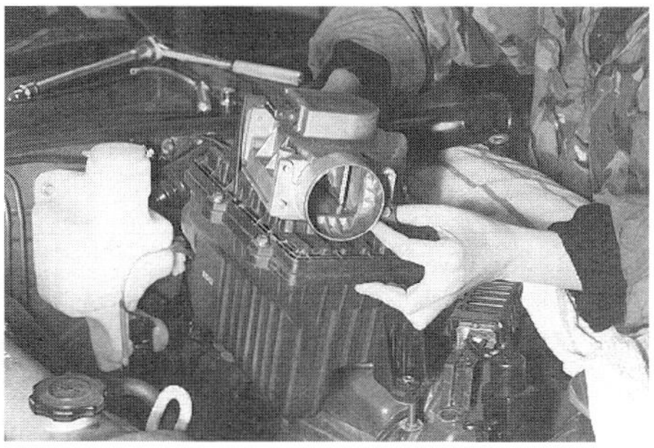
38/28b ... removing aircleaner.

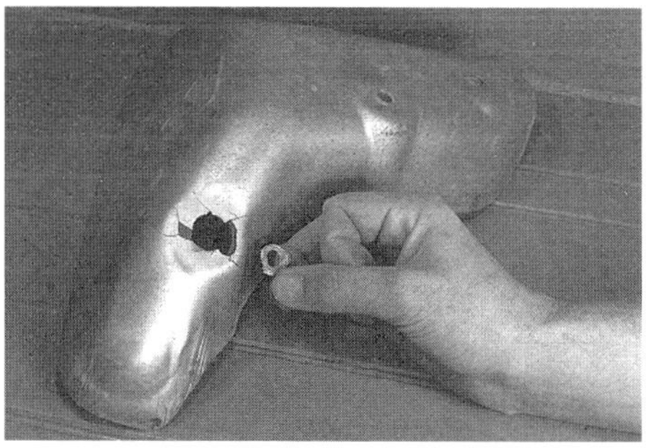
38/29 Broken heatshield.

suffered the combined effects of heat and vibration; when we removed it, a section round one of the bolt holes broke away.

30 You now need to detach the oxygen sensor, after disconnecting its wiring connector which you'll find to the rear of the cylinder head. The manifold can then be removed after slackening the nine mounting nuts - we recommend that you apply penetrating oil to the threads to ease removal.

31 + When installing the manifold, use a new gasket, and after it is in position, swing the

38/30 Apply penetrating oil to nuts.

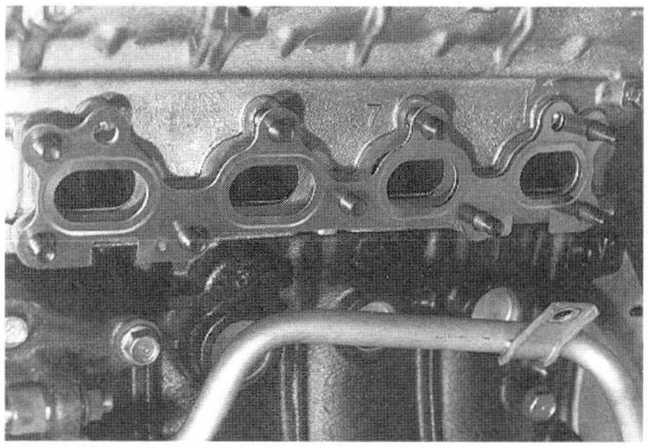
38/31a Use a new gasket when ...

38/31b ... fitting manifold.

38/31c Correctly fitted manifold.

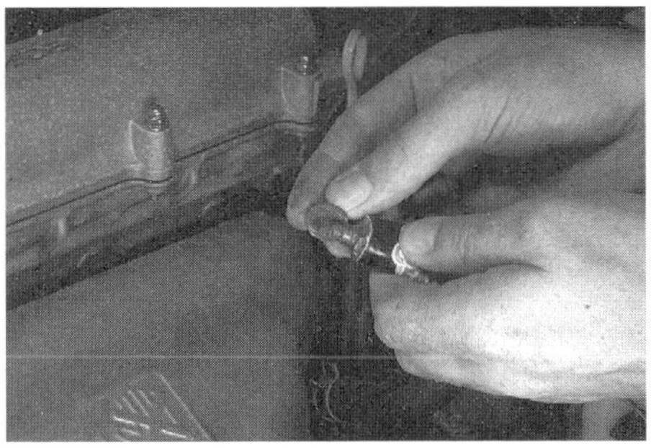

38/32a Apply copper grease to bolt threads.

38/32b Large washer secures broken area.

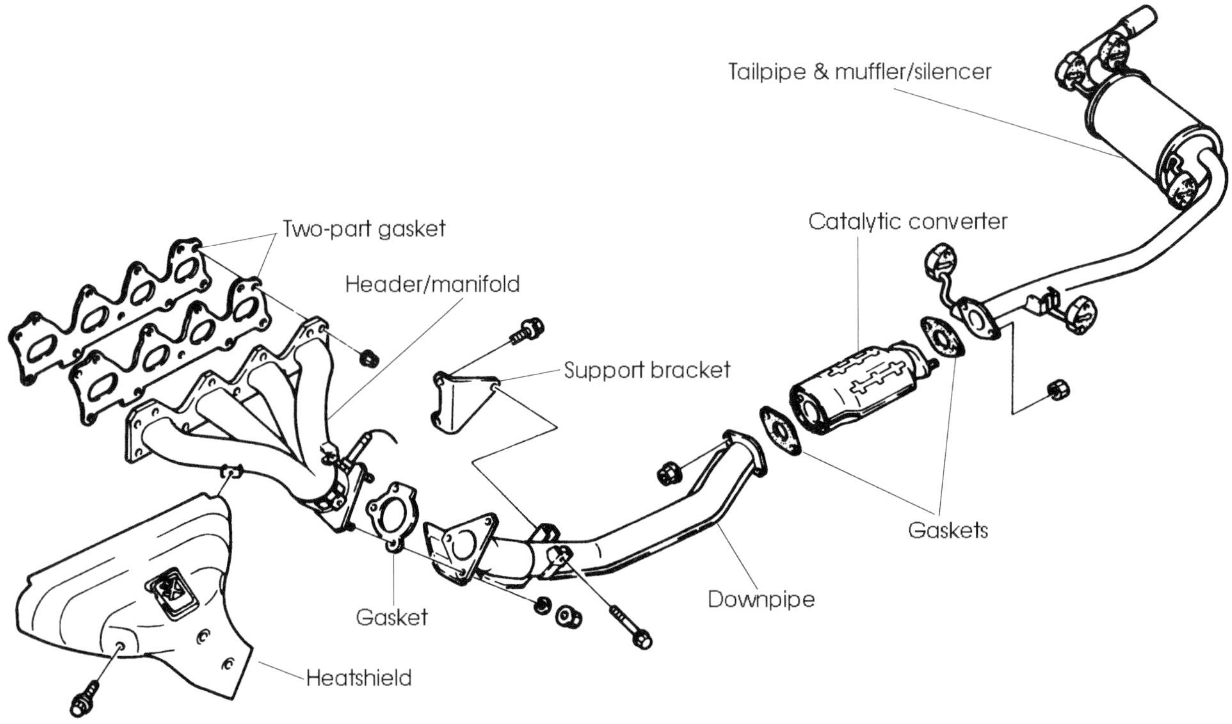

D38/1 EXHAUST SYSTEM COMPONENTS.

coolant pipe bracket over its stud before fitting the mounting nuts. These should be tightened evenly and progressively to 38-46 Nm (3.9-4.7 kgf m / 28-34 lbf ft). Fit and reconnect the oxygen sensor.

32 + When you fit the manifold heatshield, use copper grease on the retaining bolt threads to prevent them from seizing in the manifold brackets - this could cause you problems later if ignored. We did an emergency repair on our damaged heatshield, using a large washer to reinforce the broken area until a replacement could be obtained and fitted.

33 To conclude this sequence, install the air cleaner casing / plenum chamber and reconnect the airflow meter wiring and air hose.

6

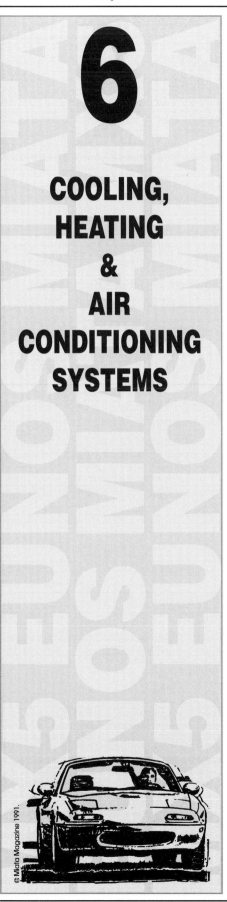

COOLING, HEATING & AIR CONDITIONING SYSTEMS

1. INTRODUCTION

The Miata/MX5 uses a conventional cooling system in which the water-based coolant is circulated around the engine by a small centrifugal pump. Engine heat is taken up by the coolant and passed back to the radiator, where air passing though the radiator matrix cools it again, the hot air venting away from the engine bay helped by the airstream moving past the car. To a large extent, cooling happens as a fringe benefit of the car's motion, but is supplemented by an electric cooling fan which will cut in at a predetermined temperature to blow air through the radiator matrix. This ensures adequate cooling in very hot temperatures, or while in slow-moving traffic.

During cold weather, the interior of the car is heated by a similar system in reverse; hot coolant from the engine is diverted through the heater matrix below the dash panel, and air is passed through it to extract heat to warm the passenger compartment. The heater control allows the occupants to control a combination of recirculated and fresh air, and to boost the incoming air with an electric fan.

An optional air conditioning system is available. This works pretty much like a domestic refrigerator. An engine-driven compressor circulates a freon-based R-12 refrigerant through the condenser - effectively another radiator - mounted in the nose of the car. This is designed to dump unwanted heat into the passing airstream, backed up by an electric fan. The coolant is piped to the cooling unit mounted under the facia. Here air is passed through the evaporator to cool the car interior, the coolant absorbing the interior heat. The warmed and gaseous refrigerant is then pumped back to the condenser, where it cools and liquefies, and the cycle is repeated.

Where electrical tests are specified in this chapter, Mazda color coding is followed. The codes and their meanings are as shown in the accompanying table.

6

2. ENGINE COOLANT - TOPPING-UP & CHANGING

☞ 1/1, 2 & 6/1.

Warning! If the engine has been run within the last hour or so, the engine coolant will be hot and under pressure. Removing the radiator filler or coolant reservoir caps can result in the water boiling as pressure is released, resulting in scalding steam

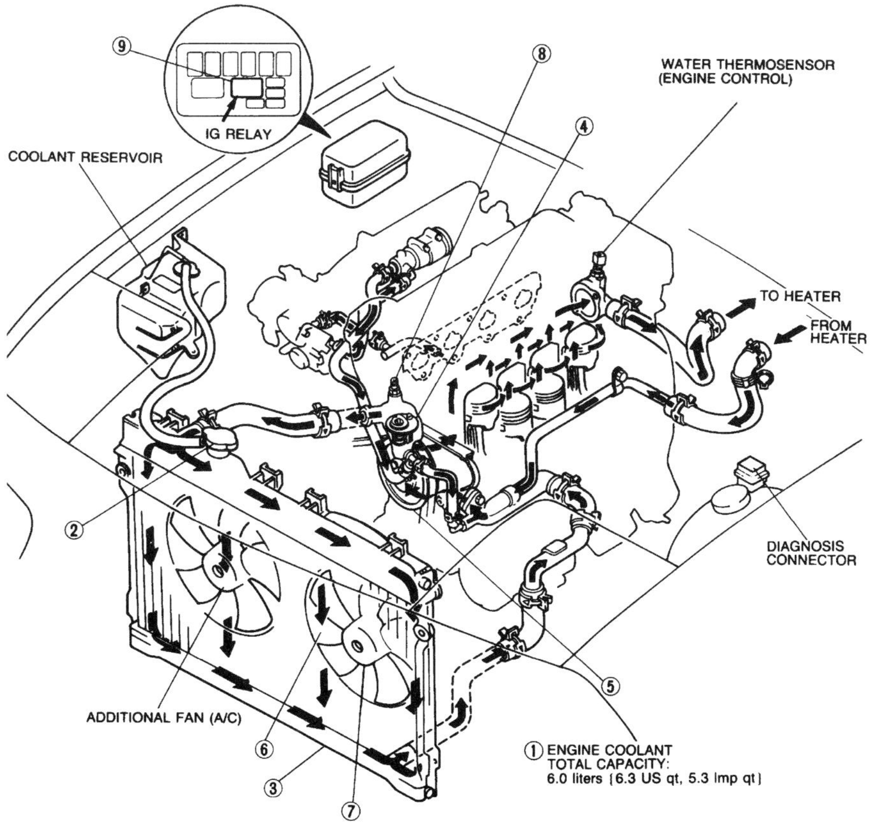

D1/0 THE COOLING SYSTEM (SHOWING COOLANT FLOW)
1 Coolant capacity. 2 Radiator pressure cap. 3 Radiator. 4 Thermostat. 5 Water pump (behind pulley). 6 Standard fan. 7 Fan motor (behind fan hub). 8 Coolant thermoswitch. 9 Position of fan relay.

CODE	COLOR	CODE	COLOR
B	Black	O	Orange
BR	Brown	P	Pink
G	Green	R	Red
GY	Gray	V	Violet
L	Blue	W	White
LB	Light blue	Y	Yellow
LG	Light green		

T6/0 WIRING COLOUR CODES.

being ejected. Always allow the engine to cool before removing either cap. Wear eye protection, gloves and overalls for safety. Place some rag over the radiator cap and turn it slowly counterclockwise until it reaches the first stop position. Wait until pressure has vented before removing the cap completely.

1 The engine coolant level should be checked and topped up regularly as required - we suggest that you give the level a quick visual check on a weekly basis. The check should be carried out with the engine cold, to avoid any risk of scalding (see warning above).

2 Check that the radiator coolant level is just below the filler neck, and that the coolant level in the reservoir is between the **FULL** and **LOW** level marks. Add only pre-mixed coolant to adjust the levels as necessary.

MIXING ENGINE COOLANT

3 It is important to use coolant made up in the correct proportions from distilled or demineralized water and ethylene glycol antifreeze. Never use tap water or you risk corrosion and scale deposits in the cooling system. Never use alcohol-based or methanol-based antifreeze.

4 To check the existing coolant mixture you will need a thermometer and a coolant hydrometer. The specific gravity of the coolant mixture varies according to ambient temperature and the water / antifreeze ratio. The recommended proportions for frost protection down to various air temperatures is shown in the table.

2/2 Topping-up radiator.

Coolant protection down to	Water (%)	Antifreeze (%)	Specific gravity at 20°C (68°F)
-16°C (3°F)	65	35	1.054
-26°C (-15°F)	55	45	1.066
-40°C (-40°F)	45	55	1.078

T2/4 COOLANT MIXTURE PERCENTAGES.

5 Note the point made above about how ambient temperature will affect the specific gravity. The accompanying graph illustrates this relationship.

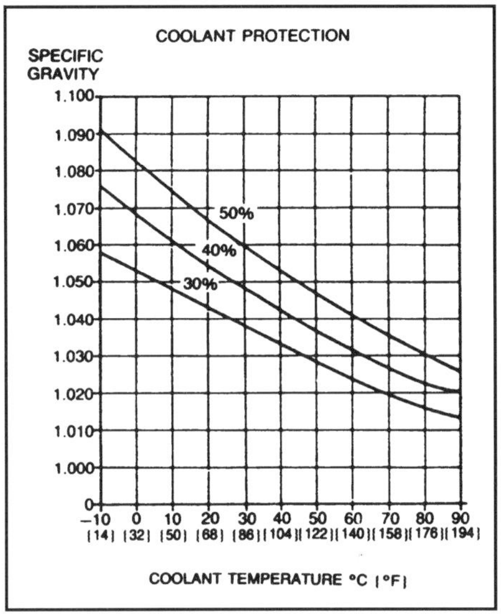

D2/5 COOLANT PROTECTION GRAPH.

6 Having checked the specific gravity required for operation in your area, mix the appropriate proportions of antifreeze and distilled / demineralized water in a clean container. Store the mixture in a sealed plastic drum or similar for use when topping up the cooling system.

TOPPING UP THE COOLING SYSTEM

7 Before adding fresh coolant, check the general condition of the existing coolant. Look for signs of scale buildup around the filler neck, and also for signs of oil contamination. If the coolant is dirty or contaminated, you should drain the system, flush it out with a hose, and then add fresh coolant. Note that if oil contamination is present, this may indicate a failed seal or gasket in the engine, especially if there has been a significant coolant loss recently. If the head gasket, for example, blows between the cooling system passages and one of the combustion chambers, combustion pressure may well force coolant out of the system and cause the oil contamination of the remainder. Always investigate and monitor such incidents closely - you could avoid more expensive repair bills if you act quickly.

CHANGING THE COOLANT

8 The engine coolant should be changed at the specified intervals, or more frequently if there have been signs of contamination or deterioration of the existing coolant (see above). This task should be undertaken with the engine cold. The cooling system capacity is 6.0 liters (6.3 US qt / 5.3 Imp qt), so you will need a drain container of at least this capacity.

9 + Remove the radiator filler cap and position the drain container below the drain plug on the underside of the radiator. Loosen and remove the plug and allow the coolant to drain.

2/9a Unscrew radiator drain plug ...

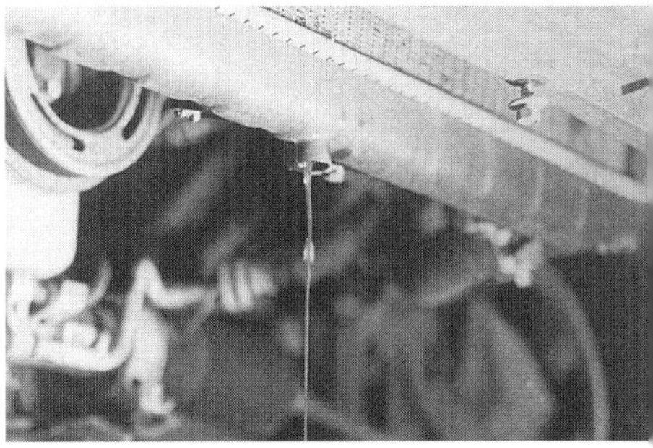

2/9b ... let coolant drain into receptacle.

10 Place a hose in the radiator filler neck and allow the system to flush through for a while, until the emerging water is completely clear, then allow the system to drain completely. While this is taking place, remove, empty and fit the coolant reservoir, washing out any dirt or sediment at the same time. Fit the drain plug and tighten it securely.

11 Add fresh coolant to the radiator until the level is just below the filler neck. Run the engine at idle for a while with the radiator cap removed. When the top hose feels hot to the touch, top up to bring the coolant level to just below the filler neck and fit the radiator cap. Top up the coolant reservoir to between the **FULL** and **LOW** marks.

3. COOLING SYSTEM - CHECKING & TESTING

☞ 1/1, 2 & 6/1.

Warning! If the engine has been run within the last hour or so, the engine coolant will be hot and under pressure. Removing the radiator filler or coolant reservoir caps can result in the water boiling as pressure is released, resulting in scalding steam being ejected. Always allow the engine to cool before removing either cap. Wear eye protection, gloves and overalls for safety. Place some rag over the radiator cap and turn it slowly counterclockwise until it reaches the first stop position. Wait until pressure has vented before removing the cap completely.

1 Check the cooling system components visually for signs of leakage or deterioration. System leaks are sometimes obvious, with dried coolant streaks indicating the source of the problem. Sometimes, though, the fault is less easily located. Tiny pinhole leaks from the radiator matrix are often hard to spot. These can be due to deterioration of the matrix due to corrosion, or from physical damage such as stone impacts or crash damage.

2 Other causes of leakage from the system include wear or damage of the radiator pressure cap (or dirt caught under the sealing washer). Problems of this type mean that cooling system pressure cannot be maintained, and at atmospheric pressure there will be coolant loss due to evaporation or boiling of the coolant. Finally, do not forget the problem of head gasket failure mentioned above - this can cause mysterious losses of coolant, sometimes without oil contamination of the remainder.

3 If you have a problem of this type, the easiest and best solution is to have the cooling system pressure tested to highlight the source of the trouble. Many garages and gas stations will perform this type of check at little cost. If you are pretty certain that the radiator cap is at fault, you could consider just fitting a new one to eliminate this as a possible cause of the trouble.

4. COOLING SYSTEM - HOSE REPLACEMENT

☞ 1/1, 2 & 6/1.

Warning! If the engine has been run within the last hour or so, the engine coolant will be hot and under pressure. Removing the radiator filler or coolant reservoir caps can result in the water boiling as pressure is released, resulting in scalding steam being ejected. Always allow the engine to cool before removing either cap. Wear eye protection, gloves and overalls for safety. Place some rag over the radiator cap and turn it slowly counterclockwise until it reaches the first stop position. Wait until pressure has vented before removing the cap completely.

1 The main hoses associated with the cooling system are the large bore top and bottom hoses connecting the engine to the radiator. There are additional smaller bore hoses which relate to the heater and engine management system, and these too can leak - all are described in the course of this section. Hoses deteriorate in time due to natural ageing and the effects of heat. Before they get so bad that a hose bursts or starts leaking, it should be replaced. Start by draining the cooling system ☞ 6/2.

2 Each hose is secured by a steel clip at each end. These are freed by grasping the tangs on the clip and squeezing them together with a pair of pliers. The clip can then be slipped along the hose until it is free of the stub. The hose can now be worked off the stub, using a flat bladed screwdriver to push it off, rather than attempting to pull the hose (this has the effect of tightening the hose on the stub and rarely succeeds in shifting it). If the hose has been in place for some time it may well be stuck. You can help free it by working a small electrical screwdriver between the stub and the hose, where access permits. As a last resort, make sure you have the correct replacement hose ready to fit, then cut off the old one by slitting it lengthways with a craft knife - take care not to cut into the stub. Clean off any traces of the old hose from the stub before fitting the new one.

TOP HOSE REMOVAL

3 + The top hose connects the thermostat housing to the top stub of the radiator, and is the easier of the two main hoses to reach. **Caution!** Behind the top hose is a smaller hose which connects the intake manifold airvalve to the thermostat housing. On our project car, the clip on this hose had started to wear a hole in the top hose. Check the position of this clip carefully.

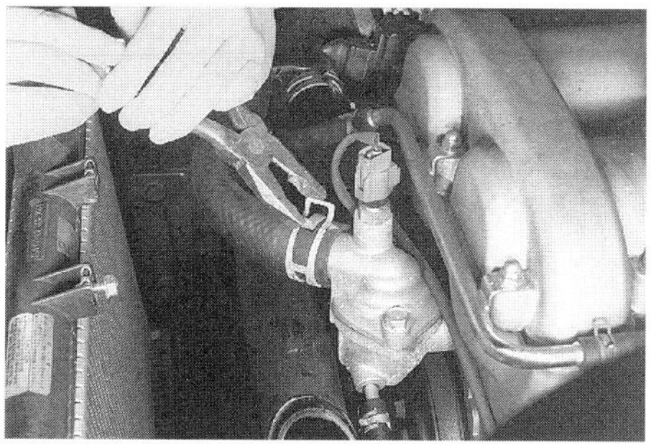

4/3a Release the spring clip ...

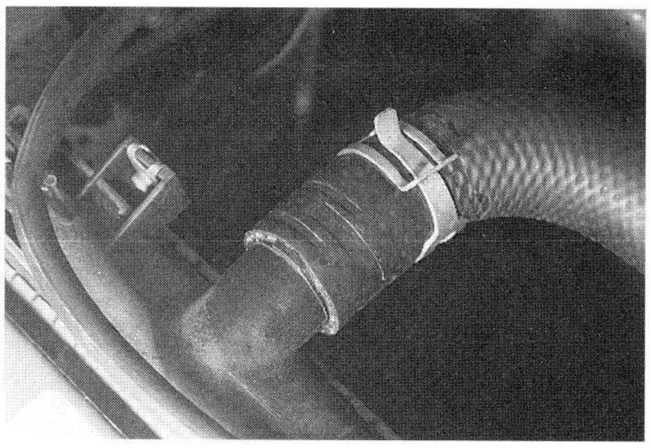

4/3b ... move it back along the hose ...

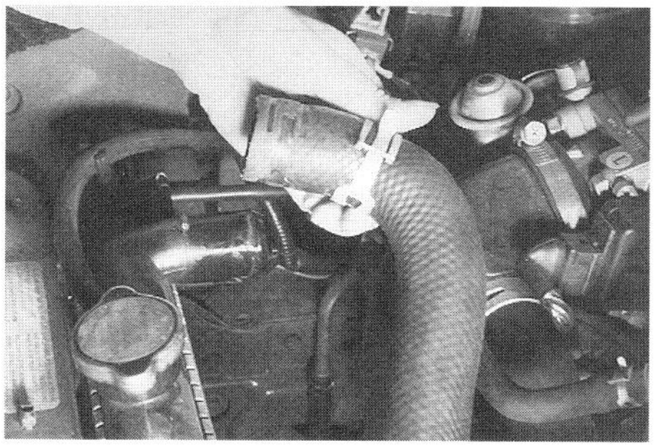

4/3c ... and slide hose off stub.

BOTTOM HOSE REMOVAL

4 The bottom hose connection consists of two short hose sections with a metal pipe between them. These are less easy to reach, being partially hidden below the exhaust manifold (header) and, where fitted, the power steering pump. You may just about be able to remove and fit this assembly from the top of the engine bay, but most likely you will need access from below. This will require the car to be jacked up and supported on safety stands and the plastic undertray detached. For information on jacking and supporting the car see ☞ 1/3.

5 Remove the undertray as follows, noting that all fixings have 10 mm heads. Remove the three sheet metal screws from the front of the tray. Next, remove the bolt next to the suspension upper wishbone on each side of the car, the bolt on the side of the chassis member in the wheelarch from each side and, finally, the nut on each side holding both the tray and front valence stay. Once the nut is removed the stay can be pulled off the stud and moved sufficiently to leave clearance for removal of the undertray. We suggest that you fit all fasteners finger-tight for safe keeping once you've removed the undertray.

6 + With the undertray out of the way, free the hose ends at the radiator stub and at the block end, removing the two hoses with the metal pipe still in place. On cars with power steering, there is a plastic cable tie holding the pump hose to the bottom hose - free this by pulling back on the locking tab with your finger nail. Once the bottom hose assembly is removed you can separate the two hoses and metal pipe in relative comfort on the workbench.

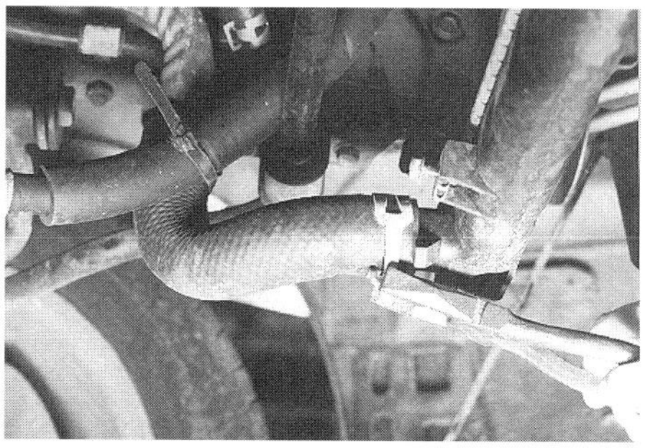

4/6a Release bottom hose at radiator ...

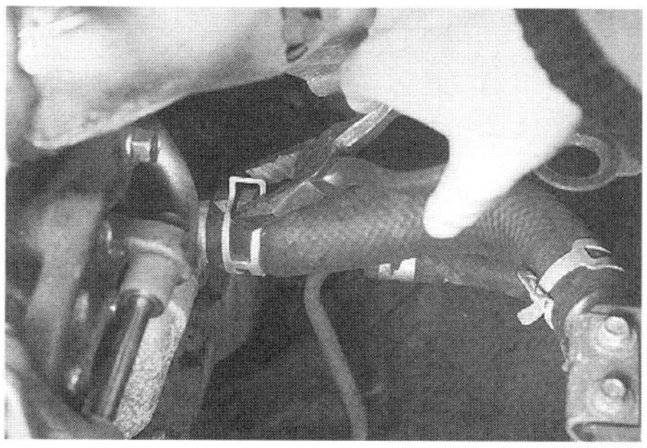

4/6b ... and cylinder block ends.

COOLANT INLET CASTING AND HOSE CONNECTIONS

7 At the front left-hand side of the block there is a casting through which engine coolant is passed from the bottom hose into the engine cooling system passages. It is not easy to reach this - it will be partially covered by the power steering and / or air conditioning pumps, but you should not normally need to disturb this component between engine overhauls.

8 Connected to an elbow at the front of the casting is a small hose which runs up to the thermostat housing. If you need to replace this, free the hose after releasing the retaining clips as described above.

4/8 Release clip.

HEATER HOSE CONNECTIONS

9 A metal pipe runs back from the coolant inlet casting, the back end being secured on one of the exhaust manifold studs. This is the heater return pipe, the hose connection to which can be reached at the back of the engine compartment. The other end of the hose connects to the heater outlet stub at the firewall. The heater hoses are easy to reach at the firewall end, and are secured by the usual clips.

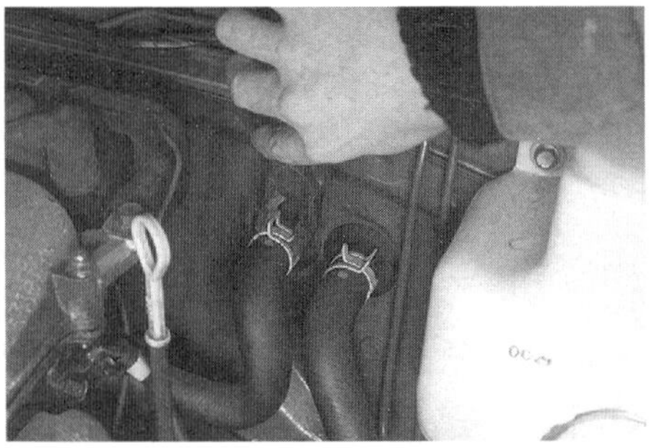

4/9 Release heater hoses at firewall stubs.

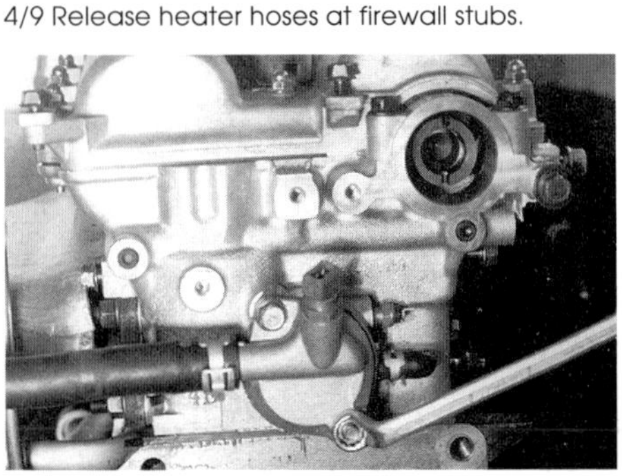

4/10 Release outlet cover.

10 The heater inlet hose is connected from the outlet cover on the back of the block to the heater inlet stub at the firewall. Access to the engine end of this hose will require removal of the ignition coil assembly. The outlet cover itself is retained by one 12 mm bolt and one 12 mm nut, should removal be required. The cover also carries the water thermosensor.

AIRVALVE HOSE CONNECTIONS

11 The final secondary hoses are those associated with the intake manifold airvalve. Water is fed to the airvalve via small bore hoses from the ISC valve on the underside of the throttle body, this in turn being fed through the intake manifold itself. The return from the airvalve is by way of another small bore hose which connects to the thermostat housing.

12 After fitting the new hose(s), refill the cooling system (☞ 6/2) then fit the filler cap and run the engine to allow the system to pressurize. Check carefully for leaks.

5. RADIATOR - REMOVAL & INSTALLATION

☞ 1/1, 2 & 6/1.

1 Start by raising the front of the car sufficiently to permit safe access below the engine compartment. You need enough room to work underneath when removing the undertray and disconnecting the radiator bottom hose connections ☞ 1/3. Isolate the electrical system by disconnecting the battery negative (-) terminal after first having disarmed the audio unit's security system. **Warning!** When loosening the negative (-) terminal take great care not to short the tool you are using across the positive (+) terminal (for more information ☞ 7).

2 Moving to the underside of the car, the next job is to remove the plastic undertray as follows, noting that all fixings have 10 mm heads. Remove the three sheet metal screws from the front of the tray. Next, remove the bolt next to the suspension upper wishbone on each side of the car, the bolt on the side of the chassis member in the wheelarch from each side and, finally, the nut on each side holding both the tray and front valence stay. Once the nut is removed the stay can be pulled off the stud and moved sufficiently to leave clearance for removal of the undertray. We suggest that you fit all fasteners finger-tight for safe keeping once you've removed the undertray.

3 Removing the electric fan (there will be an extra fan mounted on the right side of the car on models fitted with air conditioning) from the radiator. First release the electrical wire from the clip in the fan housing by pulling back the catch on the side of the clip and thereby releasing the wire retainer. The electrical connector block can now be separated by pushing the outer catch inwards and pulling the two halves apart.

4 + The electric fan housing is fixed to the radiator body by four 10 mm bolts, threaded into spring clips. Note: you may find, as we did, that the bottom retaining bolts and their clips are con-

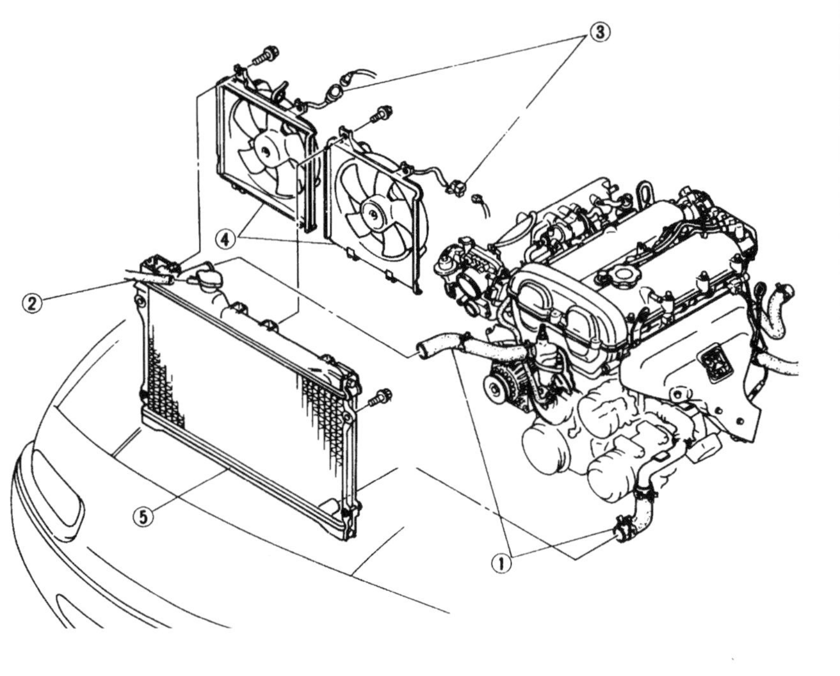

D5/1 RADIATOR REMOVAL SEQUENCE
1 Release hoses. 2 Release overflow pipe. 3 Release fan electrical connections. 4 Remove fan/s. 5 Remove radiator.

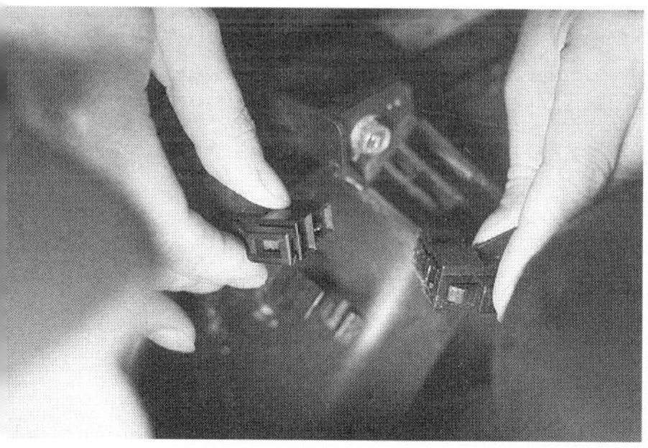

5/3 Release fan electrical connector.

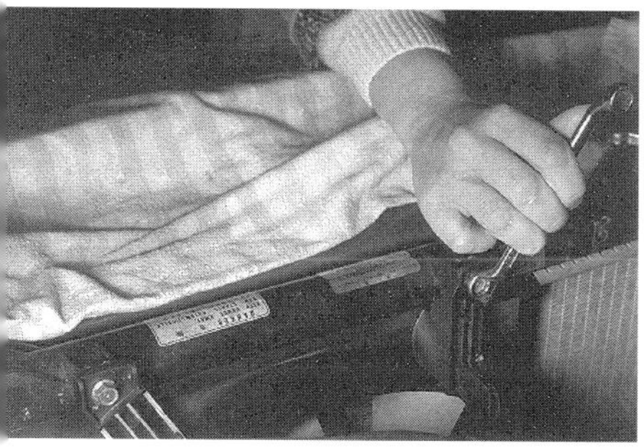

5/4a Unscrew fan fixings ...

/4b ... and lift fan away from radiator.

iderably corroded. If this is the case, a soaking with enetrating oil some time before the bolts are emoved will help. Once the two top bolts have een removed and the two bottom bolts loosened, he cooling fan assembly can be lifted away from he car.

Remove the radiator top hose by squeezng the ears of each spring clip with pliers and noving the clips back until they stop clamping the nion. The hose can then be worked off of both the adiator union and the thermostat housing union. aution! Behind the top hose there is a small ubber coolant hose which goes from the thermotat housing to the manifold airvalve. This, too, has spring clip which, on our car, was digging into the ack of the top hose and actually beginning to cut hole. If you find the same, reposition the offendng clip and, if necessary, replace the damaged ose.

Note: you may find that coolant hoses re difficult to release from metal stubs and pipes - e did, even though our project car was less than wo years old. The problem is caused by a combiation of very tight-fitting pipes and metal corroon. Generally it is better to push the hoses off than pull them. Often, working a screwdriver into and around the joint - taking care not to gouge either hose or union stub - helps; simultaneously squirting silicone based water repellent lubricant such as WD40 will help greatly, too. If the hose simply refuses to budge, carefully slit it lengthways along the union joint with a craft knife, taking care not to gouge the union stub. This method means, of course, that you'll have to buy a new hose.

7 Next remove the bottom hose after releasing the plastic tie holding the power steering pump hose against the radiator hose. To release the tie pull back the locking tab with a finger nail and then slide the tail of the tie through the clip. The bottom hose can be removed after releasing both of its spring clips and working the hose off of its unions. Easier said than done, but persevere and the hose will come free.

8 Remove the overflow pipe from its union just beneath the radiator filler cap.

9 Remove the two 12 mm headed bolts towards the top and on each side of the radiator. Once two screws have been removed the radiator can be lifted upward out of its bottom brackets and removed from the car. Store in a safe place.

10 Once the radiator has been removed,

5/9 Lift radiator out of bottom brackets.

check it carefully for signs of damage. Bent fins on the radiator matrix can be carefully straightened using a small screwdriver, but take care not to overdo this or you will probably end up causing a leak. Remove dead bugs and leaves by brushing them off the matrix or, better still, with a high-pressure hose. If you have a lot of problems with stones or debris getting in through the air intake at the front of the car, you may want to consider fitting one of the aftermarket grilles available for the Miata/MX5.

11 If you discover serious corrosion or damage, you have two options; repair or replacement. Radiator repairs are specialist work, and there are companies specializing in this type of work in most towns. The best course of action is to check the price of a new radiator, then take the damaged one to a repair specialist for assessment and repair if it proves economic to do so.

12 When installing the radiator, make sure that all hose connections are secure (you might consider fitting new hoses while you have easy access to do so). Refill the cooling system (☞ 6/2) and then run the engine for a while to check for leaks.

6. THERMOSTAT - REMOVAL, TESTING & INSTALLATION

☞ 1/1, 2 & 6/1.

1 The thermostat senses water temperature and opens and closes in response to changes. At low temperatures, the valve remains closed, and water is shut off from the radiator. This causes the engine to reach operating temperature quickly, reducing engine wear. As normal temperatures are reached, the valve opens to permit water circulation through the radiator. Note that most thermostats fail in the open position - an abnormally long warm-up period often signifies this. On the Miata/MX5, the engine management system will try to compensate by prolonging the warm-up mixture settings, and you may not notice any problem. If your heater seems to take forever to start working, and your fuel consumption seems abnormal, check out the thermostat.

2 Start by draining the engine coolant ☞ 6/2. Isolate the electrical system by disconnecting the battery negative (-) terminal after first having disarmed the audio unit's security system, if applicable. **Warning!** When loosening the negative (-) terminal take great care not to short the tool you are using across the positive (+) terminal (for more information ☞ 7). Unplug the temperature switch wire from the switch on the top of the thermostat cover. Disconnect the radiator top hose at the thermostat end.

3 + Undo and remove the two 12 mm bolts holding the thermostat cover to the thermostat housing. Once they have been removed the cover can be pulled away from the housing, but be careful as it will come away suddenly once the gasket releases.

4 **Caution!** Do not use a sharp instru-

6/3a Unscrew two 12mm bolts ...

6/3b ... remove the thermostat cover and ...

6/4 ... lift the themostat from its housing.

ment to lever the cover from the housing. Note: the right-hand cover retaining screw also holds a hose bracket. With the cover removed the thermostat can be lifted from its housing.

5 Check the thermostat visually - if it is obviously damaged or leaking, fit a new one.

6 You can check the thermostat operation by heating it in water. Suspend the unit in the water, together with a thermometer, so that they are clear of the sides of the container. Heat the water to the prescribed temperatures and test

Opening commences at	80.5-83.5°C (177-182°F)
Thermostat fully open at	95°C (203°F)
Maximum lift (fully open)	8.5 mm (0.33 in)

T6/6 CHECKING THERMOSTAT OPERATION.

performance against the accompanying table. You can accept a little variation from the table's figures, but if significantly outside the values given, fit a new thermostat.

7 When installing the thermostat, check that the gasket faces of the housing and cover are clean, using a solvent cleaner or a blunt scraper to remove any residual gasket material. Fit the cover using a new gasket, noting that the green printed face should be towards the thermostat. Tighten the cover bolts to 19-25 Nm (1.9-2.6 kgf m / 14-19 lbf ft). Reconnect the top hose, making sure the hose clip is secure. Reconnect the temperature switch wire. Fill the cooling system and then run the engine to check for leaks.

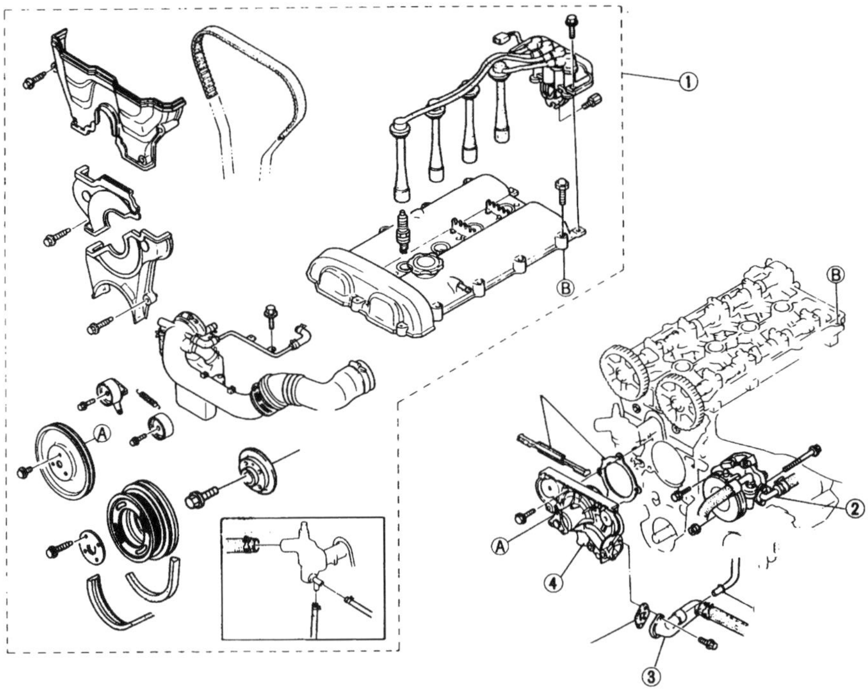

D7/2 WATER PUMP REMOVAL SEQUENCE
1 Remove all of these items, including the timing belt. 2 Power steering pump (if fitted). 3 Water inlet casting. 4 Water pump.

7. WATER PUMP - REMOVAL & INSTALLATION

☞ 1/1, 2 & 6/1.

1 The water pump is unlikely to be a source of problems unless the cooling system has become badly contaminated with scale, or the pump bearings have been damaged by wear or by water leaking past the shaft seal. Should this occur, you will probably find that the coolant level drops significantly. You can check this by leaving a sheet of cardboard under the engine bay when the car is parked overnight. Residual pressure in the cooling system will mean that the pump will continue to leak, and signs of leakage below the front of the engine will help confirm the fault. This check will also pinpoint the leak if it is from another source, such as a damaged hose.

2 Access to the water pump is by no means easy. It is mounted on the front of the engine block, just below the cylinder head joint. To reach the pump for removal, you will first need to carry out the following operations.

- *Isolate the electrical system by disconnecting the battery negative (-) terminal after first having disarmed the audio unit's security system, if applicable.* ***Warning!*** *When loosening the negative (-) terminal take great care not to short the tool you are using across the positive (+) terminal (for more information ☞ 7)*
- *Drain the engine coolant (☞ 6/2)*
- *Remove the intake hose (worm-drive hose clip at each end)*
- *Remove the plastic intake pipe (10 mm bolt to alternator bracket, release ratchet clip on side of resonance chamber, then disengage from throttle body.*

3 You now need to remove the external drivebelts for the alternator, power steering and air conditioning systems (as fitted to your vehicle) ☞ 2. With these removed, you should now detach the ignition coil assembly and plug leads, the cambox cover, the timing belt covers and the timing belt. If your car has power steering, the pump must be detached from its mounting, but can be left connected to its hoses. Move it clear of the front of the engine, holding it in place with wire to avoid straining the hoses. Disconnect the water inlet pipe from the side of the water pump, leaving it attachec to its hoses. Tie it clear of the pump.

4 Having finally got to the water pump itself it can be removed after releasing the four 12 mm mounting bolts. The pump may well be stuck in place by the gasket - use a hide mallet, or a block of wood and a hammer to jar it free. On no accoun lever the pump body or you will probably damage the gasket faces or pump body.

5 If the pump is worn or damaged, you wi have to fit a new one. In common with mos manufacturers, Mazda specifically advise that the pump should not be dismantled.

6 When installing the pump, use a new mounting gasket, and tighten the mounting bolts evenly to 19-25 Nm (1.9-2.6 kgf m / 14-19 lbf ft). Use a new gasket on the water inlet pipe, tightening its mounting bolts to the same torque figure as the pump body. Fit the various components removed to gain access to the pump ☞ 2.

7 After refilling the cooling system (☞ 6/2

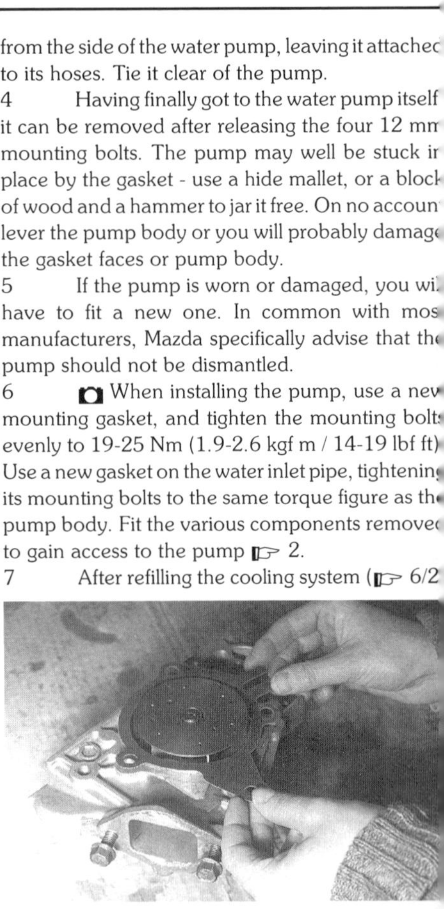

7/6 Fit a new water pump gasket.

reconnect the battery negative (-) lead and run the engine. Check carefully for leaks after the cooling system has warmed up and become pressurized. Check, and if necessary top up, the cooling system.

8. RADIATOR FAN/S - TESTING, REMOVAL & INSTALLATION

☞ 1/1, 2 & 6/1.

1 The radiator is cooled primarily by air forced through the matrix from the air intake at the nose of the car while it is in motion. However, in hot ambient temperatures, and especially in heavy traffic, the natural airflow has to be supplemented by an electrically operated fan. This is mounted immediately to the rear of the radiator. The fan is controlled by the water thermoswitch which is screwed into the top of the thermostat cover.

2 In the event that you suspect a fault with the fan, it can be checked as follows. **Warning!** The fan operates during this test - keep hands and loose clothing well away from the fan area during the test. Open the diagnostic cover and locate terminals **GND** and **TFA**. Connect these terminals together with an insulated jumper wire. Turn the ignition switch on and check that the fan operates. If the fan runs with the jumper in place, the fault is most likely to be in the water thermoswitch (*skip to paragraph* 3). If not, turn the ignition switch off and check the wiring connections, then repeat the test. If the fan is still inoperative, remove the fan assembly and check motor operation (*skip to paragraph 5*).

THERMOSWITCH OPERATION

3 Remove the radiator cap (*see precautions* ☞ 6/2). Hold a thermometer in the radiator so that the bulb is just below the water level. Start the engine and allow it to run so that the coolant warms up. The fan should cut in when the temperature reaches approximately 91°C (196°F). If the fan does not run, check the thermoswitch as follows.

4 With the radiator cap still removed, unplug the thermoswitch wiring connector and unscrew the switch from the top of the thermostat cover. Suspend the switch and a thermometer in a pan of water (keep the switch terminals dry). Connect an ohmmeter or continuity tester across the switch terminals, then begin heating the water. Below 84°C (183°F) no continuity should be indicated, while above 91°C (196°F) continuity should be shown. If the switch fails to work as specified, fit a new one. Install the thermoswitch using a new O-ring to which a drop of coolant has been applied to lubricate it during fitting. Tighten the switch to 5.9-8.8 Nm (60-90 kgf cm / 52-78 lbf in).

FAN MOTOR TESTING

5 Disconnect and remove the vehicle battery (☞ 7) and check that it is fully charged (or use a spare car battery for this check). Disconnect the fan motor wiring. Connect the battery and an ammeter as shown in the accompanying illustration. The fan should operate smoothly and draw 5.3-6.5 amps. If this is not the case fit a new fan motor. **Warning!** Take care not to short the two

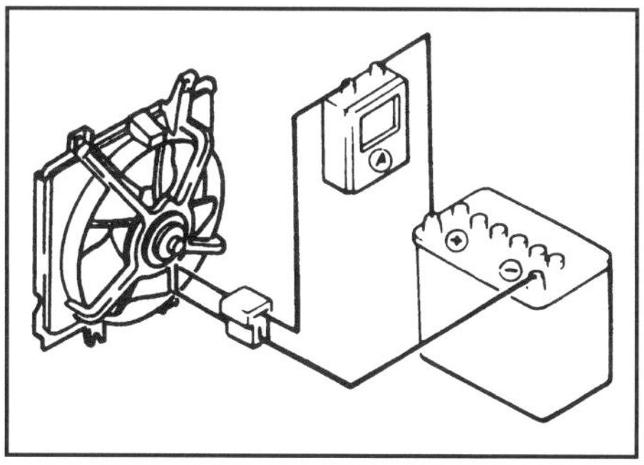

D9/5 TESTING THE FAN MOTOR.

battery wires.

FAN MOTOR REMOVAL AND INSTALLATION

6 Isolate the electrical system by disconnecting the battery negative (-) terminal after first having disarmed the audio unit's security system, if applicable. **Warning!** When loosening the negative (-) terminal take great care not to short the tool you are using across the positive (+) terminal (for more information ☞ 7). Release the electrical wire from the clip in the fan housing by pulling back the catch on the side of the clip and thereby releasing the wire retainer. The electrical connector block can now be separated by pushing the outer catch inwards and pulling the two halves apart.

7 The fan housing is fixed to the radiator body by four 10 mm bolts, threaded into spring clips. Note: you may find, as we did, that the bottom retaining bolts and their clips are considerably corroded. If this is the case, a soaking with penetrating oil some time before the bolts are removed will help. Once the two top bolts have been removed and the two bottom bolts loosened, the cooling fan assembly can be lifted away from the car.

8 With the assembly removed, unscrew the central nut which secures the fan unit to the motor shaft. Pull the fan off the shaft, then unscrew and remove the three motor mounting bolts to free the motor from the cowling. When installing the motor, tighten the mounting bolts to 3.9-4.9 Nm (40-50 Kgf cm / 35-43 lbf in). Fit the fan to the motor spindle, tightening the retaining nut to 1.5-2.5 Nm (15-25 kgf cm / 13-22 lbf in). Fit the cowling to the radiator, tightening the mounting bolts to 7.8-11 Nm (80-110 kgf cm / 69-95 lbf in).

FAN RELAY TESTING

9 Another possible cause of the fan failing to operate normally is that the fan relay has broken. This relay is housed in the fusebox on the right side of the engine compartment, its location being shown on the fusebox cover. Unplug and remove the relay and check for continuity between terminals **A** and **C** (no continuity should be shown) and terminals **B** and **D** (continuity should be shown).

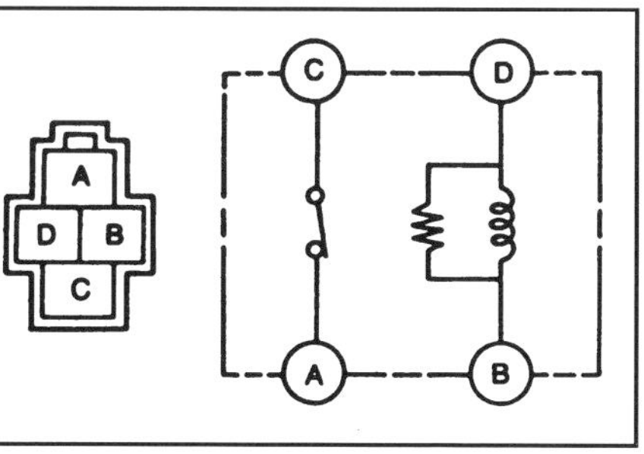

D8/9 FAN RELAY TEST (1).

10 Next, apply battery voltage across terminals **D** and **B** and check continuity between terminals **A** and **C**. With battery voltage applied as described, you should get a continuity reading (and you should hear a click as the relay operates). If the results obtained do not correspond with those described, fit a new relay.

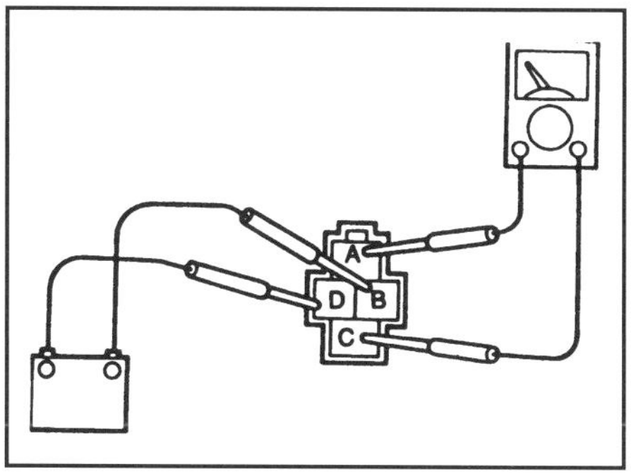

D8/10 FAN RELAY TEST (2).

9. HEATING & VENTILATION SYSTEM - HOW IT WORKS

☞ 1/1, 2 & 6/1.

1 The car interior is heated by hot coolant diverted through a heater matrix from the main cooling system. A slider on the heater control panel regulates the matrix temperature by controlling the flow of hot coolant through it. A second slider regulates the proportions of fresh and recirculated air by varying the position of a flap inside the heater unit. A third slider control selects how the air is distributed inside the vehicle, again using flap valves in the heater unit.

2 Connected by trunking to the heater unit, an electrically operated blower unit forces air through the matrix and into the passenger compartment according to the control settings. The blower motor has three operating positions, selected by a rotary switch on the control panel. A resistor assembly within the blower unit is used to control motor speed according to the switch setting.

3 The entire heating and ventilation system is mounted inside the car, behind the dash panel. The coolant system connections are accessible from the engine compartment, but removal of the heater unit will require removal of the entire dash panel first. The blower motor is easily accessible after the glovebox has been removed, and it is possible to remove the control panel after releasing the operating cables, again requiring removal of the glovebox, plus the steering column access cover. Unusually, the blower unit is protected by a

resettable circuit breaker housed in the internal fusebox, below the dash panel.

10. BLOWER UNIT - ELECTRICAL TESTS

☞ 1/1, 2 & 6/1.

CHECKING THE CIRCUIT BREAKER

1 If the blower unit fails to operate, the first thing to check is the circuit breaker. This will be found in the fusebox below the dash panel. On left-hand drive cars, the fusebox is mounted above the dead pedal on the left side of the car. In the case of right-hand drive vehicles, it is mounted above the accelerator pedal. In both cases, you can get to the fuses without any dismantling, but the location makes access awkward. First remove the two screws which secure the access panel below the steering column, then unclip the panel. You will need to slide the driver's seat right back and lie across it with your head in the footwell to be able to see the fusebox, and you will find that a flashlight will prove useful.

2 Open the fusebox cover and locate the circuit breaker - it will be found at the center of the

10/2 Circuit breaker location in fusebox.

unit. Check whether the red button has popped out, indicating that a fault has occurred and that the circuit breaker is open. If it has, try pressing it in (don't hold it in the closed position). It is possible that a momentary fault triggered the circuit breaker, and depressing the button may restore operation. If the button pops straight back out when you switch on the ignition and blower switch, however, you will need to investigate and repair the problem before it can be reset. An intermittent fault may mean that the breaker can be reset, but that it will pop out again when the fault next shows up.

CHECKING THE BLOWER MOTOR VOLTAGE

3 Remove the two sheet metal screws which secure the glovebox hinges to the hinge bar. Open the glovebox and lift it out of the dash panel. With the glovebox out of the way you have good access to the blower unit. Looking at the underside of the unit, locate the motor wiring connector which is close to the circular end of the motor body. Unplug the wiring connector and identify terminal **L** which you will find nearest the connector key. Using a voltmeter or multimeter, connect the meter negative (-) probe to ground and measure the

WIRE	VOLTAGE	ACTION REQUIRED
L/R (1-pin)	12 volts	OK - check voltage on wire L/W
	0 volts	Fit new blower motor
L/W	12 volts	OK - check L/R (4-pin connector)
	0 volts	Fit new resistor block assembly
L/R (4-pin)	12 volts	OK - check voltage on wire L/G
	0 volts	Fit new resistor block assembly
L/G	12 volts	OK - check voltage on wire L/Y
	0 volts	Fit new resistor assembly
L/Y	12 volts	OK - check blower switch voltage
	0 volts	Fit new resistor block assembly

T10/3 BLOWER RESISTOR BLOCK VOLTAGES.

voltage at terminal **L** with the ignition switch turned on and the blower switch at position 4 (maximum). You should read 12 volts. If not, there is a break in the wiring between the connector and the blower motor circuit breaker. If it checks out OK, check the resistor block terminal voltages to locate the faulty component as described below.

CHECKING THE RESISTOR BLOCK TERMINAL VOLTAGES

4 Locate the two wiring connectors (one single pin with L/W wire, and one four pin) - they are clipped to the side of the blower casing. Separate the connectors, check that the blower switch is off, and turn the ignition switch on. Using a voltmeter, check the terminal voltages on the wiring harness side of the connector following the table.

5 If the above checks have shown that the

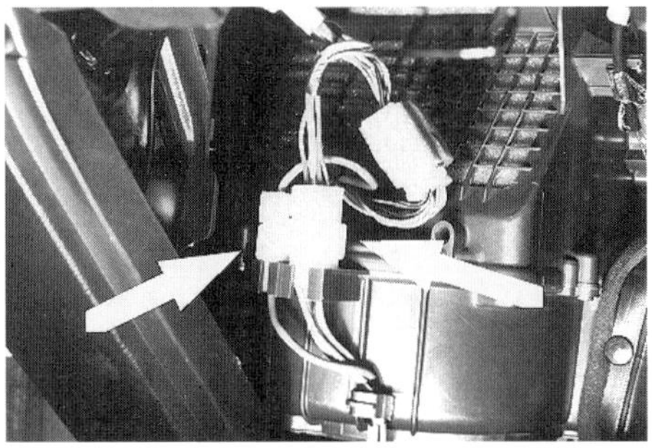

10/4 Blower wiring connectors.

resistor block or the blower motor are at fault, they should be replaced as required (☞ 6/11, 12). If the problem appears to lie with the blower switch, remove the control unit from the dash panel (☞ 6/15), then turn the ignition switch on and set the blower switch to the 4th (highest) position (leave the switch connector in place). Using a voltmeter, check the voltage between the black ground wire to the blower switch and ground. If 12 volts is shown, there is a fault between the switch and ground. You can confirm this by turning the ignition switch off and removing the switch connector. Check the black wire for continuity to ground and rewire if required.

6 If the last check showed 0 volts on the black ground wire, turn the ignition switch on, set the blower switch to off, and make the checks shown in the accompanying table with the wiring

WIRE	VOLTAGE	ACTION REQUIRED
L/W	0 volts	Check wire between switch and resistor
	12 volts	OK - move to L/R wire check
L/R	0 volts	Check wire between switch and resistor
	12 volts	OK - move to L/G wire check
L/G	0 volts	Check wire between switch and resistor
	12 volts	OK - move to L/Y wire check
L/Y	0 volts	Check wire between switch and resistor
	12 volts	Fit new blower switch

T10/6 BLOWER SWITCH TERMINAL VOLTAGES.

connected.

7 The above checks test the electrical operation of the heater system, with the obvious exception of the blower motor itself. This can be tested quite simply by unplugging the two-pin connector at the base of the motor housing, and connecting the motor directly to a 12 volt supply - use the Mazda's battery or a spare if you have one. **Warning!** Take care not to short the battery wires together. The motor should run normally when you do this. If not, fit a new motor (it cannot be dismantled for repair). For details on motor removal ☞ 6/12.

11. BLOWER UNIT - RESISTOR BLOCK CHECKING, REMOVAL & INSTALLATION

☞ 1/1, 2 & 6/1.

CHECKING

1 Before testing the resistor block, check that the motor is functioning normally ☞ 6/10/7. To gain access to the blower assembly, remove the two sheet metal screws which retain the glovebox hinges to the hinge bar and lift it away. If the blower motor runs normally when wired direct to an external battery, separate the two connectors which are clipped to the blower casing. **Warning!** Take care not to short the battery wires together.

2 Using a multimeter set to the X1000 range (or an ohmmeter) check for continuity between the single pin connector terminal and each of the four-pin connector terminals in turn, working on the blower unit side of the two connectors. No particular resistance figure is specified, but there should be continuity shown in each case. A lack of continuity shows that one of the resistors in the block has failed and the unit must be replaced. This usually corresponds with failure of the blower to operate on one of the switch settings.

REMOVAL AND INSTALLATION

3 + If you need to replace the resistor block, it is secured by two sheet metal screws to the

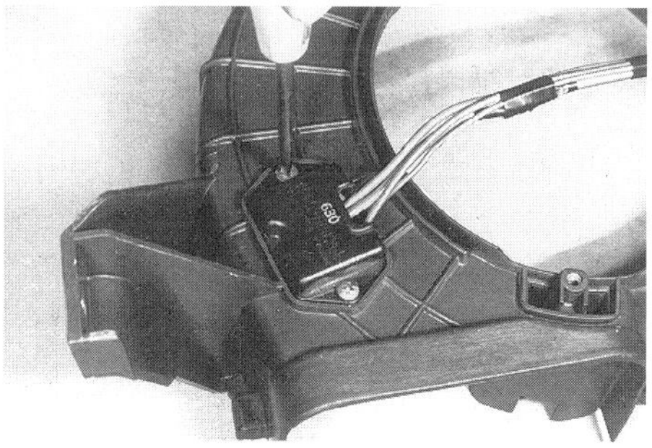

11/3a Unscrew the two retaining screws ...

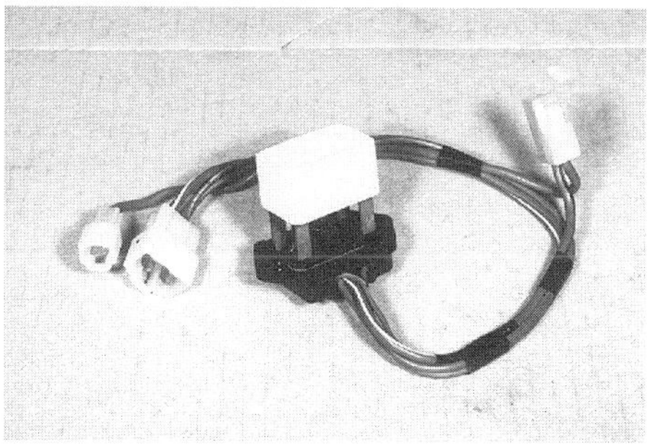

11/3b ... and lift the blower resistor from casing.

underside of the blower casing. Once these have been removed and the connectors slid out of their clips on the casing, the resistor block can be lifted away. Fit the new block to the underside of the casing, securing it with its screws, then fit the connectors to their clips and reconnect the wiring. Check that the blower system works normally before fitting the glovebox.

12. BLOWER MOTOR - CHECKING, REMOVAL & INSTALLATION

☞ 1/1, 2 & 6/1.

CHECKING

1 If you need to check or remove the blower motor, start by removing the two screws which retain the glovebox hinges to the hinge bar and then lift away the glovebox. The resulting aperture gives easier access to the blower assembly.

2 The blower motor can be tested quite simply by unplugging the two-pin connector at the base of the motor housing, and connecting the motor directly to a 12 volt supply (☞ 6/10/7) - use the Mazda's battery or a spare if you have one. The motor should run normally when you do this. **Warning!** Take care not to short the battery wires together.

REMOVAL AND INSTALLATION

3 If the motor is inoperative, you will have to fit a new one; it is not possible to dismantle or repair it. Unplug the single motor wiring connector from the underside of the motor casing then remove the three sheet metal screws which retain the blower motor unit to the bottom of the blower casing. The motor and its integral fan can now be lifted away.

4 Fit the new motor to the underside of the blower casing - noting that it only fits in one position - and tighten the retaining screws evenly. Reconnect the motor wiring and check that the blower works on all settings before installing the glovebox.

13. BLOWER UNIT - REMOVAL & INSTALLATION

☞ 1/1, 2 & 6/1.

1 Given the easy access to the blower motor and resistor block, it is hard to imagine any real need to remove the complete unit, other than for general access to the area around the unit. Apart from the blower motor and resistor block covered in the preceding sections, the blower unit consists of the main casing and a flap valve arrangement used to select either fresh air or recirculated air or a mixture of the two. This is operated from the control unit at the center of the dash panel.

2 To remove the unit, first detach the glovebox by removing the two sheet metal screws which secure the hinges to the hinge bar. The glovebox can then be lifted out of the dash panel, leaving a large access aperture.

3 Working in the footwell area, trace the control cable back to the spring clip which anchors the cable outer to the unit. Pop this out of the clip, then unhook the wire loop from the operating lever. Disconnect the two wiring connectors from the side of the unit (there is no need to disconnect the wiring which runs down to the blower motor). The unit can be removed from the car after releasing the two 10 mm nuts and single 10 mm bolt which secure it to its mounting points below the dash panel. On standard cars, note that the trunking linking the blower unit to the heater unit should be disconnected after withdrawing the plastic pin which anchors it. On air conditioned cars, the A/C cooling unit fits in place of the trunking, the join between it and the blower unit being secured by an over-center clip band. Flip the tab of the clip forward to free the connection.

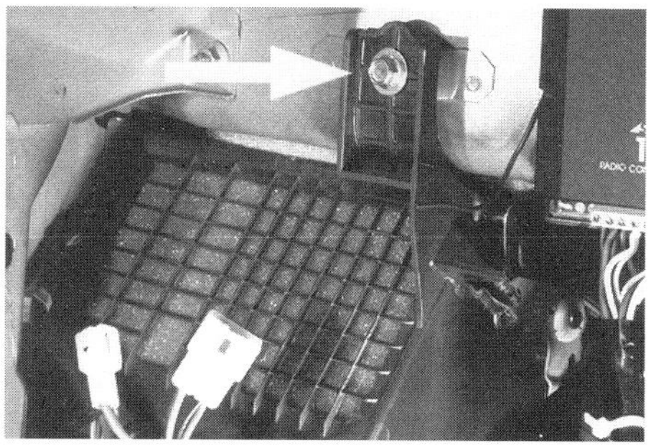

13/3a Blower unit upper mounting.

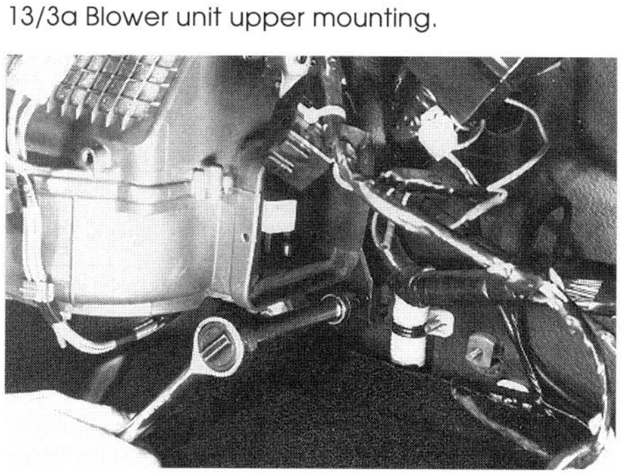

13/3b One of blower unit lower mountings.

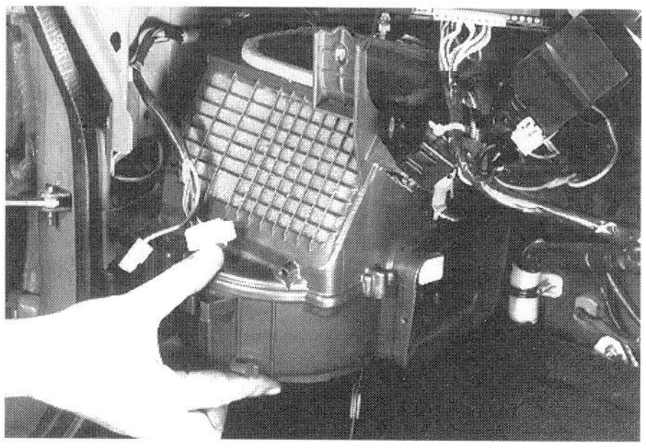

13/3c Lift out blower unit.

4 There is little that you can do with the unit once removed, but it's worth checking the operation of the flap valve arrangement. If you operate this by hand you will see how the mechanism has a cam arrangement which seals the flap firmly at each end of its travel. This relies on the foam layer on each side of the flap, the resilience of which allows the cam system to obtain a good seal. We can envisage that ageing of the foam might lead to deterioration of the seal - you may be able to recondition the flap by purchasing some thin foam sheeting from a hardware store and sticking it to each side of the flap, once the remains of the old foam have been cleaned off. Check with the foam supplier that the adhesive used is suitable for use on plastic materials. Note that a similar foam seal is fitted around the aperture at the top of the casing which connects to the fresh air inlet. The flap can be removed from the unit after releasing the single screw which retains the operating link.

5 When installing the unit, tighten the fasteners evenly to avoid distorting the plastic housing. Reconnect the operating cable, noting that the **REC/FRESH** lever on the control panel should be set to **FRESH** before the cable is connected. Check that after the cable has been connected the mechanism moves fully between the **REC** and **FRESH** positions when the control lever is operated. Reconnect the wiring connectors and check blower operation on all settings. Check that the trunking / air conditioning cooling unit joint is secure, then install the glovebox.

14. HEATER UNIT - REMOVAL, INSPECTION AND INSTALLATION

☞ 1/1, 2 & 6/1.

REMOVAL

1 The heater unit is installed below the dash panel at the center of the car, access for its removal requiring removal of the dash panel assembly; a complicated procedure not to be undertaken lightly. We know of no workarounds here. Access to the operating cables, one on each side of the unit, is possible through the glovebox aperture and by removing the access cover below the steering col-

umn. Replacement of the cables ☞ 6/15.

2 Drain the cooling system (☞ 6/2), noting the safety precautions regarding the risk from steam or hot coolant unless the engine is cold. You now need to remove the dash panel from the car. As mentioned above, this is a time consuming and complex procedure - be sure that you leave ad-

> *Oh no! The heater's leaking...*
> *If you ever have the misfortune of having the heater matrix spring a leak on you while driving, you can minimize damage if you act quickly. First, pull off the road so that you can work on the car in safety. As quickly as you can, open the hood and wrap thick rag over the radiator cap, then turn it counterclockwise to the first stop to release cooling system pressure - this will slow the leak to a trickle and you can then work more calmly. It is a good idea to allow the cooling system to cool down for a while - take this time to mop up inside the car as best you can.*
> *When the system is cool enough to handle safely, use pliers to slide back the clips which secure the hoses to the heater stubs at the firewall. Work the pipes off the stubs with a screwdriver blade. If you have something in the car that you can push into the open ends of the hoses (maybe a couple of large bolts or rods) do so, then refit the clips to secure and close the hose ends.*
> *Otherwise, trace the hoses back to where they connect to the water thermosensor housing on the back of the engine, and to the return pipe which runs forward below the exhaust manifold. You now need to connect the two pipe ends together. Use the pipe from the thermosensor housing, bending it round to connect to the return pipe end, having first removed its hose. Don't worry too much about kinking the hose - the object is to take the heater out of the cooling system so that engine cooling can be maintained.*
> *Once you've done this, try to find water to top up the cooling system (use the water in the screen washer reservoir if you need to), then refit the radiator cap and run the engine to check for leaks. If all is well, you can continue your journey - the car can be used like this until you can get a new matrix fitted.*

equate time for the job. If you know that you need to fit a new unit, you should have this ready to be fitted, or the car will have to remain off the road until you obtain a new one. Removal and installation procedure for the dash panel ☞ 10/4.

3 Once the dash panel has been removed, the heater unit is relatively easy to deal with. From the engine compartment, locate the two hose connections to the heater stubs which project through the firewall. Using pliers, squeeze the ears of the hose clips and slide them along the hoses, clear of the stubs. Use a screwdriver blade to push each hose off its stub, marking one stub and hose to ensure that they are fitted correctly. Allow any residual water to drain out of the stubs.

4 Inside the car, the heater control cables will have been detached during removal of the dash panel. Remove the trunking (standard cars) by pulling out the small pin which retains it. On air conditioned models, release the heater to cooling unit by flipping the tab of the over-center clip which secures the joint between the two.

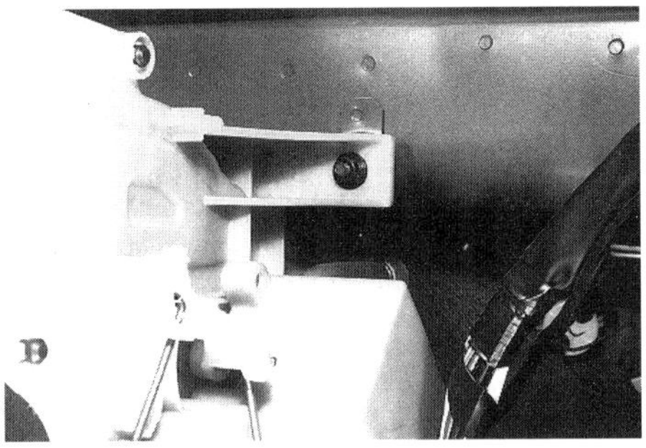

14/4a One of heater unit top mountings.

Remove the two 10 mm nuts at the top rear of the heater unit and the single 10 mm nut at the lower front. The unit is now free to be removed, but before pulling the stubs back through the firewall, try to tip the unit back a little to empty excess water. We also suggest that you put some rag over the carpet - there will be some water spillage and this may contain sediment that could cause staining.

DISMANTLING AND INSPECTION

5 The heater unit is handed depending on

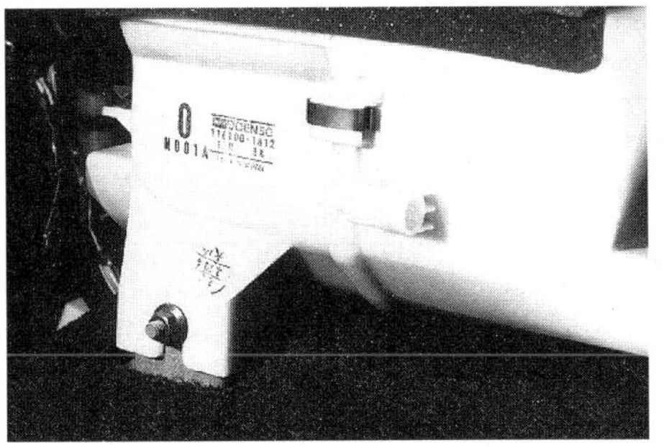

14/4b Heater unit lower mounting.

whether the car is left- or right-hand drive. On left-hand drive models, the heater matrix is fitted from the left, while on right-hand drive cars it fits from the right. The various linkages are handed accordingly. The linkages and the various flap valves in the unit are great fun to play around with - it's worth doing so before you start any dismantling so that you form a picture of how they operate - this could help during assembly.

6 You need to remove the linkages from each side of the unit before the heater matrix can be removed. The arrangement is shown in the line drawing accompanying this section - study this carefully before you start to avoid confusion later! Remove the linkages and put them to one side, preferably marked left and right side for identification.

7 Separate the casing halves after prying off the spring clips which secure the join. Place some rag over the clips as you lever them off to prevent their escape. With the unit on its side, separate the casing halves, trying to leave the flap valves in position in the lower half. Release the heater matrix pipe clamps and lift the matrix out of the casing.

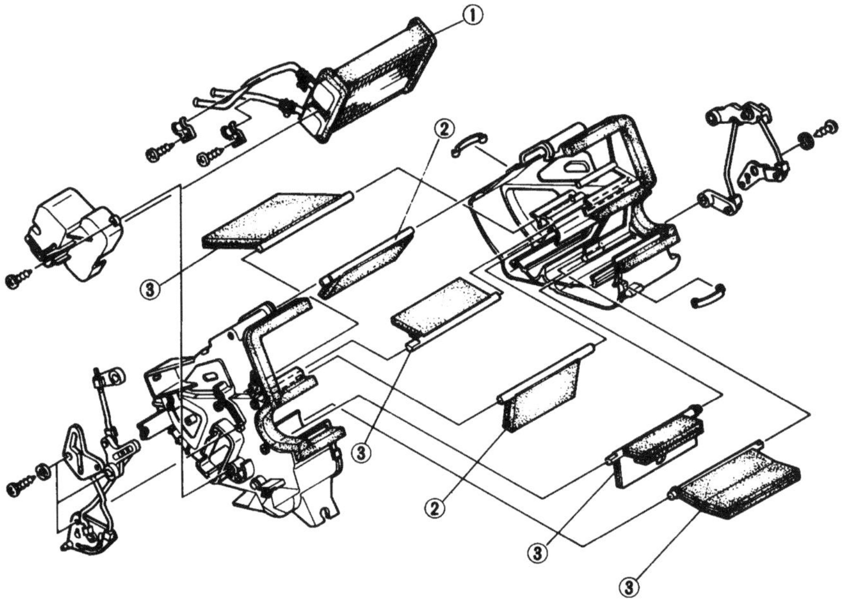

D14/6 EXPLODED VIEW OF THE HEATER UNIT
1 Heater matrix. 2 Air blend flaps. 3 Airflow control flaps.

8 The heater matrix is the vital component in the unit, and should be closely scrutinized. Accumulated debris on the outside of the matrix can be removed by washing or blowing it through with compressed air. Check carefully for signs of leakage. We would recommend that even a slight leak is good cause for fitting a new unit. Remember how long it took you to get at the heater unit, and ask yourself whether you want to go through the procedure again. No? - nor us. Also consider the hassle if the heater suddenly sprang a major leak in service, and the damage to the car's interior that might be caused.

9 Connect a garden hose to one of the matrix stubs and run water through it. This will probably expel some sediment, but the important thing to check is that the water flows freely. If the matrix is restricted, it is probably partially blocked - poor heater function would suggest this. If so, the best option is again to fit a new matrix.

10 We suggest that you do not disturb the operating linkage without good cause. There is provision for coarse adjustment on some of the link rods - these have threaded ends held in plastic clips - but this is intended for the initial setup of the flap interconnection during assembly of the unit, not later adjustment. If you do need to disturb the linkages, we suggest that you place the assembly on a sheet of paper and trace around it as an assembly template. In the case of adjustable link rods, mark their position with paint or typist's correcting fluid before you remove them, and duplicate exactly this setting during assembly.

11 The flap valves can be left in the casing unless you need to remove them for some reason. If you do, make a sketch of their positions and mark the visible end of each one to assist you during assembly. If possible, remove just one flap at a time to avoid confusion. The flaps and casing should not normally require attention though, if the foam covering on the flaps has begun to break up, the selection of the various vent outlets will be a little imprecise. You could consider fitting new foam - try a hardware store for thin foam sheeting and a suitable adhesive.

REASSEMBLY AND INSTALLATION

12 Fit any of the vent flaps removed, checking that they are fitted in their correct relative positions and move freely. Install the heater matrix and fit the pipe securing clips. Close the two halves of the housing, guiding the vent flaps into position before securing the two halves with the spring clips. Fit the operating linkages at each end of the unit, checking that the vent flaps locate correctly and that, when assembly is complete, the mechanism operates normally.

13 When installing the unit in the car, feed the heater stubs through the firewall and locate the lugs over the mounting studs. Tighten the fixing nuts securely, but do not overtighten. Reconnect the trunking or cooling unit connection (depending on the equipment fitted to your car). Reconnect the heater pipes to the stubs in the engine compartment and fit the securing clips.

14 Reassemble and install the dash panel (☞ 10/4). When connecting the heater unit cables, set the control sliders as follows. Set the top slider (temperature blend control) to the maximum position (fully to the right). Set the bottom slider (airflow mode control) to VENT (fully to the left). After reconnecting the cables, check that both the above controls move smoothly and fully through their complete range.

15. HEATER CONTROL ASSEMBLY - REMOVAL, INSPECTION & INSTALLATION

☞ 1/1, 2 & 6/1.

1 📷+ If access to the heater control assembly is required it is necessary to remove the rear console and the center console. Isolate the electrical system by disconnecting the battery negative (-) terminal after first having disarmed the audio unit's security system, if applicable. **Warning!** When loosening the negative (-) terminal take great care not to short the tool you are using across the positive (+) terminal (for more information ☞ 7). Remove the two screws securing the glovebox hinges to the hinge bar and lift the glovebox away. On the driver's side of the car, remove the two

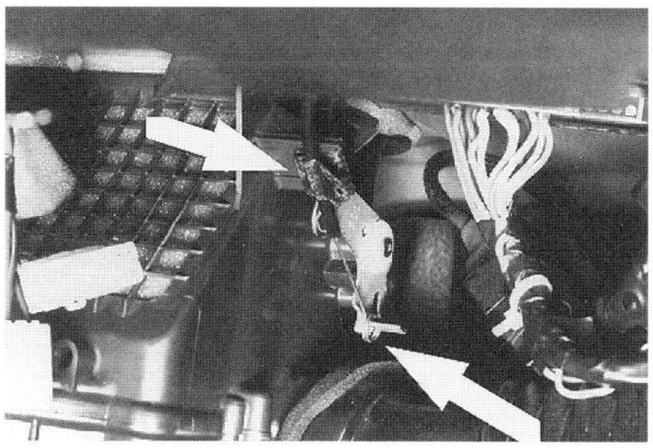

15/1a Blower unit control cable mounting.

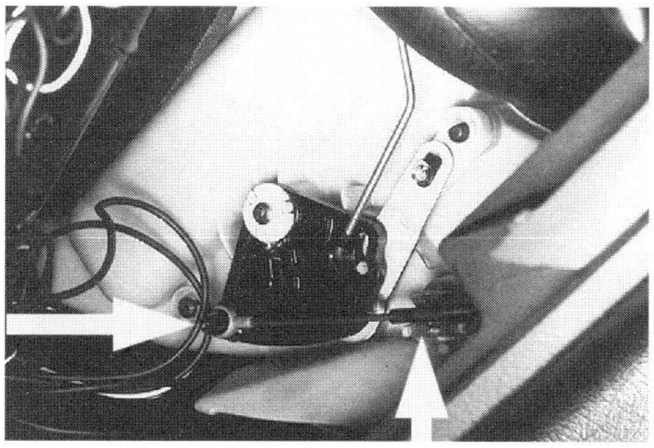

15/1b One of heater unit cable mountings.

screws securing the access panel below the steering column, then unclip and remove the panel. Working through the apertures on each side of the dash panel, trace and disconnect the heater control cables. One of the three connects to the blower unit, the remaining two connect on each side of the heater unit. Unclip each cable outer from its support, and unhook the outer from the operating lever end.

REAR CONSOLE REMOVAL

2 Open the storage box at the back of the rear console and remove the two sheet metal screws from the base. Lift out the ashtray, and remove the single sheet metal screw from the recess below it. Now, remove the two sheet metal screws, one on each side, which secure the front of the console. Unscrew the gearshift knob. The console can now be removed, noting that you will have to disengage the fuel filler release lever as it is lifted out, and that the ashtray light connector and (where fitted) the window winder switch connector should be separated to permit removal. Put the screws and gearshift knob in the storage box and place the unit to one side.

CENTER CONSOLE PANEL AND HEATER CONTROL UNIT REMOVAL

3 To get access to the center console fixing screws you need to remove the two eyeball vents at the top of the unit. This is no easy task - the vents are secured from the back by two spring clips and there is no means of access to them. The only removal method is to pry the vents out using a screwdriver, and a certain amount of cosmetic damage to the console panel and vent surround is almost inevitable. We spent a considerable amount of time getting the vents out of the project car, and concluded that the fixing arrangement is designed for ease of assembly, but not ease of subsequent removal. We suggest that before starting this operation you look at the photographs we took of the vents so you can see how they are retained ☞ 10/4.

4 Use the thinnest flat-bladed screwdriver you have, introduce the tip between the vent surround and the panel recess, pushing it in at around 45° as far as it will go. If you can, use something between the screwdriver and the panel to minimize damage to the surface by spreading the load. Whatever you use will have to be very thin - try a strip cut from a drinks can. Gradually push back on the screwdriver until the vent pops out of the recess.

5 When you attempt removal you will probably think, as we did, that the vent will not come out in one piece. You certainly have to apply an undesirable amount of force, and unless you have much lighter clips than the ones we found on our car, both the panel and the vent assembly will distort quite badly during the removal operation. That said, the vents did eventually come out, leaving slight marking on them and the panel, but with no further damage.

6 An alternative removal method is to thread some fairly strong cord or string through the vent louvres. You need to loop the cord around the vent, so use a length of wire to hook the cord and pull it back through. Grasp the ends of the cord and pull hard, while supporting the panel with your free hand. The vent should pop out. We should mention that we did not try this method ourselves, but suspect that you may need to wrap some rag around your hand to prevent the cord from cutting into your skin.

7 With the eyeball vents removed, remove the two sheet metal screws which pass upwards through the vent recesses to secure the top of the

panel. At the bottom, there are two further screws securing the panel to a metal support bracket fixed to the transmission tunnel - these should also be removed. The panel can now be pulled away slightly, but there will be further wiring to disconnect before it can be removed completely.

8 The wiring connections behind the center console panel vary according to the country in which the car was sold, and depend on various options or aftermarket items fitted. The top of the panel carries the eyeball vents, and between them, the switches for the hazard lights and the headlight lifter. The heater control assembly comes next, but below that a number of options may be fitted. Our project car had aftermarket alarm sensors, plus a removable Clarion stereo radio/cassette unit and an analog clock fitted - other options include various stereo systems, with or without CD players. Our best advice here is to move the panel away carefully, check the wiring connections on the back and disconnect them, noting the position and type of each connector. Depending on the installation on your car, you may find that you don't need to separate all of the connectors to get access to the heater controls, but if you do access will be easier.

9 With the panel out of the way you'll find that the heater control unit is retained by four sheet metal screws (these may not be fitted on all cars). Once these have been removed, the control unit will be loose in the center console recess, located over pegs in the plastic moulding. Pull the unit toward you, feeding the control cables through from under the dash panel as you do - they are quite stiff and will tend to snag. Once you can reach behind the unit, locate and unplug the blower switch wiring connectors and lift it away.

INSPECTION

10 + If cable replacement was your object in removing the control unit, you can go ahead and do it at this stage. Each cable is secured by a clamp to the control unit, the inner wire being attached by either a circular eye or by a simple stepped end to its lever. The knobs on the lever ends just pull off the levers, and the levers themselves are retained by screws and guide blocks. Our photographs plus the exploded view of the unit will help you identify how it all fits together, but it is quite complex. We suggest that you study how the lever system operates before dismantling anything - the levers use a neat arrangement which makes the ends slide across their travel instead of moving through a small arc as you would expect, and this makes for a little extra complication. We further recommend that you deal with one lever assembly and cable at a time to avoid any confusion.

11 + To remove the blower switch, pull off the lever and switch knobs and unclip the front panel from the unit. Carefully peel away the thin facia plate - this has a self-adhesive backing.

12 Underneath you'll find an interesting piece of clear plastic with tiny prisms on the front surface. This is a light guide carrying illumination from a nearby light to the back of the switch surround - the prisms ensure even lighting.

13 + Lift the light guide out to reveal the two screws which secure the switch. Remove the screws to free the switch, unclipping the wiring connector from the back of the control assembly.

14 Finally, whatever else you do while the unit is out, we recommend that you check all the bulbs and replace any that are burned out - there would be a lot of work to be done all over again if you missed this opportunity and noticed the problem later.

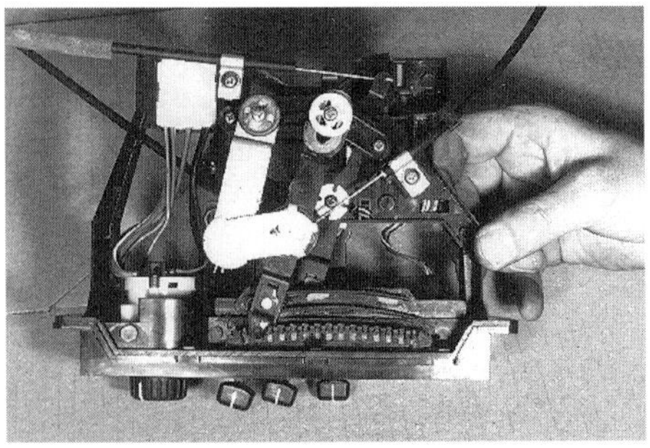

15/10a Two cables at top of control unit ...

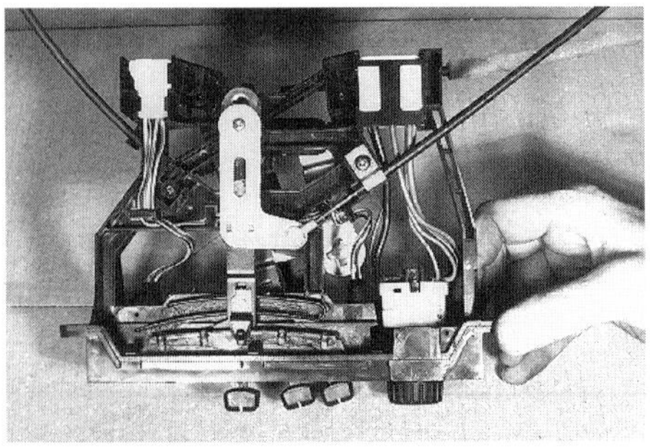

15/10b ... and one underneath.

15/11a Unclip the front panel ...

15/11b ... peel off the thin facia plate ...

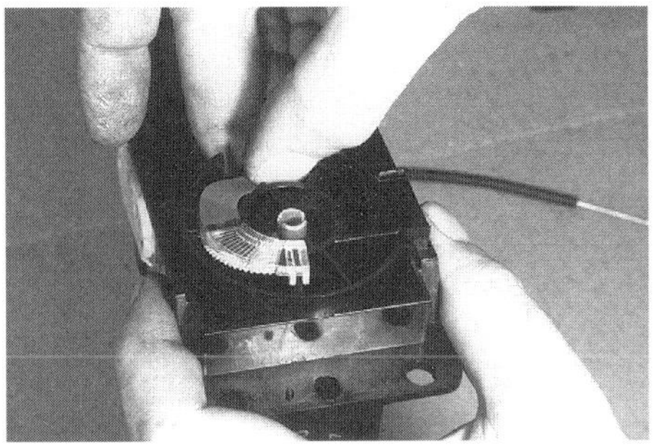

15/12 ... lift out light guide prism ...

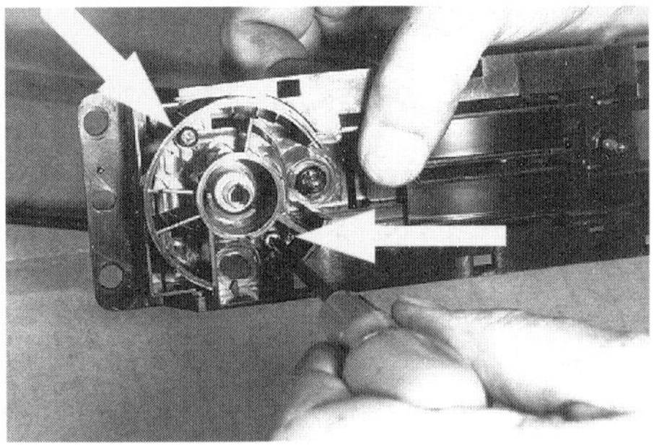

15/13a ... unscrew two securing screws ...

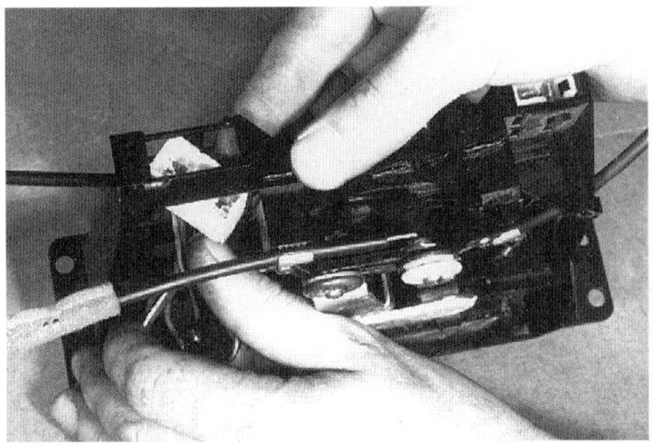

15/13b ... and release the wiring connector.

Position		a	b	c	d	e	f	g	h
Blower switch	OFF								
	First	○						○	
	Second			○				○	○
	Third					○		○	○
	Fourth		○					○	○
A/C switch	OFF								
	ON	○			○				
		○					○		

○—○ : Indicates continuity
○-▶|-○ : Indicates diode

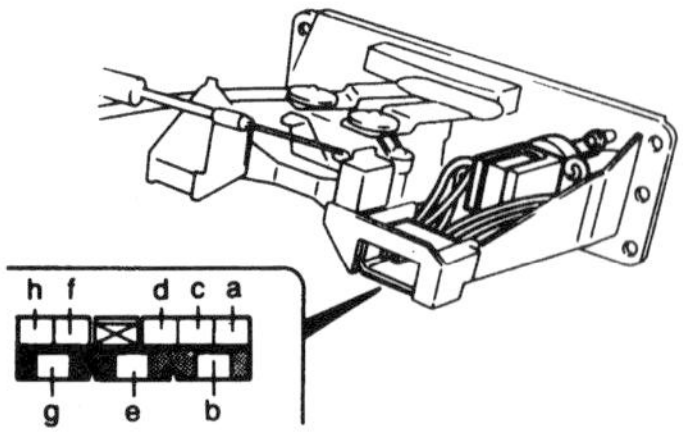

T&D15/16 CHECKING BLOWER & AIR-CONDITIONING SWITCH.

CHECKING THE BLOWER & AIR CONDITIONING SWITCH

15 The operation of the blower / air conditioning switch can be checked after the heater control assembly has been removed as described above.

16 Use a continuity checker or a multimeter set to a resistance range to check for continuity at the various switch positions. These are shown in the accompanying diagram and table. Note that in the case of the air conditioning switch (where fitted) there are diodes fitted between the terminal pairs. This means that continuity should be shown in one direction, with no continuity if the test probes are reversed.

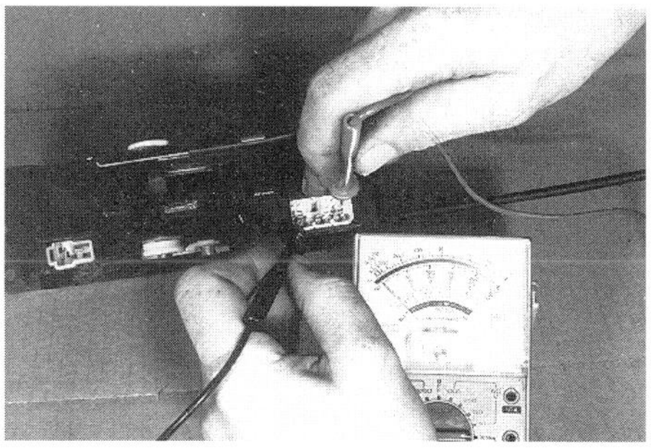

15/16 Testing blower & a/c switch.

INSTALLATION

17 Check that the control unit is reassembled correctly and that the control sliders and cables operate normally. Fit the light guide in the front of the unit, then clip the front panel into place and fit the slider and switch knobs. Install the control unit in the center console, connecting the wiring connectors and feeding the control cables into position. The cables cannot easily be connected incorrectly; the longest cable runs to the blower unit (**REC/FRESH** control), while the remaining two have different ends and fit either side of the heater unit.

18 Before you connect the cables, you should set up the control sliders as follows: Set the top slider (temperature blend control) to the maximum position (fully to the right). The center slider (**REC/FRESH** control) should be set to **FRESH**, or fully to the right. Set the bottom slider (airflow mode control) to **VENT** (fully to the left). After reconnecting the cables, check that the above controls move smoothly and fully through their complete range. Once you are satisfied the controls operate normally, secure the unit with the four sheet metal screws (where fitted).

19 You can now install the center console front panel, remembering to reconnect the wiring to the stereo (don't forget the antenna cable), the clock, the hazard light/headlight lifter switches and any other accessories installed in the panel. Make sure that you route the wiring correctly and that it does not become trapped as the panel is fitted. We strongly suggest that, before finally securing the panel, you check the operation of all electrical switches and accessories - don't forget how difficult removal of the eyeball vents was! Only when you are sure that these are operating correctly should you fit the two retaining screws through the eyeball sockets, and the two lower screws securing the panel to the transmission tunnel bracket.

20 Before installing the eyeball vents, we suggest spraying a little WD40 or a similar silicone-based lubricant on the outer surface - this might help a little if they need to be removed at a later date. Pop the vents back into their sockets (note how easily they install - you might assume that they are not fitted correctly, but just try pulling them out again). Fit the steering column access panel and the glovebox. Install the rear console, remembering to reconnect the ashtray light wire and, where fitted, the window winder switch connector. Secure the rear console with the two front screws, the single screw in the ashtray recess, and the two screws through the base of the storage box. Fit the ashtray.

16. AIR CONDITIONING SYSTEM - CHECKING

☞ 1/1, 2 & 6/1.

Warning! Skin contact with R-12 refrigerant contained in the air conditioning system could result in frostbite.

Warning! Combustion of R-12 refrigerant will produce the toxic gas phosgene (carbonyl chloride, or $COCL_2$).

Warning! Discharge to the atmosphere of R-12 refrigerant is **ILLEGAL** in most countries, and immoral in all.

Warning! Under no circumstances attempt disconnection of any part of the air conditioning system at home (see *'Precautions'* below).

1 As mentioned at the start of this chapter, air conditioning is offered as an option on all Miata/MX5s. The system, where fitted, integrates almost seamlessly with the existing heating and ventilation installation; the compressor mounts on the left side of the engine and is connected by pipes and hoses to the cooling unit and condenser (radiator) which is secured to the front of the cooling system radiator. An additional electric fan is fitted to improve the airflow through the double radiators, the additional fan being switched by a dedicated air conditioning system thermosensor.

2 Inside the car, the pipework to and from the condenser passes through the firewall and into the cooling unit, which is mounted under the dash panel, on the passenger side of the car. This unit simply replaces the plastic ducting used on non-air conditioned cars and connects directly between the heater and blower units.

PRECAUTIONS

3 Almost any mechanical work on the air conditioning system requires that the freon-based refrigerant is first discharged into a commercial recovery unit, and that the system is later charged and its operation tested properly. **Under no circumstances** should the system be allowed to vent to the atmosphere. In every responsible country in

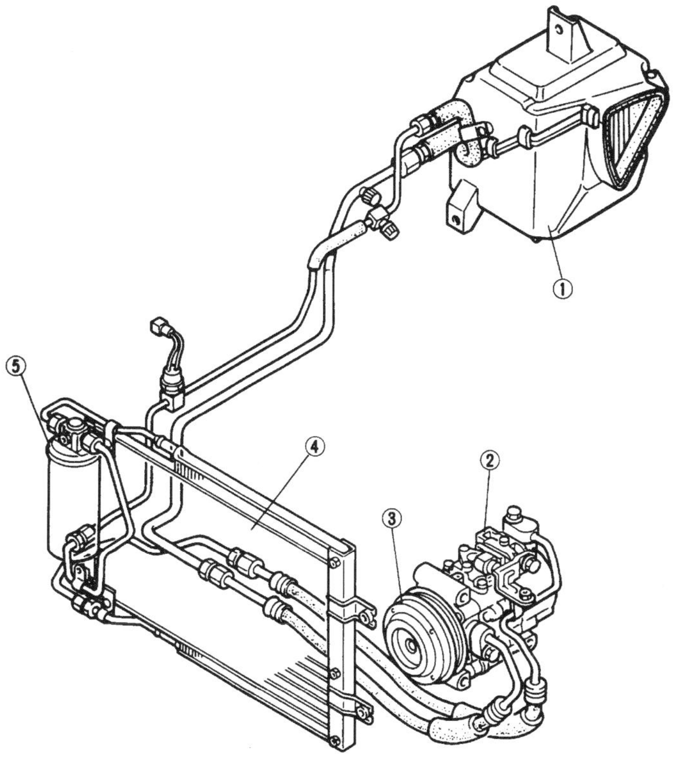

D16/1 AIR CONDITIONING SYSTEM

1 Cooling unit. 2 Compressor. 3 Magnetic clutch & pulley. 4 Condenser. 5 Receiver/drier.

the world this is illegal, and is a practice that we would in no way condone.

4 You should also be aware of the risk of personal injury posed by contact with the refrigerant; any contact with the skin will result in localized frostbite, and suitable protective clothing must be worn at all times. Also, contact between the R-12 refrigerant and flame will produce phosgene, an extremely toxic gas. Given the high cost of the equipment required to handle the refrigerant, and the attendant health and safety risks, we consider that all such work should be carried out professionally, either by a suitably equipped Mazda dealer, or by a qualified air conditioning specialist.

5 We regret that we are unable to cover mechanical procedures in greater depth, but feel that personal safety and environmental considerations preclude this. This section covers preliminary checks of peripheral equipment only.

VISUAL CHECK OF REFRIGERANT CHARGE

6 A quick check of the refrigerant charge can be made by opening the hood and observing the sight glass which is located on top of the receiver/drier unit and visible through the circular access hole in the panel in front of the radiator.

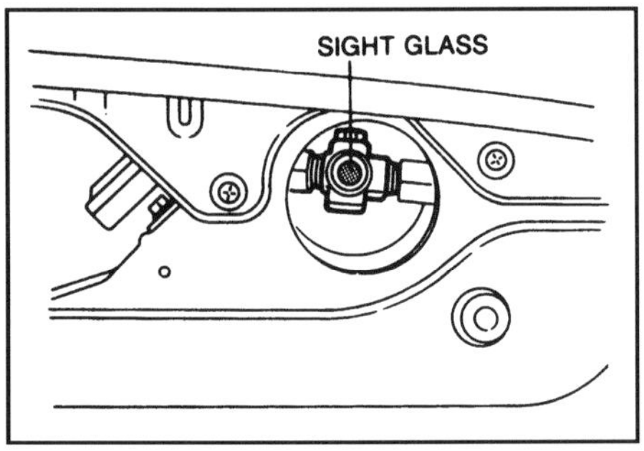

D16/6 LOCATION OF A/C SIGHT GLASS IN FRONT PANEL OF ENGINE COMPARTMENT.

7 Start the engine, and run it at a fast idle for a few minutes. Meanwhile, the air conditioning should be run at maximum cooling. Check the refrigerant visible in the sight glass. If the charge is correct, no bubbles should be seen. Bubbles in the refrigerant indicate insufficient charge.

8 Immediately the air conditioning is turned off, the refrigerant in the sight glass should foam, then become clear. If there is no foaming, the refrigerant charge is excessive. If you find indications that the refrigerant charge is incorrect, have the system checked professionally and recharged as required.

CHECKING THERMOSWITCH OPERATION

9 The thermoswitch monitors the temperature of the evaporator in the cooling unit, the switch contacts being open below 0°C (32°F) and closed above this temperature. To check the operation of the switch, remove the glovebox by unscrewing the two sheet metal screws which retain it to the hinge bar. Lift away the glovebox to reveal the cooling unit mounted between the blower and heater units.

10 Start the engine and allow it to idle for a few minutes, with the air conditioning switch turned off, and the blower set to maximum. After a few minutes, turn off the blower switch and stop the engine. Locate and disconnect the thermoswitch connector at the heater side of the cooling unit. Connect a continuity tester or a multimeter set to a resistance range to the switch terminals. A continuity reading should be indicated. If the engine is now run again, with the air conditioning switched on, the thermoswitch contacts should open as the cooling unit reaches 0°C (32°F). If the results are not as indicated, have the cooling unit removed and the thermoswitch checked further and replaced if required.

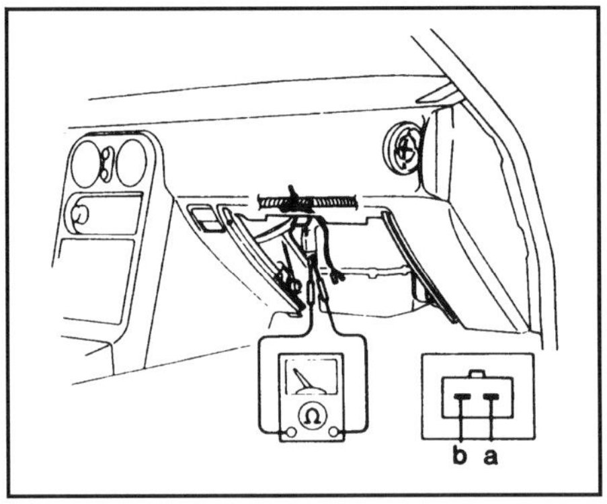

D16/10 CHECKING THERMOSWITCH AT CONNECTOR.

CHECKING THE SYSTEM FITTINGS AND REFRIGERANT LINES

11 Check the cooling system components and refrigerant lines, paying particular attention to any sign of staining around any of the pipe or hose unions. If staining is noted, a leak is indicated, and the car should be taken to a Mazda dealer or air conditioning specialist for testing with a gas leak tester. If necessary, have the system discharged, the faulty joint, union or line replaced, and the system recharged and tested.

CHECKING THE CONDENSER COOLING FAN

12 The condenser cooling fan is essentially the same as the normal cooling system fan, except it is mounted on the right-hand side of the radiator: it can be dealt with in the same way as the other fan ☞ 2/8. **Warning!** The fan operates during this test - keep hands and loose clothing well away from the fan area during the test and do not short the battery wires together. When checking fan operation, connect the battery as follows: with the wiring connector held with the key uppermost, connect the battery positive (+) terminal to the left-hand connector pin and ground the right-hand pin to the battery negative (-) terminal. No current figure is specified, but the motor should run smoothly. If replacement is indicated ☞ 6/8.

CHECKING THE AIR CONDITIONING RELAY

13 If the air conditioning system refuses to operate, it is possible that the air conditioning relay is faulty.

14 Unplug the relay and carry out the resistance check, following the terminal identification and continuity readings shown in the accompanying line drawing and table. Note that where a diode is indicated in the table, you should find continuity in one direction and no continuity if the meter probes are reversed. If not as specified the relay must be replaced. If it checks out normally, go on to the next step.

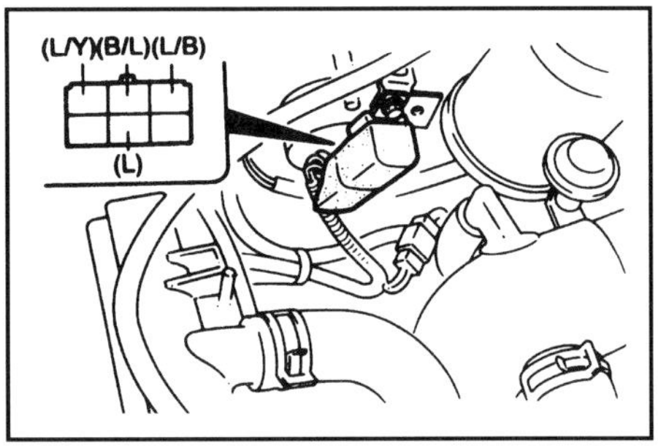

D16/14A A/C RELAY LOCATION AND WIRE COLOUR CODES.

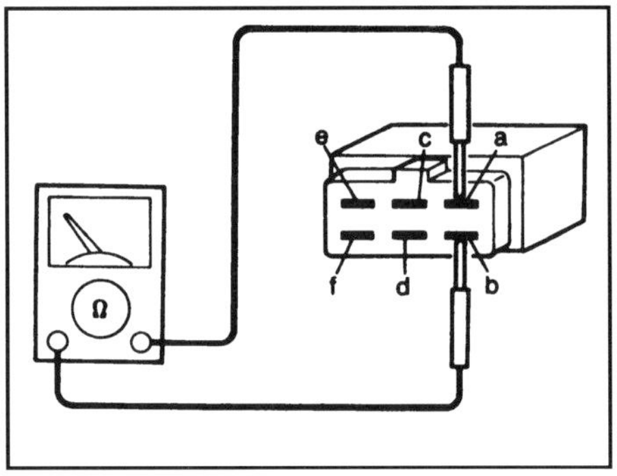

D16/14B A/C RELAY CONTINUITY CHECK 1.

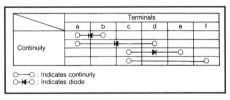

	Terminals					
	a	b	c	d	e	f
Continuity	○─◄	─○				
	○──	──	◄──	──○		
			○──	─►─	──○	
			○──	──	──	──○

○──○ : Indicates continuity
○─◄─○ : Indicates diode

T16/14 A/C RELAY CONTINUITY CHECK 1.

15 Connect a 12 volt battery to the relay, the positive (+) lead to terminal **d**, and the negative lead to terminal **a**. With the battery connected as described, there should be continuity between terminals **c** and **e** of the relay. If this is not the case, fit a new relay. **Warning!** Take care not to short the battery wires together.

MAGNETIC CLUTCH CHECKS

16 The air conditioning compressor operation is controlled by a magnetic clutch, which is switched on under certain operating conditions: the air conditioning and blower switches must be turned ON and the engine must be running. This information is sensed by the ECU, which estab-

lishes a ground circuit to the air conditioning relay. The relay operates, applying battery voltage to the magnetic clutch. The clutch is then locked up and the system operates. It should also be noted that the clutch operation is effectively controlled by the ECU, and that is in turn dependent on engine load conditions to some extent.

17 If the magnetic clutch appears to be inoperative, check the following items in sequence:

- *Check the WIPER 20A fuse housed in the fusebox in the engine compartment.*
- *Check the 20A AD FAN fuse housed in the fusebox behind the steering column access panel.*

If either of the fuses has burned out check the wiring for shorts and repair as necessary before fitting a new fuse.

18 If the fuses check out OK, open the hood and disconnect the magnetic clutch switch (B/R) wire at the single pin connector next to the headlight lifter motor on the left side of the car. Turn on the blower and air conditioning switches, then check for battery voltage between the B/R wire and ground. If you read 12 volts, continue the sequence as described below - if not, skip to *paragraph 21*.

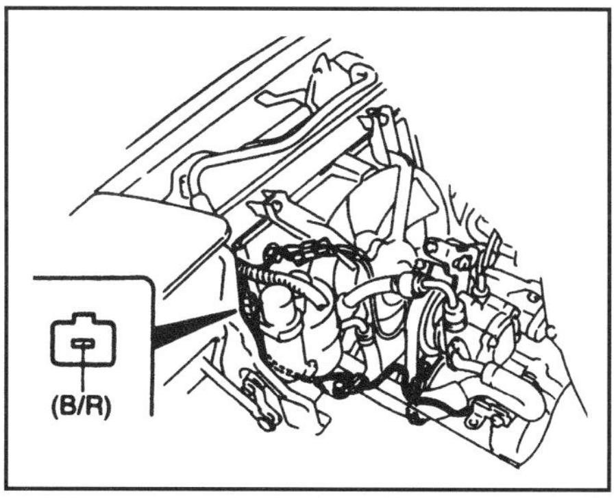

D16/18 CHECKING VOLTAGE AT A/C MAGNETIC CLUTCH SINGLE PIN CONNECTOR.

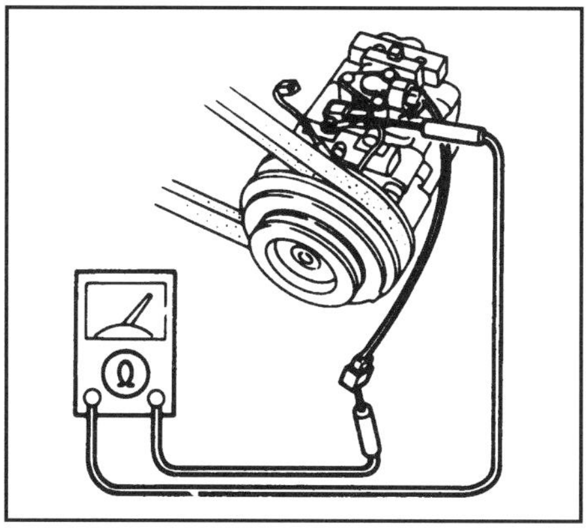

D16/19 CHECKING THERMOSWITCH CONNECTOR CONTINUITY.

19 Refer to the accompanying line drawing and disconnect the thermoswitch connector. Check the continuity of the switch. If there is no continuity, the switch should be replaced. If continuity is found move on to the next step.

20 Refer to the accompanying line drawing and disconnect the magnetic clutch wire at the compressor. Check for continuity between the wire terminal and ground, using an ohmmeter or multimeter set to the X1000 range. If there is no continuity, you will have to get a new magnetic clutch fitted by a Mazda dealer.

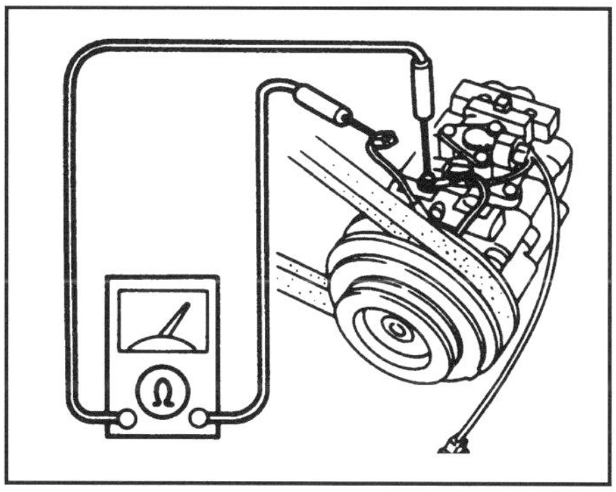

D16/20 CHECKING CONTINUITY OF A/C MAGNETIC CLUTCH CONNECTOR AT COMPRESSOR.

21 Refer to the accompanying line drawing and the following table. Check for battery voltage on the air conditioning relay terminal connector terminals, noting that the engine must be running, and the air conditioning and blower switches turned **ON** during these checks. (If you find a fault on the L/G wire, check the wire connection between the **AD FAN 20A** fuse and the **A/C** (air conditioning) relay. If a fault is evident on the L/G wire, check between the **WIPER 20A** fuse and the **A/C** relay).

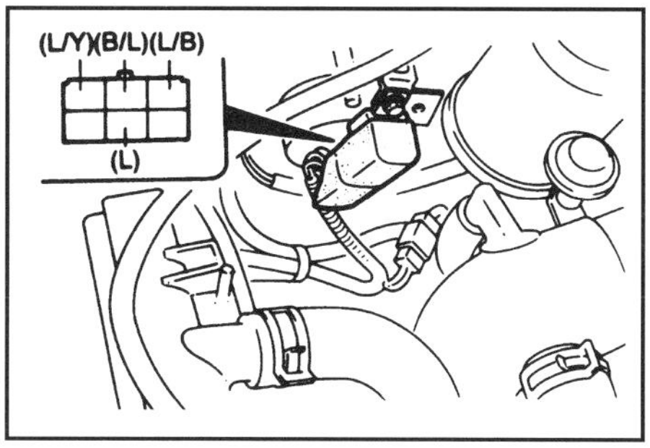

D16/21 CHECKING VOLTAGE AT A/C RELAY TERMINALS.

Wire	Volts	Action
B/L	12	Check pressure switch
	0	Check wire L/Y
L/Y	12	Check wire L/G
	0	Repair wire L/G
L	12	Check wire L/B
	0	Repair wire L/G
L/B	12	Get ECU checked
	0	Fit new A/C relay

T14/21CHECKING VOLTAGE AT A/C RELAY

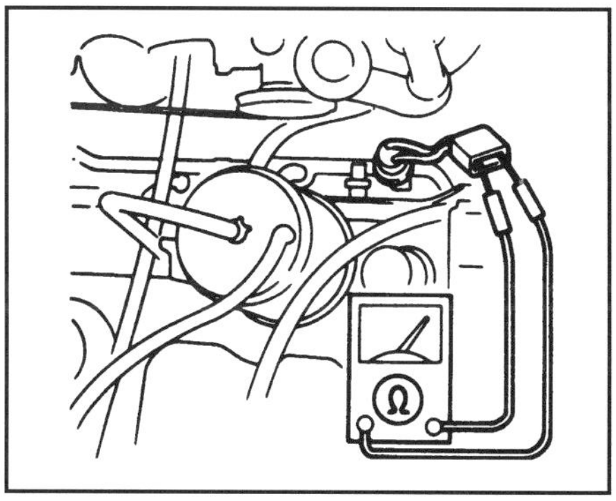

D16/22 CHECKING CONTINUITY BETWEEN REFRIDGERANT PRESSURE SWITCH WIRE TERMINALS.

22 The final check in this sequence is to check for continuity between the refrigerant pressure switch wiring terminals. Refer to the accompanying line drawing and disconnect the wiring connector. If continuity is found, check for a wiring fault between the A/C relay and the pressure switch, and between the switch and the magnetic clutch.

23 If you are unable to diagnose and correct the fault from the above sequence, you will have to have the system checked by a Mazda dealer, who will be able to perform a refrigerant pressure test as a final check of the switch condition, and who will also be able to fit a new switch if necessary.

AMERICAN/ENGLISH GLOSSARY OF AUTOMOTIVE TERMS

American	English
A-arm	Wishbone (suspension)
Antenna	Aerial
Axleshaft	Halfshaft
Back-up	Reverse
Barrel	Choke/venturi
Block	Chock/wedge
Box end wrench	Ring spanner
Bushing	Bush
Clutch hub	Synchro hub
Coast	Freewheel
Convertible	Drop head
Cotter pin	Split pin
Counterclockwise	Anti-clockwise
Countershaft	Layshaft (of gearbox)
Crescent wrench	Open-ended spanner
Curve	Corner
Dashboard	Facia
Denatured alcohol	Methylated spirit
Dome lamp	Interior light
Driveaxle	Driveshaft
Driveshaft	Propeller shaft
Fender	Wing/mudguard
Firewall	Bulkhead
Flashlight	Torch
Float bowl	Float chamber
Freeway, turnpike, etc.	Motorway
Frozen	Seized
Gas tank	Petrol tank
Gas pedal	Accelerator pedal
Gasoline (gas)	Petrol
Gearshift	Gearchange
Generator (DC)	Dynamo
Ground	Earth (electrical)
Header/manifold	Manifold (exhaust)
Heat riser	Hot spot
High	Top gear
Hood	Bonnet (engine cover)
Idle	Tickover
Intake	Inlet
Jackstands /Safety stands	Axle stands
Jumper cable	Jump lead
Keeper	Collet
Kerosene	Paraffin
Knock pin	Roll pin
Lash	Freeplay/Clearance
Latch	Catch
Latches	Locks
License plate /tag plate	Number plate
Light	Lamp
Lock (for valve spring retainer)	Split cotter (for valve cap)
Lopes	Hunts
Lug nut	Wheel nut
Metal chips or debris	Swarf
Misses	Misfires
Muffler	Silencer
Oil pan	Sump
Open flame	Naked flame
Panel wagon/van	Van
Parking light	Sidelight
Parking brake	Handbrake
Piston pin or wrist pin bearing/bush	Small (little) end bearing
Piston pin or wrist pin	Gudgeon pin
Pitman arm	Drop arm
Power brake booster	Servo unit
Primary shoe	Leading shoe (of brake)
Prussian blue	Engineer's blue
Pry	Prise (force apart)
Prybar	Crowbar
Prying	Levering
Quarter window	Quarterlight
Recap	Retread
Release cylinder	Slave cylinder
Repair shop	Garage
Replacement	Renewal
Ring gear (of differential)	Crownwheel
Rocker panel	Sill panel
Rod bearing	Big-end bearing
Rotor/disk	Disc (brake)
Secondary shoe	Trailing shoe (of brake)
Sedan	Saloon
Setscrew, Allen screw	Grub screw
Shift fork	Selector fork
Shift lever	Gearlever/gearstick
Shift rod	Selector rod
Shock absorber, shock	Damper/shocker
Snap-ring	Circlip
Soft top	Hood
Spacer	Distance piece
Spare tire	Spare wheel
Spark plug wires	HT leads
Spindle arm	Steering arm
Stablizer or sway bar	Anti-roll bar
Station wagon	Estate car
Stumbles	Hesitates
Tang or lock	Tab
Taper pin	Cotter pin
Teardown	Strip(down)/dismantle
Throw-out bearing	Thrust bearing
Tie-rod (or connecting rod)	Trackrod (of steering)
Transmission	Gearbox
Troubleshooting	Fault finding/diagnosis
Trunk	Boot
Tube wrench	Box spanner
Turn signal	Indicator
Valve lifter	Tappet
Valve lifter or tappet	Cam follower or tappet
Valve cover	Rocker cover
VOM (volt ohmmeter)	Multimeter
Wheel cover	Roadwheel trim
Wheel well	Wheelarch
Whole drive line	Transmission
Windshield	Windscreen
Wrench	Spanner

7

ELECTRICAL SYSTEM

1. INTRODUCTION

For a little car, the Miata/MX5 sure has a big electrical system. When we set about producing this book, we decided against the conventional approach of putting every electrical subsystem and component together in one chapter. For one thing, it would have been a huge and complicated part of the book and confusing to try to work from, plus we reasoned that you would want to know the fuel system electrical checks and details along with the other fuel system information, instead of having to flip from one part of the book to the other. In this chapter, then, we look at the purely electrical items like the charging and starting systems plus lighting and signalling. If you've just turned to this chapter with an electrical problem and you don't find it described here, refer to the other chapter of the book which deals with that subject in detail.

Life, of course, is never that simple. On the Miata/MX5, subsystems interconnect to a large degree, each having the engine management system in common. For example, you may have turned to this chapter to try to work out why the air conditioning fan won't run. Mostly, this will be covered in *chapter 6*, but it just might be refusing to run because of an ECU problem, which you will find covered by *chapter 5*. We're sorry about this, but it is down to the nature of the car rather than us being obscure.

2. ELECTRICAL SYSTEM - PROCEDURES & PRECAUTIONS

1 Before you tackle work on the electrical system, you should read through this section which will give you some procedural hints and some important information that could save you damaging components or assemblies. Remember that the car depends on the ECU to function - if this unit, or subsidiary electronic units, is damaged by bad testing procedures, you could immobilize the car and land yourself with a major repair bill. **Note**: throughout this chapter the symbol $\mathbf{V_B}$ means battery votage and $\mathbf{V_0}$ means zero voltage.

ISOLATING THE ELECTRICAL SYSTEM

2 In general, you should isolate the electrical system before commencing work. This avoids any risk of damage to the electronic components or to your test equipment. Before you do so, note that most optional and aftermarket stereos are security coded - if the power supply to the unit is interrupted, and you don't have the security code number for the unit, it won't operate when the supply is restored. While this means that the unit is effectively worthless to a thief, it also means that if you isolate the system without deactivating the security system, you've got problems - see below.

3 With the stereo security system deactivated, open the trunk and remove the battery cover. Using a 10 mm crescent or box end wrench, slacken the battery negative (-) terminal clamp, and pull the lead off the terminal post. If you decide

2/3 Disconnect battery negative terminal.

to use a socket for this, be very careful that the extension bar does not short against the positive (+) terminal - this is normally protected by a plastic cover. You don't need to remove the remaining lead, but always make sure you disconnect the negative (-) ground cable first whenever you deal with battery disconnection, and always fit this lead last during installation.

DEACTIVATING THE STEREO SECURITY SYSTEM

4 As mentioned above, the Mazda accessory stereo system, and most aftermarket systems, are equipped with security coding as an antitheft measure. The procedures we describe here are for the Mazda stereo system which was specially developed for the Miata/MX5 by Panasonic. Most other systems are similar (our car's Clarion system was) but you should refer to the manufacturer's literature for details on setting, activating and deactivating particular security systems. Be warned that if you have bought a used car, you **must** have the security system information, even if you never want to disconnect the battery - even if the supply is lost through a flat battery, the security system will come into operation and you could wind up with an inoperative stereo.

5 With the Mazda/Panasonic unit, you enter a four-digit code number into the unit. Once the number is entered and the security system activated, the unit will not operate after any interruption to the power supply. You get three chances of getting the code right - fail on the third attempt and the unit is permanently disabled and has to be replaced by the unit manufacturer.

6 When power is reconnected, the LCD display will show **CODE**, indicating the need to enter the code number. You enter this using the preset channel buttons 1-4. In each case, you press the button once to select the digit to be entered, then press it again as required to increment the number; for example, if your code is 2468, press channel 1 three times, channel 2 five times, channel 3 seven times and channel 4 nine times.

7 To deactivate the security system (worth doing if you are doing a number of checks requiring disconnection and reconnection of the battery) proceed as follows. Switch the unit off and turn the ignition switch to the **ACC** position so that the time is displayed on the unit's LCD. Push down the **REW** and **FF** buttons until the LCD shows four bars. Now input the unit's code number as de-

7

scribed in paragraph 6. Next, push down and hold **REW** and **FF** for about two seconds until a beep is heard and **CODE** is displayed on the LCD - this will flash for around five seconds and then the time display will resume. Note that if the LCD displays '**Err**' (error), go back to the beginning of this paragraph and go through the procedure again, remembering that you only get three attempts before the unit shuts down for good.

ELECTRICAL TEST EQUIPMENT

8 Work on the electrical system will require a few pieces of equipment in addition to normal hand tools - we're not getting into oscilloscope territory here, just basic additions to your toolkit, which you may well have already.

9 You will need a simple test lamp arrangement which you can make up yourself using easily obtained materials. The basic requirement is for a 12 volt bulb rated at between 1.4 and 3.4 watts (don't exceed this value, or you could damage electronic circuits). Connect to it two test leads. Ideally, get a bulb in a bulbholder, like an accessory warning lamp from an auto part store - this will prevent the bulb getting damaged in use and make connection of the leads easier. If you want to make a professional job of it, buy a couple of probe leads (the finer the probes the better) from an electronics hobby shop like Radio Shack, and attach these to the test lamp. As an alternative, most auto parts stores will sell you a ready-made tester - these are often in the form of a screwdriver shaped tester with a built-in lamp, and a single test lead and probe.

10 Many of the tests need either an ohmmeter or a voltmeter. We use an inexpensive multimeter for this, which allows us to do both volts and ohms tests and, as a bonus, can check current (amps) and has a continuity checker in the form of a buzzer. This last feature is great - you can check for continuity without having to look at the meter; indispensable in awkward or confined spaces. We get by with the standard probes supplied with the meter, but finer probe ends would be useful for getting in the back of the wiring connectors - some of these have very small terminal pins and you risk damage if the probes are too big. Again, pick these up at electronic hobby stores. One word of warning - never do resistance or continuity checks while the car's battery is connected. If you make a mistake, you can zap your meter.

11 You will also need one or two jumper wires. These are simple insulated wires with either probe or miniature clip ends which allow you to make temporary connections during testing. You can improvise these with odd lengths of electrical wire, but we reckon it is worth buying proper jumper wires, again from an electronics hobby shop.

WIRING CONNECTORS

12 You will find many types of these around the Miata/MX5. Most are superficially similar, with varying numbers of pins. They differ in design and pin configuration to prevent you from making incorrect wiring connections. You should always check this, especially when disconnecting more than one section of wiring, or you will end up wasting a lot of time when you come to install the wiring later - no matter how easy it looks when you start, it can look confusing in a couple of hours time.

13 Most connectors have a latching arrangement which stops them from coming apart in service. In most cases, they also have some sort of key built in so they can only be assembled one way. To separate the connector halves, find the latch tab and either depress or lift it (depending on the design) then grasp the connector halves and pull them apart, Never, ever tug the wiring when doing this, or you may damage the wiring or connector pins. When closing connectors, make sure you hear them click shut, indicating that they are properly latched.

14 Some of the electrical tests are made with the connector separated (for example, switch continuity checks) while others require the connector to be assembled. This dictates how and where you use the meter probes. In general, you should insert the probes from the *back* of the connector wherever possible - this minimizes the risk of damaging the terminals. An exception to this rule is waterproof connectors - where these are used, you cannot access the back, and tests have to be made from the front of the connector.

15 A special case is the diagnosis connector, which you will encounter many times when working on various electrical systems on the car. This unit will be found under the hood on the left side of the car. It has a hinged cover, clearly marked '**DIAGNOSIS CONNECTOR**', and inside the lid is a chart showing the terminal identification. The primary use of this connector is to hook up Special Service Tools (SSTs) for self-diagnosis procedures. You can, however, get by with a simple jumper wire in many cases - we will indicate this in the text where it is possible and describe the terminals to be jumped. To avoid damage to the diagnosis connector terminals (which might make subsequent SST connection impossible) you should always fit jumpers into the service hole of the terminal, not into the main terminal hole - see the accompanying illustration for details.

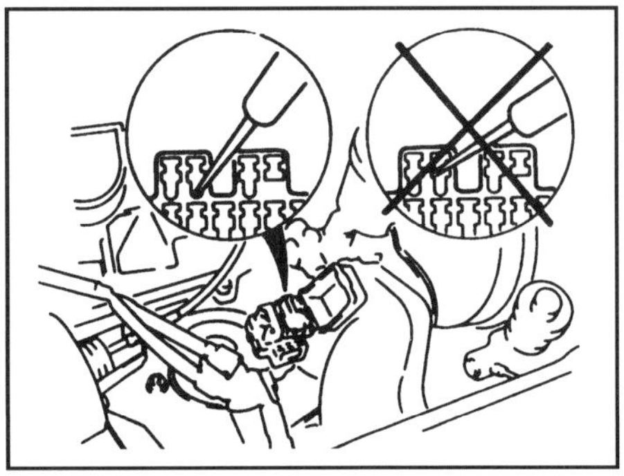

D2/15 HOW TO INSERT JUMPER WIRE.

16 When checking connectors, always make a point of pulling gently on each wire to ensure that it is secure in the connector body. Each terminal pin is latched into the plastic body by a small tang: you will need to depress this if you ever need to remove a terminal for replacement or checking. To do this, insert a fine metal blade down the center of the terminal, passing it under the terminal spring tang, until the locking tab can be pushed down. Hold the tab in this position and gently pull on the wire to withdraw the terminal. When installing the terminal, ensure that it latches securely in the connector - you may need to adjust the tab a little to get this to happen. We use a set of jeweller's screwdrivers to reach and release the locking tabs.

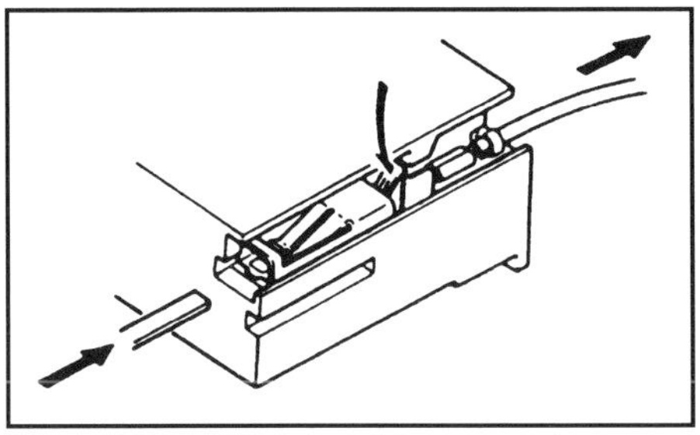

D2/16 RELEASING WIRES FROM CONNECTORS.

WIRING AND COLOR CODING

17 The Mazda's wiring is color coded to make tracing and troubleshooting easier, and to assist identification. We have stuck to Mazda's abbreviations throughout this book, so that there should be no confusion on this point. The wire colors and their abbreviations are shown in this table:

CODE	COLOR	CODE	COLOR
B	Black	O	Orange
BR	Brown	P	Pink
G	Green	R	Red
GY	Gray	V	Violet
L	Blue	W	White
LB	Light blue	Y	Yellow
LG	Light green		

T2/17 WIRE COLOUR CODES.

Note: where more than one color is indicated, for example LB/Y, the main wire color is shown first (light blue) and the second, or tracer, color is shown after the slash (yellow). Physical tracing of an individual wire is next to impossible on a system of this complexity (we reckoned that some of the main harness sections we encountered must have held a hundred or more individual wires, all tightly bound into a harness, but spurring off here and there. You can check continuity between each end of a wire, but you can't be certain of its route through the harness. If you come across a broken wire, your only alternative to fitting a new harness section is to cut off each end of the wire in question, and to add a new wire to bypass the damaged one.

18 In fairness, modern wiring is of such high quality that you would be unlucky to experience problems in the life of the car. In most cases any fault will be found at the wire ends - usually at the connector terminal, or will turn out to be a component failure. If you do find an internally broken or intermittent wire, try to trace the route of that part of the harness, and tape a new wire of the same size and, preferably, of the same color as the original to the outside of the harness with PVC electrical tape.

19 If you need to add wiring to the car, try to do it intelligently. When fitting accessory items it is tempting to do the minimum of dismantling to get access, and this invariably means that later access to some part of the car will be difficult because of straggling wires. Try to use connectors of the type already used on the car, so that panels or assemblies can still be removed for servicing. Be aware that if you patch into existing wiring using Scotchloks or similar connectors, you may be imposing too much load on that circuit or fuse. Patching in like this is just about unavoidable, but be intelligent about it - for example, if you hook into the instrument panel lighting circuit to run the rear window demister on your new hardtop, you will be drawing power through a 10A fuse, so don't be surprised when it blows.

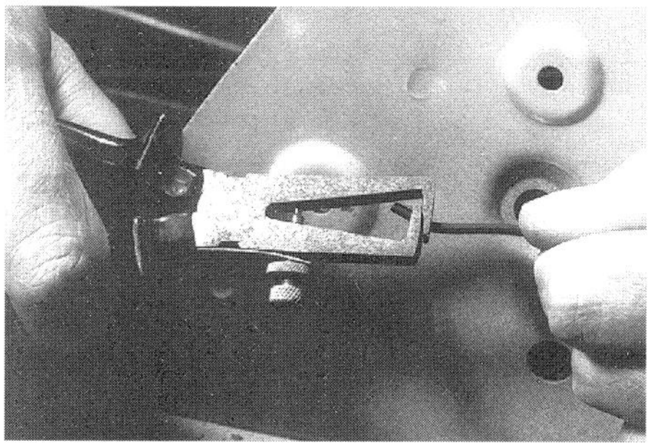
2/20a Bare end of wire ...

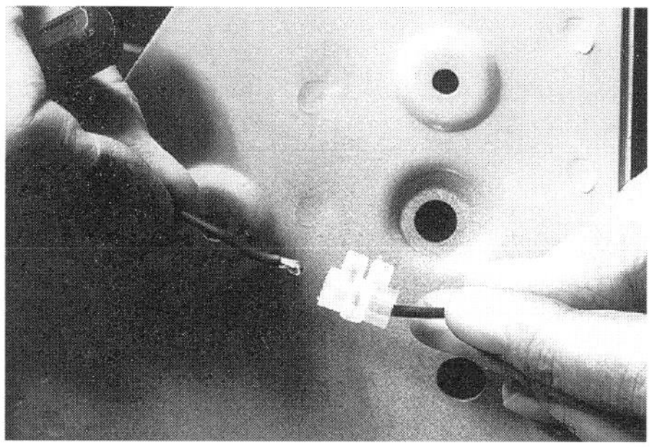
2/20b ... insert in connector ...

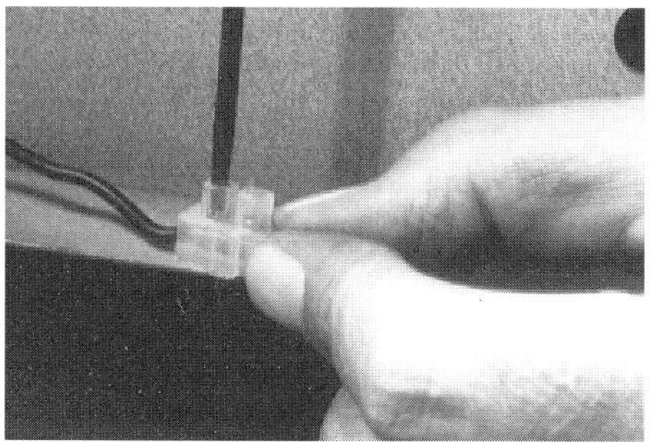
2/20c ... and tighten retaining screw.

20 If you need to cut an accessory wire in the course of removing other components, you should reconnect it in a way that allows for subsequent dismantling. We prefer to use screw-type connectors. Cut the wire and bare the ends using an insulation stripping tool. Fit the bared ends into the connector and tighten the screws to secure them.

FUSES AND RELAYS

21 The electrical circuits are protected by fuses (or in the case of the heater blower motor, a circuit breaker). Note that if a fuse burns out, you should always investigate the fault and repair it before fitting a new fuse. For more information see *section 3* of this chapter, and individual details in subsequent sections of this, and other, chapters.

22 In addition to the fuses, there are numerous relays around the vehicle. Some of these are operated by the ECU, allowing it to handle higher currents than it would otherwise be capable of doing. Others simply react to switch operation, doing the actual switching work while imposing no significant load on the switch contacts. We will be coming across these throughout this, and other, chapters.

3. FUSES & RELAYS - LOCATION, REMOVAL & REPLACEMENT

☞ 1/1, 2 & 7/2.

1 Most of the electrical subsystems on the Miata/MX5 are protected by their own fuse. All cars have at least two fuse boxes. One is mounted in the engine compartment, near the right fender (Mazda call this the **Main Fuse Block**). It has a hinged lid carrying a label which identifies the fuses in it - the exact arrangement varies according to where the car was sold and what electrical options are fitted.

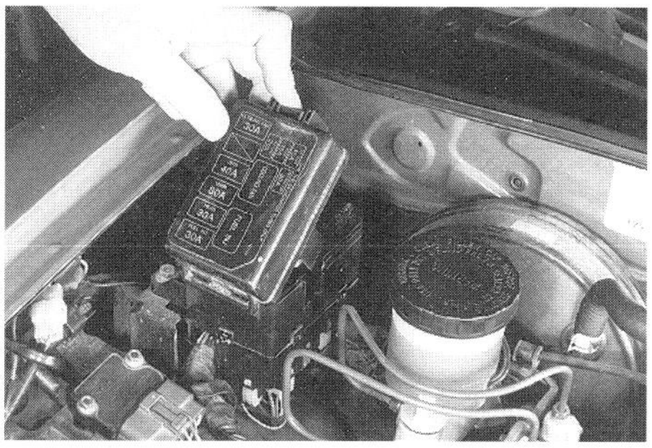
3/1a Lid identifies fuse positions.

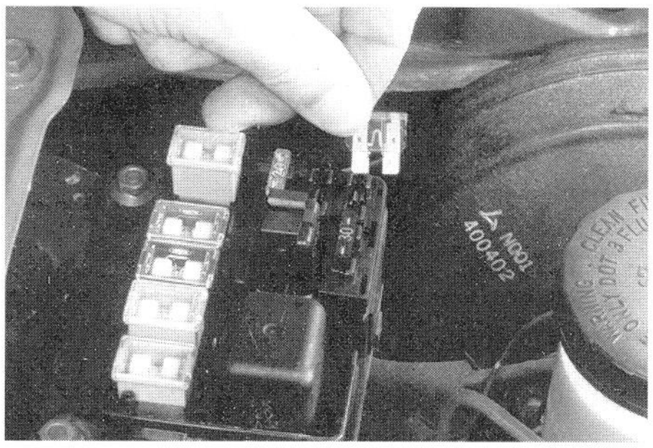
3/1b A typical fuse.

2 A second fuse box will be found in the passenger compartment and can be reached after removing the access panel which covers the steering column (the panel is secured by two cross-head screws, and is clipped into the dash panel). Mazda call this **Fuse Box No. 1** - note that in addition to various fuses it also houses a resettable

3/2a Heater circuit breaker.

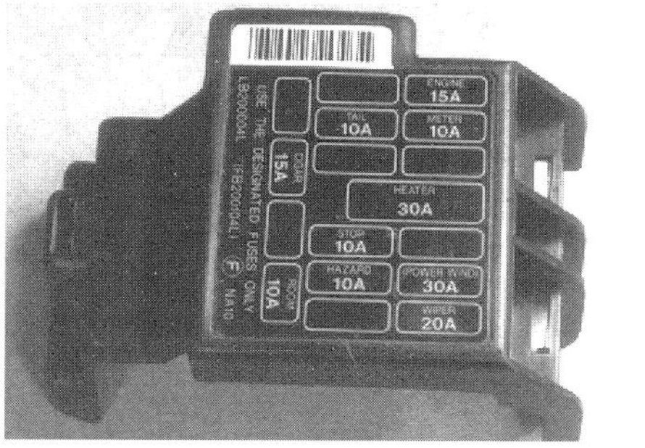

3/2b Lid identifies fuse positions.

circuit breaker, which protects the heater blower circuit.

3 Many cars have another small fuse box in the trunk, near the base of the radio antenna (**Fuse Box No. 2**). This contains fuses for the power antenna and rear window defroster (where these are fitted).

4 If a fuse burns out in service, the usual cause will be either a short circuit (where the associated component or wiring has contacted direct to ground) or an overload, for example, where the loading on a fused circuit exceeds the rated capacity of the fuse. On our car, we could find only one spare fuse, clipped into the lid of Fuse Box No. 1. We suggest that you might like to obtain a selection of fuses and stow them in the tool recess trunk, along with a selection of spare bulbs.

5 The contents of the Main Fuse Block (engine compartment) and Fuse Box No. 1 (under dash panel), excluding relays, is as shown in the tables accompanying this text. Don't be put off by the apparently endless list of fuses - we've attempted to produce a table for each fuse box, showing which fuse protects which circuit for North America, the UK and Continental Europe. As you'll see, the fuse arrangement for North American cars

Fuse ID	Rating	Circuit details
HEAD	30A	Headlight relay and switch (except Europe, LHD models).
INJ	30A	UK/North America: Alternator, Air Bag diagnostic module (where fitted). Europe, LHD models: EGI main relay.
MAIN	80A	All circuits except those protected by FUEL INJ (30A), HAZARD (30A) and RETRACTOR (30A).
BTN	40A	North America: TNS relay, Headlight switch. UK: Headlight switch. Europe LHD: Retractor switch, Alternator
COOLING FAN	30A	North America / UK: EGI main relay, Cooling fan relay. Europe LHD: Cooling fan relay only.
(AIR BAG)	10A	North America: Backup battery for air bag system
(AD FAN)	20A	Air conditioning relay (where A/C system fitted)
ST SIGN	10A	North America: Inhibitor relay, Circuit opening relay. UK: Circuit opening relay. Europe: Circuit opening relay.
RETRACTOR	30A	Headlight retractor relay
ABS	60A	Anti-lock brake system (where fitted)

T3/1 MAIN FUSE BOX/BLOCK DETAILS (LOCATED IN ENGINE COMPARTMENT).

FUSE	AMPS	PROTECTED CIRCUIT
ENGINE	15A	EGI main relay and cooling fan relay
METER	10A	Instrument panel, turn signal switch. (Timer and buzzer unit, Cruise control main switch - where fitted)
(AIR BAG)	15A	Diagnostic module (where fitted)
(POWER WIND)	30A	Power window switch (where fitted)
WIPER	20A	Blower switch, wiper switch (+ Wiper motor, washer switch, Europe LHD models)
(HEAD CLEANER)	20A	Headlight cleaner relay, switch and motor (Europe LHD models)
(HORN)	10A	Horn switch, relay and horn (Europe LHD models)
(R FOG)	10A	Rear fog light switch, Headlight levelling actuator and Retractor relay (Europe LHD)
ROOM	10A	ECU, (all models) Interior lamps and door switch (Europe LHD models) Key reminder switch and Audio unit (North America models)
CIGAR	15A	Cigarette lighter (all models). Audio Unit (North America models)
TAIL LH	10A	Tail light (LH) Panel light control switch, Position lights, ECU (Europe LHD models)
TAIL RH	10A	License plate light, Tail Light (RH) - Europe LHD models
TAIL	10A	Tail light, license plate light, (UK & North America models) ECU, Position lights (UK models) Side marker lights, Parking lights (North America models)
MAIN LH	10A	Headlight (High beam, LH) Passing light (LH) - Europe LHD models only
MAIN RH	10A	Headlight (High beam, RH) Passing light (RH) - Europe LHD models only
DIM LH	10A	Headlight (Low beam, LH) - Europe LHD models only
DIM RH	10A	Headlight (Low beam, RH) - Europe LHD models only
STOP	10A	Stoplight switch, Horn switch (UK and North America) Cruise control unit (North America models)
HAZARD	10A	Turn & Hazard flasher unit (UK and North America only)

T3/2 FUSE BOX 'NUMBER 1' DETAILS (LOCATED ON FOOTWELL SIDE IN PASSENGER COMPARTMENT).

and those sold in the UK is broadly similar, while vehicles sold in continental Europe differ in many of the fuse locations and functions. Note also that cars with power antennas and rear window defrosters (hard tops only) also have the small two-fuse unit in the trunk mentioned earlier - both fuses are rated at 20A.

6 + The fuse box mounted under the dash panel (Fuse Box No. 1) has a puller tool clipped into its lid, together with a single spare fuse. This device allows you to grip and remove or install the flat type fuses - they can be hard to grasp with the fingers because they are fitted closely together. If a fuse has burned out as the result of an overload, disconnect the battery negative (-) terminal, after

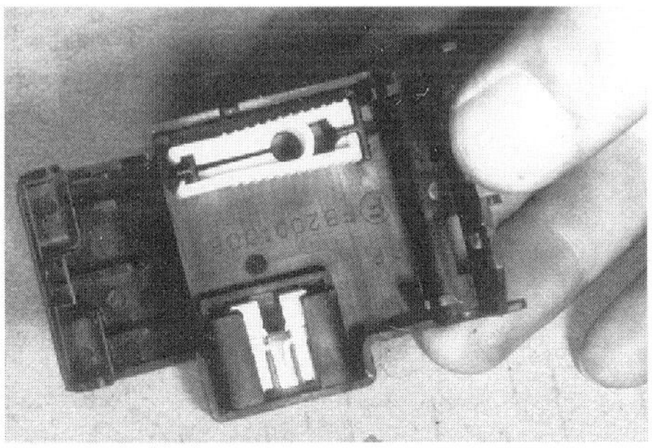

3/6a Spare fuse & fuse gripping tool in lid.

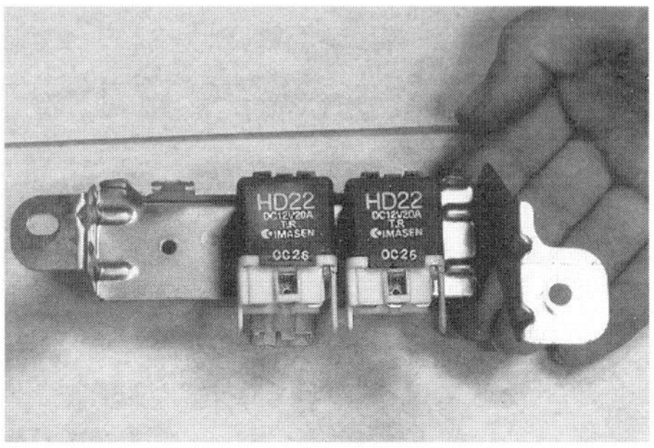

3/9a Relay mounting panel.

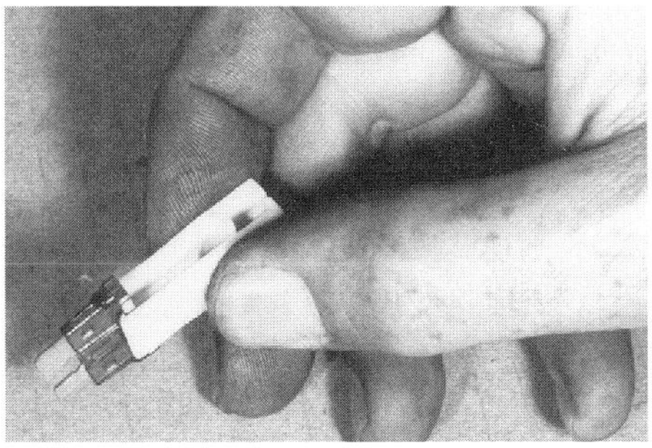

3/6b Fuse gripping tool in action.

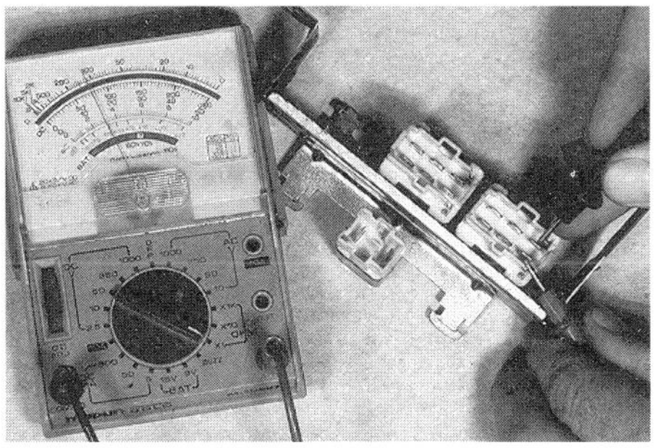

3/9b Testing relay with Multimeter.

disabling the stereo security system. Remove the damaged fuse with the puller and install a new fuse of the same rating. If the new fuse fails as soon as the circuit which it protects is used, you will have to trace and rectify the fault before normal operation is restored; refer to the appropriate section of this, and other chapters for details of the individual circuits and their components, for information on testing.

7 The circuit breaker (30A) used to protect the heater blower circuit is a special case. If this is overloaded, it breaks the circuit, the small red button at the center popping out to show that this has occurred. Try resetting the breaker by pressing the button in, then run the blower to see if it now operates normally. If the button pops out again, you should refer to *chapter 6* for information on checking this circuit.

RELAYS

8 There are numerous relays around the car. In the main, these perform the actual switching of circuits in response to control from manual switches or from the ECU. The majority of the relays are of two types; either normally open (NO) or normally closed (NC). The NO relays leave the circuit broken unless power is applied to them, while the NC type maintain the circuit until power is applied. In addition, there are specialist relays, such as the turn signal/hazard warning relay, that do more than just switch something on or off - in this case the relay flashes the turn signal lights in response to the turn signal switch setting or hazard switch setting.

9 The relays will be found in a number of main locations. All cars have the EGI and Cooling Fan relays housed in the main fuse block in the engine compartment. In addition, there is a bank of relays mounted above the left fender, again reached from the engine compartment. The relays found here depend on the country in which the car was sold. Further individual relays will be found under the dash panel. Again, the exact arrangement depends on the country in which the vehicle was sold. Refer to the accompanying illustrations for details.

10 Specific details on the location and testing of the various relays will be found in the various sections of this chapter, and also in other chapters where this is relevant - most of the data on relays associated with the Engine Management System, for example, will be found in *chapter 5*. Note that when dealing with relays, always isolate the electrical system before removing them (remember to disable the stereo security system before disconnecting the battery negative (-) cable), and handle them carefully - dropping a relay on a hard surface can damage it.

4. CHARGING SYSTEM - PRELIMINARY CHECKS

☞ 1/1, 2 & 7/2.

1 The charging system comprises the alternator and rectifier, the regulator, the battery and the associated wiring. **Caution!** Before attempting any dismantling work on the charging system, note that the stereo security system should be disabled and the battery isolated by disconnecting the negative (-) terminal connection.

2 When dealing with charging system problems, it should be noted that the condition of the battery is of great significance. The Miata/MX5 is

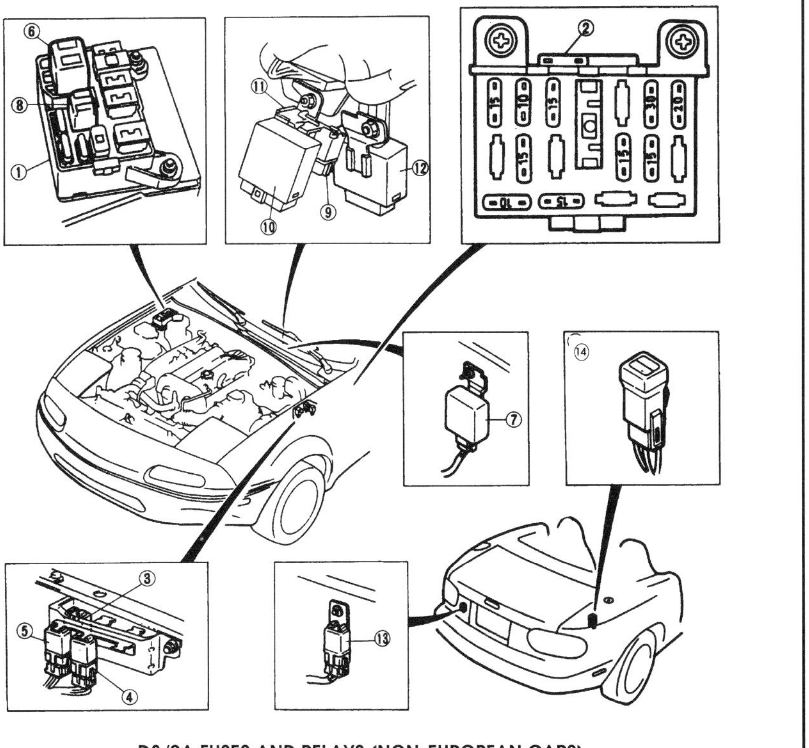

D3/9A FUSES AND RELAYS (NON-EUROPEAN CARS)
1 Main fusebox/block. 2 Fusebox 'Number 1'. 3 Headlight relay. 4 TNS relay. 5 Headlight retractor relay. 6 EGI main relay. 7 Rear window defroster timer unit. 8 Cooling fan relay. 9 Horn relay. 10 Turn & hazard warning flasher unit. 11 Timer & buzzer unit. 12 DRL control unit. 13 Rear window defroster relay. 14 Power antenna relay.

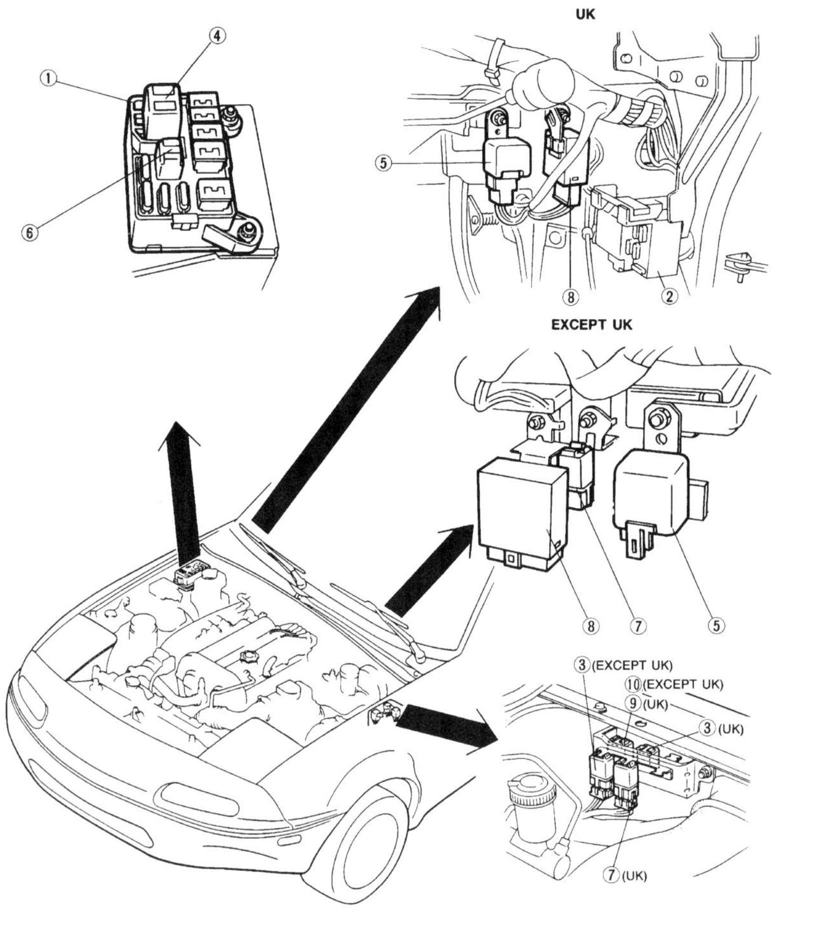

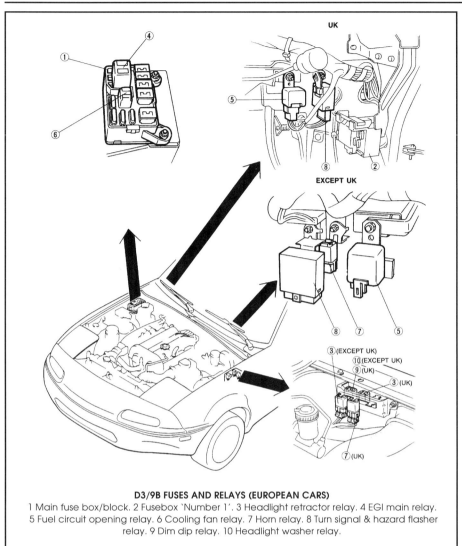

D3/9B FUSES AND RELAYS (EUROPEAN CARS)
1 Main fuse box/block. 2 Fusebox 'Number 1'. 3 Headlight retractor relay. 4 EGI main relay. 5 Fuel circuit opening relay. 6 Cooling fan relay. 7 Horn relay. 8 Turn signal & hazard flasher relay. 9 Dim dip relay. 10 Headlight washer relay.

fitted with a battery which is tiny by normal automotive standards. It was developed specifically for the car - so specifically, in fact, that you can't even purchase an identical replacement unit from Mazda or other sources (if you need to fit a new battery, you will have to obtain an equivalent unit, and install it using a special kit from Mazda - more on this later).

3 The battery, though technically advanced and commendably compact and lightweight, has a limited capacity when compared with more conventional units. This means that it is very easy to wind up with a flat battery should you accidentally overload the system. If the car is difficult to start, for example, you'll find that you won't be able to crank the engine for long before the battery gives up on you. Equally, if the charging system is performing inadequately, the normal electrical demands on the system may exceed the charge rate, so any fall-off in charging performance will have to be investigated and rectified promptly.

4 We recommend that you keep a set of jump leads in the trunk (you can stow these on the recess which runs forward from the right side of the trunk). These can get you out of trouble if you're ever stuck with a flat battery, and if you have automatic transmission on your car, you should consider them essential - you can't push-start an auto. Also, a spare battery is worth having. This doesn't need to be a Miata/MX5 battery - in fact a standard car battery would be better. If you have another car, you could use its battery as your spare, or you could keep a second battery in the garage (keep it fully charged in case you need to jump start your Miata/MX5). You'll find a spare battery valuable for both emergency starting and for extending the car's battery capacity during maintenance and testing operations.

JUMP-STARTING YOUR MIATA/MX5

5 If you have starting problems, try eliminating the battery as the cause of the fault by using a spare battery hooked up with jump leads. Open the trunk, and remove the battery cover to get access to the terminal posts. If you are jumping from a battery installed in another vehicle, position it so that the battery is within reach of the jump leads, but make sure that the two vehicles don't touch each other. (This is a precaution in case the other vehicle uses a positive (+) ground electrical system - you can accidentally weld cars together this way, and you will certainly cause damage to one or other of the vehicles' electrical systems).

6 Connect the red jump lead between the positive (+) terminal posts of both batteries, then carefully connect the black jump lead between the two negative (-) terminals. Be very careful not to ground any of the lead clamps while you are doing this - access around the Mazda's battery is severely restricted. If the car now starts normally, you know that the problem lies with the Miata/MX5 battery. It may just need charging (☞ 7/5), but if the fault happens repeatedly, you should check out the charging system (☞ 7/6).

7 If you succeed in getting the car started, leave the leads connected for a couple of minutes while the engine is running - this will allow the Miata/MX5's battery to charge up a little. Turn off the ignition switch, then carefully remove the jump leads, starting with red, or positive (+) lead, then the black, or negative (-) lead. Again, be very careful not to ground any of the clamps while you do this.

8 The above procedure will usually get you moving if you are stuck on the roadside with a discharged battery, but note that if the charging system is not working correctly, the effect will be limited. Try to get the car home using minimal electrical power. Once the engine is running, it requires minimal electrical power, but the lights,

BUYING JUMP LEADS

If you need to buy a set of jump leads, it is worth buying the best you can afford. Cheap jump leads have poor quality clamps, and the cable used usually has several thick strands of aluminum wire. We've used these in the past and they're not really worth having - You will spend as much time repairing these leads as you do using them. The leads fracture easily, which means that they present a high resistance when you try to jump start with them - the poor quality clamps exacerbate the problem. You can tell if the leads are conducting the starting current well. If they get hot, you are wasting energy heating the cables, instead of using it to turn the starter motor.

Quality jump leads are easy to spot - they have heavy, well-made clamps, and the cables are flexible instead of stiff like the aluminum leads. If you look at where the leads attach to the clamps, you'll see a thick bunch of fine copper strands. The more strands and the thicker the bunch, the better the quality. Note also that access above the battery terminal posts on the Miata/MX5 is restricted - try to find leads with short clamps which will fit under the bodywork without risk of shorting.

wipers and other electrical systems will soon drain the battery again if the charging system is down. You may get by during daylight, but you won't get far at night like this.

9 Whenever you've had to jump start your car, charge the battery as soon as possible, and monitor its condition regularly for a while. If the battery goes flat repeatedly, check that the charging system is functioning normally (☞ 7/6). If this is OK, the problem lies with either a tired battery (check and replace if required) or it indicates that you may be exceeding the capacity of the charging system in some way. A good example is the rear window defroster circuit. This uses a lot of power, and if left on continuously would soon flatten the battery - this is why it has a timer circuit. You can impose similar loads on the system without realizing it. If you do a lot of stop/start driving, or spend a lot of your journey in heavy, slow-moving traffic, the normal drain of the lights and wipers, plus the heater blower and stereo, may be just too much for the system to keep up with.

5. BATTERY - CHECKING, CHARGING & REPLACEMENT

☞ 1/1, 2 & 7/2.

Warning! Although the battery is semi-sealed and maintenance-free, note that the battery electrolyte is extremely corrosive. Take care not to drop or damage the battery casing. Take care to avoid eye or skin contact during handling (use disposable plastic gloves and eye protection). If electrolyte splashes on the skin, wash immediately with copious amounts of water and get medical assistance if burning is noted. If splashes enter the eyes, wash immediately with copious amounts of water and summon immediate medical assistance. Contact between electrolyte and clothing will quickly cause damage - wash immediately in water to minimize.

1 If you have a battery problem, the first thing to do is to remove it from the car for checking - it is a good idea to perform this as a regular maintenance check anyway. First disable the stereo security coding system ☞ 7/2.

2 Open the trunk and remove the cover over the battery. It is held in place by snap fasteners to the trunk floor carpet. Taking care to avoid shorting them to ground, remove the battery leads, disconnecting the negative (-) lead first, followed by the positive (+) lead. Each terminal is clamped in place - use a 10 mm wrench to release it.

5/2 Remove batt. cover and disconnect leads.

3 Using a 10 mm wrench or socket, remove the two bolts which secure the battery end bracket and lift this away. Unscrew and remove the single 10 mm clamp nut and unhook the upper part of the clamp from the threaded rod. The clamp mechanism can be removed by rotating it toward the center of the trunk and unhooking it.

4 + Pull off the nearest of the two vent hoses from the end of the battery vent manifold. The battery can now be lifted partway out of its recess, and the remaining vent hose disconnected. Lift the battery out of the trunk and place it on the bench for examination and charging.

5/4a Pull off outer vent hose ...

5/4b ... move battery ...

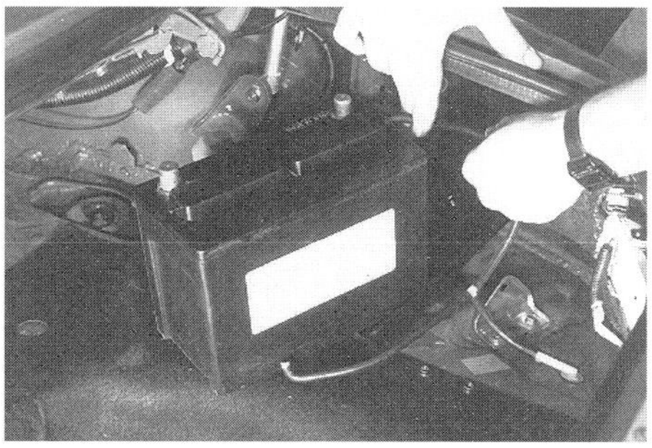

5/4c ... and then remove second vent hose.

5 The Miata/MX5 battery is of a semi-sealed design, this being dictated by its location in the trunk where any loss of electrolyte into the trunk would cause problems. Even so, be wary of signs of leakage. If found it may be that the battery casing has been damaged, in which case a new battery must be fitted. If electrolyte has leaked into the trunk, you must remove and neutralize any traces, or serious corrosion will result. With luck, any leakage will be confined in the plastic tray which the battery sits in.

6 You will need to wash the affected area

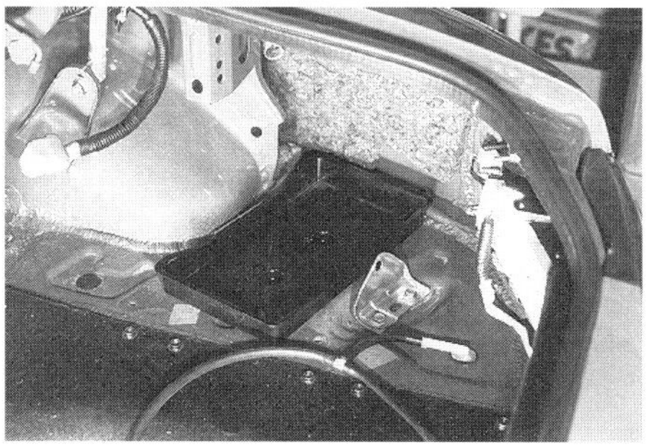

5/5 Battery tray is important.

with an alkaline solution to neutralize the acidic electrolyte. Make up a solution of warm water to which a couple of tablespoons of sodium bicarbonate have been added and dissolved. You can get sodium bicarbonate from pharmacies and general stores, where it is sold as a raising agent for home baking. The solution will fizz as it contacts the electrolyte. **Warning!** Don't breathe the fumes produced, and wear eye and skin protection throughout the operation.

7 If the battery is undamaged, wipe over its casing with a rag or paper wipe dampened with the sodium bicarbonate solution. This will clean the casing and remove any acid residue. The terminal posts can be cleaned using abrasive paper or a small wire brush (or you can buy special cleaning tools from auto parts stores). Once clean, coat the terminals with petroleum jelly or battery terminal grease to prevent corrosion - don't use regular grease for this.

BATTERY VOLTAGE CHECK

8 You can check battery condition by using a voltmeter (or a multimeter set on the appropriate range). Connect the meter negative (-) probe to the battery negative terminal, and the positive (+) probe to the battery positive terminal.

9 A reading of more than 12.6 volts shows that the battery is in good condition. If you get a reading between 12.0-12.6 volts, skip to *paragraph 10*. If the voltage reading is below 12 volts, make a note of the reading then perform a quick charge at 20A for the time specified below (see notes on charging rates below).

Battery voltage	***Charging period***
Less than 11 volts	*75 minutes*
11.0-11.5 volts	*50 minutes*
11.5-12.0 volts	*30 minutes*

5/8 Testing the battery.

After quick-charging, recheck the voltage. If it is still below 12 volts, you should fit a new battery. If above 12 volts, proceed as described below.

10 Go through the normal recharging procedure described below. If the battery voltage remains below 12.4 volts, you need to fit a new battery. If it is now above 12.4 volts, but you still experience repeated flat batteries, check the charging system ☞ 7/6.

BATTERY CHARGING

Warning! Excessively high charging rates could explode the battery due to gas buildup. Any form of charging releases hydrogen and oxygen from the battery. This is a potentially explosive mixture - keep well away from any potential source of ignition, and make sure the charging area is well ventilated. When handling the battery, take care to avoid short circuits - they can be dramatic and dangerous.

11 The standard S46A24L(S) battery fitted to all new Miata/MX5s should normally be recharged at 3A or less. This slow charging procedure is always preferable where time allows. If you need to fast-charge the battery as described above, never exceed 20A, and note that repeated fast charging shortens battery life. If the battery becomes hot to the touch during charging, discontinue charging and allow it to cool down, or reduce the charge rate.

12 The accompanying graph shows the relationship between charging rates and the time required for recharging - for example a battery discharged to 10.8 volts would take just under 4 hours to recharge fully at 10A, or nearly 13 hours at 3A. It is always preferable to use a current-controlled charger if possible - if you intend to buy a charger, try to get one of these units if you can. A current-controlled charger allows you to set the charge rate. Cheaper voltage-controlled units find their own charging current - the current starts out high, then slowly falls back to zero as the battery reaches full charge. With this type of charger it is harder to gauge how long you need to perform the charging operation.

13 Noting the precautions outlined above,

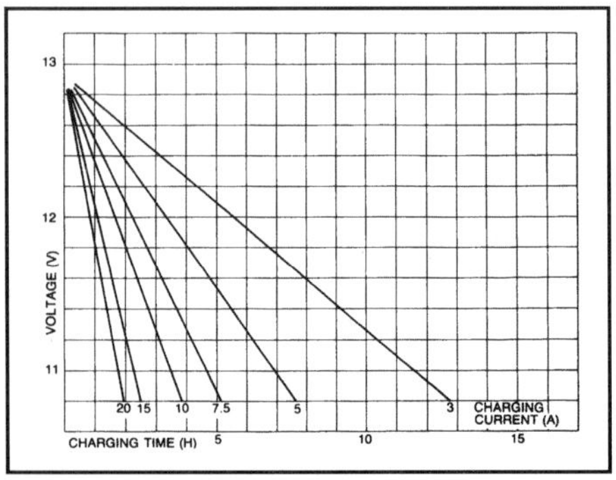

T5/12 OPTIMUM BATTERY CHARGING RATES.

check that the battery terminals are clean, then connect the charger clamps to the battery terminal posts, negative (-) to negative, and positive (+) to positive. Switch on the charger at the selected rate and charge for the prescribed amount of time. On cheaper units, just switch on and charge until the charger meter falls to zero, then disconnect the charger and recheck the voltage of the battery. Resume charging for a while if required.

14 When charging is complete, check the battery voltage as described earlier. If you are unable to get the battery up to or above 12 volts, it indicates that it is at or nearing the end of its useful life.

BATTERY INSTALLATION

15 With the battery clean and fully charged, place it in its tray in the trunk, remembering to install the vent hoses as it is maneuvered into position. Reassemble and secure the clamp (do not overtighten it). Install the end bracket, then connect the battery leads, positive (+) lead first, negative (-) lead last. Take care not to short the battery to ground with the wrench during installation. Install the battery cover.

INSTALLING A NEW BATTERY

16 As we mentioned above, you cannot purchase a straight replacement battery for the Miata/MX5. The official replacement unit is physically larger, and you will also need an installation kit to suit the new unit - ask for the Mazda battery replacement kit, Part No. NAY1 56 020A, or equivalent at your Mazda dealer. The kit consists of a new battery tray, plus a new clamp and clamp bolt. **Caution!** Do not install any battery that just happens to fit the mounting area. The correct battery must have a vent manifold, or electrolyte vapor will be released into the trunk in service.

17 To install the replacement battery, you will first need to remove the battery clamp bolt anchor plate, turn it through 180°, and the reinstall it. The position of the battery end bracket has to be changed as shown in the accompanying drawing. Install the new battery tray, then fit the new battery, connecting the vent pipes to the manifold stubs. Secure the battery using the new clamp arrangement from the fitting kit. Finally, you will need to trim part of the battery cover to fit the new battery - the accompanying drawing shows the area to be cut off. You can cut the material using heavy duty scissors or a craft knife.

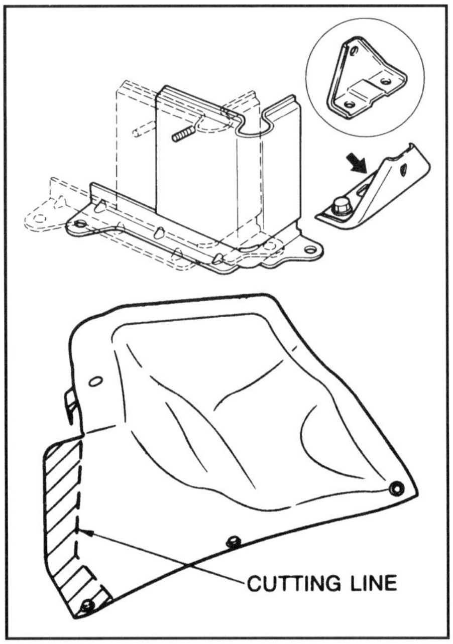

D5/17 MODIFICATIONS TO BRACKETS AND COVER IN ORDER TO FIT LARGER BATTERY.

6. CHARGING SYSTEM - TROUBLESHOOTING

☞ 1/1, 2 & 7/2.

1 In the event of charging system problems, run through the troubleshooting chart below. This gives you a sequence of checks, indicating the expected result of each one, and the next item to check, depending on the result obtained. Battery checking procedure ☞ 7/5 Alternator checks ☞ 7/7. Alternator drivebelt tension adjustment and belt replacement ☞ 2/4. Dark current checks ☞ 7/7.

STEP 1: CHECK THAT BATTERY VOLTAGE IS ABOVE 12.6 Volts	YES: MOVE TO STEP 2
	NO: CHECK BATTERY CONDITION
STEP 2: WITH IGNITION SWITCH ON, CHECK ALTERNATOR TERMINAL VOLTAGES	OK - MOVE TO STEP 3
	NOT OK - CHECK ALTERNATOR WIRING
STEP 3: START ENGINE, AND CHECK THAT ALTERNATOR WARNING LAMP GOES OFF	YES: MOVE TO STEP 4
	NO: CHECK ALTERNATOR
STEP 4: CHECK ALTERMATOR DRIVEBELT CONDITION AND TENSION	OK - MOVE TO STEP 5
	NOT OK - RENEW OR ADJUST DRIVEBELT
STEP 5: CHECK THAT DARK CURRENT LEVEL IS NORMAL	OK - CHARGING SYSTEM NORMAL
	NOT OK - CHECK FOR SOURCE OF LEAKAGE

T6/1 CHARGING SYSTEM TROUBLESHOOTING.

7. ALTERNATOR - CHECKING

☞ 1/1, 2 & 7/2.

CHECKING THE TERMINAL VOLTAGES

1 You need to check the alternator terminal voltages with the unit installed and connected normally. Access is restricted, but you should just about be able to get in there with a meter probe. Connect the meter negative (-) probe to a convenient ground, then check each of the three alternator terminals in turn, using the positive probe. You need to make the checks three times; initially, with the ignition switch OFF, then with the switch ON, and finally with the switch ON and the engine at idle.

2 If the readings you get are incorrect, check

IGNITION SWITCH POSITION	OFF	ON	IDL
Terminal	APPROX. VOLTAGES		
B	12V	12V	14V
L	0V	1V	14V
S	12V	12V	14V

T7/1 ALTERNATOR TERMINAL VOLTAGES.

the wiring connections between the alternator, battery, regulator and ignition switch. If these appear loose, damaged or corroded, repair or replace them as required, then recheck the voltages.

CHECKING ALTERNATOR OPERATION

3 Start the engine and check whether the alternator warning light on the instrument panel goes off. The alternator has a self-diagnosis function which means that the light stays on if:

a) the switch (S) circuit is open.
b) there is no output voltage.
c) The field circuit is open.
d) The battery (B) circuit is open, or
e) The output voltage is too high.

If you find that the warning light stays on, it indicates one of the above conditions - you will either have to fit a new or reconditioned unit, or remove, test and repair the existing alternator (☞ 7/8). Before you do either check and adjust drivebelt tension - or fit a new belt if the existing one is worn (☞ 2/4) - then check whether this has resolved the problem.

CHECKING THE DARK CURRENT

4 This has nothing to do with mystical practices - it refers to the residual current flow still taking place when everything that can be is switched off. While the car is parked, a small current still flows to systems like the ECU and audio circuits. In normal circumstances, the current drawn is very small, the maximum allowable figure being 20mA. You can check this by disconnecting the battery negative lead (disable the stereo security system first), and checking between the negative (-) terminal and the removed lead.

5 If the current exceeds that mentioned above, you will need to track down the cause of the excess leakage - a formidable task with an electrical system of this complexity. The best bet is to start by disconnecting each of the car's fuses in turn, checking the current drawn while each one is removed. If you find that the reading drops to normal when one of the fuses is out, you can then concentrate on checking the circuits which it protects. Areas to check are damp wiring connections, damaged wiring (though you would normally expect this to have burned out the fuse) and finally shorted or damaged electrical components, such as a sticking relay, or possibly an alternator or related charging system fault.

8. ALTERNATOR - REMOVAL, OVERHAUL & INSTALLATION

☞ 1/1, 2 & 7/2.

REMOVAL

1 If you need to work on the alternator, the first step is to remove it from the car. It is awkwardly located on the right side of the engine, partially covered by the intake manifold. Note that for the sake of clarity, many of the photographs illustrating the removal and installation procedures were taken with the engine out of the car. To improve access, you will need to do a little preliminary dismantling. Start by disconnecting the battery negative (-) terminal, having first disabled the stereo security system (where fitted). Never skip battery disconnection - the heavy battery cable connection at the alternator is always live unless this has been done.

2 From the front of the engine compartment, disconnect the ISC valve and water thermoswitch connectors. Where fitted, disconnect the power steering switch connector. Release the clip which secures the air pipe and resonance chamber assembly to the throttle body and pull it off the connecting stub. As it comes away, disconnect at the air pipe end the smaller air hose which runs to the ISC valve stub on the underside of the throttle body. Slacken the clip which secures the intake hose to the air pipe and remove the air pipe to gain access to the alternator.

3 Refer to the accompanying drawing and disconnect the alternator wiring. The heavy battery cable attached to terminal '**B**' is retained by a 10 mm nut, the remaining two cables sharing a plug-in connector. If you intend to teardown the alternator after removal, we suggest that you slacken

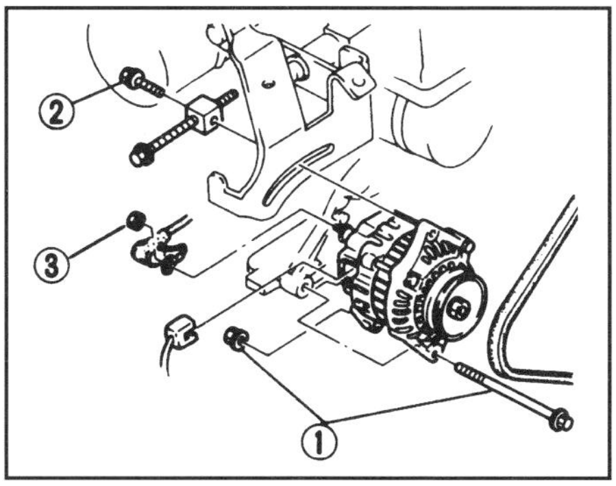

D8/2 ALTERNATOR MOUNTING DETAILS.
1 Swivel bolt. 2 Adjuster lock bolt. 3 10 mm terminal nut.

the pulley center 22 mm nut at this stage. With luck there will be enough friction in the drivebelt to allow you to do this, but if it won't come free, don't worry - we'll deal with it later.

4 With the wiring free, slacken the mounting bolt 14 mm nut on the underside of the alternator, and the adjuster lock 12 mm bolt which is located near the top of the unit - the head faces towards the rear of the car. Back off the adjuster bolt, then remove it, together with the block and bolt so that the drivebelt can be disengaged. The mounting bolt can now be removed and the alternator lifted out of the car. From here on, you have

8/4a Slacken the swivel bolt ...

8/4b ... slacken adjuster lock bolt ...

8/4c ... lift from bracket and then ...

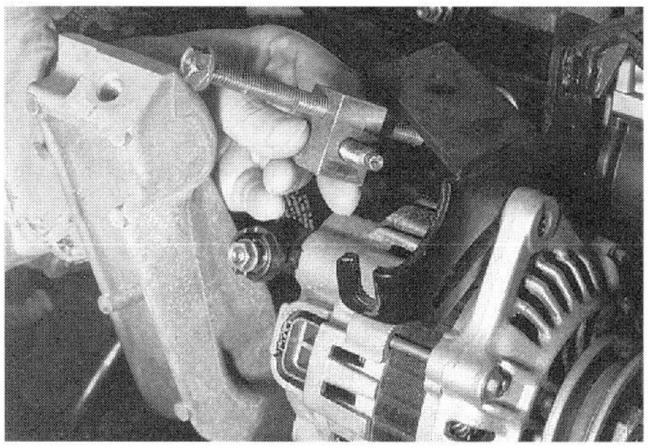

8/4d ... remove adjuster & drivebelt ...

8/4e ... remove pivot bolt & lift away alternator.

a choice; either overhaul the unit yourself, as far as is practical, or check your local auto-electrical specialists for availability of service exchange units.

5 Frankly, we would go for a new or reconditioned unit every time, given the difficulty of access to the alternator, and the limited scope for home repairs. If you fit a new unit, or one which has been professionally overhauled, you can expect long and troublefree service. Superficially, a teardown and rebuild of the alternator looks easy, but in reality you can get into real difficulties here. We left Wally, our Technical Adviser, to overhaul our project car's alternator...

TEARDOWN

6 First thing to do is to remove the 22 mm pulley nut - if you managed to slacken it while it was still in the car you can skip this paragraph. You need to hold the pulley somehow while the nut is removed. You may be able to do this using a vise fitted with soft jaws, but be very careful that you don't crush and distort the pulley. A better way is to wrap an old drivebelt around the pulley and clamp that in your vise, keeping it as tight as you can. This will grip the pulley evenly and you can unscrew and remove the nut and its spring washer.

8/6 Remove pulley nut.

7 With the pulley nut and spring washer removed, the pulley comes off in two halves followed by a spacer. Next, remove the four 8 mm through bolts which hold the unit together. Carefully lift away the end cover (pulley end), leaving the rotor sitting in the remaining casing half - push on the rotor shaft end to separate the two halves. Inside the (pulley end) casing is the main rotor bearing, held in place by a square retainer plate. The plate can be removed after unscrewing the four crosshead screws which secure it, and the old bearing drifted out of the casing using a socket of around 15 mm.

8/7 Unscrew & remove thru bolts.

8 Wally's next move was to pull the rotor out of the remaining casing half - as he did so the rotor shaft moved clear of the brushes, which popped out under spring pressure. Despite appearances, Wally failed to find a way to remove the stator assembly or the brush holder / rectifier unit without causing damage - this means big problems later. As far as we can tell, the stator can be pulled out of the casing, and the brush holder and rectifier assembly released after removing the retaining screws. However, Wally couldn't get ours apart, and discretion being the better part of valor, decided to quit before he did any damage.

8/8 The dismantled alternator.

9 Wally's problems were just beginning at this point. To get the rotor back into the casing, you have to hold the brushes back against spring pressure while the rotor is fitted. Unfortunately, the back of the casing is blind - there is no apparent method of doing this. In the end, Wally drilled a small access hole in the end of the casing center, and used a length of welding wire to hold the brushes back while he slid the rotor back into position.

10 What we think should happen is that the stator windings should be pulled out of the casing, and the brush plate and rectifier assembly released by removing the external retaining screw as they are withdrawn. We have to confess that we never really resolved this problem - if you have had more success with an alternator teardown than Wally did, we would like to hear how you did it.

INSPECTION

11 The first thing to do is to assess the overall condition of the alternator. If something catastrophic has happened, and the rotor and/or stator are obviously trashed, further work would be academic - it's time to say 'Hi!' to your Mazda dealer or auto electrical specialist.

12 Check the rotor windings for signs of damage. If they appear burned or the shellac coating is beginning to break up, you will need to get the stator rewound - again, check local auto-electrical specialists for price and availability, and compare this with the cost of a new Mazda part. Even if the windings look OK, check for shorting with an resistance check. At 20°C (68°F) you should find a resistance of 3.5-4.5 , measuring between the two slip rings. Next, check for grounding of the windings by checking the resistance between each slip ring and the steel core of the rotor. No continuity should exist. If your windings are outside the specified range, or shorted to ground, you should fit a new or reconditioned rotor.

13 Now turn your attention to the stator windings. Again, these must be undamaged, and there should be continuity between the stator leads. There must be no continuity between the stator leads and the metal core. If the stator does not meet these criteria, fit a new one.

14 Inspect the brushes for wear. If they have worn down to or near the wear limit (indicated by the rectangular surround of the Mitsubishi logo) you should fit new ones. We would suggest that it might be worth fitting new brushes as a precaution anyway, unless they are almost unworn.

15 You are supposed to check the brush spring pressure at this stage. With the brush projecting by 2 mm from the holder, the standard reading should be 3.1-4.3 N (320-440 g / 11.3-15.5 oz) and the service limit is 1.6-2.4 N (160-240 g / 5.6-8.5 oz). If you have some way of determining this, then check it by all means. We suggest that it might be good policy to fit new springs along with the brushes.

16 Finally, check the rectifier assembly, referring to the accompanying drawing. Note that in this test you are checking for continuity of the

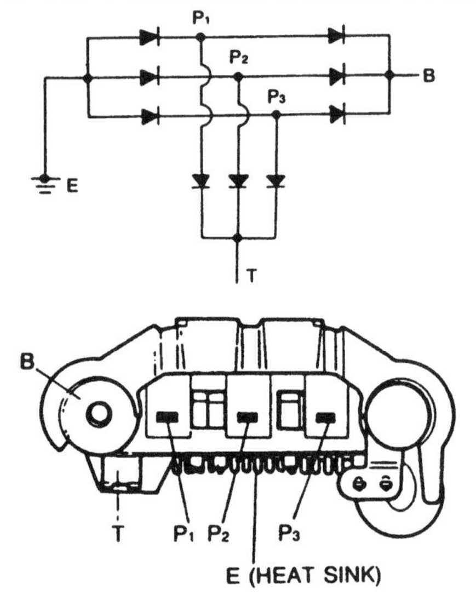

Negative (Black)	Positive (Red)	Continuity
E	P1, P2, P3	Yes
B		No
T		No
P1, P2, P3	E	No
	B	Yes
	T	Yes

D8/16 ALTERNATOR RECTIFIER - TESTING DIODES.

rectifier diodes. For each pair of terminals, check for continuity, then reverse the meter leads and repeat the test. You should read continuity in one direction only. If in any of the checks you find continuity both ways, or no continuity either way, the diode has burned out and the rectifier should be replaced.

REBUILD

17 Fit the brush holder and rectifier unit as-

sembly over the end of the rotor, checking that the brushes fit correctly over the slip rings - use a small screwdriver to lift the brushes over the slip rings as the rotor is slid home. Install the assembly into the casing, tightening the external screw which retains the brush holder and rectifier to 5.9-9.8 N (60.0-100.0 kgf cm / 52-87 lbf in). Fit the other casing half and install the long through bolts, tightening them to 2.6-6.4 N (30.0-65.0 Kgf cm / 26-56 lbf in).

18 Fit the spacer, the alternator pulley, spring washer and 22 mm nut. Hold the pulley using an old drive belt while the nut is tightened to 59-98 N (6.0-10.0 kgf m / 26-56 lbf ft). Check that the pulley can be turned smoothly and easily before installing the rebuilt unit.

INSTALLATION

19 Install the alternator in the car, fitting the fixing bolts finger tight at this stage. Set the adjuster bolt to give the correct amount of free play in the drive belt, measured between the alternator and crankshaft pulleys under moderate pressure (98 N / 10 kg / 22 lb). If a new belt is being fitted, set the free play to 8-9 mm (0.31-0.35 in). If a used belt is being fitted, the correct free play is 9-10 mm (0.35-0.39 in).

20 You can also set the drivebelt by tension, if you have a belt tension gauge. If you use this method, set a new belt to 491-589 N (50-60 kg / 110-132 lb). If the belt is used, set the tension to 422-491 N (43-50 kg / 95-110 lb).

21 Reconnect the battery cable, making sure the nut is covered by its protective boot. Reconnect the two-pin connector. Install the air pipe and reconnect the ISC valve and water thermosensor wiring. Fit the battery negative terminal and check that the alternator operates normally - the warning light on the instrument panel should go out once the engine is running.

9. STARTER SYSTEM - DESCRIPTION & CHECKS

☞ 1/1, 2 & 7/2.

1 The starter motor/magnetic switch (solenoid) assembly is mounted on the bellhousing/ engine backplate on the right side of the engine. A heavy cable runs from the battery positive terminal to the B terminal on the magnetic switch. The magnetic switch contacts are normally open, but when the ignition switch is turned to the **START** position, current is applied to the S (switch) terminal of the unit.

2 In the case of North American market cars with manual transmissions, an interlock switch is fitted, meaning that the circuit is not completed unless the clutch pedal is depressed. Where an automatic transmission is fitted, a starter inhibitor switch prevents starting unless the transmission is shifted into **PARK** or **NEUTRAL**.

3 When the circuit is made, the magnetic switch pulls the starter pinion into engagement with the starter ring on the engine flywheel, and closes the heavy contacts which allow current to flow

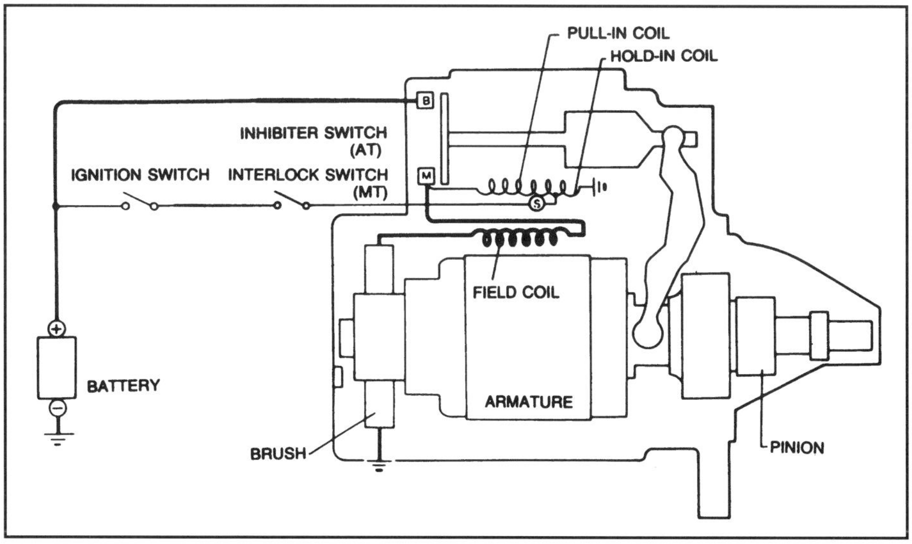

D9/3 STARTER MOTOR COMPONENT LAYOUT AND ELECTRICAL SYSTEM.

through the starter motor, and the engine is cranked. As soon as the ignition key is released, it returns to the **IDLE** position and power is disconnected to the magnetic switch. This in turn cuts power to the motor and pulls the starter pinion out of engagement with the flywheel. The accompanying drawing shows the basic starter circuit. Note that the inhibitor switch (4A/T) applies to automatic transmission models, and the interlock switch (M/T) is fitted to US market manual transmission models.

INITIAL CHECKS

4 If you experience starting problems, always check the battery before you do anything else (☞ 7/5). If the problem persists with a fully charged battery, proceed as described below.

5 Have an assistant operate the ignition switch. You should hear a click from the starter magnetic switch (solenoid) indicating that it is operating. If you do, you will need to remove the starter motor for further checks ☞ 7/10. If no click is heard, proceed as described below.

6 Connect a voltmeter with the positive (+) probe to the magnetic switch S terminal and the negative (-) probe to ground. Have your assistant operate the ignition switch once more, and check that you read battery voltage (approx 12V). If battery voltage is shown, remove the starter motor for further checks on it and the magnetic switch (☞ 7/10). If no voltage is shown ☞ 7/9/7 (manual trans, USA), ☞ 7/9/8-11 (auto trans), ☞ 7/9/12 (manual trans, except USA)

INTERLOCK SWITCH - USA, MANUAL TRANSMISSION MODELS

7 Working in the footwell on the driver's side, check for battery voltage between the starter side of the starter interlock switch and ground when the starter is operated. The switch is attached to the left side of the clutch pedal support and should not be confused with the centrally mounted clutch switch. If battery voltage is present, check the wiring and connections between the interlock

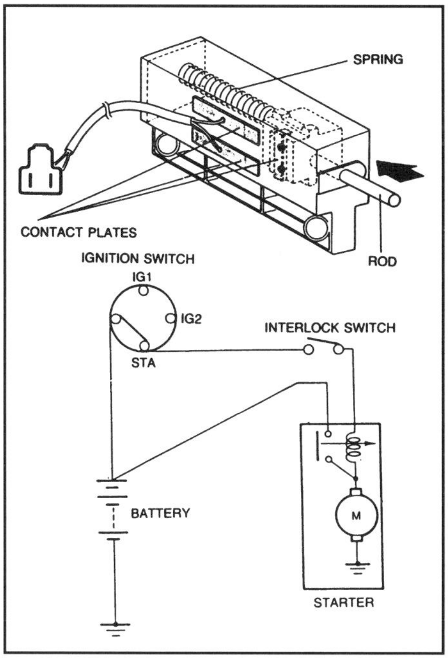

D9/7 STARTER INTERLOCK LAYOUT AND ELECTRICAL SYSTEM.

switch and the starter magnetic switch and repair or replace as necessary. If no voltage is read, check for battery voltage on the ignition switch side of the interlock switch. If the switch has failed, fit a new one, otherwise trace back and repair the wiring between the ignition and interlock switches.

INHIBITOR SWITCH - AUTOMATIC TRANSMISSION MODELS

8 The inhibitor switch on auto transmission models provides an interlock with the starter system, ensuring that the engine may only be started while **P** (Park) or **N** (Neutral) are selected. In addition, the inhibitor switch also operates the backup (reversing) lights, and if you have noticed

that the backup lights operate in anything other than reverse gear, you have a good indication that there is an inhibitor switch problem. The inhibitor switch is adjustable - if you find that sometimes the starter fails to work, try moving the shifter back and forth slightly. If you find that you can get the starter working this way, you should check the inhibitor switch adjustment.

9 To check the inhibitor switch you will need to jack the vehicle and place it securely on safety stands so that you can work underneath ☞ 1/3. Check that you have deactivated the stereo security system, then disconnect the battery negative (-) cable to isolate the electrical system.

10 The inhibitor switch is located on the right side of the transmission casing, around the shift shaft boss. Trace back and separate the two wiring connectors. The 3-pin connector (Black/yellow and Red/green wires plus a blank) relates to the backup (reversing) light function, the remaining 2-pin connector being the interlock wiring. Check continuity on the 2-pin connector while your assistant moves the shifter through the various positions. You should read continuity while **P** and **N** are selected, no continuity in the other positions. Check the backup (reversing) light wires for continuity, which should exist only while **R** (reverse) is selected. If the switch does not operate at all, you will need to fit a new one. If the switch operates, but the continuity readings do not coincide with the **P** and **N** and **R** shift positions, you need to adjust the switch.

11 Inhibitor switch adjustment ☞ 4/22.

12 If the above checks have not resolved the starter fault, check the wiring and connections between the battery, starter motor and ignition switch. If no fault can be found, you will have to remove the starter for testing.

10. STARTER MOTOR - REMOVAL, TESTING, OVERHAUL & INSTALLATION

☞ 1/1, 2 & 7/2.

REMOVAL

1 Check that you have deactivated the stereo security system, then disconnect the battery negative (-) cable to isolate the electrical system. Working through the engine compartment, disconnect the starter wiring - one spade/Lucar type terminal which is latched and, under a rubber cover, a 12 mm nut. Free the starter motor support bracket by removing the single 14 mm bolt which fixes it to the engine block (remove the bracket from the motor once you've got the assembly out of the car). You'll find access is pretty restricted - the motor is masked by the intake manifold.

2 Working under the car (☞ 1/3), remove the two upper mounting bolts and the single lower bolt and nut which secure the motor to the bellhousing. The motor can now be pulled forward until it disengages from the ring gear and maneuvered out of the car.

TESTING

3 Clamp the motor in the vise using soft jaws. Do not overtighten the vise - just tighten enough to hold it firmly in place. Using a spare battery (or remove the battery from the car) check motor operation as follows. Connect a set of jump leads, battery positive (+) to the **S** terminal on the motor, and the battery negative (-) terminal grounded to the motor body - this should operate the magnetic switch. You should hear a click as the

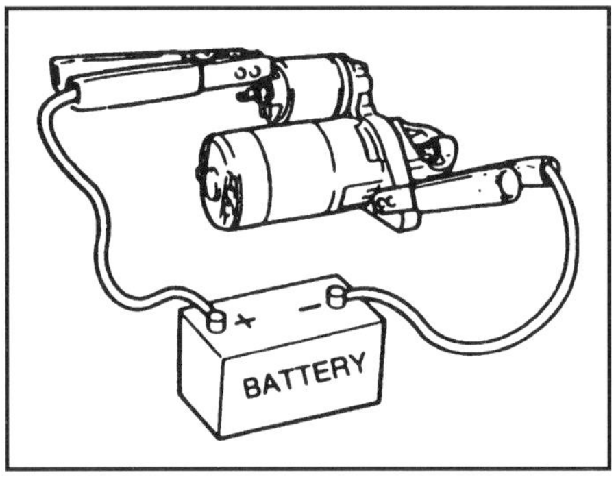

D10/3 TESTING STARTER MOTOR.

solenoid operates. If the magnetic switch fails to operate, it should be checked as described later in this section.

4 With the battery connected as described above, measure the gap between the outer face of the starter pinion and its stop with feeler gauges. The correct gap is 0.5-2.0 mm (0.02-0.08 in). If you need to adjust the gap setting, this can be done by fitting or removing shims between the magnetic switch (solenoid) and the motor casing,

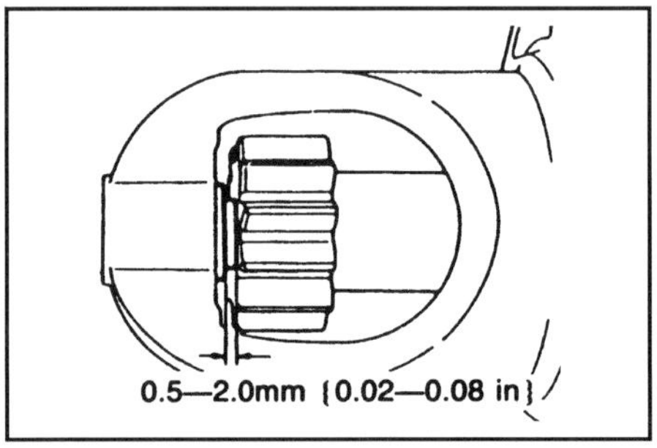

D10/4 CHECKING PINION GAP.

the adjustment requiring removal of the magnetic switch as described later.

5 Check the pinion return by disconnecting the motor wire from the magnetic switch **M** terminal, and applying the positive jump lead to the terminal (not the wire) and grounding the body. Pull the pinion out using a screwdriver and check that it holds in this position. Now disconnect the battery and check that the pinion returns to its normal position.

6 To check the motor no-load operation you will need an ammeter capable of reading up to around 100A, a dc voltmeter, a small switch, some electrical wire, a set of battery jump leads and a fully charged car battery. You need to make up the test rig shown in the accompanying drawing. Use the jump leads between the battery and the motor, connecting the circuit through the ammeter (**A**)

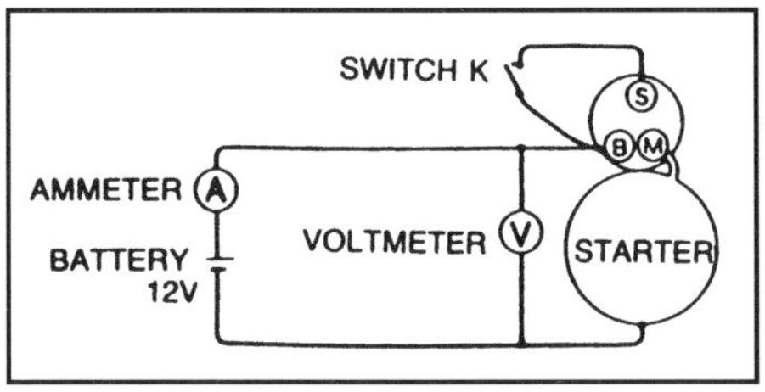

D10/6 NO-LOAD TEST.

and connecting the voltmeter (**V**) between terminal **B** and ground. Use the wire to connect the switch between terminals **B** and **S** of the magnetic switch.

7 When the switch is operated, the motor should run, drawing a current of 60A or less, and showing 11.5 volts on the voltmeter. The motor speed should be around 6,600 rpm or more - largely academic since it is next to impossible to check this at home, but you should get the impression that it runs smoothly and quite fast. If the operation of the motor seems sluggish, or if the current drawn is unusually high or low, the motor needs attention.

OVERHAUL

8 Before you start dismantling the motor for further testing and repairs, give some thought to the best way to approach this. If the motor is generally worn out or obviously burnt out, you might want to consider getting a new or reconditioned motor, or purchasing a used motor from a wrecker (scrapyard). This could save you a lot of time and work, and may be more cost effective than attempting repair of a damaged motor yourself. Remember that if you need to get the motor rewound, or the armature needs machining, you'll end up getting this work done by an auto electrical specialist anyway, in which case you may as well take the complete, assembled motor in for repair.

9 Note also that if the starter pinion teeth are worn, it is likely that similar wear of the starter ring gear has probably taken place. Using a flashlight and a small mirror, you may just be able to check this. If the ring gear is worn, fitting a replacement means removing the engine or transmission - you may want to leave this task until it gets to be a real problem (details ☞ 3/8/76-77).

10 + Remove the nut which secures the braided copper cable to the lower terminal on the magnetic switch. Lift off the cable terminal and refit the nut on the terminal. Remove the two magnetic

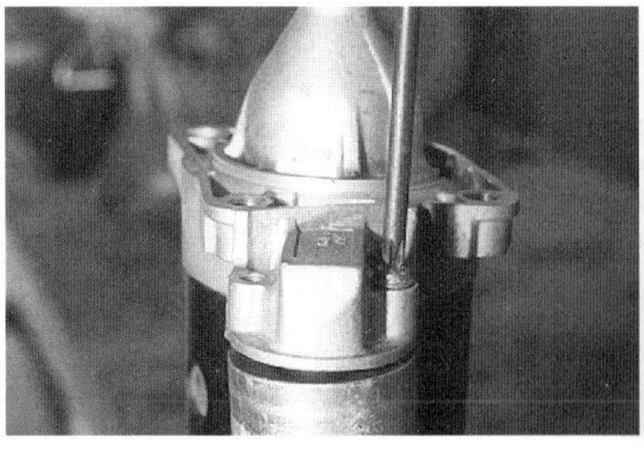

10/10a Remove switch body ...

10/10b ... detach switch core from nylon lever.

10/10c Component parts of switch.

10/11 Remove thru bolts & front cover.

switch retaining crosshead screws and lift away the switch body. The switch core will remain attached to the forked end of the drive pinion lever - lift it away and tip the switch body up to displace the core return spring.

11 If the motor support bracket is still attached to the motor body, remove it. Below the bracket, what appears to be two projecting studs with 8 mm nuts are in fact the motor through bolts. Unscrew and remove these, then lift away the motor front cover and drive pinion lever, disengaging it from the pinion groove. The pinion lever can be removed from the front cover after displacing the metal plate and seal which cover the pivot.

12 Remove the two retaining screws from the motor end cover and remove the cover, noting that the brush plate assembly should be left in position on the armature if possible. Note also that there are loose shim washers on the brush end of the armature - retain these and fit them in the order they were removed during assembly. Disengage the brush plate assembly from the armature and remove the armature from the motor yoke.

13 Use a multimeter or continuity checker to test for insulation between the commutator segments and the core and spindle of the armature. If you find continuity at any point, fit a new armature or see whether you can get the old one reconditioned.

14 Examine the commutator for wear or damage. Light discoloration and minor damage can be corrected by cleaning the commutator with fine sandpaper. Wrap the paper round the commutator and turn the armature until a bright, smooth finish is restored. In cases of more severe damage, have the armature set up in a lathe and remove the minimum amount of metal possible to restore the surface of the commutator segments. Note that if the repair work would result in the commutator

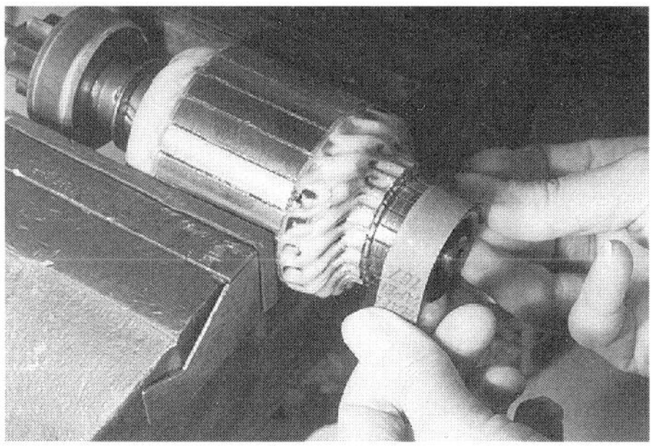

10/14 Cleaning the commutator.

diameter being reduced to 30.8 mm (1.21 in) or less, the armature should be scrapped and a new one fitted.

15 Check that the commutator runout is within limits. Set the armature up on V-blocks or between lathe centers, and use a dial gauge (DTI) to measure commutator runout. The service tolerance is 0.03 mm (0.001 in) or less. Again, minor damage can be corrected by machining the commutator in a lathe, but more severe damage will mean a new armature.

16 + After working on the commutator, check the depth of the grooves between each segment. If these are less than 0.2 mm (0.008 in) you will need to recut them. You can make up your own recutting tool from a section of used hacksaw blade. Find the end where the teeth point back towards you as you hold the blade - this will be the cutting end, so wrap some tape around the other end to form a handle. Now grind the sides of the blade flat until it is a good fit in the commutator grooves. Undercut the grooves by drawing the tool along each one until you achieve the specified undercut of 0.5-0.8 mm (0.020-0.031 in), then repeat the process on the remaining grooves. Use a little fine sandpaper to remove any burring that

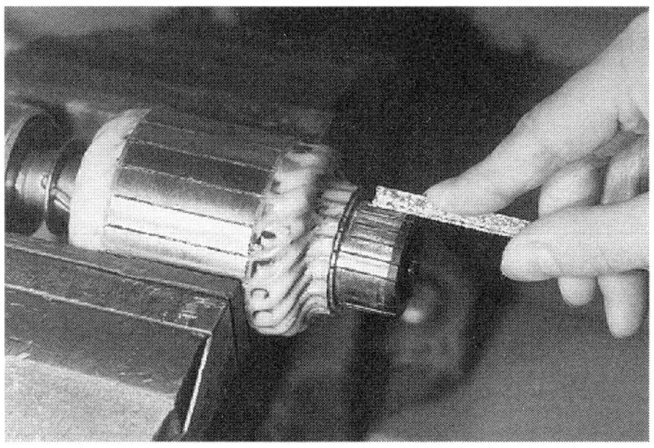

10/16a Undercutting commutator insulators ...

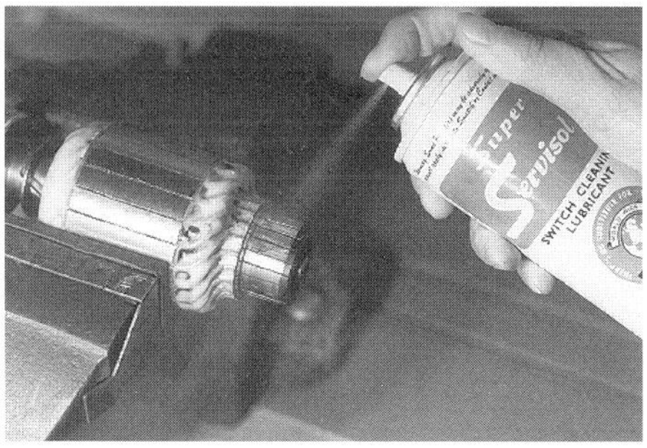

10/16b ... use switch cleaner to clear debris.

results, then clean the commutator with switch cleaner.

17 Moving to the motor body, check for continuity between the brushes and the yoke (field coil) terminals. If the circuit is broken you will need to fit a new or reconditioned unit. Don't attempt removal of the yoke assembly from the motor casing - it needs to be installed using a jig to ensure correct alignment and centering. Similarly, if either field coil is loose, get a new or reconditioned yoke assembly. Check the insulation between the yoke and the motor body - if you find continuity, the yoke assembly will have to be reconditioned or replaced.

18 The magnetic switch (solenoid) can be checked for continuity between terminals **S** (switch terminal) and **M** (motor terminal). If there is a break in continuity, fit a new switch. Next check that there is insulation between the **S** terminal and the switch body. If insulation has broken down, fit a new switch.

19 Check the brush holder assembly for shorting between each brush and the holder plate. If there is continuity indicated, fit a new brush holder assembly.

20 Measure each brush for wear. If worn to or beyond the limit (bottom of the box surrounding the Mitsubishi logo) fit new brushes. The standard brush length is 17 mm (0.67 in) and the wear limit is 11.5 mm (0.45 in). Given the inaccessibility of the motor, we would suggest fitting new brushes irrespective of condition, and this should always be done if the commutator has been skimmed.

21 Fit the armature through the motor yoke and reposition the brush holder assembly over the commutator, lifting each brush into place with a small screwdriver. Apply a little grease to the bearing, fit any shims found on dismantling and install the motor end cover, fitting the two small

10/21 Position brush holder over commutator.

screws to secure the brush holder.

22 Install the front cover, ensuring that the drive pinion lever engages correctly and that the metal plate and seal over its pivot have been installed. Fit the motor through bolts and tighten them to 3.8-7.1 Nm (39-72 kgf cm / 34-62 lbf in).

23 Install the magnetic switch core, hooking it over the lever fork. Fit the core return spring into the switch body and fit the assembly over the core end. Fit the two switch securing screws, tightening them to 4.1-7.5 Nm (42-77 kgf cm / 36-67 lbf in). Reconnect the braided copper cable to the lower switch terminal.

INSTALLATION

24 When installing the starter motor assembly, tighten the mounting bolts and nut evenly to 37-52 Nm (3.8-5.3 kgf m / 27-38 lbf ft). The bolt holding the bracket halves together should be tightened to 16-23 Nm (1.6-2.3 kgf m / 5.0-7.2 lbf ft), and the bracket mounting bolt to 37-52 Nm (3.8-5.3 kgf m / 27-38 lbf ft). Reconnect the motor wiring, securing the heavy battery cable by tightening the retaining nut to 10-12 Nm (105-120 kgf cm / 91-104 lbf in). Temporarily reconnect the battery and check that the motor works normally before lowering the car to the ground.

11. IGNITION SWITCH - TESTING, REMOVAL & INSTALLATION

☞ 1/1, 2 & 7/2.

Warning! Take care when working on the steering column area in cars equipped with air bags. This system contains an explosive charge which deploys the bag when triggered electrically. Note that triggering can take place even if the car's battery is disconnected (the system has its own backup battery). We suggest that you disable the air bag system by disconnecting the clock spring wiring connectors before working in this area. For a full description of this procedure ☞ 7/50.

1 The ignition switch is housed in a two-piece housing attached either side of the steering column. The precise details of this fitting differs according to market and equipment. Our UK specification car was a non-air bag model fitted with a Momo steering wheel. Air bag-equipped models have a different steering wheel and column switch arrangement, and a different housing. Canadian models employ a different steering wheel, but the switch housing looks similar to ours. The procedure described here relates specifically to the arrangement found on our project car - you may encounter slight variations with yours.

2 Disable the stereo security system then isolate the electrical system by disconnecting the battery negative (-) lead. On the underside of the column switch housing, remove the three sheet metal screws and the single machine screw which pass through the housing halves. The two sheet metal screws nearest you, and the machine screw, which screws into the underside of the ignition switch, are easily seen, but there is a third deeply recessed screw fitted into a tunnel near the back of the housing (Note: this arrangement may differ on air bag-equipped cars).

3 Once the retaining screws have been removed, pull the housing halves apart. The two halves clip together, and care should be taken when separating them not to break off the small guide pins around the edge of the join.

4 Unplug the wiring connector on the back of the switch unit. Using a continuity tester or a multimeter, check the switch continuity at the various settings, referring to the table. If the switch does not operate as specified in the table, or if some of the switch settings are intermittent, fit a new switch.

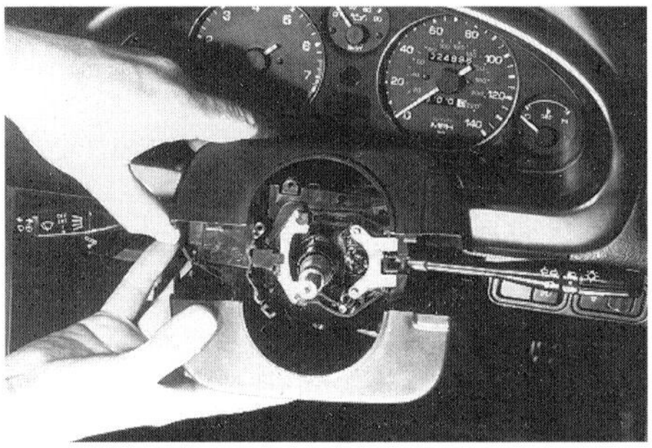

11/3 Separating column switch housing halves.

5 The switch can be removed from the end of the steering lock assembly after removing the retaining screw. When the new switch has been installed and the wiring connector fitted, temporarily reconnect the battery and check switch operation before installing the housing halves.

Position	Terminal							
	B1	B2	ACC	IG1	IG2	ST	K1	K2
LOCK							O—	—O
ACC	O—		—O				O—	—O
ON	O—	O—	—O—	—O	—O		O—	—O
START	O—	O—		—O		—O	O—	—O

O—O: Indicates continuity

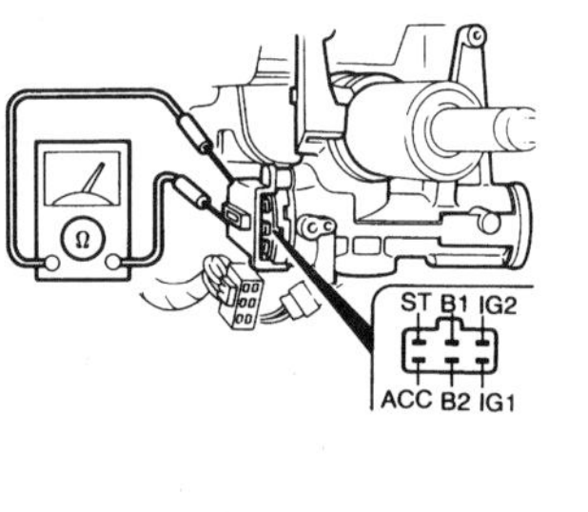

D&T11/4 IGNITION SWITCH TERMINAL IDENTIFICATION & CONTINUITY TEST TABLE.

12. COMBINATION SWITCH - REMOVAL, INSPECTION & INSTALLATION

☞ 1/1, 2 & 7/2.

Warning! Take care when working on the steering column area in cars equipped with air bags. This system contains an explosive charge which deploys the bag when triggered electrically. Note that triggering can take place even if the car's battery is disconnected (the system has its own backup battery). We suggest that you disable the air bag system by disconnecting the clock spring wiring connectors before working in this area. For a full description of this procedure ☞ 7/50.

USA (INC. AIR BAG-EQUIPPED) CARS

1 Disable the stereo security system then isolate the electrical system by disconnecting the battery negative (-) lead. The switch operation can be checked without dismantling if you first remove the inspection panel which covers the steering column. Trace back and separate the relevant connector, then proceed as described below:

2 + + Refer to the accompanying circuit diagrams and tables, and check for continuity at the switch positions and terminals indicated. If continuity is not as shown, the normal course of action is to fit a new combination switch. Before you do so, it is worth removing the old switch and spraying the switch contacts with a silicone-based switch cleaner/lubricant to see if this improves switch operation.

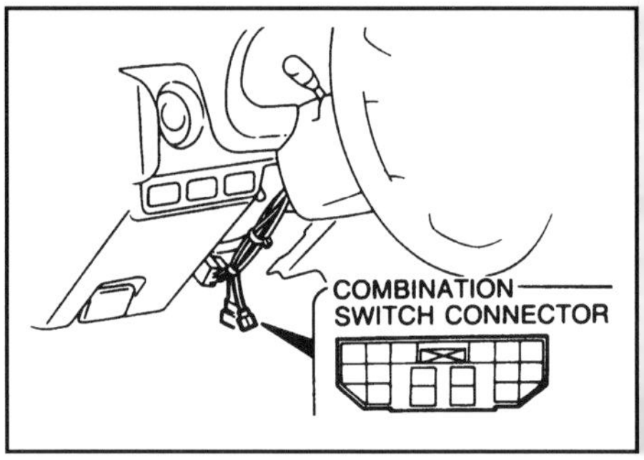

D12/2A COMBINATION SWITCH CONNECTOR LOCATION.
(see overleaf for testing procedures).

3 If you need to remove the switch, note that you must first remove the switch housing ☞ 7/11. Next remove the steering wheel ☞ 8/11 (**Warning!** Take care to disable the air bag system before you remove the wheel and note that during installation the clock spring connector for the air bag unit must be set correctly before the wheel is fitted).

CARS WITHOUT AIRBAGS

4 Disable the stereo security system then isolate the electrical system by disconnecting the battery negative (-) lead. The combination (steering column) switch assembly is covered by the two-piece housing, to expose the switch ☞ 7/11/1-3.

5 Although you can now see the switch assembly, the four wiring connectors are on the

back of the unit and remain inaccessible unless the steering wheel is removed and the switch assembly is slid back along the steering column. Remove the steering wheel ☞ 8/11.

6 With the steering wheel removed, slide off the turn signal switch cancelling sleeve and spring from the end of the steering column. Slacken the clamp screw on the underside of the switch unit so that the unit is loose on the column. Reach over the top of the switch unit and pull the plastic tab toward you so that the locating pin is disengaged from the column (the tab is hard to see from the driver's seat - you get a better view through the windshield). The switch can now be slid off the column and the four switch connectors unplugged from the back. These are all locked in place and can be freed by depressing the locking tabs.

7 Refer to the accompanying circuit diagrams and tables, and check for continuity at the switch positions and terminals indicated. Note that the diagrams and tables marked **LHD** relate to Continental Europe and Canadian market models, while the **RHD** references relate to UK

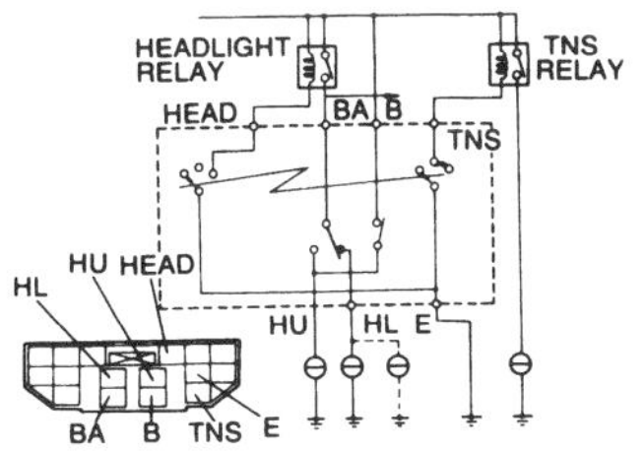

Position		E	HL	HU	TNS	HEAD	BA	B
Headlight	Low beam	O				O		
		O			O			
			O				O	
	High beam	O				O		
		O			O			
				O			O	
Passing				O				O
Tail, Parking		O			O			

O—O: Indicates continuity

D&T12/2B TESTING LIGHTS, DIMMER AND PASSING SWITCH (USA).

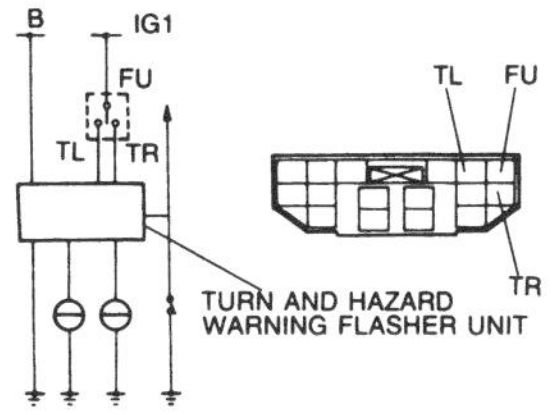

Switch	FU	TL	TR
Left	O	O	
Right	O		O

O—O: Indicates continuity

D&T12/2C TESTING TURN SIGNAL SWITCH (USA).

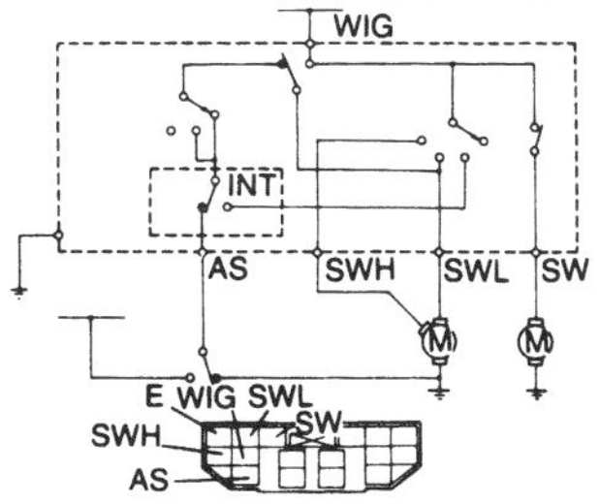

Position		One touch	AS	WIG	SWL	SWH	INT	SW
Wiper switch	OFF	OFF	O		O			
		ON		O	O			
	INT		O		O			
				O			O	
	I (Low)			O	O			
	II (High)			O		O		
Washer switch ON				O				O

O—O: Indicates continuity

D&T12/2D TESTING WINDSHIELD WIPER AND WASHER SWITCH (USA).

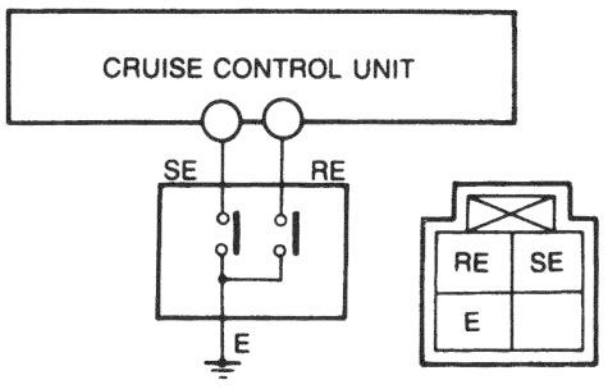

Position	SE	RE	E
SET/COAST	O		O
RESUME/ACCEL		O	O

O—O: Indicates continuity

D&T12/2E TESTING CRUISE CONTROL SWITCH (USA).

12/6a Slide off turn signal cancelling sleeve ...

12/6b ... and spring ...

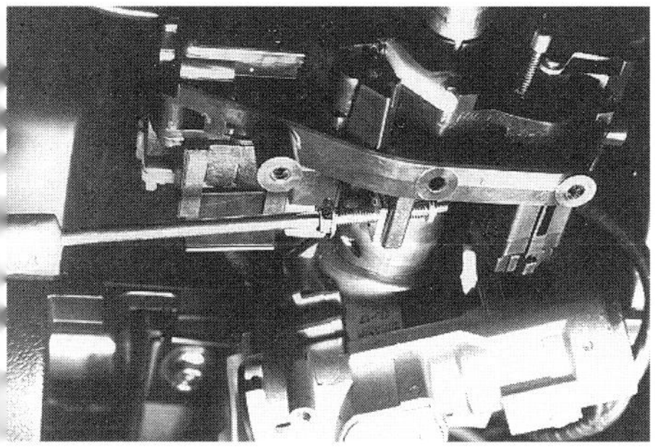

12/6c ... slacken clamp screw ...

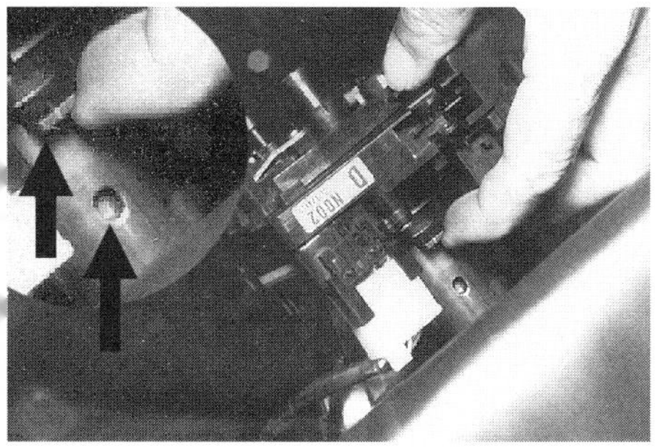

12/6d ... lift locking pin & remove switch body.

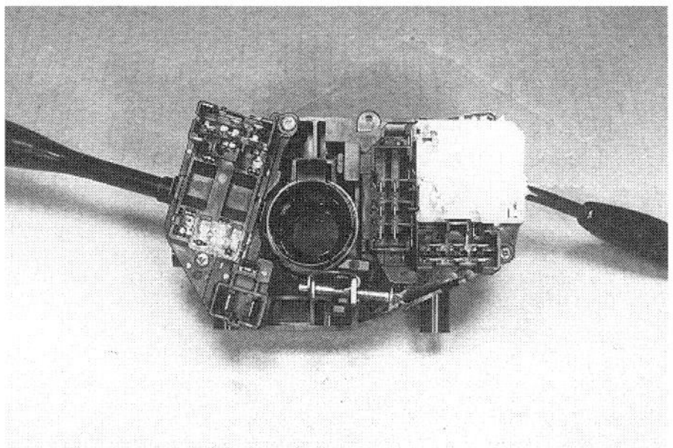

12/7a The combination switch.

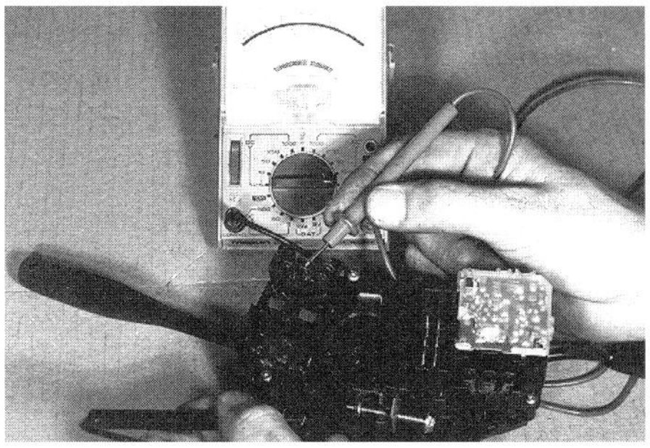

12/7b Testing continuity between terminals.

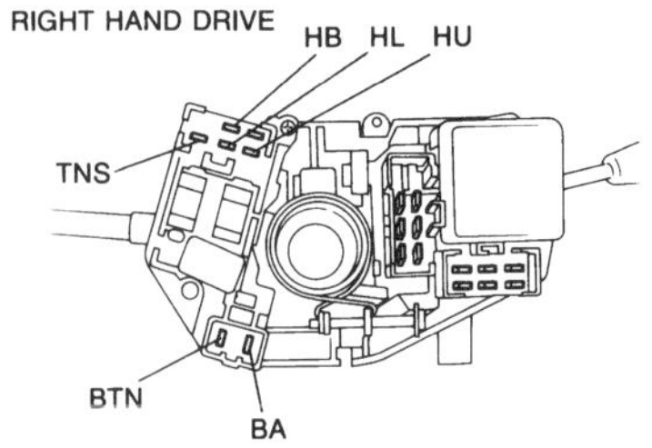

Position \ Terminal		HB	HL	HU	BA	BTN	TNS
Headlight	Low beam	O				O	O
			O		O		
	High beam	O				O	O
				O	O		
Passing				O	O		
Tail, Parking						O	O

O—O: Indicates continuity

D&T12/7A TESTING LIGHTS, DIMMER AND PASSING SWITCH (RHD).

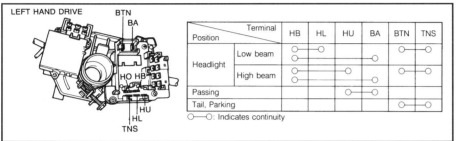

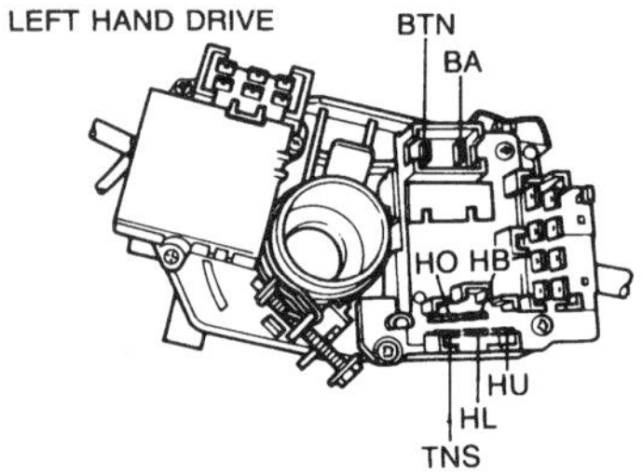

Position \ Terminal		HB	HL	HU	BA	BTN	TNS
Headlight	Low beam	O	O			O	O
		O			O		
	High beam	O		O		O	O
		O			O		
Passing				O	O		
Tail, Parking						O	O

O—O: Indicates continuity

D&T12/7B TESTING LIGHTS, DIMMER AND PASSING SWITCH (LHD).

Position \ Terminal	FU	TL	TR
Left	O	O	
Right	O		O

O—O: Indicates continuity

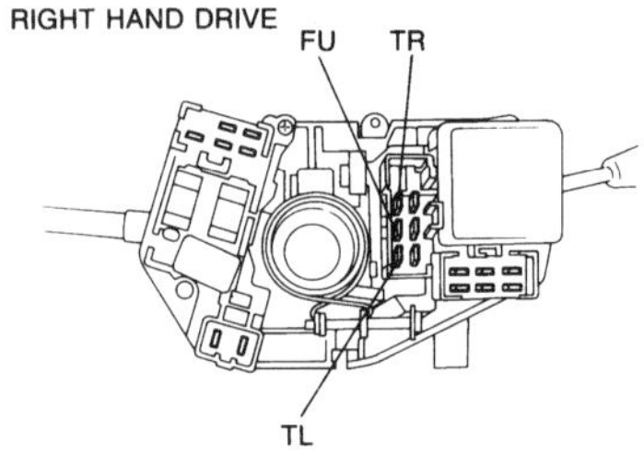

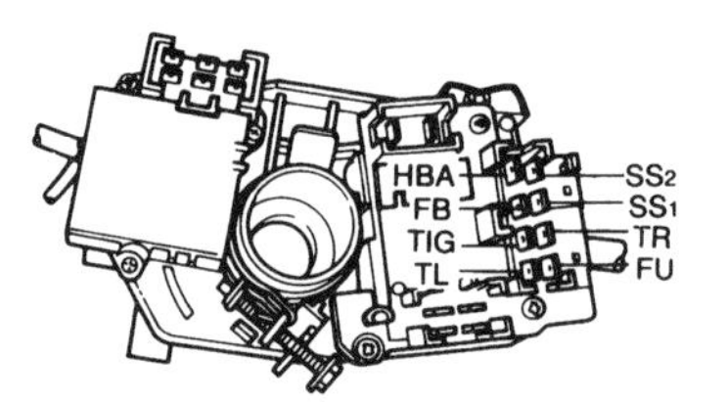

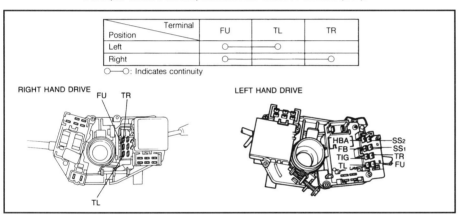

D&T12/7C TESTING TURN SIGNAL SWITCH.

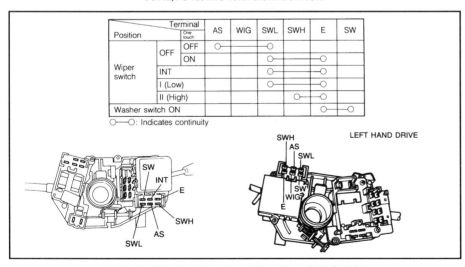

Position \ Terminal		One touch	AS	WIG	SWL	SWH	E	SW
Wiper switch	OFF	OFF	O		O			
		ON			O		O	
	INT				O		O	
	I (Low)				O		O	
	II (High)					O	O	
Washer switch ON							O	O

O—O: Indicates continuity

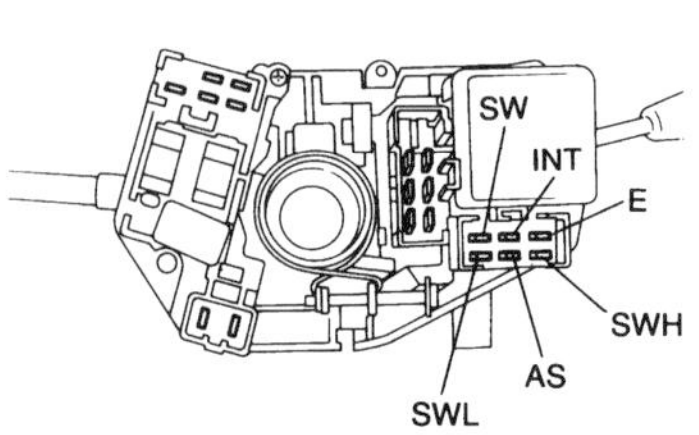

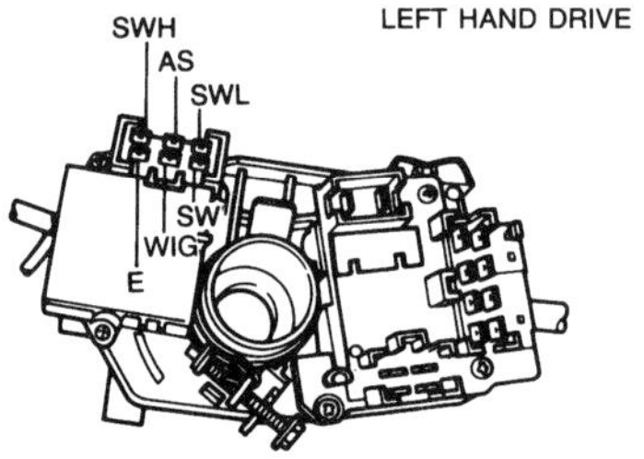

D&T12/7D TESTING WINDSHIELD WIPER AND WASHER SWITCH.

cars only. If continuity is not as shown, the normal course of action is to fit a new combination switch.

8 + Before you do so, it is worth spraying the switch contacts with a silicone-based switch cleaner/lubricant to see if this improves switch operation. You can remove each switch block

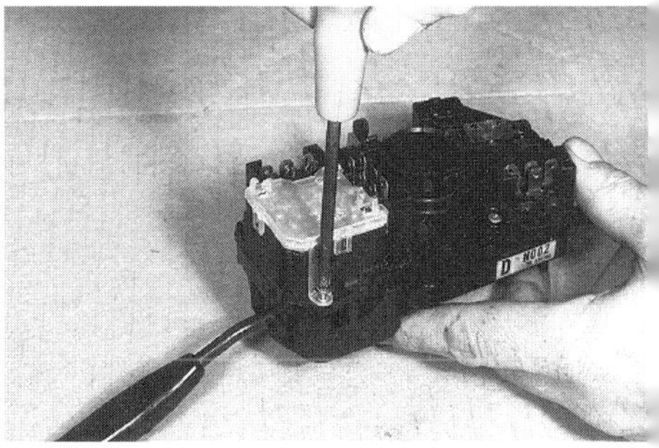

12/8a Remove securing screws ...

12/8b ... and lift switch block.

12/8c Again, remove screws ...

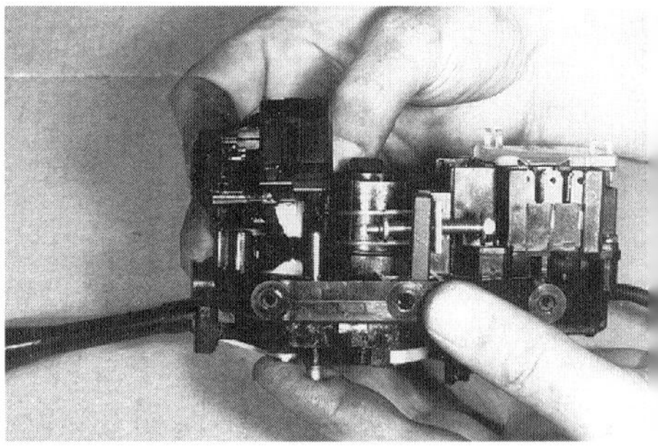

12/8d ... and lift second switch block.

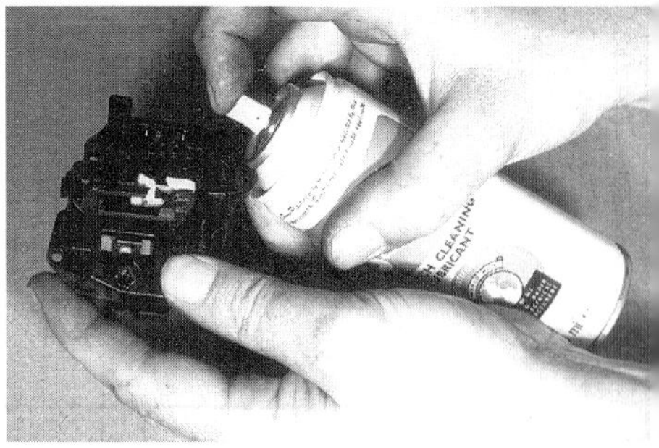

12/8e Use switch cleaner on contacts.

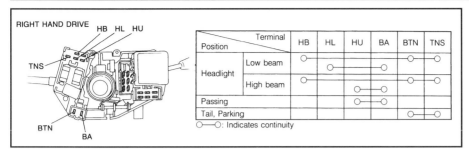

assembly by releasing the retaining screws to get better access to the contacts.

9 When installing the switch, slide it partway over the column and fit the switch connectors. Push the unit forward so that the locking pin snaps home. Tighten the clamp screw on the underside of the unit. This is a good time to temporarily reconnect the battery and check switch operation. If all is well, install the turn signal cancelling sleeve and spring, positioning it to coincide with the drive holes in the steering wheel. Install the steering wheel (☞ 8/11), then fit the switch housing.

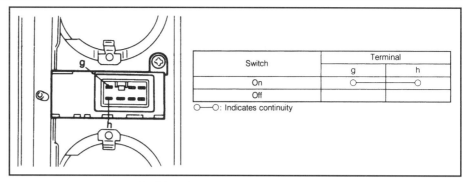

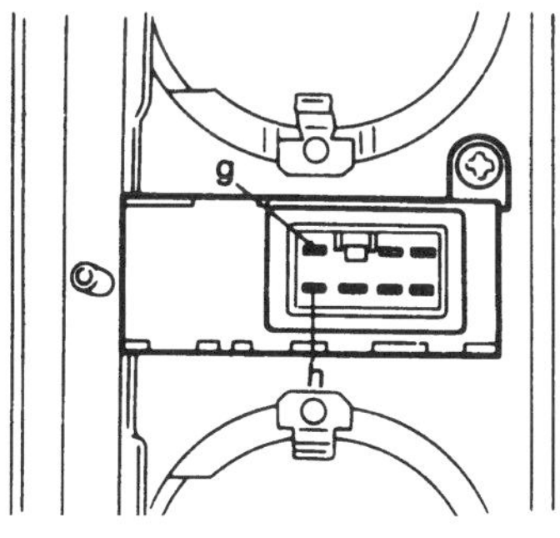

Switch	Terminal	
	g	h
On	O—	—O
Off		

O—O: Indicates continuity

D&T13/2B TESTING HAZARD WARNING SWITCH.

13. H/LIGHT RETRACT & HAZ. WARN. SWITCH - REMOVAL, CHECKING & INSTALLATION

☞ 1/1, 2 & 7/2.

1 This switch assembly is located centrally in the dash panel, between the eyeball vents. Disable the stereo security system then isolate the electrical system by disconnecting the battery negative (-) lead. Access to the switch requires removal of the center section of the dash panel ☞ 10/4. With the dash panel center section removed, un-

13/1 Switch is secured by screws.

plug the wiring connector and free the switch unit by removing the mounting screw.

2 + + Using a continuity tester or multimeter, check the operation of the switches, referring to the accompanying illustration for details of terminal identification and continuity between them. If not as specified, you will have to install a new switch; it is not possible to dismantle or repair the switch if it is faulty.

3 Fit the new switch and secure it with its screw, Move the dash panel center section into position and fit the wiring connector. At this stage, temporarily reconnect the battery and check switch operation, before installing the dash panel center section and eyeball vents.

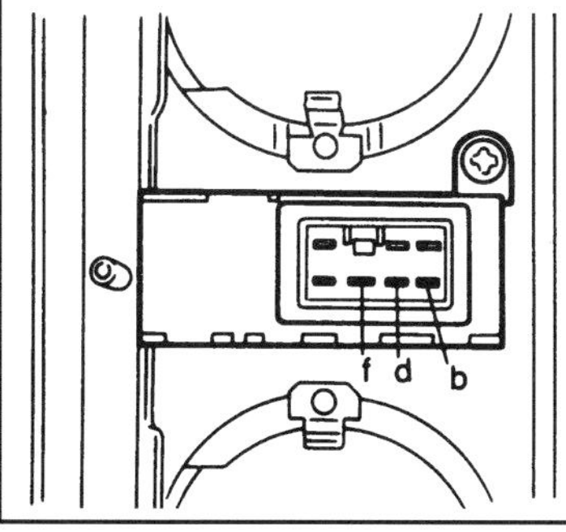

Switch	Terminal		
	b	d	f
Off	O—	—	—O
On		O—	—O

O—O: Indicates continuity

D&T13/2A TESTING HEADLIGHT RETRACTOR SWITCH.

14. INSTRUMENT PANEL - REMOVAL, INSPECTION & INSTALLATION

☞ 1/1, 2 & 7/2.

Warning! Take care when working on the steering column area in cars equipped with air bags. This system contains an explosive charge which deploys the bag when triggered electrically. Note that triggering can take place even if the car's battery is disconnected (the system has its own backup battery). We suggest that you disable the air bag system by disconnecting the clock spring wiring connectors before working in this area. For a full description of this procedure ☞ 7/50.

REMOVAL

1 Disable the stereo security system then isolate the electrical system by disconnecting the battery negative (-) lead. On the underside of the column switch housing, remove the three sheet metal screws and the single machine screw which pass through the housing halves. The two sheet metal screws nearest you, and the machine screw, which screws into the underside of the ignition switch, are easily seen, but there is a third deeply recessed screw fitted into a tunnel near the back of the housing (Note: this arrangement may differ on air bag-equipped cars).

2 Once the retaining screws have been removed, pull the housing halves apart. The two halves clip together, and care should be taken when separating them not to break off the small guide pins around the edge of the join.

3 + Remove the two sheet metal screws which retain the instrument panel housing. These are fitted from the front edge of the housing and pass upwards to secure it to the dash panel. Once you've released the screws, the housing can be pulled back until it disengages from the dash panel. The back of the housing is held by three metal clips

14/3a Remove two sheet metal screws ...

14/3b ... then disengage the instrument housing.

on the dash panel and is located by a long plastic pin.

4 + With the housing out of the way, you have clear access to the four screws which secure the instrument panel. Remove the screws and pull the panel towards you. As it moves away from the dash, unplug the instrument panel connectors - there are two of these, one at top left and one at top right - each is secured by a locking tab. The panel can now be pulled back further, but is still held by the speedometer drive cable. This is secured on the back of the instrument panel by

14/4a The instrument panel is held by 4 screws.

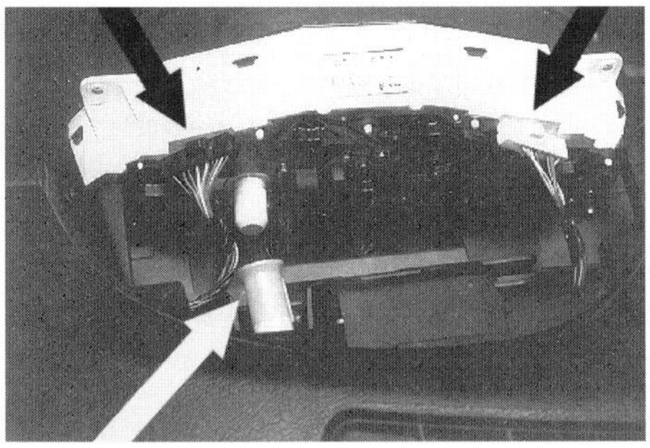

14/4b Release speedo cable and connectors.

14/4c Carefully lift the panel away.

(you guessed it) a locking tab. Press this in and pull the cable off the back of the speedometer, then lift the instrument panel away.

5 + Individual gauges are screwed to the panel from the back, and can be removed after you've unclipped the lens from the front of the instrument panel. - see the accompanying diagram (D14/4) for details.

BULB REPLACEMENT

6 With the instrument panel removed, you have access to the back for bulb replacement. We suggest that you check all the bulbs while the

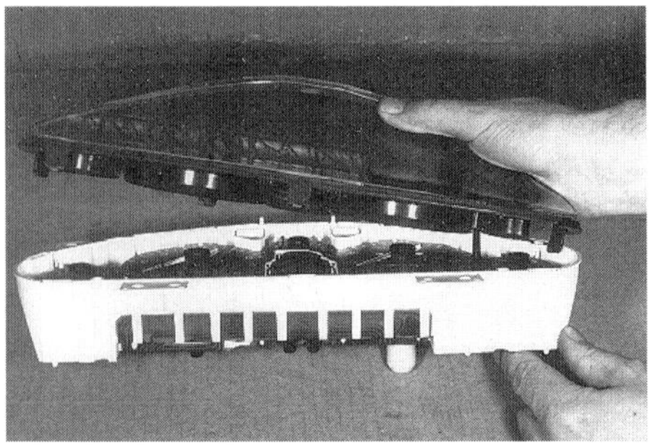

14/5a Unclip lens from front of panel.

14/5b Individual instruments now accessible.

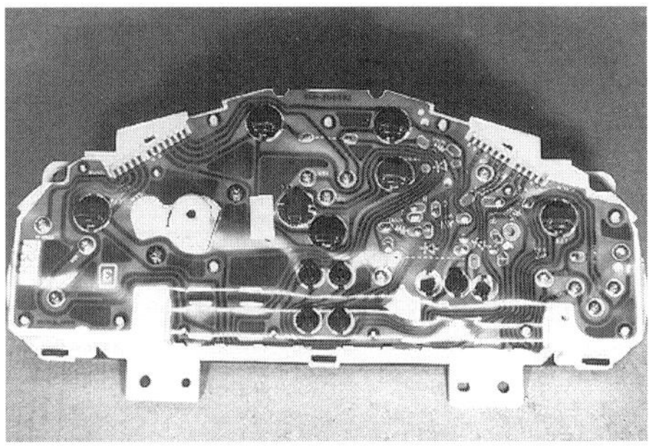

14/5c Printed circuit and bulb holders.

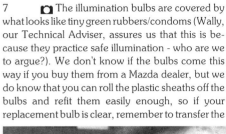

14/6 Twist bulb holder to remove.

unit is out of the car - you may have one or more burned out bulbs which you haven't noticed. The bulb holders are removed by twisting them counterclockwise - they can then be removed together with the bulb. Note that most of the holders are black, but there are several green ones - these contain the illumination bulbs which are themselves colored.

7 The illumination bulbs are covered by what looks like tiny green rubbers/condoms (Wally, our Technical Adviser, assures us that this is because they practice safe illumination - who are we to argue?). We don't know if the bulbs come this way if you buy them from a Mazda dealer, but we do know that you can roll the plastic sheaths off the bulbs and refit them easily enough, so if your replacement bulb is clear, remember to transfer the

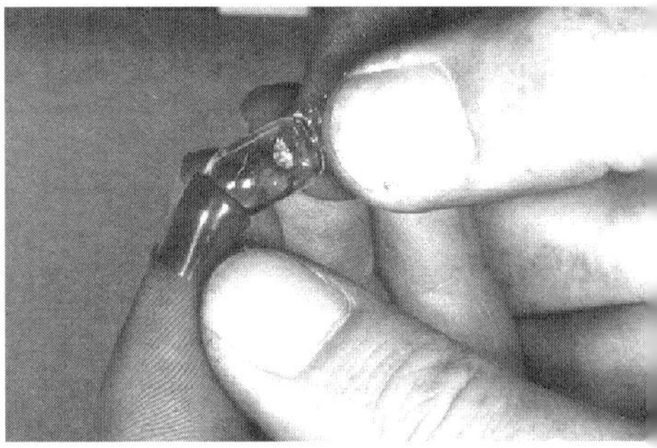

14/7 Some of the bulbs wear tiny condoms!

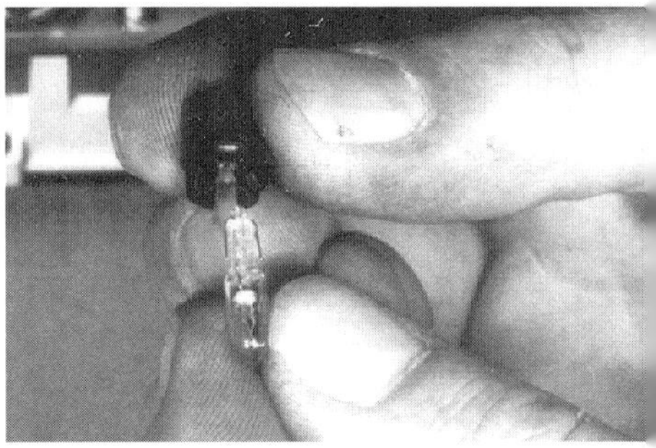

14/8 Capless bulbs are a push fit in holders.

colored sheath before you fit it.

8 The bulbs are of the capless type, and are a push-fit in the holders. When you remove or fit them, make sure that the fine wire contacts do

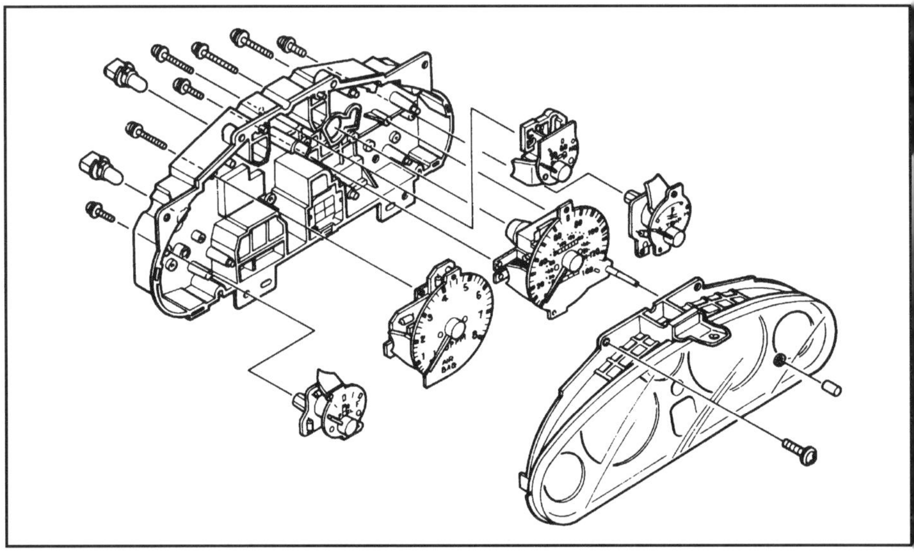

D14/4 INSTRUMENT PANEL AND INSTRUMENT DETAIL.

not get pushed out of alignment, or the bulb will not work. Note when purchasing replacement bulbs that there are two different physical sizes and various wattages. All are 12 volt and rated at 1.2W or 3.4W (except the air bag warning lamp, which is rated at 2W).

9 The exact arrangement of warning and illumination lamps varies according to the country in which the car was sold - on most models you will find at least one unoccupied warning lamp recess on the back of the panel, and the bulbs have different functions, depending on market. We suggest that you remove bulb holders individually, noting where on the panel it was fitted, to avoid confusion later (if you are unsure about whether a bulb was fitted to a particular hole in the panel, look for indentations in the soft copper tracks around the hole - the unused holes will be unmarked).

SPEEDOMETER

10 If you suspect that the speedometer has failed, it is worth noting that if the speedometer is not reading, but the odometer and trip meters continue to work, the instrument head can be considered to be at fault (drive is obviously reaching the unit but it has broken internally). The speedometer can be checked by inserting a small screwdriver in the back of the drive connection and spinning it with the fingers - if the needle moves, you can be fairly confident that the instrument is intact and that the fault lies in the drive cable.

11 If the cable appears to be broken, you will need to raise the car onto safety stands (☞ 1/3) so that you can reach the lower connection at the transmission. This can then be detached by holding the hexagon end with a crescent wrench and unscrewing the knurled retaining ring with pliers. To allow the upper end of the cable to pass through the firewall, you need to push out the large plastic cup through which the cable passes.

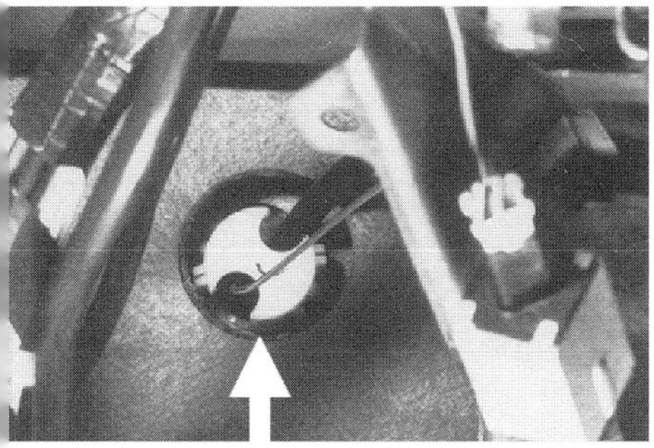

14/11 Speedo cable holder in firewall.

12 Once you have removed the cable, any break is likely to be immediately obvious - they normally break at either end. If the cable is unbroken, check that it turns smoothly and without undue resistance. If it jerks badly when it is turned, this usually indicates that the cable is kinked and that it should be replaced - a wavering speedometer needle often indicates this problem. When installing the cable, remember to snap the plastic cup at the upper end back into its hole in the firewall.

13 The instrument head is held in the panel moulding by two screws, located either side of the projecting drive connection. If you are uncertain about its condition, you can in theory get the unit checked on a speedometer tester by your Mazda dealer, though normally they usually work fine, or not at all. The instrument head is installed by placing it in the panel recess and tightening the securing screws evenly.

TACHOMETER

14 You can check tachometer faults using a test tachometer hooked up to the instrument panel connectors. Alternatively, if you know another Miata/MX5 owner, ask whether you can swap instrument panels to check whether the fault lies in the tachometer or its wiring. If the test (or substitute) tachometer reads engine speed normally, you will know that the fault lies in the wiring to the instrument - check back from the instrument panel connectors to the igniter unit. If you need to replace the instrument, it is held in the panel by screws from the back.

WATER TEMPERATURE GAUGE

15 The water temperature gauge operation can be checked without removing the instrument panel. With the engine cold, disconnect the wiring from the water thermosensor (temperature gauge sender) on the top of the thermostat housing. Connect the positive probe of an ohmmeter to the sensor terminal, and the negative probe to ground (earth). The meter should indicate a resistance of around 183 .

16 Start the engine and note the reading as the engine warms up. You are unlikely to reach the maximum engine temperature, but on US and UK market cars this should be 20 , and for Canadian and Continental Europe models it should be 18 . Despite the specified figures, if you can see that the sensor resistance falls off as temperature rises, it is unlikely that the sensor is at fault - if they fail they usually cease to operate at all.

17 Check back along the sensor wiring (Black/blue) between the sensor connector and the **2I** terminal at the instrument panel connector. A reading of continuity indicates that the wire is intact, infinite ( ) resistance indicates a break in the wire, and continuity between the wire and ground indicates a short. If required, repair the wire or bypass it using a new wire of the same size and, preferably, color taped to the harness.

18 If it looks like the gauge is broken, you can get this checked on an SST by your Mazda dealer - take in the instrument panel assembly for this check. Alternatively, you could simply substitute a known good gauge to check whether yours has failed (ask a Miata/MX5 owning friend to let you swap instrument panels to check this).

FUEL GAUGE

19 As with the temperature gauge, much of the fuel gauge testing can take place without removing the instrument panel. The procedure starts with tests on the sender unit in the fuel tank, and a certain amount of dismantling is required to get access to this. To get meaningful results from the check, try to start out with an empty fuel tank, but have ready enough fuel to fill the tank during the check. You will need to lift the carpet on the deck to the rear of the seats and remove the fuel pump / sender access panel ☞ 5/16.

14/19 Remove this access panel.

20 Disconnect the wiring connector at the fuel pump / sender flange, and connect an ohmmeter (or a multimeter set to an appropriate resistance range) positive probe to the yellow wire terminal of the connector, and ground the negative (-) probe.

21 With an empty tank, you should get a reading of around 95 . As the sender moves to the full position, the reading should fall to 7 . Try filling the fuel tank (**Warning!** - take the usual fire precautions here, and make sure you have adequate ventilation while the tank is open and being filled) and as the tank fills, check that the resistance read on the meter falls back to the lower figure.

22 You can expect the meter needle to fluctuate through the test, as the sender wiper contact moves across the variable resistance (rheostat) windings - don't interpret this as a fault unless the reading stays at (infinity) for a significant part of the range, denoting broken or corroded rheostat windings. If you read infinite resistance ( ) or no resistance throughout the test, the sender can be considered inoperative.

23 If you have diagnosed a sender fault, you should install a new unit, after removing the fuel gauge / sender assembly ☞ 5/16. Before you rush out to buy a new unit to replace an intermittent one, we suggest that you try spraying switch cleaner into the sender unit and then working the float arm through its travel a few times. Hook up the ohmmeter as described above and recheck the resistance reading as you move the arm. With a little luck, you may have cleaned the contact surfaces enough to restore normal operation.

24 If the sender checks out OK, test continuity on the wire from the sender unit and the instrument panel (yellow wire on the fuel pump / sender connector to terminal 1a (yellow wire) at the instrument panel connector. A reading of continuity indicates that the wire is intact, infinite ( ) resistance indicates a break in the wire, and continuity between the wire and ground indicates a short. If required, repair the wire or bypass it using a new wire of the same size and, preferably, color taped to the harness.

25 If you have got this far in the sequence, it looks like the gauge itself may be the problem. You

can get this checked out by your Mazda dealer by taking in the instrument panel assembly - the check requires an SST. Alternatively, you could simply substitute a known good gauge to check whether yours has failed (ask a Miata/MX5 owning friend to let you swap instrument panels to check this).

OIL PRESSURE GAUGE

26 The oil pressure gauge operation can be checked without removing the instrument panel. With the engine cold, disconnect the wiring from the oil pressure sensor. This is located below the intake manifold, above the oil filter. Connect the positive probe of an ohmmeter to the sensor terminal, and the negative probe to ground (earth). The meter should indicate a resistance of around 52 .

27 Start the engine and note the reading as oil pressure builds. You may not reach the maximum pressure resistance, but this should be 16 . Despite the specified figures, if you can see that the sensor resistance falls off quickly as oil pressure rises, it is unlikely that the sensor is at fault - if they fail they usually cease to operate at all. If the sensor proves to be faulty, it can be removed by unscrewing and a new one installed.

28 Check back along the sensor wiring (Yel-

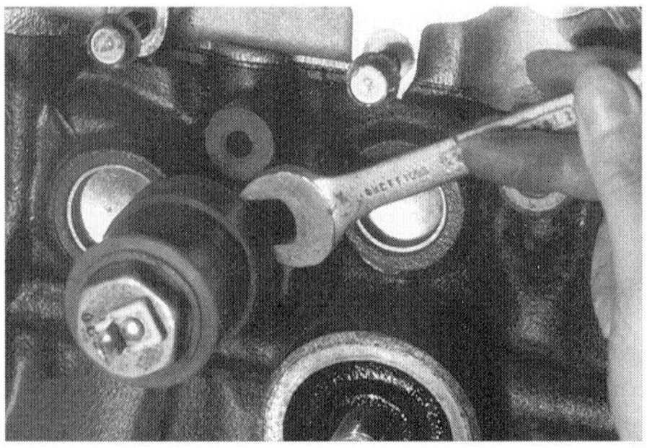

14/27 Removing oil pressure sensor.

low/red) between the sensor connector and the **2b** terminal at the instrument panel connector. A reading of continuity indicates that the wire is intact, infinite ( ) resistance indicates a break in the wire, and continuity between the wire and ground indicates a short. If required, repair the wire or bypass it using a new wire of the same size and, preferably, color taped to the harness. You should also check that the gauge is grounded correctly - check the black (**2j**) terminal to ground.

29 If it looks like the gauge is broken, you can get this checked on an SST by your Mazda dealer - take in the instrument panel assembly for this check. Alternatively, you could simply substitute a known good gauge to check whether yours has failed (ask a Miata/MX5 owning friend to let you swap instrument panels to check this).

GENERAL CHECKS

30 Before installing the instrument panel, check that the flexible printed circuit on the back of the unit is in good condition. There is no obvious reason why this should ever get damaged, but if the circuit gets bent sufficiently, the tracks may become broken. Check for corrosion on the copper tracks where bulb holders and the two wiring connectors contact them. You can use switch cleaner to ensure a good contact and to prevent damage from corrosion. If the tracks are already corroded, this can be removed with careful use of a pencil eraser to restore a clean polished finish, which can then be protected with switch cleaner / lubricant. If the corrosion is bad, or if the printed circuit is damaged, fit a new one.

INSTALLATION

31 Check that all bulb holders are secure and that the instruments have been fitted correctly. Position the unit over the steering column and reconnect the speedometer drive cable and the two wiring connectors. Place the unit against the dash panel and fit the four screws, tightening them evenly. Clip the surround in place, then fit the steering column (combination) switch housing. Check the operation of the gauges, warning lamps and instrument illumination.

15. WARNING LAMPS, SWITCHES & SENSORS - LOCATION & TESTING

1/1, 2 & 7/2.

1 The various warning lamps are housed in the instrument panel - for details on removal, bulb replacement and installation 7/14. If you have a single inoperative warning lamp the chances are that the bulb has burned out - always check this first. If all warning lamps are inoperative, this suggests that the associated fuse (**METER 10A**) has burned out. If a warning lamp stays on all the time, it is either doing its job of warning you of a fault, or the warning lamp circuit concerned has a fault. Individual circuit checks are described below.

BRAKE WARNING CIRCUIT

2 If the brake warning lamp comes on, you should stop the car immediately and check the brake fluid level. If this is below the **MIN** level on the reservoir, check the cause of the level drop (badly worn brake pads or a hydraulic leak 9. **Warning!** This is a potentially dangerous situation - do not drive the car until you have checked the hydraulic system and pads.

3 If there is no fault in the brake system, check the operation of the parking brake switch - you can just about get to this on the side of the parking brake lever. If you find access difficult, remove the single screw holding the brake lever

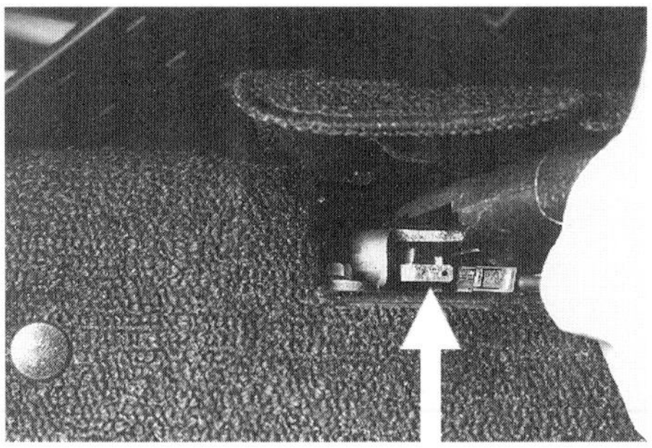

15/3 Parking brake switch from above.

cover in place, and remove it by pulling the two halves apart - you will need to pull back the carpet around the lever base - this is held by a velcro pad.

4 Check for continuity between the switch terminal and ground. With the lever fully released, you should read zero continuity. There should be continuity when the lever is raised by one notch. If the readings are not as described, either adjust the switch or fit a new one as necessary.

5 If the parking brake circuit and brake system check out OK, this leaves the fluid level sensor as prime suspect.

HAZARD WARNING INDICATOR LIGHT CIRCUIT (NOT FITTED ON ALL MODELS)

6 If the hazard warning light circuit operates normally, but the indicator light in the instrument panel does not come on, it is pretty certain that the bulb has burned out. Check and replace the bulb as necessary. If the fault persists, check back from the indicator light to the hazard warning / turn signal relay. For some reason, Mazda do not detail this connection on their circuit diagrams, but we're pretty sure that the indicator light is connected by an orange wire to the relay.

OVERDRIVE INDICATOR LIGHT CIRCUIT (AUTO TRANSMISSION MODELS)

7 We have very little information on this circuit, other than advice to check the bulb if the light fails to operate and replace it if it is burned out. If the problem remains unresolved after replacing the bulb, check back from the instrument panel **1j** terminal (Blue/black wire) to the overdrive ON/OFF switch. The switch can be checked after the rear console has been removed 11.

8 Disconnect the wiring connector. With the switch side of the connector held with the key uppermost, check for continuity between the top left and top right terminals. You should get continuity when the switch is released, and no continuity when it is depressed - if not, the shift knob should be replaced.

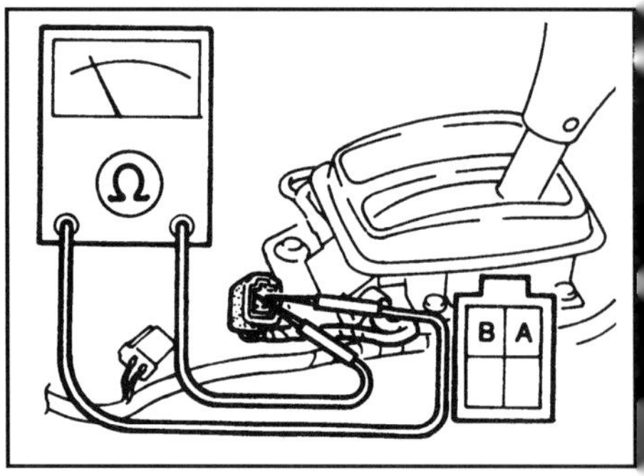

D15/8 TESTING OVERDRIVE SWITCH.

9 To check the overdrive cancel solenoid, you will need to raise the car and support it on safety stands, and then drain around 2 pints / 1 liter of transmission fluid. Disconnect the solenoid wiring and remove it from the transmission casing for testing.

10 Check the solenoid by applying battery voltage across its terminals. If it is working correctly,

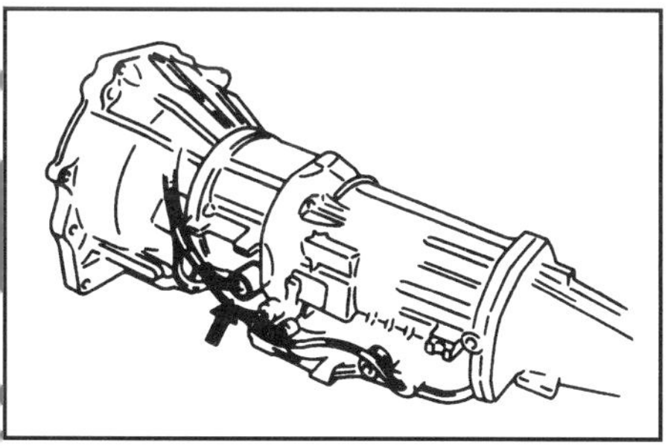

D15/9 LOCATION OF OVERDRIVE CANCEL SOLENOID.

the oil passage at the end of the solenoid should close and then open again when the battery is disconnected. Replace the solenoid if this is not the case. When installing a new or used solenoid, use a new O-ring and lubricate it with a little ATF before fitting it to the transmission casing. Lower the car to the ground and top up the ATF to the correct level ☞ 2.

11 The 4AT (automatic transmission) control unit should be checked as follows. Locate the unit after removing the access panel over the steering column. You need to check the unit terminal voltages with the unit connected, using the voltmeter probes through the back of the connector. The main thing to check is the power to the unit. Connect the meter positive (+) probe to terminal **1a**, and the negative (-) probe to terminal **1b** (ground). With the ignition switch on, you should read battery voltage. The terminal positions and the voltage readings dependent on the associated switch settings will be found in the accompanying table.

SEATBELT WARNING CIRCUIT (WHERE FITTED)

12 Locate the timer and buzzer unit after removing the access panel over the steering column. We can't swear to the exact location of the unit - it is amongst a group of relays mounted under the dash panel. If the unit operates as normal, of course, you can track it down by operating the buzzer, otherwise, refer to the accompanying drawing for location details.

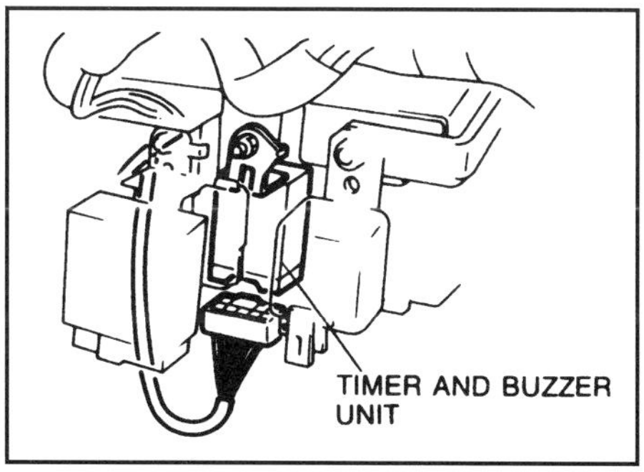

D15/12 LOCATION OF SEATBELT TIMER & BUZZER UNIT.

13 If the light remains on for more than six seconds after the ignition switch is turned on, check the unit as follows. Unplug the wiring connector from the unit and turn on the ignition switch. If the instrument panel warning light comes on, check the wiring between the unit and the warning lamp (LG wire to terminal **1b** on the instrument panel wiring connector). If the light does not come on, you need to fit a new timer and buzzer unit.

14 If the light fails to operate when the ignition switch is turned on, ground terminal **J** at the back of the timer and buzzer unit (with the wiring connected). Check that the light comes on when you turn on the ignition switch. If the light comes on, check the ground wire from the unit to the chassis, and repair or replace it as required. If the light does not illuminate, move on to step 15.

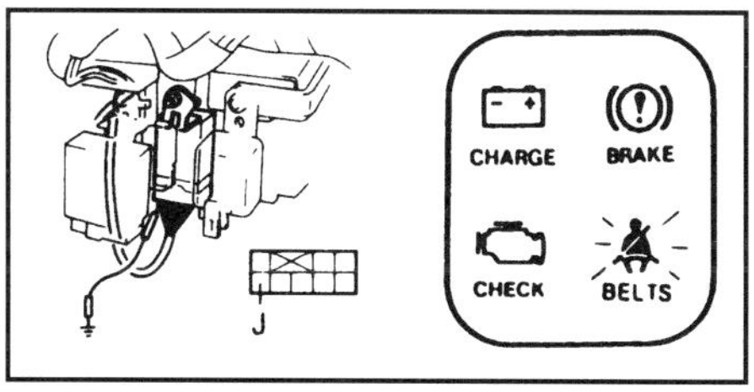

D15/14 GROUND TERMINAL 'J'.

15 Next, ground terminal **D** as described above. If the warning light comes on when the ignition is switched on, you will have to fit a new timer and buzzer unit. If the light does not come on, check the warning light bulb, and check the wiring between the unit and the instrument panel connector.

16 Finally, you should check the seat belt buckle switches. Disconnect the wiring from the buckle and check for continuity between the connector terminals with the buckle fastened (should read no continuity) and unfastened (should read continuity). Replace the switch if not as indicated.

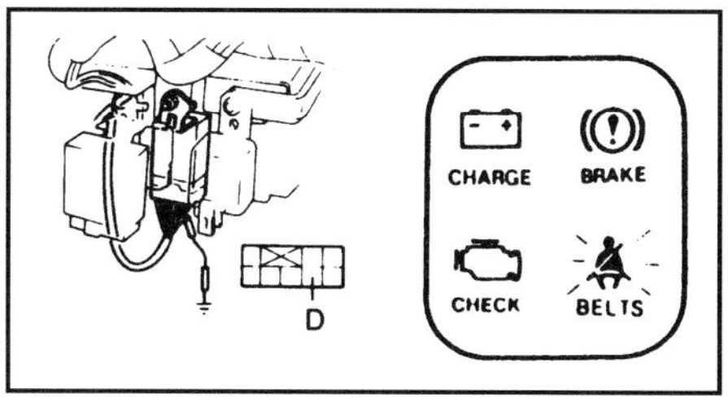

D15/16 GROUND TERMINAL 'D'.

WASHER LEVEL INDICATOR CIRCUIT (WHERE FITTED)

17 The washer level indicator light should come on when the level in the washer reservoir falls near empty. If you have a fault on the circuit, first check the bulb and replace it if it is burned out. If the fault remains, you will need to check that there is no resistance when the switch float is at its lowest

Terminal	Connected to	Voltage	Condition	VB: Battery voltage
1A (Battery power)	Battery	VB	Ignition switch ON	
		0V	Ignition switch OFF	
1B (Ground)	Battery ground	0V	Constant	
1C (Input)	OD OFF switch	VB	OD OFF switch released • OD not available	
		0V	OD OFF switch depressed • OD available	
1D (Input)	Kickdown switch	VB	Switch ON: • Throttle opening 7/8—8/8	
		0V	Switch OFF: • Other than conditions above	
1E (Input)	4-3 switch	VB	Switch ON: • Throttle opening 6/8—8/8	
		0V	Switch OFF: • Other than conditions above	
1F (Input)	Oil pressure switch	VB	Switch OFF: • 1st, 2nd, and 3rd gear positions in forward ranges • P, R, and N ranges	
		0V	Switch ON: • OD gear position	
1H (Input)	Engine control unit	Below. 1.5V	Ignition switch ON	
1J (Input)	Cruise control unit	VB	Normal conditions	
		Below. 1.5V	Set or Resume switch ON, or vehicle speed 8 km/h [5 mph] lower than preset speed (Driving vehicle: cruise control operation)	
1K (Output)	OD cancel solenoid	VB	Solenoid OFF: • OD gear position	
		Below. 1.5V	Solenoid ON: • 1st, 2nd, and 3rd gear positions in forward ranges • P, R, and N ranges	
1L (Input)	Speed sensor	1.5—7V	During driving	
		Approx. 7V or below 1.5V	Vehicle stopped	
1M (Input)	Kickdown relay	VB	Kickdown relay OFF: • Other than conditions below	
		Below. 1.5V	Kickdown relay ON: • Kickdown switch ON (throttle opening more than 7/8)	
1N (Output)	Lockup solenoid	VB	Solenoid OFF: • Lockup prohibition	Ignition switch ON
		Below. 1.5V	Solenoid ON: • Lockup	Engine running
1O	—	—	—	
1P	—	—	—	

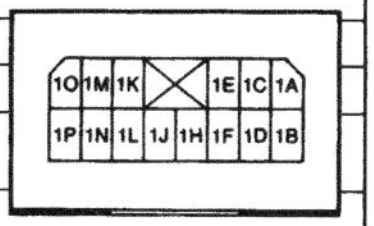

T15/11 TESTING THE 4AT (AUTOMATIC TRANSMISSION) CONTROL UNIT.

point and infinite resistance above this. If the switch has failed, you will need to fit a new one. It is a push-fit in the reservoir and can be removed after emptying the contents. If the switch and bulb are OK, check the blue wire back from the switch to terminal **1L** of the instrument panel connector.

REAR FOG LAMP WARNING CIRCUIT (WHERE FITTED)

18 If the rear fog light operates normally but the warning lamp does not come on, check first that the bulb has not burned out. If the bulb is OK and the fault remains, check back along the wiring from the instrument panel connector terminal **1c** (blue/black wire) to the switch. The switch is clipped into the dash panel and can be removed by prying it out with a small screwdriver.

16. LIGHTING SYSTEM - INITIAL CHECKS

☞ 1/1, 2 & 7/2.

1 The Miata/MX5 models come equipped with the normal range of lights - specific details vary according to the country in which the car was sold, but on the whole it's pretty much as you'd expect on any modern car. For the most part, trouble-shooting the lighting system is as you would expect - checking for burned out bulbs and testing switches, relays and wiring.

2 The use of pop-up headlights introduces a bit more electromechanical complexity than you'd find on many modern family cars; each headlight has its own motor arrangement controlled from the column switch, a separate dash panel switch and, if a problem arises, manually at the light itself. In some countries, the headlight raising system is further developed to include an automatic headlight levelling system.

3 When you are trying to track down a fault with any of the lighting circuits, give the nature of the fault some thought first. About the most common cause of problems will be a burned out bulb; if one headlight is not working on high beam, you can be pretty safe in assuming that the bulb has burned out a filament. If, on the other hand, the entire headlight circuit is down, it would be unusual for all of the related bulbs to have burned out simultaneously - you should be looking at the circuit in general starting with the fuse which protects it.

4 In the following sections we will be looking at diagnosing faults and circuit and component checks. Where more detailed testing or dismantling procedures are involved, references to the later sections of this chapter will be found in the text.

17. HEADLIGHT - CIRCUIT CHECKS (US CARS)

☞ 1/1, 2 & 7/2.

Step 1

1 Start by checking the **HEAD 30A** fuse housed in the main fuse block in the engine compartment. If the fuse has burned out, it should be replaced after you've established the cause of the failure. This may be due to a brief overload, caused by a bulb burning out, for example. If the new fuse burns out immediately the lights are switched on, you will need to investigate the headlight system wiring for shorts. If the fuse was undamaged, proceed to Step 2.

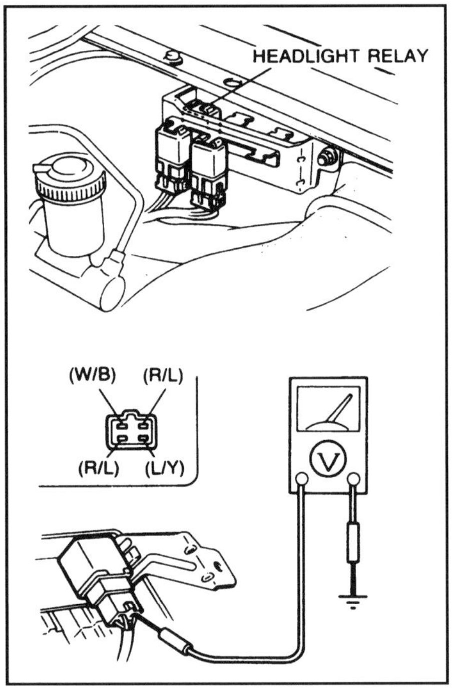

D17/2 HEADLIGHT RELAY LOCATION AND TERMINAL IDENTIFICATION (US CARS).

Step 2

2 Locate the headlight relay. This is mounted along with a number of other relays on a bracket at the left side of the engine compartment. To get access to the relay wiring connector, it is easiest to remove the bracket from the car. The following voltage checks should be made with the relay connected and with the headlights switched on. Insert the voltmeter positive (+) probe through the back of the wiring connector to the terminal to be checked, and ground the meter negative (-) probe. Note the reading shown and compare this with the table for the next diagnosis step.

Step 3

3 Locate the headlight switch connector under the dash panel (remove the access cover by removing the two retaining screws and pulling the panel away). Using the meter positive (+) probe through the back of the wiring connector (don't separate the connector halves), and the meter negative (-) probe connected to ground, turn the headlight switch on and check the voltages on the terminals indicated in the accompanying figure and table. Note the reading shown and compare this with the table for the next diagnosis step. Leave the access panel off for now - you may need to make further tests at the connector.

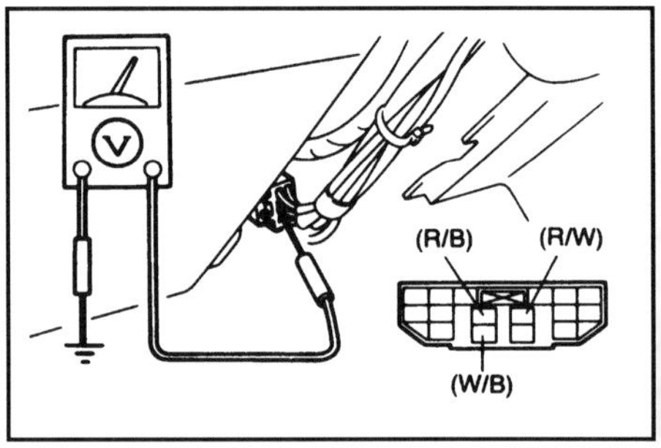

D17/3 HEADLIGHT SWITCH CONNECTOR TERMINAL IDENTIFICATION (US CARS).

Step 4

4 Check the headlight bulbs ☞ 7/27. If the

VB: Battery voltage

Terminal-wire	Voltage	Action
(W/B)	VB	Go to Step 3
	0V	Next check wire (L/Y)
(L/Y)	VB	Go to Step 6
	0V	Next check wire (R/L)
(R/L: Terminal A)	VB	Next check wire (R/L)
	0V	Repair wire (R/L) (HEAD 30A—Headlight relay)
(R/L: Terminal D)	VB	Replace headlight relay
	0V	Repair wire (R/L) (HEAD 30A—Headlight relay)

T17/2 TESTING HEADLIGHT RELAY (US CARS).

VB: Battery voltage

Wire	Headlight switch	Voltage	Action
(W/B)	—	VB	Next check wire (R/B)
		0V	Repair wire (W/B) (Headlight relay—Headlight switch)
(R/B)	Low beam	VB	Go to Step 4
		0V	Replace headlight switch
(R/W)	High beam	VB	Go to Step 4
		0V	Replace headlight switch

T17/3 TESTING HEADLIGHT SWITCH CONNECTOR (US CARS).

bulbs have burned out, replace them. If the bulbs are OK, leave the bulb connectors off and move to Step 5.

Step 5

5 With the headlight bulb wiring connectors detached from the bulb terminals, turn on the headlight switch and check the voltages on the terminals indicated in the accompanying figure and table. Note the reading shown and compare this with the table.

Step 6

6 Moving back to the headlight switch connector under the dash panel, carry out the following voltage checks. Using the meter positive (+) probe through the back of the wiring connector (don't separate the connector halves), and the meter negative (-) probe connected to ground, turn the headlight switch on and check the voltages on the terminals indicated in the accompanying figure and table. Note the reading shown and compare this with the table.

18. HEADLIGHT - CIRCUIT CHECKS (CANADIAN CARS)

☞ 1/1, 2 & 7/2.

Step 1

1 Start by checking the **HEAD 30A** fuse housed in the main fuse block in the engine compartment. If the fuse has burned out, it should be replaced after you've established the cause of the failure. This may be due to a brief overload, caused by a bulb burning out, for example.

2 If the new fuse burns out immediately the lights are switched on, you will need to investigate the headlight system wiring for shorts. If the fuse was undamaged, proceed to Step 2.

Step 2

3 Check the headlight bulbs ☞ 7/27. If the bulbs have burned out, replace them. If the bulbs are OK, leave the bulb connectors off and move to Step 3.

Step 3

4 With the headlight bulb wiring connectors detached from the bulb terminals, turn on the headlight switch and check the voltages on the terminals indicated in the accompanying figure and table. Note the reading shown and compare this with the table.

Step 4

5 Fit the headlight wiring connector(s) if removed. Remove the combination (steering column) switch housing halves (☞ 7/12) to gain access to the switch terminals. Access will not be easy - the terminals are at the back of the switch, and are only really visible through the windshield. Note that if you lift the switch locking tab after slackening the clamp screw, you may be able to pull the switch back a little to improve access.

6 Check the voltages on the terminals

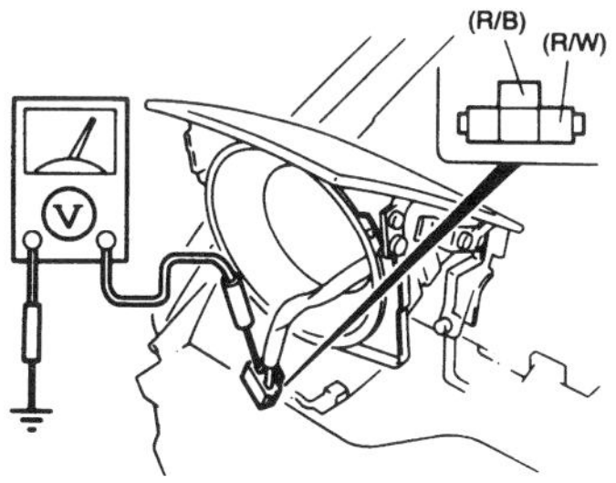

VB: Battery voltage

Headlight	Wire	Headlight switch	Voltage	Remedical Action
Left	(R/B)	Low beam	VB	Repair ground wire (B)
			0V	Repair wire (R/B) (Headlight switch—Headlight)
	(R/W)	High beam	VB	Repair ground wire (B)
			0V	Repair wire (R/W) (Headlight switch—Headlight)
Right	(R/B)	Low beam	VB	Repair ground wire (B)
			0V	Repair wire (R/W) (Headlight switch—Headlight)
	(R/W)	High beam	VB	Repair ground wire (B)
			0V	Repair wire (R/W) (Headlight switch—Headlight)

D&T17/5 TESTING THE HEADLIGHT CONNECTORS (US CARS).

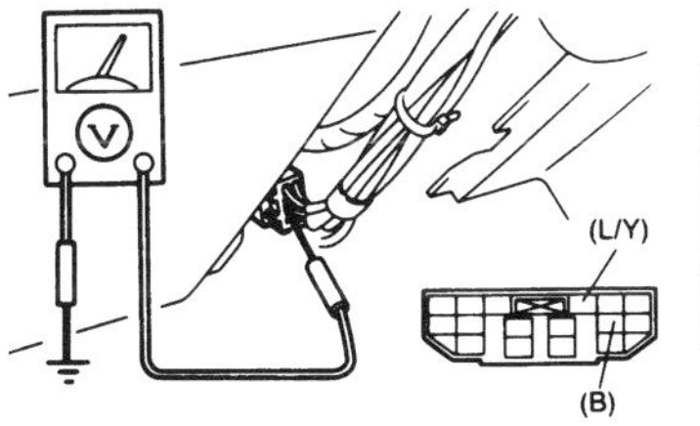

VB: Battery voltage

Wire	Voltage	Action
(L/Y)	VB	Next check wire (B)
	0V	Repair wire (L/Y) (Headlight relay—Headlight switch)
(B)	VB	Repair ground wire (B)
	0V	Replace headlight switch

D&T17/6 TESTING HEADLIGHT SWITCH CONNECTOR - HEADLIGHTS ON (US CARS).

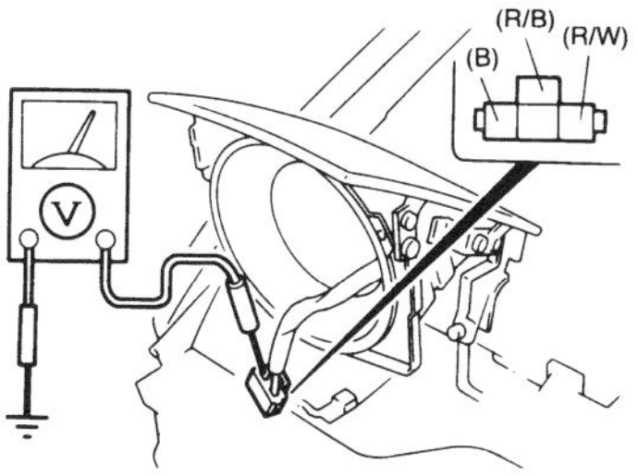

Headlight	Wire	Headlight switch	Voltage	Action
Left	(R/W)	High beam	VB	Next, check wire (R/B)
			0V	Go to Step 4
	(R/B)	Low beam	VB	Next, check wire (B)
			0V	Go to Step 4
	(B)	Any position	0V	Next, check right side
			VB	Repair ground wire (B)
Right	(R/W)	High beam	VB	Next, check wire (R/B)
			0V	Go to Step 4
	(R/B)	Low beam	VB	Next, check wire (B)
			0V	Go to Step 4
	(B)	Any position	0V	Check for poor connection of headlight connector
			VB	Go to Step 4

D&T18/4 & D&T19/4 TESTING HEADLIGHT CONNECTOR (CANADIAN/UK CARS).

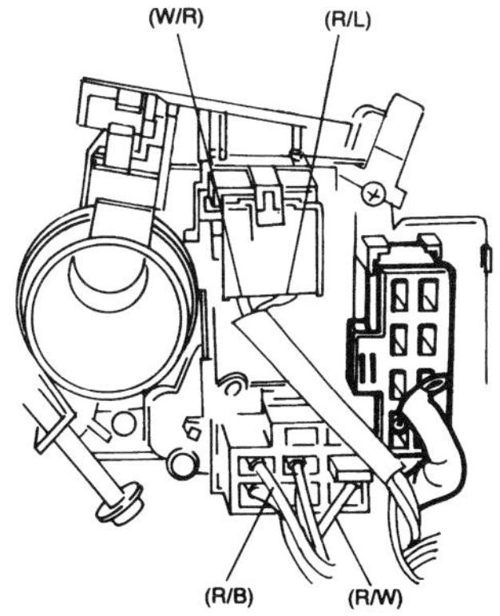

Wire	Headlight switch	Voltage	Action
(R/L)	Any position	VB	Next, check wire (W/R)
		0V	Repair wire (R/L) (HEAD 30A fuse—Headlight switch)
(W/R)	Any position	VB	Next, check wire (R/W)
		0V	Repair wire (W/R) (BTN 40A fuse—Headlight switch)
(R/W)	ON (High beam)	VB	Next, check wire (R/B)
		0V	Go to Step 5
(R/B)	ON (Low beam)	VB	Check for poor connection of headlight switch connector
		0V	Go to Step 5

D&T18/6 TESTING HEADLIGHT SWITCH TERMINAL VOLTAGES (CANADIAN CARS).

indicated in the accompanying figure and table. Note the reading shown and compare this with the table for details of the next diagnosis step. If everything checks out, leave the switch housing off and move on to Step 5.

Step 5

7 Disconnect the headlight switch connectors (see diagram) and then carry out the following continuity checks. Connect one of the meter probes to the terminals on the back of the switch, and the other probe to ground. Check for continuity on the terminals indicated in the accompanying figure and table. Note the reading shown and compare this with the table.

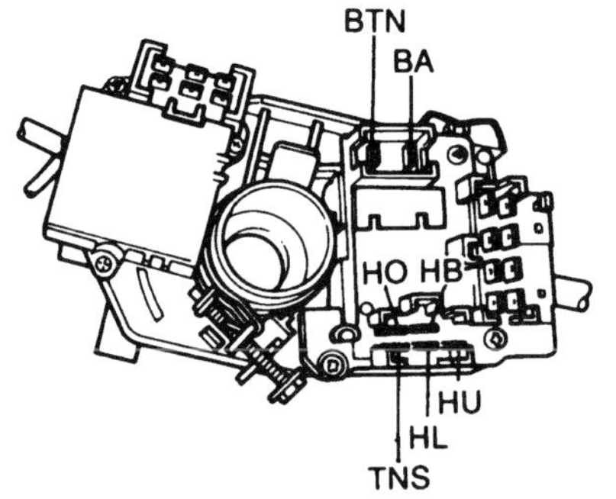

Position		Terminal: HB	HL	HU	BA	BTN	TNS
Headlight	Low beam	O	O			O	O
		O	—	—	O		
	High beam	O	—	O		O	O
		O	—	—	O		
Parking				O	O		
Tail, Parking						O	O

O—O: Indicates continuity

D&T18/7 & D&T20/7 TESTING HEADLAMP SWITCH TERMINALS CONTINUITY (EXCEPT US/UKCARS).

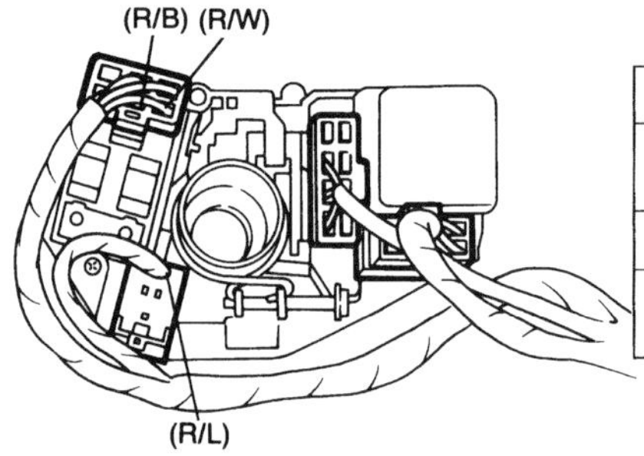

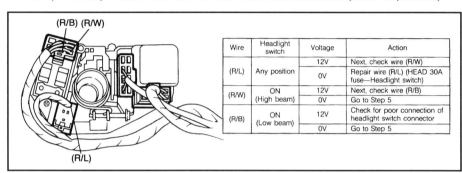

Wire	Headlight switch	Voltage	Action
(R/L)	Any position	12V	Next, check wire (R/W)
		0V	Repair wire (R/L) (HEAD 30A fuse—Headlight switch)
(R/W)	ON (High beam)	12V	Next, check wire (R/B)
		0V	Go to Step 5
(R/B)	ON (Low beam)	12V	Check for poor connection of headlight switch connector
		0V	Go to Step 5

D&T19/6 TESTING HEADLIGHT SWITCH TERMINAL VOLTAGES (UK CARS).

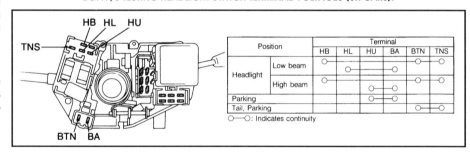

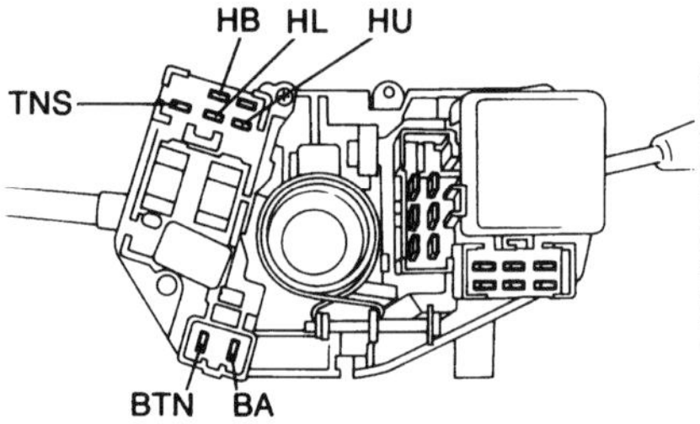

Position		Terminal: HB	HL	HU	BA	BTN	TNS
Headlight	Low beam	O	—	—	—	O	O
			O	—	O		
	High beam	O	—	—	—	O	O
				O	O		
Parking				O	O		
Tail, Parking						O	O

O—O: Indicates continuity

D&T19/7 TESTING HEADLIGHT SWITCH TERMINALS CONTINUITY (UK CARS).

19. HEADLIGHT - CIRCUIT CHECKS (UK SPEC CARS)

☞ 1/1, 2 & 7/2.

Step 1

1 Start by checking the **HEAD 30A** fuse housed in the main fuse block in the engine compartment. If the fuse has burned out, it should be replaced after you've established the cause of the failure. This may be due to a brief overload, caused by a bulb burning out, for example.

2 If the new fuse burns out immediately the lights are switched on, you will need to investigate the headlight system wiring for shorts. If the fuse was undamaged, proceed to Step 2.

Step 2

3 Check the headlight bulbs ☞ 7/27. If the bulbs have burned out, replace them. If the bulbs are OK, leave the bulb connectors off and move to Step 3.

Step 3

4 (see D&T 18/4) With the headlight bulb wiring connectors detached from the bulb terminals, turn on the headlight switch and check the voltages on the terminals indicated in the accompanying figure and table. Note the reading shown and compare this with the table.

Step 4

5 Fit the headlight wiring connector(s) if removed. Remove the combination (steering column) switch housing halves to gain access to the switch terminals ☞ 7/12. Access will not be easy - the terminals are at the back of the switch, and are only really visible through the windshield. Note that if you lift the switch locking tab after slackening the clamp screw, you may be able to pull the switch back a little to improve access.

6 Check the voltages on the terminals indicated in the accompanying figure and table. Note the reading shown and compare this with the table for details of the next diagnosis step. If everything checks out, leave the switch housing off and move on to Step 5.

Step 5

7 Disconnect the headlight switch connectors (see diagram) and then carry out the following continuity checks. Connect one of the meter probes to the terminals on the back of the switch, and the other probe to ground. Check for continuity on the terminals indicated in the accompanying figure and table. Note the reading shown and compare this with the table.

20. HEADLIGHT - CIRCUIT CHECKS (CONTINENTAL EUROPE CARS)

☞ 1/1, 2 & 7/2.

Step 1

1 Start by checking the **MAIN RH 20A**, **MAIN LH 20A**, **DIM RH 10A** and **DIM LH 10A** fuses housed in the main fuse block in the engine compartment. If any fuse has burned out, it should be replaced after you've established the cause of the failure. This may be due to a brief overload, caused by a bulb burning out, for example.

2 If the new fuse burns out immediately the lights are switched on, you will need to investigate the headlight system wiring for shorts. If the fuse was undamaged, proceed to Step 2.

Step 2

3 Check the headlight bulbs ☞ 7/27. If the bulbs have burned out, replace them. If the bulbs are OK, leave the bulb connectors off and move to Step 3.

Step 3

4 With the headlight bulb wiring connectors detached from the bulb terminals, turn on the headlight switch and check the voltages on the terminals indicated in the accompanying figure and table. Note the reading shown and compare this with the table.

Step 4

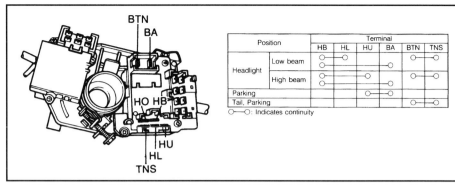

5 Fit the headlight wiring connector(s) if removed. Remove the combination (steering column) switch housing halves (☞ 7/12) to gain access to the switch terminals. Access will not be easy - the terminals are at the back of the switch, and are only really visible through the windshield. Note that if you lift the switch locking tab after slackening the clamp screw, you may be able to

pull the switch back a little to improve access.

6 Check the voltages on the terminals indicated in the accompanying figure and table. Note the reading shown and compare this with the table for details of the next diagnosis step. If everything checks out, leave the switch housing off and move on to Step 5.

Step 5

7 (see D&T 18/7) Disconnect the headlight switch connectors (see diagram) and then carry out the following continuity checks. Connect one of the meter probes to the terminals on the back of the switch, and the other probe to ground. Check for continuity on the terminals indicated in the accompanying figure and table. Note the reading shown and compare this with the table.

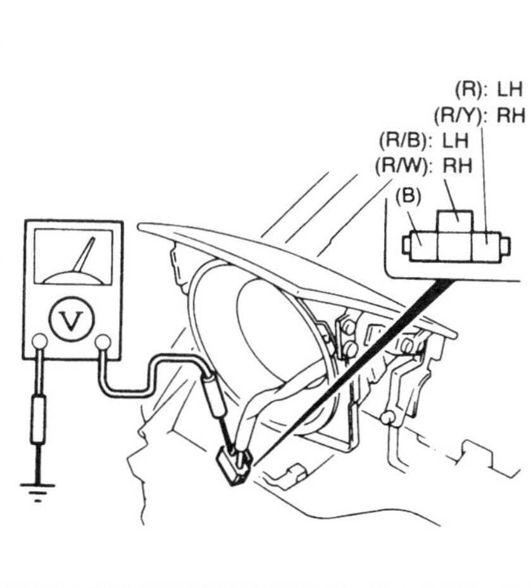

Headlight	Wire	Headlight switch	Voltage	Action
Left	(R)	High beam	12V	Next, check wire (R/B)
			0V	Go to Step 4
	(R/B)	Low beam	12V	Next, check wire (B)
			0V	Go to Step 4
	(B)	Any position	0V	Next, check right side
			12V	Repair ground wire (B)
Right	(R/Y)	High beam	12V	Next, check wire (R/B)
			0V	Go to Step 4
	(R/W)	Low beam	12V	Next, check wire (B)
			0V	Go to Step 4
	(B)	Any position	0V	Check for poor connection of headlight connector
			12V	Go to Step 4

D&T20/4 TESTING HEADLIGHT CONNECTOR (CONTINENTAL EUROPEAN CARS).

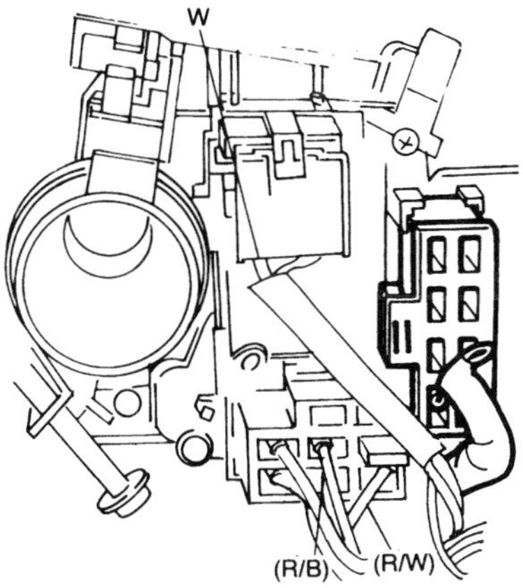

Wire	Headlight switch	Voltage	Action
(W)	Any position	12V	Next, check wire (R/W)
		0V	Repair wire (W) (MAIN 80A fuse—Headlight switch)
(R/W)	ON (High beam)	12V	Next, check wire (R/B)
		0V	Go to Step 5
(R/B)	ON (Low beam)	12V	Check for poor connection of headlight switch connector
		0V	Go to Step 5

D&T 20/6 TESTING HEADLIGHT SWITCH TERMINAL VOLTAGES (CONTINENTAL EUROPEAN CARS).

21. HEADLIGHT RETRACT SYSTEM - CHECKS

☞ 1/1, 2 & 7/2.

A: HEADLIGHT RETRACTORS INOPERATIVE ON BOTH SIDES

1 Start by isolating the exact nature of the fault by operating the headlight and retractor switches. If the retractor system operates normally when the headlight switch is turned on, skip to Step 5, if not, try operating the retractor switch. If the headlight retractor system operates, skip to Step 4, otherwise, start from Step 1 below.

Step 1

2 On US, UK and Canadian spec cars, check the **RETRACT 30A** and **HEAD 30A** fuses in the main fuse block in the engine compartment. In the case of Continental Europe spec cars, check the **RETRACT 30A** and **BTN 30A** fuses in the main fuse block. If you find a burned out fuse, fit a new fuse of the correct rating and check whether the system operates normally. If the fuse fails again, you need to check the associated wiring for shorting or damage and repair it as necessary. If the fuses prove to be in good condition, move to Step 2.

Step 2

3 If the headlights are fully or part way up, isolate the retractor circuit by unplugging the **RETRACT 30A** fuse, then retract the headlights fully using the manual control. This will be found on the top of each retractor motor - pull off the dust boot and turn the control knob clockwise until the headlight is fully down. Install the **RETRACT 30A** fuse.

4 Disconnect the wiring connector at each motor in turn. Connect a voltmeter positive (+) probe to the Red/yellow wire terminal, and the negative (-) probe to ground. Turn on the headlight and retractor switches and check for battery voltage on the Red/yellow wire (harness side of connector). If you read battery voltage, move to Step 3, if you get zero volts, skip down to Step 4.

Step 3

5 With the retractor motor wiring connectors separated as in Step 2, check for continuity between the black (ground) wire terminal and a body ground point. If continuity is shown, you will need to remove and check the retractor motor ☞ 7/26. If no continuity is shown, check, repair or replace the black ground wire as necessary. Reconnect the motor wiring connectors.

Step 4

6 Locate the retractor relay on the relay bank on the left side of the engine compartment. On US, Canadian and Continental Europe spec cars, the relay position is inner row, nearest the back (see diagram). Note that on UK cars only, the relay will be found on the outer row, second from back - you'll need to unclip the plastic cover and detach the relay bank from the car to gain access to the back of the connector. Note also that the Canadian market cars differ in the wire color positions in the connector (see diagram D&T 21/7). UK and Continental Europe cars are as shown for US models - follow the table for US spec.

7 Connect the meter negative (-) probe to ground, and then check the terminal voltages shown in the accompanying tables, noting that the retractor switch should be off, and the headlight switch turned on.

21/6a Detach relay bank cover ...

21/6b ... to access relay bank fixings.

7

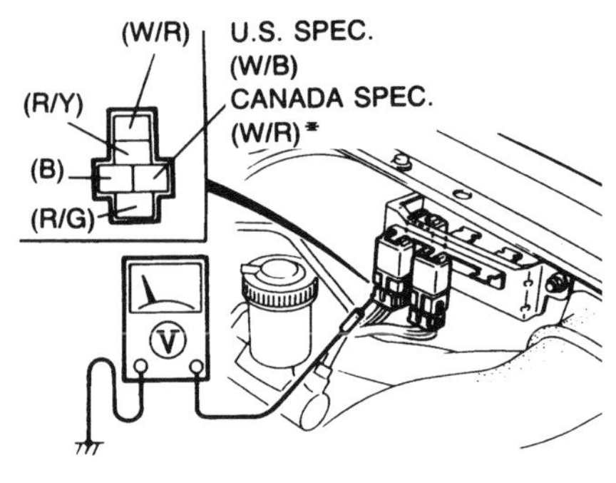

Wire	Voltage	Action
(R/G)	VB	Next check wire (W/B)
	0V	Go to Step 5
(W/B)	VB	Next check wire (B)
	0V	Repair wire (W/B) (Headlight relay—Retractor relay)
(W/R)*	VB	Next check wire (B)
	0V	Repair wire (W/R)* (Headlight switch—Retractor relay)
(B)	VB	Repair ground wire (B)
	0V	Next check wire (R/Y)
(R/Y)	VB	Repair wire (R/Y) (Retractor relay—Retractor motor)
	0V	Replace retractor motor

D&T21/7 TESTING HEADLIGHT RETRACTOR RELAY.

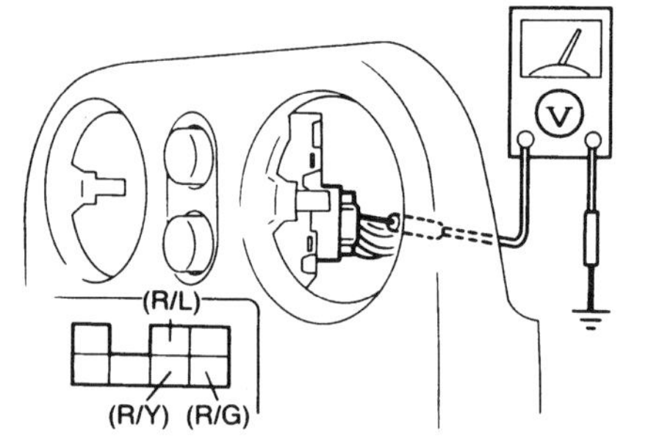

Wire	Retractor switch	Voltage	Action
(R/L)	Any position	VB	Next check wire (R/G) and (R/Y)
		0V	Repair wire (R/L) (Retract 30A—Retractor switch)
(R/G)	OFF	VB	Repair wire (R/G) (Retractor switch—Retractor motor)
		0V	Replace retractor switch
(R/Y)	ON	VB	Repair wire (R/Y) (Retractor switch—Retractor motor)
		0V	Replace retractor switch

D&T21/9 TESTING HEADLIGHT RETRACTOR SWITCH.

Step 5

8 The last check in the sequence is to test the terminal voltages at the retractor switch. Note that this will require considerable preparatory dismantling ☞ 10/3.

9 Using the voltmeter positive (+) probe through the back of the wiring connector, with the negative (-) probe connected to ground, check the terminal voltages as shown in the accompanying table.

B: HEADLIGHT RETRACTORS INOPERATIVE ON ONE SIDE ONLY

Step 1

10 In the event that one of the headlights refuses to pop up or retract, or is stuck part way, the usual cause will be something caught in the mechanism. The location of the headlights makes them prone to picking up twigs or small stones flung up by other traffic, and in cold climates, ice can build up and prevent the system operating normally. Regular lubrication of the hinges with WD40 or similar will help prevent this. If one of the headlights sticks partway open or shut, this will be indicated by the retractor warning lamp on the instrument panel staying on.

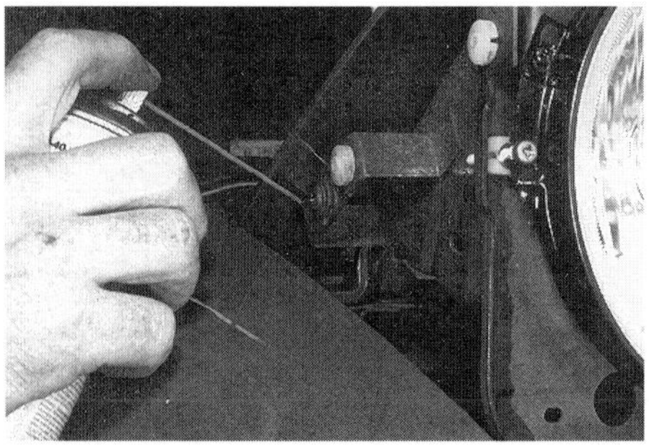

21/10 Lubricate headlamp hinges often.

11 If this happens while you are driving, stop the car and turn the ignition switch off, then remove the **RETRACT 30A** fuse from the main fuse block in the engine compartment. Pull off the protective cap, and then use the manual knob on top of the motor to raise or lower the headlight so that the obstruction can be removed, then install the fuse and check operation of the system.

Step 2

12 Remove the **RETRACT 30A** fuse as described above, then turn the manual control on the top of the retractor motor clockwise until the headlight is fully retracted. Install the fuse, then unplug the motor wiring connector from the malfunctioning retractor motor. With the headlight and retractor switches on, measure the voltage between the Red/yellow wire and ground. If no voltage is found, trace and repair the Red/yellow wire.

13 If battery voltage is read, check the black ground wire for continuity. If no continuity is shown, repair or replace the ground wire and recheck motor operation. If continuity is shown, the fault lies with the retractor motor, which should be removed and tested ☞ 7/26.

22. HEADLIGHT DIM-DIP SYSTEM - CHECKS (UK SPEC CARS)

☞ 1/1, 2 & 7/2.

1 Cars produced for the UK market are equipped with a dim-dip system. This is designed to prevent the car being driven at night with parking lights only. If the parking lights are left on, and the car is subsequently driven away, the dim-dip system automatically turns on the headlight low beams at reduced power.

2 If you experience problems with the dim-dip system, check that the retractor system is operational by turning the headlight switch on. If the retractor motors fail to operate, the fault lies in this area ☞ 7/20, 21. If the headlights pop up, but do not come on ☞ 7/16, 19.

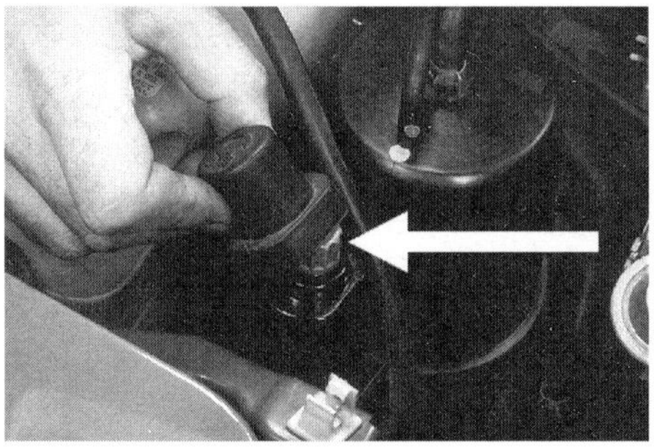

21/11 Manual headlamp retractor.

3 If the headlights function normally, the terminal voltages at the dim-dip relay need to be checked. This is located on the relay bank on the left of the car, the relay position being outer bank, rearmost. To gain access for testing, remove the relay bank from the body and turn it so that the meter probes can be inserted from the back of the wiring connector.

4 Refer to the accompanying diagram,

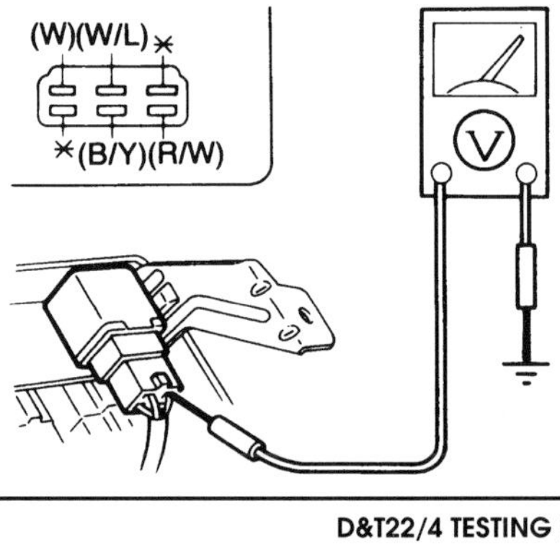

Wire	Voltage	Action
(B/Y)	12V	Next, check wire (W/L)
	0V	Repair wire (B/Y) (METER 10A fuse—Dim-dip relay)
(W/L)	12V	Next, check wire (W)
	0V	Repair wire (W/L) (Headlight switch—Dim-dip relay)
(W)	12V	Go to Step 3
	0V	Check dim-dip relay If dim-dip relay is OK, repair wire (R/W) (Dim-dip relay—Headlight)

D&T22/4 TESTING DIM DIP RELAY (UK CARS).

and check the various terminal voltages according to the table. Note that the ignition switch must be turned to **ON** for this test, and the headlight switch should be turned to the first position. If the terminal voltages check out as specified in the table, trace the white wire back from the relay to the dim-dip resistor (on bridge between air cleaner body and inner wing). Disconnect the wiring connector and check for resistance between the two resistor terminals. This should be around 1 - if the resistance found is significantly different to this, fit a new resistor.

23. HEADLIGHT PASSING LIGHT SYSTEM - CHECKS

☞ 1/1, 2 & 7/2.

1 If you experience problems with the passing light (headlight flasher) system, raise the headlights and check whether the high beams illuminate when the passing switch is operated. If not, for details of headlight circuit checks ☞ 7/16-20.

2 It appears that Austrian market cars have separate bulbs (2 X 50W) for the passing lights. We have never seen one of these cars, and Mazda don't mention where the bulbs might be located, but we guess you will if you own such a car. If you do, check and if necessary replace, the passing light bulb(s).

24. HEADLIGHT LEVELLING SYSTEM - CHECKS (GERMAN CARS ONLY)

☞ 1/1, 2 & 7/2.

Step 1

1 German market cars are equipped with a headlight levelling system controlled from a rotary switch on the dash panel. In the event of a fault in this system, check first that the **R FOG 10A** fuse in the fuse box under the dash panel is intact, and replace this and repair the associated wiring as required.

Step 2

2 If the fuse is OK, turn the headlight switch on and check the terminal voltages at the headlight levelling actuator connector, passing the meter positive (+) probe through the back of the connector and grounding the meter negative (-) probe.

Step 3

3 Remove the levelling switch from the dash panel by gently levering it out at one end with a small screwdriver. Disconnect the wiring, and check the continuity and resistances of the switch as shown in the accompanying table. If not as specified, fit a new switch.

25. HEADLIGHT BEAM - ADJUSTMENT

☞ 1/1, 2 & 7/2.

ALIGNMENT

1 Before attempting adjustment of the headlight beams, be aware that most countries have strict legislation regarding headlight settings. We suggest that you have this setting carried out professionally using a commercial headlight alignment system. In an emergency, such as after installing a new headlight, or after impact damage has affected headlight aim, proceed as described below, and have the setting verified at the earliest opportunity.

2 Carry out this check at dusk or early evening. Check that the unladen vehicle is standing on a flat, level surface, about 10 meters / 10 yards from a flat wall or a garage door. Raise the headlights (on German market cars, set the levelling control to the 0 position). Measure the height from the ground to the center of the headlight lens, and mark a horizontal line on the wall at this height.

3 Turn the light switch on and set the lights at high beam. Check that the brightest spots on the wall coincide with the line made earlier, and that the beam centers are the same distance apart as the headlights. If you need to make adjustments, turn the screw under the headlight to adjust it in a vertical plane, and the screw at the 9 O'clock position to move the light horizontally.

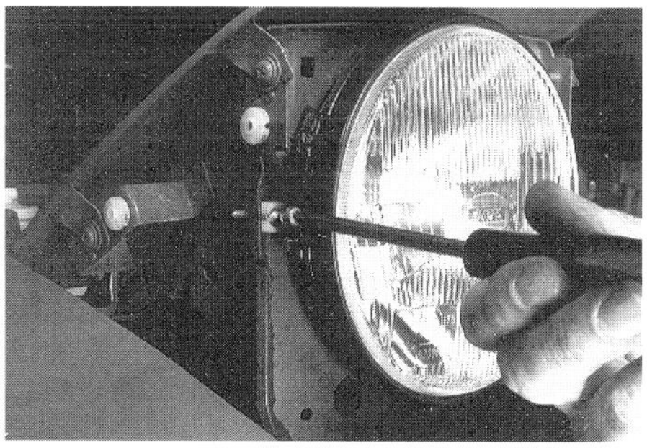

25/3 Horizontal adjustment screw.

HINGE ADJUSTMENT

4 Before making this adjustment, check that the headlights are fully retracted, then disable the stereo security system and disconnect the battery negative (-) lead. Open the hood, and locate the retractor motor arm where it connects to the retractor link. Pull off the link from its operating pin (the plastic cup will pop off if it is levered gently away with a screwdriver blade). Check that the headlight lid is flush with the surrounding bodywork (close the hood while making this check). If necessary, adjust the lid stop until the headlight is aligned correctly, then reconnect the retractor link.

26. H/LIGHT RETRACT MOTOR - CHECKING, REMOVAL, INSPECTION & INSTALLATION

☞ 1/1, 2 & 7/2.

CHECKING

1 + If you have diagnosed a fault on one of the headlight retractor motors, it can be checked as follows. Retract the headlights fully, then disable the stereo security system and isolate the battery by

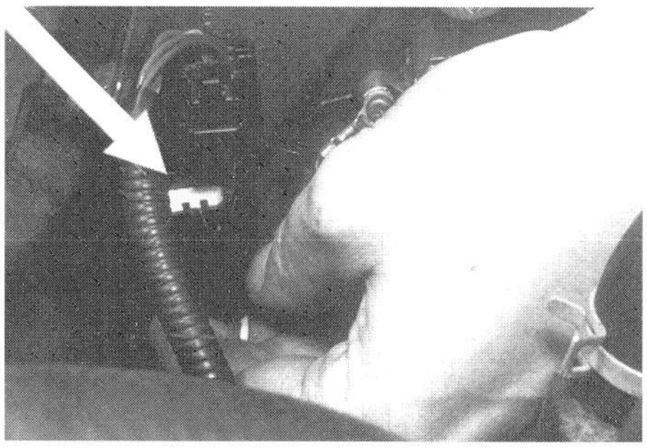

26/1a Unplug retractor wiring connector ...

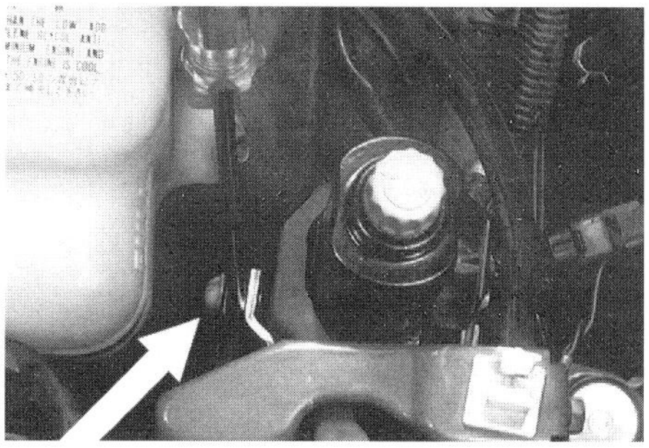

26/1b ... and lever off link.

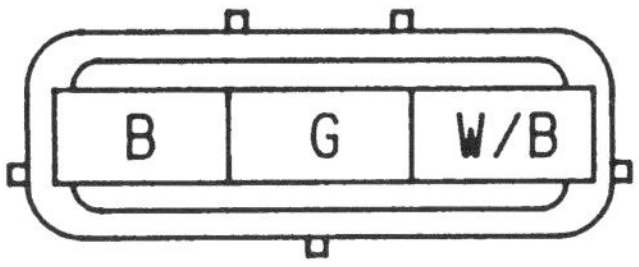

Wire	Voltage	Action
(W/B)	12V	Next, check wire (B)
	0V	Repair wire (W/B) (R. FOG 10A—Headlight leveling actuator)
(B)	12V	Repair wire (B) (Headlight leveling actuator—Body ground)
	0V	Go to Step 3

D&T24/2 TESTING HEADLIGHT LEVELLER ACTUATOR CONNECTOR (GERMAN CARS).

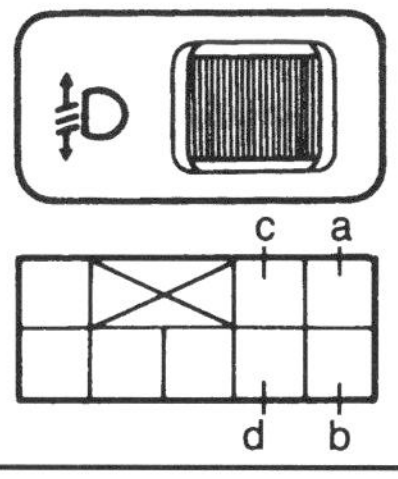

Switch	Terminal			
	a	b	c	d
0	O—	—O	O—	—O
1	O—	—O	O-ʌʌʌ-	-O 300Ω
2	O—	—O	O-ʌʌʌ-	-O 560Ω
3	O—	—O	O-ʌʌʌ-	-O 1.6 kΩ

O—O: Indicates continuity
O-ʌʌʌ-O: Indicates resistance

D&T24/3 TESTING HEADLIGHT LEVELLING SWITCH (GERMAN CARS).

detaching the negative (-) cable. Open the hood, and locate and separate the motor wiring connector. Using a screwdriver blade, push off the retractor link from the motor arm.

2 Refer to the accompanying diagram, and check motor operation by connecting an external 12 volt battery as follows. Connect the battery negative (-) lead to the motor connector **a**

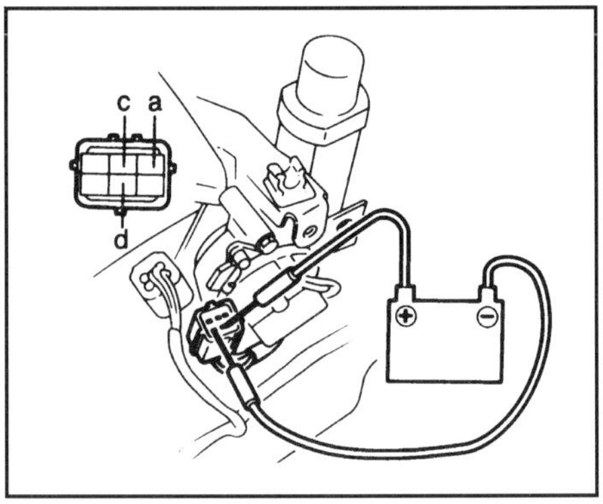

D26/2 TESTING HEADLIGHT RETRACTOR MOTOR CONNECTOR.

terminal, then touch the battery positive (+) lead to the **c** terminal. The motor should run to the raised position. Now move the battery positive (+) lead to the **d** terminal. The motor should return to the retracted position. If the motor fails to operate, it should be removed as described below.

REMOVAL

3 + With the battery and wiring connectors disconnected, and the retractor link still off the motor arm as described above, you can remove the motor as described below. First, remove any

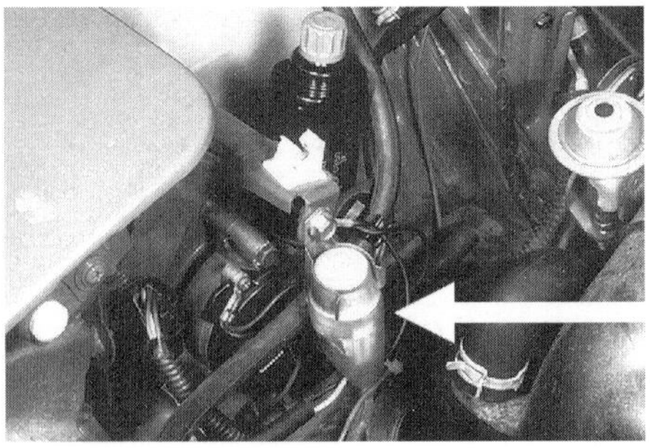

26/3a Remove foglight relay (if fitted) ...

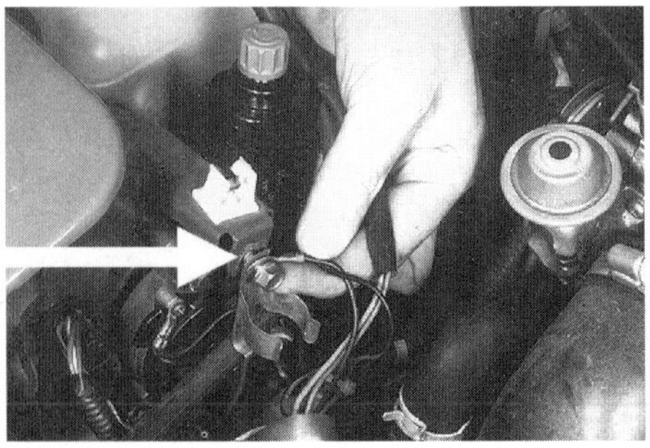

26/3b ... disconnect wiring ...

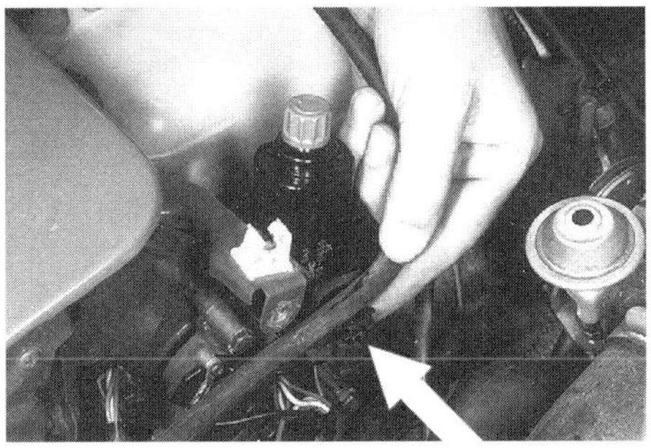

26/3c ... and move hoses.

fittings obstructing motor removal. On our UK spec project car, we had to remove the following items. On the right side the fog lamp relay was unclipped from its bracket, the bracket and ground wires freed, and the radiator to reservoir hose was disconnected from its bracket on the side of the motor. On the left side, the power steering reservoir (where fitted) needs to be released and moved to one side for access. On other market models, and depending on options and accessories fitted, you may need to detach or move other items to get access to the motor.

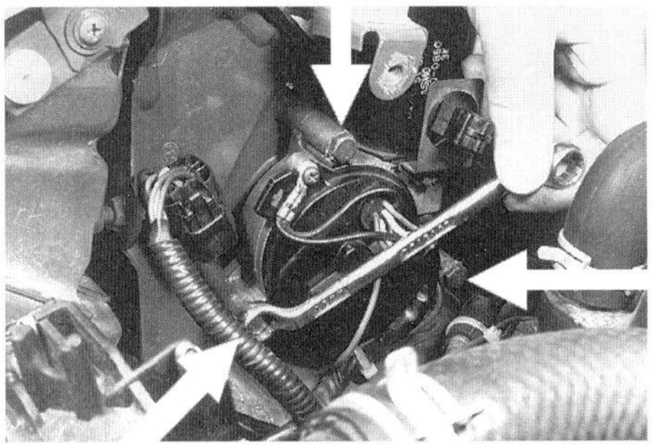

26/4 Remove motor securing bolts.

4 Once you have sufficient working access, remove the three 10 mm bolts which secure the motor to its mounting and maneuver it clear of the headlight area. We found that we could not remove all three bolts fully due to space restrictions - in fact they are intended to remain in position in the motor body holes, and have plastic washers to prevent them from dropping out as the motor is removed.

Inspection

5 In theory, if the motor fails to run during the check described above, it should be discarded and a new unit fitted. This is certainly the easiest solution, but we thought that we would check out any alternatives. We found that it is perfectly possible to dismantle and reassemble the motor. While you cannot get replacement parts for the motors from Mazda, you might be able to find suitable brushes at an auto-electrical specialist, who could also carry out any repair work to the windings and commutator. It is also quite possible that the fault is due to dirt or oxidation, in which case a good cleanup may get it working again. So, if the motor is otherwise scrap, why not give it a try? Finally, remember that you might be able to obtain a serviceable motor from a wreckers yard (scrapyard) at a considerable saving on the cost of a new unit.

6 + The first area to check is the contacts and switch rotor under the circular end cover. Remove the two securing screws and lift the cover off, noting that one of the screws carries a ground wire tag. Under the cover you will find three small spring contacts which run on copper tracks on the rotor. Check the contacts and the tracks for corrosion and oxidation. You can clean these after removing the grease with a solvent-moistened rag. We find that a pencil eraser will restore the surface without causing scoring. To make sure that the

26/6a Remove securing screws and ...

26/6b ... lift cover off.

26/6c Note sealing ring.

contacts are pressing firmly on the rotor, bend them outwards slightly. When everything looks clean and shiny, apply some silicone grease to the rotor. Check, and if necessary replace, the O-ring on the cover, then refit it and check whether the motor now operates normally.

7 The motor itself can be dismantled after pulling off the manual operating knob at the end of the motor armature and removing the two cross-head screws holding the motor body to the gearbox. As you pull the motor body away, the armature will probably come with it, pulling out from the

brush assembly. Remove the armature from the body (it will be held by the pull of the permanent magnets in the body) noting the shims on the outer end of the armature spindle - keep these safe and in the correct order. There is also a tiny bearing ball fitted to the inner end of the spindle - retrieve this and keep it safe.

8 Use a multimeter or continuity checker to test for insulation between the commutator segments and the core and spindle of the armature. If you find continuity at any point, you will need to fit a new motor (it is unlikely to be worth attempting to get the armature rewound).

9 Examine the commutator for wear or damage. Light discoloration and minor damage can be corrected by cleaning the commutator with fine sandpaper. Wrap the paper round the commutator and turn the armature until a bright, smooth finish is restored. In cases of more severe damage, have the armature set up in a lathe and remove the minimum amount of metal possible to restore the surface of the commutator segments. There are no specified service limits for the commutator, but if the repair work would result in its diameter being reduced by an appreciable amount, the motor should be scrapped and a new one fitted.

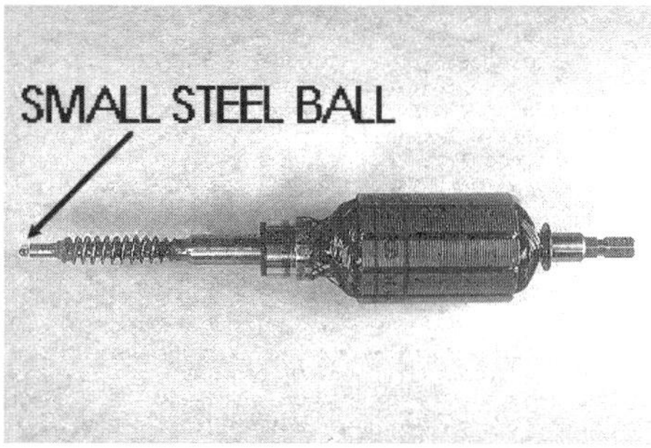

26/9 Armature: check the commutator carefully.

10 Check that the commutator runout is acceptable. Set the armature up on V-blocks or between lathe centers, and use a dial gauge (DTI) to measure commutator runout. Again, we have no service limits for this, but if the runout is greater than about 0.03 mm (0.001 in), either correct this by skimming in a lathe, or scrap the motor and fit a new one.

11 After working on the commutator, clean out the grooves between each segment. You can make up your own cleaning/recutting tool from a section of used hacksaw blade. Find the end where the teeth point back towards you as you hold the blade - this will be the cutting end, so wrap some tape around the other end to form a handle. Now grind the sides of the blade flat until it is a good fit in the commutator grooves. Undercut the grooves by drawing the tool along each one until you achieve a small undercut, then repeat the process on the remaining grooves. Use a little fine sandpaper to remove any burring that results.

12 If the brushes are worn down appreciably, you might like to try an auto-electrical specialist, who can probably supply something suitable as a replacement. You may not get an exact fit, so check this and if necessary file the brushes to fit the holder, then solder them into the brush plate (or you could get the supplier to do this for you).

13 + When you assemble the motor, you will need to hold the brushes back in their holders while you fit the armature in place. We used the plastic sleeve that protects the ends of new spark plugs. Slit the sleeve lengthways and slip it into the center of the brush holder to retain the brushes. Put a small dab of grease in the hole on the inner end of the armature and stick the bearing ball in place. Slide the armature into position, removing the sleeve as the brushes are in place over the commutator. Fit the shims to the armature outer end.

26/13a Using a sleeve to hold back brushes.

26/13b Slide the armature into place.

14 When you fit the motor body, be aware that the magnets inside it will try to pull the armature out of the gearbox. You can prevent this by applying pressure on the operating arm so that the armature resists pulling out - you will need to experiment to find the correct amount of pressure to apply - it needs to be just less than that required to turn the armature.

15 Fit the body over the armature and install the retaining screws, tightening them evenly. Fit the manual knob over the armature end. There is an adjuster screw and locknut at the commutator end of the motor unit - this permits adjustment for armature lash, the screw bearing on the steel ball in the end of the armature. If movement seems excessive, slacken the locknut and turn the screw inwards until it just contacts the ball. Back it off slightly to give just perceptible movement and secure the locknut. Now repeat the check described in paragraph 2. If the motor now runs as it should, you've just saved the cost of a new one.

26/15 Adjusting armature endfloat/lash.

INSTALLATION

16 Before installing the new or rebuilt motor, check that the mounting bolts are held in place by their plastic washers - there is not enough room to fit them through the mounting holes later. We recommend that you use copper grease on the threads - they are exposed to water and road dirt in use, and ours had begun to corrode badly.

17 Position the motor and tighten the three 10 mm mounting bolts evenly. Snap the connecting link back onto the motor arm and reconnect the wiring connector. It is a good idea to temporarily reconnect the car's battery and check motor operation at this stage. Finally, reconnect and install any components removed to give access to the motor.

27. HEADLIGHT UNIT - REMOVAL, INSTALLATION & BULB REPLACEMENT

☞ 1/1, 2 & 7/2.

1 On all cars other than German models, bulb replacement is carried out after removing the headlight unit from its housing. If you own a German market car, skip to the end of this section.

2 + Start by raising the headlights by operating the retractor switch. Remove the two screws on each side of the assembly and lift away the plastic headlight surround. Slacken the three small crosshead screws which secure the headlight

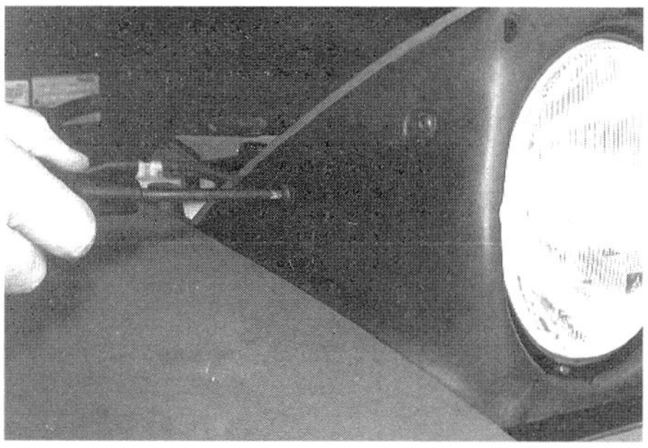

27/2a Remove the headlight surround ...

27/2b ... remove 3 headlight retaining screws ...

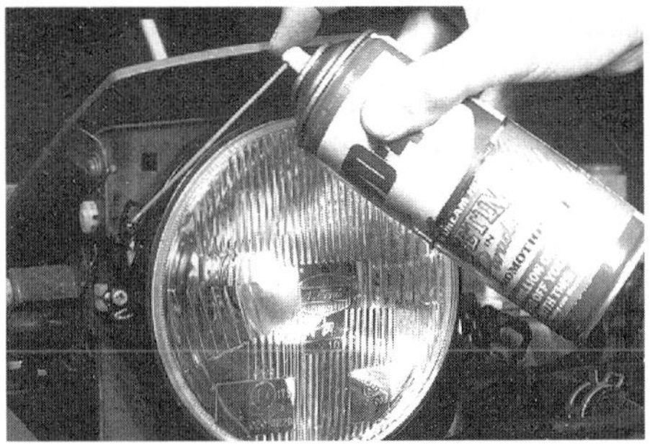

27/2c ... use penetrating oil if screws corroded.

unit to its mounting, using a little WD40 or similar to deal with corroded threads if required (Note: do not disturb the headlight adjustment screws - you need to slacken the three black-finished screws spaced equally around the unit). Turn the unit so that the screws pass through the enlarged slots, and lift it out of its mounting.

3 + Unplug the headlight wiring connector and lift the unit away. Pull off the dust boot from the back of the bulb. Disengage the wire clip which retains the bulb and remove it from the headlight unit. **Warning!** The quartz halogen bulb gets extremely hot in use - take care to allow it time to cool down before handling. Never touch the bulb envelope with the fingers or skin acids may etch into it - only handle the bulb by the metal parts.

4 Install the bulb in the headlight (it will only fit in the correct position) and secure the retaining clip. Fit the dust boot, noting that the **TOP** mark must be positioned uppermost. Fit the wiring connector, then reposition the unit, checking that the screw heads fit through the enlarged holes. Turn the unit to lock it in place, then secure the screws.

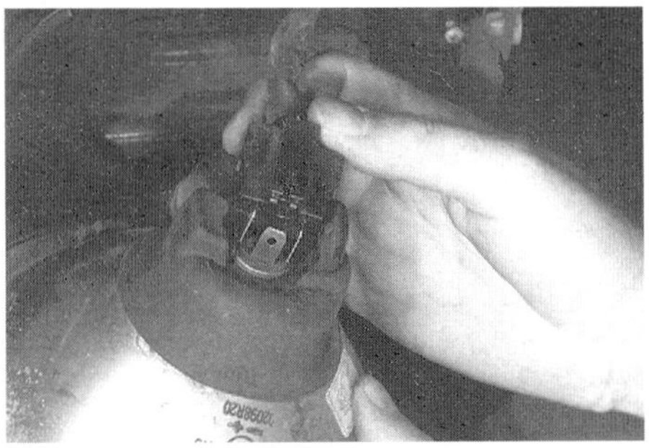

27/3a Unplug wiring connector ...

27/3b ... pull off dust boot ...

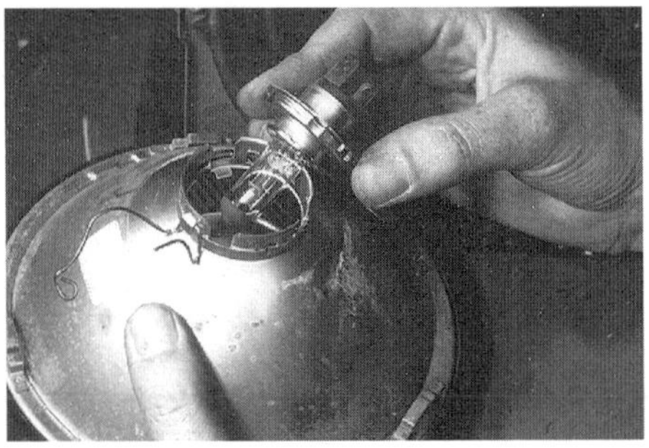

27/3c ... release clip & remove bulb.

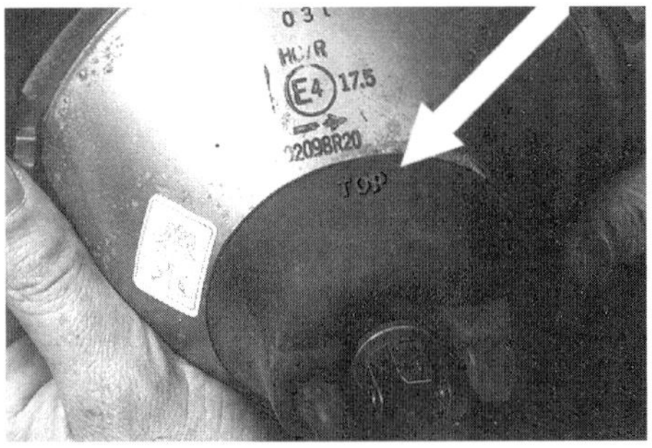

27/4 Make sure dust boot is right way up.

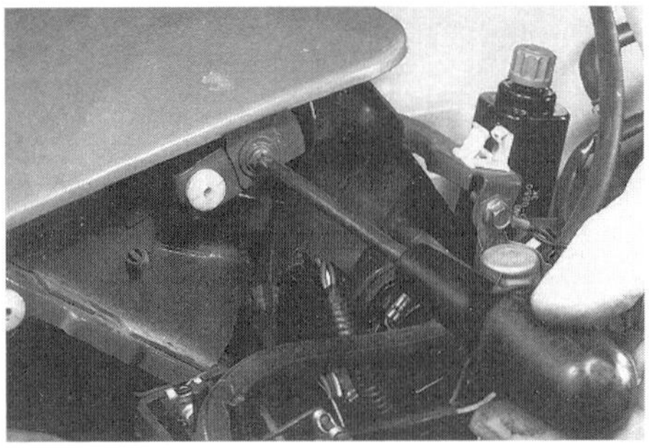

27/5 Lid is retained by 2 screws.

German models only

5 Access to the bulb is gained by removing the headlight lid from the hinge assembly. This is retained by two screws on each side. Once the lid has been removed, the bulb can be removed and installed as described above, working through the top of the assembly.

28. TAIL, S/MARKER & L/PLATE LIGHT - TROUBLESHOOTING (US CARS)

☞ 1/1, 2 & 7/2.

1 In the event of problems with the above system, proceed as described below, following each step in the checking sequence to identify the cause of the fault.

Step 1

2 Remove the access panel below the steering column and open the lid of the fuse box (Fuse Box No.1) below the dash panel. Remove the **TAIL 15A** fuse using the removal tool and check whether it is burned out. If it is, fit a new fuse and recheck operation. If the new fuse burns out, check the associated wiring for damage and shorts to ground, repairing or replacing damaged wires as necessary.

Step 2

3 With the headlight switch turned on, measure the terminal voltages of the TNS relay, which is mounted on the relay bank on the left side of the engine compartment. Refer to the accompanying drawing and table for details of terminal locations, the voltage reading expected and the next step to move to in the check sequence.

Step 3

4 Check the condition of the bulb(s) in the affected lights, referring to the bulb replacement procedures described later in this chapter. If a burned out bulb is found, fit a new one of the correct rating and check the operation of the system. If no burned out bulbs are discovered, check the wiring to the affected unit for continuity, repairing or replacing damaged wires as necessary.

Step 4

5 Disable the stereo security system and disconnect the battery negative (-) cable to isolate the electrical system. Remove the access panel below the steering column and separate the wiring connector from the steering column switch. Check the resistances of the various switch positions, following the accompanying table. If not as specified, fit a new combination switch ☞ 7/12.

29. TAIL, S/MARKER & L/PLATE LIGHT - TROUBLESHOOTING (CANADIAN CARS)

☞ 1/1, 2 & 7/2.

1 In the event of problems with the above system, proceed as described below, following each step in the checking sequence to identify the cause of the fault.

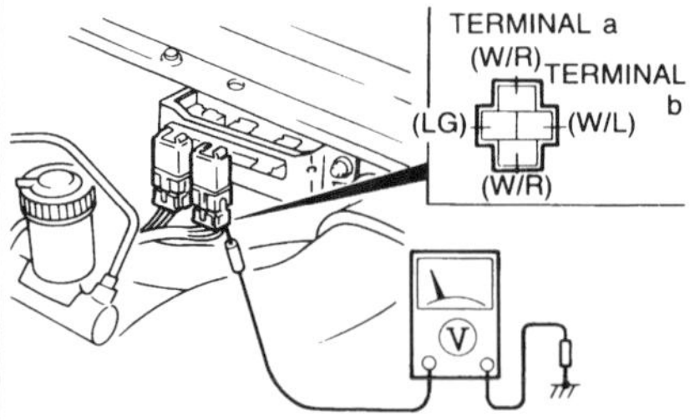

Wire	Voltage	Action
(W/L)	VB	Go to Step 3
	0V	Next check wire (LG)
(LG)	VB	Go to Step 4
	0V	Next check wire (W/R: Terminal a)
(W/R) Terminal a	VB	Next check wire (W/R: Terminal b)
	0V	Repair wire (W/R) (TAIL 15A fuse — TNS relay)
(W/R) Terminal b	VB	Replace TNS relay
	0V	Repair wire (W/R) (TAIL 15A fuse — TNS relay)

D&T28/3 TESTING TNS RELAY (US CARS).

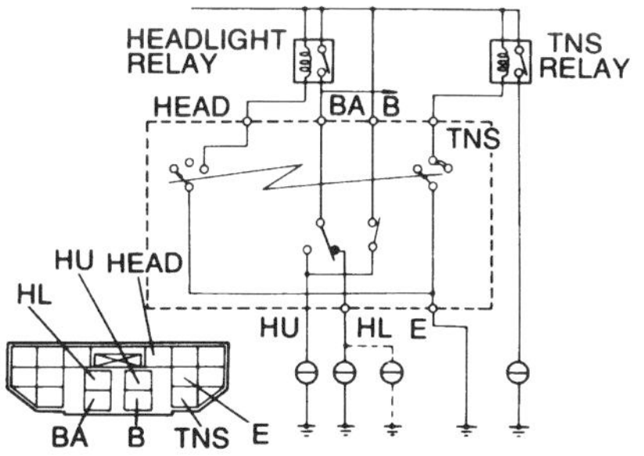

Position		E	HL	HU	TNS	HEAD	BA	B
Headlight	Low beam	O	—	—	—	O		
		O	—	—	O			
			O	—	—	—	O	
	High beam	O	—	—	—	O		
		O	—	—	O			
				O	—	—	O	
Passing				O	—	—	—	O
Taillights, Parking		O	—	—	O			

O——O: Indicates continuity

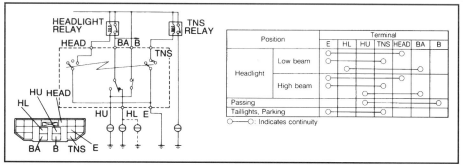

D&T 28/5 TESTING COMBINATION SWITCH TERMINALS FOR CONTINUITY (US CARS).

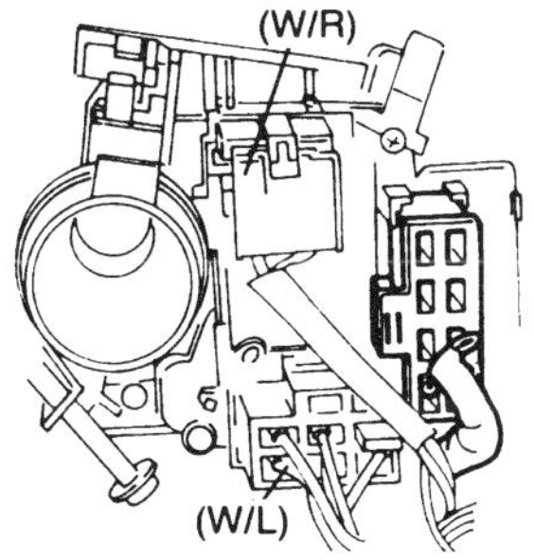

Wire	Voltage	Action
(W/R)	VB	Next check wire (W/L)
	0V	Repair wire (W/R) (TAIL 15A fuse — combination switch)
(W/L)	VB	Repair the wiring harness (Combination switch — body ground of each light)
	0V	Replace headlight switch

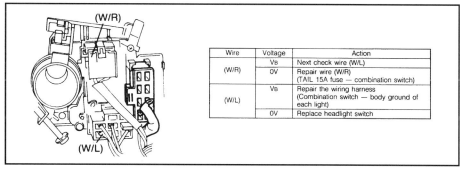

D&T29/5 TESTING SWITCH TERMINAL VOLTAGES (CANADIAN CARS).

Step 1

2 Remove the access panel below the steering column and open the lid of the fuse box (Fuse Box No.1) below the dash panel. Remove the **TAIL 15A** fuse using the removal tool and check whether it is burned out. If it is, fit a new fuse and recheck operation.

3 Remove the **BTN 40A** fuse from the fuse block in the engine compartment and check its condition, fitting a new fuse if required. If either new fuse burns out, check the associated wiring for damage and shorts to ground, repairing or replacing damaged wires as necessary.

Step 2

4 Remove the combination (steering column) switch housing halves (☞ 7/12) to gain access to the switch terminals. Access will not be easy - the terminals are at the back of the switch, and are only really visible through the windshield. Note that if you lift the switch locking tab after slackening the clamp screw, you may be able to pull the switch back a little to improve access.

5 With the headlight switch turned on, check the voltages on the terminals indicated in the accompanying figure and table, passing the meter positive (+) probe through the back of the wiring connector, and grounding the negative (-) probe.

30. TAIL, PARKING & L/PLATE LIGHT - T/SHOOTING (UK & CONT. EURO CARS)

☞ 1/1, 2 & 7/2.

1 In the event of problems with the above system, proceed as described below, following each step in the checking sequence to identify the cause of the fault.

Step 1

2 On UK spec cars, remove the **BTN 40A** and **TAIL 10A** fuses from the fuse block in the engine compartment and check their condition, fitting a new fuse if required. If either new fuse burns out, check the associated wiring for damage and shorts to ground, repairing or replacing damaged wires as necessary.

Step 2

3 Remove the combination (steering column) switch housing halves (☞ 7/12) to gain access to the switch terminals. Access will not be easy - the terminals are at the back of the switch, and are only really visible through the windshield. Note that if you lift the switch locking tab after slackening the clamp screw, you may be able to pull the switch back a little to improve access.

4 + + With the headlight switch turned on, check the voltages on the terminals indicated in the accompanying figure and table, passing the meter positive (+) probe through the back of the wiring connector, and grounding the negative (-) probe.

31. DAYTIME RUNNING LIGHT (DRL) CIRCUIT - T/SHOOTING (CANADIAN CARS)

☞ 1/1, 2 & 7/2.

1 The Canadian spec cars are equipped with daylight running lights which should operate whenever the vehicle is driven with the headlights switch turned off (unless the turn signals or hazard warning lights are on, or the parking brake applied). The system operation can be checked as follows.

2 **Warning!** Before going further place wood blocks each side of the wheels to prevent the car from rolling. Start the engine and allow it to idle, then release the parking brake. The running lights should illuminate. Note that if the turn signal switch is operated, the lights on that side should flash, while the remaining lights stay on constantly. Operating the hazard lights should override the running lights.

3 If the system does not work as described above, and the turn signal and hazard warning light systems are functioning normally, follow the check sequence described next.

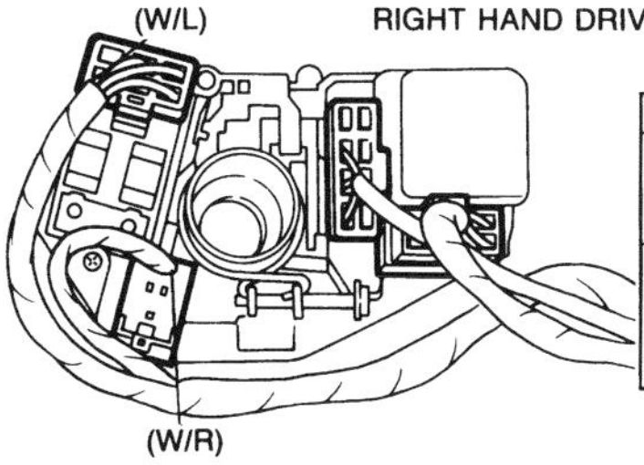

Wire	Voltage	Action
(W/R)	12V	Next check wire (W/L)
	0V	Repair wire (W/R) (BTN 40A fuse — combination switch)
(W/L)	12V	Repair the wiring harness (Combination switch — body ground of each light)
	0V	Replace headlight switch

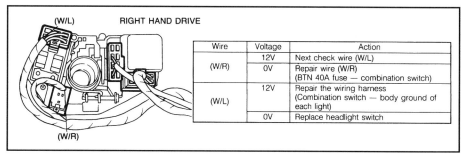

D&T30/4A TESTING SWITCH TERMINAL VOLTAGES (EURO RHD CARS).

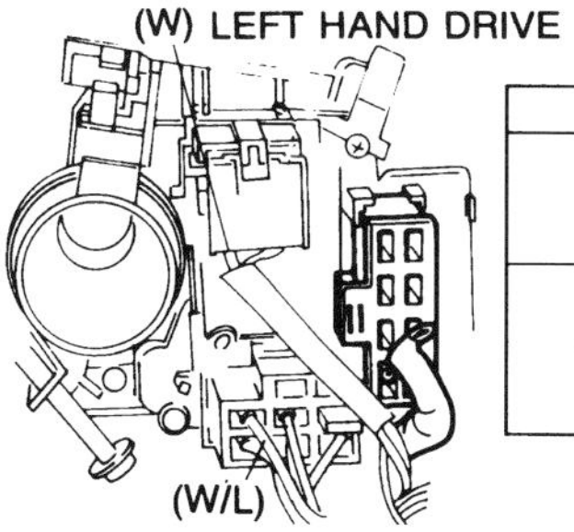

Wire	Voltage	Action
(W)	12V	Next check wire (W/L)
	0V	Repair wire (W/R) (MAIN 80A fuse — combination switch)
(W/L)	12V	Repair the wiring harness (Combination switch — body ground of each light)
	0V	Replace headlight switch

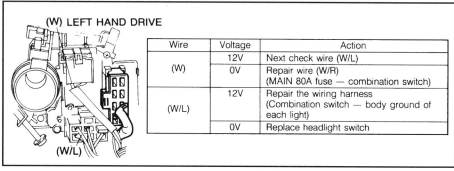

D&T30/4B TESTING SWITCH TERMINAL VOLTAGES (EURO LHD CARS).

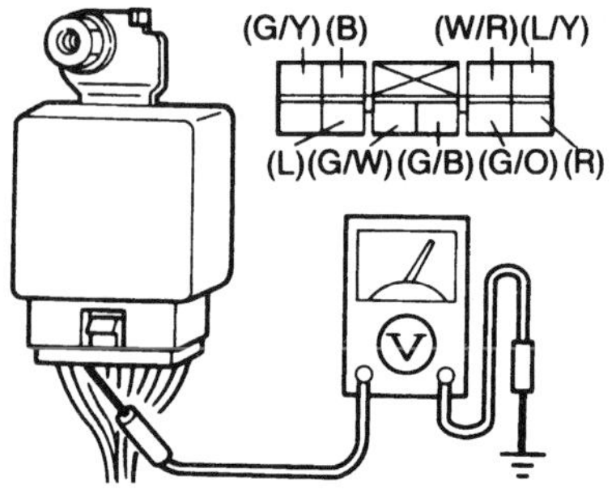

Wire	Connected to	Test condition	Specification	Action
(L)	WIPER 20A fuse	Constant	VB	Repair wire (L) (WIPER 20A—DRL unit)
(B)	Ground	Constant	0V	Repair wire (B) (DRL unit—Body ground)
(R)	Parking brake switch	Parking brake released	VB	Go to Step 2
(W/R)	Headlight switch	Headlight switch off	0V	Go to Step 3

D&T 31/5 TESTING DRL UNIT TERMINAL VOLTAGES (CANADIAN CARS).

Step 1

4 Remove the access panel below the steering wheel to gain access to the relays mounted below the dash panel. Locate the DRL unit (there are several relay units in this area - check the wire colors against the accompanying diagram (D&T31/5) to confirm the identity of the DRL unit).

5 With the ignition switch turned on and the wiring connected to the DRL unit, measure the terminal voltages, referring to the accompanying drawing and table for terminal identification, expected voltage readings and suggested action. Use the meter positive (+) probe through the back of the wiring connector, and ground the negative (-) probe.

Step 2

6 Remove the single screw which secures the two halves of the parking brake lever plastic cover. Separate and remove the cover halves to gain access to the parking brake switch. Using a continuity tester or multimeter, check for continuity between the switch terminal and ground. With the lever fully released, there should be no continuity, while continuity should be indicated if the lever is pulled up one notch or more.

7 If the continuity check produces the specified result, check the wiring back from the parking brake switch to the DRL unit (L/Y wire leaving the switch, R as it enters the DRL unit) and repair or rewire as necessary. If the expected test result is not obtained, adjust or replace the parking brake switch.

Step 3

8 Remove the combination (steering column) switch housing halves (☞ 7/12) to gain access to the switch terminals. Access will not be easy - the terminals are at the back of the switch, and are only really visible through the windshield. Note that if you lift the switch locking tab after slackening the clamp screw, you may be able to pull the switch back a little to improve access.

9 Check for continuity between the **BTN** and **TNS** terminals on the switch (see accompanying diagram for location). With the headlight switch turned on, continuity should be shown, while there should be no continuity with the switch turned off. If not as specified, fit a new headlight switch. If the unit checks out as specified, trace back and repair as necessary the W/R wire between the switch and the DRL unit.

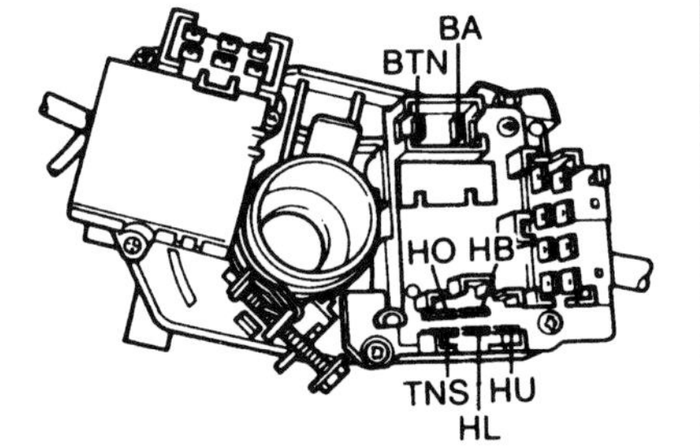

D31/9 HEADLIGHT SWITCH CONNECTOR TERMINAL IDENTIFICATION (CANADIAN CARS).

10 If the DRL system operates but does not cancel when it should, first check which switch setting is faulty as follows. **Warning!** Place wood blocks each side of the wheels to prevent the car from rolling. Start the engine and allow it to idle, then release the parking brake. The running lights should illuminate. Start the checking procedure as follows:

Step 1

11 If the DRL system does not cancel when the headlight switch is turned on, begin checking the system from Step 2. If the system does not cancel when the turn signal or hazard warning switch is turned on, begin checking the system from Step 4. If the DRL system fails to cancel when the parking brake is applied, skip down to Step 5.

Step 2

12 With the ignition and headlight switches turned on, check the voltage between the DRL unit W/R terminal and ground. If you read battery voltage, the DRL unit should be replaced. If zero volts is read, move to Step 3.

Step 3

13 Remove the combination (steering column) switch housing halves (☞ 7/12) to gain access to the switch terminals. Access will not be easy - the terminals are at the back of the switch, and are only really visible through the windshield. Note that if you lift the switch locking tab after slackening the clamp screw, you may be able to pull the switch back a little to improve access.

14 Check for continuity between the **BTN** and **TNS** terminals on the switch. With the headlight switch turned on, continuity should be shown, while there should be no continuity with the switch turned off. If not as specified, fit a new headlight switch. If the unit checks out as specified, trace back and repair as necessary the W/R wire between the switch and the DRL unit.

Step 4

15 Turn on the ignition and hazard light switches. Measure the voltage between the DRL unit G/B terminal and ground, then check between the G/W terminal and ground. In each case, the reading should alternate between 12V and 0V. If the reading is not as described, check back along the wiring to the turn signal/hazard warning relay and repair as required. If the reading is correct, replace the DRL unit.

Step 5

16 Turn on the ignition switch and check the voltage on the DRL **R** terminal while operating the parking brake lever. With the lever pulled up by one notch or more, 0V should be shown. If this is not the case, move to Step 6, otherwise, fit a new DRL unit.

Step 6

17 Remove the single screw which secures the two halves of the parking brake lever plastic cover. Separate and remove the cover halves to gain access to the parking brake switch. Using a continuity tester or multimeter, check for continuity between the switch terminal and ground. With the lever fully released, there should be no continuity, while continuity should be indicated if the lever is pulled up one notch or more.

18 If the continuity check produces the specified result, check the wiring back from the parking brake switch to the DRL unit (L/Y) wire leaving the switch, (**R** as it enters the DRL unit) and repair or rewire as necessary. If the expected test result is not obtained, adjust or replace the parking brake switch.

32. DAYTIME RUNNING LIGHT (DRL) UNIT - TROUBLESHOOTING (CANADIAN CARS)

☞ 1/1, 2 & 7/2.

1 The DRL unit should be removed from the car for these checks, which will require a 12 volt battery, some jumper leads, a voltmeter and an

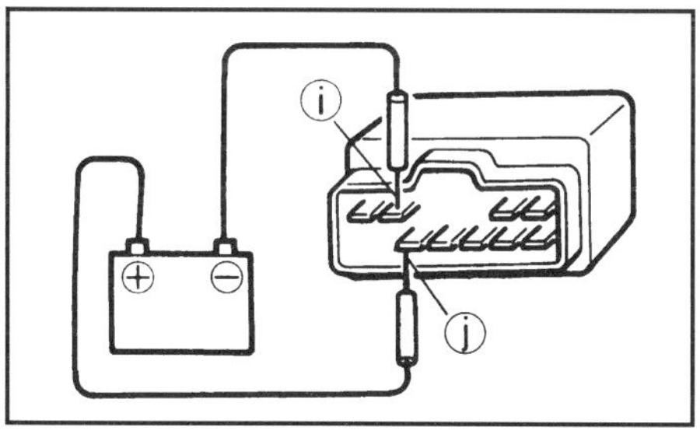

D32/1 APPLY 12 VOLTS TO 'J' & GROUND 'I' DURING FOLLOWING TESTS UNLESS OTHERWISE INDICATED.

ohmmeter (or a multimeter). Note that throughout the test sequence, unless advised otherwise, terminal **j** should be connected to battery positive (+), and terminal **i** should be connected to battery negative (-). In the various checks, you will need to apply 12V (battery positive) to one of the terminals under test and ground another, while taking voltage readings at other terminals.

2 With the unit set up as described above, apply 12V to terminal **c**, and then check the voltage readings at terminals **d** and **k**. In both cases, battery voltage should be shown. If the readings obtained are not as specified, replace the DRL unit.

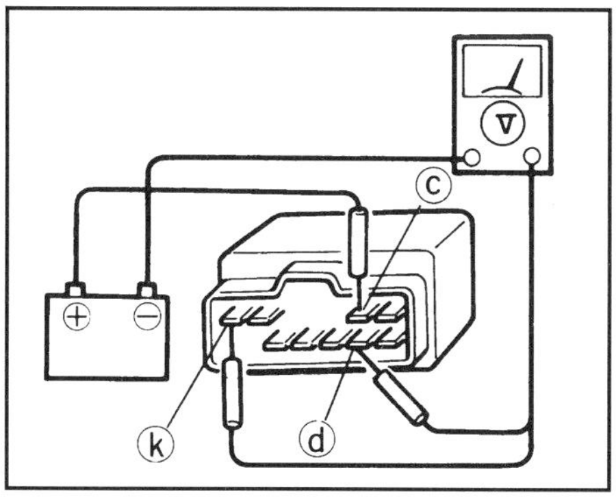

D32/2 DRL UNIT TEST 1.

3 Disconnect the 12V supply to terminal **c** and apply it to terminals **f** and **h**. Again, in both cases, battery voltage should be shown. If the readings obtained ar not as specified, replace the DRL unit.

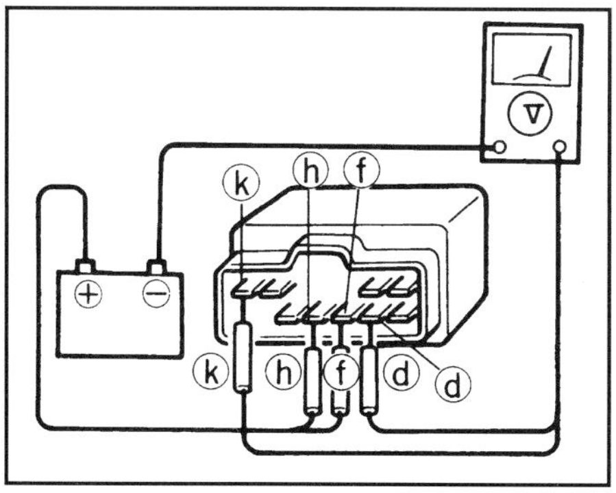

D32/3 DRL UNIT TEST 2.

4 Next, disconnect the 12V supply from terminals **f** and **h**, and then ground terminal **b**.

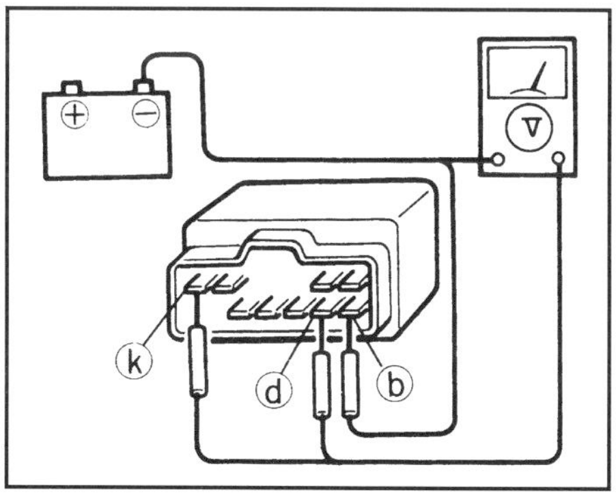

D32/4 DRL UNIT TEST 3.

Check the voltage at terminals **d** and **k**. Once again, battery voltage should be indicated, and if not as specified, the unit should be replaced.

5 Finally, perform a continuity check between terminals **d** and **f**, and then between terminals **h** and **k**. In both cases, continuity should be shown; if not, a new DRL unit should be fitted.

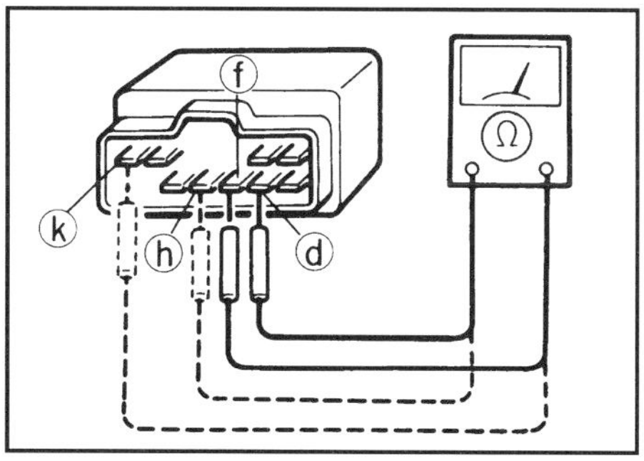

D32/5 DRL UNIT TEST 4.

33. STOP (BRAKE) LIGHT CIRCUIT - TROUBLESHOOTING

☞ 1/1, 2 & 7/2.

1 If the stop lights are completely inoperative, the first thing to check is the fuse. On US and Canadian spec cars, this is the **STOP 15A** fuse housed in the fuse box under the dash panel - you will need to remove the steering column access cover to reach the fuse. On UK and Continental Europe models, the **STOP 10A** fuse will be found in the main fuse block in the engine compartment. If the fuse has burned out, fit a new one and check the operation of the stop lights. If the fuse burns out again, check through the associated wiring and repair any short discovered.

2 If the fuse checked out OK and the fault persists, turn on the ignition switch and check the voltages on the brake light switch as follows. Connect the meter negative (-) probe to ground, then introduce the positive (+) probe through the back of the wiring connector to each terminal in turn. There should be battery voltage on the (W/G) wire at all times, with battery voltage showing on the (G) wire only when the brake pedal is depressed. If not as specified, check the switch wiring or fit a new switch as required.

33/2 Location of brake light switch.

3 If the switch is working normally, check the condition of the bulbs. If they are burned out, fit new ones and check the operation of the brake light system again.

4 If the bulbs are intact and the fault remains, the problem lies in the wiring back to the rear light units. Check the voltage at the rear light unit wiring connector (G) and (B) with the ignition switch turned on and the brake pedal depressed. Battery voltage should be shown on both terminals. If it is not, check the (G) wire back to the switch, and the (B) wire ground connection, and repair or rewire as necessary. On US spec cars with high-mount brake lights at the center of the trunk lid, check the bulb and wiring to the light unit.

5 If only one brake light is affected, the most likely cause is a burned out bulb, and you should always check this first. If this does not rectify the problem, check the wiring connections and voltages as described in the previous paragraph.

34. T/SIGNAL & HAZARD WARNING SYSTEM - T/SHOOTING (US & CAN. CARS)

☞ 1/1, 2 & 7/2.

1 Where the turn signal warning lamp on the instrument panel flashes rapidly, this almost invariably means a burned out bulb in one of the turn signal lights, or an open circuit in the associated wiring - always check this before moving to the check sequence described below.

Step 1

2 Check the **HAZARD 15A** fuse in the fuse box under the dash panel, removing the access panel to reach it. If the fuse has burned out, fit a new one, having checked the wiring for shorts or damage.

Step 2

3 Locate and remove the turn signal/hazard warning unit from under the dash panel, working through the access hole around the steering column after removing the access panel.

4 Refer to the accompanying table and diagram for details of terminal identification and location. Using an ohmmeter or a multimeter set to the X1000 range, check for continuity between the terminals as indicated in the table. If not as specified, fit a new turn signal/hazard warning unit, if OK, reconnect and move to Step 3.

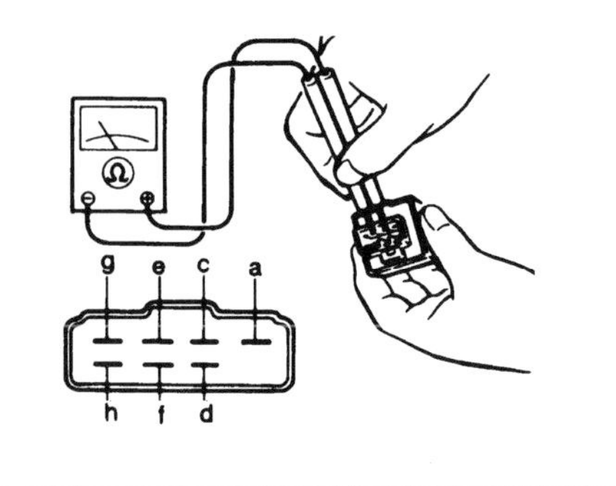

Terminal + −	Continuity	Terminal + −	Continuity	Terminal + −	Continuity
a — c	X	d — e	X	f — g	X
a — d	X	d — f	X	f — h	X
a — e	○	d — g	X	g — a	X
a — f	○	d — h	X	g — c	X
a — g	X	e — a	X	g — d	X
a — h	X	e — c	X	g — e	X
c — a	○	e — d	X	g — f	X
c — d	○	e — f	X	g — h	X
c — e	○	e — g	X	h — a	○
c — f	○	e — h	X	h — c	○
c — g	○	f — a	X	h — d	○
c — h	○	f — c	X	h — e	○
d — a	X	f — d	X	h — f	○
d — c	X	f — e	X	h — g	○

○: Indicates continuity X: No continuity

D&T34/4 TESTING FLASHER UNIT.

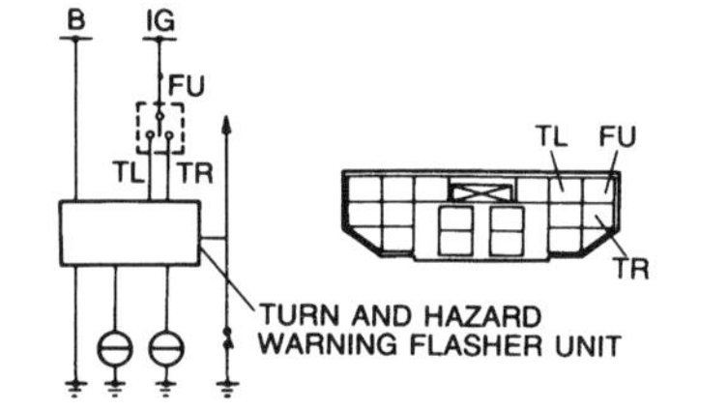

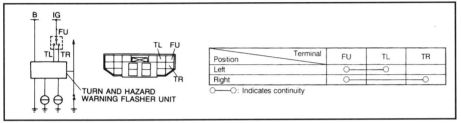

Position \ Terminal	FU	TL	TR
Left	○—	—○	
Right	○—	—	—○

○—○: Indicates continuity

D&T34/5 TESTING TURN SIGNAL SWITCH CONNECTOR TERMINALS.

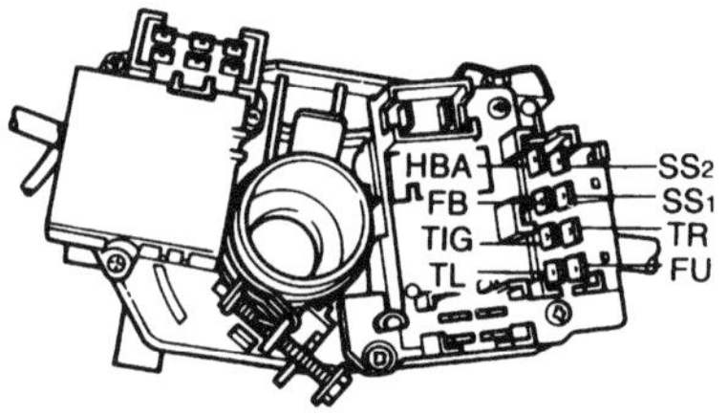

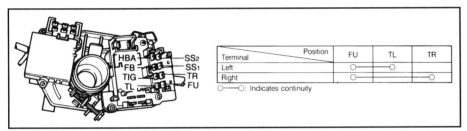

Terminal \ Position	FU	TL	TR
Left	○—	—○	
Right	○—	—	—○

○—○: Indicates continuity

D&T34/7 TESTING TURN SIGNAL SWITCH TERMINALS.

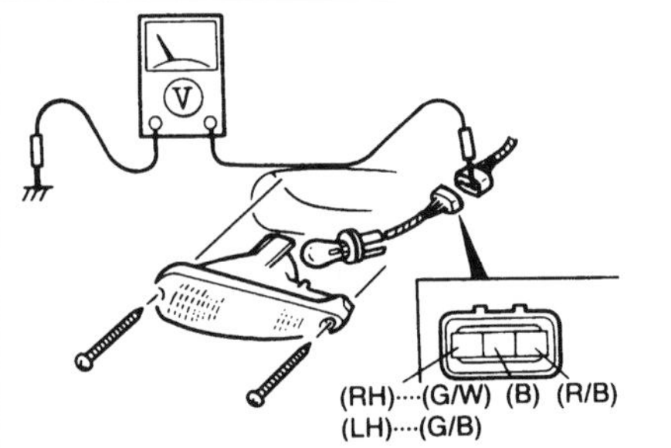

Wire	Condition	Voltage	Action
(B)	Constant	VB	Repair wire harness (Flasher unit — Body ground)
		0V	Next, check wire (G/R)
(G/R)	Turn signal switch right position	VB	Next, check wire (G/Y)
		0V	Repair wire harness (Turn signal switch — Flasher unit)
(G/Y)	Turn signal switch left position	VB	Next, check wire (B/R)
		0V	Repair wire harness (Turn signal switch — Flasher unit)
(B/R)	Constant	VB	Go to Step 7
		0V	Repair wire harness (HAZARD 15A fuse — Flasher unit)

D&T34/10 TESTING FLASHER UNIT CONNECTOR TERMINALS.

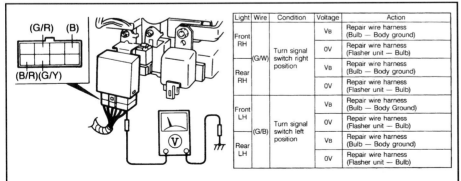

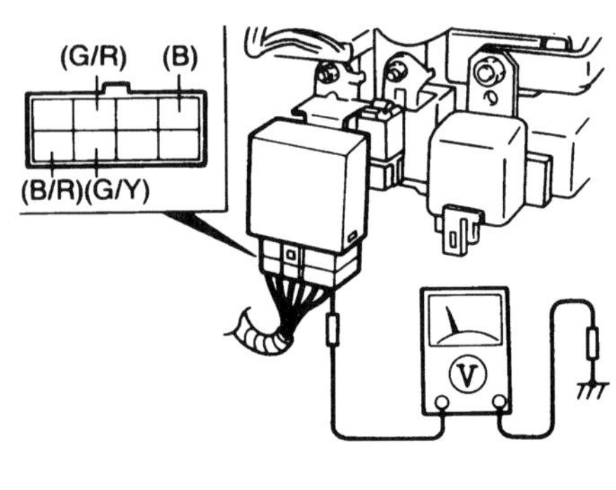

Light	Wire	Condition	Voltage	Action
Front RH	(G/W)	Turn signal switch right position	VB	Repair wire harness (Bulb — Body ground)
			0V	Repair wire harness (Flasher unit — Bulb)
Rear RH			VB	Repair wire harness (Bulb — Body ground)
			0V	Repair wire harness (Flasher unit — Bulb)
Front LH	(G/B)	Turn signal switch left position	VB	Repair wire harness (Bulb — Body Ground)
			0V	Repair wire harness (Flasher unit — Bulb)
Rear LH			VB	Repair wire harness (Bulb — Body ground)
			0V	Repair wire harness (Flasher unit — Bulb)

D&T34/11 TESTING TURN SIGNAL LIGHT CONNECTOR TERMINALS.

Step 3

5 **US spec cars:** With the steering column access panel removed, locate and separate the turn signal switch connector. Use a continuity tester or ohmmeter to check terminal connections as shown in the accompanying drawing and table. If not as specified, fit a new switch. If the switch checks out as being normal, reconnect the wiring and move to Step 4.

6 **Canadian spec cars:** Remove the combination (steering column) switch housing halves (☞ 7/12) to gain access to the switch terminals. Access will not be easy - the terminals are at the back of the switch, and are only really visible through the windshield. Note that if you lift the switch locking tab after slackening the clamp screw, you may be able to pull the switch back a little to improve access.

7 Use a continuity tester or ohmmeter to check terminal connections as shown in the drawing and table. If not as specified, fit a new switch. If the switch checks out as OK, reconnect the wiring and move to Step 4, but leave the switch housing removed for now.

Step 4

8 Check the condition of the turn signal light bulbs - if any are burned out, replace them. Move to Step 5.

Step 5

9 With the ignition switch turned on, check the voltage on the (B/Y) wire at the turn signal switch connector (leave the connector assembled during this check). You should read battery voltage - if not, check and repair the wiring between the **HAZARD 15A** fuse and the switch. If you read battery voltage, move to Step 6.

Step 6

10 With the wiring connector in place, measure the terminal voltages at the turn signal/hazard warning unit connector, referring to the accompanying drawing and table.

Step 7

11 Disconnect each of the turn signal light wiring connectors in turn, and check the voltage as shown in the accompanying table.

Step 8 - Canadian spec cars only

12 Check the terminal voltages at the DRL

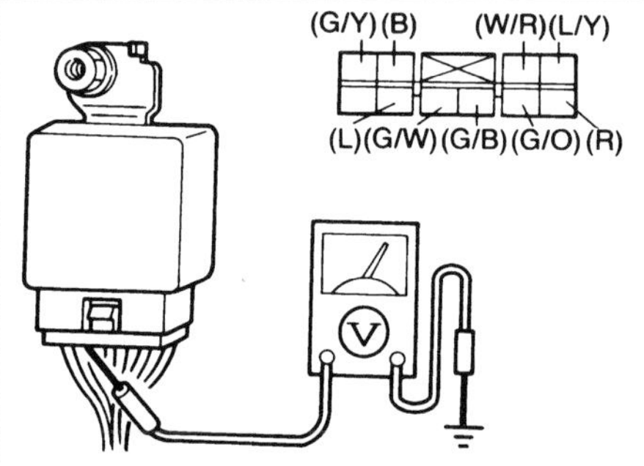

D34/12 TESTING DRL UNIT TERMINALS.

unit connector, pushing the positive (+) probe through the back of the connector, and grounding the negative (-) probe. The terminal positions are indicated in the accompanying drawing.

13 Turn on the ignition switch and set the turn signal switch to the right position, then check the voltage on the (G/W) wire. If zero voltage is shown, check the (G/W) wire back to the flasher unit and repair or replace it as necessary. If battery voltage is shown, check the reading on the (G/Y) wire.

14 If zero voltage is shown on the (G/Y) wire, check the DRL unit ☞ 7/31. If battery voltage is shown, check the (G/Y) wire back to the associated turn signal light and repair or rewire as required.

15 Next, set the turn signal switch to the left position, then check the voltage on the (G/B) wire. If zero voltage is shown, check the (G/B) wire back to the flasher unit and repair or replace it as necessary. If battery voltage is shown, check the reading on the (G/O) wire.

16 If zero voltage is shown on the (G/O) wire, check the DRL unit ☞ 7/31. If battery voltage is shown, check the (G/O) wire back to the associated turn signal light and repair or rewire as required.

Hazard warning system checks

17 If the fault is confined to the hazard warning system, check for burned out bulbs first. If the bulbs are OK, remove and check the hazard warning switch ☞ 7/13. Next, with the switch removed, check the terminal voltages at the wiring connector.

18 You should read battery voltage at the (O) wire. If not, check the wire back to the turn signal/ hazard warning unit and repair or rewire as required.

19 Next, check the voltage on the (B) ground wire. If you find battery voltage, check and repair the ground connection. If the system still fails to operate, fit a new turn signal/hazard warning unit.

35. T/SIGNAL & HAZARD WARNING SYSTEM - T/SHOOTING (UK & CONT. EURO CARS)

☞ 1/1, 2 & 7/2.

1 Note: where the turn signal warning lamp on the instrument panel flashes rapidly, this almost invariably means a burned out bulb in one of the turn signal lights, or an open circuit in the associated wiring - always check this before moving to the check sequence described below.

Step 1

2 **Continental Europe cars**: check the **HAZARD 30A** fuse in the fuse box under the dash panel, removing the access panel to reach it. If the fuse has burned out, fit a new one, having checked the wiring for shorts or damage.

3 **UK cars**: check the **HAZARD 10A** fuse located in the main fuse block in the engine compartment. If the fuse has burned out, fit a new one, having checked the wiring for shorts or damage.

Step 2

4 Locate the turn signal/hazard warning unit under the dash panel, working through the access hole around the steering column after removing the access panel.

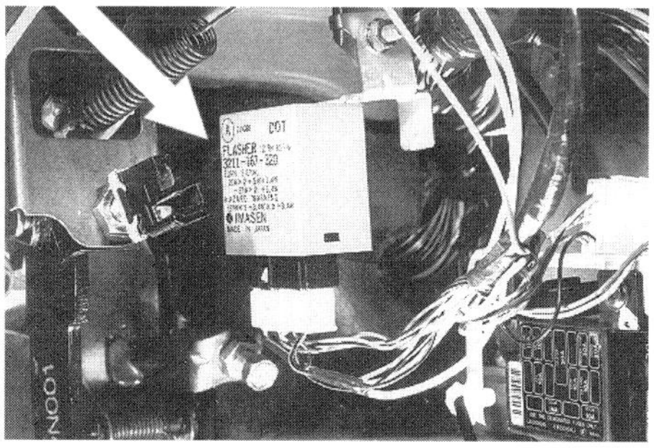

35/4 Location of flasher unit (rhd cars).

5 Refer to the accompanying table and diagram for details of terminal identification and location. Using a voltmeter or a multimeter set to the voltage range, check the terminal voltages as indicated in the table. If not as specified, follow the directions in the table for information on the next step in the checking procedure.

Step 3

6 Check the condition of the turn signal light bulbs - if any are burned out, replace them. Move to Step 4.

Step 4

7 Turn on the hazard light switch, then check the terminal voltages on the turn signal/ hazard warning unit as shown in the accompanying table and diagram.

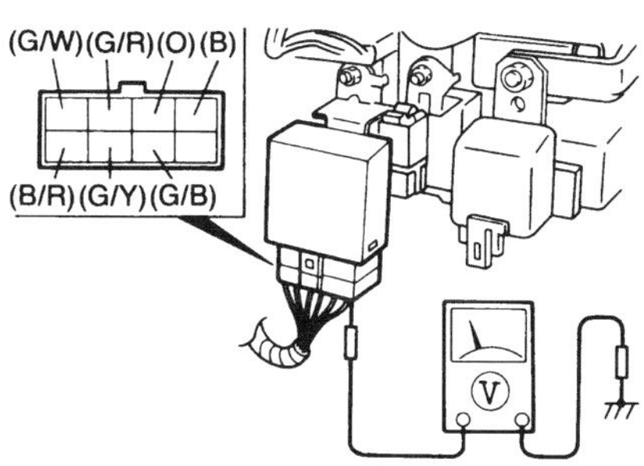

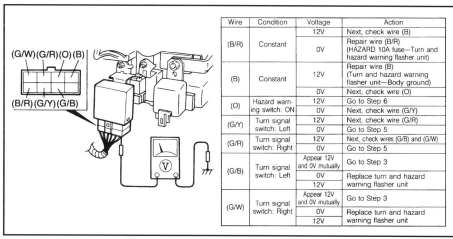

Wire	Condition	Voltage	Action
(B/R)	Constant	12V	Next, check wire (B)
		0V	Repair wire (B/R) (HAZARD 10A fuse—Turn and hazard warning flasher unit)
(B)	Constant	12V	Repair wire (B) (Turn and hazard warning flasher unit—Body ground)
		0V	Next, check wire (O)
(O)	Hazard warning switch: ON	12V	Go to Step 6
		0V	Next, check wire (G/Y)
(G/Y)	Turn signal switch: Left	12V	Next, check wire (G/R)
		0V	Go to Step 5
(G/R)	Turn signal switch: Right	12V	Next, check wires (G/B) and (G/W)
		0V	Go to Step 5
(G/B)	Turn signal switch: Left	Appear 12V and 0V mutually	Go to Step 3
		0V 12V	Replace turn and hazard warning flasher unit
(G/W)	Turn signal switch: Right	Appear 12V and 0V mutually	Go to Step 3
		0V 12V	Replace turn and hazard warning flasher unit

D&T35/5 TESTING FLASHER UNIT CONNECTOR TERMINAL VOLTAGES (EURO CARS).

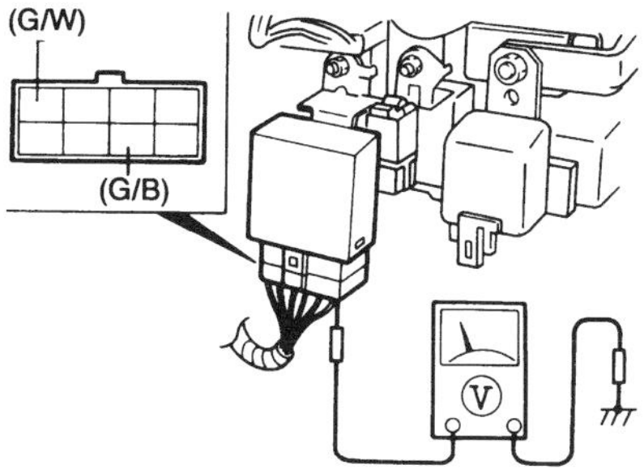

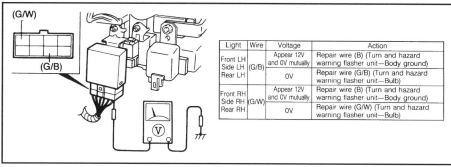

Light	Wire	Voltage	Action
Front LH Side LH Rear LH	(G/B)	Appear 12V and 0V mutually	Repair wire (B) (Turn and hazard warning flasher unit—Body ground)
		0V	Repair wire (G/B) (Turn and hazard warning flasher unit—Bulb)
Front RH Side RH Rear RH	(G/W)	Appear 12V and 0V mutually	Repair wire (B) (Turn and hazard warning flasher unit—Body ground)
		0V	Repair wire (G/W) (Turn and hazard warning flasher unit—Bulb)

D&T35/7 TESTING FLASHER UNIT CONNECTOR TERMINAL VOLTAGES - HAZARD WARNING SWITCH 'ON' (EURO CARS).

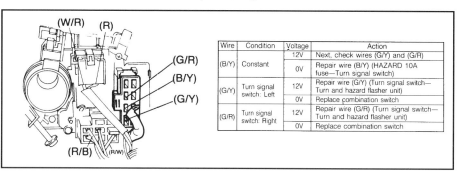

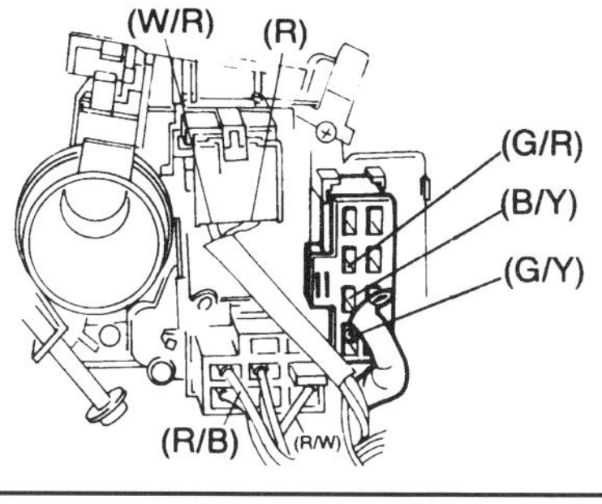

Wire	Condition	Voltage	Action
(B/Y)	Constant	12V	Next, check wires (G/Y) and (G/R)
		0V	Repair wire (B/Y) (HAZARD 10A fuse—Turn signal switch)
(G/Y)	Turn signal switch: Left	12V	Repair wire (G/Y) (Turn signal switch—Turn and hazard flasher unit)
		0V	Replace combination switch
(G/R)	Turn signal switch: Right	12V	Repair wire (G/R) (Turn signal switch—Turn and hazard flasher unit)
		0V	Replace combination switch

D&T35/9 TESTING TURN SIGNAL SWITCH CONNECTOR TERMINAL VOLTAGES (EURO CARS).

Step 5

8 Remove the combination (steering column) switch housing halves (☞ 7/12) to gain access to the switch terminals. Access will not be easy - the terminals are at the back of the switch, and are only really visible through the windshield. Note that if you lift the switch locking tab after slackening the clamp screw, you may be able to pull the switch back a little to improve access.

9 Use a voltmeter or multimeter to check terminal voltages as shown in the accompanying drawing and table. If not as specified, fit a new switch.

Step 6

10 With the wiring connector in place, measure the terminal voltages at the turn signal/ hazard warning unit connector, referring to the accompanying drawing and table.

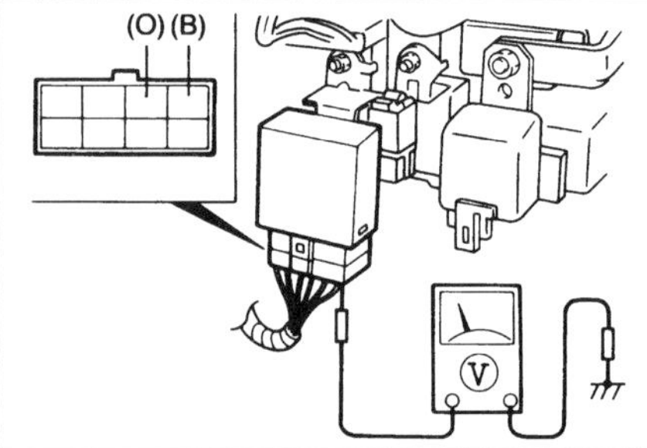

Wire	Condition	Voltage	Action
(B)	Hazard warning switch: ON	12V	Repair wire (B) (Hazard warning switch—Body ground)
		0V	Next, check wire (O)
(O)		12V	Replace hazard warning switch
		0V	Repair wire (O) (Turn and hazard warning flasher unit—Hazard warning switch)

D&T35/10 TESTING FLASHER UNIT CONNECTOR TERMINAL VOLTAGES (EURO CARS).

Hazard warning system checks

11 If the fault is confined to the hazard warning system, check for burned out bulbs first. If the bulbs are OK, remove and check the hazard warning switch ☞ 7/13. Next, with the switch removed, check the terminal voltages at the wiring connector.

12 You should read battery voltage at the (O) wire. If not, check the wire back to the turn signal/ hazard warning unit and repair or rewire as required.

13 Next, check the voltage on the (B) ground wire. If you find battery voltage, check and repair the ground connection. If the system still fails to operate, fit a new turn signal/hazard warning unit.

36. BACKUP (REVERSING) LIGHT SYSTEM - TROUBLESHOOTING

☞ 1/1, 2 & 7/2.

1 If you have problems with the backup/ reversing lights, always check bulb condition before you do anything else. If one light only has failed, you know that the system is operating normally, but that the non-functioning bulb has either burned out, or the wiring to it is damaged. If both lights are inoperative, check the **METER 10A** fuse. Fit a new fuse if necessary, and check whether the lights operate normally. If the fuse burns out again, check for a short in the wiring.

2 If the bulbs and fuse are intact, check for battery voltage at the rear light unit connector. With the ignition switch turned on and reverse selected, you should read battery voltage between the (R/G) wire and the (B) ground wire. If not, try grounding the (B) wire terminal to a sound chassis ground point - if the light then works, you need to check and repair the (B) wire ground connection.

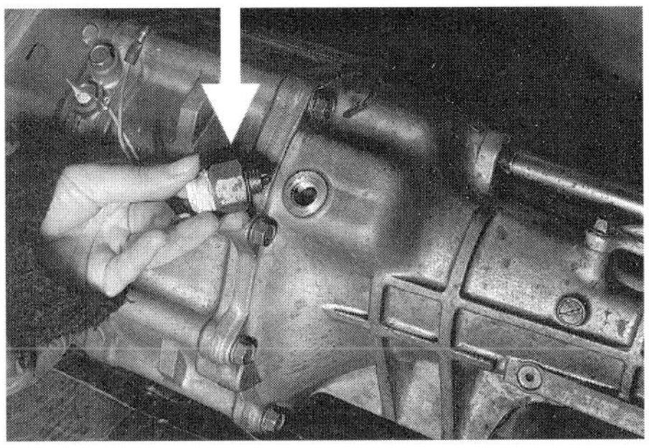
36/3 Reversing light switch (man trans cars).

3 If you still read zero volts on the (R/G) wire, you will need to check the switch operation. On manual transmission cars, the switch is located on the tail extension of the transmission, just to the left of the centerline. If the switch does not read continuity when reverse is selected (and zero continuity in all other positions) fit a new switch. If the switch checks out OK, check the wiring connections between the **METER 10A** fuse and the switch, and then back from the switch to the light units.

4 On automatic transmission cars, the backup / reversing lights are operated by the inhibitor switch, and this may require adjustment. Check that, with the ignition switch turned on, the lights do not flash on at some point as the shift lever is moved through its travel. If so, the need for adjustment is indicated ☞ 4/22.

37. TAIL LIGHT UNIT - BULB REMOVAL & INSTALLATION & LENS REPLACEMENT

☞ 1/1, 2 & 7/2.

1 + The tail and brake light bulbs can be removed after their shared bulb holder assembly has been unclipped from inside the trunk. The turn signal bulb holder is fitted separately and can be removed by turning it counterclockwise. Check that any replacement bulbs are of the correct voltage and wattage, noting that the wattage details vary according to the country in which the car was originally sold. The bulbs are standard bayonet fitting - press them slightly inwards, then turn them counterclockwise to release them from their holders.

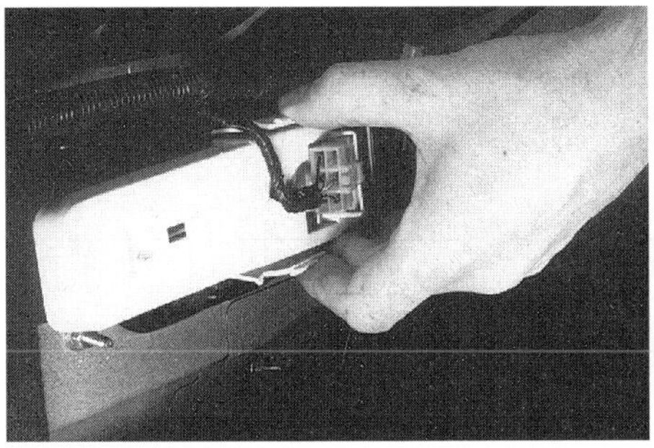
37/1a Unclip bulb holder from rear of light ...

37/1b ... and remove tail/brake light bulbs.

37/1c Turn signal bulb holder twists out.

2 + In the event of damage to the light unit, it can be removed from the car after detaching the bulb holder assembly as described above. Where fitted, unclip and remove wiring clips from the projecting end of the mounting studs, then unscrew the four 10 mm nuts to allow the unit to be removed from the car. Take care not to damage the foam seal, which can be peeled off the back of the unit.

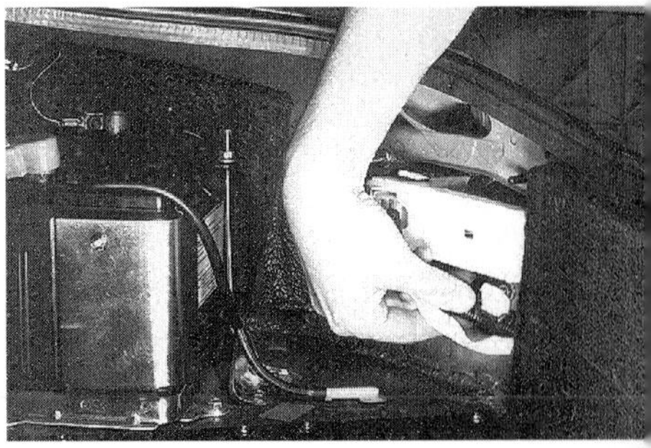
37/2a Free wire clips & remove bulb holder ...

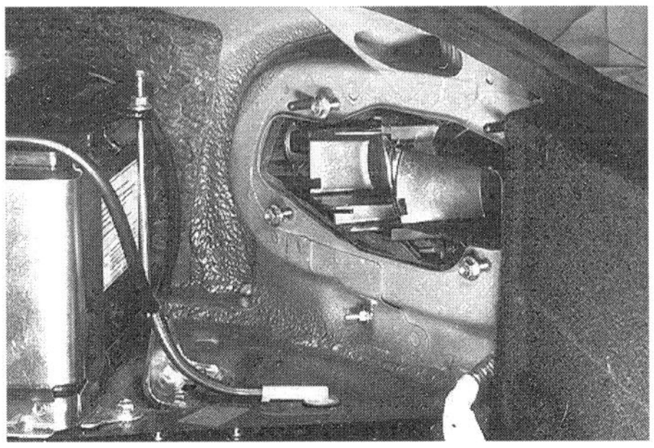
37/2b ... remove nuts from four mounting studs ...

37/2c ... remove light unit ...

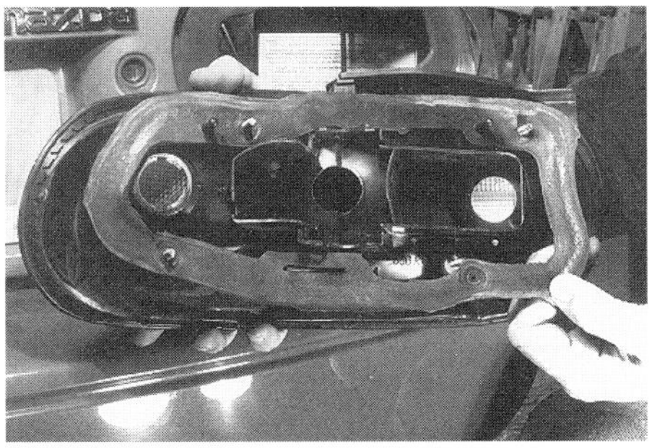
37/2d ... and foam seal.

3 If the lens has been damaged in an accident, it is possible to fit a new one once any remaining fragments of the old lens have been removed. The lens is bonded to the light unit with a hot-melt adhesive, and this can be softened by careful use of a hot air gun (the whole assembly is made of plastic, so don't overdo the heating).

4 If the old lens is more or less intact, insert a wood rod (or a small hammer handle) through one of the light apertures and use this to push the lens away from the unit. Where only fragments of lens remain, pick these off the unit with a screwdriver blade. When removing the lens, try to leave the hot-melt adhesive in place if you can - it can then be re-used to hold the new lens - just soften the adhesive with the hot air gun and press the new lens into place, making sure it beds firmly around the outer edge.

5 If you were unable to reuse the hot-melt adhesive, remove all traces of it from the unit, then apply a bead of suitable adhesive to retain the new lens. Mazda recommend **Uni-sealer** (8531 77 739) for this purpose. We have found that on similar jobs, a clear silicone-rubber RTV gasket compound is just about unbeatable; it sticks the new lens securely in position, stays resilient, and is totally waterproof. If you use RTV sealant, apply a thin bead all the way round the unit sealing face and let it stand for about 5 minutes. Press the lens onto the sealant, and then leave it to harden for a while - preferably overnight.

6 Before fitting the unit back into the car, you should check that the lens seal is watertight by partially immersing the unit in water. Fit the unit back into its recess and fit the retaining nuts, tightening them evenly to avoid stressing the plastic unit. Fit any wiring guide clips by pressing them over the projecting thread ends, then clip the bulb holder back into place.

38. FRONT COMBINATION LIGHT UNIT - BULB REPLACEMENT

☞ 1/1, 2 & 7/2.

1 Access to the front combination light bulbs requires removal of the light unit. Remove the two screws which retain the light unit to the body and lift it away. Release the bulb holders by twisting them counterclockwise.

2 + The smaller of the two bulbs is of the capless type and can be removed from its holder by pulling. The larger turn signal bulb can be removed by depressing it slightly and turning it counterclockwise.

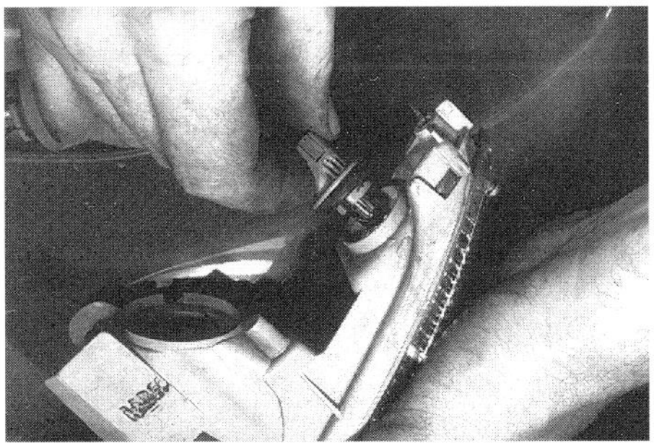
38/2a Twist out bulbholder and ...

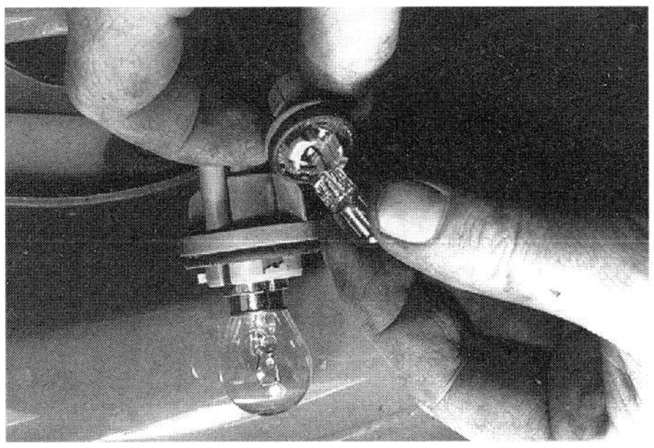
38/2b ... pull out capless sidelight bulb.

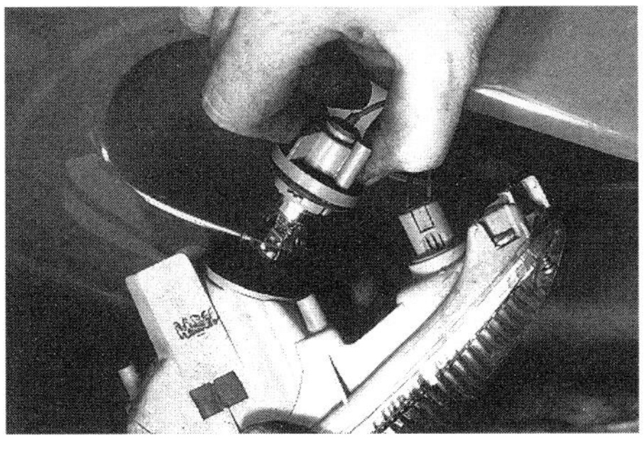
38/2c Twist out bulb holder and ...

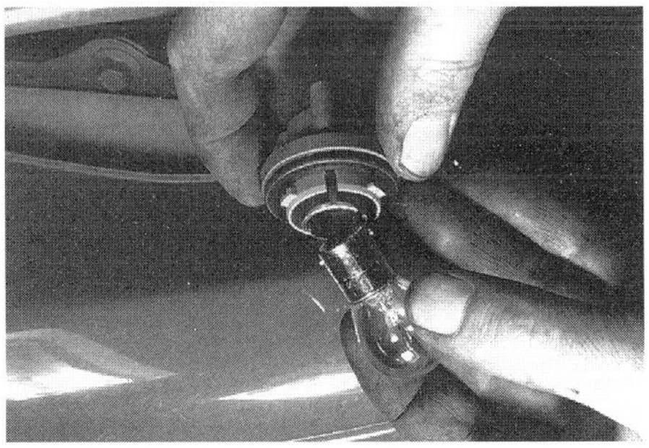
38/2d ... twist out larger turn signal bulb.

3 When fitting new bulbs, make sure that you use replacements of the correct rating. When installing the unit, fit the retaining screws and tighten them evenly. Do not overtighten.

39. SIDE MARKER LIGHT UNIT - BULB REPLACEMENT (WHERE FITTED)

☞ 1/1, 2 & 7/2.

1 Access to the side marker light bulbs requires removal of the affected light unit. Remove the two screws which retain the light unit to the body and lift it away. Note that cars sold in some markets have a reflector in place of the side marker light. Release the bulb holder by twisting them counterclockwise.

2 The bulb is of the capless type and can be removed from its holder by pulling. When fitting new bulbs, make sure that you use replacements of the correct rating. When installing the unit, fit the retaining screws and tighten them evenly - do not overtighten.

39/1 S/marker light lens/reflector held by screws.

40. TURN SIGNAL SIDE REPEATER LIGHT UNIT - BULB REPLACEMENT (WHERE FITTED)

☞ 1/1, 2 & 7/2.

1 + Access to the side repeater light bulbs requires removal of the affected light unit. Using a screwdriver covered with tape to prevent paint damage, and placing a piece of card between the blade and the car body, gently pry out the unit from

the back edge. Release the bulb holders by twisting them counterclockwise.

2 The bulb is of the capless type and can be removed from its holder by pulling it gently. When fitting new bulbs, make sure that you use replacements of the correct rating. When installing the unit, check that it snaps back securely in its recess.

41. LICENSE PLATE LIGHTS - BULB REPLACEMENT

☞ 1/1, 2 & 7/2.

1 Access to the license plate light bulbs on UK and Continental European cars requires removal of the affected light unit as follows. Remove the two screws which pass through the lens and light unit into the bodywork of the car. Lift away the lens and lower the unit so that the bulb can be reached.

2 The bulb is of the capless type and can be removed from its holder by pulling it gently. When fitting new bulbs, make sure that you use replacements of the correct rating. When installing the unit, check that it is positioned correctly, then fit the two screws to secure the unit and lens, taking care

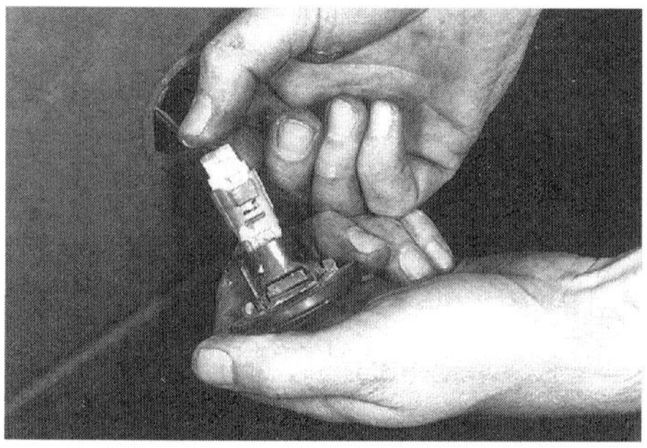

40/1a Pry light unit from body ...

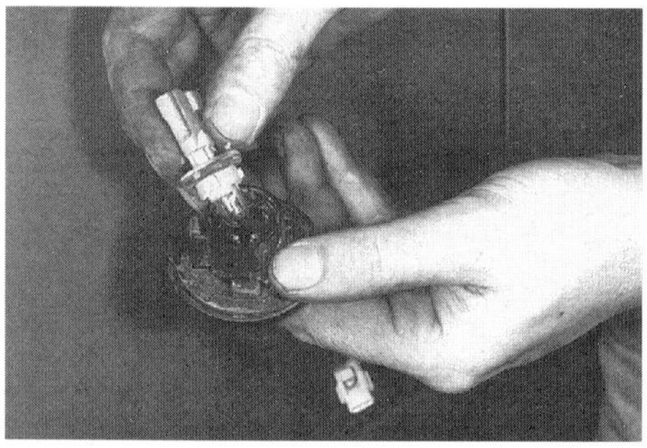

40/1b ... to access bulb.

not to overtighten.

3 The procedure for US and Canadian spec cars is similar although the lights may be differently positioned.

42. REAR FOG LIGHT - BULB REPLACEMENT (WHERE FITTED)

☞ 1/1, 2 & 7/2.

1 Remove the two screws which pass through the lens and into the light unit. Lift away

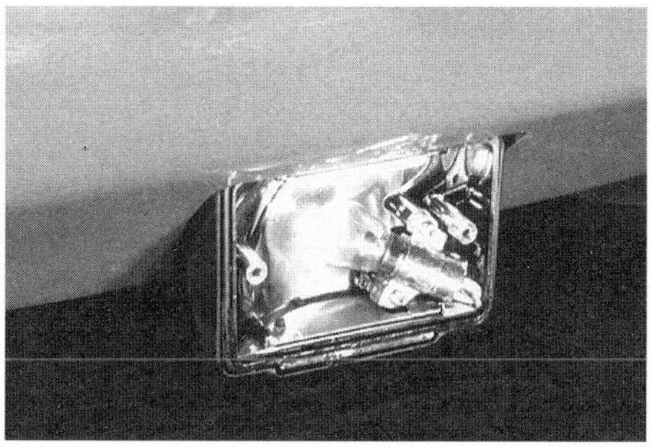

42/1 Bulb accessible after lens removed.

the lens so that the bulb can be reached.

2 The bulb can be removed from its holder by pushing it inwards slightly, then turning it counterclockwise. When fitting a new bulb, make sure that you use a replacement of the correct rating. When installing the lens, check that it is positioned correctly, then fit the two screws to secure the lens to the light unit, taking care not to overtighten.

43. DRIVING / FRONT FOG LIGHT UNITS - BULB REPLACEMENT (WHERE FITTED)

☞ 1/1, 2 & 7/2.

1 + The driving / front fog lights are mounted inside the air intake at the nose of the car. To gain access to the bulbs, remove the two screws which retain the outer lens assembly to its casing and lift it away. Remove the two screws which secure the light unit, lift it out slightly and disconnect the wiring. Release the bulb by disengaging the wire clip which retains it in the back of the reflector.

2 + Fit the new bulb, turning it to align it in the holder. Fit the retaining clip, then reconnect

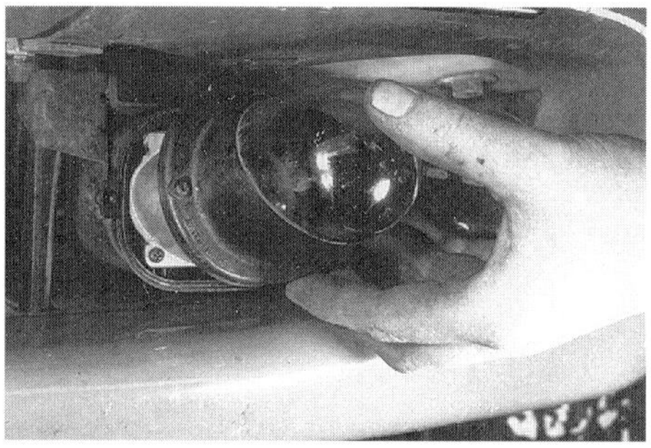

43/1a Remove outer lens ...

43/1b ...lift out light unit & disconnect wiring.

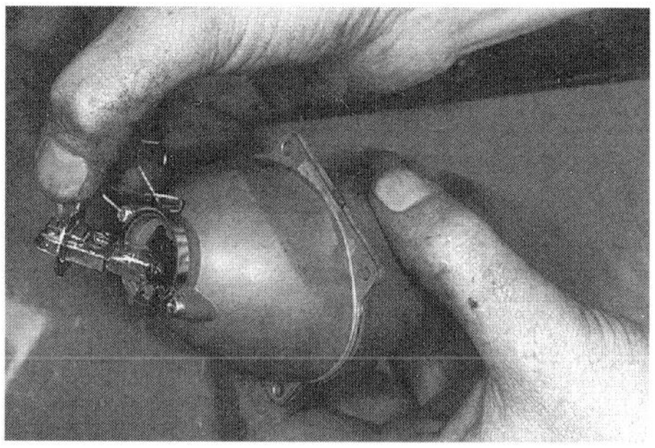

43/2a Align new bulb in its holder ...

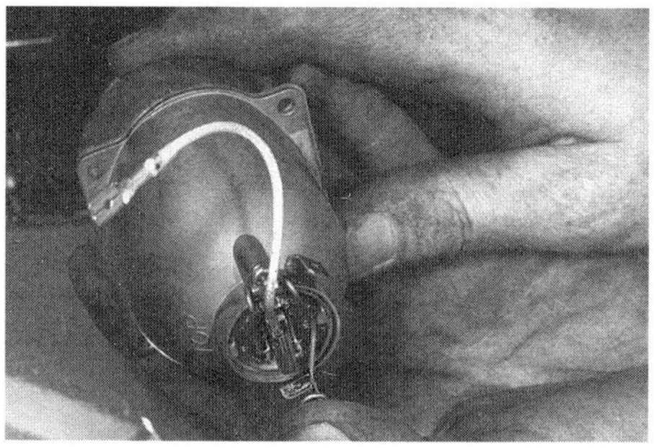

43/2b ... & secure with wire clip.

the wires to the unit. Install the unit in its casing and tighten the retaining screws evenly. Fit the outer lens assembly

44. INTERIOR LIGHTS - CHECKS & BULB REPLACEMENT

☞ 1/1, 2 & 7/2.

1 Standard Miata/MX5s have two interior lights, mounted each side of the vertical centre panel of the dash. Each unit has a three position switch, allowing it to be turned off completely, turned on manually, or operated by the two door switches. On many cars, you may find extra map reading lights added to the system. Our car had an alarm system fitted, and this had meant the fitting of an extra switch on the trunk lid. For all such accessory fitments, refer to the manufacturer's instructions for wiring details.

2 + If one of the lights is not working, the most likely cause is a burned out bulb. Check this by removing the light unit from the dash panel, using a small screwdriver to pry it out of its recess. Turn the unit over and unclip the festoon-type bulb. If it is burned out, clip a new bulb of the

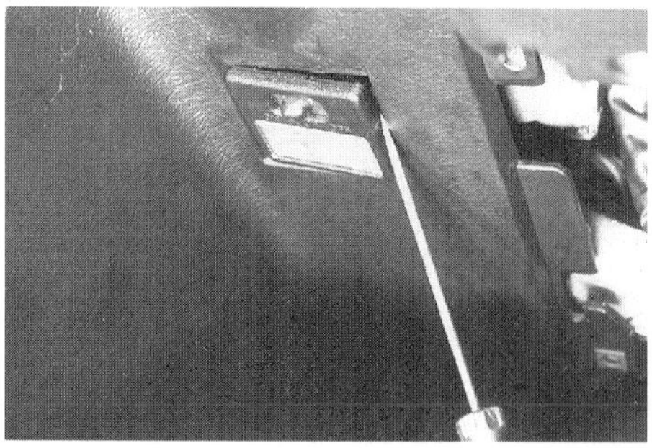

44/2a Pry light unit from dash panel ...

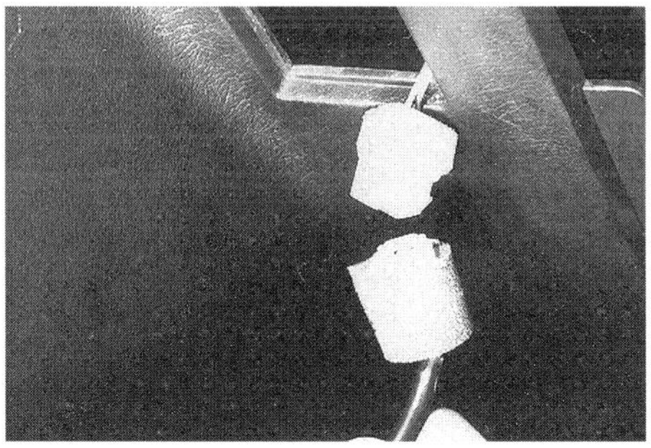

44/2b ... unplug connector ...

44/2c ... and remove festoon-type bulb.

correct rating into place.

3 If both lights are inoperative in any switch position, check the **ROOM 10A** fuse, replacing it if it is burned out. If the new fuse burns out, check the wiring between the fuse, lights and door switches, repairing or rewiring any shorted section.

4 + If the operation of the door switches is suspect, remove the switch from the car after unscrewing its mounting screw. Disconnect the switch from its wire, and check for continuity between the switch terminal and mounting plate. Continuity should exist while the switch is released,

44/4a Pin-type switch in trunk lid.

44/4b Wiring of door switch (trim removed).

with no continuity shown while it is depressed. If not as described, fit a new switch. Our photograph shows the back of the switch and its wiring with the interior trim removed. Our project car had an additional, similar switch fitted as part of the alarm system, this being fitted to the trunk lid.

Ashtray light

5 + There is a further minor interior light in the form of the ashtray light in the center console. If this is not working, check first that it is not simply obscured with cigarette ash - it is right in line for this to happen. If you need to fit a new bulb, you will

44/5a Ashtray light unit is secured by a screw.

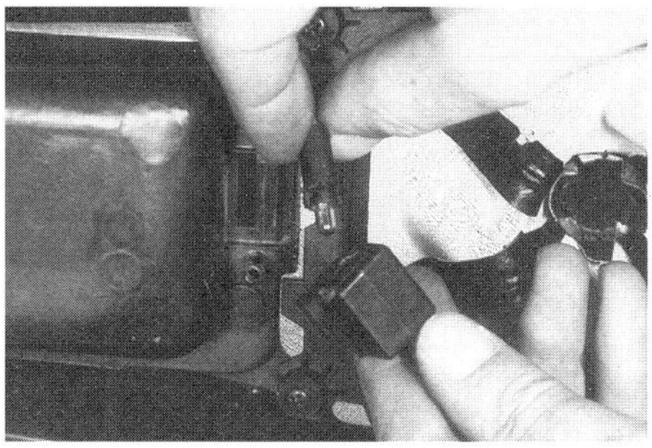

44/5b Pull out bulb holder & remove bulb.

have to remove the center console ☞ 7/13. The bulb holder is retained from the underside of the console by a single screw and a locating peg.

45. PANEL LIGHT CONTROL SWITCH - TESTING (WHERE FITTED)

☞ 1/1, 2 & 7/2.

1 The panel lighting intensity can be regulated using this rotary switch, on models so equipped. To check its operation, pop the switch control out of the dash panel (use a screwdriver blade to gently pry it out). Turn the headlight switch on, and set the panel light control switch to its Max. position, then use a voltmeter to check the terminal voltages as shown in the accompanying illustration and table.

2 Next, disconnect the panel light control switch, and use a car battery, with the positive (+) terminal connected to terminal **d** of the switch, and the battery negative (-) connected to switch terminal **g**. Connect the voltmeter positive (+) probe to the switch terminal **a**, and ground the negative (-) probe to the battery negative (-) terminal.

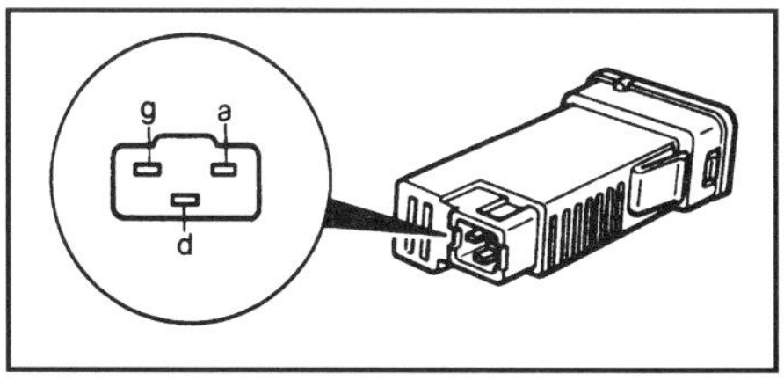

D45/2 PANEL LIGHT CONTROL SWITCH TERMINAL IDENTIFICATION.

3 Check the voltage reading on the meter. With the switch at minimum, approx. zero volts should be shown, increasing to around 10 volts at the maximum position. If this is not the case, fit a new switch unit.

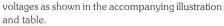

46. HORN - TESTING & REPLACEMENT

☞ 1/1, 2 & 7/2.

US SPEC CARS

Step 1

1 Check the condition of the **STOP 15A** fuse. If it has burned out, fit a new fuse and check horn operation. If the fuse burns out immediately, check the horn wiring for shorts, repairing or rewiring as necessary.

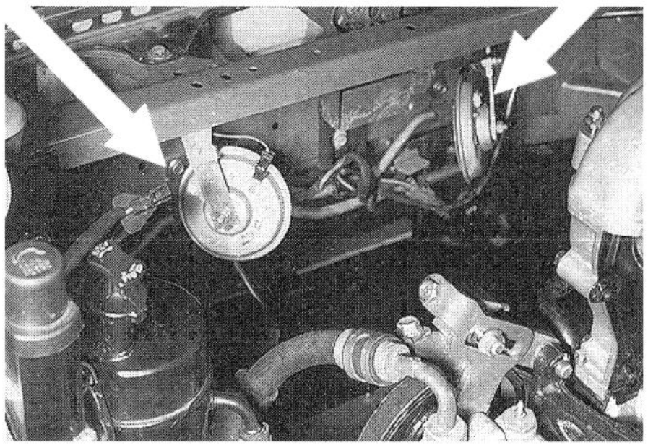

46/2 Horn location (radiator removed).

Step 2

2 Disconnect the wiring connectors from

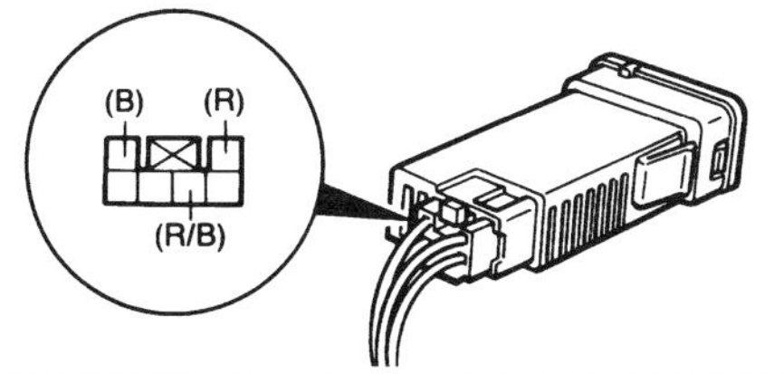

Wire	Voltage	Action
(B)	0V	Next check wire (R/B)
	Other 0V	Repair wire (B) (Panel lamp control switch — Body ground)
(R/B)	VB	Next check wire (R)
	0V	Repair wire (R/B) (TAIL 15A fuse — Panel lamp control switch)
(R)	0V	Repair wiring harness (Panel lamp control switch — Each lamp)
	Other 0V	Replace panel lamp control switch

D&T45/1 TESTING PANEL LIGHT CONTROL SWITCH CONNECTOR TERMINAL VOLTAGES.

the horn units. Using a 12 volt battery, connect the battery positive (+) terminal to the horn terminal, and ground the horn body to the battery negative (-) terminal. If the horn sounds, move to step 3. If not, fit a new horn. The horn units are each retained by a single mounting bolt in the nose of the car, and are not easy to reach with the radiator in position.

Step 3

3 Remove the access panel below the steering column and trace the horn to horn relay wire (G/O). Ground the wire and note if the horn sounds. If it does, move to Step 4. If not, skip to Step 6.

Step 4

4 **Warning!** This test requires the removal of the air bag module. This system contains an explosive charge which deploys the bag when triggered electrically. Note that triggering can take place even if the car's battery is disconnected (the system has its own backup battery). You will need to disable the air bag system by disconnecting the clock spring wiring connectors before working in this area ☞ 7/50.

5 With the air bag module removed (☞ 7/60), check for continuity between the horn switch connector and the steering column. If either horn switch is pressed, continuity should exist, with no continuity while it is released. If the switches do not work as described, they will have to be replaced along with the steering wheel as an assembly. If the switches check out OK, move to step 5.

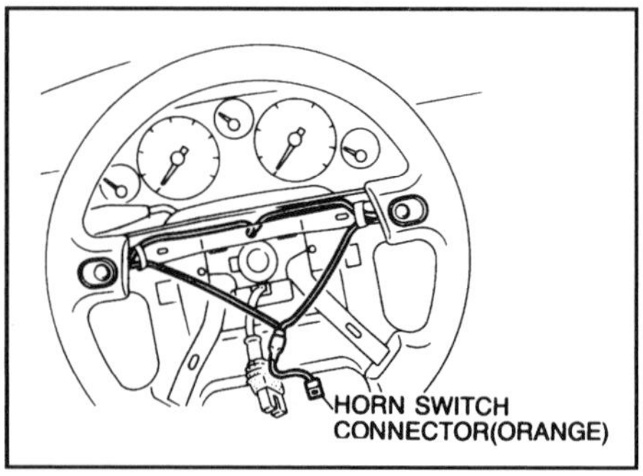

D46/5 THE HORN SWITCH CONNECTOR.

Step 5

6 Check continuity of the horn switch connector as shown in the accompanying drawing. If you read zero continuity, you will need to fit a new combination switch assembly ☞ 7/12. If continuity is shown, check and repair the (G/O) wire between the horn relay and the clock spring connector.

7 Once these checks and any repairs have been carried out, install the air bag module ☞ 7/60. Check that the air bag system is functioning correctly, as indicated by the warning light.

Step 6

8 Ground the (G/O) wire terminal at the horn relay, then check the terminal voltages as shown in the accompanying diagram and table.

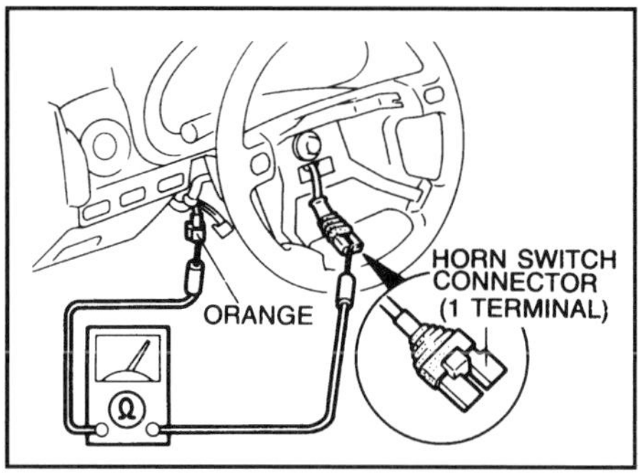

D46/6 THE HORN SWITCH CONNECTOR TERMINAL.

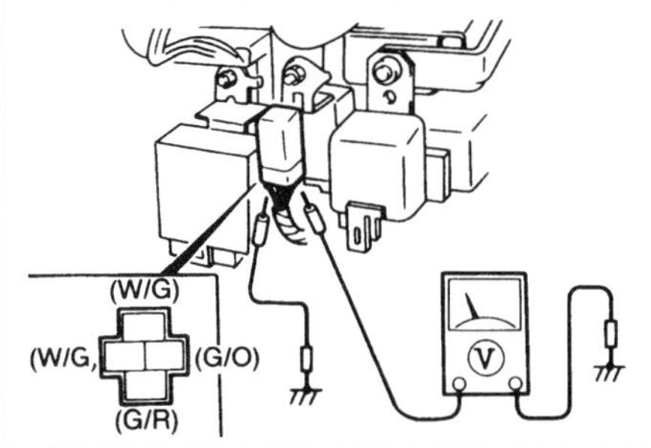

Wire	Voltage	Action
(G/W) Terminal A	VB	Next check wire (G/W) of terminal D
	0V	Repair wire (G/W) (STOP 15A fuse — Horn relay)
(G/W) Terminal D	VB	Next check wire (G/R)
	0V	Repair wire (G/W) (STOP 15A fuse — Horn relay)
(G/R)	VB	Repair wire (G/R) (Horn relay — Horn)
	0V	Replace horn relay

D&T46/8 TESTING HORN RELAY CONNECTOR TERMINAL VOLTAGES.

CANADIAN SPEC CARS

Steps 1-3

9 Follow the procedure described for US spec cars.

Step 4

10 Remove the steering wheel ☞ 8/11. Use a continuity tester or multimeter to check the operation of the switch. If defective, replace the horn switch and steering wheel as an assembly.

Step 5

11 Ground the (G/O) wire terminal at the horn relay, then check the terminal voltages as shown in Step 6 (US spec cars).

UK AND CONTINENTAL EUROPE SPEC CARS

Step 1

12 Check the condition of the **STOP 10A** fuse. If it has burned out, fit a new fuse and check horn operation. If the fuse burns out immediately, check the horn wiring for shorts, repairing or rewiring as necessary.

Step 2

13 Disconnect the wiring connector from the horn. Using a 12 volt battery, connect the battery positive (+) terminal to the horn terminal, and ground the horn body to the battery negative (-) terminal. If the horn sounds, move to Step 3. If not, fit a new horn. The horn is retained by a single mounting bolt.

Step 3

14 Use a jumper wire to ground the (G/O) wire terminal at the horn relay. If the horn sounds,

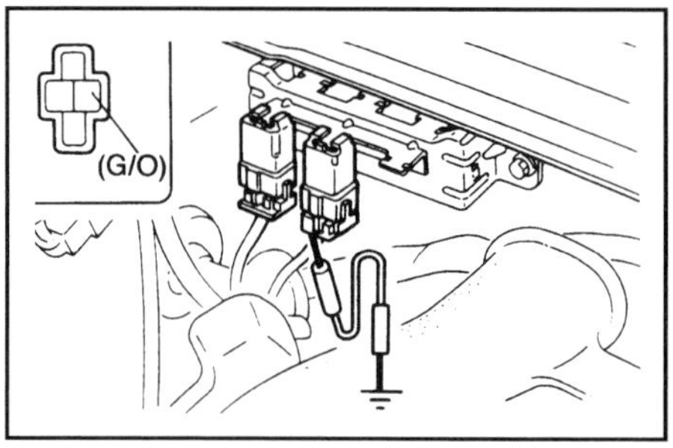

D46/14 TESTING HORN RELAY CONNECTOR.

check and repair the (G/O) wire between the horn switch and the horn relay. If the horn does not sound, move to Step 4.

Step 4

15 With the (G/O) wire terminal at the horn relay grounded as described in Step 3, measure the terminal voltages of the horn relay (wiring connected) as shown in the accompanying table and diagram.

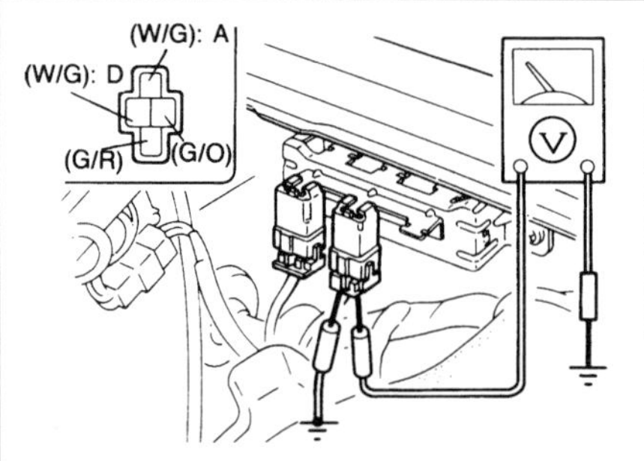

Wire	Voltage	Action
(W/G) Terminal A	12V	Next check wire (W/G) of terminal D
	0V	Repair wire (W/G) (STOP 10A fuse — Horn relay)
(W/G) Terminal D	12V	Next check wire (G/R)
	0V	Repair wire (W/G) (STOP 10A fuse — Horn relay)
(G/R)	12V	Repair wire (G/R) (Horn relay — Horn)
	0V	Replace horn relay

D&T46/15 TESTING HORN RELAY CONNECTOR TERMINAL VOLTAGES.

47. REAR WINDOW DEFROSTER - CHECKING & REPAIR (WHERE FITTED)

☞ 1/1, 2 & 7/2.

1 The rear window defroster is available as part of the factory hardtop option. The system is operated by the defroster switch (incorporated in the heater switch assembly).

2 The defroster element is connected to the electrical system from the **HEATER 30A** fuse via a 10A fuse in the secondary fuse box located in the trunk. In the event of a fault in the defroster system, follow the checking procedure described below.

Step 1

3 Check the **HEATER 30A** fuse in the main fuse box, and the **R.DEF 10A** fuse in the secondary fuse box in the trunk, near the antenna mounting. If either fuse has burned out, fit a new one of the correct rating and check the defroster. If the new fuse burns out, check back through the wiring and repair any shorted section. If the fuses are OK, move to Step 2.

Step 2

4 Remove the defroster relay from its mounting in the trunk and check for continuity between terminals 3 and 4 (see accompanying diagram for terminal identification). If continuity is found, the relay is defective and a new one must be fitted.

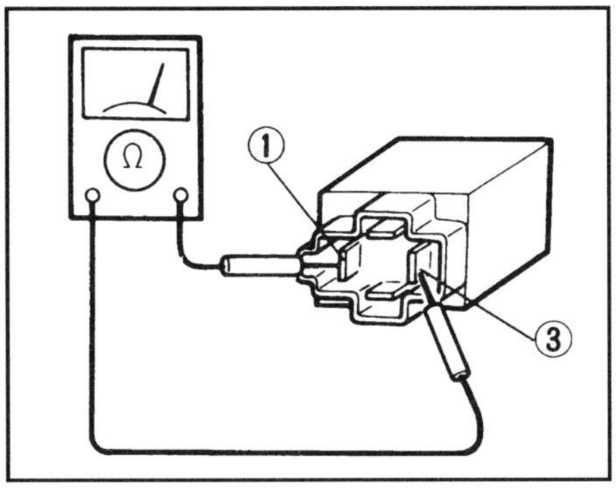

D47/4 TESTING DEFROSTER RELAY (1).

5 If no continuity is shown, connect a 12 volt car battery as follows. Connect the battery positive (+) terminal to relay terminal 1, and connect the battery negative (-) terminal to relay terminal 2. Repeat the continuity check between terminals 3 and 4. This time, continuity should be shown. If not, replace the relay. If continuity is shown and the fault persists, move to Step 3.

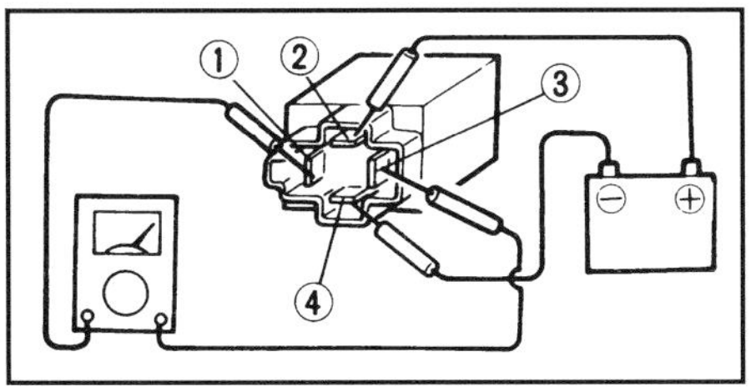

D47/5 TESTING DEFROSTER RELAY (2).

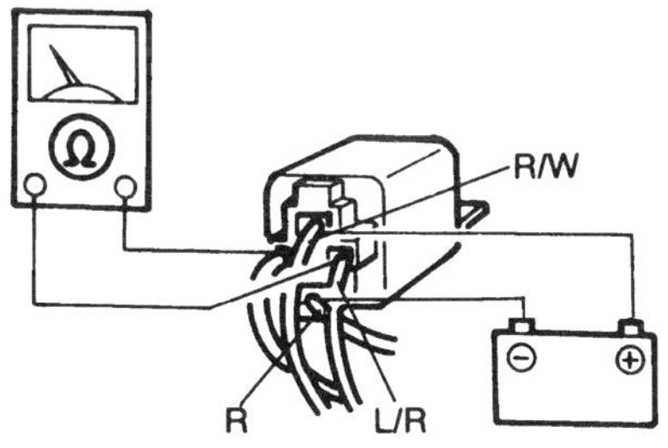

Wire	Voltage	Action
(L/B)	VB	Next, check voltage at wire (B/W)
	0V	Repair wire harness (HEATER fuse—Relay)
(R)	VB	Next, check voltage at wire (W/Y)
	0V	Repair wire harness (DEFOG fuse—Relay)
(R/W)	VB	Go to Step 4
	0V	Go to Step 5

D&T47/6 TESTING DEFROSTER RELAY CONNECTOR TERMINAL VOLTAGES.

Step 3

6 Turn on the ignition and defroster switches. With the defroster relay connected to its wiring, measure the terminal voltages as indicated in the accompanying diagram and table.

Step 4

7 Check whether the heater blower operates when set to its first position. If it does, move to Step 5. If not, check and repair as necessary the wiring between the switch assembly and the rear window defroster timer unit.

Step 5

8 Measure the voltage at the rear window defroster element connector terminals as shown in the accompanying diagram and table. If these checks fail to resolve the problem, replace the rear window defroster timer unit.

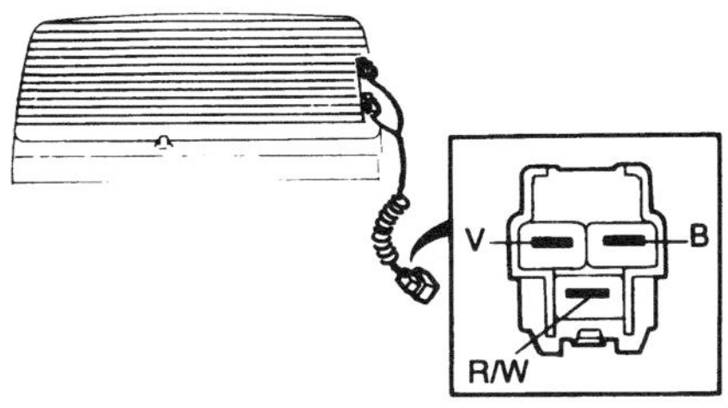

Wire	Voltage	Action
(V)	VB	Next, check voltage at wire (R/W)
	0V	Repair wiring harness (Defroster—Defroster timer unit)
(R/W)	VB	Next, check voltage at wire (B)
	0V	Repair wire harness (Relay—Defroster)
(B)	VB	Repair wire harness (Defroster—Body ground)
	0V	Repair defroster filament

D&T47/8 TESTING DEFROSTER ELEMENT CONNECTOR TERMINAL VOLTAGES.

CHECKING THE DEFROSTER ELEMENT

9 With the ignition and defroster switches turned on, check with a voltmeter the voltage at the center of each filament of the defroster element. Connect the meter negative (-) probe to ground, then touch the positive (+) probe to the center of each filament in turn.

10 Normally, you should expect a reading of around 6 volts at the filament center. If it is significantly higher than this, a short circuit is indicated. If the reading is low or zero (a more common fault) the filament may be broken.

11 Examine the filament closely, looking for signs of a break. You can confirm this by checking the voltage on each side of the suspected break - there will be a marked difference if there is a break.

REPAIRING THE DEFROSTER ELEMENT

12 If you discover a break in one of the defroster filaments, it is possible to repair it using a special conductive paint containing silver. You can get this through your Mazda dealer (Part No. 2835 77 600) or from most auto parts stores or electronic hobby shops.

13 Clean the area to be repaired with paint thinner or ethyl alcohol to remove any grease or dirt. Mask the glass on each side of the filament, then apply the paint across the break. Leave the paint to dry for at least 24 hours before using the defroster (we suggest that you remove the **R.DEF 10A** fuse to prevent accidental operation). If you're in a hurry, you can accelerate the drying process by using a hot air gun or a hairdryer to heat the area to around 60°C (140°F), in which case it will be safe to use the defroster after 30 minutes or so at this temperature. **Caution!** Don't localize the heat too much, especially in cold weather.

48. CRUISE CONTROL SYSTEM - SELF-DIAGNOSIS FUNCTION

☞ 1/1, 2 & 7/2.

1 The cruise control unit incorporates a self-diagnosis facility which can greatly reduce the time needed to pinpoint a system fault. If you experience problems with the cruise control system, you can either get your Mazda dealer to check the system for you, or you can attempt diagnosis yourself. No exotic tools are needed for this, but you need to understand how to read the self-diagnosis data. To perform the self-diagnosis procedure, you will need a 12 volt 1.4W test lamp connected to two fine probes. Don't use a bulb with a higher wattage than this or you will risk damage to the cruise control unit.

2 Locate the cruise control unit, which you'll find behind the kick panel in the passenger side footwell. Connect the test light to the cruise control unit connector terminals **f** and **d**, noting that

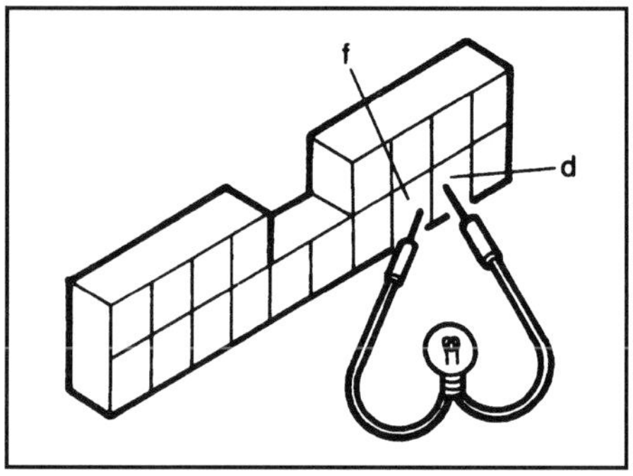

D48/2 TEST LIGHT ACROSS CRUISE CONTROL CONNECTOR TERMINALS.

the probes should be pushed gently through until they contact the terminals. (There is no terminal on the wiring connector side of the **d** terminal - you need to push the probe through until it contacts the terminal in the cruise control unit).

3 When the self-diagnosis procedure is initiated, any fault will be indicated by the test light flashing, the number of flashes, their duration and the gap between flashes denoting a fault code number, a little like morse code.

4 Codes between 01 and 09 are indicated by short flashes, each lasting 0.4 seconds, with a 0.4 second gap between them. After the flash sequence, the light will go out for an interval of 4 seconds, and the code will then repeat. If, for example, you see five short flashes followed by a four second gap, the unit is transmitting code 05.

5 Codes from 10 upward have a different flash pattern. First, the 10 digit is denoted by flashes of 1.2 seconds duration separated by a gap of 0.4 seconds. There is then an interval of 1.6 seconds before the units are transmitted as described above, and finally the cycle break interval of 4 seconds, after which the code is sent again. So, if you see two 1.2 second flashes, followed by a gap of 1.6 seconds, and then two 0.4 second flashes followed by the four second cycle break, the unit is transmitting code 22. This is easier to see in practice than to describe - refer to the accompanying diagram for a graphic representation of the last example.

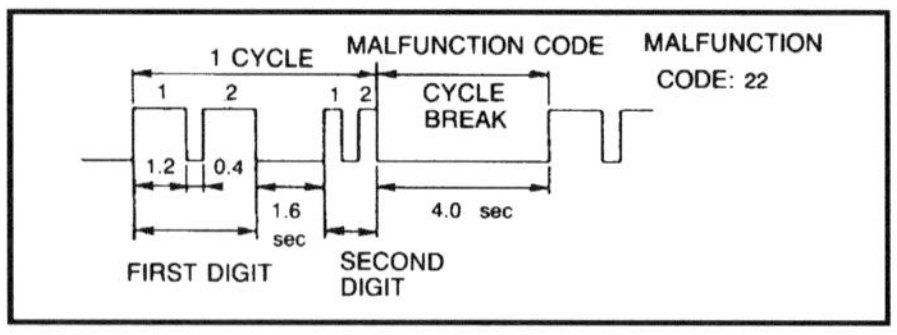

D48/5 ILLUSTRATION OF FAULT CODE.

6 Ok, that's the theory - let's give it a try. Connect up the test light and then turn on the ignition switch. Turn the cruise control system on by pressing the **MAIN** switch - the indicator light should come on. Now press and hold the **RESUME/ACCEL** control for at least three seconds. The test light should come on for 3 seconds then go out for 2 seconds, indicating that the cruise control self-diagnosis procedure has been initiated.

7 If there is a fault present, the test light will begin transmitting it in the code sequence we described above. Watch the test light and note the sequence of flashes, and then determine from this the code being sent by the unit. The code sequence will repeat, so don't worry if you don't get it first time around. Note that if there is more than one fault present, the codes will be shown in numeric sequence - *ie*. 05 first, then 09. Now, what does it all mean?

8 The fault codes, their meaning and the area(s) you need to check are described below:

Code 01 *- Indicates defective wiring between the actuator and the cruise control unit, or between the cruise control unit and the stoplight switch (check and repair the wiring). It could also indicate a defective actuator (check and replace as necessary) or a defective stoplight switch (check and replace as necessary).*

Code 05 *- Indicates STOP fuse burned out (replace) or a wiring fault between the cruise control unit and the fuse (check and repair).*

Code 07 *- Indicates that both stoplight switches are on simultaneously (check).*

Code 11 *- Indicates defective SET/COAST or RESUME/ACCEL switches (check and replace as necessary).*

Code 15 *- Indicates defective cruise control unit (check and replace if required).*

9 This next set of checks relates to the cruise control switches and sensors, and requires exactly the same test setup as the last test. Start by pressing the **MAIN** switch (indicator light should go off) to reset the cruise control system, then initiate the next test sequence by turning the ignition switch on, and operating the **MAIN** and **RESUME/ACCEL** switches simultaneously (the **MAIN** indicator light should come on). In these tests, we will be operating each of the cruise control switches in turn and looking for a specific code displayed by the test light. If the code is flashed correctly, the switch concerned is operating normally. If the light fails to flash, the switch requires attention. **Note**: On automatic transmission cars, move the shift lever to **D** or **R** before starting these tests.

10 Press the **SET/COAST** switch. The test light should send the code 21. If it fails to do so, check the cruise control switch and replace it as required ☞ 7/12.

11 Press the **RESUME/ACCEL** switch. The test light should send the code 22. If it fails to do so, check the cruise control switch and replace it as required ☞ 7/12.

12 Press down the brake pedal. The test light should send the code 31. If it fails to do so, check the stop light switches and replace them as required ☞ 7/33.

13 On automatic transmission cars, set the shift lever to **P** or **N**. The code 35 should be indicated. If this is not the case, check, adjust or replace the inhibitor switch ☞ 4/23.

14 On manual transmission cars, depress the clutch pedal. Again, code 35 should be shown. If not, check the clutch switch for continuity and replace it if defective.

15 Finally, drive the car at more than 25 mph (40kph) and check that code 37 is displayed. If it is not, the speed sensor should be checked ☞ 7/49. If this is working normally, check for faults in the wiring to the cruise control system.

16 After you have completed this diagnosis check, note that the cruise control system will be inoperative until the procedure is cancelled. This can be done by either pressing the **MAIN** switch so that the indicator light goes out, or by driving the car at more than 10 mph (16kph).

17 Using the above self-diagnosis checks, you should have some idea of where the problem lies. If you are unable to isolate the fault using this procedure, go through the full troubleshooting sequence ☞ 7/49.

49. CRUISE CONTROL SYSTEM - TROUBLESHOOTING

☞ 1/1, 2 & 7/2.

1 In this section we will be running through the full troubleshooting sequence for the cruise control system. Before stating the sequence, check that the **METER 10A** fuse which protects the system is OK. If it has burned out, fit a new fuse of the correct rating and see if the system now operates normally. If the fuse burns out again, check the associated wiring for shorts.

Step 1

2 Turn on the ignition and cruise control **MAIN** switch and verify that the indicator light comes on. If the light comes on, skip to Step 3, otherwise, move to Step 2.

Step 2

3 Using a small screwdriver, pry the cruise control main switch out of the dash panel and unplug the wiring connector. Using a continuity tester or multimeter, check continuity across the switch terminals as shown in the accompanying diagram and table. If the switch is not working as specified, fit a new one. If the switch is OK, check and repair as necessary the wiring between the switch, the **METER 10A** fuse and the switch ground

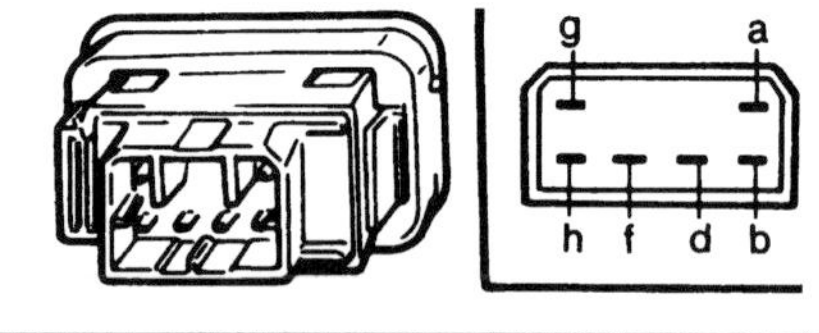

Position	Terminals a	b	d	f	g	h
Neutral			O—	—O	O—	—O
Off					O—	—O
On	O—	——	—O—	—O	O—	—O
		O—	——	—O		

O——O: Indicates continuity

D&T49/3 TESTING CRUISE CONTROL SWITCH TERMINALS CONTINUITY.

connection.

Step 3

4 Locate the cruise control unit, which you'll find behind the kick panel in the passenger side footwell. Leave the wiring connector in place, and use a multimeter to check the terminal voltages as described below, referring to the accompanying diagram for details of the terminal positions (note that these differ between automatic and manual transmission cars). Connect the meter negative (-) probe to ground, then check each wire in turn with the positive (+) probe.

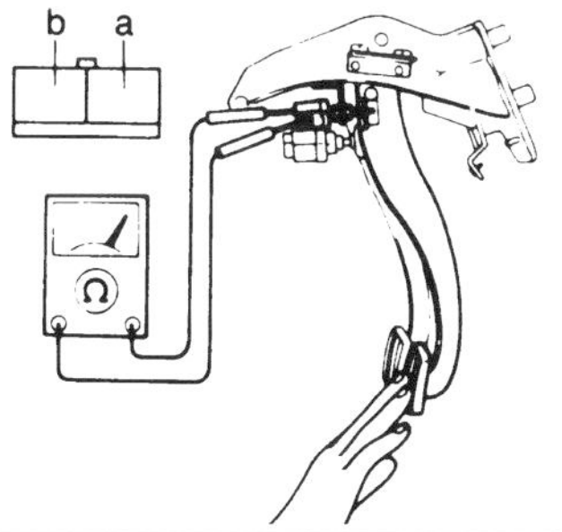

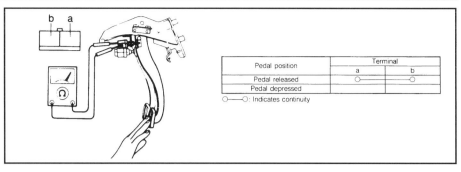

Pedal position	Terminal a	Terminal b
Pedal released	O———	———O
Pedal depressed		

O——O: Indicates continuity

D&T49/15 TESTING BRAKE LIGHT SWITCH TERMINAL CONTINUITY.

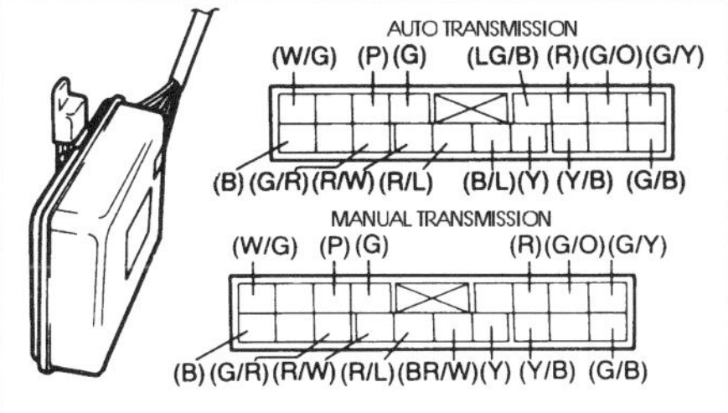

D49/4 CRUISE CONTROL CONNECTOR TERMINAL IDENTIFICATION.

5 **Terminal a (G/Y) - Actuator:** With the cruise control main switch off, zero volts should be read. With the switch on, you should read 9 volts. If the readings are other than these, check the actuator as follows.

6 Working in the engine compartment, trace and separate the actuator wiring connector. Use an ohmmeter or multimeter to check the actuator solenoid resistances according to the accompanying diagram and table.

7 If the resistances are not as shown, fit a new actuator. If the resistances check out OK, disconnect the actuator cable at the accelerator pedal, start the engine and allow it to idle.

8 Using a spare battery, apply battery voltage to the terminals indicated in the accompanying diagram and table and check that the actuator responds as indicated. If it does not work as shown, fit a new actuator.

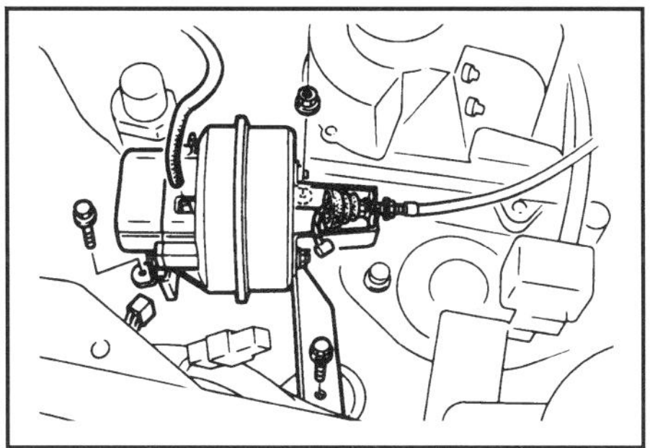

D49/9B ACTUATOR REMOVAL.

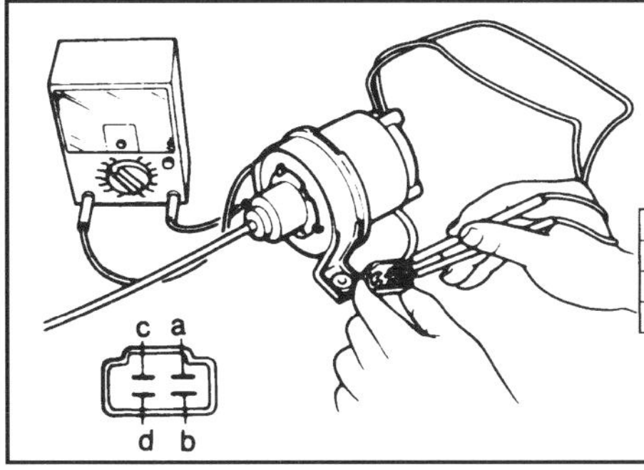

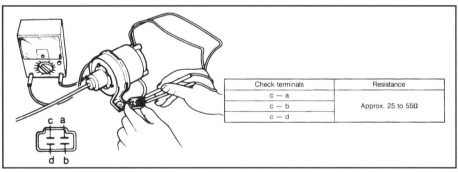

Check terminals	Resistance
c — a	Approx. 25 to 55Ω
c — b	
c — d	

D&T49/6 TESTING ACTUATOR SOLENOID TERMINAL RESISTANCES.

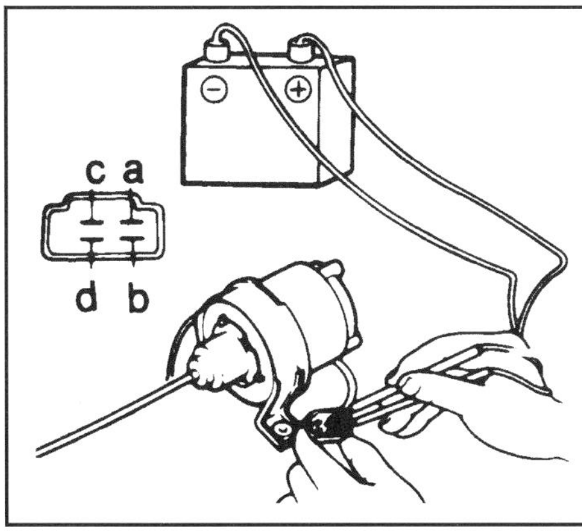

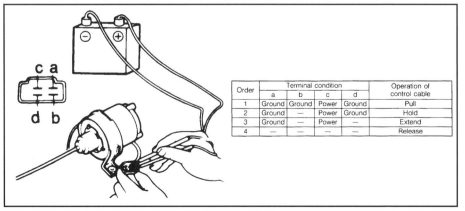

Order	Terminal condition a	b	c	d	Operation of control cable
1	Ground	Ground	Power	Ground	Pull
2	Ground	—	Power	Ground	Hold
3	Ground	—	Power	—	Extend
4	—	—	—	—	Release

D&T49/9A TESTING EFFECT OF BATTERY VOLTAGE ON ACTUATOR TERMINALS.

9 + Disconnect the cable from the actuator and pry off the vacuum hose. Remove the two bolts and single nut which retain the actuator assembly and lift it away. When installing the new unit, adjust the cable free play to 1-3 mm (0.04-0.12 in) and check that the vacuum hose is reconnected.

10 **Terminal b (G/B) - Actuator:** With the cruise control main switch off, zero volts should be read. With the switch on, you should read 9 volts. If the readings are other than these, check the actuator as described above.

11 **Terminal c (G/O) - Actuator:** With the cruise control main switch off, zero volts should be read. With the switch on, you should read 9 volts. If the readings are other than these, check the actuator as described above.

12 **Terminal e (R) - MAIN switch:** With the cruise control main switch off, zero volts should be read. With the switch on, you should read 12 volts. If the readings are other than these, check the (R) wire between the cruise control unit and main switch and repair or rewire as necessary.

13 **Terminal f (Y/B) - MAIN switch:** With the cruise control main switch off, zero volts should be read. With the switch on, you should read 12 volts. If the readings are other than these, check the (Y/B) wire between the cruise control unit and main switch and repair or rewire as necessary.

14 **Terminal g (LG/B) - AT control unit:** With the ignition switch off, zero volts should be read. With the switch on, you should read 12 volts. If the readings are other than these, check the AT control unit by substituting a new one, or have the unit checked out by a Mazda dealer.

15 **Terminal h (Y) - Brake switch:** With the brake pedal depressed, zero volts should be read. With the pedal released, you should read 9 volts. If the readings are other than these, check the switch for continuity after disconnecting the switch wiring. Continuity should be shown while the pedal is released, with zero continuity when it is depressed. If not as described, fit a new switch.

16 **Terminal j (B/L) - Inhibitor switch (automatic transmission cars):** With **N** or **P** selected, zero volts should be read. In any other position, you should read 5 volts. If the readings are other than these, check the inhibitor switch 7/9.

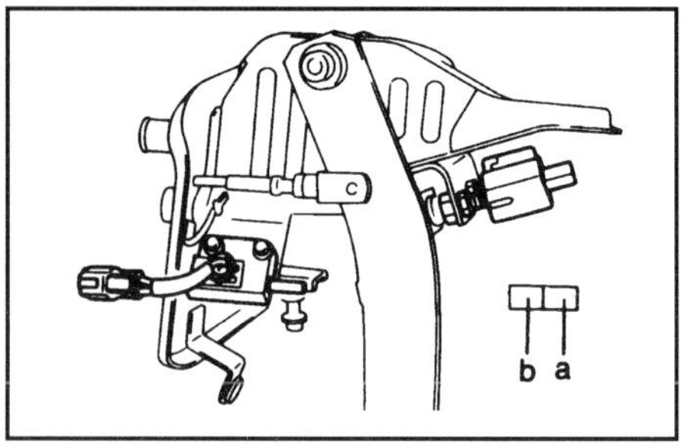

D49/17 TESTING CLUTCH SWITCH TERMINAL CONTINUITY.

17 **Terminal j (BR/W) - Clutch switch (manual transmission cars):** With the clutch pedal depressed, zero volts should be read. With the pedal released, you should read 12 volts. If the readings are other than these, check the switch for continuity after disconnecting the switch wiring. Continuity should be shown while the pedal is depressed, with zero continuity when it is released. If not as described, fit a new switch.

18 **Terminal l (R/L) - Cruise control switch (SET and COAST switches):** With the **MAIN** switch on, 12 volts should be read. Leave the **MAIN** switch on, and then turn on the **SET** switch. The reading should drop back to zero volts.

19 If not as described, remove the knee protector panel and disconnect the combination switch wiring connector. Use a continuity tester or multimeter to check the switch terminal continuity as shown in the accompanying diagram and table. If the switch is defective, fit a new one. If it checks out OK, check back for wiring damage or shorts between the switch and the cruise control unit.

20 **Terminal m (G) - Stoplight switch:** With the brake pedal depressed, 12 volts should be read. With the pedal released, you should read zero volts. If the readings are other than these, check the switch for continuity after disconnecting the switch wiring. No continuity should be shown while the pedal is released, with continuity indicated when it is depressed. If not as described, fit a new switch.

21 **Terminal n (R/W) - Cruise control switch (RESUME and ACCEL switches):** With the **MAIN** switch on, 12 volts should be read. Leave the **MAIN** switch on, and then turn on the **RESUME** switch. The reading should drop back to zero volts.

22 (see D&T49/19) If not as described, remove the knee protector panel and disconnect the combination switch wiring connector. Use a continuity tester or multimeter to check the switch terminal continuity as shown in the accompanying diagram and table. If the switch is defective, fit a new one. If it checks out OK, check back for wiring damage or shorts between the switch and the cruise control unit.

23 **Terminal o (P) - Actuator:** With the cruise control MAIN switch off, zero volts should be read. With the switch on, you should read 9 volts. If the readings are other than these, check the actuator as described above.

24 **Terminal p (G/R) - Speed sensor:** If you have access to a rolling road, check that while the rear wheels are turning, the voltage reading alternates between zero and 5 volts (or drive the car slowly and have an assistant check the voltage readings for you).

25 If the results are not as indicated, remove the instrument panel ☞ 7/14. Connect a continuity tester or multimeter between terminals **2f** and **2d** of the instrument panel wiring connector. Using a small screwdriver, turn the speedometer drive shaft and verify that continuity is indicated four times during each revolution of the shaft. If not, you will have to fit a new sensor. We are not certain about this, but it would appear that the sensor is supplied as part of the speedometer assembly - check this with you local Mazda dealer.

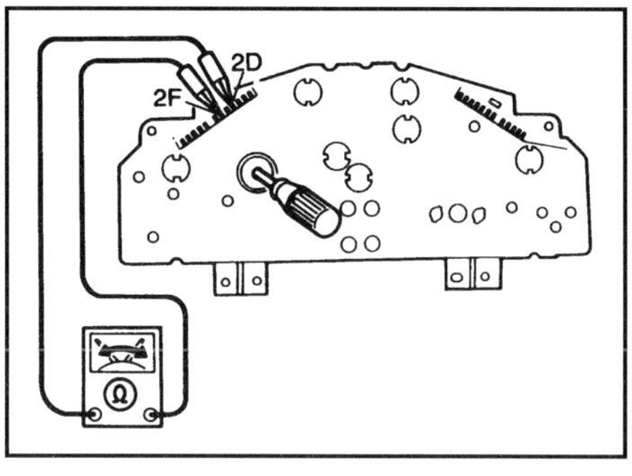

D49/25 TESTING THE SPEEDO SPEED SENSOR.

26 **Terminal s (W/G) - Battery:** Check for battery voltage (12 volts) between the (W/G) wire terminal and ground. If not as described, check the (W/G) wire back to the **STOP 15A** fuse and repair or rewire as necessary.

27 **Terminal t (B) - Ground:** Check for continuity between this terminal and a chassis ground. If continuity is not shown, repair or rewire terminal t to restore the ground connection.

50. AIR BAG SYSTEM - DESCRIPTION & WORKING PROCEDURES

☞ 1/1, 2 & 7/2.

DESCRIPTION

1 On models equipped with this system, an air bag module mounted on the steering wheel provides the driver with additional crash protection. The system is operated by sensors at the front of the vehicle. In the event of frontal impact, the 'S' sensor and any one of the three 'D' sensors combine to trigger the air bag.

2 The air bag is fired by an explosive charge in response to an electrical trigger signal. This signal is normally provided by the vehicle's electrical system, but in the event of fuse or wiring damage during the impact, a backup battery mounted under the diagnostic module is sufficient to trigger deployment. The diagnostic module monitors the air bag system and warns the driver of malfunctions through a warning light in the instrument panel.

WORKING PROCEDURES

3 **Warning!** The air bag system is operated by an explosive charge and is potentially dangerous if triggered accidentally. Note that before attempting any work on the system, you should deactivate the stereo security system, then disconnect the battery negative (-) lead to isolate the car's electrical system. You must also disconnect the clock spring connectors below the steering column to isolate the air bag module from the backup battery. The clock spring connectors are colored orange and blue and are interlocked. You need to disconnect the smaller orange connector before it is possible to unplug the blue connector. Failure to observe these precautions could result in personal injury.

4 **Warning!** Under no circumstances attempt

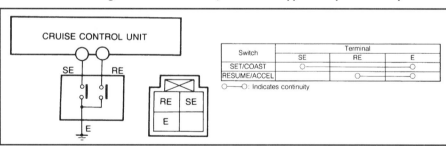

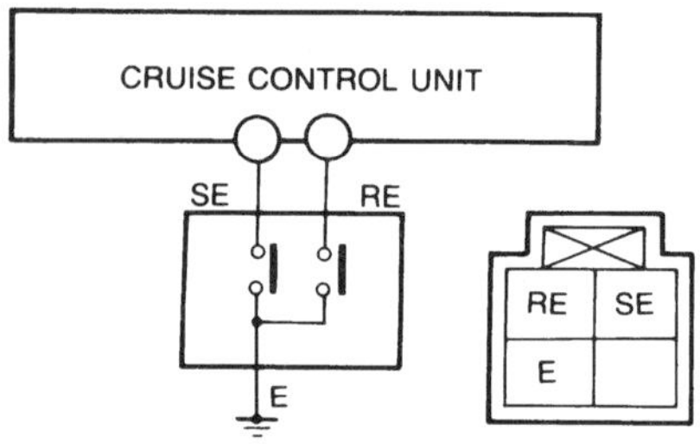

Switch	Terminal SE	Terminal RE	Terminal E
SET/COAST	○		○
RESUME/ACCEL		○	○

○——○: Indicates continuity

D&T49/19 & D&T49/22 TESTING COMBINATION SWITCH CONNECTOR TERMINALS CONTINUITY.

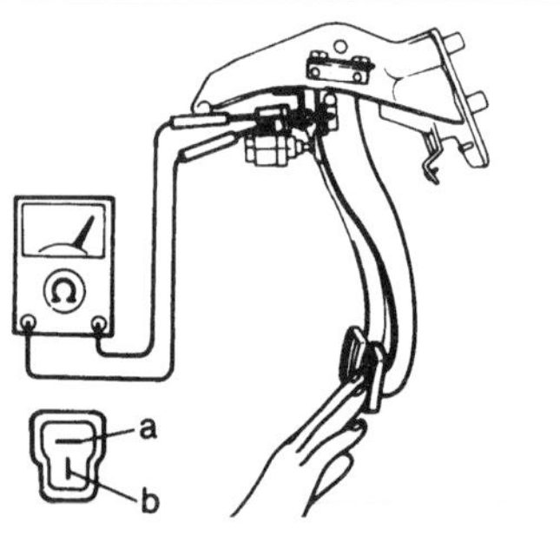

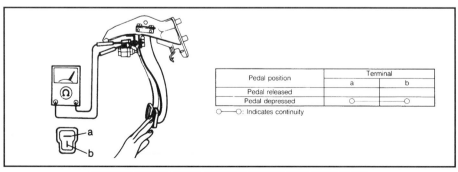

Pedal position	Terminal a	Terminal b
Pedal released		
Pedal depressed	○	○

○——○: Indicates continuity

D&T49/20 TESTING BRAKE LIGHT SWITCH TERMINAL CONTINUITY.

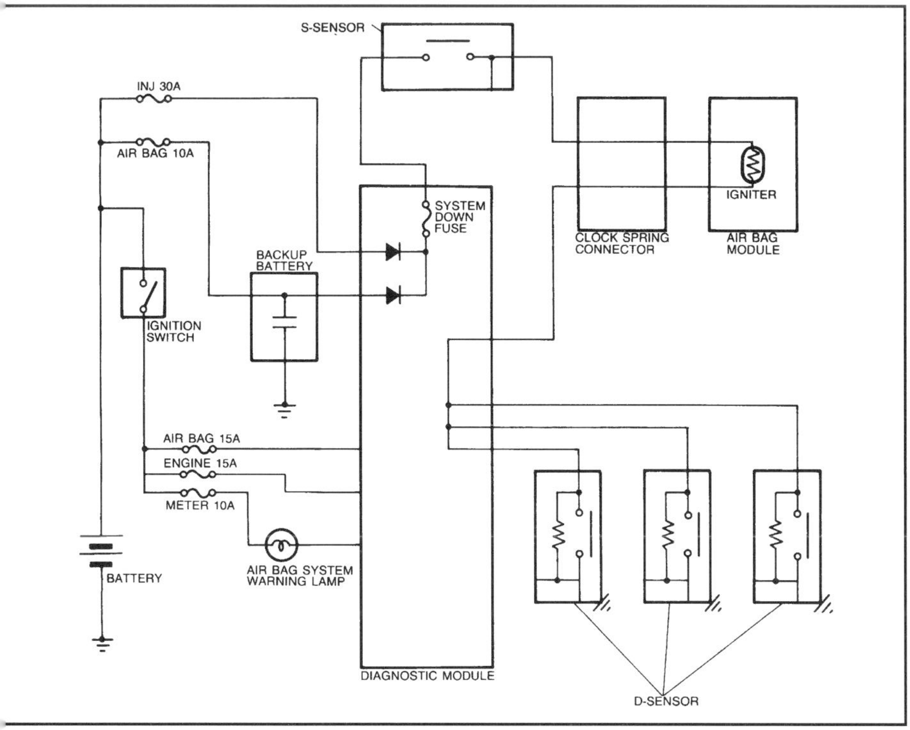

D50/2 THE AIRBAG ELECTRICAL SYSTEM.

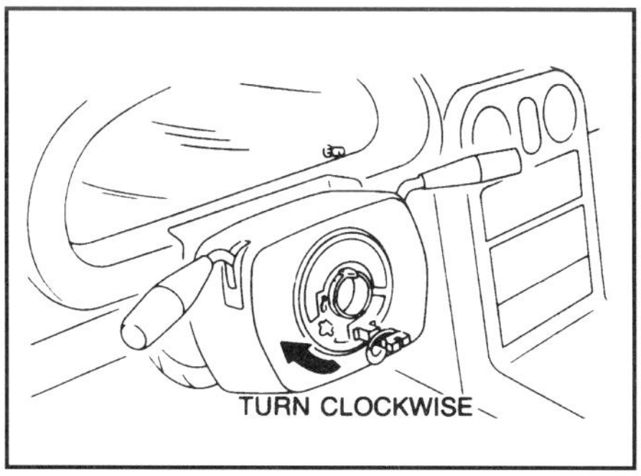

D50/12A TURN CLOCK SPRING CONNECTOR CLOCKWISE UNTIL IT STOPS ...

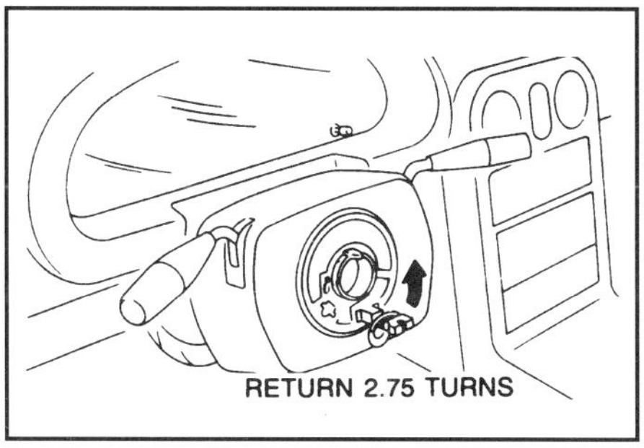

D50/12B ... TURN THE CONNECTOR ANTICLOCKWISE EXACTLY 2.75 TURNS ...

o dismantle the air bag module or any other ystem component. If a fault is diagnosed, replace he component as an assembly.

5 **Warning!** Under no circumstances attempt o repair damaged wiring. If a damaged wire or erminal is discovered, replace the affected harness ection.

6 **Warning!** Under no circumstances attempt o diagnose faults on the air bag module using an hmmeter or multimeter. These could generate nough current to trigger the explosive charge.

7 **Warning!** When handling a live air bag nodule, do so with the trim side away from you to ninimize injury in the event of accidental deploy-nent. Place the module with the trim side facing ıpward - this will prevent the module being thrown nto the air if accidentally deployed.

8 **Warning!** If you have reason to handle a leployed air bag module, be aware that it contains odium hydroxide deposits. This substance is a esidue produced by the gas-generating combus-ion process and is caustic. Always wear appropri-te clothing (gloves, coveralls and safety glasses) vhen handling a deployed air bag.

9 **Warning!** When disposing of a deployed ir bag, do so in a responsible manner. Seek advice rom your local authority about the best way to deal afely with this task, or ask your Mazda dealer to rrange disposal for you.

10 **Warning!** In addition to the major safety precautions outlined above, note following proce-dures which **must** be adhered to when working on he air bag system.

CRASH SENSORS

11 The crash sensors are extremely sensi-ive to correct alignment during installation. In the

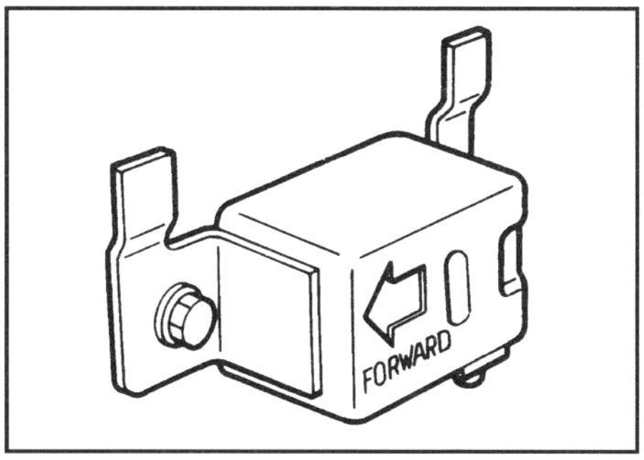

D50/11 A CRASH SENSOR UNIT.

event of any accident damage to the bodywork, even if the air bag did not deploy, the sensors should be checked carefully during repair work. Always disconnect the car's battery and the clock spring connectors before disturbing the sensors (see above). If the sensor mounting area is de-formed, detach the sensor and repair the body damage, then reinstall the sensor, taking note of fitting direction markings. Make sure that the mount-ing area is clean and that there is a good ground contact with the mounting bolts, or the sensor may not work in the event of an accident.

CLOCK SPRING CONNECTOR ADJUSTMENT

12 + If the steering wheel is removed, it is essential that the clock spring connector is adjusted correctly during installation or the connector may not work correctly or be damaged. With the front wheels facing straight ahead, turn the clock spring connector gently clockwise until it stops (do not force it past the stop or you will damage it). Turn the connector counterclockwise by exactly 2.75 turns.

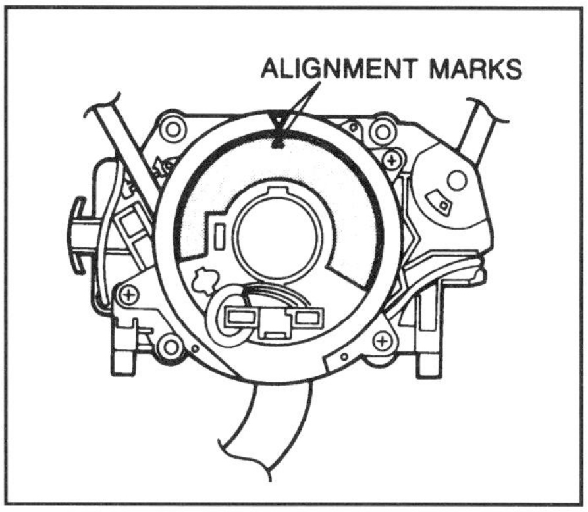

D50/12C ... ALIGN MARKS ON CONNECTOR & HOUSING.

Check that the marks are at the top of the connec-tor and its housing align - adjust if necessary.

SYSTEM CHECK AFTER REPAIR WORK

13 Whenever the air bag system has been worked on, check that the instrument panel warn-ing light indicates that the system is functioning normally. The light should come on for around six seconds each time the ignition is switched on, and then go out. If the light fails to go out or flashes, there is a problem with the system. If the light does not come on, check for a burned out fuse, wiring damage or a burned out warning light bulb.

14 Check also that the horn operates after disturbing the air bag module. If it does not, isolate the car's battery and disconnect the clock spring connectors to disable the air bag system, remove the air bag module and check the horn wiring connections.

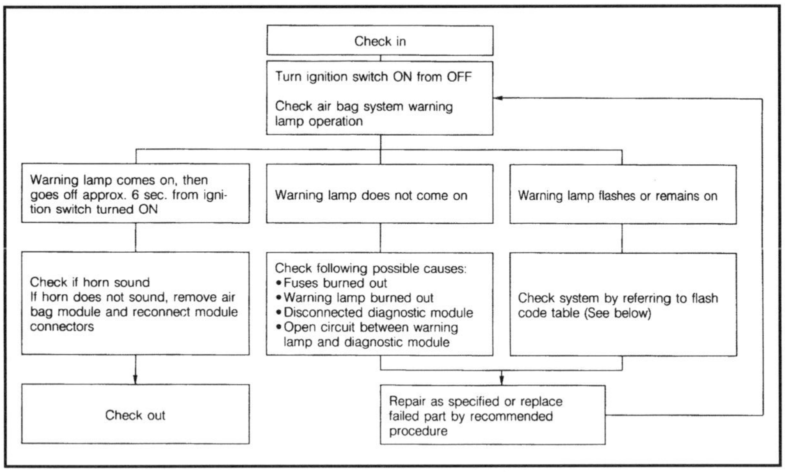

D51/2 AIR BAG SYSTEM TROUBLESHOOTING FLOWCHART.

Priority	Flash code	Possible cause
1	Remains ON	Faulty diagnostic module or poor connection of diagnostic module connector
2	Flashes three times	Open circuit or poor connection of power source circuit
3	Flashes five times	Faulty D-sensor (D-sensor remains ON)
4	Flashes ten times	Faulty diagnostic module (System-down fuse burned)
5	Flashes four times	Faulty S-sensor
6	Flashes six times	Faulty air bag module or poor connection of clock spring connector
7	Flashes seven times	Poor ground of wiring harness
8	Flashes eight times	Poor ground of D-sensor
9	Flashes nine times	Open circuit between diagnostic module and D-sensor
10	Flashes two times	Poor ground of all D-sensors

T51/2 AIR BAG FLASH CODE TABLE.

51. AIR BAG SYSTEM - TROUBLESHOOTING

☞ 1/1, 2 & 7/2 & 7/50.

1 **Warning! Before attempting any work on the system, read carefully precautions and working procedures** ☞ 7/50. Follow the diagnosis sequence described below until you identify the specific fault and repair or replace components and wiring as indicated. Note that if there is more than one fault, these will be indicated in order of priority. Note also that if an audible alarm is heard when the ignition switch is turned on, a simultaneous warning lamp failure and air bag system fault is indicated; check the warning lamp bulb and replace it if required, before continuing the checks.

PRELIMINARY CHECKS

2 Preliminary checks should be carried out as described by the accompanying flowchart:

3 Once the flash code has been identified, refer to the appropriate section for detailed diagnostic and repair information.

52. AIR BAG SYSTEM FAULT - WARNING LAMP REMAINS ON

☞ 1/1, 2 & 7/2 & 7/50.

Probable cause: fault in diagnostic module or poor wiring connection to module.

1 Disconnect the battery negative (-) lead to isolate the electrical system. Remove the knee protector and disconnect the orange and blue clock spring connectors ☞ 7/50.

2 Check that the wiring connectors to the air bag system diagnostic module are secure, then reconnect the air bag system clock spring connectors and battery negative (-) lead and recheck the system. If the fault persists, fit a new diagnostics module.

53. AIR BAG SYSTEM FAULT - WARNING LAMP FLASHES 3 TIMES

☞ 1/1, 2 & 7/2 & 7/50.

Probable cause: fault in power supply to system.

1 Disconnect the battery negative (-) lead to isolate the electrical system. Use a voltmeter to measure battery voltage. If below 9 volts, check and charge the battery (☞ 7/5). If battery voltage is above 9 volts, proceed as described below.

2 Check the **INJ 30A** and **AIR BAG 10A** fuses in the main fuse block in the engine compartment. Check the **AIR BAG 15A** and **ENGINE 15A** fuses in fuse box No. 1 (under dash panel). If any fuses are burned out, replace them and check the system again. If the fuse(s) fail again, check the associated wiring for a short to ground. If the fuses ar OK, proceed as follows.

3 Disconnect the battery negative (-) lead to isolate the electrical system. Remove the knee protector and disconnect the orange and blue clock spring connectors ☞ 7/50. Check the connection to the backup battery below the diagnostic module.

4 If the backup battery connection is OK unplug the wiring connector and temporarily reconnect the vehicle battery. Check the voltage between the backup battery connector (G/R) wire and ground - battery voltage should be indicated. If zero volts are shown, replace the wiring harness to the backup battery.

5 Disconnect the vehicle battery negative (-) terminal to isolate the electrical system. Unplug the diagnostic module connectors, and temporarily reconnect the vehicle battery. Refer to the accompanying diagram and table, and check the terminal voltages as indicated.

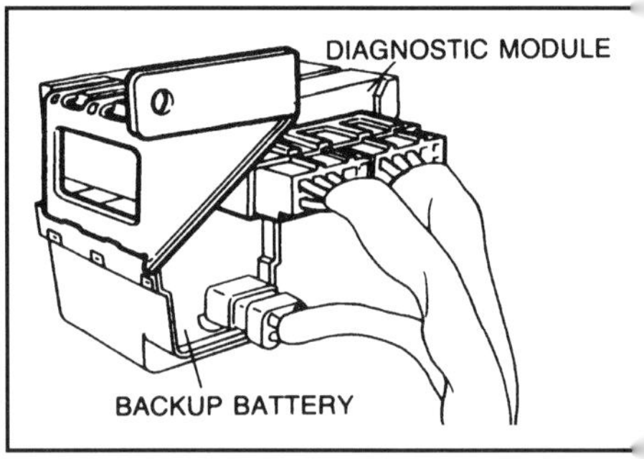

D53/3 CONNECTION TO BACK-UP BATTERY.

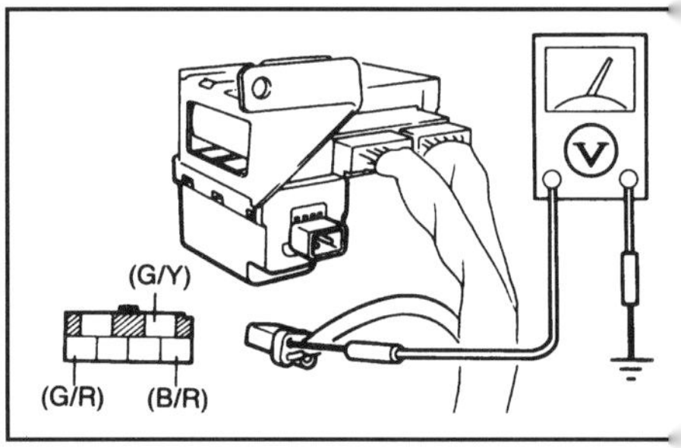

D53/4 TESTING CONNECTOR TERMINAL VOLTAGE.

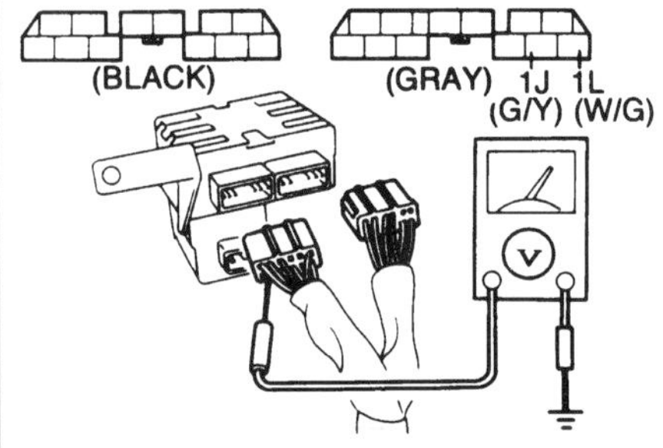

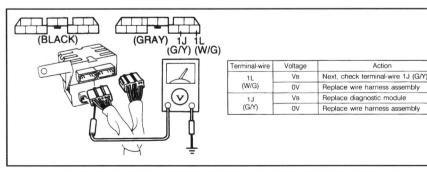

Terminal-wire	Voltage	Action
1L (W/G)	VB	Next, check terminal-wire 1J (G/Y)
	0V	Replace wire harness assembly
1J (G/Y)	VB	Replace diagnostic module
	0V	Replace wire harness assembly

D&T53/5 TESTING DIAGNOSTIC MODULE CONNECTOR TERMINAL VOLTAGES.

54. AIR BAG SYSTEM FAULT - WARNING LAMP FLASHES 5 OR 9 TIMES

☞ 1/1, 2 & 7/2 & 7/50.

robable cause: faulty 'D' sensor.

Disconnect the battery negative (-) lead to solate the electrical system. Remove the knee rotector and disconnect the orange and blue lock spring connectors ☞ 7/50.

Disconnect the three 'D' sensor connec- or (**LH**, **CNT** and **RH**) and measure the resistance f each unit. The correct resistance figure is ap- roximately 1.2 k . If significantly outside this gure, replace the sensor.

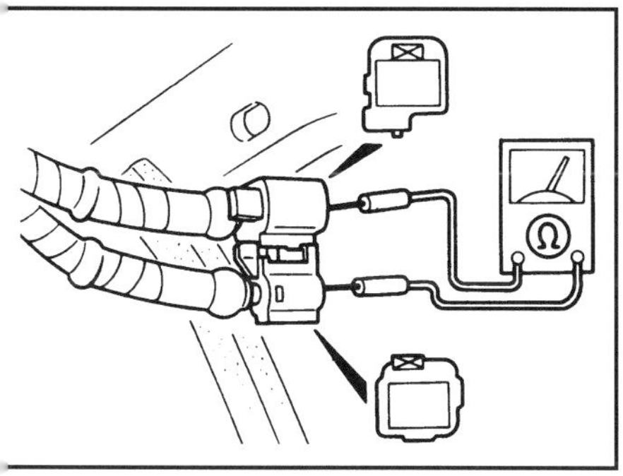

D54/2 & D55/2 TESTING 'D' SENSOR RESISTANCE.

If the sensor resistances were cor- ect, reconnect their wiring connectors and discon- ect the diagnostic module connectors. Check the esistances of the connector terminals as shown in e accompanying diagram and table.

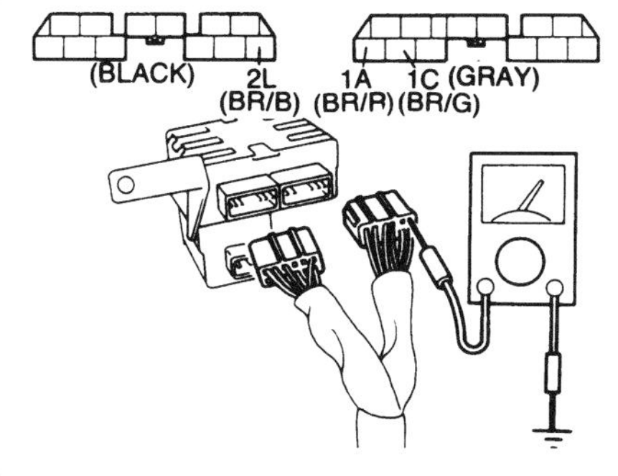

Terminal-wire	Resistance	Action
1C (BR/G)	Approx. 1.2 kΩ	Next, check terminal-wire 1A (BR/R)
	Other 1.2 kΩ	Replace wire harness
1A (BR/R)	Approx. 1.2 kΩ	Next, check terminal-wire 2L (BR/B)
	Other 1.2 kΩ	Replace wire harness
2L (BR/B)	Approx. 1.2 kΩ	Replace diagnostic module
	Other 1.2 kΩ	Replace wire harness

D&T54/3 & D&T55/3 TESTING DIAGNOSTIC MODULE CONNECTOR TERMINAL RESISTANCES.

55. AIR BAG SYSTEM FAULT - WARNING LAMP FLASHES 10 TIMES

☞ 1/1, 2 & 7/2 & 7/50.

robable cause: faulty diagnostic module SYSTEM DOWN fuse burned out).

Disconnect the battery negative (-) lead to olate the electrical system. Remove the knee rotector and disconnect the orange and blue lock spring connectors ☞ 7/50.

(see D54/2) Disconnect the three 'D' ensor connector (**LH**, **CNT** and **RH**) and measure e resistance of each unit. Correct resistance is pproximately 1.2 k . If significantly outside this figure, replace the sensor, then skip to *paragraph 4*. If the sensors are OK, move on to *paragraph 3*.

3 (see D&T54/3) If the sensor resistances are correct, reconnect their wiring connectors and disconnect the diagnostic module connectors. Check the resistances of the connector terminals as shown in the accompanying diagram and table.

4 Reconnect the diagnostic module wiring, the clock spring connector wiring and the battery negative (-) terminal. Turn on the ignition switch and monitor the warning lamp. If it flashes 10 times again, replace the diagnostic module.

56. AIR BAG SYSTEM FAULT - WARNING LAMP FLASHES 4 TIMES

☞ 1/1, 2 & 7/2 & 7/50.

Probable cause: faulty 'S' sensor.

1 Disconnect the battery negative (-) lead to isolate the electrical system. Remove the knee protector and disconnect the orange and blue clock spring connectors ☞ 7/50.

2 Disconnect the diagnostic module connectors. Refer to the accompanying diagram for details of terminal positions, and check for continuity between the two (G/W) wire terminals **2B** and **2D**. If no continuity is shown, replace the diagnostic module wiring harness. If continuity is found, leave the wiring connectors off and move to *paragraph 3*.

3 Refer to the accompanying diagram for details of terminal positions, and check for continuity between the **1E** wire terminal of the wiring connectors and a chassis ground point. If continuity is shown, move to *paragraph 4*. If there is no continuity, skip to *paragraph 6*.

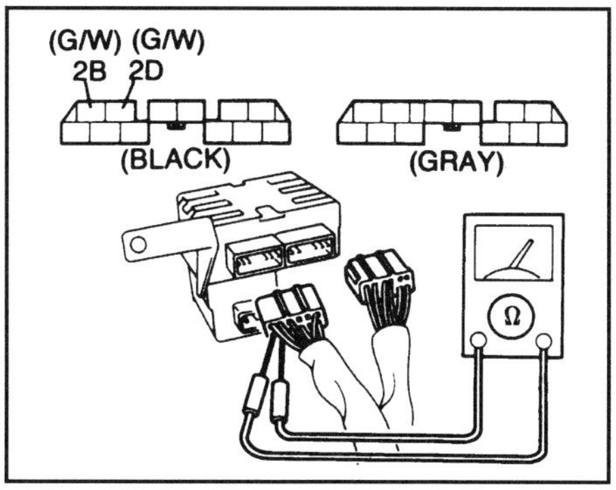

D56/2 TESTING DIAGNOSTIC MODULE CONNECTOR TERMINAL CONTINUITY.

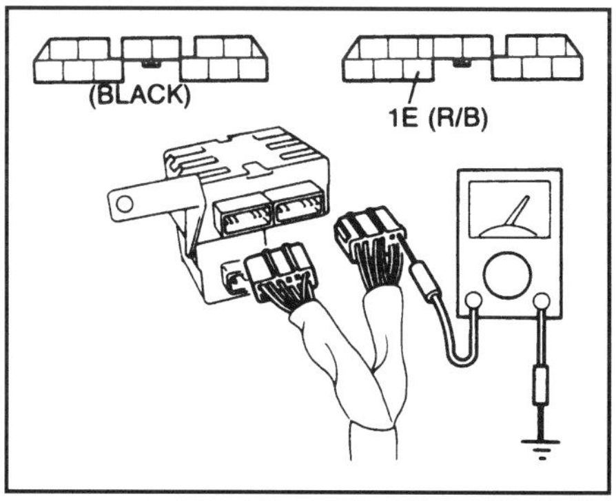

D56/3 TESTING CONNECTOR TERMINAL/GROUND CONTINUITY.

4 Refer to the accompanying diagram for details of terminal positions, and check for continuity between the **1H** (G/B) and **2C** (G) wire terminals of the wiring connectors. If continuity is shown, skip down to *paragraph 8*. If there is no continuity, move to *paragraph 5*.

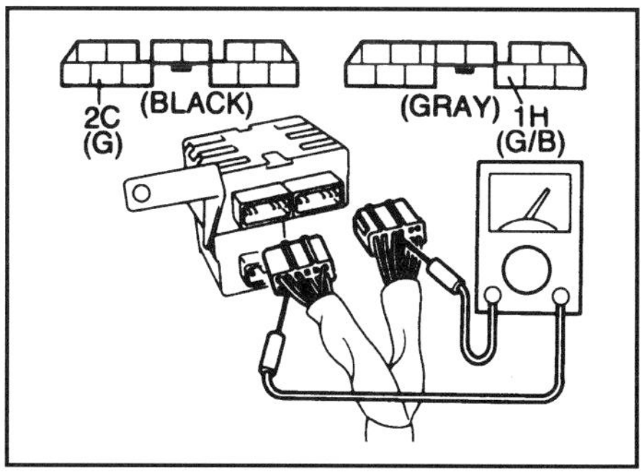

D56/4 TESTING DIAGNOSTIC MODULE CONNECTOR TERMINAL CONTINUITY.

5 Disconnect the 'S' sensor wiring connectors. Refer to the accompanying diagram for details of terminal positions, and check for continuity between the **(b)** and **(e)** wire terminals of the wiring connectors. If continuity is shown, replace the wiring harness. If there is no continuity, replace the 'S' sensor.

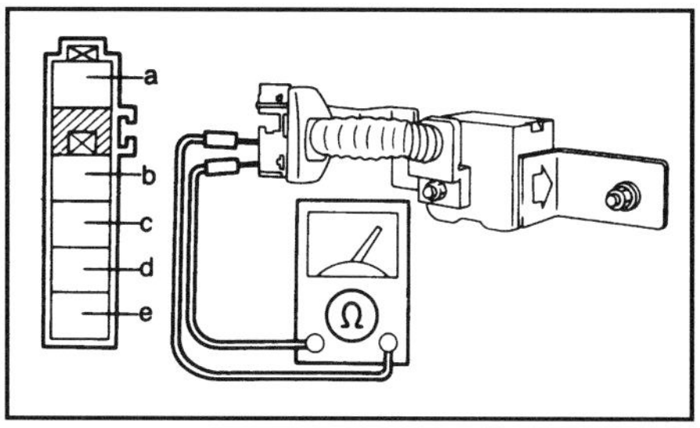

D56/5 TESTING 'S' SENSOR TERMINAL CONTINUITY.

6 Check the security of the 'S' sensor mounting, making sure that there is good contact between the sensor and ground through the mounting bracket and bolt. Clean the area with abrasive

7

paper, and check that the mounting bolts are tightened securely.

7 Disconnect the 'S' sensor wiring connectors. Refer to the accompanying diagram for details of terminal positions, and check for continuity between the sensor connector **(a)** wire terminal. If continuity is shown, replace the wiring harness. If there is no continuity, replace the 'S' sensor.

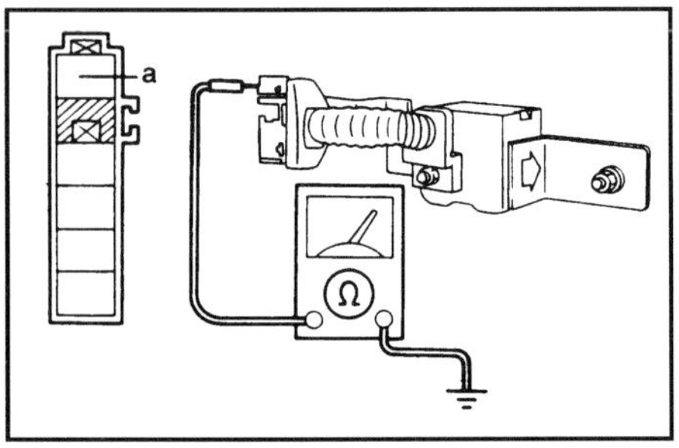

D56/7 TESTING 'S' SENSOR TERMINAL/GROUND CONTINUITY.

8 Disconnect the diagnostic module wiring connector. Refer to the accompanying diagram for terminal location details, and check for continuity between the **2B** (G/W) terminal in the wiring connector and a chassis ground. If there is continuity shown, replace the wiring harness. If no continuity is shown, refer back to *paragraph 6*.

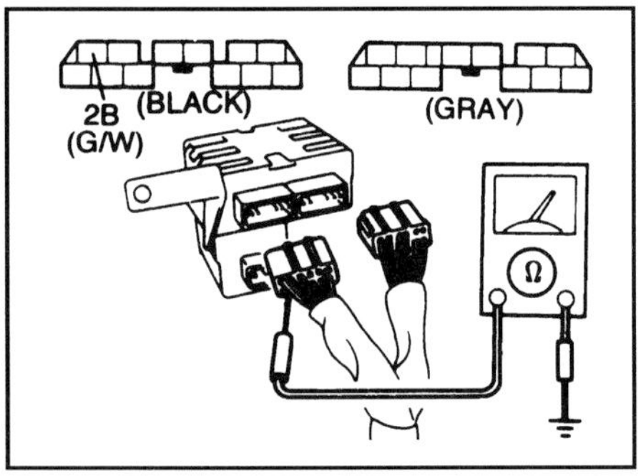

D56/8 TESTING DIAGNOSTIC MODULE CONNECTOR TERMINAL/GROUND CONTINUITY.

57. AIR BAG SYSTEM FAULT - WARNING LAMP FLASHES 6 TIMES

☞ 1/1, 2 & 7/2 & 7/50.

Probable cause: faulty air bag module, or poor clock spring connector contact.

1 Disconnect the battery negative (-) lead to isolate the electrical system. Remove the knee protector and check the orange and blue clock spring connectors for security. If loose or disconnected, reconnect them properly. If the connections are OK, move to *paragraph 2*.

2 Disconnect the orange and blue clock spring connectors. Remove the four air bag module mounting nuts from the back of the steering wheel and lift away the module.

3 Check for continuity between the clock spring connector wiring as shown in the accompanying diagram. If continuity is not shown on both

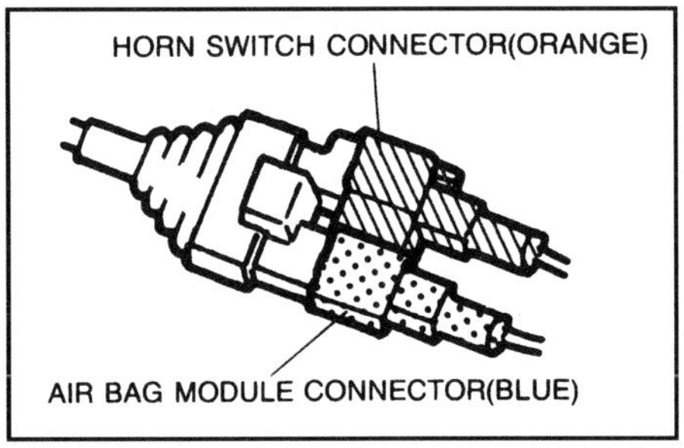

D57/1 CHECK THAT CLOCK SPRING CONNECTIONS ARE GOOD.

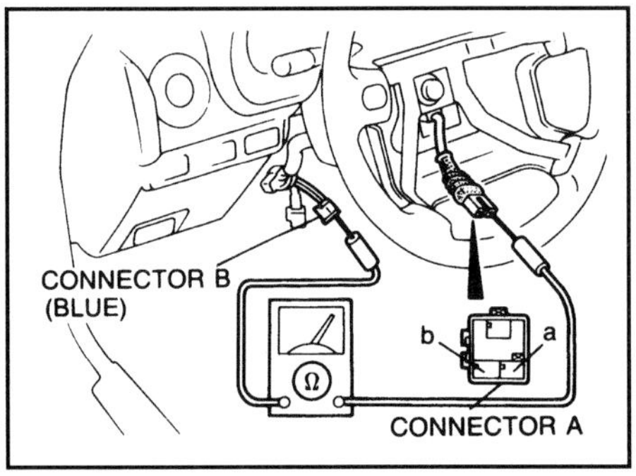

D57/3 TESTING CLOCK SPRING CONNECTORS (BLUE) TERMINAL CONTINUITY.

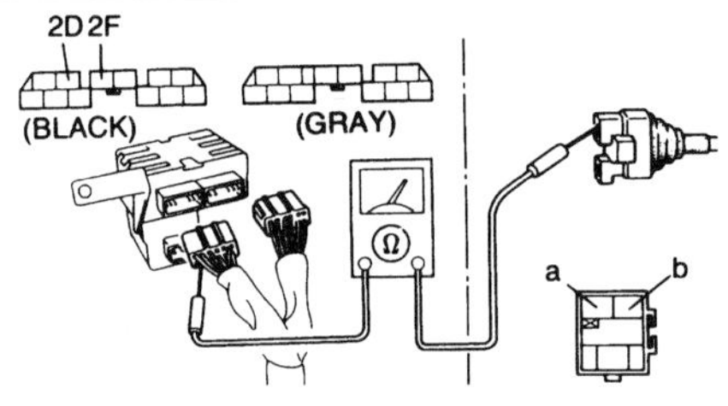

Terminal-wire (Diagnostic module — Clock spring connector)	Continuity
(2D : G/W)—(a : R)	Yes
(2F : G/Y)—(b : G/Y)	Yes

D&T57/4 TESTING DIAGNOSTIC MODULE/CLOCK SPRING CONNECTORS CONTINUITY.

terminal connections, you will have to fit a new clock spring connector as part of the combination switch assembly ☞ 7/12. If the wiring checks out OK, move on to *paragraph 4*.

4 Disconnect the diagnostic module connectors and check for continuity in the harness between the module and clock spring connector as shown in the accompanying diagram and table. If not as specified, replace the wiring harness, otherwise move to *paragraph 5*.

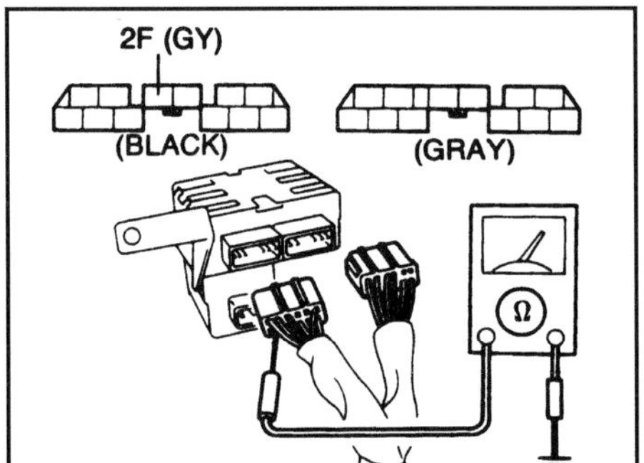

D57/5 TESTING MODULE CONNECTOR TERMINAL/GROUND CONTINUITY.

5 Check for continuity between the diagnostic module wiring connector terminal **2F** and a body ground, as shown in the accompanying diagram. If continuity is found, replace the wiring harness. If no continuity is found, fit a new air bag module.

58. AIR BAG SYSTEM FAULT - WARNING LAMP FLASHES 2 OR 8 TIMES

☞ 1/1, 2 & 7/2 & 7/50.

Probable cause: poor ground contact of 'D' sensor

1 Disconnect the battery negative (-) lead to isolate the electrical system. Remove the knee protector and disconnect the orange and blue clock spring connectors. Unplug the diagnostic connector wiring, and check for continuity between the connector terminals (wiring side) and a chassis ground point - see accompanying diagram for details of terminal positions. Check the **2J** terminal (BR/Y) first. If no continuity is shown, skip to *paragraph 2*. Next, check the **2H** (BR/W) terminal. If no continuity is shown, skip down to *paragraph 3*. Finally, check the **2E** (BR) terminal. If no continuity is shown, skip to *paragraph 4*, otherwise replace the diagnostic module.

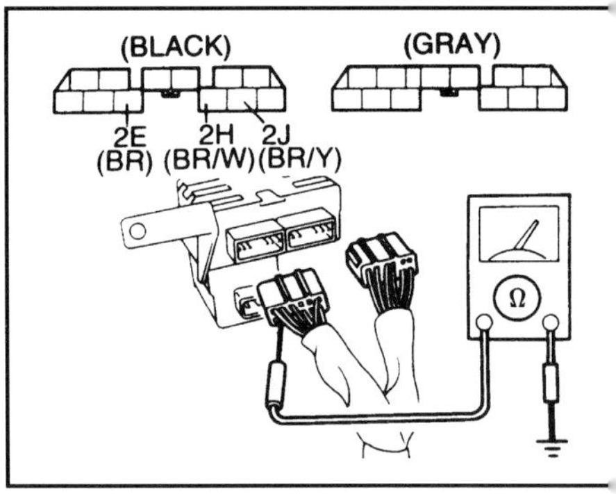

D58/1 TESTING DIAGNOSTIC MODULE CONNECTOR TERMINAL/GROUND CONTINUITY.

2 Disconnect the 'D' sensor **RH** (right hand) connector and check for continuity between the sensor connector terminals and ground. If continuity is shown, replace the wiring harness, otherwise skip down to *paragraph 5*.

3 Disconnect the 'D' sensor **CNT** (center) connector and check for continuity between the sensor connector terminals and ground. Refer t

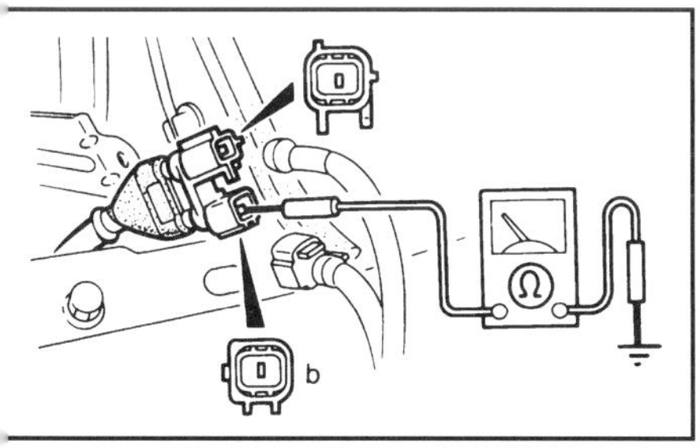

D58/2 TESTING 'D' SENSOR CONNECTOR TERMINAL/GROUND CONTINUITY.

he diagram accompanying *paragraph 2* for con-ection details. If continuity is shown, replace the viring harness, otherwise skip down to *paragraph* 5.

4 Disconnect the 'D' sensor **LH** (left-hand) connector and check for continuity between the ensor connector terminals and ground. Refer to he diagram accompanying *paragraph 2* for con-ection details. If continuity is shown, replace the viring harness, otherwise skip down to *paragraph* 5.

5 Check that all three 'D' sensors are mounted ecurely and in good contact with the car body. Clean and tighten the mounting area and recheck vhether the warning lamp flashes. If the fault emains unresolved, replace the affected sensor.

59. AIR BAG SYSTEM FAULT - WARNING LAMP FLASHES 7 TIMES

☞ 1/1, 2 & 7/2 & 7/50.

Probable cause: poor ground contact of wiring harness.

1 Disconnect the battery negative (-) ead to isolate the electrical system. Remove the nee protector and disconnect the orange and blue clock spring connectors. Unplug the diagnostic connector wiring, and check for continuity be-ween the connector terminals (wiring side) and a chassis ground point - see accompanying diagram or details of terminal positions.

60. AIR BAG MODULE - REMOVAL, INSTALLATION & DISPOSAL

☞ 1/1, 2 & 7/2 & 7/50.

REMOVAL AND INSTALLATION

1 **Warning!** If you need to remove an air bag module, refer to the operating procedures and safety precautions ☞ 7/50.

2 Disconnect the battery negative (-) lead to isolate the electrical system. Remove the knee protector and disconnect the orange and blue clock spring connectors.

3 Slacken and remove the four air bag mounting nuts from the back of the steering wheel, and lift the module away from the wheel. Handle and dispose of the removed module safely.

4 Install the new module on the steering wheel. Fit the mounting nuts and tighten them evenly to 39-49 Nm (4.0-5.0 kgf m / 29-36 lbf ft).

5 Reconnect the clock spring connectors and the battery negative cable, and check that the air bag system warning lamp comes on for six seconds when the ignition switch is turned on. If the lamp stays on or flashes, for fault finding information ☞ 7/51-59.

DISPOSAL

6 **Warning!** It is very important to note that you should never, under any circumstances, dispose of an undeployed air bag. The air bag remains potentially dangerous until the explosive charge has been fired, and even then, the caustic residues in the bag require careful handling. Note that this applies where the vehicle itself is to be scrapped - it is dangerous to allow the vehicle to be crushed or otherwise destroyed until the air bag has been deployed and disposed of separately.

7 **Warning!** Controlled deployment must be carried out in the open, using a Mazda special service tool (SST). The SST itself must be checked for safe operation before use. We figure that no-one is likely to have one of these tools handy, and so recommend (as do Mazda themselves) that you contact the nearest Mazda agent for advice about how to deal with this situation.

8 **Warning!** If you have reason to deal with a deployed air bag, note that the module (not the deployed bag) gets extremely hot during deployment and must not be touched for 15 minutes after deployment. Do not allow water to come into contact with the deployed air bag.

9 **Warning!** Wear coveralls, safety glasses and gloves when handling the deployed air bag. Wrap the deployed bag in a vinyl refuse bag, seal the top, and then dispose of it safely - get advice from your local authority or Mazda dealer about safe disposal methods.

10 **Warning!** Wash your hands and protective clothing after handling the deployed air bag.

61. AIR BAG SYSTEM DIAGNOSTIC MODULE - REMOVAL & INSTALLATION

☞ 1/1, 2 & 7/2 & 7/50.

1 Disconnect the battery negative (-) lead to isolate the electrical system. Remove the knee protector and disconnect the orange and blue clock spring connectors.

2 Disconnect the diagnostic module and backup battery wiring connectors. Remove the diagnostic module and backup battery mounting bracket nuts and remove the module and battery as an assembly.

3 Fit the new assembly over the mounting studs and tighten the retaining nuts securely. Reconnect the wiring connectors, then reconnect the clock spring connector wiring and install the battery negative (-) lead.

62. AIR BAG SYSTEM SENSORS - REMOVAL & INSTALLATION

☞ 1/1, 2 & 7/2 & 7/50.

Warning! Before attempting to remove any sensor, disconnect the battery negative (-) lead to isolate the electrical system. Remove the knee protector and disconnect the orange and blue clock spring connectors ☞ 7/50.

'D' SENSORS

1 There are a total of three 'D' sensors, one on each side of the car behind the front section of the fenders, and a third near the nose of the car. To gain access to the side sensors, remove the plastic shields from the underside of the fender, working from the wheelwell (arch). The shields are retained by bolts and a selection of plastic panel clips.

2 Disconnect the sensor wiring connector inside the car, working under the dash panel. On the right side of the car, temporarily detach the fuse block to improve access - on the left side the relay bank needs to be detached. Feed the wiring through the firewall, and remove the sensor wiring clips back to the sensor.

3 Remove the two bolts which retain each sensor and lift it away from the car with its wiring harness. When installing the sensors, observe the front markings on each unit. Make sure that the ground connection between the unit and the body is clean - if the ground contact is poor or intermittent, the sensor will not operate correctly. If required, clean the area with abrasive paper, and then apply a film of petroleum jelly (Vaseline) to inhibit corrosion. Install the mounting bolts and tighten them to 8.8-12.7 Nm (90-130 kgf cm / 78-113 lbf in).

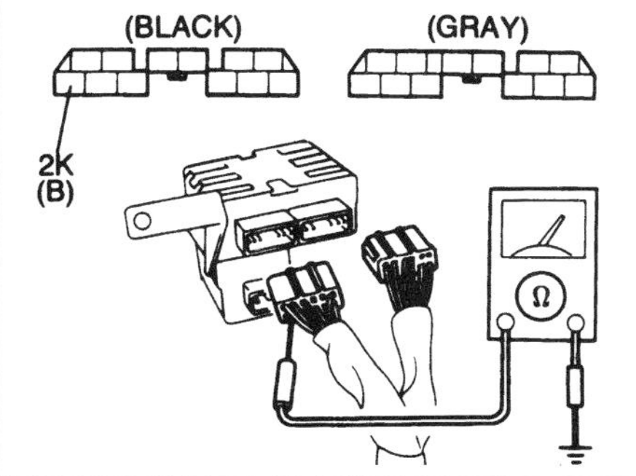

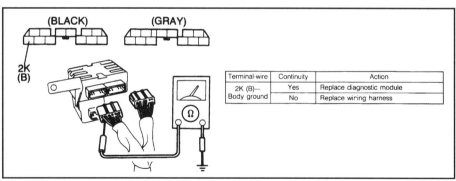

Terminal-wire	Continuity	Action
2K (B)— Body ground	Yes	Replace diagnostic module
	No	Replace wiring harness

D&T59/1 TESTING DIAGNOSTIC MODULE CONNECTOR TERMINAL/GROUND CONTINUITY.

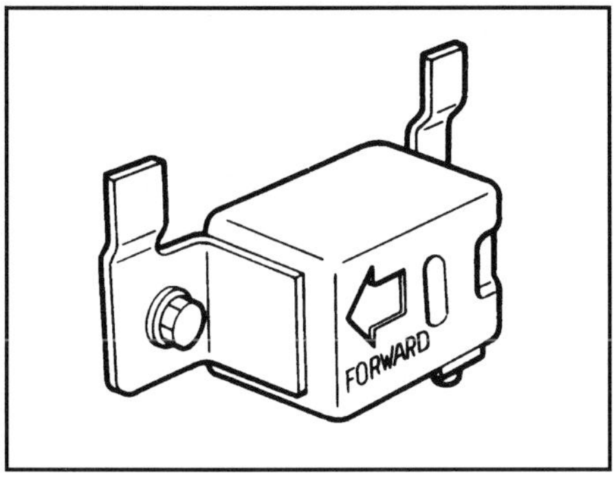

D62/3 CHECK CONDITION OF 'D' (CRASH) SENSOR UNITS.

4 Feed the wiring back through the firewall and install the wiring clips. Reconnect the sensor wiring connectors, the clock spring connectors and the battery negative (-) cable, then turn on the ignition switch. Check that the air bag system warning lamp comes on for 6 seconds and then goes out - if it remains on, or flashes, a system fault is indicated ☞ 7/50-59. If all is well, temporarily disconnect the battery negative (-) lead to isolate the electrical system and disconnect the orange and blue clock spring connectors to disable the air bag system while installation of the remaining parts removed during dismantling is completed.

63. AIR BAG SYSTEM CLOCK SPRING CONNECTOR - REMOVAL & INSTALLATION

☞ 1/1, 2 & 7/2 & 7/50.

Warning! Before attempting to remove the clock spring connector and combination switch assembly, disconnect the battery negative (-) lead to isolate the electrical system. Remove the knee protector and disconnect the orange and blue clock spring connectors ☞ 7/50.

1 The clock spring connector is an integral part of the combination switch, and if a fault is found, it will require a new switch assembly to be fitted ☞ 7/12.

2 If the switch assembly is disturbed for any reason, or if the steering wheel has been removed, it is essential that the clock spring connector is adjusted during installation ☞ 7/50.

64. WINDSHIELD WIPER & WASHER SYSTEM - TROUBLESHOOTING

☞ 1/1, 2 & 7/2.

Wiper inoperative in high or low position - US spec cars.

1 Check the **WIPER 20A** fuse. If it has blown, try fitting a new fuse and see whether the wiper now operates normally. If the fuse burns out again, check the wiper system wiring for shorts, and repair or rewire as necessary.

2 Remove the access panel below the steering column and check for battery voltage at the (L) wire at the combination switch wiring connector with the ignition switch turned on. If no voltage is shown, check back and repair the wiring between the **WIPER 20A** fuse and the switch connector.

3 Next, check for battery voltage at the combination switch wiring connector, again with the ignition switch turned on. You should read battery voltage on the (L/W) wire with the wiper switch set to **LO**, and on the (L/R) wire with the switch set to HI. If battery voltage is not indicated, check the (L/W) and (L/R) wires back from the switch to the motor.

4 If the fault persists, check the wiper motor ☞ 7/65.

Wiper inoperative in high or low position - Canadian spec cars.

5 Check the **WIPER 20A** fuse. If it has blown, try fitting a new fuse and see whether the wiper now operates normally. If the fuse burns out again, check the wiper system wiring for shorts, and repair or rewire as necessary

6 Check for battery voltage at the (L) wire at the wiper motor wiring connector with the ignition switch turned on. If no voltage is shown, check back and repair the wiring between the **WIPER 20A** fuse and the motor connector.

7 Check the wiper motor ☞ 7/65.

8 Next, check for continuity at the combination switch wiring connector ☞ 7/12. You should read continuity between the motor and switch ends of the (L/W) and (L/R) wires. If continuity is not indicated, check the (L/W) and (L/R) wires back from the switch to the motor.

9 Check for continuity between the wiper switch connector (B) wire terminal and a chassis ground. If continuity is not shown, check and repair or rewire the (B) wire.

10 If the fault persists, check the wiper switch for continuity ☞ 7/12.

Wiper inoperative in high or low position - UK and Continental Europe spec cars.

11 Check the **WIPER 20A** fuse. If it has blown, try fitting a new fuse and see whether the wiper now operates normally. If the fuse burns out again, check the wiper system wiring for shorts, and repair or rewire as necessary.

12 Check for battery voltage at the (L) wire at the wiper motor wiring connector with the ignition switch turned on. If no voltage is shown, check back and repair the wiring between the **WIPER 20A** fuse and the motor connector.

13 Next, check for battery voltage at the wiper motor wiring connector, again with the ignition switch turned on. You should read battery voltage on the (L/W) wire with the wiper switch set to **LO**, and on the (L/R) wire with the switch set to HI. If battery voltage is not indicated, check the (L/W) and (L/R) wires back from the switch to the motor.

14 Disconnect the wiper switch 6-pin connector at the combination switch (access details ☞ 7/12) and check continuity between the (B) wire and ground. Repair or rewire the ground connection as necessary.

15 If the fault persists, check the wiper motor switch for continuity ☞ 7/12.

Wipers do not park correctly when turned off- US and Canadian spec cars.

16 With the ignition switch turned on, check for battery voltage on the (L) wire at the wiper motor wiring connector. If zero volts is indicated, check and repair the (L) wire between the motor and fuse. If battery voltage is shown, check the motor ☞ 7/65.

Wipers do not park correctly when turned off- UK and Continental Europe spec cars.

17 With the ignition switch turned on, check for battery voltage on the (L) wire at the wiper switch (combination switch) wiring connector. If zero volts is indicated, check and repair the (L) wire between the switch and fuse. If battery voltage is shown, check for continuity between the motor wiring connector (B) wire and ground, If there is no continuity shown, check the motor brush plate assembly ☞ 7/65. If you read continuity, check the wiper motor ☞ 7/65.

Intermittent wipe function inoperative - US and Canadian spec cars.

18 Check for continuity between the wiper motor wiring connector (B) wire and ground. If no continuity is found, repair or rewire the motor ground connection. If you read continuity, check the wiper switch (combination switch) ☞ 7/12.

Intermittent wipe function inoperative- UK and Continental Europe spec cars.

19 Disconnect the wiper switch 6-pin connector at the combination switch and check for continuity between the (B) wire and ground. If no continuity is found, repair or rewire the switch ground connection, and check the brush plate assembly ☞ 7/65. If you read continuity, check the wiper switch (combination switch) ☞ 7/12.

One-touch function inoperative - all cars.

20 Check the operation of the wiper switch in all positions ☞ 7/12.

Wipers will not switch off - all cars.

21 Check the operation of the wiper switch in all positions ☞ 7/12. Check for damage to the wiper motor wiring. Check the motor brush plate assembly ☞ 7/65.

Windshield washer system inoperative - US spec cars.

22 If motor can be heard running, check reservoir water level - top up as required. Check for blocked washer jet - clear using a pin or fine wire.

23 Remove the access panel below the steering column and check for battery voltage at the (L/O) wire at the combination switch wiring connector with the ignition and washer switches turned on. If no voltage is shown, check the combination switch operation ☞ 7/12.

24 Check for battery voltage on the (L/O) wire at the washer motor connector, again with the ignition and washer switches on. If zero volts are indicated, check and repair the wiring between the switch and motor.

25 Disconnect the motor wiring connector and check for continuity between the (B) wire and ground. If no continuity is shown, repair or rewire the motor ground connection. If continuity is shown, check the washer motor ☞ 7/67.

Windshield washer system inoperative - Canadian spec cars.

26 If motor can be heard running, check reservoir water level - top up as required. Check for blocked washer jet - clear using a pin or fine wire.

27 Check for battery voltage on the (L) wire at the washer motor connector, with the ignition and washer switches on. If zero volts are indicated, check and repair the wiring between the fuse and motor.

28 Check the washer motor ☞ 7/67.

29 Check for continuity between the motor and switch ends of the (L/O) wire - repair or rewire as required if continuity is not found.

30 Disconnect the wiper switch 6-pin wiring connector and check for continuity between the (B) wire and ground. If no continuity is shown, repair or rewire the ground connection. If continuity is shown, check the washer switch operation ☞ 7/12.

Windshield washer system inoperative - UK and Continental Europe spec cars.

31 If motor can be heard running, check reservoir water level - top up as required. Check for blocked washer jet - clear using a pin or fine wire.

32 Check for battery voltage on the (L) wire at the washer motor connector, with the ignition and washer switches on. If zero volts are indicated, check and repair the wiring between the fuse and motor.

33 Check the washer motor ☞ 7/67.

34 Check for battery voltage at the (L/O) wire terminal at the wiper switch 6-pin connector, with the ignition switch and washer switch on. If zero volts is indicated, repair or rewire the switch to motor wiring.

35 Disconnect the wiper switch 6-pin wiring connector and check for continuity between the (B) wire and ground. If no continuity is shown, repair or rewire the ground connection. If continuity is shown, check the washer switch operation ☞ 7/12.

Windshield washer system operates when switch is released - all cars.

36 Check switch operation ☞ 7/12. Check for shorted wiring between switch and motor.

65. WINDSHIELD WIPER MOTOR - CHECKING, REMOVAL, O/HAUL & INSTALLATION

☞ 1/1, 2 & 7/2.

CHECKING

1 You can check the motor operation using a spare 12 volt car battery (or use the Mazda's battery after disabling the stereo security system and removing it from the trunk). You will need a couple of test leads with probe ends connected to the battery terminals.

2 Connect the negative (-) battery terminal to the motor body, then apply the positive (+) probe to the following terminals, referring to the accompanying drawing for details.

3 On US, UK and Continental Europe spec

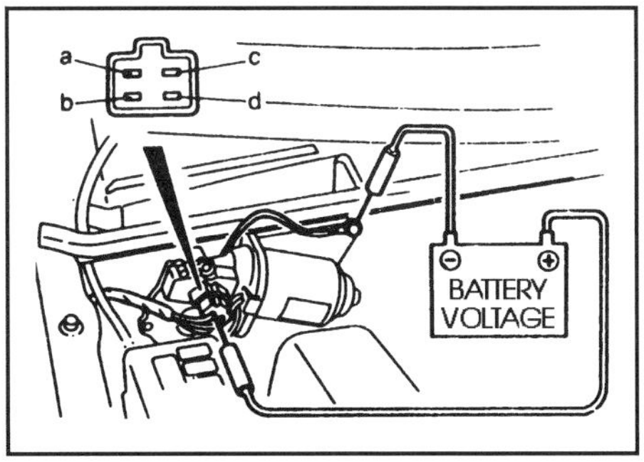

D65/2 TESTING MOTOR OPERATION.

cars, the wipers should run at low speed when the probe is connected to terminal **a**, and at high speed when connected to terminal **c**. On Canadian spec models, the terminal connections should be reversed - **a** = high speed and **c** = low speed.

4 If the motor does not work as specified during this check, the official solution is to fit a new motor. We, of course, decided to take ours apart - you probably won't be able to get parts from a Mazda dealer, but you may be able to fix the fault by cleaning the commutator or fitting new brushes. Wally, our Technical Adviser, asks us to point out that the photographs show our right-hand drive project car - on left-hand drive cars everything is reversed, but otherwise similar. Wally says to hold the book in front of a mirror if you are working on a LHD model - great if you can read mirror writing!

REMOVAL

5 + Start by disconnecting the motor wiring connector. You now need to disconnect the linkage from the motor arm to the wiper mechanism. This is reached from behind the panel carrying the motor; you can free the link by levering it gently away with a screwdriver blade - the plastic socket will pop off the pin end on the motor arm. You can now release the three mounting bolts and lift the motor away, feeding the motor arm through the panel hole. Note that depending on the country in which the car was originally sold, and on options fitted, you may need to remove other units to allow the motor to be removed. On US spec cars, for

65/5a Unplug motor's wiring connector ...

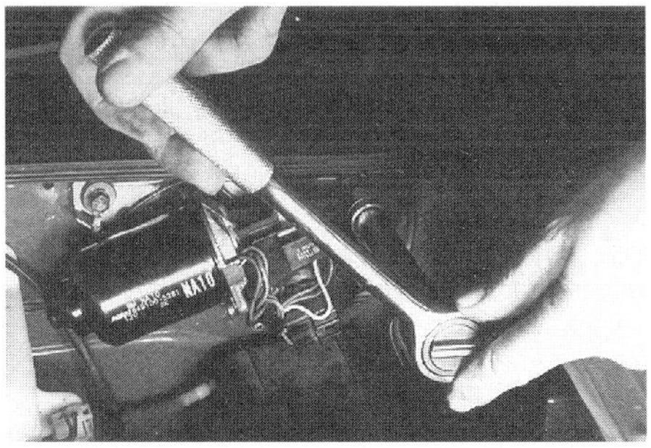

65/5b ... and undo mounting bolts.

example, you will usually need to detach the fuse block from its mounting to make room.

OVERHAUL

6 Remove the three screws which retain the gearbox end cover and lift it away. Inside, you will find the plastic gear in which are embedded contact tracks. On the cover are three spring contacts which operate on the tracks. The spring contacts transfer power to the motor brushes, their position deciding whether the motor is under power or not. Note that if these contacts are not working correctly, the motor may not run, or the parking function may be inoperative.

7 If you have dismantled the motor because of such problems, you can clean the contacts and tracks after removing the grease with a solvent-moistened rag. We find that a pencil eraser will restore the surface without causing scoring. To make sure that the contacts are pressing firmly on the rotor, bend them outwards slightly. Install the cover and reconnect the wiring, then check if the motor operates normally.

8 The motor itself can be dismantled after removing the two crosshead screws holding

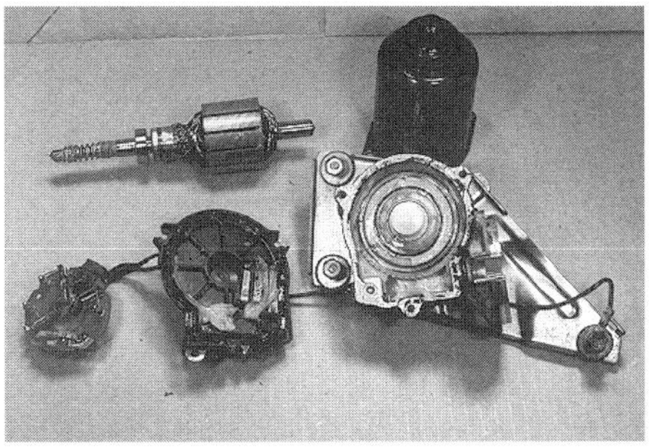

65/8 Disassembled wiper motor.

the motor body to the gearbox. As you pull the motor body away, the armature will probably come with it, pulling out from the brush assembly. Remove the armature from the body (it will be held by the pull of the permanent magnets in the body) noting the bearing ball fitted to the end of the spindle - retrieve this and keep it safe.

9 Use a multimeter or continuity checker to test for insulation between the commutator segments and the core and spindle of the armature. If you find continuity at any point, you will need to fit a new motor (it is unlikely to be worth attempting

to get the armature rewound).

10 Examine the commutator for wear or damage. Light discoloration and minor damage can be corrected by cleaning the commutator with fine sandpaper. Wrap the paper round the commutator and turn the armature until a bright, smooth finish is restored. In cases of more severe damage, have the armature set up in a lathe and remove the minimum amount of metal possible to restore the surface of the commutator segments. There are no specified service limits for the commutator, but if the repair work would result in its diameter being reduced by an appreciable amount, the motor should be scrapped and a new one fitted.

11 Check that the commutator runout is acceptable. Set the armature up on V-blocks or between lathe centers, and use a dial gauge (DTI) to measure commutator runout. Again, we have no service limits for this, but if the runout is greater than about 0.03 mm (0.001 in), either correct this by skimming in a lathe, or scrap the motor and fit a new one.

12 After working on the commutator, clean out the grooves between each segment. You can make up your own cleaning/recutting tool from a section of used hacksaw blade. Find the end where the teeth point back towards you as you hold the blade - this will be the cutting end, so wrap some tape around the other end to form a handle. Now grind the sides of the blade flat until it is a good fit in the commutator grooves. Undercut the grooves by drawing the tool along each one until you achieve a small undercut, then repeat the process on the remaining grooves. Use a little fine sandpaper to remove any burring that results.

13 If the brushes are worn down appreciably, you might like to try an auto-electrical specialist, who can probably supply something suitable as a replacement. You may not get an exact fit, so check this and if necessary file the brushes to fit the holder, then solder them into the brush plate (or you could get the supplier to do this for you). Note that the brush plate carries an internal fuse. We have no information about this fuse, but if it has blown it is presumably as a result of a dead short in the motor, or because the motor has been stalled by some obstruction in the mechanism. We suggest that you try an auto-electrical specialist for advice in the event that the fuse needs replacing.

14 + When you assemble the motor, you will need to pull the brushes back in their holders while you fit the armature in place. If you leave the ends of the brush springs unhooked while you fit the armature, this is relatively easy to do - but don't

65/14a Leave brush springs unhooked ...

65/14b ... feed armature into place ...

omit to hook the spring ends into place afterwards.

65/14c ... and tighten brushplate screws.

It is helpful to leave the brush baseplate loose unt the armature has been fed into position, afte which the two securing screws should be fitted. Pu a small dab of grease in the hole on the end of th armature and stick the bearing ball in place.

15 When you fit the motor body, be awar that the magnets inside it will try to pull the arma ture out of the gearbox. You can prevent this b applying pressure on the operating arm so that th armature resists pulling out - you will need t experiment to find the correct amount of pressur to apply - it needs to be just less than that require to turn the armature.

16 Fit the body over the armature and insta the retaining screws, tightening them evenly. Nov repeat the check described in paragraph 1-3. If th motor now runs as it should, you've just saved th cost of a new one.

INSTALLATION

17 + Install the motor on its mounting an fit the three retaining bolts, tightening them evenl to 6.9-9.8 Nm (70-100 kgf cm / 61-87 lbf in). If th motor has been dismantled, it is likely that th operating arm will be in the wrong position fo

65/17a Torque tighten 3 fixing bolts.

65/17b Operating arm in park position.

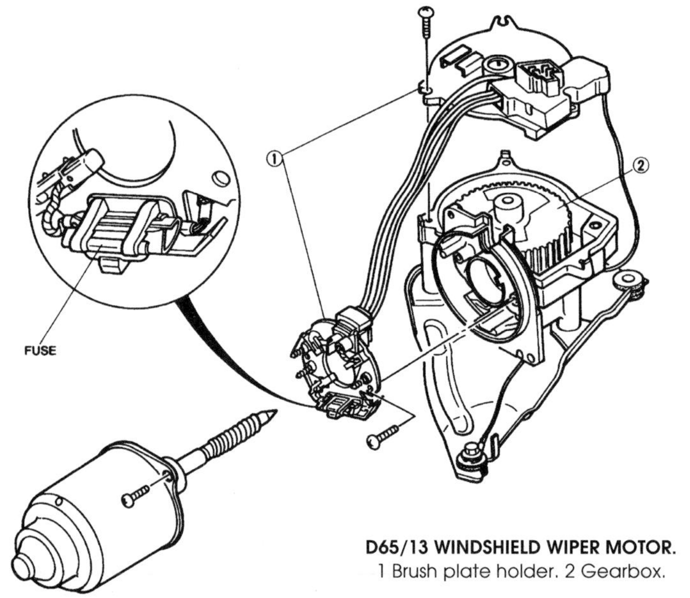

D65/13 WINDSHIELD WIPER MOTOR.
1 Brush plate holder. 2 Gearbox.

reconnection. To remedy this, reconnect the wiring connector - if the position was wrong, the motor should run until the right position is achieved and then park as shown in the accompanying photograph (Note: RHD shown). Install the wiper mechanism connecting link by snapping it over the head of the motor arm pin.

18 Fit any components removed to make access easier during removal, then check the operation of the wipers under all switch positions.

66. WINDSHIELD WIPER MECHANISM - REMOVAL, INSTALLATION & ADJUSTMENT

☞ 1/1, 2 & 7/2.

1 + To release the wiper arms from their spindles, pry out the plastic plugs from the lower end of the arm, then remove the flanged nut which secures the arm to the spindle. Note the position of the wiper blade in relation to the screen (this is usually obvious unless the screen is unusually clean. The arm can now be pulled off - you may need to twist it a little to get it free.

2 If you need to remove the linkage, start

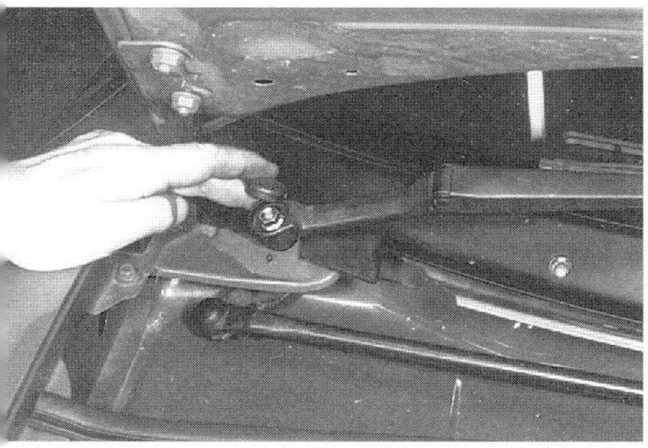

66/1a Pry off plastic cover ...

66/1b ... remove flanged nut ...

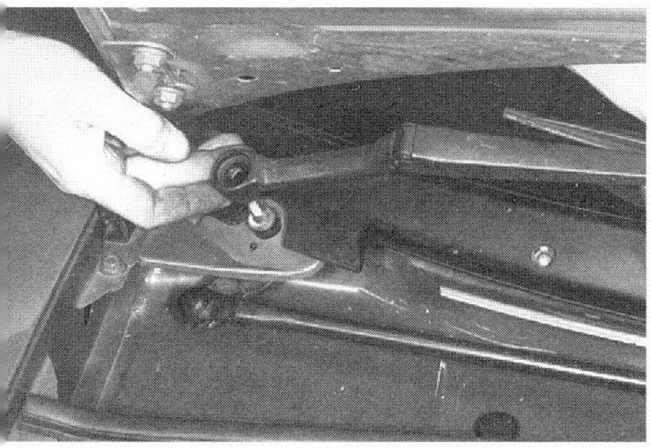

66/1c ... lift arm from spindle.

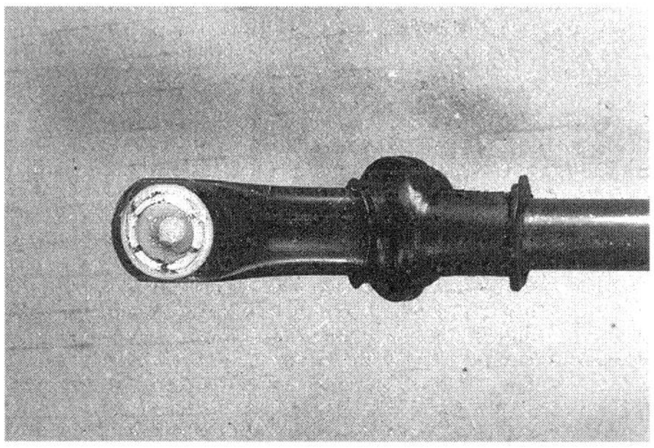

66/2 Nylon cup of wiper link arm.

by removing the arms as described above, then disconnect the link from the motor end by levering it off with a screwdriver blade - the cup-shaped link is snapped in place over the round head on the motor arm. The remaining link connections can be removed in the same way.

3 The wiper gearboxes are each retained by two bolts fitted from above, and can be removed once the bolts have been released and the connecting links detached. Alternatively, you can remove the links and gearboxes as an assembly. The problem here is that the gearbox mounting bolts are covered by what Mazda describe as the 'cowl grille' - the windshield lower trim panel. This is held in place by crosshead screws, but the screw heads are covered by plastic caps which are incredibly difficult to remove.

4 + The caps have small tangs which locate and latch them into the panel. To remove them, you need to introduce a curved tool under the edge of the panel to depress the tangs so that the caps pop out - you can't lever them out from above. We made up a tool with a piece of mild steel (see photograph, which shows the tool and the removed panel) - you may be able to modify an old screwdriver to do the same job. Pass the tool under the lip of the panel and feel around with the end until you locate the tang. Now push fairly hard, keeping your hand over the cap to prevent it flying off at high speed (Wally managed to lose two of our car's caps during removal ...).

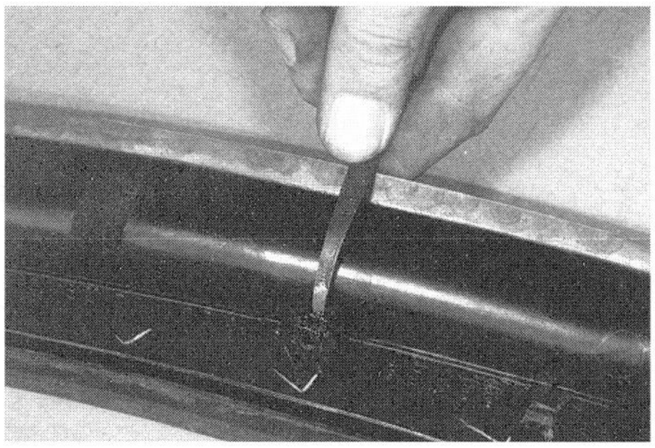

66/4a Cap removal tool demo (trim panel out).

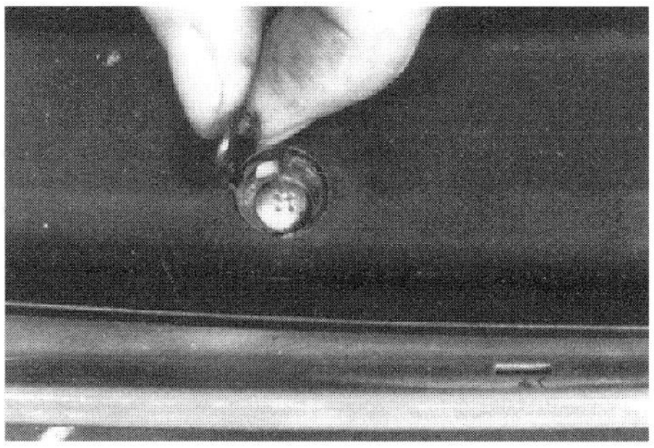

66/4b Screws accessible once caps removed.

5 + With the caps removed, you can unscrew the panel retaining screws and lift the panel away to reveal the wiper gearbox mounting bolts. On the passenger side there is a plastic cover which covers the blower air intake. There is no specific need to remove this, but if you wish to do so, it is retained by a row of four black crosshead

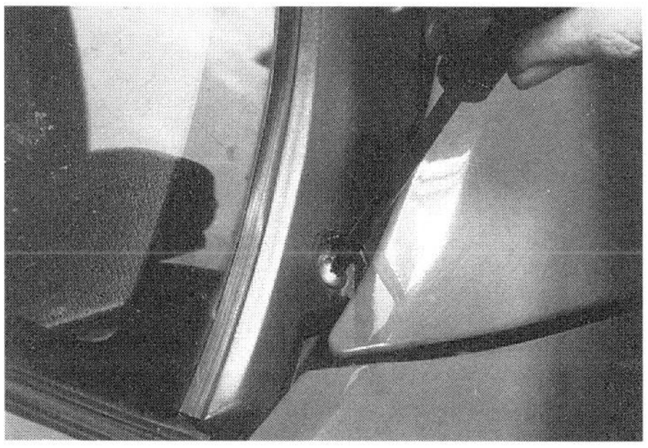

66/5a Unscrew panel retaining screws ...

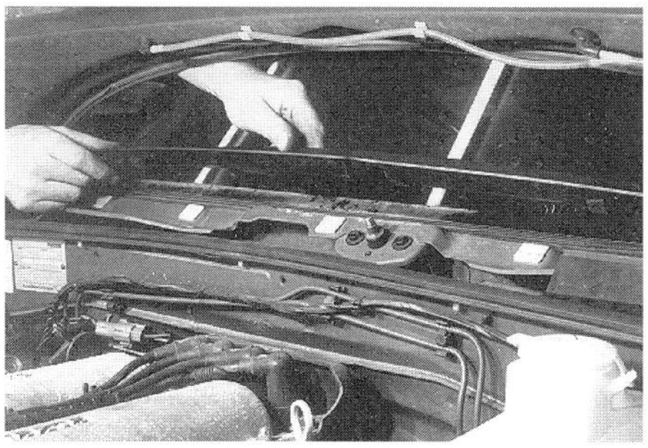

66/5b ... lift panel away ...

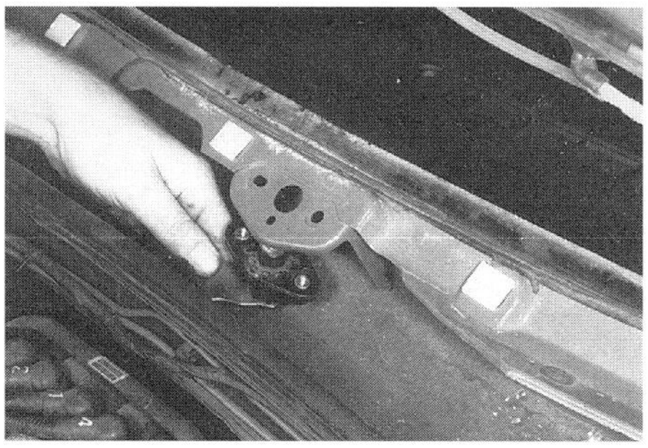

66/5c ... remove bolts to free link gearboxes.

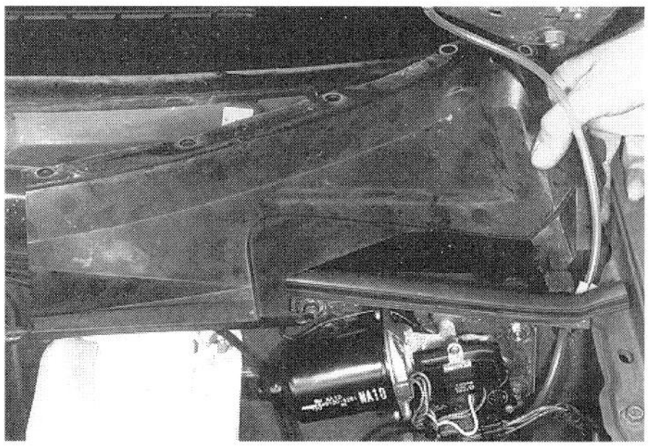

66/5d This panel gives access to blower intake.

screws along the lower edge of the windshield, a single small silver screw near the fender, and a couple of clips into the firewall. Remove the bolts and withdraw the gearboxes and linkage - the rods can be freed by prying the ends off the gearbox crank pins.

6 When installing the gearboxes, tighten the mounting bolts to 6.9-9.8 Nm (0.7-1.0 kgf m / 5.1-7.2 lbf ft). Fit the cowl grille (trim panel), snapping the caps back in place after the screws have been tightened. Snap the connecting links back into place, where these were removed. Fit the wiper arms (the one with the tiny airfoil fits on the driver's side) and tighten the flange nuts provisionally. Check the arm height setting, comparing it with the accompanying drawing. After making any necessary adjustment to the arm position, tighten the flanged nuts down to 9.8-14 Nm (1.0-1.4 kgf m / 7.2-10.0 lbf ft) and fit the plastic caps.

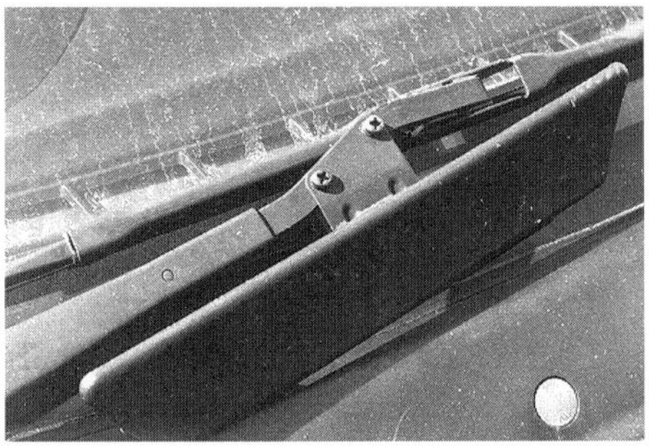
66/6 Wiper with airfoil goes on driver's side.

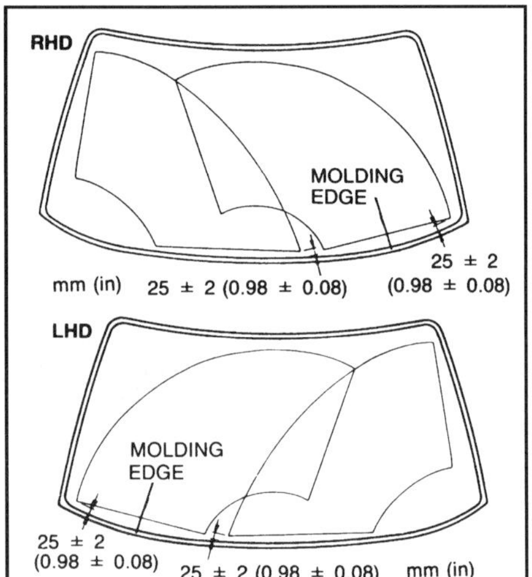

D66/6 WIPER ADUSTMENT DIAGRAM.

67. WINDSHIELD WASHER PUMP MOTOR - TESTING & REPLACEMENT

☞ 1/1, 2 & 7/2.

1 The washer pump motor (and reservoir tank) design and location vary somewhat according to specification and options fitted, but in each case the motor is attached to or very near the reservoir. In most cases, the motor snaps into a recess on the reservoir, and can be removed by pulling it away and disconnecting the wiring. (Wally discovered that if the tank is full when you do this, it empties itself inside the engine compartment). Other tank designs have the motor bracketed on the outside, but the principle is pretty similar.

2 Check the pump motor operation by connecting its two terminals to an external battery - if the motor runs, it is OK, if it doesn't, fit a new one. We suggest that you take your dead pump unit along when purchasing a new one to make sure that you get one of the same design.

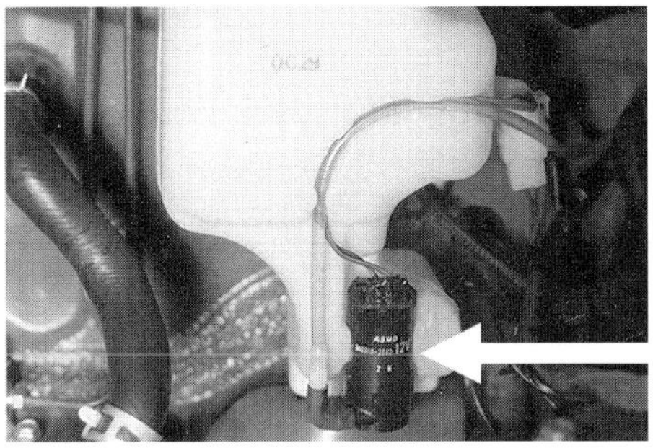
67/1 Windshield washer pump.

68/1 Clear jet nozzles with a pin or thin wire.

68. HEADLIGHT WASHER SYSTEM - TROUBLESHOOTING

☞ 1/1, 2 & 7/2.

1 If the pump runs but no water emerges from the jets, check that the washer jets are clear, using a pin or fine wire to clear any obstruction. You can release the jet from the hood by squeezing together the locking tabs on the underside if removal is necessary. Check the **HEAD CLEANER 20A** fuse. If it has blown, try fitting a new fuse and see whether the headlight washer system now operates normally. If the fuse burn out again, check the washer system wiring fo shorts, and repair or rewire as necessary.

2 At the relay bank on the left side of th engine compartment, locate the headlight cleane relay (location details ☞ 7/3). Check for batter voltage on the (R/Y) wire with the headlight retrac tor switch on. If no voltage is found, check anc repair the wiring between the relay and the switch

3 Turn the ignition switch on to the ACC position, and check for battery voltage on the (G wire at the relay connector. If zero volts is shown check the (G) wire back to the fuse and repair o rewire as necessary.

4 If you have not located the fault a this point, check the relay continuity, referring tc the accompanying diagram and table for details.

5 Next, check for continuity betwee terminals **c** and **d** as shown in the accompanyin diagram and table, while applying 12 volts tc terminals **a** and **b**. If the above checks do not give the expected results, fit a new relay.

6 Check for battery voltage on the (Y/B terminal of the headlight cleaner switch. If batter voltage is not present, check back along the wirin

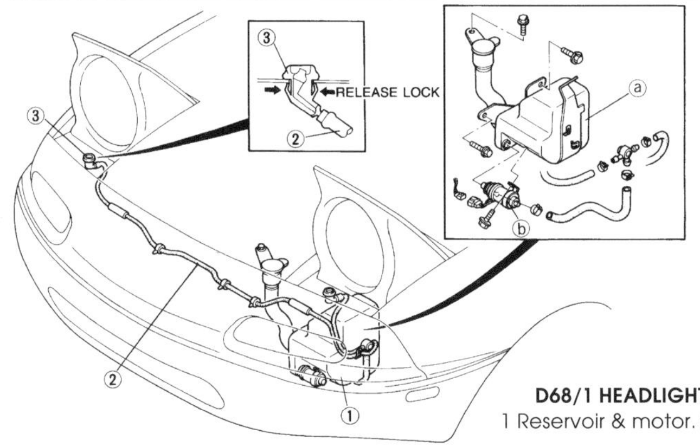

D68/1 HEADLIGHT WASHER SYSTEM.
1 Reservoir & motor. 2 Piping. 3 Jet nozzle.

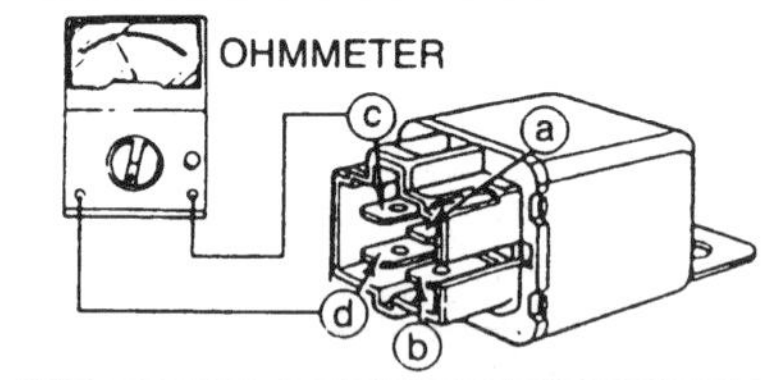

Terminal	Continuity
a—b	Yes
c—d	No

D&T68/4 TESTING HEADLIGHT WASHER RELAY TERMINAL CONTINUITY (1).

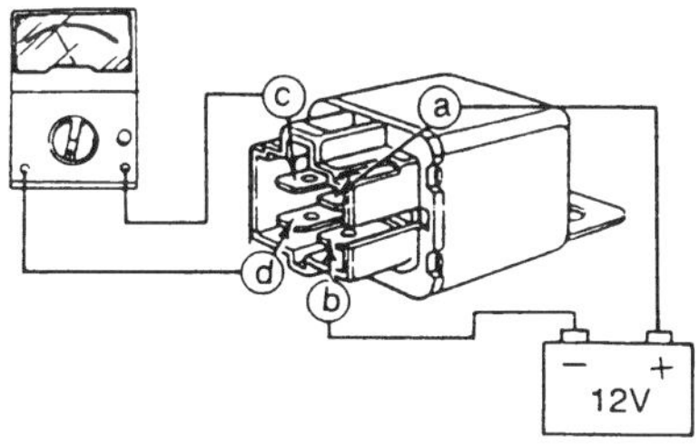

Terminal	Continuty
c—d	Yes

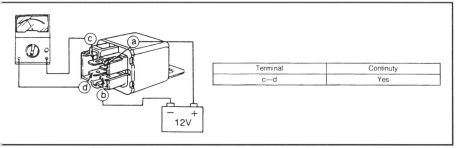

D&T68/5 TESTING HEADLIGHT WASHER RELAY TERMINAL CONTINUITY (2).

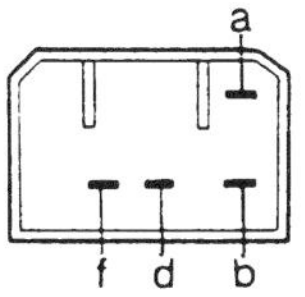

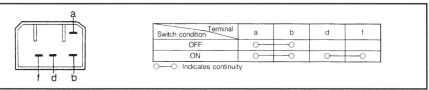

Switch condition \ Terminal	a	b	d	f
OFF	O—	—O		
ON	O—	—O	O—	—O

O—O: Indicates continuity

D&T68/7 TESTING HEADLIGHT WASHER SWITCH TERMINAL CONTINUITY.

between the switch and the relay.

7 Referring to the accompanying diagram and table, check the headlight cleaner switch continuity. If not as shown, replace the switch.

8 Check continuity between the headlight cleaner switch connector (B) wire terminal and a chassis ground point. If no continuity is shown, repair or rewire the (B) ground wire.

9 With the retractor and headlight switches on, check for battery voltage on the (Y/W) terminal of the headlight cleaner motor. If battery voltage is not present, check back along the wiring between the motor and the relay.

10 Check continuity between the headlight cleaner motor connector (B) wire terminal and a chassis ground point. If no continuity is shown, repair or rewire the (B) ground wire.

11 Disconnect the motor wiring connector. Referring to the accompanying diagram for terminal positions, apply 12 volts (+) to the motor **a** terminal and ground the **b** terminal. If the motor fails to operate, fit a new one.

69. CIGARETTE LIGHTER - REMOVAL & INSTALLATION

☞ 1/1, 2 & 7/2.

1 The cigarette lighter is mounted in the dash panel. If it stops working, check the **CIGAR 15A** fuse, fitting a new one if it has blown. Check what is inside the lighter body - kids love to stuff things in there, and if what they stuffed into yours was aluminum foil, you may have found out what blew the fuse. Poke around with a screwdriver to dislodge the crud and vacuum it out. If the heating coil has burned out, this is pretty easy to replace - pull out the old one, push in the new one. Done.

2 If haven't solved the problem at this stage, either quit smoking or keep a Zippo in the glovebox (you can probably get a really nice one with the Miata logo on it). Even those cheap plastic disposables aren't so bad - but fitting a new lighter body in the dash panel just isn't worth the hassle.

3 OK, so you *really need* to have the dash-mounted lighter working - well don't say we didn't warn you. Before you go any further, remove the access panel under the steering column (two screws and unclip it). Feel behind the dash panel and see if you can reach the lighter unit. See - we told you! We reckoned that if we had six-inch long fingers with about three extra knuckle joints we could have done it. ET could probably reach it easily, but then he could always light the cigarette with his finger anyway, if he smoked.

4 + You might try prying out the interior light above the cigarette lighter as another, limited, means of access. The aperture is too small to get your hand in (though if you can find the kid who put the aluminum foil into the lighter and burned it out, his hand might fit). You need to wiggle the lighter body around and push it out of the dash panel. As the lighter body comes out of the recess, disconnect the wiring connector and remove it. If you need to remove the plastic surround and metal cup, reach behind and squeeze the ears of the plastic surround and push it out, then remove the cup.

69/4a Unplug wiring connector ...

69/4b ... push lighter body thru dash ...

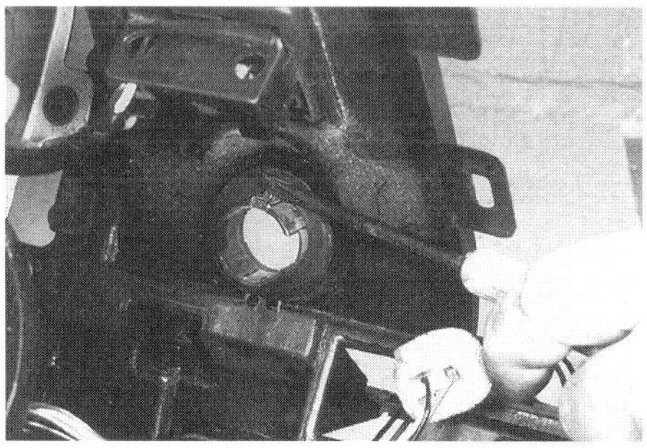

69/4c ... depress locking tabs & push out sleeve.

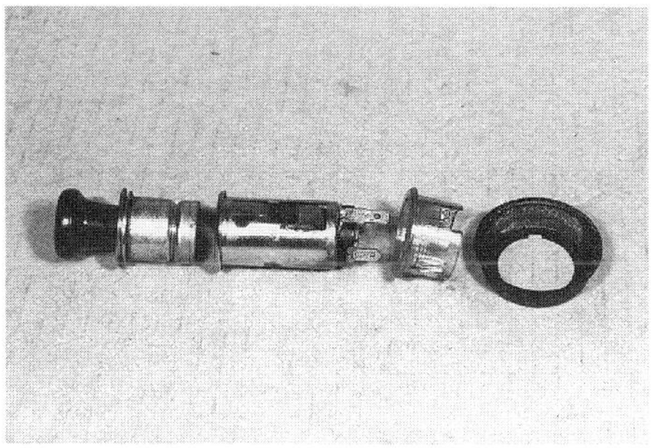

69/4d Component parts of the cigarette lighter.

5 Clean everything up before you install the new body. Fit the metal cup and plastic surround. Clip the wiring connector in place on the lighter body and slide it home. Now check that it works.

6 So how did we get those shots of the inside of the dash panel? Easy. We took the dash panel out of the car - nothing's too much trouble for our readers!

70. AUDIO SYSTEM - CHECKING, REMOVAL, INSTALLATION & TROUBLESHOOTING

☞ 1/1, 2 & 7/2.

1 The type of audio installation in your car will depend on where and when you bought it. In the US, Miatas are supplied with a Panasonic audio system as standard. This was specially designed for the Miata, and appears to vary in detail according to model year. Note also that the installation details depend on which accessories or options may have been specified on original purchase.

2 The base model system comprises an AM/FM/cassette stereo featuring an integral digital clock and anti-theft security coding, with door speakers and a manual antenna. A matching accessory compact disc (DC) player can be installed in the slot provided below the base unit, and headrest speakers and a power antenna can be added to the system if required - these form part of various

option packages which may have been fitted when the car was first supplied, though it is likely that similar third-party add-ons may well have been fitted on other cars.

3 As an optional upgrade package, Mazda's Sensory Sound System may have been specified. This features upgraded door and headrest speakers, additional tweeters in the door edge panels and bass transducers in the seats. The package is designed to augment the standard installation to give better top-down performance.

4 Outside the US, the permutations of audio equipment are less well defined, and you are likely to encounter almost any brand of stereo, with varying levels of refinement. Our UK-spec project car, for example, was equipped with a Clarion security-coded AM/FM/cassette stereo with door speakers, but no headrest speakers. We were not the original owners of the car from new, so cannot say if this was supplied by the original dealer, fitted later or a replacement for a failed original system.

5 Given the wide variety of installation options, we felt it would be pointless to attempt to offer specific coverage. Instead, we will describe general checks and installation details applicable to just about any car stereo system. That way, you should find this section helpful even if you have a car fitted with a stereo system completely unconnected with Mazda; it is quite usual for owners to wish to upgrade from the standard system, and sadly, to have to fit a new unit after the original has been stolen. The accompanying diagram shows a typical installation.

SECURITY

6 Depending on your neighborhood, we feel that you would be crazy to drive your Miata/MX5 without a good quality alarm system, particularly where the usual convertible top is fitted. The car is very vulnerable to break-ins; you don't even need to get past the door lock to get in if you have a knife. Though most car stereos have a security coding feature, they still get stolen, even if the thief has to abandon them when he finds that he is unable to get the unit to work.

7 In the case of many of the standard and option systems, the main stereo unit is located in the dash center panel, which has to be removed to get the unit out. Thieves are unlikely to spend time removing this carefully, so if the stereo gets ripped out, you will often have collateral damage to deal with as well. You may argue that the insurance will take care of it, but every time someone loses their stereo, insurance rates get forced up. Since that includes yours and ours, even if it was someone else's stereo, we think that alarm systems are good news.

8 Despite the risk of damage to the center panel in the event of theft, it is preferable to install any aftermarket system as described above. If the unit fixings are not accessible, it means that removal will be more difficult for the thief, and the additional time involved creates a useful deterrent effect. You should also fit prominent window stickers on the car underlining the fact that the stereo is security coded and that an alarm is fitted (even if this is untrue) - this may be enough to deter the casual thief.

AUDIO SYSTEM TROUBLESHOOTING

9 Problems can be divided into three main groups; unit problems, speaker problems and antenna problems. The first thing to do if you have problems with your stereo system is to determine which part of the system is to blame. The checklist below will give you a good start with this:

Nothing works

- *Check that the unit is turned on, and that power is available to it - turn the ignition switch to **ACC**.*
- *Check if the antitheft system has been activated. If **CODE** or a similar message is displayed, you need to enter the security code for your unit. Refer to the manufacturer's literature for details of this procedure and see section 2 of this chapter for more details on Mazda-supplied systems.*
- *If you see **Err** displayed, you will need to get the unit reset or exchanged by the supplier.*
- *If the unit shows nothing on the display, you will need to remove it and check the wiring connections at the back, the associated wiring and the fuse.*

System works on one channel only

- *Check the position of the balance control - it may have been accidentally knocked to the fully left or fully right position.*
- *Check the speaker wiring, working from the connector on the back of the unit to the individual speaker(s). Reconnect, repair or replace as necessary.*
- *Check the speaker(s). The resistance across the speaker terminals should be 4 - if significantly outside this, you will need to install new speaker(s).*

System fails to operate when playing cassettes

- *Check the unit control settings and try playing a known good tape.*
- *Check for dirt or oxide buildup in the tape player mechanism. Use a quality head cleaner tape and see if problem is resolved.*
- *Try playing a tape with the volume turned right back. Listen for the sound of the tape running in the player unit; if no sound is heard, the drive belt may have broken. (Consult Mazda dealer or car audio specialist).*
- *If no tape will load into the unit, replace the unit or have it repaired or serviced.*

Radio inoperative but system operates normally with cassettes

- *If the radio is completely inoperative, or there are bad static or interference problems, check the antenna and antenna connections, working along the antenna lead from the audio unit antenna socket to the antenna itself.*
- *Check for continuity between the antenna and a body ground; no continuity should be shown, and if the antenna is grounded, a new one should be installed.*
- *Check that the antenna base is securely grounded. If no continuity is shown, or there is intermittent or poor contact, check for corrosion. Clean the contact area and protect from further corrosion with petroleum jelly (Vaseline) before tightening the antenna mounting.*
- *If you are unable to resolve the fault, have the unit checked by a Mazda dealer or car*

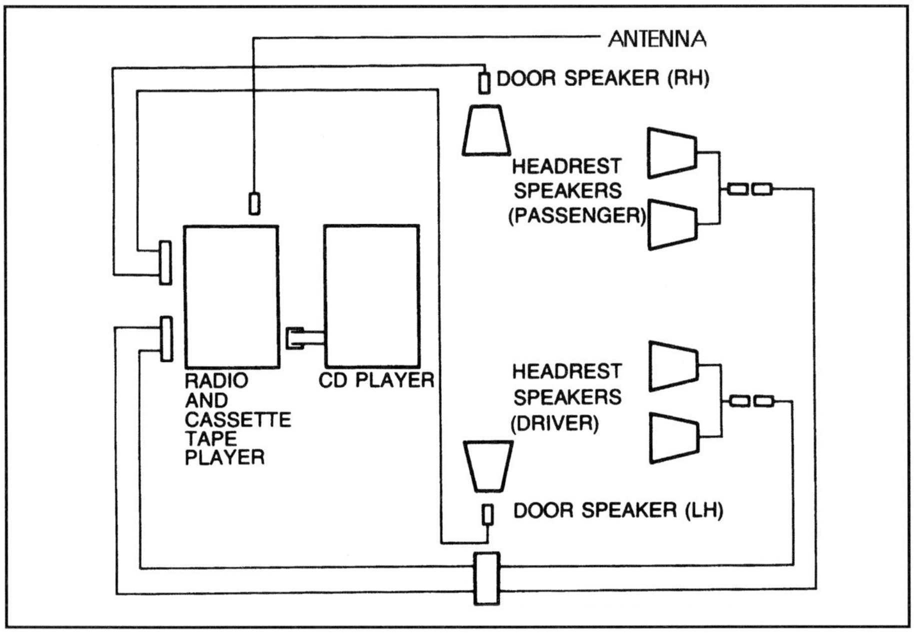

D70/5 TYPICAL MIATA/MX5 AUDIO SYSTEM.

audio specialist.

CD player inoperative - disc will not load
• *Try another disc - if the original disc was dirty or damaged, the unit will reject it.*
• *Check the remaining audio system - if this is OK, have the CD player section checked and repaired by a Mazda dealer or car audio specialist.*

CD skips during play
• *This can be caused by the car driving over a rough road surface.*
• *If skipping occurs on a particular disc only, it may be dirty or damaged.*
• *If skipping occurs randomly, or while the car is stationery, have the unit checked professionally (may be a tracking fault).*

AUDIO UNIT - REMOVAL AND INSTALLATION

10 Whatever the system fitted, it will normally be housed in the recess provided in the center section of the dash panel - there is nowhere else you could easily fit an audio unit in the car. With all security-coded audio units, you must disable the security system (or have ready the security code) before you disconnect the battery negative (-) terminal to isolate the electrical system. Never work on the audio system while the electrical system is live or you risk accidental grounding and damage to the unit or the car's wiring. For more information on security coding ☞ 7/2.

11 Unless the unit has been mounted very strangely, you will have to remove the dash center panel to gain access to the unit mounting screws: procedure ☞ 10/3.

12 With the front of the unit accessible, remove the mounting screws and draw the unit out of its recess. As it comes out, you will need to disconnect the wiring connections. These will vary according to the unit fitted. In many cases, an adaptor arrangement will have been used to patch a nonstandard unit into the Mazda wiring connectors. On original equipment installations, the Mazda wiring will connect directly to the unit. In most cases, a separate ground wire connection will be found, and there is always an antenna lead connection to the unit.

13 Installation is relatively straightforward. The main considerations are that you check that all wiring connections are securely made, paying particular attention to ground wire connections. We suggest that you power up and check the operation of the unit before you secure it in its recess and install the center panel.

MANUAL ANTENNA - REMOVAL AND INSTALLATION

14 The standard manual antenna fitment is mounted in the trunk. The lower end of the unit is retained by a single 10 mm nut to a bracket in the trunk, while the top of the unit can be freed after unscrewing the slotted chrome retainer on the outside of the car. The antenna itself can be unscrewed and removed from the base unit - worth doing to avoid vandalism while the car is parked.

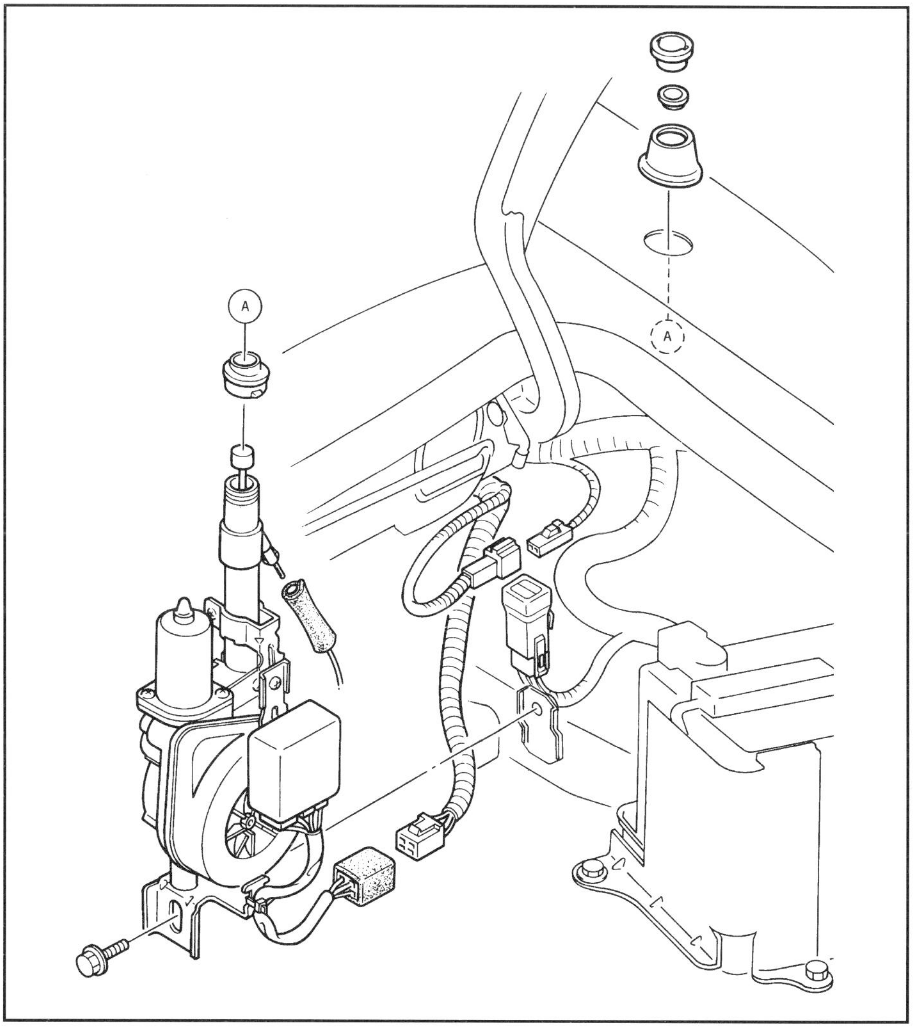

D70/17 POWER ANTENNA.

15 To remove the antenna from the car, first unscrew and remove the antenna mast from the base unit, then unscrew the chrome retainer ring. Unplug the antenna lead in the trunk, then remove the single nut at the base and lift the assembly away. Note the installation sequence of the chrome retainer, the rubber bush and the ground plate on the underside of the body.

16 When installing the antenna, check that the mounting points are clean and corrosion-free to ensure a good ground contact. Use petroleum jelly (Vaseline) to prevent subsequent corrosion problems. Check that the plug from the antenna is firmly inserted in its socket.

POWER ANTENNA - DESCRIPTION, REMOVAL AND INSTALLATION

17 The power antenna supplied as an option is fitted in much the same way as the manual version, but has additional wiring connections from the small fuse box in the trunk. The unit comprises the antenna, the motor and associated gearbox and drive rack and the relay unit. When connected to a compatible audio unit, the antenna raises automatically when the audio unit is turned on, and retracts when it is turned off.

18 The mounting nut on the top of the unit has slots either side of the antenna mast end, and can be unscrewed using snap ring pliers. With the ignition switch turned to the **ON** or **ACC** positions, turn the radio on, and the antenna mast will be pushed out of the unit body and can be removed.

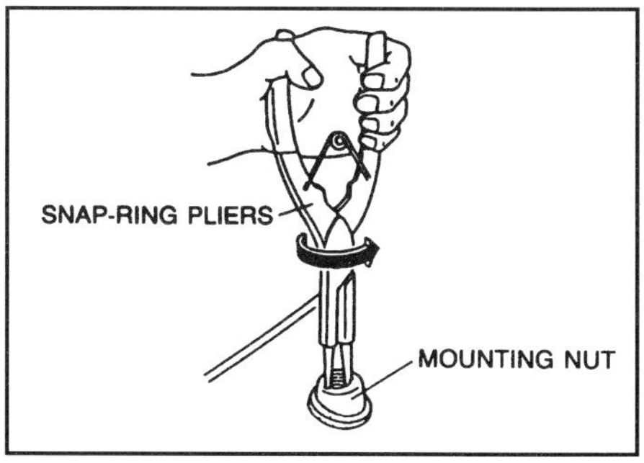

D70/18 MOUNTING NUT CAN BE UNSCREWED WITH SNAP-RING PLIERS.

19 If there have been problems with antenna system operation, check the end of the plastic rack

for damage; there should be a smooth taper on the end of the rack end (opposite side to the teeth). If the rack end is damaged or broken, the end will have remained inside the motor, in which case you will have to fit a new motor unit.

20 To install the mast, turn the radio switch off and, as the rack is retracted into the unit, guide the mast into position. Fit the mounting nut, then operate the radio switch to check that the antenna extends and retracts normally.

21 If the antenna seems mechanically sound, but does not operate normally, either the motor unit or the relay may have failed. These are best checked by substitution. If you have a Miata-MX5 owning friend with a power antenna, try swapping motor units and relays to identify the faulty part, or have your Mazda dealer track this down for you.

HEADREST SPEAKERS - REMOVAL AND INSTALLATION

22 The headrest speakers, where fitted, are set in the foam of the seat headrest. You can reach these by folding back the lip of the seat cover which conceals a zipper around the headrest. Open the zipper and remove and disconnect the speakers as required. Note the routing of the speaker cable which runs down the back of the seat under the seat cover to a two-pin wiring connector.

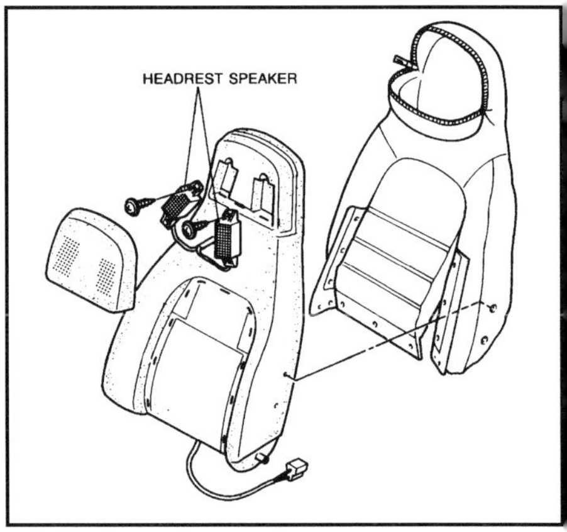

D70/22 HEADREST SPEAKER INSTALLATION.

8

SUSPENSION & STEERING

© Miata Magazine 1991.

1. INTRODUCTION

The Miata/MX5 is equipped with fully independent suspension front and rear. The suspension on all four wheels is of the double wishbone type. The suspension wishbones are carried on rubber bushed pivots supported on the ends of transverse subframes, or crossmembers. The lower pivots are adjustable using eccentrics, permitting adjustment of the caster and camber angles. This system provides servicing adjustment, as well as allowing for the application of nonstandard geometries for competition purposes.

Suspension is provided in the form of double-acting gas charged shock absorber struts, around which are mounted coil springs. Body roll is controlled by front and rear torsional stabilizer bars (anti-roll bars).

2. WHEEL ALIGNMENT - PRELIMINARY CHECKS

☞ 1/1, 2.

1 As we mentioned above, Mazda have built in comprehensive adjustment facilities for the suspension and steering. This does not mean that you need to adjust the suspension on a regular basis - the adjustment facility is there primarily to allow the correct standard alignment settings to be restored after new suspension parts have been fitted or as wear occurs. Mazda put in a lot of work developing and optimizing the car's suspension geometry, and departure from the standard settings will normally cause more problems than it solves.

2 It may be, however, that you need to apply different settings if you intend to use the car in competition, where ride comfort can be ignored in favor of optimum handling. Also, the fitting of nonstandard suspension parts may call for revised suspension geometry - if this is necessary, then consult the supplier of the parts for detailed setup instructions.

3 When checking wheel alignment, it is assumed that the tires are in serviceable condition and correctly inflated, that the wheel bearings are within specification and that the steering joints are unworn. The car should be checked on smooth, level ground. Note that the fuel tank should be full, the engine coolant and oil levels should be normal, and the spare wheel, jack and tools should be in their normal positions in the trunk. There should be no luggage or occupants in the car.

4 In addition to normal hand tools, you will need some sort of alignment gauge. It is possible to check and adjust toe-in using a simple beam-type tracking gauge of the type sold by most automotive tool stores. We feel that most proprietary tracking gauges would work on the Miata/MX5, but we cannot be certain of this - we suggest that you check that the proposed gauge will work on the car before you disturb any alignment settings. We also describe a simple checking method which only requires accurate measurement between lines made on the tires - this is Mazda's official checking method.

5 Checking and adjusting camber and caster angles is a little more complex. The adjustment procedure itself is not too difficult, but since adjustable suspension of this type is relatively rare on road cars, you may find a suitable gauge difficult to source. Given that you will only rarely need to check and adjust these settings, you might consider this alternative. If you need to disturb the suspension settings, for example, due to the need to teardown the suspension for other work, you can mark the current settings during the teardown, and simply return them to the marked positions during installation. This method may not be 100% accurate, but it will be close enough to allow you to drive the car - slowly - to the nearest tire specialist or Mazda dealer, who will be able to fine-tune the settings if necessary. We detail the adjustment procedure below for the benefit of owners with access to the necessary equipment, and who are familiar with its use.

6 Before starting the geometry checks, bounce the car on its suspension a few times to check suspension efficiency and to settle the car in its normal position. When you push down on each corner of the car, it should bounce back up and settle quickly - excessive bouncing indicates wear in the suspension units and this should be investigated and rectified before proceeding.

7 You now need to measure and note down the exact distance between the fender brim and the center of each wheel. The difference in height on each side of the car must not exceed 10 mm (0.39 in). The rear of the car should sit slightly higher than the front - but this must not exceed 10-30 mm (0.39-1.18 in). If you find a discrepancy during this check, you should look at the suspension springs, which may have become permanently compressed through normal wear. Note also that wear or deterioration in the suspension pivots can cause height irregularities.

8 Before you start work on caster or camber angle checks and adjustments, we strongly recommend that you first spray releasing fluid or WD40 onto the suspension cam bolts, so that subsequent adjustment is made easier. There are two of these to each wheel, at the lower wishbones, where they attach to the crossmember. Similarly, if you need to adjust toe-in, clean and lubricate the ball joint threads after sliding back the dust boots. You can just about get to the required areas without jacking the car (but take care not to get the fluid on the brake parts).

3. WHEEL ALIGNMENT - CHECKING & ADJUSTMENT

☞ 1/1, 2.

FRONT WHEELS, TURNING RADIUS

1 Having carried out preliminary checks (☞ 8/2), place the front wheels on a turning radius gauge and measure the maximum steering angle by turning the steering from lock to lock. Measuring from the straight ahead position, each wheel should move inwards by 37° 23' ± 2° and outwards by 32° 32' ± 2°. If adjustment is required, slacken the clip which secures the dust boot to each tie rod end (if

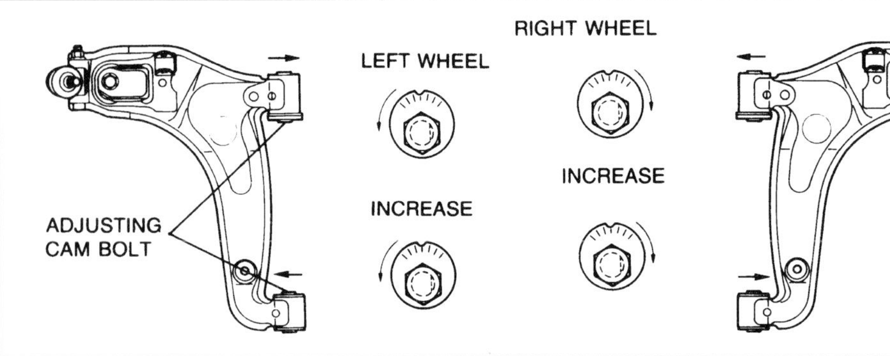

Caster	Left wheel		Right wheel	
	Front cam	Rear cam	Front cam	Rear cam
Increase	Counter-clockwise	Counter-clockwise	Clockwise	Clockwise
Decrease	Clockwise	Clockwise	Counter-clockwise	Counter-clockwise

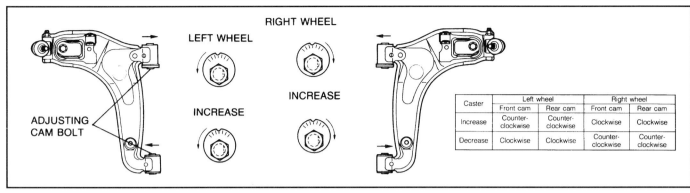

D&T3/9 FRONT WHEEL CASTER ADJUSTMENT.

fitted) and slide the boots inwards. Apply some releasing fluid or WD40 to the tie rod threads and slacken the 17 mm locknuts. Using a 20 mm crescent wrench / open ended spanner, turn the tie rods equally until the specified steering angle is achieved. Before securing the locknut and fitting the dust boot, perform the toe-in check described below. Once the setting is correct, tighten the locknuts securely. (Mazda specify a torque wrench setting of 34-39 Nm (3.5-4.0 Kgf m / 25 - 29 lbf ft) - you may need to improvise a little to achieve this. Spray the area covered by the dust boot with WD40 to prevent corrosion of the tie rod threads, then fit the dust boots and tighten the retaining clips.

FRONT WHEELS, TOE-IN (TRACKING) ADJUSTMENT

2 Perform the toe-in adjustment check described below whenever the turning radius, caster or camber has been adjusted, or if unusual tire wear characteristics indicate that the tracking is set incorrectly. Note that you should check the turning radius adjustment (☞ 8/3/1) before adjusting the tracking.

3 Raise the front of the car so that the front wheels are just clear of the ground, supporting the body by placing stands below the front jacking points (☞ 1/3). We suggest that you use small strips of wood between the stands and the jacking points to protect the paint finish.

4 Either use a proprietary tracking gauge to check the toe-in, following the manufacturers instructions, or use the following method. First, mark the tread area centerline of each tire by turning the wheel by hand while marking a line with chalk. Support the chalk by holding it against a block placed in front of the tire so that you get an even, unbroken line around the tire. Now measure the distance between the two lines at the front and rear of the tires, ensuring that the measurement is made at the same height each side of the tire.

5 The measurement should be 3 ± 3 mm (0.12 ± 0.12 in) greater at the rear of the tire than at the front, indicating that the wheels toe-in by this amount. If your tracking gauge reads in degrees, the specified setting is 0° 18' ± 18'. If the measurement obtained is outside these limits, adjust the tracking as follows.

6 Release the clip which secures the dust boot (if fitted) to each tie rod end and slide the boots away from the steering rack so that the tie rod is free to turn. Apply some releasing fluid or WD40 to the tie rod threads at the outer ends of the tie rods and slacken the ball joint 17 mm locknuts. Using a 20 mm crescent wrench / open ended spanner, turn the left and right tie rods by the same amount, until the prescribed toe-in is achieved. Note that both tie rods have right-hand threads, and so they must be turned in opposite directions when making this adjustment. Each full revolution of the tie rod alters the toe-in by about 7 mm (0.28 in).

7 Once the setting is correct, tighten the locknuts securely. (Mazda specify a torque wrench setting of 34-39 Nm (3.5-4.0 Kgf m / 25 - 29 lbf ft). Spray the ends of the tie rods with WD40 to prevent corrosion of the tie rod threads, then fit the dust boots to the steering rack and fit the retaining clips.

FRONT WHEELS, CASTER ANGLE ADJUSTMENT

8 Set up the camber/caster angle test rig, following the maker's instructions, and check the caster angle. The specified range is 4° 26' ± 45', with no more than 1° difference between the two sides.

9 Refer to the accompanying diagram and table for details of cam movement and effect. Slacken the cam bolt 17 mm locknuts just enough to permit the bolts to be turned - too much slack will introduce error here. Turn the front and/or the rear 17 mm cam bolts in the direction indicated to obtain the correct setting. Leave the locknuts loose until you have checked the camber angle. **Note: one graduation on the front cam alters the caster angle by about 22' and the camber angle by about 25'. Moving the rear cam by one graduation alters the caster angle by about 22' and the camber angle by about 2'.**

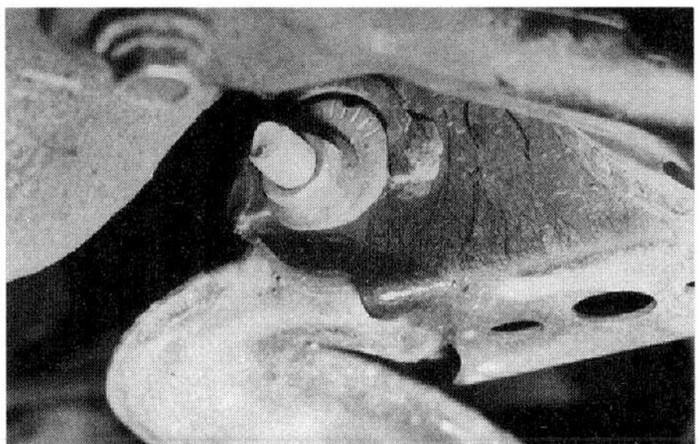

3/9 Wishbone adjustment cam.

FRONT WHEELS, CAMBER ANGLE ADJUSTMENT

10 Check and adjust toe-in and caster angle before making this check. Refer to the accompanying diagram and table for details of cam movement and effect. With the 17 mm cam bolt locknuts slackened just enough to permit the 17 mm bolts to be turned - again, too much slack will introduce error - adjust the camber angle as follows. Turn the front and rear cam bolts by an equal amount in opposite directions to obtain the correct setting. **Note: one graduation on the front cam alters the caster angle by about 22' and the camber angle by about 25'. Moving the rear cam by one graduation alters the caster angle by about 22' and the camber angle by about 2'.**

11 If you are unable to make the camber angle adjustment within the range provided by the cams, go back to the caster angle adjustment sequence and reposition the cams to give enough range for the camber adjustment sequence. After you have adjusted the caster and camber angles, tighten the cam bolt locknuts to 93-113 Nm (9.5-11.5 kgf m / 69-83 lbf ft). Finally, recheck the toe-in as described above - any adjustment of caster or camber angle will have had some effect on this setting.

REAR WHEELS, TOE-IN ADJUSTMENT

12 Set up the camber/caster angle test rig, following the maker's instructions, and check the rear wheel toe-in. The specified range is 3 mm ± 3 mm (0.12 ± 0.12 in).

13 Refer to the accompanying diagram and table for details of cam movement and effect. Slacken the 17 mm cam bolt locknuts just enough to permit the bolts to be turned - too much slack will introduce error. Turn the front and/or the rear 17 mm cam bolts in the direction indicated to obtain the correct setting. Leave the locknuts loose until you have checked the camber angle. **Note: one graduation on the front cam alters the toe-in by about 2.8 mm (0.11 in) and the camber angle by about 15'. Moving the rear cam by one graduation alters the toe-in by about 2.8 mm (0.11 in) and the camber angle by about 6'.**

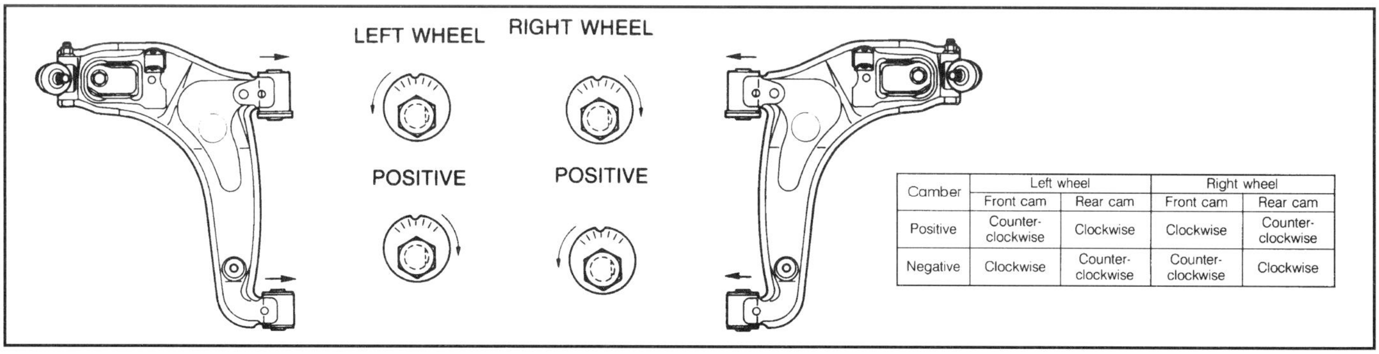

Camber	Left wheel		Right wheel	
	Front cam	Rear cam	Front cam	Rear cam
Positive	Counter-clockwise	Clockwise	Clockwise	Counter-clockwise
Negative	Clockwise	Counter-clockwise	Counter-clockwise	Clockwise

D&T3/10 FRONT WHEEL CAMBER ADJUSTMENT.

REAR WHEELS, CAMBER ANGLE ADJUSTMENT

14 Check and adjust rear wheel toe-in before making this check. Refer to the accompanying diagram and table for details of cam movement and effect. With the 17 mm cam bolt locknuts slackened just enough to permit the bolts to be turned - too much slack will introduce error here, adjust the camber angle as follows. Turn the front and rear 17 mm cam bolts by an equal amount in opposite directions to obtain the correct setting. **Note: one graduation on the front cam alters the toe-in by about 2.8 mm (0.11 in) and the camber angle by about 15'. Moving the rear cam by one graduation alters the toe-in by about 2.8 mm (0.11 in) and the camber angle by about 6'.**

15 If you are unable to make the camber angle adjustment within the range provided by the cams, go back to the rear wheel toe-in adjustment sequence and reposition the cams to give enough range for the camber adjustment sequence. After you have adjusted the toe-in and camber angle, tighten the cam bolt locknuts to 73-95 Nm (7.4-9.7 kgf m / 54-70 lbf ft).

4. SHOCK ABSORBER & SPRING (FRONT) - REMOVAL, O/HAUL & INSTALLATION

☞ 1/1, 2.

REMOVAL

1 Position the vehicle on a smooth, level surface and apply the parking brake. Place wood chocks back and front of the rear tires. Remove the front hub caps, and loosen the wheel nuts by one turn. Raise the front of the car and support on safety stands (☞ 1/3). Unscrew the wheel nuts and remove the wheel.

2 Locate the end of the stabilizer bar (anti-roll bar) and remove the 14 mm nut, bolt and spring washer which secure it to the link rod. As the bolt is removed, the stabilizer bar may move slightly, but it's not under a great deal of pressure.

3 You now have to separate the suspension upper ball joint. Start by straightening and withdrawing the cotter pin / split pin which secures the ball joint castellated nut. Keep the cotter pin / split pin as a pattern - you will need to fit a new one of the correct size during assembly. Remove the 21 mm ball joint nut, then, using a proprietary ball joint separator or Mazda's special tool, release the ball joint pin from its tapered hole in the knuckle.

4 Access around the ball joint is restricted, making the official tool (SST 49 0118 850C) very desirable - we tried a couple of proprietary separators and found it impossible to get them in position. Eventually we used a wedge-type separator, driving the forked taper of the tool between the upper wishbone and knuckle. This works, but you have to take care not to damage the

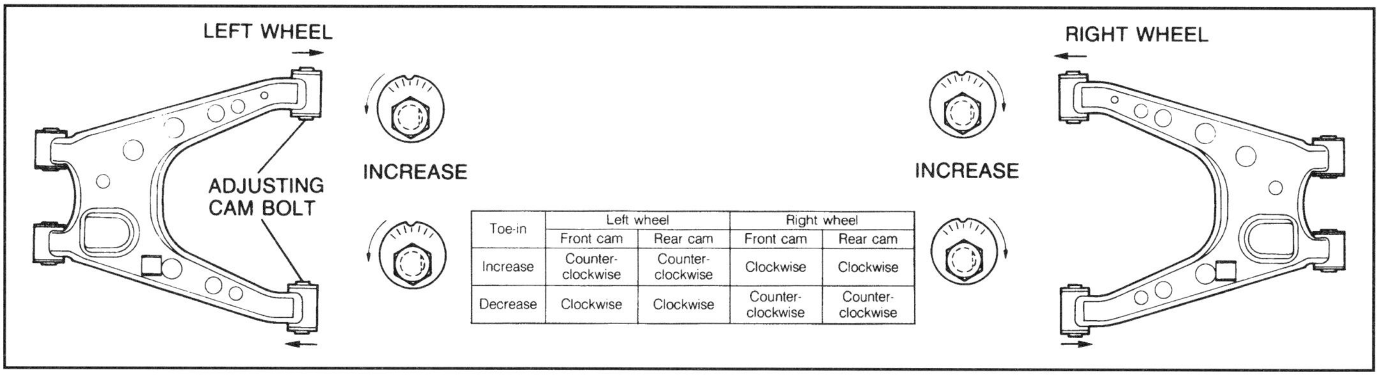

Toe-in	Left wheel		Right wheel	
	Front cam	Rear cam	Front cam	Rear cam
Increase	Counter-clockwise	Counter-clockwise	Clockwise	Clockwise
Decrease	Clockwise	Clockwise	Counter-clockwise	Counter-clockwise

D&T3/13 REAR WHEEL TOE-IN ADJUSTMENT.

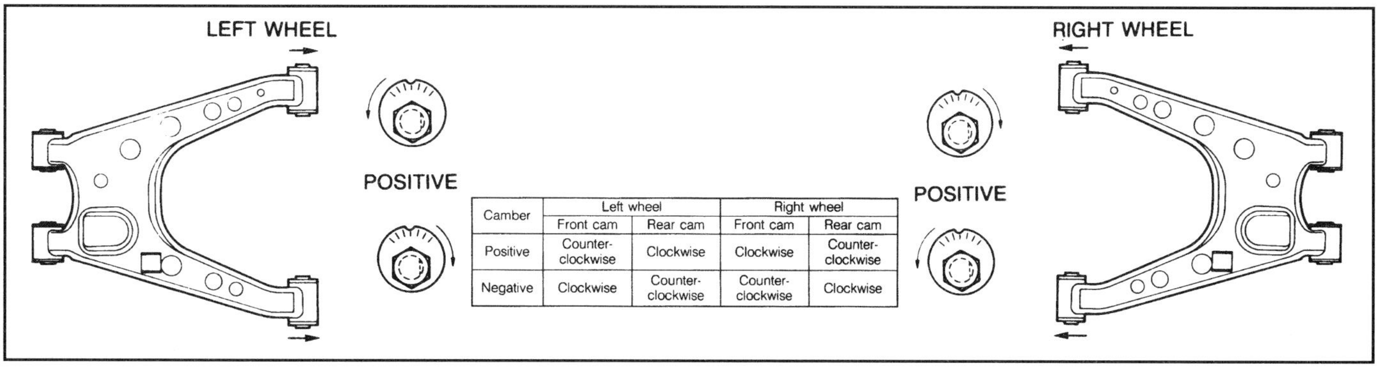

Camber	Left wheel		Right wheel	
	Front cam	Rear cam	Front cam	Rear cam
Positive	Counter-clockwise	Clockwise	Clockwise	Counter-clockwise
Negative	Clockwise	Counter-clockwise	Counter-clockwise	Clockwise

D&T3/14 REAR WHEEL CAMBER ADJUSTMENT.

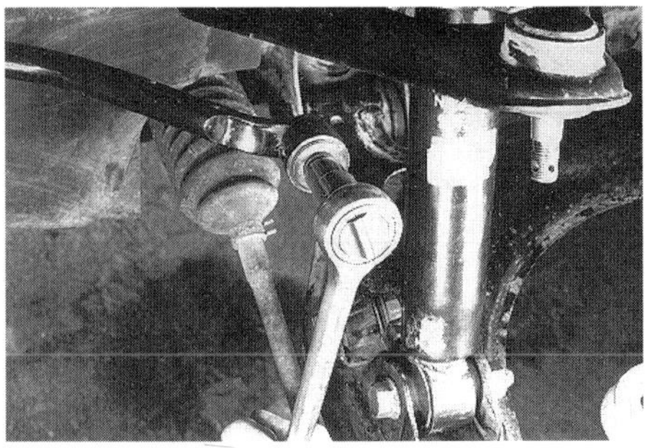

4/2 Undo the stabilizer bar link.

4/4 Release the top ball joint.

ball joint or its dust boot. Note that Mazda recommend the dust boot is replaced each time disassembly takes place, in which case damage to the old boot will not be a problem.

5 If all else fails, try screwing the nut onto the threads upside down, positioning the nut so it is flush with the pin end to protect the threads. Now tap the pin end sharply with a hammer to shock the tapered joint apart, remove the nut, and separate the joint. Again, access is difficult, and you must take great care not to damage the pin end - if you do you will have to replace the upper wishbone and ball joint as an assembly.

6 Working inside the engine compartment, locate the two 14 mm nuts on either side of the suspension top mount dust cap. Remove the two nuts to free the upper end of the suspension unit. **Warning!** Do not remove the large central nut which is covered by the dust cap - if you do, the strut unit will separate under considerable pressure from the suspension spring and become firmly wedged in place - you could also suffer injury as the whole thing flies apart.

7 + Moving back to the underside of the fender, mark the position of the lower wishbone pivot bolts in relation to the crossmember as a guide during installation, using typist's correction fluid or paint marks. If you fail to do this, you will have to set up the suspension from scratch, which takes a lot of time and can only be done using the correct tools. Remove the suspension unit lower mounting bolt, nut and spring washer. Slacken the lower wishbone pivot bolts so that the wishbone can be pushed down slightly, then disengage the upper end of the suspension unit, thread it out of the upper wishbone and remove it to the workbench. Note: do not push down too far on the lower wishbone or you may strain the brake hose.

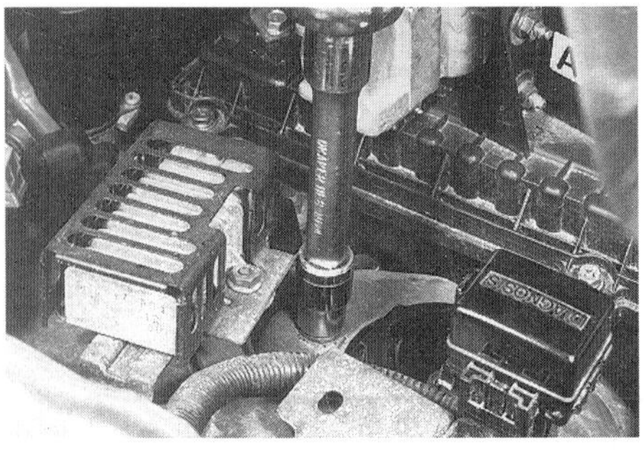

4/6 The strut top is secured by two nuts.

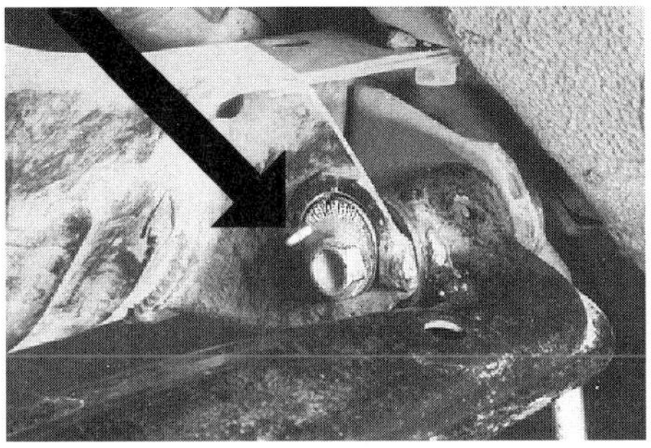

4/7a Mark position of bolt cams before removal.

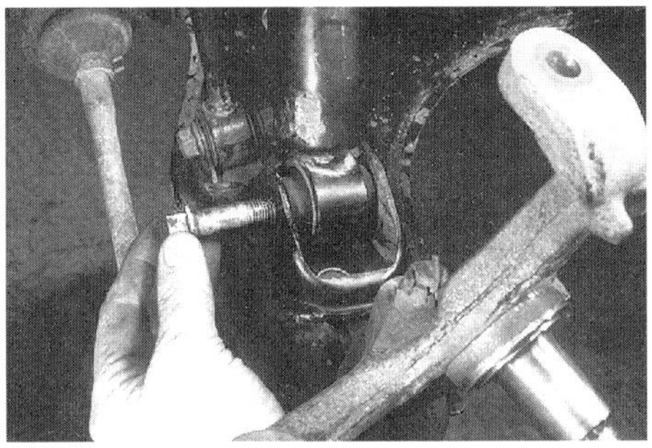

4/7b Withdraw strut lower mounting bolt.

4/7c Pull strut thru top wishbone.

TEARDOWN

8 Clamp the unit in a vise, using soft jaws to protect the paint finish on the spring. Unscrew the 17 mm center nut by a couple of turns, but on no account remove it. Using a commercially available suspension spring compressor (or SSTs 49 G034 102, 49 G034 103 and 49 G034 101) compress the suspension spring until it can be turned freely on the shock absorber. Take care when assembling the compressor. Follow the maker's instructions, and be sure that it is seated securely before compressing the spring.

4/8 Compress the suspension spring.

9 + With the spring safely compressed, unscrew and remove the center nut, lift away the upper mounting plate, then remove the spring and compressor tool. Note the position of the paint mark on the spring coils; the purpose of the mark is to identify the spring rate, but it is preferable to fit the spring facing in the same direction. In the case of the front springs, the identification paint mark is red (manual transmission) or white (automatic transmission), the automatic models requiring slightly heavier springs. Carefully decompress the spring completely and remove it from the tool for cleaning and examination. Pull off the dust boot to reveal the shock absorber body.

4/9a Remove centre nut & mounting plate ...

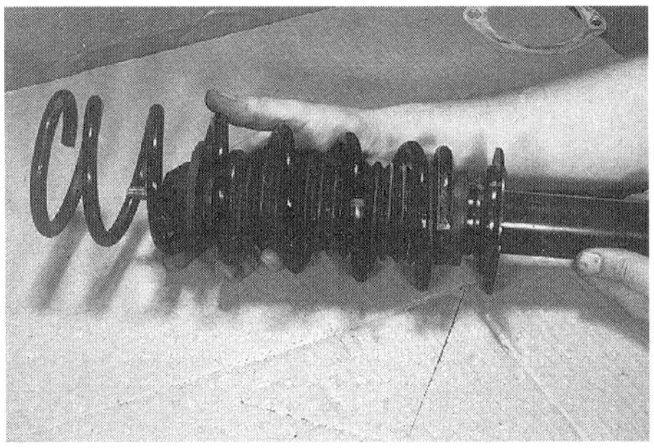

4/9b ... release compressor & remove spring.

CHECKING

10 Before cleaning the shock absorber, check carefully for signs of damper oil leakage. A very light misting of oil on the shock absorber body around the damper rod seal is normal and acceptable - the units work hard in service, and a tiny amount of oil is almost certain to escape. There should not be an appreciable amount of leakage, however, and if you can see that oil has been

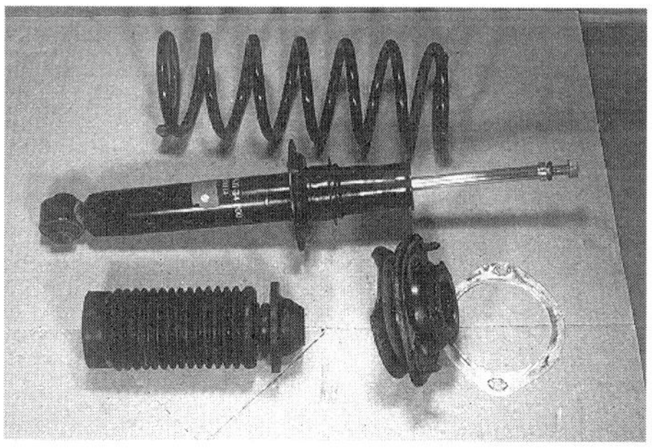
4/10 Suspension strut components.

running down the shock absorber body, it is time to fit a new set.

11 If there is no sign of leakage, clean the shock absorber, then check its operation. The unit is filled with gas at low pressure. When compressed by hand, you should be able to feel the damping effect, and when released the unit should move smoothly back to the extended position. If the action of the unit is abnormally stiff or noisy, or if it fails to extend to its normal position, the need for replacement is indicated.

12 Clean off the spring and measure its free length. This should be 282.5 mm (11.12 in). Mazda do not provide a minimum length figure, but in time the springs will weaken, and the free length will be less than the prescribed figure. If the springs have shortened appreciably, you should consider fitting a new pair, particularly if you've noticed any abnormality in the suspension operation.

13 When new shock absorber units and / or springs are to be fitted, note that they should be replaced as pairs, not individually, or you may suffer suspension imbalance as a result.

14 + Assemble the spring compressor and compress the spring sufficiently for it to be fitted to

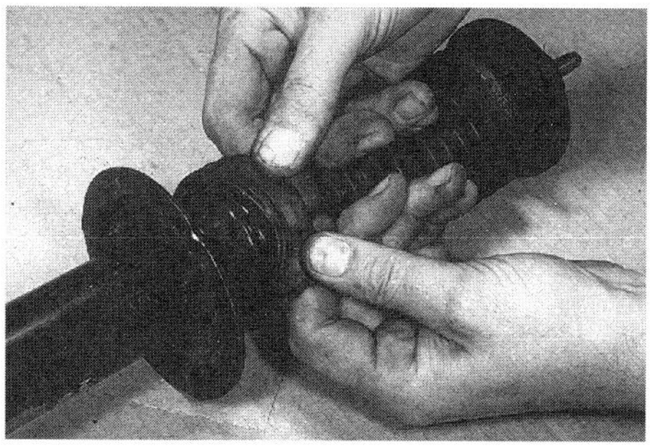
4/14a Refit shock absorber dust boot ...

4/14b ... recompress spring (carefully!) ...

4/14c ...fit mounting plate & centre nut.

the shock absorber. Remember to fit the spring with the paint mark in the same position as it was prior to removal. Fit the dust boot over the shock absorber, making sure that it fits over the locating collar correctly. Fit the compressed spring over the shock absorber, followed by the top mounting plate. Fit the spring washer and nut to the end of the damper rod and tighten by hand.

15 Gradually release the spring compressor, which can be removed once the shock absorber is under spring tension. Clamp the top mounting plate in a vise and tighten the damper rod nut to 31-46 Nm (3.2-4.7 kgf m / 23-34 lbf ft). Finally, clamp the unit upside down by the top plate in a vise (use soft jaws). Fit a screwdriver or smooth metal bar through the lower mount, and turn the unit so that the lower eye and upper mounting studs lie on the same axis.

INSTALLATION

16 Before commencing installation, check the suspension ball joint dust boot for deterioration or damage. If replacement is required, you will have to remove the upper wishbone to do the job, so now is a good time to get on with it (☞ 8/6).

17 Install the plastic gasket over the top of the suspension unit. Position the suspension unit, passing the lower end through the hole in the upper wishbone. You will need to push the wishbone down slightly so that the unit can be maneuvered into place, but don't overdo it - you could strain the brake hose. Fit the suspension unit lower mounting bolt (head towards the rear of the car) and fit the spring washer and nut finger-tight at this stage. Position the suspension unit top mounting and fit the two retaining nuts from inside the engine compartment. If you have difficulty positioning the unit, the small scissor jack supplied with the car's toolkit can be used to raise the assembly a little.

4/17 Don't forget plastic gasket.

18 Realign the link rod and stabilizer (anti-roll) bar, again using the car's jack if you need to, then fit the mounting bolt (head faces outwards). Fit the spring washer and nut finger-tight. Next, position the suspension upper ball joint pin in its tapered hole in the knuckle. Place a block of wood over the top of the ball joint and tap it reasonably hard to seat the taper. This will allow the nut to be fitted and tightened. (If the ball joint turns during tightening, tap it once more and try again. Get the nut as close as you can to the specified torque figure of 41-62 Nm (4.2-6.2 kgf m / 30-46 lbf ft) noting that the hole through the pin end must align

4/18 Lock nut with new cotter (split) pin.

with one of the castellations. Fit a new cotter pin / split pin, bending the ends over to secure the nut. Fit the roadwheel and tighten moderately the wheel nuts.

19 Jack the front of the car (☞ 1/3) so that the safety stands can be removed, then lower it so that its weight is taken on the suspension. This ensures that the suspension components are in the normal running positions before final tightening. You will need access to the fasteners which were slackened during removal, so we suggest that you temporarily fit the roadwheels, then use fabricated steel ramps under the front wheels to obtain working clearance.

20 Check carefully the position of the lower wishbone pivot bolts, referring to the alignment marks made during the teardown. Turn the bolts until the marks are correctly aligned, then tighten the pivot nuts to 83-103 Nm (8.5-10.5 kgf m / 61-76 lbf ft).

21 + Tighten the suspension unit bottom mounting bolt nut to 73-93 Nm (7.4-9.5 kgf m / 54-69 lbf ft), and the upper mounting nuts to 29-36 Nm (3.0-3.7 kgf m / 22-27 lbf ft). Fit the plastic cap over the suspension unit upper mounting plate center. Finally, check-tighten the roadwheel nuts

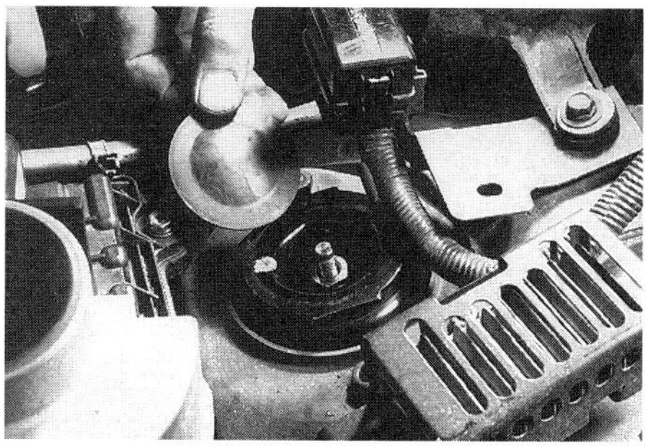
4/21 Refit dust cover if it was removed.

(specified torque is 88-118 Nm (9.0-12.0 kgf m / 65-87 lbf ft). That's about it. If you made sure that the lower wishbone pivot bolts were fitted in *exactly* the same positions as they were before removal, the suspension geometry should be unchanged. Note, however, that Mazda recommend the settings should be checked (☞ 8/3).

5. WISHBONE (LOWER, FRONT) - REMOVAL, O/HAUL & INSTALLATION

☞ 1/1, 2.

REMOVAL

1 Position the vehicle on a smooth, level surface and apply the parking brake. Place wood chocks back and front of the rear tires. Remove the front hub caps, and loosen the wheel nuts by one turn. Raise the front of the car and position safety stands under the jacking points at the front of each sill (☞ 1/3). Unscrew the wheel nuts and remove the wheel.

2 Locate the end of the stabilizer bar (anti-roll bar) and remove the 14 mm nut, bolt and spring washer which secure it to the link rod. As the bolt is removed, the stabilizer bar may move slightly, but it's not under a great deal of pressure. Next, you should remove the suspension unit lower mounting 17 mm nut, bolt and spring washer. Push out the bolt to free the lower end of the suspension unit.

3 You now have to separate the suspension lower ball joint. Start by straightening and withdrawing the cotter pin / split pin which secures the ball joint castellated nut. Keep the used pin as a pattern - you will need to fit a new one of the same size during assembly. Remove the ball joint 21 mm nut, then, using a proprietary ball joint separator or Mazda's special tool, release the ball joint pin from its tapered hole in the knuckle.

4 + Access around the ball joint is restricted, making the official tool (SST 49 0727 575) very desirable - we tried a couple of proprietary separators and found it impossible to get them in position. You can cheat a little here, but only if you know that you don't need to change the ball joint - leave the ball joint attached to the steering knuckle, and instead remove the single 17 mm bolt which secures the rear of the ball joint casting to the wishbone. You can just get to this with the suspension unit pushed back a little, through the cutout in the top surface of the wishbone. Next, remove the outer 17 mm pivot bolt which fits horizontally

5/4a This bolt and ...

5/4b ... this one secure ball joint casting.

through the two components. Once the bolts are removed, you can swing the knuckle and hub clear of the wishbone with the ball joint undisturbed.

5 If you have used the cheat described above, you can leave the steering and suspension lower ball joints attached to the knuckle, unless they specifically require attention. If you need to detach the lower ball joint from the steering knuckle, you may now have enough room to use a wedge-type separator, driving the forked taper of the tool between the lower wishbone and the steering knuckle. This will work, given the right tool, but you have to take care not to damage the ball joint or its dust boot. (Of course, if the joint is worn out, it won't matter if you wreck it during removal).

6 If all else fails, try screwing the nut onto the threads upside down, positioning the nut so it is flush with the pin end to protect the threads. Now tap the pin end sharply with a hammer to shock the tapered joint apart, remove the nut, and separate the joint. Again, access is difficult - you may need to use a drift to reach the pin end. If you need to remove the steering ball joint from the knuckle, a similar technique can be employed, but normally this too can be left attached to the steering knuckle.

7 Mark the position of the lower wishbone pivot bolts in relation to the crossmember as a guide during installation, using typist's correction fluid or paint marks. If you fail to do this, you will have to set up the suspension from scratch, which takes a lot of time. Once you have marked the position of both bolts, remove the nuts and tap out and remove the pivot bolts. Pull the wishbone clear of the crossmember, and fit the bolts in their respective positions in the crossmember for safe keeping.

CHECKING AND OVERHAUL

8 Clean off the wishbone, and check for damage. If you find signs of cracking, rusting or impact damage, fit a new one - attempted repairs are inadvisable on suspension parts.

9 If the wishbone is serviceable, you should fit new mounting bushes before installing it. You can press the old bushes out using a socket, but you will need something to press them into. The official method is to use a couple of SSTs (49 B034 201 and 49 N028 201). These are support blocks which you position together on one side of the mounting bush bores. Place a large socket on the other side of the bush, clamp the assembly in a vise, and jack the bush out by tightening the vise.

10 We made up our own support block from a 50 mm / 2 in long (approx) section of scaffold tube - any thick-walled steel tubing with an internal bore of a little over 40 mm will do fine. You need to make sure that the lip at the end of the bush will fit into the support block. One way to do this is to cut a notch out of the wall of the block. The lip can be guided in by turning the block and feeding it in with a small screwdriver. You should make sure that it is not trapped by the block, especially during installation, or the lip will tear off.

11 Once you are sure that everything is positioned correctly, start winding the vise down to

5/11 Push out wishbone bush.

force the bush out into the support block. Note that the bush is a very tight fit - use some rubber lubricant or WD40 to ease removal, working it under the lips at the edges of the bush. Even with lubricant, you will have to exert a lot of pressure to get the bush moving. We used a sturdy old 4 1/2 inch engineers vise - it worked, but we grew concerned about its health during the removal process. If you have doubts about your vise's ability to withstand this sort of pressure, it may be worth getting a local engineering shop to press out the old bushes and fit the new ones for you.

12 + Installing the new bushes is done using the support block and socket in much the same way. We employed a socket into which had been fitted a short bolt, the bolt acting as a pilot to hold it square and prevent any risk of it slipping out under pressure. This time the support block is needed only to allow the bush to protrude a little during fitting before the natural resilience of the rubber lets it settle back square in the bore. Use rubber lubricant or a little soapy water to ease fitting, and make sure that the bush is positioned centrally in its bore.

13 Turning our attention to the lower ball

5/12a Removed bush & 'special' tool.

5/12b Lubricate bush as it's pushed into place.

joint, the official procedure is to remove the old dust boot, re-grease and fit a new one as part of any overhaul. The boot has a metal rim which is a tight fit on the ball joint. To remove it, you have to chisel it off, taking great care not to chisel the joint while you are doing so. This effectively destroys the boot, so have a new one ready before you start chiselling. Once the boot has been removed, clean off the old grease and apply some fresh lithium-based general purpose grease to the joint in the area covered by the dust boot.

14 Time for the next SST (49 H028 301 Installer, dust boot). This tool is essentially a short tube with a double diameter lip at the end. The seal fits into the tool and is then pressed onto the ball joint. If you don't happen to have the tool, you will need to use a socket or an odd piece of tubing to press the dust boot onto the joint. It can be done this way, but it is easy to damage the boot without the tool.

15 You should now check the ball joint condition by measuring the torque required to turn the ball joint pin. You can either use the appropriate SST (49 0180 510B attachment) and the Mazda approved pull scale, or improvise this check. The specified rotational torque is 0.5-1.5 Nm (5-15 kgf cm / 4.3-13 lbf in) and the pull scale reading using the SST should be 4.9-14.7 N (0.5-1.5 kg / 1.7-3.3 lb).

16 If you want to do this check without having the SST mentioned above, we suggest that you get a steel strip and drill two holes exactly 12 inches apart. Enlarge one hole so you can just fit it over the end of the ball joint pin and secure it by fitting the castellated nut. As you tighten the nut, the strip will be pulled firmly down onto the pin taper. Now hook a spring balance to the remaining hole, and check that you need to exert the specified rotational torque before it moves.

17 Oops, nearly forgot! Mazda say that before you do the above torque test you should shake the ball joint five times ... (Yes, seriously). We have a number of theories about why this should be done, our best guess is that it might ward off evil spirits.

INSTALLATION

18 + The assembled wishbone can now be installed, remembering that the pivot bolts are fitted so that the two bolt heads face each other across the gap in the wishbone. Fit the eccentric washers and nuts, fingertight only at this stage. If the ball joint is still attached to the steering knuckle,

5/18a Slide wishbone into place ...

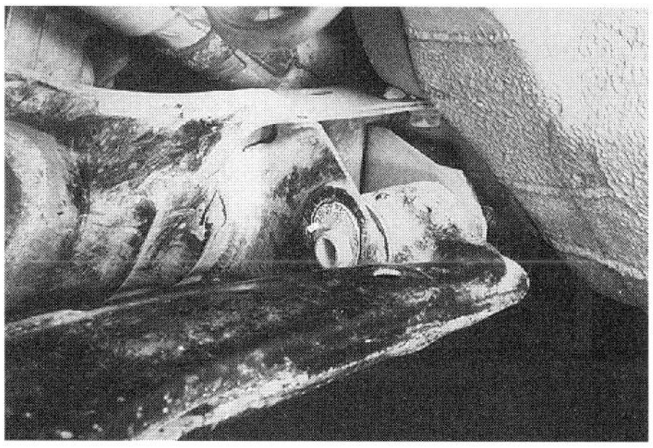

5/18b ... position cams correctly.

5/18c Secure ball joint casting (if removed).

slide it back into the end of the wishbone, tightening the vertical mounting bolt to 73-93 Nm (7.4-9.5 kgf m / 54-69 lbf ft). The horizontal mounting bolt is fitted with the head facing forward, and should be tightened to the same torque figure.

19 If you separated the lower ball joint from the steering knuckle, clean its taper and reposition the pin end through the tapered hole in the knuckle. Place a block of wood below the head of the ball joint, then give it several sharp upward blows to seat it in the knuckle. You should now be able to fit the castellated nut, tightening it to the lower end of its torque range of 58-77 Nm (5.8-7.9 kgf m / 43-57 lbf ft). If the pin turns, reseat it and continue tightening. Check to see if any one of the castellations align with the hole in the ball joint pin - if necessary, tighten the nut a little more until a new cotter pin / split pin can be fitted. Bend over the ends of the pin to secure the nut, trimming off any excess with wire cutters.

20 If you separated the steering ball joint from the steering knuckle during the teardown, check that the ball joint taper is clean, then fit it to the steering knuckle, tapping it sharply into position so that the pin is gripped in the tapered hole. Fit the castellated nut, then tighten it to the lower end of the 29-44 Nm (3.0-4.5 kgf m / 22-33 lbf ft) torque range. If the pin turns during tightening, tap it again to seat the taper and try again. Check whether the hole through the pin aligns with a pair of castellations, and tighten further if required until it does line up. Fit a new cotter (split) pin and bend the ends over to secure the nut.

21 Fit the suspension unit lower mounting bolt (head towards the rear of the car) and fit the spring washer and nut finger-tight at this stage. If you have difficulty positioning the unit, the small scissor jack supplied with the car's toolkit can be used to raise the assembly as required. Realign the link rod and stabilizer (anti-roll) bar, again using the car's jack if you need to, then fit the mounting bolt (with the head facing outwards). Fit the spring washer and nut finger-tight.

22 Jack the front of the car (☞ 1/3) so that the safety stands can be removed, then lower it so that its weight is taken on the suspension. This ensures that the suspension components are in the normal running positions before final tightening. You will need access to the fasteners which were slackened during removal, so we suggest the use of fabricated steel ramps under the front wheels to obtain this.

23 Check carefully the position of the lower wishbone pivot bolts, referring to the alignment marks made during the teardown. Turn the bolts until the marks are correctly aligned, then tighten the pivot nuts to 83-103 Nm (8.5-10.5 kgf m / 61-76 lbf ft).

24 Tighten the suspension unit bottom mounting bolt nut to 73-93 Nm (7.4-9.5 kgf m / 54-69 lbf ft). Finally, check-tighten the roadwheel nuts (specified torque is 88-118 Nm (9.0-12.0 kgf m / 65-87 lbf ft). That's about it. If you made sure that the lower wishbone pivot bolts were fitted in *exactly* the same positions as they were before removal, the suspension geometry should be unchanged. Note, however, that Mazda recommend the settings should be checked (☞ 8/3).

6. WISHBONE (UPPER, FRONT) - REMOVAL, O/HAUL & INSTALLATION

☞ 1/1, 2.

REMOVAL

1 Position the vehicle on a smooth, level surface and apply the parking brake. Place wood chocks either side of the rear tires. Remove the front hub cap/s, and loosen the wheel nuts by one turn. Raise the front of the car and position safety stands under the jacking points at the front of each sill (☞ 1/3). Unscrew the wheel nuts and remove the wheel/s.

2 Moving to the underside of the car, the next job is to remove the plastic undertray from beneath the front of the engine - access to the upper wishbone pivot bolts is restricted, and you will need to get the undertray clear to improve access. All fixings are 10 mm. First, remove the three sheet metal screws from the front of the tray. Then remove the bolt next to the upper wishbone

on each side of the car, the bolt on the side of the chassis member in the wheelwell from each side and, finally, the nut on each side holding not only the tray but also the front valence stay. Once the nut is removed the stay can be pulled from the stud and moved out of the way to give enough clearance to remove the plastic undertray, It's recommended that you put all of the screws and the two nuts back in place finger-tight once the tray is removed.

3 Next, you should remove the suspension unit lower mounting 17 mm nut, bolt and spring washer. Push out the bolt to free the lower end of the suspension unit.

4 You now have to separate the suspension upper ball joint. Start by straightening and withdrawing the cotter pin / split pin which secures the ball joint castellated nut. Keep the old pin as a pattern - you will need to fit a new one of the same size during assembly. Remove the ball joint 21 mm nut, then, using a proprietary ball joint separator or Mazda's special tool, release the ball joint pin from its tapered hole in the knuckle.

5 Access around the ball joint is restricted, making the official tool (SST 49 0118 850C) very desirable - we tried a couple of proprietary separators and found it impossible to get them in position. Eventually we used a wedge-type separator, driving the forked taper of the tool between the upper wishbone and knuckle. This works, but you have to take care not to damage the ball joint or its dust boot.

6 If all else fails, try screwing the nut onto the threads upside down, positioning the nut so it is flush with the pin end to protect the threads. Now tap the pin end sharply with a hammer to shock the tapered joint apart, remove the nut, and separate the joint. Again, access is difficult, and you must take great care not to damage the pin end - if you do you will have to replace the upper wishbone and ball joint assembly.

7 Slacken and remove the pivot bolt 21 mm nut and its spring washer. You can now withdraw the pivot bolt towards the front of the car, noting that if it has become corroded in place, it will help to apply some releasing fluid or WD40, leaving it to soak in for a while before attempting removal. Once you have pulled the pivot bolt free the wishbone can be maneuvered off the suspension unit and withdrawn.

CHECKING AND OVERHAUL

8 Clean off the wishbone, and check for damage. If you find signs of cracking, rusting or impact damage, fit a new one - attempted repairs are inadvisable on suspension parts. Check the pivot bolt bore through the crossmember end, sliding the bolt into position and checking for free play. If this is excessive, try fitting a new pivot bolt. In extreme cases, the bore through the crossmember may be worn, in which case you will have to consider fitting a new crossmember. Turning our attention to the upper ball joint, check for excessive wear by manipulating the ball joint pin. If you can feel free play, the joint should be considered unserviceable. Similarly, if the joint is stiff and notchy, or if it rattles when you shake it, it's broke. The good news is that you get a free ball joint with every upper wishbone purchased, the bad news is that the upper ball joint is an integral part of the wishbone, so if the ball joint is worn out, don't waste any more time on the wishbone.

9 If the wishbone (and the ball joint) is serviceable, you should fit new mounting bushes before installing it. You can press the old bushes out using a socket, but you will need something to press them into. The official method is to use an SST (49 B034 201). This is a support block which you position on one side of the mounting bush bores. Place a large socket on the other side of the bush, clamp the assembly in a vise, and jack the bush out by tightening the vise. It is possible to fabricate your own support block ☞ 8/5/10.

10 The procedure for removing and installing the bushes is exactly the same as that described for the lower wishbone ((☞ 8/5/9-12) except the bushes are slightly different, having a head which fits to the outside of the wishbone. Press the old bushes out from between the wishbone mounting bores, and fit the new ones from the outer edges of the bores.

11 Before fitting the wishbone, note that it is official procedure to remove the old dust boot, regrease the joint and fit a new boot as part of any overhaul. The boot has a metal rim which is a tight fit on the ball joint. To remove it, you have to chisel it off, taking great care not to damage the joint while you are doing so. This effectively destroys the boot, so have a new one ready before you start. Once the boot has been removed, clean off the old grease and apply some fresh lithium-based general purpose grease to the joint in the area covered by the dust boot.

12 To fit the new dust boot you will need to use a 30 mm socket to press it onto the joint. Take care that you press the boot onto the joint squarely and evenly, or you will damage the metal rim of the boot, making installation impossible. Do not use excessive force - the boot should be pressed into place until it just contacts the seat on the joint. After installation, check that there is no more than 1 mm (0.04 in) clearance between the boot and the joint seat.

13 You should now check the ball joint condition by measuring the torque required to turn the ball joint pin. You can either use the appropriate SST (49 0180 510B attachment) and the Mazda approved pull scale, or improvise this check. The specified rotational torque is 0.4-1.2 Nm (4-12 kgf cm / 3.5-10.0 lbf in) and the pull scale reading using the SST should be 3.9-11.8 N (0.4-1.2 kg / 2.9-8.8 lb).

14 If you want to do this check without having the SST mentioned above, we suggest that you improvise as follows. Get a steel strip about an inch wide, and drill two holes exactly 12 inches apart. Enlarge one hole so you can just fit it over the end of the ball joint pin and secure it by fitting the castellated nut. As you tighten the nut, the strip will be pulled firmly down onto the pin taper. Now hook a spring balance to the remaining hole, and check that you need to exert the specified rotational torque before it moves.

15 As with the lower ball joint, Mazda say that before you do the above torque test you should shake the ball joint five times. (This is driving us nuts, why should it be shaken *five* times? - what happens if you shake it four times, or six ... We still haven't figured out a sane explanation for this; Wally scoffed at our suggestion about warding off evil spirits - he says that maybe it compensates for gravitational anomalies).

16 OK, we're ready to install the wishbone. Thread it over the suspension strut and fit it back into position; then slide in the pivot bolt. We suggest that you coat the bolt in molybdenum grease before you fit it. Fit the spring washer and nut, tightening lightly at this stage.

17 Position the suspension upper ball joint pin in its tapered hole in the knuckle. Place a block of wood over the top of the ball joint and tap it reasonably hard to seat the taper. This will allow the nut to be fitted and tightened. (If the ball joint turns during tightening, tap it once more and try again. Get the nut as close as you can to the lower end of the specified torque range of 41-62 Nm (4.2-6.2 kgf m / 30-46 lbf ft) noting that the hole through the pin end must align with one of the castellations. Tighten a little more as required until the holes line up, then fit a new cotter pin / split pin, bending the ends over to secure the nut.

18 Fit the suspension unit lower mounting bolt (head towards the rear of the car) and fit the spring washer and nut finger-tight at this stage. If you have difficulty positioning the unit, the small scissor jack supplied with the car's toolkit can be used to raise the assembly as required. Fit the roadwheel and tighten the wheel nuts.

18 You can now fit the plastic undertray. You will need to get to the pivot bolt and nut heads to check-tighten them in a while, but this is just about possible with the undertray in place. Temporarily fit the roadwheels, then jack the front of the car so that the safety stands can be removed, lowering it so that its weight is taken on the suspension. This ensures that the suspension components are in the normal running positions before final tightening. You will need access to the fasteners which were slackened during removal, so we suggest the use of fabricated steel ramps under the front wheels to achieve this.

19 Tighten the suspension unit bottom mounting bolt nut to 73-93 Nm (7.4-9.5 kgf m / 54-69 lbf ft). Tighten the upper wishbone pivot bolt to 118-138 Nm (12.0-14.0 kgf m / 87-102 lbf ft). Finally, check-tighten the roadwheel nuts (specified torque is 88-118 Nm (9.0-12.0 kgf m / 65-87 lbf ft). Note that Mazda recommend the suspension alignment settings should be checked (☞ 8/3).

7. STABILIZER BAR (FRONT) - REMOVAL, CHECKING & INSTALLATION

☞ 1/1, 2.

REMOVAL

1 Position the vehicle on a smooth, level surface and apply the parking brake. Place wood

chocks either side of the rear tires. Remove the front hub caps, and loosen the wheel nuts by one turn. Raise the front of the car and position safety stands under the jacking points at the front of each sill (☞ 1/3). Unscrew the wheel nuts and remove the wheels.

2 Moving to the underside of the car, the next job is to remove the plastic undertray from beneath the front of the engine. All fixings are 10 mm. First, remove the three sheet metal screws from the front of the tray. Then remove the bolt next to the upper wishbone on each side of the car, the bolt on the side of the chassis member in the wheelwell from each side and, finally, the nut on each side holding not only the tray but also the front valence stay. Once the nut is removed the stay can be pulled from the stud and moved out of the way to give enough clearance to remove the plastic undertray, It's recommended that you put all of the screws and the two nuts back in place finger-tight once the tray is removed.

3 Working underneath the car, locate the two support brackets which retain the stabilizer bar to the underside. Remove the two 12 mm bolts which secure each bracket and remove the brackets, leaving the rubber support blocks in place on the stabilizer bar for now. Remove the bolt, nut and spring washer which secures each of the two stabilizer bar control links to the lower wishbones and remove the stabilizer bar and links from the vehicle. The links can be removed from the stabilizer bar ends by releasing the 14 mm nut, bolt and spring washer which retains them. Before removing the rubber support blocks from the stabilizer bar, check that the alignment marks which indicate the correct position of the blocks are clearly visible - if not, mark the bar with paint or typist's correction fluid as a guide during installation.

CHECKING

4 The stabilizer bar is unlikely to require replacement unless accident damaged or a high performance unit is being installed. If the stabilizer bar has been bent or twisted, or is badly corroded, it should be replaced. Check the stabilizer bar control links for signs of similar damage, and check the condition of the rubber bushes at each end. If these are obviously worn or deteriorated, fit new links. Check the stabilizer bar support blocks for wear or deterioration, replacing them if obviously worn or damaged (wear in the blocks can produce mysterious clanks and rattles from the suspension).

INSTALLATION

5 Position the rubber support blocks on the stabilizer bar, making sure that they line up with the alignment marks you made during removal. Fit the control links to the ends of the stabilizer bar, bolt heads outwards, leaving the nuts loose for now. Reposition the assembly under the car, fitting the control link to lower wishbone bolts, nuts and spring washers with the bolt heads facing the front of the car. Tighten the nuts finger-tight only at this stage.

6 Jack the front of the car (☞ 1/3) so that the safety stands can be removed, then lower it so that its weight is taken on the suspension. This ensures that the suspension components are in the normal running positions before final tightening. You will need access to the fasteners which were slackened during removal, and also room to install the undertray, so we suggest the use of fabricated steel ramps under the front wheels to achieve this.

7 Tighten the control link nuts to 36-54 Nm (3.7-5.5 kgf m / 27-40 lbf ft). Reposition the stabilizer bar brackets over the rubber support blocks, ensuring that these have not moved on the stabilizer bar (check the alignment marks). Fit and tighten the mounting bolts to 18-26 Nm (1.8-2.7 kgf m / 13-20 lbf ft). Finally, reposition the plastic undertray and fit the numerous 10 mm fasteners to retain it.

8. CROSSMEMBER (FRONT) - REMOVAL & INSTALLATION

1 The front suspension attaches to a fabricated steel subframe, or crossmember, attached to the car's bodyshell. The subframe also provides engine mounting points, and in theory it is possble to remove the engine, transmission, suspension and steering as one big assembly.

2 In reality, such a procedure would be pretty much impossible outside of a full commercial workshop. You would need a vehicle lift at the very least, and sufficient space overhead to lift the car clear of this major assembly. It is also doubtful if carrying out this procedure successfully would convey any particular advantage to the home mechanic; it is really just a convenient way of putting cars together on an assembly line.

3 If you need to remove just the crossmember and the steering/suspension parts, note that you will first need to jack the car well clear of the ground and support it on safety stands. You will also need an engine crane or hoist which will reach over the top of the engine bay so that the weight of the engine and transmission can be supported while the crossmember is detached and removed.

4 Our considered advice here is don't bother - on balance, it is probably best not to attempt removal of this assembly. We looked into this on our project car, and in the end could see lots of problems and few advantages to doing this. The only time we envisage this being a realistic working technique would be in the context of a full structural restoration; a little beyond the scope of this book.

5 The suspension and steering parts can be worked on without disturbing the crossmember, as can the engine and transmission. If the crossmember itself requires attention, it is likely to be as a result of impact damage, in which case professional help will be needed anyway (if your car's crossmember is bent, we wouldn't care to think about how the body looks!). You'll need to get the car checked out on a body jig, either by a Mazda dealer or a reputable body shop.

6 Similarly, if rusting is the reason for removal, we suggest that you get the car checked out professionally. In reality, we suspect that the rest of the car will have been eaten away to nothing long before rust gets to be a problem in this area.

9. STEERING (MANUAL) - DESCRIPTION

The Miata/MX5 is equipped with conventional rack-and-pinion steering. Depending on which option was chosen when the car was ordered, this will be either manually-operated or speed-sensitive power steering, the latter being described and covered in detail later in this chapter.

Turning motion from the steering wheel is transmitted down a collapsible steering column to an intermediate shaft. The shaft has universal joints at each end, allowing an indirect line between the column and steering rack.

Inside the rack, the intermediate shaft turns a small pinion, which in turn drives the rack from side to side as the steering is operated. Motion from the rack ends is conveyed by articulated tie-rods terminating in steering ball joints attached to the steering knuckles. The effective length of the tie-rod is adjustable to permit the correct amount of front wheel toe-in to be set.

10. STEERING (MANUAL) - CHECKING

☞ 1/1, 2.

1 Preliminary checks on the steering can be carried out without a teardown. Sit in the driver's seat with the front wheel in the straight ahead position, and gently turn the wheel to and fro to gauge the amount of free play before any slack in the steering mechanism is taken up. You can gauge this better by leaning out of the car and noting when the road wheel begins to move. Allowable free play at the steering wheel rim is 0-30 mm (0-1.18 in) before the road wheels begin to move. Excessive play normally indicates wear in the steering ball joints, steering column universal joints or the rack mechanism. Less likely causes are loose steering column clamps or rack mountings.

2 Next, try pulling the steering wheel left and right, then up and down, at right angles in relation to the steering column. There should be no play felt here. If there is, check for wear in the steering column and joints and check the security of the steering wheel and the clamps at the upper and lower ends of the intermediate shaft.

3 The final check requires the car to raised so that the front wheels are clear of the ground. Position the vehicle on a smooth, level surface and apply the parking brake. Place wood chocks front and back of the rear tires. Raise the front of the car and position safety stands under the jacking points at the front of each sill (☞ 1/3). Turn the steering from lock to lock at least five times to settle the steering components. While doing so, note any unusually slack or tight spots which might indicate wear or damage in the intermediate shaft joints or the rack mechanism, possibly as a result of impact damage. If noted, these faults should be investigated and rectified.

4 If the steering is abnormally stiff with the wheels clear of the ground, the rack mechanism

may be at fault, or the steering ball joints may be badly worn or damaged. Hook a pull scale (spring balance) to the outer edge of one of the steering wheel spokes and check the effort needed to turn the wheel during one complete revolution. This should be in the range 4.9-29.4 N (0.5-3.0 kg / 1.1-6.6 lb), so a fair amount of latitude is available, but if it is outside these limits a problem is indicated.

11. STEERING WHEEL & COLUMN REMOVAL, CHECKING & INSTALLATION

☞ 1/1, 2.

REMOVAL

1 Before attempting steering wheel removal on cars equipped with air bag modules ☞ 7/50. **Warning!** If the air bag module is handled incorrectly it may be deployed accidentally causing damage or injury.

2 ☞ 7/60 describes the correct removal and installation procedure for air bag modules, however, before starting work, note that the steering wheel should not be removed needlessly. If you simply need to remove the column assembly, remove the air bag module for safety (see below) but leave the wheel attached to the steering column. Note that you will have to remove the wheel to allow the combination (steering column) switch to be removed from the column.

3 On all cars, start by disabling the stereo security system and then isolate the electrical system by disconnecting the battery negative (-) terminal ☞ 7/2).

4 **Air bag equipped cars.** Remove the access panel below the steering column (unclip it from the dash panel - see diagram) and locate the air bag clock spring wiring connector assembly. These connectors, colored orange and blue for identification, are interlocked. You need to unlatch and separate the smaller orange connector before you can disconnect the blue connector. Once these have been disconnected, the air bag module is safe from accidental triggering from the backup battery. The air bag module can now be removed from the steering wheel, again observing the safety precautions (☞ 7/50). Remove the four module mounting nuts from the back of the wheel and remove the air bag module, storing it in a safe place, face upwards.

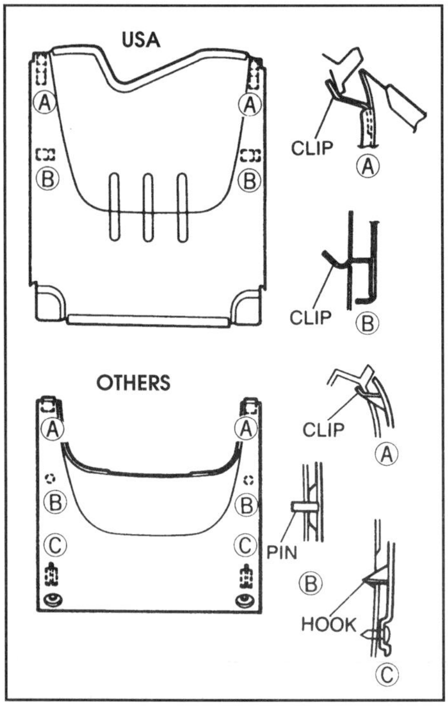

D11/4 ACCESS PANEL REMOVAL DETAILS.

5 + **Non-air bag equipped cars.** If steering wheel removal is required, remove the moulded safety cover at the center of the steering wheel. On some wheel types this is secured from the back by screws. On our UK spec project car, a Momo wheel was fitted, and the cover simply clipped over the spokes of the steering wheel. If a central horn switch is fitted, pry it out with a small screwdriver and disconnect the switch wire.

6 **All models.** If the steering wheel is to be removed, check that the road wheels are positioned straight ahead and that the steering wheel spokes are level. Although not strictly essential, we marked the relationship of the wheel and column end with paint to avoid any problems with alignment during installation - though this becomes irrelevant if both the steering wheel and the column are removed. Slacken and remove the central retaining 21 mm nut. You will now need a puller to draw the wheel off the steering column splines. The exact design of the puller is dependent on the type of steering wheel fitted - you will need to find something which can be attached securely to the wheel and having a center bolt that can be used to jack against the end of the column. Note that under no circumstances should you try shocking the wheel free by striking the end of the column - you can easily collapse the column by doing this.

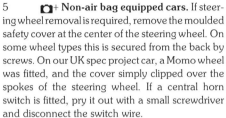

11/5a Pry out horn button or central cover.

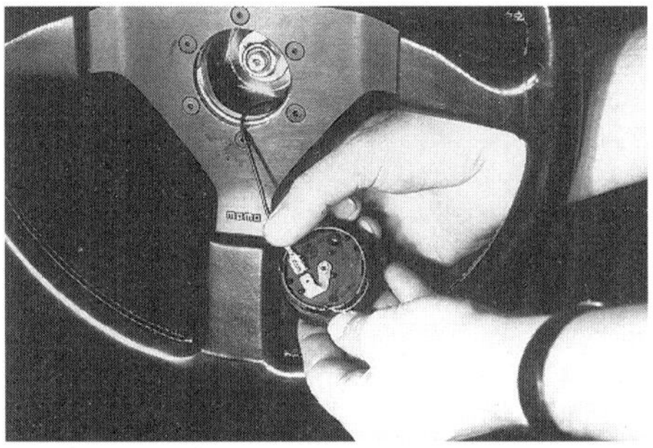

11/5b Disconnect electrical terminal.

11/6 Remove steering wheel retaining nut.

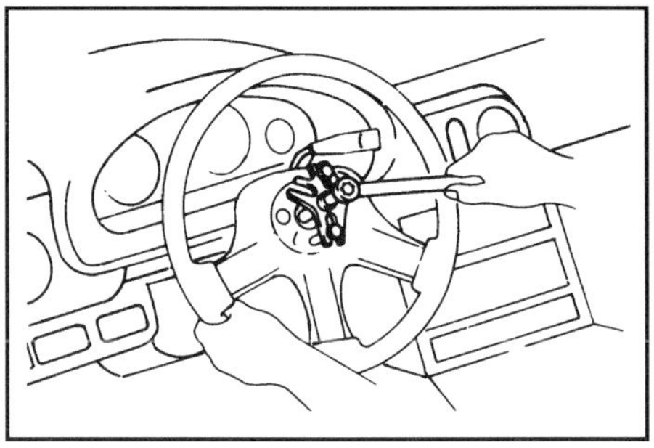

D11/6 USING PULLER TO REMOVE STEERING WHEEL.

7 Wally, our Technical Adviser, encountered problems in removing the Momo steering wheel without damage using the method described by Mazda. He tried using a puller lodged below the aluminum spokes, but when the center bolt was tightened, the pressure crushed the pressed steel retainer ring which locates the horn switch. In the end, we removed the countersunk socket screws which retain the wheel to the wheel boss, removed the horn switch retainer ring, installed the wheel again, and then used the puller to draw it off the column. Depending on the arrangement you find on your car, you may need to adopt a similar method to avoid damage.

8 The next step is to remove the combination switch assembly. Start by removing the screws from the underside of the switch housing. On our non-air bag car, the housing was held by three sheet metal screws and a single machine screw. There are two sheet metal screws near the outer edge of the housing, with the third of these screws deeply recessed in a tunnel near the inner edge. Next to the tunnel is the machine screw, which screws into the underside of the ignition switch assembly. Once the screws are removed, the housing halves can be pulled apart, taking care not to damage the rather small locking tangs. Note that on other cars you may discover minor variations in the housing design.

9 On our project car, the combination switch was located on the column by a small locking tab and secured by a screw clamp however it's possible there may be fixing variations. Start removal by sliding off the turn signal cancelling collar and its spring. Working under the switch unit, slacken the clamp screw until the switch can be moved slightly on the column. Next, reach over the

top of the switch until you can pull back on the plastic tab to free the locking peg from the column (you can see this more easily if you look down on the switch through the windshield).

10 Pull the switch back until the switch wiring connectors can be reached and removed. Each of these is locked in place and can be unplugged after the locking tab has been pressed or lifted according to the design of connector. The switch assembly can now be slid off the column.

11 + Unplug the ignition switch wiring, and on automatic transmission cars, free the ignition switch interlock cable. Working below the dash

11/11a Separate two parts of lower cover.

11/11b Release lower mounting bracket.

panel, locate and separate the two halves of the cover which protects the lower end of the column. The two cover halves snap together and can be separated by pulling them apart. Below the cover you will find the clamp bolt which secures the intermediate shaft coupling to the steering column. Slacken and remove the clamp 12 mm bolt, then remove the two 10 mm nuts which secure the steering column lower mounting bracket to the firewall to free the lower end of the column. (Arrowed in the photograph. Note that one of the bracket holes is slotted, so you don't need to remove its nut completely, though we found it easier to do so).

12 Moving to the upper end of the column, slacken and remove the two 12 mm bolts which secure the column upper bracket to the underside of the dash panel. The column assembly can now be pulled back into the car until the intermediate shaft coupling splines drop free, then lifted out. Take care not to snag the wiring as you remove the unit.

CHECKING

13 + Do not attempt to remove the steering lock unit from the column unless it needs to be

11/12 Release upper bracket.

11/13a Centre punch lock bolt and then ...

11/13b ... drill, prior to using a stud extractor.

replaced. If removal is necessary, you will have to find a way of releasing the shear-head security bolts which retain it. Either center punch and then drill out the heads of the bolts, and then use a stud extractor to unscrew the bolt shanks, or chisel a slot in the heads and unscrew them with a screwdriver. Note that you will need to obtain a pair of replacement shear-head bolts during installation. Fit the lock in position and tighten the bolts evenly until the heads shear off.

14 Examine the column assembly for signs of wear or damage. If the column bearing is worn, or if it feels stiff or uneven when turned, you should

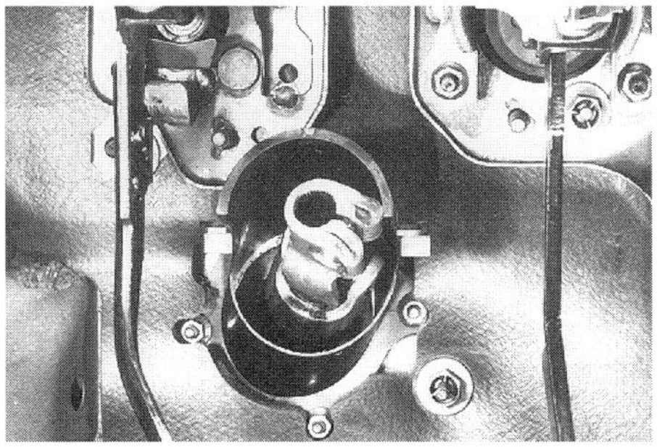

11/14 Check clamp spline for wear/damage.

fit a new column assembly - it is not considered repairable by Mazda. Check the overall length of the column inner shaft. If outside the range 603.7 - 605.7 mm (23.77 - 23.85 in) it is possible that impact damage sometime in the past may have partially collapsed the column. Again, fit a new one. If wear or damage to the splines at either end of the shaft is noted, replacement is again the only option. If wear is noted , you should also check the intermediate shaft splines for wear and replace this too, where necessary.

INSTALLATION

15 Position the column assembly, guiding the splined end into engagement with the intermediate shaft coupling. Fit and tighten to 18-26 Nm (1.8-2.5 kgf m / 13-20 lbf ft) the column lower bracket nuts, then fit the upper mounting bolts, tightening them to 16-23 Nm (1.6-2.3 kgf m / 12-17 lbf ft). Install the column / intermediate shaft clamp bolt and tighten it to 18-26 Nm (1.8-2.5 kgf m / 13-20 lbf ft).

16 + Reconnect the ignition switch wiring, and on automatic transmission cars, fit the interlock cable, tightening the clamp bolt to 4.2-6.2 Nm

11/16a Fit spring, followed by the turn signal ...

11/6b ... cancelling sleeve/cam - pins outward.

(43-63 kgf cm / 37-55 lbf in). Install the steering column switch and reconnect the wiring connectors. Fit the turn signal cancelling sleeve and spring (if applicable). Fit the combination switch housing.

17 + When installing the steering wheel, check that the road wheels are in the straight ahead position and that the steering wheel spokes are level before fitting the wheel boss over its splines. (Where the wheel was removed without disturbing the column assembly, check the alignment marks made during removal). Where applicable, check that the pins on the turn signal cancelling sleeve

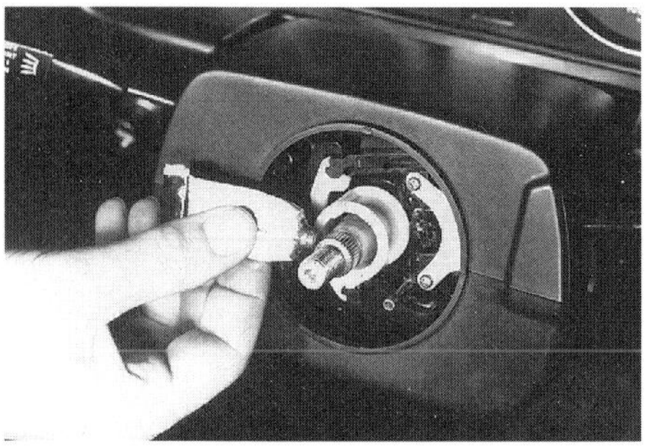

11/17a Apply copper-based grease to splines.

11/17b Lubricate horn ring tracks.

locate in the holes on the back of the steering wheel boss. On air bag equipped cars, you now have to set up the clock spring connector ☞ 7/50/12.

18 The steering wheel can now be fitted, noting that it helps to apply a little copper grease to the splines to make subsequent removal easier.

19 Tighten the steering column nut to 39-49 Nm (4.0-5.0 kgf m / 29-36 lbf ft). Where fitted, install the air bag module, tightening the retaining nuts evenly. Reconnect the clock spring wiring connectors (orange and blue) then temporarily reconnect the battery and check that the horn operates normally. If not, remove the air bag module and check the wiring connections, having first isolated the battery and clock spring wiring connectors.

20 On non-air bag cars, reconnect and install the central horn switch (where fitted). Install the steering wheel safety cover, clipping it in position or securing it with screws, according to the type fitted.

11/18 Align correctly & refit steering wheel.

11/19 Torque tighten retaining nut.

12. TIE ROD BALL JOINT & RACK DUST BOOT - REMOVAL & INSTALLATION

☞ 1/1, 2.

1 Position the vehicle on a smooth, level surface and apply the parking brake. Place wood chocks either side of the rear tires. Remove the front hub cap/s, and loosen the wheel nuts by one turn. Raise the front of the car and position safety stands under the jacking points at the front of each sill (☞ 1/3). Unscrew the wheel nuts and remove the wheel/s.

2 Straighten and remove the cotter pin / split pin which secures the tie rod ball joint 17 mm castellated nut. You will find this easier if you use releasing fluid to help deal with any buildup of rust and dirt around the pin. You will need to fit a new pin during assembly, but keep the old one for now as a pattern. Slacken and remove the ball joint nut.

3 Using a proprietary ball joint separator or the appropriate SST (49 0118 850C), free the ball joint from its tapered hole in the steering knuckle. You may find, as we did, that many proprietary separators will not fit easily in the gap between the joint and the knuckle. You may be able to separate the joint using a wedge-type separator driven between the two parts, but you have to be careful to avoid damage to the ball joint if you intend to reuse it - the dust boot will almost certainly get damaged, but you should in theory replace this anyway. Another removal method involves screwing the castellated nut back onto the pin end upside down until it is flush with the end of the pin - this protects the pin threads from damage. Using a hammer on the pin end, strike it sharply to jar the taper free. We found that this method worked fine on our project car. Unscrew the nut and separate the joint.

12/3 Invert nut and tap sharply to break joint.

4 Clean off the tie rod to remove all traces of road dirt and rust. Make a reference mark across the tie rod locknut and the tie rod threads as a guide during installation, using paint or typist's correction fluid. Slacken the 17 mm locknut by a half turn, then hold the tie rod with a 12 mm wrench and unscrew the ball joint (20 mm) from its end. If you're removing the rack end dust boot/ gaiter, you'll also need to remove the tie rod ball joint locknut.

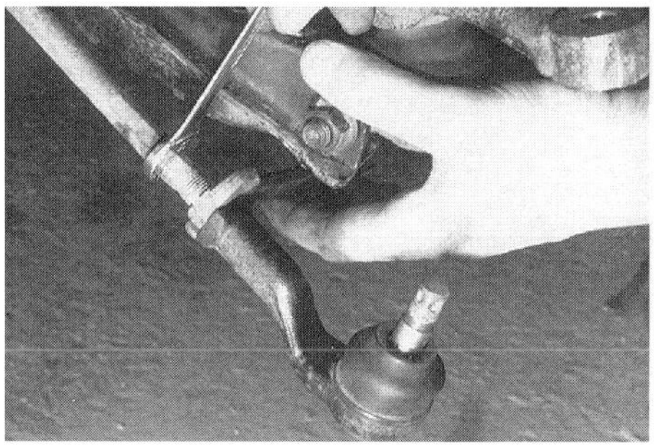

12/4 Hold tie-rod & slacken locknut.

5 If your replacing the steering rack dust boot/gaiter clean the tie rod thoroughly with a wire brush - but don't erase the tie rod ball joint reference marks!. Release the clips which secure the dust boot to the steering rack and the tie rod, and slide off the dust boot and the clips. Clean up the exposed rack ball joint and apply multipurpose lithium-based grease to it, then slide a new dust boot - complete with new clips - along the tie rod and into position. Tighten the boot retaining clips.

6 If the tie rod end ball joint is obviously unserviceable, it should be discarded and a new one fitted. However, if you wish to replace its boot, first remove the old boot by clamping the ball joint in a vise and carefully chiselling off the boot - it has a metal retaining ring which will be a tight fit on the joint rim. Take great care not to damage the joint during boot removal. Clean off any remaining grease around the area normally covered by the boot, then repack the joint using a general purpose lithium-based grease. To fit the new boot, you will need another SST (49 1243 785) to press it into place. This tool is essentially a short tube with a double diameter lip at the end. The seal fits into the tool and is then pressed onto the ball joint. If you don't happen to have the tool, you will need to use a socket or an odd piece of tubing to press the dust boot onto the joint. It can be done, but it is easy to damage the boot without the tool, so take care.

7 Screw the tie rod ball joint locknut onto the tie rod (if removed) followed by the new or overhauled steering ball joint. Align the marks made during removal and lock the ball joint in position by tightening the locknut to 29-44 Nm (3.0-4.5 kgf m / 22-33 lbf ft).

8 Check that the ball joint taper is clean, then fit it to the steering knuckle, tapping it sharply into position so that the pin is gripped in the tapered hole. Fit the castellated nut, then tighten it to the lower end of the 29-44 Nm (3.0-4.5 kgf m / 22-33 lbf ft) torque range. If the pin turns during tightening, tap it again to seat the taper and try again. Check whether the hole through the pin aligns with a pair of castellations, and tighten further if re-

12/8 Tighten ball joint nut & fit cotter/split pin.

quired until it does line up. Fit a new cotter (split) pin and bend the ends over to secure the nut.

9 **Caution!** Once you've completed assembly, you MUST check and adjust the steering angle and toe-in ☞ 8/3.

13. STEERING RACK (MANUAL) - REMOVAL, O/HAUL & INSTALLATION

☞ 1/1, 2.

REMOVAL

1 Position the vehicle on a smooth, level surface and apply the parking brake. Place wood chocks either side of the rear tires. Remove the front hub cap/s, and loosen the wheel nuts by one turn. Raise the front of the car and position safety stands under the jacking points at the front of each sill (☞ 1/3). Unscrew the wheel nuts and remove the wheel/s.

2 Moving to the underside of the car, the next job is to remove the plastic undertray from beneath the front of the engine. All fixings are 10 mm. First, remove the three sheet metal screws from the front of the tray. Then remove the bolt next to the upper wishbone on each side of the car, the bolt on the side of the chassis member in the wheelwell from each side and, finally, the nut on each side holding not only the tray but also the front valence stay. Once the nut is removed the stay can be pulled from the stud and moved out of the way to give enough clearance to remove the plastic undertray, It's recommended that you put all of the screws and the two nuts back in place finger-tight once the tray is removed.

3 The next task is to free the steering ball joints from the steering knuckles (☞ 8/12) - you can leave them attached to the tie rods at this stage but note that, before you release the ball joints, the 'wheels' should be turned to the straight ahead position, and all subsequent work should be carried out without moving the steering wheel if possible. **Warning!** On models with air bags if the wheel is moved after the intermediate shaft to steering rack joint has been separated, you MUST reset the clock spring connector ☞ 7/50/12.

4 📷 Working underneath the car, or via the engine compartment, locate the 12 mm pinch bolt at the base of the steering column intermediate shaft where it fits inside the flexible coupling to the steering rack. There is a reference groove in the intermediate shaft end. Check that a corresponding paint mark is visible on the rack side of the flexible joint, and make a new one if it is not easily visible. Slacken and remove the pinch bolt (note that the shaft end is notched - you can't disconnect the shaft until the bolt is fully withdrawn).

13/4 Pinch bolt at base of steering column.

5 Remove the four rack mounting 14 mm bolts, leaving the rack mounting clamps attached to the rack at this stage. The rack assembly can now be lifted and moved forward to disengage it from the intermediate shaft. Once clear, pull the rack assembly out from the driver's side.

OVERHAUL

6 It is possible to teardown and repair the rack, but a number of special tools are required and it's a complex procedure. We don't usually avoid describing tasks just because they're difficult but, in this case, we seriously doubt that a rack rebuild is a cost effective do-it-yourself proposition when so many specialists offer reconditioned exchange units off the shelf. Our advice - and even Wally agrees! - is to buy an exchange unit from a reputable company.

INSTALLATION

7 When installing the rack assembly, lift it into position and check that the steering ball joints will align with their holes on the steering knuckles. If necessary, turn the pinion until they are correctly positioned, and check that the reference marks on the intermediate shaft and pinion splines coincide. **Warning!** On US cars with steering wheel air bags, the steering wheel should not have been moved since the rack was removed. If this has happened, you MUST adjust the clock spring connector ☞ 7/50/12.

8 Fit the mounting bolts, tightening them evenly and progressively to 46-59 Nm (4.7-6.0 kgf m / 34-43 lbf ft).

9 Check that the ball joint tapers are clean, then fit each ball joint to its steering knuckle, tapping it sharply into position so that the pin is gripped in the tapered hole. Fit the castellated nut, then tighten it to the lower end of the 29-44 Nm (3.0-4.5 kgf m / 22-33 lbf ft) torque range. If the pin turns during tightening, tap it again to seat the taper and try again. Check whether the hole through the pin aligns with a pair of castellations, and tighten further if required until it does line up. Fit a new cotter (split) pin and bend the ends over to secure the nut.

10 Once you've completed assembly, check and adjust the steering angle and toe-in ☞ 8/2, 3.

14. STEERING (POWER) - DESCRIPTION

On cars equipped with the power steering option, the manual rack and pinion system is supplemented by hydraulic pressure generated by the power steering pump. The engine-driven pump circulates ATF (automatic transmission fluid) under pressure to the rack assembly, the effect of the power assistance rising in response to engine speed, giving much of the feel of a manual system without the physical effort.

The adoption of power steering allows the gear ratio of the rack to be changed, and on power steering cars, 2.8 turns of the steering wheel moves the road wheels from lock to lock, rather than the 3.38 turns required on manual steering models.

Working on the power steering system is broadly similar to dealing with the manual steering system, with the obvious additional considerations of the power steering pump and associated hydraulic lines.

15. STEERING (POWER) - FLUID LEVEL CHECK & AIR BLEEDING

☞ 1/1, 2.

1 📷 Fluid level in the power steering fluid reservoir should be checked periodically according to the maintenance schedule, and whenever abnormal steering operation is suspected. Note that low fluid level or air in the hydraulic system can result in excessive steering effort being required, or abnormal noise from the steering system. Pull out the combined filler plug and dipstick, and check that the fluid level lies between the high and low marks. If you need to add fluid, use only **ATF Dexron®II** or **M-III**.

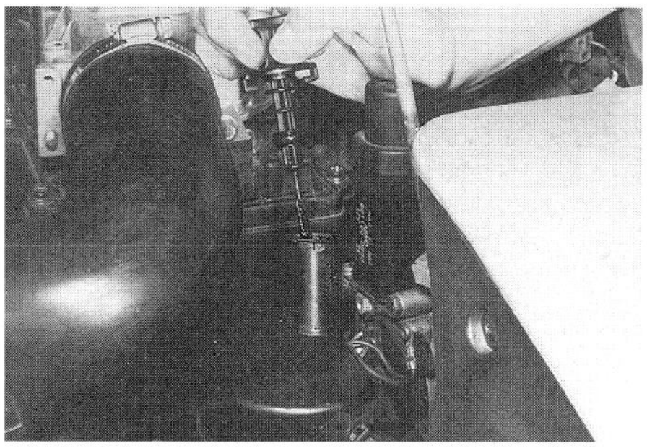

15/1 Power steering reservoir dipstick.

2 To bleed air from the hydraulic system, jack the front of the car so the wheels are just clear of the ground and support the car on safety stands placed under the front jacking points (☞ 1/3).

3 With the engine off, turn the steering fully to the left and then back to the right several times, and check whether the fluid level in the power steering fluid reservoir drops. If it does, top up the fluid in the reservoir and repeat this procedure until the level remains stable.

4 Next start the engine and allow it to idle.

8

Turn the steering wheel fully to the left and then back to the right several times, and check whether the fluid level in the power steering fluid reservoir drops or becomes foamy. If it does, top up the fluid in the reservoir as necessary, then repeat the procedure until the level remains stable, indicating that any air has been expelled.

16. STEERING (POWER) - CHECKING FOR LEAKS

☞ 1/1, 2.

1 In the event of power steering problems, it is a good idea to check the system for possible leakage at the points arrowed in the accompanying drawing. Note that in the case of rhd models, there will be slight differences in the pipe routing due to steering arrangement - see the photographs accompanying this chapter for details. Start by jacking the front of the car so the wheels are just clear of the ground and supporting it on safety stands placed under the front jacking points (☞ 1/3).

2 Start the engine and let it idle. Turn the steering from lock to lock a few times, then hold it at full lock in each direction to place the system under pressure. **Caution!** Do not keep the steering fully turned for more than 15 seconds or damage may result. Check for signs of leakage as shown in the drawing. If leakage is found, check and tighten the affected union, or replace worn or damaged hoses as required.

17. STEERING (POWER) - PRESSURE CHECK

☞ 1/1, 2.

1 + To perform this test, you will need a thermometer and the SSTs shown in the accompanying illustration. These are unlikely to be available to most owners, and we would suggest that you get the check done by your Mazda dealer, who should have the necessary equipment. The pressure test rig should be connected at the power steering pump as indicated in the drawing, noting that the power steering pump hose connections should first be marked to ensure correct reconnection after the test is completed. Assemble the SSTs, tightening the hydraulic connections to 39-49 Nm (4.0-5.0 kgf m / 29-36 lbf ft).

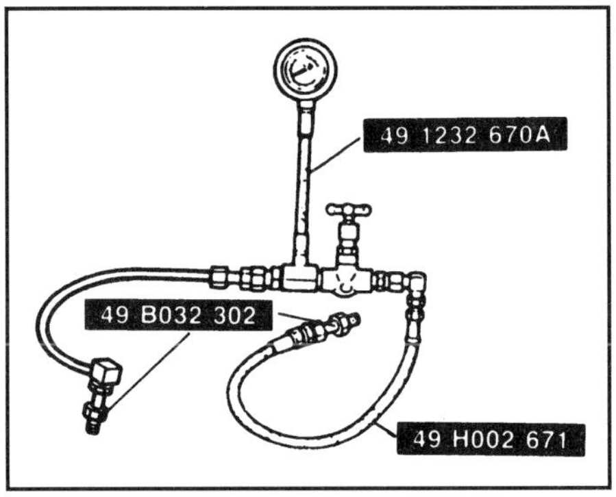

D17/1A ASSEMBLE PRESSURE GAUGE AS SHOWN.

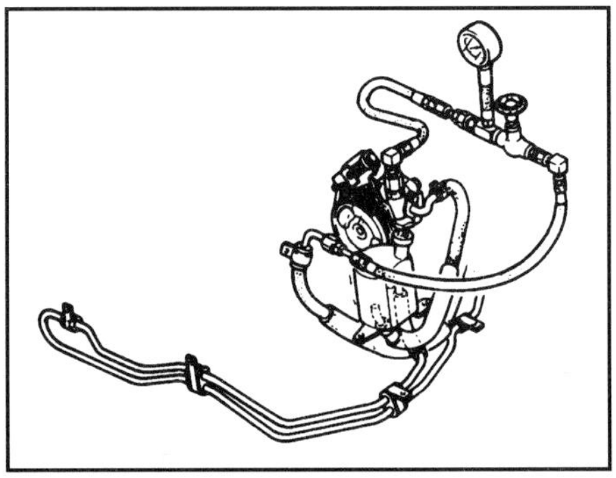

D17/1B CONNECT TO POWER STEERING SYSTEM AS SHOWN.

2 Start by jacking the front of the car so the wheels are just clear of the ground and supporting it on safety stands placed under the front jacking points(☞ 1/3).

3 Open the test rig valve fully. Start the engine and let it idle. Bleed any air from the system ☞ 8/15. Place the thermometer in the power steering fluid reservoir, then hold the steering at full lock in each direction until the fluid temperature rises to 50-60°C (122-140°F). **Caution!** Do not keep the steering fully turned for more than 15 seconds or damage may result.

4 Next, close the test rig valve fully and raise engine speed to 1000-1500 rpm and note the pressure reading on the gauge. **Caution!** Do not keep the valve closed for more than 15 seconds or the fluid temperature may become excessive, damaging the pump. The specified pressure is 7603-8339 kPa (77.5-85.0 kg cm2 / 1102-1209 psi). If pressure is low, try adjusting the pump drive belt tension. If this fails to improve the pressure reading, a new pump should be fitted.

5 Open the test rig valve fully, and turn the steering wheel, holding it at full lock in each direction while noting the system pressure reading. **Caution!** Do not keep the steering fully turned for more than 15 seconds or damage may result. The specified pressure is 7603-8339 kPa (77.5-85.0 kg cm2 / 1102-1209 psi). If the pump pressure is OK, but the system pressure reading is low, wear or damage in the steering rack assembly is indicated.

6 After completing the checks described above, turn off the ignition switch and disconnect the test rig. Reconnect the pressure hose to pump union, ensuring that it is correctly aligned using the marks made during removal. Tighten the union nut to 31-47 Nm (3.2-4.8 kgf m / 23-35 lbf ft). Bleed the air from the power steering system ☞ 8/15.

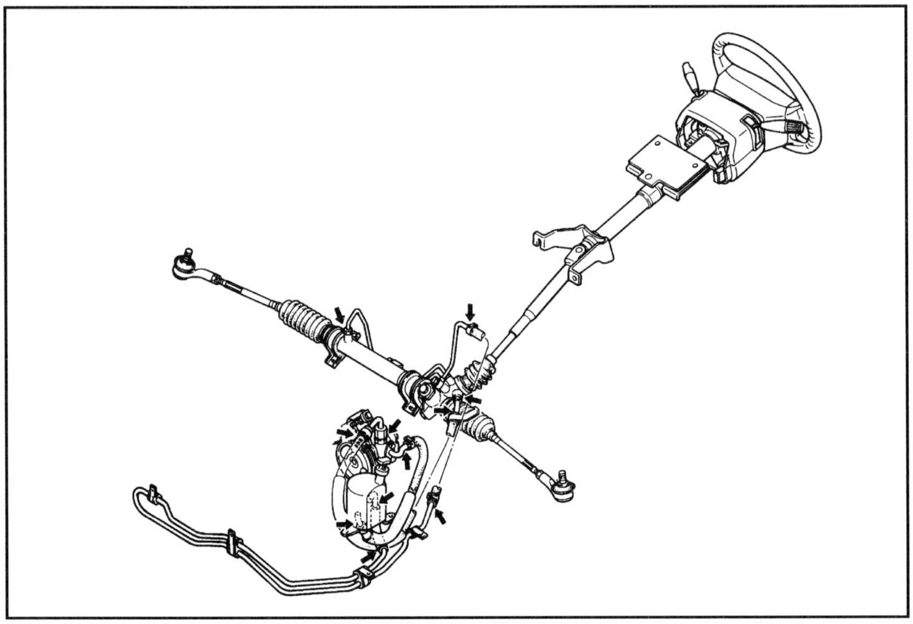

D16/1 POINTS IN THE POWER STEERING HYDRAULIC SYSTEM WHERE LEAKAGE IS MOST LIKELY TO OCCUR.

18. STEERING (POWER) - CHECKING

☞ 1/1, 2.

1 Preliminary checks on the steering can be carried out without a teardown. Sit in the driver's seat with the front wheel in the straight ahead position, and gently turn the wheel to and fro to gauge the amount of free play before any slack in the steering mechanism is taken up. You can gauge this better by leaning out of the car and noting when the road wheel begins to move. Allowable free play at the steering wheel rim is 0-30 mm (0-1.18 in) before the road wheels begin to move. Excessive play normally indicates wear in the steering ball joints, steering column universal joints or the rack mechanism. Less likely causes are loose steering column clamps or rack mountings.

2 Next, try pulling the steering wheel left and right, then up and down, at right angles in relation to the steering column. There should be no play felt here. If there is, check for wear in the steering column and joints and check the security of the steering wheel and the clamps at the upper and lower ends of the intermediate shaft.

3 The final check requires the car to be raised on safety stands so that the front wheels are clear of the ground ☞ 1/3. With the engine running, turn the steering wheel from lock to lock until the fluid temperature in the reservoir reaches 50-60°C (122-140°F) - you can check this using a thermometer inserted into the reservoir. While turning the steering wheel, note any unusually slack or tight spots which might indicate wear or damage in the intermediate shaft joints or the rack mechanism, possibly as a result of impact damage. If noted, these faults should be investigated and rectified.

4 If the steering is abnormally stiff with the wheels clear of the ground, the rack mechanism may be at fault, or the steering ball joints may be badly worn or damaged. With the power steering fluid at the specified temperature and the engine idling, hook a pull scale (spring balance) to the outer edge of one of the steering wheel spokes and check the effort needed to turn the wheel from left to right. This should be in the range 23.5-35.3 N (2.4-3.6 kg / 5.3-8.0 lb). If it is outside these limits a problem is indicated. Check the fluid level in the reservoir and bleed any air from the system ☞ 8/15. Check also for fluid leakage (☞ 8/16) and check the system pressure (☞ 8/17).

19. STEERING RACK (POWER) - REMOVAL, O/HAUL & INSTALLATION

☞ 1/1, 2.

REMOVAL

1 Position the vehicle on a smooth, level surface and apply the parking brake. Place wood chocks front and back of the rear tires. Remove the front hub caps, and loosen the wheel nuts by one turn. Raise the front of the car and position safety stands under the jacking points at the front of each sill (☞ 1/3). Unscrew the wheel nuts and remove the wheels.

2 Moving to the underside of the car, the next job is to remove the plastic undertray from beneath the front of the engine. All fixings are 10 mm. First, remove the three sheet metal screws from the front of the tray. Then remove the bolt next to the upper wishbone on each side of the car, the bolt on the side of the chassis member in the wheelwell from each side and, finally, the nut on each side holding not only the tray but also the front valence stay. Once the nut is removed the stay can be pulled from the stud and moved out of the way to give enough clearance to remove the plastic undertray, It's recommended that you put all of the screws and the two nuts back in place finger-tight once the tray is removed.

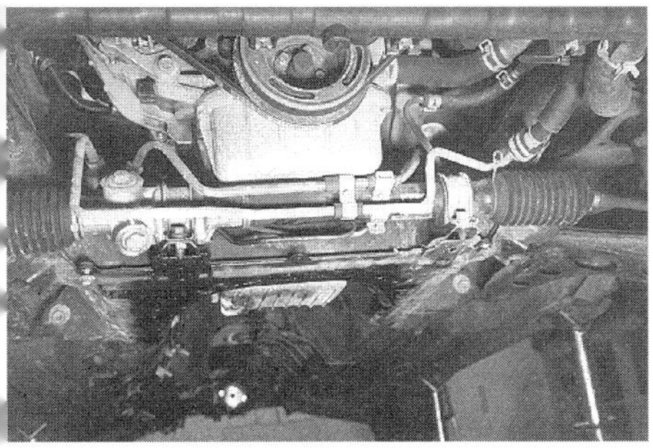

19/2 The rack layout of a rhd car with PS.

3 The next task is to free the steering ball joints from the steering knuckles (☞ 8/12) - you can leave them attached to the tie rods at this stage but note that, before you release the ball joints, the 'wheels' should be turned to the straight ahead position, and all subsequent work should be carried out without moving the steering wheel if possible. **Warning!** On models with air bags, if the wheel is moved after the intermediate shaft to steering rack joint has been separated, you MUST reset the clock spring connector ☞ 7/50/12.

4 Working underneath the car, or via the engine compartment, locate the 12 mm pinch bolt at the base of the steering column intermediate shaft where it fits inside the flexible coupling to the steering rack. There is a reference groove in the intermediate shaft end. Check that a corresponding paint mark is visible on the rack side of the flexible joint, and make a new one if it is not easily visible. Slacken and remove the pinch bolt (note that the shaft end is notched - you can't disconnect the shaft until the bolt is fully withdrawn).

19/5 Pressure pipe & return hose (rhd).

5 Mark the positions of the pressure pipe and return hose where they connect to the rack assembly - these will act as a positional guide during installation. The pressure pipe is also retained by a bracket to the car body on the left side of the rack - release this by removing the single 12 mm retaining bolt.

6 On rhd cars, there are two large bore metal pipes which pick up the pump hose connections on the left side of the car, conveying the hydraulic fluid to the right side of the unit. The feed and return pipes are bracketed together, with a clamp retaining the assembly to the center of the rack - this should be freed to allow the pipes to be disengaged from the rack.

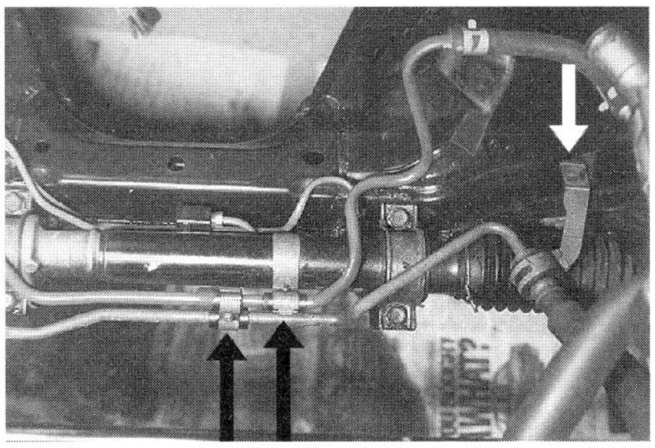

19/6 Release these clamps (rhd).

7 Using a small container to catch any ATF which will spill as the pipe unions are disconnected, free the connections (17 & 12 mm) at the rack end and tie the pipes clear of the working area, having plugged the open ends to keep dirt out of the hydraulic system.

8 Remove the four rack mounting 14 mm bolts, leaving the rack mounting clamps attached to the rack at this stage. The rack assembly can now be lifted and moved forward to disengage it from the intermediate shaft. Once clear, pull the rack assembly out from the driver's side.

OVERHAUL

9 It is possible to teardown and repair the rack, but a number of special tools are required and it's a complex procedure. We don't usually avoid describing tasks just because they're difficult but, in this case, we seriously doubt that a rack rebuild is a cost effective do-it-yourself proposition when so many specialists offer reconditioned exchange units off the shelf. Our advice - and even Wally agrees! - is to buy an exchange unit from a reputable company.

INSTALLATION

10 When installing the rack assembly, lift it into position and check that the steering ball joints will align with their holes on the steering knuckles. If necessary, turn the pinion until they are correctly positioned, and check that the reference marks on the intermediate shaft and pinion splines coincide. **Warning!** On US cars with steering wheel air bags, the steering wheel should not have been moved since the rack was removed. If this has happened, you MUST adjust the clock spring connector ☞ 7/50/12.

11 Fit the mounting bolts, tightening them evenly and progressively to 46-59 Nm (4.7-6.0 kgf m / 34-43 lbf ft).

12 Reconnect the power steering pump pressure and return lines, tightening the pipe unions to 31-47 Nm (3.2-4.8 kgf m / 23-35 lbf ft). Fit the pressure pipe support bracket to the body, tightening its retaining bolt to 18-26 Nm (1.8-2.7 kgf m / 13-20 lbf ft).

13 Check that the ball joint tapers are clean, then fit each ball joint to its steering knuckle, tapping it sharply into position so that the pin is gripped in the tapered hole. Fit the castellated nut, then tighten it to the lower end of the 29-44 Nm (3.0-4.5 kgf m / 22-33 lbf ft) torque range. If the pin turns during tightening, tap it again to seat the taper and try again. Check whether the hole through the pin aligns with a pair of castellations, and tighten further if required until it does line up. Fit a new cotter (split) pin and bend the ends over to secure the nut.

14 Once you've completed assembly, check for fluid leaks (☞ 8/16) and bleed air from the system (☞ 8/15). Note that you should also check and adjust the steering angle and toe-in ☞ 8/2, 3.

20. STEERING PUMP (POWER) - REMOVAL & INSTALLATION

☞ 1/1, 2.

1 Slacken the power steering pump mountings (14 mm) **A**, **B** and **C** (see drawing later in this section) and back off the belt tension adjuster bolt so that the drivebelt can be lifted off the pump pulley. Note that the pump pulley has holes to permit access to the mounting bolt nut - you may need to turn the engine slightly to align these.

2 Using paint or typist's correction fluid, make

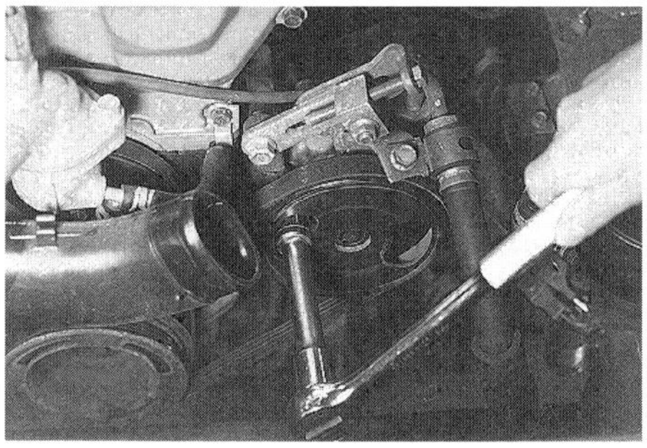

20/1 Access to pivot bolt is thru pulley.

a reference mark on the pressure pipe union nut and the adjacent adaptor to act as an alignment guide during installation. Position a rag to catch any oil spills, then slacken the pressure pipe 22 mm union nut. Free the pipe support bracket by removing its single mounting bolt and lodge the pipe clear of the pump, having covered the open end of the pipe to keep dirt out.

3 Disconnect the pressure switch wiring connector from the top of the pump. Squeeze together the return hose clip and slide it along the hose, clear of the union stub. Work the hose off the stub and plug the end to keep dirt out, then lodge the hose clear of the pump. Remove the mounting bolt nut and the belt tensioner to mounting bracket bolt and lift the pump away.

4 When installing the pump, fit the mounting fasteners loosely - you will need to adjust drivebelt tension before they are tightened. Fit the return hose and secure it by sliding the hose clip back into position. Reconnect the pressure pipe, aligning the marks made during removal. Tighten the union down to 31-47 Nm (3.2-4.8 kgf m / 23-35 lbf ft), then fit the pipe support bracket bolt, tightening it to 18-26 Nm (1.8-2.7 kgf m / 13-20 lbf ft). Reconnect the pressure switch wiring connector.

5 Fit the drivebelt over the pulley and check belt tension adjustment. Referring to the accompanying drawing, turn the adjuster bolt **D** until the prescribed deflection figure is reached. With a used belt, it should be possible to depress the belt at the middle of the upper run, using moderate hand pressure of around 98 N (10 kg / 22 lb), by 9-10 mm (0.35-0.39 in). With a new belt, the deflection setting should be 8-9 mm (0.31-0.35 in). If you have a belt tension gauge, note that the specified tension for a used belt is 422-491 N (43-50 kg / 95-110 lb) and for a new belt, 491-589 N (50-60 Kg / 110-132 lb).

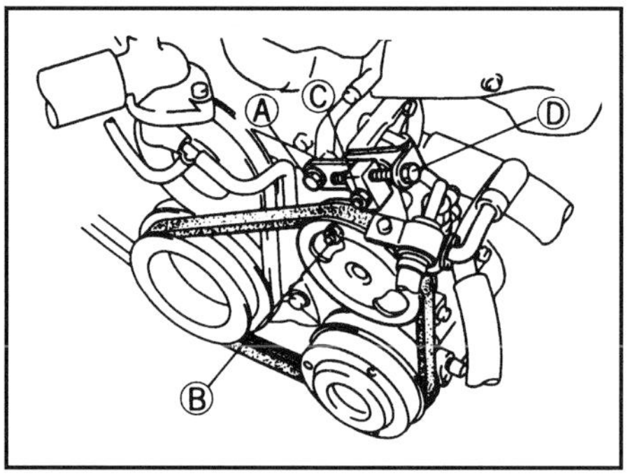

D20/5 POWER STEERING PUMP FIXINGS & ADJUSTMENT (SEE TEXT).

6 Once you have set the belt tension / deflection as described above, tighten bolt **A** and nut **B** to 36-54 Nm (3.7-5.5 kgf m / 27-40 lbf ft), and the adjuster block nut **C** to 19-25 Nm (1.9-2.6 kgf m / 14-19 lbf ft).

21. STEERING PUMP (POWER) - TEARDOWN, O/HAUL & REASSEMBLY

☞ 1/1, 2.

TEARDOWN

1 Before starting work on pump disassembly, plug the pressure pipe and return pipe openings to exclude dirt, then clean off the pump with a degreasing solvent. Note that you will require a set of new O-rings during reassembly - these should be obtained before you start. Teardown the pump as described below, laying out the removed parts on clean newspaper.

2 Remove the two 10 mm bolts which retain the return hose union to the pump body and remove the union and its O-ring. Unscrew the pressure switch body (19 mm) and remove it and the O-ring, spring and valve body and pin.

3 Unscrew the pressure pipe connector from the pump body and tip out the control valve and spring. Working through the slots in the pump pulley, remove the two bolts which retain the adjuster bracket and lift it away.

4 Release the four 10 mm bolts which retain the pump end cover and lift it and its O-ring away. Take care not to lose the small dowel pins from the cover. The cam ring, rotor and blades and the side plate can now be removed for checking.

OVERHAUL

5 Clean the pump components carefully, checking for any signs of dirt or obstructions which may have been impeding its operation. Check the pump body and end cover for signs of wear or cracking - if found, a new pump should be fitted.

6 Check the condition of the pump internal components (cam ring, rotor & blades and the side plate for signs of wear. A bright, polished appearance of the working surfaces is normal and to be expected, but signs of more severe wear indicate the need for replacement.

7 Check the fit between the rotor and each blade, which should be a light sliding fit. No specific clearance is given by Mazda, but if the pump pressure was low and there is excessive clearance between these parts, the resulting leakage is likely to have been causing the loss of pressure.

8 Examine the control valve and spring, carefully removing any dirt which may have built up. If the valve is cracked or badly worn, or if the spring is damaged, they should be replaced.

REASSEMBLY

9 Check that the pump components are completely clean, then reassemble the pump as follows, using a little clean ATF to lubricate the moving parts during installation, and fitting new O-rings throughout. Clamp the pump body lightly in soft vise jaws with the pulley end downwards. Fit the side plate into pump body, then install the pump rotor, noting that the identification mark must face upwards.

10 Next, fit the cam ring with the identification mark facing downwards (into the pump body). Slide each of the rotor blades into position, noting that the rounded edge should face outwards, towards the cam ring surface.

11 Check that the dowel pins are in place in the end cover, then install it on the pump body. Fit the cover bolts and tighten them evenly and progressively to 18-22 Nm (1.8-2.2 kgf m / 13-16 lbf ft). Remove the pump body from the vise.

12 Install the pump adjuster bracket, securing it with the two mounting bolts fitted via the slots in the pulley. Tighten the bolts to 29-39 Nm (3-4 kgf m / 22-29 lbf ft).

13 Assemble the control valve, spring and pressure pipe union, remembering to fit new O-rings. Tighten the union to 49-69 Nm (5-7 kgf m / 36-51 lbf ft). Install the pressure switch components, tightening the switch down to 25-29 Nm (2.5-3.0 kgf m / 18-22 lbf ft).

14 Finally, fit the return hose union, tightening its two mounting bolts to 5.9-9.8 Nm (0.6-1.0 kgf m / 4.3-7.2 lbf ft). Note that after the rebuilt pump is installed, be sure to bleed any air from the system and check the ATF level after doing so ☞ 8/15.

22. SHOCK ABSORBER & SPRING (REAR) - REMOVAL, O/HAUL & INSTALLATION

☞ 1/1, 2

REMOVAL

1 Position the vehicle on a smooth, level surface and apply the parking brake. Place wood chocks front and back of the front tires. Remove the rear hub cap/s, and loosen the wheel nuts by one turn. Raise the rear of the car and position safety stands under the jacking points at the rear of each sill (☞ 1/3). Unscrew the wheel nuts and remove the wheel/s.

2 + Position the scissor jack from the Miata/MX5's trunk under the lower wishbone, using wood blocks under the jack as required. Raise the jack so that it is just contacting the underside of the wishbone. Remove the stabilizer bar control link to wishbone 14 mm nut, bolt and spring washer. If the bolt won't pull thru, raise or lower the

2/2a Place car's own jack under wishbone.

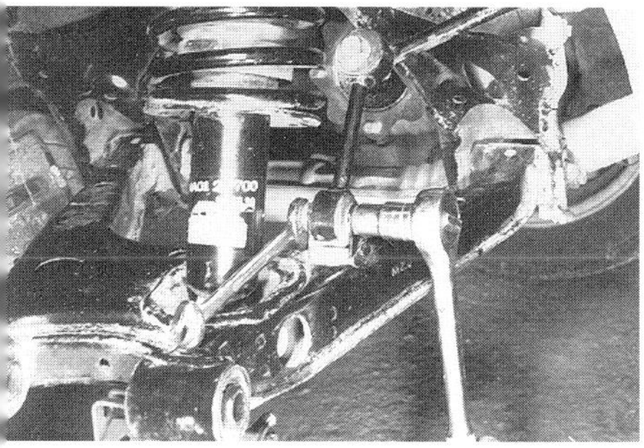

2/2b Release stabilizer bar link.

2/2c Withdraw strut lower mounting bolt.

ack a little until it can be withdrawn easily. Remove he suspension unit lower mounting 17 mm bolt, vhich can be accessed though a hole at the rear of he wishbone. Again, make any necessary height djustment with the jack to allow the bolt to be vithdrawn.

3 Working inside the trunk, remove the uspension unit top mounting 14 mm nuts (two per uspension unit), noting that on the left side of the ar you will first need to detach the pressed steel over which conceals the fuel filler pipes. **Warning!** Do not remove the large central nut which is overed by the dust cap - if you do, the unit will separate under considerable pressure from the suspension spring and become firmly wedged in place - you could also suffer injury as it flies apart.

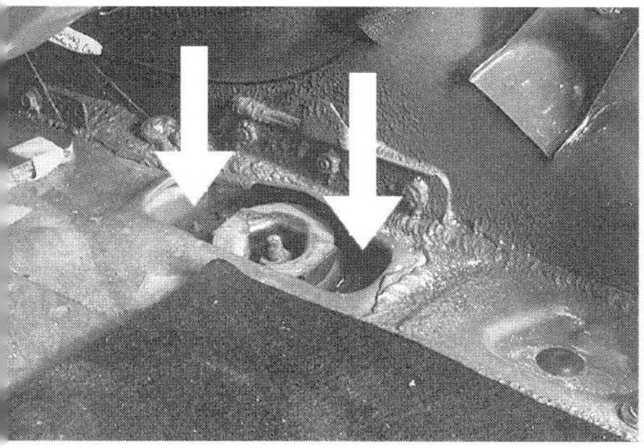

2/3 Suspension strut top mounting nuts.

4 Lower the scissor jack to allow the suspension assembly to assume its natural position (it will be under light pressure due to the elasticity of the suspension rubber bushes). You may just about have enough room to pull the unit downward and disengage it - try pushing down a little on the suspension to increase clearance.

5 If you need to obtain more clearance, the official procedure is to slacken off the upper wishbone pivot nut and the lower wishbone cam bolt locknuts to allow the suspension to be lowered, but note that this will require the suspension geometry to be checked and adjusted after installation. If you wish to use this method, first mark the position of the cam bolts so that their setting can be restored during installation. Note also that if the wishbone pivots are disturbed, you will need to arrange final tightening of the pivot cam and stabilizer bar fasteners when the car has been lowered onto its wheels. This ensures that the rubber bushes are not under tension. Be aware that this will pose access problems unless you are using full commercial workshop facilities - access is limited when the car is standing on the ground.

22/4 Lower jack to release strut.

6 Our alternative method is to detach the 14 mm pivot bolt which connects the upper wishbone to the suspension upright. The lower wishbone and the upright can then be moved sufficiently to allow the suspension unit to be disengaged at its top mounting, then lifted away from the lower wishbone. (Note that our photographs show the suspension upright and brake detached - we removed these for photographic access, and they do not need to be disturbed in real life). This method requires a little more maneuvering when the unit is removed, but will require less work later.

OVERHAUL

7 The rear suspension unit is functionally identical to the front unit, and can be dealt with in exactly the same way (☞ 8/4/10-15). There are specification differences - note that in the case of the rear springs, the identification paint mark is blue (manual transmission) or orange (automatic transmission), the automatic models requiring slightly heavier springs.

INSTALLATION

8 Check that the mounting areas and the various bolt threads are clean. Use a wire brush to clean the bolt threads and lubricate them with copper or molybdenum grease. Reposition the suspension unit and slide the lower mounting bolt into place. Fit the upper mounting nuts fingertight at this stage.

9 If you used our removal method, fit the suspension unit to upper wishbone pivot bolt (head towards the rear of the car), spring washer and nut. Reconnect the stabilizer bar control link to lower wishbone bolt. Once everything is loosely assembled, tighten the suspension unit upper mounting nuts to 29-36 Nm (3.0-3.7 kgf m / 22-27 lbf ft), and the lower mounting bolt to 73-93 Nm (7.4-9.5 Kgf m / 54-69 lbf ft). The control link to wishbone pivot bolt nut should be tightened to 36-54 Nm (3.7-5.5 kgf m / 27-40 lbf ft). The upper wishbone to suspension upright pivot bolt nut is tightened to 46-67 Nm (4.7-6.8 kgf m / 34-49 lbf ft). Because the suspension pivots were not disturbed and the cam bolt adjustment has not been lost, this is about all you need to do using this method, and the car can be lowered to the ground once the wheels have been installed. Once on the ground, tighten the wheelnuts to 88-118 Nm (9.0-12.0 kgf m / 65-87 lbf ft). Remember to install the pressed steel cover inside the trunk.

10 If you used the Mazda removal method, fit the suspension unit, installing the mounting nuts and lower bolt loosely. Reconnect the stabilizer bar control link, again leaving the bolt and nut fingertight. You now need the car to be lowered onto its wheels for final tightening of the suspension-related fasteners, so fit the road wheels. If, like us, you don't have a proprietary vehicle lift, access when the car is lowered to the ground will be difficult.

11 The car has to be resting on its wheels so that the suspension adopts its normal position, and should be level. The best way of achieving this without restricting access is to arrange the car so that all four wheels are supported on fabricated steel ramps. Once resting on its wheels, position the lower wishbone cam bolts so that the reference marks made during the teardown are aligned, and then tighten the nuts to 73-95 Nm (7.4-9.7 kgf m / 54-70 lbf ft). The upper wishbone pivot bolt nuts should be tightened to 46-67 Nm (4.7-6.8 kgf m / 34-49 lbf ft). Torque tighten the remaining fasteners ☞ 8/22/9.

12 Note that because the suspension geometry was disturbed during this procedure, you should check and adjust the settings (they should be reasonably close if you remembered to make reference marks during the removal process, and realigned these during installation) ☞ 8/2, 3.

23. WISHBONE (LOWER, REAR) - REMOVAL, O/HAUL & INSTALLATION

☞ 1/1, 2.

REMOVAL

1 Position the vehicle on a smooth, level surface and apply the parking brake. Place wood chocks front and back of the front tires. Remove

the rear hub cap/s, and loosen the wheel nuts by one turn. Raise the rear of the car and position safety stands under the jacking points at the rear of each sill (☞ 1/3). Unscrew the wheel nuts and remove the wheel/s.

2 Position the scissor jack from the Miata/ MX5's trunk under the lower wishbone, using wood blocks under the jack as required. Raise the jack so that it is just contacting the underside of the wishbone. Remove the stabilizer bar control link to wishbone 14 mm nut, bolt and spring washer. If the bolt won't pull thru, raise or lower the jack a little until it can be withdrawn easily. Remove the suspension unit lower mounting 17 mm bolt, which can be accessed though a hole at the rear of the wishbone. Again, make any necessary height adjustment with the jack to allow the bolt to be withdrawn.

3 Next, you need to remove the lower wishbone to suspension upright 17 mm pivot bolt. We ran into problems here, and it seems highly likely that you will find the same problem on your car. The pivot bore in the suspension upright is partially open at the inner edge, and this means that part of the bolt shank is exposed to all of the road dirt thrown up by the wheels (Why, Mazda?).

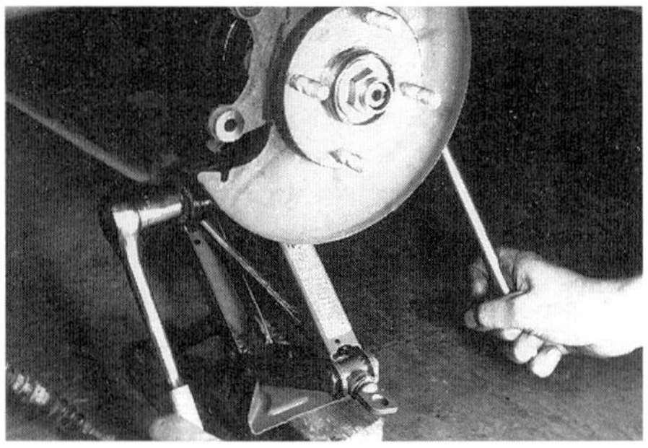

23/3 Slacken & remove lower pivot bolt.

This in turn causes the bolt shank to corrode quite badly, which makes removal of the bolt difficult.

4 Try to remove as much of the corrosion as you can before trying to get the bolt out, and soak it in penetrating fluid. The only thing you can do now is try to drive the bolt out without damaging the thread. Run the nut onto the thread so that it lies flush with the bolt end, then use a hide or rubber hammer to drive it out. The presence of the nut will help stop the threaded end from distorting. Once the nut contacts the wishbone you will have to remove it and use a brass drift to knock the bolt the rest of the way through the wishbone.

5 Using paint or typist's correcting fluid, mark the positions of the cam bolts which secure the wishbone to the crossmember - this will minimize the task of setting up the suspension geometry during installation. Remove the cam bolt 17 mm nuts, push out the bolts and lift out the lower wishbone.

OVERHAUL

6 Clean off the wishbone, and check for damage. If you find signs of cracking, rusting or impact damage, don't bother with further work on the wishbone - you will need to fit a new one.

23/5 Mark positions of bolt cams.

Warning! Repairs to suspension parts are inadvisable for reasons of safety.

7 If the wishbone is serviceable, you should fit new mounting bushes before installing it. The procedure for removing and installing the bushes is essentially the same as described for the front wishbone ☞ 8/5.

INSTALLATION

8 Before starting installation, spend some time cleaning up the lower wishbone to suspension upright pivot bolt, or fit a new one. If you plan to reuse the old one, clean off any remaining corrosion with abrasive paper and check that it slides through the wishbone and upright bores easily.

9 Position the wishbone against the crossmember and fit the cam bolts, noting that the heads should face each other (front bolt head facing rearwards, rear bolt head facing forwards). Fit the eccentric washers and nuts, but do not tighten at this stage. Lift the wishbone, guiding the suspension unit lower mounting into its recess and fitting the mounting bolt fingertight.

10 Grease the lower wishbone to suspension upright pivot bolt and slide it through the

23/10 Cover exposed bolt with sticky grease.

wishbone and upright, fitting the nut fingertight. We packed the open area of the upright with the thickest, stickiest grease we could find, in the hope that this will prevent further corrosion problems - we suggest that you do likewise.

11 If you have difficulty positioning the wishbone while fitting the suspension unit or pivot bolts, the small scissor jack supplied with the car's toolkit can be used to raise the assembly as required. Realign the link rod and stabilizer (anti-roll) bar, again using the car's jack if you need to, then fit the mounting bolt (with the head facing outwards). Fit the spring washer and nut finger-tight.

12 You now need to lower the car onto its wheels (☞ 1/3) for final tightening of the suspension-related fasteners, so fit the road wheels. If, like us, you don't have a vehicle lift, access when the car is lowered to the ground will be difficult.

13 The car has to be resting on its wheels so that the suspension adopts its normal position, and should be level. The best way of achieving this without restricting access is to arrange the car so that all four wheels are supported on steel ramps.

14 Once resting on its wheels, position the lower wishbone cam bolts so that the reference marks made during the teardown are aligned, and then tighten the nuts to 73-95 Nm (7.4-9.7 kgf m / 54-70 lbf ft). Tighten the suspension unit lower mounting bolt to 73-93 Nm (7.4-9.5 Kgf m / 54-69 lbf ft). The control link to wishbone pivot bolt nut should be tightened to 36-54 Nm (3.7-5.5 kgf m / 27-40 lbf ft), and the lower wishbone to suspension upright pivot bolt nut to 63-75 Nm (6.4-7.6 kgf m / 46-55 lbf ft). Tighten the wheelnuts to 88-118 Nm (9.0-12.0 kgf m / 65-87 lbf ft).

15 Note that because the suspension geometry was disturbed during this procedure, you should check and adjust these settings (they should be reasonably close if you remembered to make reference marks during the removal process, and realigned these during installation) ☞ 8/2, 3.

24. WISHBONE (UPPER, REAR) - REMOVAL, O/HAUL & INSTALLATION

☞ 1/1, 2

REMOVAL

1 Position the vehicle on a smooth, level surface and apply the parking brake. Place wood chocks front and back of the front tires. Remove the rear hub cap/s, and loosen the wheel nuts by one turn. Raise the rear of the car and position safety stands under the jacking points at the rear of each sill (☞ 1/3). Unscrew the wheel nuts and remove the wheel/s.

2 Position the scissor jack from the Miata/ MX5's trunk under the lower wishbone, using wood blocks under the jack as required. Raise the jack so that it is just contacting the underside of the wishbone. Remove the upper wishbone to suspension upright 14 mm bolt, nut and spring washer. If the bolt seems tight, raise or lower the jack a little until it can be withdrawn easily. Remove the two upper wishbone 14 mm pivot bolt nuts and spring

24/2 Remove upper wishbone pivot bolts.

washers, then push out and remove the bolts. The wishbone can now be withdrawn from the car.

OVERHAUL

3 The upper wishbone can be overhauled in the same way as described for the lower wishbone ☞ 8/23/6-7. There are only two rubber bushes to be replaced and, again, these can be removed and installed using the technique described for the front wishbone bushes ☞ 8/5, 6.

INSTALLATION

4 When installing the wishbone assembly, lubricate the pivot bolts with molybdenum or copper grease, and install them so that their heads face towards each other. Fit the nuts and spring washers fingertight at this stage. Install the upper wishbone to suspension upright bolt, nut and spring washer, again fingertight only. Note that the bolt head faces towards the rear of the car.

5 You now need to lower the car (☞ 1/3) onto its wheels for final tightening of the suspension-related fasteners, so fit the road wheels. If, like us, you don't have a proprietary vehicle lift, access when the car is lowered to the ground will be difficult. The car has to be resting on its wheels so that the suspension adopts its normal position, and should be level. The best way of achieving this without restricting access is to arrange the car so that all four wheels are supported on fabricated steel ramps.

6 Once the car's resting on its wheels, tighten the upper wishbone pivot bolt nuts and the upper wishbone to suspension upright pivot bolt nut to 46-67 Nm (4.7-6.8 kgf m / 34-49 lbf ft). Tighten the wheelnuts to 88-118 Nm (9.0-12.0 kgf m / 65-87 lbf ft).

25. STABILIZER BAR (REAR) - REMOVAL, CHECKING & INSTALLATION

☞ 1/1, 2.

REMOVAL

1 Position the vehicle on a smooth, level surface and apply the parking brake. Place wood chocks back and front of the front tires. Access to the stabilizer control links is easier with the road wheels removed - pry off the rear hub caps, and loosen the wheel nuts by one turn. Raise the rear of the car and position safety stands under the jacking points at the rear of each sill (☞ 1/3). Remove the wheel nuts and lift the wheels away.

2 Working under the rear of the car, remove the stabilizer bar control link 14 mm nuts and bolts. There may be a little tension in the stabilizer bar which could make removal of the bolts difficult. If this is the case, position the scissor jack from the Miata/MX5's trunk under the lower wishbone, using wood blocks under the jack as required. Raise the jack so that it is just contacting the underside of the wishbone, then adjust the angle of the suspension so that the control link bolts can be pushed out.

3 The stabilizer bar can now be detached from the crossmember by removing the two brackets and bushes, these each being retained by two 14 mm bolts.

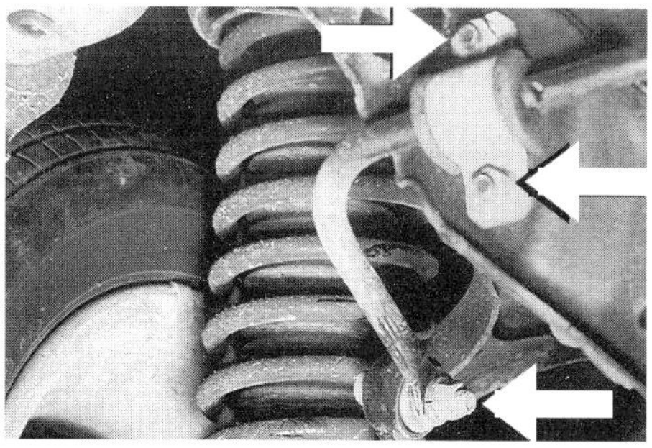

25/2 Stabilizer bar link & mounting nuts.

CHECKING

4 Check the stabilizer bar for signs of damage or corrosion. It is unlikely to require replacement unless as a result of accident damage or if a high performance unit is being fitted. If the stabilizer bar has been bent or twisted, or is badly corroded, it should be replaced. Check the stabilizer bar control links for signs of similar damage, and check the condition of the rubber bushes at each end. If these are obviously worn or deteriorated, fit new links. Check the stabilizer bar support blocks for wear or deterioration, replacing them if obviously worn or damaged (wear in the blocks can produce mysterious clanks and rattles from the suspension).

INSTALLATION

5 Position the rubber support blocks on the stabilizer bar, making sure that they line up with the alignment marks as shown in the accompanying drawing. Fit the control links to the ends of the stabilizer bar, bolt heads outwards, leaving the nuts loose for now. Reposition the assembly under the car, fitting the control link to lower wishbone bolts, nuts and spring washers with the bolt heads facing the front of the car. Tighten the nuts finger-tight only at this stage.

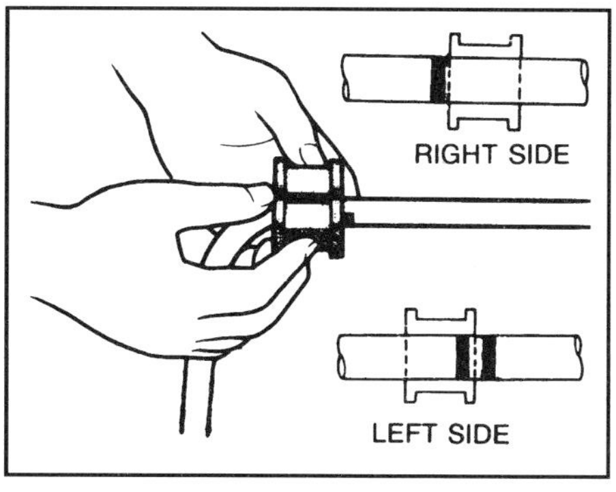

D25/5 ALIGN BUSHES WITH MARKS ON BAR.

6 You now need to lower the car onto its wheels for final tightening of the suspension-related fasteners, so fit the road wheels. If, like us, you don't have a proprietary vehicle lift, access when the car is lowered to the ground will be difficult. The car has to be resting on its wheels so that the suspension adopts its normal position, and should be level. The best way of achieving this without restricting access is to arrange the car so that all four wheels are supported on fabricated steel ramps.

7 Once resting on its wheels, tighten the stabilizer bar bracket bolts to 20-28 Nm (2.0-2.9 kgf m / 14-21 lbf ft). Tighten the control link bolts to 36-54 Nm (3.7-5.5 kgf m / 27-40 lbf ft). If the wheels were removed for access, tighten the wheelnuts to 88-118 Nm (9.0-12.0 kgf m / 65-87 lbf ft).

26. CROSSMEMBER (REAR) - REMOVAL, CHECKING AND INSTALLATION

☞ 1/1, 2.

1 This operation is complicated, even if you have access to a 2-post vehicle lift and a transmission jack. Without this equipment we would advise you to consider having the work done professionally. We're not saying that you can't do it at home, but it will entail a lot of work. Read through the procedure first, and then decide for yourself if you want to attempt it. The most likely reason for crossmember removal is after severe accident damage, in which case we suggest that the job is carried out by a body shop who will have facilities to check and realign any body damage.

REMOVAL

2 The first task is to get the whole car raised high enough for access to the underside. We did this a number of times on the project car, and evolved a systematic method of raising the vehicle safely using normal domestic workshop equipment ☞ 1/3. Once you're satisfied that the car is raised sufficiently to give reasonable access, and that it is totally secure on its safety stands, remove the rear wheels. Disable the stereo security system, then open the trunk and disconnect the battery negative (-) terminal to isolate the electrical system ☞ 7/2.

3 You need to drop the exhaust system clear of the underside of the car to get access to the PPF and propshaft (actually, you may be able to get by if you just remove the main silencer, but access is much better with the system out of the way, and it takes little extra time to do). Disconnect the front downpipe, then free the system from the hangers and lift it away. If you have trouble unhooking the hangers, push a screwdriver through the hanger in line with the pin, and use it like a tire lever to work the hanger over the head of the pin. For a detailed explanation of the removal procedure ☞ 5/38.

4 Remove the propshaft ☞ 4/2/12-14.

5 The next step is to remove the Power Plant Frame (PPF). Unless you have access to SST 49 0259 440, which prevents oil leakage from the transmission housing when the propeller shaft coupling is detached, you will need to drain the oil from the transmission ☞ 2/10.

6 Remove the PPF (power plant frame) ☞ 4/2/16-23.

7 What we will be doing here is supporting the rear crossmember as an assembly on a normal hydraulic trolley jack, and lowering it from under

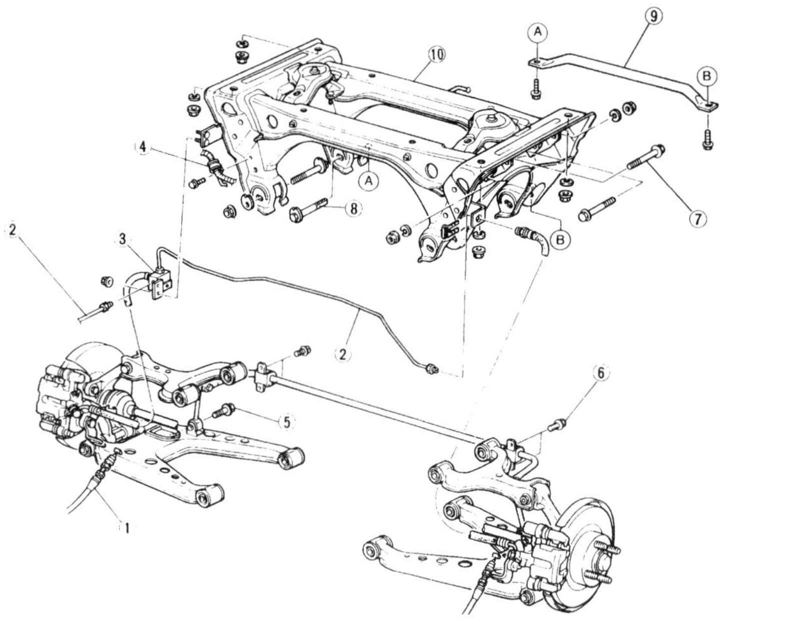

D26/1 REAR SUSPENSION & CROSSMEMBER DETAIL.
1 Parking brake cable. 2 Brake pipe. 3 Distributor block. 4 Battery cable bracket. 5 Strut lower mounting bolt. 6 Stabilizer bracket & bolts. 7 Wishbone pivot bolt. 8 Pivot bolt/cam. 9 Performance bar. 10 Rear crossmember.

the car. As well as the jack, you will need a couple of assistants, one on each side of the crossmember, to steady and support it as it is lowered and to help maneuver it out.

8 From inside the car, back off the parking brake adjuster to allow plenty of slack in the cable. You can turn the hexagonal adjuster with a screwdriver; you'll find the adjuster at the side of the parking brake lever. At the wheel ends of the parking brake cable, slacken the 14 mm cable locknut and disengage the cable adjuster from its bracket. You can now free the cable inner from the operating lever and disengage the cable assembly. Repeat this procedure on the remaining wheel.

9 Working below the car, disconnect the brake pipe which runs back from the front of the car at its 10 mm union with the distributor block. Free the pipe end, and plug the distributor block thread and cap the pipe end to keep dirt out of the hydraulic system. Release the distributor block by removing two 10 mm nuts. Disconnect the square-section guide which carries the battery cables and wiring along the crossmember and lodge them clear of the working area. On each side of the car, remove the suspension unit lower mounting bolt from the lower wishbone, passing a 17 mm socket through the access hole (when you remove the crossmember the suspension units will be left hanging from their top mountings, reducing the weight and overall height of the crossmember assembly).

10 📷+ Position a wheeled hydraulic jack below the differential housing, making sure that the finned area sits squarely in the jack pad. Raise the jack slightly to take the weight of the crossmember assembly. Working from each side of the car through the wheelwell (arch), slacken and remove the crossmember fasteners - it helps if you detach the plastic undershield at the front of the wheelwell. On each side there are two 19 mm headed nuts at the front and rear mounting points, with a single 19 mm headed bolt between the two. (The center bolt may not be fitted on all cars). You will need a fairly long socket extension to reach them, the center bolt being accessed through the gap in the upper wishbone. As you remove the fasteners, note that the crossmember will come free, and you should have an assistant at each side to steady it and prevent it from toppling off the jack.

26/10a Remove this undershield ...

26/10b ... then remove these nuts & bolt .

11 Slowly lower the jack, with your assistants guiding it downwards on each side. As it moves down, keep a close eye on the wiring, brake lines, fuel lines and parking brake cables - these are easily strained if they get caught up as the crossmember descends. Note that if your car is wired differently to ours, or if aftermarket wiring has been added in the vicinity of the crossmember, you may need to disconnect or reroute it.

12 Once the crossmember has been lowered enough to clear the body, it can be removed from the rear of the car. Wheel it out on the jack, with your assistants steadying each end. You will need to arrange some kind of support for the crossmember by positioning strong crates or pieces of lumber under the lower wishbones. **Warning!** Make sure that it sits securely and is in no danger of toppling off the supports.

CHECKING AND REPAIR

13 Once removed from the car, the suspension components can be removed from the crossmember as described elsewhere in this chapter. To remove the driveshafts and differential assembly ☞ 4/13, 15.

14 Check the crossmember for signs of damage or corrosion. If bad corrosion is noted, or if there are any signs of cracking or impact damage, fit a new crossmember. **Warning!** Although it is theoretically safe to carry out minor repairs by welding, this must be done professionally and at the operator's discretion - remember that this component fundamentally affects the safe operation of the vehicle.

15 While the crossmember is out of the car, check the body underside closely, and carry out any rustproofing work while you have good access in this area. We further recommend that you check the fuel tank closely - this can only be removed with the crossmember out of the way, so if there is any doubt about the condition of the tank, now would be a good time to fit a new one ☞ 5/15.

16 After checking the crossmember, install the removed suspension and transmission parts, referring to the appropriate sections of this chapter for procedural details. For information on driveshaft and differential casing installation ☞ 5/13, 15.

INSTALLATION

17 Reposition the rear crossmember and carefully jack it back into position, checking that nothing gets trapped or strained as it is raised. Install the crossmember mounting bolts and nuts, tightening them evenly to 93-117 Nm (9.5-11.9 kgf m / 69-86 lbf ft). Where they were removed, make sure that you guide the bottoms of the suspension units into their recesses in the lower wishbones. Fit the suspension unit lower mounting bolts and tighten them to 73-93 Nm (7.4-9.5 kgf m / 54-69 lbf ft).

18 Fit the brake distributor block, tightening the mounting nuts to 13-22 Nm (1.3-2.2 kgf m / 9.4-16 lbf ft). Fit and secure the brake pipe unions,

then bleed the hydraulic system at each rear caliper - you may need to bleed the front ones too if you can't get a hard pedal. ☞ 9/2. Fit the wiring harness / battery cable guide to the crossmember. Fit the brake cables, if removed, and secure their locknuts. Check and adjust the parking brake ☞ 9/20. Check that any accessory wires disconnected during removal are reconnected properly.

19 From beneath the car put the PPF in place by sliding it forward onto its mounting on the right side of the transmission, then pushing it up around the side of the differential unit until it slides onto its mounting. Note: you may have to lift the propeller shaft flange end of the differential slightly to get the PPF to slide into engagement. The end of the PPF with round drillings is the differential end.

20 With the PPF roughly positioned, install the two 17 mm-headed bolts that pass through the lower flange of the PPF, up through the transmission casing and then screw into the top flange of the PPF. For the moment, these bolts should be left finger-tight.

21 Move to the rear end of the PPF and install the 17 mm through bolts that clamp the PPF to the side of the differential casing. Fit the bolt without a collar first, followed by the bolt with the collar. It's suggested that you spray the shanks of both bolts with WD40 or similar silicone-based lubricant as they seem prone to corrosion. You may need to lift the nose of the diff casing a little to align the holes in the differential casing and the PPF. Tighten the two bolts snugly but not fully at this stage.

22 Move once again to the forward end of the PPF and install the transmission extension housing support bracket between the PPF and the tailhousing of the transmission. If you've used a jack to support the transmission, and it's in the way, you should remove it before installing the bracket. Hold the bracket in place above the lower flange of the PPF and finger-tighten the 17 mm retaining bolt. Insert the two 14 mm bolts that secure the bracket to the transmission tailshaft and, once again, tighten them finger-tight. You may need to lift the tail of the transmission slightly to make the bracket align with the threaded holes in the transmission casing. Tighten the two 17 mm PPF to transmission side bolts to a torque of 115 Nm (11.5 kgf m / 85 lbf ft).

23 Next, tighten the PPF to differential 17 mm side bolts to the same torque. Make sure the collar on the forward bolt is properly engaged in the recess in the PPF.

24 Move to the tailshaft support bracket and tighten the 17 mm bolts to the same torque as the other 17 mm bolts. Then tighten the bracket's 14 mm bolts to a final torque of 45 Nm / 4.5 kgf m/ 35 lbf ft.

25 Fit the speedometer drive to the transmission.

26 Start to secure the loom by fixing its support bracket to the side of the transmission with the short, sheet metal screw provided.

27 Work your way along the PPF, pushing each loom retaining clip into place as you go. Note that the first clip, at the engine end, is at the top of the PPF and the second clip about halfway down the side of the frame. The following clips run along the frame about two thirds of the way down on the right-hand side, while the last two clips, at the axle end of the PPF, are at the top.

28 Toward the rear end of the PPF there is a ground/ earth wire sprouting from the loom which should be re-secured to the PPF by tightening its 10 mm retaining bolt. Note: before fastening the ground/ earth strap clean the eye and the contact area of the PPF with emery paper. Smear both with petroleum jelly (Vaseline) and then replace and tighten the screw.

29 Rub engine oil over the section of the propshaft that enters the transmission tailhousing and engages with the transmission mainshaft splines. This ensures that the transmission tailshaft oil seal is well lubricated.

30 Slide the front end of the propshaft into the tail end of the transmission unit: you may have to rotate the propshaft just a little to allow the splines to engage. Then, lift up the rear end of the propshaft and engage its flange with the differential drive flange, lining up the marks you made when the propeller shaft was removed. Fit the four bolts and nuts (nuts toward the front of the car) and tighten to a torque of 29 Nm (2.9 kgf m / 21 lbf ft). **Warning!** If the spring washers show any signs of having become flattened, they should be replaced. Note: you'll need to apply the parking brake in order to stop the propshaft rotating when you try to torque the nuts.

30 Now's a good time to refill the transmission with oil if it has been emptied. Manual transmission: first check that the 24 mm drain plug is tight, then remove the filler plug halfway up the left hand side of the transmission case. Add 2 liters (0.43 Imp gal / 0.52 US gal) of the approved gear oil and then replace and tighten the filler plug. If the transmission oil was not emptied, check oil level and top up as necessary ☞ 2/8. On automatic transmission cars, remember to check the transmission fluid level after installation is complete ☞ 2/9.

31 Fit the exhaust system ☞ 5/38/16-24.

32 That's about it. Mazda recommend that the rear suspension adjustment is checked and reset ☞ 8/2, 3. We suggest that you get the alignment checked by a tire specialist or by a Mazda dealer.

© Miata Magazine 1990.

AMERICAN/ENGLISH GLOSSARY OF AUTOMOTIVE TERMS

American	English
A-arm	Wishbone (suspension)
Antenna	Aerial
Axleshaft	Halfshaft
Back-up	Reverse
Barrel	Choke/venturi
Block	Chock/wedge
Box end wrench	Ring spanner
Bushing	Bush
Clutch hub	Synchro hub
Coast	Freewheel
Convertible	Drop head
Cotter pin	Split pin
Counterclockwise	Anti-clockwise
Countershaft	Layshaft (of gearbox)
Crescent wrench	Open-ended spanner
Curve	Corner
Dashboard	Facia
Denatured alcohol	Methylated spirit
Dome lamp	Interior light
Driveaxle	Driveshaft
Driveshaft	Propeller shaft
Fender	Wing/mudguard
Firewall	Bulkhead
Flashlight	Torch
Float bowl	Float chamber
Freeway, turnpike, etc.	Motorway
Frozen	Seized
Gas tank	Petrol tank
Gas pedal	Accelerator pedal
Gasoline (gas)	Petrol
Gearshift	Gearchange
Generator (DC)	Dynamo
Ground	Earth (electrical)
Header/manifold	Manifold (exhaust)
Heat riser	Hot spot
High	Top gear
Hood	Bonnet (engine cover)
Idle	Tickover
Intake	Inlet
Jackstands /Safety stands	Axle stands
Jumper cable	Jump lead
Keeper	Collet
Kerosene	Paraffin
Knock pin	Roll pin
Lash	Freeplay/Clearance
Latch	Catch
Latches	Locks
License plate /tag plate	Number plate
Light	Lamp
Lock (for valve spring retainer)	Split cotter (for valve cap)
Lopes	Hunts
Lug nut	Wheel nut
Metal chips or debris	Swarf
Misses	Misfires
Muffler	Silencer
Oil pan	Sump
Open flame	Naked flame
Panel wagon/van	Van
Parking light	Sidelight
Parking brake	Handbrake
Piston pin or wrist pin bearing/bush	Small (little) end bearing
Piston pin or wrist pin	Gudgeon pin
Pitman arm	Drop arm
Power brake booster	Servo unit
Primary shoe	Leading shoe (of brake)
Prussian blue	Engineer's blue
Pry	Prise (force apart)
Prybar	Crowbar
Prying	Levering
Quarter window	Quarterlight
Recap	Retread
Release cylinder	Slave cylinder
Repair shop	Garage
Replacement	Renewal
Ring gear (of differential)	Crownwheel
Rocker panel	Sill panel
Rod bearing	Big-end bearing
Rotor/disk	Disc (brake)
Secondary shoe	Trailing shoe (of brake)
Sedan	Saloon
Setscrew, Allen screw	Grub screw
Shift fork	Selector fork
Shift lever	Gearlever/gearstick
Shift rod	Selector rod
Shock absorber, shock	Damper/shocker
Snap-ring	Circlip
Soft top	Hood
Spacer	Distance piece
Spare tire	Spare wheel
Spark plug wires	HT leads
Spindle arm	Steering arm
Stablizer or sway bar	Anti-roll bar
Station wagon	Estate car
Stumbles	Hesitates
Tang or lock	Tab
Taper pin	Cotter pin
Teardown	Strip(down)/dismantle
Throw-out bearing	Thrust bearing
Tie-rod (or connecting rod)	Trackrod (of steering)
Transmission	Gearbox
Troubleshooting	Fault finding/diagnosis
Trunk	Boot
Tube wrench	Box spanner
Turn signal	Indicator
Valve lifter	Tappet
Valve lifter or tappet	Cam follower or tappet
Valve cover	Rocker cover
VOM (volt ohmmeter)	Multimeter
Wheel cover	Roadwheel trim
Wheel well	Wheelarch
Whole drive line	Transmission
Windshield	Windscreen
Wrench	Spanner

9 BRAKES, WHEELS & TIRES

1. BRAKE SYSTEM - INTRODUCTION & ON-VEHICLE CHECKS

The Miata/MX5 uses a conventional hydraulic disc brake system, supplemented by a vacuum servo unit (power brake unit) which employs engine vacuum to enhance braking effort. A cable-operated parking brake is used, acting on the rear wheels. The main sections of this chapter relate to the standard hydraulic brake system and parking brake system.

Some models are fitted with an anti-lock brake system (ABS) which monitors braking and modulates braking effort to reduce the risk of wheels locking and a skid developing. The ABS system is described in the later sections of this chapter, though it should be noted that the scope for owner maintenance and repair of the ABS system is extremely limited.

You can determine quite a lot about the condition of the braking system while driving the car, and you should make a note of any suspected brake problems as they arise. Unusual noises, generally poor brake operation, or pulling to one side are all indicative of the need for further investigation.

When dismantling parts of the hydraulic system, it is good practice to make some provision for covering line (pipe) ends and blocking hydraulic passages to keep dirt out. The line ends can be protected by using small plastic caps to cover them - these caps often come fitted to replacement parts and are normally discarded - we like to keep a few handy in the workshop for jobs like these. We've also used short lengths of plastic tube blanked off with small bolts - not as neat as the caps, but it keeps out the dirt. The passages in the hydraulic components can again be plugged with those small caps, or you could try golf tees for this.

Warning! When adding fluid, use only hydraulic fluid conforming to **SAE J1703** or **FMVSS 116, DOT 3** or higher. Never use any other type of fluid or oil in the hydraulic system or damage to the seals will result, and you stand a good chance of the brakes failing in service.

Warning! Brake friction materials normally contain a proportion of asbestos, which is hazardous if inhaled as dust. When working on the brakes, wear protective clothing and a dust mask. Work in a well-ventilated area. Never use compressed air to clean brake parts. Use a commercially available brake cleaner and paper wipes or rags during cleaning, and dispose of the rags or wipes safely after use - DO NOT reuse them.

2. BRAKE HYDRAULIC SYSTEM - TOPPING UP & AIR BLEEDING

☞ 1/1, 2 & 9/1.

CHECKING AND TOPPING UP THE FLUID LEVEL

1 The fluid level in the brake master cylinder reservoir should be monitored on a regular basis. In normal circumstances, the level will drop almost imperceptibly as the brake pads wear down, and the hydraulic system compensates for this by repositioning the caliper pistons. A sudden drop in fluid level will require immediate investigation - it indicates a leak somewhere in the system. Note that although there is a fluid level warning system fitted, this should be considered an emergency warning system only - don't wait until the light comes on before checking the fluid level.

2 Periodic topping up of the reservoir is normal and acceptable. The fluid level should be maintained between the **MAX** and **MIN** level lines in the reservoir body. If you need to top up, first pack some rag around the underside of the reservoir to catch any accidental spills. **Caution!** Hydraulic fluid will damage and discolor painted and plastic parts. If you do accidentally spill any fluid, wipe it up immediately, and wash the area with warm water and detergent to prevent damage.

2/2 Topping-up brake master cylinder.

3 **Warning!** When adding fluid, use only hydraulic fluid conforming to **SAE J1703** or **FMVSS 116, DOT 3** or higher. Never use any other type of fluid or oil in the hydraulic system or damage to the seals will result, and you stand a good chance of the brakes failing in service.

AIR BLEEDING

4 Air bleeding is the procedure used to remove air bubbles from the hydraulic system. If present in the hydraulic system, air will reduce braking efficiency significantly. Unlike hydraulic fluid, air is highly compressible and much of the braking effort is wasted in compressing the gases, instead of operating the brakes.

5 It is important to find out how the air got in there in the first place. If you have recently dismantled any part of the hydraulic system, it may be that minute bubbles in the system have simply joined together to form one or more larger bubbles, and the bleeding process will eliminate them.

6 If the problem is recurrent, air must be entering the system somehow. This is often caused by seal failure, usually in the master cylinder. It is not uncommon for a worn master cylinder seal to hold up fine under pressure, but to allow air to be drawn in during the return stroke. If this is the case, bleeding will probably help in the short term, but the problem will soon reappear. The answer is to overhaul the master cylinder.

7 Air can also be introduced as a result of repeated heavy braking which has caused the brake calipers to heat up abnormally. Any water

(from atmosphere) in the fluid will boil under the heat generated by heavy braking and will result in bubbles forming in the system. It should be noted that this problem is most likely to occur where the fluid in the system is old. Hydraulic fluid gradually absorbs moisture from the air over time, and this is why the fluid must be changed at the specified intervals.

8 To carry out the bleeding procedure, you will need a supply of fresh brake fluid (never use old or used fluid). You will also need a bleed tube (available from auto parts stores), a glass or plastic jar and a brake wrench. We strongly recommend that you use the correct type of 8 mm wrench for this - a brake wrench is basically a hexagon pattern box-ended wrench with a slot to allow it to pass over the brake line, and which will fit snugly on the bleed screw. Mazda can supply a wrench as an SST (49 0259 770B), or a commercially available equivalent. If you try using a crescent wrench, you will probably damage the screw hexagon - it is very small and, invariably, tight. You will also need an assistant during the bleeding procedure.

9 Before you can start work, you'll need to slacken the wheel nuts by one turn each, then jack the car and support it on safety stands positioned under the jacking points at each end of the rockers/sills (☞ 1/3). Remove the wheel nuts and lift the wheels away. Remove the dust caps from the bleed screws on the top of each caliper and carefully clean the area around them. Start the bleeding procedure at the wheel furthest from the master cylinder, and work forwards (*i.e.*: lhd - r/right, r/left, f/right, f/left; rhd - r/left, r/right, f/left, f/right).

10 Fit the bleed tube over the ball of the bleed screw and place the free end of the tube into a jar to which sufficient fluid has been added to submerge the tube end. Using the brake wrench, slacken the bleed screw very slightly. Install your

2/10 Bleeding air from brake hydraulic system.

assistant in the driver's seat. He or she will be operating the brake pedal while you open or close the bleed screw, so it is important you agree on a system of commands so that you each know what the other is doing.

11 The secret to the bleeding operation is to keep the system under pressure whenever the bleed screw is open; you want your assistant to maintain that pressure while you control the bleeding using the bleed screw. Have your assistant apply pressure to the brake pedal, and yell "READY!" when they have done so. Gradually open the bleed screw - your assistant will note that the pedal moves down as the fluid flows out. As soon as the pedal reaches the end of its stroke, your assistant should yell "DOWN!" or something similar to indicate this to you. Close the bleed screw and yell "CLOSED!" to your assistant, who should then release the pedal and reapply pressure (and yell "READY!" again).

12 In this way, you both know exactly what is going on at any given time, and the system remains under constant pressure - air cannot be drawn in accidentally. You should repeat the cycle about 10 times, then pause and top up the reservoir. You will find that after about 20 strokes, any air will have been expelled. You can monitor this by watching for bubbles in the bleed tube. Once all traces of air have gone, you can close the bleed screw, remove the tube, wipe up any fluid spills and fit the dust cap. Move on to the next caliper and repeat the process.

13 When you have bled the air from all four calipers, check brake operation by depressing the pedal. It should feel firm, with no signs of sponginess when pressed down. Make a final check of the level of fluid in the reservoir, topping it up to the **MAX** line before fitting the cap. When you've completed the bleeding operation collect the expelled fluid and dispose of it safely - never tip it down a drain or onto the ground. Your local authority will be able to advise on safe (and legal) disposal procedures.

3. BRAKE SYSTEM HYDRAULIC FLUID - REPLACEMENT

☞ 1/1, 2 & 9/1.

1 The brake hydraulic fluid should be changed at the intervals specified in the service schedule (☞ 2) or whenever you have reason to suspect that the fluid is contaminated or degraded through age. The procedure is essentially similar to the bleeding procedure (☞ 9/2) so set up the car and equipment as described.

2 You need to remove most of the old fluid from the reservoir. This can be done using a suction pump, if you have one. Alternatively, open one of the bleed screws with the bleed tube and jar in position, and pump the brake pedal repeatedly until the level falls to the bottom of the reservoir. Don't keep pumping beyond this point or you will introduce air to the brake lines.

3 Fill the reservoir with new hydraulic fluid conforming to **SAE J1703** or **FMVSS 116, DOT 3** or higher. Starting from the caliper furthest from the master cylinder and working round the car to the nearest, bleed each line in turn until fresh fluid emerges from the bleed tube. There will normally be a slight but perceptible color change as the new fluid begins to flow. Remember to pause after about 10 pedal strokes and top up the reservoir - if the level falls too low, air will enter the system and you will have to bleed this out. When all four calipers have been bled through, check that the pedal feels firm when operated, then install the dust caps and lower the car to the ground. Make a final check of the level of fluid in the reservoir, topping it up to the **MAX** line before fitting the cap.

4. BRAKE LINES (PIPES) - CHECKING & REPLACEMENT

☞ 1/1, 2 & 9/1.

RIGID LINES

1 The metal brake lines and the brake hoses should be examined at regular intervals as specified in the maintenance schedule (☞ 2) or whenever a leak is suspected.

2 Before you can start work, you'll need to slacken the wheel nuts by one turn each, then jack the car and support it on safety stands positioned under the jacking points at each end of the rockers/sills (☞ 1/3). You need to raise the car sufficiently to allow you clear and safe access underneath. Remove the wheel nuts and lift the wheels away.

3 Working back from the master cylinder, check each brake line carefully for signs of leaks or damage. In the case of the metal lines, look for physical damage or corrosion - if found, the line(s) will have to be replaced. Check the flexible hoses to each caliper for signs of deterioration such as splits or bulges, or cracking of the casing material. Again, if any deterioration is noted, fit a new hose.

4 If you need to fit a new brake line, it is preferable to have the new line ready to install before work starts - that way you can check that the new line will fit exactly, and make any minor adjustments by carefully bending the line (take care not to overdo this, or you risk kinking the line and collapsing the line walls). Where the official replacement line is unavailable, most garages can make up a suitable line for you, but this normally requires the old line to be removed first so that it can be used as a pattern.

5 Unclip the line from the plastic support clips along its length, then unscrew the 10 mm line union at each end to free it. In cases of severe corrosion, it is not uncommon for the line to be frozen (seized) inside the union, in which case it is likely that the line will twist off as the union is unscrewed - this is no real problem if you were intending to fit a new line anyway. As the union is freed, there will be a little fluid leakage. Don't worry too much about this, but use some rag to catch the spills.

6 Position the new line and screw the unions loosely into position with your fingers. Clip the line along its length, checking that it is routed correctly. Finally, tighten the line unions securely, but do not overtighten. The recommended torque setting for the line unions is 13-22 Nm (1.3-2.2 kgf m / 9.4-16.0 lbf ft). Bleed the hydraulic system ☞ 9/2.

FLEXIBLE HOSES

7 + Where a brake flexible hose is to be removed, slacken the 10 mm flare nut while the union is still gripped in the body bracket. Using pliers or vise grips, withdraw the retaining spring clip to release the line union from the body bracket

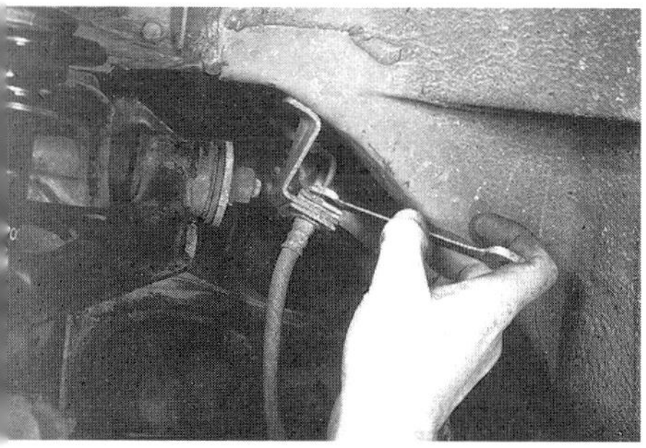

4/7a Loosen the flare nut ...

4/7b ... then pull out the spring clip.

inish undoing the rigid line's flare nut and then unscrew the hose union 12 mm banjo bolt at the caliper end and remove the hose.

3 Install the new hose, using new copper washers at the caliper end. Make sure the banjo union locating peg engages correctly, then tighten the banjo union bolt to 22-29 Nm (2.2-3.0 kgf m / 16.0-22 lbf ft). Fit the flexi hose's 'nut' into the recess under the body bracket and then push the spring clip into place. Connect the rigid line by screwing the flare nut into the flexi hose union - start the thread with your fingers. **Warning!** Be sure that the hose is positioned so that suspension or steering movement will not cause it damage. Bleed air from the system ☞ 9/2.

5. BRAKE PEDAL - REMOVAL, INSTALLATION & ADJUSTMENT

☞ 1/1, 2 & 9/1.

REMOVAL AND INSTALLATION

1 If you need to remove the brake pedal, you'll find it easier if you first detach the access panel under the steering column; remove the two retaining screws and unclip it from the dash panel.

2 The first thing to do is to free the pushrod clevis from the pedal. This pivots on a clevis pin, which is secured by an R-pin (spring clip). Pull out the R-pin and displace the clevis pin to free the pushrod.

3 Remove the pedal pivot bolt 14 mm nut and spring washer. The bolt can now be pulled out to free the pedal from its pivot. As you withdraw the pedal, unhook the return spring.

4 Check the pedal pivot bolt, sleeve and bushes, the return spring and the clevis pin for wear or damage, replacing them as necessary. Prior to installation, apply copper or molybdenum grease to all moving parts

5 When installing the pedal, tighten the pivot bolt nut to 20-34 Nm (2.0-3.5 kgf m / 14-25 lbf ft) and check that the pedal moves smoothly through its travel. Reconnect the pedal return spring, then fit the pushrod, installing the clevis pin to retain it and securing this with the R-pin. Check and adjust the pedal as described below.

ADJUSTMENT

6 Check the distance between the center of the upper surface of the pedal pad and the carpet

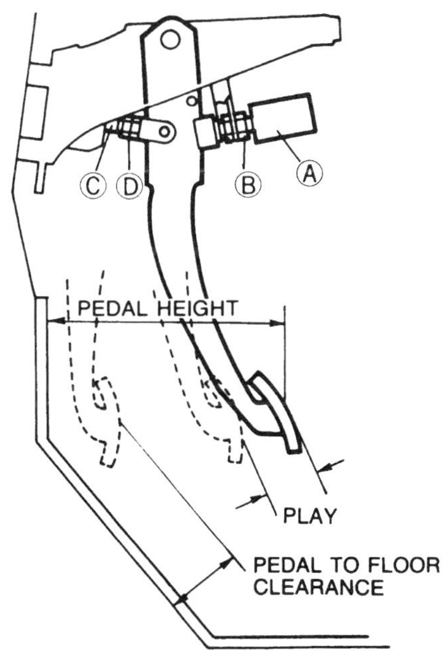

D5/6 BRAKE PEDAL HEIGHT ADJUSTMENT.
A Brake light switch body. B Adjuster nut. C Master cylinder pushrod. D Locknuts.

on the firewall (see diagram). The specified pedal height setting is 171-181 mm (6.93-7.13 in). If adjustment is required, disconnect the stoplight switch wiring connector (A), back off the switch 17 mm locknuts (B), and unscrew the switch (21 mm) until it is clear of the pedal.

7 Working behind the pedal, slacken the pushrod locknuts (D), then rotate the pushrod (C) to obtain the prescribed pedal height.

8 Operate the brake pedal a few times to release any residual vacuum in the servo, then depress the pedal by hand until resistance is felt, indicating pedal free play. The pedal play should be 4-7 mm (0.16-0.28 in). If required, make any necessary correction by adjusting the pushrod (C), then secure locknuts (D).

9 Screw in the stoplight switch body until the switch plunger just contacts the pedal, then turn it a further half turn. Secure the locknuts (B) and reconnect the wiring connector. Turn on the ignition switch and check that the stoplights are working normally.

10 The pedal to floor clearance can be checked, though this is not an adjustable clearance - insufficient clearance indicates the presence of air in the hydraulic system. To check this, you need to apply a specified pressure, 589 N (60 kg / 132 lb) to the pedal. Quite how you do this is another matter. (Wally, our Technical Adviser on this project, suggests that you might use a set of bathroom scales, placing a wood block between the scales and the pedal. We guess it might work, but then again, Wally *was* in a bar when he suggested this method ...).

11 If you find a way to apply the correct pressure (or just guess at it and press the pedal pretty hard) the pedal to floor clearance, without carpet in place, is 95 mm (3.74 in). As we mentioned above, insufficient clearance suggests the presence of air in the hydraulic system. Bleed the system (☞ 9/2) and try the check again.

6. BRAKE MASTER CYLINDER & SERVO - REMOVAL, INSTALLATION & ADJUSTMENT

☞ 1/1, 2 & 9/1.

1 In addition to your normal hand tools, to carry out this job you will need a supply of rags (in case of hydraulic fluid spills) and a brake wrench. Mazda can supply a brake wrench as an SST (49 0259 770B), or you can use a commercially available equivalent. Some small plastic caps to cover the ends of the brake lines would be a good idea. (These often come on replacement parts and are normally discarded - we like to keep a few handy in the workshop for jobs like these.) The main part of this section relates to non-ABS cars. If your car is fitted with ABS, look at the details on ABS models near the end of the section and use these notes in conjunction with the main text.

2 If you intend to overhaul or replace either the master cylinder, servo unit or both, you will need to check and adjust the servo unit pushrod to master cylinder clearance during installation. On non-ABS cars, this operation requires a depth gauge tool (SST 49 F043 001) and a hand operated vacuum pump with gauge. If your car has ABS fitted, you will need the vacuum pump, plus a different depth gauge (SST 49 B043 001). In addition, on ABS models, you will also require a special socket wrench (SST 49 B043 004) and a lock tool (SST 49 B043 003) **Warning!** If you don't have access to these tools, you'll have to get a Mazda dealer to carry out the work for you. We do not recommend that you proceed without the correct tools - we know of no alternative method of setting up this clearance, and it is important that it is set up correctly. If you are on really good terms with your dealer, you may be able to borrow the tools, otherwise, take the servo unit and master cylinder in for the adjustments to be made.

MASTER CYLINDER REMOVAL

3 Unplug the master cylinder reservoir level warning switch wiring connector. Disconnect the brake lines at the master cylinder and at the proportioning bypass (brake compensator) valve, using rag to mop up any spills. One of the lines connects to a banjo union bolted to the side of the master

cylinder: disconnect this by removing the 14 mm union bolt.

4 Note that the bypass valve mounting arrangement varies between cars of different specification. Most have the valve bracketed on the right-hand side of the master cylinder. On our project car, the valve is mounted on the other side of the master cylinder and is positioned in line with it. The basic line connection details are the same, however, as are union sizes at 10 mm.

5 If you find that the reservoir is gradually emptying itself now that the lines are off, either plug the outlet hole, or place a small drain container under the master cylinder and allow it to empty.

6 Remove the two 12 mm nuts and spring washers which retain the master cylinder and the bypass valve bracket to the vacuum servo unit (power brake unit). Lift away the valve and its bracket, then remove the master cylinder.

VACUUM SERVO (POWER BRAKE) UNIT REMOVAL

7 Remove the master cylinder as described in the preceding steps. Working inside the car, detach the access panel under the steering column; remove the two retaining screws and unclip it from

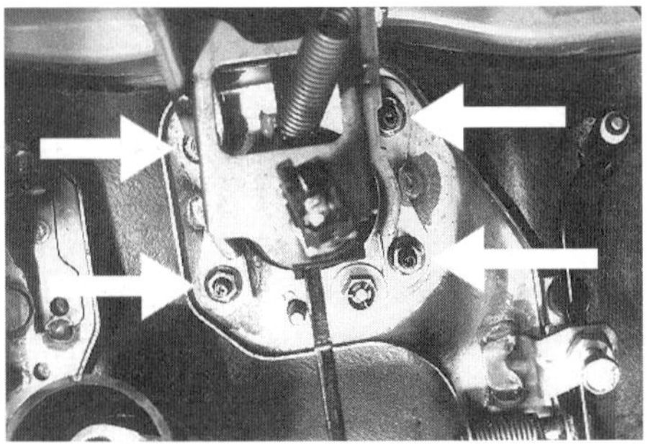

6/8 Four nuts secure the servo unit.

the dash panel.

8 Next, you need to free the pushrod clevis from the pedal. This pivots on a clevis pin, which is secured by an R-pin (spring clip). Pull out the R-pin and displace the clevis pin to free the pushrod. Around the pedal bracket, you'll see the four 12 mm nuts which secure the servo unit. Remove these and move back to the engine compartment.

9 Pull off the vacuum hose at the servo and vacuum line connections, then remove the servo unit.

VACUUM SERVO (POWER BRAKE) UNIT INSTALLATION

10 Check that the servo unit and firewall gasket surfaces are clean and dry. Fit a new gasket, using a gasket sealant. Have an assistant hold the unit in place while you fit the four retaining nuts and spring washers from inside the car. Tighten these evenly and progressively to 19-25 Nm (1.9-2.6 kgf m / 14-19 lbf ft).

11 Lubricate the pushrod clevis pin with grease, then install it to retain the pushrod clevis to the pedal end. Fit the R-pin to secure the clevis pin.

12 Moving back to the engine compartment, you need to check the servo unit pushrod to master cylinder clearance at this point. Place the depth gauge (SST 49 F043 001) over the end of the master cylinder as shown in the diagram, and turn the center screw until it just touches the end of the piston.

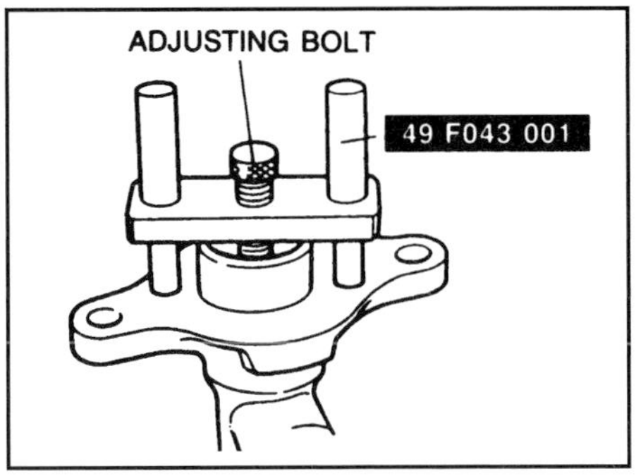

D6/12 TURN ADJUSTMENT BOLT UNTIL IT BOTTOMS IN PISTON.

13 Connect the vacuum pump to the stub on the servo unit, and apply 500 mmHg (19.7 inHg) vacuum to the unit. Turn the depth gauge round and fit it over the end of the servo unit, so that the head of the adjuster screw is immediately above the pushrod end. There should be no clearance between the screw head and pushrod. If there is, or if there is less than zero clearance, slacken the pushrod locknut and adjust the pushrod until zero clearance is obtained. Tighten the locknut to secure the setting. Note that when set as described, this will provide the specified 0.1-0.4 mm (0.004-0.016 in) clearance between the pushrod and master cylinder piston when the servo is installed.

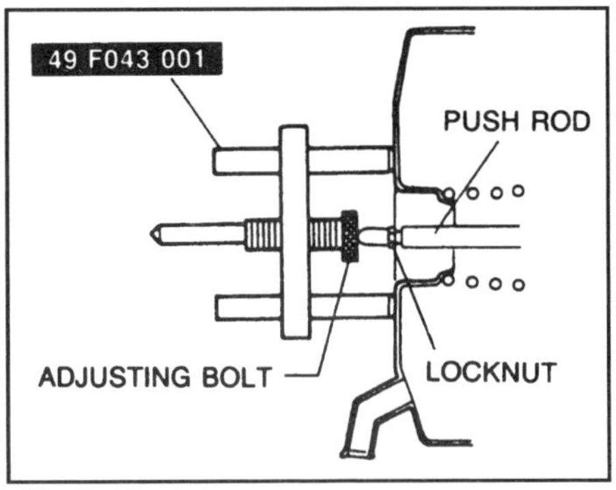

D6/13 MEASURE THE CLEARANCE BETWEEN PUSHROD AND TOOL.

14 After setting the pushrod clearance as described above reconnect the vacuum hose, noting the fitting direction marking on it (the hose contains a one-way check valve and must be fitted correctly). Secure the hose connections by sliding the hose clips into position over the hose ends.

MASTER CYLINDER INSTALLATION

15 Reposition the master cylinder and the bypass valve and bracket assembly, securing them with the two mounting nuts and spring washers. Tighten the nuts to 9.8-16.0 Nm (1.0-1.6 kgf m / 7.2-12.0 lbf ft)

16 Reconnect the brake lines, using new copper washers on the single banjo union, and tightening the union bolt to 20-29 Nm (2.0-3.0 kgf m / 14.0-22.0 lbf ft). Reconnect the remaining line unions, tightening them to 13-22 Nm (1.3-2.2 kgf m / 9.4-16.0 lbf ft). Plug in the fluid warning switch wiring connector. Wipe away any residual fluid spillage around the master cylinder.

17 Fill the reservoir with fresh brake fluid and bleed the system (☞ 9/2), noting that because air has been introduced near the master cylinder, it may take a while to bleed through. When bleeding is completed, have your assistant press down the brake pedal as hard as possible for a minute or two and check the disturbed connections for signs of leakage.

SPECIAL NOTES: ABS-EQUIPPED CARS

18 In general, the procedure for dealing with the master cylinder and servo unit on cars with ABS fitted is as described above, with the following exceptions -

19 During master cylinder removal, note that the line connections differ slightly - the master cylinder and servo unit used are similar, but specific to ABS cars.

20 When installing the master cylinder check the master cylinder to servo unit pushrod clearance as follows. Using SST 49 B043 001, turn the nut fully clockwise to retract the gauge rod. Mount the tool on the servo unit, securing it with the master cylinder mounting nuts, tightening them to 9.8-15.7 Nm (1.0-1.6 kgf m / 7.2-11.6 lbf ft).

21 Connect the vacuum pump to the servo unit vacuum stub and apply 500 mmHg (19.7 inHg) vacuum to the unit. Turn the gauge nut counterclockwise until the gauge rod can be felt to

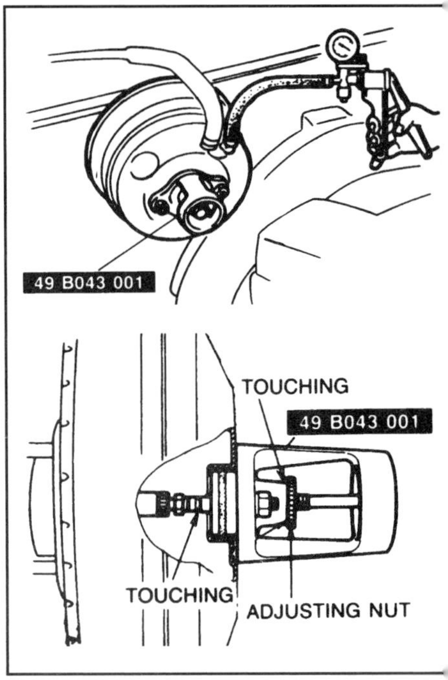

D6/20&21 MOUNT THE TOOL ON THE SERVO BODY AND ADJUST UNTIL GAUGE ROD TOUCHES

›e just touching the servo unit pushrod - push the ːnd of the rod gently to confirm that it is just seated, ınd that no free play exists.

:2 Remove the gauge from the servo unit, aking care not to move the gauge nut as you do so. nvert the gauge and place it over the end of the naster cylinder. Do not press hard on the tool or ou will get a misleading reading - the gauge rod hould just bottom in the piston end. Refer to the ccompanying diagram and check for clearance at B) between the gauge nut and body, and at (C) etween the gauge body and the master cylinder, ısing feeler gauges.

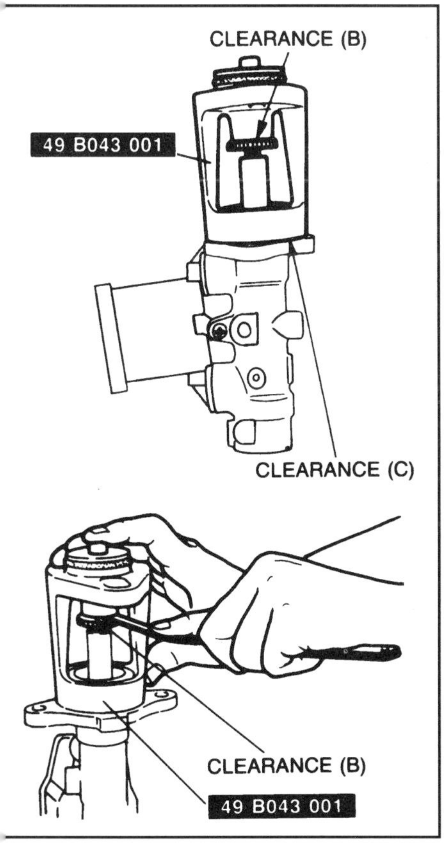

D6/22&23 MOUNT THE TOOL ON THE MASTER CYLINDER TO MEASURE CLEARANCE. ADJUST PUSHROD IF NECESSARY.

:3 Ideally, there should be zero clearance ıt either (B) or (C). If you measure any clearance ıt (B), the servo pushrod is too short, if clearance s found at (C), the pushrod is too long. Either way, ou need to adjust it.

:4 Assemble the remaining two special ools, the socket wrench (SST 49 B043 004) and ock tool (SST 49 B043 003) on the servo unit as hown in the diagram.

:5 If you read a clearance at (B) above, turn he socket wrench to lengthen the pushrod by the mount of clearance measured. Note that the ushrod threads will become tight after a certain mount of movement. This is intentional, and revents the pushrod from loosening. Do not turn he adjuster beyond this point.

:6 If clearance was found at (C) in the above check, measure the height of the gauge rod at (D1) as shown in the accompanying diagram.

27 Fit the gauge on the master cylinder, and turn the gauge nut until the rod just contacts the piston end (do not turn it further or you will get an incorrect reading). Measure the resulting changed height of the gauge rod (D2), then subtract (D1) from (D2). The resulting measurement gives the amount by which the servo unit pushrod needs to be shortened. Using the tools as described in paragraphs 24-25 above, adjust the servo pushrod length.

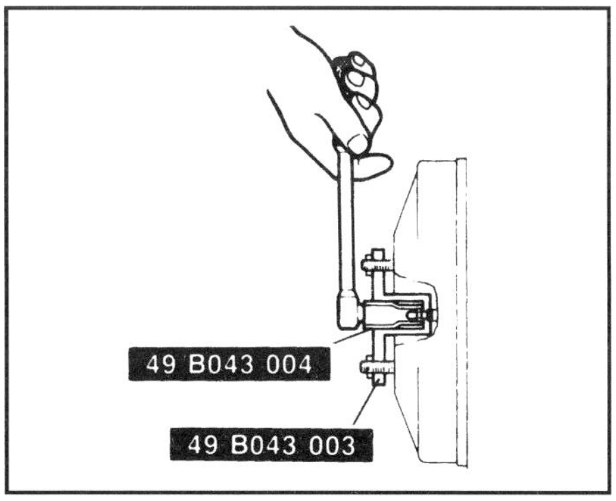

D6/24 FIT TOOLS TO SERVO UNIT AS SHOWN.

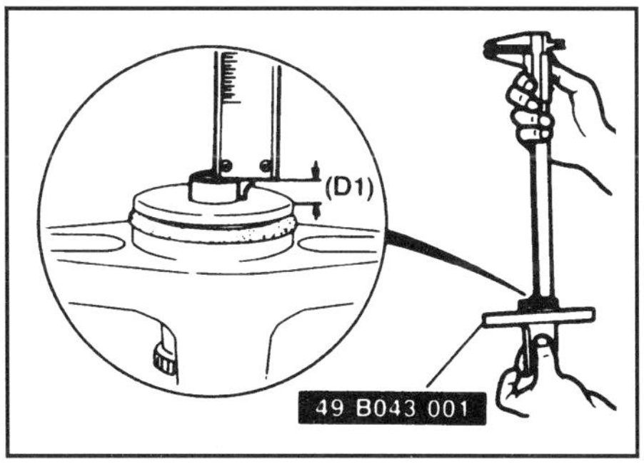

D6/26 USE A VERNIER GAUGE TO MEASURE HEIGHT OF GAUGE ROD (D1).

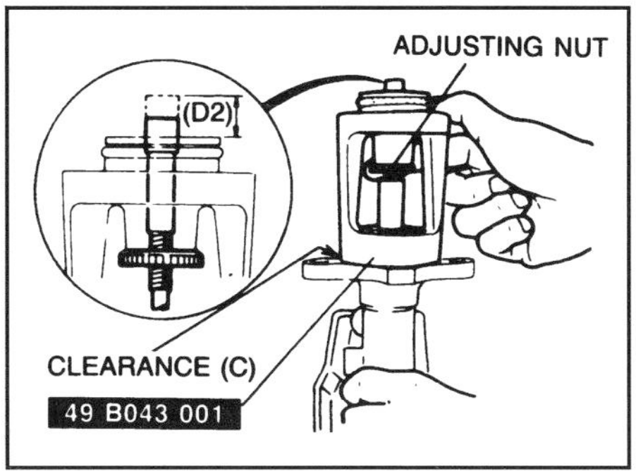

D6/27 MEASURE THE HEIGHT OF GAUGE ROD (D2).

7. BRAKE MASTER CYLINDER - OVERHAUL

☞ 1/1, 2 & 9/1.

1 The master cylinder and servo unit fitted to non-ABS and ABS-equipped cars are similar in construction, with a few detail variations - these are described in the text. Remove the master cylinder ☞ 9/6.

2 If you intend to overhaul either the master cylinder, servo unit or both, you will need to check and adjust the servo unit pushrod to master cylinder clearance during installation. On non-ABS cars, this operation requires a depth gauge tool (SST 49 F043 001) and a hand operated vacuum pump with gauge.

3 If your car has ABS fitted, you will need the vacuum pump, plus a different depth gauge (SST 49 B043 001). In addition, on ABS models, you will also require a special socket wrench (SST 49 B043 004) and a lock tool (SST 49 B043 003)

4 **Warning!** If you don't have access to the above tools, you'll have to get a Mazda dealer to carry out the work for you. We do not recommend that you proceed without the correct tools - we know of no alternative method of setting up this clearance, and it is important that it is set up correctly. If you are on really good terms with your dealer, you may be able to borrow the tools, otherwise, take the servo unit and master cylinder in for the adjustments to be made.

5 Before starting any dismantling work, check the operation of the fluid level sensor as follows. Connect an ohmmeter or continuity tester to the sensor terminals. With fluid present in the reservoir (above the **MIN** level mark), there should be no continuity indicated. If you now empty the fluid, continuity should be shown. If the sensor does not operate correctly, a new one should be fitted. Note that the above check can be carried out with the master cylinder in place, but you will need some kind of pump or siphon arrangement to drain the fluid from the reservoir. **Warning!** Don't try to start a siphon effect by sucking on the tube.

MASTER CYLINDER OVERHAUL

6 With the fluid emptied from the reservoir, remove the single screw which retains the reservoir to the master cylinder, then remove it by pulling it out of the rubber sealing bushes in the body. The seals, which should be replaced during assembly, can be removed from the master cylinder. Pull out and remove the fluid level sensor, then invert the reservoir and tap it on a hard surface to dislodge the filter screen and lower block.

7 On non-ABS cars, remove the small stop screw and its O-ring from the underside of the master cylinder body. On ABS-equipped models, the equivalent stop screw is much longer, and is fitted from the side of the cylinder.

8 Remove the snap ring (circlip) from the end of the master cylinder body. On ABS-equipped cars, there is a spacing washer behind the snap ring which should also be removed.

9 The primary and secondary piston assemblies should now be displaced by their springs and can be removed. If you have difficulty in removing them, wrap some rag around the master cylinder to catch any fluid spray, then apply compressed air to an outlet drilling to push the piston assembly out of the body. On no account pry or lever the assembly out or damage will result.

10 The overhaul kit you have purchased will

contain all of the new components which should be included in the rebuild. However, if the kit is universal or multiple application, it may contain redundant parts as far as your car's master cylinder is concerned - follow the kit manufacturer's instructions.

11 Clean the dismantled parts which will be reused using only clean hydraulic fluid or methylated spirit. Never use general purpose degreasing solvents or gasoline to clean brake parts - these can attack and damage the seals, or cause contamination of the hydraulic fluid after reassembly and installation.

12 Check the surface of the cylinder bore, and the outer surfaces of the pistons for wear or damage. They should be clean and smooth, with no signs of scoring or corrosion. Although it is possible to hone damaged bores, our strong recommendation is that brake cylinders with damaged bores should be replaced.

13 When reassembling the master cylinder, have a container with a little fresh hydraulic fluid handy. Lubricate the seals, pistons and cylinder bore as the pistons are installed. Fit the secondary piston into the cylinder bore, pushing it home with a screwdriver against spring pressure (take care not to scratch the cylinder wall or damage the seals during installation).

14 On non-ABS cars, push the secondary piston fully home, then secure it with the stop screw, using a new O-ring. Tighten the stop screw to 1.96-2.45 Nm (20-25 kgf cm / 17.4-21.7 lbf in). On ABS-equipped cars, the piston must be installed so that the slot in its side aligns with the stop screw hole. Push the piston fully inwards, and secure it with the stop screw, using a new O-ring. Tighten the stop screw to 0.7-1.0 Nm (7.0-10.0 kgf cm / 6.1-8.7 lbf in). On both types, check that the piston moves normally, and that it is retained by the stop screw.

15 Lubricate and install the primary piston assembly and fit the snap ring (and spacer washer, ABS-equipped cars only) to retain it. Lubricate and fit new rubber sealing bushes into the holes in the cylinder, then install the reservoir assembly, fitting the single screw to secure it, tightening it to 0.98-1.47 Nm (10-15 kgf cm / 8.7-13.0 lbf in). If it was removed, install the fluid level sensor. Fit the master cylinder ☞ 9/6.

8. BRAKE SERVO - CHECKING (IN-SITU)

☞ 1/1, 2 & 9/1.

1 You can make a number of checks on the servo unit without dismantling it. Start by depressing the brake pedal several times to release any residual vacuum. Hold the pedal down while starting the engine. As soon as the engine starts, the pedal should move down slightly if the unit is operating correctly.

2 Next, run the engine for a minute or two and then stop it. Depress the brake pedal using normal braking force, and note how far down it moves. Release and reapply the brake several times, noting how far it moves each time. If the servo is working normally, the pedal stroke should decrease with successive applications.

3 Finally, start the engine and depress the pedal with normal braking pressure. Hold the pedal in this position and stop the engine. Keep the brake applied for about 30 seconds, during which time the pedal should not move.

4 If the above checks indicated abnormal operation, disconnect the servo unit vacuum hose and remove it from the car. The hose contains a one-way check valve - note the arrow mark on the hose which indicates the fitting direction (arrow should point away from the servo unit). Examine the hose for signs of splits or holes. If damaged in any way it should be replaced.

5 The check valve operation can be verified by blowing through the hose. Air should pass only in the direction indicated by the arrow. If the valve allows air to pass in both directions, or if it obstructs flow in both directions, fit a new vacuum hose.

6 Install the vacuum hose, making sure it is pushed fully over the mounting stubs and that it is installed in the correct direction. Slide the retaining clips over the hose ends, ensuring that they seat firmly. Repeat the above checks to verify that the unit is now operating correctly.

7 If the above checks failed to resolve a servo fault, you will need to get the servo checked out by a Mazda dealer. The official method is to use vacuum, hydraulic pressure and pedal depression force gauges to check the operation of the unit in detail. In reality, most dealers would check by substituting a known good unit.

9. BRAKE PROPORTIONING BYPASS VALVE - CHECKING (IN-SITU)

☞ 1/1, 2 & 9/1.

1 The brake proportioning bypass valve (let's just call it the bypass valve for convenience) has the job of maintaining the correct balance of braking effort between the front and rear wheels. This is important because as braking effort increases, the car's center of mass transfers forward, so proportionally less effort needs to be applied to the rear brakes. If this were not the case, there would be a tendency for the rear wheels to lock and skid under moderate to heavy braking.

2 To check the operation of the bypass valve you need to connect two hydraulic pressure gauges to measure the relative pressures of the system from the master cylinder, and to the rear brakes

9/1 Location of brake proportioning valve (rhd).

after passing through the bypass valve. If you suspect that the bypass valve is not operating normally, we suggest that you have your Mazda dealer perform this check for you, either using gauges or by substitution. In practice, these valves rarely give trouble.

10. BRAKE PADS (FRONT) - WEAR CHECK

☞ 1/1, 2 & 9/1.

1 Before you can start this check, you'll need to slacken the front wheel nuts by one turn each then jack the front of the car and support it on safety stands positioned under the jacking points at each end of the rockers/sills (☞ 1/3). You need to raise the car sufficiently to allow you clear and safe access underneath. Remove the wheel nuts and lift the wheels away.

2 There is an inspection hole at the back of each caliper, through which the pad condition can be checked without dismantling. You may find it easier if you first turn the steering so that you can view the back edge of the caliper more easily. On a new pad, the friction material is 9.5 mm (0.37 in) thick, the service limit being 1.0 mm (0.04 in). On

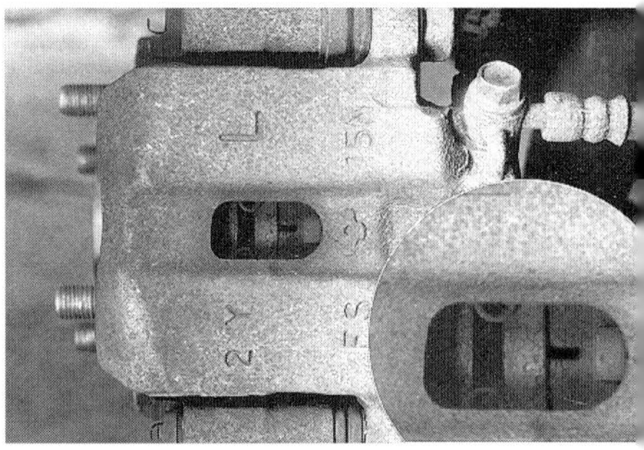

10/2 Disc pad wear check.

our project car, the service limit was denoted by a slot in the friction surface - this may not be present on all pads.

3 **Warning!** It is dangerous to allow the pads to wear beyond the service limit. Not only is there a danger of the disc surface getting damaged by metal-to-metal contact, but the friction material also acts as a heat barrier between the brake disc and the hydraulic system. If this heat barrier is ineffective, you could find that sustained, heavy braking heats the caliper enough to boil the fluid, leading to brake failure.

4 If one or both pads is at or near the service limit, you should replace all four on the 'axle' as a set ☞ 9/11. Note that exaggerated uneven wear of one pad denotes a caliper problem - you should check that the caliper can slide freely on its support during the pad replacement operation.

11. BRAKE PADS (FRONT) - REMOVAL AND INSTALLATION

☞ 1/1, 2 & 9/1.

Warning! Brake friction materials normally contain a proportion of asbestos, which is hazardous nhaled as dust. When working on the brakes, wear ›rotective clothing and a dust mask. Work in a well-'entilated area. Never use compressed air to clean ›rake parts. Use a commercially available brake :leaner and paper wipes or rags during cleaning, ınd dispose of the rags or wipes safely after use -)O NOT reuse them.

ı Before starting work, you should have eady a replacement set of four pads, together with he backing shims and anti-rattle clips. These are upplied by Mazda as a set. With the front of the car acked and supported on safety stands (☞ 1/3) ınd the wheels removed as described above, pro-

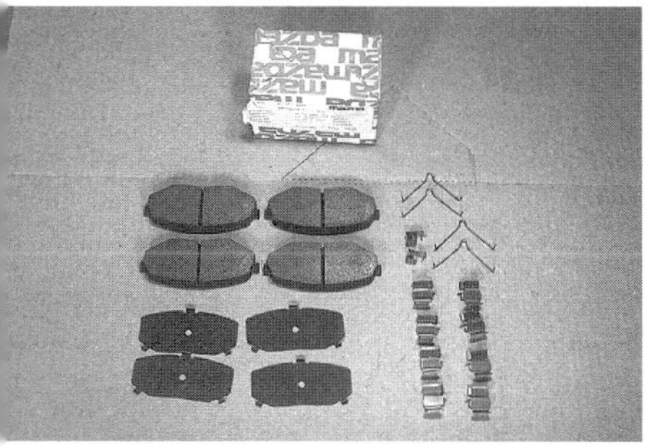
1/1 Components of disc pad replacement set.

eed as follows -

2 + Working from the inner face of the :aliper, slacken and remove the 12 mm caliper ower mounting bolt. This has a long plain shank on vhich the caliper body slides. Withdraw the bolt, hen pivot the caliper upwards and clear of the ›ads. You can either tie the caliper clear of the pads ınd mounting bracket, or disengage the caliper rom the upper mounting by pulling it inward. If ou disengage the caliper, tie or lodge it clear of the vorking area, taking care not to strain the hydraulic ıose. Clean the pivot pin ends and apply copper-

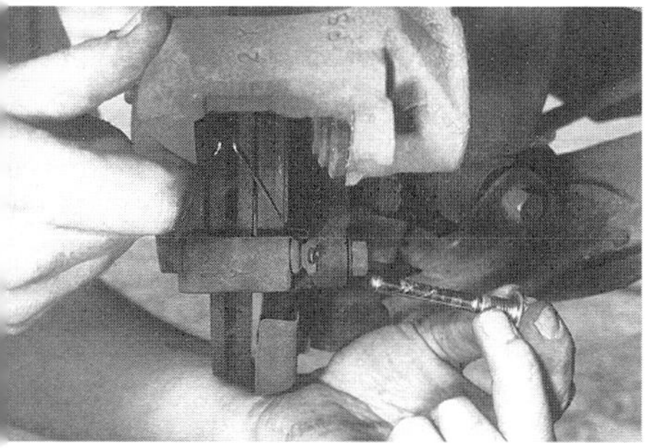
1/2a Remove caliper lower mounting bolt ...

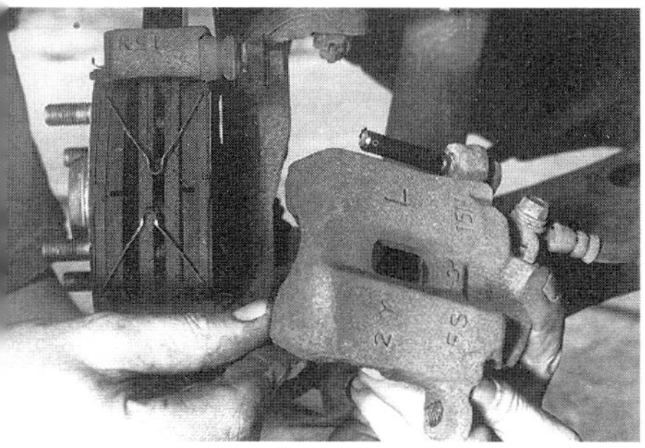
1/2b ... swing caliper up & off.

based brake grease prior to installation - it is important that the caliper assembly can slide freely on the pins.

3 If you intend to fit new pads, the caliper piston must be pushed back into the body to make room (the piston will have gradually crept forward to compensate for wear in the old pads). You can get an SST for this (49 0221 600C), but you may find that thumb pressure will be sufficient. Alternatively, place a tire lever or a similar flat steel strip against the piston end to prevent damage, and gently lever the piston back with a screwdriver. Keep an eye on the fluid level in the reservoir while you do this - it may move back above the **MAX** level line, in which case you will need to remove the excess.

4 + Before removing the old pads, take note of the way they and their shims/clips are fitted in the caliper bracket. On our project car, there were two V-shaped springs fitted between the two pads, hooked into holes in the pad backing, and anti-rattle clips attached to the bottom edge of each pad. Mazda do not show the springs or the anti-rattle clips in their literature, though they were certainly supplied with the new pad set - it may be that they are not used on all models, or that they

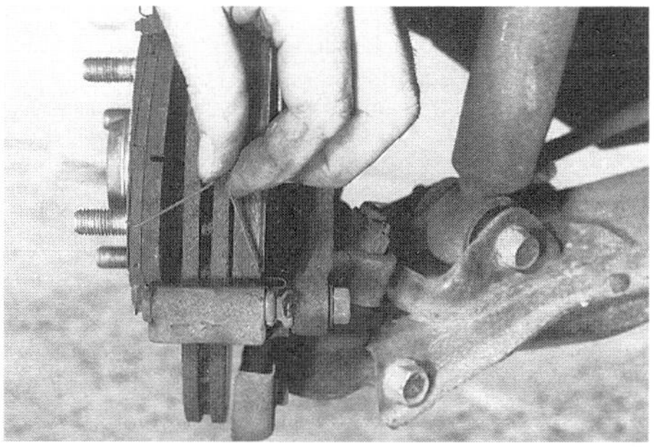
11/4a Remove springs ...

11/4b ... lift out pads with anti-rattle clips.

have been introduced as a modification to eliminate brake noise in service. Note also that the condition of the brake discs must be checked before the new pads are installed - see below for details. If the disc condition is acceptable, run a file around the edge of the disc to remove the buildup of scale which will have appeared outside the swept area of the disc, or this will prevent the new pads seating correctly.

5 + Fit the backing plates to the new pads, checking that they clip securely over the pad edges. Fit the anti rattle clips to the bottom lip of each pad.

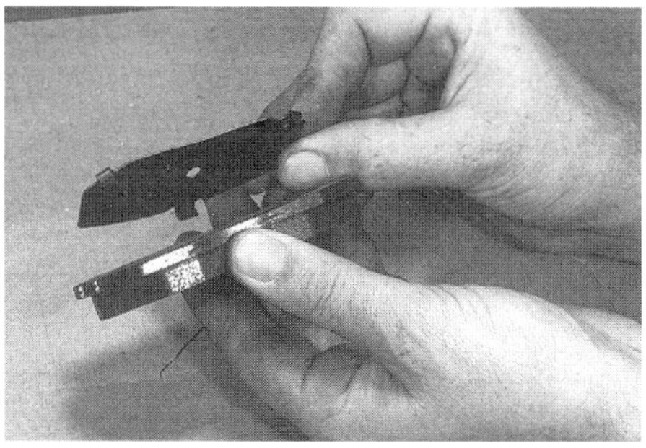
11/5a Fit backing plates to pads ...

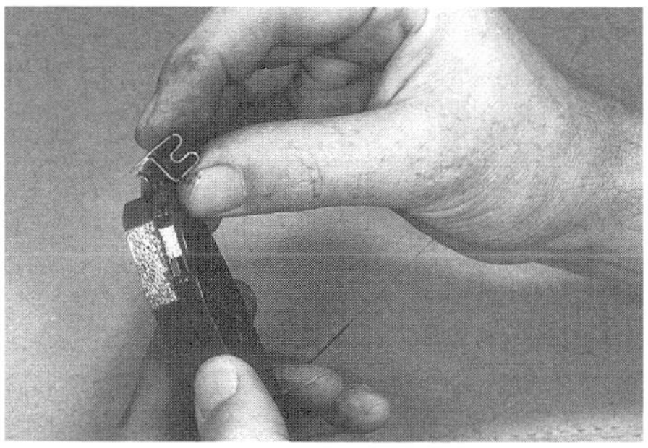
11/5b ... followed by anti-rattle clips ...

11/5c ... and shims to caliper body.

Clip the new anti-rattle shims to the caliper mounting bracket. When installing the pads, apply copper-based brake grease to both sides of the pad backing plates, to the sliding surfaces of the pads and to the contact points of anti-rattle clips and shims. **Warning!** Use the grease sparingly, and never apply any other type of grease, or it will end up melting - ruining the new pads and putting you in danger of brake failure.

6 You don't need to remove the caliper mounting bracket from the steering knuckle during pad replacement, but if you have disturbed it for any reason, tighten the mounting bolts to 49-69

11/6 If applicable, tighten bracket bolts.

Nm (5.0-7.0 kgf m / 36-51 lbf ft).

7 + Place the pads in position on the mounting bracket and carefully hook the V-shaped springs into the holes at the pad ends. Hold the assembly in position, then swivel the caliper body down over the bracket to retain them. Fit the remaining mounting bolt, then check tighten both to 78-88 Nm (8.0-9.0 kgf m / 58-65 lbf ft).

8 Once the new pads have been fitted on both wheels, operate the brake pedal repeatedly to readjust the caliper piston to the new pads. Fit the road wheels and lower the car to the ground. Road test the car to check brake operation, and remem-

11/7a Place pads into the mounting bracket ...

11/7b ... apply grease to backing plates ...

11/7c ... fit springs.

ber to use the brakes as gently as possible for the first 100 miles or so to allow the new friction surfaces to bed in properly.

12. BRAKE DISC (FRONT) - CHECKING, REMOVAL & INSTALLATION

☞ 1/1, 2 & 9/1.

Warning! Brake friction materials normally contain a proportion of asbestos, which is hazardous if inhaled as dust. When working on the brakes, wear protective clothing and a dust mask. Work in a well-ventilated area. Never use compressed air to clean brake parts. Use a commercially available brake cleaner and paper wipes or rags during cleaning, and dispose of the rags or wipes safely after use - DO NOT reuse them.

1 Before starting this operation, you'll need to remove the front wheels for access. Slacken the front wheel nuts by one turn each, then jack the front of the car and support it on safety stands positioned under the jacking points at each end of the rockers (☞ 1/3). You need to raise the car sufficiently to allow you clear and safe access underneath. Remove the wheel nuts and lift the wheels away.

2 Working from the inner face of the caliper, slacken and remove the 10 mm caliper lower mounting bolt. Withdraw the bolt, then pivot the caliper upwards and clear of the pads. Disengage the caliper from the upper mounting by pulling it inward, then tie or lodge it clear of the working area, taking care not to strain the hydraulic hose.

3 While you don't need to remove the pads from the caliper bracket, you'll find that they will fall out anyway - make a note of their position on the bracket, the arrangement of stainless shims and clips, and also the V-shaped pad springs, where fitted, then remove them and place them to one side (☞ 9/14 for more details).

4 Remove the two 14 mm bolts which secure the caliper bracket to the steering knuckle and lift it away. The disc is now free to be lifted off the hub - but leave it in position until you have checked the runout.

5 Temporarily fit two of the wheel nuts to secure the disc on the hub. Position a dial gauge so that the probe touches the outer face of the disc near the outer edge, and zero the gauge. Turn the disc through one revolution and note the runout indicated. This must be 0.1 mm (0.004 in) or less - if it exceeds this figure, a new disc must be fitted.

6 Examine the disc visually for signs of wear or scoring. If damaged, the disc surface will rapidly destroy the pads, and should be replaced to avoid this. Check general wear with a micrometer. The standard thickness is 18 mm (0.71), and the discs should be replaced as a pair if either has worn to 16 mm (0.63 in) or less. If the disc is serviceable, use a file to remove the scale buildup on the outer edge of the disc before installing it.

7 Place the disc over the front wheel studs. Install the caliper bracket, tightening the retaining bolts to 49-69 Nm (5.0-7.0 kgf m / 36-51 lbf ft).

12/6 Measure disc thickness with a micrometer.

Warning! If new discs were fitted, you must als install new pads, irrespective of the amount of wea on the old ones - the pad surfaces will have worn to the profile of the old discs and, if refitted, wi wear the new discs unevenly and will not make fu surface contact. Install the pads, shims, clips an springs, then install the caliper itself ☞ 9/11, 13

13. BRAKE CALIPER (FRONT) - REMOVAL & INSTALLATION

☞ 1/1, 2 & 9/1.

Warning! Brake friction materials normally con tain a proportion of asbestos, which is hazardous inhaled as dust. When working on the brakes, wea protective clothing and a dust mask. Work in a well ventilated area. Never use compressed air to clea brake parts. Use a commercially available brak cleaner and paper wipes or rags during cleaning and dispose of the rags or wipes safely after use DO NOT reuse them.

1 Before you can commence removal slacken the front wheel nuts by one turn each, the jack the front of the car and support it on safet stands positioned under the jacking points at eac end of the rockers (☞ 1/3). You need to raise th car sufficiently to allow you clear and safe acces underneath. Remove the wheel nuts and lift th wheels away.

2 Working from the inner face of th caliper, slacken and remove the 12 mm calipe lower mounting bolt. This has a long plain shank o which the caliper body slides. Withdraw the bol then pivot the caliper upwards and clear of th pads. Next, disengage the caliper from the uppe mounting by pulling it inward. Take care not t strain the hydraulic hose.

3 If you intend to dismantle the caliper afte

13/2 Remove caliper lower mounting bolt.

removal, you will need to make a decision abou the method of piston removal at this stage (☞ 9 14 for details). If the caliper is not to be dismantled fit a hose clamp on the caliper hose to prevent flui leakage, then slacken and remove the hose unio bolt to free the hose.

4 When installing the caliper, fit the hos union using new copper sealing washers and mak ing sure that the union locating pin fits into its hol in the caliper body. Fit the union bolt and tighten provisionally, leaving the hose clamp in place a this stage.

13/4 Check pin and tighten banjo union.

13/5 Slide caliper onto upper mounting pin.

5 Assemble the pads, shims and springs on the caliper bracket ☞ 9/11. Apply grease to the end of the upper mounting pin. Fit the caliper over the upper mounting pin and pivot it down over the pad assembly. Grease the lower mounting bolt and install it, tightening it to 78-88 Nm (8.0-9.0 kgf m / 58-65 lbf ft). Next, tighten the hose union bolt to 22-29 Nm (2.2-3.0 kgf m / 16-22 lbf ft) and remove the hose clamp.

6 Before the road wheels are installed, bleed the brake system (☞ 9/2), then pump the brake pedal several times to settle the piston and pads in their correct positions.

14. BRAKE CALIPER (FRONT) - OVERHAUL

☞ 1/1, 2 & 9/1.

1 Remove the caliper from the steering knuckle (☞ 9/13), but don't disconnect the brake hose yet. You need to give some thought at this stage as to how you will get the caliper piston out of its bore. If you have a compressed air supply, you can use this to remove the piston after the caliper has been disconnected from the hose. We found it easier to use the hydraulic system to jack the piston out before the hose was disconnected. Place a wood strip across the caliper opening to prevent the piston being pushed out too far, and wrap the caliper in rag to catch any fluid spills.

2 Support the caliper in your hand, keeping fingers well clear of the caliper opening. Have an assistant pump gently on the brake pedal. With each stroke, the piston will edge out of the caliper. Proceed slowly as the dust boot begins to stretch out flat - the piston will pop gently out of its bore and will be retained by the dust boot. Pumping should stop immediately at this point, or you will risk forcing the boot off, showering you and the caliper in hydraulic fluid. Install a hose clamp on the caliper hose to prevent fluid draining out, then remove the hose union bolts and disconnect the caliper from the hose.

3 Working over a drain tray, lift the edge of the dust boot and tip out the piston, allowing the fluid in the caliper to drain out. Wipe off any excess fluid, then carefully remove the piston seal, using a small screwdriver to work it out of its groove - take care not to scratch the caliper bore while doing this. Put the dust boot and seal to one side - they will be replaced by new parts during reassembly. Remove the bleed screw, then clean the screw, piston and caliper body in a dish of denatured alcohol or methylated spirit. Use compressed air to blow through the caliper passages and the bleed screw drillings.

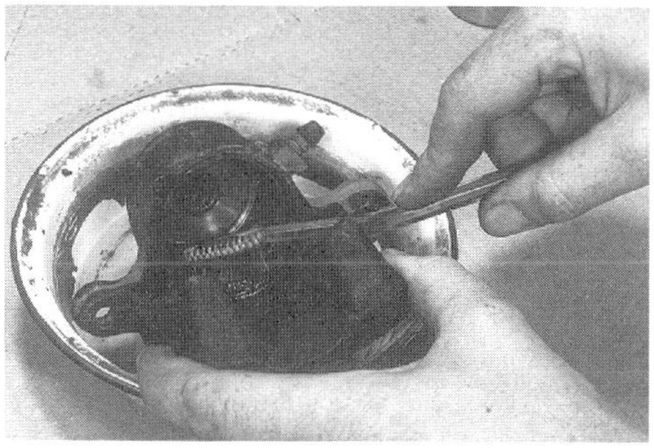

14/3 Clean caliper parts thoroughly.

4 When everything is cleaned up, check the piston and bore surfaces for wear or corrosion damage. If the hydraulic system is kept well maintained, with regular fluid changes, the problem of internal corrosion is unlikely to occur. If neglected, however, the fluid will gradually absorb moisture from the air, and this will allow corrosion to take place. Dirt in the fluid will also cause wear problems. Once the caliper surfaces are damaged and fluid leakage has occurred, you have no other choice but to fit a new caliper unit.

5 + If the piston and bore are serviceable, fit a new piston seal into its groove in the caliper bore, lubricating it with fresh hydraulic fluid during installation. Lubricate the dust seal with hydraulic fluid and fit it into its groove in the caliper bore. Slide the piston part way into the caliper, working the dust seal over it. As the piston is pushed home, check that the dust seal engages over the piston groove. Install the bleed screw loosely at this stage.

6 Install the caliper (☞ 9/13), noting that you will then need to bleed the hydraulic system ☞ 9/2. Get an assistant to press down and hold the brake pedal while you check carefully for signs of leaks.

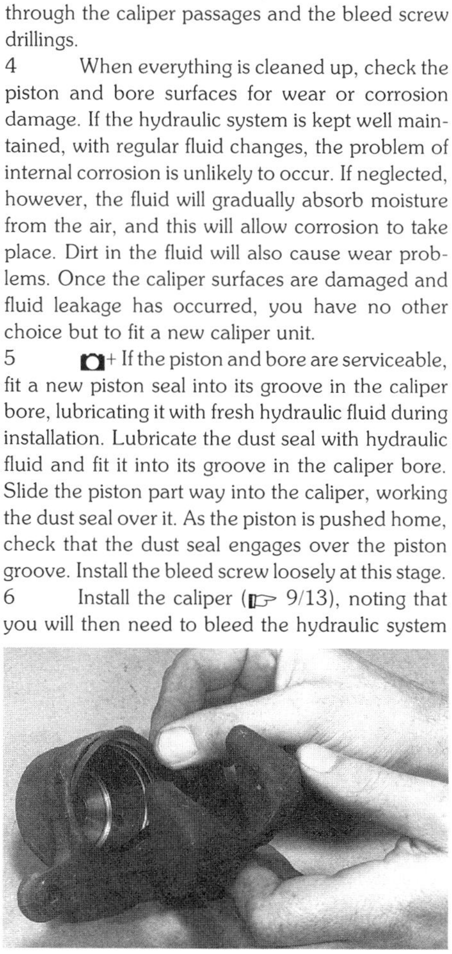

14/5a Fit new piston seal into groove ...

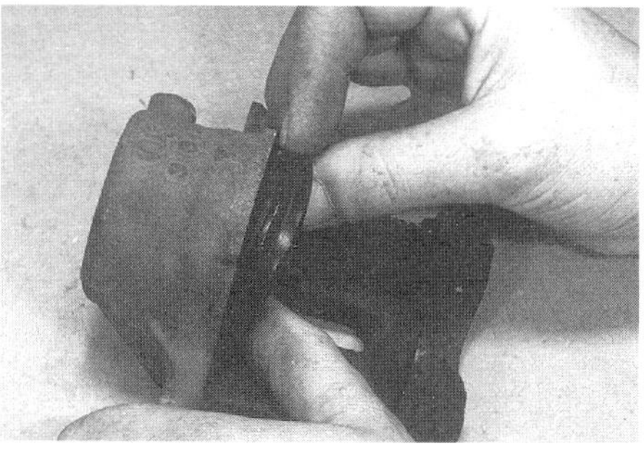

14/5b ... then fit dust seal ...

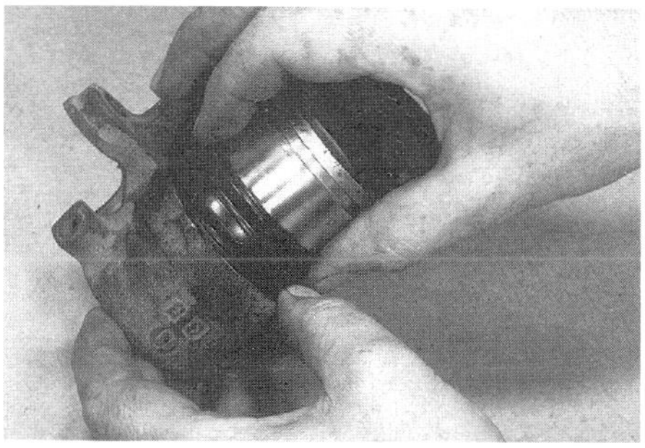

14/5c ... followed by piston.

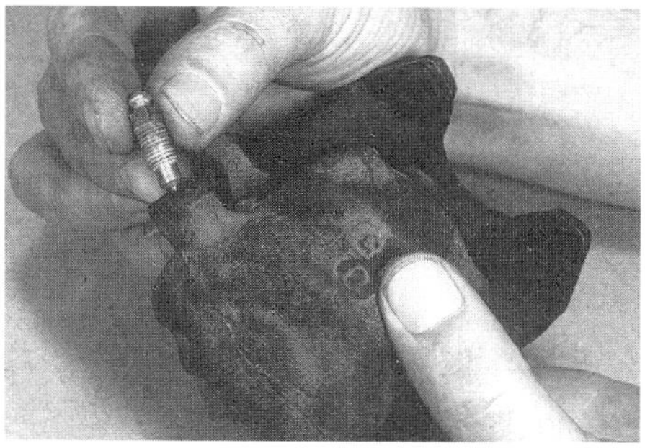

14/5d Fit bleed valve.

15. BRAKE PADS (REAR) - WEAR CHECK

☞ 1/1, 2 & 9/1.

1 Before you can start this check, you'll need to slacken the rear wheel nuts by one turn each, then jack the rear of the car and support it on safety stands positioned under the jacking points at each end of the rockers (☞ 1/3). You need to raise the car sufficiently to allow you safe working access around the rear wheelwells (arches). Remove the wheel nuts and lift the wheels away.

2 There is an inspection slot at the back of each caliper, through which the pad condition can be checked without dismantling. On a new pad, the friction material is 8.0 mm (0.31 in) thick, the service limit being 1.0 mm (0.04 in). On our car, the pads had a groove across the center which denoted the wear limit - this may not be the case on all replacement pads. The accompanying photograph shows a new pad next to a fairly worn one for

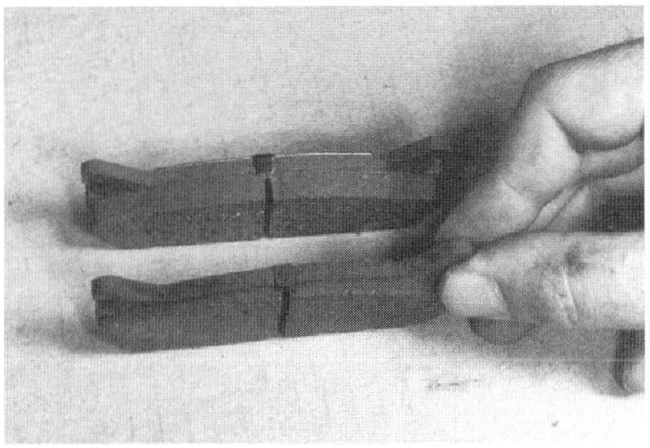

15/2 Comparison of new & part worn pads.

comparison purposes.

3 **Warning!** It is dangerous to allow the pads to wear beyond the service limit. Not only is there a danger of the disc surface getting damaged by metal-to-metal contact, but the friction material also acts as a heat barrier between the brake disc and the hydraulic system. If this heat barrier is ineffective, you could find that sustained, heavy braking heats the caliper enough to boil the fluid, leading to brake failure.

4 If one or both pads is at or near the service limit, you should replace all four on the axle as a set ☞ 9/16. Note that exaggerated uneven wear of one pad denotes a caliper problem - you should check that the caliper can slide freely on its support during the pad replacement operation.

16. BRAKE PADS (REAR) - REMOVAL & INSTALLATION

☞ 1/1, 2 & 9/1.

Warning! Brake friction materials normally contain a proportion of asbestos, which is hazardous if inhaled as dust. When working on the brakes, wear protective clothing and a dust mask. Work in a well-ventilated area. Never use compressed air to clean brake parts. Use a commercially available brake cleaner and paper wipes or rags during cleaning, and dispose of the rags or wipes safely after use - DO NOT reuse them.

1 Before starting work, you should have ready a replacement set of four pads, together with the backing shims and anti-rattle clips. These are supplied by Mazda as a set. The pad set is shown in the photograph, together with the caliper and mounting bracket. With the car jacked and supported on safety stands (☞ 1/3), proceed as follows -

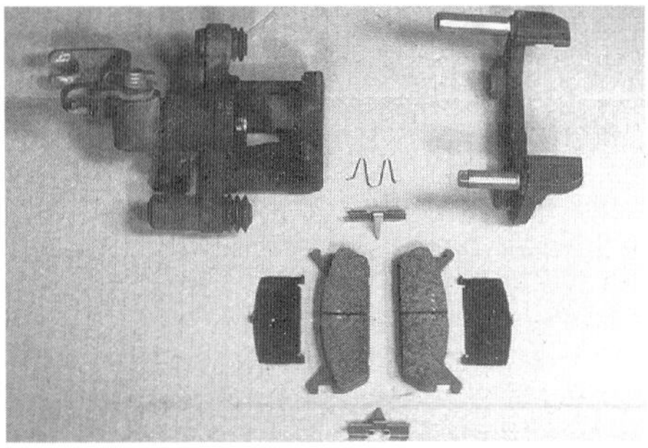

16/1 Component parts of brake caliper.

2 + Working from the inner face of the caliper, remove the 14 mm plug bolt and copper washer which cover the piston adjuster screw. Introduce a 6 mm Allen key through the adjuster hole, then turn it counterclockwise to back off the piston - turn the adjuster back until it stops. Keep an eye on the fluid level in the reservoir while you do this - it may move back above the **MAX** level line, in which case you will need to remove any excess. The plug and adjuster screw hole are not easy to see with the caliper installed - our photographs show it removed for clarity.

3 The caliper lower mounting bolt is

16/2a Remove plug ...

16/2b ... and use Allen key to pull piston back.

16/3 Remove cap from lower mounting.

covered by a black plastic cap, which should be pulled off the bolt head (ours was surprisingly reluctant to come off and had to be twisted quite hard to release its grip on the bolt head). Once the cap is removed, slacken and remove the 10 mm caliper lower mounting bolt. This has a long plain shank on which the caliper body slides.

4 Withdraw the bolt, then pivot the caliper upwards and clear of the pads. You can either tie the caliper clear of the pads and mounting bracket, or disengage the caliper from the upper mounting by pulling it inward. If you disengage the caliper, tie or lodge it clear of the working area, taking care not to strain the hydraulic hose. Note that because the parking brake cable is rather stiff, you will have to wrestle with it a little to find a position it will happily stay in - it helps to release the parking brake lever or you could disconnect the parking brake cable to take the pressure off a little.

5 It is a good idea at this stage to clean the pivot pin ends and apply copper-based brake grease ready for installation - it is important that the caliper assembly can slide freely on the pins: if it sticks, uneven pad wear and poor brake operation will result.

6 Before removing the old pads, take note of the way they and their shims and clips are fitted in the caliper bracket. On our project car, there was an M-shaped spring fitted between the two pads hooked into holes in the top edges of the pad backings, and stainless anti-rattle clips attached to the top and bottom of the caliper bracket, on which the pads slide. Each pad had a steel backing shim clipped to it. We assume that all cars will use this or a similar arrangement.

7 Note also that the condition of the brake discs must be checked before the new pads are installed - see below for details. If the disc

16/7 Removing rust scale from disc edge.

condition is acceptable, run a file around the edge of the disc to remove the buildup of rust scale which will have appeared outside the swept area of the disc, or this will prevent the new pads seating correctly.

8 + You don't need to remove the caliper mounting bracket from the suspension upright during pad replacement, but if you have disturbed it for any reason, tighten the mounting bolts to 49-69 Nm (5.0-7.0 kgf m / 36-51 lbf ft). We recommend that you use a thread locking compound on the mounting bolts for security.

9 + Fit the backing plates to the new

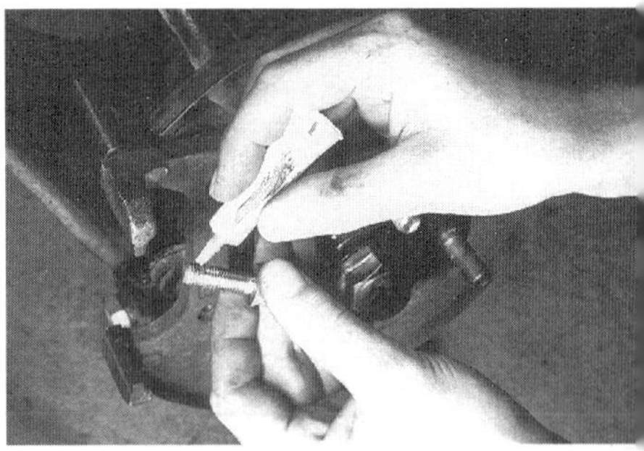

16/8a Apply locking compound ...

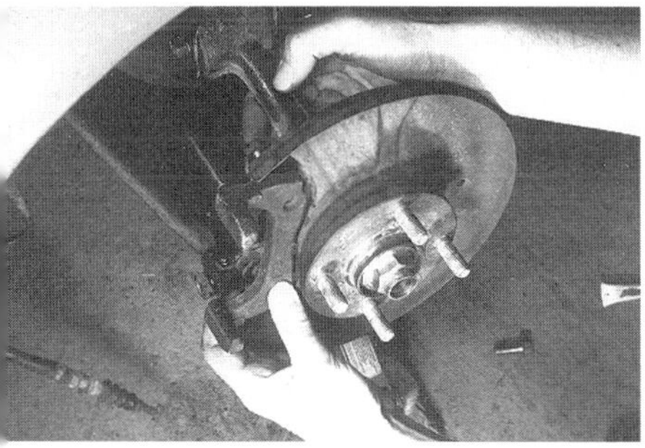

16/8b ... before fitting caliper bracket bolts.

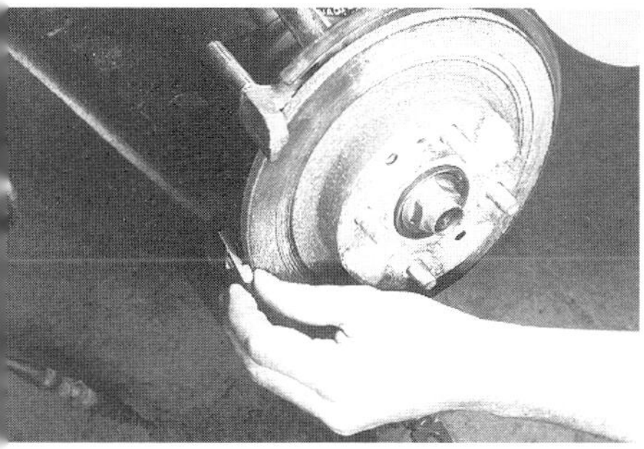

16/9a Fit anti-rattle shims to caliper bracket ...

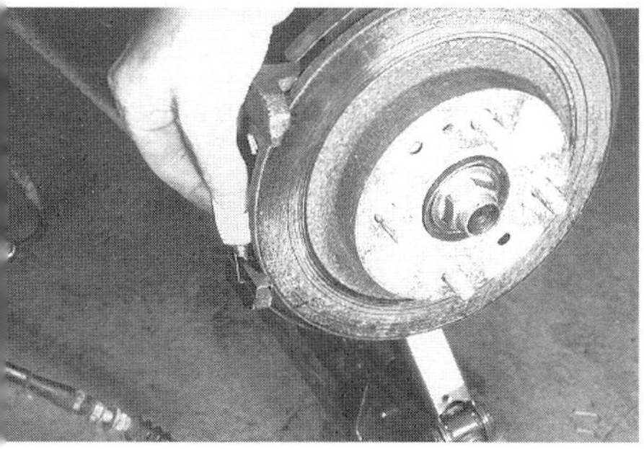

16/9b ... apply copper grease to contact areas.

pads, checking that they clip securely over the pad edges. Clip the new anti-rattle shims to the top and bottom edges of the caliper mounting bracket. When installing the pads, apply copper-based brake grease to both sides of the pad backing plates, to the sliding surfaces of the pads and to the contact points of anti-rattle shims/clips. **Warning!** Use the grease sparingly, and never apply any other type of grease, or it will end up melting and ruining the new pads, and putting you in danger of ineffective brakes.

10 + Place the pads in position on the mounting bracket and carefully hook the M-shaped

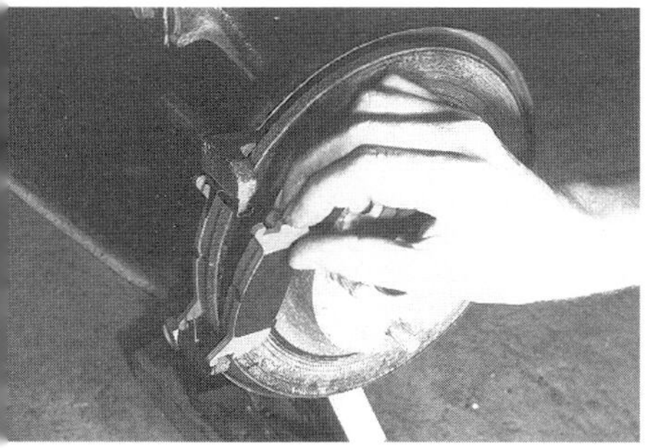

16/10a Place pads in position ...

16/10b ... fit springs ...

16/10c ... slide caliper onto top pin ...

16/10d ... lower caliper & fit mounting bolt.

spring into the holes at the pad upper ends. Hold the assembly in position, then swivel the caliper body down over the bracket to retain them. Fit the mounting bolt, then tighten it to 34-39 Nm (3.5-4.0 kgf m / 25-29 lbf ft).

11 With the new pads in place, turn the piston adjuster clockwise until the pads just touch the disc surface, then back off the adjuster by 1/3 turn. Next, operate the brake pedal repeatedly to seat the new pads. Check that the hub can be turned without significant brake drag.

12 You should not confuse brake drag with the inevitable drag from the transmission. If you are

16/11 Adjust piston position.

unsure, note the amount of effort required to turn the hub with the piston adjuster backed right off, then carry out the adjustment and check if extra drag has been introduced. If necessary, repeat the adjustment operation until satisfactory.

13 Fit the road wheels and lower the car to the ground (☞ 1/3). Road test the car to check brake operation, and remember to use the brakes as gently as possible for the first 100 miles or so to allow the new friction surfaces to bed in properly.

17. BRAKE DISC (REAR) - CHECKING, REMOVAL & INSTALLATION

☞ 1/1, 2 & 9/1.

Warning! Brake friction materials normally contain a proportion of asbestos, which is hazardous if inhaled as dust. When working on the brakes, wear protective clothing and a dust mask. Work in a well-ventilated area. Never use compressed air to clean brake parts. Use a commercially available brake cleaner and paper wipes or rags during cleaning, and dispose of the rags or wipes safely after use - DO NOT reuse them.

1 Before starting this operation, you'll need to remove the rear wheels for access. Slacken the rear wheel nuts by one turn each, then jack the rear of the car and support it on safety stands positioned under the jacking points at each end of the rockers (sills) (☞ 1/3). You need to raise the car sufficiently to allow you clear and safe access underneath. Remove the wheel nuts and lift the wheels away.

2 Examine the disc visually for signs of wear or scoring. If damaged, the disc surface will rapidly destroy the pads, and the disc should be replaced to avoid this. Check general wear with a micrometer. The standard thickness is 9 mm (0.35), and the discs should be replaced as an axle pair if either has worn to 7 mm (0.28 in) or less. If the disc is serviceable, use a file to remove the rust scale buildup on the outer edge of the disc before installing it.

3 Temporarily fit two of the wheel nuts to secure the disc on the hub. Position a dial gauge so that the probe touches the outer face of the disc near the outer edge, and zero the gauge. Turn the disc through one revolution and note the runout indicated. This must be 0.1 mm (0.004 in) or less - if it exceeds this figure, a new disc must be fitted.

REMOVAL AND INSTALLATION

4 Remove the caliper body from its mounting bracket and tie it clear of the working area ☞ 9/16. While you don't really need to remove the pads from the caliper bracket, you'll find that they will probably fall out anyway - make a note of their position on the bracket, the arrangement of shims, and also the M-shaped pad spring, then remove them and place them to one side. It is not necessary to remove the caliper bracket.

5 When installing the disc, if the caliper bracket was removed for any reason, tighten the retaining bolts to 49-69 Nm (5.0-7.0 kgf m / 36-51 lbf ft). Place the disc over the rear wheel studs, then

install the pads ☞ 9/16. **Warning!** If new discs were fitted, you must also install new pads, irrespective of the amount of wear on the old ones - the pad surfaces will have worn to the profile of the old discs, and if refitted, will wear the new discs unevenly and will not make full surface contact.

18. BRAKE CALIPER (REAR) - REMOVAL & INSTALLATION

☞ 1/1, 2 & 9/1.

Warning! Brake friction materials normally contain a proportion of asbestos, which is hazardous if inhaled as dust. When working on the brakes, wear protective clothing and a dust mask. Work in a well-ventilated area. Never use compressed air to clean brake parts. Use a commercially available brake cleaner and paper wipes or rags during cleaning, and dispose of the rags or wipes safely after use - DO NOT reuse them.

1 Before starting this operation, you'll need to remove the rear wheels for access. Slacken the rear wheel nuts by one turn each, then jack the rear of the car and support it on safety stands positioned under the jacking points at each end of the rockers/sills (☞ 1/3). You need to raise the car sufficiently to allow you clear and safe access underneath. Remove the wheel nuts and lift the wheels away.

2 Fit a hose clamp to the caliper hose, then slacken and remove the hose union bolt. Working from the inner face of the caliper, remove the 14 mm plug bolt and copper washer which cover the piston adjuster screw. Introduce a 6 mm Allen key through the adjuster hole, then turn it counterclockwise to back off the piston - turn the adjuster back by one or two turns so that the pads are no longer held close to the disc surface. As the

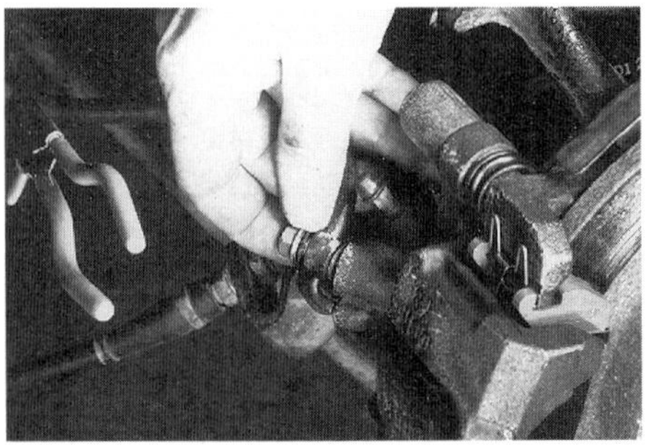

18/2 Remove the hose banjo union bolt.

piston moves back, hydraulic fluid will be expelled from the hose union hole - use some rag to catch the fluid spills, and keep the fluid well away from the disc and pads.

3 Check that the parking brake is off, then slacken the cable adjuster locknut at the wheel end by one or two turns so that the cable can be disengaged from the slotted bracket which carries it. Disengage the cable inner from the operating arm and lodge it clear of the caliper.

4 The caliper lower mounting bolt is covered by a black plastic cap, which should be pulled off the bolt head (ours was surprisingly reluctant to come off and had to be twisted quite hard to release its grip on the bolt head). Once the cap is removed, slacken and remove the 10 mm caliper lower mounting bolt. This has a long plain shank on which the caliper body slides. Withdraw the bolt, then pivot the caliper upwards and clear of the pads. Disengage the caliper from the upper mounting by pulling it inwards towards the center of the car.

5 It is a good idea at this stage to clean the pivot pin ends and apply copper-based brake grease ready for installation - it is important that the caliper assembly can slide freely on the pins, and if it sticks, uneven pad wear and poor brake operation will result.

6 Unless they are worn, there is no need to remove the pads from the caliper bracket - you can hold them in place with a rubber band or some wire until the caliper is installed. There is no particular need to remove the caliper mounting bracket from the suspension upright during caliper removal.

7 When installing the caliper, it is good practice to apply copper-based brake grease to both sides of the pad backing shims, to the sliding surfaces of the pads and to the anti-rattle shims. **Warning!** Use the grease sparingly, and never apply any other type of grease, or it will end up melting - ruining the pads and putting you in danger of brake failure.

8 Place the pads in position on the mounting bracket and carefully hook the M-shaped spring into the holes at the pad upper ends. Hold the assembly in position, then swivel the caliper body down over the bracket to retain them. Fit the mounting bolt, then tighten it to 34-39 Nm (3.5-4.0 kgf m / 25-29 lbf ft). Reconnect the parking brake cable and tighten the locknuts to 16-23 Nm (1.6-2.3 kgf m / 12-17 lbf ft). Fit the brake hose union using new copper sealing washers, and checking that the locating pin fits into the hole in the caliper body. Tighten the union bolt to 22-29 Nm (2.2-3.0 kgf m / 16-22 lbf ft).

9 Once the caliper is installed, temporarily fit two of the wheel nuts to hold the disc in place. Turn the piston adjuster clockwise until the pads just touch the disc surface, then back off the adjuster by 1/3 turn. Bleed the brake hydraulic system to remove the air introduced when the system was disconnected ☞ 9/2. Operate the brake pedal repeatedly to seat the pads. Check that the hub can be turned without significant brake drag.

10 You should not confuse brake drag with the inevitable drag from the transmission. If you are unsure, note the amount of effort required to turn the hub with the piston adjuster backed right off, then carry out the adjustment and check if extra drag has been introduced. If necessary, repeat the adjustment operation until satisfactory.

11 Fit the road wheels and lower the car to the ground (☞ 1/3). Road test the car to check brake operation, and remember that if new pads were fitted as part of the overhaul, the brakes should be used as gently as possible for the first 100 miles or so to allow the new friction surfaces to bed in properly.

19. BRAKE CALIPER (REAR) - OVERHAUL

☞ 1/1, 2 & 9/1.

Warning! Brake friction materials normally contain a proportion of asbestos, which is hazardous if inhaled as dust. When working on the brakes, wear protective clothing and a dust mask. Work in a well-ventilated area. Never use compressed air to clean brake parts. Use a commercially available brake cleaner and paper wipes or rags during cleaning, and dispose of the rags or wipes safely after use - DO NOT reuse them.

1 Start by removing the brake caliper ☞ 9/18. Clean off any road and brake dirt from the outside of the caliper using some denatured alcohol (methylated spirit) or brake cleaner. Remove the 14 mm plug bolt from the back of the caliper to gain access to the piston adjuster. Using a 6 mm Allen wrench, turn the adjuster screw clockwise until it moves freely. When the piston is free of the adjuster it can be pulled out of the caliper.

2 Working over a drain tray, lift the edge of the dust boot and tip out the piston, allowing the fluid in the caliper to drain out. Wipe off any excess fluid, then carefully remove the piston seal, using a small screwdriver to work it out of its groove - take care not to scratch the caliper bore while doing this. Put the dust boot and seal to one side - they will be replaced by new parts during reassembly. Remove the bleed screw, then clean the screw, piston and caliper body in a dish of denatured alcohol or methylated spirit. Use compressed air to blow through the caliper passages and the bleed screw drillings.

3 When everything is cleaned up, check the piston and bore surfaces for wear or corrosion damage. If the hydraulic system is kept well maintained, with regular fluid changes, the problem of internal corrosion is unlikely to occur. If neglected, however, the fluid will gradually absorb moisture from the air, and this will allow corrosion to take place. Dirt in the fluid will also cause wear problems. Once the caliper surfaces are damaged and fluid leakage has occurred, you have no other choice but to fit a new caliper unit.

4 + Note that the automatic adjuster mechanism inside the piston is not repairable, and there is little to be gained by removing it, other than access for cleaning being a little easier. If you do remove it, make a careful note of the direction in which it was fitted, and install it in the same position. The adjuster thread can be seen inside the

19/4a Auto adjuster fits inside piston.

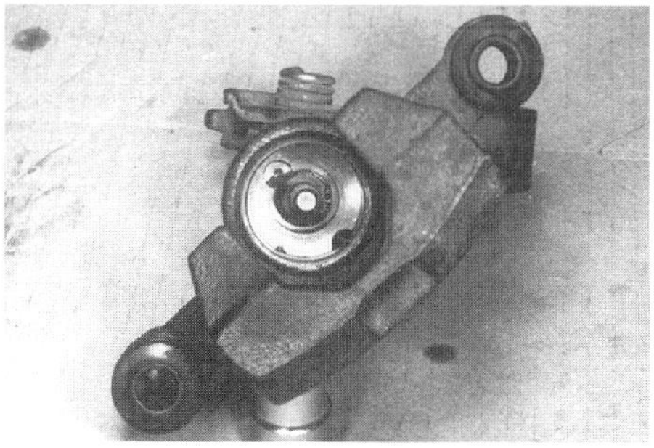

19/4b At end of the bore is splined adjuster.

caliper bore - take care not to lose the small plastic adjuster pinion which can fall out of its hole in the caliper if the plug is left out.

5 + If the piston and bore are serviceable, fit a new piston seal into its groove in the caliper bore, lubricating it with fresh hydraulic fluid during installation. Lubricate the dust seal with hydraulic fluid and fit it into its groove in the caliper. Slide the piston into the caliper, working the dust seal lip over the piston.

6 + You will need some sort of tool to help work the seal lip around the piston, and we

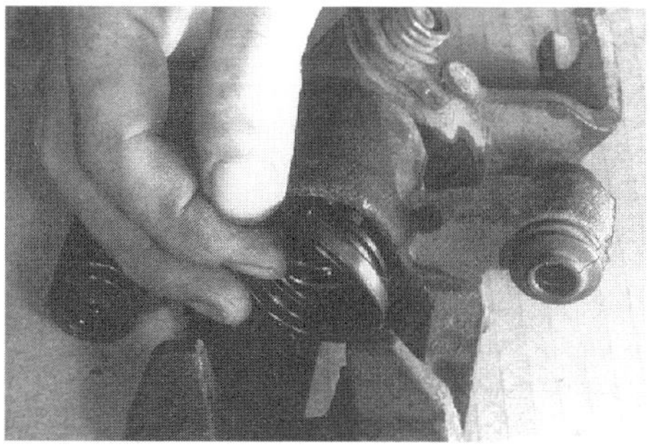

19/5a Fit new seal & dust cover ...

19/5b ... & slide piston into place ...

19/6a ... this 'special' tool helps to locate seal ...

19/6d ... and is made from a paper clip!

used a modified paperclip to do this (see photo). Push the piston in until the adjuster screw contacts the mechanism, then use the Allen wrench to wind it fully back into the caliper (turn it counterclockwise). Install the bleed screw loosely at this stage.

7 Install the caliper, setting the piston adjustment as described in the text (☞ 9/18). Bleed the hydraulic system (☞ 9/2) then check that when the brake pedal is held down hard, for a minute or so, that there are no signs of leakage.

20. PARKING BRAKE - CHECKING & ADJUSTMENT

☞ 1/1, 2 & 9/1.

1 If the parking brake is to work efficiently, it must be adjusted correctly. The adjustment can be checked and set as follows. Press the brake pedal several times and release it. Check that the parking brake stroke is between 5 and 7 notches when the lever is pulled up with a force of 98 N (10 kg / 22 lb). Use a spring scale to apply the prescribed force.

2 If adjustment is required, place blocks front and back of the front wheels, then jack the rear of the car and support it on safety stands positioned under the jacking points at the rear end of the rockers/sills (☞ 1/3). You need to raise the rear of the car sufficiently to allow the rear wheels to rotate.

3 + Remove the plastic cover which is fitted around the parking brake lever. This is secured by a single screw, and once this is removed the two cover halves can be snapped apart and lifted away from the lever. Using a screwdriver or a nut spinner, turn the hexagonal adjuster clockwise to reduce cable free play, setting the adjustment so that the brake is completely off when released, and on by the time the lever has been pulled up by the

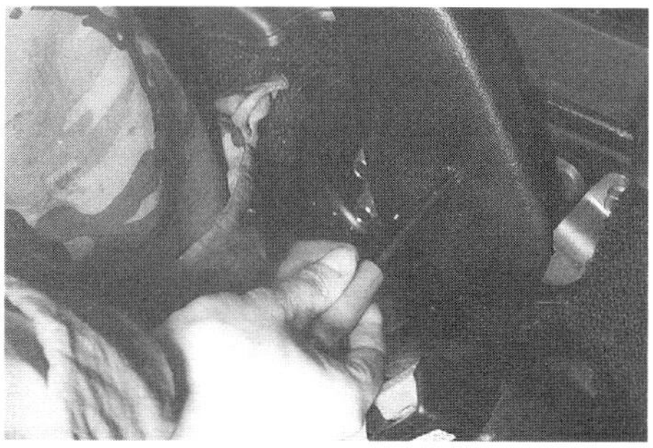

20/3a Remove securing screw and ...

20/3b ... separate two parts of cover.

20/3c Adjuster is alongside lever base ...

20/3d ... turn with screwdriver or wrench.

prescribed 5-7 notches.

4 Check by turning the rear wheels that the brakes do not drag when the parking brake is released. Do not confuse brake drag and transmission drag - remember that when you rotate the rear wheel you are also turning the driveshaft and differential, so some resistance is to be expected. If you find it impossible to eliminate brake drag, check that this is not due to incorrect adjustment of the caliper piston, or to a fault in the main brake system.

5 After adjusting the parking brake, check that the switch is correctly adjusted. With the

20/5 Parking brake switch adjustment.

ignition switch turned on, the warning light in the instrument panel should be off when the lever is released, and should come on after the lever is raised by one notch. If necessary, slacken the switch fixing screw and adjust the switch position until the switch operates as described.

6 Lower the car to the ground (☞ 1/3).

21. PARKING BRAKE LEVER - REMOVAL, CHECKING & INSTALLATION

☞ 1/1, 2 & 9/1.

1 Work on level ground and place blocks front and back of the front wheels, then release the parking brake. Remove the single crosshead screw which passes through the parking brake lever. This secures the two halves of the lever cover, passing through a boss formed inside the larger outer section. The boss in turn fits through a hole in the lever. With the screw removed, pull apart the cover halves, lifting the smaller section nearest the transmission tunnel clear, then disengaging the outer section from the lever and removing it.

2 Slide off the spring clip which secures the cable adjuster, then unscrew and remove the adjuster from the cable end, working between the lever and the transmission tunnel. Disconnect the brake switch wiring connector. Remove the three 12 mm bolts which retain the lever to the transmission tunnel and lift it away.

3 Check the mechanism for visible signs of damage such as cracking - if found, fit a new lever assembly. Similarly, if the ratchet mechanism is worn and the brake cannot be operated reliably, it makes sense to fit a new one.

4 Install the mechanism on the transmission tunnel, tightening the mounting bolts to 19-26 Nm (1.9-2.6 kgf m / 14-19 lbf ft). Reconnect the brake switch wire, turn on the ignition switch, and check that the parking brake warning light is off when the lever is fully released, and that it comes on when the lever is raised by one notch. If not as described, slacken the single screw which retains the switch and slide it in its mounting slot until it operates correctly. Note that the switch end should just contact the lever with the brake off.

22. PARKING BRAKE CABLE - REMOVAL, CHECKING & INSTALLATION

1 Slacken the rear wheel nuts by one turn each. Jack the rear of the car and support it on safety stands positioned under the jacking points at each end of the rockers/sills (☞ 1/3). You need to raise the car sufficiently to allow working access underneath. Remove both rear wheels.

2 Once the car is raised sufficiently and is supported securely on safety stands, slide underneath and check the area where the two main cables connect to the compensator link next to the PPF in the transmission tunnel recess. If the short cable from the lever to the link requires attention, it should be disconnected at the lever (☞ 9/21). If it is good condition it can be left undisturbed.

3 At each rear wheel, slacken the 14 mm

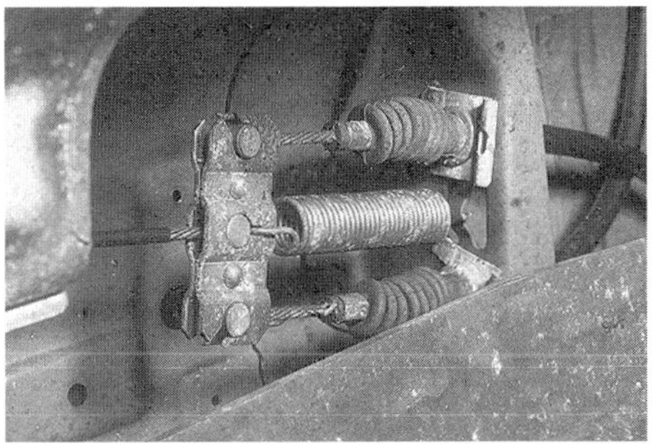

22/2 Parking brake compensator mechanism.

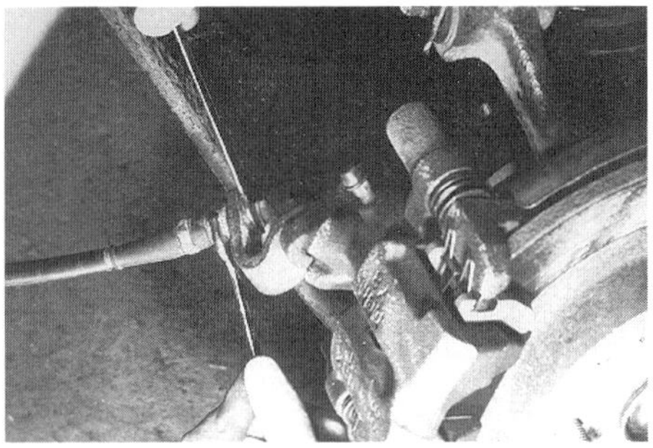

22/3 Free cable from brake caliper bracket.

locknuts which secure the cable outer to the caliper bracket. Disengage the cable from the bracket slot, then unhook the cable end from the operating arm. Move back to the center of the car's underside, pull off the clips which retain the cable outer, and disengage the cable end from the compensator link. The two main cables can now be threaded out from the underside of the car and removed. If the short front cable requires attention, have an assistant guide the cable through from inside the car and remove it.

4 If any of the cables is broken, or if there are signs of fraying cable strands or corrosion, it should be replaced. The compensator link at the end of the front cable should move freely. This component balances the pull from the lever equally between the two main cables, and if frozen (seized) in position by rusting, braking will be out of balance. Check the two main cables, making sure that the inner wire moves freely. Again, rusting can prevent full movement at the wheel end leading to an imbalance.

5 Lubricate the cables before installing them. Pull back the dust boots at the front end of the cables, and make up temporary funnels using the corner cut from a plastic bag. Push the cable through the bag and secure it with electrical tape, then hang the cable up with the funnel at the top. Pour a little gear oil into the funnel and leave it until it runs through the cable. Remove the funnel and fit the dust boot. Alternatively, you can use a proprietary cable oiler for this job - try your local motocross dealer - they are widely used in dirt bike circles. Coat the exposed section of the front cable with grease, and similarly lubricate the compensator.

6 When installing the new (or newly-lubed) cables, reroute them in the same positions as they occupied prior to removal. Hook the front ends onto the compensator and install the retaining clips which secure the cable outer. Reconnect the cables at the wheel end, setting the locknuts so that the compensator lies at right angles to the front cable. The compensator will take care of small imbalances between the two rear cable adjustments, but it helps if it is set up correctly initially. Set up the parking brake lever adjustment ☞ 9/20.

7 Lower the car to the ground ☞ 1/3.

23. ABS (ANTI-LOCK BRAKE SYSTEM) - CHECKING

☞ 1/1, 2 & 9/1.

1 The ABS system fitted on some cars consists of sensors on all four wheels which are monitored by the ABS control unit, housed next to the ECU below a panel in the passenger side footwell. If the system senses that one or more wheels are beginning to skid during braking, the control unit, working though the hydraulic unit mounted on the firewall, releases braking pressure momentarily, pulsing the brake on and off. This happens very rapidly, keeping the wheel turning and stopping the skid from developing.

2 In use, the driver will not normally be aware of the system, until braking on a wet or slippery surface. When the ABS system begins to operate, a slight pulsation will be felt through the brake pedal, and slight vibration will be felt in the steering and through the car body. As the speed falls to around 4 mph (6 kph), you may be aware of the ABS pump motor running for a few seconds as the system self-diagnosis function operates. This is quite normal, and indicates that the system is functioning as intended. If these indicators are not present, and the car skids when braking on loose or slippery surfaces, it is a reasonable assumption that all is not well with the ABS system.

3 The big problem from the enthusiast owner's perspective, is that it is just about impossible to do anything to the ABS system without a lot of expensive equipment. Mazda produce a really neat ABS tester for dealer use. This connects to the ABS control unit, and when activated, runs the diagnostic procedure, prompting the operator to perform the required tests and indicating, through its LCD panel, the next check in the sequence with messages informing which component should be checked further. A superb piece of design, but you are helpless without it.

4 Work on the ABS system also requires a number of SSTs to allow the various system components to be removed and installed. We feel that the only realistic way to deal with the ABS system is to have a Mazda dealer carry out the work for you. **Warning!** Without the necessary equipment it would be dangerous to tamper with this system.

24. WHEELS AND TIRES - CHECKING

1 The Miata/MX5 is equipped with light aluminum alloy wheels fitted with tubeless radial tires. The tires and wheels have a significant effect on the car's handling and roadholding, and should be

checked regularly as detailed below. Note also that if you have reason to suspect possible damage, as might be caused by running over an object in the road, or accidentally curbing the wheels, make a point of checking for damage as soon as possible.

2 Once each week, make a point of checking over each wheel and tire. Check the tire generally for wear, splits or other damage, and for foreign objects like stones or nails embedded in the tire treads. The tire condition and tread wear limit laws vary from one country to another, and you should be aware of and conform with local laws applicable to your car. In addition to these requirements, the tires must be replaced when the tread depth falls to 1.6 mm (0.063 in) or less, or whenever the tread has worn down enough to reach the wear indicator bars at any point.

TREAD WEAR

3 While checking the tread, take note of how the tread is wearing - this can tell you a lot about potential tire and suspension problems. The accompanying diagram shows exaggerated examples of different types of tire wear.

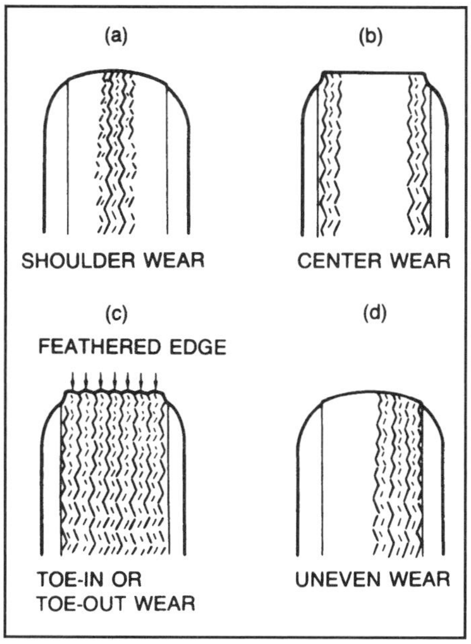

D24/3 EXAMPLES OF TYRE WEAR - SEE TEXT FOR KEY.

4 In example (a) **SHOULDER WEAR**, typical effects of underinflation are shown. If the air pressure in the tire is inadequate, the tire's contact with the road surface will mean greater pressure on the edges of the tire than at the center, and this type of damage will result. If the tire pressures are always as specified, the problem may just be down to over-enthusiastic cornering. Note also that failure to rotate the tires to even out wear may result in the tire wearing in this way.

5 Example (b) **CENTER WEAR** shows the result of the opposite problem - overinflation of the tires. If the pressures are too high, the tread becomes convex in contact with the road, and accelerated wear of the center of the tread will result. Again, failure to rotate the tires to even out wear may result in center wear problems.

6 In (c) **FEATHERED EDGE**, the edges of the tire tread blocks have become feathered in one direction. This is caused by the twisting action on the tread that takes place where the toe-in is set incorrectly. As the tread rolls against the road surface, one side is pulled harder against the surface and wears quickly. As the wheel turns further and the tread resumes its normal position, the opposite side is left higher than the worn side, giving the feathered appearance.

7 If as in (d) **UNEVEN WEAR**, one side of the tread is worn down, you have a suspension geometry problem and should get the camber, caster and toe-in checked. If the problem persists, you may have a general suspension problem - worn pivots or suspension units, for example. If the unevenness shows up as excessive wear at one point on the tire's rotation, check for wheel imbalance or excessive runout on the brake disc. Bear in mind also that a really dramatic panic stop or skid will literally wear miles off the tire at one point only.

TIRE DAMAGE

8 While checking for tread wear, look out for stones, nails or other items embedded in the tire. If found, pry out the object with an old screwdriver or similar tool. Modern tire construction methods give us tires which are pretty resistant to punctures, but if an object has penetrated the tire sufficiently for it to be punctured (you should hear the leak hissing as the object is pulled out) mark the site of the puncture, then fit the spare and get the damaged tire repaired or replaced.

9 Examine the tire tread and both sidewalls (don't forget the inner wall!) for splits, cuts or bulges. Splits or cuts are usually caused by running over road debris - steel strapping from packing cases is a common culprit. Bulges in either the tread or sidewall denote a structural failure of the tire casing, and in extreme cases you may find the casing plies, fine steel strands, sticking out of the tire. If you find damage of this type, again, install the temporary spare and get a new tire fitted.

25. WHEEL CHANGING (WITH CAR'S TOOLKIT) & TIRE ROTATION

☞ 1/1, 2 & 9/1.

WHEEL REMOVAL AND INSTALLATION

1 + The usual reason for needing to remove and fit a tire is in the event of a puncture. If you think that you may have a puncture, pull over as quickly as possible, and try to find a flat area off the road if you can. Inside the trunk you will find the temporary spare wheel. Release the wing bolt which retains it to the trunk floor, lift the wheel out and remove its cover. Lift the lid of the storage compartment at the left side of the trunk and take out the tool roll and the jack. The jack is retained by another wing bolt. Note the jack's position - it will only go in one way, and it is not too obvious which this is.

25/1a Unscrew bolt & lift spare from trunk.

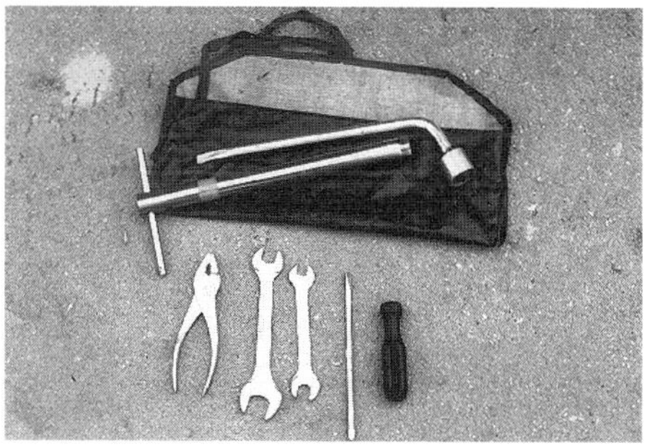

25/1b Get out car's standard toolkit.

25/1c Remove jack & brace from trunk.

25/2a Pry off hub cover & use lug wrench ...

25/2b ... & extension to loosen lug nuts.

2 Try to find something to block the front wheel on the side opposite the puncture, particularly if the car is on a sloping surface. Moving to the punctured tire, pry off the hub cap - the wheel nut wrench has a tang on one end for this, or you can use a screwdriver. Use the wrench to slacken each wheel nut by one turn, using the tube wrench in the toolkit as an extension to the wheel nut wrench handle to get better leverage.

3 Position the jack under the side jacking point nearest the punctured tire. The jacking points are reinforced areas at each end of the rockers (sills) - marked by two small cutouts in the base seam - and the jack has a slot in the lifting pad to fit over the reinforced seam. Raise the jack until the tire is clear of the ground, then remove the wheel nuts and lift off the punctured wheel. Fit the temporary spare wheel and tighten the wheel nuts provisionally, then lower the car to the ground. Tighten the wheel nuts to 88-118 Nm (9-12 kgf m (65-87 lbf ft). If you are doing this on the roadside, tighten the nuts with the wheel nut wrench as hard as you can by *hand* pressure using the wheelbrace from the toolkit.

25/3a Position jack between cutouts, then ...

25/3b ... raise until wheel clear of ground ...

25/3c ... remove lug nuts & lift off wheel ...

25/3d ... fit spare, tighten nuts & lower car.

4 **Warning!** The temporary spare wheel is just that - TEMPORARY, and is for emergency use only. Observe the speed restrictions marked on the spare wheel while it is in place, and get the punctured tire fixed as soon as you can.

25/4 Spare in place - **Warning!** See text.

TIRE ROTATION

5 At intervals specified in the maintenance schedule (☞ 2) the wheels should be rotated on the car to even out tire wear. Slacken all wheel nuts by one turn, then jack one side of the car and support it on safety stands positioned under the jacking points at each end of the rockers (☞ 1/3). You need to raise the car sufficiently to allow both wheels on one side to be removed.

6 Remove and exchange the front and rear wheels on each side of the car. Lower the car to the ground (☞ 1/3) and tighten the wheel nuts to 88-118 Nm (9-12 kgf m (65-87 lbf ft). Check and adjust the tire pressures.

26. TIRE PRESSURES - CHECKING & ADJUSTING

1 Tire pressures need to be maintained regularly, and should be checked when the tires are cold. It is preferable to check these at home, after the car has been standing for some hours. Not only will this mean that the tires are at the right temperature, you will also be using the same gauge for checking pressures each time - gas station gauges can vary in accuracy.

2 You can buy pocket pressure gauges at auto parts stores, and if you don't have compressed air in your garage, you can use either a footpump, or a small electric compressor to inflate the tires.

3 The specified tire pressure (front and rear) for standard tires is 177 kPa (1.8 kgf cm2 / 26 psi). In the case of the temporary spare tire, inflate to 412 kPa (4.2 kgf cm2 / 60 psi).

27. TIRE FITTING & WHEEL BALANCING

TIRE REMOVAL AND FITTING AND TIRE REPAIRS

1 This should always be done by a tire specialist using professional tire changing equipment. The wheel must be balanced after the new tire has been installed. There is no good reason to attempt tire replacement at home - without the right facilities you will probably damage the wheel rim and it's unlikely that you will get the tire seated correctly.

2 If you need to get a punctured tire repaired use a reputable tire dealer. He will be able to advise whether a repair is possible or legal in your area, and will be able to fit a new tire if repair is out of the question.

WHEEL BALANCE

3 It is important that the wheels are accurately balanced each time a tire is fitted - any good tire specialist will do this automatically, or at least ask if you require the wheel to be balanced. You should also get wheel balance checked if you notice vibration or shimmying while driving the car. Sudden imbalance may occur after impact damage to the wheel, or if a balance weight has come loose and flown off. The maximum allowable imbalance at the rim edge is 10 g (0.35 oz).

4 Note that there should be no more than two balance weights fitted to the inner or outer faces of the wheel, and that the combined weight of any balance weights fitted must not exceed 100 g (3.5 oz). If the wheel won't balance within these limits, the tire should be removed and repositioned on the rim; all wheels and tires have heavy spots, and if the two coincide, the imbalance may be too great for countering with balance weights. The weights used must be of the type designed for use on aluminum rims, or the wheel may be damaged when they are fitted. The weights must not protrude more than 3 mm (0.12) from the rim edge.

28. WHEELS - MAINTENANCE

1 The standard aluminum wheels are tough, but require a degree of care if they are to be kept in good condition. Remove road dirt by washing, never while the wheel is dry, or you will scratch the wheel finish. Salt, in particular, is bad for aluminum wheels - if they come into contact with salt water or road salt from winter roads, wash this off as soon as you can to prevent corrosion. In winter, wipe (**Warning!** Do not spray) over the wheel with a rag soaked in WD40 or similar to leave a protective film on the wheel surface.

2 **Warning!** Accident damage should always be checked professionally - impact with rocks or other debris may damage the wheel, but this may not be obvious through visual examination. Consult your Mazda dealer, or a wheel and tire specialist for advice. Curbing the wheels can cause damage and distortion. If suspected, jack the car and support it on safety stands (☞ 1/3) so that the

wheels can be spun, then check runout at the wheel rim using a dial gauge. If this exceeds 2.0 mm (0.079 in) in the horizontal plane, or 1.5 mm (0.059 in) vertically, the wheel should be replaced.

29. WHEEL HUBS & BEARINGS - CHECKING & OVERHAUL

☞ 1/1, 2 & 9/1.

FRONT HUB - CHECKING

1 Position the vehicle on a smooth, level surface and apply the parking brake. Place wood chocks front and back of the rear tires. Remove the front hub caps, and loosen the wheel nuts by one turn. Raise the front of the car with a jack positioned at the center of the front crossmember and position safety stands under the jacking points at the front of each rocker (sill) (☞ 1/3). Unscrew the wheel nuts and remove the wheel.

2 Remove the brake caliper (☞ 9/13), leaving it connected to the hydraulic hose, and tie it clear of the hub with a length of wire. Be careful not to press the brake pedal while the caliper is removed - it is a good idea to push a wooden wedge into the caliper jaw to prevent the piston moving in this eventuality. Lift away the brake disk.

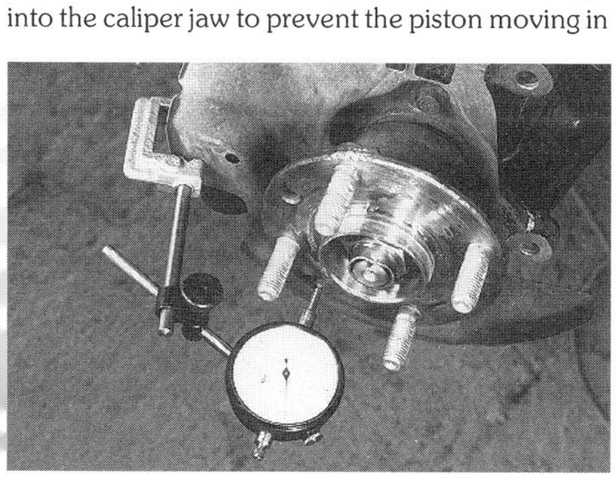

29/3 Testing wheel bearing lash/freeplay.

3 Assemble a dial gauge, using a clamp or magnetic base to mount it on the pressed steel dust cover. Position the gauge pointer so that it just touches the hub surface, and zero the gauge.

4 Move the hub laterally by hand and note the wheel bearing play indicated. If this exceeds the maximum allowable play of 0.05 mm (0.002 in) action is required. Start by checking and re-torquing the hub nut: it will help to fit the wheel/s and lower the car to the ground (☞ 1/3) to do this. If the play is still outside specification, you will have to fit a new hub unit -

FRONT HUB - REMOVAL AND INSTALLATION

5 Position the vehicle on a smooth, level surface and apply the parking brake. Place wood chocks front and back of the rear tires. Remove the wheel trim (where fitted) and pry out the metal dust cap which covers the hub nut. On our project car, the dust cap proved to be surprisingly tight. In the end we used an old wood chisel to remove it - the thin blade was able to work behind the cap flange and allowed us to lever it off - you may need to remove the road wheel to permit access.

6 With the cap out of the way, you can set about slackening the hub nut. This is staked into a groove in the stub axle, and you need to straighten out the staked area so that the nut can be turned. We found that a square-section drift could be used to do this. Be absolutely certain that you relieve the staking fully - you will want no extra resistance when removing the nut.

29/5 Remove the hub dust cap.

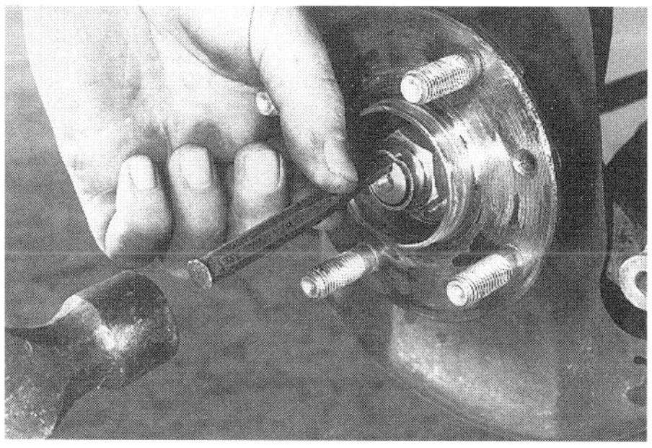

29/6 Use narrow chisel to release staking.

7 The hub nut will be found to be extremely tight - it is torqued down to 167-216 Nm (17-22 kgf m / 123-159 lbf ft) during assembly. You will need a 29 mm socket to fit the nut. This is an unusual size and unlikely to be found in most socket sets - we used a 1 1/8 in AF socket, which fitted fine.

8 Because the nut is so tight, we found that normal 1/2 in drive accessories were of little use - our 1/2 in drive T-bar simply bent when we tried to shift the nut. We eventually resorted to 3/4 in drive equipment, and slid a length of tubing over the T-bar to get extra leverage. This also explains why we are describing the slackening procedure with the road wheel still on the car - you need to keep everything as rigid as possible so you can apply sufficient pressure to the nut. Slacken the nut by about one turn only at this stage, then loosen the wheel nuts by one turn each.

9 Raise the front of the car with a jack positioned at the center of the front crossmember and position safety stands under the jacking points at the front of each rocker (sill) (☞ 1/3). Unscrew the wheel nuts and remove the wheel.

10 You can now remove the hub nut completely and slide the hub unit off the stub axle. Note that it is not possible to dismantle the hub further - if the bearings are worn, you will have to replace them as part of the hub unit. On cars equipped with ABS, there is a slotted rotor fitted to the back of the hub. Do not attempt removal of this without good reason - the rotor cannot be reused if removed. If a new rotor needs to be fitted, note that two SSTs and a press are needed - have the job carried out by a Mazda dealer.

29/10 Withdraw the hub from the stub axle.

29/11 Backplate is secured by three bolts.

11 Note also that once the hub has been removed it is possible to detach the brake disc dust cover. This is retained on the steering knuckle by three bolts - if you have reason to remove it, note that the bolts should be tightened to 16-23 Nm (1.6-2.3 kgf m / 12-17 lbf ft) during installation. We would recommend the use of thread locking compound on the bolts.

12 During installation, fit the hub unit over the stub axle, then secure it using a **new** locknut. Tighten the nut to 167-216 Nm (17-22 kgf m / 123-159 lbf ft). Note that it is important to torque this nut down to the recommended pressure - this preloads the wheel bearings correctly. If necessary, borrow or hire a torque wrench capable of reaching these pressures - many home-use wrenches won't reach the prescribed figure. It may help to fit the wheel and lower the car to the ground ☞ 1/3.

29/12 Torque tighten the hub nut: phew!

13 + Finally, stake the collar section of the hub nut into the stub axle groove, making sure that the staking lies at least 0.5 mm (0.02 in) into the

29/13a Stake the hub nut and ...

29/13b ... tap the dust cap into place.

groove. Fit the dust cap, tapping it home with a hide or rubber faced hammer. Lower the car to the ground (☞ 1/3), fit the dust cover and tighten the wheel nuts.

REAR HUB - CHECKING

14 Position the vehicle on a smooth, level surface and temporarily apply the parking brake. Place wood chocks front and back of the front tires, then release the parking brake. Remove the rear hub caps, and loosen the wheel nuts by one turn. Raise the back of the car with a jack positioned at the center of the differential casing and position safety stands under the jacking points at the back of each rocker (sill) (☞ 1/3). Unscrew the wheel nuts and remove the wheel.

15 Remove the brake caliper (☞ 9/18) leaving it connected to the hydraulic hose, and tie it clear of the hub with a length of wire - the caliper mounting can be left attached to the suspension upright. You may find it difficult to tie the caliper clear with the parking brake cable attached. If so, you can disconnect the cable ☞ 9/22. Be careful not to press the brake pedal while the caliper is removed - it is a good idea to push a wooden wedge into the caliper jaw to prevent the piston moving in this eventuality. Lift away the brake disc.

16 Assemble a dial gauge, using a clamp or magnetic base to mount it on the pressed steel dust cover. Position the gauge pointer so that it just touches the hub surface, and zero the gauge.

17 Move the hub laterally by hand and note the wheel bearing play indicated. If this exceeds the maximum allowable play of 0.05 mm (0.002 in) action is required. Start by checking and re-torqueing the hub nut: fitting the wheel and lowering the car to the ground may help ☞ 1/3. If the play is still outside specification, you will have to fit a new hub bearing.

REAR HUB - REMOVAL

18 Position the vehicle on a smooth, level surface and apply the parking brake. Place wood chocks front and back of the front tires. Remove the rear hub caps, then slacken the rear hub nut as follows. The nut, which secures the outer end of the driveshaft, is staked into a groove in the driveshaft end, and you need to straighten out the staked area of the nut so that it can be unscrewed. We found that a square-section drift could be used to do this. Be absolutely certain that you relieve the staking fully - you will want no extra resistance when removing the nut.

19 The hub nut will be found to be extremely tight - it is torqued down to 216-294 Nm (22-30 kgf m / 159-217 lbf ft) during assembly. You will need a 29 mm socket to fit the nut. This is an unusual size and unlikely to be found in most socket sets - we used a 1 1/8 in AF socket, which fitted fine.

20 Because the nut is so tight, we found that normal 1/2 in drive accessories were of little use - our 1/2 in drive T-bar simply bent when we tried to shift the nut. We eventually resorted to 3/4 in drive equipment, and slid a length of tubing over the T-bar to get extra leverage. This also explains why we are describing the slackening procedure with the road wheel still on the car - you need to keep everything as rigid as possible so you can apply sufficient pressure to the nut to shift it. Slacken the nut by about one turn only at this stage, then loosen the wheel nuts by one turn each.

21 Raise the rear of the car with a jack positioned under the differential housing and position safety stands under the jacking points at the rear of each rocker (sill) (☞ 1/3). Unscrew the wheel nuts and remove the wheel.

22 Detach the brake caliper from the suspension upright (☞ 9/18) leaving it connected to the brake hose. The caliper should be tied back

29/22 Tie caliper out of harm's way.

with a length of wire or string so that it is clear of the working area and no strain is placed on the hose. You'll find that the parking brake cable makes this difficult, and if necessary, you should disconnect the cable.

23 Position the jack from the Miata/MX5's trunk under the lower wishbone, using wood blocks under the jack as required. Raise the jack so that it is just contacting the underside of the wishbone. Slacken and remove the upper wishbone to suspension upright 14 mm mounting bolt. If the bolt won't slide out easily, raise the jack slightly to

29/23 Remove upper pivot bolt.

release any pressure from the suspension.

24 Remove the hub nut from the end of the driveshaft, then pivot the suspension upright downwards to allow the driveshaft end to be disengaged. The driveshaft splines can be a tight fit in the hub. To free the splines, fit the hub nut so that it lies flush with the shaft end, then drive it out using a hammer and a drift. Take care to avoid damaging the driveshaft end. On cars fitted with ABS, take care not to damage the ABS rotor which is fitted to the end of the driveshaft outer ball joint.

25 Next, you need to remove the lower wish-

29/24 Pull hub & backplate off driveshaft.

bone to suspension upright 17 mm pivot bolt. We ran into problems here, and it seems highly likely that you will encounter the same difficulty on your car. The pivot bore in the suspension upright is partially open at the inner edge, and this means that part of the bolt shank is exposed to all of the road dirt thrown up by the wheels (why, Mazda?). This in turn causes the bolt shank to corrode quite badly, which makes removal of the bolt difficult - the corroded center section will not pass through the suspension upright.

26 Try to remove as much of the corrosion as you can before trying to get the bolt out, and soak it in penetrating fluid. The only thing you can do now is to try to drive the bolt out without damaging the thread. Run the nut onto the thread so that it lies flush with the bolt end, then use a hide or rubber hammer to drive it out. The presence of the nut will help stop the threaded end from getting distorted. Once the nut contacts the wishbone you will have to remove it and use a brass drift to knock the bolt the rest of the way through the wishbone. Once the bolt has been removed, the suspension upright and hub can be removed to the workbench for further dismantling.

REAR HUB - OVERHAUL

27 Once the suspension upright and hub assembly have been removed from the car, you will need to make a decision about how to proceed from here. To dismantle the assembly further, Mazda recommend a range of SSTs and a press, and you may decide that it is more effective to take the assembly to a Mazda dealer for the new bearing and seal to be fitted. We found that we could just about get by using a selection of sockets in place of the SSTs, using them to drive out the various components.

28 From the back of the upright, pry out

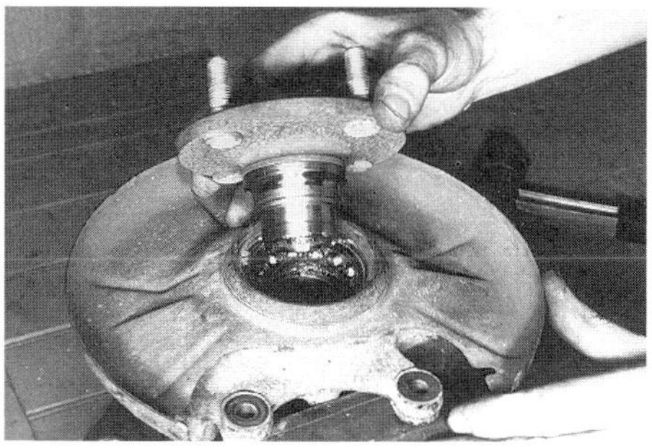

29/28 Pull the hub from the race.

and discard the seal - you will have to fit a new one during installation. Using a suitable socket as a drift, tap out the hub from the upright. You will probably find that the bearing inner race remains on the hub shaft. To get this off you will need a proprietary bearing puller - you may be able to hire this from a tool hire specialist. If necessary, start the race moving on the hub using a chisel, then assemble the puller and draw it off.

29 Remove the large snap ring which retains the bearing in the suspension upright. Support the upright on wood blocks with the brake disc

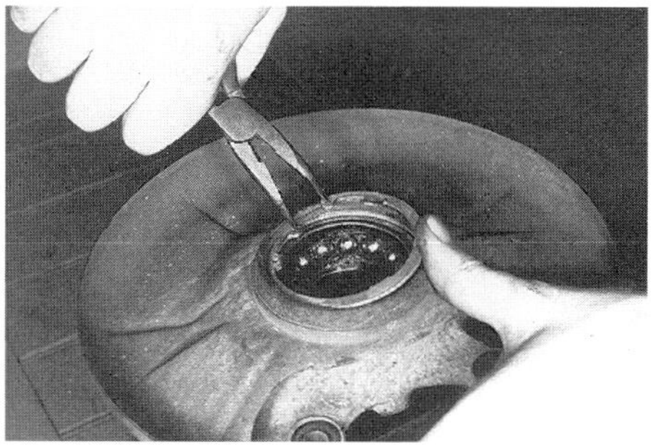

29/29 Remove the large snap ring/circlip.

dust cover downwards - check that the upright is supported by its central boss, not on the dust cover. Using a large socket as a drift, drive out the bearing from its bore in the upright. Clean the upright assembly to remove all traces of dirt and grease.

30 The dust cover must not be removed unless it is essential - note that it cannot be re-used once removed. If you need to replace the dust cover, first mark its position in relation to the upright with a paint mark, and make a similar mark

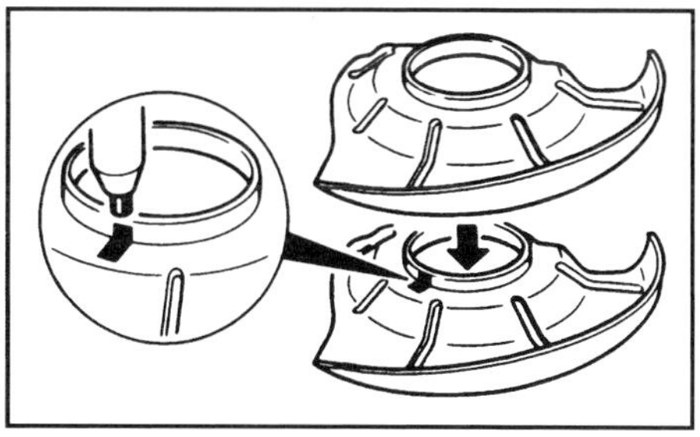

D29/30 MARK THE NEW DUST COVER IN EXACTLY THE SAME PLACE AS THE OLD.

29/32 Tap the hub into position.

in exactly the same position on the new dust cover. Tap off the old cover, then fit the new one, using a section of tubing to tap it into position. Make sure that you align the position marks correctly.

31 Install the new bearing in the upright, using a large socket or tube to drive it into position. It is preferable to press the bearing home if you can - if you have a large vise, use this to wind the bearing into place, taking care to ensure that it enters its bore squarely.

32 Secure the bearing using a new snap ring, then tap the hub into position through the bearing. Carefully press the new grease seal into its recess at the back of the upright.

REAR HUB - INSTALLATION

33 Before starting installation, spend some time cleaning up the lower wishbone to suspension upright pivot bolt, or fit a new one. If you plan to reuse the old one, clean off any remaining corrosion with abrasive paper and check that it slides through the wishbone and upright bores easily.

34 Grease the lower wishbone to suspension upright pivot bolt and slide it through the wishbone and upright, fitting the nut fingertight. We packed the open area of the upright with the thickest, stickiest grease we could find, in the hope that this will prevent further corrosion problems - we suggest that you do likewise.

35 Pivot the upright upwards, feeding the driveshaft through as you do so. Fit a new hub nut and tighten it provisionally. Install the upper wishbone to upright pivot bolt and nut, noting that if you have difficulty positioning the wishbone while fitting the suspension unit or pivot bolts, the small scissor jack supplied with the car's toolkit can be used to raise the assembly as required.

36 Tighten the lower wishbone to suspension upright pivot bolt nut to 63-75 Nm (6.4-7.6 kgf m / 46-55 lbf ft), and the upper wishbone to suspension upright pivot bolt nut to 46-67 Nm (4.7-6.8 kgf m / 34-49 lbf ft).

37 Install the brake caliper and reconnect the parking brake cable, if this was removed ☞ 9/18. Fit the roadwheel, provisionally tightening the nuts. Lower the car to the ground (☞ 1/3), then tighten the wheelnuts to 88-118 Nm (9.0-12.0 kgf m / 65-87 lbf ft).

38 You now need to torque the hub nut to 216-294 Nm (22-30 kgf m / 159-217 lbf ft). Using the socket and accessories used during removal, plus a suitable torque wrench, tighten the nut to the prescribed figure. You may need to borrow or hire a truck-type torque wrench for this - most automotive wrenches do not reach the required pressures. It is important that you tighten down to within this range, however, because this applies the correct bearing preload.

39 Once the hub nut is secure, stake the collar into the groove on the driveshaft end using a punch or chisel. The staking should lie at least 0.5 mm (0,02 in) below the shaft diameter. Fit the dust cover and tighten the wheel nuts.

30. WHEEL STUDS - REMOVAL & INSTALLATION

☞ 1/1, 2 & 9/1.

1 The wheel studs are fitted through from the back of the front or rear hub, and removal and installation will require the removal of the relevant hub ☞ 9/29.

2 The studs are pressed into position in the hub, and should not be removed without good cause - once removed, the studs cannot be reused.

3 The usual reason for removal is in the event of breakage or thread damage. This can be due to overtightening of the wheel nuts, but is more commonly the result of trying to remove the wheel nuts after the stud threads have corroded through neglect.

4 You will need to remove the old or broken stud in a press, and the new stud must also be pressed into position. Unless you have access to a press, you may prefer to entrust this operation to a Mazda dealer or engineering shop.

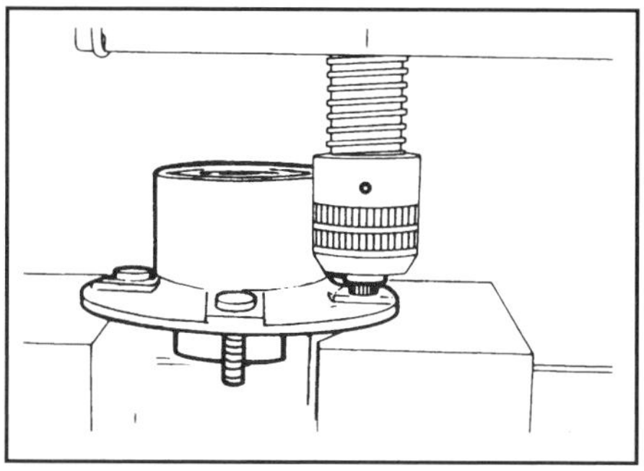

D30/4 PRESS NEW BOLTS INTO HUB FLANGE.

AMERICAN/ENGLISH GLOSSARY OF AUTOMOTIVE TERMS

American	English
A-arm	Wishbone (suspension)
Antenna	Aerial
Axleshaft	Halfshaft
Back-up	Reverse
Barrel	Choke/venturi
Block	Chock/wedge
Box end wrench	Ring spanner
Bushing	Bush
Clutch hub	Synchro hub
Coast	Freewheel
Convertible	Drop head
Cotter pin	Split pin
Counterclockwise	Anti-clockwise
Countershaft	Layshaft (of gearbox)
Crescent wrench	Open-ended spanner
Curve	Corner
Dashboard	Facia
Denatured alcohol	Methylated spirit
Dome lamp	Interior light
Driveaxle	Driveshaft
Driveshaft	Propeller shaft
Fender	Wing/mudguard
Firewall	Bulkhead
Flashlight	Torch
Float bowl	Float chamber
Freeway, turnpike, etc.	Motorway
Frozen	Seized
Gas tank	Petrol tank
Gas pedal	Accelerator pedal
Gasoline (gas)	Petrol
Gearshift	Gearchange
Generator (DC)	Dynamo
Ground	Earth (electrical)
Header/manifold	Manifold (exhaust)
Heat riser	Hot spot
High	Top gear
Hood	Bonnet (engine cover)
Idle	Tickover
Intake	Inlet
Jackstands /Safety stands	Axle stands
Jumper cable	Jump lead
Keeper	Collet
Kerosene	Paraffin
Knock pin	Roll pin
Lash	Freeplay/Clearance
Latch	Catch
Latches	Locks
License plate /tag plate	Number plate
Light	Lamp
Lock (for valve spring retainer)	Split cotter (for valve cap)
Lopes	Hunts
Lug nut	Wheel nut
Metal chips or debris	Swarf
Misses	Misfires
Muffler	Silencer
Oil pan	Sump
Open flame	Naked flame
Panel wagon/van	Van
Parking light	Sidelight
Parking brake	Handbrake
Piston pin or wrist pin bearing/bush	Small (little) end bearing
Piston pin or wrist pin	Gudgeon pin
Pitman arm	Drop arm
Power brake booster	Servo unit
Primary shoe	Leading shoe (of brake)
Prussian blue	Engineer's blue
Pry	Prise (force apart)
Prybar	Crowbar
Prying	Levering
Quarter window	Quarterlight
Recap	Retread
Release cylinder	Slave cylinder
Repair shop	Garage
Replacement	Renewal
Ring gear (of differential)	Crownwheel
Rocker panel	Sill panel
Rod bearing	Big-end bearing
Rotor/disk	Disc (brake)
Secondary shoe	Trailing shoe (of brake)
Sedan	Saloon
Setscrew, Allen screw	Grub screw
Shift fork	Selector fork
Shift lever	Gearlever/gearstick
Shift rod	Selector rod
Shock absorber, shock	Damper/shocker
Snap-ring	Circlip
Soft top	Hood
Spacer	Distance piece
Spare tire	Spare wheel
Spark plug wires	HT leads
Spindle arm	Steering arm
Stablizer or sway bar	Anti-roll bar
Station wagon	Estate car
Stumbles	Hesitates
Tang or lock	Tab
Taper pin	Cotter pin
Teardown	Strip(down)/dismantle
Throw-out bearing	Thrust bearing
Tie-rod (or connecting rod)	Trackrod (of steering)
Transmission	Gearbox
Troubleshooting	Fault finding/diagnosis
Trunk	Boot
Tube wrench	Box spanner
Turn signal	Indicator
Valve lifter	Tappet
Valve lifter or tappet	Cam follower or tappet
Valve cover	Rocker cover
VOM (volt ohmmeter)	Multimeter
Wheel cover	Roadwheel trim
Wheel well	Wheelarch
Whole drive line	Transmission
Windshield	Windscreen
Wrench	Spanner

10

INTERIOR

1. INTRODUCTION

This chapter relates to the interior details of the car, mainly within the passenger compartment area. It covers most aspects of the interior, but we found that we ran into a problem when it came to the soft top. Is this part of the interior or the body of the car? Eventually, we decided that it, and the hard top, should be covered in *chapter 11*.

Having made that decision, you may be surprized that we've dealt with the door internal components in this chapter. We figured that since the door trim was definitely part of the interior, we may as well go on to cover items like the door window and catch assemblies. 'External' aspects of the door will be found in *chapter 11*.

2. CONSOLE (REAR) REMOVAL - CHECKING & INSTALLATION

☞ 1/1, 2.

REMOVAL

1 + Open the storage box at the back of the rear console. Remove the two screws from the base. Lift out the ashtray, and remove the single screw from the recess below it. Unscrew the gearshift knob (manual transmission cars). Remove the two screws, one on each side, which secure the front of the console.

2 The console can now be removed as follows. Lift the front of the unit, guiding the gearshift lever boot over the lever end (manual transmission). On cars equipped with automatic transmission, the shift lever indicator panel occupies the cutout in the console where the shift lever boot is fitted on manual transmission models, and the console just lifts away.

3 Once clear, move the unit forward to disengage the fuel filler release lever as the console is lifted. The ashtray light connector and (where fitted) the window winder switch connector should be separated to permit removal of the console. Put the screws and gearshift knob in the storage box, close the lid and place the unit to one side.

CHECKING

4 There is nothing of great interest in the center console itself - the usual reason for removing it is to get access to some other component. Center console fittings include the ashtray light and window winder switches (if fitted): for detail ☞ 11.

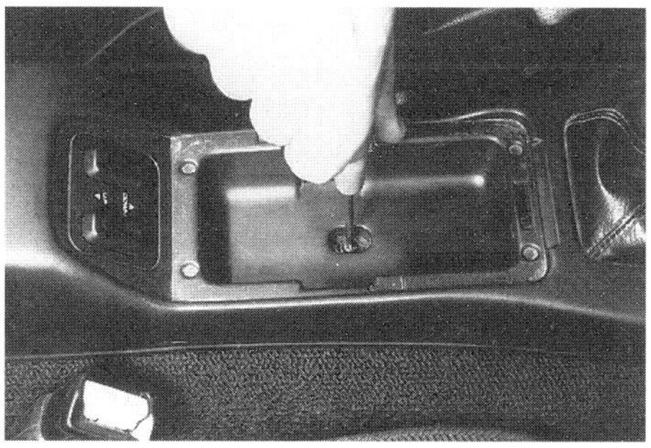

2/1a There's a screw beneath the ashtray.

2/4 Two screws secure lock.

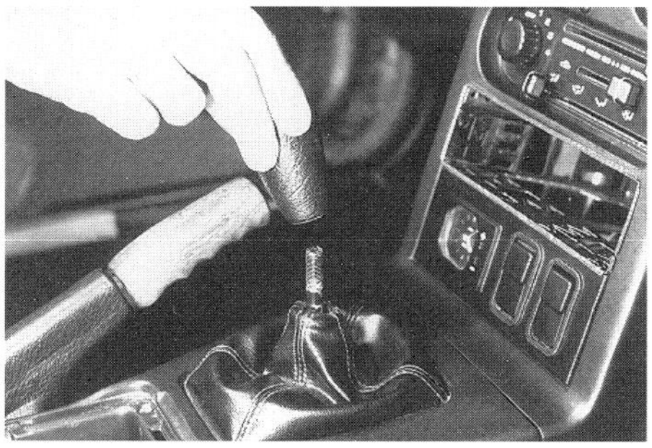

2/1b Unscrew gearshift knob.

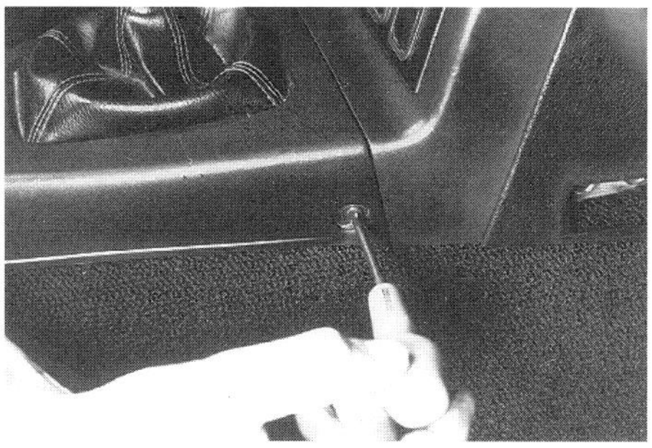

2/1c There's a screw on each side at the front.

From the underside of the console you also have access to the storage compartment lock mechanism. This is retained to the underside of the console by two crosshead screws.

INSTALLATION

5 When installing the rear console, remember to reconnect the ashtray light wire and, where fitted, the window winder switch connector. Position the back of the console, ensuring that the fuel filler release lever passes through the cutout at the rear. Lower the console over the gearshift lever, guiding the lever through the boot in the case of manual transmission cars.

6 Secure the rear console with the two front screws, the single screw in the ashtray recess, and the two screws through the base of the storage box. Fit the ashtray, and on manual transmission cars, screw the gearshift knob onto the shift lever.

3. DASH CENTER PANEL - REMOVAL & INSTALLATION

☞ 1/1, 2.

1 Before the dash center panel can be re-

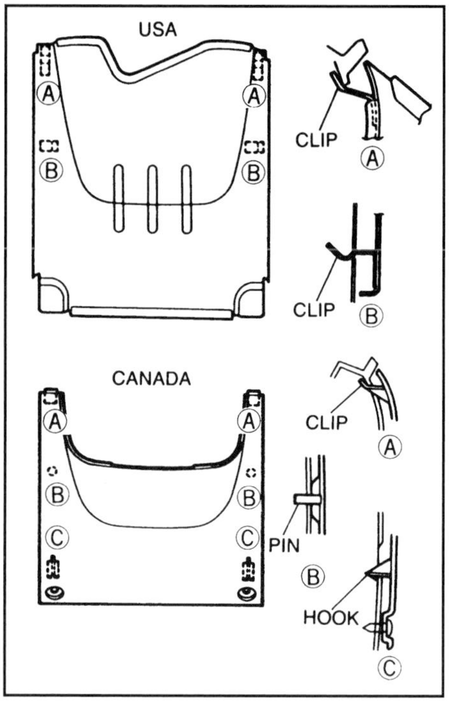

D3/2&D4/3 ACCESS PANEL FITTING DETAIL.
Note that the majority of non-US cars have same fixings as Canada cars.

moved you will first have to remove the rear console ☞ 10/2. To prevent any risk of short circuits, disconnect the battery negative (-) terminal to isolate the electrical system, having first disabled the stereo security system (where applicable) ☞ 7/2.

2 Remove the two screws securing the glovebox hinges to the hinge bar and lift the glovebox away. On the driver's side of the car,

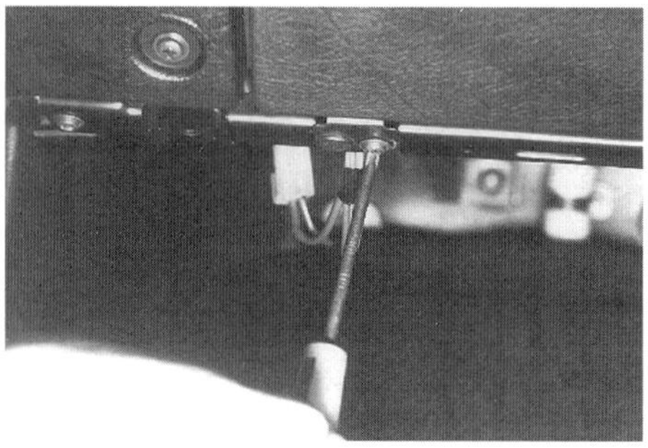

3/2 Remove screws securing hinges.

remove (where fitted) the two screws securing the access panel below the steering column, then unclip and remove the panel. Note that there are two basic types of access panel used, and these are shown in the accompanying diagram - the non-US cars use the same type as fitted to Canadian market cars.

3 + Working through the apertures on each side of the dash panel, trace and disconnect the heater control cables. One of the three connects to the blower unit located immediately behind the glovebox, the remaining two connect on

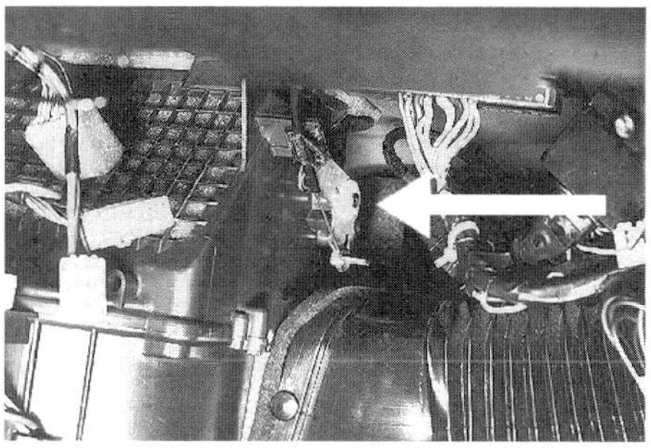

3/3a Blower unit cable connection.

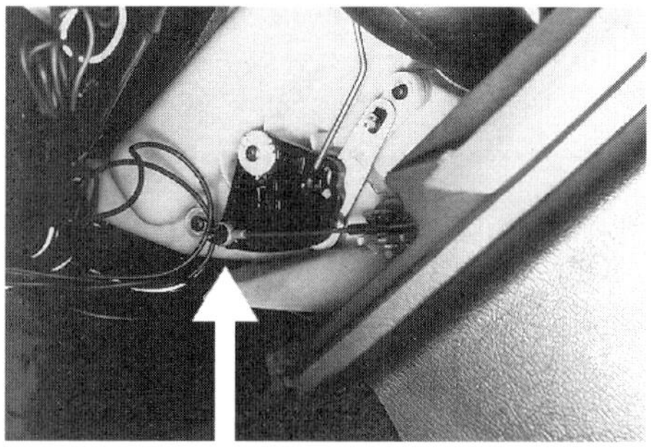

3/3b Heater unit cable connection.

each side of the heater unit which is mounted behind the dash center panel. Unclip each cable outer from its support, and unhook the outer from the operating lever end.

4 To get access to the centre panel fixing screws you need to remove the two eyeball vents at the top of the unit. This is no easy task - the vents are secured by two spring clips from the back, and there is no means of external access to them.

5 The original removal method described by Mazda is to pry the vents out using a screwdriver, and a certain amount of cosmetic damage to the center panel and vent surround is almost inevitable. We spent a considerable amount of time getting the vents out of the project car, and concluded that the fixing arrangement is designed for ease of assembly, but not ease of subsequent removal.

6 We suggest that before starting this operation you look at the photograph we took of the back of the vent so you can see what you are dealing with. There are two small metal clips, one each side of each vent. Note that you cannot reach the clips to release them while the center panel is in position (and you can't remove the centre panel until you've removed the vents ...).

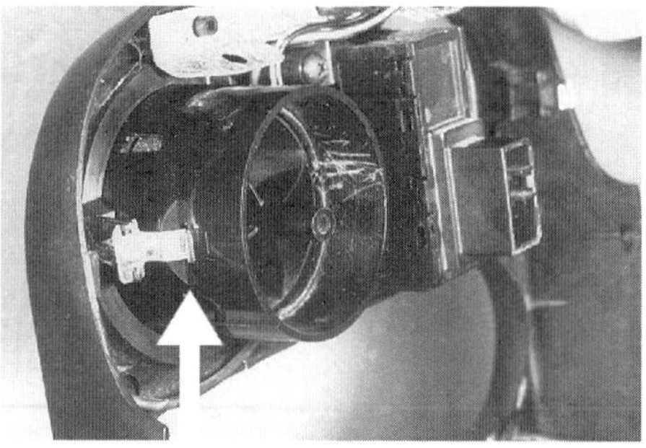

3/6 Detail of eyeball vent securing clip.

3/7 Use screwdrivers to pry vent out.

7 Use a pair of the thinnest flat-bladed screwdrivers you have, introduce the tips on each side of the vent, between the vent surround and the panel recess. Push them in at around 45° as far as they will go. If you can, use something between the screwdriver and the panel to minimize damage to the surface by spreading the load. Whatever you use will have to be very thin - try a strip cut from a drinks can, or a strip of plastic. Gradually lever back on the screwdrivers until the vent pops out of the recess.

8 When you attempt removal you will

3/8 Wally's prybar method - don't take seriously!

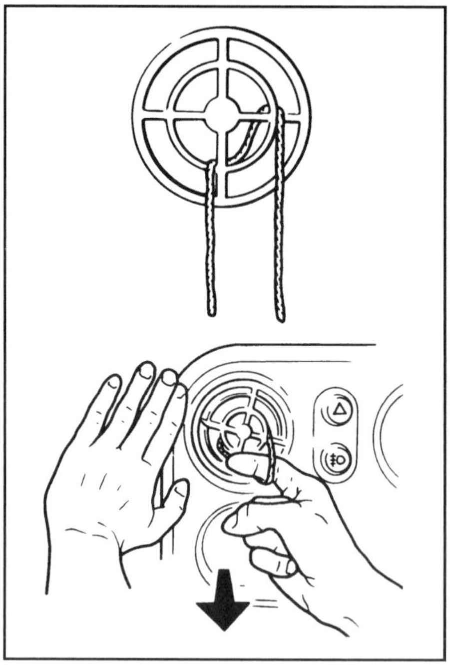

D3/9 ANOTHER VENT REMOVAL METHOD.

probably think, as we did, that the vent will not come out in one piece. You certainly have to apply an undesirable amount of force, and unless you have much lighter clips than the ones we found on our car, both the panel and the vent assembly will distort quite badly during the removal operation. That said, the vents did eventually come out, leaving marks on them and the panel, but with no further damage - unless you have someone like Wally, our Technical Adviser, that is. Please note that we cannot recommend his removal method (see photograph)!

9 Mazda describe an alternative removal method using a length of cord. This should be looped around the vent louvers as shown in the accompanying diagram. Feed the cord in through one of the vent slots, then use a piece of wire to hook the end of the cord and pull it back through. Tie the ends of the cord to form a loop. Once the cord is in place, support the center panel with one hand and pull hard on the cord to pop the vent out of the panel.

10 With the vents removed, remove the two sheet metal screws which pass upwards through the vent recesses to secure the top of the center panel to the main dash panel assembly.

3/10 Remove screw at top of each vent.

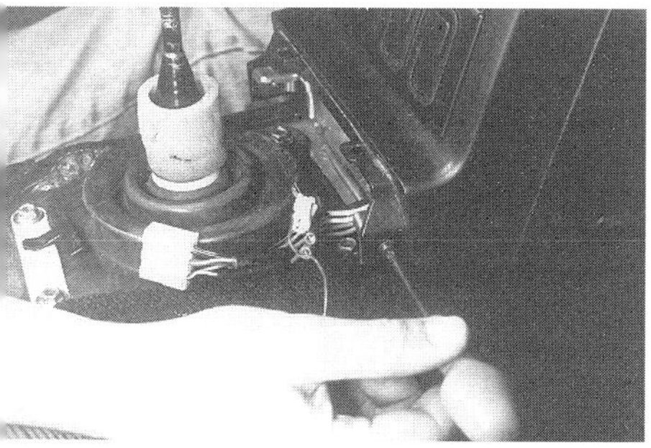

3/11a Remove two screws at unit base ...

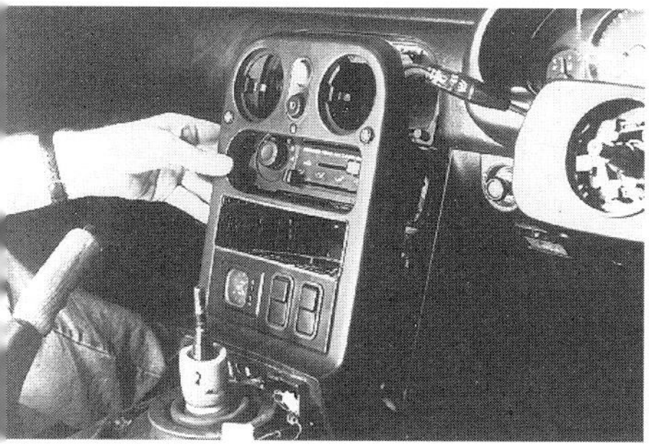

3/11b ... and ease console away.

11 + At the bottom, there are two further screws securing the panel to a metal support bracket fixed to the transmission tunnel - these should also be removed, leaving the metal bracket in place. The panel can now be pulled away slightly, but there will be further wiring to disconnect before it can be removed completely.

12 The wiring connections behind the center panel vary according to the country in which the car was sold, and on what combination of options or aftermarket items are fitted. The top of the panel carries the eyeball vents and between them, the switches for the hazard lights and the headlight lifter. Our project car had aftermarket alarm sensors fitted on this part of the panel.

13 The heater control assembly comes next, but below that, a number of options may be fitted. Our project car had a removable Clarion stereo radio/cassette unit fitted, and below this was a panel carrying an analog clock and two accessory switch blanks - other options include various stereo systems, with or without CD players. The arrangement you find on your car may differ from ours, and the stereo may need to be removed before or after the center panel is released, depending on the type of installation. Some stereo units are removable for security purposes, in which case the main unit should be unplugged and the wiring connections to the mounting bracket dealt with as the panel is detached.

14 Our best advice here is to move the panel away carefully, check the wiring connections on the back and disconnect them, noting the position and type of each connector. We suggest that you use colored electrical tape, or a permanent marker pen, to code the wiring connector halves as they are separated. This will make installation quick and foolproof.

15 Once the center panel wiring has been disconnected, pull the panel gently toward you, feeding the heater control cables through from the access panel and glovebox apertures if they snag. Again, depending on accessory items fitted, there may be ground tag connections to be released - our car had two, attached to one of the bottom bracket screws. Once all wiring has been freed, the panel can be removed. (For information on the various components carried on the center panel ☞ 6 & 7)

16 Finally, whatever else you do while the unit is out, we recommend that you check all the bulbs and replace any that are burned out or beginning to blacken - there would be a lot of work to be done all over again if you missed this opportunity and noticed the problem later.

INSTALLATION

17 When installing the center panel, position it in front of its mounting point on the dash panel, connecting the wiring connectors and feeding the heater control cables into position. The cables cannot easily be connected incorrectly; the longest cable runs to the blower unit (**REC/FRESH** control), while the remaining two have different ends and fit either side of the heater unit.

18 Before you connect the cables, you should set up the control sliders as follows: set the top slider (temperature blend control) to the maximum position (fully to the right); the center slider (**REC/ FRESH** control) should be set to **FRESH**, or fully to the right; set the bottom slider (airflow mode control) to **VENT** (fully to the left). After reconnecting the cables, check that the above controls move smoothly and fully through their complete range.

19 You can now install the centre panel, remembering to reconnect the wiring to the stereo (don't forget the antenna cable), the clock (where fitted), the hazard light/headlight lifter switches and any other accessories installed in the panel. Make sure that you route the wiring correctly, and that it does not become trapped as the panel is fitted.

20 We strongly suggest that before finally securing the panel, you check the operation of all electrical switches and accessories - don't forget how difficult removal of the eyeball vents was! Only when you are sure that these are operating correctly should you fit the two retaining screws through the eyeball sockets, and the two lower screw securing the panel to the transmission tunnel bracket. Do not forget to fit any ground wires that were removed.

21 Before installing the eyeball vents, we suggest spraying a little WD40 or a similar silicone-based lubricant on the outer surface - this might help a little if they need to be removed at a later date. Pop the vents back into their sockets (note how easily they install - you might assume that they are not fitted correctly, but just try pulling them out again). Fit the steering column access panel and the glovebox.

4. DASH PANEL ASSEMBLY - REMOVAL, CHECKING & INSTALLATION

☞ 1/1, 2.

REMOVAL

1 Removal of the dash panel is a complex operation, and you should allow plenty of time to complete it - remember that the car is out of action until it is installed and everything is working correctly again. We spent nearly six hours working on ours, though we were photographing the process, and we spent a lot of time working out the best method of doing things. We would estimate that you should allow around three hours. You should carry out the work under cover, so that you can fold the soft top or remove the hard top before work commences.

2 Start by removing the rear console and the dash center panel ☞ 10/2, 3. On non-airbag cars, remove the steering wheel (☞ 8/11), then remove the combination switch housing and the combination switch (☞ 7/12). On air bag cars, leave the steering wheel in place so as not to disturb the air bag module, removing it together with the steering column.

3 + (D3/2) If still in place, remove the access panel below the steering column - this is secured by two screws near the bottom edge, and can be unclipped once these have been removed. The exact details of the access panel vary according to market - US specification cars have a different

10

4/3a Remove lower securing screws and ...

4/3b ... then release panel from clips.

design to our UK project car and others, but the fitting method is similar.

4 On US market cars equipped with air bag systems, locate the blue and orange wiring connectors from the air bag system clock spring connector. Note that these use a double latching arrangement - to disconnect them you need to remove the smaller orange connector before it is possible to disconnect the larger blue one. **Warning!** Do not omit to disconnect these connectors as, until the connectors have been separated, the air bag system remains armed and may be deployed accidentally - even with the car's battery disconnected.

5 On all cars, remove the steering column assembly from the car. In the case of air bag-equipped cars, the steering wheel and combination switch should be left attached to the column assembly. On all other models, the wheel and switch are removed first, as described earlier. For full details of the column removal (☞ 8/11).

6 Remove the two sheet metal screws which retain the instrument panel housing. These are fitted from the front edge of the housing, and pass upwards to secure it to the dash panel. Once you've released the screws, the housing can be pulled back until it disengages from the dash panel.

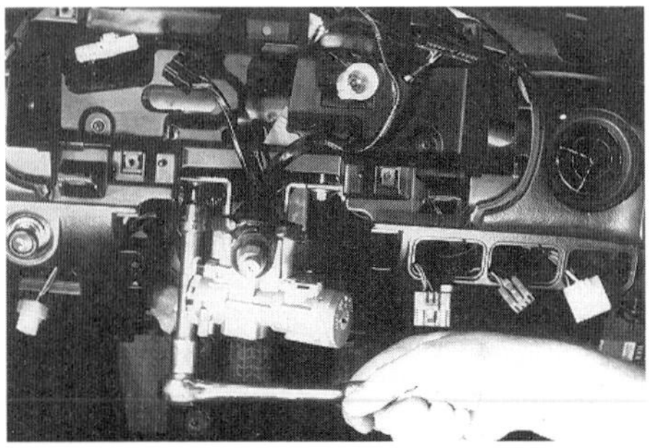

4/5 Release column top mountings.

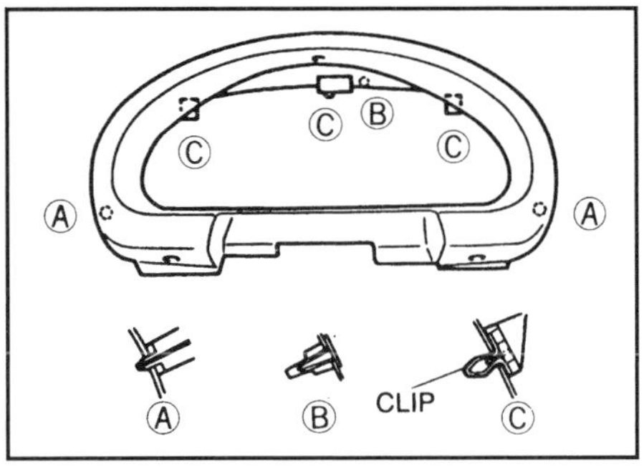

D4/6 INSTRUMENT PANEL HOUSING FIXING DETAIL.

The back of the housing is held by three metal clips on the dash panel, and is located by a long plastic pin.

7 With the housing out of the way, you have clear access to the four screws which secure the instrument panel. Remove the screws and pull the panel towards you. As it moves away from the dash, unplug the instrument panel connectors - there are two of these, one at top left and one at top right - each is secured by a locking tab. The panel can now be pulled back further, but is still held by the speedometer drive cable. This is secured on the back of the instrument panel by (you guessed it) a locking tab. Press this in and pull the cable off the back of the speedometer, then lift the instrument panel away.

8 Free the hood release knob from the lower edge of the dash panel after slackening the locknut which retains it. Move the knob and cable clear of the dash panel so that it does not get caught during dash removal.

9 You now need to pry off the small rectangular access covers which hide the dash panel fasteners. Note that the covers are directional - one end has a deep hook which locates on the edge of the dash panel, with a smaller clip at the back edge. The covers should unclip easily, but if they don't pop out when you insert the screwdriver blade, they may have been fitted incorrectly - try inserting the blade from the opposite edge to check this.

10 On each side of the dash panel, right next to the doors, you will find two covers. Lift the rear edge of each cover with a screwdriver and lift it away. There are two similar covers located on the dash panel center section, one on each side, and a further single cover at the center top of the dash panel, close to the windshield.

11 + The dash panel mounting bolts should be removed at this stage. Start with the 10 mm bolts fitted at the top center of the dash panel (one bolt) and on each side of the panel near the door openings (two on each side). Next, remove the four 14 mm bolts which retain the center section (two bolts on each side). The dash panel should now be lying loosely in position in the car.

12 As the dash panel is removed from the car it will be necessary to disconnect the electrical wiring. This is not as complicated as it seems at first

4/8 Slacken locknut to free hood release pull.

4/9 Pry off screw covers.

4/10 Pry cover from top centre of dash panel.

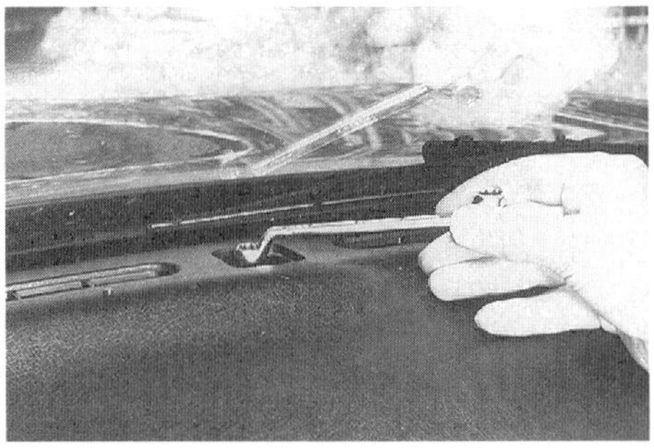

4/11a Unscrew top centre bolt ...

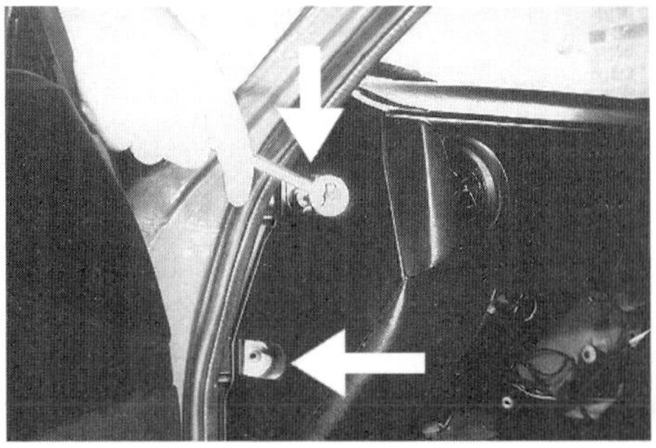

4/11b ... followed by those near doors ...

4/11c ... then these each side of trans tunnel.

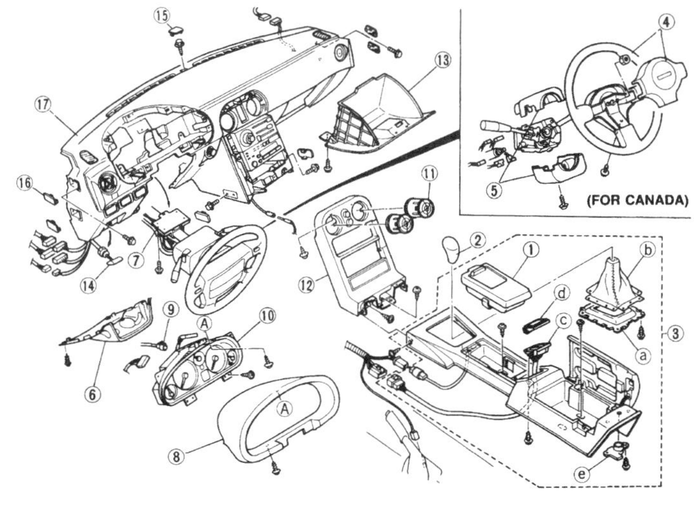

D4/20 DASH PANEL & CENTER CONSOLE DETAIL.
1 Ashtray. 2 Gearshift lever knob. 3 Rear console. (a mounting plate. b lever boot. c window lift switch. d optional cover. e lock body). 4 Steering wheel & horn push cover (except US). 5 Switch cover (except US). 6 Access panel (varies). 7 Steering column. 8 Instrument panel cover. 9 Speedo cable. 11 Eyeball airvent. 12 Center console. 13 Glove box. 14 Hood (bonnet) release handle. 15 Screw cover trim. 16 Screw cover trim. 17 Dash panel.

sight; the dash panel is obviously prewired during manufacture, and simply connected to the electrical system as it is installed. You will need to check the exact wiring connection details on your particular car, since this varies according to the market and options fitted, plus any accessory item which may have been added.

13 It is not entirely obvious which wiring connectors need to be separated, and which can be left undisturbed. We found that the best method was to gently lift the dash panel and move it back into the car - that way you can see clearly which connectors are impeding removal. It is very useful to have assistance at this stage of the removal sequence - the dash panel assembly is not heavy, but it needs careful manipulation during removal.

14 Don't be too concerned about getting the connectors confused - although many appear similar, they are readily differentiated by the wire colors, number of terminal pins and keys, and are not easily reconnected wrongly. It is useful, but not essential, to mark the connectors with pvc electrical tape or paint dots of different colors - this will speed up installation by making it immediately obvious which connectors go where.

15 On our UK-market project car we found that, on the driver's side, there are a group of three foam-wrapped connectors of different sizes, one of which is colored green and the rest white. These lie inboard of the steering column.

16 A second section of the loom terminates in four connectors running to the combination switch, and these will already have been disconnected; one black 6-pin, one white 8-pin, with only three terminal pins in use, a white 6-pin with five terminals and one blank, and a right-angled black 2-pin connector. Note that these will be entirely different on US spec cars which use a different combination switch.

17 A third subsection of the dash panel wiring runs to the bank of switches outboard of the steering column. On our car, two of the three connectors were physically identical, but were colored black and white to correspond with the back of the switch to which they were connected.

18 On the passenger's side of the car the only wiring connection needing attention was that to the heater blower unit. Note that on our car, we found that the aftermarket alarm system complicated removal a little - we had to cut one or two wires during removal, and these were subsequently reconnected using a terminal strip.

19 You are quite likely to encounter similar minor problems where accessory items have been added to the car - most will have been installed without removal of the dash panel. If you do need to disconnect accessory wiring, make a written note of the various connections, and where there is a risk of confusion during installation, mark the wires and / or connectors for identification using PVC tape.

20 When you have identified and separated the various wiring connectors, lift the dash panel up and back into the car. Make a final check around the back of the dash for any missed wiring connections, then lift the assembly out of the car, placing it on some soft cloth to protect the surface from scratches until it is needed again.

CHECKING

21 + With the dash panel removed you have access to the various assemblies like the heater unit and air conditioning unit (where fitted), as well as to the inside of the dash panel itself. The accompanying photographs show a general view of the car interior with the dash panel removed, plus closer shots of the driver's and passenger's side. These depict a UK market (RHD) car - other

4/21a Components accessible once dash out.

4/21b Rhd right hand detail and ditto ...

4/21c ... left. (Alarm components non-standard).

market models will be broadly similar, though most will of course be LHD versions.

22 The main dash panel molding is carried on a tubular steel fabricated subframe, which both supports the panel and adds to the rigidity of the body. In the event of impact damage severe enough to have damaged the subframe and surrounding bodywork, it is likely that the plastic molding will have sustained damage too. If this is the case, you will need specialist attention from a body shop, who will have to check the body alignment and install a new dash panel assembly as part of the

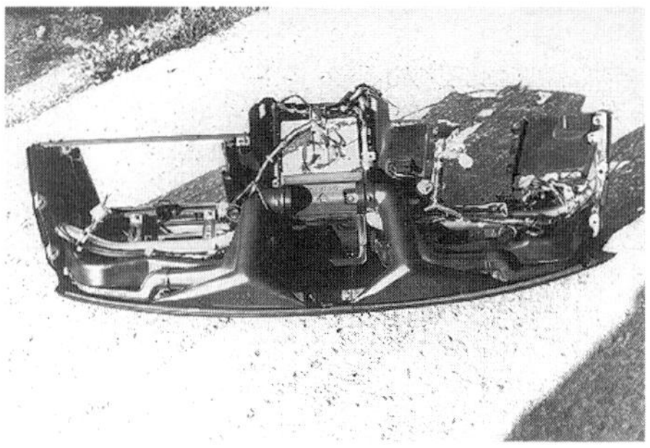

4/22 Detail of dash construction.

vehicle repair.

23 Minor components housed inside the dash panel can be removed or replaced as necessary; for example, this is a great time to fit a new cigarette lighter, if required - the lighter is difficult to remove and install while the dash panel is in the car (☞ 7/69).

24 If you need to remove such items, note carefully how any associated wiring is routed and duplicate the routing when installing the new part - it is preferable to avoid changes in routing because the wiring may become trapped or damaged

4/24 Note wiring routes & ground terminals.

when the dash panel is installed later. Note also the ground (earth) tag connections which will be found at the end of the dash subframe; these should be checked for security, noting that poor ground connections may result in electrical circuits operating intermittently.

25 + Check over the air ducts which are mounted inside the dash panel. These are lightweight ABS moldings which carry air to the defroster slots from the heater unit at the center of the under-dash area. The ducts slot together and are held (very loosely) in place by raised pips and ribs. Check that these sections are correctly engaged. If

4/25a Check air duct connections carefully ...

4/25b ... they could be taped for extra security.

necessary, you can improve the joints by taping around them.

INSTALLATION

26 Before you commence installation, we recommend that you spend a little time preparing the wiring connectors on the car side to simplify the process. Again, there will be some variation between cars built for different markets, but the point of this exercise is to position the connector ends so that they line up with the dash panel connectors when the unit is installed. You may find it easier to lay the dash panel across the seats so that you can check and compare the connector halves side-by-side.

27 With the aid of an assistant where possible, lift the dash panel into position, and start reconnecting the wiring - don't fit any mounting bolts at this stage. Pay careful attention to the routing of each section of wiring so that it is in no danger of being trapped when the dash is fastened in place.

28 Where switches are fitted into the dash panel, pop the switches out of their recesses and feed the related connector through the switch aperture. Connect each switch to the wiring, then snap the switch back into the dash panel.

4/28 Pry switches out and unplug connectors.

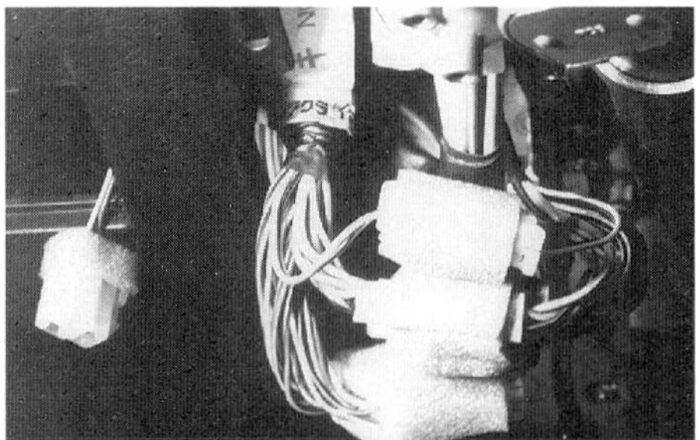

4/29 Some connectors are foam wrapped.

29 With the dash panel general wiring, check each connector for wire color, terminal positions and keys, and for any identification marks made during removal. Connect each one in turn, ensuring that they latch properly, and check carefully behind the dash to make sure that none have been missed. Don't forget any accessory wiring which you may have encountered during removal.

30 When you are confident that you have reconnected all the wiring, the dash panel can be fixed in position. Fit the 10 mm bolts at the outer edges of the panels, next to the door openings (two on each side of the car), plus the single 10 mm bolt at the center of the dash panel, immediately below the windshield. Next, fit the 14 mm bolts (two on each side) either side of the dash panel center section. Fit all the bolts fingertight at first so that minor positional adjustments can be made, then tighten down the 10 mm bolts to 7.8-12 Nm (80-120 kgf cm / 69-104 lbf in) and the 14 mm bolts to 36-54 Nm (3.7-5.5 kgf m / 27-40 lbf ft).

31 Clip the plastic covers over the dash panel mounting bolts, taking note of the direction markings; the covers will fit facing either way, but subsequent removal will be made more difficult if

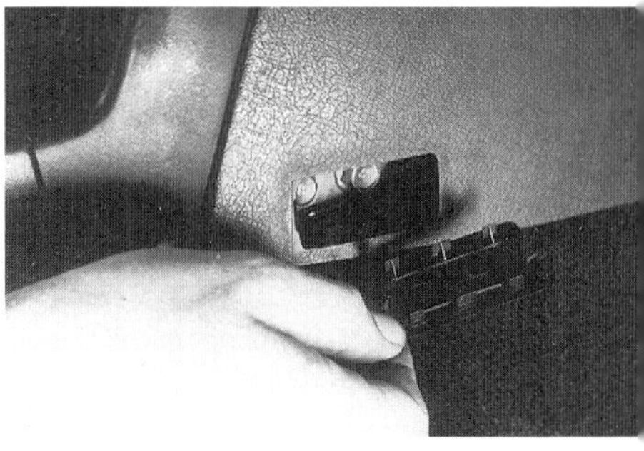

4/31 Screw cover trims clip into place.

positioned incorrectly.

32 Fit the hood release control knob, securing it by tightening the locknut firmly.

33 Install the dash center panel assembly (☞ 10/3), noting that the heater control cables must be fed into position and connected as the panel is installed. We suggest that you do not install the eyeball vents at this stage; if you need to remove the center panel or the dash panel to correct an installation problem it will be easier to do so with the vents removed.

34 Reposition the instrument panel, connecting the speedometer drive cable and the instrument panel wiring connectors as it is fitted. Once connected, fit and tighten the four retaining screws. Fit the instrument panel surround, clipping it in position and securing it with its two retaining screws.

35 Install the steering column and wheel (if removed) ☞ 8/11. During installation, check the dash panel wiring routing and rearrange this if necessary to prevent wiring getting trapped. Where appropriate (non-airbag cars), install the combination switch assembly and connect its wiring. On air bag-equipped cars, the combination switch and steering wheel are normally removed with the steering column assembly; check and reconnect

the clock spring wiring connectors. **Warning!** The clock spring connector adjustment of air bag cars must be checked ☞ 7/50/12.

36 Install the rear console assembly, remembering to reconnect any associated wiring connections (ashtray light, power window switches, etc).

37 This is a good point at which to temporarily reconnect the car's battery and check the operation of the electrical systems. If you find a problem, check and resolve this before proceeding further. Once everything is working correctly, install the glove box and steering column access panel. Finally, snap the eyeball vents into place.

5. INTERIOR TRIM - REMOVAL & INSTALLATION

☞ 1/1, 2.

1 In addition to the dash panel, dash center panel and rear console assemblies described in the preceding sections, the remaining metalwork in the car is concealed by plastic trim panels. In some cases these are purely cosmetic coverings, though some also conceal other mechanisms or serve a protective function. It is also useful to be able to remove the trim panels to give better access for rustproofing.

2 Note that the exact fixing methods seemed to differ on our car from those described by Mazda, and we assume that there have been some modifications during the production run of the car, and that detail differences will exist between cars built for different markets.

FRONT HEADER RAIL TRIM, SUN VISORS & INTERIOR MIRROR

3 The front header trim covers the top section of windshield surround between the two A-pillars. To remove it, first unclip the plastic cover which conceals the interior mirror mounting - this snaps over the mirror base and is a tight fit. Remove the sheet metal screws and remove the mirror. Next, remove the soft top locating cups which are held in place by 6.6 mm Torx screws. The cups are adjustable via slotted mounting holes - make a note of their positions. Now remove the sun visors, each being retained by two sheet metal screws. Once these fittings have been detached, lift the header trim at one end until the retaining clip snaps free. Continue working along the trim, noting that the clips are quite tight. When you have installed the trim and external fixings, check that the soft top locating cups are set up correctly (close the top and check this) then tighten the Torx screws to secure them.

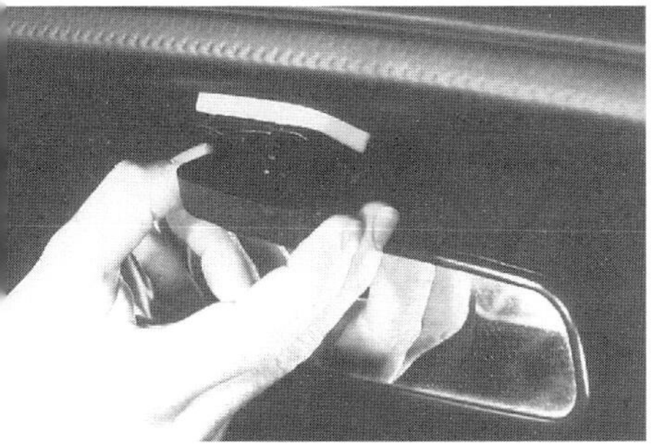

5/3a Remove mirror mounting trim ...

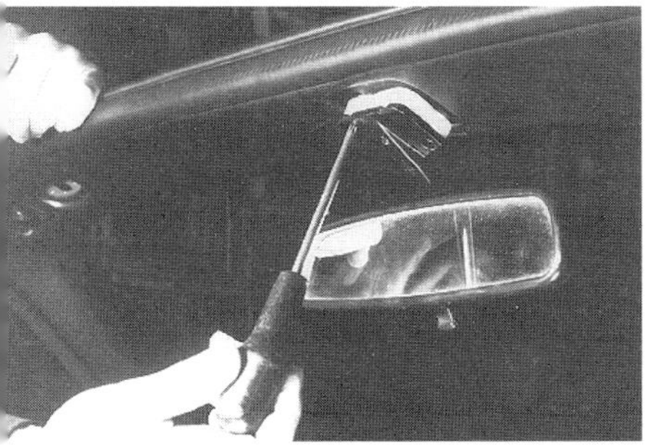

5/3b ... and unscrew securing screws.

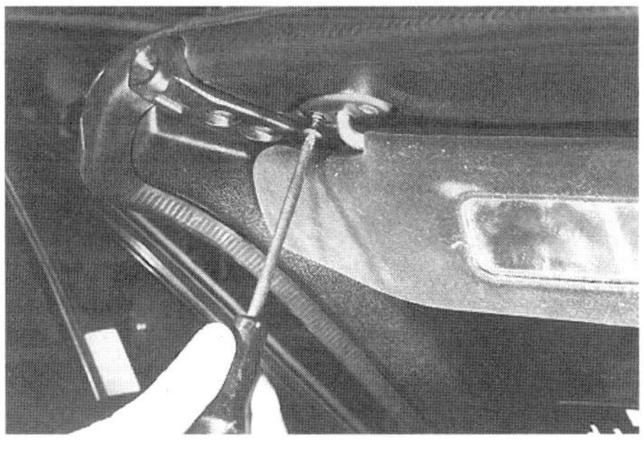

5/3c Sun visors held by 2 screws each.

5/3d Torx screws hold latch cups.

5/3e Lift away header rail trim panel.

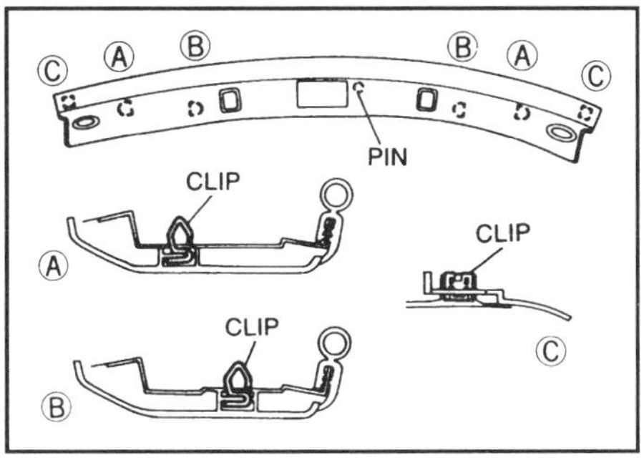

D5/3 HEADER RAIL TRIM FIXING DETAIL.

A-PILLAR TRIM

4 The A-pillar trim covers the two A-pillars (A-posts) on either side of the windshield. Before you can remove the individual trim panels, you will need to pull off the door seal in the vicinity of the relevant trim. Beware of body mastic! Unclip the trim section working from the top down. Once the clips are free, disengage the locating peg near the top and lift away lower end of the trim section where it hooks into the A-pillar. Note that the metal clips hook onto the trim section and may drop off as you pull the trim away - check that these are retrieved. When installing the A-pillar trim, check that it locates correctly around the ends of the header trim, and check that the door seal is snapped back into position correctly.

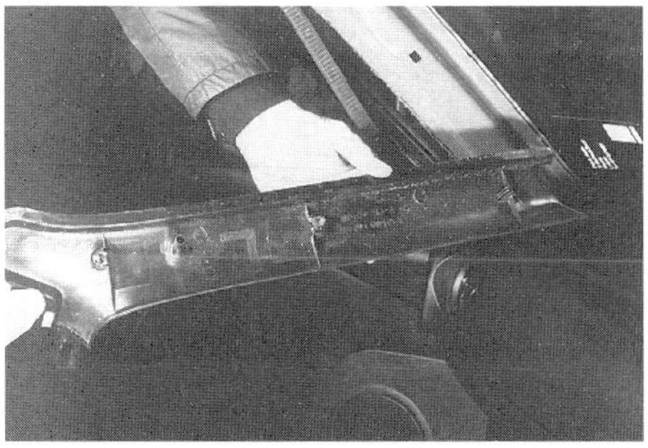

5/4a Unclip A-pillar trim.

5/4b Clips hook into these cups.

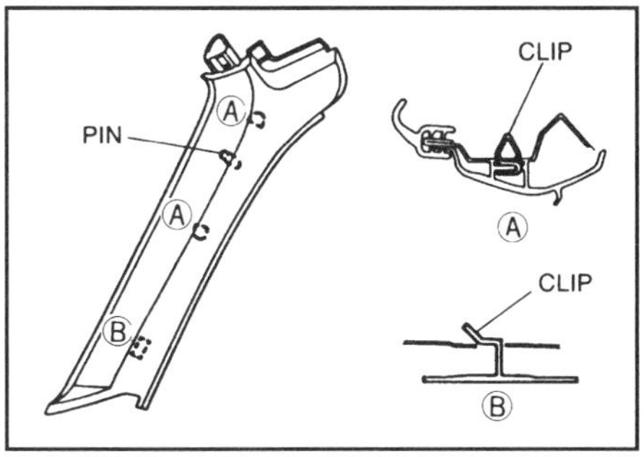

D5/4 A-PILLAR TRIM FIXING DETAIL.

FRONT SIDE (FOOTWELL) TRIM

5 The front side trim is located for-

10

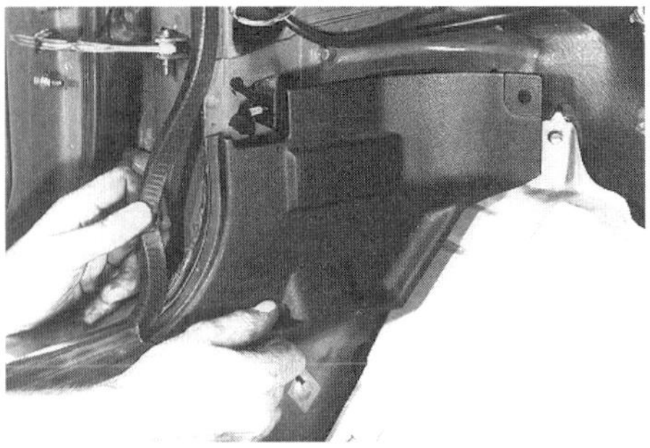

5/5 Peel back door seal to release trim.

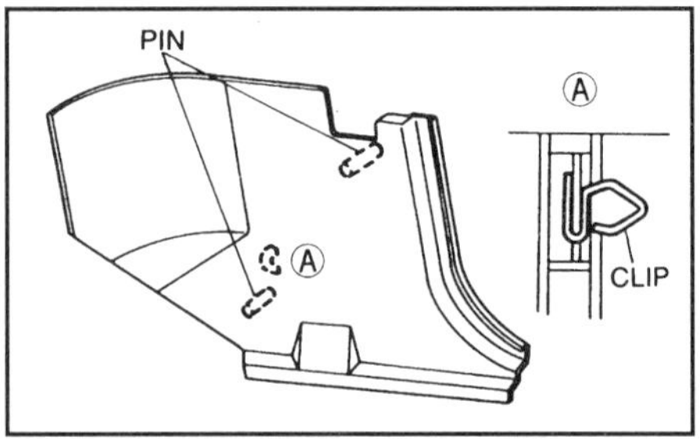

D5/5 FRONT (FOOTWELL) SIDE TRIM FIXING DETAIL.

ward of the door opening on the outer sides of the footwells. The trim section clips into place and is located by small pins. Note also that the back edge of the trim is retained by the door seal, which clips over it. The forward top edge is secured by a threaded plastic retainer clip. To remove and install the trim section you will need to peel away the section of door seal which covers the trim edge.

6 On cars equipped with aftermarket scuff plates, these may also impede removal; on our project car we needed to free the scuff plate screws to allow the trim section to be removed.

SCUFF PLATE

7 The scuff plate is fitted over the raised seam which runs across the bottom of the door openings, protecting the seam and surrounding paintwork from damage by the driver's and passenger's feet. The standard scuff plate is secured by two spring clips and a single locating pin and may be removed by pulling upwards.

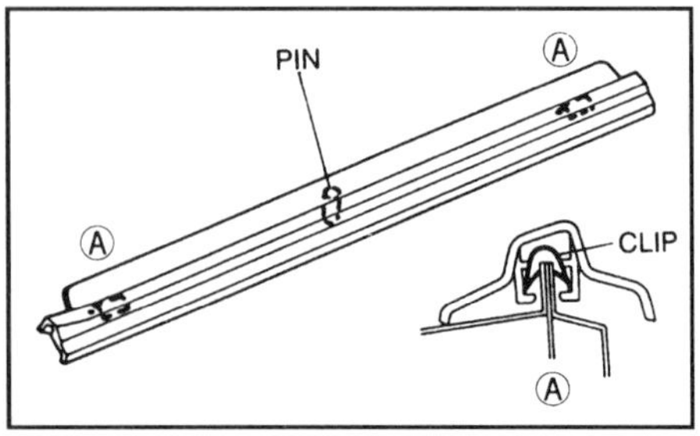

D5/7 SCUFF PLATE (STANDARD) FIXING DETAIL.

8 Many Miata/MX5s will have been fitted with aftermarket scuff plates which are much wider, and do a better job of protection. On our project car, these were held by sheet metal screws, and the outer edges appeared to have been secured with impact adhesive. (We had no good reason to remove the scuff plates completely, and so decided to avoid risking cosmetic damage by pulling them off).

QUARTER TRIM

9 The quarter trim panels cover the rear quarters of the car interior, running from the back edge of the door opening around to the package shelf, and providing a housing for the seat belt mechanisms.

10 To remove a quarter trim panel, start by removing the hard top location stop which is secured by two 6.6 mm Torx screws. You should really use a Torx wrench on these screws, though we found it possible to shift them using Allen wrenches - a 5 mm Allen wrench is a little slack, while a 6 mm wrench may be too tight - you'll have to experiment with your own set to find a snug fit. If the screws on your car prove to be tight, don't risk damaging the screw heads - get the correct Torx wrench.

5/10 Hardtop locating pad fixed by Torx screws.

11 Next, remove the finishing piece at the top corner of the door opening. This is held in place by a single crosshead screw plus a 10 mm headed set screw.

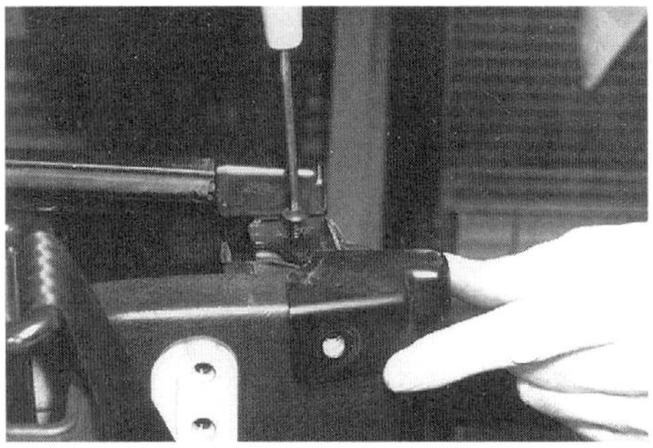

5/11 Remove screw, lift away trim panel.

12 + From the edge of the trim panel just to the rear of the seatbelt top mounting point, unclip and remove the small closing section to provide a gap though which the belt can be passed. You will also need to pull out the clip-in plastic loop through which the belt passes - free this from the trim, leaving it loosely in place around the belt.

13 On the side of the trim panel, free the single plastic clip, lifting the center section using a small screwdriver, and then lifting the fastener out of its hole. Remove the 10 mm set screw adjacent to the clip.

5/12a Unclip & remove closing section.

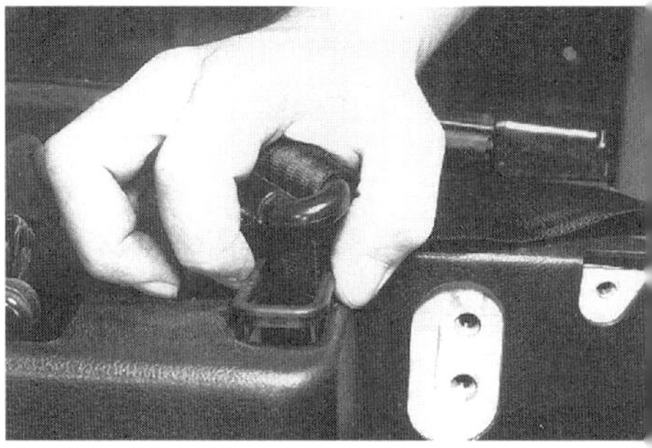

5/12b Release belt aperture trim.

5/13 Remove plastic clip and screw.

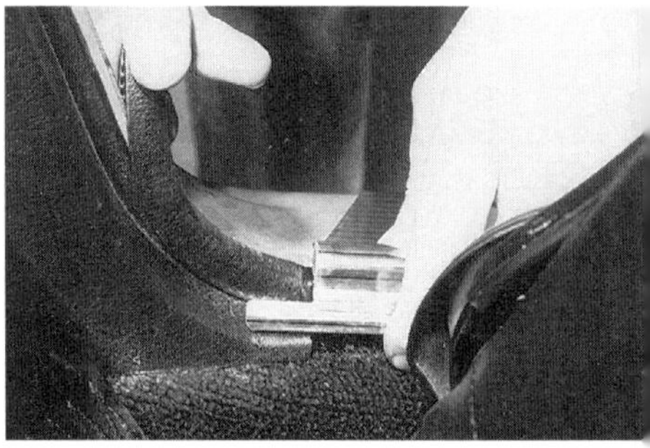

5/14 Pull away door seal to release trim.

14 Pull away the door seal where it covers the edge of the trim. On our car, which had aftermarket scuff plates, we also needed to release the scuffplate screws - this allows the bottom of the trim to be freed. The rest of the trim edge is tucked under the carpet edge and comes free easily.

15 Lift the panel and move it forward, remembering to feed the seatbelt through the slot at the back of the trim.

16 When installing the quarter trim panel, position it in the car, simultaneously feeding the seatbelt through the slot provided, then clip the

5/15 Remove panel feeding s/belt thru slot.

plastic loop into the panel and install the closing section at the back edge.

17 Fit the plastic clip and set screw on the side of the panel, then fit the finishing piece, securing it with its sheet metal screw and set screw. Check that the edge of the panel is located properly (you may have to lift the carpet a little to cover the edge) and clip the door seal back in position.

18 If the scuff plate screws were slackened, they should be tightened at this stage. Finally, fit the hard top location stop and secure it with its two Torx screws.

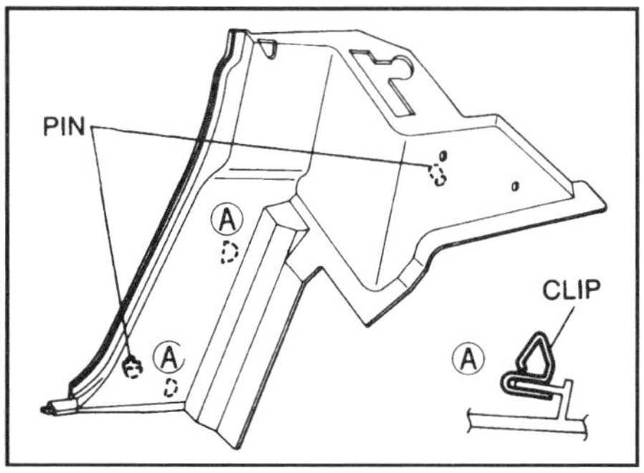

D5/18 QUARTER TRIM FIXING DETAILS.

DOOR SPEAKER AND GRILLE

19 The door speakers are recessed into the front lower corner of each door and are covered by a separate grille trim panel. The panel is secured by four plastic clips which push through holes in the door skin. The grille can be removed by pulling it away from the door - it helps to get the fingers under the grille near the clip to be freed, working around the grille until all four clips have been displaced.

20 + Once the grille has been detached, it is possible to remove the speaker after its three

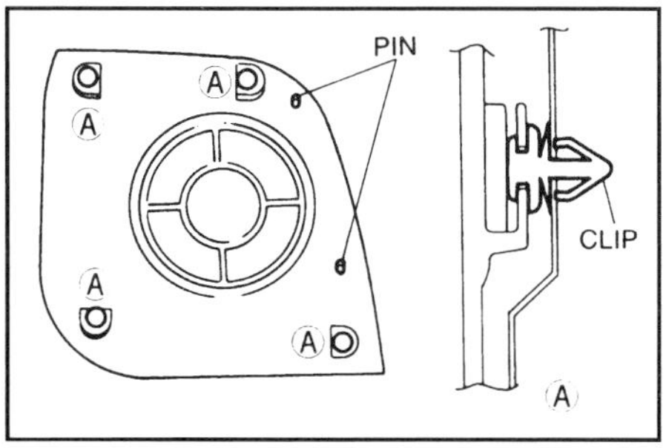

D5/19 SPEAKER TRIM FIXING DETAIL.

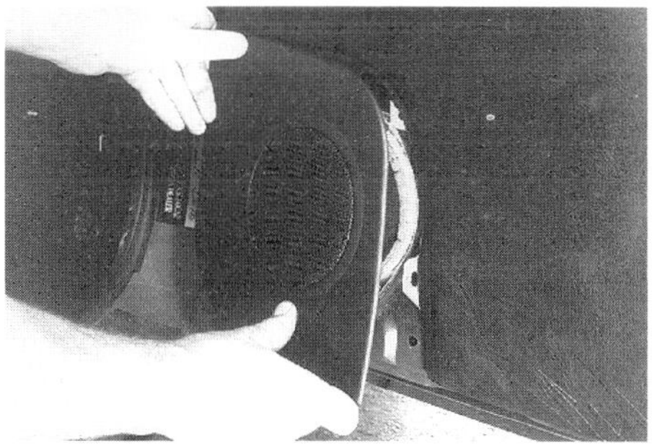

5/19 Unclip speaker cover panel.

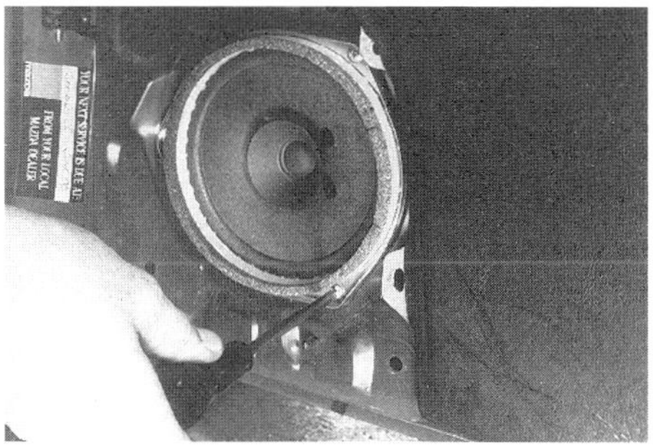

5/20a Speaker is held by screws ...

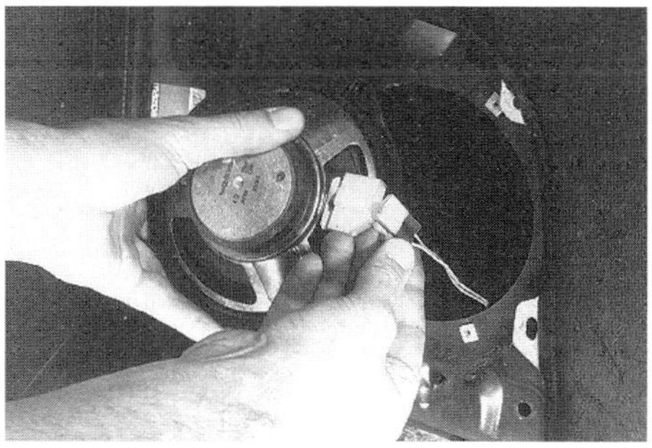

5/20b ... & needs to be unplugged from wiring.

mounting screws have been removed. As you lift it away, disconnect the speaker wiring connector.

DOOR TRIM

21 The door trim panel covers a number of access holes in the inner door skin and so provides the means of access to the door catch and lock mechanism, mechanical or electric window regulators and, where fitted, the central locking solenoid.

22 Disable the stereo anti-theft system and then disconnect the battery negative cable to isolate the electrical system ☞ 7/2.

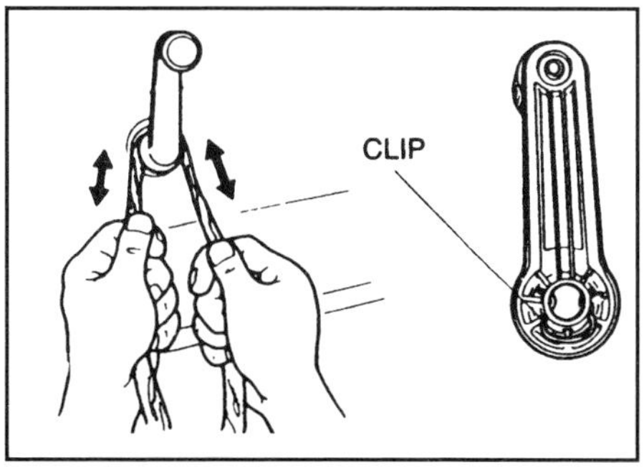

D5/23 HANDLE REMOVAL METHOD.

23 On manual window cars, start by removing the regulator handle. This is secured on its shaft by a spring clip, and the easiest removal method is to loop a strip of rag around the base of the handle, pulling the loop of rag so that it is forced between the handle and its base (escutcheon).

24 Further pressure on the loop will displace the clip and the handle can be pulled off.

25 On all cars, pull off the door speaker grille as described above. You now need to remove the armrest, which is secured by three crosshead screws, the uppermost of which is hidden under a small trim plug. Pry out the plug with a small

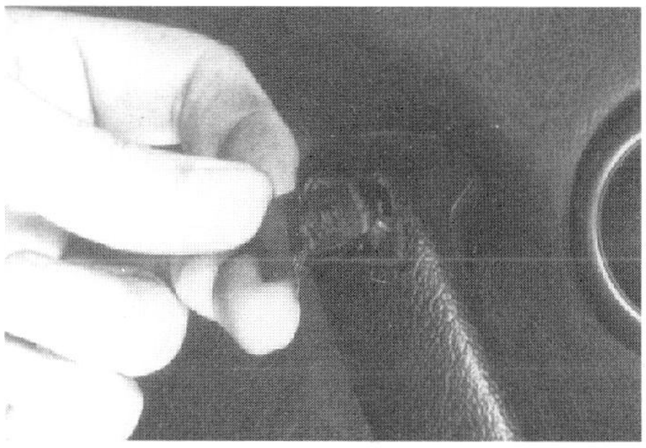

5/25 Pry out screw cover trim.

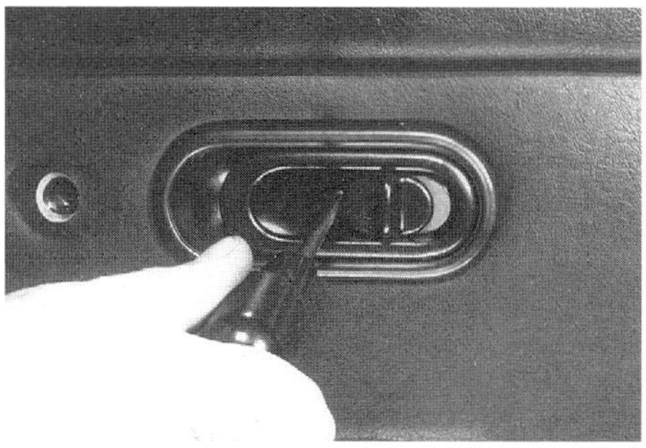

5/26a Remove securing screw & then ...

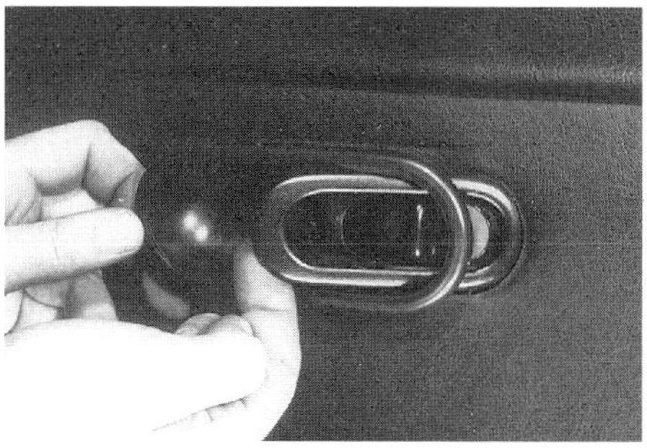

5/26b ... slide off handle surround trim.

screwdriver, then remove the three screws and lift the armrest away.

26 + Remove the single small crosshead screw which retains the interior door handle surround. Lift the handle about half way, then maneuver the surround over the handle and remove it.

27 The door trim is now held in place by plastic peg clips around its front, lower and rear edges. Work your hand between the trim and the door and begin popping the clips out of the door. Once all the clips are free, lift the trim slightly to unhook its top edge and remove it.

10

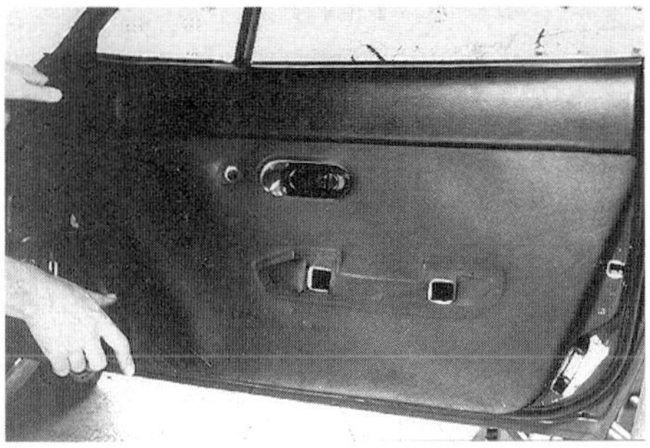

5/27 Once unclipped the door trim lifts off.

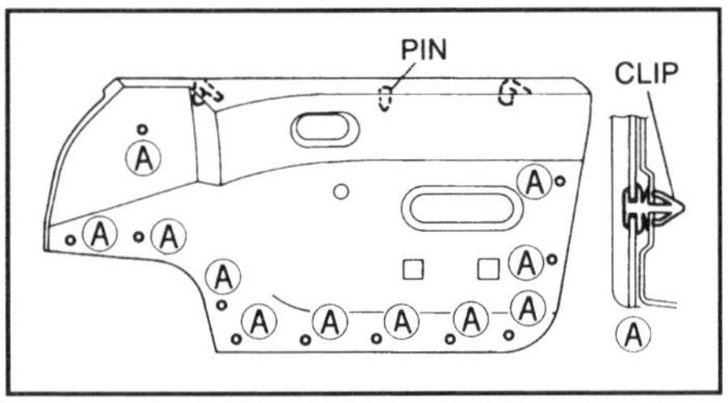

D5/27 DOOR TRIM PANEL FIXING DETAIL.

28 Below the door trim, you will note a plastic sheet covering the door apertures; if you need access to the door interior, you will need to remove this.

29 Start by removing the interior door handle. This is secured by three crosshead screws, and you will need to free the ends of the lock and latch rods. The easiest way of doing this is to disconnect the lock rod at the door end and the latch rod at the handle end. The rods are secured by swivel clips. Unclip these from the rod ends and turn them through 90° until the rod end can be lifted out.

30 Check that nothing else will impede removal (on our car, one of the screw receptor clips

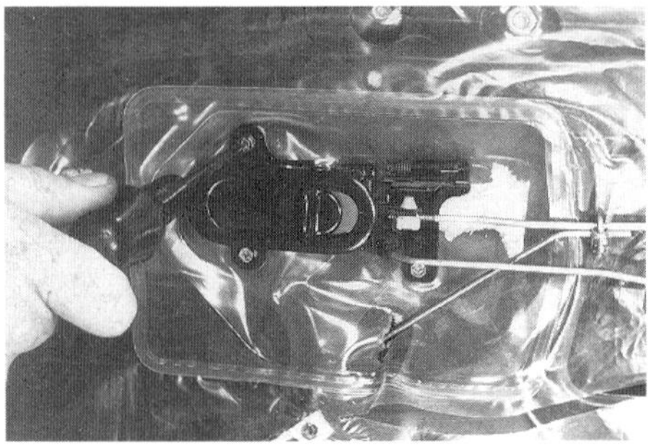

5/29 Unscrew door handle retaining screws.

had been pushed through the sheet by mistake). Note also that where aftermarket central locking has been added, you may find, as we did, that the solenoid control rod runs outside of the sheet. If you have to detach the rod, and like ours it is clamped to the door locking rod, mark the relationship of the two rods before releasing the clamp.

31 The plastic sheet is held by very sticky black mastic, and you will need somewhere clean to put it when removed. We recommend that you place it face down on a plastic garbage bag for this - it will allow you to reuse the mastic, and the bag can be disposed of after use.

32 Take care during removal to avoid contact between the mastic and your clothes, or the car upholstery or paintwork. In case of accidental contact, hand cleaner will remove the mastic from your hands, and a proprietary tar remover will get it off paintwork or fabrics - refer to the manufacturer's directions when using these products, and always test on a small, unobtrusive area for discoloration effects before using it on the actual stain.

33 If the sheet is torn or holed, you should fit a new one. Either purchase one from your Mazda dealer, or make one up using industrial grade polyethylene sheeting. You can use the old sheet as a template for cutting the new one, but note that the original is shaped to fit the door skin contours, and your home-brewed equivalent may not fit quite as well. Use proprietary automotive mastic to stick the new sheet in place, after removing the old mastic with Stoddard solvent (white spirit).

34 When fitting the plastic sheet, position it carefully along the top edge and check that it lines up across the door skin - it will be obvious if this is not the case. Pass the door latch and lock rods through the sheet, positioning the foam sealing pad over the holes in the sheet. If you needed to

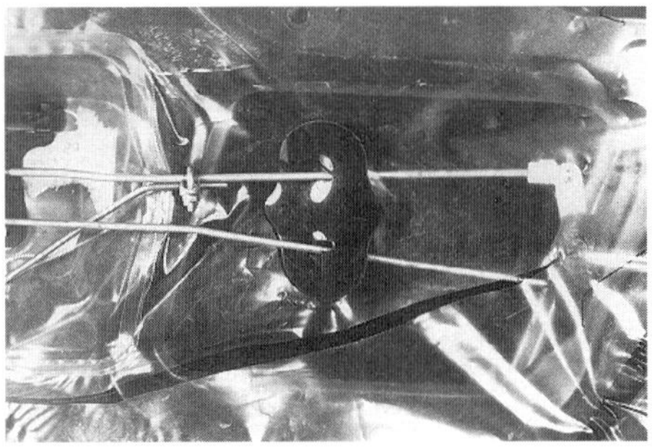

5/34 Don't forget foam sealing pad.

disconnect the central locking control rod, now is the time to reconnect it, passing it through the plastic sheet and aligning the marks made during removal before securing the clamp. Press the sheet down onto the mastic in key areas, such as where screws pass through the sheet into the door, before smoothing the sheet down evenly across the door.

35 Hook the door trim on along its top edge, then pivot it down against the door skin. Press around the rear, lower and front edges until the pins have all snapped home. Position the speaker grille and press this home until the four pins have locked in place.

36 On cars with manual window regulators, install the handle, positioning it 45° off vertical and facing forwards when the glass is fully raised. Check that the window raises and lowers normally.

37 Lift the interior door handle slightly and slide the surround into position. Release the handle and fit the single screw which locates the surround.

38 Fit the armrest, tightening the three crosshead screws evenly, and remembering to fit the trim plug which conceals the upper screw head. Reconnect the battery and check the operation of the electric window and central locking systems, where these are fitted

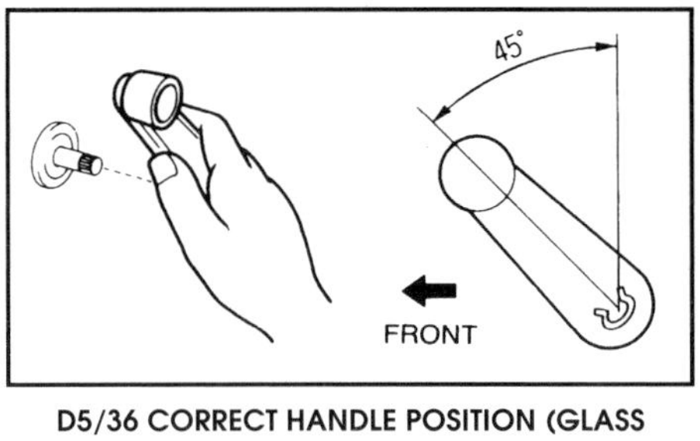

D5/36 CORRECT HANDLE POSITION (GLASS RAISED).

6. DOOR GLASS & LIFTER MECHANISM - REMOVAL & INSTALLATION

☞ 1/1, 2.

REMOVAL

1 Wind down the door glass to about 190 mm (7.5 in) from the fully open position - this will roughly position the glass ready for removal, but further adjustment may be needed later. Disable the stereo security system and then disconnect the battery negative (-) lead to isolate the electrical system (☞ 7/2). Remove the door trim and plastic sheet ☞ 10/5.

2 You now need to remove the front beltline molding - the weather seal which fits around the glass at the top of the door. Pry out the plastic pins at the front and back ends of the molding where it wraps around the ends of the door, using a screwdriver blade to lever them out. Next, prepare a small screwdriver by wrapping some PVC tape around the shaft.

3 + Using the protected screwdriver (and taking great care to minimize the risk of paint damage in such a conspicuous area), carefully lift the edge of the beltline molding seal lip on the

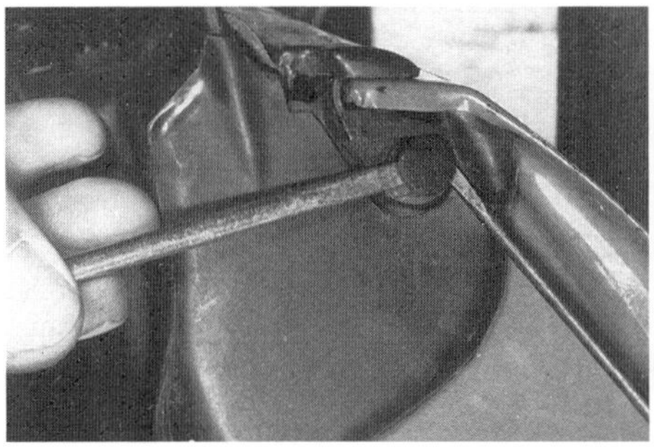

6/2 Pry out molding securing pins.

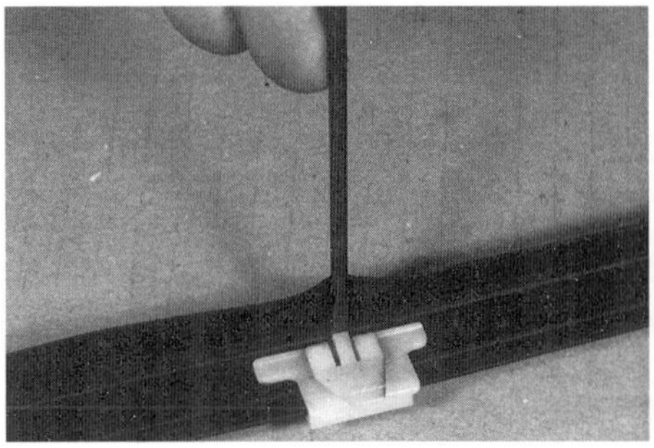

6/3a Tab release demo (molding removed).

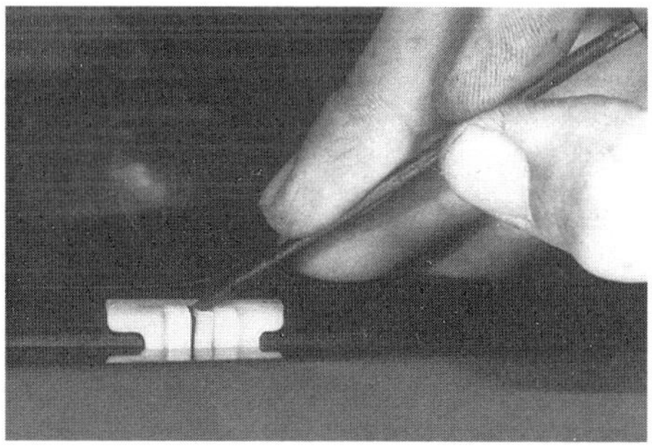

6/3b Lift molding & release each clip.

outside of the door. If you peer underneath the lip, you should be able to make out one or more of the retaining clips. At the center of each one is a locking tab, which you need to depress with the screwdriver blade. Gently depress the tab and the clip will pop out of the door recess. Repeat this procedure on the remaining clips and lift the molding away. Our photographs show the method of depressing the central tabs with the molding removed and during removal.

4 To minimize the amount of final adjustment required after installation, mark the position of all bolt heads in relation to the door inner skin, and the nuts on the underside of the door. You can use paint for this, or as we did, typist's correcting fluid (it's easily visible and dries fast). Mark around the edge of the bolt head or nut so that its position can be duplicated during installation

5 Remove the two glass stops which are retained by a single bolt each, either side of the regulator mechanism. The bolts can be reached through oval access holes near the top of the door skin - you identify the two bolts concerned by pee-ing down through the top of the door - you will see where the two stops are. Hold each stop in turn,

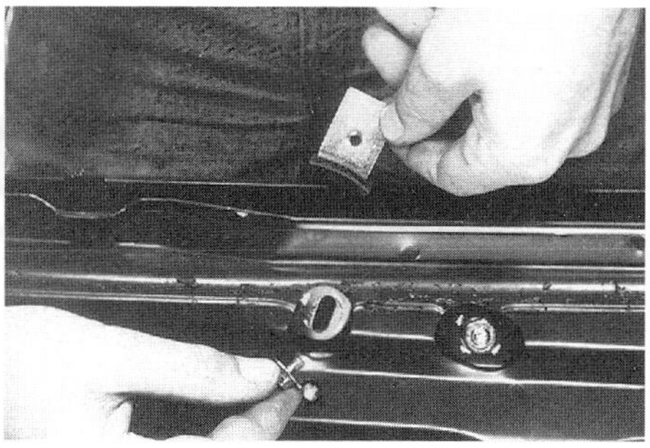

6/5 Remove glass stops.

remove the fixing bolt, and lift the stop out of the door.

6 Check the position of the glass in relation to the door. The glass is secured by three crosshead screws to the regulator mechanism, two of which can be reached through the large aperture nearest the back edge of the door, and there is an oval hole for access to the third screw at the front of the regulator mechanism. If you need to reposition the glass so that the front screw aligns with the access hole, on manual window cars, fit the handle and move the glass up or down until this screw is visible through the access hole. On cars with power windows, temporarily reconnect the battery, and use the power window switch to position the glass as described.

7 Have an assistant remove the three screws while you support the glass. Once the screws have been removed, lift the glass clear of the regulator mechanism and out of the door cavity. Place the glass safely out of harm's way on some soft cloth until it is needed again.

8 The rear glass guide can now be removed if required, again having made sure that its fasteners are marked for position beforehand. Once

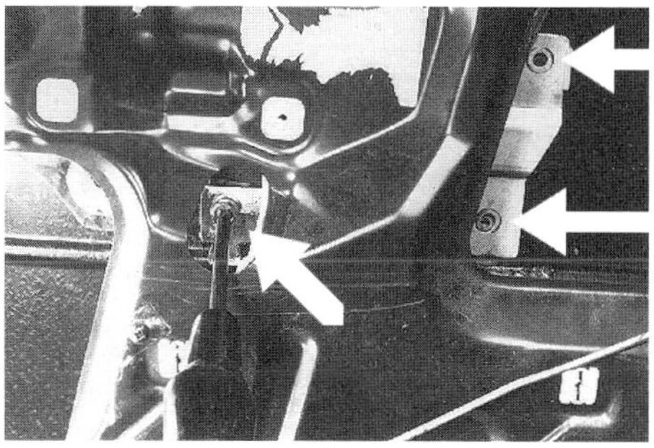

6/7 These 3 screws support the glass.

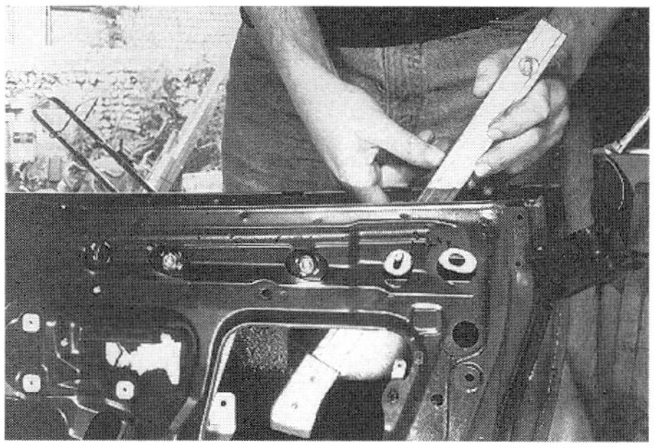

6/8 Slide out rear glass guide.

the upper and lower fixing nuts have been removed, the guide can be lifted out through the top of the door.

9 + The regulator mechanism is similar on both manual and power window versions, and is removed as an assembly with the regulator gearbox or motor assembly. Remove the three 10 mm flanged nuts which retain the gearbox / motor assembly to the door inner skin. Note that the mounting points differ between manual and power models, but this does not affect removal (manual winder mounting holes arrowed on photograph). On power window cars, disconnect the motor

6/9a Three nuts hold motor (arrows: see text).

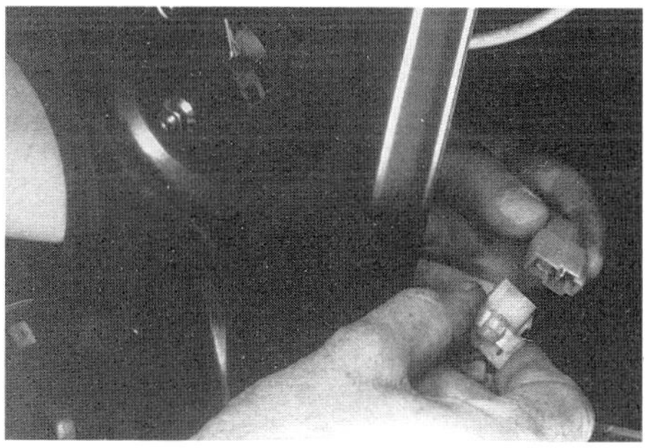

6/9b Unplug power lift motor wiring.

wiring connector.

10 + Feel along the cables inside the door skin and locate the cable guide clips - these push through holes in the door skin and should be displaced after noting their relative positions. The regulator mechanism can now be freed by releasing the two nuts at the top (accessible through holes in the door skin) and two further nuts on the lower edge of the door. Raise the mechanism slightly, then feed it down through the center aperture in the door skin, followed by the regulator gearbox / motor assembly.

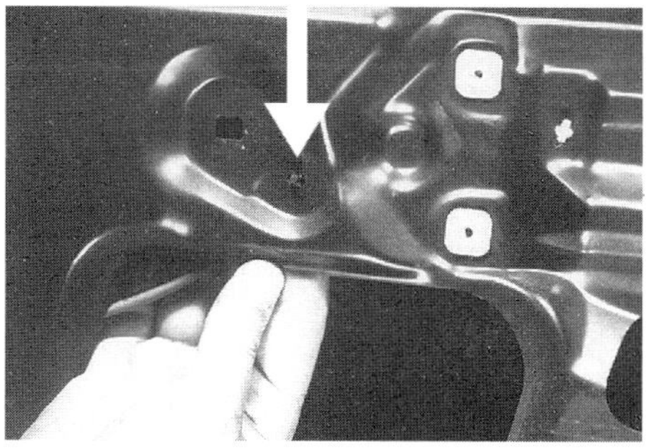

6/10a Feel for the cable clips.

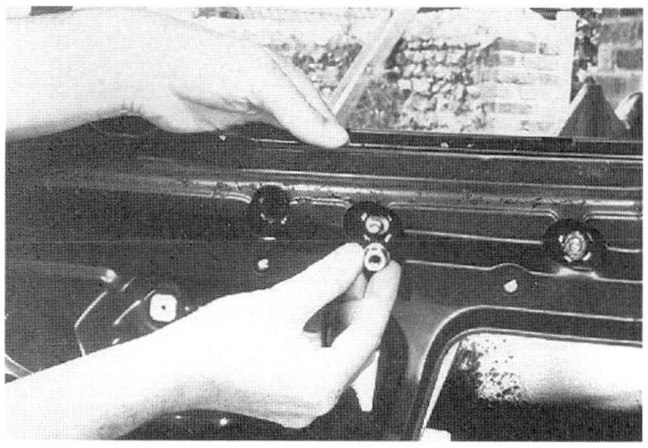

6/10b Release regulator securing nuts ...

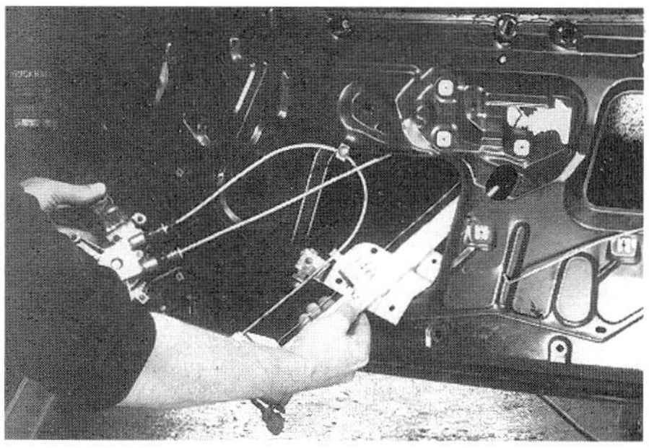

6/10c ... then pull regulator from door.

INSTALLATION

11 During installation, you should fit the removed regulator components and the window glass, making reference to the positioning marks made around the fasteners during removal. This will mean that the assembly is set up more or less exactly as it was prior to removal, but note that you may need to carry out final adjustment of the glass (☞ 10/9). Start by installing the rear glass guide (if it was removed) and provisionally tighten the mounting bolts, noting the positioning marks made during removal.

12 + Feed the regulator mechanism, together with the gearbox / motor assembly attached on its cables, through the center door aperture. Position the regulator studs through the mounting holes in the door and provisionally tighten the four mounting nuts, observing the position marks made during removal. Fit the gearbox / motor assembly and tighten the three mounting nuts to 8.8-13.0 Nm (90-130 kgf cm / 78-113 lbf ft). Clip the cable guide clips into their holes in the door skin.

13 If you have simply removed and installed the regulator assembly, it will be correctly positioned for installation of the window glass. If, however, the mechanism has been dismantled or

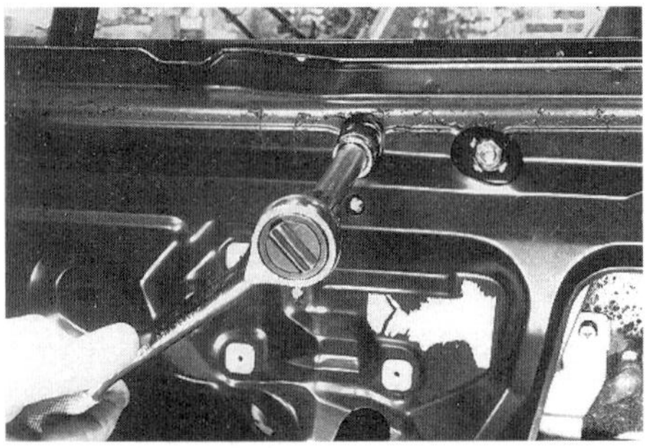

6/12a Secure regulator loosely in position.

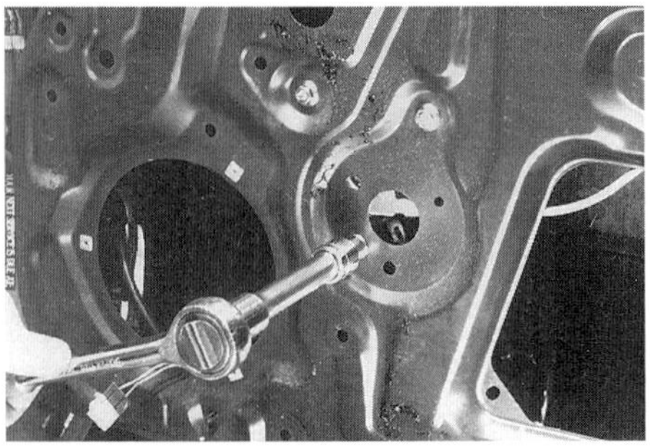

6/12b Secure motor or manual lift.

moved, you will need to check that the front mounting point in the mechanism is correctly aligned with the access hole in the door skin - if this is not the case you will be unable to fit the fixing screw. This procedure was described earlier (☞ 10/6/6), and should be repeated if necessary.

14 Lower the window glass through the aperture at the top of the door, engaging the glass guide posts in their channels. Align the fixing holes with the regulator mechanism, then fit and tighten evenly the three fixing screws. It is advisable to have some help at this stage, though you can just

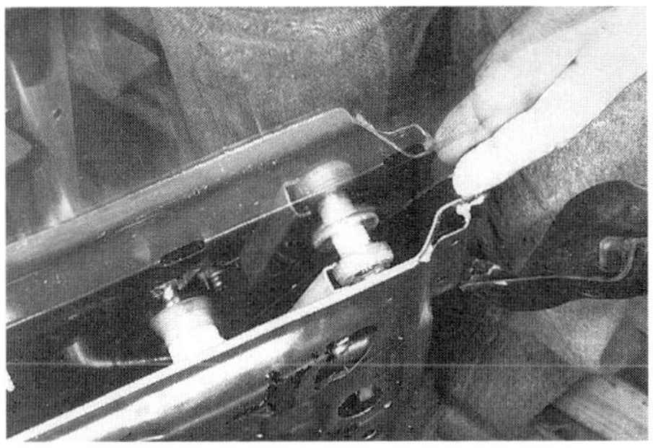

6/14 Slide glass guides into channels.

about get by unaided.

15 Fit the glass upper stops through the top of the door, securing them with their mounting bolts in the position indicated by the marks you made during removal. Do this carefully, because the stop positions have a significant effect on the fit of the glass against the soft / hard top weatherstrip.

16 Check the glass adjustment ☞ 10/9. The amount of work this will entail is dependent on whether you made reference marks during dismantling, and whether new parts have been installed. If you have simply removed and installed the existing parts using reference marks during the dismantling operation, you should only need to check the adjustment - if this was correct before you disassembled the glass and regulator, and you have worked to the reference marks made, there should be no need to set the adjustment from scratch.

17 Once you have carried out the adjustment check, tighten the regulator, stop and guide fasteners to 22-27 Nm (2.2-2.8 kgf m / 16-20 lbf ft). Install the door trim components ☞ 10/5/26 on.

7. WINDOW LIFT SYSTEM (POWER) - CHECKING & OVERHAUL

☞ 1/1, 2.

1 The power window lift system is an option which will be found on a good number of Miata/MX5s. In essence this is a motorized version of the manual regulator arrangement, differing only in the use of an electric motor system to raise and lower the door window glass. The motors are controlled from two switches housed in the rear console.

2 In the event of problems with the power window system, the likely cause is either an electrical problem or failure of the regulator mechanism cables - these convey movement between the motor unit and the regulator mechanism. The nature of the fault is likely to be self-evident; if a cable has broken, you will still hear the motor running when the switch is operated, but the glass will not move. (The glass may well have dropped open if the closing cable has broken). If both windows are inoperative, check the **P.WINDOW 30A** fuse. If this has burned out, check the wiring for a short circuit and repair as necessary, then fit a new fuse.

3 If you suspect a cable fault, or if the problem is confined to one side only, start checking inside the affected door after removing the door trim ☞ 10/5. If you discover a broken cable, you will need to remove the glass, followed by the regulator mechanism and motor as an assembly ☞ 10/6. Skip down to the *'Regulator overhaul and cable replacement'* heading.

4 In the case of electrical problems, check the operation of the motor unit as follows. Disconnect the motor wiring connector, and connect a spare car battery to the motor terminals - battery positive (+) to terminal **a** and battery negative (-) to terminal **b**. The motor should operate. Now reverse the battery connections and verify that the motor runs the other way. If the motor does not run, or works intermittently, you will need to fit a new unit.

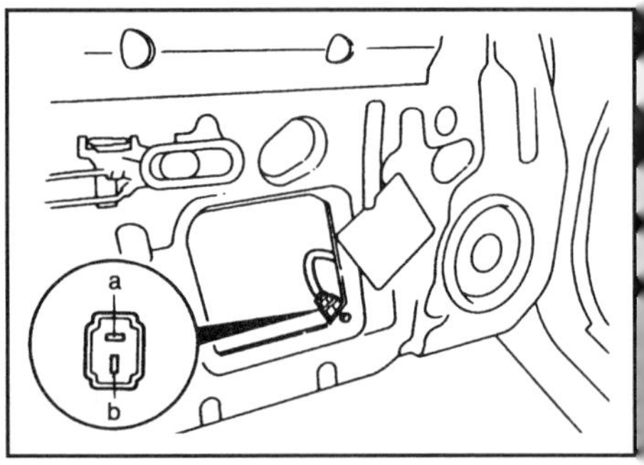

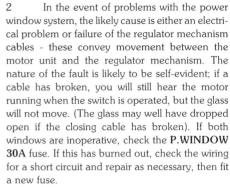

D7/4 POWER LIFT MOTOR TERMINAL IDENTIFICATION.

5 + If the motor checks out OK, trace the wiring back to the switch panel in the rear console unit - you will need to remove the console ☞ 10/2. Disconnect the switch wiring and check switch continuity as shown in the accompanying diagram and table. If the switch is faulty, fit a new unit.

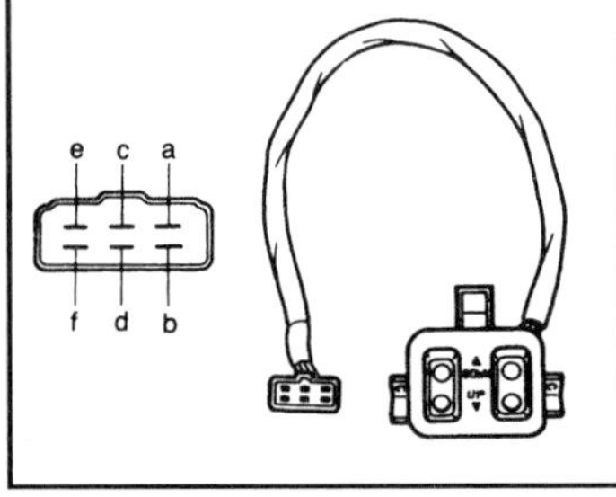

Switch	Driver side				Passenger side			
Position \ Terminal	a	b	c	d	a	b	e	f
UP	○		○		○		○	
		○		○		○		○
OFF		○	○	○		○	○	○
DOWN	○			○	○			○
		○	○			○	○	

○—○: Indicates continuity

D&T7/5A POWER WINDOW SWITCH CONTINUITY TESTING.

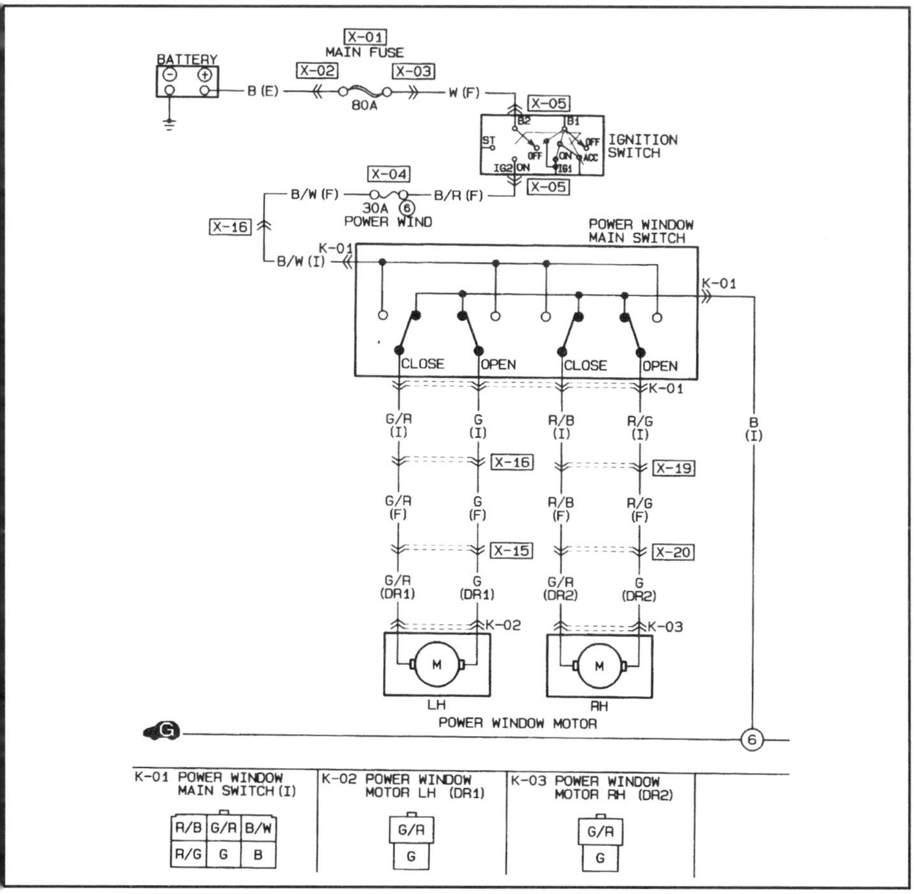

D7/5B POWER WINDOW LIFT ELECTRICAL CIRCUIT.

REGULATOR OVERHAUL AND CABLE REPLACEMENT

6 With the motor unit and regulator removed as an assembly (☞ 10/6), start dismantling the unit on the bench. Before you start work, lay the assembly out and note how it all fits together. In particular, note how the cables cross over each other - this looks like it might be wrong, but is in fact intentional. The accompanying photographs depict the mechanism from a right-hand door, viewed from both sides, for reference purposes.

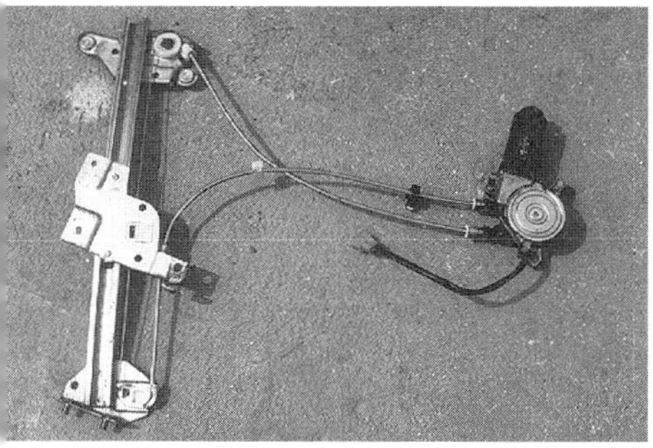

7/6a Both sides of regulator and motor ...

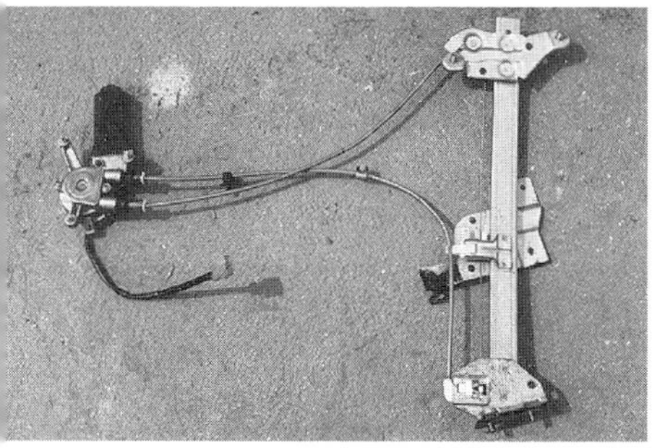

7/6b ...note cable runs & crossover.

7 The lower cable from the motor unit (the UP cable) runs to the top of the regulator to a stop. From here the inner cable runs around a pulley and down to the sliding glass bracket. The motor upper cable (the DOWN cable) runs to the combined stop and guide block at the bottom of the regulator, the inner cable then connecting to the glass bracket. Note also that you need to have the glass bracket positioned roughly midway along its travel - we started out with ours at the lower extreme of its travel and discovered that it's impossible to get the cables disconnected because they are covered by the lower end of the guide. Finally, note that the 'DOWN cable' is significantly longer than the 'UP cable', and this is a good guide during installation - to make life even easier, mark one cable and its attachment points on the motor and regulator with paint dots or typist's correction fluid.

8 To free the cables, start by unhooking the 'UP cable' inner from the pulley at the top of the regulator - there is enough give in the system to allow this. The cable outer sits in a plastic stop which pushes over a metal tab, and can be lifted off.

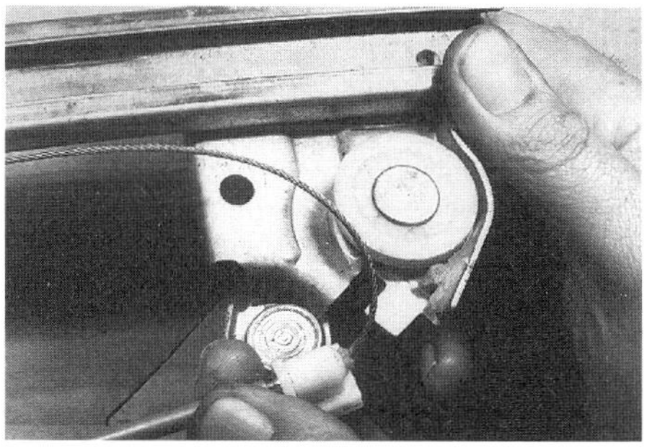

7/8 Pull cable stop from metal tab.

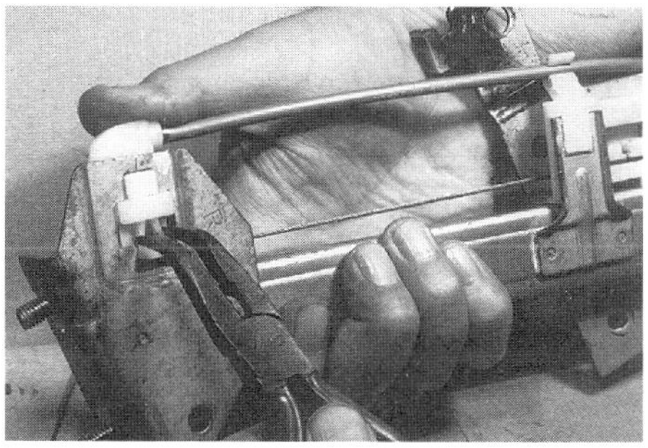

7/9a Squeeze tabs to ...

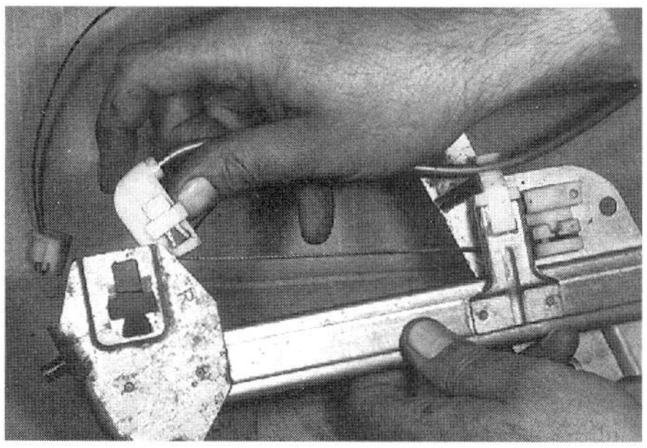

7/9b ... release guide/cable stop block.

9 Next, unclip the combined guide and stop from the lower end of the regulator. This has two tabs which retain it, and it can be slid out when these have been compressed.

10 The two inner cables will now be relatively slack, and you can unhook them from their shared anchor point on the glass bracket. Lift each cable end and feed it through the slot in the anchor block.

11 Moving to the motor end of the system,

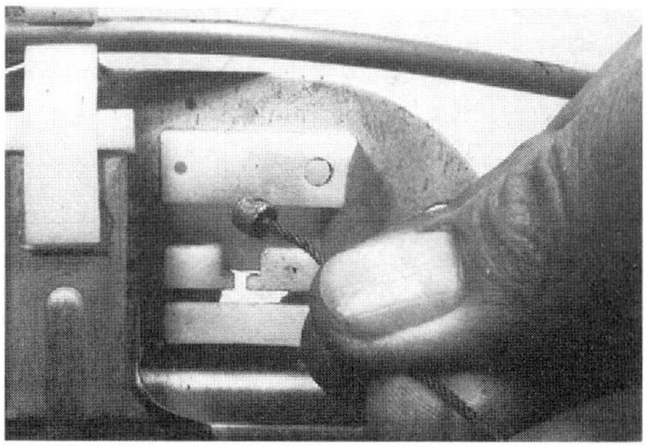

7/10 Release both cables from anchor point.

you will note that the two cables enter the motor gearbox casting through spring-loaded stops which seat in black plastic adjusters. Inside the gearbox housing, each cable is wound 2 1/2 times around the capstan before being anchored on one side. The capstan is driven off a square-section shaft from the motor gearbox.

12 Remove the two screws which retain the D-shaped capstan cover and remove it. The capstan will be seen in its recess in the gearbox casting and can be lifted out. Beware! As you lift out the capstan, the inner cable ends will spool off it, so as it comes away grasp the cable ends between finger and thumb to prevent this happening. Unwind each cable in turn and unhook its end from the capstan to free it.

13 This is about as far as you will want to go with the teardown - you won't get motor parts, and given the relative inaccessibility of the motors, if you have a motor fault, fit a new one. Even if the cables are intact, check them closely. If you see any sign of fraying or other damage, fit a new one to avoid subsequent failure in service.

14 Fit the end of the (longer) DOWN cable through the hole in the motor gearbox casting nearest the motor body, and the shorter UP cable

7/13 Basic motor unit. Replace if faulty.

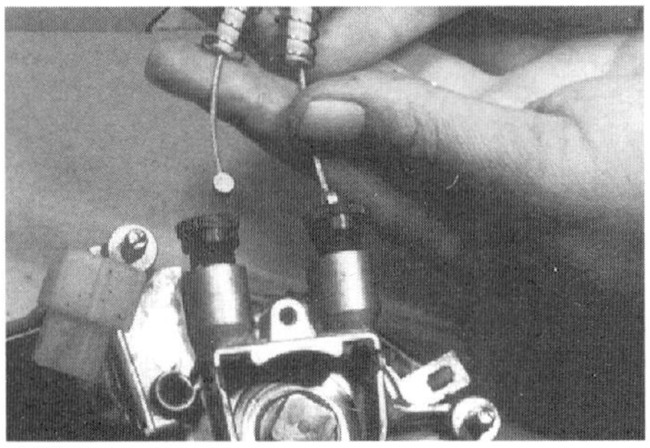

7/14 Slide cable ends thru ferrules - see text.

through the remaining hole.

15 + Attach the cable ends to their holes in the capstan, the UP cable end being uppermost and visible when the capstan is installed (the capstan will only fit one way). Note that each cable should be wound 2 1/2 turns around the capstan, the UP cable running counterclockwise and the DOWN cable running clockwise. Hold the cables between finger and thumb to prevent them unwinding again.

16 + Grease the capstan and cables thoroughly, then install the capstan assembly in its

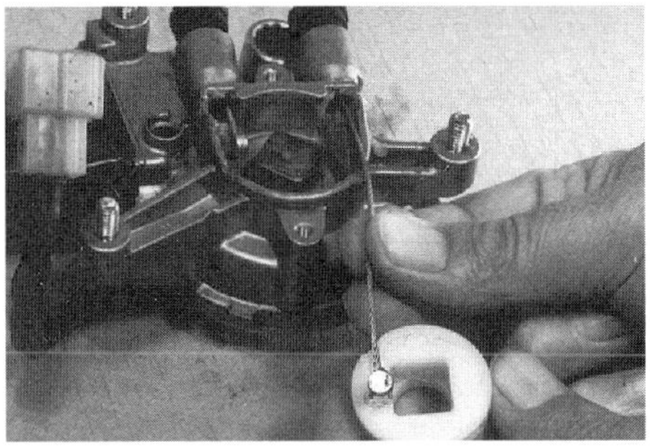

7/15a Place cable end in capstan recess ...

7/15b ... 2.5 turns around capstan ...

7/15c ... repeat with second cable ...

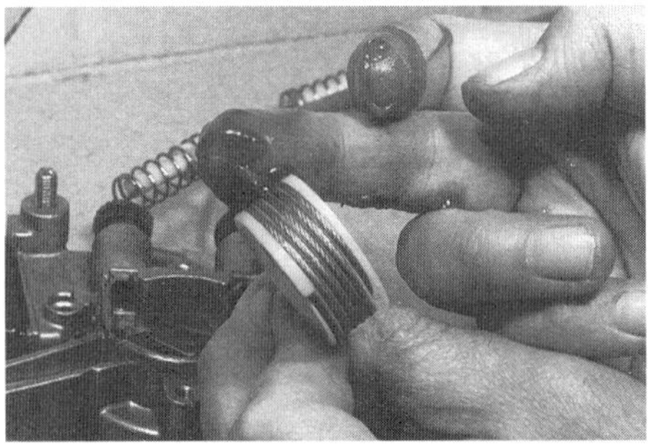

7/16a ... grease cables & capstan then fit ...

7/16b ... capstan & secure with cover.

recess. Fit the capstan cover and secure it with its two screws. The black plastic adjusters provide coarse initial adjustment and probably won't need to be disturbed - on our project car they were very tight in their threads, so take care if you do need to reset them.

17 + Hook both cable ends onto the glass bracket. Feed the DOWN cable inner through the slot in the side of its combined stop and guide block, then fit the block into its hole in the base of the regulator, snapping it home until the tabs lock it in position. Connect the DOWN cable inner end to the block on the glass bracket. Attach the UP

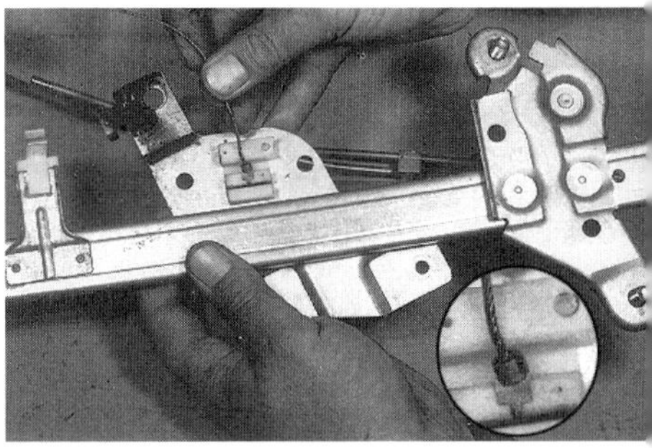

7/17a Hook both cables into anchor.

7/17b Fit stop, run cable around pulley.

cable end to the other side of the block, then fit the upper stop over its locating tab and run the cable around the pulley - the springs at the motor end allow enough movement to facilitate this.

18 Before you install the assembly, we suggest that you temporarily reconnect the battery and motor wiring and check that the mechanism runs smoothly throughout its range. If you do this, take care not to get your fingers in the way - the mechanism is quite powerful and you could get hurt. When you're satisfied that all is well, install the mechanism and motor in the door ☞ 10/6.

8. WINDOW LIFT SYSTEM (MANUAL) - CHECKING & OVERHAUL

☞ 1/1, 2.

1 As we mentioned in the preceding section, there really isn't much difference between the manual and power window systems. On the manual version, the winder motor and gearbox are replaced by a manual equivalent operated manually by a handle.

2 We should come clean at this point and admit that we have not worked on a manual

system. However, the regulator mechanism is identical, and as far as we can tell, the connection/disconnection details for the cables at the drive end are the same. Refer to coverage of the power lift system (☞ 10/7), making allowances for the absence of the motor and gearbox unit.

9. DOOR GLASS - ALIGNMENT CHECKS & ADJUSTMENT

☞ 1/1, 2.

1 Before you attempt to adjust the door window glass, be certain that it *is* the glass which requires adjustment. If you have just dismantled and overhauled the window winder mechanism or have fitted new parts in the door, then this is quite possible, but bear in mind that other factors can affect the seal between the glass and the hard top or soft top; if the window mechanism has not been disturbed, check the door adjustment (☞ 11/9), the weatherstrip and overall roof alignment on soft top cars (☞ 11/15) and the hard top alignment/fitting (☞ 11/14). If you are changing from a hard top to a soft top or vice versa, it's probable that you will need to check the glass adjustment

2 With the window wound fully up, check the fit of the glass against the weatherseal. This is made of soft foam section and will permit a degree of misalignment, but the edge of the glass should touch evenly all round. If the top edge of the glass is too high or too low, you need to look at vertical adjustment. If the angle of the glass in relation to the opening is wrong, you have a horizontal adjustment problem. It is a good idea to mark the existing position of the glass on the weatherseal before you alter any adjustments. Remove the door trim and associated components ☞ 10/6. Also, familiarize yourself with the glass stop bolt and guide bolt positions.

VERTICAL ADJUSTMENT

3 To alter the vertical position of the glass, you need to reposition the two stops which limit the upward travel of the glass. Wind the glass down a fraction, slacken the two stop bolts and move the stops to the required position, then tighten the bolts. Now wind the window fully up and check that it is correctly positioned. Repeat the procedure until the glass is aligned correctly. The official adjustment position is to set the glass so that the top edge is positioned 7.4-11.4 mm (0.29-0.45 in) from the inside of the weatherseal retainer. Note that this measurement is made with the weatherseal removed. The glass edge should be equidistant from the retainer across the top edge.

HORIZONTAL ADJUSTMENT

4 This adjustment is made by slackening the window regulator and glass guide nuts on the bottom edge of the door, and altering the angle of both components. This has the effect of changing the angle of the glass in relation to the weatherstrip. Position the guides so that the glass touches the weatherstrip evenly around the opening. After adjustment, check that the glass moves smoothly throughout its travel, and that it seals correctly.

FORE-AND-AFT ADJUSTMENT

5 This adjustment controls the angle of the side edges of the glass in relation to the weatherseal. Adjustment is made after slackening the nuts securing the top of the regulator and glass guides, and moving them to alter the fore-and-aft angle. Note that this adjustment may affect the vertical and horizontal settings.

ADJUSTMENT CHECKS

6 If you have adjusted the glass, you need to check the following points before final tightening and installation of the door trim and fittings. With the weatherstrip detached;

- *The glass should contact both stops simultaneously as the glass is raised.*
- *The glass must be correctly positioned when fully closed.*

Install the weatherstrip, then verify that;

- *The glass raises and lowers smoothly with the door closed.*
- *The weatherstrip is aligned correctly.*
- *The weatherstrip is mounted correctly.*

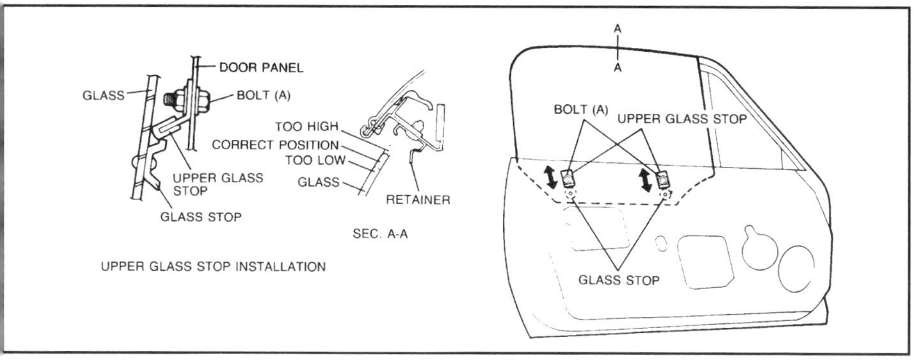

D9/3 DOOR GLASS ALIGNMENT DETAILS.

10. DOOR LATCH AND LOCK ASSEMBLY - REMOVAL, OVERHAUL & INSTALLATION

REMOVAL

1 Before attempting to work on the door latch or lock assemblies, you will need to remove the door trim components (☞ 10/5) and set the window glass fully up. Once you've done this, make sure that you have disabled the stereo security system, then disconnect the battery negative (-) lead to isolate the electrical system (☞ 7/2).

2 With the door trim and the inner plastic sheet removed, you will be able to see the interior door handle and the control rods which run back to the door latch mechanism inside the door. The upper rod controls door locking, and runs back to a bellcrank, which in turn connects through a curved rod to the door latch mechanism. The lower rod operates the door latch itself and connects directly to the mechanism.

3 Disconnect the upper rod at the bellcrank end, and the lower rod at the interior door handle end. The rod ends are retained by plastic swivel clips - unclip them from the rod and turn through 90° until the rod end can be disengaged. The clips can be left in position.

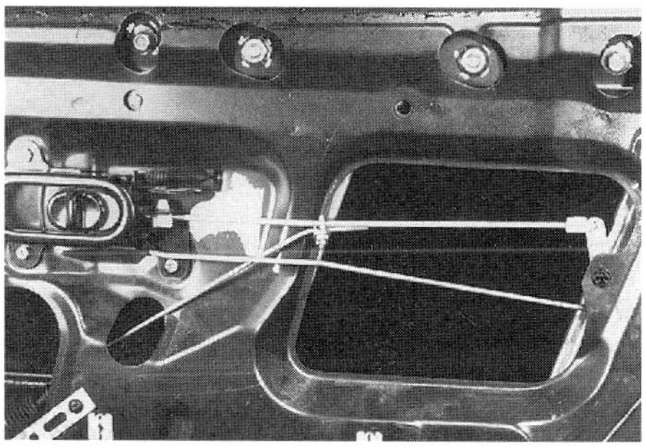

10/2 Control rods (inc.non-std electric lock).

4 On our project car, aftermarket central locking was fitted, and a third rod was connected from the central locking solenoid to the middle of the upper (locking) rod where it was clamped in position. If you encounter a similar arrangement, mark the relationship between the two rods with an indelible pen or paint marker, then remove the clamp to disengage the extra rod.

5 Remove the three screws which retain the interior door handle assembly to the door inner skin, using a crosshead screwdriver or 8 mm nut spinner, and lift the assembly away.

6 The door latch mechanism and the exterior door handle are both removed from inside the door, working through the apertures in the inner skin. It is not easy to see exactly how they are interconnected, and even less easy to disconnect the rods running between them. We found that the best method was to release the fasteners holding each assembly to the door, and to disconnect the rods as they were maneuvered out of the door.

7 Remove the three countersunk screws which secure the latch to the back edge of the door, working from the outside. The latch can now be maneuvered partway out of the door, but is still connected by two rods to the exterior handle and a third to the bellcrank.

8 + Reach up into the door cavity to the back of the exterior handle and free the end of the thinner of the two rods which run up from the latch. This is secured by another plastic swivel clip. Now disconnect the thicker rod at the latch end. This rod is threaded, and is secured by a plastic clip. It can be repositioned to give rough adjustment, so mark the relationship of the rod and the clip with paint

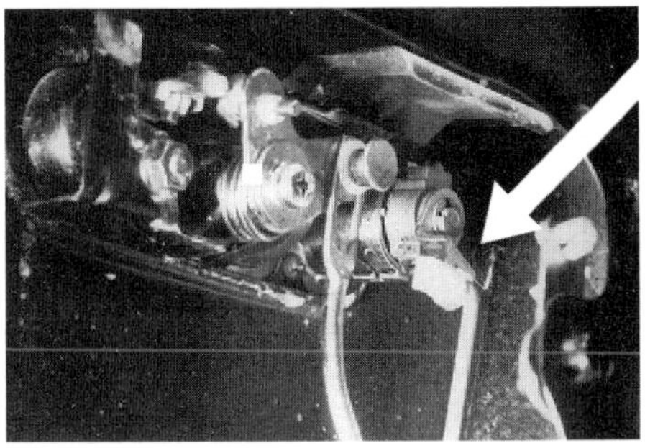

10/8a Swivel clip arrowed.

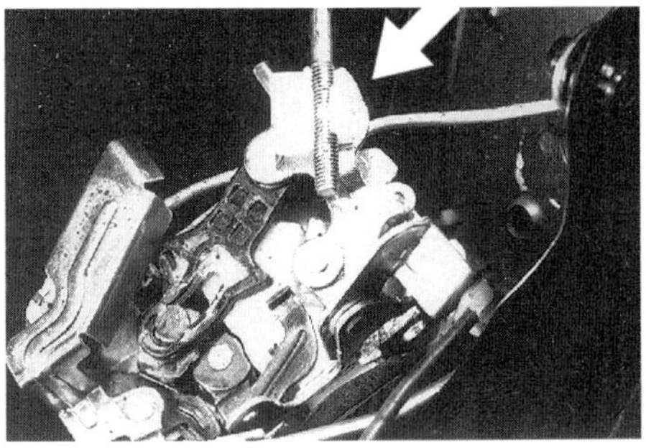

10/8b Adjustable clip arrowed.

before disconnecting it.

9 Feel inside the door skin and locate the latch end of the bellcrank. This has a similar plastic swivel clip to those described earlier, and this should be disconnected at the latch end, leaving the rod attached to the bellcrank. The bellcrank will allow enough movement for this to be achieved. The latch mechanism is now free and can be removed from the door.

10 Working through the door aperture, and through the nearby access hole, remove the two 10 mm nuts which retain the exterior handle to the bracket inside the door. The handle can now be displaced and removed, feeding the remaining rod through the door outer skin as you do so.

11 The only part of the mechanism remaining in place is the bellcrank, which will not normally require attention. If you do need to remove it, it is held in place by a plastic mounting, which can be released by squeezing together the locating tabs.

OVERHAUL

12 We suggest at this stage that you temporarily reassemble the connecting rods between the latch and exterior handle so you can see how the mechanism works, and to make installation a little less puzzling. There is little point in attempting further general dismantling, but if there is a problem with either assembly, you may be able to figure it out and rectify it. It is a good idea to clean the assemblies (try using switch cleaner) and to lubricate the moving parts.

13 + The most likely item to fail is the lock cylinder, and this can be removed after the wire retainer clip has been removed using a small screwdriver blade. Note that if you need to fit a new barrel, try to get one which matches the remaining locks on the car, or replace all of the cylinders with identical units, or you will have to carry an assortment of keys with you.

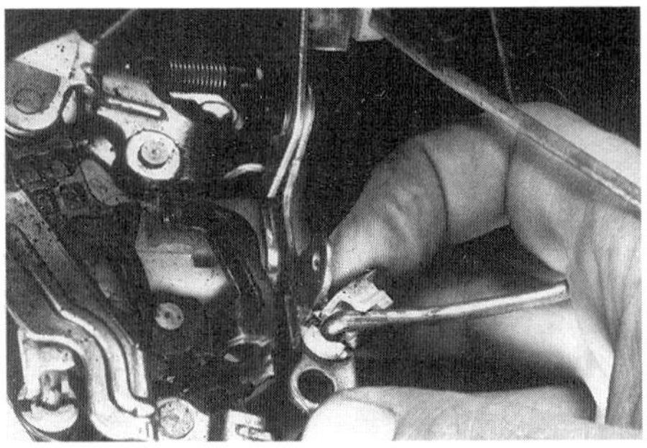

10/9 Latch end swivel clip.

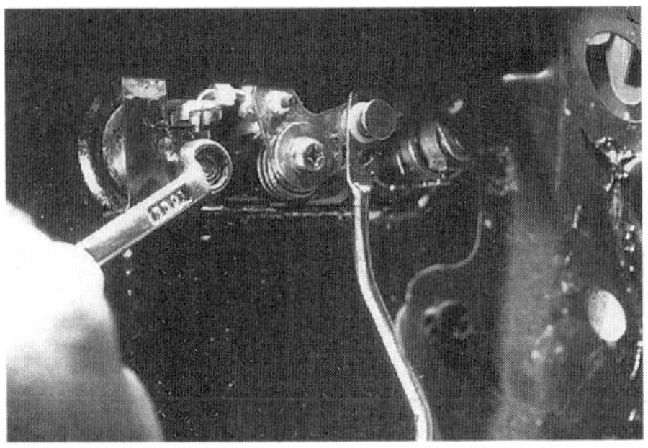

10/10 Handle/lock mechanism fixed by nuts.

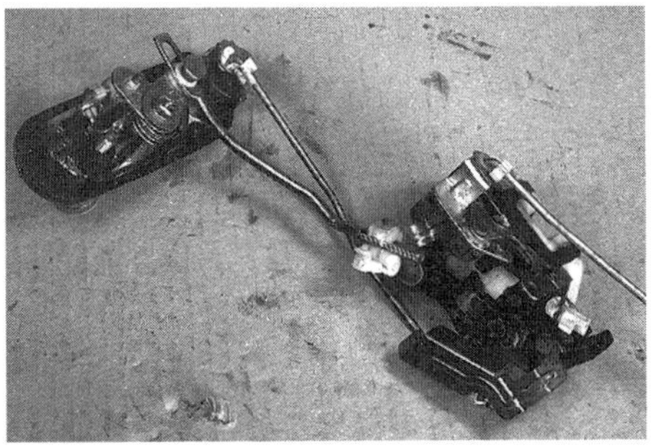

10/12 Control rods temporarily reassembled.

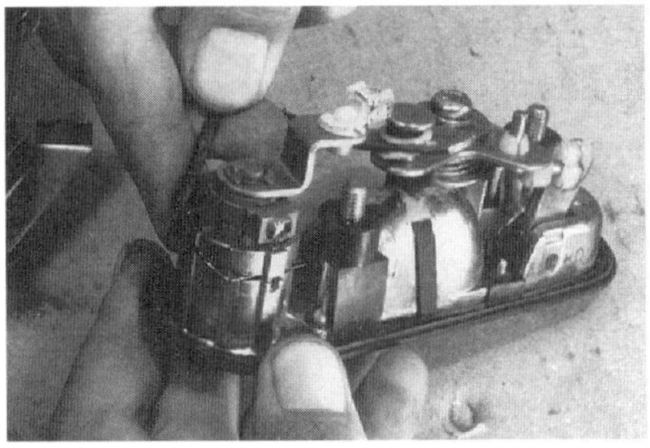

10/13a Release spring clip ...

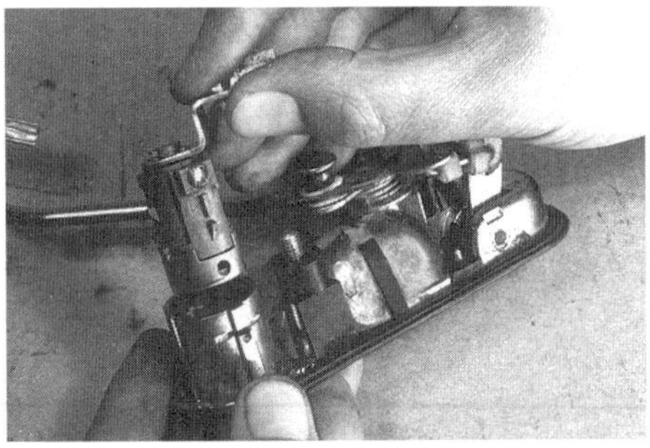

10/13b ... & withdraw lock barrel.

INSTALLATION

14 Install the exterior handle, securing it with its two nuts, which should be tightened to 7.8-11.0 Nm (80-110 kgf cm / 69-95 lbf in).

15 Reassemble the various link rods between the exterior handle and the door latch, remembering to align the paint marks made on the threaded rod end and its retainer. Reconnect the latch to bellcrank rod.

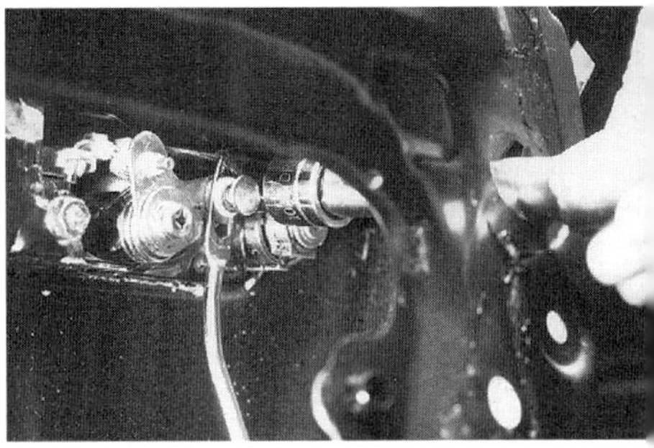

10/14 Torque tighten handle/lock fixing nuts.

10/17 How it should look.

16 Install the latch assembly, tightening the mounting screws to 4.2-6.2 Nm (43-63 kgf cm / 40-55 lbf in).

17 To give you some idea of how it all looks when fitted, we got our Technical Adviser, Wally, to photograph the assembly in the door. It may not be a truly great photograph, but like Wally said, *you* try getting your head, floodlights and a 35 mm camera inside a Miata/MX5 door!

AFTERMARKET CENTRAL LOCKING

18 + Although not strictly a part of this

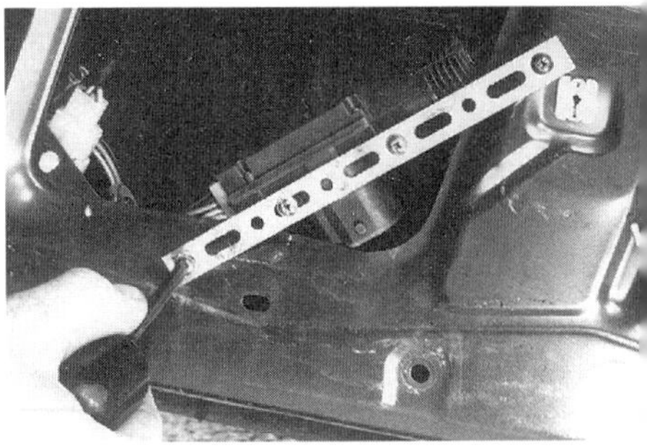

10/18a Electric lock mounted on metal strap.

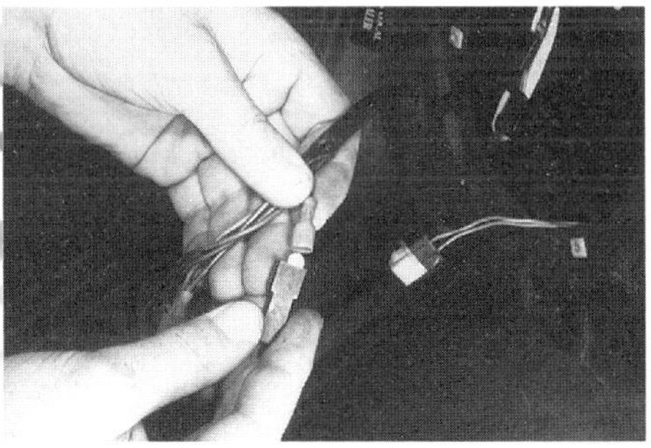

10/18b Connect & route non-std wiring carefully.

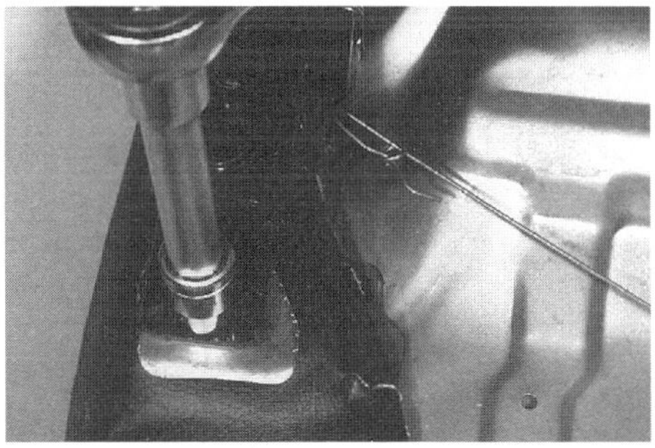

11/3 Check security of seat runners.

11/5b Remove knuckle retaining bolts.

manual, our car had a pretty typical add-on central locking system fitted as part of an alarm installation. As we mentioned earlier, this connects to the locking rod from the interior handle, the solenoid being mounted as shown inside the door skin. One point worth noting - if you add any electrical item inside the door, make sure that any wiring is well away from the window mechanism: it, or the accessory, may be damaged as the window glass is raised and lowered.

11. SEATS - REMOVAL, CHECKING, O/HAUL & INSTALLATION

☞ 1/1, 2.

Warning! Take care when working on the seat components - especially in areas where pressed steel parts are normally covered by trim or upholstery. Some of these parts have razor-sharp edges - ask Wally, he still carries the scars.

REMOVAL

1 The seats are retained by four 14 mm bolts which pass through the seat runners into the floor of the car. The bolts used are unusual in that the hexagon heads are slightly tapered. It is important that you use a close fitting wrench or socket during removal, or the hexagon will be damaged. We suggest that you use only a hexagon pattern socket or box wrench - a conventional bi-hexagon socket is more likely to slip.

2 On cars equipped with the optional headrest speakers, trace and disconnect the speaker wiring connector. Slide the seat right back, and remove the two front mounting bolts. Now slide the seat forward and tip the seat back as far forward as you can to improve access to the rear mounting bolts. Remove the bolts and lift the seat out of the car.

CHECKING

3 Check the security of the seat runners after inverting the seat. If they have worked loose, the mounting bolts can be tightened after positioning the runners so that the bolt heads can be accessed through the holes provided. Check that the runners move smoothly. If they seem stiff in operation, use aerosol grease to lubricate them, taking care not to get overspray on the upholstery. Check the operation of the recliner mechanism (**Warning!** Watch out - the seat back is strongly spring loaded!).

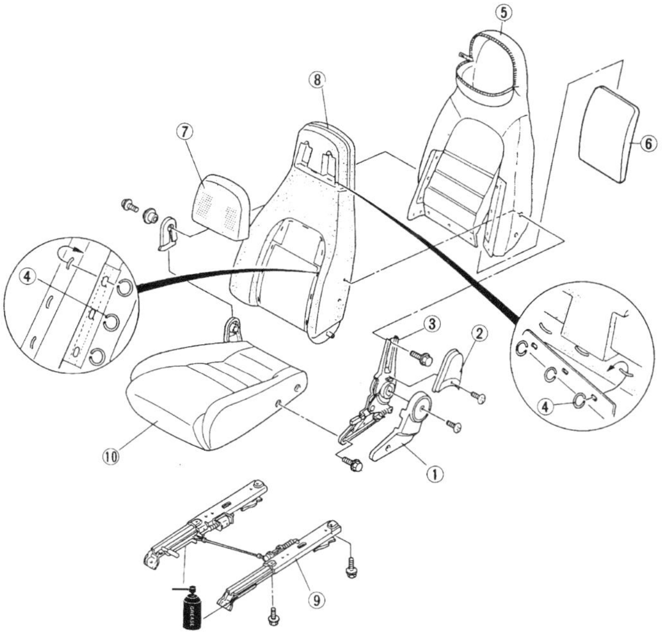

D11/5 SEAT CONSTRUCTION DETAIL.
1 Knuckle cover trim. 2 Side cover trim. 3 Recliner knuckle (hinge). 4 Hog ring. 5 Seat cover. 6 Lumbar pad. 7 Speaker cover. 8 Backrest frame. 9 Seat runner/slide. 10 Seat cushion/squab.

OVERHAUL

4 Seat teardown for overhaul is as follows. Position the runners so that you can reach the mounting bolts through the access holes. Remove the runners and adjuster lever as an assembly, noting the arrangement of the link wire which runs between the two latch mechanisms. Apart from cleaning and greasing the runner assemblies, you can do little else to repair them. If they are damaged or distorted, fit new runner assemblies.

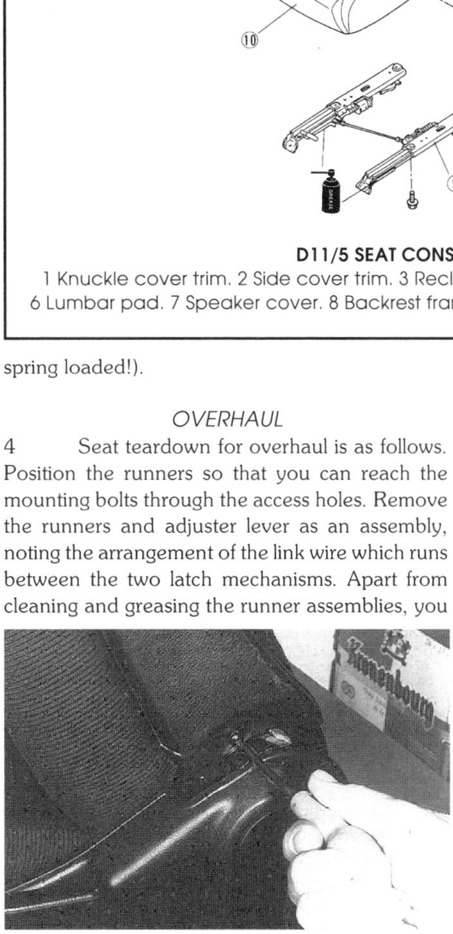

11/5a Remove screw, then side cover.

5 The accompanying drawing shows how the seat components fit together. You need to detach the knuckle from the outer side of the seat to separate the seat back from the seat cushion. Start by removing the crosshead screw which retains the side cover and lift the cover away. You can now remove the 14 mm bolts with ease, but the recliner knuckle cover is a different can of worms altogether ...

6 First, remove the two crosshead screws which secure the plastic cover. In the illustration, it looks as if the lower cover will just lift away. It might on your car, in which case, great. On ours, the cover was different, and couldn't be maneuvered over the recliner lever. We had to twist and turn the cover so that we could get the knuckle unbolted. It is possible, but not easy. Refer to the accompanying photos. Start by turning the cover so that the front bolt can be removed - this is pretty easy to do. The rear bolt, however, requires the cover to be twisted upwards for access. Slacken

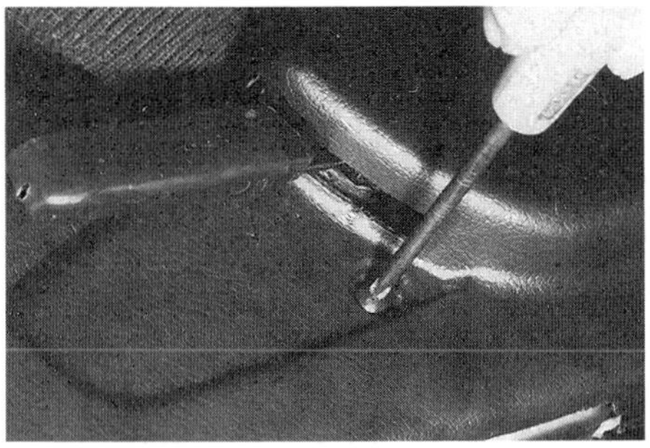

11/6a Remove trim retaining screw.

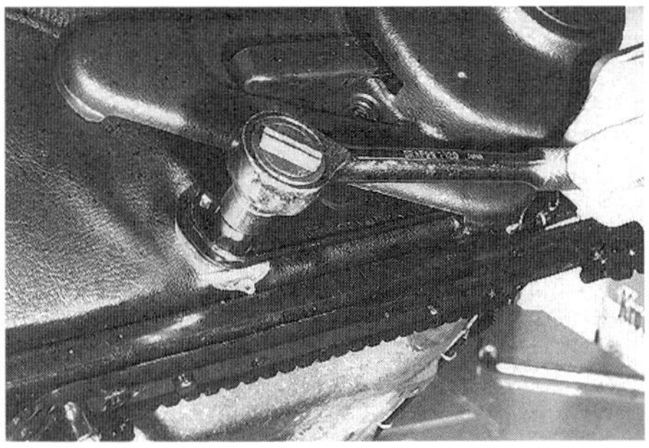

11/6b Twist cover to give access to bolt ...

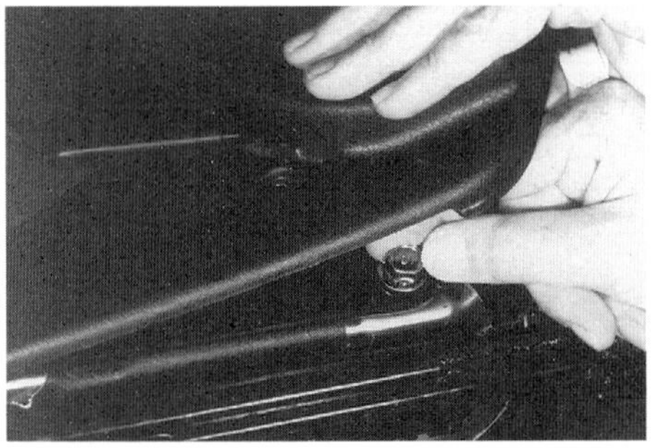

11/6c ... at each end.

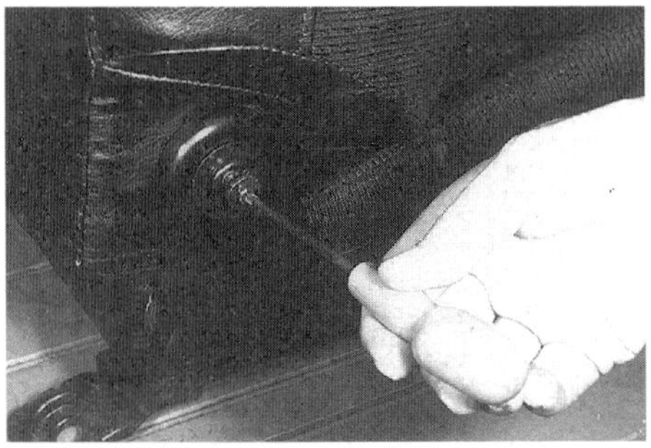

11/7a Remove screw and collar ...

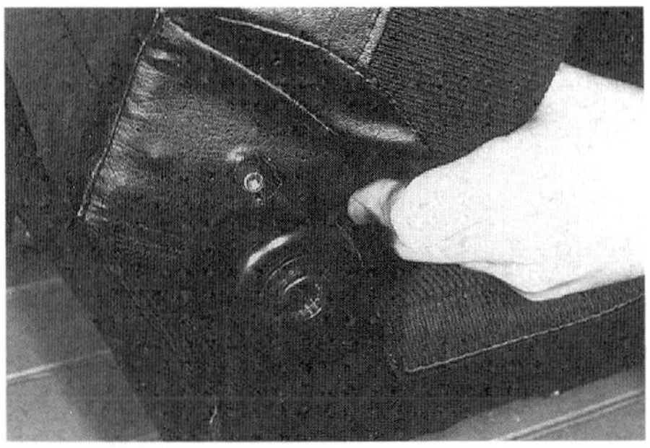

11/7b ... & pry out bush to release seat back.

11/7c This is as close as you can get.

the bolt with a crescent or box-end wrench, then remove it with your fingers.

7 Once you've got the knuckle detached, the inner side of the seat is secured on a short pivot pin. Remove the screw and collar, then pry out the headed bush and slide off the cover, the seat back can be disengaged and removed. Don't even think about trying to take the recliner mechanism apart - you can't, and even if you did, the heavy spring used would be impossible to retension. If it's broken, fit a new one.

8 If you need to do so, the seat covers

11/8 Open/close hog rings with pliers.

can be removed after releasing the hog rings which retain them. Use pliers to remove the rings, which can be kept and reused. The top of the seat back cover has a concealed zipper. This can be undone to allow you access to the headrest speaker recesses. The recesses are there on all cars, so you could install your own speakers if you can find suitable units to fit the small recesses. Note also that a removable lumbar support pad is fitted in the seat back.

9 When reassembling the seat, fit the covers, if removed, and secure them with the hog rings. Reassemble the inner pivot and cover and fit the securing bolt. You will need to reverse the wrestling process to fit the knuckle on the outer side of the seat. Tighten the knuckle mounting bolts to 34-56 Nm (3.5-5.7 kgf m / 25-41 lbf ft).

INSTALLATION

10 Check that the seat runners are secure on the seat base, and that they lie parallel. Tip the seat back fully forward. Lower the seat into the car and fit the rear mounting bolts. Slide the seat fully rearward and recline the seat back. Fit the front mounting bolts. Tighten all four bolts to 38-51 Nm (3.9-5.2 kgf m / 28-38 lbf ft). Where fitted, reconnect the headrest speaker wiring.

12. CARPETS - REMOVAL & INSTALLATION

☞ 1/1, 2.

1 Before the main carpet section can be removed, you will first need to remove the following:

Seats (☞ 10/6)
Dash panel assembly (☞ 10/4)
Heater unit (☞ 6/14)
Package shelf carpet (see following text)
Front side trim, scuff plates, and quarter trim (☞ 10/5)

2 Start by removing the package shelf carpet. This is secured by a couple of crosshead screws and cup washers, two round plastic stops secured by crosshead screws, plus numerous plastic clips around the edge of the carpet. When removing the clips, use a pair of screwdriver blades or cranked needle-nosed pliers under the head of the pin and lever each one out. Don't be tempted to pull on the carpet - it will just pull off over the head of the pin. Remove the section of carpet

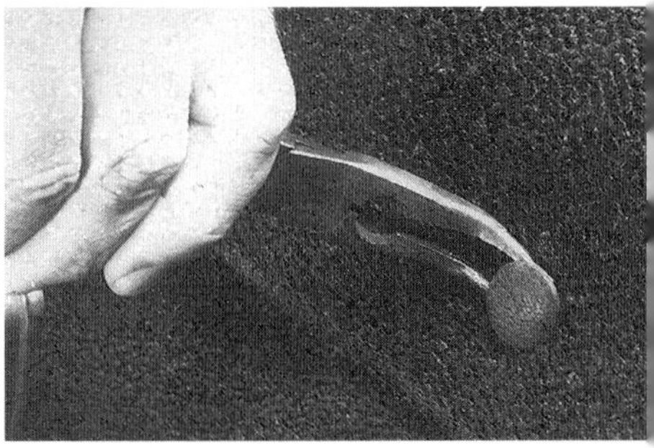

12/2 Clips can be released by cranked pliers.

which covers the bodywork behind the seat backs, again by pulling out the plastic pins which secure it.

3 Remove the remaining items listed above. With the interior of the car clear, remove the footrest from the driver's side footwell (two 10 mm nuts) and the dash center panel lower mounting bracket (two sheet metal screws). Lift the main carpet away, checking for any missed obstructions as you do so. It is likely that there will be minor variations between models of different years or markets, and further minor dismantling may be needed if interior fixtures are impeding removal.

4 When installing the carpet, make sure

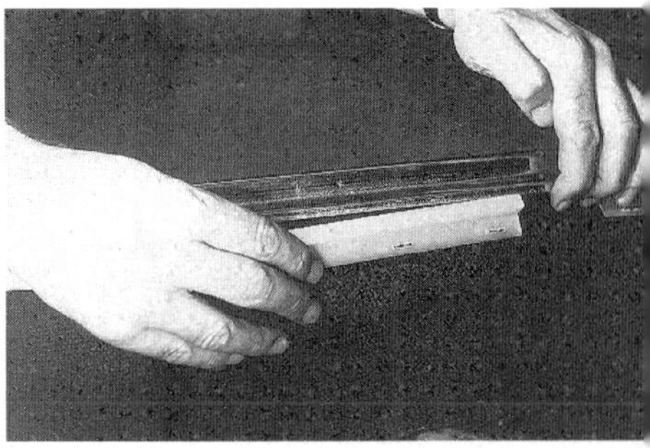

12/4 Hook channel over metal seam.

that it sits flat in the car, and that the edges are correctly positioned. At each door opening there is a plastic channel section which hooks over the seam edge - fit this, then secure the carpet at this point with the scuff plates. Once you are satisfied that the carpet is positioned correctly, install the components removed for access, referring to the relevant chapters and sections mentioned above for fitting details and tightening torques. In view of the work needed to remove the carpet, we would recommend that you consider fitting small floormats in each footwell where wear is heaviest. If you do this, be sure that pedal movement is not obstructed.

13. TRUNK CARPET & TRIM - REMOVAL & INSTALLATION

☞ 1/1, 2.

1 + The trunk carpet can be removed after the spare wheel has been lifted out and the two plastic nuts and the snap fasteners which retain the battery cover have been released and the cover removed. When installing the carpet, make sure it aligns correctly around the spare wheel fixing point and battery area, and that the cover section over the tool well on the left side of the car fit properly.

2 + There is a pressed steel access cover concealing the fuel filler and vent hoses. This can be detached after unclipping the jack handle and removing the 10 mm bolts which retain it. There is no need to remove the trunk carpet for access.

3 + At the very back of the trunk there is a molded trim cover across the back panel. This is held by plastic clips, and these must be released by lifting the center section of the clip (it looks like a plastic rivet head sitting in a cup washer) with a small screwdriver blade. Once lifted, grasp the whole pin and withdraw it. Repeat this procedure on the remaining clips and lift the trim cover away. Again, no other parts of the trunk trim affect its removal or installation.

13/1d ... and lift out battery cover.

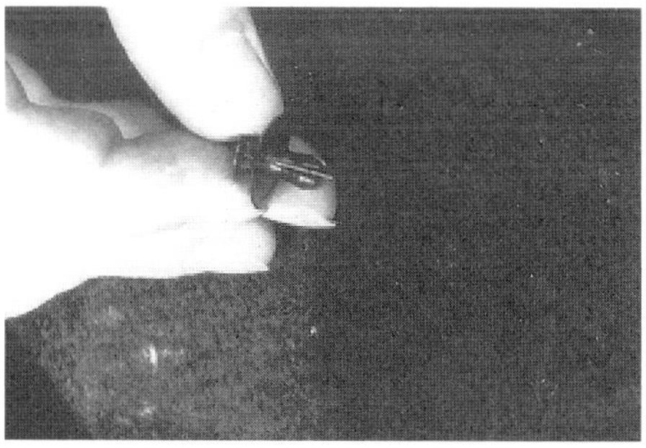
13/3b ... then pull out clip body.

14. SEATBELTS - REMOVAL, CHECKING & INSTALLATION

1 To gain access to the seatbelts you must first remove the rear quarter trim ☞ 10/5. On cars so equipped, trace and disconnect the seatbelt warning switch wiring connector.

2 + Pry off and remove the plastic cover which conceals the head of the upper mounting bolt. Slacken the bolt using a 17 mm socket. Once again, there appears to be variation between various models and markets of the spacer and washer arrangement used here - make a careful note of the order in which these are fitted. Note that it is likely that belts from different suppliers may be fitted, and this may affect the details of the mounting arrangement.

3 + Remove the 17 mm mounting bolt which secures the inertia reel mechanism to the

10

13/1a Remove spare wheel ...

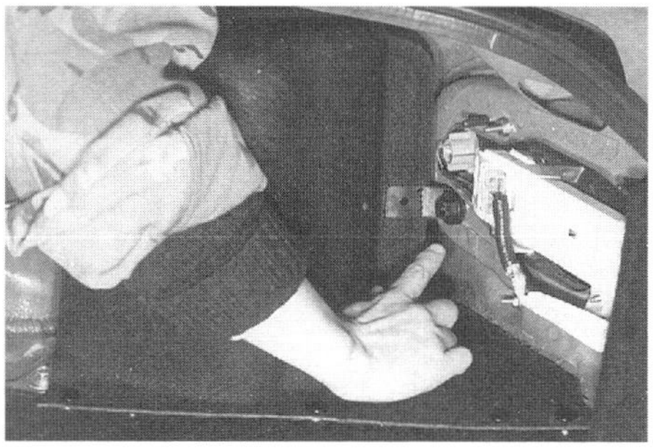
13/1b ... release this 'nut' and ...

13/1c ... this one, release studs at base ...

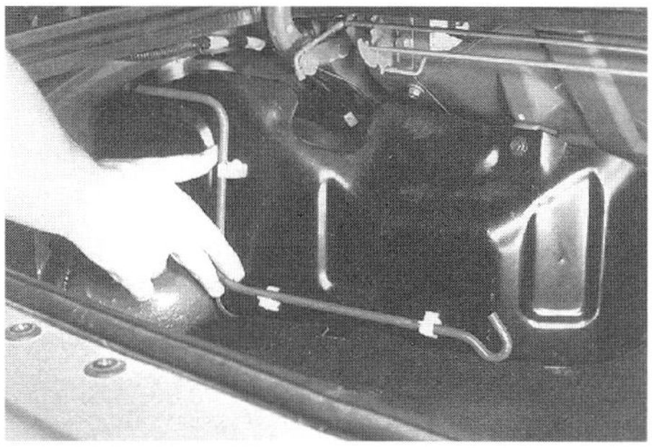
13/2a Remove jack handle from clips & ...

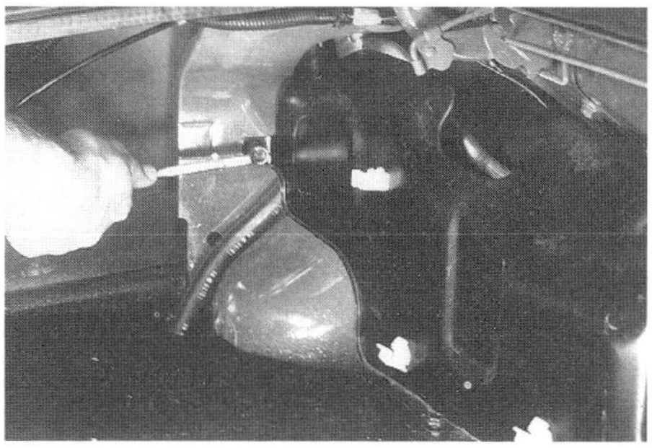
13/2b ... then remove access panel bolts.

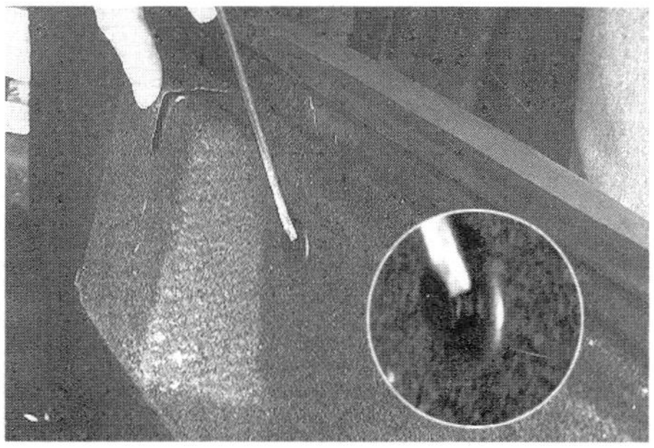
13/3a Use screwdriver to pry up clip center ...

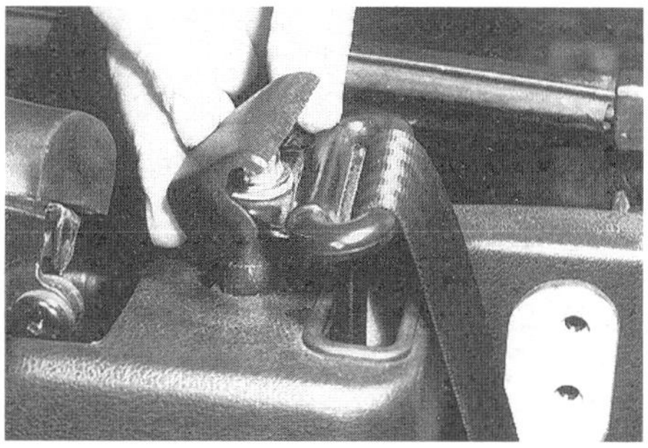
14/2a Remove covering trim ...

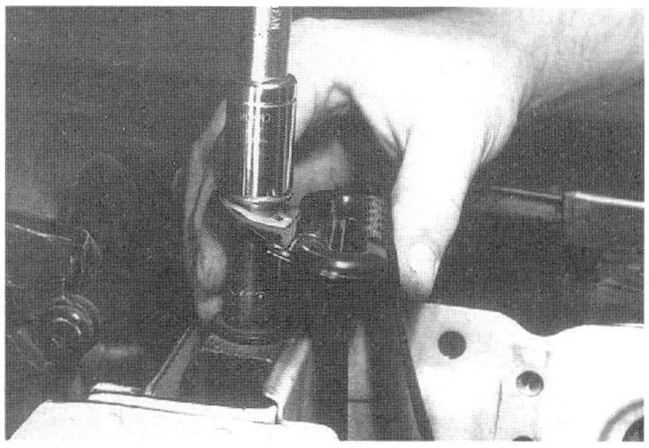
14/2b ... & unscrew top anchor bolt.

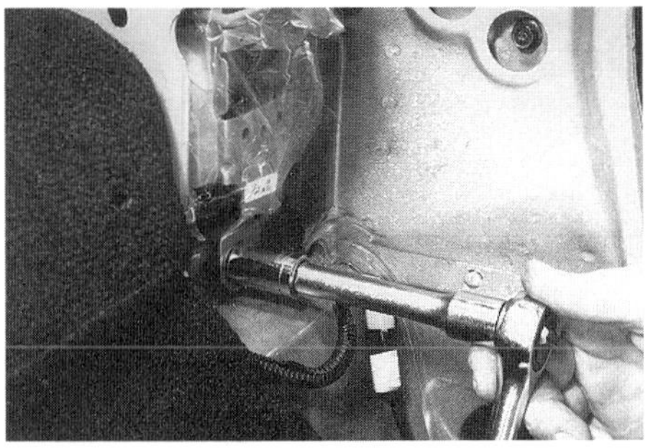

14/3a Remove the inertia reel's anchor bolt ...

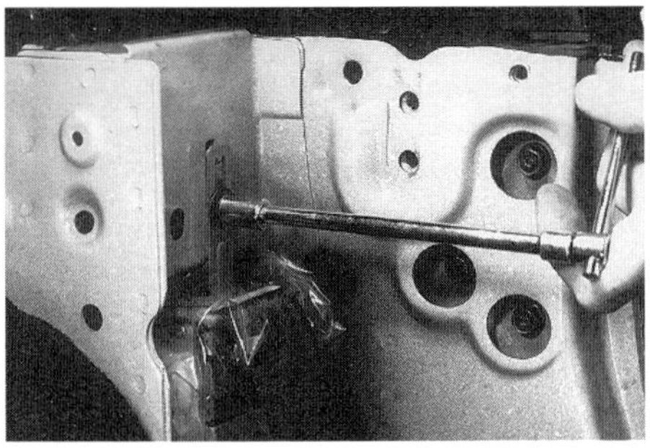

14/3b ... followed by alignment bolt ...

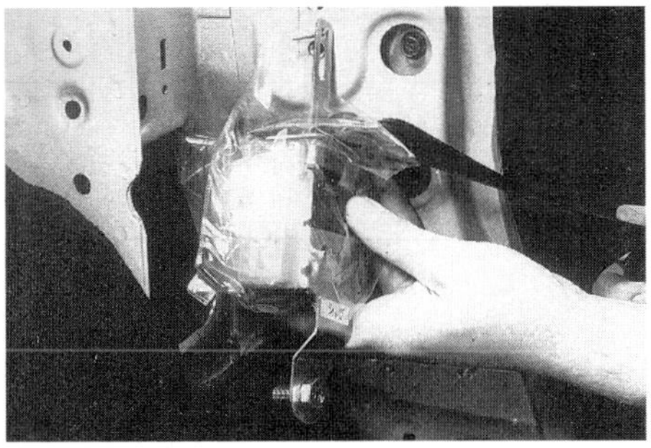

14/3c ... then lift away inertia reel.

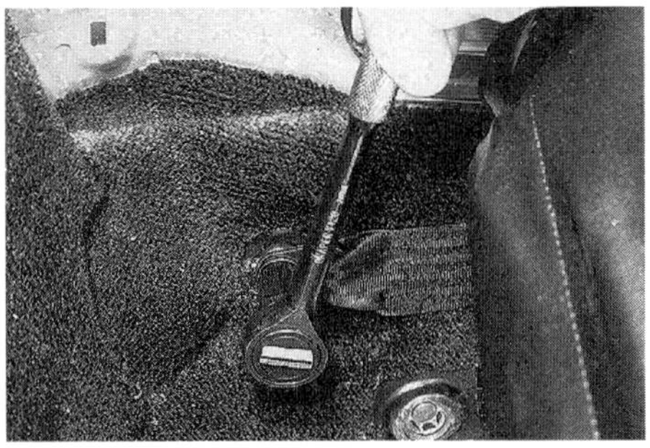

14/3d Final anchor bolt is on side of tunnel.

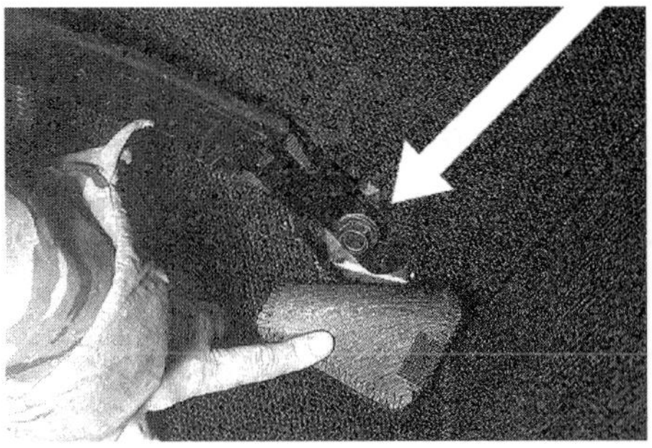

14/4 Buckle section has single anchor bolt.

body recess, followed by the smaller 10 mm bolt which aligns the mechanism at the top. Free the lower end of the belt by removing the 17 mm fixing bolt, again noting the arrangement of spacers used.

4 If removal is necessary, the buckle section can be freed by unscrewing the 17 mm mounting bolt which secures it to the transmission tunnel. As the buckle is removed, note the order of the spacer and washers used.

5 **Warning!** Once removed, the seatbelt mechanism must not be dismantled or interfered with - if there is a fault in the inertia reel mechanism, or if the belt webbing is frayed or cut, a new seatbelt must be installed. Check that the reel mechanism allows the belt to extend smoothly and easily when it is pulled gently with the mechanism held upright. Next, check that the reel mechanism locks if the belt is pulled out quickly or jerked, or when the reel mechanism is inclined at 30° or more from the vertical position. If this is not the case, fit a new belt.

6 Check that the buckle mechanism latches positively and reliably. If your car has seatbelt warning switches in the buckle mechanism, check the switch for continuity between the connector terminals. You should read continuity while the belt is released and no continuity when it is buckled.

7 When installing the belt assembly, fit the spacers and washers in the same order as they were removed. Tighten all of the 17 mm bolts to 38-78 Nm (3.9-8.0 kgf m / 28-58 lbf ft). Install the rear quarter trim and connect the seatbelt warning switch wiring (where fitted). Check that the belt operates normally.

© Miata Magazine 1990.

11

BODY

1. INTRODUCTION

This chapter relates to the main body assembly and the various panels and doors which form part of it, plus items like the convertible top and optional hard top. We cover all areas of repair and overhaul appropriate to the enthusiast and which can be dealt with at home using normal tools and equipment - major body repairs on any car require specialist facilities, and as such should be left to a Mazda dealer or body shop.

The Miata/MX5 features a conventional unitary body constructed from welded steel pressings. On the underside of the body, the engine, transmission and front suspension assembly are mounted via a fabricated steel crossmember or subframe. At the back of the car, a second subframe carries the rear axle and suspension components. The two subframes are linked by the PPF ('Power Plant Frame').

The visible parts of the bodyshell comprise of various hinged, welded and bolt-on panels; the doors, the hood (bonnet) and trunk (boot) lids, plus the front and rear bumper assemblies. Most of the visible body area is of steel construction, though items like the bumpers are of color-matched plastic. Many aftermarket add-on body parts will be made from plastic moldings too.

2. BODY - MAINTENANCE & COSMETIC CARE

WHY MAINTENANCE MATTERS

1 Maintenance is very much the keyword where the car's body is concerned, especially if you want to be your own mechanic. As we mentioned above, major body repairs will require specialist equipment, and as such are outside the scope of most enthusiasts. If you intend to keep your Miata/MX5 in prime condition, the answer is regular maintenance. This will not just enhance the value of your car, it will help you keep an eye on any developing problem so that you can have it put right *before* it gets too expensive.

2 Body repairs have always posed a problem for the enthusiast owner, and the Miata/MX5 is no different in this respect. With just about any other part of the car, you can repair or replace it to keep the car running well. The bodyshell should be regarded as a single large component to which all the other mechanical assemblies are attached, and it is vital that this component in particular does not need to be replaced; when a car reaches the point at which the bodyshell has corroded badly or has sustained serious accident damage, economics usually dictate that it gets scrapped.

3 While you could probably get your Mazda dealer to order up a new body for you, the sheer cost and time involved in transferring all the other parts across would probably make this option unrealistic. (A little like replacing all the walls in your house - theoretically possible, but unworkable in practice). Next time you pass a wrecker's yard, just consider how and why all those cars got in there - the chances are that it was due to corrosion or damage to the body.

4 The simple answer to body maintenance is regular attention. You should wash the bodywork regularly to keep the paint in good condition - this is the first-line defense against corrosion. Washing will remove visible road dirt, and more importantly, the invisible chemical pollutants which will dull and damage the finish if ignored. Of equal importance is regular polishing. This seals the paint and protects it from attack from pollutants and chemicals. These two operations are especially important on modern cars - the types of paints used now are more environmentally-friendly but, seemingly, less durable than the older paints were.

WASHING

5 Wash the car using plenty of water - a hose or domestic pressure wash is ideal for this. Alternatively, use water from a bucket, but remember to change it regularly before the dirt turns it into an abrasive. To avoid any risk of damage to the paint finish, soak the bodywork thoroughly to soften the film of dirt, then gently hose it away using a soft brush or a sponge to agitate the dirt and loosen it. Don't scrub at the paintwork during this stage, or you will cause tiny scratches to form, dulling the finish.

6 By all means use a detergent additive in moderation - this will help shift the greasy road dirt which builds up where the car is used in areas of high traffic density (in other words, just about everywhere). Beware of using too much detergent or you will remove any body wax as well as the dirt. Whatever method and solution you use for the job, wash the car on an overcast day if possible, or park it in the shade while you work; if the sun is shining on the car and the paintwork heats up, you'll find that you will have problems with spotting as the water keeps drying out too fast.

7 All external parts of the car should be cleaned in this way, including the plastic body parts, the hard or convertible top and the wheels. Follow up by rinsing thoroughly with clean water. When rinsing down, check how the water lies on the hood or trunk lid - if it forms small beads, the wax coating is still good, while a continuous film tells you that it's time to wax the car. The paintwork can be dried off using an old (clean!) towel to prevent marking from the water droplets - some owners may prefer to use a traditional chamois leather; expensive, but effective. You may wish to try out some of the newer synthetic chamois leathers (the old ones were next to useless, but we hear that they've got better).

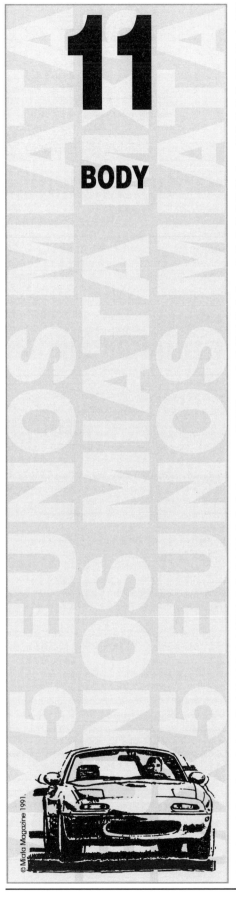

8 In the case of the wheels, note that they are lacquer-coated; don't use abrasive cleaners or you will damage the lacquer film and then rapid corrosion will set in. Never, ever, use a wire brush to clean them. If your car has signs of peeling lacquer, or damage has resulted from stone chips, have the wheels blasted and re-lacquered professionally before the alloy surface gets pitted by corrosion. If you encounter stubborn staining or marking of the wheels, you could try one of the specialist products formulated for use on alloy wheels. Check with the

store that it will not damage the protective lacquer coating before use.

9 Don't forget the wheel wells (wheelarches) or the lower edges of the rockers (sills) during regular washes. These areas are easily overlooked, and this explains why they are often the first areas to suffer corrosion problems - don't just deal with the easy-to-reach parts, or you'll get a nasty surprise when you do get round to them. Pay special attention to the lip which lies inside the edge of many panels. These are here to give strength and rigidity. Unfortunately, they also provide tiny ledges where dirt can often build up unnoticed until the paint begins to blister.

10 Inside each wheel well you'll notice plastic liners attached with 10 mm bolts. Be aware that road dirt can get behind these and build up - this can lead to corrosion problems if left too long. It is a good idea to remove the liners once in a while and clean out any buildup of dirt, especially to the rear of the wheels where most of it gets thrown by the tires. You can guard against corrosion here (and elsewhere) by applying a wax-based underbody coating before the liners are reinstalled.

11 Don't forget that road dirt contains all kinds of pollutants, many of which are corrosive. In temperate areas where the winter roads are salted to clear snow, salt corrosion is a real problem. If you drive your car all year round and live in such an area, during winter you need to wash the bodywork at least as often as during summer.

POLISHING

12 We recommend that you wax your car at least twice a year, or whenever water stops forming droplets on the hood. Spring and Fall are the best times - that way you get protection from summer sun and winter rain and snow. Polishing takes a little time to do, especially if you use a traditional, quality wax. On the other hand, we are talking about the Miata here, not a 30 foot RV - so you can afford to lavish attention on the body.

13 The choice of polish is up to you. There the are hi-tech wax-in-30-seconds products, and wax-as-you-wash additives. We've used them, and don't rate them very highly. The way we figure it, if the instant wax products work, why are there still expensive, labor-intensive traditional waxes on sale ... Take our advice, and use a traditional nonabrasive paste or cream body wax - you'll work hard a couple of times a year, but the rest of the time you can rest easy about your paint.

14 As with washing, waxing should be carried out on a dull day, or under shade, **never** in full sun or while the bodywork is still hot. Be sure to use really soft, clean rag for polishing and buffing the paint. Work on a small area at a time (we like to complete one panel at a time and then move to the next - that way, nothing gets missed). Apply the wax sparingly with a light circular action - if the paint has not been waxed for a long time and it soaks in, apply a little more. When it has dried to a white color, use a clean rag to buff to a good finish. Don't skip seams and crevices - they need waxing more than the flat areas. Finally, hand waxing is always preferable to using a power polisher. Frankly, on the Miata/MX5, you don't need anything else.

VINYL TRIM CLEANERS AND POLISHES

15 These products are great for cleaning items like the convertible top, dash panel, interior trim and the various body seals and the like. They make these parts look like new and offer a degree of protection from sun damage and chemical attack. We have used 'Armor All' and 'Son of a Gun' to good effect. (Those of you who reside in prime convertible top country, where the sun always shines, may prefer to seek out specialized products which may offer better sun protection - the black interior of the car builds up heat in a big way on a sunny day). This type of cleaner also works well on tire sidewalls.

TAR SPOTS

16 Road tar spotting on your paint can be removed using a proprietary solvent. Always follow the maker's directions, and we further suggest you try out the product on an unobtrusive area first to check for paint discoloration. Note that tar spots are much easier to remove from waxed paintwork than neglected and faded paint.

COLOR RESTORERS

17 Most of these products are fine abrasives, designed to remove the surface layer of the paint to expose the unoxidised layer below. If you need to use them, do so sparingly, or you could cut through to the primer or bare metal - and the paint finish on the Miata/MX5 is none too thick. On the whole, steer clear. That said, if you've just bought a used Miata with dull paint at a bargain price - try a color restorer before booking a paint job - you could be pleasantly surprised. You might also like to try one of the color-impregnated waxes - these are designed to cover minor scratches and blemishes in the paint finish. In either case, follow the maker's directions for use, and with any abrasive restorer or wax, don't rub too hard, especially near panel edges.

3. PAINTWORK - DAMAGE REPAIR

☞ 1/1, 2.

1 Your car is almost certainly going to suffer from at least minor cosmetic damage during its life. In the case of the Miata/MX5, one of the most vulnerable areas is the nose of the car. The rounded design with its integrated bumpers looks great, but unfortunately is very prone to stone chips. Small stones, flung up by passing traffic, can hardly fail to cause damage if they impact with the front of the car.

2 Like washing and waxing, preventative maintenance beats having to repair paint damage. A popular method of avoiding stone chips on the nose of the car is to fit a front mask or 'bra'. These vinyl covers attach to the nose of the car, usually just forward of the headlight covers, and fend off the worst of the flying debris. We have no personal experience of these devices, but if you can live with the way it makes your car look, then it will probably keep the paint underneath looking good for longer.

3 If you do use a front mask, you might find it worth removing and checking for dirt and moisture underneath once in a while - if this builds up, you may find that it tends to damage the paint anyway. This can also occur with luggage packs which strap directly onto the trunk lid. (We have experienced problems like this with motorcycle tank bags, which are made of similar materials. The airflow tends to blast rain and road dirt underneath where it gets trapped and acts like a cutting compound - beware!)

4 The lower edge of the car is vulnerable to stone chip damage from the car's own wheels. This can be reduced by installing mud guards (mud flaps). These are available as Mazda accessories or through Mazda specialists. We would suggest that you use the correct type in preference to the one-size-fits-all guards sold in most auto parts stores - the fit and appearance will be a lot better. In the case of the European specification car, the tail of the car is protected by factory-fitted flaps around the back edge of the rear wheel wells. These are color-impregnated to match the rest of the body. While we feel that the car looks better without them, they doubtless help protect the bodywork. If you like the sound of these items, you could try ordering a set through your Mazda dealer.

5 If damage has already occurred, you'll want to do something about it quickly: especially if bare metal is exposed. The best place to buy touch-up paint is from a Mazda dealer - that way you should get a good color match, and you can be certain that the paint will be safe to use on all body parts, steel or plastic. Before you can apply the paint you will need to rub down the area around the chip or scratch with fine rubbing compound to smooth the edge of the scratch and to remove old body wax. Note that if the car has been waxed with a silicone-based product, you may need to wipe the area with a special solvent to remove it before the paint will stick. If you think you may have problems here, ask a paint specialist for advice on what to use.

6 Where the damaged area has exposed bare steel, you will need to apply a primer. Remove any surface corrosion with fine abrasive paper, and apply a rust-inhibiting primer, or use a rust-killing coating, followed by regular primer. Be warned that if you leave traces of rusting in the damaged area, it will break through the repair in time. If the paint damage is deep, use a fine filler paste or stopper to fill the deepest areas before starting with the paint stage. Leave the filler layer just a little lower than the paint surface - if necessary, use fine abrasive paper to rub down any high spots.

7 Using a fine brush, apply a thin coat of paint to the damaged area and allow it to dry. Repeat as often as necessary to bring the level of the new paint slightly higher than the surrounding paint, then leave it to harden fully - this takes around two weeks. You can then use the rubbing compound to blend the new paint in with the old, finally sealing the repair by waxing the area.

4. BODY - DAMAGE REPAIR & PAINTING

☞ 1/1, 2.

1 In this section we are looking at what to do in the event of relatively minor body damage - the sort of thing that happens to everyone's car once in a while in the parking lot or driveway. If the damage is more severe, and there is any possibility of hidden structural damage, forget about home repairs and get the car checked out by a Mazda dealer or reputable body shop - don't risk lives by trying to save money.

ASSESSING THE DAMAGE

2 The exact nature of minor impact damage will be dependent on what area of the car is affected. In the case of plastic or composite panels, light impacts may have produced no visible signs of damage, in which case you need carry out no repair work at all, though you should check for underlying damage which may not be outwardly apparent. This is especially important after front-end or rear-end impact, where the bumper may appear unmarked, but underlying deformation of the supporting structure may have occurred. If you are unsure about this, you should seek professional advice. If plastic panels have split or shattered, the best option is to fit a new one. Repairing this type of material is not easy, though some professional body shops may have facilities for such repairs. Once again, seek expert opinion about this.

3 What you do about minor bumps and scrapes depends on the extent of the damage and your ability and facilities. Never forget that, while it might be well within your capabilities to fix the damage, you may find that it works out cheaper to get a professional job done if you would otherwise need to spend out heavily on body repair materials and tools.

4 Another thing you need to consider is the potential effect on the car's resale value. Poor quality body repairs are usually pretty obvious under professional scrutiny, and may mean a lower trade-in price. If this would be the result of home repair, you may actually be costing yourself money in the longer term.

5 Before you do anything else, examine the damaged area carefully. You need to assess the full extent of the damage, and that means checking for underlying deformation of any supporting structure. Where you are dealing with a closed section, or a double-skinned area, this may not be easy, but whatever else you do, never just cover up the external damage without making sure that it does not extend to other components. Note that the repair procedures we describe here assume that the damage is superficial, and that the underlying body structure is not affected

6 The exact method of repair will depend on the type of damage. Shallow scrapes which have not pushed the panel line out by more than about an eighth of an inch (3 mm) can usually just be prepared, filled and painted, while deeper gouges and dents will have to be pulled out first. If the metal has been holed, the gap will have to be bridged with perforated metal mesh or glassfiber matting before you can fill the resulting depression - you will need to take this into account when purchasing repair materials.

PULLING OUT DENTS

7 A professional body shop will use equipment and skills unavailable to the home enthusiast to deal with deformed body panels, and in many cases will be able to reshape the damaged panel without needing to apply much filler. The best the amateur can do is to try to get the panel as close as possible to the original shape, using whatever tools come to hand. The trick is to avoid pulling the metal out too far - it needs to lie around an eighth of an inch (3 mm) below the eventual repaired surface.

8 If you can get behind the damaged area, use a hammer to tap the dent outward. Aim to get as close as you can to the original shape with the minimum number of blows. Note that the metal will stretch as you work, and you need to minimize this problem. If the dent is on a relatively flat area, you may be lucky and find that it will pop out to its original shape quite easily. On more complicated or heavily curved areas this is less likely, and more work will be required. It helps to hold a heavy wood block on the outside of the dent as you strike the inside of the area - this helps ensure that the dent comes out evenly and stretching is minimized.

9 Where access behind the dent is difficult (in our experience, there is some universal law of physics which dictates that all dents will occur right above a closed box section) you will need to pull the dent out from the front. Body shops will use a slide hammer to do this. If you have one, you can do the same, otherwise improvise with sheet metal screws. Drill several holes through the panel inside the dent area, and screw the sheet metal screws into them, leaving the heads well above the metal surface. You can now grasp the screw heads with a self-locking wrench (vise grip or similar) and pull the dent out. A carpenter's hammer with a claw end can also be useful here.

10 📷+ When the dent is as close as you can get it to the original shape, run your hand across it and check for high spots. If you need to, tap these inwards carefully so that no metal area lies above the proposed final surface. Note that this check is important - if you have high spots, you will never be able to get the repair close to the original contours.

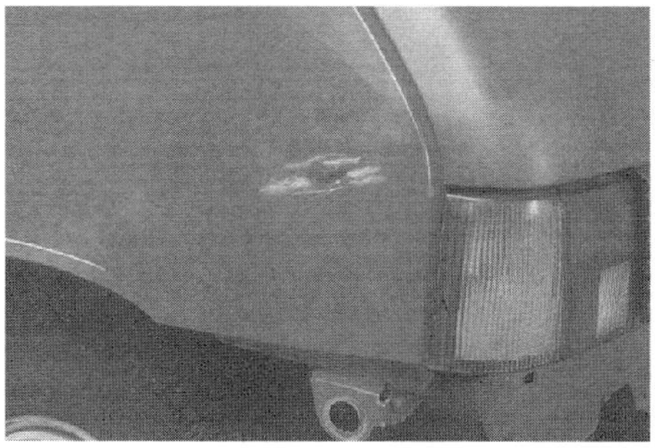

4/10a Typical minor dent.

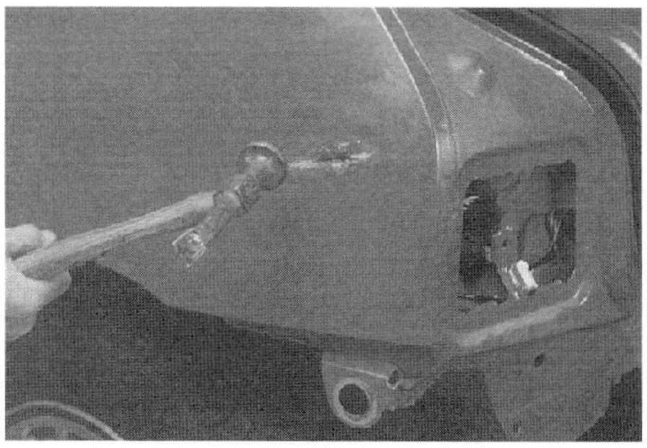

4/10b First give dent enough depth for filler.

REPAIRING HOLED OR GASHED AREAS

11 📷 If the repair includes a hole, you will need to deal with this before you start filling. If rust has caused the problem, you must remove all traces, or the corrosion will continue and push the filler out of the repaired area. Wire brush or sandpaper the rusted metal until all rust has been removed. You will need to wear gloves, a dust mask and eye protection while doing this. Remove paint from the damaged area, feathering the surrounding paint edge using fine sandpaper. You will need to provide a key which the filler can grip, so roughen the dent area using a body file, or score the metal with an old screwdriver. Also note that drilling small holes will help. The surface needs to be quite rough to provide a key for the filler paste - using a drill or polisher fitted with a coarse abrasive disc will speed up this process for large areas.

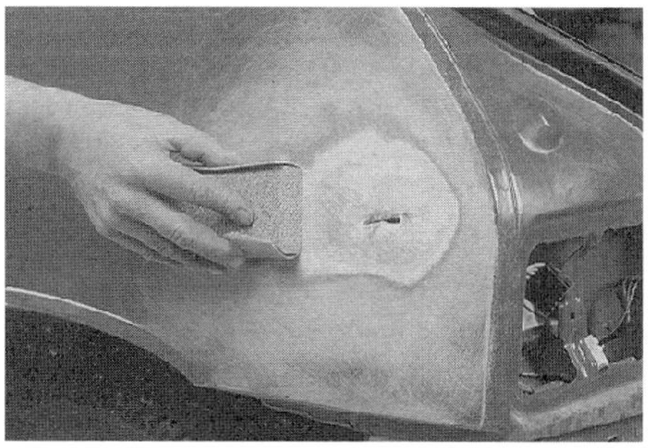

4/11 Remove paint from damaged area.

12 📷 Apply a rust removing gel or liquid to kill any traces of rust remaining on the metal, and remember to treat the inside of the panel too - the paint and any underbody coating will probably have flaked off during the impact. Read the directions on the packaging and take appropriate pre-

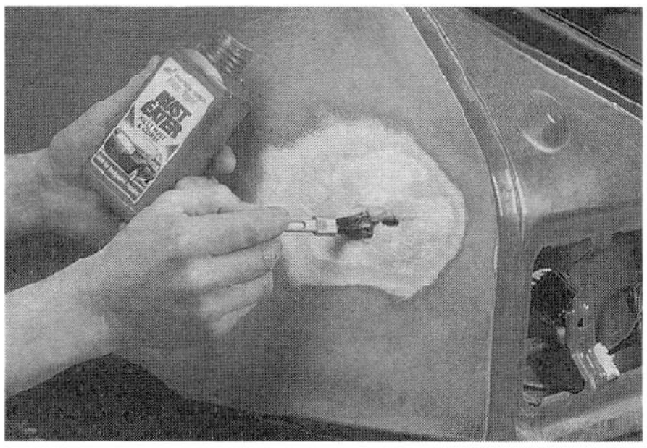

4/12 Treat bare metal & rust with rust killer.

cautions when handling these products, which are corrosive.

13 To bridge small holes or gashes, cut a piece of perforated metal mesh (supplied with most repair kits) to the required shape, and 'glue' this in position with dabs of filler paste. Note also that the quantities of filler and hardener need to be measured accurately - too much or too little hardener may result in the mixture setting too quickly, or not at all. Make sure that the mesh fits the contours of the dent, and that it does not protrude above the surface. Wait for a while to allow the filler paste to harden and secure the mesh.

14 + Alternatively, some repair kits include glassfiber matting and a liquid resin. These materials are a little trickier to work with, but will permit you to follow intricate contours more faithfully. The matting is cut to shape with scissors, and then the damaged area is coated with resin to which a hardener has been added. Press the matting onto the resin coat, and check that any fibers projecting above the finished surface are removed before the resin sets hard. Use an old paintbrush dipped in resin to stipple the matting down and to remove any trapped air bubbles. Depending on the extent of the hole, you may need to build up several layers

4/14a Cut fiberglass mat to right size & shape.

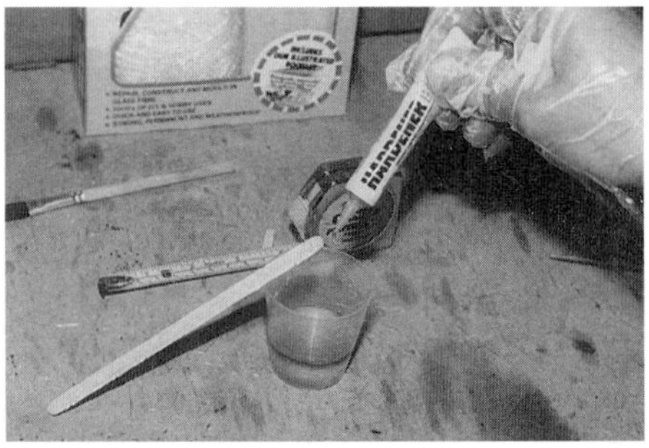

4/14b Mix hardener into resin.

to complete the repair. You should allow the initial layer to dry hard for an hour or so before adding successive layers - this will give you a firm surface on which to build.

15 **Warning!** Follow the maker's directions when using these products, noting safety instructions and handling precautions. You should wear gloves when working with resins, hardeners and glassfiber, and always ensure adequate ventilation. Note also that the quantities of resin and hardener need to be measured accurately - too much or too little hardener may result in the resin setting too quickly, or not at all. If using the glassfiber method, leave the repair to harden before moving on to filling.

FILLING

16 By now, the repaired area should begin to look a little more car-shaped, and you are ready to apply the filler to reprofile the surface. Following the maker's directions, mix up an appropriate amount of filler paste and hardener. Don't be tempted to mix too much at once, or it will begin to harden before you have chance to apply it. Try instead to build up the repair in layers.

4/16 Mix appropriate amount of filler & hardener

17 Use a plastic spreader (normally included in the repair kit) to spread paste over the dented area. As each layer dries hard (usually around 20 minutes) check that you have left no high spots - if you need to, use a body file or a Surform tool to remove these. Try to end up with a smooth surface which conforms as closely as possible to the finished profile and level. Although the filler can be worked with hand tools when it has hardened, it is obviously preferable if you have the minimum amount of sanding to carry out.

4/17 Build filler layer-by-layer.

SANDING

18 The filled area now needs to be shaped and sanded smooth. You can do this using progressively fine grades of sandpaper, or a silicon-carbide 'wet-or-dry' paper wrapped round a sanding block. If you need to remove a lot of filler, use a power sander or drill motor fitted with an abrasive disc. We suggest that you finish the work by hand, however, because it is very easy to remove too much material with power tools. Whatever method you use, wear eye protection and a dust mask.

19 The wet type papers allow you to rinse

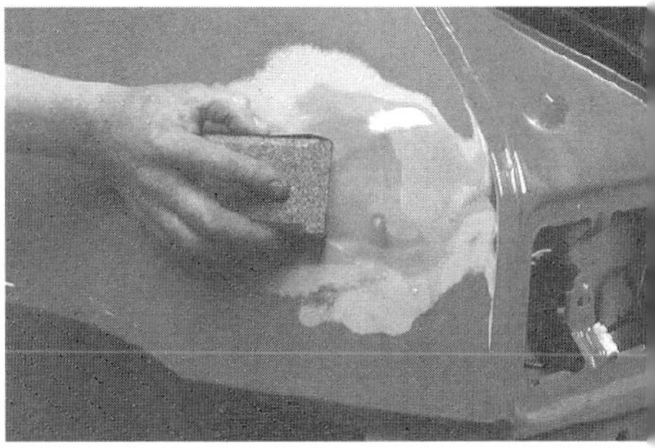

4/18 Abrasive paper creates smooth surface.

away the filler debris, and so last longer than plain sandpaper. Also, by working with a wet surface, any steps or hollows show up well. While the work area is wet, sight along it to check the surface profile every so often. Note that you will need to ensure that the repair is completely dried out before you can apply paint. If you're in a hurry, a hairdrier helps this process.

PAINTING

20 Note: painting operations require a clean environment, comfortable temperatures (around 20°C / 68°F or higher) low humidity and no wind, bugs or flies. Spraying paint seems to bring out the suicidal element in the bug population. At the slightest scent of thinner, they come from miles around to hurl themselves at fresh, wet paint, and then crawl around for a while before dying, stuck firmly in your new paint. There is no point trying to remove them if this happens - you'll still need to repair the resulting craters in the paint. It follows that you are likely to get better results in your garage. The work area should be really clean before you start - remove any sources of dust, and damp down the floor with a fine water spray just before spraying commences.

Warning! Although this sequence assumes the use of spray cans, rather than professional spraygun equipment, if you do decide to borrow or hire such equipment, be careful that you get the right type of paint. Seek expert advice on this, and on no account use professional two-pack paint. Many of these types of paint are isocyanate-based, requiring a full body suit and air-fed mask. Don't try using this type of paint at home - it could kill you if you inhale it. Your paint supplier will need to know the car's paint code details, and you should also explain your facilities and level of experience so that he can advise you on safe usage procedures.

21 Once any necessary repairs have been made and the filled area has dried thoroughly, you can start painting. For this you will need primer, plus a top coat to match the original paint finish. The paint color of the car is identified by a sticker on the underside of the hood.

22 Most owners will be using aerosol cans of paint for this job, and these can be obtained through Mazda dealers. You will also need a can of primer (aerosol spray or brush type), masking tape and some newspaper, plus some very fine abrasive paper and paint cutting compound.

23 Make absolutely sure that the filled area

has been rubbed down smooth, and that no holes or low spots are left in the filler surface; don't waste time or paint until you are certain that you've got this right. Check by feel rather than by eye - it tends to be more reliable in detecting faults in the surface. The repaired area should be feathered into the surrounding paint, and you should not be able to feel the join between them - if you can, you still have work to do. The surrounding paint must be clean and free from any trace of body wax - you can buy solvents which will remove any wax from the surface. Note that unless the wax is removed, the new paint will not adhere properly, and may form pinholes as it pulls away from the wax.

24 Mask off the surrounding area to protect it against overspray. Wherever possible, mask up to a natural boundary line, such as a seam or moulding edge. This will make any slight color variation less obvious. You should remove any trim, plus items like lights or badges, in the area to be painted so that the new paint will cover these areas too. When complete, the lights, trim or whatever can be fitted, covering and disguising the new paint edge. Don't try to mask off removable items - it looks terrible because you will be able to see the edge of the new paint film at these points. Apply the sheets of newspaper to the surrounding bodywork, securing their edges with strips of masking tape.

25 + Following the directions on the can, brush or spray on the primer coat, making sure that all bare metal is covered. While the primer coat is wet and glossy, sight across the repair, looking for any defects in the surface. The gloss surface will help to identify any rippled or sunken areas. If necessary, wait until the primer coat has dried and apply further filler coats or knifing putty to build up such areas, then sand down and repeat the primer coat.

26 Once the primer has been applied satisfac-

4/25a Mask off area and apply primer.

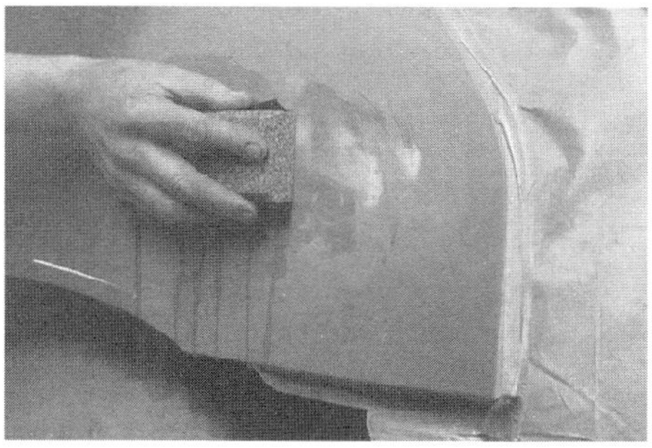

4/25b Sand primer &, if necessary, fill ...

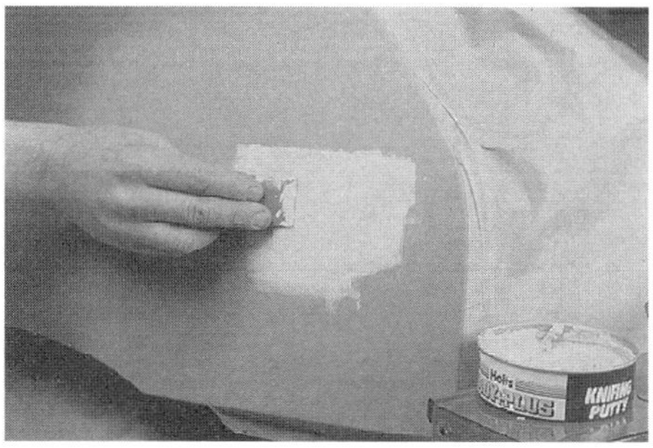

4/25c ... small holes with filler or knifing putty.

torily, leave it to dry thoroughly for several hours. Now use a very fine wet-and-dry type abrasive paper (around 400 grade or finer) to rub down the primer coat. The paper should be used wet, rinsing it regularly in clean water to remove excess paint from the surface. A small amount of detergent in the water will help here.

27 When the primer surface is completely smooth to the touch, wipe down with a lint-free rag and plenty of clean water, then allow the area to dry. You can speed this up by using a heat gun or fan heater. Immediately before you spray on the top coat, wipe over the surface with a tack rag (available from paint suppliers) to remove any tiny dust specs.

28 Agitate the paint can for at least one minute to mix the paint thoroughly. The paint can needs to be held with the nozzle about 8-10 inches from the surface (check this on the can). Start moving the can across the surface, and as it reaches the edge of the area to be sprayed, depress the nozzle. Keep the can moving slowly and evenly, checking that the nozzle to surface distance remains constant. Note that it is easy to find that you are moving the can through an arc. Don't do this or

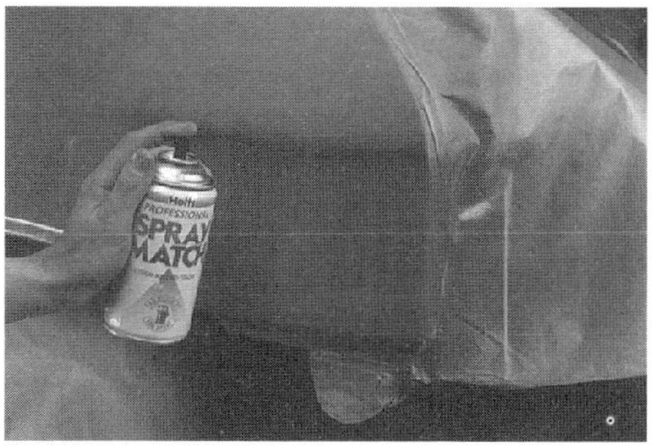

4/28 Colour coat in thin layers.

the paint will be applied unevenly, and may sag or run at the center of the arc, where the nozzle got too close to the surface.

29 As you reach the far side of the area being sprayed, release the button. Move back to the start point and repeat the process, this time a little lower down so that the bands of paint just overlap. Repeat the sequence until the area is covered.

30 At this stage, the paint film will look semi-transparent. This is correct - don't be tempted to try to apply the paint too thickly or the film will run or sag. If this happens, you must allow it to dry

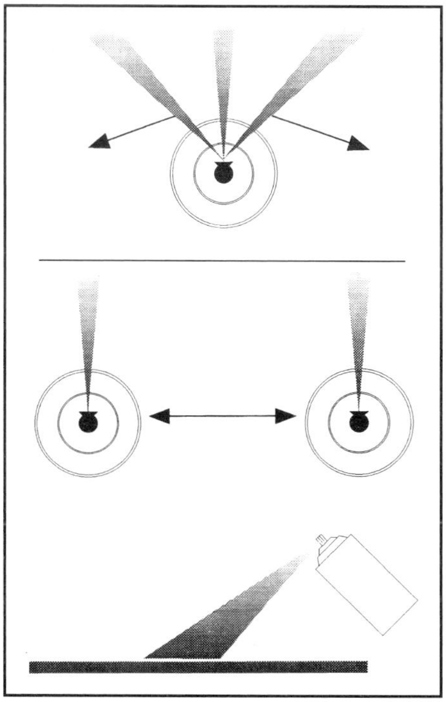

D4/28 SPRAYING TECHNIQUES.
Top: don't swivel the spray can. Centre: Do keep the spraycan parallel to the workpiece. Bottom: For horizontal surfaces spray from angle of 45 degrees, but otherwise use same techniques. (courtesy Davann).

completely, then rub it down and start over. What you need to do is to apply a thin even film. Allow this to dry for about 15-20 minutes, then apply a second coat. Continue in this way until the paint coat is even and opaque. Don't worry too much if the finish seems a little rough and has a dull appearance; you can deal with this later using a rubbing compound. Let the new paint dry for an hour or so, then remove the masking.

FINISHING

31 By now you will have got rid of the dent, and the damaged area should be looking a lot better. Your new paint will probably look a little flat and dull - it is difficult to get a good gloss from a spraycan, so don't get too despondent about it if this is your first attempt at body repair . Don't be in a hurry to polish the new paint; it needs around two weeks to cure and harden completely. For now, install any trim or other items removed and just use the car as normal for a while.

32 + After waiting for at least two weeks, you can set to work with rubbing compound. This is a fine abrasive paste which will remove any roughness on the paint surface and produce a good gloss finish. Work carefully, taking care not to rub through the new paint. Once you have a smooth, gloss surface, apply a wax coat to seal and protect the new paint. Depending on your care in preparation and the accuracy of the color match, the repair should be pretty well invisible. Remember that some damage remains at the back of the repair though - we suggest that you use a wax-type

11

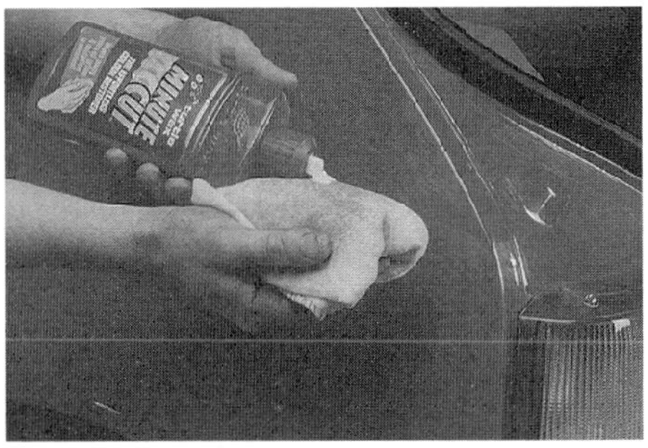

4/32a Rubbing compound smooths paint.

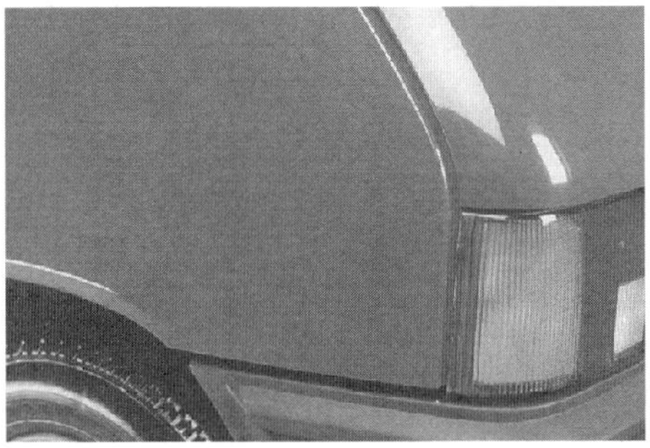

4/32b Magic! Your Mazda's become a Peugeot!

underbody sealant to prevent further corrosion taking place.

5. HOOD (BONNET) - REMOVAL & INSTALLATION

☞ 1/1, 2.

REMOVAL

1 You will need an assistant during this operation. Open the engine hood (bonnet) and support with its stay. Protect the paintwork around the engine compartment with thick cloth (old towels are ideal) - this will prevent expensive cosmetic damage if the hood slips during removal or installation.

2 Disconnect the windshield washer jet pipework at the first union by pulling on the pipe and moving it to and fro until the pipe is free. You may find that it helps to push the pipe off its stub using a screwdriver blade.

3 Mark the relative position of the hood and hinge on each side of the car with a marker pen so that the hood can be exactly realigned when refitted. If you are fitting a new hood, you can ignore this step, but alignment will need to be carried out more carefully.

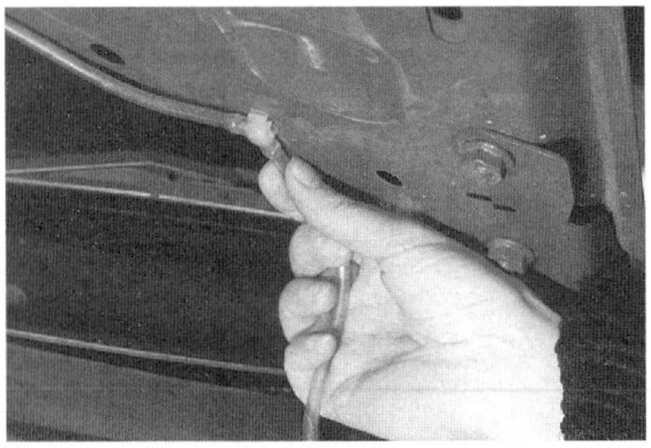

5/2 Disconnect washer pipe at union.

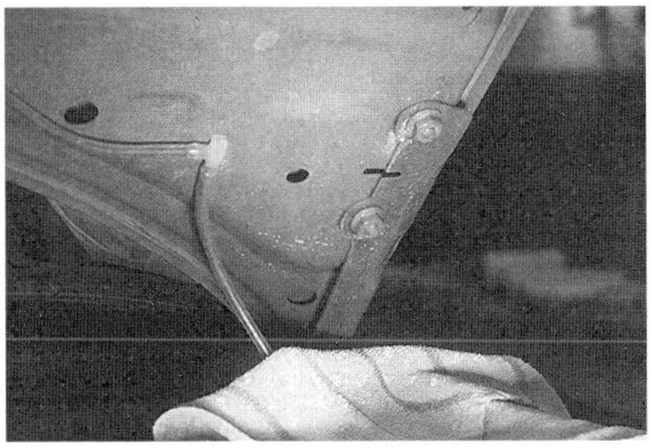

5/3 Mark hinge positions.

4 With an assistant holding the hood steady, release the two 14 mm nuts on each side and then carefully lift the hood away from the car. Replace the four nuts finger-tight on the projecting studs for safekeeping and then store the hood safely until it is required again.

5 + If required, you can remove the hood support stay by pulling back the outer tag of its nylon swivel clip and levering the clip open with a screwdriver blade. After this the stay can be pulled out of the clip and removed from the car. Note that if you need to detach the hood hinges from the body, you'll need to remove the front fenders to gain access to the mounting bolts ☞ 11/12.

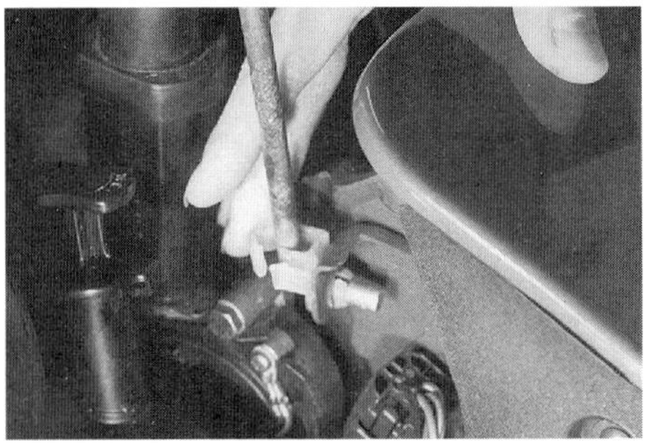

5/5a Clip retains hood support stay.

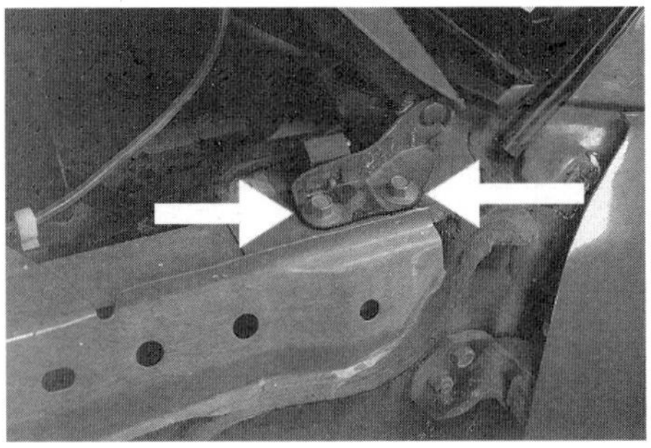

5/5b Hinge removal requires fender off.

INSTALLATION

6 The gold colored end of the stay with the longer leg fits in the hinge clip. The clip is located high on the left chassis rail, just behind the headlight assembly. Make sure the nylon clip is open and pass the leg of the stay through the circular section of the clip and metal bracket, then close the latch over the vertical section of the stay. Lay the stay across the front of the engine compartment and fix the other end into its clip.

7 With the help of an assistant carefully position the hood so that its rear corners are wedged into the gap on each side of the car between the windshield lower rail and the fender (wing). Quickly lift the hinges and push them over the protruding studs on the underside of the hood and then tighten the two 14 mm nuts on each side finger-tight. Prop the hood open with its stay.

8 If you made positional marks on the hinges during removal, manipulate the hood/hinge relationship until the marks realign and then tighten the 14 mm nuts to 19-25 Nm (1.9-2.6 kgf m /14-19 lbf ft). Repeat the process with the second hinge. If you are fitting a new hood, there will of course be no positional marks, and you'll have to slide the hood backwards and forwards in the hinges until you are able to close the hood and obtain even gaps all the way around, then tighten the retaining nuts.

9 The correct clearances around the hood are as follows. On each side, there should be a gap of 5 ± 1.5 mm (0.2 ± 0.06 in). Along the front edge, you should have a clearance of 5 ± 1.0 mm (0.2 ± 0.04 in). Make sure that the hood does not contact the surrounding bodywork while closed, or when being opened or shut.

10 **Warning!** After installing the hood, especially if a new hood has been fitted, you should check, and if necessary adjust, the hood latch and safety latch mechanism. Adjust the latch by slackening the mounting bolts and aligning it so that it contacts the striker on the underside of the hood. Tighten the two mounting bolts and single nut to 7.8-11 Nm (80-110 kgf cm / 69-95 lbf in).

11 Reconnect the windshield washer pipe to the pipework union stub on the underside of the hood.

6. TRUNK LID, FITTINGS & REAR PANEL - REMOVAL & INSTALLATION

☞ 1/1, 2.

Warning! The trunk lid is supported on strong torsion springs (balance springs) fixed between the two hinges. You won't need to disturb these to remove the trunk lid, but you will need to release tension on the springs if the trunk lid hinges are to be removed. Take care when doing this or you could be injured.

TRUNK LID REMOVAL & INSTALLATION

1 Open the trunk lid fully. Mark around the outline of the hinge where it attaches to the trunk lid as a guide during installation. We use typist's correction fluid for this, or you could use paint or a marker pen. On cars so equipped, disconnect the wiring to the hi-mount brake light mounted on the trunk lid so that it does not impede removal.

2 Remove the four 10 mm nuts which secure the trunk lid to its hinges. The lid is not especially heavy, but we suggest that you have some assistance as the nuts are removed - note that if the lid slips during removal, it will probably

6/2 Four nuts fix hood to hinges.

damage the paint forward of the trunk opening.

3 When installing the trunk lid, hold it in position against the hinges and install the four retaining nuts loosely. Align the marks made during removal, then provisionally tighten the nuts. If you forgot to mark the hinge positions, or if you are fitting a new or refinished lid, you will need to align the lid in relation to the opening.

4 Lower the lid and check the gap on all sides. This should be 5 ± 1.2 mm (0.2 ± 0.05 in). If necessary, make any minor position adjustments, making sure that the gap is even on all sides, then tighten the nuts to 7.8-11 Nm (69-95 lbf in). Check that the trunk closes and latches correctly, and if necessary check the adjustment of the latch mechanism as described below. Where appropriate, reconnect the hi-mount brake light wiring.

TRUNK LATCH - REMOVAL, INSTALLATION & ADJUSTMENT

5 With the trunk lid raised for access, remove the trunk end trim panel. This is retained by numerous plastic fasteners. To remove them, lift the center pin with your fingernails or a small screwdriver, then pull the fasteners out to free the panel. For more information on these devices ☞ 1/2.

6 The trunk lid latch mechanism is secured by two 10 mm bolts, which also provide adjustment of the latch position. Before removing the bolts, mark around the mechanism with a marker pen or paint, as an alignment guide.

7 Feel along the operating rod to the lock barrel assembly. Swing the plastic clip away from the rod and unhook the end from the barrel lever.

8 + Remove the two latch mechanism fixing bolts, and lift it out of the trunk together with the operating rod. The striker hook can be re-

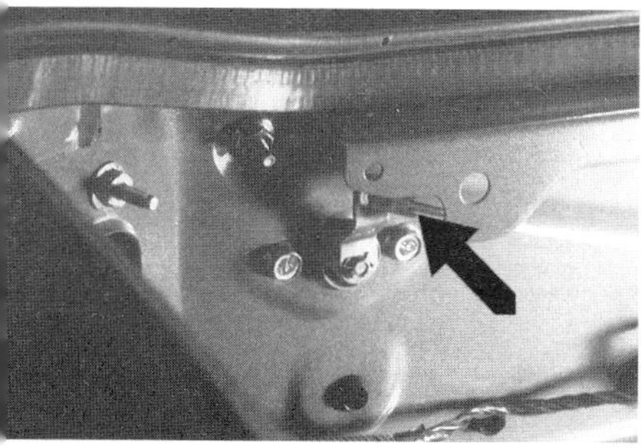

6/7 Operating rod fixed by clip.

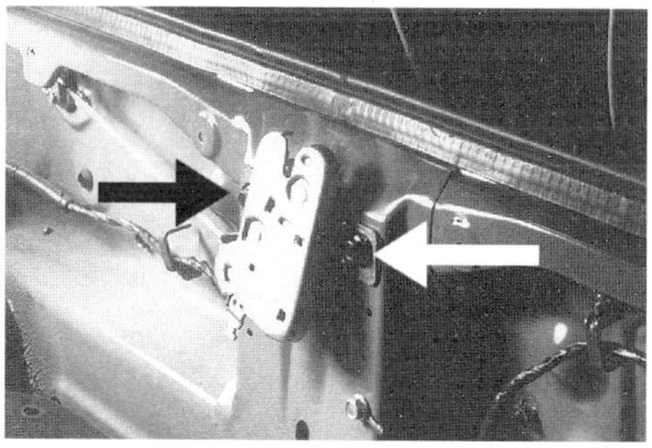

6/8a Latch held by 2 bolts ...

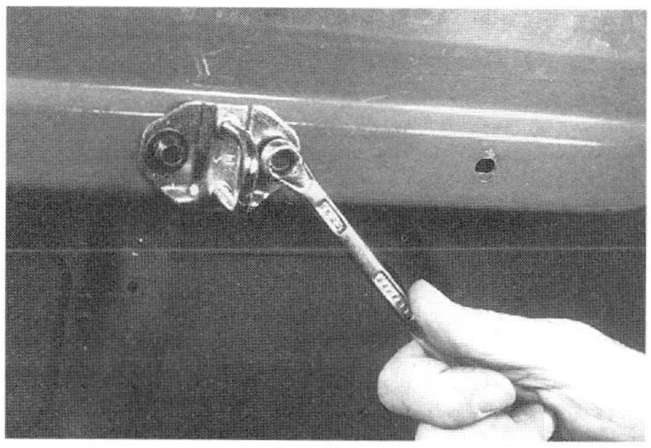

6/8b ... as is striker hook.

moved from the underside of the trunk lid by releasing the two 10 mm fixing bolts. For details on removing and installing the lock barrel assembly ☞ 11/6/12.

9 When fitting the latch mechanism, or when making adjustments, note that some early Miata/MX5 cars had problems with the rubber cushions on the underside of the trunk lid. Up to the fall of 1989, these were 14 mm deep, and made operation of the latch difficult - you needed to press down on the trunk lid to allow the latch to operate easily. This can be misinterpreted as bad adjust-

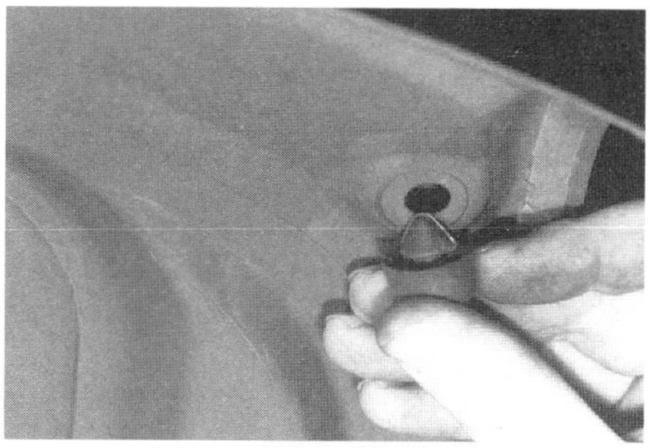

6/9 Rubber cushions pull out.

ment of the latch, when in fact you should first fit the later 12 mm cushions before you attempt any adjustment corrections.

10 With the latch installed in the car and the bolts tightened lightly, reconnect and secure the operating rod at the lock barrel end. **Caution!** If you forget to do this and close the trunk lid, opening it again will be very difficult ...

11 Lower the trunk lid and check that the striker hook meets the latch at the correct angle and position. Tighten the latch bolts, then check that the trunk lid closes easily. You need to be able to have the lid shutting completely, but without requiring excessive effort on the key to release it. You will have to work on a trial and error basis to achieve this, checking and then repositioning the latch as required.

REAR FINISHER (LICENSE PLATE) PANEL AND TRUNK LOCK BARREL - REMOVAL

12 If you need to remove the lock barrel assembly, note that you will first need to detach the rear combination light units, and then the finisher panel, from the back of the car. Start by removing the trunk end trim and disconnecting the latch operating rod from the lock barrel unit (☞ 11/6/7). Unplug the combination and license plate light wiring connectors inside the trunk, then remove the combination lights ☞ 7/37.

13 + With the lights removed, you will be able to access the four 10 mm nuts at each end of the finisher panel - these are accessed from inside the trunk. The center of the panel is held by four screws (non-US models), and you will need to remove the license plate to reach these. On our car (and, no doubt on many others), the license plate was secured by self-adhesive foam pads - remem-

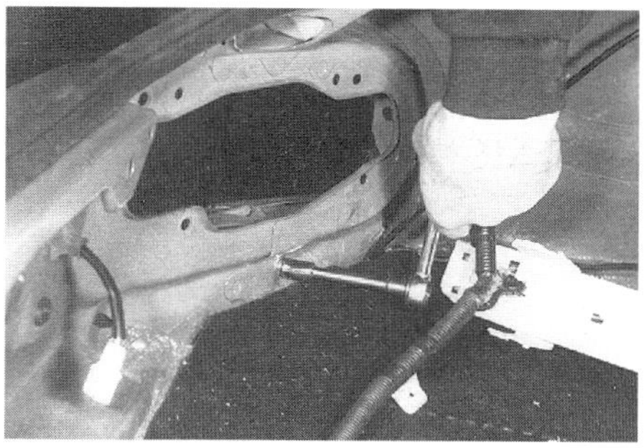

6/13a Release finisher panel nuts ...

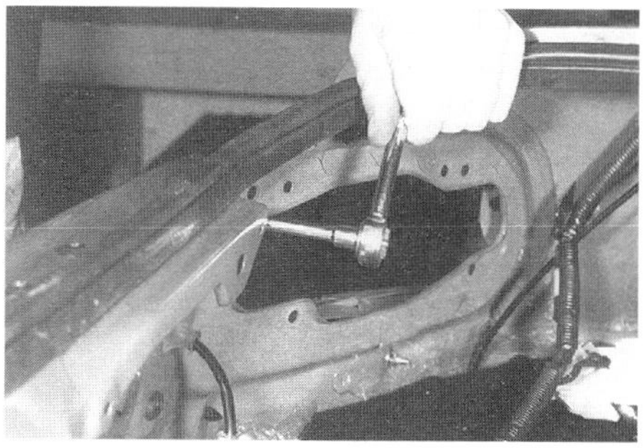

6/13b ... some of which are recessed.

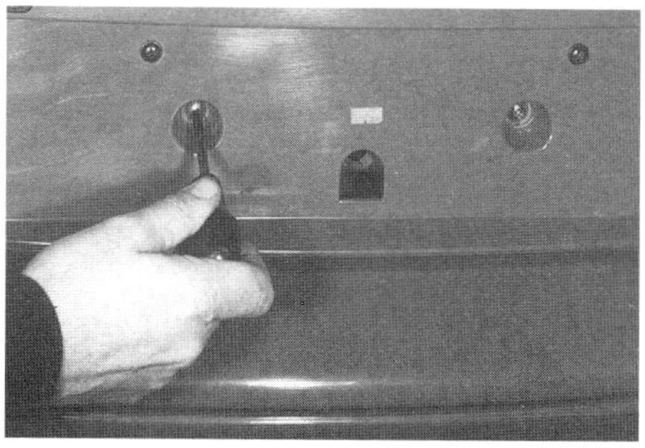

6/13c These screws hidden by license plate.

11

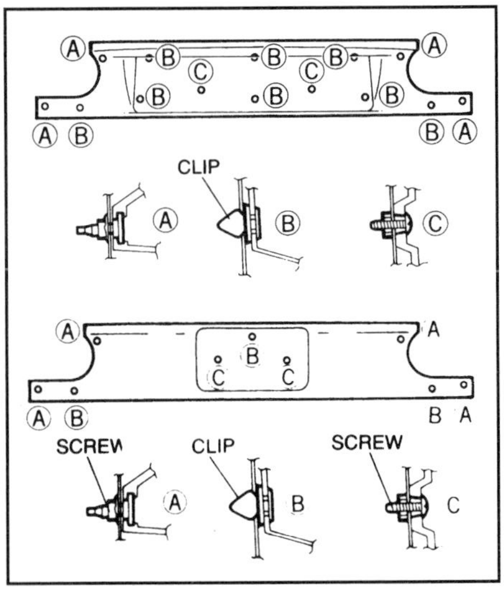

D6/13 DEPENDING ON THE SHAPE OF THE REAR FINISHER (LICENSE PLATE) PANEL, THE FIXINGS ARE DIFFERENT.

ber that you'll need new pads to reinstall. Note that the US type rear finisher differs from most in detail - a different shaped license plate recess is used, and the clips which locate the panel vary accordingly. The two drawings which accompany this text illustrate the two types of panel, and their respective fixing arrangements.

14 + Once the screws have been removed, unclip and remove the finisher. The clips are held in slots on the inner face of the finisher, and push through panel holes. To reduce the risk of damage, squeeze together the clip ends using pliers and working from inside the trunk - the clips will then pull out easily. You'll find that the center clips are hard to reach; they are covered by a welded section inside the trunk. You can depress the clip tangs

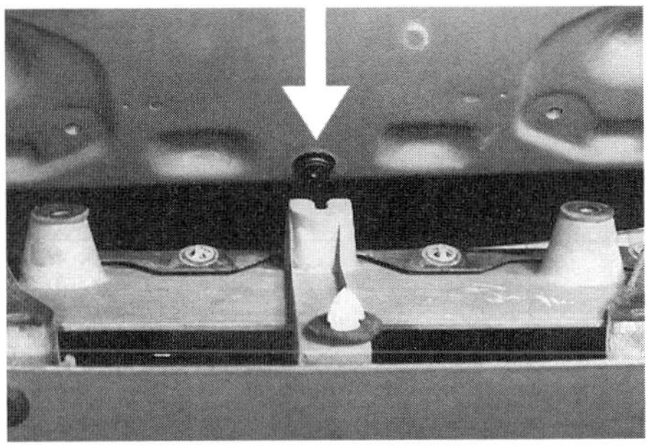

6/14c ... lift panel to free it from this clip.

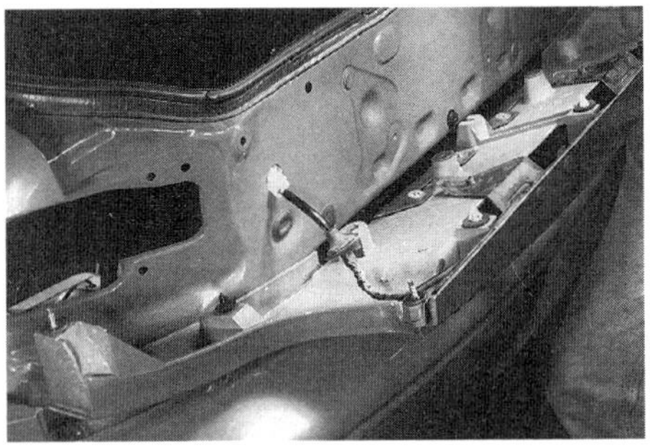

6/14d Free grommet & pull wiring thru.

with a screwdriver blade to help free them. On our car we found that we could release all but the lower center clip this way - we freed the rest, then unhooked this last clip from the panel by lifting it slightly, leaving the clip attached to the body. Before you lift the panel away, locate and disconnect the license plate wiring inside the trunk. The lights plus a short section of harness need to be fed through the panel hole as the rear finisher panel is removed.

15 + With the trunk end trim and rear finisher panel out of the way, you can detach the

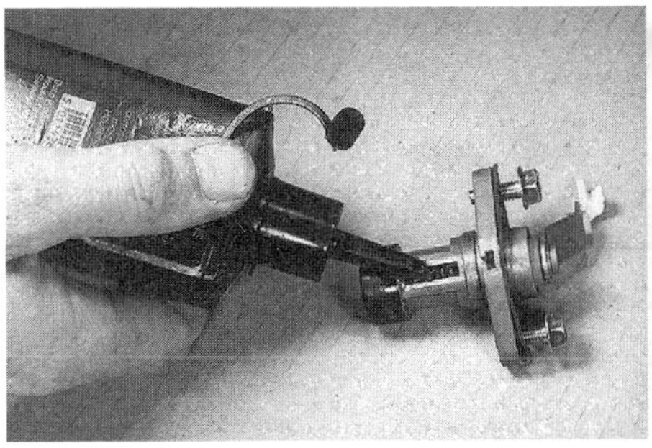

6/15c Lubricate lock before installing.

lock barrel unit. This is retained by two 10 mm fixing bolts which can be unscrewed from inside the trunk. With the bolts removed, maneuver the barrel assembly away from the body. Before reinstalling the lock barrel assembly, or in the event of stiff operation, note that you can lubricate the lock mechanism by applying machine oil through the slot on the underside of the unit.

TRUNK LID BALANCE SPRINGS - REMOVAL, INSTALLATION & ADJUSTMENT

Warning! The trunk lid is supported on strong torsion springs (balance springs) attached between the two hinges. Take care when working on the springs or hinges or you could be injured.

16 Open the trunk lid and arrange some method of supporting it while the springs are released - Wally (our technical adviser) discovered that if you omit to do this, the trunk lid falls on your head as you release the spring pressure. If you don't have someone like Wally around to support the trunk lid with his head, you can use a length of wood as a prop. Also, note that the retainer at the center of the two springs should be unclipped to free them before they are removed at each end.

17 + Wrap the blade of a strong screw-

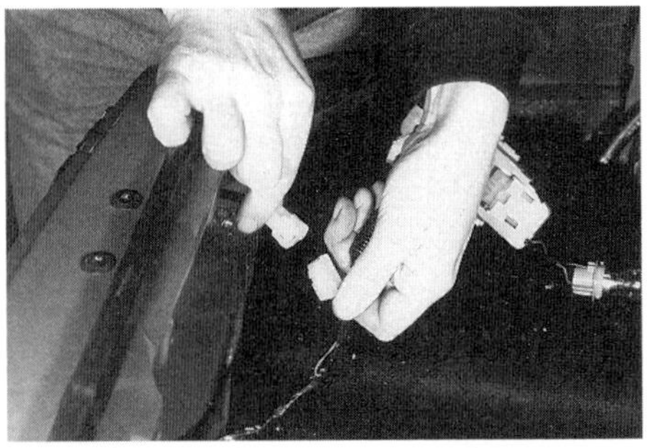

6/14a Disconnect license plate light wiring.

6/15a Unscrew 2 fixing bolts ...

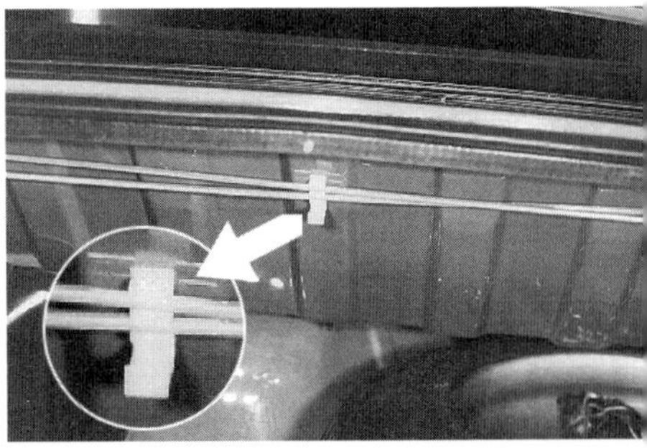

6/16 Central spring retainer/anti-rattle clip.

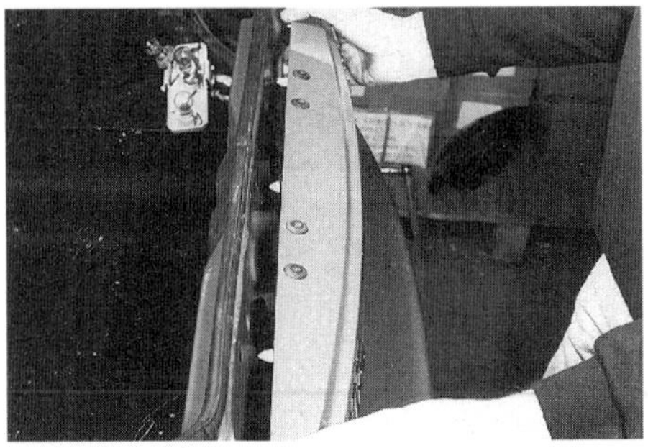

6/14b Free accessible clips & pull out panel ...

6/15b ...& then pull out the lock unit.

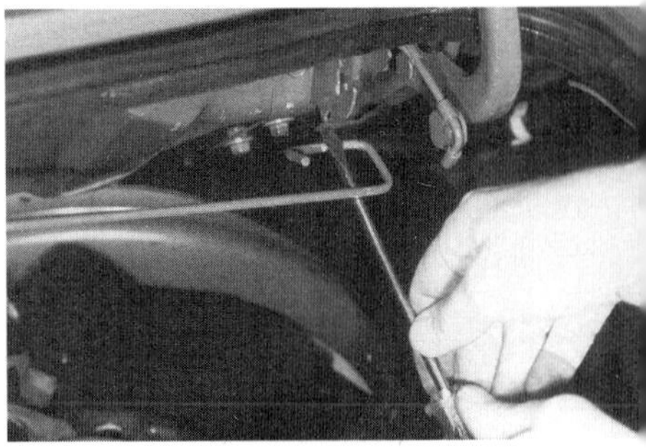

6/17a Release spring tension at anchor end ...

6/17b ... then disengage from hinge lever.

driver with pvc tape to prevent paint damage. Hook the blade through the looped end of the spring and lever upwards to disengage it. Take care when doing this - the springs are strong; carefully rotate the screwdriver to release pressure in the spring. Once spring tension has been released, disengage and remove it from the fixed end.

18 When installing the springs, note that you can adjust them to alter the balance, or 'lift', effect on the trunk lid, especially where the springs have weakened with age. However, before you adjust the springs, check that the problem is

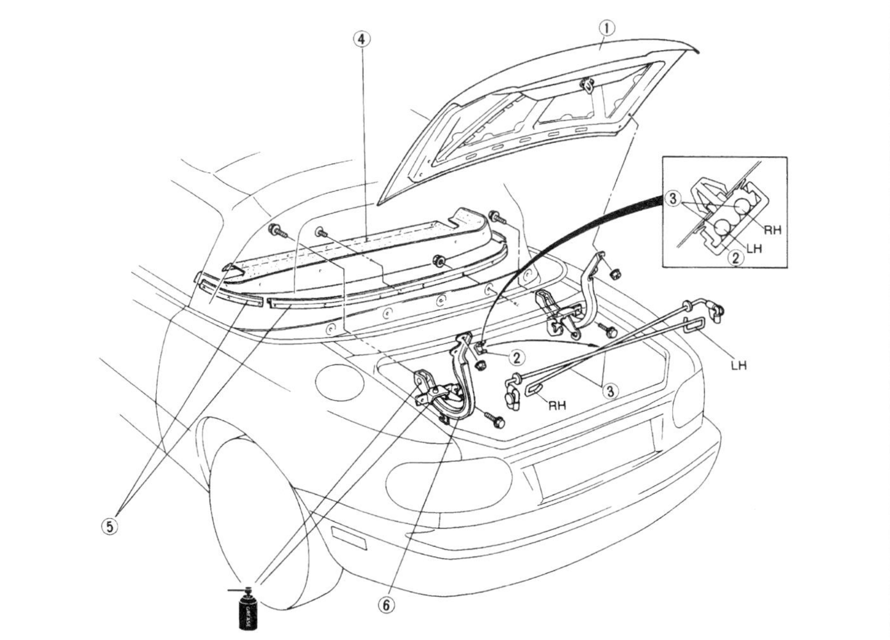

D6/20 TRUNK LID COMPONENTS.
1 Trunk lid. 2 Central spring retainer. 3 Balance springs (x2). 4 Rear package shelf trim. 5 Set plates. 6 Hinge.

6/18 Use screwdriver to adjust spring tension.

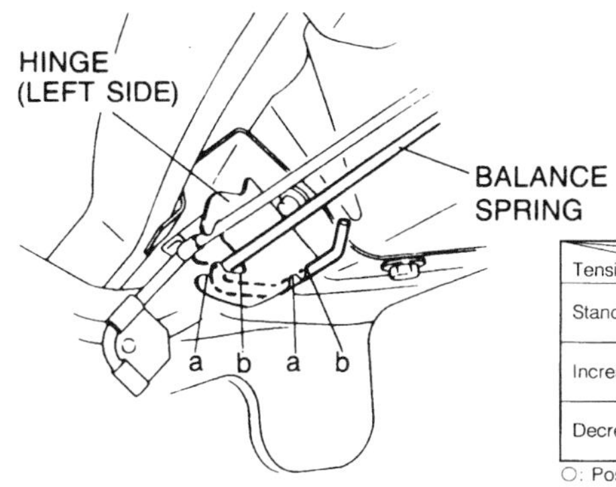

Tension	Hinge \ Set position	a	b
Standard	Left side		○
	Right side	○	
Increase	Left side	○	
	Right side	○	
Decrease	Left side		○
	Right side		○

○: Position

D&T6/18 SPRING TENSION ADJUSTMENT DETAIL AND TABLE.

not due to stiffness or lack of lubrication of the hinges. The lift pressure is varied by moving the hooked end of the spring to one of two positions, as illustrated.

TRUNK LID HINGES - REMOVAL & INSTALLATION

19 If you need to remove the trunk lid hinges, first detach the trunk lid and release and remove the balance springs as described above. The hinge-to-body fasteners are accessed from inside the car. You will need to remove the convertible top's set plate to gain access to them. You don't need to remove the top completely for this - just detach the rear edge with the top raised but unfastened, and lift the lower section to get at the bolts and nuts ☞ 11/16.

20 When installing the hinges, fit the mounting bolts and nuts loosely in position at first, then tighten them to 7.8-11 Nm (80-110 kgf cm / 69-95 lbf ft). Install the balance springs and trunk lid. Check, and if required adjust, the balance spring settings and trunk lid position. Check that the lid closes correctly and adjust the latch position if required.

7. FUEL FILLER CABLE & LID - REMOVAL, INSTALLATION & EMERGENCY LID OPENING

☞ 1/1, 2.

1 The fuel filler release lever in the back of the rear console is connected to the filler lid by a cable.

2 In the event of a cable breaking, your first problem is going to be opening the filler lid until you can install a new cable. You can reach the underside of the lid and its catch through the trunk.

3 At the catch you will find a small plastic trigger which allows you to release the filler lid manually. You'll find it easier to use your left hand to reach in and locate the trigger. Once you find it, pull it back to open the lid. Our photograph shows this with the cable and catch removed to show the trigger location.

4 When installing a new cable, start by removing the rear console so that you can reach the release lever ☞ 10/2.

5 With the console removed, you can reach the lever. Remove the two 10 mm mounting

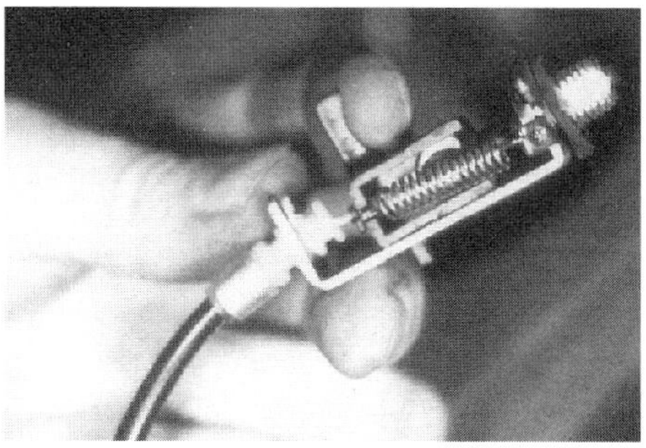

7/3 This trigger manually releases catch.

7/5 Release lever fixed by two bolts.

bolts and lift the lever assembly so that the cable can be disconnected. To get the old cable out (and the new one in) you'll need to remove the carpet from the package area behind the seats ☞ 10/12.

6 Remove the sheet metal screws which retain the long access panel which runs the width of the package area. You'll be able to see the filler release cable clipped to the body. Unhook the cable from its clips - you should be able to reach these from the access hole and from inside the trunk, but if you find it difficult to reach the clips, you can remove further access panels in the pack-

7/6 Cable clips.

age area.

7 When working inside the trunk area, you will need to remove the metal panel which conceals the fuel filler and vent hoses - it's secured by 10 mm bolts. With the panel detached, you'll be able to reach the remainder of the cable which is clipped in place. With the filler lid open, remove the 14 mm nut and washer which retain the catch and withdraw it.

8 + Thread the new cable into place and connect it at the operating lever and catch ends. Install the catch and release lever, and check that the mechanism operates normally, then clip the

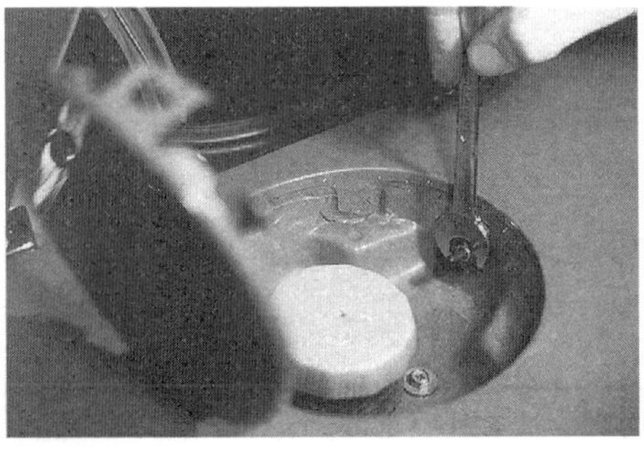

7/7 Catch retained by single nut.

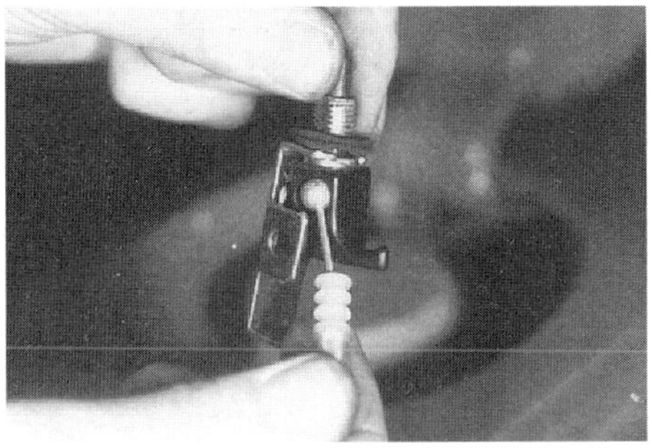

7/8a Fit cable nipple into catch & ...

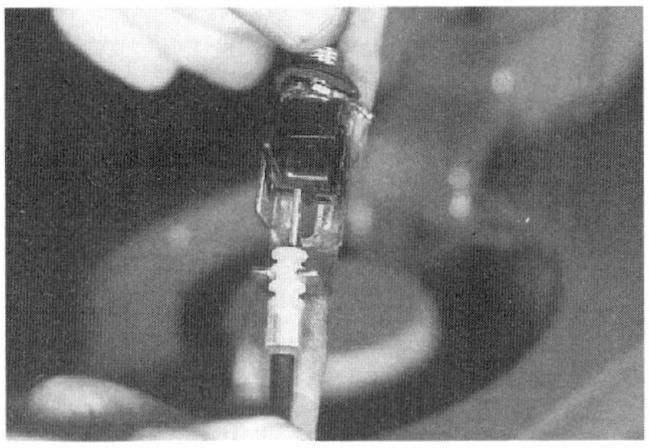

7/8b ... select appropriate groove in cable stop.

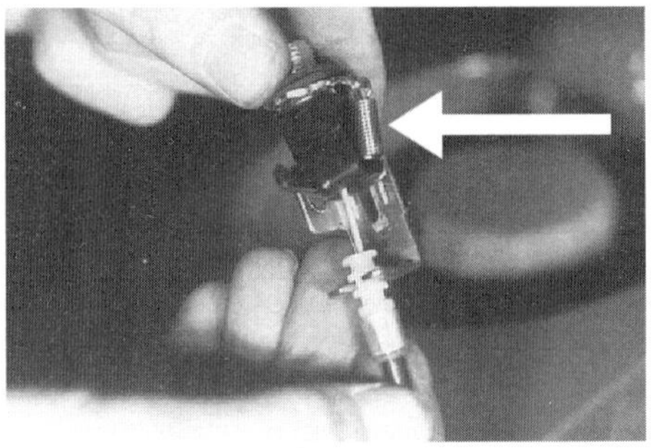

7/8c Make sure return spring is in place.

cable in place and install the removed access panels and carpet before fitting the rear console. If you find that you need to adjust the cable at any time, note that at the catch end there are three locating grooves on the cable stop. Select the best groove of the three to adjust the cable length (the center groove is normally used). Check that the small return spring is correctly attached.

9 The filler lid hinge is secured by two screws accessed from inside the filler well. If you need to fit a new lid, check that it fits correctly in the recess. In particular, make sure that it opens and closes without rubbing on the surrounding paintwork. If necessary, you can make minor adjustments by judicious bending of the hinge.

8. DOOR MIRROR - REMOVAL & INSTALLATION

☞ 1/1, 2.

1 The door mirrors are secured by screws to the doors. To reach the screws, you'll need to pry up the cover around the mounting. Use a small screwdriver blade wrapped with pvc tape to prevent paint damage. Slide the blade into the recess

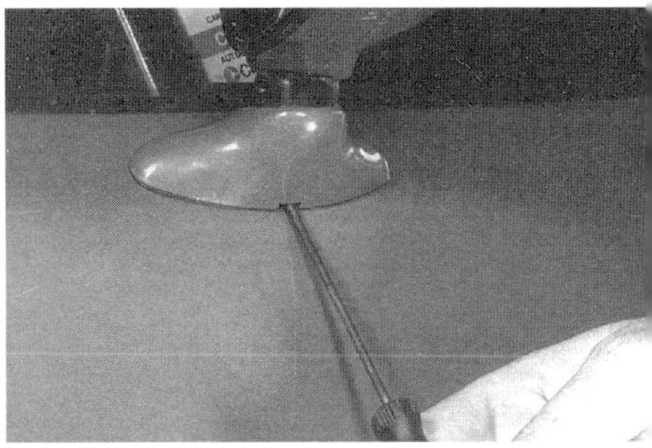

8/1 Spring the cover free & twist ...

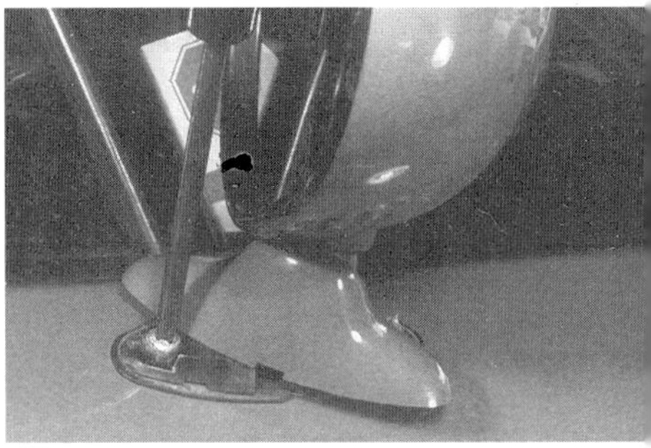

8/2 ... to access securing screws.

at the base of the cover and carefully lever it upward until the cover springs free of the base.

2 Turn the base cover slightly until you can get to the mounting screw heads. The cover will not turn far, but will move enough to allow the screws to be removed.

3 When installing the mirror, check that the mounting screws are tight, then snap the cover back into place against the door.

9. DOOR - REMOVAL, INSTALLATION & ADJUSTMENT

☞ 1/1, 2.

1 Before starting work, obtain the security code for the stereo unit, or disable the security system, then disconnect the battery negative lead to isolate the electrical system ☞ 7/2.

2 If you need to remove the check mechanism from the door first remove the speaker panel, door trim panel and the plastic screen beneath it to give access to the check mechanism ☞ 10/5/19 on.

3 Tap out and remove the check mechanism pin from its anchor point in the door

9/3 Tap out check strap pin.

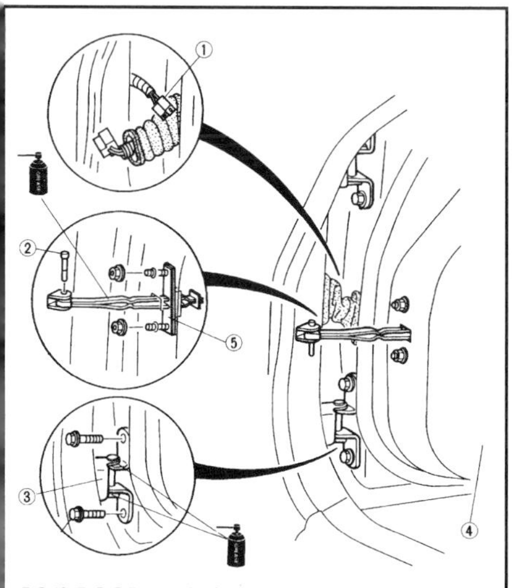

D9/3 DOOR HINGES, CHECK STRAP & WIRING.
1 Wiring connector. 2 Check strap pin.
3 Hinge detail. 4 Door. 5 Check strap detail.

opening. The hollow pin is tapered, and can be removed by tapping it upward and pulling it out with pliers. You don't need to remove the mechanism from the door during door removal, but wire the check mechanism to prevent it getting pushed back into the door accidentally. If you need to remove it for repair or replacement, remove the check mechanism by unscrewing the mounting nuts at the door end, and removing the mechanism from inside the door.

4 Pull back the boot from the body end to expose the door wiring. Separate the wiring connector. Note that where accessory wiring has been added, it may well need to be traced back to the nearest connection point inside the door and separated. The accompanying photograph illus-

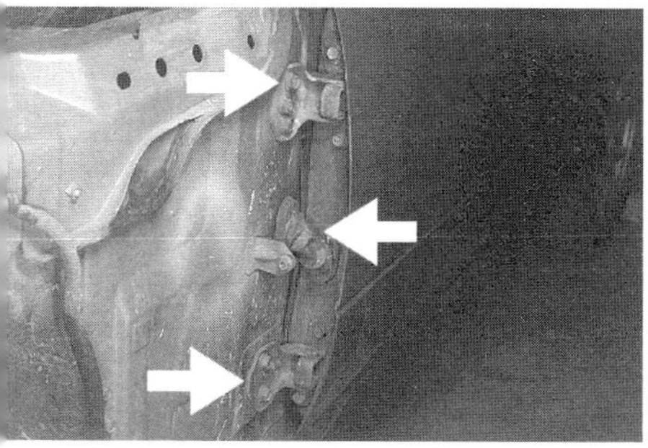

9/4 Hinges & wiring boot (fender removed).

trates the hinge-to-door and hinge-to-body bolts, and the wiring boot. Note that the fender is shown removed for clarity - you don't need to remove the fender to work on the door.

5 With an assistant supporting the weight of the door, slacken and remove the door hinge 12 mm bolts and then lift the door away. Place it on some cloth to prevent damage to the paint along the lower edge.

6 If you need to remove or repair the internal door components ☞ 10/6-10.

7 When installing the door, tighten the hinge bolts provisionally, reconnect the wiring and wiring boot, and secure the check mechanism.

8 Carefully close the door and check that it aligns normally - look for alignment along body molding lines as a guide. If you need to adjust the door, slacken the hinge bolts enough to permit movement, then set the door to give a gap of 5 ± 1 mm (0.2 ± 0.04 in) between the back edge and the door opening. Check that the gap is even down the back edge of the door. Tighten the hinge bolts to

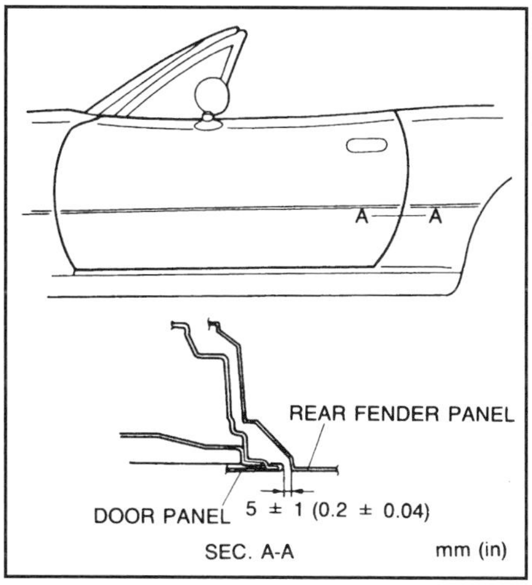

D9/8 CORRECT DOOR GAP.

22-30 Nm (2.2-3.1 kgf m / 16-22 lbf ft).

9 If the door striker adjustment is incorrect, loosen the mounting screws and move the striker vertically until the door closes correctly. Tighten the screws to 18-26 Nm (1.8-2.7 kgf m / 13-20 lbf ft).

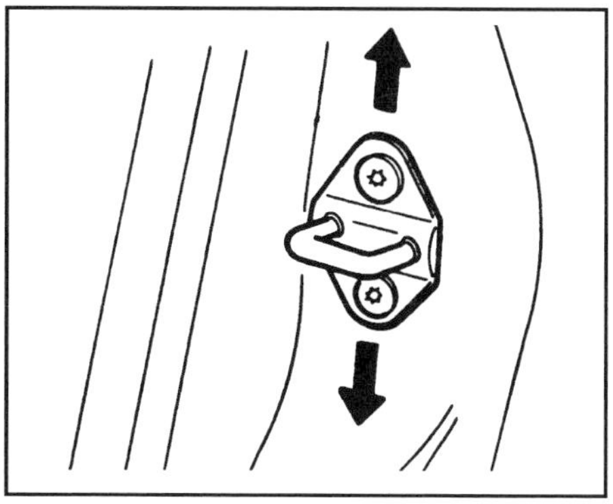

D9/9 DOOR STRIKER ADJUSTMENT.

10 Check the adjustment of the door wedge - this locates the door in its closed position. If necessary, slacken the screws and alter the vertical adjustment. Tighten the screws to 4.2-6.2 Nm (43-63 kgf cm / 37.3-54.7 lbf in).

10. BUMPER (REAR) - REMOVAL & INSTALLATION

☞ 1/1, 2.

1 Before you start work on bumper removal, decide which parts of the assembly you need to remove - this will determine your working method. If you are going to remove the complete bumper assembly, you can leave the finisher panel in place. If you intend to remove just the molded plastic tailpiece, or fascia, as Mazda describe it, you can leave the main bumper structure undisturbed, but note that you will need to remove the rear finisher panel before you can start work ☞ 11/6.

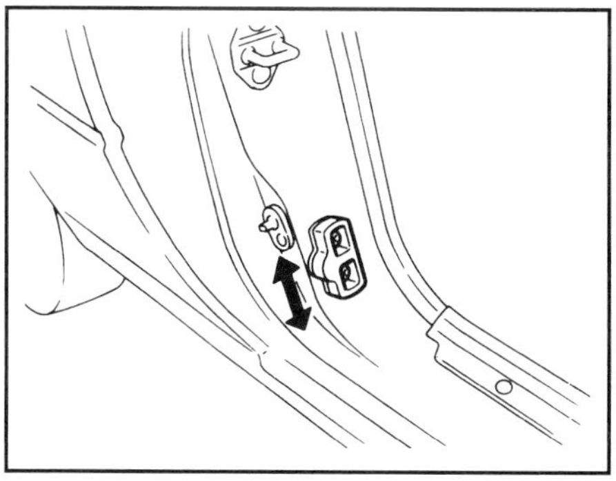

D9/10 DOOR WEDGE ADJUSTMENT.

2 Before you begin work, we suggest that you get the underside of the car and the rear wheel wells pressure-washed to remove accumulated road dirt - this will make the removal procedure much less messy. The first requirement is to raise the back of the car to give access to the fasteners on the underside of the body and bumper. You can either raise the car on fabricated steel ramps, or jack the car and support it on safety stands ☞ 1/3.

3 On European spec cars, you will have to detach the rear flaps. These are fitted to the rear of the rear wheel well and are designed to fend off mud splashes on the rear wings and bumper. Owners of cars not fitted with these flaps should skip down to paragraph 5.

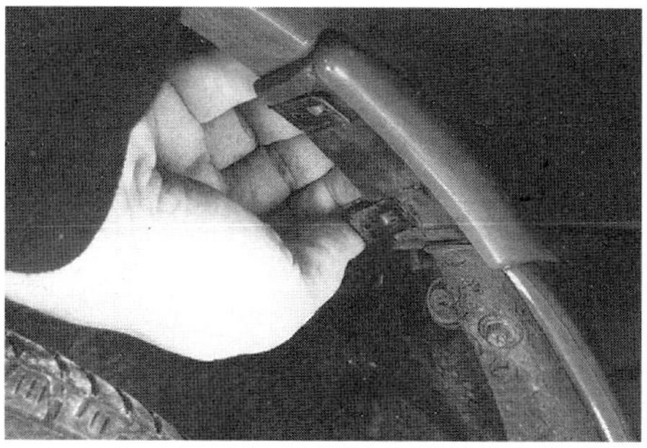

10/4a Upper flap held by clips ...

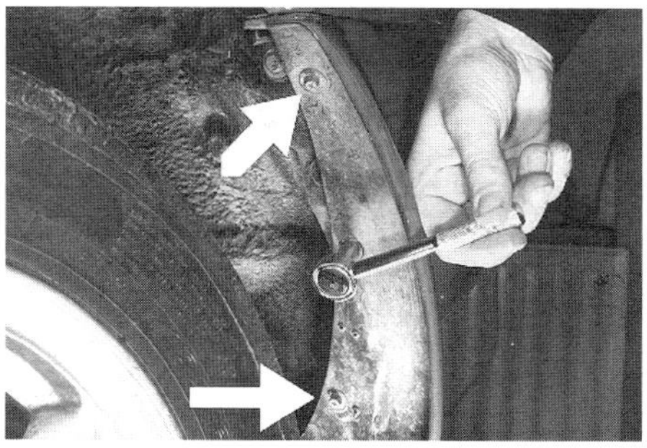

10/4b ... lower by screws.

4 + Each rear flap is in two parts. The short upper section can be removed by pulling off the two flat clips which clamp it to the body seam. The longer lower section is secured by four machine screws with 8 mm hexagon heads, screwed into clips attached to the bumper. Three of the screws are fitted horizontally into the leading edge of the bumper, with a fourth fitted from the underside. Remove the screws, lift away the flap and place it to one side.

5 + On all cars, remove the plastic splash shields. These are fitted in the rear of the wheel well to close the gap between it and the bumper. Each shield is held by three hexagon-headed sheet metal screws. Next, remove the two sheet metal screws which retain each bumper end to the body and wheel well extension - these both fit vertically from below the forward edge of the bumper, one top and bottom at each side of the assembly.

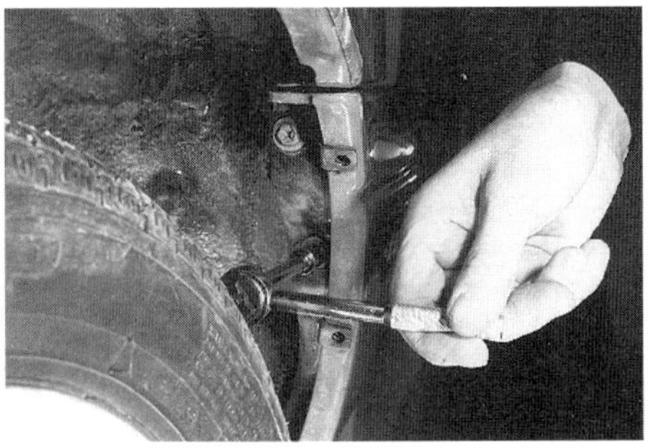

10/5a Splash shield held by screws.

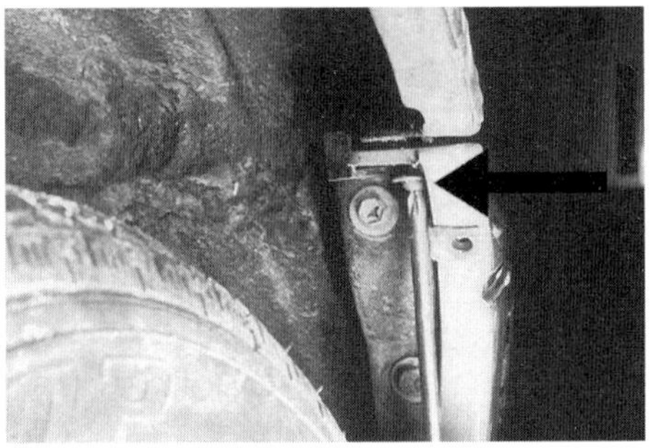

10/5b This screw and this ...

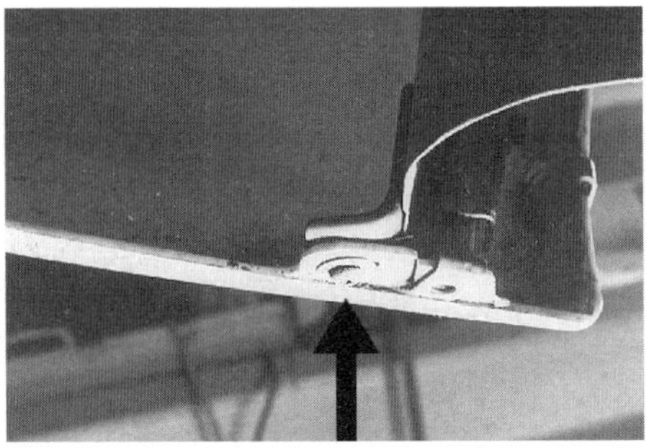

10/5c ... one, fix bumper ends.

6 On cars with a rear foglight fitted near the lower edge of the bumper, you need to disconnect the wiring. This is attached to the harness inside the trunk. Separate the connector, and push it and its boot through the panel hole so that it does not impede removal of the bumper. You may need to remove the trunk end trim and open the access panel to the jack recess for access, depending on how the wiring is routed on your car.

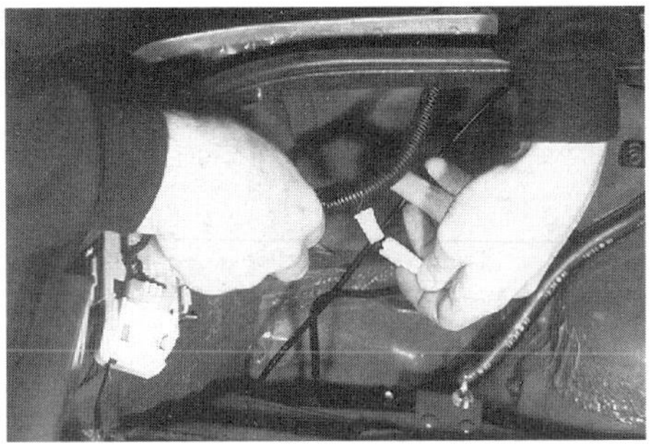

10/6 Disconnect rear foglight wiring.

7 On cars, plus any others fitted with illuminated side marker lights in the sides of the bumper, trace back and disconnect the wiring. The lights and connecting wiring are removed with the bumper, but you need to separate the connector to the main harness inside the trunk and feed the connector and boot through the panel hole during removal. You may need to remove the trunk end trim and open the access panel to the jack recess for access, depending on how the wiring is routed on your car.

8 The bumper assembly should now be retained only by the main mountings. Check that the assembly is free at each end - we think that we've described all of the fittings, but you may encounter slight variations for specific markets.

9 + Working under the back of the car, slacken and remove the eight 14 mm nuts which retain the bumper assembly to the reinforced turrets which project down from the body. Some of these are partly concealed by the exhaust system, and you'll find that removal will be easier if you use a short socket extension. Note that the bumper will come free when you do this, so have some help ready to support it. The assembly is lightweight, but you won't be able to support it and remove the nuts from below at the same time. Pull the assembly back and clear of the body, checking that it or any associated wiring does not get snagged. Place the assembly on some soft cloth to protect it from damage.

10/9a Remove securing nuts ...

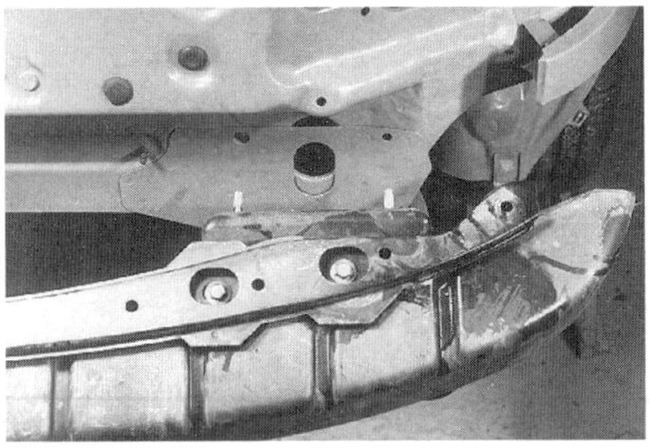

10/9b ... and lift bumper away making ...

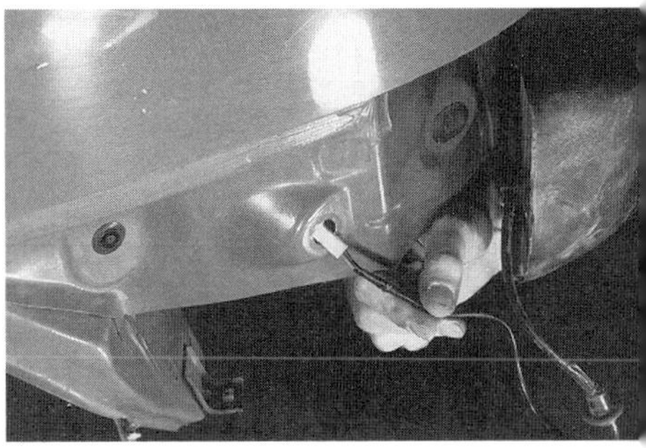

10/9c ... sure wiring is withdrawn too.

10 + To detach the rear fascia molding from the supporting structure, you need to remove the plastic retainers which fit along the top and bottom edges. Before you do this, detach the side

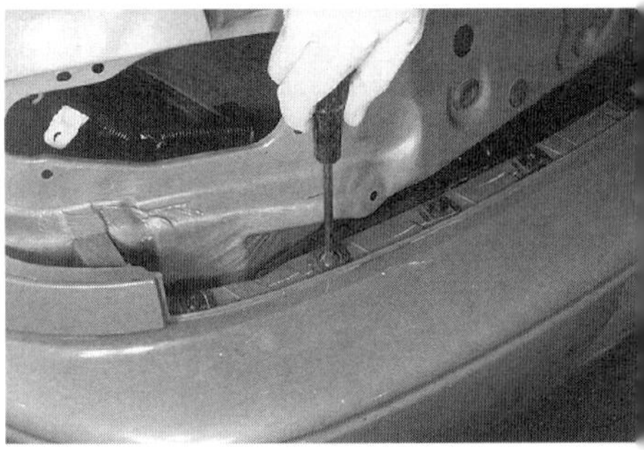

10/10a Release centre screw and ...

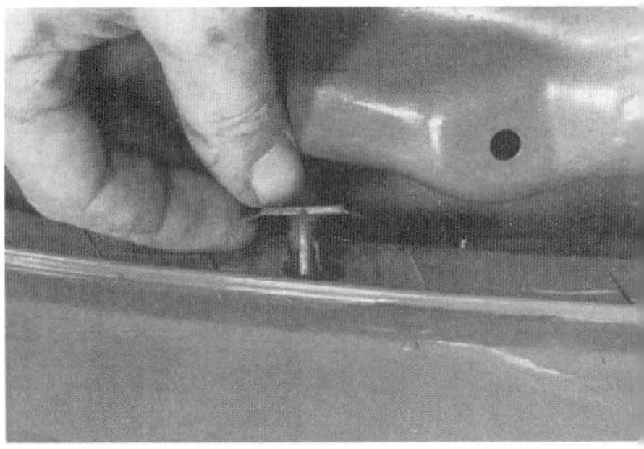

10/10b ... then pull out each retainer ...

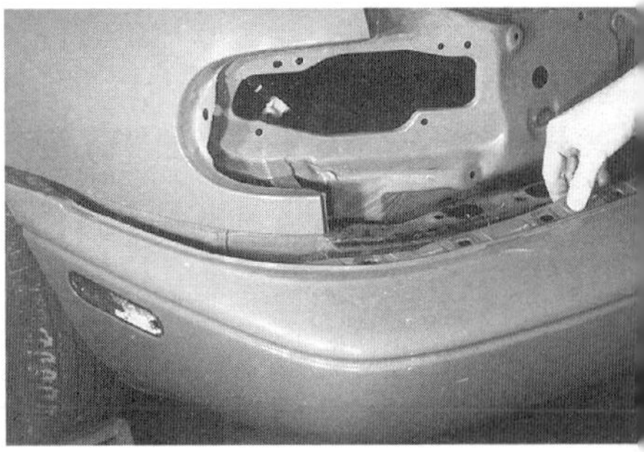

10/10c ... to free the rear fascia molding.

marker lights and wiring (where fitted). Unscrew each of the cross-headed screws, then pull the rectangular retainers out to free the fascia. If you need to do this without removing the bumper from the car, you can do so after removing the rear finisher panel ☞ 11/6.

11 ☐+ 🔲 The metal retainer strip can be removed from the top edge of the bumper reinforcement if necessary (two bolts) as can the bumper set plates and stays.

12 The most usual reason to be removing the bumper is in the aftermath of a rear-end impact, 'though we know they also get sun-bleached. Just

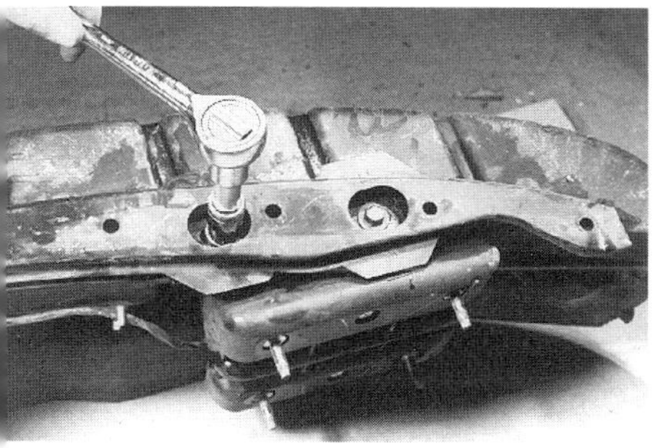

10/11a Two bolts hold retainer strip each side ...

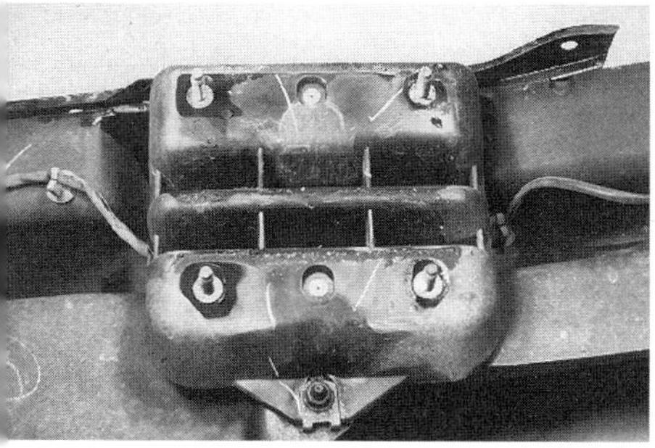

10/11b ... then single nut holds set plate.

about all of the bumper assembly is made up of molded plastic parts, designed to absorb low-speed impact energies, and to deform under harder impact to prevent damage to the vehicle structure. You'll need to examine the bumper parts closely to check for impact damage - most likely this will not be readily apparent during casual checking. Even where the bumper reinforcement and stays appear to be the right shape, look out for white patches which may indicate stress areas. If you have any doubts, fit new parts.

13 ☐ You also need to examine the turrets which support the bumper stays. These are sub-

10/13 Full rearward nudity!

stantial steel fabrications, and we would be surprised if they *ever* got damaged! Even if the turrets themselves are tough, we note that they attach to the regular-gauge steel box-section under the trunk floor. These sections are much lighter in construction and would bend or deform easily under moderate impact forces, so check these especially carefully, looking for indications of bending or rippling of the steel. If you think that there might be damage in this area, we recommend that you get this checked out by a Mazda dealer or a professional body shop - don't take chances with safety.

14 ☐ When assembling the bumper, note that the two bolts which secure the retainer strip to the bumper reinforcement should be tightened to 16-23 Nm (1.6-2.3 kgf m / 12-17 lbf ft). Fit the fascia panel over the bumper reinforcement and secure it with the plastic retainers, pushing them in position. They are locked in place by the center screws. We must confess to having trouble with these on our car - screwing them in didn't seem to work too well. We concluded that the 'screws' are simply pressed or tapped into place during initial assembly, and this approach seemed to work better for us during installation. Check that the side marker wiring harness is correctly positioned (where

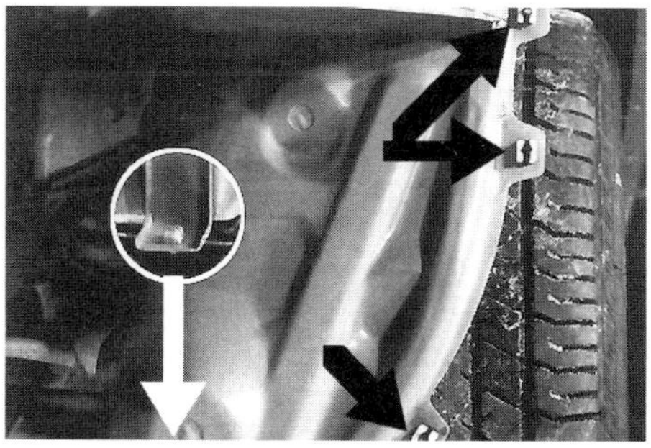

10/14 Check that threaded clips present.

fitted) before installing the bumper. Check also that the various threaded clips are correctly positioned around the edge of the inner wheelwell extension.

15 Installing the assembled bumper is quite straightforward, but note that you'll need assistance to hold it in position while you fit and tighten the mounting nuts. Start by positioning the assembly with one person on each side - that way you can make sure that the bumper ends fit correctly around the body, particularly around the wheelwells. Remember to feed rear side marker/rear fog lamp wiring through the body hole and to snap the boot into the hole to seal it. Once in place, have your assistant hold it there while you climb underneath and fit the eight mounting nuts. These should be tightened evenly to 16-23 Nm (1.6-2.3 kgf m / 12-17 lbf ft).

16 Fit the two sheet metal screws which retain the ends of the bumper at the wheelwells. The top screw is fitted up into the hollow locating peg, while the lower screw fits into the lug at the bottom of the wheel arch extension.

17 Fit the splash shields which close the gap between the bumper and the wheel arch. Each one is secured by three sheet metal screws, threaded into inserted clips on the body.

18 On cars which use them, install the additional rear flaps. Each lower section is held by four machine screws which thread into body clips. Position the short upper section and retain it with the two spring clips to the body seam. Note that in addition to the clips, a strip of self-adhesive foam positions these sections. Use commercially-available adhesive foam for this, or alternatively, coat the back of the section with silicone-rubber RTV sealant, position the section, then fit the clips.

19 Where appropriate, reconnect the side marker light wiring and install the marker lights in the fascia panel. On European cars with a rear fog light, reconnect the wiring in the trunk. On all cars, install any removed trim parts and check that all lights work normally.

11. BUMPER (FRONT) - REMOVAL & INSTALLATION

☞ 1/1, 2.

REMOVAL

1 🔲 Start by raising the headlights, then disconnect the battery negative (-) lead to isolate the electrical system ☞ 7/2. Open the hood and support it with its stay.

2 Pry off the front wheel hubcaps, and slacken the lug nuts by one turn each. Raise the front of the car and support it securely on safety stands, then remove the lug nuts and lift the wheels away ☞ 1/3.

3 ☐ Remove the front license plate holder. This will vary in design according to the type and shape of the plate used in each country, but the Mazda support bracket is held by two 10 mm nuts under the top edge of the air intake at the nose of the car. Slacken and remove the nuts (after pulling off the protective caps, where fitted) and remove

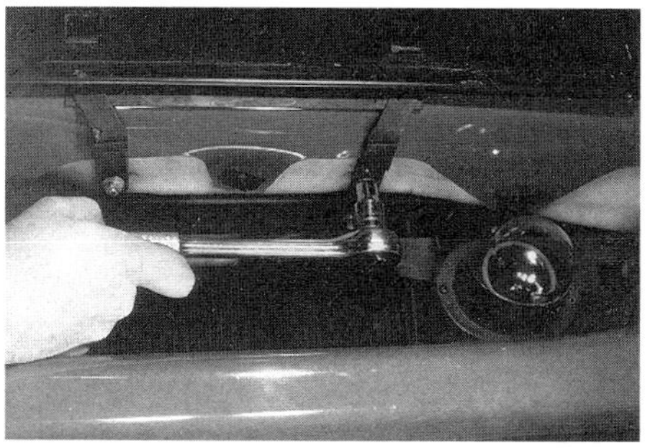

11/3 Bracket held by two nuts.

the bracket and plate as an assembly. Note that the projecting studs are attached to plates fitted from above the opening - push these out and remove them, storing them with the plate and nuts.

4 On cars with front side marker lights, remove the two screws which secure each light to the bumper fascia, pull out the lights and disconnect the wiring. On other cars with plain reflectors at this location, these may be left in position.

5 ☐ Remove the front combination lights (two crosshead screws) and unplug the bulb holders, which can be left in position. You may wish to

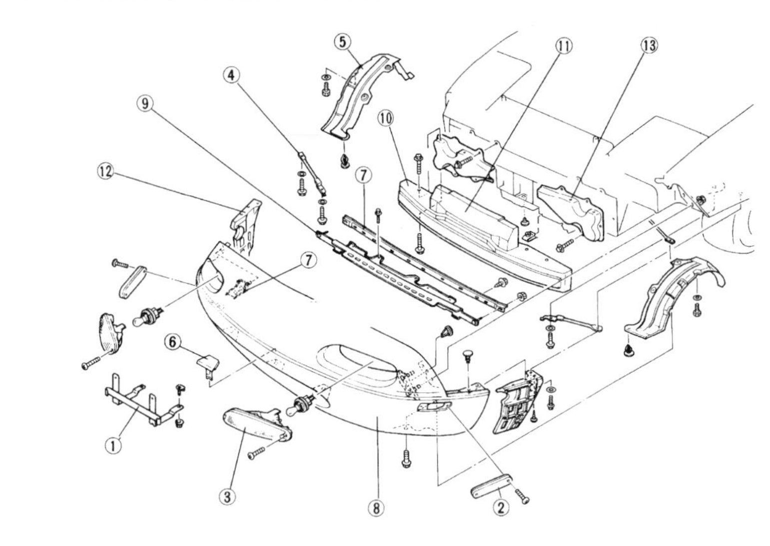

D11/1 FRONT BUMPER DETAIL.
1 License plate holder. 2 Light or reflector unit. 3 Light unit. 4 Fender stay. 5 Liner. 6 Fascia molding grille retainers. 7 Set plate. 8 Front bumper fascia molding. 9 Retainer. 10 Bumper reinforcement. 11 Spacer. 12 Retainer. 13 Bumper mounting bracket.

11/8b ... pull foglights from grille opening.

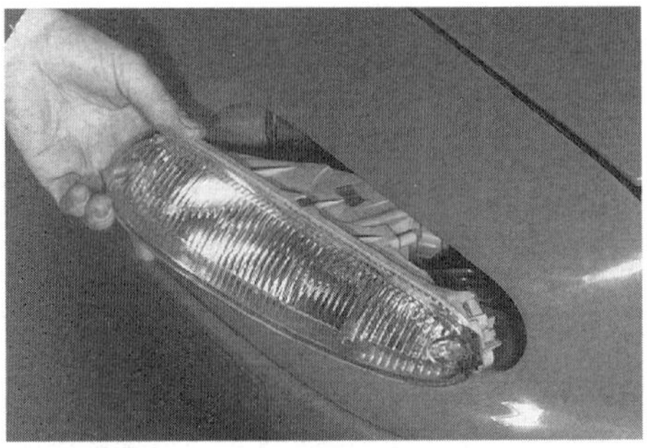

11/5 Remove combination light & unplug wiring.

11/7Liner held by screws & plastic fasteners.

remove the bulbs to prevent accidental breakage ☞ 7/38.

6 Working in each wheel well in turn, remove the two stays which locate and support the bumper assembly. These are each retained by a 10 mm bolt at each end. You may find that it helps to apply a little releasing fluid to overcome any corrosion on the threads.

7 Next, remove the liners from the wheel wells. These are lightweight plastic moldings secured around the lip of the well by 10 mm headed screws, and to the inner wheel arch panel by two-piece plastic fasteners. The fasteners used have plastic crosshead screws at the center which need to be removed before the outer, flanged section can by pried out and removed. You may find, as we did, that you need to lever gently under the flange of the fastener so that it grips the screw threads, which can then be gently unscrewed and removed. Check each fastener as you remove it. If it is worn or distorted, fit a new one during installation.

8 + Moving to the air intake, if your car has the optional fog/driving lights fitted, these need to be detached. Each light is mounted on a bracket, held at each end by a 10 mm nut. Remove the nuts, pull the light out of the intake and disconnect the wiring, then place it to one side. The mounting studs are loose in the nose, located by flat metal plates reached from above. Push these out and place the studs with the removed lights.

9 + Along the lower edge of the intake are three trapezoidal plastic plates - these form the heads of locating pins which secure the fascia molding. These need to be removed. Note that each one is locked by small tangs on the lower end of the pins - it is preferable to squeeze these tangs together with snipe-nosed pliers to facilitate removal. At the top of the intake, you'll find three plastic crosshead retainers; these should be re-

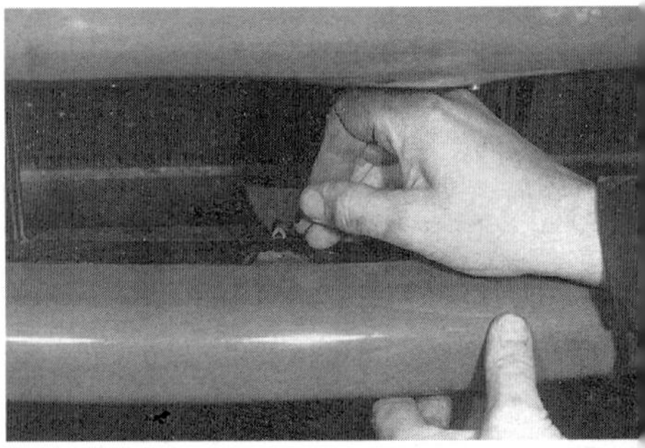

11/9a Three retainers in base of grille & ...

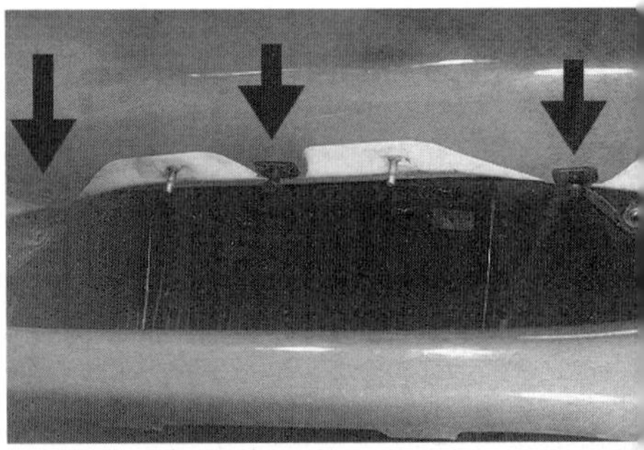

11/9b ... three at the top.

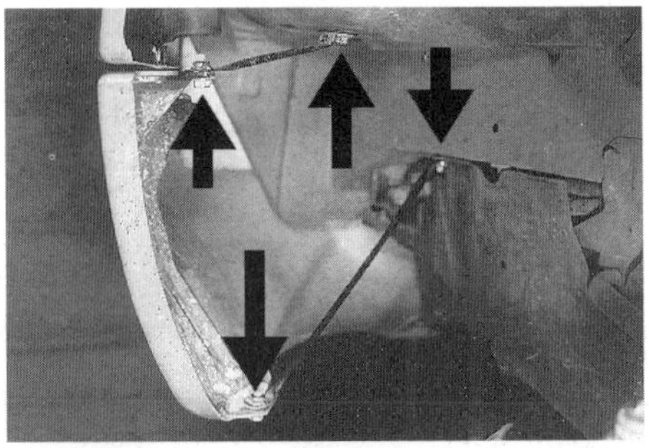

11/6 Stays are bolted at each end.

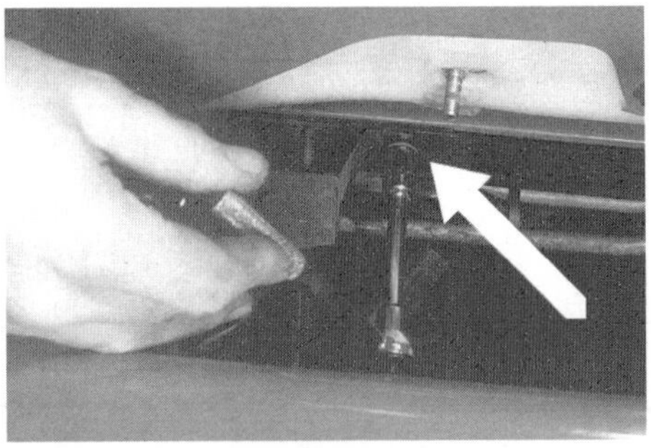

11/8a Remove fixing nuts and ...

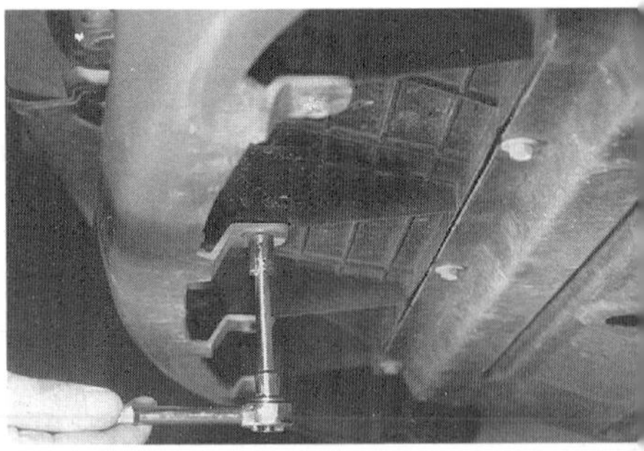

11/9c Four bolts secure base of fascia molding.

moved to free the fascia panel from the supporting structure. Finally, remove the four 10 mm bolts which secure the lower edge of the fascia to the underside of the car.

10 + Just inside the hood opening, you'll find a steel retainer plate which attaches the bumper assembly to the body. Remove the six 10 mm bolts which retain it, plus the single 10 mm nut at each end of the retainer - you'll need to lift the rubber plate a little to reach these.

11 Moving back to the wheel wells, remove the two 10 mm nuts which secure the bumper assembly to the outer supports. On our car these

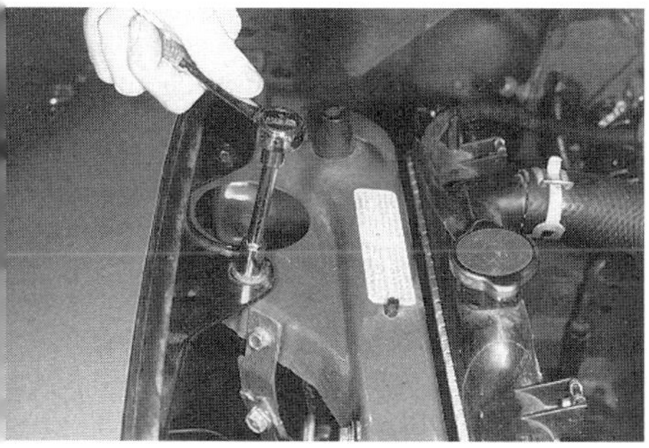

11/10a The retainer plate is held by bolts, two ...

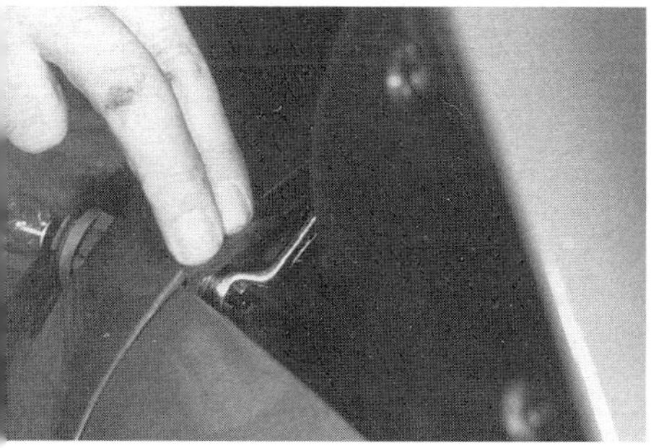

11/10b ... are well hidden.

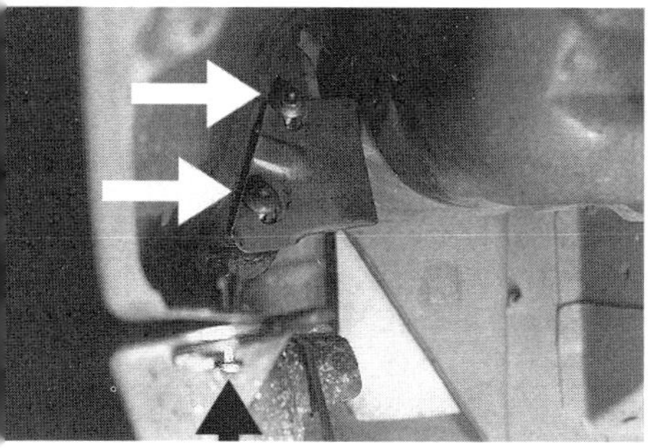

11/11 Fender fixed to supports by two nuts.

had corroded quite badly, so we soaked them in releasing fluid rather than risk breaking the studs during removal. Next, release the sheet metal screw which secures the extreme edge of the bumper on each side of the car.

12 You can now remove the front fascia from the car. Ideally, you should have assistance during this stage to make sure nothing gets snagged up as you pull it away. You will need to guide the outer ends of the fascia away from the support brackets as the unit is removed.

13 If required, the set plate and weather seal

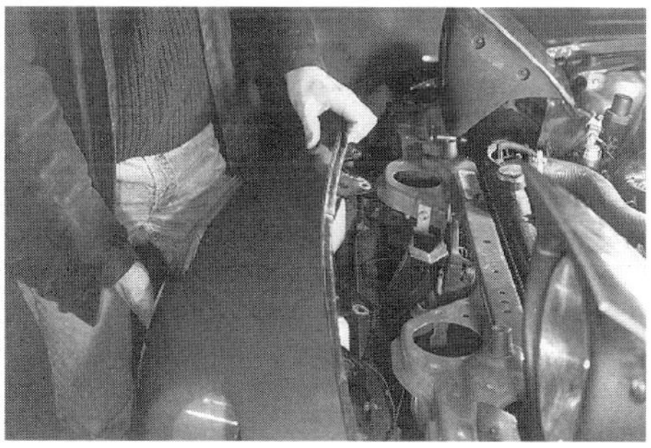

11/12 Lift away the front fascia molding.

can be removed from the fascia. This is in two sections and each is retained by sheet metal screws. Note how the sections overlap at the center, and that each is located over small plastic pegs. The retainers at the outer ends of the fascia can also be removed if needed.

14 The bumper reinforcement takes the form of a plastic molding bolted to the two pressed steel brackets at the front of the body. Above the reinforcement is a styrofoam 'spacer' section, which on our car was taped in position, and was removed with the reinforcement. Remove the eight shoul-

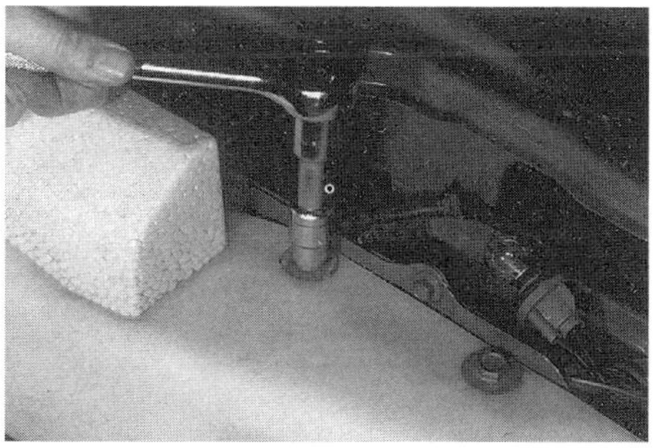

11/14 Bumper reinforcement held by 8 bolts.

dered bolts and lift the assembly away.

CHECKING

15 The most usual reason for removing the bumper is in the aftermath of impact damage, 'though we know they also get sun-bleached. Just about all of the bumper assembly is made up of molded plastic parts, designed to absorb low-speed impact energies, and to deform under harder impact to prevent damage to the vehicle structure. This means that in some circumstances, little external evidence of the impact will be visible, but you should examine the bumper parts closely to check for telltale signs - most likely this will not be readily apparent during casual checking. Even where the bumper reinforcement appears to be the right shape, look out for white patches which may indicate stress areas. If you have any doubts, fit new parts.

16 You also need to examine the bumper brackets. These can be unbolted and new ones installed if they have become bent, but check carefully for damage to the underlying bodywork. If this has been damaged or distorted, get professional help with the repair. If you think that there might be damage in any related area, we recommend that you get this checked out by a Mazda dealer or a professional body shop - don't take chances with safety.

INSTALLATION

17 Where they were removed, install the bumper brackets and the bumper reinforcement. Each is secured by bolts which need to be tightened to 16-23 Nm (1.6-2.3 kgf m / 12-17 lbf ft).

18 Before installing the fascia assembly, check that the retainers at each end are correctly installed, and that the set plate / weatherstrip sections are in position. In the case of the latter, note that you can't easily reach the screws with the fascia installed.

19 Carefully position the fascia assembly, checking that nothing is stopping it from aligning with the surrounding bodywork. Make sure that you don't trap the combination light wiring during installation. Fit the two nuts on each side to the studs projecting through the flange in the front of the wheel well. Tighten the retaining nuts to 7.8-12.0 Nm (80-120 kgf cm / 69-104 lbf in).

20 Secure the retainer plate to the body just inside the hood opening, tightening the bolts to 7.8-12.0 Nm (80-120 kgf cm / 69-104 lbf in). Fit and tighten the nut at each end of the retainer / set

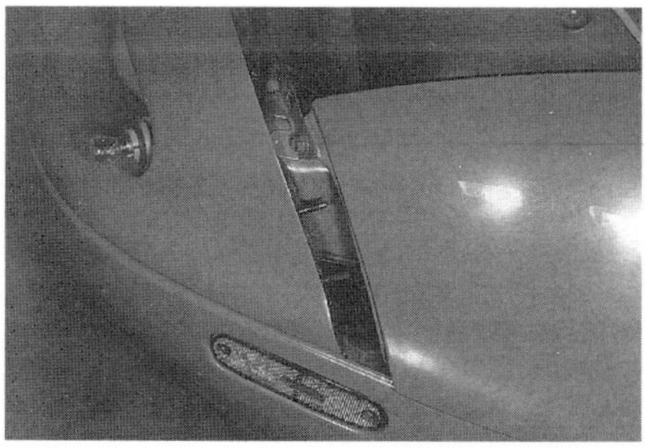

11/19 Carefully reposition the fascia molding.

plate assembly.

21 + Fit the three trapezoidal retainers in the air intake opening, then fit the fog/driving lights (where fitted) and the license plate. Reconnect and install the front combination lights and front side marker lights (where fitted).

22 Working in each wheel well in turn, install the inner liners, then fit the two stays. Reconnect the battery and check that the lights work correctly. Fit the wheels, tightening the lug nuts handtight.

23 Jack the car and remove the safety stands, then lower it to the ground and check tighten the lug nuts before fitting the hub caps ☞ 1/3.

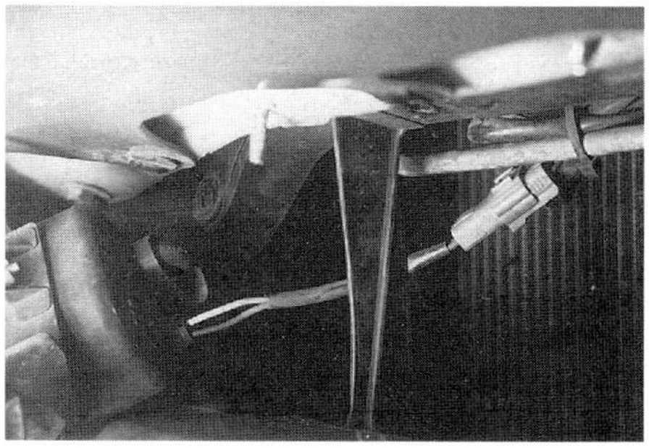

11/21a Reconnect foglight wiring ...

11/21b ... and secure foglights in position.

12. FENDER (WING) (FRONT) - REMOVAL & INSTALLATION

☞ 1/1, 2.

1 The Miata/MX5's front fender is a bolt-on item, which means that minor scrapes and bumps in this area are best dealt with by bolting on a new panel. You will need to get the new panel painted to match your car, but in most cases you'll get better results this way than attempting to repair and paint the old panel. If you are careful during installation (and have allowed the new paint to harden thoroughly) you can avoid the hassle of masking and spraying the new panel by getting it painted first - that way, even the hidden areas get a coat of paint.

2 Apart from one bolt, you can get at all of the fender fastening points without disturbing other bodywork. The problem of the remaining bolt is that it is hidden under the front bumper fascia, so you will need to remove the front bumper (☞ 11/11) before you can remove the damaged fender.

3 📷+ With the bumper assembly removed, start removing the fender bolts - all have 10 mm hexagon heads. There are two at the bottom edge of the fender, just below and forward of the door opening. The next is concealed in the door opening, near the beltline, so you'll need the door part open for access. Use a quarter or three eighths inch drive socket here, to avoid damaging the paint on the door edge.

4 📷+ Next, remove the five bolts along the top edge of the fender, accessible with the hood raised (the bolt nearest the front of the car is the one normally covered by the front bumper). You now need to remove the turn signal side repeater light (European cars) by popping it out of its hole in the fender and unplugging the wiring connector. Hidden in the recess between the back edge of the fender and the body is the final fixing, a single nut which is normally concealed by the wheel arch liner. You will need several extension bars to allow a socket to reach the nut, which should be slackened by several turns but left attached to its stud.

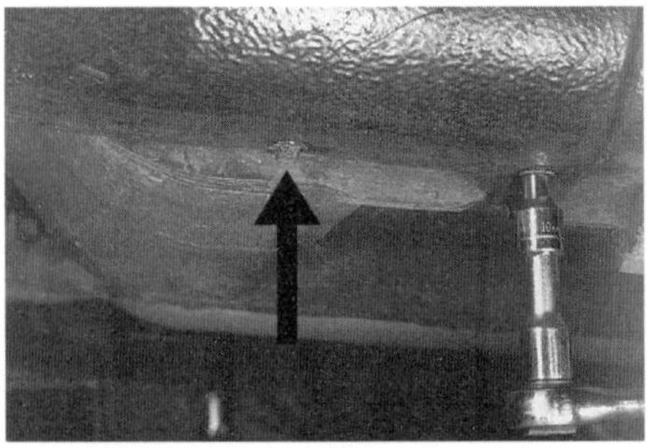

12/3a Two bolts secure lower part of fender.

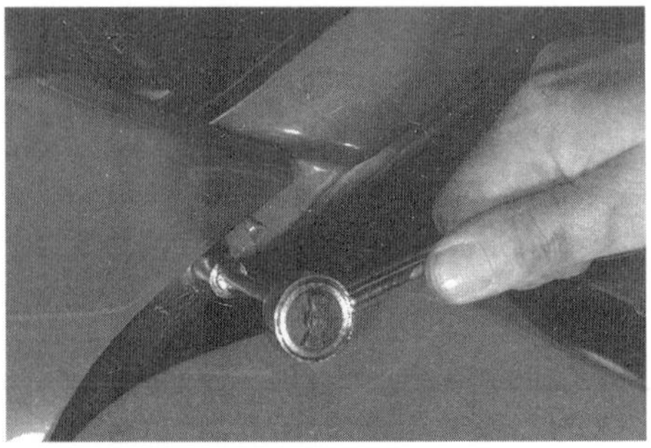

12/3b One bolt concealed in door opening.

12/4a Release bolts along fender top ...

12/4b ... this one at the front ...

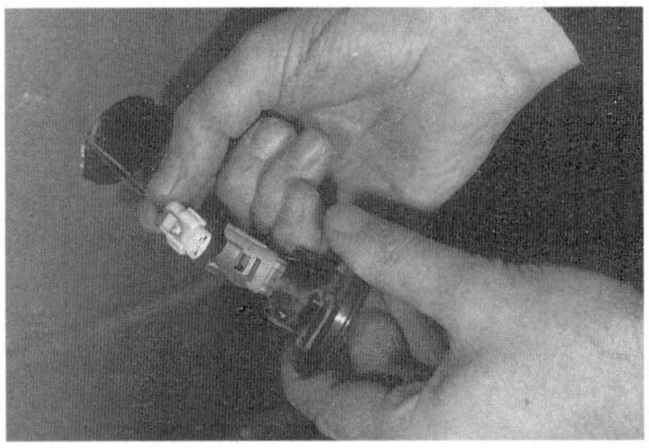

12/4c ...remove and disconnect side repeater ...

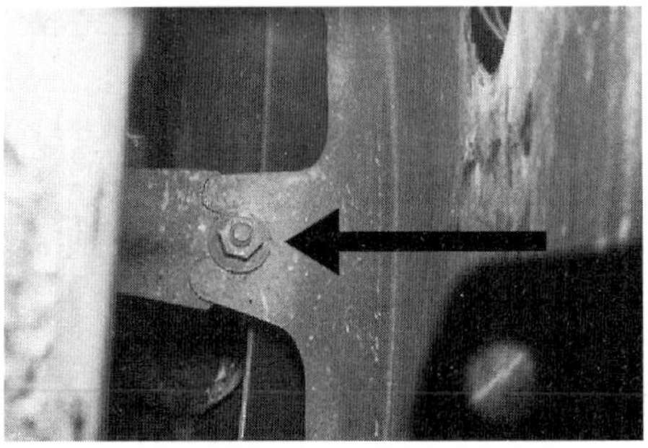

12/4d ... leaving just one nut, right at the back ...

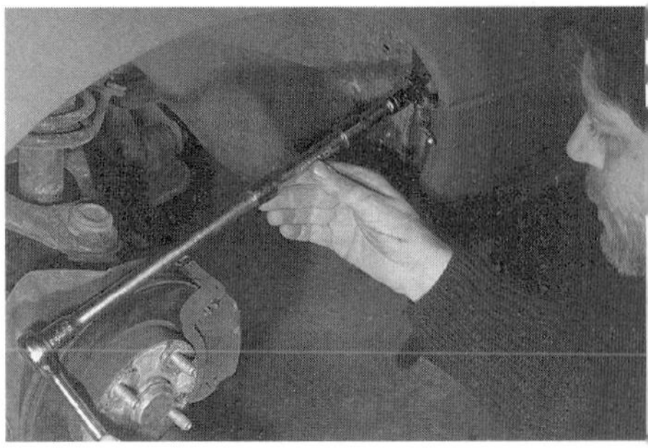

12/4e ... for which you'll need several extensions.

5 📷 The remaining fixing points are shared with the bumper, and so will have already have been dealt with. Lift the fender away, taking care not to gouge surrounding paint on the sharp edges of the panel.

6 When installing the fender, note that if it is the original panel, you need only align it so that the bolts fit with the unpainted areas at the flanges to ensure a good fit. If it is a new panel, we suggest that you use only an original Mazda part, or you may experience fitting or alignment problems.

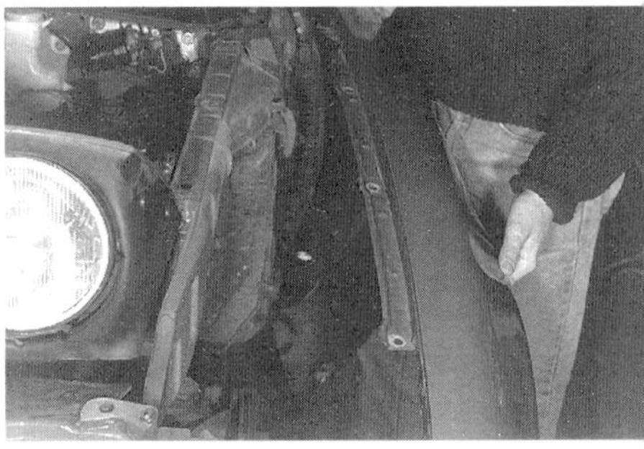

12/5 Lift the fender away.

7 Fit and tighten loosely all of the fixing bolts, then check the fit against the door and hood. Make any minor adjustments, then tighten the fixing bolts, checking that any shared fixing points with the bumper mountings will align correctly. Finally, install the bumper assembly, checking the fit between it and the new panel.

8 We noted with some surprise that there is a bad potential rust trap area at the bottom of the fender, where it curves under the car. Generally, Mazda have done a good job of avoiding this kind of design problem, but in this instance it is just as bad as its European forebears of twenty years ago.

9 Road dirt (and, of course, any salt used during winter) is flung into the void between the fender and body through gaps between the liner and fender. There is a wedge-shaped cavity formed between the panels near the bottom, and the two panels eventually touch along the lower edge. This means that the dirt is trapped between the fender and the body.

10 There is no way to flush this out once it builds up, and it will certainly cause corrosion to take place in time. The problem is compounded because the well below the windshield discharges into this space, and because there is nowhere for the water to go, this compacts the dirt between the panels.
11 You could minimize this problem by removing the wheel well liner and the lower fender bolts so that it can be bent outward slightly and the dirt flushed out with a hose or pressure washer. We recommend that maybe once a year you apply a wax-based underbody coating to this area before the fender bolts are tightened and the liner installed. This is a real chore to do, but will be worthwhile if you plan on keeping the car for a while. If Mazda had designed-in a small drainage gap, the problem would not have arisen, but as things stand - beware of rusting in this area.

13. WINDSHIELD - REMOVAL & INSTALLATION

☞ 1/1, 2.
1 The windshield (and the rear windshield, in the case of cars fitted with hard tops) is located in a recess in the body and sealed in position with a mastic compound, the join area being concealed with trim components. Removal and installation should not be undertaken at home - special tools and sealants will be required, and it is very easy to break the glass if the wrong removal or fitting technique is employed. We suggest that you take the car to a Mazda dealer, or to one of the many companies specializing in vehicle glass - this is the most economic way of dealing with this eventuality.
2 The most usual reason for glass replacement is as a result of accident damage or vandalism. Check your insurance before you do anything else - in many instances, your insurance may cover glass damage, though this may not be the case in some countries or states. If you have glass cover, contact one of the approved specialists listed by the insurers.
3 If your car's screen breaks while driving, pull over as quickly as you can. If your vision is obscured, wind down the door glass so that you can see better. **Warning!** Do not attempt to punch out the damaged screen. This usually results in serious injury to the hand, and you'll be covered in flying glass if you should succeed in breaking through the screen.
4 If your car is fitted with a laminated screen, it will most likely crack from the point of impact, but will remain in one piece and generally unobscured. Toughened glass screens, on the other hand, tend to shatter into tiny cubes, making vision difficult.
5 If you have no option but to remove the damaged screen yourself, cover the hood and the interior of the car with sheets to catch the debris, and wear gloves and eye protection when removing the remaining glass. Be absolutely certain that you have removed all traces of glass from the car interior and from the hood, and take care to avoid glass entering vents. If possible, use an industrial vacuum cleaner to ensure that all glass fragments are removed from the car interior.
6 In some countries and states it may be permissible to fit a temporary plastic screen until you can get a new one fitted. These are made of clear plastic sheeting, and so will soon become scratched in use, especially if the wipers are used; they should be regarded as an emergency measure only and a glass screen must be installed as soon as possible. Some drivers carry one of these screens in the trunk for just such emergencies, though we suspect that most Miata/MX5 owners will have more pressing demands on trunk space.

14. HARD TOP - INSTALLATION & ADJUSTMENT

☞ 1/1, 2.
1 Mazda offer a hard top option for the Miata/MX5, and it is this standard item that we refer to in this section. Note that there are a number of third-party hard tops available. These normally use a similar mounting arrangement to the factory top, but you should refer to the manufacturer's instructions for specific information when dealing with these parts.
2 Most Miata/MX5 owners will wish to use the hard top option through the winter months, and will probably install the soft top during summer. The hard top also offers greater vehicle security in high-risk areas. Installing and removing the hard top should be regarded as a two-person operation - the top is not especially heavy, but it is too cumbersome to maneuver into place alone, without risking damage to the top or body.
3 If you have no choice but to remove and fit the top unaided, you should consider purchasing one of the miniature hoists produced for this purpose. These allow you to suspend the top from your garage, drive the car into position, and then lower the top safely into place on the car.
4 After installing the hard top, you should check the various latch adjustments and check the fit of the top in relation to the body and doors. In the most part, these adjustments and checks will be found below - the latches and weatherstrips are generally similar to those used on the convertible top ☞ 11/15.
5 Specific to the hard top only is the rear deck latch assembly. This secures the back edge of the hard top, and controls its position in relation to the windshield header. If the top is misaligned, remove the small screw which secures the rear deck latch cover plate and hinge it open. Install the top and check its fit with the surrounding panels and the windshield header.
6 If you need to adjust the latch, slacken the mounting plate bolts sufficiently to permit the assembly to move, then adjust its position until a good fit is obtained. Tighten the bolts to 18-26 Nm (1.8-2.7 kgf m / 13-20 lbf ft), then close the cover and fit the retaining screw. Recheck the adjustment, making sure that the top now latches in the correct position.

15. CONVERTIBLE TOP - REMOVAL, INSTALLATION & ADJUSTMENT

☞ 1/1, 2.

REMOVAL

1 Miata/MX5 owners are justifiably proud of the fit and functionality of the factory convertible top; it is well designed and manufactured, opens and shuts easily, and keeps out the rain well; it is notable that many more expensive cars are sadly lacking in this respect. If and when the time comes that you need to remove the top, here's how to do it.
2 Start work inside the car with the top up. We found that it is easier if you remove the seats to give you better access, or at least to adjust them fully forward and to tip the seat backs forward. You will need to remove the carpet which covers the luggage area and the vertical firewall which runs behind the seat. These sections are retained by plastic clips and also by two stops which are retained by screws. For more information ☞ 10/12.
3 You now need to remove the two quarter trim panels. These cover the rear quarters of the car interior, running from the back edge of the door opening around to the package shelf, and providing a housing for the seat belt mechanisms.
4 Start by removing the hard top location

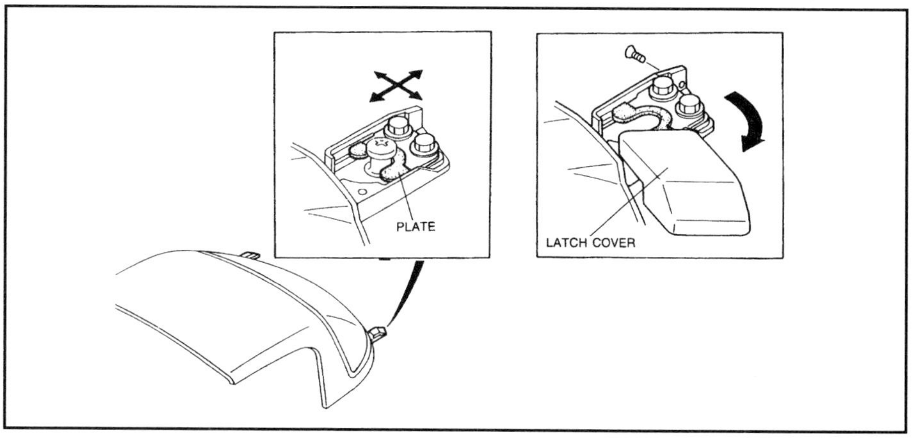

D14/6 HARDTOP LATCH ADJUSTMENT.

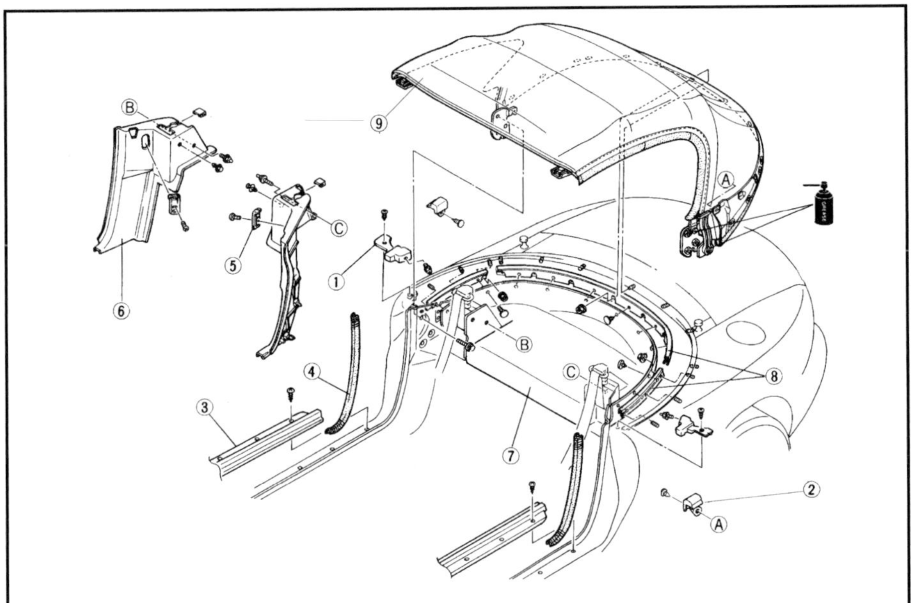

D15/1 CONVERTIBLE TOP DETAIL.
1 Beltline cover trim. 2 Beltline protector. 3 Rocker door sill scuff plate. 4 Door seal. 5 Striker plate. 6 Rear quarter trim panel. 7 Rear package shelf trim. 8 Set plates. 9 Convertible top.

stop which is secured by two 6.6 mm Torx screws. You should really use a Torx wrench on these screws, though we found it possible to shift them using Allen wrenches - a 5 mm Allen wrench is a little slack, while a 6 mm wrench may be too tight - you'll have to experiment with your own set to find a snug fit. If the screws on your car prove to be tight, don't risk damaging the screw heads - get the correct Torx wrench.

5 Next, remove the finishing piece (beltline cover) at the top corner of the door opening. This is held in place by a single crosshead screw fitted from the top plus a 10 mm headed set screw fitted from the side. Next, remove the beltline protector. This is a short trim section and is secured just inside the body opening by a single plastic pin retainer. Note that this pin also passes through the convertible top's rain rail.

6 From the edge of the trim panel just to the rear of the seatbelt top mounting point, unclip and remove the small closing section to provide a gap though which the belt can be passed. You will also need to pull out the clip-in plastic loop through which the belt passes - free this from the trim, leaving it loosely in place around the belt.

7 On the side of the trim panel, free the single plastic clip, lifting the center section using a small screwdriver, and then lifting the fastener out of its hole. Remove the 10 mm set screw adjacent to the clip.

8 Pull away the door seal where it covers the edge of the trim. On our car, which had aftermarket scuff plates, we also needed to release the scuff plate screws - this allows the bottom of the trim to be freed. The rest of the trim edge is tucked under the carpet edge and comes free easily.

9 Lift the panel and move it forward, remembering to feed the seatbelt through the slot at the back of the trim, then lift it away. Remove the remaining quarter trim panel to provide access to the main convertible top mounting area.

10 + You now need to free the back edge of the convertible top. This is secured by a three-piece set plate arrangement, each section of which is retained by 10 mm nuts. Remove the nuts and pull the set plate sections of the mounting studs. You can now free the back edge of the top by carefully pulling it away from the studs. You need to tip the lower edge of the top away from the body until the lip disengages from the top's rain rail section - do not force this or the top may be

15/10a Remove the securing nuts, followed ...

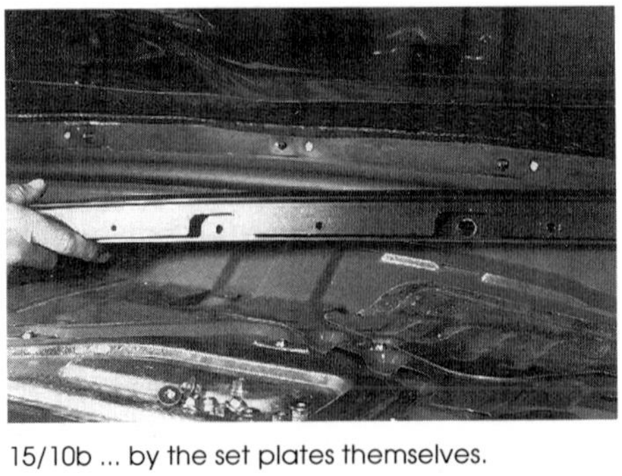

15/10b ... by the set plates themselves.

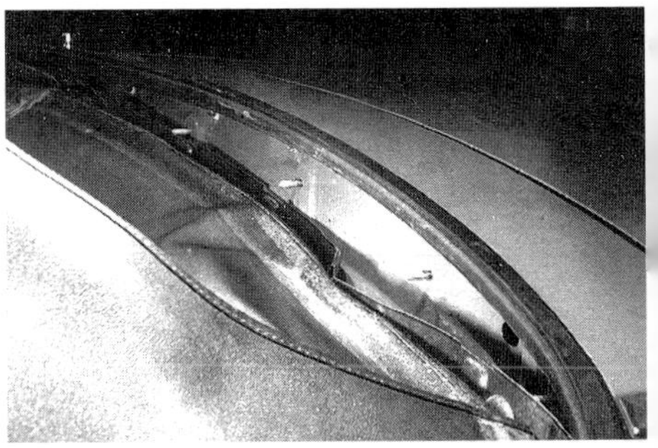

15/10c Carefully pull the softtop from the studs.

damaged.

11 Release the convertible top's front latches, but don't fold the top. Unzip the rear window and lay it flat, then carefully fold the top.

12 Have an assistant to help you from this stage onward. Remove the three bolts which secure the main hinge plate (Mazda call this a link bracket) to the body. The top will remain in place, located by pins on each side. Grasp each side of the convertible top, lift it slightly and disengage it from the locating pins. The assembly can now be lifted away from the body.

INSTALLATION

13 With the help of an assistant, lift the folded top assembly into position, making sure that the link bracket hooks over the locating pins on each side. Check that the extended rain rail molding on each side is positioned correctly - this is brittle and easily damaged if forced into place or mishandled, and if damaged, rain will get into the car. Once it is positioned correctly, fit the retaining bolts and tighten them to 19-25 Nm (1.9-2.6 kgf m / 14-19 lbf ft). Note that the link bracket should be resting on the locating pins - there should be no clearance between them.

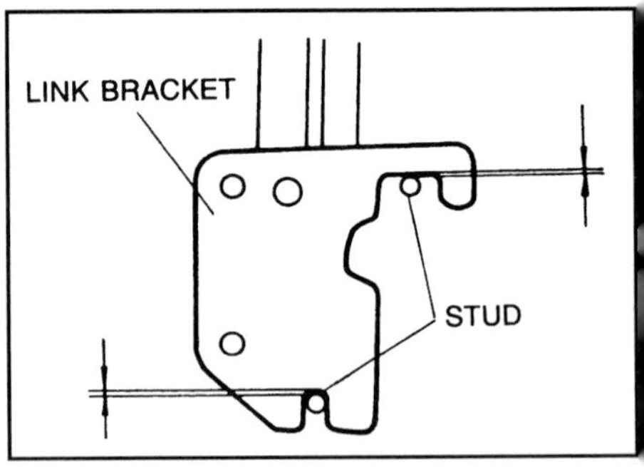

D15/3 THERE SHOULD BE NO CLEARANCE BETWEEN LINK BRACKET & PINS.

14 Part-open the top, but do not latch it at the front. Fit the back edge of the top over the row of studs at the back of the luggage area. Note that it is important that the rain rail section hooks under the projecting lip, or rain will leak into the car. We suggest that you check this from the outside - you should be able to run a finger along the rubber lip edge to make sure that it sits over the rain rail. Fit the set plate sections over the studs and tighten the nuts to 7.8-11 Nm (80-110 kgf cm / 69-

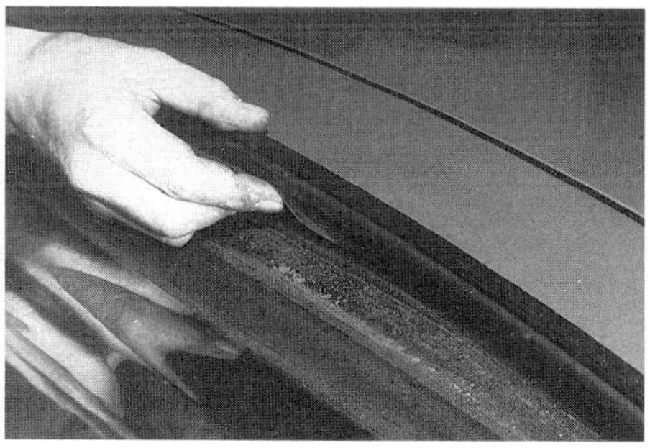

15/14 Make sure rain rail is behind this lip.

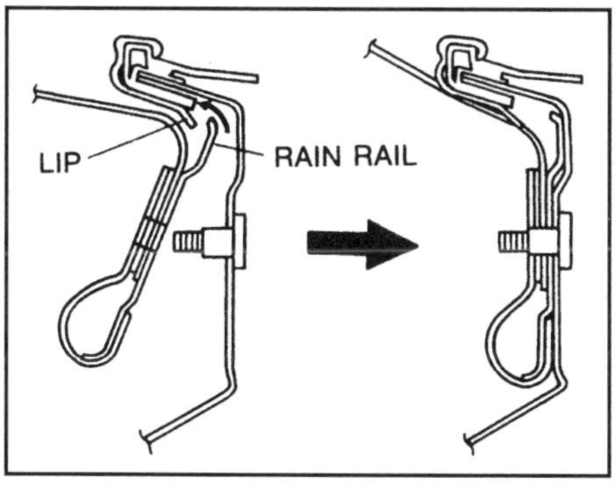

D15/14 CORRECT INSTALLATION OF THE BELTLINE MOLDING.

95 lbf in).

15 Fit the quarter trim panels, remembering to feed the seatbelt webbing through the slot at the rear. Note that the pip-headed set screws should be tightened to 6.9-9.8 Nm (70-100 kgf cm / 61-87 lbf in). Clip the closing piece into the gap to the rear of the seatbelt webbing and install the plastic loop through which the belt passes.

16 Install the beltline covers and beltline protectors. Again, note that the pip-headed set screws should be tightened to 6.9-9.8 Nm (70-100 kgf cm / 61-87 lbf in). Fit the hard top stops and tighten the Torx screws which retain them to 9.8-15 Nm (100-150 kgf cm / 37-55 lbf in). Fit the door weatherseal and scuff plates.

ADJUSTMENT

Note. These adjustments also apply to the optional hard top.

17 The top latch can be adjusted to increase or decrease the clearance between the windshield header and the convertible top or optional hard top. This is achieved by turning the adjuster nut inside the latch assembly after folding back the protector.

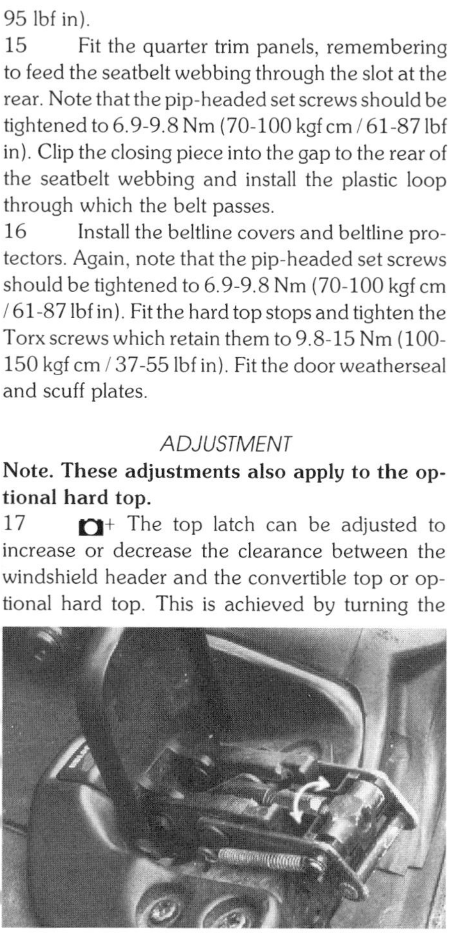

15/17a Softop latch adjustment.

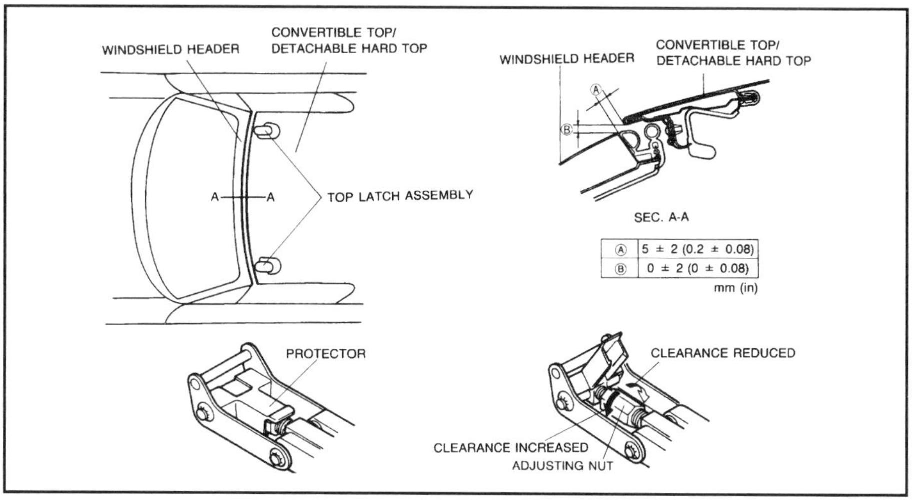

D15/18 CONVERTIBLE TOP TENSION ADJUSTMENT.

18 Turning the nut clockwise reduces clearance, while turning it counterclockwise increases clearance. The specified clearances between the top and the header are as shown in the accompanying drawing. Note that you should lock the adjustment setting afterwards by closing the protector.

15/17b We couldn't eradicate all uneveness.

19 On cars fitted with hard tops, similar side latches are fitted, and these can be adjusted in the same way as the top latches. Turning the adjuster clockwise will tighten the fit of the latch, while conversely, turning it counterclockwise will loosen the fit. For information on the rear deck latch (hard tops) ☞ 11/14.

16. CONVERTIBLE TOP REAR WINDOW & RAIN RAIL - REMOVAL & INSTALLATION

☞ 1/1, 2.

REMOVAL

1 Like just about every other convertible top, the one fitted to the Miata/MX5 employs a flexible plastic rear window. This can be unzipped from the main top fabric, allowing it to be folded down flat without creasing the window. Care when stowing the top will extend its life considerably, but eventually the window material will become

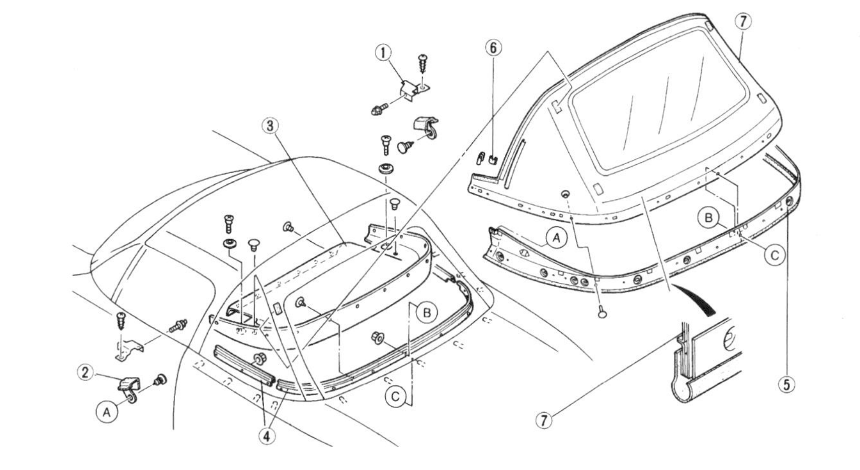

D16/1 CONVERTIBLE TOP REAR WINDOW SECTION DETAIL.
1 Beltline cover trim. 2 Beltline protector. 3 Rear package shelf trim. 4 Set plates. 5 Rain rail. 6 Zipper stop. 7 Rear window section.

scratched and opaque. When this occurs, the window section can be detached without having to remove the convertible top entirely. The removal procedure should be started with the window unzipped and folded flat, and the convertible top lowered fully.

2 Referring to the accompanying drawing, remove the beltline covers. These are each retained by a single sheet metal screw fitted from the top, plus a pip-headed 10 mm bolt fitted from the side. Next release the beltline protectors, which are secured by a plastic pin pushed into the body from the package area. The pin is not easy to spot - it is tucked away in the extreme corner of the soft top well area. The pin also passes through and secures the ends of the rain rail, which needs to be removed a little later in the procedure.

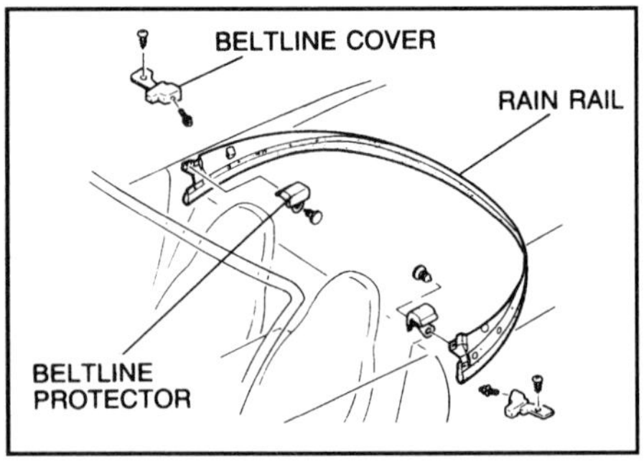

D16/2 BELTLINE COVERS, PROTECTORS & RAIL.

3 Raise the convertible top, but do not latch it to the windshield header. Remove the rear package shelf trim (carpet). This is retained by a row of plastic pins around the back edge - these push into the convertible top set plates. There are further pins along the front edge, plus a couple on the flat package area. You also need to remove the two round stops which are retained by cross-headed screws.

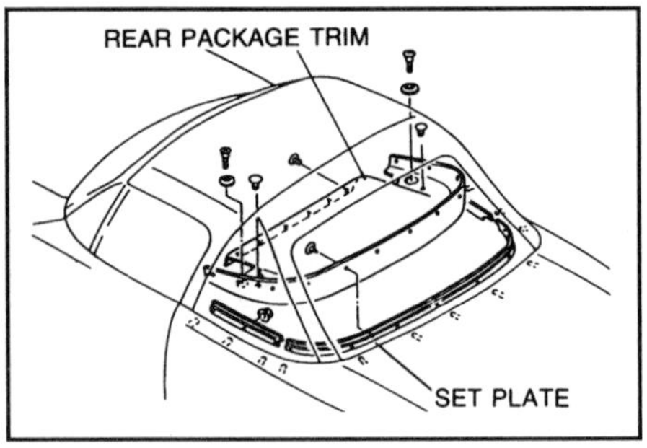

D16/3 REAR PACKAGE SHELF TRIM & SETPLATES.

4 Remove the 10 mm nuts which retain the convertible top's set plate sections which retain the top along the sides and back. The set plate comes away in three sections.

5 Just next to the seatbelt turrets you will find the end of the rain rail, riveted to the convertible top link assembly (main hinge). Using a 4 mm (0.16 in) approx. drill, carefully drill out the heads of the two rivets so that the front edge of the rain rail can be detached from the convertible top's mechanism.

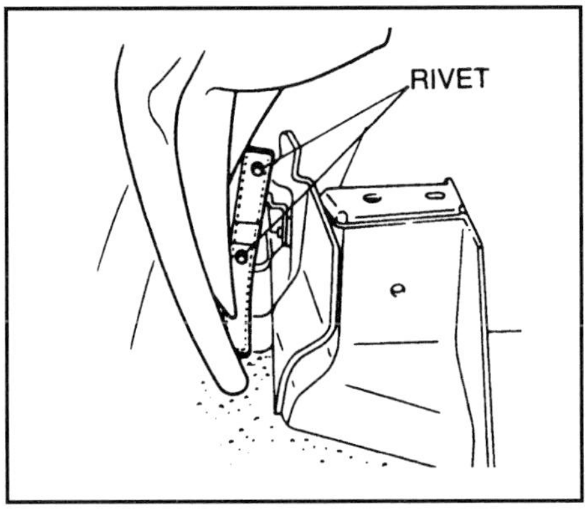

D16/5 DRILL OUT THESE RIVETS.

6 Moving to the outside of the car, lay some old towels or similar around the body opening to form a protective cover. Free the rain rail from the body by pulling it off the mounting studs. Note that the rail is made of thin plastic and is easily torn if mishandled.

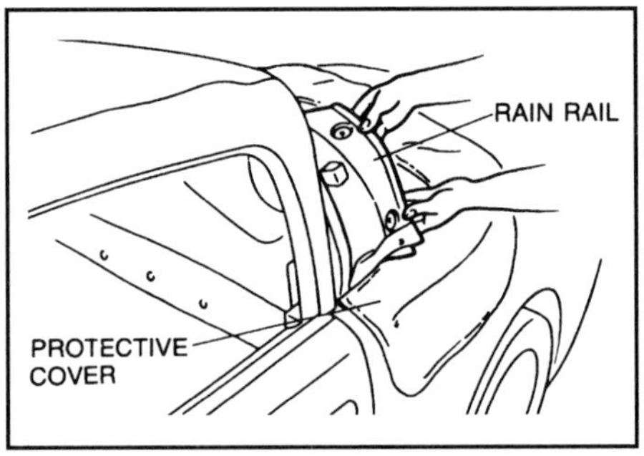

D16/6 REMOVE RAIN RAIL.

7 Using a pair of sharp side cutters, carefully remove the rivets from the rain rail, taking care not to damage the rail while doing so. Once all the rivets have been cut, remove the rain rail from the top and place it to one side.

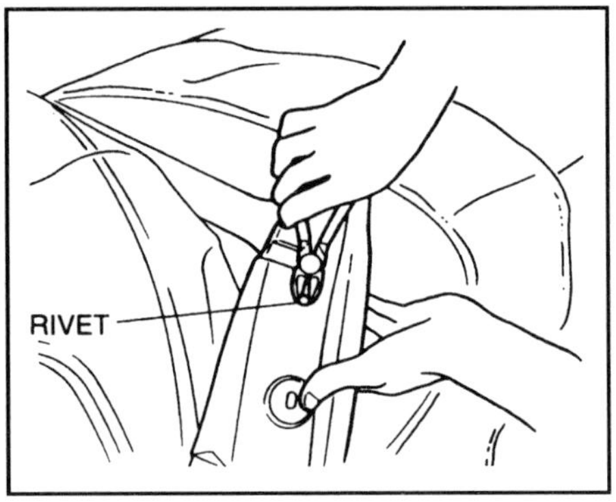

D16/7 REMOVE RIVETS WITH A CUTTER.

8 Using the cutters, remove the rivets from the edge of the rear window section, again taking care not to damage the window surround fabric.

9 Locate the ends of the rear window zipper. Using paint, mark the position of the zipper stops and the relative positions of each side of the zipper, as a guide during installation. Carefully

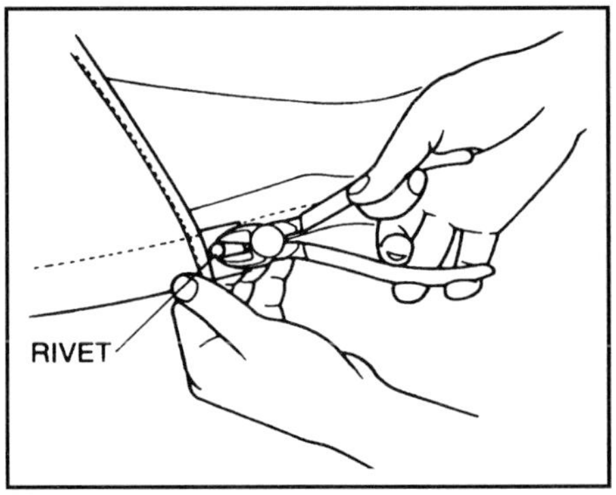

D16/8 REMOVE RIVETS WITH A CUTTER.

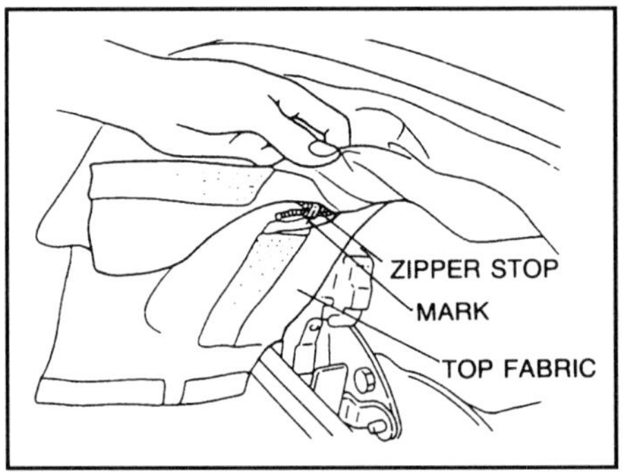

D16/9 REMOVE THE ZIPPER STOPS.

remove the stops, retrieving them for reuse during installation. The zipper may now be separated completely and the rear window section detached from the convertible top; pull off the pull tab and retain it for use during installation.

INSTALLATION

10 Clean and degrease the rain rail using ethyl alcohol, then cover the rivet holes in the rail using small pieces of pvc electrical tape. The tape pieces need to be about 20 x 20 mm (0.8 x 0.8 in).

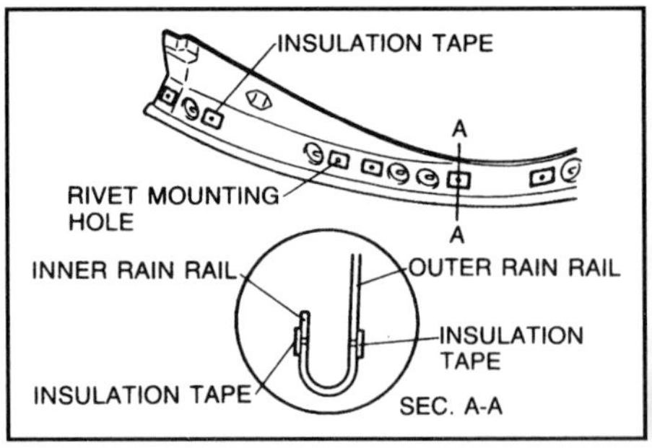

D16/10 COVER RIVET HOLES WITH PVC TAPE.

11 Position the window section in the back of the convertible top. Align the zipper ends, then engage the zipper pull tab over the ends of the zipper and zip the window into the convertible top. Check that the window section is correctly positioned and that the convertible top is not pulled out of shape. If necessary, remove the pull tab and realign the zipper ends to correct any misalignment.

12 Fit the zipper stops, positioning them as indicated by the paint marks made during removal.

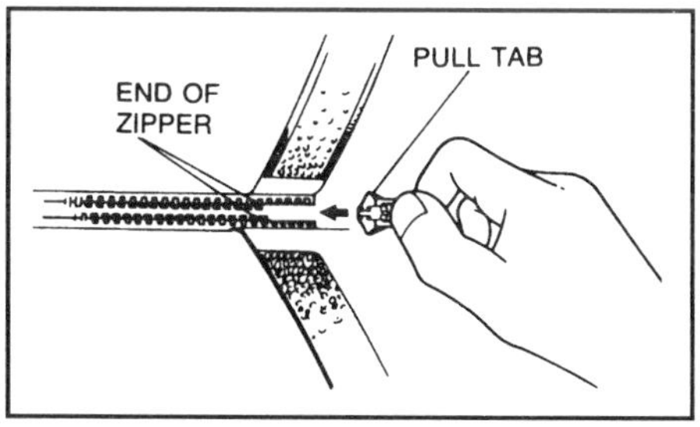

D16/11 ZIP WINDOW INTO PLACE.

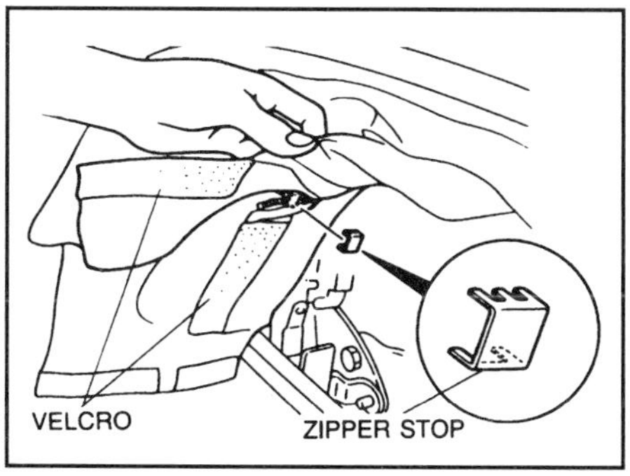

D16/12 INSTALL ZIPPER STOPS.

Close the join between the top and window sections by pushing together the Velcro pads.

13 Assemble the rain rail, top fabric and window fabric as shown in the accompanying drawing, positioning the assembly over the body studs. Note the order in which the various elements are fitted, and that the loop of the rain rail encloses the fabric sections. Position the set plates over the studs, working from the left, and fit the nuts fingertight.

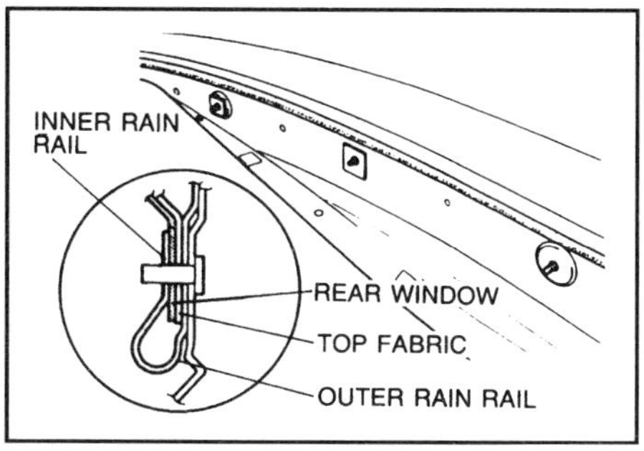

D16/13 FIT SOFTOP OVER STUDS.

14 Unzip the rear window and lower the convertible top fully. Install the beltline protectors,

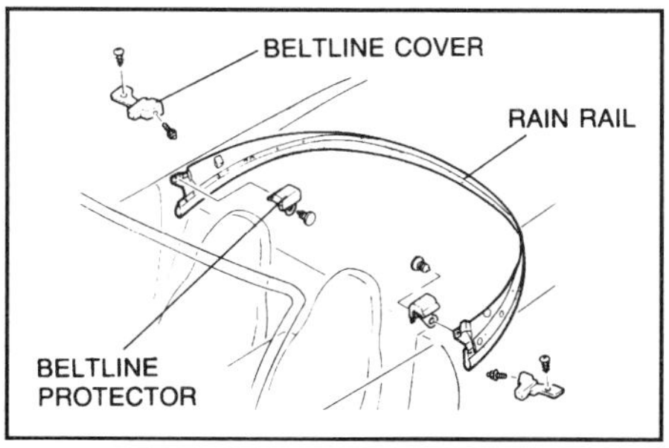

D16/14 FIT BELTLINE COVERS & PROTECTORS.

ensuring that the fixing pins pass through the ends of the rain rail. Install the beltline covers, securing each one with the single sheet metal screw and single pip-headed set screw. Now raise the top, latching it to the windshield header, and zip the window into place.

15 Working inside the car, tighten down the set plate nuts, pulling them down evenly and progressively to a torque setting of 8.8-12 Nm (90-120 kgf cm / 78-104 lbf in). Rivet the ends of the rain rail to the link assembly on each side of the car.

16 Install the rear package trim, securing it with its plastic pins and the two round stops. Make a final check of the alignment of the convertible top and rear window section. If any adjustment is needed, realign the zipper.

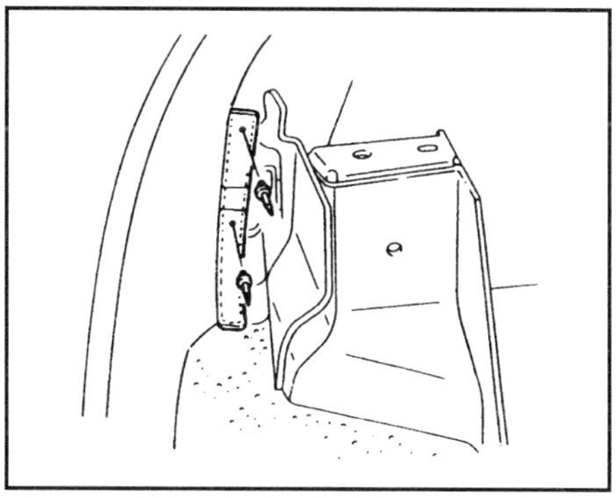

D16/15 RIVET FABRIC TO LINKS.

17. CONVERTIBLE TOP FABRIC - REMOVAL & INSTALLATION

☞ 1/1, 2.

1 It is possible to completely dismantle the convertible top to permit a new fabric section to be fitted or to allow the mechanism to be repaired or replaced. Whether you choose to do so is another matter - the procedure is complicated, and without previous experience in this type of work, you could end up with a badly-fitting top.

2 If you do not feel confident about your abilities and facilities, we suggest that you consider removing the top as described above and having a Mazda or trim specialist carry out the necessary repair or overhaul for you - that way it is somebody else's problem if the repaired top does not fit correctly. Either way, start out by removing the complete top ☞ 11/15.

17/3 Lay top upside-down on soft surface.

3 Open up the top and lay it upside down on a soft surface. You could do this on a bench covered in thick cloth, though a grassed area works well enough for this if the weather is good. Before you start, have ready a marker pen, some self-adhesive labels and some tie-on labels so that each part can be clearly marked - there are a lot of them, and it will get very confusing if you skip this.

4 Remove the weather strip sections, the set plate and the weatherstrip retainers, marking each part as it is removed. Note that you should paint-mark the retainers and screws as a position guide during installation

5 Using a 4 mm drill, remove the ten rivets which secure the top fabric to the link assembly. Remove the screws which secure the end plates to the link assembly and remove them.

6 With the rear window unzipped and the top folded loosely, free the top fabric from the link assembly.

7 Grasp the edge of the top fabric where it attaches to the front header and peel it back - it is secured by double-sided tape. Remove the screws which retain the ends of the top fabric tensioner cable springs and disconnect them from the link assembly.

8 Part unfold the top and position it with the header rail upwards. Using a 4 mm drill, drill out the rivets as shown in the drawing to free the front ends of the tensioner cables.

9 Peel back the Velcro at the rear bow. Wrap a screwdriver blade with pvc tape to prevent damage, then carefully bend back the bow retainers to release the fabric from them.

10 Free the tensioner cables from the cable guides, then detach the top fabric and cables from the link assembly. Unthread the cables from the top fabric.

17/11a Lube frame joints with WD40 or similar.

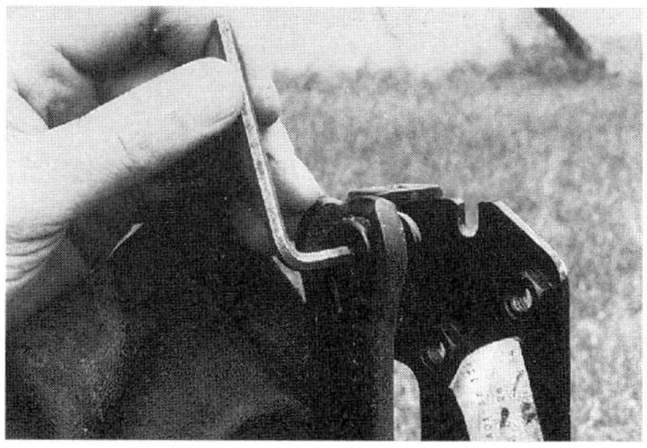

17/11b Tighten any loose joints.

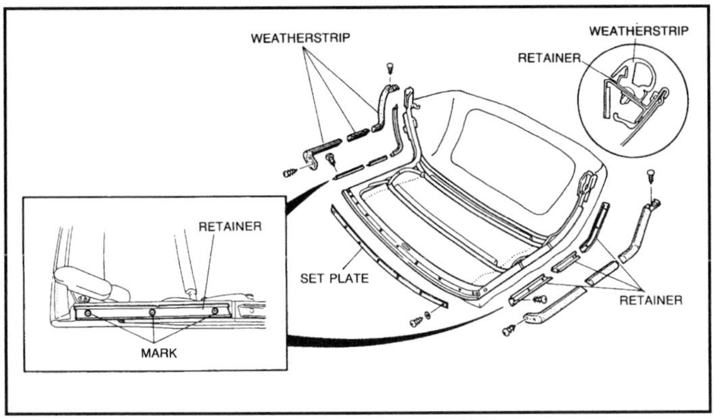

D17/4 CONVERTIBLE TOP DETAIL.

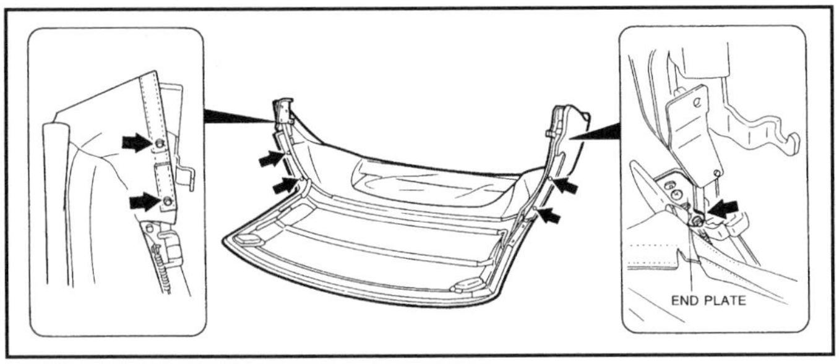

D17/5 REMOVE SCREWS & ENDPLATES FROM LINK ASSEMBLY.

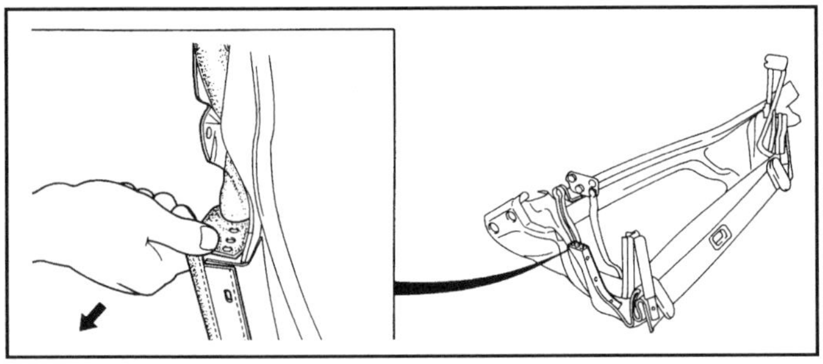

D17/6 DETACH THE FABRIC FROM THE LINK ASSEMBLY.

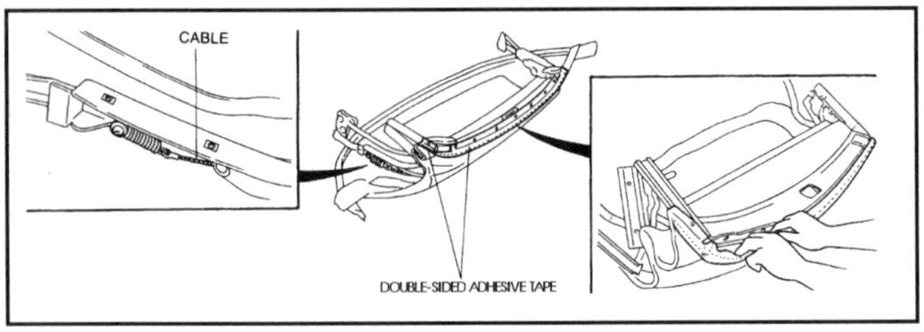

D17/7 REMOVE SCREWS & DISCONNECT CABLES FROM LINKS.

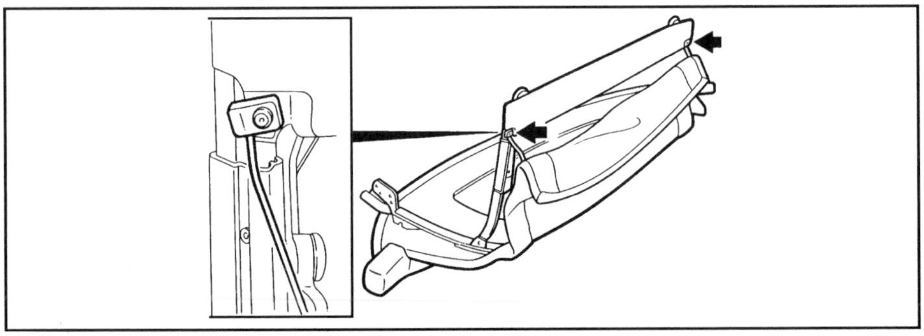

D17/8 DRILL OUT LINK ASSEMBLY RIVETS.

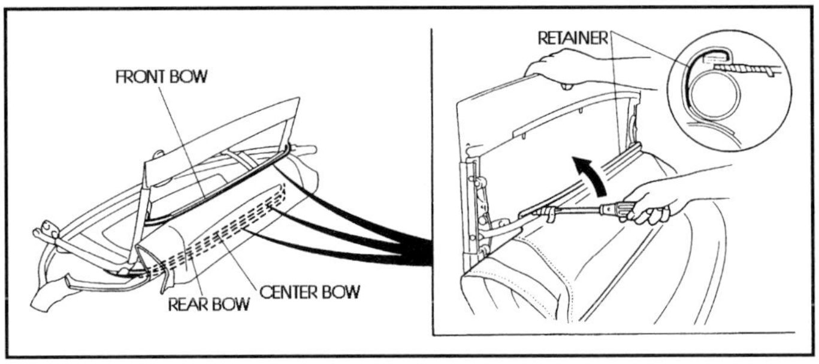

D17/9 DETACH FABRIC FROM BOW RETAINER.

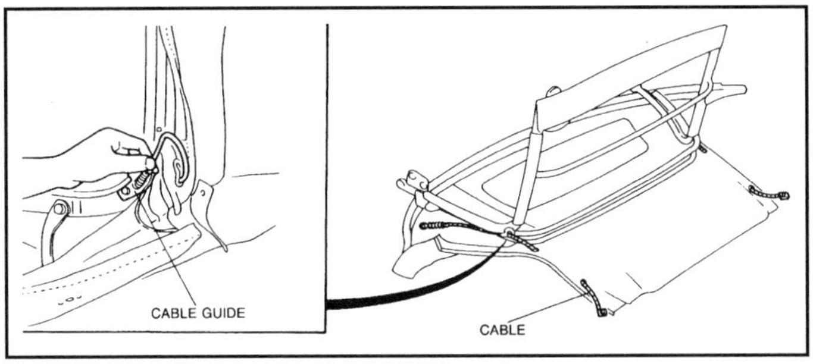

D17/10 REMOVE CABLES FROM GUIDES & FABRIC & CABLES FROM LINKS.

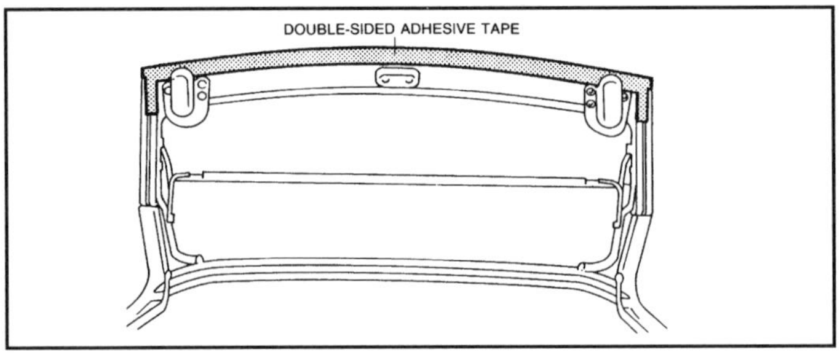

D17/11 APPLY DOUBLE-SIDED TAPE TO FRONT HEADER.

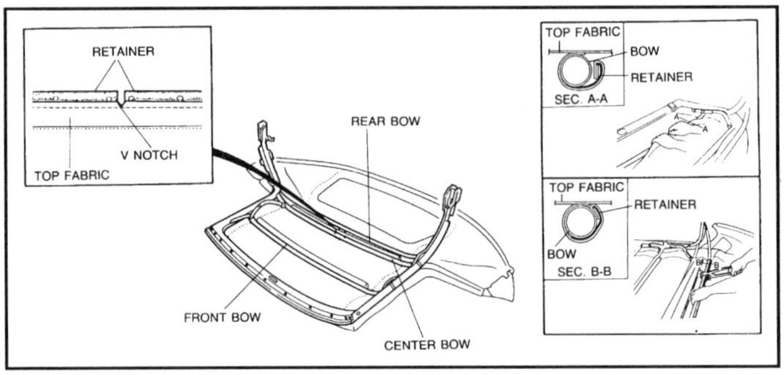

D17/13 FIX FABRIC TO REAR BOW WITH VELCRO.

INSTALLATION

11 Check over the link mechanism, lubricating the joints with WD40 or similar, and also tightening any loose joints. Remove all traces of the original double-sided tape from the front header. Degrease the header with ethyl alcohol and allow it to dry, then apply new double-sided tape to the shaded areas as shown in the drawing.

12 Thread the tensioner cables through the top fabric, then lay the top on a soft surface and place the link assembly over it.

13 Cover the jaws of a pair of water pump pliers with pvc tape to prevent damage to the link

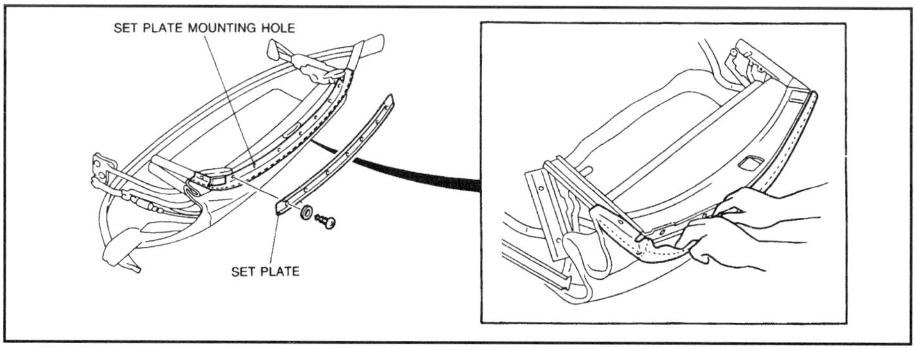

D17/14 FIT THE SET PLATE TO THE LINK ASSEMBLY.

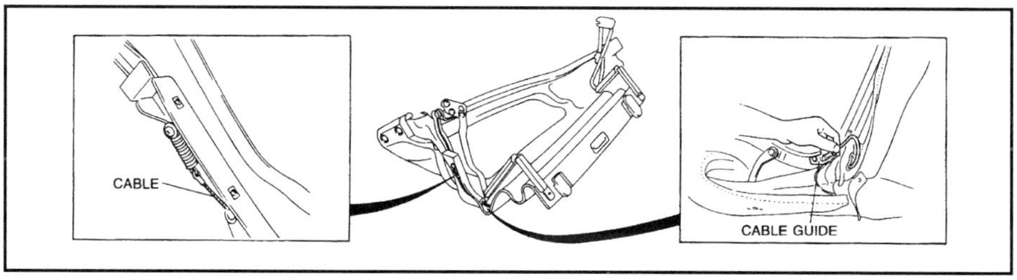

D17/15 PASS CABLES THRU GUIDES & FIT THEM TO LINKS.

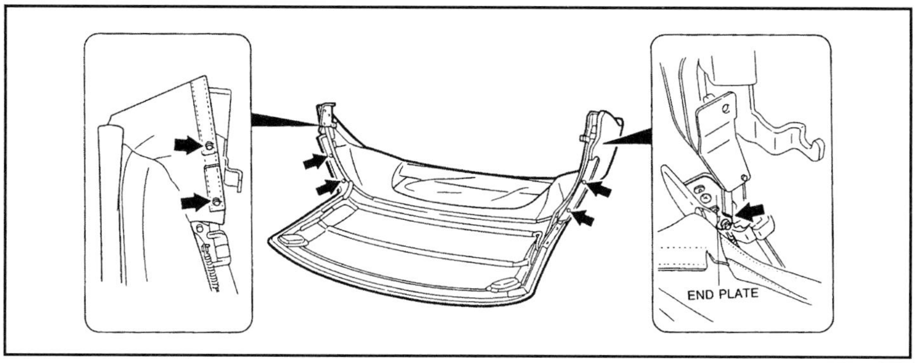

D17/16 FASTEN THE TOP FABRIC TO THE LINKS.

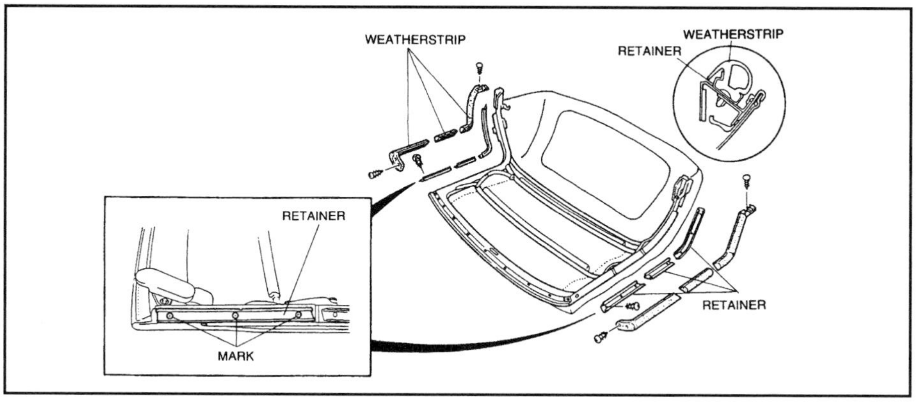

D17/17 FIT WEATHERSTRIP RETAINERS & WEATHERSTRIPS.

assembly and top. Starting at the rear bow, align the center of the retainer with the V-notch in the fabric. Hook the end of the top fabric strip over the end of the retainer, then squeeze the retainer shut using the protected pliers. Repeat this procedure on the center and front bows. Secure the top fabric to the rear bow with the Velcro pads.

14 Rivet the front ends of the tensioner cables to the header strip. Turn the assembly over for access, then secure the fabric to the header with the double-sided tape. Take your time with this or the fabric will get puckered during fixing. Pull off a little of the backing paper at a time and don't stretch the fabric. Now position the set plate and secure it with its screws to the header.

15 With the top unfolded halfway, feed the tensioner cables through the cable guides, then secure them at the back by screwing the springs to the link assembly.

16 Fit the top fabric over the end of the link assembly, and align the fabric and end plates with the holes in the link assembly. Secure the plates and fabric with 10 new rivets.

17 Install the weatherstrip retainers, aligning the paint marks made during removal, then fit the weatherstrips in their correct positions in the retainers.

18 Install the convertible top, and check that it operates correctly, that the rear window can be zipped and unzipped normally, and that it aligns correctly, and that the fit between the door glass and weatherstrips is correct.

18. CONVERTIBLE TOP - FABRIC REPAIRS

☞ 1/1, 2.

1 If your car's convertible top develops holes or gets torn, it can (within reason) be repaired. You will need some repair sheet (Mazda: NAYI R1 211), adhesive (Mazda: K180 W0 313 or equivalent) and some ethyl alcohol for cleaning the damaged area.

2 If the damage is a small tear, you need to clean around the damaged area with ethyl alcohol on the inside of the top fabric.

3 Now cut a piece of repair sheet slightly larger than the tear, and apply a thick coat of adhesive to both parts (the adhesive should be applied to the *inside* of the top fabric - this is where you will fix the repair sheet material).

4 After the adhesive has been left for a few minutes, press the repair sheet firmly onto the inside of the top fabric. Leave the repair to dry fully before using the car - ideally overnight.

5 If you have a large or jagged hole to deal with, you will need to cut out the damaged part and replace it with a section of repair sheet. This operation is easier if you have an assistant. You will need a piece of lumber to cut against, a craft knife or scalpel and a straightedge.

6 Place a piece of repair sheet on the outside of the top material so that it covers the damaged area. Have your assistant hold the lumber under the area to be cut out, then using the craft knife and the straightedge, cut through the repair sheet and top fabric together. You should cut out a rectangular area which encloses the damage.

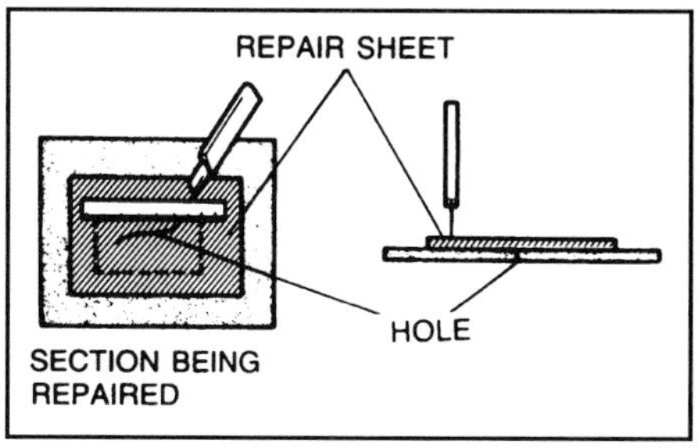

D18/6 CUT THRU REPAIR PATCH & TOP FABRIC.

7 The result should be a rectangular hole in the top, and a repair patch which exactly matches

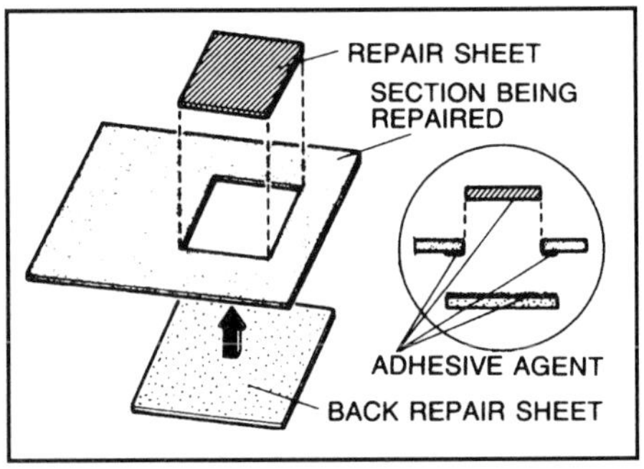

D18/8 BACKING MUST BE BIGGER THAN PATCH.

this. Do this very carefully, and the repair will be just about invisible when completed. It is worth trying to match the direction of the 'grain' of the top fabric and repair material when cutting the repair section.

8 Cut out another rectangle of the repair sheet material, slightly larger than the hole, to be used as a backing sheet. Degrease the top fabric and repair sheet sections with ethyl alcohol. Apply a thick film of adhesive to the inside of the top material, to the backing sheet, and around the hole edges. Leave the adhesive to start drying for a few minutes, then fit the backing sheet from inside the car and press the repair piece into the hole from the outside. Press all parts together firmly, then allow to dry for as long as possible before using the car - preferably overnight.

12

UNDERBODY & RUSTPROOFING

1. INTRODUCTION

This chapter describes how to keep the body structure of your Miata/MX5 in good shape. The body chapter deals with the visible aspects of the body: here we consider the hidden areas which impart strength and rigidity to the car.

Like all contemporary cars, the Miata/MX5 is based on a unitary body made up from welded steel panels. This method of construction utilizes the body panels themselves as an intrinsic part of the car's structure. Each panel in isolation is relatively frail, but once combined into a unified structure it provides great strength with relatively low weight, a little like an eggshell. Also like an eggshell, the body only maintains its structural integrity while it remains intact; once rust gets a hold, or in the event of impact damage deforming the structure, it becomes weakened, and eventually dangerous.

Repairs to the body structure require skill and experience if they are to be performed safely. It is no good just patching over rust with sheet steel, especially on a car like the Miata/MX5, which was designed to be driven hard, placing extra stress on the body as well as the suspension and steering parts attached to it.

In the following pages, we deal with the best methods of preserving the body structure in safe condition. We also describe how to check the body in the event of a suspected structural fault. We don't tell you how to go about welded repairs, and we recommend that you entrust this type of repair work to a Mazda dealer or professional repair shop.

2. RUSTPROOFING - WHY IT'S A GOOD IDEA

1 At first sight, this section may seem to you to have a pretty dumb title - after all, we all know that cars eventually rust away and die, and rustproofing seems like a good idea if it slows the process down. We would like you to consider, however, what can be achieved by rustproofing, and what can't. The car as supplied is adequately protected to survive for some years in reasonable conditions, but like all modern vehicles is not exactly over-endowed with paint, especially in the hidden areas not immediately visible.

2 If you intend that the car should survive intact well beyond the manufacturer's corrosion warranty period, you may wish to improve on the corrosion prevention measures already taken by Mazda. In part, the need to do this will depend on where you live; a car used in warm and predominantly dry climates will probably last well without further intervention, but the same car operating close to the sea, or in temperate climates where the roads are salted during winter, will corrode a lot faster.

3 If you bought your Miata/MX5 new and intend to trade up in a year or two, you might not consider this extra work to be worthwhile; the car is unlikely to start rusting away for several years, and you will derive no benefits from having had the work done. If, on the other hand, you are a Miata nut who intends never to be parted from your pride and joy, the earlier you carry out this preventative work, the better the car will last - and if you do sell, your car will keep its value better. Always keep in mind that rustproofing is entirely a preventative operation - no amount of rustproofing will repair already damaged bodywork.

4 You have options when it comes to rustproofing. In many areas, there are specialists who will do this work for you. This is fine if you use an established company who offer guaranteed work; many operate a system where you need to take the car in for checking and additional work at regular intervals. If you choose this option, read the small print carefully before you sign anything. Remember that you will be paying for work that is largely impossible to check, and there is a good chance that a small rustproofing operation may have gone out of business well before any problems or failures show up. You should also beware of contacts which obligate you to have additional extensive treatments carried out over a period of years: this can get expensive.

5 You can do the same kind of work yourself, using commercially available rustproofing kits. This has a couple of advantages. Firstly, it is cheaper. Secondly, you know with absolute certainty that the work has been carried out correctly. On the down side, it is a messy job, and requires time and patience to do properly - you may find that you never get around to repeat treatments or checks.

3. RUSTPROOFING PROCEDURE

☞ 1/1, 2.

PREPARATION

1 The first thing be aware of is that the Miata/MX5 has a complex body structure. In most conventional sedan bodies, the roof and its supporting pillars form an important part of the structure. With any convertible body design, the absence of an integral roof structure compromises the unitary design, and this has to be compensated for by additional strengthening elsewhere. Between the hidden structural members and the external body panels lie cavities, mostly closed by access panels and trim. This means that, after preliminary cleaning, you will need to dismantle areas of the car to be able to gauge the condition of the body.

2 To conduct a full assessment of the condition of your car, you will need to clean it thoroughly, and this includes the underbody and areas like the wheel wells (arches). We suggest that you use a pressure-wash facility for this. Note that hot pressure washing or steam cleaning will also tend to remove the existing underbody wax layer. This is not a problem, and could be considered advantageous, if you intend to rustproof the car completely, but don't leave the car unprotected after removing this coating. Cold pressure washing should not affect any wax rustproofing materials and can therefore be used safely.

3 Note that if you intend to carry out a full check of the condition of the body, the necessary dismantling work will also provide access for rust-

proofing, so you may as well carry out any remedial work as part of your check. This being the case, we suggest that you gather together the necessary tools and materials. The main requirement is for a quantity of rustproofing fluid. The best choice here is for one of the wax-based products sold for this purpose. These are widely used by automotive manufacturers, and have largely replaced the earlier bituminous coatings.

4 You should be able to obtain a suitable product through your auto parts store, and in many cases you will be able to buy a kit containing the fluid, plus application tools. These normally include some sort of hand pump plus a long-reach probe and nozzles for coating the insides of box sections and body cavities. Check your kit to see if you have enough of the fluid to carry out a full rustproofing job - you may need to buy extra in some cases. Depending on how meticulous you are, and how heavily you apply the product, you'll need 1-2 gallons (5-10 liters) of the rustproofer. You'll also need a couple of old paint brushes for spot application of the rustproofing fluid, plus an assortment of bungs and some pvc tape for sealing up any holes made during the procedure. A small flashlight - if possible with a flexible gooseneck head - will also be invaluable for checking inside the box sections and cavities.

5 Once the car is clean and dry, you need to jack it as high as possible and support it on safety stands to allow clear access to the underbody - on no account get under the car until you are certain that it is supported securely. The road wheels need to be removed for access to the wheelwells. For details of jacking and supporting the car ☞ 1/3

6 Many of the body cavities are effectively sealed from the outside of the car, but you can usually get to them from the inside. Beneath the carpet and trim panels lie numerous holes and apertures which allow easy access to most of these closed sections. With the interior of the body exposed in this way, you can see how the various body cavities are formed. Using a small flashlight and perhaps a dentist's mirror, try to assess the condition of the internal surfaces. It is in these areas that the manufacturer's protection is at its weakest, and which will benefit most from rustproofing. We recommend that you remove the seats, carpets and interior trim to facilitate this ☞10/5 & 10/11.

7 📷 The external surfaces of the underbody and the wheelwells are easily checked. Wear eye protection to avoid getting dirt in your eyes, and use a wire brush to remove any residual road dirt. You will find that the wheel wells contain plastic liners, or splash shields. These are retained by a mixture of sheet metal screws and the ubiquitous plastic fasteners which you'll find throughout the car. Remove the liners so that you can check behind them, and remove any accumulated dirt.

MAIN ROCKER (SILL) SECTIONS

8 The lower body is strengthened by the rocker sections which run between the two wheelwells. These are complex structures which contribute greatly to the longitudinal rigidity of the car, and which are particularly vulnerable to corrosion if left untreated. Moisture inside the sections can cause rusting to start off unseen, and this will only be apparent when it breaks through the external surfaces. Don't confuse this with surface rusting which may have taken place as the result of stone chips on the outside. If the external paint finish is damaged, you will need to repair the damage before you go any further ☞ 11/3, 4.

9 At the front of the rocker sections, the body panels are overlapped by the rear lower edges of the front fenders. What starts out as a cavity at the back of the wheel arch narrows down until the fender and underlying body panel are in close contact producing a particularly bad rust trap. Dirt from the front wheels gets past the liners and then builds up in this area. To add to the problem, rain running down from the windshield drains off through this cavity, which having no intentional outlet, means that the dirt (and any road salt) gets compacted at the lower edge.

10 If the winter roads are salted in your area, we estimate that serious corrosion will be evident after a few years. To clear this area, you'll need to detach the two bolts which retain the rear lower edge of the fender so that it can be pulled away slightly (you don't need to remove the fender entirely - the lower edge will flex enough to allow it to be cleaned out). You can then pressure-wash the area to flush out any dirt and salt. If the lower part of the fender is showing signs of rust penetration, this will almost certainly be caused by dirt and salt trapped in this area. If this is noted, you should detach the fender completely to allow full check of the underlying body - this will probably have started rusting too, and measures should be taken to repair any damage ☞ 11/12.

11 📷+ Working inside the car, locate all suitable injection points through which the rustproofing coat can be applied. You'll find access holes along the rocker sections and on the sides of the footwell area. If access permits, use a flashlight to check for signs of rust inside the section. Insert the probe into the rocker section, and apply an even coat of wax rustproofing fluid along its length. The best technique is to push the probe as far down the cavity as it will go, and then pump fluid through it as it is withdrawn. When the rustproofing fluid is first applied it is fairly thin, and may drip out from under the car for a while. You might want to place some newspaper or cat litter under the car to catch the drips. After a while the solvent will evaporate and the coating will dry to a sticky wax finish.

12 📷 Before you install the wheel arch liners, apply a good coat of the wax rustproofing fluid from each end of the rocker section. Working from the rear wheel arch, you can access the back of the rocker section - coat everything in sight with the fluid. At the front, apply a thick coat to the body and to the inside of the fender, especially where the two come into contact towards the bottom edge. You can either spray or brush the fluid onto these areas.

LONGITUDINAL BOX SECTIONS

13 📷 Running parallel to the rockers you will find two longitudinal box sections. These are designed to make the floor more rigid, but have little

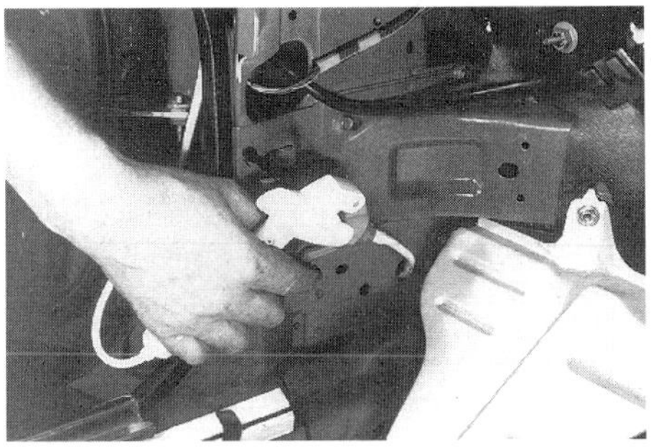

3/11b ... spray head inside rockers (sills).

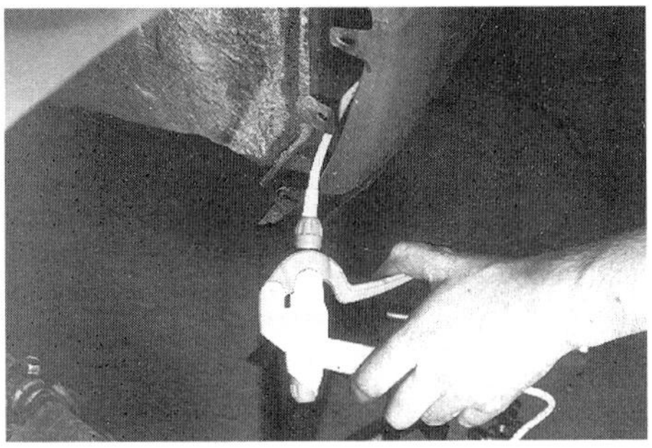

3/12 Clean inside fender & apply rustproofer.

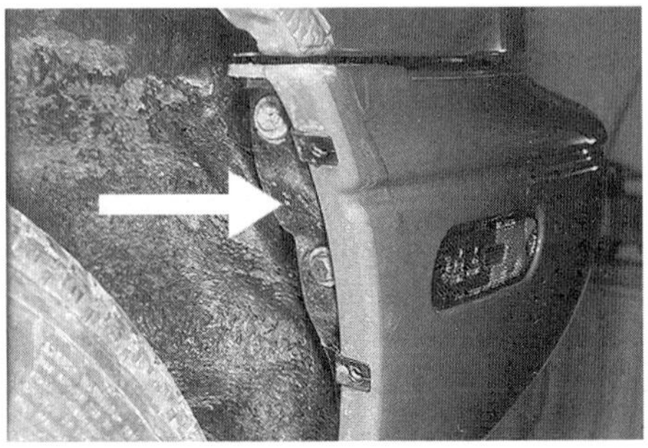

3/7 Remove splash shields to gain access.

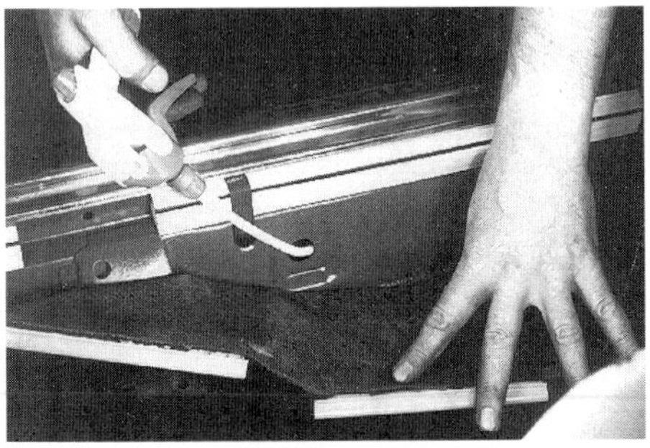

3/11a Use these existing holes to get ...

6/13 Access to longitudinal box members.

other function. If you look closely, you'll note that they are made from thin gauge sheet steel, and if you ever try to jack the car on these box sections they will most likely collapse. Check that all drain holes are clear, and that there is no buildup of dirt inside the sections (use a high-pressure hose to flush out any dirt, then allow the section to dry out thoroughly). Use the wax-based rustproofing fluid to seal the inside of the box sections and prevent rusting. Note that if you have reason to remove the rear trim panel from the back of the car, you have good access to the open ends of these box sections. Again, the probe can be fed into the end of the section and slowly withdrawn as the fluid is applied.

REAR BODY CAVITIES

14 There are a number of complex cavities formed around the back of the car, and in particular behind the outer body panels formed by the rear fenders. You can get to these once the rear quarter trim panels have been removed, and also from the top if the convertible top is removed ☞ 10/5 & 11/15.

15 With the quarter trim panels out of the way a large access hole is revealed, and this offers a good access point for rustproofing; in fact you can reach just about anywhere from here using a flexible probe and a little ingenuity.

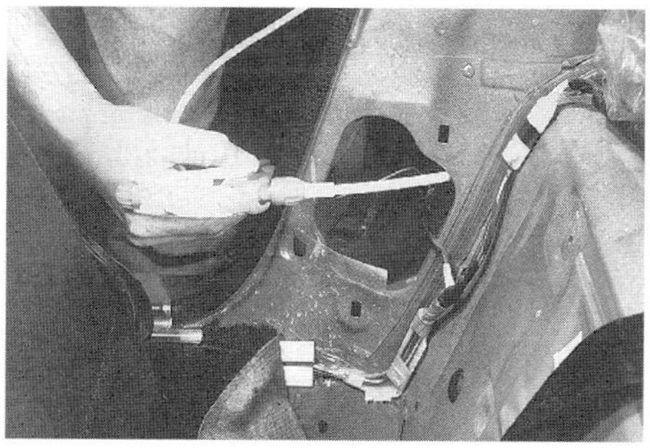

3/15 Removal of quarter panels gives access.

16 + If you have also removed the convertible top, you will have access to a number of holes around the back edge of the package area though which you can feed your rustproofing probe.

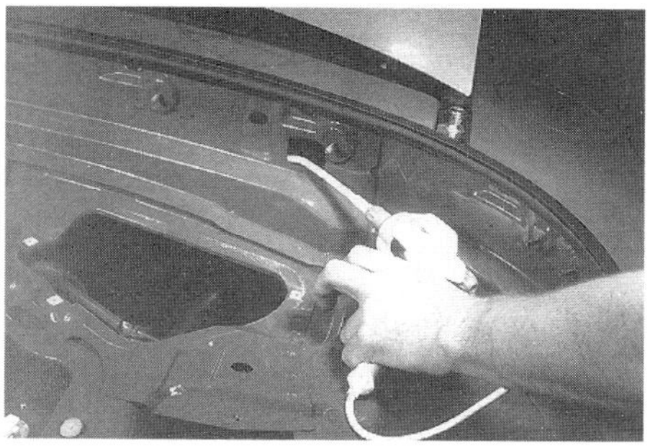

3/16a You need to remove the convertible ...

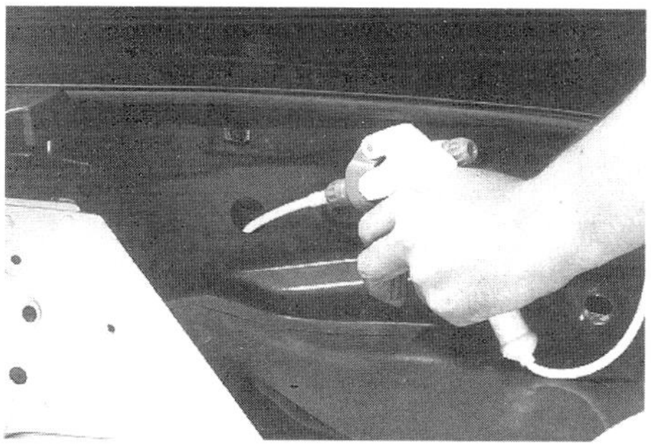

3/16b ... top to reveal these access points.

17 + Note also the two rain drip trays located near the convertible top mounting points. These are connected by large-diameter hoses to outlets under the car, and these can be withdrawn to give additional rustproofing access points. Working under the car, pull out the large grommet which locates the bottom of each hose, then withdraw the drip tray and hose for access. When you have completed the rustproofing, install the drip trays and hoses, then install the grommets.

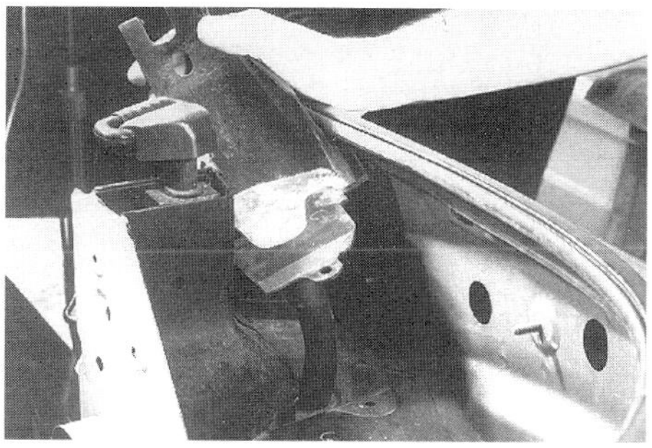

3/17a Pull out drain tube, and then apply ...

3/17b ... rustproofer thru hole.

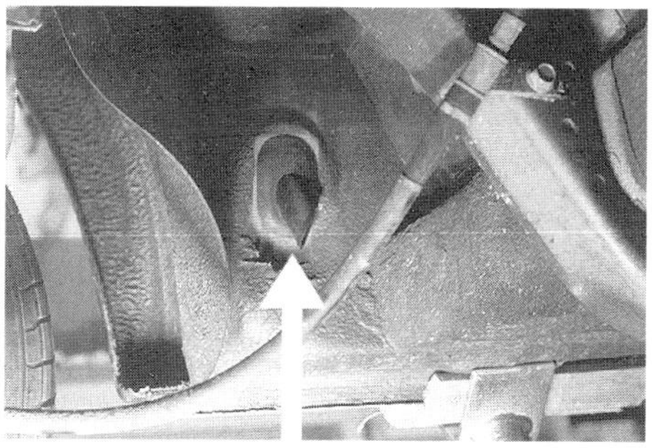

3/17c Make sure this drain outlet is not blocked.

18 Additional access to the area above and around the fuel tank can be gained after removing the pressed steel access panels in the package area. With these removed, you can reach any remaining internal cavities.

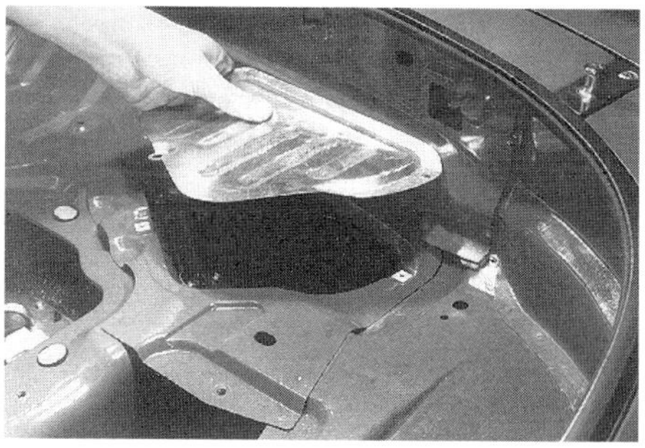

3/18 Removal of covers reveals fuel tank area.

DOORS

19 The interiors of the doors should be checked periodically and rustproofed as required. Things to check are that you keep the rustproofing fluid off the glass (ensure that the door glass is wound fully up) and that any drain holes remain unobstructed - check and remove any dirt from inside the door before starting, and check that the waxy proofing material does not block off these essential outlets . To get access to the door interiors, remove the interior trim panel and the plastic sheet behind it ☞ 10/5.

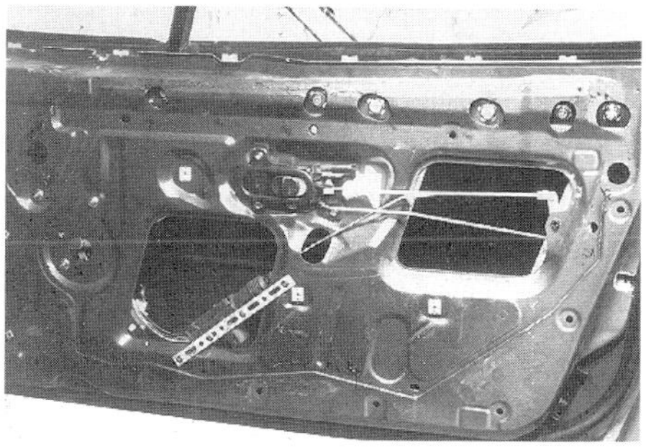

3/19 Trim removal gives access to door interior.

20 Apply an even coat of rustproofing fluid around the inside of the door. Don't worry about getting this on the door mechanism or wiring - it will help protect and lubricate these areas too.

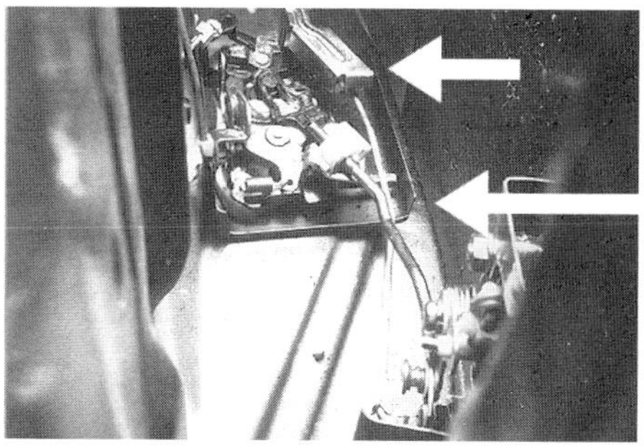

3/20 Make sure fluid runs into all seams.

OTHER AREAS

21 Apart from the specific areas for antirust treatment discussed above, apply rustproofing fluid to all other minor closed sections (*eg*: hood and trunk lid reinforcing box sections). In general, these are accessible after preliminary dismantling as described earlier. If there is no obvious access point available, you can make your own by drilling an access hole, which can then be closed by inserting

12

a suitable plastic plug. Be careful when doing this - it is easy to accidentally damage wiring or other parts hidden behind a panel. In general, we could find no areas where access through existing holes or cutouts was not possible.

22 Be on the lookout for rustproofing opportunities when doing other jobs on the car. For example, whenever you remove a light unit, take the time to apply some rustproofing fluid to any body areas this exposes - that way you will eventually cover all areas of the car.

23 The pressed steel suspension wishbones and crossmembers are well worth rustproofing. All these components have suitable access holes for the rustproofer spray probe. **Warning!** Take care not to spray rustproofing fluid on brake components, particularly discs and pads.

24 Before installing the removed trim and lowering the car to the ground, apply a film of rustproofing fluid to the whole of the underside of the car and around the wheelwells. When doing this, protect areas like the brakes and exhaust system from accidental overspray by masking with paper or rags.

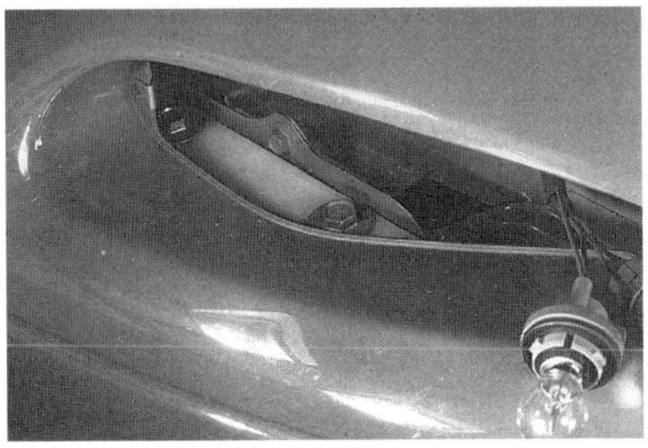

3/22 An opportunity to apply rustproofer.

25 Finally, rustproof minor areas around the car with WD40 or similar silicone-based spray. Items like the headlight surrounds and lids will be protected and lubricated in this way, as will electrical connectors and other small mechanical parts. WD40 does not dry to a thick, waxy consistency, and while this means that it is less permanent, it is useful in more visible areas.

3/25 Silicone spray protects light adjusters.

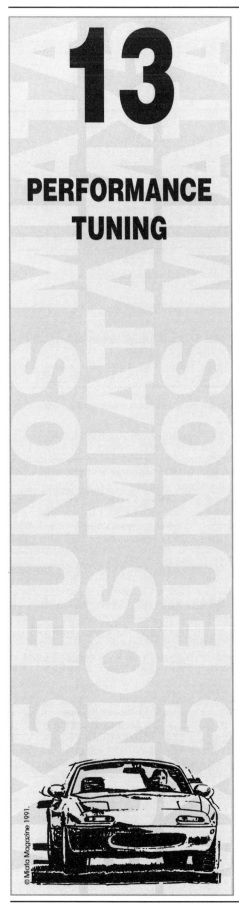

13
PERFORMANCE TUNING

© Miata Magazine 1991.

1. INTRODUCTION

In this chapter we take a brief look at the mechanical tuning possibilities for the Miata/MX5. Like any other car, it is perfectly possible to improve the performance of specific mechanical areas by adding aftermarket equipment. Inevitably, though, there is a price to be paid in terms of financial outlay and in loss of flexibility.

The Miata/MX5 is a pretty well-developed vehicle designed for a specific purpose, unlike the average sedan which is compromised to a much greater extent; the sedan needs to be all things to all owners. Inevitably, this means that it turns out pretty bland. The Miata/MX5, on the other hand, is a sports roadster pure and simple, and this clear definition has allowed its designers to tune the standard car for this specific role.

The singular nature of the Miata/MX5 is what makes the car a delight to drive; it doesn't *need* to be good at lugging five people and their luggage or towing a trailer, so it makes no attempt at this. Instead, it concentrates on moving one or two people with little or no luggage in the most enjoyable way it can.

It also scores over its European predecessors in terms of refinement and integration. The application of 90s' technology to the classic roadster concept, backed by a serious R&D budget, has resulted in a degree of harmonization undreamed of a decade or so ago - no flaking chrome or occasional electrical functionality here. The car works as a package; the engine, transmission and suspension parts complement each other to a high degree, and this means that adding aftermarket parts presents a real risk of making the car worse instead of better.

That said, the Miata/MX5 is an individual car, and the individuals who buy them will invariably hanker for even more individuality - the large aftermarket which already exists around this car underlines this demand. If you want to uprate your car our advice is to think carefully about exactly what it is that you want to achieve, read all you can on the available conversions and modifications and get as much independent advice as you can. This way, you'll end up with a *genuine* improvement.

One other point. The engine in Miata/MX5 form is configured as a pure sportscar power unit. It is designed to be able to take 6500 rpm shifts when you are really looking for its maximum power: if you habitually shift at 5000 rpm you're losing 21 horses ...

2. TUNING PARTS - SOURCES

1 There are many potential sources of tuning parts and accessories for the Miata/MX5 including Mazda. A few items may be obtainable from auto parts stores, but in general you will need to deal with a specialist supplier. We don't propose to attempt to list all the Miata/MX5 specialists worldwide - there are too many of them, and we have no intention of getting into a situation where we appear to be recommending (or omitting to mention!) suppliers who we have never had dealings with. Where we mention specific suppliers, they are major players in the Miata/MX5 world who have helped in the preparation of this book by supplying us with information about their products. We have included some addresses at the end of the book.

2 We suggest that you start out by joining an owners club. Of these, the biggest and best is undoubtedly the Miata Club of America, staffed by people very close to the development of the Miata, and whose excellent publication, *Miata Magazine*, carries a wealth of reviews and advertisements for the latest Miata goodies. We would rate this as the definitive source for all things Miata, and as such, warrants membership wherever you happen to live in the world.

3 There are other national and local clubs catering for the Miata scattered around the world. Our suggestion would be to start off with the Miata Club of America, and then to track down and join any local organization. A list of known clubs appears at the end of the book.

4 Other sources for Miata parts and accessories will be found in the general motoring press, which is also a good source of reviews of aftermarket products. Check for product reviews at the newsstand - if a Miata-related part is reviewed in a particular issue, you'll almost certainly find various suppliers advertising.

5 Talk to other Miata owners about any proposed modification or improvement. If you can track down another owner who has done the same or a similar modification, you'll pick up a lot of information which could save you unnecessary time and expense when you do the work on your car. Other owners will also have opinions about suppliers, tuners and specialists. If this is on the basis of personal experience, take note. If it is one of those 'this happened to a friend of a friend' type stories, take it with a pinch of salt.

6 Finally, be wary of modifying your car in any way if it is under warranty from Mazda. Unauthorized changes may invalidate your warranty, even if not directly responsible for some later failure. Obviously, Mazda-approved or supplied add-ons should not have this effect.

3. TUNING - IMPORTANT CONSIDERATIONS

1 Before you start bolting on performance parts, give some thought to the effect that they will have on the rest of the car. As we mentioned earlier, the stock Miata is a well-balanced car. This means that items like the tires, brakes and suspension complement the standard engine. If you bolt a turbocharger to your Miata, you will upset this balance; the stock suspension, brakes and tires may no longer be adequate for the improved power output. A substantial increase in the engine's power output will put additional strain on all driveline components, especially the clutch. Uprated after market clutch kits are available from several sources.

2 You should discuss these considerations with your proposed supplier. If the supplier knows and cares about what he is doing, he will be happy

to run through any other modifications which need to be made as a result of fitting his supplied engine parts - if he shows no interest in your questions, go elsewhere for your engine parts.

3 Be wary of modifying the suspension on your Miata. Just about anything you do here will make the car less comfortable to drive in, and you could easily spend a lot of time and money on suspension parts and hate the result. Unless you plan to race the car, the benefits of suspension modifications don't really square with the expense. Frankly, the stock setup is really very good and quite adequate for 95% of us, so be very sure that you really need to make these changes. Of course, you'll need to keep this in mind if you start out on engine tuning; a big increase in engine power may force you to uprate the suspension, whether you like it or not.

4 You should also check out the legality of any proposed modification. Depending on where you live, non-factory parts, or items affecting emissions levels may well be illegal. Our advice here is to check this carefully before you invest time and money. In the US in particular, a perfectly acceptable modification in one state could get you into trouble in another. Germany also has very stringent legislation governing non-factory parts. Be aware, too, that failure to disclose performance modifications to your car's insurers could nullify the insurance cover you thought you had.

MIATA CLUB ENGINE TUNING MENU

5 The Miata Club of America is in an excellent position to evaluate all of the tuning options currently available, and it does so as performance tuning is a popular subject with its members. The club has reached the conclusion that, because of the standard engine's high efficiency, you have to consider spending a considerable amount of money to see a substantial power increase - although the first 10 horsepower is relatively cheap. The following four stage menu shows the club's recommendations with cost in US dollars (remember the relative cost will have changed if you've had this book on the shelf for some time!) -

Phase 1 (+ 10 HP for under $250)
Jackson Racing or K&N replacement air filter.
Aftermarket final muffler (silencer).
Splitfire spark plugs (they have a split electrode).
Advance ignition timing to 14 degrees BTDC.

Phase 2 (+ 15 HP for under $400)
HKS Power Flow air filter system.
Aftermarket final muffler.
Splitfire spark plugs.
Advance ignition timing to 14 degrees BTDC.

Phase 3 (+ 20 HP for under $800)
Jackson Racing Cold Air induction system.
Aftermarket final muffler.
Aftermarket exhaust header (manifold).
Splitfire spark plugs.
Advance ignition timing to 14 degrees BTDC.

Phase 4 (+ 50 HP for under $2000)
Sebring Supercharger.

4. TUNING - ENGINE MODIFICATIONS

1 Mazda's B6 engine is used in the Miata/MX5, and has been around for some time. It is a tough and well-developed unit, for which there are numerous engine tuning parts and accessories available from an equally wide variety of sources. Exactly how you go about modifying the standard unit needs to be thought out carefully, from both the cost and legal viewpoints.

BETTER BREATHING

2 One reasonably low-cost option is to improve the airflow through the engine. This need not affect the operation of the engine management system, and can yield a modest but cost effective power increase. Typically, mid-range power and throttle response can be improved without detrimental effect on the car's driveability - an important consideration if you intend to keep the car usable as regular transport.

3 There are several main areas of interest here. The easiest area for attention is the stock air cleaner element which is quite restrictive. Fitting a washable K&N filter in place of the standard part is claimed to give a power increase of around 2 HP, and has the advantage of being reusable; you just wash out the element and re-oil it. Jackson Racing also offer a similar filter. Best of all, a new filter is an inexpensive upgrade. The HKS Power Flow is an improved intake system, while the Jackson Racing Cold Air induction system can yield up to 12 HP.

4 Your next step upward in improving the stock intake system should be the Jackson Racing Cold Air Intake. The standard air intake is deep in the engine compartment where temperatures are very high: cooler air is denser and, therefore, gives better performance. The Jackson system comprises new intake trunking which draws air from in front of the radiator where it is no warmer than ambient temperature. The kit comes complete with a high flow air filter and all components needed for installation. You'll need to reposition

4/4 Jackson Racing's Cold Air Intake system.

the standard airflow meter and extension wiring for this purpose is included. The Miata Owner's Club of America rates this modification as the 'best bang for the buck' you can make. It should be worth between 4 HP and 12 HP. For US owners EPA certification is expected.

5 By way of an experiment, the Miata Owner's Club of America installed a pair of SU HS4 carburettors on a Miata. Apparently, the car ran "Great!" and achieved zero to 60 mph (96.5 kph) in 8.2 seconds. Some racers are reported to be using single Weber 45DCOE or twin 40DCOE installations.

4/5 Twin SUs on a Miata/MX5!

EXHAUST SYSTEM IMPROVEMENTS

6 Getting more, and cooler, air into the engine is one aspect of the airflow equation - getting it out again is another consideration. The standard header (manifold) arrangement is pretty good, but can be improved upon, as can the stock muffler which restricts the exhaust gases a little. It is possible to fit aftermarket parts to enhance exhaust performance, while retaining the oxygen sensor and catalytic converter; this maintains driveability and legality in most areas.

7 The first thing to change is the header (exhaust manifold). In the factory design four separate steel exhaust pipes run from the head flange and combine into a single, large diameter, pipe at the flange next to the transmission bellhousing. In the case of aftermarket performance headers, pairs of pipes are combined next to the transmission bellhousing. Two separate pipes then run under the car, eventually combining into one pipe as the system reaches the catalytic converter.

8 The purpose of this is to make the transition from four separate exhaust pipes down to one more gradual, easing the passage of the gases leaving the cylinders and so imposing less restriction to the flow. Additionally, the pipe lengths are carefully chosen to produce a negative pressure wave which help scavenge more of the burnt gases from the cylinders, and this in turn means that more fuel/air mixture is admitted on the next induction stroke. This effect is strongest at a particular engine speed, and so the 'boost' to performance is localized around this speed. The art is to make best use of the effect by choosing this speed carefully.

9 When shopping for a header, try to read up any relevant road tests, and compare which header offers performance improvements at what engine speed. You also need to consider build quality, and to this end try to look at the header

before you buy. The best systems generally have fewest welds, and are finished with a aluminum/ ceramic coating. This makes for longevity and helps minimize heat loss into the engine compartment; both desirable attributes. The Miata Club likes the Jackson Racing progressive diameter header which gives good mid and top end torque and produces around 4 extra horses.

10 Almost any aftermarket muffler is worth around 3 HP, albeit at the expense of a little more exhaust noise. You may not wish to replace the stock unit right away, though you should consider this if the original muffler wears out. In conjunction with a perfoımance header, you should obtain a noticeable overall improvement.

ENGINE MODIFICATIONS

11 Traditionally, engine tuning meant sophisticated reworking of the engine internals to produce more power. In its day, this was a perfectly reasonable approach, but in recent years, the standard production power unit has itself become very much more sophisticated, reducing the margin for improvement. In effect, the cost of extracting just a little more power from the already-tuned standard engine has become too great for road use. In many areas, the standard parts are about as good as you could get anyhow. It is still possible to polish and hone an engine, but unless you are using the car for racing, and are looking to shave fractions of seconds off your lap times, our advice is to forget it.

12 While the days of polishing and reworking the cylinder head may be gone for all but serious racers, you can still consider modifying the camshafts as part of an engine overhaul. Camshafts with modified lift and duration are available and, in terms of overall power output, will produce the goods. As usual, though, there is a price to pay for more power, and in this case it comes in the form of poorer low-speed driveability.

13 A full race cam would make the car totally unusable on public roads and such profiles are intended for use only on the race circuit, where niceties like the engine's ability to idle don't matter. A 'Sport' cam is as radical as you will want to go for road use, and is a compromise between the race and road cam profiles. If you are a diehard tinkerer, you may also be interested in installing adjustable cam sprockets. These permit ultra-fine adjustment of the cam timing, though the advantage that this is likely to offer on a road car is open to debate.

14 You can also get lightened flywheels (or you could get yours lightened by a specialist engine tuning shop). The removal of weight makes for snappier acceleration, the down side is a rougher feel to the engine, and an increased tendency for the engine to falter and stall at idle. By removing the weight, you effectively reduce the mass and therefore the flywheel's ability to do its job; namely to smooth out engine power impulses and to carry the engine over the odd misfire.

15 Honing the internal walls of the intake manifold may improve power in an otherwise unrestricted engine. The Extrude Hone Company offer a fluid honing system to achieve the desired effect. At the time of writing, the Miata Club is evaluating this process and will report its findings in the club magazine.

5. TUNING - ELECTRONIC MODIFICATIONS

1 The possibilities offered by electronic tuning are generally as interesting as those offered by mechanical tuning. In effect, the Miata's engine is capable of more than it delivers, but its power output and delivery are shaped electronically by the ECU. It is quite possible to alter the characteristics of just about any ECU-controlled engine by re-chipping the ECU (we've heard that the Miata/ MX5's ECU does not readily lend itself to rechipping), this replaces the factory setup with custom parameters which can have a dramatic effect on performance.

2 This type of modification is completely uncondoned by Mazda, of course, and will almost certainly void your warranty. More importantly, you may find that it is illegal on emissions or other grounds in your area, so investigate this before taking this option.

3 We do not know of any company specializing in rechipping the Miata/MX5, but any reputable business working in this field should be able to assist you. We would keep clear of any company offering cheap deals on chips, especially if they are unknown to you and operating by mail order - make sure that the company you deal with is reputable and technically competent. Check the car magazines for articles on rechipping, or ask around at race shops; the people who know what they're doing will be well-known in race circles.

4 You may luck out and find a company who have already done work on the Miata/MX5 ECU, and if so they may be able to offer you an uprated chip off the shelf. More likely, you will need to have them dyno the car to establish the current setup, and then to program new settings into a fresh chip. Having a dyno check carried out is good policy anyway. This will give you a datum point showing the current state of tune of your engine, and any subsequent modifications can then be checked against this.

5 Once the power and torque curves for your engine have been plotted on a dyno, you can make decisions regarding which aspects of tuning you need to address. This way, you'll get proven (and customized) settings specifically for your car, but you'll need to be prepared to pay; the equipment these guys use costs serious money, so hourly rates will be significant.

6. TUNING - TURBOCHARGING & SUPERCHARGING

1 If you rely on atmospheric pressure to push air into the engine's cylinders, there comes a point at which no amount of easing the way will get a bigger volume in and out. If you want more power still, you need something to force air into the engine at greater than atmospheric pressure, and this is exactly what these devices do.

2 Turbochargers and superchargers do basically the same job in different ways. A turbocharger uses waste energy, in the form of the exhaust gases, to spin a turbine at very high speed. On the other end of the turbine's spindle is a vane-type compressor. This forces air though the intake system, packing more combustion mixture into the cylinders. A supercharger does the same job, but is mechanically driven from the engine (usually from the crankshaft pulley), instead of being powered by the exhaust system. In recent years, the turbo has taken over from the supercharger to such an extent that superchargers are now extremely rare, while turbos are almost commonplace.

3 Until comparatively recent years, the turbo was a rare beast outside of race tracks and similar specialized arenas - the turbos that used to be available were exquisitely expensive, and tended to blow engines apart. Over the last decade in particular, turbo technology and control systems have improved beyond recognition, and it is now quite possible to fit a turbo to just about anything, enhancing the performance dramatically, without any detrimental effect on engine wear.

4 The Miata works very well indeed when fitted with a turbo, and many owners have wondered just when Mazda would get around to releasing a factory turbo model. The answer to this is, probably never. This is due to a number of considerations, including the perceived market niche occupied by the Miata. As it stands, the car is an affordable fun car. Add a turbo, and it suddenly becomes a different beast; fast, expensive to build and expensive to insure.

5 Meanwhile, the aftermarket turbo wizards have not been sitting around. There are a wide range of turbo options available for the car, and these differ widely in their effect on the performance envelope. You could opt for a no-holds-barred performance oriented setup, transforming the relatively civilized Miata into a real street racer. At the other extreme is the noteworthy UK-designed BBR turbo system. This particular setup is so carefully integrated into the Miata's design that Mazda (in the UK) treat it as an official option, which can be fitted by Mazda dealers before the car is handed over to its new owner; turbo power, and full Mazda warranty intact! The BBR unit is available in kit form in some markets, but does require engine removal for installation. Engine output is boosted by around 40 HP when the unit's boosting intake pressure to 5.5 psi: fuel management is controlled by an auxiliary computer. At the time of writing, BBR had obtained 50 State EPA approval for their turbo in the US.

6 + The American company Cartech makes a nice turbo kit for the Miata/MX5 too. Though not EPA approved (at the time of writing), the Cartech unit can be installed with the engine in-situ and can give a nicely torquey extra 40 HP. Fuel management is by a variable fuel pressure regulator.

7 Turbo systems are theoretically owner-installable, (assuming you are technically competent to do so) but usually benefit from professional installation. You should be aware that in some cases, the engine needs to come out of the car as part of the installation procedure, and that a dyno

6/6a Cartech's turbo & intercooler =185bhp.

6/6b Cartech's knock sensor allows extra boost.

check before and after installation is a good idea. Having the manufacturer or supplier do the installation means that it is done properly, and that the engine and turbo are set up correctly. If you do decide to carry out your own installation, be sure to follow the manufacturer's directions closely; mistakes made in setting up the turbo, particularly excessive boost pressures, could cause serious engine damage.

8 At the time of writing only one purpose-designed, EPA-50 US state approved supercharger installation was available for the Miata/

6/8 Neat Sebring Supercharger installation.

MX5. Jointly developed by Miata Club engineers and the Eaton Corporation the kit is sold under the name Sebring Supercharger and is distributed by Downing/Atlanta. The unit mounts above the exhaust header and draws air through a repositioned throttle body. Running a boost of 6 psi the supercharger increases power by 50 HP. The Miata Club of America tells us that installation takes less than 3 hours and that the sealed-for-life unit is expected to have a service life of 150,000 miles or more. We are hoping to obtain one of these kits and cover installation, in detail, in a future edition of this manual. TUV approval was being sought at the time of writing.

9 Nelson Superchargers also market a supercharger kit based around a Paxton unit. Nelson say the unit is smog legal in 50 US States and gives 45% more power. At the time of writing we have no more information.

10 We would advise you to get all the literature on the various systems on sale, and if possible, talk to owners who have had your chosen conversion done - another good reason for joining an owner's club. Also, talk to your insurance company about the effect that the turbo or supercharger will have on your insurance rates. Be warned that a lot of insurers dislike even factory turbos, and may refuse to insure cars equipped with aftermarket systems. Also, remember that your factory warranty will almost certainly be partly or completely voided by the addition of a turbo or supercharger.

7. TUNING - BRAKES, SUSPENSION & STEERING

BRAKES

1 As mentioned above, the factory brake, suspension and steering systems on the Miata/MX5 are about as good as you'll get on a production car, and for this reason you may wish to leave well alone. If, however, you have made significant changes to the engine power output, or if the prime use for your particular Miata is on the race track, you may need to look into improvements in these areas.

2 The standard brake setup includes a power brake unit (servo), eliminating the addition of such a unit as a quick and easy upgrade. The first step in brake improvement, and the one which will prove least costly, is to fit uprated pads. These use harder friction material (often sintered metal) and are more resistant to fade than the standard type. The downside is that comparatively high pedal pressure will be required for a given braking effort.

3 The feel and precision of the brakes can be improved by removing any 'give' in the hydraulic lines. This occurs mostly because of the natural elasticity of the brake hoses, so it is these parts which will need uprating. The answer to the problem is braided stainless brake hoses. These have a woven stainless steel outer covering which is highly resistant to giving under hydraulic pressure. Normally, the inner part of these hoses is made from thin-walled PTFE tubing, giving a much thinner hose overall. This type of hose is much more expensive than the original type, but lasts almost forever. You may be able to purchase a hose set from a Miata specialist, or alternatively, you could have a custom set made up by a race shop.

4 When installing the uprated hoses, you will need to dismantle the brake system, and the opportunity should be taken to change the brake fluid - this in itself can improve brake performance. This would also be a good time to consider a change to synthetic brake fluid. If you do so, you should first overhaul the working parts of the hydraulic system (calipers and master cylinder) and flush the system through to remove all traces of the original fluid.

5 The above enhancements should be enough for all but the most demanding conditions. If you really need to go further than this, be warned that it is going to cost real money. Depending on how far you wish to go, you may have to install new discs, calipers and master cylinder, and the revised arrangement may also require you to change to a 15 inch wheel size. We understand that a conversion is available from Rod Millen Motorsports which utilizes brake parts from Mazda's RX7 turbo, but have no experience of this conversion in practice.

SUSPENSION & STEERING

6 The Miata offers numerous opportunities for modification of the suspension system. The steering system, on the other hand, does not really come into the area of direct modification, though changes to the suspension, wheels and tires will all have some effect here. Before you embark on suspension modifications, be sure of your intentions. Remember that, compared to the average car, your Miata/MX5 already has pretty harsh 'sporty' suspension. If you regularly embark on long journeys in your car, you may find that the modified suspension gets to be less enjoyable after a couple of hundred miles.

7 As was discussed in the earlier chapter of this manual, the suspension system is unusual in that the upper and lower wishbones are carried on eccentric pivots, allowing fine adjustment of the caster, camber and toe settings front and rear. Probably the least expensive form of suspension tuning would be to modify these settings slightly to favor the conditions under which the car is normally operated. This option also has the advantage that the spring rates and travel are not affected, so ride comfort will remain pretty much as standard.

8 To do this you'll need access to sophisticated alignment equipment, and for this reason you should have any such work carried out professionally. Ideally, try to find a race shop which is familiar with the car, and discuss your requirements with them. They will be able to advise whether the proposed adjustment will achieve what you wish to do, or whether more radical modification may be needed.

9 Alternatively, discuss the proposed changes with your Mazda dealer - if they have experience of setting up the car for competition use, they may be able to help with the changes. Note also that most tire suppliers are equipped to carry out this type of adjustment, though you will need to be able to specify exactly what settings you want. It is useful to discuss this with other owners who race or have modified their own Miatas/MX5s. Any adjustments made in this way should be considered refinements of the basic setup to suit your personal preferences; you won't achieve radical changes this way. When you have got the car set up just how you want it, make a note of all of the geometry settings for future reference.

10 Many owners have modified their Miata suspension more radically than just tweaking the basic settings. The idea is to emphasize specific

characteristics to suit your driving style and local operating conditions. As we mentioned earlier, any such change brings with it a cost in terms of ride comfort and the ability of the suspension to deal with minor irregularities of the road surface, but if you want ultimate handling, this may be a price you are prepared to pay.

11 The first area for change, certainly for owners of US market cars, are the stabilizer bars. The stock items are designed as a compromise between handling and comfort, and by fitting heavier stabilizer (anti-sway) bars you can favor the former over the latter. On European cars, slightly heavier stabilizers come as standard. This modification will significantly reduce body roll, allowing the car to corner quicker. Note that as well as the ride becoming harsher, you may find that the suspension is less flexible on poor surfaces; you may find that the change makes the car slower and less predictable in some situations. As well as Mazda's own Finish Line product, Jackson Racing, Rod Millen and Racing Beat are respected suppliers of aftermarket stabilizer bars. At the time of writing, the Miata Club says that Jackson make the most comfortable bars, while the Rod Millen and Racing Beat units are more aggressive.

12 Adjustable stabilizer bar links with harder bushes will also sharpen up handling.

13 The standard shocks are widely acknowledged as being pretty good, and unless your car's have worn out, or you are racing your car, you are unlikely to need to change them. The stock springs are also perfectly adequate for most owners, though there are plenty of aftermarket options here. By changing the springs you can lower the car, thus reducing its center of gravity, making it quicker through tight turns. You may need to modify the suspension bump stops a little, and remember that if you reduce suspension travel,

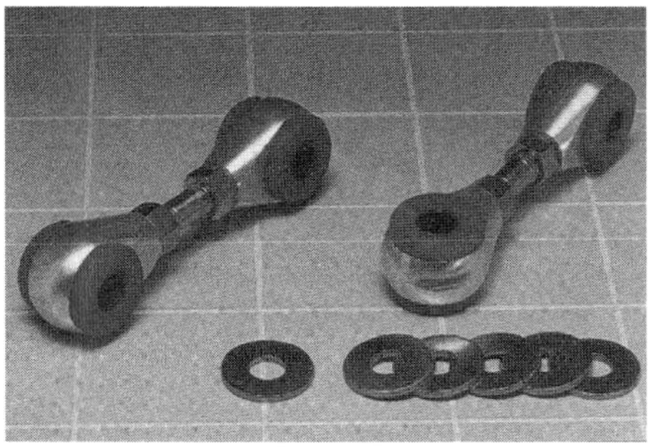

7/12 Racing Beat's stabilizer links.

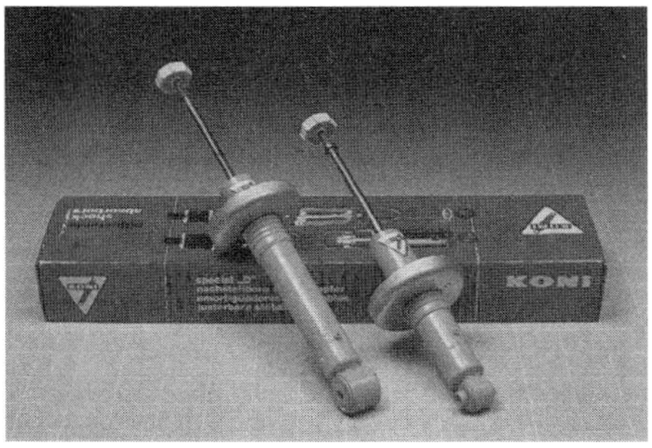

7/13 Racing Beat's replacement s/absorbers.

you'll lose out on comfort. Aftermarket springs can also have different spring rates than standard, again, stiffening the suspension, which makes for tighter handling.

14 The Miata Club has some experience of spring conversions and tells us that shortened springs can cause the suspension to bottom-out, damaging bump stops and subframe members. The club recommends aftermarket strut units with adjustable spring seats: this way you can have a lowered car but retain standard length springs. Koni and GAB make suitable units and we're told that Konis at the lowest spring seat position and

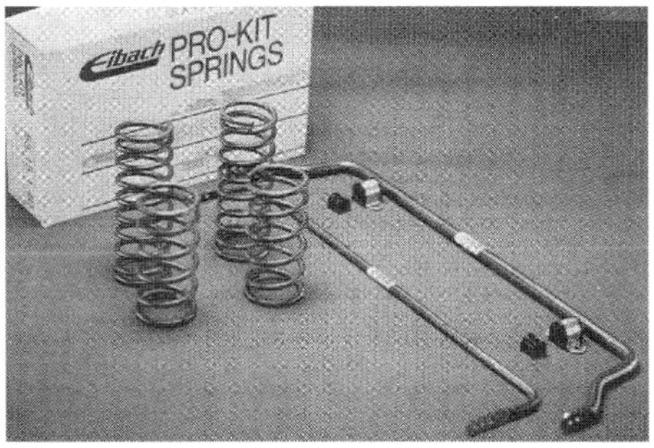

7/15 Pacific's uprated spring & stabiizer bar kit.

softest damper setting give a near stock ride with improved handling.

15 If you decide to opt for a suspension upgrade, it makes sense to purchase one of the recognized packages. These will contain all you need for the upgrade, and will have been developed and tested to ensure that the various parts work together harmoniously. Unless you are certain about what you are doing, beware of purchasing the various parts separately; you can easily wind up with suspension which is badly matched and which makes the car worse to drive instead of better.

8. TUNING - WHEELS & TIRES

1 Most Miatas/MX5s are sold with 7-spoke Minilite look-alike wheels, for which there are numerous replacement options. There is also a steel wheel option, which in our experience has not proved too popular. Regardless of the type of wheel used, all are of the same diameter and section. The standard diameter is 14 in, with a section of 5.5 in. It is possible to go up in rim section a little (though too much will mean that you get problems with the tire fouling the body), but the standard offset of 45 mm should not be changed if possible.

2 You can also go up a size in diameter to 15 in, this change being implemented together with a change to lower profile tires to maintain the effective rolling circumference of the tire. This will result in the preservation of gearing accuracy, but with a stiffer tire sidewall, giving sharper handling. It should be noted that if you use 15 in rims, you should not fit tires of the standard aspect ratio; not only will this mess up the car's overall gearing, you'll find that the speedometer will read low, and you'll run the risk of the tires fouling the body.

3 If you decide to shop for new wheels or tires, bear in mind that you'll want to maintain or improve the unsprung weight of the car. The standard wheels weigh in at only 12 lb or so, plus the weight of the tires fitted. If possible, go for wheels which reduce this weight, but on no account go for wheels which increase it. It is all too easy to buy wheels which look great, but weigh in at a higher

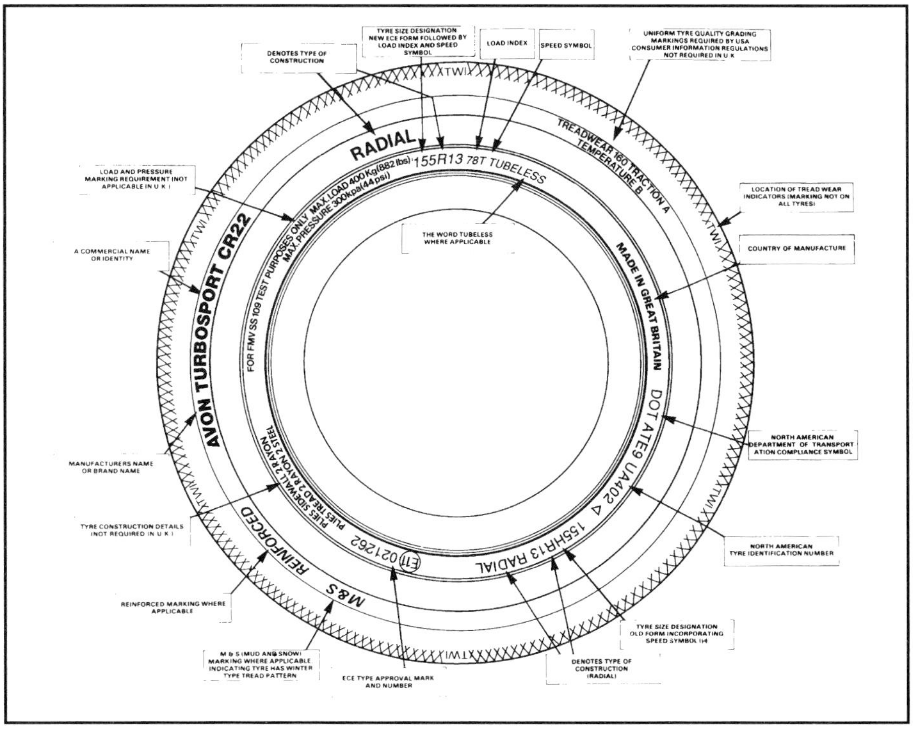

D8/1A THERE'S A LOT OF INFORMATION ON A TIRE SIDEWALL. THESE ARE STANDARD MARKINGS.

figure; check this before buying.

4 Unsprung weight is very important to the way the suspension operates, particularly on a light car like the Miata. It is the relationship between the unsprung weight (wheels, tires, brakes, and a proportion of the weight of the suspension and driveshafts) and the sprung weight (the rest of the car, plus occupants and luggage) which matters. The lower the percentage of unsprung weight, the better and more responsive your car's suspension will be, and the better the car will ride. It is easy to achieve this on a Cadillac, harder on a Miata. In simple terms, the lighter the unsprung components are, the less inertia they have, and the quicker they will react to changing road conditions.

5 The choice of tire is very subjective, and also dependent on what is on offer locally. We talked to a number of manufacturers, who each offered recommendations about the correct type of tire and size from their range. Without going into specifics, the tire manufacturer's recommendations varied somewhat from Mazda's in some cases. This is because each manufacturer bases its recommendations on its own test results. As a general rule, avoid fitting oversize tires, and if you do, get advice from the manufacturer concerned. Normally, you should not go up by more than one size - if you do, you may find that the tire fouls the body, and that handling is impaired.

6 If you change to a wider rim section, you will normally increase the tire section accordingly, but again you'll need to be careful that the tire does not foul the body at full lock or at the extremes of suspension travel. A wider tire tread will provide better grip on good road surfaces in dry conditions, but remember that this may not be the case on wet roads. The increased surface area means less contact pressure, and on a wet surface this can cause the car to skid or aquaplane more easily.

7 In fine-tuning your choice of tire size, you may arrive at slightly different sections for the front and rear tires. This is fine, except that you cannot then rotate the tires from front to rear as is normally the case. Also, note that changes in tire sizes and pressure settings will also produce slightly different handling characteristics, making the car understeer more or less according to the nature of the changes. For this reason, it's a good idea to be guided by the the tire maker's experience when making changes. Most tire companies are happy to offer advice and information on their products.

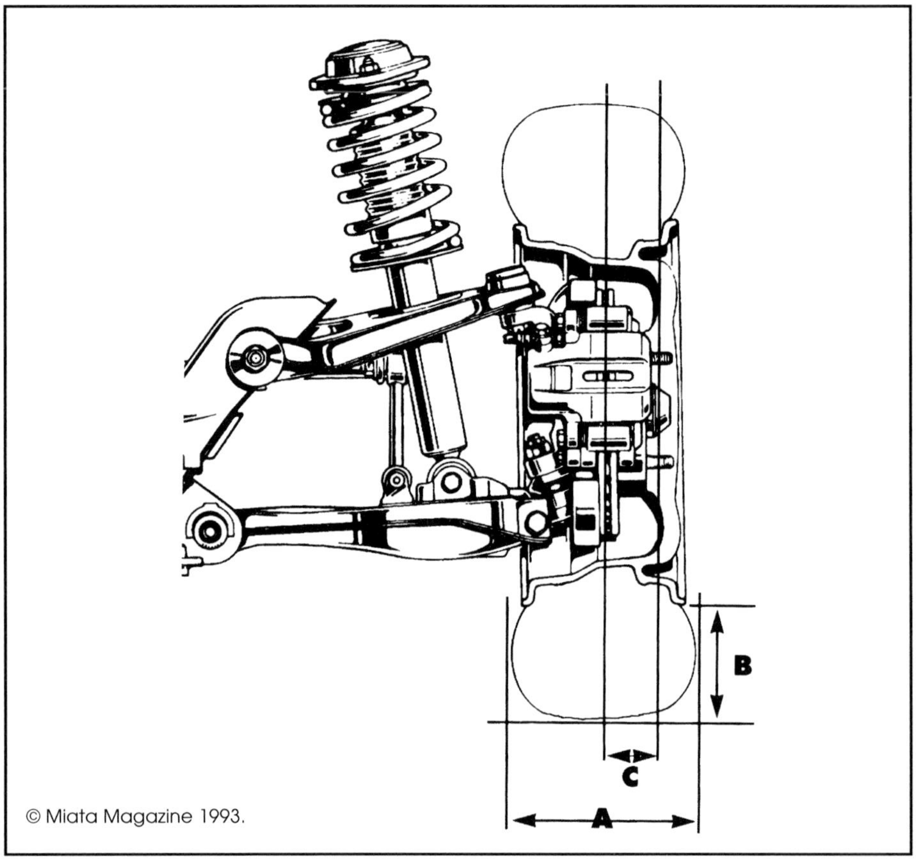

D8/1B TIRE ASPECT RATIO AND WHEEL OFFSET EXPLAINED

A Tire section width in millimeters (eg 185). B Tire section height (expressed as a percentage of width: eg a 185/60 tire has a width of 185 mm and a height equal to 60% of that width). C Wheel offset (in millimeters).

14 COSMETIC ACCESSORIES

1. INTRODUCTION

It is possible that the Miata/MX5 is even more fun to dress up with aftermarket body parts than it is to drive. The sheer volume of accessory parts produced for this car is little short of bewildering - and this is just the Miata/MX5-specific stuff.

To some extent, items already covered in chapter 13 fall into the 'cosmetic' category as much as they do to the more serious mechanical tuning arena. Objectively, for example, there may be little practical justification for changing the car's wheels, but on the other hand, this can make *your* car stand out from the crowd - after all, who wants to drive something as individual as a Miata/MX5, only to find that everyone else in your street had the same idea?

To find out what is available, may we once again recommend the Miata Club of America's *Miata Magazine* - an excellent reference source for Miata/MX5 accessory advertisers, and which also includes regular reviews and comparisons of many aftermarket parts.

2. COSMETIC ACCESSORIES - INTERIOR

1 You could spend forever adding accessory items to the Miata/MX5's interior. Items on offer range from novelty items to complete re-trim packages. Most owners consider the Miata/MX5 interior to be about right, if a little austere; but it is certainly in keeping with the 'European sports roadster' theme which the car evokes.

2 Individual accessory items, like drink can holders, key fobs and custom shift knobs, make acceptable gifts for the Miata/MX5 owner - check out the aftermarket advertisers for a bewildering range of such items, along with Miata/MX5 clothing and die-cast models.

3 Storage space is always at a premium on the Miata/MX5, so anything which adds to this has got to be good news. The possibilities are limited here, but it is possible to get an add-on storage unit which attaches behind the seat back to hold small items like cassettes and CDs. This may seem like a weird place to store these items, being pretty much inaccessible while driving, but it does mean that they are stowed out of sight while the car is parked - good security feature, though not as good as locking them in the trunk.

4 In sunnier areas, another practical item is a steering wheel & dash cover. The standard dash, being black, gets incredibly hot if the car is parked with the top up, and these covers help keep the heat levels down and provide some protection against sun damage of the dash fabric. They also help to hide your expensive stereo from prying eyes.

2/3 Mazda's behind seat storage bag.

5 You can uprate your car's interior trim as far as your taste and bank balance permit. Add-ons range from practical items like custom rocker protectors (door sill scuff plates) and floor mats, to full leather interior trim kits and wood dash trim upgrades. Moving your Miata/MX5 up into Jaguar territory does not come cheap, but the results are impressive.

2/5 Rod Millen's wood dash kit.

6 You can change the factory seats for aftermarket items if you so wish - all the major players in the seat market seem to make something to suit. The problem here is that the stock seats are good enough to make you question the need to upgrade. Like wheel upgrades, however, the best is available if you want it badly enough.

7 The viability of changing the steering wheel is dependent on where you live; some cars come with airbags, which more or less rules out wheel changes for these cars. European specification models are supplied with Momo steering wheels as standard (though the Momo logo on the center horn push is hidden under foam trim!) so you may consider upgrading to be superfluous. Be warned that if you do decide to change the steering wheel, you may experience some difficulty obtaining a wheel with the correct amount of dish.

8 Moving away from the pure accessory areas, you may also wish to add items which were not originally specified as options on your car. There are many options for central locking, alarm and cruise control add-ons if your car missed out on these. Also available is an electrically operated remote trunk release. This might seem like overkill, but it beats having to keep going back to the ignition lock to get your keys every time you need something from the trunk.

9 Staying with the trunk, you may wish to add to the trunk trim a little. The Miata/MX5 is very vulnerable to unsecured items in the trunk flying around and denting the body panels. This is due to the inside of the rear left fender being completely exposed and to the type of fast cornering that the Miata/MX5 encourages. You can purchase an add-on to protect this area. We recommend that you put something there to protect the body, even if it is only a carpet offcut glued inside the panel.

14

3. COSMETIC ACCESSORIES - EXTERIOR

1 It seems strange to consider how many hours the designers and engineers at Mazda put into achieving the classic roadster body shape of the Miata/MX5. After all that work, what do the owners want? Body kits!

2 Of course, most Miata/MX5 owners are more than content with the stock body shape, and in reality, most body kits are primarily enhancements of the basic design. Really, it is a case of the aftermarket designer saying *'It looks great, but why is there no air dam or spoiler?'*

3 The result is that you can get an amazing range of body kits and individual add-on body parts for the Miata/MX5. In some instances, these are just physical manifestations of items which got dropped from Mazda's own original design. We are thinking here of the hard boot cover which fits over the folded convertible top. A similar idea was played around with during the design stage, but never saw production. The aftermarket manufacturers have simply recognized how this item fits into the overall design, and are now offering their own versions.

4 Rear deck spoilers are another popular accessory body part that look as if they should have been part of the original concept. Again, these come in a range of shapes and designs, and properly fitted and color-matched, blend in seamlessly with the original bodywork.

3/4 Rod Millen's Club Sport Aero-Cover.

5 + More radical reworking of the Miata/MX5's shape is quite possible, by adding other items which subtly alter or enhance the lines of the car. There is demonstrably a strong demand for this type of customizing, illustrated by the variety of body kits with different front air dam and rocker extension shapes, emanating from just about every country where the car is sold.

3/5a Mazda's Finish Line body kit ...

3/5b ... and same kit from rear.

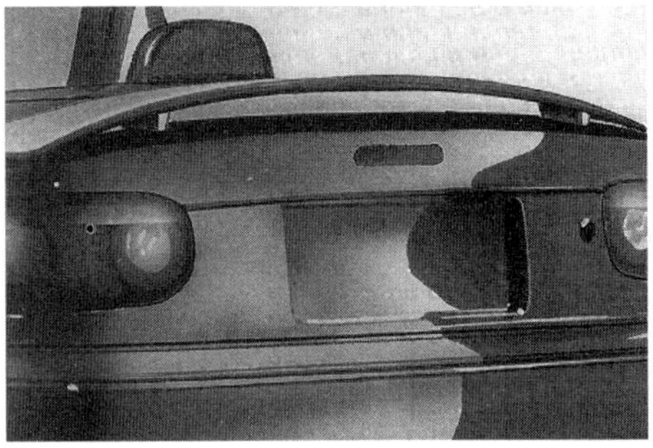

3/5c Mazda's Finish Line Rear Aerospoiler.

3/5d Racing Beat body kit.

3/5e Pacific body kit.

6 If you are thinking about adding any of these kits, you need to consider a number of factors. Firstly, does the price of the kit reflect good manufacturing quality and fit. A cheap and badly manufactured body part will take forever to install, and may never look like an integral part of the car, while a carefully-crafted part will look as if Mazda simply forgot to install it themselves.

7 Most body parts are available finished in primer or color matched. The decision here may depend on the age of your car. If more than a year or two old, your car's paint may have begun to age and fade, and if the new parts are matched to the original color code, they will look a completely different color when installed. On the other hand, if you buy the parts in primer finish, you'll have the additional expense of getting them painted to match the car. In some cases, a full professional repaint may be the only solution to getting an accurate color match.

8 Also find out how the panels mount. In many cases they attach with sheet metal screws to the Miata/MX5's body. This means that you won't be able to get rid of the panels easily should you tire of them, and if you are looking on your car as being a classic of the future, drilling holes in the body does nothing to maintain its originality.

9 In addition to the full body kits, there are smaller and more subtle exterior add-ons. An example of this is the rear wheelwell (wheelarch) mud flaps which come as standard on European cars. These are available as aftermarket items for US owners, and though we feel that the car looks much better without them, they do undoubtedly keep dirt off the tail of the car.

10 'Luggage' and 'Miata/MX5', as any owner will tell you, is a contradiction in terms. The first time you look into a Miata/MX5 trunk, your mind turns to thoughts of folding toothbrushes. What little space there is gets eaten up by the spare wheel and the battery, and the remaining space is a very strange shape.

11 If you travel with a passenger, you will already have come round to the notion of carrying with you soft, squashable possessions only. Soft luggage is about all you will fit into the trunk, so forget about suitcases. If you intend to do any serious travelling, you will need to improve your car's luggage capacity, however.

12 One option is to use one of the custom-made soft luggage systems designed to bungee onto the trunk lid. These are fine if you are very careful about what you carry and how you pack - hard or heavy items near the base of the bag will dent the trunk lid. Also, beware of the bag shifting while you drive - any trace of dirt between the trunk lid and luggage will scour into your car's paint. **Warning!** Under emergency braking or in a head on collision, luggage carried on the rear deck could fly forward and strike the car's occupants.

13 An alternative would be to use a traditional trunk lid rack (just like they did in the 50s and 60s). These clamp onto the trunk lid, providing a hard luggage grid to which you can lash your bags and cases. With all such luggage systems, be aware

3/13 Mazda's Finish Line Deck Rack.

that your rearward vision just about vanishes. **Warning!** Under emergency braking or in a head on collision, luggage carried on the rear deck could fly forward and strike the car's occupants.

4. COSMETIC ACCESSORIES - ENGINE

1 To make the engine look good you can fit a chromed cover over the cambox and, if you wish, bright red silicone plug leads. Of course, braver souls can remove the existing cambox and polish the aluminum until it gleams, just like Alfa owners do. However, unless you take great care to seal the polished alloy with a suitable lacquer, you're gonna have to polish that cambox often ...

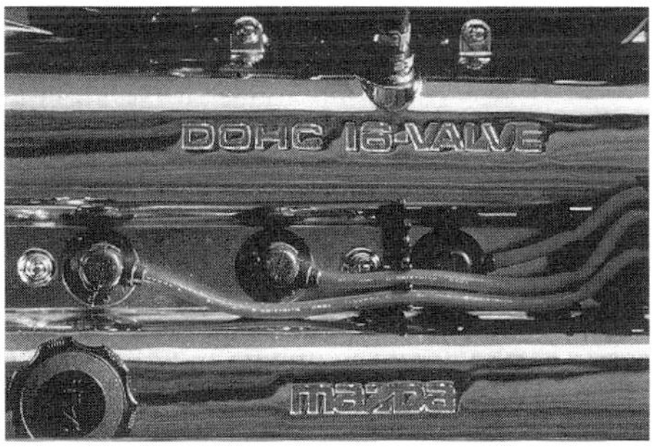

4/1 Mazda's Finish Line chrome cambox cover.

AMERICAN/ENGLISH GLOSSARY OF AUTOMOTIVE TERMS

American	English
A-arm	Wishbone (suspension)
Antenna	Aerial
Axleshaft	Halfshaft
Back-up	Reverse
Barrel	Choke/venturi
Block	Chock/wedge
Box end wrench	Ring spanner
Bushing	Bush
Clutch hub	Synchro hub
Coast	Freewheel
Convertible	Drop head
Cotter pin	Split pin
Counterclockwise	Anti-clockwise
Countershaft	Layshaft (of gearbox)
Crescent wrench	Open-ended spanner
Curve	Corner
Dashboard	Facia
Denatured alcohol	Methylated spirit
Dome lamp	Interior light
Driveaxle	Driveshaft
Driveshaft	Propeller shaft
Fender	Wing/mudguard
Firewall	Bulkhead
Flashlight	Torch
Float bowl	Float chamber
Freeway, turnpike, etc.	Motorway
Frozen	Seized
Gas tank	Petrol tank
Gas pedal	Accelerator pedal
Gasoline (gas)	Petrol
Gearshift	Gearchange
Generator (DC)	Dynamo
Ground	Earth (electrical)
Header/manifold	Manifold (exhaust)
Heat riser	Hot spot
High	Top gear
Hood	Bonnet (engine cover)
Idle	Tickover
Intake	Inlet
Jackstands /Safety stands	Axle stands
Jumper cable	Jump lead
Keeper	Collet
Kerosene	Paraffin
Knock pin	Roll pin
Lash	Freeplay/Clearance
Latch	Catch
Latches	Locks
License plate /tag plate	Number plate
Light	Lamp
Lock (for valve spring retainer)	Split cotter (for valve cap)
Lopes	Hunts
Lug nut	Wheel nut
Metal chips or debris	Swarf
Misses	Misfires
Muffler	Silencer
Oil pan	Sump
Open flame	Naked flame
Panel wagon/van	Van
Parking light	Sidelight
Parking brake	Handbrake
Piston pin or wrist pin bearing/bush	Small (little) end bearing
Piston pin or wrist pin	Gudgeon pin
Pitman arm	Drop arm
Power brake booster	Servo unit
Primary shoe	Leading shoe (of brake)
Prussian blue	Engineer's blue
Pry	Prise (force apart)
Prybar	Crowbar
Prying	Levering
Quarter window	Quarterlight
Recap	Retread
Release cylinder	Slave cylinder
Repair shop	Garage
Replacement	Renewal
Ring gear (of differential)	Crownwheel
Rocker panel	Sill panel
Rod bearing	Big-end bearing
Rotor/disk	Disc (brake)
Secondary shoe	Trailing shoe (of brake)
Sedan	Saloon
Setscrew, Allen screw	Grub screw
Shift fork	Selector fork
Shift lever	Gearlever/gearstick
Shift rod	Selector rod
Shock absorber, shock	Damper/shocker
Snap-ring	Circlip
Soft top	Hood
Spacer	Distance piece
Spare tire	Spare wheel
Spark plug wires	HT leads
Spindle arm	Steering arm
Stablizer or sway bar	Anti-roll bar
Station wagon	Estate car
Stumbles	Hesitates
Tang or lock	Tab
Taper pin	Cotter pin
Teardown	Strip(down)/dismantle
Throw-out bearing	Thrust bearing
Tie-rod (or connecting rod)	Trackrod (of steering)
Transmission	Gearbox
Troubleshooting	Fault finding/diagnosis
Trunk	Boot
Tube wrench	Box spanner
Turn signal	Indicator
Valve lifter	Tappet
Valve lifter or tappet	Cam follower or tappet
Valve cover	Rocker cover
VOM (volt ohmmeter)	Multimeter
Wheel cover	Roadwheel trim
Wheel well	Wheelarch
Whole drive line	Transmission
Windshield	Windscreen
Wrench	Spanner

15

TROUBLE-SHOOTING

INTRODUCTION

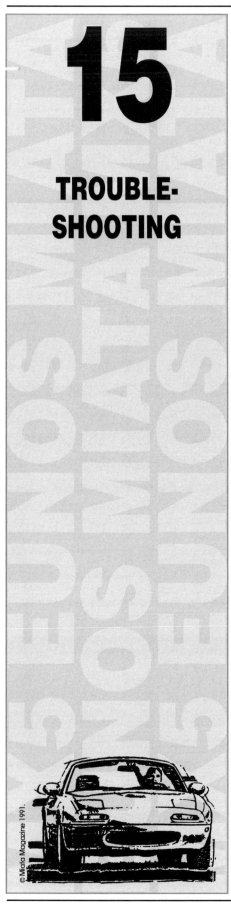

This part of the book is not intended to be an exhaustive guide to troubleshooting. In many respects, that is what much of the rest of the book is about and, like all modern cars, the Miata/MX5 is just too complex to summarize all possible problems in a few pages.

What we are attempting to do here is to offer a few helpful pointers in the event of something going wrong on the road, or if you can't get the car started. Inevitably, this is going to be pretty generalized, but we hope that it provides a starting point.

When you've identified the general area of a suspected fault, we strongly recommend that you refer to the related chapter. Not only will this cover diagnostic checks and procedures in greater detail than is possible here, it also includes important safety and procedural information which you should not overlook.

You'll find that some of the chapters are heavily troubleshooting oriented. In areas like the fuel, ignition and engine management systems, the majority of the main text is concerned with diagnosing faults. This is a necessary way of presenting this information, because these systems, each of which is complex in its own right, are heavily interrelated.

If we could offer just one piece of essential advice on the subject of troubleshooting in the event of a roadside breakdown, it would be to pull off the road and to read through the relevant part of this chapter, and then to refer to the appropriate part of this book before you even lift the hood. If you know what you are looking for, you are more than halfway to solving the problem.

ENGINE WON'T START OR STOPS SUDDENLY

ENGINE REFUSES TO CRANK WHEN ATTEMPTING TO START

• Incorrect gear selected and starter system locked out. Make sure that the transmission is in neutral (manual transmission) or Park, (automatic transmission) and try again.

• Battery discharged. The Miata/MX5 has a battery of limited physical size and capacity which is easily discharged if the accessory circuits, like the audio system and lights, are used extensively while the engine is not running. Try jump-starting from a backup battery. If engine now starts normally, remove, test and recharge the car's battery.

• If a discharged battery is a recurrent problem, check the charging system - watch for alternator warning light indicating a fault in this component. Frequent, short or low-speed journeys can exceed the charging system's ability to compensate for the heavy drain on the battery made during starting. Also, old and tired batteries have little reserve capacity. If your battery is more than about three years old, it may be due for retirement.

• If engine will not crank with a fully charged battery, the starter magnetic switch (solenoid) may be damaged or inoperative. Listen for a click from the magnetic switch on the starter motor as the ignition key is turned to the START position. No click usually means trouble here.

• Other possible causes are problems with the interlock switch (manual transmission) or inhibitor switch (automatic transmission).

• Check for broken or damaged wiring connections between the ignition switch, battery and starter motor. If the battery terminals or leads get hot, abnormally high resistance is indicated - check the connections.

• If everything else checks out, remove and test the starter motor.

• Sometimes, a starter motor develops a 'dead' commutator segment. If the motor stops in the wrong place, it won't work next time you try it. This can show up as an intermittent (and very annoying) fault.

The above checks cover the most likely causes of this type of fault. Don't forget, though, that a seriously damaged engine is unlikely to start! If your engine went bang, stopped and now refuses to crank, a major engine fault may have occurred. Get the car trailered to your home or a garage for attention.

ENGINE CRANKS VERY SLOWLY WHEN ATTEMPTING TO START

• Battery may be partly discharged. Try jump-starting from a backup battery. If the engine now starts normally, remove, test and recharge the car's battery.

• Check for damaged or corroded wiring connections between the ignition switch, battery and starter motor, paying particular attention to the heavy-duty cable connections at the battery and starter motor. High resistances here may allow other parts of the system to function normally, but won't be able to provide the high current needed for starting. If the wires or terminals get hot when attempting to start the car, a high resistance is indicated. Dismantle, clean and assemble using petroleum jelly (Vaseline) on the connections.

• Remove and test the starter motor. If you can, eliminate the motor as a source of trouble by substituting a known good motor. If your starter motor is suspect, get it reconditioned or fit a new one.

• Wrong grade engine oil in very cold conditions.

ENGINE CRANKS NORMALLY, BUT DOES NOT START

• Fuel tank empty. No, really, it *does* happen! Check it out, even if the gauge tells you that you have plenty of gas - gauges go wrong sometimes.

• Fuel, ignition or control system malfunction. This could be any number of individual faults and careful and systematic diagnosis is needed. Chapter 5 deals with this in detail. You need to establish that the plugs are sparking and that fuel is reaching the engine.

• Abnormally low engine compression. If the engine is badly worn or damaged, it may not have enough compression to allow normal combustion to take place.

• Exhaust tailpipe blocked.

ENGINE DIFFICULT TO START WHEN COLD

• Fuel, ignition or control system malfunction. This could be any number of individual faults and careful and systematic diagnosis is needed. Chapter 5 deals with this in detail. If the engine management system is getting the wrong information, starting may be difficult or impossible.
• Summer grade (low RPV) fuel in use producing poor atomization. Change to winter grade fuel if you are operating the car in cold conditions.
• Condensation on the plug leads can allow the ignition spark to ground out instead of sparking at the plug electrodes. Dry the leads carefully and try again.
• Spark plugs in poor condition.
• Battery in poor condition.
• If you accidentally flood the engine, floor the gas pedal and crank the engine. This shuts off the injector system and allows the flooding to clear.

ENGINE DIFFICULT TO START WHEN WARM

• Fuel, ignition or control system malfunction. This could be any number of individual faults and careful and systematic diagnosis is needed. Chapter 5 deals with this in detail.
• Vapor lock in the fuel system due to winter grade (high RPV) fuel. Change to summer grade fuel in warm operating conditions.
• If you accidentally flood the engine, floor the gas pedal and crank the engine. This shuts off the injector system and allows the flooding to clear.

ENGINE STARTS BUT WON'T RUN NORMALLY

ENGINE IDLE ERRATIC OR ROUGH

• Fuel, ignition or control system malfunction. This could be any number of individual faults and careful and systematic diagnosis is needed. Chapter 5 deals with this in detail.
• Check the spark plugs. Plugs are cheap and it is worth fitting a new set to see if this resolves the problem. Plugs can malfunction even if they look great.
• Damaged or aged plug caps or leads. As these components get old, the gradually become less efficient, and can build up high resistances. The easiest way to check this is to fit new parts.
• Fuel contaminated with dirt or water. If you have got dirty fuel in your tank, the in-line filter will take care of a certain amount, but will eventually allow water to pass through, or dirt to block the flow of fuel. Refer to chapter 5, and flush out the tank and fit a new filter.
• Malfunctioning or damaged fuel injectors.
• Intake system leak. This will cause erratic fuel/air mixture. Often characterized by squealing or hissing noise around source of leak.
• Incorrect ignition timing. This may be due to misinformation fed to engine control system from sensor(s).

ENGINE STALLS

• Fuel, ignition or control system malfunction. This could be any number of individual faults and careful and systematic diagnosis is needed. Chapter 5 deals with this in detail.
• Idle speed too low. May be due to incorrect signal fed to ECU from power steering or air conditioning systems, or other sensor fault.

ENGINE HESITATES OR STUMBLES DURING ACCELERATION

• Fuel, ignition or control system malfunction. This could be any number of individual faults and careful and systematic diagnosis is needed. Chapter 5 deals with this in detail.
• Damaged or aged plug caps or leads. As these components get old, they gradually become less efficient, and can build up high resistances. The easiest way to check this is to fit new parts.
• Fuel contaminated with dirt or water. If you have got dirty fuel in your tank, the in-line filter will take care of a certain amount, but will eventually allow water to pass through, or dirt to block the flow of fuel. Refer to chapter 5, and flush out the tank and fit a new filter.
• Blocked or dirty fuel injectors. Parts stores sell cleaning chemicals which you can add to fuel and these will work if blockage is not too serious. Chapter 5 has more information on injectors.

ENGINE SURGES DURING CRUISE

• Fuel, ignition or control system malfunction. This could be any number of individual faults and careful and systematic diagnosis is needed. Chapter 5 deals with this in detail.
• Clutch slipping. This can allow engine speed to rise and fall independent of road speed.

ENGINE LACKS POWER

• Fuel, ignition or control system malfunction. This could be any number of individual faults and careful and systematic diagnosis is needed. Chapter 5 deals with this in detail.
• Incorrect ignition timing, or other ignition system malfunction.
• Low tire pressures. The extra drag can make it seem like engine power is down.
• Brake drag. The drag can make it seem like engine power is down.
• Clutch slip (manual transmission). If engine speed rises as the accelerator pedal is pressed down, but road speed stays the same or drops, your clutch is slipping.
• Transmission problem (automatic transmission). Limp the car home if you can, but get the transmission checked urgently.

ENGINE RUNS ROUGHLY DURING DECELERATION (BACKFIRING IN EXHAUST)

• Fuel, ignition or control system malfunction. This could be any number of individual faults and careful and systematic diagnosis is needed. Chapter 5 deals with this in detail.
• Exhaust system fault or damage allowing air leakage.
• Intake system air leak.

ABNORMAL FUEL CONSUMPTION

• Fuel, ignition or control system malfunction. This could be any number of individual faults and careful and systematic diagnosis is needed. Chapter 5 deals with this in detail.
• Changed operating conditions (numerous short journeys, traffic holdups, etc).
• Heavy use of gas pedal to compensate for other factors (dragging brakes, low tire pressures, engine wear).

CLUTCH PROBLEMS

CLUTCH SLIPPING

• Clutch disc worn. Fit a new clutch assembly.
• Clutch disc friction material glazed (heat damaged).
• Clutch disc contaminated with oil. Fit a new clutch after rectifying any oil leak.
• Clutch cover diaphragm spring weak or damaged.
• Incorrect pedal lash (free play) adjustment.

CLUTCH JUDDER

• Worn or damaged clutch cover.
• Worn or damaged clutch disc.
• Friction material loose or broken.
• Clutch disc contaminated with oil. Fit a new clutch after rectifying any oil leak.
• Flywheel surface damaged.
• Loose or damaged engine mountings.

CLUTCH NOISE

• Noise during engagement. Severe wear of clutch disc friction material allowing metal-to-metal contact.
• Noise during initial pedal movement. Worn or damaged release bearing.
• Excessive crankshaft lash (end play).
• Worn or damaged pilot bearing.

TRANSMISSION (MANUAL) PROBLEMS

GEAR ENGAGEMENT DIFFICULT OR NOISY

• Air in clutch hydraulic system. Bleed system to remove air.
• If problem is recurrent after air has been bled from system, check for worn clutch master/release cylinder seals.
• Incorrect clutch pedal lash (free play) adjustment.
• Clutch disc failure.
• Wear or rusting of clutch disc splines causing disc to jam on shaft.
• Clutch cover failure - broken diaphragm spring.
• If pedal travels to floor with little or no resistance, check for complete hydraulic system failure indicated by pool of fluid in vicinity of leak (pipe fracture or total failure of seal).
• If hydraulic system intact, mechanical failure of

the clutch, clutch release fork or bearing is indicated.

- If the car has been stored for a long period, the clutch disc may have become frozen on the flywheel by rust. You can usually shock the clutch free by towing the car slowly in gear with the clutch pedal depressed.
- Insufficient transmission oil present (transmission will sound noisy and harshness or vibration may be noted).
- Transmission oil degraded or contaminated.
- Worn or damaged bearings in transmission.
- Worn or damaged transmission synchronizer ring or cone.
- Excessive axial play on transmission gearshaft(s).
- Worn or damaged shift (extension housing) mechanism.

Note. The Miata/MX5 is known to have a baulky change from 1st to 2nd when cold: this is quite normal. Some early cars have a particularly bad problem which is the subject of a dealer fix: your dealer will advise you appropriately. The Miata Club of America has found that using synthetic oil in the transmission produces smoother shifts.

TRANSMISSION JUMPS OUT OF GEAR

- Weak or broken detent spring.
- Worn or damaged shift fork.
- Worn clutch hub or sleeve.
- Worn or damaged gears.
- Worn or damaged bearings.
- Excessive gear backlash.
- Worn or damaged shift (extension housing) mechanism - gear not selecting correctly.

UNUSUAL NOISES

- Insufficient oil present.
- Oil degraded or contaminated.
- Worn or damaged bearings.
- Worn or damaged gear teeth.
- Excessive gear backlash.

ABNORMAL VIBRATION

- Worn or damaged engine/transmission mountings.
- Incorrectly mounted or loose power plant frame (PPF).
- Worn or damaged bearings.

TRANSMISSION (AUTOMATIC) PROBLEMS

GENERAL

- In the event of a problem with the automatic transmission, your options are limited. In Chapter 4 we describe a number of checks and tests relating to the operation of the transmission, but full diagnosis or repairs will require help from an automatic transmission specialist or a Mazda dealer. Have the car trailered to the repairer - don't attempt to tow it or you will almost certainly damage the transmission.

A transmission specialist will need to have the complete car with the transmission in place to be able to locate and identify the fault, so don't think that you can help by removing the transmission.

FINAL DRIVE PROBLEMS

ENGINE RUNS NORMALLY, AND GEARS ENGAGE, BUT CAR DOES NOT MOVE

- Driveshaft or differential unit internal failure. This is not a common problem, but if it does occur you may get this symptom. Have someone look under the car while the engine is running and the transmission is in gear (but DON'T get under or too near the car!) If the propshaft can be seen turning, a fault of this type is indicated.

ABNORMAL NOISE OR VIBRATION

- Lack of differential oil.
- Worn or damaged driveshaft joints.
- Loose or damaged propshaft.
- Worn or damaged differential ring gear and/or pinion.
- Worn differential bearings.
- Loose or worn engine/transmission mountings.
- Loose, worn or damaged PPF mountings, or damaged PPF.

COOLING SYSTEM PROBLEMS

STEAM EJECTED FROM UNDER THE HOOD

- Sudden failure of cooling system hose or connection. Pull over and wait until escape of steam subsides, then open the hood carefully and locate source of leak. Allow engine to cool fully before attempting repair or you could suffer serious burns. If damage is to cooling system hose, fit a new hose, top up with fresh coolant, then run the engine to check repair.
- Sudden failure of heater hose or connection. If the leak is in one of the heater hoses, you can take the heater out of the coolant circuit as a get-you-home measure. This is described in Chapter 6.
- Radiator failure. This may have been caused by a stone or other debris hitting the radiator core, or by failure due to internal corrosion. Fit a new radiator.
- Radiator cap failure. If the radiator cap has become aged or damaged, it may allow a pressure leak. If this happens, the coolant will boil at a lower temperature and will escape as steam. Wait until the system cools right down, then fit a new cap and check that the problem is resolved.
- Radiator fan or thermoswitch failure. If the fan system fails to operate at the preset temperature, the coolant may overheat and boil. Check and replace the affected parts.
- Coolant frozen. Although this sounds crazy, if the coolant freezes in the system, you can get local overheating and boiling elsewhere in the system. This will not occur if the correct water/antifreeze mix is used.

STEERING AND SUSPENSION PROBLEMS

CAR WANDERS OFF LINE

- Wheel alignment incorrect.
- Suspension geometry incorrect (impact damage or incorrect adjustment).
- Incorrect tire pressures.
- Tire worn or damaged.
- Wheel damaged (impact damage).
- Wheel lug nuts loose.
- Worn hub bearing.
- Weak or broken suspension spring, or damaged shock absorber.
- Different types of tire on same axle.

EXCESSIVE STEERING FREE PLAY

- Worn steering column or intermediate shaft joints.
- Worn steering joint.
- Steering rack mountings loose or damaged.
- Worn suspension bushes.

STEERING EXCESSIVELY STIFF OR HEAVY (MANUAL STEERING)

- Low tire pressures.
- Frozen (seized) steering joint.
- Wear or damage in steering rack.
- Worn or frozen (seized) steering column joints.
- Misalignment of steering column or linkages as a result of impact damage.

STEERING EXCESSIVELY STIFF OR HEAVY (POWER STEERING)

(See above, then check the following additional points).

- Loose or broken power steering pump drivebelt.
- Low power steering fluid level, or air in system.
- System leaks.
- Inadequate system pressure.

WHEEL (FRONT) WOBBLE OR VIBRATION

- Front wheels and tires out of balance.
- Front wheels damaged or distorted.
- Wheel lug nuts loose or broken wheel stud.
- Worn or damaged suspension components.
- Front brake disc distorted or damaged.
- ABS system fault.

WHEEL (REAR) WOBBLE OR VIBRATION

- Rear wheels and tires out of balance.
- Rear wheels damaged or distorted.
- Wheel lug nuts loose or broken wheel stud.
- Worn or damaged suspension components..
- Rear brake disc distorted or damaged.
- ABS system fault.
- Propshaft joints worn or damaged.
- Driveshaft or driveshaft joints worn or damaged.

CAR ROLLS EXCESSIVELY OR WALLOWS IN CORNERS

- Wear or damage of suspension components.
- Worn or damaged shock absorbers.
- Weak or broken suspension springs.
- Worn or damaged stabilizer bar or mounting.

ABNORMAL TIRE WEAR

- Tire pressures or steering geometry incorrect.
- Suspension geometry incorrect.
- Use of vehicle on poor road surfaces.
- Excessively hard driving or braking.

ABNORMAL SMELLS, NOISES OR VIBRATION

FUEL SMELLS IN OR AROUND CAR

- Damaged or leaking fuel system or evaporative emission system parts.
- Charcoal canister overflow (evaporative emission control system malfunction).
- Leaking emergency gas container (if carried in car).
- Fuel, ignition or control system malfunction.

SMELL OF BURNING

- Electrical fault. If suspected, stop immediately and isolate electrical system by disconnecting battery leads. Locate and rectify fault before reconnecting supply.
- Engine overheating. Allow engine to cool down completely, then check coolant level and fan operation.
- Leaking exhaust manifold or system connection (take note of unusual exhaust noise - try blocking end of exhaust pipe and check that pressure builds up quickly. No buildup indicates a system leak)
- Trim or flammable item in contact with exhaust system.
- Oil contamination of catalytic converter. Identify and rectify leak before fitting new converter.
- Brake(s) overheating. May be caused by repeated heavy brake use, in which case stop and allow to cool down. Check pads for glazing. Can also be caused by fault in brake system causing brakes to drag, or by leaving parking brake applied.
- Clutch slipping. Excessive clutch slip will overheat the friction material. Allow to cool, then proceed cautiously to minimize slipping. Repair clutch as soon as you can.
- Automatic transmission fault. Can lead to overheating of transmission oil. Get transmission checked out to avoid possible costly damage.
- Minor fire in trim or upholstery. Can be caused by cigarette dropped inside the car. Stop and extinguish any such problems before the fire takes hold. Note that fire can spread rapidly, especially with soft top down.

ABNORMAL SULFUR SMELL FROM EXHAUST

- High sulfur fuel in use. Change to low sulfur brand.
- Over-rich fuel supply.

ENGINE NOISES

PREIGNITION: PINGING OR KNOCKING WHILE ENGINE UNDER LOAD

- Incorrect ignition timing.
- Incorrect fuel grade.
- Engine overheating.
- Buildup of carbon deposits in engine.
- Intake air leak.
- Damaged or malfunctioning engine control system or related subsystem.

LIGHT TAPPING OR RATTLING NOISES

- Excessive valve lash (worn or damaged hydraulic lash adjuster, degraded engine oil).
- Worn or damaged camshaft bearings.
- Worn valves or valve guides.
- Piston slap (excessive piston/bore clearances).
- Worn or damaged piston pin bearing.

RUMBLING OR KNOCKING NOISES

- Regular deep knocking noise: Conrod bearing (big end) failure. Usually worse when engine is lightly loaded, and for a few seconds when first started (until normal oil pressure is attained).
- Rumbling and vibration: main bearing failure. Usually worse when engine under load. Oil pressure may read low.

SQUEALING OR SCREECHING FROM UNDER HOOD

- Drivebelt slipping (usually when under load, worse in damp or wet weather. Try to note when it happens - if when turning steering wheel, for example, it may be due to added load on power steering pump).

EXHAUST SYSTEM NOISES

- System loose or connection leaking.
- Damaged or rusted exhaust system.
- Contaminated or obstructed system causing excessive back-pressure.
- Rattling or loose heatshield.
- Damaged or broken mounting or hanger.

DRONING OR RUMBLING FROM WHEEL AREA

- Worn or damaged wheel bearings.
- Worn or damaged differential bearings.
- Differential oil loss.
- Differential ring gear/pinion wear or damage.
- Differential bearing wear or damage.

CLUTCH NOISES

- Badly worn clutch disc (metal-to-metal grinding during take-up).
- Worn release bearing (squealing during pedal operation).
- Damaged clutch cover/diaphragm spring (rattles or other noise during pedal operation).

SUSPENSION NOISES

- Worn suspension bushes (knocking or rattling noises on irregular surfaces).
- Loose or worn stabilizer mountings/bushes (knocking or rattling noises on irregular surfaces).
- Rusted or frozen suspension pivots (creaks or groaning as suspension parts move).
- Shock absorber shaft bent.

BRAKE SYSTEM PROBLEMS

POOR BRAKE PERFORMANCE

- Pads contaminated with water. Allow to dry out.
- Air in hydraulic system. Bleed system.
- Hydraulic fluid old or contaminated with moisture. Change fluid.
- Brake pads excessively worn or damaged. Fit new pads.
- Brake pads glazed (heat damaged). Check pads for wear - fit new pads as necessary, or remove glazed surface.
- Brake pads contaminated with oil or grease. Resolve source of leak, then fit new pads.
- Brake pads contaminated with hydraulic fluid. Overhaul or fit new caliper(s), then fit new pads.
- Brake pads of wrong specification fitted (pad material may be too hard). If in doubt, fit genuine Mazda pads.
- Master cylinder wear or damage. Overhaul or replace.
- Caliper wear or damage. Overhaul or replace.
- Power brake unit (servo) fault.
- Power brake unit (servo) vacuum hose or check valve fault.
- Deterioration of brake hose(s).
- Malfunctioning Proportioning Bypass Valve (PBV).

BRAKES PULL TO ONE SIDE

- Pad(s) worn, damaged or contaminated on one side.
- Disc surface worn, distorted or damaged.
- Incorrect operation of automatic adjuster mechanism (rear caliper only).
- Caliper damaged or inoperative.
- Damaged or obstructed brake line.
- Incorrect wheel alignment.
- Incorrect tire pressures.

BRAKES DRAGGING

- Insufficient pedal free play.
- Obstructed return port in master cylinder.
- Pad(s) jammed or sticking.
- Caliper damaged or piston sticking.
- Brake disc - excessive runout or damage.
- Parking brake applied or out of adjustment.

EXCESSIVE PEDAL MOVEMENT

- Incorrect free play adjustment.
- Air in hydraulic system.
- Disc distorted or damaged (can result in excessive clearances between pads and disc surfaces).

BRAKE NOISE OR VIBRATION

- Pad(s) worn down to backing metal. Check disc for damage. Fit new pad(s) and disc(s) as required.
- Foreign material embedded in pad surface(s). Check pads and discs for damage, Fit new pads and discs as required.
- Loose caliper mounting bolts - check and retighten.

• Pad squeal. Apply copper grease to back of pads.

Anti-lock braking system (ABS) malfunction
• Refer to Mazda dealer for diagnosis and rectification.

PARKING BRAKE INEFFECTIVE
• Mechanism out of adjustment.
• Cable broken.
• Cable rusted or jammed with road dirt.

ELECTRICAL PROBLEMS

BATTERY BECOMES DISCHARGED FREQUENTLY
• Excessive 'dark current' load from accessory systems.
• Battery failing internally.
• Charging system fault (check if warning light is on).
• Alternator drivebelt loose or slipping.
• Fault in accessory system (such as aftermarket alarm or stereo).

BATTERY BECOMES OVERCHARGED
• Damaged charging system (faulty regulation).

HEADLIGHTS DIM OR INOPERATIVE
• Headlight lens dirty (this does happen - raise the lights manually to check!)
• Blown bulb or fuse.

15

CLUBS

ANNUAL EUROPEAN MEETING

Ed Goedert
International Meeting Organiser
Route D'Arlon 98
L-8008 Strassen
Luxembourg.

Note. This International meeting is held annualy around the end of May. (The '94 event was in Schwartzenberg, Austria).

AUSTRALIA

Peter Randell
4 Ventnor Avenue
West Perth 6005 W
Australia

Ms A. Kehl
11/108 Crimea Road
Marsfield, NSW, 2122
Australia

Mr M. Finlay
PO Box 183
South Melbourne, Victoria, 3205
Australia

Mr B. Williams
PO Box 34
Uraidla, SA, 5142
Australia

Ms B. Lewis
92 Whatley Crescent
Mount Lawley, WA, 6050
Australia.

AUSTRIA

Renato Zappela,Gessellshaft MBH
Hermannga A 1071 Wien
Austria

BELGIUM

Dominique De Rauw
Turnhoutsebaah 100
B-2970 Schilde
Belgium

CANADA

Bob Varey
1540 Falconcrest Drive
Pickering, Ontario
L1V 4Z4
Canada

Bruce Alger
1636 Broadview Road NW
Calgary, Alberta
T2N 3H1
Canada

Norio Nakayama
1110-1060 Alberni Street
Vancouver, BC
V6E 1A3
Canada

Kay Walker
PO Box 288
Brentwood Bay, BC
VO5 1A0
Canada

GERMANY

Daniel Alexander Brose
Gotenstrasse 14
5300 Bonn 2
Germany

Reiner Goernert
Peter Hannweg Strasse 94
8510 Fuerth
Germany

JAPAN

Katsuyuki Sataki
5-61-21 Ujinci Miuki
Minami-Ku
Hiroshima
Japan

NETHERLANDS

Hedwig M. Taminiau
Arnhemse Bovenweg 295
3971 MJ Driebergen
Netherlands.

NEW ZEALAND

Norman Johston
PO Box 6864 Wellesley St
Auckland
New Zealand

SOUTH AFRICA

Gus Weddepohl
PO Box 8163
Johannesburg 2000
South Africa

SWITZERLAND

Prezgaj Olivera
Stettemerstrasse 149
CH-8207 Schaffhausen
Switzerland

USA

Miata Club of America
PO Box 759
Lilburn
GA 30226
USA

Note. The club has many local chapters throughout the USA.

SPECIALIST SUPPLIERS

BBR
Oxford Road
Brackley
Northants NN13 5DY
England
(Turbocharger)

Cartech
11723 Warfield
San Antonio
TX 78216
USA
(Turbocharger)

Jackson Racing
Suite E
16371 Gothard Street
Huntington Beach
CA 92647
USA
(Performance tuning parts & accessories)

Downing Atlanta
5096 Peachtree Road
Atlanta
GA 30341
USA
(Supercharger)

Racing Beat
1291 Hancock Street
Anaheim
CA 92807
USA
(Performance tuning parts & accessories)

Rod Millen Motorsport
7575 Reynolds Circle
Huntington Beach
CA 92647
USA
(Performance tuning parts & accessories)

Nelson Superchargers
3724 Overland Avenue
Los Angeles
CA 90034
USA
(Supercharger)

Pacific Auto Accessories Inc
5882 Machine Drive
Huntington Beach
CA 92649
USA
(Performance tuning parts & accessories)